1203

1203

HUXFORD'S
PAPERBACK
VALUE GUIDE

Bob & Sharon Huxford

COLLECTOR BOOKS
A Division of Schroeder Publishing Co., Inc.

The current values in this book should be used only as a guide. They are not intended to set prices, which vary from one section of the country to another. Auction prices as well as dealer prices vary greatly and are affected by condition as well as demand. Neither the Author nor the Publisher assumes responsibility for any losses that might be incurred as a result of consulting this guide.

On the Cover:

L'Amour, Louis. *Kilkenny*. Ace S-82. Very Good-Fine. $75.00.

Cain, James M. *Double Indemnity*. Avon 60. Very Good-Fine. $35.00.

Cheyney, Peter. *Dark Street Murders*. Avon 764. Very Good-Fine. $10.00

Conklin, Groff, edt. *Possible Worlds of SF*. Berkley G-3. Very Good-Fine. $7.50.

Hammett, Dashiell. *Dead Yellow Women*. Dell 308. Very Good-Fine. $50.00

Jessup, Richard. *The Deadly Duo*. Dell First A194. Near Fine. $10.00.

Lomax, Bliss. *Rusty Guns*. Hillman 33. Very Good-Fine. $10.00.

Dutourd, Jean. *A Dog's Head*. Lion 196. Very Good-Fine. $37.50.

Dickens, Charles. *A Christmas Carol*. Pocket 29. Very Good- Fine. $25.00.

Queen, Ellery. *The Dragon's Teeth*. Pocket 459. Very Good-Fine. $15.00.

Cohen, Octavus Roy. *Don't Ever Love Me*. Popular Library 332. Very Good. $22.50.

Cohen, Octavus Roy. *More Beautiful Than Murder*. Popular Library 427. Near Fine. $37.50.

Kerouac, Jack. *On The Road*. Signet D1619. Very Good-Fine. $30.00.

Books on the cover courtesy of

Buck Creek Books

Introduction

In 1939 when paperback books began to be mass-produced, a whole new world opened up for readers. Previously only best-selling books reached the hands of avid fans; now millions could afford the small twenty-five cent books. When we realize that this period was before the age of mass communication, the paperback book was truly a great innovation. Today these early editions are eagerly sought after by collectors.

This book contains the values of nearly 25,000 paperback books. These prices reflect not just one person's opinions but actual market dealings around the country. Scores of the nation's largest dealers sent us their current lists of books for sale, and prices from large book auctions have been included as well. All sources will be clearly identified, a factor you'll want to consider as you use this book to evaluate your holdings.

As you will see, not only is our book a price guide but a buying and selling catalog as well. This is a concept that has worked well in our companion publication, *Huxford's Old Book Value Guide*. Through the inclusion of dealer codes, you'll be able to make contacts for books you would like to purchase. Even if the book has already sold, the contact you make will be valuable to you. Many book dealers keep files of titles wanted by collectors and will usually be happy to let you know when they acquire something they know you're in the market for. Our dealers' codes are explained in the section called Book Sellers, Auction Galleries, and Their Codes.

In regard to values, it is our intention that this book be used simply as a guide, a learning tool, a place to start for the new collector. It cannot substitute for hands-on experience. The field is too vast and varied for one book to cover. There are too many directions one's interest might take for us to encompass them all. But we have attempted to put you in touch with the market by including not only major dealers nationwide, but periodicals, auction houses, paperback shows and fairs, and other services directed solely toward the paperback collector as well.

How To Use This Book

Our format is very simple. Listings are alphabetized first by the name of the author. If more than one book is listed for a particular author, each title is listed alphabetically under his or her name. Dual-title books are indicated by the use of a slash mark between the two authors' names.

The description line further contains the date (when known), publisher's number, edition (first printing, paperback original, etc.), cover artist (or type of art), condition codes, and the source. When pseudonyms are known, names have been cross-referenced. (Consult the section titled Pseudonyms for more information.)

Abbreviations

/ ....dual title or author	edt..................................editor	MTI ....movie tie-in
Ad ....adult	F ....fine	My ....mystery
Av ....adventure	Fa ....fantasy	NF............................near fine
Auto ....autobiography	Fi ....fiction	NFi...........................nonfiction
Bio.......................biography	G ....good	PBO.........paperback original
bwc ....black & white cover	gga....................good girl art	prtg.................print, printing
c/ ....cover art or artist	Hi ....history	SF ....science fiction
cc ....color cover	Ho ....horror	sgn ....signed
Cr ....crime	Hu ....humor	TVTI ....TV tie-in
De.........................detective	inscr......................inscribed	VG.......................very good
edn ....edition	intl...........................initialed	We..........................western

Book Buyers

In the back of this book is a listing of scores of collectors and dealers who are actively looking to buy particular titles, examples of their favorite genre, or books by a certain publisher needed to round out their collections. As those of us interested in the hobby already know, as you buy for yourself, you invariably find that you have duplicates for sale. Or since you first started buying, your interests may have changed, and some of the books that you've purchased may no longer 'fit' into your library. If this is the case, refer to that section.

If you sell your books to a dealer, you should expect to receive no more than 50% of the values listed in this book, unless the dealer has a specific buyer in mind for some of your material. In most cases, a dealer will pay less than 50% of retail for a book to stock. Some dealers prefer exchanging used paperbacks instead of buying outright. When you make your contact, be sure to list your books by author, full title, publisher, date, and edition. Indicate condition, noting any defects on cover or contents. Please, do not send lists of books for appraisal.

If you need to ship your books by mail, first wrap each individually. Never use newspaper for the inner wrap, since newsprint tends to rub off. (It may, however, be used as a cushioning material within the outer carton.) Pack books in padded bags or small corrugated boxes; these may be purchased at most post offices or office supply stores. Place these bags or boxes in a large sturdy box. Here's where you can use that newspaper. Pack the space between the two containers with enough wadded up paper to keep your books from shifting in the mail. Be sure to use a good shipping tape to seal it. Tape reinforced with nylon thread is preferable, as it will not tear. Books shipped via the US Postal Service may be sent special fourth class book rate, which may be lower than parcel post, but delivery may be slower.

How To Succeed As a Paperback Collector

Reasons for Collecting: People collect paperbacks for a wide variety of reasons. Some collect books by a particular author. You might choose to become a collector of the novels of Earl Stanley Gardner or Agatha Christie, for instance, and you may or may not decide to expand your collection to include titles written under the pseudonyms used by the particular author you've chosen. Some collectors focus on cover art and illustrations by such artists as James Avati, Jeff Jones, or Frank Frazeta.

On the other hand, topic may be the deciding factor. Sexology and erotica are often avidly sought by collectors. Personally, you may want to zero in on other genre: mystery, television or movie tie-ins, Westerns, historical adventures, horror, crime, detective stories, or science fiction.

Some collections are based on titles from a particular publisher and may be directed toward collecting everything that company has published. Often they may focus on low-number series such as 'the first 500 Avons,' 'all Dell Books with map-back covers,' or 'all cover variants of the first 300 Pocket Book titles.'

As a collector, you might find yourself fascinated (as I am) with the histories of obscure paperback houses and join the group of paperback collectors who are also historians and bibliographers. As you can see, collectors come with all sorts of interests and motivations, yet still there are many potentially 'collectible' books around that can be bought at reasonable prices.

How To Recognize a Collectible Paperback: Perhaps we need to distinguish between 'collectible' and 'valuable.' There are many interesting books that actually have little market value, yet for one reason or another they catch your eye. Who knows! If you're lucky, you may find yourself a 'pioneer' in some new corner of the field. What makes a paperback valuable? Like most, the paperback market is driven by forces of supply and demand. But because demand depends on so many overlapping factors, there is no easy formula for determining value. In fact, were we to take all of the complexities of evaluation into account, a guide of this sort would be a virtual impossibility. As it is, any price guide is at best just that, a guide. It can't replace the accumulated knowledge that gives paperback 'experts' an edge. But you can go a long way in this game simply by following a few basic principles.

There are, as I suggested above, lots of reasons for a book to be interesting to the collector — cover art, author, publisher, genre, and so forth. A book that exhibits several desirable factors is likely to be more valuable than one, for example, written by a popular author, yet with very little else to its credit, simply because the demand for it is likely to be greater. It has the potential to attract a wider range of buyers. All things being equal, a scarce book will be more valuable than a common one, but certainly this is not always true. For instance, a scarce book on roller derby might not generate as much demand as a more common erotic title, simply because it holds the interest of only a handful of collectors.

The same terms apply to the critera of age. In general, older books are more interesting to collectors, and older printings are more desirable. Paperback originals — books that never appeared in a hardcover edition — are the 'first editions' of the paperback world with interest in paperback printings following closely behind. But other factors may upset this simple rule of thumb. Certainly a signed second printing may be more valuable than an unsigned first. And a later edition with particularly fine cover art may generate greater demand. If there is a single trick to finding valuable paperbacks, it is learning enough to begin to see which books are interesting in various, multiple ways.

The Importance of Learning To Judge Condition: As is true with any item of ephemera, time and use takes a toll on paperback books, and the collector needs to learn how to assess damage and wear in relation to value. This is often a matter of personal standards; and an especially rare or desirable book, even if the condition is less than one would like, will carry a price tag disproportionately higher than a more common title. (You'll find more information dealing with condition later on.)

To Sum It Up: There is no way to succeed in collecting paperbacks except to play the game for awhile and learn the rules. If you stick with it, keep your eyes and ears open, and aren't put off by the occasional bit of library research, you'll quickly find that you're accumulating expertise. You'll know the 'look' of a collectible paperback, and you'll develop a collection of important names — authors, titles, artists, publishers, etc. — that will do you good service at the oddest of times. That's much of the joy of collecting books — knowing that you can 'read' the outsides of them just as well as you can the insides!

Contributed by Shawn P. Wilbur, %Pauper's Books, 206 N Main St., Bowling Green, OH 43402-2420

Condition and Grading

Terminology varies somewhat from dealer to dealer. Generally, 'fine' or 'mint' are the highest grades used and refer to a book that is **as new**, with no defects. The grades then range down, sometimes using '+' and/or '-' symbols. 'Very good' indicates a nice collectible book with several small-to-moderate defects. A book graded 'good -' or less is not considered collectible, except, perhaps, as a 'filler' copy within a collection until a better replacement copy can be found.

The nature of defects found in collectible paperbacks is varied. All defects result in a lower grade down from from an otherwise fine book. Here are some common defects that you might see mentioned in catalogs.

Bumps: These usually appear on book corners. At their most extreme, they would crease or warp the book from cover to cover. A mild bump may appear as a very slight bend with loss of sheen to the cover near the point of impact.

Chips or nicks: These often occur at the top or bottom of the spine; the removal of a small area of color or actual cover stock.

Corner clip: The removal of a triangular corner of the book cover.

Corner creases, splits or tears

Darkening or fading: These problems may occur to covers, spine, or interior pages. Most commonly spines are faded by sun exposure and interior pages excessively browned and brittle due to age.

Front cover lift: This sometimes happens when books were bound too tightly causing the cover to curl slightly.

Glass ring or cup ring marks: These are visible on the covers of books carelessly used as coasters.

Lam lift or lam peel: Refers to the thin clear film bonded to the color image on many early paperback books. As the books age and are rubbed against one another this lamination begins to peel back at the edges.

Loose pages

Missing pages

Reading creases: Lengthwise creases on the spine or on the covers adjacent to the spine which result from flattening the book when it is opened.

Remainder marks: A general term for a physical change made to the book by a publisher, distributor or bookseller to indicate that the book is nonreturnable. Some of these methods include the use of rubber stamps (on covers or page ends), blind-embossing stamps, rounded and/or clipped corners, a neat saw cut to an edge, a punch hole through the cover, and marker stripes to the page ends.

Scrapes: These occur when a book edge is dragged over a sharp object creating a series of scuffs that remove color.

Scuffing: This may simply refer to a very slight dulling of covers caused from being rubbed along a shelf or against another book, all the way to a more serious bruise that may have removed color from the covers.

Spine roll: The spine has been bent lengthwise and is not at right angles to the covers.

Sticker pull: Discoloration or actual removal of cover color caused by pulling off a price sticker.

Store Stamp or S/S: These often appear on front end papers.

Tape repairs

Warping: Books are misshapen; this may occur from misbinding, poor storage or handling, and sometimes from water damage.

Water Damage: Sometimes visible on covers and often on pages or page edges. Discoloration of tinted page edges may also occur.

Writing: May be on covers, spine, or interior made by a marker, ballpoint pen, or pencil. This may also refer to obliteration of the original cover price as well as rewritten cover prices, owners' signatures and/or underlining.

We have limited our grading to four basic levels — fine, near fine, very good, and good — on a scale of one to ten, good being no more than a two (unless the book in question is very expensive and hard to find, in which case it might rate a four), very good a five, near fine an eight, and fine a ten. Plus and minus symbols are also used. Generally speaking, all things being equal, if you can find a value for a book in (for example) fine condition, then it is a simple matter of arithmetic to determine that the same book in only very good condition would be worth only half as much (remember our scale, five being half of ten). Or, knowing the value of a book in near fine condition, compute the value of one only very good by multiplying the first value by five-eights, and so forth. Remember, this only applies to books from the same edition. You cannot determine the price of a second edition by comparing it to the suggested value of a paperback original, for instance.

Terms That Describe Edition

There are several terms used in the paperback book trade to indicate various types of editions. To the novice, this may be confusing.

Paperback original — this is a book that did not originally appear as a hardcover edition.

First paperback edition or first paperback printing — books issued after the hardcover version (or in pulps and digests).

First edition thus — a book that may be (1) a collection of short stories that never before have appeared together in book form; (2) a retitled book by its original publisher or a new company; or, (3) a reissue of the original book text with new cover art.

First printing — the number of books of a title originally in print. If it sold out, the publisher would follow up with a subsequent number of books, called a second printing, etc. (All things equal, the value of a subsequent printing is much less than a first.)

In general, paperback originals or first paperback printings of a work originally appearing in pulps or digests are more valuable than first paperback editions issued after the hardcover version.

A paperback original (also called PBO, original, or first edition) may be determined by looking on the back of the title page for any previous publishing history. In some cases, the cover may say 'original' or 'first book publication.' Also, check the back of the title page for 1st printing information. The best indication of this is when prior publishing history refers only to a hardback edition. Each publisher has their own way of providing a publishing history, so it is sometimes difficult to determine the printing. For example: Dell and Pocket Books are very good with this information; Gold Medal often gives only the original copyright date.

Courtesy of Black Ace Books

Paperback Auctions

Several of the major dealers regularly conduct mail and telephone auctions of the rarer, more highly desirable paperback books. A typical auction works this way: potential bidders are sent the auction catalog a few weeks ahead of time. The catalog consists of photographs of each book to be sold along with basic information about the book and notes concerning its defects and condition.

Participants may mail or telephone their bids. Mail bids are usually accepted up until the closing day of the auction. Telephone bidders are given the 'current high bid' on each book they wish to bid on. They are required to bid at least 10% above the current high bid. They may phone back as often as they like to check the status of their bids and increase them if they wish to do so. At the stated closing time of the auction, the phone bidding may continue until there is a 5-minute pause without a phone call, then the auction officially ends. There is no way to determine if you have 'won' a book or not until after the auction has ended, because you never know who the final bidder was. Someone may have phoned in just after you with a higher bid.

An option available in some auctions is to allow 'maximum bids.' This means that you authorize the dealer to continuously top existing bids on the book you want by 10% until your maximum is reached. It saves you both time and effort by eliminating the need to make repeated phone calls to check the status of your bids.

As an example: If you call and find that the high bid on the book you want is $10.00, you say 'I'll raise that 10% with a maximum bid of $25.00.' You become high bidder at that point with your $11.00 bid ($10.00 plus 10%). If another caller then bids $15.00, the dealer tops that with your next bid of $16.50 ($15.00 plus 10%). Then another bid may come in at $20.00. Your bid tops that at $22.00. This would continue up to your maximum bid of $25.00, unless someone 'jumped over' your maximum. You could, of course, call back and raise your maximum bid at any time. Of course, if no one went over your original bid, you would get the book for $11.00.

Most dealers will continue to send their auction lists free of charge to those who bid regularly, whether or not those bidders are successful. A fee will sometimes be charged to those who do not bid and wish to use the lists for reference purposes only. Results from the dealer's previous auction are listed in the current auction catalog. Prices realized from most major auctions are listed annually in *Paperbacks at Auction*, published by Gorgon Books.

Courtesy of Black Ace Books

Periodicals and Publications

Black Ace Books
1658 Griffith Park Blvd.
Los Angeles, CA 90026
213-661-5052
Issues a helpful guide, *Vintage Paperback Collecting*, to define collecting terms, what makes a paperback collectible, and how auctions are operated; also includes information about book fairs and other references. Available for $2 with quantity discounts available

Books Are Everything
P.O. Box 5068
Richmond, KY 40475
606-624-9176
Books Are Everything Magazine subscription: $25 US or $36 foreign per year; contains over 100 photos per issue

Dime Novel Round-Up
Edward T. Le Blanc
87 School St.
Fall River, MA 02720-3425
Subscription: $10 for 6 issues per year

Gorgon Books
21 Deer Lane
Wantagh, NY 11793
516-472-3504
Issues annual report, *Paperbacks at Auction*, listing actual prices realized

Paper Collector's Marketplace
P.O. Box 128
Scandinavia, WI 54977-0128
Subscription: $17.95 per year for 12 issues

Paperback Parade
%Gryphon Publications
P.O. Box 209
Brooklyn, NY 11228-0209
718-646-6126
Issued bimonthly, $30 per year, $6 for sample issue; inquire about other available publications

Paper Pile Quarterly
Ada Fitzsimmons, Publisher/Editor
P.O. Box 337
San Anselmo, CA 94979-0337
Subscriptionin US and Canada $12.50 per year

Paperback, Pulp &
Comic Collector
% Zardoz Books
20 Whitecroft
Dilton Marsh, Westbury
Wilts, England BA13 4DJ
phone or FAX (0373) 865371
Issued quarterly, $35 year by international money order made payable to Zardoz Books; Visa and Mastercard are also accepted. For a history of postwar British paperback publishing, contact them for information on ordering their book, *The Mushroom Jungle*.

Paperback Previews
P.O. Box 6781
Albuquerque, NM 87197
505-345-5925
This service informs collectors about forthcoming paperbacks and potential best-sellers; it is not a book club; yearly subscription is $15 for 12 issues with money-back refund on unused subscription if not completely satisfied

Smallbooks, the list for
paperback people
% Pauper's Books
Shawn P. Wilbur/aka 'bookish'
206 N Main St.
Bowling Green, OH 43402-2420
419-352-2163.
This list provides a forum for people with a serious interest in paperbound books to discuss 'paperback culture' with like-minded folks. Some topics will be collecting, archival issues, publishing history, bibliographic queries, bookselling, distribution, and publishing technologies along with may others.

Paperback Shows and Fairs

Paperback shows feature the merchandise of many established dealers as well as the 'once-a-year' collector/dealer. Author and illustrator book signings are a popular feature at many of these shows. The scarce, more desirable books are sometimes bought up quickly by those who are wise enough to arrive early. On the other hand, those buyers who come late, near the end of the show, may often find treasures that can be purchased at reduced prices.

The following listing includes annual shows devoted primarily (or exclusively, in some cases) to collectible paperbacks.

Los Angeles Area: Paperback Collectors Show and Sale; held in March or April in Mission Hills, California. For information contact Tom Lesser (818) 349-3844 or Black Ace Books (213) 661-5052.

Portland, Oregon: Annual Lancecon; held third weekend of August. For information call Lance Casebeer (503) 232-4280.

London, England: UK Paperback and Pulp Bookfair; held in October. For information phone Peter Chapman at (D1144) 0634-53157 or Maurice Flangan, %Zardoz Books, 200 Whitecroft, Dilton Marsh, Wilts, England, BA13 4DJ.

New York City: Annual Collectible Paperback Expo; held in October. For information call Gorgon Books at 516-472-3504 or Gryphon Publications at 718-646-6126.

Cleveland, Ohio: Paperback Book and Collectable Paper Show; held in October. For information phone Dave Bosco at 216-271-5915.

Courtesy of Black Ace Books

Acknowledgements

The editors and staff take this opportunity to express our sincere gratitude and appreciation to each person, dealer and auction house who has contributed catalogs, lists, photos, and invaluable advisor information for the preparation of this guide.

The American Dust Company
47 Park Court
Staton Island, NY 10301

Americana Books
David Moloan
P.O. Box 14
Decatur, IN 46733

Dan Baumgartner
2675 Cloverlawn Dr.
Grants Pass, OR 97527

Black Ace Books
Rose Idlet, Tony Scibella &
Joe McCabe
1658 Griffith Park Blvd.
Los Angeles, CA 90026

Books Are Everything
R.C. & Elwanda Holland
P.O. Box 5068
Richmond, KY 40475

Buck Creek Books
Nancy & Howard Mancing
838 Main St.
Lafayette, IN 47901

For Collectors Only
2028B Ford Pkwy. Dept. 136
St. Paul, MN 55116

Gorgon Books Co.
102 Jo Anne Dr.
Holbrook, NY 11741

Gryphon Publications
Gary Lovisi
P.O. Box 209
Brooklyn, NY 11288

Graham Holroyd
19 Borrowdale Dr.
Rochester, NY 14626

Michel Lanteigne, Bookseller
5468 St. Urbain #4
Montreal, Quebec H2T 2X1
Canada

Jeff Patton
3621 Carolina St. NW
Massillon, OH 44646-3201

Joseph Patton, Rare Books
Box 95
Galax, VA 24333

Pauper's Books
206 N Main St.
Bowling Green, OH 43402-2420

Jeffrey L. Pressman, Bookseller
3246 Ellie St.
Oakland, CA 94608

Raintree Books
Jeff Davis
432 N Eustis
St. Eustis, FL 32726

Roger Reus
9412 Huron Ave.
Richmond, VA 23294

Tom Rolls
3 Sunset Dr.
Greencastle, IN 46135

Marvin Sommer
Box 442, Bridge Station
Niagara Falls, NY 14305

Shawn P. Wilbur
451 Thurstin, Apt. 304
Bowling Green, OH 43402

Zardoz Books
20 Whitecroft,
Dilton Marsh, Westbury,
Wilts, England BA13 4DJ

Book Sellers and Auction Houses

As you will see, each of our listings include a code identifying the dealer list or auction catalog that was the source of that particular line of information. Each code will contain a letter of the alphabet and a number. (See the corresponding name and address file that follows.) You'll also be able to see at a glance whether the given price is an auction price (an 'a' will follow the code to indicate auction) or a dealer's asking price (indicated by a 'd.') Pricing is a delicate matter. Though auction prices of antiques and collectibles in general are usually regarded to be 'wholesale' (there are always exceptions), in the realm of paperbacks, it would seem that many times prices realized *exceed* the recommendations of many price guides. This is usually because the books are vintage and in exceptionally fine condition. Since they are seldom found in such good shape, collectors vie to own them. The simple, basic law of supply and demand applies, and as a result prices often soar.

We encourage you to contact our dealers if you find they have titles you're looking for. If they no longer have the book in stock, ask them to keep your name on file and contact you should they find another copy. If you write to them, please include a SASE for their convenience, and if you call and get their machine, tell them to call back collect. They will appreciate your courtesy, and so will we. We may be adding more dealers in the future, so if you're currently sending out lists of books for sale and would like to be considered, please call.

A1
Allen
10218 Dovercrest
St. Louis, MO 63128

A2
The American Dust Company
47 Park Court
Staten Island, NY 10301

A3
Americana Books
P.O. Box 14
Decatur, IN 46733

A4
Ardent Books
1110 Park Dr.
Ft. Lauderdale, FL 33312
305-792-8845 or FAX 305-467-0959

A4
Attic Books
707 S Loudoun St.
Winchester, VA 22601

B1
Dan Baumgartner
2675 Cloverlawn Dr.
Grants Pass, OR 97527

B2
Ben Franklin Bookshop
Michael Houghton
318 N Broadway
Upper Nyack, NY 10960

B3
Black Ace Books
1658 Griffith Park Blvd.
Los Angeles, CA 90026
313-661-5052

B4
Book Rack
4840 Irvine Blvd., #108
Irvine, CA 92720
714-669-1844

B5
Buck Creek Books, Ltd.
838 Main St.
Lafayette, IN 47901
317-742-6618

B6
Books Are Everything
R.C. & Elwanda Holland
P.O. Box 5068
Richmond, KY 40475
606-624-9176

C1
Cameron's Book Store
336 SW 3rd Ave.
Portland, OR 97204

C2
Chagnon
448 Jackson Ave.
Peru, IN 46970

C3
Don Crawford
3210 Eastlake
Elkhart, IN 46514
219-264-2784

C4
Darby Curtis
229 Broadway
Jackson, OH 45640

D1
Arnie Davis
HCR 72, Box 3418
E Waterboro, ME 04030
207-247-4222

D2
L.D. Dick
P.O. Box 3711
Bartlesville, OK 74006-3711
918-335-2179

F1
Robert Fisher
1631 Sheridan St.
Williamsport, PA 17701

F2
For Collectors Only
2028B Ford Parkway
Dept. 136
St. Paul, MN 55116

F3
A. Forbes
225 Cleveland Ave.
Syracuse, NY 13208

F5
Footstool Detective Books
3148 Holmes Ave. S
Minneapolis, MN 55408-2629

G1
Andrew Geppi
1718-G Belmont Ave.
Baltimore, MD 21207

G2
Michael Gerlicher
1375 Rest Point Rd.
Orono, MN 55364

G3
Jim Goodrich
P.O. Box 3035
Albuquerque, NM 87190

G4
Gorgon Books Co.
102 Jo Anne Dr.
Holbrook, NY 11741
516-472-3504

G5
Grave Matters-Mysteries by Mail
P.O. Box 32192
Cincinnati, OH 45232

G6
Green Lion Books
2402 University Ave. W; Suite 409
St. Paul, MN 55114

G7
Gryphon Publications
Gary Lovisi
P.O. Box 209
Brooklyn, NY 11288

H1
Graham Holroyd
19 Borrowdale Dr.
Rochester, NY 14626
716-225-4879

I1
Island Books
P.O. Box 19
Old Westbury, NY 11568
516-759-7818

I2
Linwood Ipock
301 S Mineral Springs Rd.
Durham, NC 27703

J1
J.&J. Books
P.O. Box 847
Nicholasville, KY 40340-0847

K1
A.F. Kokol
5 Jamaica Ave.
Plainview, NY 11803

L1
Michel Lanteigne, Bookseller
5468 St., Urbain #4
Montreal, Quebec H2T 2X1
Canada

L2
Ed Le Blanc
87 School St.
Fall River, MA 02720

L3
Thomas M. Lesser
19947 Vintage St.
Chatsworth, CA 91311

M1
Robert A. Madle
4406 Bester Dr.
Rockville, MD 20853

M2
Hazel McLane
116 Driftwood Dr.
Elizabeth City, NC 27909

M3
Brian McMillan Books
1429 L Ave.
Traer, IA 61264

M4
Montclair Book Center
221 Glenridge Ave.
Montclair, NJ 07042
201-783-3630

M5
Mordida Books
P.O. Box 79322
Houston, TX 77279
713-467-4280

M6
Wayne Mullins-Books
Rt. 4, Box 367
Wetumpka, AL 36092

M7
Lynn Munroe Books
P.O. Box 1736
Orange, CA 92668

M8
Murder by the Book
1281 N Main St.
Providence, RI 02904

M9
Murphy's Books
3113 Bunker Hill Rd.
Marietta, GA 30062-5421

M10
My Bookhouse
122 S Washington
Tiffin, OH 44883

P1
Pandora's Books
P.O. Box 54
Neche, ND 58265

P2
Paper Treasures
9595 Congress St.
New Market, VA 22844

P3
The Paperback
1500 W Littleton
Littleton, CO 80120

P4
Paperbacks for Collectors
Jim Kovacs
P.O. Box 2121
Borrego Springs, CA 92004
619-767-5589

P5
Passaic Book Center
594 Main Ave.
Passaic, NJ 07055

P6
Jeff Patton
3621 Carolina St. NW
Massillon, OH 44646-3201

P7
Joseph Patton Rare Books
Box 95
Galax, VA 24333
703-744-3572

P8
Pauper's Books
206 N Main St.
Bowling Green, OH 43402-2420
419-352-2163

P9
Pelanor Books
7 Gaskill Ave.
Albany, NY 12203

P10
Popek's
R.D. 3, Box 44C
Oneonta, NY 13820
607-432-8036

P9
Jeffrey L. Pressman, Bookseller
3246 Ettie St.
Oakland, CA 94608
510-652-6232

R1
Raintree Books
Jeff Davis
432 N Eustis St.
Eustis, FL 32726
904-357-7145

R2
Roger Reus
9412 Huron Ave.
Richmond, VA 23294

R3
Rockaway Books
P.O. Box 1508
Woodbridge, VA 22193

R4
Rogofsky
Box 107
Glen Oak, NY 11004

R5
Tom Rolls
3 Sunset Dr.
Greencastle, IN 46135

R6
Wallace A. Robinson Books
R.D. #6, Box 574
Meadville, PA 16335

S1
Science Fiction +
P.O. Box 10696
Rochester, NY 14610-0696

S2
Science Fiction Collectibles
P.O. Box 1715
Rahway, NJ 07065

S3
Bob Scherl
P.O. Box 7124
Van Nuys, CA 91409
818-780-2072

S4
Sebert's Books
P.O. Box 325
Mt. Nebo, WV 26679

S5
Skyline Books & Records Inc.
13 W 18th St.
New York City, NY 10011

S6
Marvin Sommer, Bookseller
Box 442, Bridge Station
Niagara Falls, NY 14305

T1
Tattered Cover Book Shop
2023 Boston Pike
Richmond, IN 47374
317-935-6293

T2
Three Sinister Characters
4523 Browne St.
Omaha, NE 68104

T3
C. Townsend
44 Edgedale Dr. NW
Calgary, Alberta T3A 2R4
Canada

V1
The Vintage Paperback Exchange
8821 Cardinal Ct.
Laurel, MD 20723
301-369-0484

W1
J. Waters
Box 459
Morristown, AZ 85342

W2
Welch
Box 2004
Independence, MO 64055

W3
Mike Weng
5401 69th Ave.
Milan, IL 61264

W4
West's Booking Agency
Antiquarian Books
P.O. Box 406
Elm Grove, WI 53122

Z1
Zardoz Books
20 Whitecroft
Dilton Marsh, Westbury
Wilts, England
BA13 4DJ

AARONS, Edward S. *Art Studio Murders.* MacFadden 50-198. VG. G5d. $3.00

AARONS, Edward S. *Assignment Amazon Queen.* 1974. Gold Medal M 2904. 1st edn. My. F. F2d. $10.00

AARONS, Edward S. *Assignment Amazon Queen.* 1974. Gold Medal M 2904. 1st prtg. My. VG+. W2d. $3.50

AARONS, Edward S. *Assignment Angelina.* Gold Medal 322. VG. B3d. $6.00

AARONS, Edward S. *Assignment Angelina.* Gold Medal 749. VG. B3d. $4.00

AARONS, Edward S. *Assignment Ankara.* 1966. Gold Medal D 1630. 4th prtg. My. VG. W2d. $3.50

AARONS, Edward S. *Assignment Bangkok.* 1972. Gold Medal 3343. 1st edn. My. F. F2d. $10.00

AARONS, Edward S. *Assignment Black Gold.* 1975. Gold Medal P 3354. 1st prtg. My. VG. W2d. $3.50

AARONS, Edward S. *Assignment Budapest.* 1966. Gold Medal D 1653. 1st prtg. c/Barye: gga. VG. P7d. $4.50

AARONS, Edward S. *Assignment Budapest.* 1957. Gold Medal 707. PBO. NF. B6d. $12.00

AARONS, Edward S. *Assignment Burma Girl.* Gold Medal R 2165. My. NF. B5d. $5.00

AARONS, Edward S. *Assignment Burma Girl.* Gold Medal 1091. VG+. B3d. $6.00

AARONS, Edward S. *Assignment Burma Girl.* Gold Medal 560. VG. B3d. $4.00

AARONS, Edward S. *Assignment Cairo Dancers.* 1965. Gold Medal D 1983. My. G+. W2d. $2.50

AARONS, Edward S. *Assignment Carlotta Cortez.* 1963. Gold Medal D 1373. 2nd edn. My. VG+. B5d. $4.50

AARONS, Edward S. *Assignment Carlotta Cortez.* 1966. Gold Medal D 1692. 1st prtg. VG. P7d. $4.50

AARONS, Edward S. *Assignment Ceylon.* Gold Medal 13583. 5th prtg. My. VG+. W2d. $3.25

AARONS, Edward S. *Assignment Ceylon.* 1973. Gold Medal 2888. 1st edn. My. F. F2d. $10.00

AARONS, Edward S. *Assignment Cong Hai Kill.* 1966. Gold Medal D 1695. My. VG+. B4d. $3.25

AARONS, Edward S. *Assignment Girl in the Gondola.* Gold Medal 1398. VG+. B3d. $4.50

AARONS, Edward S. *Assignment Helene.* 1973. Gold Medal T 2681. My. VG+. W2d. $4.00

AARONS, Edward S. *Assignment Helene.* 1959. Gold Medal 863. 1st prtg. PBO. c/gga. VG. P7d. $5.00

AARONS, Edward S. *Assignment Karachi.* 1962. Gold Medal R 2231. My. F. B4d. $3.00

AARONS, Edward S. *Assignment Karachi.* Gold Medal 1237. NF. B3d. $5.00

AARONS, Edward S. *Assignment Lili Lamaris.* 1966. Gold Medal D 1707. 4th prtg. My. VG. W2d. $3.25

AARONS, Edward S. *Assignment Lili Lamaris.* Gold Medal D 2209. My. VG. B5d. $3.00

AARONS, Edward S. *Assignment Madeleine.* Gold Medal T 2461. My. F. W2d. $4.00

AARONS, Edward S. *Assignment Madeleine.* 1958. Gold Medal 799. VG. B3d. $5.00

AARONS, Edward S. *Assignment Madeleine.* 1958. Gold Medal 799. 1st edn. c/gga. My. F. F2d. $12.50

AARONS, Edward S. *Assignment Maltese Maiden.* 1972. Gold Medal T 2635. 1st prtg. My. VG. W2d. $3.50

AARONS, Edward S. *Assignment Manchurian Doll.* Gold Medal D 1778. My. VG. B5d. $3.50

AARONS, Edward S. *Assignment Manchurian Doll.* 1963. Gold Medal 1364. VG+. B3d. $5.50

AARONS, Edward S. *Assignment Mara Tirana.* 1968. Gold Medal D 1920. c/gga. My. VG+. B4d. $3.00

AARONS, Edward S. *Assignment Mara Tirana.* Gold Medal 2378. VG. B3d. $4.00

AARONS, Edward S. *Assignment Moon Girl.* Gold Medal 30355. My. VG. W2d. $3.75

AARONS, Edward S. *Assignment Nuclear Nude.* Gold Medal 2000. VG. B3d. $4.00

AARONS, Edward S. *Assignment Palermo.* 1966. Gold Medal D 1753. c/gga. My. VG. B4d. $2.75

AARONS, Edward S. *Assignment Palermo.* Gold Medal T 2630. My. VG+. B5d. $4.00

AARONS, Edward S. *Assignment Sorrento Siren.* 1963. Gold Medal M 2875. 1st prtg. My. G+. W2d. $3.75

AARONS, Edward S. *Assignment Star Stealers.* 1970. Gold Medal 3249. My. VG+. W2d. $4.25

AARONS, Edward S. *Assignment Stella Marni.* Gold Medal 666. VG. I1d. $4.00

AARONS, Edward S. *Assignment Suicide.* 1968. Gold Medal D 1944. 6th prtg. My. VG. W2d. $3.50

AARONS, Edward S. *Assignment Sulu Sea.* 1966. Gold Medal D 1654. 1st prtg. VG. P7d. $4.50

AARONS, Edward S. *Assignment Sulu Sea.* 1968. Gold Medal D 1967. VG+. B3d. $4.00

AARONS, Edward S. *Assignment Sulu Sea.* 1964. Gold Medal K 1497. PBO. My. VG. B5d. $5.00

AARONS, Edward S. *Assignment Sumatra.* 1974. Gold Medal 3139. 1st edn. My. F. F2d. $10.00

AARONS, Edward S. *Assignment to Disaster.* Gold Medal K 1534. My. VG+. B5d. $4.00

AARONS, Edward S. *Assignment to Disaster.* Gold Medal T 2640. c/Elaine. VG+. M6d. $5.00

AARONS, Edward S. *Assignment to Disaster.* Gold Medal 491. VG. B3d. $4.50

AARONS, Edward S. *Assignment Tokyo.* 1971. Gold Medal T 2390. c/oriental. My. VG+. B5d. $5.50

AARONS, Edward S. *Assignment White Rajah.* 1970. Gold Medal R 2202. 1st prtg. My. VG. W2d. $4.00

AARONS, Edward S. *Assignment Zoraya.* 1966. Gold Medal D 1631. 3rd prtg. My. VG. W2d. $4.00

AARONS, Edward S. *Assignment Zoraya.* 1969. Gold Medal R 2071. My. VG. B5d. $3.00

AARONS, Edward S. *Don't Cry, Beloved.* Gold Medal T 2626. My. VG. W2d. $3.50

AARONS, Edward S. *Don't Cry, Beloved.* 1952. Gold Medal 239. 1st edn. c/gga. Th. F. F2d. $25.00

AARONS, Edward S. *Escape to Love.* Gold Medal 258. VG. B3d. $5.00

AARONS, Edward S. *Gift of Death.* 1964. MacFadden 50-193. My. G+. B5d. $2.50

AARONS, Edward S. *Gift of Death.* 1964. MacFadden 50-193. My. VG. B4d. $3.00

AARONS, Edward S. *Girl in the Gondola.* 1964. Gold Medal R 2054. c/gga. My. VG. B4d. $2.00

AARONS, Edward S. *Girl on the Run.* Gold Medal R 2142. My. G+. W2d. $2.50

AARONS, Edward S. *Hell to Eternity.* Gold Medal K 1455. c/B Phillips. Fi. VG. B5d. $3.50

AARONS, Edward S. *Hell to Eternity.* 1960. Gold Medal 1023. MTI. VG+. B3d. $4.00

AARONS, Edward S. *Hell to Eternity.* 1960. Gold Medal 1023. 1st edn. c/gga. My. F. F2d. $10.00

AARONS, Edward S. *I Can't Stop Running.* 1951. Gold Medal 166. 1st edn. c/gga. My. F. F2d. $10.00

AARONS, Edward S. *Million-Dollar Murder.* 1969. Gold Medal R 2162. 1st prtg. VG. P7d. $4.00

AARONS, Edward S. *Million-Dollar Murder.* 1950. Gold Medal 110. 1st edn. c/gga. F. F2d. $14.00

AARONS, Edward S. *Nightmare.* 1963. MacFadden 50-171. c/J Podwill. My. VG. B5d. $3.00

AARONS, Edward S. *No Place To Live.* MacFadden 50-225. VG. G5d. $3.00

AARONS, Edward S. *Three's a Shroud.* 1959. Gold Medal 896. 1st prtg. c/Barye: gga. VG. P7d. $5.00

AARONS, William B. *Assignment Mermaid.* 1979. Gold Medal 14203. 1st prtg. My. VG. W2d. $3.00

AARONS, William B. *Assignment Tiger Devil.* 1977. Gold Medal 13811. 1st prtg. My. VG+. W2d. $4.00

AARONS, William B. *Assignment Tyrant's Bride.* 1986. Gold Medal 14371. 1st prtg. My. VG+. W2d. $3.25

AARONS, William B. *Assignment 13th Princess.* 1977. Gold Medal 13919. 1st prtg. My. VG+. W2d. $3.25

ABBEY, Kieran. *Beyond the Dark.* Dell 93. VG. B3d. $7.50

ABBOT, Anthony. *About Murder of the Circus Queen.* Popular. 1st pb. VG. M1d. $20.00

ABBOT, Anthony. *Creeps.* Dell 88. G. G5d. $4.50

ABBOT, Anthony. *Murder of a Startled Lady.* 1944. Avon Murder My 25. VG+. B3a #22. $26.65

ABBOT, Anthony. *Murder of a Startled Lady.* 1944. Avon Murder My 25. 1st edn. PBO. VG+. B6d. $30.00

ABBOT, Anthony. *Murder of Clergyman's Mistress.* 1950. Popular 286. VG+. B3a #24. $16.50

ABBOT, Anthony. *Murder of the Circus Queen.* Popular 159. G+. G5d. $7.50

ABBOT, Anthony. *Murder of the Circus Queen.* Popular 159. 1st pb. c/Belarski. VG. B6d. $12.50

ABBOT, Anthony. *Murder of the Clergyman's Mistress.* Popular 286. 1st pb. My. VG. B6d/I1d. $12.00

ABBOTT, A.C. *Wild Blood.* 1951. Gold Medal 208. VG. P6d. $6.00

ABBOTT, Sheldon. *His Second Wife.* 1964. Saber 68. 1st edn. c/gga. F. F2d. $12.50

ABELL, Elizabeth edt. *American Accent.* 1954. Ballantine 75. 1st edn. F. F2d. $8.00

ABELL & GREENE. *First Love.* Bantam 503. NF. B3d. $5.00

ABELL & GREENE. *Stories for Here & Now.* Bantam 914. VG+. B3d. $5.00

ABELL & GREENE. *Stories of Sudden Truth.* Ballantine 19. VG. B3d. $3.50

ABELS & SMITH edt. *Best Stories From Mademoiselle.* Popular W 1111. VG+. B3d. $5.00

ACKERMAN, Forrest J. edt. *Best SF for 1973.* 1973. Ace 91360 SF. VG. B5d. $3.00

ADAMS, Bill. *Bedroom Tramp.* 1962. Playtime 603. 1st edn. F. F2d. $10.00

ADAMS, Cleveland F. *Black Door.* 1952. Popular 426. 1st edn. PBO. c/gga. scarce. NF. B6a #75. $41.00

ADAMS, Cleveland F. *Contraband.* Signet 902. NF. I1d. $8.00

ADAMS, Cleveland F. *Crooking Finger.* 1946. Dell 104. c/Gregg. My. VG. P6d. $8.00

ADAMS, Cleveland F. *No Wings on a Cop.* Harlequin 256. VG. B3d. $8.00

ADAMS, Cleveland F. *Private Eye.* Signet 850. VG. I1d. $3.00

ADAMS, Cleveland F. *Private Eye.* 1951. Signet 850. c/L Kimmel: gga. G+. P6d. $2.00

ADAMS, Cleveland F. *Sabotage.* Signet 936. reprint. VG. B6d. $9.00

ADAMS, Cleveland F. *What Price Murder.* 1952. Popular 456. c/gga. My. VG. P6d. $4.00

ADAMS, Clifton. *Colonel's Lady.* 1952. Gold Medal 230. PBO. c/Ross. We. VG. B6d. $4.50

ADAMS, Clifton. *Desperado.* 1950. Gold Medal 121. PBO. We. VG. B3d/B6d. $6.00

ADAMS, Clifton. *Gambling Man.* 1955. Gold Medal 533. PBO. c/McCarthy. scarce. NF. B6a #80. $43.00

ADAMS, Clifton. *Grabhorn Bounty.* 1966. Ace F 404. We. VG. B4d. $6.00

ADAMS, Clifton. *Renegade.* Badger LW 35. VG. B3d. $6.00

ADAMS, Clifton. *Stranger in Town.* 1965. PB Library 50-824. 2nd edn. c/C Hantman. We. VG. B5d. $3.00

ADAMS, Clifton. *Sundown.* Badger LW 59. VG+. B3d. $8.00

ADAMS, Clifton. *Wild Ones.* Badger LW 52. VG. B3d. $6.00

ADAMS, Douglas. *Hitchhikers' Guide to the Galaxy.* 1981. Pocket 52721. 21st prtg. SF. VG+. W2d. $3.50

ADAMS, Douglas. *Life, the Universe, & Everything.* 1982. Pan 26738. SF. VG+. B5d. $4.00

ADAMS, Douglas. *Life, the Universe, & Everything.* 1983. Pocket 46726. SF. F. W2d. $4.00

ADAMS, Douglas. *Long Dark Tea-Time of the Soul.* 1990. Pocket 69404. SF. VG. W2d. $3.25

ADAMS, Fay. *To Love, To Hate.* 1953. Gold Medal 333. PBO. VG. B6d. $7.00

ADAMS, Henry. *Democracy.* 1968. Airmont CL 164. Fi. VG+. B5d. $3.50

ADAMS, Hunter. *Tiger by the Tail.* 1977. Pinnacle 523-230646-2. Man From Planet X #2. c/Bruce Minney. VG+. P6d. $2.00

ADAMS, Joey. *Curtain Never Falls.* 1950. Popular 285. c/Earle Bergey: gga. VG. P6d. $5.50

ADAMS, John Paul. *We Dare You To Solve This.* Berkley G 454. F. I1d. $6.00

ADAMS, Robert. *Castaways in Time.* 1982. Signet 11474. SF. VG+. W2d. $3.25

ADAMS, Robert. *Coming of the Horseclans.* Pinnacle 662. PBO. F. B6d. $10.00

ADAMS, Robert. *Patrimony.* 1980. Signet E 9179. SF. G+. W2d. $2.50

ADAMS, Robert. *Swords of the Horseclans.* Pinnacle 991. PBO. F. B6d. $10.00

ADAMS, Robert. *Woman of the Horseclans.* 1983. Signet AE 2575. 1 prtg. Horseclans #12. SF. VG+. W2d. $3.00

ADAMS, S.H. *Canal Town.* Dell F 51. VG. B3d. $4.50

ADAMS, S.H. *Night Bus.* Dell Dimer 3. VG. B3d. $6.00

ADAMS, S.H. *Sunrise to Sunset.* Bantam 1107. VG+. B3d. $4.50

ADAMS, S.H. *Tambay Gold.* Dell 20. VG. B3d. $6.00

ADAMS, T. *Hotel Nurse.* Ace D 583. PBO. VG+. B3d. $5.00

ADAMS/DIDELOT. *Many Ways of Death.* Belmont 50-645. VG+. B3d. $4.50

ADAMSON, J. *Living Free.* MacFadden 75-105. VG. B3d. $4.00

ADDAMS, Charles. *Drawn & Quartered.* Pocket 50058. VG+. B3d. $5.50

ADDAMS, Charles. *Drawn & Quartered.* 1964. Pocket 50-058. Hu. F. B4d. $8.00

ADDAMS, Charles. *Homebodies.* Pocket 50-062. VG+. B3d. $5.50

ADDAMS, Charles. *Homebodies.* 1965. Pocket 50-062. 1st prtg. TVTI. G+. R5d. $4.50

ADDAMS, Charles. *Nightcrawlers.* Pocket 50-060. VG. B3d. $4.00

ADDAMS, Kay. *Queer Patterns.* Beacon B 259. VG. I1d. $9.00

ADDEO & GARVIN. *Fortec Conspiracy.* 1969. Signet T 3832. SF. NF. B4d. $2.75

ADDY, Ted. *Dutch Schultz Story.* 1962. Monarch 323. 1st edn. c/photo. Bio. F. F2d. $15.00

ADDY, Ted. *Dutch Schultz Story.* 1962. Tower 44-129. PBO. NF. B6d. $7.50

ADLER, Allen. *Terror on Planet Ionus.* 1966. PB Library 52941. 1st edn. PBO. VG. P9d. $1.50

ADLER, Bill edt. *Letters From Camp.* MacFadden 35-113. c/Hoff. VG+. B3d. $3.00

ADLER, Bill edt. *Robert F Kennedy Wit.* 1968. Berkley S 1634. Nfi. NF. B5d. $4.50

ADLER, Polly. *House Is Not a Home.* Popular G 140. VG. B3d. $4.00

ADLON, Arthur. *Adam's Women.* 1962. Beacon B561F. PBO. Ad. G+. B5d. $3.00

ADLON, Arthur. *Crazy Street USA.* Chariot 127. VG+. B3d. $5.50

ADLON, Arthur. *Her Sister's Husband.* 1963. Lancer Domino 72-698. 1st edn. c/gga. F. F2d. $12.00

ADLON, Arthur. *Love Kitten.* 1961. Chariot 188. PBO. VG+. B6d. $8.00

ADLON, Arthur. *Prince of Poisoners.* 1960. Chariot CB 134. PBO. c/gga. VG. P6d. $5.50

ADLON, Arthur. *Seduction of Denby Martin.* Beacon 787. PBO. VG+. B3d. $8.00

ADLON, Arthur. *Strange Seduction.* Beacon B564F. NF. I1d. $8.00

ADLON, Arthur. *Two-Timing Wife.* 1964. Imperial 701. 1st edn. F. F2d. $8.50

ADRIAN, Jack. *Deathlands: Pilgrimage to Hell.* 1986. Gold Medal 62501. SF. VG+. W2d. $3.50

AGEE, Doris. *Edgar Cayce on ESP.* PB Library 64 122. VG. B3d. $4.00

AGEE, James. *Letters of James Agee.* 1963. Bantam S 2646. 1st prtg. VG. P7d. $3.50

AGNES, Lucy. *Hancock.* 1948. Pocket 520. c/gga. F. VG. B4d. $3.00

AHERN, Jerry & Sharon. *Freeman.* 1986. Bantam 26174. SF. G. W2d. $2.50

AHERN, Jerry. *Battle Begins.* 1988. Dell 20099. 1st prtg. Defender #1. My. VG. W2d. $3.00

AHERN, Jerry. *Earth Fire.* 1984. Zebra 01405. Survivalist #9. SF. NF. B5d. $6.50

AHERN, Jerry. *Overload.* 1987. Zebra 02070. Survivalist #15. SF. NF. B5d. $5.50

AHERN, Jerry. *Prophet.* 1984. Zebra 01339. Survivalist #7. SF. VG+. B5d. $5.50

AHERN, Jerry. *Pursuit.* 1986. Zebra 01877. Survivalist #13. SF. NF. B5d. $6.50

AHERN, Jerry. *Rebellion.* 1985. Zebra 01676. Survivalist #12. SF. VG+. B5d. $5.50

AHERN, Jerry. *Reprisal.* 1985. Zebra 01590. Survivalist #11. SF. VG+. B5d. $5.50

AHERN, Jerry. *Savage Horde.* 1983. Zebra 01243. Survivalist #6. SF. NF. B5d. $6.50

AHERN, Jerry. *Takers.* 1984. Gold Medal 62401. SF. F. W2d. $4.25

AHERNE, Owen. *Man on Fire.* 1957. Avon T 177. MTI. c/Bing Crosby: photo. VG. B4d. $2.75

AHRIMAN, Seth. *Ring-a-Ding.* 1962. France 3. 1st edn. c/gga. F. F2d. $15.00

AINSWORTH, Vera. *Passionate Jungle.* 1966. Publishers Export 1115. Ad. NF. B5d. $5.00

AIRD, Catherine. *Parting Breath.* 1983. Bantam 23668. 1st prtg. My. F. W2d. $4.00

AKERS, Alan Burt. *Manhounds of Antares.* 1974. DAW UY 1124. 1st prtg. SF. VG. W2d. $3.50

AKERS, Alan Burt. *Savage Scorpio.* DAW 285. 1st prtg. F. S1d. $6.00

AKERS, Alan Burt. *Suns of Scorpio.* 1973. DAW UQ 1049. SF. VG. W2d. $3.75

AKERS, Alan Burt. *Suns of Scorpio.* 1974. Orbit 7815. SF. VG. B5d. $3.50

AKERS, Alan Burt. *Swordships of Scorpio.* 1973. DAW 81. 1st edn. PBO. G. P9d. $1.25

AKERS, Alan Burt. *Tides of Kregen.* DAW 204. 1st edn. G. P9d. $1.00

AKERS, Alan Burt. *Transit to Scorpio.* 1972. DAW 33. PBO. c/T Kirk. SF. VG. B5d. $2.50

AKERS, Alan Burt. *Warrior of Scorpio.* 1973. DAW 65. 1st prtg. PBO. c/Kirk. VG. P7d. $4.00

AKIN, Jim. *Walk the Moons Road.* 1985. Ballantine. 1st edn. F. M1d. $4.00

ALAIN. *Yoga for Perfect Health.* Pyramid 659. c/photo. VG+. B3d. $4.50

ALBAN, Anthony. *Catharsis Central.* 1969. Berkley X 1687. SF. VG. W2d. $4.00

ALBAN, Anthony. *Day of the Shield.* 1973. Berkley N 2275. 1st prtg. SF. VG+. R5d. $3.00

ALBEE, George Sumner. *Girl on the Beach.* 1953. Dell 1st Edn 4. PBO. c/Bobertz. VG+. B6d. $9.00

ALBERT, Jay. *Sign Here, Lover.* Beacon 151. VG. B3d. $8.00

ALBERT, Jay. *Stranger in Her Bed.* 1963. Beacon B 593F. PBO. Ad. VG+. B5d. $5.50

ALBERT, Marvin H. *All the Young Men.* 1960. Cardinal C 389. 1st prtg. VG. R5d. $1.50

ALBERT, Marvin H. *Do Not Disturb.* 1965. Dell 2117. 1st prtg. VG. R5d. $2.50

ALBERT, Marvin H. *Duel at Diablo.* 1966. Gold Medal K 1666. 1st prtg. G+. R5d. $2.00

ALBERT, Marvin H. *Lie Down With Lions.* Gold Medal 519. VG. B3d. $5.00

ALBERT, Marvin H. *Long White Road.* 1960. Pyramid G 532. c/M Crair. Nfi. VG. B5d. $3.50

ALBERT, Marvin H. *Midnight Sister.* 1989. Gold Medal 13163. 1st prtg. My. VG. W2d. $3.00

ALBERT, Marvin H. *Move Over, Darling.* 1963. Dell 5859. 1st prtg. VG. R5d. $1.75

ALBERT, Marvin H. *My Kind of Game.* 1962. Dell B 232. 1st edn. De. F. F2d. $15.00

ALBERT, Marvin H. *Outrage.* 1964. Pocket 50-104. 1st prtg. VG. R5d. $3.00

ALBERT, Marvin H. *Palm Springs Weekend.* 1963. Dell 6813. 1st edn. MTI. c/Connie Stevens: photo. F. F2d. $8.00

ALBERT, Marvin H. *Party Girl.* 1958. Gold Medal 808. MTI. VG. B3d. $5.00

ALBERT, Marvin H. *Party Girl.* 1958. Gold Medal 808. 1st prtg. G+. R5d. $3.50

ALBERT, Marvin H. *Reformed Gun.* Gold Medal 856. VG+. B3d. $5.00

ALBERT, Marvin H. *Renegade Posse.* Gold Medal 826. VG+. B3d. $5.00

ALBERT, Marvin H. *Strange Bedfellows.* 1965. Pyramid R 1132. 1st prtg. G+. R5d. $2.75

ALBERT, Marvin H. *That Jane From Maine.* 1959. Gold Medal 846. 1st prtg. G+. R5d. $5.50

ALLRED & KUWAHARA. *Kamikaze.* Ballantine 244. PBO. NF. B3d. $5.50

ALLYSON, K. *Daisies in a Chain.* Brandon House 6082. VG+. B3d. $4.50

ALMAN, David. *World Full of Strangers.* Signet 803. VG. B3d. $4.00

ALPERT & KNIGHT. *Playboy's Sex in Cinema #2.* Playboy 16159. 2nd edn. VG+. B3d. $8.00

ALPERT & KNIGHT. *Playboy's Sex in Cinema #3.* 1973. Playboy 16333. 1st edn. c/Sophia Loren: color photo. F. F2d. $15.00

ALTER, Robert Edmond. *Carny Kill.* Black Lizard. F. G5d. $5.00

ALTER, Robert Edmond. *Swamp Sister.* Black Lizard. F. G5d. $5.00

ALTER, Robert Edmond. *Thieves Like Us.* 1968. Avon S 325. PBO. My. F. F2d. $30.00

ALTH, Max. *Wicked & the Warped.* Berkley G 161. VG+. I1d. $9.00

AMBLER, Eric. *Coffin for Demitrios.* Dell D 201. VG. B3d. $3.50

AMBLER, Eric. *Coffin for Demitrios.* 1943. Pocket 232. My. VG+. B4d. $5.00

AMBLER, Eric. *Coffin for Dimitrios.* 1964. Dell 1303. 1st prtg. My. VG+. R5d. $3.00

AMBLER, Eric. *Coffin for Dimitrios.* 1943. Pocket 232. 1st pb. NF. M1d. $10.00

AMBLER, Eric. *Epitaph for a Spy.* Pennant 3. c/gga. VG. B3d. $4.50

AMBLER, Eric. *Journey Into Fear.* 1960. Dell D 343. 1st prtg. My. VG+. R5d. $4.00

AMBLER, Eric. *Journey Into Fear.* 1943. Pocket 193. My. VG. B5d. $5.00

AMBLER, Eric. *Judgment on Deltchev.* 1964. Bantam F 2781. 1st prtg. My. VG+. R5d. $3.00

AMBLER, Eric. *Judgment on Deltchev.* Pocket 887. VG. G5d. $3.00

AMBLER, Eric. *Light of Day.* 1964. Bantam F 2780. 1st prtg. MTI. My. VG. R5d. $2.25

AMBLER, Eric. *Mask of Dimitrios.* Pan 114. VG. B3d. $7.00

AMBLER, Eric. *Passage of Arms.* 1961. Bantam F 2246. 1st prtg. My. G+. R5d. $1.50

AMES, Delano. *Murder Begins at Home.* 1951. Dell 552. c/Robert Stanley. My. VG+. B3d. $6.00

AMES, Delano. *Nobody Wore Black.* Dell 579. VG+. B3d. $4.50

AMES, Delano. *She Shall Have Murder.* Dell 493. VG. B3d. $4.50

AMES, H.P. *Hell Bent.* 1958. Beacon B 163. 1st prtg. c/gga. VG. P7d. $8.50

AMES, Robert. *Dangerous One.* 1954. Gold Medal 435. PBO. c/Meese. My. NF. B6d. $15.00

AMIS, Kingsley. *Anti-Death League.* 1967. Ballantine U 6114. 1st prtg. My. G+. R5d. $1.50

AMIS, Kingsley. *Green Man.* 1971. Ballantine 02326. 1st prtg. My. VG+. R5d. $2.50

AMIS, Kingsley. *James Bond Dossier.* 1966. Pan X 561. Nfi. VG. P1d. $7.50

AMIS, Kingsley. *New Maps of Hell.* 1960. Ballantine 479K. VG+. I1d. $6.00

AMIS, Kingsley. *New Maps of Hell.* 1960. Ballantine 479K. 1st pb edn. F. M1d. $10.00

AMIS, Kingsley. *New Maps of Hell.* 1963. Four Square 863. Nfi. VG. P1d. $10.00

AMIS & CONQUEST. *Spectrum #2.* Berkley F 950. 1st prtg. F. S1d. $6.50

AMIS & CONQUEST. *Spectrum #3.* 1965. Berkley X 1108. 1st prtg. SF. VG+. R5d. $5.00

AMIS & CONQUEST. *Spectrum #4.* Berkley S 1272. 1st prtg. VG. S1d. $4.00

AMIS & CONQUEST. *Spectrum #5.* Berkley 51595. VG. P9d. $1.50

AMIS & CONQUEST. *Spectrum #5.* Pan 02236. SF. VG. B5d. $4.00

AMIS & CONQUEST. *Spectrum.* 1963. Berkley. 1st pb. NF. M1d. $7.00

AMMONS, Pat. *Faithful to None.* 1962. Beacon B 483F. PBO. c/Darcy. Ad. VG. B5d. $6.50

AMOS, Alan. *Jungle Murder.* 1944. Adventure Novel 24. 1st pb. My. VG+. B6d. $9.00

AMSBARY, Mary Anne. *Caesar's Angel.* 1953. Signet S 1080. Fa. VG. B4d. $2.00

ANDERSON, Ben. *Wild Oats.* 1961. Chariot 178. PBO. VG+. B6d. $9.00

ANDERSON, Chester. *Butterfly Kid.* 1967. Pyramid X 1730. VG+. B4d. $10.00

ANDERSON, Chester. *Butterfly Kid.* 1967. Pyramid X 1730. 1st pb. F. M1d. $20.00

ANDERSON, Chester. *Pink Palace.* Gold Medal 1374. VG+. B3d. $8.00

ANDERSON, Colin. *Magellan.* 1972. Berkley S 2262 c/skull. SF. VG+. B5d. $3.50

ANDERSON, Edward. *Hungry Men.* 1959. Pyramid G 456. 1st edn. PBO. c/Kunstler: gga. F. F2d. $15.00

ANDERSON, Edward. *Spinster & the Boys Next Door.* Barclay 7298. c/photo. VG+. B3d. $4.50

ANDERSON, Edward. *Your Red Wagon (Thieves Like Us).* Bantam 350. MTI. VG+. B3d. $7.00

ANDERSON, Edward. *Your Red Wagon.* 1948. Bantam 350. MTI. c/F Granger & C O'Donnell. We. G+. B5d. $3.00

ANDERSON, Edward. *Your Red Wagon.* 1948. Bantam 350. MTI. F. B4d. $9.00

ANDERSON, K. *Nine Maneaters & One Rogue.* Panther 638. VG+. B3d. $8.00

ANDERSON, M. *Her Mother's Husband.* 1960. Newsstand Library U 134. 1st edn. c/gga. De. F. F2d. $15.00

ANDERSON, Oliver. *Maidens in the Midden.* 1951. Avon 391. Fa. VG+. B4d. $7.50

ANDERSON, Poul. 1963. Pyramid F 818. 2nd edn. G. P9d. $1.00

ANDERSON, Poul. *After Doomsday.* 1962. Ballantine 579. PBO. c/Brillhart. SF. VG. B5d. $5.00

ANDERSON, Poul. *Beyond the Beyond.* 1969. Signet 3947. 1st edn. VG. P9d. $2.00

ANDERSON, Poul. *Brain Wave.* 1960. Ballantine F393K. 2nd edn. c/R Powers. SF. VG+. B5d. $6.50

ANDERSON, Poul. *Brain Wave.* Ballantine 01889. 4th edn. VG. P9d. $1.25

ANDERSON, Poul. *Brain Wave.* 1954. Ballantine 80. PBO. c/Powers. NF. B3d. $8.00

ANDERSON, Poul. *Brain Wave.* 1954. Ballantine 80. 1st edn. PBO. F. M1d. $10.00

ANDERSON, Poul. *Brain Wave.* 1954. Ballantine 80. 1st prtg. G+. S1d. $4.00

ANDERSON, Poul. *Broken Sword.* 1971. Ballantine 02107. c/sgn. NF. B3d. $10.00

ANDERSON, Poul. *Broken Sword.* 1971. Ballantine 02107. 1st edn. Ad/Fa. F. M1d. $5.00

ANDERSON, Poul. *Conan the Regal.* 1980. Bantam 13831. 1st prtg. F. S1d. $5.00

ANDERSON, Poul. *Corridors of Time.* 1966. Lancer 73-505. VG+. B3d. $4.50

ANDERSON, Poul. *Corridors of Time.* 1969. Lancer 74-742. 2nd prtg. SF. F. W2d. $5.50

ANDERSON, Poul. *Day of Their Return.* 1975. Signet Y 6371. 1st edn. PBO. VG. P9d. $1.75

ANDERSON, Poul. *Enemy Stars.* 1965. Berkley F 1112. SF. VG. B4d/B5d. $3.00

ANDERSON, Poul. *Enemy Stars.* 1959. Berkley G 289. 1st prtg. SF. G. R5d. $1.00

ANDERSON, Poul. *Ensign Flandry.* Ace 20724. NF. P9d. $1.50

ANDERSON, Poul. *Ensign Flandry*. 1967. Lancer 73-677. 1st edn. PBO. SF. F. F2d. $7.00

ANDERSON, Poul. *Ensign Flandry*. 1967. Lancer 73-677. 1st edn. PBO. VG. P9d. $2.00

ANDERSON, Poul. *Explorations*. 1981. Pinnacle 48517. SF. VG+. W2d. $3.25

ANDERSON, Poul. *Golden Slave*. Avon T 388. PBO. c/sgn. VG+. B3d. $7.00

ANDERSON, Poul. *Golden Slave*. 1959. Avon T 388. 1st edn. F. F2d. $15.00

ANDERSON, Poul. *Guardians of Time*. 1960. Ballantine 422K. PBO. c/R Powers. SF. VG+. B5d. $6.50

ANDERSON, Poul. *Guardians of Time*. 1960. Ballantine 422K. PBO. VG. B3d. $5.00

ANDERSON, Poul. *Guardians of Time*. 1960. Ballantine 422K. 1st edn. NF. M1d. $10.00

ANDERSON, Poul. *High Crusade*. 1964. MacFadden 50-211. c/Powers. SF. VG. B5d. $4.50

ANDERSON, Poul. *High Crusade*. 1968. MacFadden 60-349. 2nd prtg. SF. VG. W2d. $4.00

ANDERSON, Poul. *Knight of Ghosts & Shadows*. Signet Y 6725. 1st edn. PBO. G. P9d. $1.00

ANDERSON, Poul. *Last Viking #3*. 1980. Zebra 89083. SF. F. W2d. $4.00

ANDERSON, Poul. *Let the Spacemen Beware*. 1963. Ace F 209. 1st edn. SF. F. F2d. $8.00

ANDERSON, Poul. *Long Way Home*. 1978. Ace 48922. 2nd edn. SF. NF. B5d. $5.00

ANDERSON, Poul. *Long Way Home*. 1981. Ace 48924. SF. F. W2d. $4.00

ANDERSON, Poul. *Midsummer Tempest*. Ballantine 24404. 1st prtg. F. S1d. $3.00

ANDERSON, Poul. *Nebula Award Stories Four*. 1971. Pocket 75646. SF. VG+. W2d. $3.75

ANDERSON, Poul. *Night Face*. Ace 57451. 3rd edn. c/M Whelan. SF. NF. B5d. $4.50

ANDERSON, Poul. *Night Face*. 1978. Ace. F. M1d. $5.00

ANDERSON, Poul. *No World of Their Own*. 1955. Ace D 550. NF. M1d. $8.00

ANDERSON, Poul. *No World of Their Own*. 1955. Ace D 550. 1st edn. SF. F. F2d. $10.00

ANDERSON, Poul. *No World of Their Own*. 1955. Ace D 550. 2nd edn. G. P9d. $2.00

ANDERSON, Poul. *Orbit Unlimited*. 1963. Pyramid F 818. 2nd edn. reprint. SF. VG. B4d. $2.75

ANDERSON, Poul. *Orbit Unlimited*. 1961. Pyramid G 615. 1st edn. SF. F. F2d. $12.00

ANDERSON, Poul. *Orbit Unlimited*. 1961. Pyramid G 615. 1st prtg. VG. S1d. $6.50

ANDERSON, Poul. *Orion Shall Rise*. 1984. Pocket 82842. SF. VG. W2d. $4.00

ANDERSON, Poul. *Queen of Air & Darkness*. 1973. Signet Q 5713. SF. VG+. B4d. $2.50

ANDERSON, Poul. *Rebel Worlds*. 1969. Signet. 1st pb. NF. M1d. $7.00

ANDERSON, Poul. *Rogue Sword*. 1960. Avon T 472. PBO. VG+. B3d. $4.50

ANDERSON, Poul. *Rogue Sword*. 1960. Avon T 472. 1st edn. c/sgn. F. F2d. $20.00

ANDERSON, Poul. *Satan's World*. 1973. Corgi 09184. 2nd prtg. SF. VG. R5d. $1.75

ANDERSON, Poul. *Satan's World*. 1970. Lancer 74-698. SF. VG. W2d. $4.00

ANDERSON, Poul. *Satan's World*. Lancer 75-388. VG. P9d. $1.00

ANDERSON, Poul. *Shield*. 1963. Berkley F 743. 1st edn. c/Powers: gga. SF. F. F2d. $12.50

ANDERSON, Poul. *Star Fox*. 1966. Signet P 2920. c/sgn. VG. B3d. $3.00

ANDERSON, Poul. *Star Fox*. 1966. Signet P 2920. SF. F. W2d. $3.00

ANDERSON, Poul. *Star Ways*. 1963. Ace D 568. SF. F. W2d. $8.00

ANDERSON, Poul. *Strangers From Earth*. 1961. Ballantine 483K. PBO. c/Powers. SF. VG. B5d. $5.00

ANDERSON, Poul. *Strangers From Earth*. 1961. Ballantine 483K. 1st edn. NF. M1d. $10.00

ANDERSON, Poul. *Tales of the Flying Mountains*. 1971. Collier 01626. 1st prtg. VG. P7d. $5.00

ANDERSON, Poul. *Three Hearts & Three Lions*. Avon G 1127. 1st prtg. G. S1d. $2.00

ANDERSON, Poul. *Three Hearts & Three Lions*. 1962. Avon G 1127. 1st edn. PBO. SF. F. F2d. $7.00

ANDERSON, Poul. *Three Worlds To Conquer*. Pyramid R 994. 1st prtg. VG. S1d. $5.00

ANDERSON, Poul. *Three Worlds To Conquer*. 1964. Pyramid R 994. PBO. c/Gaughan. SF. VG+. B5d. $6.50

ANDERSON, Poul. *Three Worlds To Conquer*. 1968. Pyramid X 1875. c/Jack Gaughan. SF. VG+. B4d. $3.00

ANDERSON, Poul. *Time & Stars*. 1965. MacFadden 60206. SF. VG. W2d. $4.50

ANDERSON, Poul. *Time & Stars*. 1970. MacFadden 75330. 2nd prtg. SF. G+. W2d. $3.25

ANDERSON, Poul. *Trader to the Stars*. Berkley F 1284. 1st prtg. VG. S1d. $4.00

ANDERSON, Poul. *Trouble Twisters*. 1967. Berkley X 1417. SF. VG+. W2d. $6.00

ANDERSON, Poul. *Twilight World*. 1983. Tor 48561. SF. F. W2d. $3.50

ANDERSON, Poul. *Un-Man/Mankshift Rocket*. Ace F 139. VG+. I1d. $5.00

ANDERSON, Poul. *Vault of the Ages*. 1969. Ace Z 5161. SF. G. W2d. $2.00

ANDERSON, Poul. *Vault of the Ages*. 1978. Berkley. 1st pb. F. M1d. $6.00

ANDERSON, Poul. *Virgin Planet*. 1960. Beacon 270. 1st prtg. c/Stanley: gga. VG. M6d. $12.50

ANDERSON, Poul. *War of the Wing-Men*. Ace G 634. NF. M1d. $7.00

ANDERSON, Poul. *War of the Wing-Men*. 1967. Ace G 634. SF. VG+. B4d. $3.00

ANDERSON, Poul. *We Claim These Stars*. Ace G 697. 1st prtg. VG. S1d. $3.00

ANDERSON, Poul. *World Without Stars*. 1978. Ace 91706 2nd edn. SF. VG. B5d. $3.00

ANDERSON, Poul. *World Without Stars*. Ace F 425. NF. M1d. $6.00

ANDERSON, Poul. *World Without Stars*. 1966. Ace F 425. 1st prtg. SF. G+. R5d. $2.25

ANDERSON, Poul. *World Without Stars*. 1978. Ace 91706. 2nd prtg. SF. F. W2d. $6.00

ANDERSON, Poul. *Worlds of Poul Anderson*. 1974. Ace 91055. SF. F. W2d. $5.00

ANDERSON, Poul. *7 Conquests*. Collier 00907. 1st prtg. F. S1d. $8.00

ANDERSON, Robert. *Tea & Sympathy*. 1956. Signet 1343. 3rd prtg. VG+. R5d. $2.00

ANDERSON, Sherwood. *Dark Laughter*. 1952. Pocket 878. c/T Dunn. Fi. VG. B5d. $4.00

ANDERSON, Thomas. *Your Own Beloved Sons*. 1957. Bantam A 1570. War. VG. B4d. $2.00

ANDERSON, William. *Penelope*. 1965. Pocket. 1st pb. F. M1d. $10.00

ANDERSON & DICKSON. *Earthman's Burden*. Avon S 166. 1st prtg. VG. S1d. $4.00

ANDERSON & DICKSON. *Earthman's Burden*. 1979. Avon. F. M1d. $7.00

ANDERSON & DICKSON. *Other Worlds #30*. 1953. Perma Other Worlds 30. c/Bloch: sgn. VG. B3d. $6.00

ANDERSON & KURLAND. *Ten Years to Doomsday*. 1977. Jove A 4458. 1st prtg. SF. VG. R5d. $1.50

ANDERSON & KURLAND. *Ten Years to Doomsday.* 1964. Pyramid F 1015. PBO. c/Emsh. SF. VG. B3d/B5d. $4.00

ANDERSON & KURLAND. *Ten Years to Doomsday.* 1964. Pyramid F 1015. 1st pb. F. M1d. $15.00

ANDERSON & LEEMING. *More About Marmaduke.* Monarch 267. VG+. B3d. $4.00

ANDERSON/ANDERSON. *Makeshift Rocket/Un-Man.* Ace F 139. F. M1d. $9.00

ANDERSON/ANDERSON. *Makeshift Rocket/Un-Man.* 1962. Ace F 139. PBO. c/Emsh & Valigursky. SF. VG. B5d. $5.00

ANDERSON/ANDERSON. *Makeshift Rocket/ Un-Man.* 1962. Ace F 139. 1st prtg. G. S1d. $2.50

ANDERSON/ANDERSON. *Snows of Ganymede/War of the Wing-Men.* 1958. Ace D 303. 1st edn. My. F. F2d. $10.00

ANDERSON/ANDERSON. *Snows of Ganymede/War of the Wing-Men.* 1958. Ace D 303. 1st prtg. SF. G+. R5d. $2.75

ANDERSON/ASIMOV. *No World of Their Own/1,000-Year Plan.* 1955. Ace D 110. 1st prtg. PBO. VG+. P7d. $9.00

ANDERSON/BRUNNER. *War of Two Worlds/ Threshold of Eternity.* Ace D 335. c/Emsh. F. M1d. $20.00

ANDERSON/BRUNNER. *War of Two Worlds/Threshold of Eternity.* 1959. Ace D 335. 1st prtg. PBO. c/Emsh. VG. P7d. $6.00

ANDERSON/BULMER. *Let the Spacemen Beware/Wizard of Starship Poseidon.* Ace F 209. F. M1d. $9.00

ANDERSON/BULMER. *Let the Spacemen Beware/Wizard of Starship Poseidon.* Ace F 209. PBO. VG+. B3d. $5.00

ANDERSON/BULMER. *Mayday Orbit/No Man's World.* 1961. Ace F 104. F. M1d. $10.00

ANDERSON/BULMER. *Mayday Orbit/No Man's World.* 1961. Ace F 104. 1st prtg. SF. VG+. R5d. $5.50

ANDERSON/BULMER. *Star Ways/City Under the Sea.* Ace D 255. c/Emsh. F. M1d. $15.00

ANDERSON/BULMER. *Star Ways/City Under the Sea.* 1957. Ace D 255. c/Emsh & Valigursky. SF. VG. B5d. $6.00

ANDERSON/NORTON. *Planet of No Return/ Star Guard.* 1957. Ace D 199. F. M1d. $20.00

ANDERSON/NORTON. *Planet of No Return/Star Guard.* 1957. Ace D 199. PBO. c/Valigursky, Emsh. SF. G+. B5d. $4.00

ANDERSON/NORTON. *Planet of No Return/Star Guard.* 1957. Ace D 199. SF. VG+. W2d. $11.00

ANDERSON/SILVERBERG. *We Claim These Stars!/Planet Killers.* Ace D 407. F. M1d. $20.00

ANDERSON/TUCKER. *Earthman, Go Home!/To the Tombaugh Station.* 1960. Ace D 479. SF. VG+. B4d. $6.00

ANDERSON/TUCKER. *Earthman, Go Home!/To the Tombaugh Station.* 1960. Ace D 479. 1st edn. PBO. SF. F. F2d. $8.00

ANDRADE, Wade. *Hot Skin.* 1970. Bee Line 423Z. Ad. VG. B4d. $4.00

ANDREWS, B. *SF Movie Quiz Book.* Signet W 7948. 3rd prtg. VG. R5d. $1.50

ANDREWS, Ned. *Cowdog.* Pocket J 56. VG+. B3d. $5.00

ANDREWS, R.C. *Heart of Asia.* Harlequin 291. G+. B3d. $4.00

ANDREWS & DUNNING. *Star Trek Quiz Book.* 1977. Signet W 7497. 1st prtg. VG. R5d. $5.00

ANDRIOLA & CASSON. *Ever Since Adam & Eve.* Signet 1361. c/cartoons. VG. B3d. $4.00

ANET, Claude. *Ariane.* 1948. Signet 676. VG+. B3d. $5.00

ANET, Claude. *Love in the Afternoon.* 1957. Signet 1404. 3rd prtg. G+. R5d. $1.00

ANGELO, Tony. *Honey Hold That Scream.* 1952. Leisure Library 17. c/Heade. VG. B3a #21. $40.00

ANGELO, Tony. *Satan's Sister.* 1950. Archer Press NN. PBO. VG+. B6a #77. $61.00

ANGELO, Tony. *Sinner's Shroud.* 1950. Archer Press NN. PBO. VG+. B6a #77. $61.00

ANGLE, Paul M. edt. *Lincoln Reader.* 1954. Cardinal GC 23. Bio. VG. B4d. $1.75

ANHALT, P. *Confessions of an Author.* Brandon House 3014. VG+. B3d. $5.00

ANOBILE, Richard. *Drat!* 1969. Signet Q 3933. Hu. NF. B4d. $5.00

ANOBILE, Richard. *Mork & Mindy.* 1979. Pocket 82754. 1st prtg. SF. VG. W2d. $5.75

ANOBILE, Richard. *Star Trek II: The Wrath of Khan.* 1982. Pocket 45912. 1st edn. c/color photo: sgn/inscr. SF. F. F2d. $27.50

ANOBILE, Richard. *Star Trek II: The Wrath of Khan.* 1982. Pocket 45912. 1st prtg. VG. R5d. $5.00

ANOBILE, Richard. *Star Trek: The Motion Picture Photostory.* 1980. Pocket 83089. 1st edn. SF. F. F2d. $20.00

ANON. *Adam & Two Eves.* 1957. Beacon 152. 1st pb. c/gga. VG+. B6d. $16.50

ANON. *Art of Barbecue & Outdoor Cooking.* 1970. Bantam NE 4782. Nfi. NF. B5d. $4.00

ANON. *Bad Men & Good.* Popular 610. VG. B3d. $4.00

ANON. *Book of Grass.* 1968. Grove Press B 166. 1st pb. c/marijuana. VG+. B6d. $8.00

ANON. *Con Girl.* 1962. Midwood 143. PBO. VG+. B3d. $8.00

ANON. *Corrupter.* No Publisher NN. Ad. VG+. B5d. $6.50

ANON. *Devil's Brand.* Holloway HH 170. VG+. B3d. $6.00

ANON. *Flash Gordon #1, Massacre in the 22nd Century.* 1980. Tempo 12963. SF. F. W2d. $4.50

ANON. *Guide to American Waterfowl.* 1962. Collier 419. 1st pb. NF. B6d. $4.50

ANON. *Hunting Dogs.* 1962. Collier 420. 1st pb. NF. B6d. $5.00

ANON. *I Worked for Lucky Luciano.* Avon 568. VG. B3d. $5.00

ANON. *Indiscreet Confessions of a Nice Girl.* 1950. Lion 30. c/Michel. G+. P6d. $2.50

ANON. *Last Train to Limbo.* 1978. Playtime 16106. SF. F. W2d. $4.00

ANON. *Latex Lady.* 1964. Carousel Book 521. PBO. c/gga. rare. SF. VG. B6a #77. $53.50

ANON. *Love Toy.* Novel Library 21. VG. B3d. $15.00

ANON. *Love Toy.* 1949. Novel Library 21. 1st edn. PBO. c/gga. F. F2d. $25.00

ANON. *Madeleine.* 1955. Pyramid 175. 5th edn. c/L Marchetti. Fi. VG. B5d. $3.50

ANON. *Madeleine.* 1951. Pyramid 30. 4th prtg. VG+. B3d. $5.00

ANON. *Marijuana Murder.* 1945. Duchess NN. PBO. VG+. B6a #77. $137.50

ANON. *Movie Trivia Quiz Book.* 1982. Ventura NN. 1st prtg. VG+. R5d. $2.50

ANON. *No-Frills SF Book.* 1981. Jove 0-515-6247-2. PBO. SF. VG+. P6d. $4.00

ANON. *No-Frills SF Book.* 1981. Jove. 1st edn. F. M1d. $7.00

ANON. *Passion Pitch.* 1963. Moonglow MR 1007. Ad. VG. B5d. $4.00

ANON. *Shuttered Houses of Paris.* Venus 1048. VG+. B3d. $5.00

ANON. *Sin Studio.* Nightlight 128. VG. B3d. $4.00

ANON. *Superboy & the Legion of Super-Heroes.* 1977. Tempo 14535. SF. G+. W2d. $3.00

ANON. *What To Tell Your Children About Sex.* 1965. Pocket 50163. 8th edn. Nfi. VG+. B5d. $3.00

ANON. *Wife Trade.* 1963. Moonglow MR 1017. Ad. VG. B5d. $4.00

ANON. *23 Women.* 1952. Pyramid 46. Fi. VG. B5d. $7.50

ANSON, M. *Merry Order of St Bridget.* Brandon House 908. VG. B3d. $4.00

ANTHOLGY. *Bantam Spectra Sampler.* 1991. Bantam. 1st edn. F. M1d. $7.00

ANTHOLOGY. *Adult Version of Dracula.* 1970. Calga Publishers 808. PBO. scarce. Ad. NF. B6a #80. $82.50

ANTHOLOGY. *Adult Version of Frankenstein.* 1970. Calga Publishers 802. PBO. scarce. Ad. VG+. B6a #80. $55.00

ANTHOLOGY. *All About Girls!* Avon 357. VG+. B6d. $40.00

ANTHOLOGY. *Amazing Spider-Man.* 1966. Lancer 72-112. PBO. VG+. P6d. $6.00

ANTHOLOGY. *Amazons of the Asteroids.* Thrilling Novel 17. VG. B3d. $6.00

ANTHOLOGY. *Angry Black.* 1962. Lancer 72-625. Black. VG+. B4d. $9.00

ANTHOLOGY. *Another All About Girls.* Avon 869. VG. B3d. $5.00

ANTHOLOGY. *Anthology: October 1950.* Hollywood Detective V10. VG+. B3a #21. $55.95

ANTHOLOGY. *Apeman, Spaceman.* 1970. Berkley N 1819. 1st pb. c/Lehr. VG. B6d. $8.00

ANTHOLOGY. *Atomic Age Opens.* Pocket 340. VG. B3d. $4.50

ANTHOLOGY. *Avon Annual 1945.* 1945. Avon Annual 2. PBO. Fi. G+. B5d. $10.00

ANTHOLOGY. *Avon Fantasy Reader #7.* 1948. Avon. NF. B3a #21. $18.90

ANTHOLOGY. *Avon Ghost Reader.* 1946. Avon 90. 1st edn. F. M1d. $35.00

ANTHOLOGY. *Avon Ghost Reader.* 1946. Avon 90. 1st prtg. My. G. I1d/R5d. $5.00

ANTHOLOGY. *Avon Mystery Story Teller.* 1946. Avon 86. PBO. My. VG+. B3d. $12.00

ANTHOLOGY. *Bar the Doors!* 1946. Dell 143. PBO. c/Gregg. F. B6d. $40.00

ANTHOLOGY. *Barnabas Collins in a Funny Vein.* 1969. PB Library 62-062. PBO. SF. VG. M3d. $5.00

ANTHOLOGY. *Baseball Stars of 1950.* 1950. Lion 23. PBO. c/Doares. rare. VG. B6a #77. $50.00

ANTHOLOGY. *Beat Generation & Angry Young Men.* 1959. Dell F 84. Beat VG+. B4d. $16.00

ANTHOLOGY. *Bedside Bedlam.* 1945. Quick Reader 137. VG+. B3a #24. $11.00

ANTHOLOGY. *Believe It or Not!* 1962. Pocket 6143. Nfi. VG. B5d. $4.00

ANTHOLOGY. *Best From True.* Gold Medal 99. VG. B3d. $5.00

ANTHOLOGY. *Best of Adam Magazine.* 1962. Holloway House 106. PBO. VG+. B3d. $6.00

ANTHOLOGY. *Best of Adam Magazine.* 1962. Holloway House 106. 1st edn. F. F2d. $32.00

ANTHOLOGY. *Best of Creepy.* Tempo 12125. VG+. B3d. $6.00

ANTHOLOGY. *Beyond the End of Time.* 1952. Perma PB P 145. PBO. SF. VG. P6d. $3.00

ANTHOLOGY. *Beyond.* 1963. Berkley F 712. PBO. c/Powers. SF. G+. B5d. $3.00

ANTHOLOGY. *Beyond.* 1963. Berkley F 712. VG+. I1d. $5.00

ANTHOLOGY. *Beyond.* 1963. Berkley F 712. 1st pb. F. M1d. $8.00

ANTHOLOGY. *Big League Baseball.* 1951. Avon 307. PBO. scarce. VG+. B6a #76. $28.00

ANTHOLOGY. *Big League Baseball.* 1951. Avon 307. PBO. VG. B6d. $18.00

ANTHOLOGY. *Carol, in a Thousand Cities.* 1960. Gold Medal D 1009. VG. P6d. $4.00

ANTHOLOGY. *Cartoon Laffs.* Gold Medal 249. VG+. I1d. $5.00

ANTHOLOGY. *Celebrated Stories Made Into Movies.* 1944. Quick Reader 127. VG. P6d. $7.00

ANTHOLOGY. *Classic Cartoons Playboy: 1957-1959.* Playboy 16158. VG+. B3d. $5.00

ANTHOLOGY. *Combat!* Lion LL 127. PBO. NF. B3d. $5.00

ANTHOLOGY. *Coming, Aphrodite!* Avon 683. VG. B3d. $3.50

ANTHOLOGY. *Comments on the Kinsey Report.* Newsstand 5. VG. B3d. $6.50

ANTHOLOGY. *Crazy Mixed-Up Kids.* Berkley G 12. NF. I1d. $7.00

ANTHOLOGY. *Crossroads of Ecstasy.* Brandon House 6014. VG+. B3d. $6.00

ANTHOLOGY. *Crossword Puzzles Book Two.* 1948. Popular 150. PBO. rare. VG+. B6a #80. $154.00

ANTHOLOGY. *Crossword Puzzles.* 1946. Popular 107. PBO. rare. VG+. B6a #80. $82.50

ANTHOLOGY. *Dames, Danger, Death.* 1960. Pyramid G 504. PBO. c/Harry Schaare. G+. P6d. $2.50

ANTHOLOGY. *Damned.* 1954. Lion Library LL 6. Anth. VG+. B4d. $25.00

ANTHOLOGY. *Dead of Night.* 1957. Dell 1st Edn B 107. PBO. scarce. VG+. B6a #77. $38.50

ANTHOLOGY. *Dead of Night.* 1957. Dell 1st Edn B 107. PBO. VG. B6d. $12.50

ANTHOLOGY. *Detective & Crime Stories.* Avon 21. G. I1d. $7.00

ANTHOLOGY. *Eastern Love.* Crest 199. VG+. B3d. $6.00

ANTHOLOGY. *Eastern Shame Girl.* 1947. Avon 127. 1st pb. VG. M1d. $30.00

ANTHOLOGY. *Fantastic Four Return.* 1967. Lancer 72-169. PBO. NF. P6d. $7.00

ANTHOLOGY. *Fantastic Four.* Lancer 72-111. c/comics. VG+. B3d. $5.00

ANTHOLOGY. *Fantasy Reader #11.* Avon. c/sgn. VG+. B3d. $11.00

ANTHOLOGY. *Fantasy Reader #12.* Avon. VG. B3d. $7.00

ANTHOLOGY. *Fantasy Reader #13.* Avon. VG. B3d. $4.00

ANTHOLOGY. *Fantasy Reader #5.* 1947. Avon. c/Bloch: sgn. VG+. B3a #22. $28.45

ANTHOLOGY. *Favorite Poems.* Bantam Los Angeles 8. VG. B3d. $25.00

ANTHOLOGY. *Favorites Volume 2, #2.* Fabian. VG+. B3d. $5.50

ANTHOLOGY. *Feast of Blood-Vampire.* 1967. Avon S 277. PBO. c/Matheson. VG. B6d. $10.00

ANTHOLOGY. *Fiend.* Playboy 16122. VG. B3d. $4.00

ANTHOLOGY. *Four Fallen Women.* 1953. Dell 667. VG. B3d. $4.00

ANTHOLOGY. *Fourth Book of Crime Craft.* Corgi 717. VG. B3d. $6.00

ANTHOLOGY. *French Love Stories.* 1945. Quick Reader 144. NF. B3a #22. $22.00

ANTHOLOGY. *French Postcards.* Avon 609. VG. B3d. $4.00

ANTHOLOGY. *From the S File.* Playtime 16110. VG+. B3d. $5.00

ANTHOLOGY. *From the S File.* Playtime 16110. 1st prtg. SF. VG. W2d. $3.50

ANTHOLOGY. *Frozen Planet.* 1966. Mac-Fadden 60-229. SF. VG. W2d. $4.00

ANTHOLOGY. *Frozen Planet.* 1966. Mac-Fadden 60-229. 1st pb. F. M1d. $7.00

ANTHOLOGY. *Funny Side Up.* Dell 607. PBO. c/Fabry: cartoons. NF. VG. B5d. $4.50

ANTHOLOGY. *GI Revues: 10 Package Shows.* 1944. At Ease Volume XVI. VG+. B3a #20. $16.00

ANTHOLOGY. *Girl Possessed.* 1964. Gold Star 41. PBO. c/Barton: gga. NF. B6a #80. $73.00

ANTHOLOGY. *Girl With the Hungry Eyes.* Avon 184. SF. G. W2d. $10.00

ANTHOLOGY. *Girl With the Hungry Eyes.* 1949. Avon 184. PBO. c/Ann Cantor. scarce. Fa. VG+. B6a #75. $88.00

ANTHOLOGY. *Girl With the Hungry Eyes.* 1949. Avon 184. VG. B6d. $50.00

ANTHOLOGY. *Goddess of Space.* Thrilling Novel 20. VG. B3d. $6.50

ANTHOLOGY. *Gold Medal Treasury of American Verse.* Gold Medal 312. VG. B3d. $5.00

ANTHOLOGY. *Great Short Stories.* 1944. Quick Reader 106. VG+. B3a #21. $42.50

ANTHOLOGY. *Great Wild West.* Avon 194. VG. B3d. $5.00

ANTHOLOGY. *Gunfight at the OK Corral.* 1957. Avon 774. VG+. B3d. $6.00

ANTHOLOGY. *Gunman's Land.* Lion LL 72. c/Gross. VG. B3d. $4.50

ANTHOLOGY. *Happiest Hookers.* Playboy 16234. VG+. B3d. $5.00

ANTHOLOGY. *Harem of His Men.* Royal Books Giant 26. NF. I1d. $20.00

ANTHOLOGY. *Highlights From Yank.* Beacon 113. reprint. VG. B6d. $18.00

ANTHOLOGY. *Incredible Hulk.* 1966. Lancer 72-124. PBO. VG. P6d. $3.75

ANTHOLOGY. *Incurably Sick.* Avon F 147. VG. B3d. $3.50

ANTHOLOGY. *John Steinbeck: 13 Great Stories.* Avon Short Story 9. G+. M6d. $8.50

ANTHOLOGY. *Just My Luck.* Playboy 16297. VG+. B3d. $4.50

ANTHOLOGY. *Laughs Around the World.* Berkley G 292. VG+. I1d. $5.00

ANTHOLOGY. *Liberty Laughs.* 1944. Dell 38. PBO. c/Gregg. VG+. B6d. $75.00

ANTHOLOGY. *Man Story.* Gold Medal 102. VG+. I1d. $5.00

ANTHOLOGY. *Manhunt.* 1956. Manhunt Volume 4 No 5. PBO. NF. B6a #76. $82.50

ANTHOLOGY. *Masters of SF.* 1964. Belmont 92-606. VG. I1d. $3.00

ANTHOLOGY. *Mighty Barbarians.* 1969. Lancer 74-556. PBO. VG. P6d. $3.50

ANTHOLOGY. *More Stories in the Modern Manner.* 1954. Avon T 77. PBO. Fi. VG. B5d. $3.50

ANTHOLOGY. *My Son, the Doctor.* Gold Medal 1322. NF. B3d. $5.00

ANTHOLOGY. *National Lampoon.* Warner 75-082. NF. B3d. $5.00

ANTHOLOGY. *New Collection of Great Stories.* 1946. Avon Modern Story 33. Fi. G+. B5d. $2.50

ANTHOLOGY. *Now & Beyond.* 1965. Belmont B50-646. 1st prtg. SF. G+. R5d. $2.50

ANTHOLOGY. *Nude Croquet.* 1960. Berkley D 2034. 2nd edn. c/Maguire. Fi. VG. B5d. $4.50

ANTHOLOGY. *Nude Look.* Playboy 16141. VG. B3d. $6.00

ANTHOLOGY. *Official AAF Guide Book.* 1944. Pocket 265. c/photo. VG. P6d. $4.00

ANTHOLOGY. *Omnibus of American Humor.* 1949. Popular 170. Hu. VG. B4d. $4.00

ANTHOLOGY. *Partners in Wonder.* Avon N 416. c/Van Vogt: sgn. VG. B3d. $5.50

ANTHOLOGY. *Peeping Tom Patrol.* Playboy 16125. VG+. B3d. $4.50

ANTHOLOGY. *Phantom Ones.* 1950s. Badger SN 48. PBO. c/Fox. scarce. NF. B6a #76. $50.00

ANTHOLOGY. *Playboy's Girls of the World #3.* Playboy 16172. revised. VG. B3d. $5.00

ANTHOLOGY. *Playboy's Holiday Book.* Playboy 16185. VG. B3d. $6.50

ANTHOLOGY. *Playboy's Music Scene.* Playboy 16190. VG+. B3d. $6.00

ANTHOLOGY. *Pocket Book of Boners* 1943. Pocket 110. 17th edn. Nfi. VG. B5d. $4.00

ANTHOLOGY. *Pocket Book of Short Stories.* Pocket 91. VG+. B3d. $5.00

ANTHOLOGY. *Pocket Playboy #1.* Playboy 16194. VG. B3d. $7.00

ANTHOLOGY. *Pocket Playboy #6.* Playboy 16280. VG+. B3d. $7.50

ANTHOLOGY. *Popular Book of Western Stories.* Popular 156. VG. B3d. $4.00

ANTHOLOGY. *Puzzle It Out.* Avon T 484. G+. I1d. $5.00

ANTHOLOGY. *Rulers of Men.* Pyramid R 1227. VG. I1d. $4.00

ANTHOLOGY. *Saber Reader.* Saber Volume 1-1. VG. B3d. $4.00

ANTHOLOGY. *Saturday Evening Post Fantasy Stories.* Avon 389. VG. B3d. $6.00

ANTHOLOGY. *Saturday Evening Post Reader of Fantasy & SF.* 1963. Popular SP 331. 1st prtg. SF. G. W2d. $2.75

ANTHOLOGY. *Saturday Evening Post Western Stories.* 1951. Avon 311. VG. P6d. $5.00

ANTHOLOGY. *Saturday Review Reader.* 1951. Bantam 913. Fa. VG. B4d. $3.00

ANTHOLOGY. *Sex in Cinema #3.* Playboy 16333. 2nd edn. NF. B3d. $12.50

ANTHOLOGY. *Sex in Cinema #4.* Playboy 16334. 2nd prtg. VG+. B3d. $10.00

ANTHOLOGY. *SF & Fantasy Reader #2.* Science Fiction. VG. B3d. $4.00

ANTHOLOGY. *SF & Fantasy.* Playboy BA 0115. c/Bloch: sgn. VG. B3d. $6.00

ANTHOLOGY. *SF Reader #2.* Science Fiction. VG+. B3d. $10.00

ANTHOLOGY. *SF Reader #3.* Avon. VG. B3d. $7.00

ANTHOLOGY. *Shadow of Tomorrow.* 1953. Perma P 236. SF. VG. P6d. $4.00

ANTHOLOGY. *Ship Ahoy.* Avon 567. PBO. VG+. B3d. $6.50

ANTHOLOGY. *So You Want To Be a Star.* Playboy. VG+. B3d. $4.50

ANTHOLOGY. *Sometime Never.* 1957. Ballantine 215. PBO. c/Powers. SF. VG. B5d. $6.00

ANTHOLOGY. *Spectra Special Editions.* 1992. Bantam. 1st edn. F. M1d. $8.00

ANTHOLOGY. *Stories From Somadeva's Kathasaritsacara.* 1956. Jaico J 39. Fi. G+. B5d. $4.00

ANTHOLOGY. *Stories in the Modern Manner.* 1953. Avon AT 61. VG+. B6d. $6.00

ANTHOLOGY. *Stories in the Modern Manner.* Avon T 61. VG. B3d. $4.00

ANTHOLOGY. *Stories of Scarlet Women.* 1955. Avon T 113. PBO. c/Miller. VG. B6d. $6.00

ANTHOLOGY. *Stories of Suspense.* 1963. Scholastic 487. 2nd prtg. SF. G+. W2d. $3.00

ANTHOLOGY. *Strange Psychic Experiences.* PB Library 52-695. NF. B3d. $5.00

ANTHOLOGY. *Super Science Stories.* Lantern 50526. 1st prtg. F. S1d. $4.00

ANTHOLOGY. *Supernatural Stories #27: Featuring the Ghost Rider.* 1950s. Badger Supernatural 27. PBO. scarce. VG+. B6a #77. $50.00

ANTHOLOGY. *Supernatural Stories #43.* 1950s. Badger Supernatural 43. PBO. rare. VG+. B6a #77. $55.00

ANTHOLOGY. *Supernatural Stories #5: Featuring My Name Is Satan.* Badger Supernatural 5. VG. B3a #24. $18.15

ANTHOLOGY. *Supernatural Stories #55.* 1950s. Badger Supernatural 55. PBO. c/Fox. VG+. B6a #76. $50.00

ANTHOLOGY. *Supernatural Stories #61.* 1960s. Badger Supernatural 61. PBO. c/Fox. scarce. NF. B6a #80. $61.00

ANTHOLOGY. *Supernatural Stories #63.* 1950s. Badger Supernatural 63. PBO. c/Fox. NF. B6a #76. $50.00

ANTHOLOGY. *Supernatural Stories #65.* 1960s. Badger Supernatural 65. PBO. c/Fox. scarce. NF. B6a #80. $61.00

ANTHOLOGY. *Swords & Sorcery.* 1963. Pyramid R 950. SF. VG+. B4d. $6.00

ANTHOLOGY. *Taboo 2.* 1965. New Classics 7N760. PBO. scarce. NF. B6a #76. $48.50

ANTHOLOGY. *Tales of Love & Fury.* Avon 549. VG. B3d. $4.00

ANTHOLOGY. *Tales of the Cyhulhu Mythos Volume 2.* 1973. Ballantine. 2nd pb edn. VG. M1d. $4.00

ANTHOLOGY. *Tales of the Supernatural.* Pan 22. VG+. B3d. $15.00

ANTHOLOGY. *Tales To Be Told in the Dark.* 1960. Ballantine 380K. 1st pb. VG+. B6d. $16.50

ANTHOLOGY. *Ten Nights of Love.* 1947. Avon 128. PBO. Fi. G+. B5d. $5.00

ANTHOLOGY. *Ten Nights of Love.* 1947. Avon 128. VG. I1d. $7.00

ANTHOLOGY. *Terror at Night.* 1947. Avon 110. PBO. c/Mayers. scarce. Ho. NF. B6a #75. $133.25

ANTHOLOGY. *Terror at Night.* 1947. Avon 110. PBO. VG+. B6d. $60.00

ANTHOLOGY. *Time Untamed.* 1967. Belmont B50-781. 1st prtg. SF. G+. R5d. $3.00

ANTHOLOGY. *Times Anthology of Ghost Stories.* 1977. Corgi 10474. SF. VG. W2d. $3.25

ANTHOLOGY. *Twenty-Five Years of Harlequin.* 1974. Harlequin. Nfi. VG. P1d. $7.50

ANTHOLOGY. *Two-Fisted Detective Stories Volume 1, #3.* 1959. PBO. c/gga. NF. B6a #74. $44.00

ANTHOLOGY. *Two-Fisted Detective Stories Volume 1, #4.* 1959. PBO. c/gga. NF. B6a #74. $44.00

ANTHOLOGY. *Unexpected.* 1961. Pyramid G 590. PBO. c/Schoenherr. VG+. P6d. $7.00

ANTHOLOGY. *Various Temptations.* Avon T 109. VG. B3d. $4.00

ANTHOLOGY. *Weird & Occult #1.* Gerald Swan. G+. B3d. $7.50

ANTHOLOGY. *Weird & Occult #2.* Gerald Swan. G+. B3d. $7.00

ANTHOLOGY. *Weird & Occult #2.* Gerald Swan. VG+. B3a #24. $18.20

ANTHOLOGY. *Weird Mystery #3.* 1971. Perma Weird 3. c/Bloch: sgn. VG. B3d. $7.50

ANTHOLOGY. *Weird Show.* Playboy 16138. VG+. I1d. $12.00

ANTHOLOGY. *Western Triggers.* Bantam 200. VG+. B3d. $6.00

ANTHOLOGY. *Zacherley's Vulture Stew.* 1960. Ballantine 417K. PBO. TVTI. VC. P6d. $6.50

ANTHOLOGY. *Zane Grey's Western.* Dell NN Digest 52. c/Stanley: gga. We. VG+. B4d. $8.00

ANTHOLOGY. *10 Great Stories.* 1945. Avon Modern Story 25. Fi. G. B5d. $2.50

ANTHOLOGY. *12 Great Modern Stories.* 1944. Avon Modern Story 20. VG. B3d. $4.00

ANTHOLOGY. *12 Great Stories.* 1946. Avon Modern Story 31. Fi. G. B5d. $2.00

ANTHOLOGY. *13 Great Stories.* 1944. Avon Modern Story 15. Fi. VG. B5d. $4.00

ANTHOLOGY. *15 Short Surprise Stories.* Quick 124. VG. B3d. $6.50

ANTHOLOGY. *20 Great Ghost Stories.* 1955. Avon 630. 1st pb. VG. M1d. $12.00

ANTHOLOGY. *20 Great Ghost Stories.* 1955. Avon 630. 1st prtg. SF. G. R5d. $3.00

ANTHOLOGY. *31 Short Stories From Colliers.* Beacon 249. VG+. B3d. $5.00

ANTHOLOGY/PETTIT. *Love in a Junk/Impotent General.* Ace D 26. c/Saunders. F. G+. B5d. $6.00

ANTHOLZ, Peyson. *All Shook Up.* 1958. Ace D 306. JD. G+. P1d. $10.00

ANTHONY, Bill. *Loose Women.* 1962. Novel Book 5088. PBO. c/gga. F. B6a #74. $48.50

ANTHONY, Evelyn. *Warriors Mistress.* Hillman 134. VG+. I1d. $6.00

ANTHONY, I. edt. *Saga of the Bounty.* Dell S 22. MTI. VG+. B3d. $4.00

ANTHONY, John J. *Marriage, Sex & Family Problems.* Hillman 21. VG. B3d. $4.50

ANTHONY, Piers. *Blue Adept.* 1983. Ballantine 28214. 4th prtg. SF. F. W2d. $3.25

ANTHONY, Piers. *Castle Roogna.* 1979. Ballantine. 1st pb. F. M1d. $5.00

ANTHONY, Piers. *Centaur Aisle.* 1982. Ballantine. 1st pb. F. M1d. $5.00

ANTHONY, Piers. *Chthon.* Ballantine U 6107. PBO. VG+. B3d. $5.50

ANTHONY, Piers. *Dragon on a Pedestal.* 1983. Ballantine. 1st pb. F. M1d. $5.00

ANTHONY, Piers. *Heaven Cent.* 1988. Avon 75288. 1st edn. SF. F. F2d. $6.00

ANTHONY, Piers. *Juxtaposition.* 1983. Ballantine. 1st pb. F. M1d. $4.00

ANTHONY, Piers. *Macroscope.* 1969. Avon. 1st pb. F. M1d. $10.00

ANTHONY, Piers. *Mercenary.* 1984. Avon 87221. 11th prtg. SF. VG+. W2d. $3.25

ANTHONY, Piers. *Nightmare.* 1983. Ballantine 30456. SF. F. W2d. $4.00

ANTHONY, Piers. *Omnivore.* 1978. Avon 82362. 6th prtg. SF. F. W2d. $3.50

ANTHONY, Piers. *Omnivore.* 1968. Ballantine 72014. PBO. VG+. B3d. $5.00

ANTHONY, Piers. *Ox.* 1976. Avon 82370. 6th prtg. SF. F. W2d. $3.75

ANTHONY, Piers. *Refugee.* 1983. Avon 84194. 1st edn. SF. F. F1d. $6.00

ANTHONY, Piers. *Ring.* 1968. Ace A 19. 1st edn. F. P9d. $3.00

ANTHONY, Piers. *Source of Magic.* 1979. Ballantine. 1st pb. F. M1d. $5.00

ANTHONY, Piers. *Spell for Chameleon.* 1979. Ballantine. F. M1d. $5.00

ANTHONY, Piers. *Split Infinity.* Ballantine 28213. SF. G+. W2d. $2.75

ANTHONY, Piers. *Vale of the Vole.* 1987. Avon. 1st pb. F. M1d. $5.00

ANTHONY, Piers. *Var the Stick.* Bantam N 6948. 1st prtg. F. S1d. $4.00

ANTHONY, Piers. *Wielding a Red Sword.* 1987. Ballantine 32221. SF. F. B5d. $5.00

ANTHONY & MARGROFF. *ESP Worm.* 1970. PB Library 63-357. PBO. SF. NF. B6d. $8.00

ANTHONY & MARGROFF. *ESP Worm.* 1970. PB Library. 1st edn. F. M1d. $10.00

ANTHONY. *Silent Man.* 1950s. Cleveland 1573. PBO. We. VG+. B6d. $7.50

ANVIC, F. *His Mother's Arms.* Barclay 7296. c/photo. NF. B3d. $5.00

ANVIC, F. *His Mother's Sinful Sister.* Barclay 7318. VG+. B3d. $4.00

ANVIL, Christopher. *Day the Machines Stopped.* 1964. Monarch. 1st edn. F. M1d. $20.00

ANVIL, Christopher. *Pandora's Planet.* 1973. DAW 66. 1st edn. PBO. VG. P9d. $1.50

ANVIL, Christopher. *Warlords World.* 1975. DAW 168. 1st edn. G. P9d. $1.00

APPEL, Benjamin. *Brain Guy.* 1957. Lion LL 151. 2nd prtg. VG+. B3d. $5.00

APPEL, Benjamin. *Funhouse.* 1959. Ballantine 345K. PBO. c/B Shahn. SF. VG. B5d. $5.00

APPEL, Benjamin. *Funhouse.* 1959. Ballantine 345K. 1st edn. F. M1d. $10.00

APPEL, Benjamin. *Hell's Kitchen.* Berkley G 152. scarce. JD. VG. B6a #77. $46.75

APPEL, Benjamin. *Hell's Kitchen.* 1952. Lion 95. JD. G+. P1d. $16.50

APPEL, Benjamin. *Life & Death of a Tough Guy.* 1955. Avon T 101. PBO. scarce. JD. NF. B6a #80. $55.00

APPEL, Benjamin. *Plunder.* 1952. Gold Medal 266. PBO. c/Barye. VG. B6d. $5.00

APPEL, Benjamin. *Sweet Money Girl.* 1954. Gold Medal 385. PBO. c/Barye. VG. B6d. $5.00

APPEL, Benjamin. *Teen-Age Mobster.* Avon T 162. JD. VG. B6d. $15.00

APPEL, Benjamin. *Teen-Age Mobster.* Avon T 468. scarce. JD. VG+. B6a #76. $44.00

APPELL, George C. *Gunman's Grudge.* Lion 139. G. I1d. $3.00

APPELL, George C. *Massacre Trail.* 1955. Perma M 3013. PBO. c/Schulz. We. NF. B6d. $15.00

APPELL, George C. *Quick on the Shoot.* Dell 892. c/W George. We. VG. B5d. $3.00

APPELL, George C. *Shadow on the Border.* Ballantine 185. PBO. NF. B3d. $5.00

APPLEBY, John. *Barbary Hoard.* Dell 751. c/G Foxley. Fi. NF. B5d. $6.00

APPLEFORD, R. Duncan. *SF Inventing the Future.* 1972. Bellhaven House 303. Nfi. VG. P1d. $10.00

APPLETON, Victor. *Tom Swift & His Flying Lab.* 1977. Tempo 14602. SF. F. W2d. $4.50

APPLETON, Victor. *Tom Swift: The War in Outer Space.* 1981. Wand 42579. 1st prtg. SF. VG. W2d. $4.00

APRIL, Jack. *Feud at Five Rivers.* 1962. Pyramid F 775. 2nd edn. We. VG. B5d. $4.50

APRIL, Jack. *Feud at Five Rivers.* Pyramid 239. VG+. B3d. $5.50

ARAGONES, S. *Mad About Mad!* Signet 4304. VG+. B3d. $5.00

ARCESTE, Jean Lissette. *All Our Yesterdays.* 1978. Bantam 11350X. PBO. TVTI. c/photo. VG+. P6d. $10.00

ARCHER, Jeffrey. *Quiver Full of Arrows.* 1983. Pocket 60408. 5th prtg. My. VG. W2d. $4.00

ARCHER & LAWTON. *Sexual Conduct of the Teen-Ager.* Berkley G 200. scarce. JD. VG+. B6a #80. $27.00

ARD, William. *All I Can Get.* 1959. Monarch 124. PBO. c/gga. NF. B6a #74. $110.00

ARD, William. *And So to Bed.* 1962. Monarch 231. PBO. c/gga. VG+. B6a #74. $61.00

ARD, William. *Babe in the Woods.* 1960. Monarch 172. PBO. c/gga. VG+. B6a #74. $55.00

ARD, William. *Deadly Beloved (Root of His Evil).* Dell 991. VG. G5d. $4.00

ARD, William. *Girl for Danny.* 1953. Popular 502. PBO. c/De Soto: gga. VG+. B6a #76. $36.50

ARD, William. *Give Me This Woman.* 1962. Monarch 269. PBO. c/gga. NF. B6a #74. $92.00

ARD, William. *Hell Is a City.* Popular 756. VG. B3d. $7.00

ARD, William. *Like Ice She Was.* 1960. Monarch 147. PBO. c/gga. VG+. B6a #74. $165.00

ARD, William. *Make Mine Mavis.* 1961. Monarch 215. PBO. c/gga. VG+. B6a #74. $55.00

ARD, William. *Mr Trouble.* 1956. Popular 723. PBO. c/Johnson: gga. NF. B6a #74. $44.00

ARD, William. *No Angels for Me.* 1954. Popular 591. PBO. c/gga. scarce. NF. B6a #74. $53.00

ARD, William. *No Angels for Me.* 1954. Popular 591. PBO. c/Walter Popp: gga. VG+. B6a #76. $36.50

ARD, William. *No Angels for Me.* 1954. Popular 591. VG. B3d. $5.00

ARD, William. *Perfect Frame.* Popular 416. VG. B3d. $6.00

ARD, William. *Private Party.* Popular 569. 1st pb. G+. M6d. $12.50

ARD, William. *Private Party.* 1954. Popular 569. 1st edn. PBO. c/gga. NF. B6a #76. $42.50

ARD, William. *Sins of Billy Serene.* 1960. Monarch 152. PBO. c/gga. NF. B6a #74. $150.00

ARD, William. *Sins of Billy Serene.* 1960. Monarch 152. PBO. c/Maguire: gga. VG+. B6a #79. $55.00

ARD, William. *Wanted: Danny Fontaine (As Bad As I Am).* Dell D 364. VG. B3d. $5.00

ARD, William. *You Can't Stop Me.* 1953. Popular 526. PBO. c/gga. scarce hardboiled. VG+. B6a #74. $36.50

ARD, William. *You Can't Stop Me.* 1953. Popular 526. VG+. B3a #24. $15.51

ARD, William. *You Can't Stop Me.* 1953. Popular 526. 1st pb. VG+. B6d. $15.00

ARD, William. *You'll Get Yours.* Berkley Diamond D 2037. c/Maguire: gga. scarce. VG+. B6a #77. $24.25

ARDEN, Barbi. *Mystery at Indigo.* 1960. Berkley G 405. 1st prtg. My. VG. R5d. $3.00

ARDEN, Leon. *Savage Place.* 1958. Dell F 64. c/C Hulings. Fi. VG. B5d. $3.00

ARFELLI, Dante. *Unwanted.* 1952. Signet 984. Fa. VG+. B4d. $12.00

ARMSTRONG, Chalotte. *Dram of Poison.* Crest 191. VG. B3d/P7d. $4.00

ARMSTRONG, Chalotte. *Innocent Flower.* Pocket 427. VG. B3d. $4.00

ARMSTRONG, Chalotte. *Little Less Than Kind.* Ace G 540. VG+. G5d. $4.00

ARMSTRONG, Charlotte. *Alibi for Murder.* 1955. Pocket 1095. c/L Marchetti. My. VG. B5d. $5.00

ARMSTRONG, Charlotte. *Black-Eyed Stranger.* Pocket 880. VG. G5d. $7.00

ARMSTRONG, Charlotte. *Case of the Weird Sisters.* Ace G 510. VG. G5d. $3.75

ARMSTRONG, Charlotte. *Girl With a Secret.* 1960. Crest 382. My. VG. P6d. $1.00

ARMSTRONG, Charlotte. *Innocent Flower.* 1947. Pocket 427. 1st pb. My. NF. B6d. $15.00

ARMSTRONG, Charlotte. *Lemon in the Basket.* Crest T 1491. 1st prtg. My. VG+. R5d. $2.00

ARMSTRONG, Charlotte. *Mask of Evil.* 1958. Crest 247. 1st prtg. My. G+. R5d. $2.00

ARMSTRONG, Charlotte. *Mischief.* 1951. Pocket 805. 1st pb. My. VG. B6d. $7.50

ARMSTRONG, Charlotte. *Murder's Nest.* 1955. Pocket 1058. 1st pb. My. VG+. B6d. $12.00

ARMSTRONG, Charlotte. *Protege.* 1971. Crest T 1505. 1st prtg. My. VG. R5d. $1.25

ARMSTRONG, Charlotte. *Unsuspected.* 1967. Berkley X 1391. My. VG+. B5d. $4.00

ARMSTRONG, Charlotte. *Walk Out on Death (Catch-As-Catch-Can).* 1954. Pocket 1034. PBO. VG. G5d. $6.50

ARMSTRONG, Louis. *Satchmo.* 1955. Signet S 1245. c/S Zuckerberg. Nfi. VG. B5d. $7.50

ARNAUD, Georges. *Wages of Fear.* Avon G 1332. 3rd edn. VG. B3d. $4.00

ARNAUD, Georges. *Wages of Fear.* Avon 531. G+. G5d. $4.00

ARNO, Peter. *New Peter Arno Pocket Book.* 1955. Pocket 1087. c/P Arno: cartoons. Nfi. VG. B5d. $4.50

ARNOLD, A.F. *How To Play With Your Child.* 1955. Ballantine 105. 1st edn. c/photo. F. F2d. $7.50

ARNOLD, Alan. *Once Upon a Galaxy.* 1980. Ballantine 29075. MTI. SF. F. W2d. $5.75

ARNOLD, Edwin L. *Gulliver of Mars.* 1964. Ace F 296. F. M1d. $8.00

ARNOLD, Edwin L. *Gulliver of Mars.* 1964. Ace F 296. SF. VG. B4d. $3.00

ARNOLD, Edwin L. *Gulliver of Mars.* 1964. Ace F 296. 1st prtg. NF. S1d. $5.00

ARNOLD, Edwin L. *Gulliver of Mars.* Ace 30600. F. P9d. $2.00

ARNOLD, Elliot. *Commandos.* Harlequin 175. VG. B3d. $5.00

ARNOLD, Elliott. *Everyone Slept Here.* 1949. Signet 735. c/gga. Fa. VG+. B4d. $7.50

ARNOLD, Elliott. *Walk With the Devil.* 1952. Pocket 839. c/R Pease. Fi. VG. B5d. $4.00

ARNOLD, Pauline. *Rate Yourself.* 1958. Perma M 4084. PBO. Nfi. VG+. B5d. $3.50

ARNOLD, William. *Sheila's Daughter.* 1952. Original Digest 717. PBO. c/gga. extremely scarce. VG+. B6a #79. $82.50

ARONOWITZ & HAMILL. *Life & Death of a Man.* 1961. Lancer 72-611. Bio. VG+. B4d. $5.00

ARROW, W. *Return to Planet of the Apes #1: Visions Nowhere.* Ballantine 25122. TVTI. VG. B3d. $4.00

ARTHUR, Burt. *Black Rider.* Star Books 23. c/Gross. VG. B3d. $8.00

ARTHUR, Burt. *Buckaroo.* 1950. Signet 782. We. VG+. B5d. $5.50

ARTHUR, Burt. *Duel on the Range.* Berkley G 242. reprint. We. VG+. B6d. $10.00

ARTHUR, Burt. *Killer's Crossing.* 1953. Lion 168. PBO. c/Schulz. We. VG. B6d. $9.00

ARTHUR, Burt. *Return of the Texan.* Avon F 132. We. VG+. B5d. $3.50

ARTHUR, Burt. *Return of the Texan.* Signet 1339. VG+. B3d. $4.50

ARTHUR, Burt. *Ride Out for Revenge.* Avon T 198. MTI. VG+. B3d. $5.00

ARTHUR, Burt. *Thunder Valley.* Popular 425. VG. I1d. $4.00

ARTHUR, Burt. *Two-Gun Texan.* Lion LB 85. PBO. VG+. B3d. $5.00

ARTHUR, Ella Bently. *My Husband Keeps Telling Me Go to Hell.* Signet 1210. VG+. B3d. $5.00

ARTHUR/WORMSER & GORDON. *Drifter/ Longhorn Trail.* Ace D 92. VG. B3d. $4.50

ARTZYBASHEFF, Mikhail. *Savage.* 1951. Lion 64. 1st edn. PBO. c/gga. F. F2d. $10.00

ASBURY, Herbert. *Barbary Coast.* Cardinal C 251. NF. B3d. $4.50

ASBURY, Herbert. *Barbary Coast.* 1957. Cardinal C 251. 1st prtg. c/Hulings: gga. VG. P7d. $3.50

ASBURY, Herbert. *Barbary Coast.* Pocket 474. G+. C5d. $2.50

ASBURY, Herbert. *Barbary Coast.* Pocket 474. NF. I1d. $5.00

ASBURY, Herbert. *French Quarter.* 1949. Pocket 565. 1st prtg. c/Witt: gga. VG. P7d. $5.00

ASBURY, Herbert. *Gangs of New York.* Avon 263. VG. B3d. $4.00

ASCH, Sholem. *Apostle.* 1956. Cardinal GC 38. 1st prtg. c/James Meese. VG. P7d. $3.50

ASCH, Sholem. *Nazarene.* 1956. Cardinal GC 36. c/C Hulings. Fi. VG. B5d. $2.50

ASCH, Sholem. *Prophet.* 1958. Cardinal GC 49. 1st prtg. c/James Meese. VG. P7d. $3.50

ASHABRANNAR, Brent. *Stakes Are High.* 1954. Pennant P 64. PBO. c/C Binger. Fi. G+. B5d. $4.00

ASHABRANNAR, Brent. *Stakes Are High.* 1954. Pennant P 64. PBO. NF. B3d. $6.00

ASHBROOK, Harriette. *Purple Onion Mystery.* Penguin 626. G+. G5d. $6.00

ASHE, Gordon. *Drop Dead!* 1954. Ace D 71. 1st edn. PBO. NF. B6a #76. $45.00

ASHE, Penelope. *Naked Came the Stranger.* 1970. Dell 06297. 1st prtg. VG. P7d. $4.00

ASHE/CHAVIS. *You've Bet Your Life/Terror Package.* 1957. Ace D 221. 1st prtg. PBO. c/Tossey: gga. VG. P7d. $6.00

ASHE/SCHERF. *Drop Dead/Case of the Hated Senator.* Ace D 71. NF. I1d. $12.00

ASHE/SCHERF. *Drop Dead/Case of the Hated Senator.* 1954. Ace D 71. My. VG. B4d. $7.00

ASHMAN, Howard. *Mandrake the Magician.* 1979. Ace 51628. PBO. TVTI. VG. P6d. $3.50

ASHMAN, Howard. *Mandrake the Magician.* 1979. Ace 51628. 1st edn. TVTI. c/photo. SF. F. F2d. $7.00

ASHTON, Blair. *Deeds of Darkness.* Ace D 314. VG. B3d. $5.00

ASHTON-WARNER, Sylvia. *Spinster.* 1961. Bantam F 2228. 1st prtg. VG+. R5d. $3.00

ASIMOV, Isaac. *Alternate Asimovs.* Signet 5370. NF. P9d. $1.75

ASIMOV, Isaac. *Asimov on SF.* 1982. Avon. 1st pb. F. M1d. $7.00

ASIMOV, Isaac. *Before the Golden Age.* 1975. Crest Q 2525. 1st prtg. SF. VG. R5d. $1.75

ASIMOV, Isaac. *Buy Jupiter.* Crest 23828. SF. VG. W2d. $3.00

ASIMOV, Isaac. *Caves of Steel.* 1972. Crest P 2497. SF. G. W2d. $2.50

ASIMOV, Isaac. *Caves of Steel.* Crest T 1659. 1st prtg. G+. S1d. $2.50

ASIMOV, Isaac. *Caves of Steel.* 1955. Signet S 1240. 1st pb. c/Schulz. SF. VG. B6d. $6.00

ASIMOV, Isaac. *Collapsing Universe.* 1978. Pocket 44868. 6th prtg. SF. F. W2d. $4.50

ASIMOV, Isaac. *Currents of Space.* Gold Medal T 1541. F. P9d. $1.50

ASIMOV, Isaac. *Currents of Space.* 1966. Lancer 72-104. 1st prtg. SF. VG. R5d. $4.50

ASIMOV, Isaac. *Currents of Space.* 1953. Signet 1082. SF. VG. B5d. $4.50

ASIMOV, Isaac. *Currents of Space.* 1953. Signet 1082. VG+. I1d. $6.00

ASIMOV, Isaac. *Currents of Space.* 1953. Signet 1082. 1st edn. PBO. c/gga. SF. F. F2d. $10.00

ASIMOV, Isaac. *Currents of Space.* 1953. Signet 1082. 1st edn. PBO. G. P9d. $1.50

ASIMOV, Isaac. *Double Planet.* 1966. Pyramid. 1st pb. NF. M1d. $10.00

ASIMOV, Isaac. *Early Ashimov, Book #2.* 1974. Gold Medal P 2323. 1st edn. PBO. VG. P9d. $1.50

ASIMOV, Isaac. *Early Asimov, Book #1.* 1974. Gold Medal P 2087. SF. F. W2d. $4.00

ASIMOV, Isaac. *Earth, Our Crowded Spaceship.* Crest 23172. SF. VG. W2d. $3.50

ASIMOV, Isaac. *Earth Is Room Enough.* 1959. Bantam A 1978. 1st prtg. SF. VG. R5d. $3.00

ASIMOV, Isaac. *Earth Is Room Enough.* Crest Q 2801. SF. VG+. W2d. $3.75

ASIMOV, Isaac. *End of Eternity.* Lancer 72107. 1st prtg. G+. S1d. $4.00

ASIMOV, Isaac. *End of Eternity.* 1958. Signet S 1493. SF. VG. B5d. $4.00

ASIMOV, Isaac. *Fantastic Voyage.* 1966. Bantam H 3177. 3rd prtg. MTI. SF. G. W2d. $3.00

ASIMOV, Isaac. *Foundation & Empire.* 1966. Avon N 305. 18th prtg. SF. F. W2d. $3.50

ASIMOV, Isaac. *Foundation.* Avon 23168. 23rd prtg. SF. F. W2d. $3.25

ASIMOV, Isaac. *From Earth to Heaven.* 1972. Avon W 338. 1st prtg. Nfi. G+. W2d. $2.75

ASIMOV, Isaac. *From Earth to Heaven.* 1972. Avon 00338. SF. F. W2d. $4.00

ASIMOV, Isaac. *Gods Themselves.* 1972. Crest X 2883. SF. F. W2d. $3.75

ASIMOV, Isaac. *Hugo Winners, Volume #1.* 1973. Crest M 1811. 1st prtg. SF. G+. R5d. $1.00

ASIMOV, Isaac. *Hugo Winners, Volume #1.* Crest 2315. c/Bloch: sgn. VG. B3d. $4.00

ASIMOV, Isaac. *I, Robot.* 1970. Crest M 1966. 1st prtg. VG. P7d. $4.00

ASIMOV, Isaac. *I, Robot.* Crest Q 2829. SF. F. W2d. $5.00

ASIMOV, Isaac. *I, Robot.* 1970. Crest T 1453. 1st prtg. SF. G+. R5d. $1.25

ASIMOV, Isaac. *I, Robot.* 1956. Signet S 1282. c/Schulz. SF. G+. B5d. $4.50

ASIMOV, Isaac. *I, Robot.* 1956. Signet S 1282. 1st pb. c/Schulz. SF. VG. B6d. $6.00

ASIMOV, Isaac. *Lucky Star & the Rings of Saturn.* Crest 23462. SF. F. W2d. $4.75

ASIMOV, Isaac. *Man Who Upset the Universe.* 1955. Ace D 125. c/gga. SF. VG. B5d. $6.00

ASIMOV, Isaac. *Man Who Upset the Universe.* 1955. Ace D 125. F. M1d. $15.00

ASIMOV, Isaac. *Man Who Upset the Universe.* 1955. Ace D 125. SF. G+. W2d. $4.25

ASIMOV, Isaac. *Man Who Upset the Universe.* 1963. Ace F 216. VG. I1d. $4.00

ASIMOV, Isaac. *Martian Way.* Gold Medal 1914. NF. P9d. $1.50

ASIMOV, Isaac. *Martian Way.* Signet S 1433. VG+. I1d. $5.00

ASIMOV, Isaac. *Martian Way.* 1957. Signet. 1st pb. F. M1d. $12.00

ASIMOV, Isaac. *More Tales of the Black Widowers.* Crest 2-3375-8. 1st prtg. VG. R5d. $1.50

ASIMOV, Isaac. *Naked Sun.* 1958. Bantam A 1731. 1st pb. F. M1d. $12.00

ASIMOV, Isaac. *Nightfall & Other Stories.* Crest M 1486. 1st prtg. G. S1d. $2.00

ASIMOV, Isaac. *Nine Tomorrows.* Crest 02688. SF. F. W2d. $5.00

ASIMOV, Isaac. *Of Time & Space & Other Things.* 1975. Disc 24166. SF. VG. W2d. $3.25

ASIMOV, Isaac. *Of Time & Space & Other Things.* 1968. Lancer 74-930. Nfi. VG+. B5d. $5.00

ASIMOV, Isaac. *Opus 100.* 1970. Dell 6695. SF. VG. W2d. $5.75

ASIMOV, Isaac. *Pebble in the Sky.* Crest T 1567. 1st prtg. G+. S1d. $2.50

ASIMOV, Isaac. *Pebble in the Sky.* 1971. Crest T 1567. SF. VG. W2d. $3.50

ASIMOV, Isaac. *Rebellious Stars.* 1954. Ace D 84. SF. G. W2d. $7.00

ASIMOV, Isaac. *Rest of the Robots.* 1966. Pyramid. 1st pb. NF. M1d. $8.00

ASIMOV, Isaac. *Robots of Dawn.* 1984. Ballantine 31571. 1st prtg. SF. VG+. R5d. $2.25

ASIMOV, Isaac. *Second Foundation.* 1972. Avon N 306. 14th prtg. SF. VG+. W2d. $3.00

ASIMOV, Isaac. *Second Foundation.* 1967. Avon S237. 4th edn. SF. VG+. B5d. $3.50

ASIMOV, Isaac. *Second Foundation.* Avon T 232. VG+. B3d. $4.50

ASIMOV, Isaac. *Second Foundation.* 1983. Ballantine 30901. SF. F. W2d. $4.50

ASIMOV, Isaac. *Second Foundation: Galactic Empire.* Avon. 1st pb. G+. M1d. $4.00

ASIMOV, Isaac. *Soviet SF & More Soviet SF.* 1971-1972. Collier. 2 volumes. F. M1d. $10.00

ASIMOV, Isaac. *Space Shuttles #7.* 1987. Signet AE 5017. SF. VG. W2d. $3.75

ASIMOV, Isaac. *Stars Like Dust.* 1963. Lancer 74-815. c/E Emsh. SF. VG. B5d. $4.00

ASIMOV, Isaac. *Through a Glass Clearly.* 1978. . 42391. SF. F. W2d. $5.50

ASIMOV, Isaac. *TV 2000.* 1982. Gold Medal 24493. SF. VG+. W2d. $3.25

ASIMOV, Isaac. *Witches #2.* 1984. Signet AE 2882. SF. VG. W2d. $3.50

ASIMOV, Isaac. *2nd Foundation: Galactic Empire.* Avon T 232. c/R Powers. SF. G+. B5d. $3.00

ASIMOV, Issac. *1000-Year Plan.* Ace D 110. F. M1d. $15.00

ASIMOV/DEE. *Rebellious Stars/Earth Gone Mad.* 1954. Ace D 84. PBO. c/Valigursky. SF. G+. B5d. $7.50

ASIMOV/DEE. *Rebellious Stars/Earth Gone Mad.* 1954. Ace D 84. SF. G. W2d. $4.00

ASIMOV/DEE. *Rebellious Stars/Earth Gone Mad.* 1954. Ace D 84. 1st prtg. PBO. c/gga. VG. P7d. $9.00

ASPIRIN, Robert. *Another Fine Myth.* 1984. Ace 02360. 3rd prtg. SF. F. W2d. $4.25

ASPIRIN, Robert. *Face of Chaos.* 1983. Ace 22549. SF. VG+. W2d. $3.25

ASPIRIN, Robert. *Myth Conceptions.* 1985. Ace 55519. 2nd prtg. SF. F. W2d. $3.75

ASPIRIN, Robert. *Shadows of Sanctuary.* Ace 76027. c/sgn. VG. B3d. $5.00

ASPIRIN & ABBEY. *Thieves' World Book #1: Thieves' World.* 1982. Ace 80591. 27th prtg. SF. VG+. W2d. $3.75

ASPIRIN & ABBEY. *Thieves' World Book #11: Uneasy Alliances.* 1988. Ace 80610. 1st prtg. SF. F. W2d. $4.75

ASPIRIN & ABBEY. *Thieves' World Book #12: Stealer's Sky.* 1989. Ace 80612. SF. F. W2d. $4.75

ASPIRIN & ABBEY. *Thieves' World Book #6: Wings of Omen.* 1986. Ace 80596. 8th prtg. SF. F. W2d. $4.75

ASTOR, G. *Charge Is Rape.* Playboy 16267. VG+. B3d. $5.00

ASWELL, James. *Midsummer Fires.* 1950. Avon 247. VG+. B3d. $5.00

ATHAS, Daphne. *Fourth World.* 1957. Pyramid G 267. 1st edn. PBO. F. F2d. $7.00

ATIYAH, Edward. *Murder, My Love.* Avon 786. My. VG. B5d. $4.00

ATKINSON, D.T. *Magic, Myth & Medicine.* 1958. Premier D 69. Nfi. VG. B5d. $3.00

ATKINSON, O. *Her Life To Live.* Popular 307. c/Bergey. VG. B3d. $4.00

ATLEE, Philip. *Death Bird Contract.* Gold Medal D 1632. PBO. c/Thurston. My. VG. B5d. $3.50

ATLEE, Philip. *Death Bird Contract.* 1966. Gold Medal D 1632. PBO. VG+. B6d. $7.50

ATLEE, Philip. *Green Wound Contract.* Gold Medal D 1780. My. VG. B5d. $3.50

ATLEE, Philip. *Green Wound Contract.* 1963. Gold Medal D 1780. My. G+. W2d. $3.00

ATLEE, Philip. *Ill Wind Contract.* Gold Medal R 2087. PBO. My. VG. B5d. $3.00

ATLEE, Philip. *Irish Beauty Contract.* 1966. Gold Medal T 2628. My. NF. B4d. $2.75

ATLEE, Philip. *Kiwi Contract.* 1972. Gold Medal T 2530. My. VG+. B5d. $4.00

ATLEE, Philip. *Naked Year (Inheritors).* Lion 188. VG. B3d. $6.00

ATLEE, Philip. *Silken Baroness.* 1964. Gold Medal K 1489. c/gga. My. VG+. B4d. $4.00

ATLEE, Philip. *Silken Baroness.* 1964. Gold Medal K 1489. 1st prtg. PBO. c/Bob McGinnis: gga. VG. P6d. $3.75

ATLEE, Philip. *Skeleton Coast Contract.* Gold Medal D 1977. PBO. My. VG+. B5d. $5.00

ATLEE, Philip. *Spice Route Contract.* 1973. Gold Medal T 2697. My. G+. W2d. $3.00

ATLEE, Philip. *Star Ruby Contract.* Gold Medal D 1770. PBO. My. VG. B5d. $4.50

ATLEE, Philip. *Trembling Earth Contract.* Gold Medal R 2181. My. VG+. B5d. $4.00

AUCHINCLOSS, Louis. *Law for the Lion.* 1965. Lancer 73-437. 1st pb. c/Engel. NF. B6d. $7.50

AUCHINCLOSS, Louis. *Sybil.* 1953. Signet 1004. c/S Zuckerberg. Fi. VG. B5d. $4.00

AUGUST, John. *Advance Agent.* Popular 133. VG+. G5d. $10.00

AUGUST, John. *Advance Agent.* 1947. Popular 133. 1st pb. My. NF. B6d. $18.00

AUGUST, John. *Novice Sex Queen.* Brandon House. VG+. B3d. $5.00

AUGUST, John. *Sex in the Shadows.* Nite-Lite 203. NF. B3d. $5.00

AUSTEN, Jane. *Sense & Sensibility.* 1961. Washington Square W 151. Fi. VG. B5d. $2.50

AUSTIN, A. *Greatest Lover in World.* Hillman 110. VG+. B3d. $6.00

AUSTIN, G. *Texan-Killer.* 1955. Perma M 3001. We. B3d/B5d. $4.00

AUSTIN, Martin. *All Hungry Young Bodies.* 1967. PB Library 53-524. 1st edn. c/gga: photo. F. F2d. $10.00

AVALLONE, Michael. *All the Way.* Midwood Y 184. VG+. M6d. $8.50

AVALLONE, Michael. *And Sex Walks In.* 1963. Beacon G 679F. 1st edn. Ad. VG. F2d. $15.00

AVALLONE, Michael. *Bedroom Bolero.* 1963. Belmont 90-276. 1st edn. De. F. F2d. $20.00

AVALLONE, Michael. *Birds of a Feather Affair (Girl From UNCLE).* 1966. Signet D 3012. 1st edn. My. F. F2d. $12.50

AVALLONE, Michael. *Birds of a Feather Affair.* 1966. Signet D 3012. TVTI. c/Stephanie Powers. VG+. B4d. $3.25

AVALLONE, Michael. *Blazing Affair (Girl From UNCLE).* 1966. Signet D 3042. 1st edn. My. F. F2d. $12.50

AVALLONE, Michael. *Blazing Affair.* 1966. Signet D 3042. TVTI. c/photo. VG+. B4d. $3.25

AVALLONE, Michael. *Boris Karloff, Tales of the Frightened.* 1973. Pyramid N 3282. Ho. VG. B4d. $2.25

AVALLONE, Michael. *Case of the Bouncing Betty/Case of the Violent Virgin.* 1957. Ace D 259. 1st edn. My. VG. F2d. $25.00

AVALLONE, Michael. *Coffin Things.* 1970. Lancer 74-636. 1st prtg. c/photo. VG. P7d. $5.00

AVALLONE, Michael. *Craghold Legacy.* 1971. Beagle 94105. 1st edn. Go. F. F2d. $10.00

AVALLONE, Michael. *Crazy Mixed-Up Corpse.* 1959. Gold Medal 718. 1st edn. c/gga. De. F. F2d. $14.50

AVALLONE, Michael. *Crazy Mixed-Up Corpse.* Gold Medal 718. G. G5d. $4.00

AVALLONE, Michael. *Darkening Willows.* 1965. PB Library 52-881. 1st edn. c/sgn & inscr to fan in 1972. Go/Th. F. F2d. $17.00

AVALLONE, Michael. *Darkening Willows.* 1965. PB Library 52-881. 1st edn. Go. F. F2d. $13.00

AVALLONE, Michael. *Daughter of Darkness.* 1966. Signet 2967. 1st edn. Go. F. F2d. $10.00

AVALLONE, Michael. *Dead Game.* Perma M 3012. VG+. B3d. $7.00

AVALLONE, Michael. *Death Dives Deep.* 1971. Signet 4490. 1st edn. My. F. F2d. $10.00

AVALLONE, Michael. *Doctor's Wife.* 1963. Beacon B626F. 1st edn. Ad. F. F2d. $25.00

AVALLONE, Michael. *Doctors.* 1970. Popular 08115. 1st prtg. VG. R5d. $2.00

AVALLONE, Michael. *Fallen Angel.* 1974. Warner 75676. Satan Sleuth #1. SF. G+. W2d. $2.50

AVALLONE, Michael. *February Doll Murders.* 1967. Signet P 3152. PBO. VG. B6d. $3.50

AVALLONE, Michael. *Felony Squad.* Popular 60-8036. My. VG. B5d. $4.00

AVALLONE, Michael. *Flight Hostess Rogers.* 1962. Midwood 168. 1st edn. My. F. F2d. $30.00

AVALLONE, Michael. *Girl From UNCLE #2.* 1966. Signet D 3042. PBO. TVTI. c/photo. VG+. P6d. $3.50

AVALLONE, Michael. *Girl in the Cockpit.* 1972. Curtis 7261. PBO. VG+. B6d. $7.00

AVALLONE, Michael. *Girls in Television.* 1974. Ace 28914. 1st prtg. My. G+. R5d. $1.50

AVALLONE, Michael. *Gothic Sampler.* 1966. Award 199. 1st edn. Hu. F. F2d. $10.00

AVALLONE, Michael. *Haunted Hall.* 1970. Curtis 05004. 1st prtg. TVTI. My. G+. R5d. $1.75

AVALLONE, Michael. *Hornet's Nest.* Popular 08130. MTI. VG. B3d. $4.50

AVALLONE, Michael. *Hornet's Nest.* Popular 08130. 1st edn. c/sgn: photo. My. F. F2d. $15.00

AVALLONE, Michael. *Hornets' Nest.* Popular 08130. PBO. MTI. NF. B6d. $10.00

AVALLONE, Michael. *Horrible Man.* Curtis 07220. 1st prtg. My. G+. R5d. $1.50

AVALLONE, Michael. *Kaleidoscope.* 1966. Popular. 1st edn. My. F. F2d. $12.00

AVALLONE, Michael. *Keith the Hero.* 1970. Curtis 05005. 1st edn. TVTI. c/photo. My. F. F2d. $10.00

AVALLONE, Michael. *Kill Quick or Die.* 1971. Pinnacle P011N. 1st edn. My. F. F2d. $10.00

AVALLONE, Michael. *Krakatoa, East of Java.* 1969. Signet 3797. 1st edn. My. F. F2d. $15.00

AVALLONE, Michael. *Krakatoa, East of Jave.* Signet 3797. MTI. VG. B3d. $4.50

AVALLONE, Michael. *Last Escape.* 1970. Popular 8102. 1st edn. c/photo. My. F. F2d. $12.00

AVALLONE, Michael. *Little Black Book.* 1961. Midwood Y 135. PBO. c/Rader: gga. G+. B6d. $4.50

AVALLONE, Michael. *Little Miss Murder.* 1971. Signet T 4616. c/gga. My. VG+. B4d. $2.00

AVALLONE, Michael. *Lust Is No Lady.* 1964. Belmont 90-318. 1st edn. My. NF. F2d. $25.00

AVALLONE, Michael. *Man From Avon.* 1967. Avon G 1307. 1st edn. My. F. F2d. $20.00

AVALLONE, Michael. *Man From UNCLE.* Ace G 553. PBO. TVTI. VG. M6d. $6.50

AVALLONE, Michael. *Man From UNCLE.* 1965. Ace G 553. TVTI. c/sgn. VG. B4d. $8.00

AVALLONE, Michael. *Mannix.* 1968. Popular 60-2256. 1st prtg. TVTI. VG+. R5d. $6.00

AVALLONE, Michael. *Mannix.* Popular 60-2256. PBO. TVTI. VG. M6d. $5.00

AVALLONE, Michael. *Meanwhile Back at the Morgue.* 1960. Gold Medal 1024. 1st edn. My. NF. F2d. $12.00

AVALLONE, Michael. *Missing!* 1969. Signet T 3741. PBO. VG+. M6d. $5.00

AVALLONE, Michael. *Missing!* 1969. Signet T 3741. 1st edn. My. F. F2d. $10.00

AVALLONE, Michael. *Night Walker.* 1964. Award 124. 1st edn. scarce. Ho. F. F2d. $25.00

AVALLONE, Michael. *One More Time.* 1970. Popular 8142. c/photos. Th. F. F2d. $10.00

AVALLONE, Michael. *Satan Sleuth.* 1975. PB Library 75-678. PBO. VG. B6d. $7.50

AVALLONE, Michael. *Seacliffe.* 1968. Signet 3357. 1st edn. My. F. F2d. $6.00

AVALLONE, Michael. *Sex Kitten.* 1962. Midwood F 189. 1st edn. Ad. F. F2d. $25.00

AVALLONE, Michael. *Shock Corridor.* 1963. Belmont L 92-570. 1st edn. My. F. F2d. $15.00

AVALLONE, Michael. *Shock Corridor.* Belmont 92-570. PBO. VG. B3d. $5.50

AVALLONE, Michael. *Shoot It Again, Sam.* Curtis 07203. c/sgn. VG. B3d. $6.00

AVALLONE, Michael. *Silent, Silken Shadows.* 1965. PB Library 52-820. 1st edn. c/sgn & inscr to fan in 1972. Go/Th. F. F2d. $17.00

AVALLONE, Michael. *Silent Silken Shadows.* 1965. PB Library 52-820. 1st edn. Go. F. F2d. $10.00

AVALLONE, Michael. *Spitting Image.* 1954. Perma 289. 1st edn. My. F. F2d. $20.00

AVALLONE, Michael. *Stag Stripper.* Midwood 132. PBO. VG. B3d. $10.00

AVALLONE, Michael. *Station Six-Sahara.* 1964. Popular PC 1042. 1st edn. MTI. HA. F. F2d. $12.00

AVALLONE, Michael. *Tales of the Frightened.* Belmont 50-736. 2nd prtg. VG. B3d. $4.50

AVALLONE, Michael. *Tales of the Frightened.* Belmont 90-297. PBO. VG+. M6d. $7.50

AVALLONE, Michael. *Tales of the Frightened.* 1963. Belmont 90-297. PBO. SF. F. M3d. $12.00

AVALLONE, Michael. *Terror in the Sun (Hawaii Five-O).* Signet P 3994. G+. G5d. $4.50

AVALLONE, Michael. *Terror in the Sun.* 1969. Signet P 3994. 1st prtg. VG. R5d. $5.00

AVALLONE, Michael. *There Is Something About a Dame.* 1963. Belmont 90-293. 1st edn. c/photo. scarce. De. F. F2d. $20.00

AVALLONE, Michael. *Thousand Coffin Affair.* 1965. Ace G 553. Man From UNCLE #1. NF. G5d. $6.00

AVALLONE, Michael. *Thousand Coffins Affair.* 1965. Ace G 553. 1st edn. My. F. F2d. $9.00

AVALLONE, Michael. *Thousand Coffins Affair.* 1965. Ace G 553. 1st prtg. VG. R5d. $3.00

AVALLONE, Michael. *Violence in Velvet.* 1956. Signet 1294. 1st edn. My. F. F2d. $20.00

AVALLONE, Michael. *90 Gramercy Park.* 1965. PB Library 52-835. 1st edn. Go. F. F2d. $13.00

AVERY, A.A. *Anything for a Quiet Life.* 1946. Bantam 38. My. NF. B4d. $12.00

AVERY, A.A. *Anything for a Quiet Life.* 1946. Bantam 38. 1st pb. My. VG+. B6d. $9.00

AVERY, C. *Pay Playgirl.* Playtime 663. PBO. VG+. B3d. $6.00

AVERY, Richard. *Expendables #1, #2, #3.* 1975. Gold Medal. 1st edn. NF. M1d. $4.00

AVERY, Richard. *Rings of Tantalus.* 1975. Gold Medal P 3307. 1st prtg. SF. VG. R5d. $1.75

AVERY, Richard. *War Games of Zelos.* 1975. Gold Medal P 3430. SF. VG+. B5d. $3.50

AXELROD, George. *Beggar's Choice.* Bantam 403. VG+. B3d. $4.50

AXELROD, George. *Blackmailer.* Gold Medal 248. VG. B3d. $4.00

AXELROD, George. *Seven-Year Itch.* Bantam 1371. 2nd prtg. VG. R5d. $7.00

AYLESWORTH, John. *Fee, Fei, Fo, Fum.* Avon G 1166. PBO. SF. VG. B5d. $3.50

AYME, Marcel. *Grand Seduction (Second Face).* Crest 250. VG+. B3d. $5.00

AYME, Marcel. *Walker Through Walls.* Berkley. 1st pb. F. M1d. $6.00

AYRES, R.M. *Afterglow.* Dell 336. VG. B3d. $3.50

BAARZMAN, Ben. *Echox.* 1962. PB Library 52-130. c/R Abbett. SF. VG+. B5d. $4.00

BABCOCK, Dwight V. *Gorgeous Ghoul Murder Case.* Avon 30. G. G5d. $5.00

BABCOCK, Dwight V. *Gorgeous Ghoul Murder Case.* Avon 30. VG. I1d. $15.00

BABCOCK, Dwight V. *Gorgeous Ghoul Murder Case.* Avon 320. c/gga. NF. B6a #75. $33.00

BABCOCK, Dwight V. *Gorgeous Ghoul Murder Case.* Avon 320. F. I1d. $30.00

BABCOCK, Dwight V. *Homicide for Hannah.* 1945. Avon 68. c/P Stahr: skull. My. G+. B5d. $11.00

BACCANTE, Leonora. *Johnny Bogan.* 1952. Popular 423. c/De Soto: gga. Fa. VG. B4d. $6.00

BACH, M. *Strange Altars.* Signet T 3484. 1st prtg. F. S1d. $3.00

BACH, R. *Jonathan Livingston Seagull.* Avon 14316. NF. B3d. $10.00

BACH, R. *Stranger to the Ground.* Dell 8343. VG+. B3d. $5.00

BACHMAN, Richard; see King, Stephen.

BACHMAN & LEES. *Death in the Dolls House.* 1949. Dell 356. MTI. VG+. B4d. $10.00

BACKUS, H. & J. *Only When I Laugh.* Holloway House HH 115. VG+. B3d. $5.00

BAGBY, George. *Another Day: Another Death.* Curtis 06006. 1st pb. VG. M6d. $4.50

BAGBY, George. *Blood Will Tell.* Bantam 1226. VG. B3d. $4.00

BAGBY, George. *Coffin Corner.* Pocket 736. VG. I1d. $5.00

BAGBY, George. *Cop Killer.* 1959. Dell 997. 1st prtg. c/James Hill. VG+. B5d. $5.50

BAGBY, George. *Corpse With Sticky Fingers.* Berkley G 84. G+. G5d. $3.00

BAGBY, George. *Dead Storage.* Dell 949. NF. G5d. $5.50

BAGBY, George. *Drop Dead.* 1955. Bantam 1308. 1st prtg. My. G+. R5d. $1.75

BAGBY, George. *Give the Little Corpse a Great Big Hand.* Dell 848. c/V Kalin. My. VG. B5d. $3.00

BAGBY, George. *Give the Little Corpse a Great Hand.* Dell 848. VG+. I1d. $5.00

BAGBY, George. *Murder's Little Helper.* 1964. Cardinal 35007 My. VG+. B5d. $3.50

BAGBY, George. *Real Gone Goose.* Consul 1078. VG. B3d. $6.00

BAGBY, George. *Real Gone Goose.* 1960. Perma M 4178. c/gga. My. VG. B4d. $3.00

BAGBY, George. *Real Gone Goose.* 1960. Perma M 4178. 1st pb. c/beatnik. My. NF. B6d. $15.00

BAGLEY/JAKES. *Star Virus/Mask of Chaos.* Ace 78400. 1st prtg. G+. S1d. $2.50

BAHNSON, Agnew H. Jr. *Stars Are Too High.* 1960. Bantam A 2048. 1st prtg. SF. G+. M1d. $7.00

BAHRENBURG, Bruce. *Creation of Di Laurentiis' Kong.* Pocket 08796. PBO. MTI. VG. B3d. $5.00

BAHRENBURG, Bruce. *Creation of Dino De Laurentiis' King Kong.* 1976. Star 30006. 1st prtg. VG. R5d. $2.50

BAHRENBURG, Bruce. *Creation of King Kong.* 1976. Pocket 80796. Nfi. VG. P1d. $3.50

BAHRENBURG, Bruce. *Filming the Great Gatsby.* 1974. Berkley 02576. 1st prtg. VG. R5d. $2.50

BAILEY, Gerald Earl. *Sword of Poyana.* 1979. Berkley 04055. 1st prtg. SF. VG. R5d. $1.50

BAILEY, H.C. *Best of Mr Fortune Stories.* Pocket 190. G. G5d. $5.00

BAILEY, H.C. *Bishop's Crime.* Pony 60. VG. G5d. $11.00

BAILEY, H.C. *Twittering Bird Mystery.* Bonded Mystery 8. VG+. G5d. $10.00

BAILEY, Seth. *Hand in the Cobbler's Safe.* 1944. Bart House NN. VG. B3a #22. $22.80

BAILEY, Temple. *Pink Camellia.* Dell 178. VG. B3d. $4.50

BAILEY, Tom. *Comanche Wars.* 1963. Monarch MA 357. PBO. c/photo. Nfi. VG. B5d. $4.50

BAILLE, Peter. *Chindwin Mission.* Digit D 188. c/WWII prisoner. NF. B3a #21. $10.00

BAIR, L. *Memoirs of Casanova.* Corgi 1071. 2nd reissue. VG+. B3d. $8.00

BAIRD, Jack. *Care & Handling of Dogs.* Perma P 76. VG. I1d. $4.00

BAKER, Charles. *Blood of the Lamb.* 1951. Dell 492. 1st pb. c/Kalin. NF. B6d. $10.00

BAKER, D.V. *Strange Fulfillment.* Pyramid 681. 2nd prtg. VG. B3d. $4.00

BAKER, George. *Passion Pirate.* 1962. Bedside BB 1228. Ad. VG. B5d. $5.00

BAKER, Ledru Jr. *And Be My Love.* 1951. Gold Medal 183. PBO. c/Barye. VG+. B6d. $9.00

BAKER, Ledru Jr. *Brute Madness.* Novel Book 5033. PBO. VG+. B3d. $6.00

BAKER, Ledru Jr. *Preying Streets.* 1955. Ace S 122. PBO. c/Marchetti: gga. VG. B3d. $4.50

BAKER, Ledru Jr. *Un-Human Orgy.* 1964. Novel Book 7N711. 1st edn. F. F2d. $40.00

BAKER, S.S. *Murder -- Very Dry.* Graphic 135. VG. B3d. $4.00

BAKER, S.S. *One Touch of Blood.* Graphic 97. G+. C5d. $4.50

BAKER, Scott. *Nightchild.* 1983. Pocket 46931. F. P9d. $1.75

BAKER, Scott. *Symbiotes Crown.* 1978. Berkley 03839. PBO. SF. VG+. B6d. $3.00

BAKER, W. *Sex Cruise.* Brandon House 6501. NF. B3d. $4.50

BAKER, W.H. *Battle Song.* Sexton Blake 371. VG+. B3d. $7.00

BAKER, W.H. *Big Smear.* Sexton Blake 511. c/Parabellum. VG+. B3d. $8.00

BAKER, W.H. *Dark Mambo.* Sexton Blake 361. VG. B3d. $6.50

BAKER, W.H. *Departure Deferred.* 1966. MacFadden 50-275. 1st prtg. TVTI. G+. R5d. $2.50

BAKER, W.H. *Every Man an Enemy.* MacFadden 50-354. VG. G5d. $3.00

BAKER, W.H. *Frightened Lady.* Sexton Blake 359. VG. B3d. $7.50

BAKER, W.H. *Judas Diary.* 1969. Lancer 74-511. 1st edn. My. F. F2d. $10.00

BAKER, W.H. *Rape of Berlin.* 1967. Lancer. 1st edn. F. M1d. $8.00

BAKER, W.H. *Rape of Berlin.* 1967. Lancer 73-628. My. VG. W2d. $3.00

BAKER, W.H. *Shoot When Ready.* Sexton Blake 383. VG+. B3d. $8.00

BAKER, W.H. *Storm Over Rockall.* 1966. MacFadden 50-284. 1st prtg. VG. R5d. $3.50

BAKER, W.H. *Traitor!* 1967. Lancer 73-646. We. VG. B4d. $2.75

BAKER, Wade. *Black Magician.* 1982. Warner 30-178. 1st edn. My. F. F2d. $10.00

BAKER, Wade. *Borderland of Hell.* 1982. Warner 30-127. 1st edn. My. F. F2d. $10.00

BAKER, Wade. *Death's Door.* 1982. Warner 30-229. 1st edn. My. F. F2d. $10.00

BAKER, Wade. *Mountain of Fear.* 1981. Warner 30-064. 1st edn. My. F. F2d. $10.00

BAKER, Wade. *Only the Good Die.* 1983. Warner 30-239. 1st edn. My. F. F2d. $10.00

BAKER, Wade. *Skin Swindle.* 1983. Warner 30-227. 1st edn. My. F. F2d. $10.00

BAKER, Wade. *Vengeance Is His.* 1981. Warner 30-032. 1st edn. My. F. F2d. $10.00

BALCH/CORD. *Blind Man's Bullets/Prodigal Gun.* Ace D 208. VG. B3d. $4.00

BALCHIN, Nigel. *Anatomy of Villainy.* 1961. Four Square 352. Nfi. VG. B3d. $7.50

BALCHIN, Nigel. *Small Back Room.* 1950. Lion 31. Fa. VG+. B4d. $16.50

BALDWIN, Bates. *Sultan's Warrior.* Pocket 884. VG+. B3d. $4.50

BALDWIN, Bates. *Tide of Empire.* 1954. Avon T 72. 1st pb. c/gga. NF. B6d. $9.00

BALDWIN, Faith. *Alimony.* Dell 318. G. I1d. $3.00

BALDWIN, Faith. *Bride From Broadway.* Dell 10¢ 5. VG+. B3d. $5.00

BALDWIN, Faith. *He Married a Doctor.* 1962. Dell 3508. 1st prtg. c/Forte: gga. VG. P7d. $3.50

BALDWIN, Faith. *Heart Has Wings.* 1946. Pony 51. Fa. VG. B4d. $7.50

BALDWIN, Faith. *High Road.* Dell 445. VG+. B3d. $4.50

BALDWIN, Faith. *Hotel Hostess.* 1948. Bantam 411. c/Wm Shoyer. VG. P6d. $1.50

BALDWIN, Faith. *Manhattan Nights.* Dell 475. c/R Stanley. Fi. G+. B5d. $2.50

BALDWIN, Faith. *Men Are Such Fools.* Dell 138. VG+. B3d. $5.00

BALDWIN, Faith. *Search for Tomorrow.* Popular 60-8017. TVTI. c/photos. Fi. VG. B5d. $4.00

BALDWIN, Faith. *Skyscraper.* Dell 236. VG. B3d. $4.00

BALDWIN, Faith. *Sleeping Beauty.* 1964. Pyramid R 1079. Ro. VG+. B4d. $2.75

BALDWIN, Faith. *White Magic.* Superior Reprint M 637. G+. M6d. $4.00

BALDWIN, Faith. *Wife Vs Secretary.* Dell Dimer 30. VG+. B3d. $8.00

BALDWIN, Faith. *Wife Vs Secretary.* 1962. Dell 9541. 1st prtg. c/Ludlow: gga. VG. P7d. $3.50

BALDWIN, James. *Another Country.* 1963. Dell 0200. 1st prtg. c/Liebman. VG+. P7d. $4.50

BALDWIN, James. *Fire Next Time.* 1964. Dell 2542. 1st prtg. VG+. P7d. $4.50

BALDWIN, James. *Giovanni's Room.* 1959. Signet S 1559. VG. P6d. $2.25

BALDWIN, James. *Go Tell It on the Mountain.* 1954. Signet 1138. 1st pb. VG. B6d. $9.00

BALDWIN, Linton. *Sinners' Game.* 1954. Lion 227. PBO. c/gga. scarce. NF. B6a #76. $42.00

BALEY, Barington J. *Empire of Two Worlds.* Ace 20565. 1st prtg. VG+. S1d. $3.00

BALHAM, Joe. *Human Pipline.* 1977. Futura 7497. TVTI. VG. P1d. $5.00

BALHAM, Joe. *Snout Who Cried Wolf.* 1977. Futura 7554. TVTI. VG. P1d. $5.00

BALL, Brian N. *Regiments of Night.* 1972. DAW 19. PBO. c/K Freas. SF. VG. B5d/P7d. $4.00

BALL, Brian N. *Sundog.* 1969. Avon V 2193. 1st prtg. SF. VG+. R5d. $3.00

BALL, Brian N. *Timepiece.* 1970. Ballantine 01903. SF. G+. W2d. $3.00

BALL, J. *In the Heat of the Night.* Pan X 711. MTI. VG+. B3d. $8.00

BALLARD, J.G. *Billenium.* Berkley G-667. PBO. NF. B3d. $6.00

BALLARD, J.G. *Burning World.* 1964. Berkley F 961. 1st edn. VG. I1d. $8.00

BALLARD, J.G. *Burning World.* 1964. Berkley F 961. 1st pb. NF. M1d. $15.00

BALLARD, J.G. *Crystal World.* 1967. Berkley X 1380. SF. VG+. W2d. $4.25

BALLARD, J.G. *Drowned World.* Berkley F 1266. 2nd edn. VG. P9d. $2.00

BALLARD, J.G. *Drowned World.* 1966. Berkley F 1266. SF. VG. B5d. $4.50

BALLARD, J.G. *Drowned World.* 1966. Berkley F 1266. 1st pb. F. M1d. $20.00

BALLARD, J.G. *Drowned World.* Berkley F 655. VG+. I1d. $7.00

BALLARD, J.G. *Impossible Man.* 1966. Berkley F 1204. PBO. c/R Powers. SF. G+. B5d. $6.00

BALLARD, J.G. *Impossible Man.* 1966. Berkley F 1204. 1st pb. NF. M1d. $15.00

BALLARD, J.G. *Passport To Eternity.* 1963. Berkley 823. PBO. c/R Powers. SF. VG. B5d. $10.00

BALLARD, J.G. *Passport To Eternity.* 1963. Berkley 823. 1st pb. F. M1d. $20.00

BALLARD, J.G. *Terminal Beach.* 1964. Berkley F 928. PBO. c/Powers. SF. VG. M3d. $10.00

BALLARD, J.G. *Terminal Beach.* 1964. Berkley. 1st pb. F. M1d. $20.00

BALLARD, J.G. *Vermilion Sands.* 1971. Berkley S 1980. SF. VG. W2d. $4.00

BALLARD, J.G. *Voices of Time.* 1966. Berkley F 1243. 1st prtg. SF. VG+. R5d. $4.00

BALLARD, J.G. *Voices of Time.* 1966. Berkley. F. M1d. $15.00

BALLARD, J.G. *Wind From Nowhere.* 1966. Berkley F 1198. 2nd edn. SF. G+. B5d. $5.00

BALLARD, J.G. *Wind From Nowhere.* Berkley F 600. PBO. NF. I1d. $15.00

BALLARD, J.G. *Wind From Nowhere.* 1962. Berkley. 1st edn. F. M1d. $20.00

BALLARD, K.G. *Coast of Fear.* Curt 06039. My. G+. W2d. $3.00

BALLARD, P.D. *Age of the Junkman.* Gold Medal 714. VG. B3d. $5.00

BALLARD, P.D. *End of a Millionaire.* Gold Medal 1486. VG+. B3d. $4.50

BALLARD, S.T. *Gunman From Texas.* Popular 735. VG. B3d. $4.00

BALLARD, S.T. *Guns of the Lawless.* Popular 772. VG. B3d. $3.50

BALLARD, S.T. *High Iron.* Popular 552. VG. B3d. $4.50

BALLARD, S.T. *Incident at Sun Mountain.* Popular 492. NF. I1d. $7.00

BALLARD, S.T. *Saddle Tramp.* Popular G 249. VG. B3d. $4.00

BALLARD, S.T. *Superstition Range.* Banner B40-105. VG+. B3d. $5.00

BALLARD, W.T. *Chance Elson.* 1958. Cardinal C 277. 1st prtg. PBO. c/Marchetti: gga. VG. P7d. $5.00

BALLARD, W.T. *Dealing Out Death.* Graphic 72. VG+. B3d. $8.00

BALLARD, W.T. *Death Ride.* 1960. Gold medal 1055. 1st edn. De. F. F2d. $17.50

BALLARD, W.T. *Long Sword.* 1962. Avon G 1099. 1st edn. Hi. F. 2d. $12.00

BALLARD, W.T. *Murder Can't Stop.* Graphic 26. VG. G5d. $8.00

BALLARD, W.T. *Murder Can't Stop.* Graphic 65. VG. I1d. $4.00

BALLARD, W.T. *Package Deal.* 1957. Bantam Giant A 1600. 1st edn. PBO. VG+. P6d. $2.50

BALLARD, W.T. *Seven Sisters.* Perma M 4258. PBO. VG+. B3d. $6.00

BALLARD, W.T. *Seven Sisters*. 1962. Perma M 4258. 1st prtg. PBO. VG. P7d. $4.00

BALLARD, W.T. *Walk in Fear*. Gold Medal 259. VG. B3d. $4.00

BALLARD & LYNCH. *Showdown*. 1959. Popular G 335. We. VG. B4d. $3.00

BALLINGER, Bill S. *Beacon in the Night*. 1960. Signet S 1794. c/gga. My. VG. B4d. $3.00

BALLINGER, Bill S. *Beautiful Trap*. 1954. Signet 1134. My. VG. B5d. $4.00

BALLINGER, Bill S. *Body Beautiful*. 1950. Signet 774. 1st pb. My. G. B6d/G5d. $3.50

BALLINGER, Bill S. *Body in the Bed*. 1949. Signet 730. 3rd edn. My. VG. B3d. $3.00

BALLINGER, Bill S. *Chinese Mask*. 1965. Signet D 2715. My. F. B4d. $6.00

BALLINGER, Bill S. *Darkening Door*. Signet 1040. VG. B3d. $4.50

BALLINGER, Bill S. *Darkening Door*. 1953. Signet 1040. 1st pb. My. NF. B6d. $16.50

BALLINGER, Bill S. *Formula for Murder*. 1958. Signet 1585. PBO. My. VG. B6d. $7.00

BALLINGER, Bill S. *Longest Second*. 1959. Signet 1730. c/R Schulz. My. VG. B5d. $4.00

BALLINGER, Bill S. *Spy at Angkor Wat*. 1966. Signet 2899. 1st edn. F. F2d. $10.00

BALLINGER, Bill S. *Spy in the Java Sea*. Signet 2981. VG+. B3d. $4.50

BALLINGER, Bill S. *Wife of the Red-Haired Man*. 1958. Signet 1494. c/gga. My. VG+. B4d. $4.00

BALLINGER, W.A. *Exterminator*. 1967. MacFadden 50-342. 1st prtg. VG+. R5d. $5.00

BALLINGER, W.A. *Naked From a Well*. Softcover Library B 10635. PBO. VG. M6d. $6.50

BALLINGER, W.A. *Witches of Notting Hill*. MacFadden 50-350. Sexton Blake #2. G. G5d. $5.00

BALLINGER, W.A. *Women's Battalion*. 1967. Lancer 73-699. 1st edn. c/gga. F. F2d. $10.00

BALMER & WYLIE. *When Worlds Colide*. 1952. Dell 627. 1st prtg. G. S1d. $2.00

BALMER & WYLIE. *When Worlds Collide*. 1952. Dell 627. c/R Stanley. SF. G+. B5d. $4.50

BALMER & WYLIE. *When Worlds Collide*. 1952. Dell 627. 1st edn. PBO. F. F2d. $20.00

BALMER & WYLIE. *When Worlds Collide*. 1952. Dell 627. 1st prtg. SF. VG. R5d. $6.75

BALMER & WYLIE. *When Worlds Collide*. 1973. PB Library 74021. 6th prtg. SF. VG. W2d. $3.25

BALSIGER & SELLIER. *In Search of Noah's Ark*. 1976. Schick Sun 1544. 1st prtg. TVTI. VG. R5d. $1.75

BAMBER, George. *Sea Is Boiling Hot*. Ace 75690. c/J Gaughn. SF. VG. B5d. $4.00

BANISTER, Manly. *Conquest of Earth*. 1964. Airmont SF 7. SF. F. W2d. $6.00

BANISTER, Manly. *Conquest of Earth*. 1964. Airmont SF 7. SF. VG+. B4d. $3.00

BANKO, Daniel. *Not Dead Yet*. 1972. Gold Medal T 2581. My. VG. B4d. $2.00

BANKS, Lynne Reid. *House of Hope*. 1964. Cardinal GC 191. Fi. VG+. B5d. $3.50

BANKS, Polan. *My Forbidden Past*. 1951. Popular 319. MTI. c/Mitchum & Gardner: photo. VG+. B4d. $12.50

BANKS, Rosie M. *Navy Nurse*. 1960. Perma M 4137. Fa. NF. B4d. $3.00

BANKS, Rosie M. *Surgical Nurse*. Pocket 1243. PBO. VG+. B3d. $4.50

BANNING, Margaret Culkin. *Clever Sister*. Dell 381. Fi. VG+. B5d. $5.00

BANNISTER, William. *Counterfeit Death*. 1968. Lancer 73-710. PBO. My. VG+. B6d. $7.00

BANNON, Ann. *Beebo Brinker*. 1962. Gold Medal 1224. 1st edn. scarce. VG. F2d. $20.00

BANNON, Ann. *I Am a Woman*. Gold Medal D 833. VG. G5d. $8.00

BANNON, Ann. *Odd Girl Out*. 1957. Gold Medal Giant S 653. PBO. G+. M6d. $4.50

BANNON, Ann. *Odd Girl Out*. 1957. Gold Medal Giant S 653. 1st prtg. PBO. c/Barye Phillips. G. P6d. $2.00

BANNON, Ann. *Women in the Shadows*. 1959. Gold Medal S 919. 1st prtg. PBO. c/photo. VG. P6d. $7.50

BARBANELL, Maurice. *He Walks in Two Worlds*. 1968. Flagship 092-00837-075. c/photo. VG. P6d. $4.00

BARBERA & HANNA. *Yogi Bear Goes to College*. 1961. Dell 1st Edn B 199. PBO. F. B6d. $45.00

BARBET, Pierre. *Baphomet's Meteor*. 1972. DAW 35. c/K Thole. SF. VG+. B5d. $4.00

BARBET, Pierre. *Cosmic Crusaders*. 1972. DAW. 1st pb. F. M1d. $7.00

BARBET, Pierre. *Enchanted Planet*. 1975. DAW 156. 1st pb. F. M1d. $6.00

BARBET, Pierre. *Enchanted Planet*. 1975. DAW 156. 1st prtg. VG+. S1d. $3.00

BARBET, Pierre. *Games Psyborgs Play*. DAW 83. 1st prtg. F. S1d. $5.50

BARBETTE, J. *Final Copy*. Bantam 1076. VG+. B3d. $4.50

BARING-GOULD, W.S. *Nero Wolfe of West Thirty-Fifth Street*. 1970. Bantam S 4887. Nfi. VG. P1d. $5.00

BARKE, James. *Song in the Green Thorn Tree*. 1957. Fontana 210. Nfi. G+. P1d. $4.50

BARKER, Clive. *Books of Blood Volume #3*. 1986. Berkley 9347. F. P9d. $2.00

BARKER, Clive. *Weaveworld*. 1988. Pocket 66506. c/J Warren. SF. NF. B5d. $5.00

BARKER, M.R. *Flansoury*. 1985. DAW. 1st pb. F. M1d. $4.00

BARKER, R. *Down in the Drink*. Pan G 133. VG. B3d. $7.00

BARLEY, Rex. *Cross To Bear Proudly*. 1963. Signet P 2401. c/gga. Fa. VG+. B4d. $2.75

BARNARD, Allan. *Cleopatra's Nights*. 1950. Dell 414. PBO. c/Johnson: gga. VG. B6d. $12.50

BARNES, Arthur K. *Interplanetary Hunter*. 1972. Ace 37100. SF. VG. B5d/S1d. $3.00

BARNES, Gregory. *Homo Alley*. 1965. All Star AS 46. PBO. Ad. VG. B5d. $5.00

BARNES, John. *Sin of Origin*. 1989. World Wide 30307. 1st pb. SF. NF. B6d. $3.00

BARNES, Margaret Campbell. *King's Choice*. Dell 563. c/G Mayers. Fi. VG. B5d. $3.00

BARNES, Steven. *Kundalini Equation*. 1986. Doherty. 1st pb. NF. M1d. $4.00

BARNES & NIVEN. *Barsoom Project*. 1989. Ace 16712. PBO. c/J Burleson. SF. VG+. B5d. $4.00

BARNS, Glenn M. *Lawyers Don't Hang*. Bestseller B 175. My. G+. B5d. $4.00

BARNS, Glenn M. *Only the Losers Win*. 1968. Gold Medal D 1959. PBO. Ad. NF. B6d. $9.00

BARON, Alexander. *Golden Princess*. Bantam 1634. c/Zuckerberg. VG+. B3d. $4.50

BARON, Stanley. *End of the Line*. 1955. Ace S 91. 1st pb. Th. VG. B6d. $7.50

BARR, Donald. *Space Relations*. 1975. Crest P 2370. 1st prtg. SF. VG+. R5d. $2.00

BARR, George. *Green Phoenix*. 1972. DAW 27. 1st prtg. VG+. P6d. $2.00

BARR, George. *How Are the Mighty Fallen*. 1974. DAW 94. 1st prtg. PBO. VG+. P6d. $2.00

BARR, George. *Minikins of Yam*. 1976. DAW 182. 1st prtg. PBO. VG+. P6d. $2.00

BARR, George. *Not-World Strong.* 1975. DAW 140. 1st prtg. VG+. P6d. $2.00

BARR, Jeff. *Nobody's Children.* 1969. Brandon House 6028. PBO. VG+. P6d. $5.00

BARR, Tyrone. *Last 14.* 1960. Chariot. 1st pb. NF. M1d. $15.00

BARREN, Charles. *Seed of Evil.* 1959. Ace H 315. PBO. F. B6a. $33.00

BARRETT, M. *Murder at Belle Camille.* Boardman NN MBC. VG. B3d. $7.50

BARRETT, Michael. *Reward.* 1965. Gold Medal K 1577. MTI. VG. B4d. $3.00

BARRETT, Monte. *Smoke Up the Valley.* 1951. Popular 311. c/Samuel Cherry: gga. VG. B3d. $5.00

BARRETT, Monte. *Smoke Up the Valley.* Popular 630. VG. B3d. $4.50

BARRETT, Monte. *Sun in Their Eyes.* Popular G 137. VG. B3d. $4.50

BARRETT, Monte. *Sun in Their Eyes.* 1950. Popular 224. c/Belarski: gga. Fa. VG. B4d. $4.50

BARRETT, Monte. *Tempered Blade.* Popular 270. VG. B3d. $4.50

BARRETT, Monte. *Tempered Blade.* 1950. Popular 270. 1st edn. PBO. F. F2d. $12.00

BARRETT, Neil Jr. *Aldair, Across the Misty Sea.* 1980. DAW. 1st pb. F. M1d. $7.00

BARRETT, Neil Jr. *Aldair, Master of Ships.* 1977. DAW. 1st pb. F. M1d. $7.00

BARRETT, Neil Jr. *Aldair, the Legion of Beasts.* 1982. DAW. 1st pb. F. M1d. $7.00

BARRETT, Neil Jr. *Aldair in Albion.* 1976. DAW 195. 1st prtg. PBO. c/Kirby. VG. P7d. $4.00

BARRETT, Neil Jr. *Aldair in Albion.* 1976. DAW. 1st pb. F. M1d. $7.00

BARRETT, Neil Jr. *Stress Pattern.* 1974. DAW. 1st pb. F. M1d. $7.00

BARRETT, William E. *Empty Shrine.* 1960. Cardinal C 403. Fa. VG+. B4d. $2.00

BARRETT, William E. *Lilies of the Field.* 1963. Popular PC 1027. 1st prtg. VG. R5d. $2.00

BARRETT/BAYLEY. *Highwood/Annihilation Factor.* Ace 33710. PBO. c/Enrich & P Lloyd. SF. VG. B5d. $4.00

BARROW, R.M. *Ghost in the Lady's Boudoir.* Consol. SF. G. W2d. $10.00

BARROW, Whitney Jr. *Hold It, Florence.* Dell 786. c/W Darrow Jr: cartoons. NF. VG. B5d. $3.00

BARRY, J. *Erotic Variations.* Brandon House 1109. VG+. B3d. $6.00

BARRY, J. *Leopard Cat's Cradle.* Boardman 48. VG. B3d. $10.00

BARRY, Jerome. *Lady of Night.* Hillman 86. VG. B3d. $4.00

BARRY, Jerome. *Lady of Night.* My Novel Classic 86. VG. M6d. $7.50

BARRY, Jerome. *Murder Is No Accident.* 1960. Dell D 369. 1st prtg. My. G+. R5d. $1.25

BARRY, Joe. *Fall Guy.* 1945. Handi-Book 42. My. VG. P6d. $4.00

BARRY, Joe. *Homicide Hotel.* 1951. Phantom Book 500. PBO. VG. B6a. $73.00

BARRY, Ken. *Golden Girls.* 1962. Beacon B 474F. PBO. Ad. G+. B5d. $4.00

BARRY, Ken. *Love Itch.* 1962. Beacon B 536F. PBO. Ad. G+. B5d. $3.50

BARRY, Mike. *Detroit Massacre.* 1975. Berkley N 2793. Lone Wolf #11. My. VG. W2d. $3.50

BARRY, Ray. *Ominous Folly.* 1949. Curtis NN. PBO. scarce. SF. VG+. B6a #77. $25.00

BARRY, Winchell. *Scarlet City.* 1960. Beacon 290. 1st prtg. PBO. VG. P7d. $7.50

BARRY & KAUFMAN. *Right People.* Gold Medal 1349. VG+. B3d. $5.00

BARSTEAD, Harry. *Passionate Amazons.* 1962. All Star 528. 1st edn. c/gga. photo. My. F. F2d. $10.00

BARSTOW, Craig. *Lady of the Line.* 1961. Kozy Book 138. 1st edn. c/gga. F. F2d. $10.00

BARTDORF, S. *Broads Make the Odds.* France 13. VG+. B3d. $6.00

BARTELL, D. *Nympho Mania.* Saber SA 34. VG. B3d. $6.00

BARTHELME, Donald. *City Life.* 1971. Bantam Q 5908. 1st prtg. VG. P7d. $4.00

BARTHELME, Donald. *Unspeakable Practices, Unnatural Acts.* 1969. Bantam N 4411. 1st prtg. VG. P7d. $4.00

BARTLETT, S. *Twelve O'Clock High.* Bantam 743. MTI. VG. B3d. $4.00

BARTON, J. *Texas Rawhider.* Popular 498. VG. B3d. $4.50

BARTON, J.C. *Pay-Off.* Badger Crime 9. VG. B3d. $8.00

BARTON, M. *Blood-Stained Dime.* Bleak House 14. VG. B3d. $6.00

BARTON, William. *Plague of All Cowards.* 1976. Ace 66780. 1st edn. NF. P9d. $3.00

BARTON/PHILLIFENT. *Hunting on Kunderer/Life With Lancelot.* 1973. Ace 48245. PBO. SF. VG. B5d. $3.00

BARTONLINI, Elio. *La Signora.* 1957. Lion LB 163. c/gga. Fa. VG+. B4d. $7.50

BARWICK, James. *Shadow of the Wolf.* 1980. Ballantine 28316. 1st prtg. My. VG+. W2d. $3.75

BARZMAN, Ben. *Echo X.* 1962. PB Library 52-130. SF. VG+. W2d. $5.00

BASINGER, Jeanine. *Shirley Temple.* 1975. Pyramid 3643. 1st edn. c/photos. Bio. F. F2d. $15.00

BASINSKY, Earle. *Death Is a Cold.* 1956. Signet 1351. 1st prtg. PBO. c/Maguire. VG. P7d. $5.00

BASS, L. *Out of Darkness.* Saber SA 9. VG. B3d. $5.00

BASS, T.J. *Godwhale.* 1974. Ballantine 23712. PBO. c/Lehr. SF. NF. B6d. $10.00

BASS, T.J. *Half-Past Human.* 1977. Ballantine 2306. 1st edn. F. P9d. $2.00

BASSETT & MONATH. *Play It Yourself.* Perma M 3054. VG+. B3d. $5.00

BAST, William. *James Dean.* 1956. Ballantine 180. 1st prtg. Bio. VG. R5d. $12.50

BATES, H.E. *Hark, Hark, the Lark!* Popular G 565. VG+. B3d. $4.50

BATES, H.E. *Nature of Love.* 1955. Popular 654. G+. P6d. $1.00

BATES, H.E. *Scarlet Sword.* 1953. Popular G 127. c/gga. Fa. VG+. B4d. $7.00

BATES, H.E. *Valley of Love.* Popular 683. VG. B3d. $4.50

BATES & CONNERS. *Voyeurism '70.* Barclay 7077. VG+. B3d. $5.00

BATTLE, Roy. *Secrets of Sin.* 1971. Saber SA 230. Ad. NF. B5d. $8.00

BAUER, Steven. *Amazing Stories Volume #2.* 1986. Charter 01912. SF. G+. W2d. $4.00

BAUM, L. Frank. *Wizard of Oz.* Award CL 605. SF. VG+. W2d. $3.00

BAUM, L. Frank. *Wizard of Oz.* 1960. Crest S 395. 1st prtg. SF. VG+. W2d. $7.50

BAUM, L. Frank. *Wizard of Oz.* Gold Medal J 1883. SF. VG. W2d. $4.00

BAUM, L. Frank. *Wonderful Wizard of Oz.* 1965. Airmont C 169. SF. VG. W2d. $3.00

BAUM, Vicki. *Back Stage.* 1945. Avon 64. Fi. G+. B5d. $6.50

BAUM, Vicki. *Grand Hotel.* 1946. Bart House 28. G. P6d. $1.00

BAUM, Vicki. *One Tropical Night.* 1951. Perma P 109. c/gga. Fa. VG. B4d. $2.25

BAUME, Eric. *Yankee Woman.* 1953. Perma P 235. 1st pb. c/Schwartz: gga. VG+. B6d. $12.00

BAWDEN, N. *Odd Flamingo.* Pan 406. VG+. B3d. $8.00

BAX. Roger. *Two if by Sea.* Dell 634. c/F McCarthy. My. VG. B5d. $3.00

BAXTER, George Owen. *Horseback Hellion.* 1950. Signet 785. c/L Ross. We. VG. B5d. $4.00

BAXTER, John. *Doorway to Sin.* Pillar PB 819. VG. P6d. $2.00

BAXTER, John. *Flesh Finder.* 1963. Pillar PB 807. VG. P6d. $2.00

BAXTER, John. *SF in the Cinema.* 1970. PB Library 66-420. PBO. VG. B6d. $9.00

BAXTER, John. *Sin Pit.* Ember Book EB 915. VG. B3d. $4.00

BAXTER, John. *Unfaithful.* Avon 647. VG. B3d. $5.00

BAXTER, John. *Unfaithful.* Avon 836. VG+. B3d. $7.50

BAXTER/CARTER. *Off-Worlders/Star Magicians.* Ace G 588. F. M1d. $12.00

BAYLEY, B.J. *Empire of Two Worlds.* Ace 20565. SF. VG. B5d. $3.00

BAYLEY, B.J. *Fall of Chronopolis.* 1974. DAW 105. 1st edn. VG. P9d. $1.75

BAYLEY, B.J. *Garments of Caean.* DAW 375. 1st edn. PBO. VG. P9d. $1.50

BAYLEY, B.J. *Garments of Caean.* DAW 375. 1st prtg. F. S1d. $4.00

BAYLEY, B.J. *Grand Wheel.* DAW 255. 1st prtg. VG. S1d. $3.00

BAYLEY, B.J. *Pillars of Eternity.* 1982. DAW UE 1717. SF. F. W2d. $3.50

BAYLEY, B.J. *Zen Gun.* 1983. DAW 87997. SF. F. W2d. $3.50

BAYLEY/JAKES. *Star Virus/Mask of Chaos.* Ace 78400. PBO. c/K Freas & J Gaughn. SF. VG. B5d. $3.00

BAYLEY/JAKES. *Star Virus/Mask of Chaos.* 1970. Ace 78400. 1st edn. SF. F. F2d. $14.00

BAYNES, Jack. *Hand of the Mafia.* Crest 224. VG+. B3d. $5.00

BAYNES, Jack. *Meet Morocco Jones.* 1957. Crest 195. 1st prtg. My. G+. R5d. $2.25

BEACH, Edward L. *Submarine!* 1953. Signet S 1043. Nfi. VG. B4d. $2.00

BEACH & FORD. *Patterns of Sexual Behavior.* Ace K 128. VG. B3d. $4.00

BEAGLE, Peter S. *Fine & Private Place.* 1978. Ballantine 27627. c/D Sweet. SF. VG. B5d. $3.00

BEAGLE, Peter S. *Folk of the Air.* 1986. Ballantine. 1st pb. F. M1d. $5.00

BEAGLE, Peter S. *Last Unicorn.* 1969. Ballantine 01503. 1st edn. PBO. F. F2d. $10.00

BEAGLE, Peter S. *Last Unicorn.* 1980. Ballantine 28620. 17th prtg. SF. VG+. W2d. $3.00

BEAR, Greg. *Corona.* 1984. Pocket 47390. 1st edn. SF. F. F2d. $10.00

BEAR, Greg. *Eternity.* 1989. Popular 20547. c/R Miller. SF. NF. B5d. $4.00

BEARD, James. *Eat Better for Less Money.* 1956. Perma M 4065. Nfi. VG+. B4d. $2.00

BEARD & KENNEY. *Bored of the Rings.* 1969. Signet Y 5588. SF. F. W2d. $4.00

BEARDSLEY, Helen. *Who Gets the Drumstick.* 1968. Bantam H 3675. 1st prtg. VG+. R5d. $2.25

BEARDSLEY & GLASSCO. *Under the Hill.* 1968. Grove Press Z 1024. 1st prtg. VG. P7d. $5.50

BEATTY, J. Jr. *Have You Ever Wondered?* MacFadden 35-123. NF. B3d. $4.50

BEAUCHAMP, Loren. *Connie.* Midwood 74. c/Rader: gga. reprint. VG. B6d. $9.00

BEAUCHAMP, Loren. *Love Nest.* 1958. Midwood 7. 1st prtg. PBO. c/Nappi: gga. NF. P7d. $15.00

BEAUCHAMP, Loren. *Meg.* Midwood 30. PBO. VG+. B3d. $6.00

BEAUCHAMP, Loren. *Strange Delights.* 1962. Midwood F 145. c/Rader. VG+. B3a #24. $13.04

BEAUCHAMP, Loren. *Strange Delights.* 1962. Midwood F 145. PBO. NF. B6a #76. $68.50

BEAUCHAMP, Loren. *Wayward Widow.* 1962. Midwood F 226. PBO. c/Rader: gga. NF. B6a #75. $67.25

BEAUMONT, Charles. *Fiend in You.* Ballantine 641. 1st pb. c/Matheson & Bloch. VG. M6d. $6.50

BEAUMONT, Charles. *Hunger & Other Stories.* 1959. Bantam. 1st pb. F. M1d. $25.00

BEAUMONT, Charles. *Intruder.* 1960. Dell F 94. 1st prtg. c/Brule. VG. P7d. $6.00

BEAUMONT, Charles. *Magic Man.* 1965. Gold medal D 1586. 1st edn. SF. F. F2d. $15.00

BEAUMONT, Charles. *Night Ride & Other Stories.* 1960. Bantam A 2087. 1st edn. NF. M1d. $20.00

BEAUMONT, Charles. *Yonder.* 1958. Bantam 1759. 1st edn. SF. F. F2d. $18.00

BEAUMONT & NOLAN. *When Engines Roar.* 1964. Bantam FP 64. PBO. scarcest book Anth/19. VG+. B6a #74. $44.00

BECHDOLT, F.R. *Danger on the Border.* Century 52. VG. B3d. $8.00

BECHDOLT, F.R. *Horse Thief Trail.* 1954. Pennant P 57. We. VG. B5d. $5.00

BECK, Charles. *Wife Traders.* 1961. Beacon B 450F. PBO. Ad. VG. B5d. $6.00

BECK, Charles. *Wife Traders.* 1965. Signal City B 808X. Ad. G+. B5d. $2.00

BECK & SMEDLEY. *Honey & Your Health.* 1974. Bantam N 6522. Nfi. Nf. B5d. $4.00

BECKER, Beril. *Spitfires.* 1953. Pyramid G 86. 1st edn. PBO. c/Julian Paul: gga. VG+. B6a #75. $25.00

BECKFORD, William. *Vathek.* 1971. Ballantine 02279. 1st prtg. PBO. Ad/Fa. F. F2d/M1d. $12.00

BECKHARD, Arthur. *Albert Einstein.* 1959. Avon. c/Einstein: bw photo. Bio. G+. B4d. $2.00

BECKHARDT & BROWN. *Violators.* 1956. Popular 734. PBO. c/DeSoto. scarce. JD. VG+. B6a #74. $37.50

BEDFORD, S. *Favourite of the Gods.* Popular M 2051. c/Zuckerberg. VG+. B3d. $4.50

BEDI, Rajinder Singh. *I Take This Woman.* 1968. Orient E 6. 3rd edn. Fi. G+. B5d. $3.00

BEEBE, W. *Jungle Peace.* Armed Services F 161. VG+. B3d. $7.00

BEECH, Linda. *TV Favorites.* 1971. Scholastic 1659. TVTI. VG. P1d. $6.00

BEECH, W. *Make War in Madness.* 1965. Gold Medal D 1548. War. VG+. B4d. $4.00

BEECH, W. *Warrior's Way.* Gold Medal 1467. VG. B3d. $4.00

BEEDING, Francis. *Coffin for One.* Avon 37. VG. B3d. $6.50

BEEDING, Francis. *Coffin for One.* 1943. Avon. 1st pb. F. M1d. $35.00

BEEDING, Francis. *Heads Off at Midnight.* Popular 381. G+. G5d. $4.50

BEEDING, Francis. *Heads Off at Midnight.* Popular 381. VG+. B3d. $7.00

BEEDING, Francis. *Hell Let Loose.* 1946. Popular 71. 1st pb. c/Hoffman. My. VG. B6d. $12.50

BEEDING, Francis. *Murdered: One by One.* Popular 42. VG. B3d. $7.50

BEEDING, Francis. *Nine Waxed Faces.* Popular 268. G+. G5d. $5.50

BEEDING, Francis. *Twelve Disguises.* Popular 57. VG+. G5d. $15.00

BEHAN, Brendan. *Confessions of an Irish Rebel.* Lancer 34-102. NF. B3d. $5.00

BEKKER, C. *Luftwaffe War Diaries.* Ballantine 07124. NF. B3d. $7.50

BELBENOIT, Rene. *I Escaped From Devil's Island.* Bantam 728. VG. B3d. $5.00

BELFRAGE, S. *Freedom Summer.* Crest 908. VG+. B3d. $6.00

BELGION, Montgomery. *Reading for Profit.* 1945. Pelican A 151. Nfi. VG. P1d. $10.00

BELL, A. *Frenchie.* Kozy Book 171. VG. B3d. $4.50

BELL, Jay. *All I Can Get.* Gold Medal R 1836. PBO. G+. M6d. $5.00

BELL, Joseph N. *Man Into Orbit.* 1960. Avon G 1075. 32 photos/7 diagrams. Nfi. VG. B4d. $2.25

BELL, Josephine. *Death at the Medical Board.* 1964. Ballantine U 2158. PBO. My. NF. B6d. $15.00

BELL, Josephine. *Double Doom.* 1966. Ballantine U 2155. 1st pb. c/Lehr. My. NF. B6d. $15.00

BELL, Josephine. *Easy Prey.* 1966. Ballantine U 2156. 1st pb. c/Lehr. My. NF. B6d. $15.00

BELL, Josephine. *Murder on the Merry-Go-Round.* 1965. Ballantine U 2159. PBO. VG. B6d. $6.00

BELL, Josephine. *Room for a Body.* Ballantine U 2157. VG. B3d. $3.50

BELL, Josephine. *Room for a Body.* 1966. Ballantine U 2157. 1st pb. My. NF. B6d. $15.00

BELL, Josephine. *Upfold Witch.* Ballantine U 2154. VG. B3d. $4.00

BELL, M.H. *Whistle Down the Wind.* Four Square 904. MTI. VG. B3d. $5.00

BELL, Neal. *Gone To Be Snakes Now.* Popular 00582. SF. VG+. B5d. $4.00

BELL, Steve. *Venue of Lesbos.* 1961. News Stand Library 176. PBO. c/Bonfils. scarce. NF. B6a #74. $53.50

BELL, Steve. *Venus of Lesbos.* 1961. News Stand Library 176. 1st edn. c/gga. My. F. F2d. $15.00

BELL, Vereen. *Swamp Water.* Bantam 1225. c/George Gross. reprint. VG. B6d. $9.00

BELL, Vereen. *Swamp Water.* 1947. Bantam 97. 1st pb. Th. VG+. B6d. $8.00

BELL/HASTINGS. *Honey at Her Lips/3rd Sex Syndr.* 1962. Dollar Double 954. c/Bonfils. VG+. B3a #21. $18.15

BELLAH, J.W. *Divorce.* Popular 404. VG. B3d. $5.00

BELLAH, J.W. *Man Who Shot Liberty Valance.* Perma M 4238. PBO. MTI. VG. B3d. $5.00

BELLAH, J.W. *Man Who Shot Liberty Valance.* 1962. Perma M 4238. 1st edn. c/photo. F. F2d. $12.00

BELLAH, J.W. *Massacre.* Lion 43. VG. B3d. $5.00

BELLAH, J.W. *Reveille.* Gold Medal 646. VG. B3d. $5.00

BELLAH, J.W. *Valiant Virginians.* 1953. Ballantine 44. 1st prtg. PBO. VG. P7d. $5.00

BELLAH, J.W. *Ward 20.* 1949. Popular 195. c/Belarski. Fa. VG. B3d/B4d. $8.00

BELLAMY, Hamon. *Frenchy.* 1949. Quarter Book 39. PBO. c/gga. VG+. B6a #74. $82.50

BELLAMY, Harmon. *Flesh & Females.* 1950. Quarter Book 66. 1st edn. PBO. c/gga. scarce. VG+. B6a #77. $74.00

BELLAMY/LEINSTER. *Atta/Brain-Stealers.* 1954. Ace D 79. SF. G+. B5d. $5.50

BELLEM, Robert Leslie. *Hollywood Detective.* 1950. Hollywood Vol 10 No 5. PBO. c/Maguire: gga. scarce. VG+. B6a #80. $105.00

BELLEM, Robert Leslie. *Sleeping Nude.* Harlequin 106. rare. VG. B6a #75. $90.00

BELLMORE, Don. *Lust Shill.* Idle Hour IH 453. VG+. I1d. $5.00

BELLMORE, Don. *Lust Shuffle.* 1968. Nightstand 1878. PBO. c/gga. NF. B6a #74. $44.50

BELLMORE, Don. *Shame Sheet.* Leisure LB 656. VG+. I1d. $5.00

BELLMORE, Don. *Shame Toy.* 1963. Nightstand NB 1649. Ad. NF. B5d. $6.50

BELLMORE, Don. *Swap Fever.* 1968. Companion 587. PBO. c/gga. NF. B6a #76. $44.00

BELLMORE, Don. *Swap Klatsch.* 1969. Companion 628. PBO. c/gga. VG+. B6a #77. $82.50

BELLMORE, Don. *Swaps in Color.* Adult Books AB 1546. PBO. VG. M6d. $15.00

BELLOC, Hilaire. *But Soft: We Are Observed.* 1939. Penguin. 1st pb. NF. M1d. $15.00

BEMELMANS, L. *Hotel Splendide.* Signet 637. VG. B3d. $4.50

BEMELMANS, Ludwig. *Small Beer.* 1945. Pocket 306. Hu. VG. P6d. $4.00

BENCHLEY, N. *One To Grow On.* Pyramid 431. VG+. B3d. $4.50

BENCHLEY, Robert. *Inside Benchley.* Armed Services G 192. Nfi. G. B5d. $2.00

BENCHLEY, Robert. *My Ten Years in a Quandry.* Pocket 449. 1st pb. VG. M6d. $5.00

BENDER, William Jr. *Tokyo Intrigue.* 1956. Ace S 198. Fa. VG+. B4d. $5.00

BENDLER, S.L. *Bed Game Sinners.* 1967. Spartan 149. PBO. NF. B6d. $10.00

BENEDICT & FREEDMAN. *Mrs Mike.* 1948. Bantam 152. c/N Lannon. Fi. VG. B5d. $3.00

BENEFIELD, B. *Chicken Wagon Family.* Armed Services M 10. VG+. B3d. $5.00

BENFORD, Gregory. *Deeper Than Darkness.* 1970. Ace 14215. SF. G+. W2d. $2.50

BENFORD, Gregory. *Great Sky River.* 1988. Bantam 27318. SF. VG. W2d. $3.75

BENFORD, Gregory. *In the Ocean of Night.* 1978. Dell 13999. SF. VG. W2d. $3.50

BENGTSSON, Frans. *Long Ships.* 1957. Signet D 1391. 1st pb. c/Viking. VG. B6d. $5.00

BENJAMIN, J. *Oral Brides.* Barclay 7179. c/photo. NF. B3d. $5.00

BENJAMIN, J. *Savvy Secrets of a Teen Sex Swinger.* Barclay 7044. VG+. B3d. $5.00

BENJAMIN, J. *Sexually Aggressive Husband.* Barclay 7329. NF. B3d. $5.00

BENJAMIN, J. *Suburban Swappers.* Barclay 7121. VG+. B3d. $4.00

BENJAMIN, P. *Quick, Before It Melts.* 1964. Avon S 168. 1st pb. MTI. NF. B6d. $9.00

BENNET, G. *Gin Mill Gigolo.* Magenta 104. VG+. B3d. $5.00

BENNETT, Arnold. *Jackie, Bobby & Manchester.* 1967. Bee Line 179. 1st edn. c/photo. Nfi. F. F2d. $12.00

BENNETT, Dwight. *Lost Wolf River.* Bantam 1141. VG. B3d. $4.00

BENNETT, Dwight. *Lost Wolf River.* 1964. Lancer 70-077. 1st pb. We. NF. B6d. $9.00

BENNETT, Fletcher. *Escape Into Vice.* 1962. Playtime 611. 1st edn. c/gga. My. F. F2d. $9.00

BENNETT, Fletcher. *Lust Be My Destiny.* Playtime 621. VG. B3d. $4.50

BENNETT, Fletcher. *Moment of Desire.* 1962. Playtime 604. PBO. c/gga. VG. P6d. $5.50

BENNETT, Fletcher. *Naked Streets.* Playtime 606. VG+. B3d. $5.00

BENNETT, Fletcher. *Vice Row.* Playtime 642. PBO. VG. B3d. $5.00

BENNETT, Fletcher. *Way of a Dame.* Playtime 625. NF. B3d. $7.00

BENNETT, George. *Great Tales of Action & Adventure.* 1965. Dell 3202. 7th prtg. SF. VG. W2d. $3.50

BENNETT, Hall. *Blonde Mistress.* Pyramid 14. VG. I1d. $10.00

BENNETT, Hall. *Blonde Mistress.* 1949. Pyramid 14. 1st pb. c/gga. VG+. B6d. $18.00

BENNETT, Hall. *Call It Love.* Century 97. G+. I1d. $4.00

BENNETT, Hall. *Confessions of a Part-Time Bride.* 1945. Hanro 4. 1st pb. VG. B6d. $7.50

BENOIT, Pierre. *Atlantida.* 1964. Ace F 281. 1st prtg. c/gga. VG. P7d. $4.00

BENSEN, D.R. *Mr Horn.* 1978. Dell 15194. 1st edn. Hi. F. F2d. $15.00

BENSEN, D.R. *Swashbuckler.* 1976. Bantam 10245. 1st prtg. VG+. R5d. $2.00

BENSEN, D.R. *Unknown 5.* 1964. Pyramid R 962. SF. NF. B4d. $9.00

BENSEN, D.R. *Unknown 5.* 1964. Pyramid R 962. 1st edn. F. M1d. $12.00

BENSEN, D.R. *Unknown.* 1963. Pyramid R 851. PBO. c/J Schoenherr. forward Asimov. SF. VG. B5d. $4.00

BENSON, Ben. *Beware the Pale Horse.* 1953. Bantam 1070. c/Al Rossi: gga. My. VG. B4d. $3.00

BENSON, Ben. *Blonde in Black.* Bantam 1974. c/Barye. VG. B3d. $4.50

BENSON, Ben. *Broken Shield.* 1957. Bantam 1552. c/gga. My. VG+. B4d. $2.00

BENSON, Ben. *End of Violence.* 1960. Bantam A 2067. 1st prtg. My. VG. R5d. $2.25

BENSON, Ben. *Girl in the Cage.* Bantam 1359. NF. B3d. $5.00

BENSON, Ben. *Ninth Hour.* 1957. Bantam A 1698. 1st prtg. My. VG+. R5d. $2.50

BENSON, Ben. *Silver Cobweb.* 1956. Bantam 1468. 1st prtg. My. G+. R5d. $1.75

BENSON, Ben. *Stamped for Murder.* 1953. Pennant P4. c/A Rossi. My. VG. B5d. $5.00

BENSON, Ben. *Target in Taffeta.* 1955. Bantam 1323. 1st prtg. My. VG. R5d. $2.25

BENSON, Sally. *Junior Miss.* Pocket 332. VG+. B3d. $7.00

BENSON, Sally. *Meet Me in St Louis.* 1945. Bantam 15. Hu. NF. B4d. $9.00

BENTLEY, E.C. *Trent's Last Case.* Armed Services 3. 1st prtg. c/Hoffman. VG. P7d. $5.00

BENTLEY, E.C. *Trent's Last Case.* Ballantine F 690. 1st prtg. My. VG. R5d. $3.25

BENTLEY, E.C. *Trent's Last Case.* 1937. Penguin 78. My. VG. P6d. $3.00

BENTLEY, W.R. *Girls on the Million-Dollar Mattress.* Brandon House 6410. VG+. B3d. $5.00

BENTON, R. *Teenage Seductress.* Barclay 7231. NF. B3d. $6.00

BERCKMAN, Evelyn. *Evil of Time.* Dell 841. 1st prtg. My. VG. R5d. $2.75

BERCKMAN, Evelyn. *Strange Bedfellow.* Dell D 268. VG+. B3d. $4.00

BERCKMAN, Evelyn. *Worse Than Murder (The Beckoning Dream).* Dell 936. VG. G5d. $5.00

BERENSTAIN, Stanley & Janice. *Lover Boy.* 1959. Dell 998. c/S & J Berenstain: cartoons. Nfi. G+. B5d. $2.50

BERENSTAIN, Stanley & Janice. *Marital Blitz.* 1955. Dell 1st Edn 50. PBO. c/S & J Berenstain. NF. VG+. B5d. $5.00

BERESFORD-HOWE, Constances. *My Lady Greensleeves.* Ballantine 112. F. F2d. $6.00

BERG, Louis. *Prison Nurse.* 1959. Bantam A 2008. My. NF. M3d. $7.50

BERGER, John. *G.* 1973. Dell 02757. 1st prtg. VG. P7d. $4.00

BERGGUIST & MOORE. *Your Shot, Darling!* Graphic 84. VG. G5d. $5.00

BERGLUND, Edward edt. *Disciples of Cthulhu.* 1976. DAW. 1st pb. VG. M1d. $7.00

BERGMAN, Andrew. *Big Kiss-Off of 1944.* 1983. Perennial Library P 673. 1st prtg. c/Irving Freeman. VG. P7d. $4.50

BERGMAN, Lee. *Wackiest Ship In the Army.* 1965. Popular 50-1056. TVTI. VG. P1d. $7.50

BERGMAN, Lee. *Walk Softly, Walk Deadly.* 1963. Belmont 90-282. PBO. JD. VG. P6d. $3.50

BERGQUIST & Moore. *Your Shot, Darling!* Graphic 84. VG. G5d. $5.00

BERGSON & MCMAHON. *Widow Master.* Gold Medal 1810. VG+. B3d. $4.50

BERKLEY, Anthony. *Poisoned Chocolates Case.* Pocket 814. VG. B3d. $4.00

BERKLEY, B. *Madame.* Kozy 161. VG+. B3d. $5.00

BERKMAN, T. *Cast a Giant Shadow.* 1966. Pocket 50294. 1st prtg. VG+. R5d. $2.00

BERLITZ, Charles. *Mystery of Atlantis.* 1976. Avon 46250. 8th prtg. SF. F. W2d. $3.50

BERLYN, Michael. *Crystal Phoenix.* 1980. Bantam 13468. SF. VG. W2d. $3.75

BERLYN, Michael. *Integrated Man.* 1980. Bantam 13999. PBO. SF. VG+. B5d. $4.00

BERMAN, Harold edt. *Pocket Book of Dog Stories.* 1942. Pocket 187. PBO. c/Hoffman. VG. B6d. $5.00

BERNARD, Joel. *Thinking Machine Affair.* Ace 51704. PBO. TVTI. G+. M6d. $9.50

BERNARD, M. *Mario Lanza.* MacFadden 125113. VG. B3d. $4.00

BERNARD, Rafe. *Invaders #3, Army of the Undead.* 1967. Pyramid R 1711. TVTI. c/Roy Thinnes: photo. VG+. B4d. $6.00

BERNARD, William. *Jailbait.* 1952. Popular 1392. 2nd edn. JF. G+. P1d. $8.50

BERNARD, William. *Jailbait.* 1951. Popular 392. PBO. c/Belarski. scarce. JD. NF. B6a #74. $55.00

BERNARD & JOHNSON. *Buttercup 9.* 1966. Bee Line 127. PBO. VG+. B6d. $7.50

BERNSTEIN, Leonard. *Joys of Music.* 1967. Signet Q 3215. 1st prtg. c/photo. VG. P7d. $4.50

BERRILL, N.J. *Man's Emerging Mind.* 1957. Premier D 50. Nfi. VG+. B5d. $4.00

BERRY, James R. *Galactic Invaders.* 1976. Laser 31. 1st edn. SF. F. F2d. $12.50

BERRY, Stephen A. *Final Assault.* 1988. TOR 53189. SF. F. W2d. $3.75

BERRYMAN, Opal Leigh. *Make It on Temple Street.* 1961. News Stand Library 168. PBO. c/Bonfils: gga. NF. B6a #74. $48.50

BERRYMAN, Opal Leigh. *Make It on Temple Street.* 1961. Newsstand Library U 168. 1st edn. c/gga. Cr. F. F2d. $15.00

BERTIN, Jack. *Pyramids From Space.* Uni-Book. SF. F. W2d. $4.00

BERTO, Giuseppe. *Sky Is Red.* 1952. Signet S 971. Fi. VG. B5d. $4.00

BERWYN, J.N. *Carnal Clinic.* Corsair 208. VG. B3d. $4.00

BESAW, Victor. *Alien.* 1979. Gold Medal 4197. PBO. SF. NF. B6d. $3.00

BESSIE, Oscar. *Bonnie.* 1965. Domino Book 72-960. PBO. scarce. NF. B6a #76. $38.25

BESSIE, Oscar. *Queer Frenzy.* 1960. Tuxedo 123. 1st edn. F2d. $10.00

BESTE, R. Vernon. *Moonbeams.* 1964. Lancer 73-444. c/S Borack. My. VG. B5d. $4.00

BESTER, Alfred. *Dark Side of the Earth.* 1964. Signet D 2474. VG. I1d. $5.00

BESTER, Alfred. *Dark Side of the Earth.* 1964. Signet D 2474. 1st pb. NF. M1d. $10.00

BESTER, Alfred. *Demolished Man.* 1965. Signet D 2679. 3rd prtg. SF. F. W2d. $3.50

BESTER, Alfred. *Demolished Man.* 1959. Signet S1593. 2nd edn. SF. VG+. B5d. $5.00

BESTER, Alfred. *Demolished Man.* 1954. Signet 1105. 1st pb. SF. VG+. B6d. $8.00

BESTER, Alfred. *Demolished Man.* 1954. Signet. 1st pb. F. M1d. $15.00

BESTER, Alfred. *Rat Race.* 1956. Berkley G 19. c/Sardis. Fi. G+. B5d. $2.50

BESTER, Alfred. *Rat Race.* 1956. Berkley G 19. c/sgn. VG. B3d. $5.00

BESTER, Alfred. *Starburst.* 1958. Signet S 1524. PBO. SF. G+. B5d. $3.00

BESTER, Alfred. *Starburst.* 1958. Signet S 1524. VG. I1d. $5.00

BESTER, Alfred. *Starburst.* 1958. Signet S 1524. 1st pb. F. M1d. $15.00

BESTER, Alfred. *Stars My Destination.* 1970. Bantam H 4815. SF. VG. W2d. $3.75

BESTER, Alfred. *Stars My Destination.* 1957. Signet S 1389. PBO. c/R Powers. SF. G+. B5d. $4.50

BESTER, Alfred. *Stars My Destination.* 1957. Signet S 1389. 1st pb. NF. M1d. $10.00

BESTER, Alfred. *Stars My Destination.* 1961. Signet S 1931. 1st prtg. c/Powers. VG. P7d. $5.00

BESTER, Alfred. *Tiger! Tiger!* 1967. Penguin 2620. c/Bester: sgn. VG. B3d. $9.00

BETHANCOURT, T.E. *Mortal Instruments.* Bantam 11752. 1st prtg. F. S1d. $5.00

BETTERIDGE, D. *Spies of Peenemunde.* Corgi 745. VG. B3d. $6.00

BEVERLEY-BIDDINGS, A.R. *River of Rogues.* Pocket 946. G+. G5d. $2.00

BEYNON, John. *Harris.* 1967. Lancer 72-155. SF. VG+. B4d. $5.00

BICKHAM/PATTERSON. *Rider of the Rincon/Killer's Paradise.* Ace D 442. We. VG. B6d. $5.00

BICKHAM/WHITTINGTON. *Searching Rider/Hangman's Territory.* 1961. Ace D 510. PBO. We. VG. P6d. $4.00

BIDART, G. *Naked Witch.* 1975. Pinnacle 240529. VG+. B3d. $5.00

BIERCE, Ambrose. *Monk & the Hangman's Daughter.* 1955. Avon 628. 1st prtg. My. G+. R5d. $4.50

BIERCE, Ambrose. *Vol I: World of Horror.* Ballantine 02422. VG+. B3d. $6.00

BIGGERS, Earl Derr. *Agony Column.* 1951. Avon 337. My. VG. B4d. $5.00

BIGGERS, Earl Derr. *Behind That Curtain.* 1942. Pocket 191. c/H L Hoffman. My. VG. B5d. $8.00

BIGGERS, Earl Derr. *Black Camel.* Pocket 133. VG+. G5d. $17.50

BIGGERS, Earl Derr. *Charlie Chan Carries On.* 1975. Bantam Q 6415. 1st prtg. My. VG. R5d. $1.75

BIGGERS, Earl Derr. *Charlie Chan Carries On.* 1943. Pocket 207. 1st prtg. VG. P7d. $9.00

BIGGERS, Earl Derr. *Chinese Parrot.* Avon 344. VG. B3d. $5.00

BIGGERS, Earl Derr. *Chinese Parrot.* 1942. Pocket 168. My. G+. B5d. $7.50

BIGGERS, Earl Derr. *Chinese Parrot.* Pyramid T 1970. reprint. VG. B6d. $4.00

BIGGERS, Earl Derr. *Keeper of the Keys.* PB Library 52-208. VG. B3d. $4.50

BIGGERS, Earl Derr. *Seven Keys to Baldpate.* Popular 132. VG. G5d. $12.00

BIGGLE, Lloyd. *All the Colors of Darkness.* 1968. PB Library 53-746. 2nd prtg. SF. VG. W2d. $3.50

BIGGLE, Lloyd. *All the Colors of Darkness.* 1965. PB Library. 1st pb. F. M1d. $8.00

BIGGLE, Lloyd. *Fury Out of Time.* 1967. Berkley X 1393. 1st prtg. SF. VG. R5d. $2.50

BIGGLE, Lloyd. *Light That Never Was.* DAW 52. NF. I1d. $4.00

BIGGLE, Lloyd. *Silent Sky.* BT 51122. VG. P9d. $1.75

BIGGLE, Lloyd. *Watchers of the Dark.* Curtis 07033. 1st prtg. SF. VG+. R5d. $2.50

BIGGLE/LOWNDES. *Angry Espers/Puzzle Planet.* 1966. Ace D 485. SF. VG+. W2d. $10.00

BILL, Alfred H. *Wolf in the Garden.* 1972. Centaur 9. c/V Finlay. SF. NF. B5d. $8.50

BILL, Tom. *Gentleman of the Jungle.* Dell 456. c/R Stanley. Fi. VG. B5d. $4.00

BILL, Tom. *Iams, Jack.* Dell 457. c/H Barton. My. VG. B5d. $5.00

BILLIAS, S. *American Book of the Dead.* My 20335. c/sgn. VG. B3d. $6.00

BINDER, Eando. *Adam Link, Robot.* 1965. PB Library 52-847. 1st edn. SF. F. F2d. $10.00

BINDER, Eando. *Adam Link, Robot.* 1974. Warner 75460. 3rd prtg. SF. VG. W2d. $3.25

BINDER, Eando. *Anton York, Immortal.* 1969. Belmont B60-1033. 1st prtg. SF. VG. R5d. $2.00

BINDER, Eando. *Anton York, Immortal.* 1965. Pyramid. 1st pb. F. M1d. $7.00

BINDER, Eando. *Double Man.* Curtis 07167. 1st prtg. SF. VG. R5d. $1.50

BINDER, Eando. *Five Steps to Tomorrow.* Curtis 07106. 1st prtg. VG. S1d. $4.00

BINDER, Eando. *Impossible World.* Curtis 07113. 1st prtg. SF. VG+. R5d. $2.50

BINDER, Eando. *Lords of Creation.* 1969. Belmont B50-852. 1st prtg. SF. VG. R5d. $3.00

BINDER, Eando. *Menace of the Saucers.* 1969. Belmont. 1st edn. NF. M1d. $5.00

BINDER, Eando. *Mind From Outer Space.* Curtis 07188. 1st prtg. G. S1d. $2.50

BINDER, Eando. *Night of the Saucer.* Belmont B75-2116. 1st prtg. G+. S1d. $3.50

BINDER, O.O. *Hospital Horror.* Popular 01593. VG. B3d. $4.00

BINDER, Otto. *Avengers Battle the Earth-Wrecker.* 1967. Bantam F 3569. SF. VG. W2d. $3.75

BINDER, Otto. *What We Really Know About Flying Saucers.* 1967. Gold Medal T 1863. 1st prtg. VG. P7d. $4.00

BINGHAM, Carson. *Gorgo.* Monarch 603. MTI. VG. B3d. $4.50

BINGHAM, Carson. *Payola Woman.* Belmont 203. PBO. VG. B3d. $5.50

BINGHAM, Carson. *Run Tough, Run Hard.* 1961. Monarch 194. JD. VG. P1d. $15.00

BINGHAM, Carson. *Run Tough, Run Hard.* 1964. Monarch 487. 1st edn. c/gga. De. F. F2d. $18.00

BINGHAM, Carson. *Street Is My Beat.* 1961. Monarch MM 606. PBO. c/De Soto: gga. scarce. VG+. B6a #80. $41.00

BINGHAM, Carson. *Witch Queen of Mongo.* 1974. Avon 21378. SF. F. W2d. $4.50

BINGHAM, J. *Marion.* 1960. Pan G 368. VG. B3d. $7.50

BINGHAM, John. *Murder Off the Record.* Dell D 351. VG+. G5d. $5.50

BINGHAM, John. *Murder Plan Six.* 1962. Dell R 112. 1st prtg. My. VG+. B3d/R5d. $5.00

BINGHAM, John. *My Name Is Michael Sibley.* Dell 813. NF. G5d. $6.00

BINGHAM, John. *Night's Black Agent.* Peng C 224. VG. G5d. $3.00

BIRCH, B. *Subway in the Sky.* Four Square 149. 1st Eng edn. MTI. c/Van Johnson. VG+. B3d. $6.00

BIRD, Brandon. *Dead & Gone (Downbeat for a Dirge).* Dell 857. G+. G5d. $3.50

BIRD, Brandon. *Death in 4 Colors.* Dell 531. G+. G5d. $4.00

BIRKENFIELD, G. *Room in Berlin.* Avon 675. VG. B3d. $4.50

BIRKIN, Charles edt. *Witch-Baiter.* 1967. PB Library 52-468. SF. G+. B5d. $3.00

BISCHOFF, BROWN, & RICHARDSON. *Personal Demon.* 1985. Signet 3814. PBO. NF. B6d. $3.00

BISCHOFF, David. *Gremlins 2: The New Batch.* 1990. Avon 76061-4. 1st edn. SF. F. F2d. $8.00

BISCHOFF, David. *Infinite Battle.* 1985. Ace 37018. SF. F. W2d. $3.50

BISCHOFF, David. *Manhattan Project.* 1986. Avon 75125. 1st prtg. MTI. SF. VG. W2d. $3.25

BISHOP, C. *Quick Draw.* Bantam 108. VG+. B3d. $5.00

BISHOP, G. *Flagellation: Rod & Whip.* Viceroy 109. VG+. B3d. $5.50

BISHOP, Jim. *Day Christ Died.* 1959. Cardinal GC 73. c/T Dunn: crucifixion. NF. VG. B5d. $2.50

BISHOP, Jim. *Day Christ Was Born.* 1961. Pocket 7012. NF. VG+. B5d. $4.00

BISHOP, Jim. *Day Lincoln Was Shot.* 1956. Bantam F 1428. 1st prtg. VG. P7d. $4.00

BISHOP, Leonard. *Desire Years.* 1962. Gold medal 1247. 1st edn. JD. F. F2d. $15.00

BISHOP, Leonard. *Everlasting.* 1984. Pocket 47677. SF. VG. W2d. $3.50

BISHOP, Michael. *Ancient of Days.* 1986. TOR 53197. SF. VG. W2d. $3.50

BISHOP, Sheilah. *House With Two Faces.* 1963. Ace K 192. 1st prtg. My. G+. R5d. $1.00

BISSELL, Richard. *High Water.* 1955. Signet 1230. 1st pb. Ad. VG+. B6d. $7.50

BISSELL, Richard. *Pajama.* Signet 1129. c/Zuckerberg. VG+. B3d. $4.50

BISSELL, Richard. *River in My Blood.* 1955. Signet 1193. Fa. NF. B4d. $5.00

BISSON, Terry. *Talking Man.* 1987. Avon. 1st pb. F. M1d. $5.00

BIXBY, Jerome. *Day of the Dove.* 1978. Bantam 12017. SF. F. W2d. $17.50

BIXBY, Jerome. *Space by the Tale.* 1964. Ballantine. 1st edn. F. M1d. $10.00

BLACK, A. edt. *Devil's Coven.* 1972. New English 12441. PBO. VG+. B3d. $9.00

BLACK, Andrew. *Love Hostess.* 1963. Beacon B 664F. PBO. c/App. Ad. NF. B5d. $7.50

BLACK, Brian. *Eve Without Adam.* 1964. Beacon B 692X. Ad. VG+. B5d. $5.50

BLACK, Brian. *Jeanne.* 1963. Beacon B 623F. PBO. Ad. VG+. B5d. $5.50

BLACK, Campbell. *Wanting.* 1987. Jove 09177. 1st prtg. SF. VG+. R5d. $1.75

BLACK, Gavin. *Dragon for Christmas.* 1967. Banner. 1st pb. F. M1d. $10.00

BLACK, Gavin. *Dragon for Killing.* Banner 102. VG. B3d. $5.00

BLACK, Libbie. *Bedeviled.* Dell 344. 1st prtg. My. VG+. R5d. $6.75

BLACK, M. *Shadow of Evil.* Digit NN. Th. VG+. B3d. $7.00

BLACK, Pansy E. *Men From the Meteor.* Stellar 13. SF. F. W2d. $20.00

BLACK, Veronica. *Master of Malcarew.* Berkley S 2301. G+. G5d. $4.50

BLACK & DE PALMA. *Dressed To Kill.* 1980. Bantam 12977. 1st prtg. My. VG. R5d. $1.75

BLACK & KOLMAN. *Royal Vultures.* Perma M 4103. VG+. G5d. $3.00

BLACKBURN, John. *Bury Him Darkly.* Berkley S 1953. VG. G5d. $2.50

BLACKBURN, John. *Gaunt Woman.* Lancer 73-583. G+. G5d. $4.00

BLACKBURN, John. *Gaunt Woman.* Panther 2227. VG. B3d. $5.00

BLACKBURN, John. *Wreath of Roses.* 1966. Lancer 73-521. 1st pb. VG. B6d. $3.50

BLACKBURN, T.W. *Broken Arrow Range.* Dell 10¢ 20. VG. B3d. $4.00

BLACKBURN, T.W. *Navajo Canyon.* Pennant P 1. NF. I1d. $7.00

BLACKBURN, T.W. *Short Grass.* 1948. Bantam 207. 1st pb. c/Saunders. We. VG+. B6d. $8.00

BLACKBURN, T.W. *Sierra Baron.* Bantam 1798. MTI. VG. B3d. $4.50

BLACKSTOCK, Lee. *Woman in the Woods.* Dell D 301. VG. G5d. $5.00

BLACKWELL, Ken. *Warm Summer's Shame.* 1966. Midwood 33-745. Ad. VG. B5d. $4.50

BLAIR, Clay Jr. *Beyond Courage.* 1964. Ballantine U 2209. reprints 134. War. VG+. B4d. $2.00

BLAIR, Ken. *Starway to Lust.* 1966. Spartan 143. PBO. NF. B6d. $10.00

BLAKE, Andrew. *Love Hostess.* 1963. Beacon B664F. PBO. Ad. NF. B5d. $7.50

BLAKE, Bud. *Ever Happen To You?* 1963. Avon F 170. G+. P6d. $1.75

BLAKE, Eleanor. *Death Down East.* 1945. Penguin 571. c/Jonas. My. G+. B4d. $2.00

BLAKE, J.D. *Executive Pad.* Rapture R 217. VG+. B3d. $9.00

BLAKE, J.D. *Neon Jungle.* PEC N146. c/Blake & Neutzel: sgn. VG. B3d. $7.00

BLAKE, Nicholas. *Death & Daisy Bland.* 1960. Dell 1st Edn D 339. 1st pb. My. VG+. B6d. $12.00

BLAKE, Nicholas. *Head of a Traveler.* Pocket 742. VG. I1d. $5.00

BLAKE, Nicholas. *Penknife in My Heart.* 1960. Crest S 388. 1st prtg. My. VG+. R5d. $5.00

BLAKE, Nicholas. *Question of Proof.* Popular 123. c/Fiedler. My. VG. B4d. $6.00

BLAKE, Nicholas. *Smiler.* 1945. Popular 41. c/Hoffman. My. VG. P6d. $8.50

BLAKE, Nicholas. *Thou Shell of Death.* 1964. Berkley F 1002. 1st prtg. My. VG. R5d. $3.50

BLAKE, Nicholas. *Widow's Cruise.* Dell 9538. VG+. B3d. $4.00

BLAKE, R. *Encyclopedia of Abnormal Sex.* Brandon House 936. VG+. B3d. $6.00

BLAKE, Roger. *Caper at Canaveral.* 1963. Intimate Edn 724. PBO. c/gga. VG. P6d. $4.00

BLAKE, Roger. *Depraved Debutante.* 1962. Saber SA 28. Ad. G. B5d. $2.00

BLAKE, Roger. *Lesbianism & Single Girl.* Century. VG+. B3d. $4.50

BLAKE, Samantha. *Teacher's Revenge.* 1973. Liverpool SRS 1018. AD. VG+. B5d. $5.00

BLAKE, Stephanie. *Swap Fever.* 1974. Liverpool TNS 598. Ad. VG+. B5d. $4.50

BLAKE, Walker E. *Heartbreak Ridge.* 1962. Monarch 247. PBO. c/R Stanley. Fi. VG. B5d. $4.50

BLAKE, Walker E. *Space Egg.* 1962. Monarch 252. SF. VG+. B4d. $7.00

BLAKENEY, Jay D. *Goda War.* 1989. Ace 28855. 1st prtg. SF. VG. W2d. $3.00

BLAKESLEY, S. *Man With a Number*. Sexton Blake 278. VG+. B3d. $8.00

BLANC, Suzanne. *Green Stone*. Lancer 73-533. VG. M6d. $5.00

BLASHFIELD, Jean. *Villians of Volturnus #8*. 1983. TOR 51208. SF. VG. W2d. $3.00

BLASSINGAME, Lurton. *Sweet Cheat*. 1959. Dell A 182. 1st edn. c/gga. My. F. F2d. $20.00

BLASSINGAME, W. *J Smith Hears Death Walking*. Bart 5. VG. B3d. $7.00

BLATTY, W.P. *John Goldfarb, Please Come Home*. 1964. Crest D 763. 1st prtg. VG. R5d. $2.00

BLAYLOCK, James. *Disappearing Dwarf*. 1983. Ballantine. 1st edn. NF. M1d. $5.00

BLAYLOCK, James. *Elfin Ship*. 1983. Ballantine 29491. 2nd prtg. SF. F. W2d. $3.50

BLAYNE, S. *Terror in the Night*. Gold Medal 325. VG. B3d. $4.00

BLEDSOE, R. *Love Is Fun*. Kozy Book 153. NF. B3d. $7.00

BLEILER & DIKTY edts. *Frontiers in Space*. 1955. Bantam. 1st pb. F. M1d. $13.00

BLEILER & DIKTY edts. *Imagination Unlimited*. 1959. Berkley G 233. SF. VG. W2d. $5.00

BLIGH, Norman. *Artists' Model*. 1951. Quarter Book 94. PBO. c/Gross: gga. VG+. B6a #77. $77.00

BLIGH, Norman. *Bad Sue*. 1950. Quarter Book 50. PBO. c/gga. scarce. VG+. B6a #77. $82.50

BLIGH, Norman. *Motel Mistress*. Star Novel 763. c/gga. VG+. B6a #76. $61.00

BLIGH, Norman. *River Boat Girl*. Original Digest 740. c/Belarski. scarce. VG+. B6a #77. $85.00

BLIGH, Norman. *Soft Shoulders*. 1952. Cameo Digest 316. PBO. c/Mal Singer: gga. VG+. B6a #74. $66.00

BLIGH, Norman. *Strictly for Pleasure*. Original 702. VG. B3d. $7.00

BLIGH, Norman. *Visiting Nurse*. Original 727. PBO. VG. B3d. $10.00

BLIGH, Norman. *Wayward Nurse*. Venus 186. c/Belarski: gga. VG. B6a #76. $65.00

BLIGH, Norman. *Young Wife*. Venus 151. PBO. VG. B3d. $12.50

BLISH, James. *Best of James Blish*. 1979. Ballantine 25600. c/H Van Dongen. SF. NF. B5d. $7.50

BLISH, James. *Black Easter*. 1969. Dell. 1st pb. F. M1d. $15.00

BLISH, James. *Case of Conscience*. Arrow 637. VG+. B3d. $6.00

BLISH, James. *Case of Conscience*. 1958. Ballantine 256. PBO. c/R Powers. SF. F. M1d. $12.00

BLISH, James. *Case of Conscience*. 1958. Ballantine 256. SF. VG+. B4d. $7.00

BLISH, James. *Cities in Flight*. 1971. Avon N 187. 3rd prtg. SF. VG. W2d. $3.00

BLISH, James. *Duplicated Man*. 1964. Airmont SF 8. SF. VG. W2d. $4.50

BLISH, James. *Earthman Come Home*. 1968. Avon S 218. 5th end. SF. VG+. B5d. $3.50

BLISH, James. *ESPer*. 1958. Avon T 268. VG+. B3d. $4.50

BLISH, James. *ESPer*. 1952. Avon. 1st pb. NF. M1d. $15.00

BLISH, James. *Frozen Year*. Ballantine 197. PBO. c/Powers. VG+. B3d. $5.50

BLISH, James. *Frozen Year*. 1957. Ballantine. 1st edn. F. M1d. $10.00

BLISH, James. *Galactic Cluster*. 1959. Signet S 1719. PBO. c/P Lehr. SF. VG. B5d. $4.00

BLISH, James. *Galactic Cluster*. 1959. Signet. 1st pb. F. M1d. $13.00

BLISH, James. *Jack of Eagles*. Galaxy SF 19. VG. B3d. $4.00

BLISH, James. *Life for the Stars*. 1966. Avon G 1280. 3rd prtg. SF. VG. W2d. $3.50

BLISH, James. *Life for the Stars*. 1962. Avon. 1st pb. F. M1d. $10.00

BLISH, James. *Nebula Award Stories #5*. Pocket 77423. VG+. B3d. $5.00

BLISH, James. *New Dreams This Morning*. 1966. Ballantine U 2331. 1st edn. F. M1d. $6.00

BLISH, James. *Night Shapes*. 1962. Ballantine F 647. PBO. SF. G+. B5d. $5.50

BLISH, James. *Night Shapes*. 1962. Ballantine. 1st edn. F. M1d. $15.00

BLISH, James. *Seedling Stars*. 1959. Signet S 1622. c/P Lehr. SF. VG+. B5d. $5.00

BLISH, James. *Seedling Stars*. 1959. Signet. 1st pb. F. M1d. $20.00

BLISH, James. *So Close to Home*. 1961. Ballantine 465K. SF. VG. B3d/B5d. $5.00

BLISH, James. *So Close to Home*. 1961. Ballantine. F. M1d. $10.00

BLISH, James. *Spock Must Die!* 1970. Bantam HP 5515. 7th prtg. SF. G. W2d. $4.00

BLISH, James. *Spock Must Die!* 1972. Bantam 08075. 11th prtg. SF. VG+. W2d. $5.00

BLISH, James. *Spock Must Die!* 1978. Bantam 12589. 15th prtg. SF. VG. W2d. $4.50

BLISH, James. *Star Trek #10*. 1974. Bantam SP 8401. TVTI. SF. VG+ B5d. $4.00

BLISH, James. *Star Trek #10*. 1974. Bantam 8401. 1st edn. SF. F. F2d. $7.00

BLISH, James. *Star Trek #2*. 1968. Bantam 039. 4th prtg. SF. VG. W2d. $7.00

BLISH, James. *Star Trek #2*. 1977. Bantam 10811. 20th prtg. SF. VG. W2d. $6.00

BLISH, James. *Star Trek #3*. 1969. Bantam F 4371. TVTI. c/photo. NF. B4d. $4.00

BLISH, James. *Star Trek #3*. 1976. Bantam Q 2253. 19th prtg. SF. F. W2d. $7.00

BLISH, James. *Star Trek #5*. 1972. Bantam S 7300. 5th prtg. SF. F. W2d. $8.00

BLISH, James. *Star Trek #6*. 1972. Bantam S 7364. 1st edn. SF. F. F2d. $8.00

BLISH, James. *Star Trek #8*. 1977. Bantam 10816. 10th prtg. SF. VG. W2d. $4.50

BLISH, James. *Star Trek #9*. 1973. Bantam SP 7808. 1st edn. NF. P9d. $1.75

BLISH, James. *Star Trek*. 1967. Bantam F 3459. 4th prtg. SF. VG. W2d. $6.00

BLISH, James. *Star Trek*. 1972. Bantam S 7300. 1st edn. TVTI. SF. F. F2d. $10.00

BLISH, James. *Titan's Daughter*. 1966. Berkley F 1163. 3rd edn. VG. P9d. $1.50

BLISH, James. *Titan's Daughter*. 1961. Berkley G 507. PBO. c/Barye. SF. VG. B3d/B6d. $5.00

BLISH, James. *Titan's Daughter*. 1961. Berkley G 507. 1st edn. F. M1d. $10.00

BLISH, James. *Torrent of Faces*. Ace A 29. VG. M1d. $6.00

BLISH, James. *Triumph of Time*. 1966. Avon S 221. 3rd edn. SF. VG. B5d. $2.50

BLISH, James. *Triumph of Time*. 1958. Avon. 1st pb. F. M1d. $13.00

BLISH, James. *Vor*. 1967. Avon S 313. 2nd prtg. SF. G. B5d/W2d. $2.50

BLISH, James. *Vor*. 1958. Avon. 1st pb. F. M1d. $13.00

BLISH, James. *Warriors of Day*. Galaxy SF 16. VG+. B3d. $6.00

BLISH, James. *Warriors of Day.* 1967. Lancer 73-580. c/A Weston. SF. VG. B5d. $35.00

BLISH, James. *Where No Man Has Gone Before.* 1977. Bantam Photonovel 2. 1st edn. F. M1d. $15.00

BLISH, James. *Year 2018.* 1957. Avon T 193. 1st edn. F. M1d. $10.00

BLISH, James. *Year 2018.* 1957. Avon T 193. 1st prtg. SF. VG+. I1d/R5d. $4.00

BLISH & COHEN. *Monsters of Star Trek.* 1980. Pocket. 1st edn. F. M1d. $5.00

BLISH & GERROLD. *World of Star Trek.* 1973. Ballantine. 1st edn. F. M1d. $10.00

BLISH & GOLDIN. *Trek to Madworld.* 1984. Bantam. 3rd edn. F. M1d. $3.00

BLISH & MARSHAK. *Star Trek: The New Voyages.* 1976. Bantam. 1st edn. F. M1d. $5.00

BLISH & MCINTYRE. *Enterprise: The First Adventures.* 1986. Pocket. 1st edn. F. M1d. $4.00

BLISH & SILVERBERG. *Pair From Space.* 1965. Belmont Double. 1st edn. NF. M1d. $10.00

BLISH/SILVERBERG. *Giants in the Earth/ We, the Marauders.* 1968. Belmont B50-813. 1st prtg. SF. VG+. R5d. $5.75

BLOCH, Robert. *American Gothic.* Gold Medal 2391. c/sgn. VG. B3d. $7.00

BLOCH, Robert. *American Gothic.* 1975. Star 39813. 1st pb. Ho. VG+. B6d. $9.00

BLOCH, Robert. *Atoms & Evil.* 1962. Gold Medal S 1231. 1st edn. c/sgn. SF. F. F2d. $30.00

BLOCH, Robert. *Atoms & Evil.* 1962. Gold Medal S 1231. 1st prtg. SF. VG. R5d. $9.00

BLOCH, Robert. *Blood Runs Cold.* Popular K 18. VG. B3d. $5.00

BLOCH, Robert. *Bogey Men.* 1963. Pyramid F 839. 1st edn. F. F2d. $12.00

BLOCH, Robert. *Bogey Men.* Pyramid 839. c/sgn. VG+. B3d. $6.00

BLOCH, Robert. *Chamber of Horrors.* 1966. Award 187. PBO. c/sgn. NF. B6d. $12.50

BLOCH, Robert. *Chamber of Horrors.* 1966. Award 187. 1st edn. Ho. F. F2d. $20.00

BLOCH, Robert. *Couch.* 1962. Gold Medal S 1192. 1st edn. MTI. c/sgn. Ho. F. F2d. $30.00

BLOCH, Robert. *Couch.* Gold Medal 1192. MTI. c/sgn. VG. B3d. $6.50

BLOCH, Robert. *Dead Beat.* Popular Giant G 532. NF. I1d. $10.00

BLOCH, Robert. *Deadbeat.* 1960. Popular. 1st pb. F. M1d. $20.00

BLOCH, Robert. *Dragons & Nightmares.* 1969. Belmont B75-1060. 1st prtg. SF. VG. R5d. $7.50

BLOCH, Robert. *Dragons & Nightmares.* Tower 40119. 1st prtg. G+. S1d. $3.00

BLOCH, Robert. *Fear Today: Gone Tomorrow.* 1971. Award A 8115. SF. F. W2d. $12.00

BLOCH, Robert. *Firebug.* 1977. Corgi 10403. 1st pb. Ho/My. NF. B6d. $16.50

BLOCH, Robert. *Firebug.* 1961. Regency RB 101. c/Bloch: sgn. VG+. B3a #24. $38.50

BLOCH, Robert. *Firebug.* 1961. Regency RB 101. 1st edn. scarce. My. F. F2d. $70.00

BLOCH, Robert. *Horror 7.* 1963. Belmont 90-275. 1st edn. My. F. F2d. $25.00

BLOCH, Robert. *House of the Hatchet.* 1971. London. 2nd British edn. F. M1d. $15.00

BLOCH, Robert. *House of the Hatchet.* 1965. Tandem Book T 19. 1st UK edn. c/sgn. VG+. B6a #80. $24.25

BLOCH, Robert. *It's All In Your Mind.* 1971. Curtis 7147. PBO. c/classic. NF. B6a #74. $50.00

BLOCH, Robert. *Kidnapper.* 1954. Lion 185. 1st edn. My. NF. F2d. $85.00

BLOCH, Robert. *Living Demons.* 1967. Belmont B 50-787. 1st edn. My. F. F2d. $12.00

BLOCH, Robert. *More Nightmares.* 1962. Belmont L 92-530. 1st edn. SF. F. F2d. $25.00

BLOCH, Robert. *Night of the Ripper.* TOR 50070. 1st pb. c/sgn. NF. B6d. $15.00

BLOCH, Robert. *Night Walker.* 1964. Award. 1st pb. VG. M1d. $15.00

BLOCH, Robert. *Night World.* Crest M 1845. c/sgn. VG. B3d. $5.00

BLOCH, Robert. *Night World.* Crest M 1845. 1st prtg. G. S1d. $3.50

BLOCH, Robert. *Night World.* 1986. TOR 51570. 1st edn. c/sgn. F. B6d. $15.00

BLOCH, Robert. *Nightmares.* 1961. Belmont 233. PBO. Ho. VG. F2d. $7.00

BLOCH, Robert. *Psycho II.* Warner 90-804. c/sgn. NF. B3d. $6.00

BLOCH, Robert. *Psycho.* 1960. Crest 385. MTI. VG. B3d. $7.50

BLOCH, Robert. *Psycho.* 1960. Crest 385. 1st edn. PBO. c/sgn: photo. F. F2d. $40.00

BLOCH, Robert. *Scarf of Passion.* Avon 211. 1st prtg. My. VG. F2d. $25.00

BLOCH, Robert. *Scarf of Passion.* Avon 211. 1st edn. PBO. c/sgn. VG+. F2d. $45.00

BLOCH, Robert. *Scarf.* 1952. Avon 494. c/sgn. G+. B6d. $12.50

BLOCH, Robert. *Scarf.* Gold Medal 1727. c/sgn. VG. B3d. $5.50

BLOCH, Robert. *Scarf.* 1966. Gold Medal. 1st pb. F. M1d. $15.00

BLOCH, Robert. *Skull of the Marquis De Sade & Other Stories.* 1961. Pyramid F 1247. 1st edn. MTI. c/sgn. F. F2d. $35.00

BLOCH, Robert. *Skull of the Marquis De Sade & Other Stories.* 1961. Pyramid F 1247. 1st prtg. VG. S1d. $10.50

BLOCH, Robert. *Sneak Preview.* PB Library 64-660. c/sgn. VG. B3d. $5.00

BLOCH, Robert. *Spiderweb.* 1954. Ace D 59. PBO. c/sgn. VG+. B6d. $45.00

BLOCH, Robert. *Spiderweb.* 1954. Ace D 59. 1st edn. PBO. c/Bloch: sgn. scarce. VG+. B6a #77. $66.00

BLOCH, Robert. *Star Stalker.* 1968. Pyramid F 1869. 1st edn. My. NF. F2d. $25.00

BLOCH, Robert. *Such Stuff As Screams Are Made Of.* Dell 27996. c/sgn. VG+. B3d. $6.50

BLOCH, Robert. *Tales in a Jugular Vein.* 1965. Pyramid R 1139. 1st edn. F. F2d/ M1d. $15.00

BLOCH, Robert. *Twilight Zone the Movie.* 1983. Warner 30840. 1st prtg. VG. R5d. $2.00

BLOCH, Robert. *Will To Kill.* 1954. Ace D 67. 1st edn. My. NF. F2d. $75.00

BLOCH, Robert. *Will To Kill.* 1954. Ace S 67. PBO. c/DeSoto: sgn. extremely scarce. VG+. B6a #77. $82.50

BLOCH, Robert. *Yours Truly, Jack the Ripper.* 1962. Belmont 92-527. PBO. c/sgn. VG+. B6a #79. $68.00

BLOCH, Robert. *Yours Truly, Jack the Ripper.* 1962. Belmont 92-527. 1st edn. Ho. NF. F2d. $20.00

BLOCH/BLOCH. *Ladies' Day/This Crowded Earth.* 1968. Belmont B 60-080. PBO. SF. VG. P6d. $7.00

BLOCH/BLOCH. *Shooting Star/Terror in the Night.* 1958. Ace D 265. c/Bloch: inscr. VG+. B3a #20. $40.00

BLOCH/BLOCH. *Shooting Star/Terror in the Night.* 1958. Ace D 265. 1st edn. Ho. VG. F2d. $22.00

BLOCHMAN, Lawrence G. *Blow-Down.* Dell 156. VG. I1d. $7.00

BLOCHMAN, Lawrence G. *Blow-Down.* 1953. Dell 740. c/gga. My. VG. B4d. $3.00

BLOCHMAN, Lawrence G. *Bombay Mail.* Dell 488. 1st prtg. My. VG+. I1d/R5d. $5.50

BLOCHMAN, Lawrence G. *Death Walks in Marble Halls.* Dell 10¢ 19. G+. G5d. $7.50

BLOCHMAN, Lawrence G. *Diagnosis: Homicide.* 1951. Pocket 793. 1st prtg. c/Johnson: gga. VG. P7d. $6.00

BLOCHMAN, Lawrence G. *Midnight Sailing.* 1944. Dell 43. 1st edn. PBO. c/Gregg. rare. F. B6a #80. $165.00

BLOCHMAN, Lawrence G. *Recipe for Homicide.* Dell 833. c/V Tossey. My. VG. B5d. $3.00

BLOCHMAN, Lawrence G. *Recipe for Homicide.* Dell 833. VG+. G5d. $6.50

BLOCHMAN, Lawrence G. *See You at the Morgue.* 1952. Dell 638. c/Mike Ludlow: gga. My. VG. P6d. $1.50

BLOCHMAN, Lawrence G. *Wives To Burn.* Dell 134. G+. I1d. $5.00

BLOCHMAN, Lawrence G. *Wives To Burn.* Dell 134. VG+. B3d. $9.00

BLOCK, Lawrence. *Adolescent Sexual Behavior.* 1964. Monarch 436. 1st edn. My. F. F2d. $25.00

BLOCK, Lawrence. *Ariel.* Berkley 05169. 1st pb. VG. M6d. $4.50

BLOCK, Lawrence. *Cancelled Czech.* 1966. Gold Medal D 1747. 1st edn. My. F. F2d. $25.00

BLOCK, Lawrence. *Carla.* 1958. Midwood 8. 1st edn. c/Rader: gga. My. F. F2d. $40.00

BLOCK, Lawrence. *Death Pulls a Double-cross.* 1961. Gold Medal S 1162. 1st edn. My. F. F2d. $25.00

BLOCK, Lawrence. *Eight-Million Ways To Die.* 1983. Jove 07257. 1st prtg. VG. P7d. $3.50

BLOCK, Lawrence. *Enough of Sorrow.* 1965. Midwood 32-550. 1st edn. My. F. F2d. $25.00

BLOCK, Lawrence. *Here Comes a Hero.* 1968. Gold Medal R 2008. 1st edn. My. NF. F2d. $20.00

BLOCK, Lawrence. *Markham.* 1961. Belmont 236. 1st edn. My. NF. F2d. $20.00

BLOCK, Lawrence. *Markham.* 1961. Belmont 236. 1st edn. TVTI. c/sgn. De. F. F2d. $35.00

BLOCK, Lawrence. *Me Tanner, You Jane.* Jove 08516. 1st pb. G+. M6d. $7.50

BLOCK, Lawrence. *Mona.* 1961. Gold Medal S 1085. 1st edn. My. VG+. F2d. $20.00

BLOCK, Lawrence. *Sin Bum.* 1963. Corinth MR 472. 1st edn. My. F. F2d. $25.00

BLOCK, Lawrence. *Specialist.* 1967. Gold Medal D 1896. 1st edn. My. NF. F2d. $20.00

BLOCK, Lawrence. *Tanner's Tiger.* 1968. Gold Medal D 1940. 1st prtg. PBO. c/McGinnis: gga. VG+. P7d. $9.00

BLOCK, Lawrence. *Thief Who Couldn't Sleep.* 1966. Gold Medal D 1722. 1st edn. My. VG+. F2d. $22.00

BLOCK, Lawrence. *Two for Tanner.* 1967. Gold Medal D 1896. 1st edn. My. NF. F2d. $20.00

BLOCK, Lawrence. *When the Sacred Gin-mill Closes.* 1987. Charter 88097. 1st prtg. My. F. W2d. $3.50

BLOCK, Lawrence. *Wide Open.* 1973. Dell 9266. 1st edn. My. F. F2d. $25.00

BLOCK, Libbie. *Bedeviled.* Dell 344. VG+. G5d. $8.00

BLOCK, Thomas. *Forced Landing.* 1984. Berkley 06830. My. VG+. W2d. $3.25

BLOOD, Matthew. *Avenger.* 1959. Gold Medal 924. 1st prtg. c/Barye: gga. VG. P7d. $5.00

BLOOM, Murry Teigh. *Money of Their Own.* 1960. Ballantine F 435K. NF. VG+. B5d. $5.00

BLOOM & ULLMAN. *Naked Spur.* 1953. Pennant P 29. We. VG+. P1d. $12.50

BLOOMFIELD, Robert. *When Strangers Meet.* 1957. Pocket 1171. 1st pb. My. NF. B6d. $15.00

BLOUNT, Margaret. *Animal Land.* 1977. Avon 30130. Nfi. F. P1d. $7.50

BLUM, R. *Simultaneous Man.* Bantam N 5878. 1st prtg. F. S1d. $5.00

BLUMENTHAL, John. *Case of the Hard-boiled Dicks.* 1985. Fireside 55538. 1st prtg. PBO. NF. P7d. $7.50

BOAL, Sam. *Man From the Diner's Club.* 1963. Lancer 70-041. 1st prtg. VG. B3d/R5d. $4.00

BOARDMAN, Tom. *ABC of SF.* 1968. Avon V 2249. SF. VG. W2d. $4.00

BOARDMAN, Tom. *ABC of SF.* 1971. Avon V 2392. 2nd edn. SF. VG. B5d. $2.50

BOARDMAN, Tom. *Connoisseur's SF.* 1964. Penguin. 1st US pb. NF. M1d. $6.00

BOCCA, Al. *Easy Come Easy Go!* Scion Gangster NN. VG. B3d. $8.50

BODENHEIM, Maxwell. *Georgie May.* 1947. Avon 152. Fi. G. B5d. $2.00

BODENHEIM, Maxwell. *My Life & Loves in Greenwich Village.* 1961. Belmont 231. VG+. B4d. $9.00

BODENHEIM, Maxwell. *My Life & Loves in Greenwich Village.* 1961. Belmont 231. 1st prtg. VG. P7d. $5.00

BODENHEIM, Maxwell. *Ninth Avenue.* 1951. Avon 352. c/gga. VG. B4d. $5.00

BODENHEIM, Maxwell. *Replenishing Jessica.* Avon 191. VG. B3d. $4.00

BODIN, Paul. *All Women's Flesh.* Berkley G 559. VG. B3d. $4.00

BODIN, Paul. *Sign of Eros.* Berkley Y 580. 4th edn. VG+. G5d. $3.00

BODMER, Frederick. *Loom of Language.* Armed Services 893. Nfi. G+. B5d. $3.50

BOGAR, Jeff. *Fire Zone.* Panther 113. PBO. NF. B3d. $9.00

BOGAR, Jeff. *My Gun, Her Body.* 1952. Lion 79. 1st US edn. c/Maguire: gga. scarce. My. VG+. B6a #75. $36.50

BOGAR, Jeff. *Tigress.* 1951. Lion 72. c/gga. My. VG+. B4d. $12.50

BOGART, William. *Murder Man.* 1940s. Tech Mystery NN. 1st pb. My. VG. B6d. $4.75

BOGART, William. *Queen City Murder Case.* 1954. Phantom 608. PBO. VG+. B3a #21. $59.04

BOGART, William. *Singapore.* 1947. Century Digest 37. PBO. MTI. scarce. VG+. B6a #74. $55.00

BOHLE, Edgar. *Man Who Disappeared.* 1960. Dell 1013. My. VG. B3d/B4d. $4.00

BOILEAU & NARCEJAC. *Choice Cuts.* 1968. Bantam S 3578. My. VG. W2d. $3.75

BOILEAU & NARCEJAC. *Vertigo.* 1958. Dell 977. 1st edn. PBO. MTI. c/Maguire. F. F2d. $25.00

BOK, Edward. *Americanization of Edward Bok.* 1965. Pocket 75043. Nfi. VG. B5d. $3.00

BOK, Hannes. *Beyond the Golden Stair.* 1970. Ballantine. 1st edn. Ad/Fa. F. M1d. $12.00

BOK, Hannes. *Sorcerer's Ship.* 1969. Ballantine. 1st edn. Ad/Fa. F. M1d. $12.00

BOLAND, John. *League of Gentleman.* Beacon-Envoy 103. MTI. My. G+. B5d. $3.00

BOLIN, Gary. *Sunset Strip Sex Agent.* 1962. Intimate 705. VG+. B3a. $11.00

BOLTIN, William. *Witch on Wheels.* 1956. Beacon 128. 1st prtg. c/photo. VG. P7d. $7.50

BOLTINOFF, edt. *Howls of Ivy.* 1955. Bantam 1389. PBO. NF. B6d. $10.00

BOLTON, Johanna M. *Alien Within.* 1989. Ballantine 35541. 1st pb. SF. VG+. B6d. $3.00

BOND, Harvey. *Other World.* Priory 1053. SF. F. W2d. $4.00

BOND, Nelson S. *Exiles in Time.* 1965. PB Library 52804. SF. G+. W2d. $3.50

BOND, Nelson S. *Exiles in Time.* 1965. PB Library. 1st pb. F. M1d. $10.00

BOND, Nelson S. *No Time Like the Future.* 1954. Avon. 1st edn. F. M1d. $12.00

BOND, Richard. *Doctor's Wife.* 1966. All Star AS100. PBO. Ad. VG. B5d. $4.00

BOND/BRETT. *Kill Me With Kindness/Guilty Bystander.* Ace D 349. PBO. G+. M6d. $7.50

BOND/BRETT. *Kill Me With Kindness/Guilty Bystander.* Ace D 349. VG. M1d. $10.00

BOND/FARR. *Murder Isn't Funny/Deadly Combo.* Ace D 301. c/Barton: gga. My. VG+. B6d. $18.00

BONE, J.F. *Lani People.* 1962. Bantam J 2363. 1st prtg. SF. G+. R5d. $1.50

BONE, J.F. *Legacy.* 1976. Laser 18. PBO. c/K Freas. SF. VG+. B5d. $5.00

BONE, J.F. *Meddlers.* 1976. Laser 37. 1st edn. SF. F. F2d. $20.00

BONE & MYERS. *Gift of the Manti.* 1977. Laser 56. 1st edn. very scarce. SF. F. F2d. $50.00

BONETT, J. & E. *Dead Lion.* Pocket 738. VG. B3d. $4.00

BONETT, J. & E. *Little Sister.* Pocket 750. VG. B3d. $5.00

BONHAM, F. *By Her Own Hand.* 1963. Monarch 361. My. VG+. B4d. $6.00

BONHAM, F. *Feud at Spanish Fork.* Ballantine 357. PBO. VG+. B3d. $5.00

BONHAM, F. *Logan's Choice.* Gold Medal s 1416. VG+. I1d. $4.00

BONHAM, F. *Lost Stage Valley.* Pocket 604. VG+. B3d. $4.50

BONHAM, F. *Night Raid.* Ballantine 64. VG. B3d. $3.50

BONHAM, F. *One for Sleep.* 1960. Gold Medal 988. VG. P6d. $2.00

BONHAM, F. *Sound of Gunfire.* Dell 1st Edn A 177. c/McGinnis. VG+. B3d. $5.00

BONHAM, F. *Tough Country.* Dell 1st Edn A 150. c/Gross. VG+. B3d. $5.00

BONNAMY, Francis. *Dead Reckoning.* 1946. Penguin 584. 1st prtg. My. VG. W2d. $9.50

BONNAMY, Francis. *Murder As a Fine Art.* 1949. Signet 713. c/J Avati. My. VG. B5d. $5.00

BONNELL, James Francis. *Death Over Sunday.* Dell 19. G+. G5d. $6.00

BONNER, Michael. *Kennedy's Gold.* 1960. Avon F 184. We. VG. B4d. $2.50

BONNER, Parker. *Outlaw Brand.* Popular 603. VG. B3d. $4.50

BONNER, Parker. *Tough in the Saddle.* 1964. Monarch 452. We. VG+. B4d. $3.00

BONNER, Paul H. *Art of Llewellyn Jones.* Dell 0288. VG+. B3d. $4.00

BONNEY, Joseph. *Death by Dynamite.* 1947. Black Knight 19. 1st pb. My. G. B6d. $3.50

BOONE, J. *Backwoods Woman.* Dell 557. VG. B3d. $5.00

BOORMAN & STAIR. *Zardoz.* 1974. Signet Q 5830. 1st prtg. VG+. R5d. $2.50

BOOTH, C.G. *Murder Strikes Thrice.* Bonded 4. VG. B3d. $7.00

BOOTH, Edward. *Chains of Passion.* 1960. Newsstand U 150. Ad. G+. B5d. $3.00

BOOTH, Edward. *Deadly Desire.* 1960. Newsstand U 146. Ad. VG. B5d. $4.50

BOOTH, Edward. *Torch of Desire.* 1960. Newsstand U 139. Ad. G+. B5d. $3.00

BOOTH, Edwin. *Stranger in Buffalo Springs.* 1969. Berkley X 1728. PBO. We. VG. B6d. $4.00

BOOTH, Ernest. *With Sirens Screaming.* 1954. Pyramid 121. Fi. VG. B5d. $5.50

BOOTH, R. *Girl Stowaway.* Intimate 53. VG+. B3d. $10.00

BOOTH/HOGAN. *Jinx Rider/Walk a Lonely Trail.* Ace D 236. VG. I1d. $5.00

BOOTH/HOGAN. *Valley of Violence/Last Gun at Cabresto.* Ace F 244. PBO. VG. M6d. $4.50

BOOTH/SULLIVAN. *Hardesty/Stranger.* 1972. Ace 31739. We. NF. B5d. $5.00

BORBES, Esther. *Paradise.* Armed Services I 269. Fi. G+. B5d. $3.50

BORDEN, Lee. *Secret of Sylvia.* Gold Medal 1308. 3rd prtg. VG+. B3d. $5.00

BORDEN, Lee. *Secret of Sylvia.* Gold Medal 744. NF. I1d. $7.00

BORG, J. *Badlands Fury.* Wagonwheel 293. VG. B3d. $7.00

BORGESON & KAUFMAN. *Man & Sex.* Crest 621. VG. B3d. $4.00

BORN, Franz. *Jules Verne: The Man Who Invented the Future.* 1967. Scholastic 838. 1st prtg. Nfi. VG. W2d. $3.50

BOROWIK. *Lions Three: Christians Nothing.* 1967. MacFadden 60-302. 1st pb. F. B6d. $5.00

BOSS, S. *Someday, Boy.* Bantam 1214. VG+. B3d. $4.50

BOSTWICK, Ronald. *Iron Ring.* 1963. Avon G 1165. War. VG. B4d. $2.25

BOSWELL, James. *London Journal.* 1956. Signet D 1305. c/Hattock. Nfi. VG. B5d. $4.50

BOSWELL & THOMPSON. *Girl in Lover's Lane.* 1953. Gold Medal 334. 1st prtg. PBO. c/gga. VG. P7d. $7.50

BOSWELL & THOMPSON. *Girl in the Stateroom.* 1951. Gold Medal 180. VG+. B3a #21. $8.50

BOSWELL & THOMPSON. *Girl With the Scarlet Brand.* 1954. Gold Medal 384. 1st prtg. c/gga. VG. P7d. $9.00

BOSWELL & THOMPSON. *Girls in Nightmare House.* Gold Medal 480. PBO. VG. M6d. $9.50

BOSWORTH, Allan R. *Border Roundup.* 1947. Bantam 86. We. NF. B4d. $9.00

BOSWORTH, Allan R. *Bury Me Not.* Dell 858. VG. B3d. $4.50

BOSWORTH, Allan R. *Double Deal.* Bantam 119. PBO. VG. B3d. $4.00

BOSWORTH, Allan R. *Only the Brave.* 1955. Popular 684. c/gga. Fa. VG+. B4d. $7.00

BOSWORTH, Jim. *Speed Demon.* 1958. Ace D 267. PBO. Fi. VG. B5d. $4.50

BOTEIN, Bernard. *Prosecutor.* 1958. Cardinal C 279. 1st prtg. c/Hulings. VG+. P7d. $4.00

BOTTARI, G.L. *Untamed Passion.* Merit 352. PBO. NF. B3d. $6.00

BOTTOME, P. *Mortal Storm.* Popular 94. VG+. B3d. $5.00

BOTTUME, Carl. *Sailor's Choice.* 1952. Signet 990. Fa. VG. B4d. $3.25

BOUCHER, Anthony. *Best From Fantasy & SF 3rd Series.* 1960. Ace D 422. F. P9d. $3.00

BOUCHER, Anthony. *Best From Fantasy & SF 3rd Series.* 1968. Ace G 712. VG. B3d/S1d. $6.00

BOUCHER, Anthony. *Best From Fantasy & SF 4th Series.* Ace D 455. VG+. B3d. $5.00

BOUCHER, Anthony. *Best From Fantasy & SF 5th Series.* Ace F 105. F. S1d. $6.00

BOUCHER, Anthony. *Best From Fantasy & SF 6th Series.* 1962. Ace F 131. F. F2d/M1d. $8.00

BOUCHER, Anthony. *Best From Fantasy & SF 7th Series.* Ace F 162. F. S1d. $6.00

BOUCHER, Anthony. *Best From Fantasy & SF 8th Series.* Ace F 217. SF. VG. B5d. $4.50

BOUCHER, Anthony. *Case of the Crumpled Knave.* 1949. Popular 154. 1st edn. PBO. My. F. F2d. $20.00

BOUCHER, Anthony. *Case of the Crumpled Knave.* 1967. Pyramid R 1585. 1st prtg. VG. P7d. $4.00

BOUCHER, Anthony. *Case of the Seven Sneezes.* Dell 334. VG. B3d. $4.00

BOUCHER, Anthony. *Case of the Seven Sneezes.* 1966. Pyramid R 1542. My. VG+. B4d. $2.50

BOUCHER, Anthony. *Far & Away.* Ballantine 109. PBO. VG+. B3d. $5.00

BOUCHER, Anthony. *Far & Away.* 1955. Ballantine 109. 1st edn. SF. F. F2d. $15.00

BOUCHER, Anthony. *Pocket Book of True Crime.* 1943. Pocket 213. 1st edn. My. NF. F2d. $12.00

BOUCHER, Anthony. *Rocket to the Morgue.* Dell 591. VG+. B3d. $7.00

BOUCHER, Anthony. *Rocket to the Morgue.* 1952. Dell 591. 1st prtg. SF. F. F2d. $30.00

BOULLE, Pierre. *Bridge Over the River Kwai.* 1957. Bantam A 1677. MTI. VG+. B4d. $2.00

BOULLE, Pierre. *Garden on the Moon.* 1966. Signet P 3031. 1st prtg. SF. VG+. W2d. $5.00

BOULLE, Pierre. *Garden on the Moon.* 1966. Signet Q 5806. 2nd prtg. SF. VG. W2d. $4.00

BOULLE, Pierre. *Noble Profession.* 1964. Bantam F 2832. 1st prtg. VG+. P7d. $4.00

BOULLE, Pierre. *Planet of the Apes.* 1964. Signet D 2547. 1st edn. PBO. VG. P9d. $2.50

BOULLE, Pierre. *Planet of the Apes.* 1964. Signet P 3642. 6th prtg. SF. F. W2d. $4.50

BOUNDS, Sidney. *Robot Brains.* Uni-Book NN. 1st prtg. VG. S1d. $3.00

BOUNDS, Sydney. *Robot Brains.* 1969. MacFadden 60-410. SF. VG+. B4d. $3.00

BOURGET/DEGONCOURT. *Crime D'Amour/ Germaine.* 1953. Ace D 16. c/Barton & Saunders. VG+. B3a #21. $16.20

BOURJAILY, Vance. *Confessions of a Spent Youth.* 1961. Bantam S 2289. 1st prtg. VG. P7d. $3.50

BOURJAILY, Vance. *End of My Life.* 1962. Bantam F 2389. 1st prtg. VG+. P7d. $4.00

BOURJAILY, Vance. *End of My Life.* 1952. Bantam 1047. c/gga. Fa. VG+. B4d. $4.00

BOURKE, Vernon J. edt. *Pocket Aquinas.* 1960. Washindton Square W 575. Nfi. NF. B4d. $3.00

BOURNE, Peter. *Drums of Destiny.* Popular 237. VG+. B3d. $6.00

BOUTELL, Anita. *Cradled in Fear.* 1943. Thriller Novel 22. 1st pb. My. VG+. B6d. $9.00

BOUTLETT, John. *House Party.* 1968. New Library 425. Ad. VG+. B5d. $5.50

BOVA, Ben. *Analog Annual.* 1976. Pyramid A 4016. 1st prtg. SF. VG. W2d. $3.25

BOVA, Ben. *City of Darkness.* 1982. Berkley 05774. SF. VG. W2d. $3.00

BOVA, Ben. *Forward in Time.* 1973. Popular 8310. 1st pb. SF. NF. B6d. $3.00

BOVA, Ben. *Out of the Sun.* 1984. TOR 53210. 1st prtg. SF. VG+. W2d. $3.50

BOVA, Ben. *THX 1138.* 1971. PB Library. 1st pb. F. M1d. $15.00

BOVA, Ben. *When the Sky Burned.* Popular 00207. SF. VG. W2d. $3.50

BOWEN, Croswell. *They Went Wrong.* 1955. Bantam A 1375. 1st pb. Cr. NF. B6d. $15.00

BOWEN, John. *After the Rain.* 1959. Ballantine 284K. 1st edn. F. M1d. $10.00

BOWEN, R.S. *Hot Rod Fury.* 1963. Monarch 374. JD. F. B4d. $7.00

BOWEN, R.S. *Silent Wings.* Monarch 430. c/Schaare. VG+. B3d. $4.50

BOWER, B.M. *Pirates of the Range.* 1964. Pyramid F 1018. We. NF. B5d. $5.50

BOWER, Brock. *Late Great Creature.* 1971. Popular 0187. 1st edn. VG. P9d. $1.50

BOWER, S. *Teen Chicks Who Love Older Men.* Brandon House 6529. VG+. B3d. $4.50

BOWIE, Jim. *Scarred Leather!* 1952. Scion Western NN. VG. B3d. $8.00

BOWKER, R. *Forbidden Sanctuary.* 1982. Ballantine 29871. PBO. c/D Sweet. SF. NF. B6d. $3.00

BOWLES, Jerry. *Forever Hold Your Banner High!* 1977. Pocket 81348. TVTI. VG. P1d. $5.00

BOWLES, Paul. *Let It Come Down.* Signet 1002. VG. B3d. $4.00

BOWLES, Paul. *Up Above the World.* Pocket 75222. 1st pb. G+. M6d. $6.50

BOWLING, Jackson M. *In the Line of Fire.* Regency RB 307. VG. M6d. $7.50

BOX, Edgar. *Death Likes It Hot.* 1955. Signet 1217. VG+. I1d. $5.00

BOYCE, David. *Lady Is Lost.* Gannet NN. c/Noir. VG+. B3a. $23.10

BOYD, E.M. *Murder Wears Mukluks.* Dell 259. VG+. I1d. $6.00

BOYD, F. *Flesh Peddlers.* Monarch 133. c/Maguire. VG. I1d. $12.00

BOYD, John. *Andromeda Gun.* 1975. Berkley N 2878. SF. VG. B5d. $3.00

BOYD, John. *Last Starship From Earth.* 1969. Berkley X 1675. SF. VG. B5d. $3.00

BOYD, John. *Rakehells of Heaven.* 1971. Bantam 5479. G. P9d. $1.00

BOYD & HARRIS. *Baseball Card Book.* 1975. PB Library 72-649. PBO. VG. B6d. $15.00

BOYINGTON, Pappy. *Tonya.* 1961. Cardinal GC 115. 1st prtg. c/Barye: gga. VG. P7d. $3.50

BRACCO, Edgar Jean. *Boots & Saddles.* 1958. Berkley G 180. PBO. TVTI. We. VG+. B3d. $4.00

BRACCO, Edgar Jean. *Chattels of Eldorado.* 1955. Avon T 98. 1st prtg. c/Kinstler: gga. VG. P7d. $5.00

BRACCO, Edgar Jean. *Flight.* 1959. Berkley G291. PBO. TVTI. Fi. VG. B5d. $2.50

BRACKEEN, Steve. *Baby Moll.* Crest 206. PBO. c/Barye. VG. B3d. $4.50

BRACKEEN, Steve. *Danger in My Bloods.* Crest 316. VG. G5d. $3.00

BRACKETT, Leigh. *Big Jump.* 1987. TOR 53229. SF. VG+. W2d. $3.00

BRACKETT, Leigh. *Coming of the Terrans.* Ace G 669. PBO. VG+. B3d. $4.50

BRACKETT, Leigh. *Coming of the Terrans.* Ace 11546. 1st prtg. F. S1d. $4.00

BRACKETT, Leigh. *Eye for an Eye.* Bantam 2308. VG. B3d. $4.00

BRACKETT, Leigh. *Ginger Star.* 1979. Ballantine 28514. 3rd edn. c/B Vallejo. SF. VG+. B5d. $3.50

BRACKETT, Leigh. *Hounds of Skaith.* 1980. Ballantine 28594. 3rd edn. c/J Steranko. SF. VG+. B5d. $3.50

BRACKETT, Leigh. *Long Tomorrow.* 1962. Ace F 135. 1st edn. PBO. VG. M1d. $8.00

BRACKETT, Leigh. *Long Tomorrow.* 1974. Ballantine 24289. SF. VG+. B5d. $3.50

BRACKETT, Leigh. *Nemesis From Terra.* Ace 56940. SF. F. W2d. $5.00

BRACKETT, Leigh. *Reavers of Skaith.* Ballantine 22438. 1st prtg. F. S1d. $5.00

BRACKETT, Leigh. *Rio Bravo.* 1959. Bantam 1893. PBO. MTI. c/Barye Phillips: gga. We. G+. P6d. $12.50

BRACKETT, Leigh. *Shadow Over Mars.* 1951. World Fantasy Classic. PBO. VG+. B3a #22. $177.00

BRACKETT, Leigh. *Sword of Rhiannon.* 1967. Ace F 422. c/John Schoenherr: gga. VG+. P6d. $2.25

BRACKETT, Leigh. *13 West Street (Tiger Among Us).* Bantam 2323. MTI. c/Zuckerberg. VG. B3d. $5.50

BRACKETT/BRACKETT. *People of the Talisman/Secret of Sinharat.* 1964. Ace M 101. PBO. c/Emsh. SF. VG. B3d/M2d. $5.00

BRACKETT/COURSE. *Nemesis From Terra/Collision Course.* 1961. Ace F 123. c/Emsh. NF. M1d. $8.00

BRACKETT/DICK. *Big Jump/Solar Lottery.* 1955. Ace D 103. PBO. c/R Schulz & E Valigursky. SF. G+. B5d. $17.50

BRACKETT/HAMILTON. *Nemesis From Terra/Battle for the Stars.* 1989. TOR 55960. SF. F. W2d. $5.00

BRACKETT/HOWARD. *Sword of Rhiannon/Conan the Conqueror.* 1953. Ace D 36. PBO. c/R Shulz & N Saunders. SF. G+. B5d. $17.50

BRACKETT/HOWARD. *Sword of Rhiannon/Conan the Conqueror.* 1953. Ace D 36. SF. VG+. M3d. $45.00

BRACKETT/SILVERBERG. *Nemesis From Terra/Collision Course.* 1961. Ace F 123. PBO. c/E Emsh & E Valigursky. SF. VG+. B5d. $6.50

BRACKETT/SILVERGERG. *Nemesis From Terra/Collision Course.* 1961. Ace F 123. 1st prtg. G. S1d. $3.00

BRACKETT/WALLIS. *Alpha Centauri-or Die!/Legend of Lost Earth.* Ace F 187. F. M1d. $8.00

BRACKETT/WILLIAMS. *Galactic Breed/Conquest of the Space Sea.* 1955. Ace D 99. c/Valigursky. VG+. B6d. $15.00

BRACKETT/WILLIAMS. *Galactic Breed/Conquest of the Space Sea.* 1955. Ace D 99. 1st prtg. PBO. c/gga. SF. VG. B5d/P7d. $10.00

BRADBURY, Edward. *Barbarians of Mars.* 1968. Lancer 72-127. 1st edn. VG. P9d. $1.50

BRADBURY, Edward. *Barbarians of Mars.* 1966. Lancer 72-127. SF. F. W2d. $5.50

BRADBURY, Edward. *Blades of Mars.* 1966. Lancer 72-122. 1st edn. F. M1d. $12.00

BRADBURY, Edward. *Blades of Mars.* 1966. Lancer 72-122. 1st prtg. VG. S1d. $4.50

BRADBURY, Edward. *Warriors of Mars.* 1966. Lancer 72-118. 1st American edn. VG+. B3d. $4.00

BRADBURY, Edward. *Warriors of Mars.* 1966. Lancer 72-118. SF. F. W2d. $5.50

BRADBURY, Ray. *Autumn People.* Ballantine U 2141. PBO. VG. B3d. $5.00

BRADBURY, Ray. *Circus of Dr Lao.* 1956. Bantam. 1st edn. VG. M1d. $10.00

BRADBURY, Ray. *Dandelion Wine.* 1980. Bantam 14394. 10th prtg. SF. F. W2d. $4.00

BRADBURY, Ray. *Dandelion Wine.* Bantam 25236. c/sgn. VG. B3d. $6.00

BRADBURY, Ray. *Fahrenheit 451.* 1967. Ballantine U 2843. 2nd prtg. SF. VG+. W2d. $3.75

BRADBURY, Ray. *Fahrenheit 451.* 1967. Ballantine U 5060. 9th edn. MTI. c/Christie & Werner photo. VG+. B4d. $3.00

BRADBURY, Ray. *Fahrenheit 451.* 1953. Ballantine 382K. PBO. VG. B3d/I1d. $4.00

BRADBURY, Ray. *Fahrenheit 451.* 1953. Ballantine 382K. 3rd edn. G. P9d. $1.25

BRADBURY, Ray. *Fahrenheit 451.* 1953. Ballantine 41. PBO. c/Mugnaini. VG. B6d. $12.50

BRADBURY, Ray. *Fahrenheit 451.* 1977. Ballantine 27431. 45th prtg. SF. F. W2d. $3.25

BRADBURY, Ray. *Golden Apples of the Sun.* 1954. Bantam A 1241. 1st prtg. c/Binger. VG. P7d. $7.50

BRADBURY, Ray. *Golden Apples of the Sun.* 1954. Bantam A 1241. 1st prtg. SF. NF. F2d. $10.00

BRADBURY, Ray. *Halloween Tree.* 1974. Bantam. 1st pb. F. M1d. $10.00

BRADBURY, Ray. *Illustrated Man.* 1951. Bantam 991. 1st prtg. SF. F. F2d. $13.00

BRADBURY, Ray. *Illustrated Man.* 1952. Bantam 991. 1st edn. PBO. G. P9d. $2.00

BRADBURY, Ray. *Machineries of Joy.* 1970. Bantam S 5258. 8th prtg. SF. VG+. W2d. $4.25

BRADBURY, Ray. *Martian Chronicles.* 1954. Bantam 1261. 1st prtg. VG+. P7d. $6.00

BRADBURY, Ray. *Martian Chronicles.* 1980. Bantam 13179. 58th prtg. SF. VG. W2d. $3.25

BRADBURY, Ray. *Martian Chronicles.* 1951. Bantam 886. 1st edn. PBO. G. P9d. $2.00

BRADBURY, Ray. *Martian Chronicles.* 1951. Bantam 886. 1st pb. SF. VG+. B6d/R5d. $15.00

BRADBURY, Ray. *Medicine for Melancholy.* Bantam S 5268. 5th edn. SF. VG. B5d. $2.50

BRADBURY, Ray. *Medicine for Melancholy.* 1960. Bantam. 1st pb. F. M1d. $12.00

BRADBURY, Ray. *October Country.* 1956. Ballantine F 139. SF. VG. B4d. $18.00

BRADBURY, Ray. *October Country.* 1956. Ballantine F 139. 1st pb edn. F. M1d. $35.00

BRADBURY, Ray. *October Country.* 1962. Ballantine F 580. 3rd edn. G. P9d. $2.00

BRADBURY, Ray. *October Country.* Ballantine U 2139. VG. B3d. $4.00

BRADBURY, Ray. *October Country.* 1973. Ballantine 02760. 10th prtg. SF. VG. W2d. $3.25

BRADBURY, Ray. *S Is for Space.* 1970. Bantam. 1st pb. F. M1d. $10.00

BRADBURY, Ray. *Something Wicked This Way Comes.* 1963. Bantam H 2630. SF. VG+. B4d. $3.00

BRADBURY, Ray. *Something Wicked This Way Comes.* 1970. Bantam N 7202. 10th prtg. SF. VG. W2d. $3.25

BRADBURY, Ray. *Something Wicked This Way Comes.* 1963. Bantam. 1st pb. F. M1d. $15.00

BRADBURY, Ray. *Timeless Stories for Today & Tomorrow.* 1952. Bantam A 944. 1st edn. F. M1d. $15.00

BRADBURY, Ray. *Timeless Stories for Today & Tomorrow.* 1970. Bantam S 5372. 9th prtg. SF. VG. W2d. $3.25

BRADBURY, Ray. *Tomorrow Midnight.* Ballantine U 2142. VG+. B3d. $10.00

BRADBURY, Ray. *Toynbee Convector.* 1989. Bantam 27957. 1st pb. SF. NF. B6d. $3.00

BRADBURY, William. *All the Natives Are Lovers.* 1958. Newsstand 104. PBO. c/gga. VG+. B6a #76. $33.00

BRADDOCK, Joseph. *Bridal Bed.* 1962. MacFadden 50-125. NF. VG. B5d. $3.00

BRADLEY, David. *No Place To Hide.* Bantam 421. NF. B3d. $5.50

BRADLEY, Lee. *Rose of Sharon.* 1960. Fabian 133. PBO. NF. B6d. $12.00

BRADLEY, Lee. *Rose of Sharon.* Saber SAR 8. VG. B3d. $3.00

BRADLEY, M. *New American Sexual Appetites.* Brandon House 968. VG+. B3d. $5.50

BRADLEY, Marion Z. *Bloody Sun.* 1964. Ace F 303. F. M1d. $10.00

BRADLEY, Marion Z. *Bloody Sun.* 1964. Ace F 303. PBO. SF. VG. P6d. $2.00

BRADLEY, Marion Z. *Bloody Sun.* Ace 06851. SF. VG. B5d. $3.00

BRADLEY, Marion Z. *Castle Terror.* 1965. Lancer 72-983. PBO. VG. P6d. $2.00

BRADLEY, Marion Z. *City of Sorcery.* 1980. DAW. 1st edn. F. M1d. $6.00

BRADLEY, Marion Z. *Colors of Space.* 1963. Monarch 368. c/Ralph Brillhart: gga. SF. VG. P6d. $5.00

BRADLEY, Marion Z. *Darkover Landfall.* 1972. DAW. 1st edn. F. M1d. $10.00

BRADLEY, Marion Z. *Endless Voyage.* Ace 20660. PBO. Ace SF Special. SF. VG. B5d. $3.00

BRADLEY, Marion Z. *Forbidden Tower.* 1977. DAW. 1st edn. F. M1d. $8.00

BRADLEY, Marion Z. *Free Amazons of Darkness.* 1986. DAW. 1st edn. F. M1d. $7.00

BRADLEY, Marion Z. *Hawkmistress!* 1982. DAW 00762. PBO. c/JMG Shapero. SF. VG. B5d. $3.00

BRADLEY, Marion Z. *Hunters of the Red Moon.* 1973. DAW UQ 1071. SF. F. W2d. $2.75

BRADLEY, Marion Z. *Keeper's Price.* 1980. DAW. 1st edn. F. M1d. $7.00

BRADLEY, Marion Z. *Other Side of the Mirror.* 1987. DAW. 1st edn. F. M1d. $7.00

BRADLEY, Marion Z. *Sharra's Exile.* 1981. DAW. 1st edn. F. M1d. $7.00

BRADLEY, Marion Z. *Shattered Chain.* 1976. DAW. 1st edn. F. M1d. $6.00

BRADLEY, Marion Z. *Spell Sword.* 1974. DAW 119. 1st edn. F. M1d. $7.00

BRADLEY, Marion Z. *Star of Danger.* 1965. Ace F 350. NF. M1d. $8.00

BRADLEY, Marion Z. *Star of Danger.* 1965. Ace F 350. SF. G+. W2d. $3.50

BRADLEY, Marion Z. *Star of Danger.* Ace 77945. SF. VG+. B5d. $5.00

BRADLEY, Marion Z. *Storm Queen.* 1978. DAW. 1st edn. F. M1d. $6.00

BRADLEY, Marion Z. *Sword & Sorceress III.* 1986. DAW 678. 1st edn. VG. P9d. $2.00

BRADLEY, Marion Z. *Sword & Sorceress IV.* 1987. DAW 714. 1st edn. VG. P9d. $2.00

BRADLEY, Marion Z. *Sword of Chaos.* 1982. DAW. 1st edn. F. M1d. $7.00

BRADLEY, Marion Z. *Thendara House.* DAW UE 2119. F. P9d. $2.50

BRADLEY, Marion Z. *Two To Conquer.* DAW UE 1876. F. P9d. $2.00

BRADLEY, Marion Z. *World Wreckers* Ace 91170. c/K Freas. SF. VG+. B5d. $4.00

BRADLEY, Matthew. *Balzac '64 Volume I.* 1963. Jade 205. VG+. B3d. $4.50

BRADLEY, Matthew. *Balzac '64 Volume I.* 1963. Jade 205. 1st edn. F. F2d. $10.00

BRADLEY, Matthew. *Balzac '64 Volume II.* Jade 206. NF. B3d. $5.00

BRADLEY, Matthew. *Lesbian Land.* 1963. Jade 202. Ad. VG+. B5d. $7.50

BRADLEY/BRADLEY. *Dark Intruder/Falcons of Narabedla.* Ace F 273. NF. I1d. $6.00

BRADLEY/BRADLEY. *Dark Intruder/Falcons of Narabedla.* 1964. Ace F 273. F. M1d. $12.00

BRADLEY/BRADLEY. *Dark Intruder/Falcons of Narabedla.* 1964. Ace F 273. 1st prtg. SF. VG. R5d. $3.25

BRADLEY/BRADLEY. *Dark Intruder/Falcons of Narabedla.* 1972. Ace 22576. 2nd edn. c/K Freas. SF. VG. B5d. $5.00

BRADLEY/BRADLEY. *Planet Savers/Sword of Aldones.* 1962. Ace F 153. SF. F. W2d. $12.50

BRADLEY/CHANDLER. *Door Through Space/Rendezvous on a Lost World.* 1961. Ace F 117. NF. M1d. $8.00

BRADLEY/CHANDLER. *Door Through Space/Rendezvous on a Lost World.* 1961. Ace F 117. PBO. c/E Emsh. SF. VG+ B5d. $5.50

BRADLEY/CHANDLER. *Door Through Space/Rendezvous on a Lost World.* 1961. Ace F 117. 1st prtg. PBO. VG. P7d. $5.00

BRADLEY/LAUMER. *Seven From the Stars/Worlds of the Imperium.* 1962. Ace F 127. PBO. c/E Valigurdsky. SF. VG. B5d. $4.00

BRADLEY/RACKHAM. *Anything Tree/Winds of Darkover.* Ace 89250. 1st prtg. VG. S1d. $3.50

BRADLEY/RACKHAM. *Brass Dragon/Ipomoea.* Ace 37250. PBO. SF. VG+. B5d. $5.00

BRADY, Leo. *Edge of Doom.* 1949. Popular 260. MTI. c/Belarski: gga. VG. B4d. $4.00

BRADY, Matt. *Take Your Last Look.* 1954. Gold Medal 376. PBO. My. VG+. B6d. $12.50

BRADY, Matt. *Take Your Last Look.* Gold Medal 811. VG. B3d. $4.00

BRADY, Ryder. *Instar.* 1977. Ballantine 25658. SF. VG. W2d. $3.25

BRADY, Sheila. *Memoirs of an Ex-Porno Queen.* 1975. Pocket 78821. PBO. c/David Byrd. VG. P6d. $3.00

BRAHAM, Hal. *Call Me Deadly.* Graphic 152. VG. B3d. $6.00

BRAITHWAITE, E.R. *To Sir, With Love.* 1969. Pyramid T 1950. VG+. B4d. $3.00

BRALY, Malcolm. *Felony Tank.* Gold Medal S 1075. PBO. VG. M6d. $6.50

BRALY, Malcolm. *It's Cold Out There.* 1966. Gold Medal D 1683. c/gga. Fa. VG. B4d. $2.75

BRAMAH, Ernest. *Kai Lung Unrolls His Mat.* Ballantine 23787. VG. G5d. $5.50

BRAMAH, Ernest. *Kai Lung Unrolls His Mat.* 1974. Ballantine. 1st edn. Ad/Fa. NF. M1d. $10.00

BRAMAH, Ernest. *Max Carrados Mysteries.* Penguin C 2158. G+. G5d. $5.50

BRANCH, Bud. *Murder Volume 2.* 1957. No 1. PBO. scarce. NF. B6a #74. $61.00

BRANCH & WATERS. *Diamond Head.* Dell D 127. VG+. B3d. $4.50

BRAND, Christianna. *Cat & Mouse.* 1951. Avon 385. Hu. VG. B4d. $5.00

BRAND, Christianna. *Fog of Doubt.* Dell 881. VG+. B3d. $6.00

BRAND, Christianna. *Green for Danger.* 1965. Bantam F 2858. 1st prtg. My. VG. R5d. $1.50

BRAND, Kurt. *Cosmic Traitor.* 1973. Ace 66009. Perry Rhodan 26. SF. F. B5d. $6.00

BRAND, Max. *Alcatraz, the Wild Stallion.* 1961. Pocket 6092. We. VG+. B5d. $4.00

BRAND, Max. *Border Guns.* 1954. Pocket 991. 1st pb. c/Newquist. We. NF. B6d. $12.50

BRAND, Max. *Border Kid.* 1947. Pocket 491. 1st prtg. c/Keller. VG. P7d. $5.50

BRAND, Max. *Brother of the Cheyennes.* 1949. Signet 757. 1st pb. We. VG+. B6d. $12.00

BRAND, Max. *Calling Dr Kildare.* 1961. Dell R 123. 1st prtg. c/Miller: gga. VG. P7d. $4.00

BRAND, Max. *Dr Kildare Takes Charge.* 1962. Dell 1983. 1st prtg. c/Schaare: gga. VG+. P7d. $4.00

BRAND, Max. *Fightin' Fool.* Pocket 316. VG. B3d. $5.00

BRAND, Max. *Fighting Four.* Pocket 423. VG. B3d. $3.00

BRAND, Max. *Hired Guns.* Pocket 705. VG. B3d. $4.00

BRAND, Max. *Hunted Riders.* 1950. Pocket 744. c/J Floherty. Jr. We. VG. B5d. $4.00

BRAND, Max. *Jackson Trail.* Popular 801. VG. B3d. $4.00

BRAND, Max. *King of the Range.* Pocket 584. VG+. B3d. $4.50

BRAND, Max. *Longhorn Feud.* 1948. Pocket 523. 1st prtg. c/Blaine. VG+. P7d. $6.50

BRAND, Max. *Lucky Larribee.* 1959. Cardinal C 368. 1st prtg. VG. P7d. $3.50

BRAND, Max. *Rancher's Revenge.* Popular 152. VG. B3d. $5.00

BRAND, Max. *Secret of Dr Kildare.* 1962. Dell 7712. 1st prtg. c/Miller: gga. VG. P7d. $3.50

BRAND, Max. *Silvertip's Strike.* Pocket 547. VG+. B3d. $5.00

BRAND, Max. *Smiling Desperado.* Pocket 1168. c/Gross. VG+. B3d. $5.00

BRAND, Max. *South of the Rio Grande.* Pocket 390. VG. B3d. $4.00

BRAND, Max. *Timbal Gulch Trail.* 1946. Popular 78. 1st pb. c/Hoffman. We. VG. B6d. $10.00

BRAND, Max. *Valley of Vanishing Men.* Pocket 609. G+. G5d. $2.50

BRAND, Millen. *Outward Room.* 1950. Lion 26. Fa. VG. B4d. $7.50

BRAND, Oscar. *Folksongs for Fun.* 1961. Berkley X 573. PBO. VG. P6d. $8.50

BRANDE, Dorothea. *Wake Up & Live!* 1939. Pocket 2. VG. B3a #21. $66.00

BRANDE, Dorothea. *Wake Up & Live!* 1939. Pocket 2. 2nd edn. c/L Steinberg. NF. G+. B5d. $6.50

BRANDEL, Marc. *Moron.* 1951. Avon 393. 1st pb edn. F. F2d. $15.00

BRANDNER, Gary. *Big Brain #1: The Aardvark Affair.* 1975. Zebra 89083. SF. VG. W2d. $3.50

BRANDON, Curt. *High, Wide & Handsome.* 1951. Signet 903. We. VG. B5d. $3.50

BRANDON, Michael. *Nonce.* 1953. Avon 506. 1st pb. NF. M1d. $15.00

BRANDON, Ralph. *Blind Date.* 1962. Saber SA 27. Ad. G+. B5d. $3.50

BRANDON, Ralph. *His Sisters Were Call Girls.* Saber SA 35. VG+. B3d. $5.00

BRANDON, William. *Dangerous Dead.* 1946. Handi-Book 50. 1st edn. PBO. scarce. VG+. B6a #77. $46.25

BRANDT, C. *Flight Sex '70.* Barclay 7057. VG+. B3d. $4.00

BRANDT, Tom. *Run, Brother, Run!* 1954. Popular 584. c/gga. Fa. VG+. B4d. $7.00

BRANDT, Tom. *Run, Brother, Run!* 1954. Popular 584. PBO. My. VG. B6d. $6.00

BRANDTSON, G & I. *Male & Female: Five Life-Styles.* Barclay 7353. c/photo. NF. B3d. $5.00

BRANDTSON, G. *Teens & Their Older Lovers.* Barclay 7468. VG+. B3d. $4.50

BRANNON, William. *Lady Killers.* 1951. Handi-Book 139. PBO. c/Saunders. VG+. B6a #74. $72.25

BRANSON, H.C. *I'll Eat You Last.* 1946. Bonded Mystery 5. VG. I1d. $10.00

BRAUM, M.G. *Operation Atlantis.* 1966. Berkley F 1239. 1st prtg. My. VG+. R5d. $3.25

BREAN, Herbert. *Clock Strikes 13.* Dell 758. c/G Foxley. My. VG. B5d. $4.00

BREAN, Herbert. *Collar for the Killer.* Corgi 620. VG+. B3d. $7.50

BREAN, Herbert. *Darker the Night.* Pocket 698. VG+. B3d. $5.00

BREAN, Herbert. *Hardly a Man Is Now Alive.* Dell 675. G. G5d. $3.00

BREDENBERT, Jeff. *Dream Compass.* 1991. Avon 75647. 1st edn. SF. F. F2d. $6.00

BREHAN, D. *Kicks Is Kicks.* Holloway BH 426. VG. B3d. $4.50

BREHNER, Winston. *Dream of Eden.* 1953. Signet 1011. Fi. VG. B5d. $4.00

BREIHAN, C.W. *Great Lawmen of the West.* Signet 8126. VG. B3d. $4.00

BREIT & SLONIM edts. *This Thing Called Love.* Signet 1234. PBO. VG+. B3d. $5.50

BRELIS, Dean. *Mission.* 1959. Pocket 1246. Fi. VG. B5d. $4.00

BRENNAN, Alice. *Hollywood Nurse.* Avon F 232. VG. B3d. $4.00

BRENNAN, Alice. *Nurses Dormitory.* 1962. Lancer 71-326. 1st edn. F. F2d. $7.50

BRENNAN, Dan. *Doomed Sinner.* 1961. Newsstand U 180. Ad. G+. B5d. $4.00

BRENNAN, Dan. *Naked Light.* 1957. Lion LB 147. War. NF. B4d. $12.50

BRENNAN, Dan. *No Sense of Shame.* 1963. Midwood F 322. PBO. NF. B6d. $18.00

BRENNAN, Dan. *Sleep With Me!* 1962. Novel Book 5072. PBO. c/photo. Ad. VG+. B5d. $5.00

BRENNAN, Frederick Hazlitt. *Memo to a Firing Squad.* 1944. Dell 30. My. VG. B4d. $10.00

BRENNAN, Frederick Hazlitt. *One of Our H-Bombs Is Missing.* 1955. Gold medal 498. 1st edn. scarce. SF. F. F2d. $20.00

BRENNAN, Joseph. *Nine Horrors & a Dream.* 1962. Ballantine. 1st pb edn. NF. M1d. $10.00

BRENNAN, Louis A. *Death at Flood Tide.* 1958. Dell 1st Edn A 149. 1st prtg. PBO. c/Kalin: gga. VG+. P7d. $5.50

BRENNAN, Louis A. *These Items of Desire.* 1954. Popular G 141. c/gga. Fa. VG. B3d/B4d. $5.00

BRENT, A.D. *Rackets Incorporated.* Badger CS 10. VG. B3d. $6.00

BRENT, L.W. *Lavender Love Rumble.* Brentwood 1013. VG. B3d. $4.00

BRENT, Nigel. *Leopart Died Too.* 1957. Midnight Thriller 14. VG. B3d. $7.50

BRENT, R.L. *Liquidator #1.* 1975. Award AQ 1507. 2nd prtg. My. VG. W2d. $3.25

BRENT, Simon. *Murder Unprompted.* 1984. Dell 16145. 1st prtg. My. F. W2d. $3.50

BRENTER, J.G. *Female Menagerie.* Brandon House 1161. VG+. B3d. $5.00

BRESLIN, Howard. *Hundred Hills.* 1961. Perma M 4204. 1st prtg. c/Johnson: gga. VG+. P7d. $4.50

BRESLIN, Jimmy. *World of Jimmy Breslin.* 1976. Avon 27318. 1st prtg. c/photo. NF. P7d. $4.00

BRETNOR, Reginald. *SF Today & Tomorrow.* 1975. Penguin 3921. Nfi. VG. P1d. $6.00

BRETT, L. *Alien Ones.* Tomer T 060. 1st prtg. VG. S1d. $3.50

BRETT, L. *Forbidden.* 1960s. Badger Supernatural 72. PBO. c/Fox. scarce. VG+. B6a #80. $48.50

BRETT, L. *From Realms Beyond.* Badger SN 74. VG. B3d. $6.00

BRETT, L. *Power Sphere.* Badger SF 95. VG. B3d. $8.00

BRETT, L. *They Never Come Back.* Badger SN 68. VG. B3d. $5.00

BRETT, M. *Flight of the Stiff.* Pocket 50528. VG. G5d. $3.00

BRETT, M. *Guilty Bystander.* Ace D 349. VG. B3d. $5.50

BRETT, M. *Guilty Bystander.* Digit 310. 1st Eng edn. VG. B3d. $6.00

BRETT, M. *Hot Freeze.* Popular 612. VG. B3d. $4.50

BRETT, M. *Kill Him Quickly, It's Raining.* Pocket 50517. VG. G5d. $3.00

BRETT, R. *Pagan Interlude.* Leisure 20. VG. B3d. $7.50

BREUER, Bessie. *Memory of Love.* 1949. Avon 196. 1st edn. PBO. c/Ann Cantor: gga. VG+. B6a #76. $61.00

BREUER, Bessie. *Memory of Love.* 1949. Avon 196. 1st edn. PBO. c/Cantor. VG. B6d. $18.00

BREWER, Gil. *And the Girl Screamed.* 1956. Crest 147. PBO. c/Kimmel. scarce. My. VG. B6a #80. $38.50

BREWER, Gil. *Angel.* 1960. Avon 866. 1st edn. My. NF. F2d. $10.00

BREWER, Gil. *Backwoods Teaser.* 1960. Gold Medal 950. 1st edn. My. VG. F2d. $10.00

BREWER, Gil. *Bitch.* Avon 830. PBO. VG. B3d. $5.00

BREWER, Gil. *Devil in Davos.* 1969. Ace 37598. 1st prtg. My. VG. R5d. $5.00

BREWER, Gil. *French Street.* 1951. Gold Medal 211. VG. P6d. $2.50

BREWER, Gil. *Girl From Hateville.* 1958. Zenith 7. 1st edn. PBO. c/Nappi: gga. VG+. B6a #77. $75.00

BREWER, Gil. *Hell's Our Destination.* 1953. Gold Medal 345. PBO. c/Meese. scarce. VG+. B6a #77. $49.50

BREWER, Gil. *It Takes a Thief #2.* 1969. Ace 37599. 1st edn. TVTI. My. F. F2d. $10.00

BREWER, Gil. *It Takes a Thief.* 1969. Ace 37598. 1st edn. TVTI. My. F. F2d. $10.00

BREWER, Gil. *Little Tramp.* 1957. Crest 173. PBO. c/Barye: gga. VG. B6a #77. $40.25

BREWER, Gil. *Play It Hard.* 1964. Monarch 444. 1st edn. My. F. F2d. $15.00

BREWER, Gil. *Red Scarf.* 1959. Crest 310. PBO. c/McGinnis. scarce. VG+. B6a #80. $40.25

BREWER, Gil. *Satan Is a Woman.* 1951. Gold Medal 169. 1st edn. My. NF. F2d. $15.00

BREWER, Gil. *So Rich, So Dead.* 1951. Gold Medal 196. PBO. c/Barye: gga. NF. B6a #74. $66.00

BREWER, Gil. *So Rich, So Dead.* 1951. Gold Medal 196. PBO. VG. B6d. $27.50

BREWER, Gil. *Squeeze.* 1955. Ace D 123. PBO. c/Barton. VG. B6d. $22.50

BREWER, Gil. *Sugar.* 1959. Avon T 335. 1st edn. c/gga. Cr. F. F2d. $45.00

BREWER, Gil. *Vengeful Virgin.* 1958. Crest 238. PBO. NF. B6a #80. $55.00

BREWER, Gil. *Vengeful Virgin.* 1958. Crest 238. 1st edn. My. F. F2d. $16.00

BREWER, Gil. *Wild To Possess.* 1959. Monarch 107. 1st prtg. PBO. c/Maguire: gga. VG. P7d. $10.00

BREWER, Gil. *Wild.* 1958. Crest 229. PBO. scarce. NF. B6a #76. $49.50

BREWER, Gil. *Wild.* 1958. Crest 229. 1st edn. My. VG. F2d. $12.00

BREWER, Gil. *Wild.* Gold Medal 1466. VG. B3d. $4.50

BREWER, Gil. *13 French Street.* 1959. Gold Medal 858. 5th edn. c/gga. reprint. Fa. VG. B4d. $2.00

BREWSTER, Elliot. *Temptress.* 1951. Intimate 9. 1st pb. VG. B3d. $5.00

BRICK, John. *Strong Men.* 1960. Ace G 480. 1st pb. NF. B6d. $16.50

BRICK, John. *Troubled Spring.* 1952. Popular 405. VG+. B3d. $5.50

BRICKHILL, Paul. *Dam Busters.* 1957. Ballantine 245. 3rd edn. NF. VG. B5d. $3.50

BRICKMAN, M. *Do It Yourself.* Perma M 3029. c/cartoons. VG+. B3d. $6.00

BRIDGE, Ann. *Enchanter's Nightshade.* 1967. Berkley S 1388. 1st pb. VG+. B6d. $6.00

BRIDGE, Ann. *Numbered Account.* 1964. Berkley X 903. 1st prtg. My. G+. R5d. $1.00

BRIDGES, Laurie. *Dark Forces #12: The Ashton Horror.* 1984. Bantam 26609. 4th prtg. SF. VG. W2d. $3.00

BRIFFAULT, Robert. *Carlotta.* 1949. Avon Monthly 13. PBO. NF. B6a #74. $88.00

BRIFFAULT, Robert. *Carlotta.* 1949. Avon Monthly 13. 1st edn. PBO. VG. B6d. $50.00

BRIFFAULT, Robert. *Europa.* 1950. Avon 272. F. I1d. $35.00

BRIFFAULT, Robert. *Europa.* 1950. Avon 272. VG. B3d. $4.00

BRIGGS, John. *Leonard Bernstein.* 1962. Popular SP 198. 1st prtg. c/photo. VG. B3d/P7d. $4.00

BRIGHT, Robert. *Intruders.* 1954. Perma 278. VG+. B4d. $4.00

BRILL, L. *Bedroom Game.* Softcover Library B 866. VG. I1d. $6.00

BRIN, David. *Postman.* Bantam 25704. c/sgn. NF. B3d. $8.00

BRIN, David. *Startide Rising.* 1983. Bantam. 1st pb. F. M1d. $10.00

BRIN, David. *Uplift War.* 1987. Bantam. 1st pb. F. M1d. $8.00

BRINIG, Myron. *No Marriage in Paradise.* 1950. Bantam 767. Fa. VG+. B4d. $3.00

BRINKLEY, William. *Quicksand.* 1956. Signet S 1362. Fi. VG. B5d. $4.00

BRINTON, Henry. *Purple 6.* Avon S 135. SF. VG. B5d. $2.50

BRISTER, Richard. *Kansas.* Avon 606 We. VG. B5d $4.50

BRISTER, Richard. *Law Killer.* 1959. Avon T 373. 1st edn. We. F. F2d. $12.00

BRISTER/MANNING. *Shoot-Out at Sentinel Peak/Tangled Trail.* 1954. Ace D 86. PBO. We. VG. P6d. $5.00

BRISTOW, Gwen. *Handsome Road.* 1949. Pocket 589. Fa. VG. B4d. $3.25

BRISTOW, Gwen. *This Side of Glory.* 1964. Perma M 5089. 1st prtg. VG. P7d. $3.50

BRITAIN, Sloane. *Finders Keepers.* 1965. Midwood 32-484. 2nd edn. Ad. VG. B5d. $4.00

BRITAIN, Sloane. *Insatiable.* Midwood F 320. reprint. NF. B6d. $15.00

BRITAIN, Sloane. *Insatiable.* 1960. Midwood 57. PBO. c/gga. scarce. NF. B6a #80. $55.00

BRITAIN, Sloane. *Meet Marilyn.* Midwood 284. 2nd prtg. VG. B3d. $4.50

BRITAIN, Sloane. *Meet Marilyn.* 1960. Midwood 52. PBO. c/Wagner: gga. NF. B6d. $22.50

BRITAIN, Sloane. *Needle.* 1959. Beacon 237. 1st prtg. PBO. VG+. P7d. $35.00

BRITAIN, Sloane. *Woman Doctor.* 1962. Midwood F 142. PBO. c/Rader:gga. NF. B6d. $25.00

BRITAIN/RUBEL. *Strumpet's Jungle/Any Man's Playmate.* 1962. Dollar Double 951. VG+. B3a #22. $12.10

BRITISH COMMITTEE REPORT. *Wolfenden Report.* Lancer 74-829. VG+. B3d. $4.50

BRITT, D. *Hard Sell Girls.* Brandon House 717. VG+. B3d. $10.00

BRITTON, Rod. *Sixty-Niners.* No Publisher NN. Ad. VG+. B5d. $6.50

BRITTON, S. *Unnatural.* Midwood 47. VG+. I1d. $10.00

BROCK, Glen T. *Shack Town.* Holloway House 87067. G+. M6d. $5.00

BROCK, R. *Art Masterpieces.* Perma P 62. VG. I1d. $3.00

BROCK, Stuart. *Double-Cross Ranch.* 1957. Pyramid 255. We. G+. B5d. $3.00

BROCK, Stuart. *Just Around the Coroner.* Dell 337. VG. G5d. $3.50

BRODERICK, Charles. *Loverboy.* 1963. France 34. 1st edn. c/gga. My. F. F2d. $8.50

BRODERICK, Damien. *Dreaming Dragons.* 1980. Pocket 83150. PBO. SF. NF. B6d. $3.00

BRODERICK, Damien. *Striped Holes.* 1988. Avon 75377. PBO. SF. NF. B6d. $3.00

BRODRICK, Alan Houghton. *Man & His Ancestry.* 1964. Premier T 239. Nfi. VG+. B5d. $3.50

BROME, V. *Spy.* Pyramid 379. VG+. B3d. $4.50

BROMFIELD, Louis. *Early Autumn.* 1962. PB Library 52-129. Fi. VG+. B5d. $3.50

BROMFIELD, Louis. *Great Short Novels.* 1944. Avon Modern Story 13. Fi. G. B5d. $2.00

BROMFIELD, Louis. *Man Who Had Everything.* Avon 52. VG. B3d. $5.00

BROMFIELD, Louis. *Rains Came.* 1951. Signet 904AB. c/J Avati. Fi. VG. B5d. $4.00

BROMFIELD, Louis. *Strange Case of Miss Annie Spragg.* 1956. Berkley G 36. SF. VG+. B5d. $5.00

BROMFIELD, Louis. *What Became of Anna Bolton?* 1948. Bantam 462. VG+. B3a #20. $78.05

BROMFIELD, Louis. *Wild Is the River.* Bantam 910. VG. B3d. $4.50

BROMIGE, Iris. *Rosevean.* 1965. PB Library 52-861. 1st US edn. c/Marchetti. Go. NF. B6d. $7.50

BRONTE, Emily. *Wuthering Heights.* 1944. Quick Reader 122. VG. B3a #21. $25.00

BROOKS, Barbara. *Just the Two of Us.* 1963. Midwood F 323. PBO. c/Rader. VG. B6d. $12.50

BROOKS, G.R. *This Was Joanna.* Newsstand A 10. VG. B3d. $8.00

BROOKS, John. *Big Wheel.* 1951. Pocket 767. c/L Manso. Fi. VG. B5d. $4.00

BROOKS, Win. *Shining Tides.* 1954. Pocket 984. c/T Dunn. Fi. VG. B5d. $4.00

BROSSARD, Chandler. *Bold Saboteurs.* 1954. Dell D 137. JD. VG+. P1d. $20.00

BROSSARD, Chandler. *First Time.* Pyramid 260. VG. B3d. $4.00

BROSSARD, Chandler. *Pangs of Love.* Regency RB 302. VG. B3d. $4.00

BROSSARD, Chandler. *Who Walk in Darkness.* Signet 974. 1st pb. c/Beatnik. VG+. B6d. $15.00

BROTHERS, William P. *Morrocco Episode.* 1959. Hillman 111. 1st edn. c/Maguire: gga. Th. F. F2d. $13.00

BROUGH & HOPPER. *Whole Truth & Nothing But.* 1963. Pyramid T934. c/photo. Nfi. VG+. B5d. $4.00

BROWARD, Donn. *Convention Queen.* Ace D 432. PBO. VG. B3d. $4.00

BROWN, Beth. *Wedding Ring.* Avon 97. VG. B3d. $4.00

BROWN, Calvin edt. *Reader's Companion to World Lit.* 1956. Mentor MD 179. Nfi. VG. P1d. $5.00

BROWN, Carter. *Aseptic Murders.* 1972. Signet 4961. 1st edn. De. F. F2d. $7.00

BROWN, Carter. *Black Lace Hangover.* 1966. Signet 2945. 1st edn. c/gga. F. F2d. $7.00

BROWN, Carter. *Blonde on a Broomstick.* Signet D 2831. G+. G5d. $5.00

BROWN, Carter. *Blonde.* 1958. Signet 1565. c/B Phillips. $4.00

BROWN, Carter. *Body.* 1958. Signet T 4550. 5th prtg. My. VG. W2d. $3.50

BROWN, Carter. *Bombshell.* Signet D 3097. 3rd prtg. My. G. W2d. $2.00

BROWN, Carter. *Bombshell.* 1960. Signet 1767. 1st edn. c/gga. Th. F. F2d. $10.00

BROWN, Carter. *Brazen.* 1960. Signet 1836. 1st edn. c/gga. F. F2d. $15.00

BROWN, Carter. *Bump & Grind Murders.* Signet G 2541. NF. G5d. $4.50

BROWN, Carter. *Burden of Guilt.* 1970. Signet 4219. 1st edn. c/McGinnis: gga. F. F2d. $10.00

BROWN, Carter. *Catch Me a Phoenix!* 1965. Signet 2637. 1st edn. c/McGinnis: De. F. F2d. $10.00

BROWN, Carter. *Charlie Sent Me!* 1963. Signet G 2394. 1st US edn. c/McGinnis. My. NF. B6d. $10.00

BROWN, Carter. *Clown.* Signet T 5206. VG. G5d. $3.75

BROWN, Carter. *Corpse.* Signet 1606. VG+. I1d. $5.00

BROWN, Carter. *Coven.* 1971. Signet. 1st pb. F. M1d. $8.00

BROWN, Carter. *Creative Murders.* Signet T 4520. VG. G5d. $5.00

BROWN, Carter. *Dame.* 1959. Signet 1738. c/B Phillips. My. VG+. B5d. $5.00

BROWN, Carter. *Dance of Death.* 1964. Signet 2425. 1st edn. c/gga. F. F2d. $7.00

BROWN, Carter. *Deep Cold Green.* 1968. Signet D 3623. c/gga. My. F. G5d. $7.00

BROWN, Carter. *Desired.* 1960. Signet 1764. c/B Phillips. My. F. F2d. $15.00

BROWN, Carter. *Die Anytime, After Tuesday!* Signet P 3903. VG+. G5d. $5.00

BROWN, Carter. *Dream Is Deadly.* 1960. Signet 1845. 1st edn. c/gga. Th. F. F2d. $10.00

BROWN, Carter. *Dream Merchant.* Signet Y 7031. VG+. G5d. $5.00

BROWN, Carter. *Ever-Loving Blues.* 1961. Signet S 1919. 1st edn. c/Barye. De. F. F2d. $15.00

BROWN, Carter. *Girl From Outer Space.* Signet D 2736. VG. G5d. $5.00

BROWN, Carter. *Girl in a Shroud.* 1963. Signet G 2344. c/McGinnis: gga. My. VG. B4d. $3.00

BROWN, Carter. *Good Year for Dwarfs?* 1970. Signet P 4320. 1st prtg. My. VG. W2d. $3.50

BROWN, Carter. *Graves, I Dig!* 1960. Signet S 1801. 1st edn. c/gga. My. NF. F2d. $8.00

BROWN, Carter. *Guilt-Edged Cage.* Signet S 2220. VG. G5d. $4.50

BROWN, Carter. *Had I But Groaned.* Signet D 3380. G+. G5d. $5.00

BROWN, Carter. *Hammer of Thor.* 1965. Signet D 2794. c/McGinnis: gga. My. VG. B4d. $3.00

BROWN, Carter. *Hang-Up.* 1970. Signet 4159. 1st edn. c/gga. F. F2d. $7.00

BROWN, Carter. *House of Sorcery.* Signet D 3218. VG. G5d. $3.75

BROWN, Carter. *Invisible Flamini.* Signet T 4854. G+. G5d. $5.00

BROWN, Carter. *Jade-Eyed Jungle.* 1963. Signet G 2355. c/gga. My. VG. B4d. $4.00

BROWN, Carter. *Lady Is Available.* 1963. Signet S 2244. 1 prtg. My. VG. W2d. $3.50

BROWN, Carter. *Lament for a Lousy Lover.* 1960. Signet 1856. 1st edn. De. F. F2d. $15.00

BROWN, Carter. *Loving & the Dead.* 1959. Signet 1654. 1st edn. My. F. F3d. $10.00

BROWN, Carter. *Manhattan Cowboy.* Signet T 5571. G+. G5d. $3.50

BROWN, Carter. *Million-Dollar Babe.* 1961. Signet 1909. 1st edn. My. F. F2d. $10.00

BROWN, Carter. *Mini-Murders.* 1968. Signet 3585. 1st edn. c/McGinnis: gga. F. F2d. $7.00

BROWN, Carter. *Mistress.* 1958. Signet 1594. VG. B3d/I1d. $4.00

BROWN, Carter. *Mistress.* 1958. Signet 1594. 1st edn. My. F. F2d. $10.00

BROWN, Carter. *Murder in the Key Club.* 1962. Signet 2140. 1st edn. c/McGinnis. F. F2d. $10.00

BROWN, Carter. *Murder Is a Package Deal.* 1964. Signet 2530. 1st edn. c/McGinnis. De. F. F2d. $10.00

BROWN, Carter. *Myopic Mermaid.* 1961. Signet S 1924. c/gga. My. VG+. B4d. $5.00

BROWN, Carter. *Myopic Mermaid.* 1961. Signet S 1924. c/gga. F. F2d. $13.00

BROWN, Carter. *Never-Was Girl.* 1964. Signet 2457. 1st edn. F. F2d. $10.00

BROWN, Carter. *No Tears From the Widow.* 1966. Signet D 3052. c/gga. My. VG. B4d. $4.00

BROWN, Carter. *Only the Very Rich.* Signet P 3842. VG+. G5d. $5.00

BROWN, Carter. *Only the Very Rich.* 1969. Signet 3842. 1st edn. c/McGinnis: gga. De. F. F2d. $10.00

BROWN, Carter. *Passionate.* 1964. Signet G 2537. 3rd prtg. My. G+. W2d. $3.50

BROWN, Carter. *Passionate.* 1959. Signet 1674. 1st edn. c/gga. F. F2d. $15.00

BROWN, Carter. *Play Now. Kill Later.* 1966. Signet 2906. 1st edn. c/gga. De. F. F2d. $10.00

BROWN, Carter. *Remember Maybelle?* Signet Y 6995. G+. G5d. $4.50

BROWN, Carter. *Ride the Roller Coaster.* Signet Y 6804. G. G5d. $4.50

BROWN, Carter. *Savage Salome.* Signet S 1896. VG. I1d. $4.00

BROWN, Carter. *Scarlet Flush.* 1963. Signet G 2365. c/gga. My. VG. B4d. $4.00

BROWN, Carter. *Seidlitz & the Super-Spy.* 1967. Signet D 3168. c/gga. My. VG. B4d. $4.00

BROWN, Carter. *Seven Sirens.* Signet T 4908. VG. G5d. $4.50

BROWN, Carter. *Sex Clinic.* 1971. Signet T 4658. 1st prtg. My. VG+. W2d. $3.75

BROWN, Carter. *Silken Nightmare.* Signet G 2400. VG. G5d. $4.50

BROWN, Carter. *Silken Nightmare.* 1963. Signet 2400. 1st edn. My. F. F2d. $10.00

BROWN, Carter. *So What Killed the Vampire?* 1966. Signet D 2859. VG+. G5d. $4.00

BROWN, Carter. *Stripper.* 1961. Signet 1981. 1st edn. My. F. F2d. $10.00

BROWN, Carter. *Suddenly by Violence.* 1959. Signet 1722. c/B Phillips. My. VG. B5d. $4.00

BROWN, Carter. *Swingers.* Tower 51583. VG. G5d. $3.50

BROWN, Carter. *Target for Their Dark Desire.* Signet D 3017. G. G5d. $4.50

BROWN, Carter. *Temptress.* 1960. Signet S 1817. c/gga. My. VG+. B4d. $4.00

BROWN, Carter. *Terror Comes Creeping.* 1959. Signet 1750. c/B Phillips. My. VG. B5d. $4.00

BROWN, Carter. *Tomorrow Is Murder.* 1960. Signet S 1806. c/Barye: gga. My. VG+. B4d. $3.00

BROWN, Carter. *True Son of the Beast.* Signet 4268. VG. B3d. $4.00

BROWN, Carter. *Up-Tight Blonde.* 1969. Signet S 3955. c/McGinnis: gga. My. VG. B4d. $4.00

BROWN, Carter. *Victim.* Signet 1633. VG+. I1d. $5.00

BROWN, Carter. *Wanton.* 1959. Signet 1713. 1st edn. c/gga. F. F2d. $10.00

BROWN, Carter. *Wayward Wahine.* 1960. Signet 1784. c/gga. My. VG+. B4d. $3.00

BROWN, Carter. *Wayward Wahine.* 1960. Signet 1784. 1st edn. My. F. F2d. $10.00

BROWN, Carter. *Where Did Charity Go?* 1970. Signet T 4455. c/McGinnis: gga. My. VG+. B4d. $4.00

BROWN, Carter. *White Bikini.* Signet S 2275. G. G5d. $4.50

BROWN, Carter. *Who Killed Dr Sex?* Signet D 2581. NF. G5d. $6.00

BROWN, Carter. *Wind-Up Doll.* Signet G 2413. G+. G5d. $3.50

BROWN, Dale. *Hammerheads.* 1991. Berkley 12645. 1st prtg. My. VG. W2d. $3.50

BROWN, Dee. *Calvary Scout.* Perma M 3101. PBO. VG. B3d. $4.00

BROWN, Dee. *Yellowhorse.* 1957. Ballantine 202. 1st prtg. c/Mel Crair. VG. P7d. $5.00

BROWN, Douglas. *Anne Bonny Pirate Queen.* Monarch 320. VG. B3d. $4.00

BROWN, Eugene. *Trespass.* 1953. Pocket 964. c/T Dunn. Fi. VG+. B5d. $5.00

BROWN, F. *Project Jupiter.* 1964. Digit 828. reissue. VG. B3d. $10.00

BROWN, Francis edt. *Highlights of Modern Literature.* 1954. Mentor M 104. Nfi. VG. P1d. $9.00

BROWN, Fredric. *Case of the Dancing Sandwiches.* 1951. Dell 10¢ 33. PBO. c/Stanley. rare. VG. B6a #75. $88.00

BROWN, Fredric. *Daymares.* Lancer 73-727. VG. B3d. $8.00

BROWN, Fredric. *Dead Ringer.* Bantam 1216. reprint. VG. B6d. $12.50

BROWN, Fredric. *Dead Ringer.* 1949. Bantam 361. VG. B3a #24. $18.50

BROWN, Fredric. *Dead Ringer.* 1949. Bantam 361. VG. B3d. $5.00

BROWN, Fredric. *Death Has Many Doors.* Bantam 1040. VG. B3d. $8.50

BROWN, Fredric. *Deep End.* 1954. Bantam 1215. c/Charles Binger: gga. VG. B3d. $5.00

BROWN, Fredric. *Fabulous Clipjoint.* 1948. Bantam 302. VG. B3d. $15.00

BROWN, Fredric. *Fabulous Clipjoint.* 1948. Bantam 302. 1st prtg. My. VG+. F2d. $18.00

BROWN, Fredric. *Here Comes a Candle.* 1951. Bantam 943. 1st prtg. My. F. F2d. $15.00

BROWN, Fredric. *His Name Is Death.* Bantam 1436. VG. B3d. $4.00

BROWN, Fredric. *His Name Was Death.* 1956. Bantam. 1st pb. F. M1d. $20.00

BROWN, Fredric. *Honeymoon in Hell.* 1958. Bantam A 1812. PBO. NF. M1d. $20.00

BROWN, Fredric. *Honeymoon in Hell.* 1958. Bantam A 1812. PBO. SF. VG. B6d. $15.00

BROWN, Fredric. *Honeymoon in Hell.* 1963. Bantam J 2650. 2nd edn. SF. VG. B5d. $5.00

BROWN, Fredric. *Knock Three-One-Two.* Bantam 2135. c/Barye. VG. B3d. $7.50

BROWN, Fredric. *Late Lamented.* Bantam 2030. c/Barye. VG. B3d. $5.00

BROWN, Fredric. *Lenient Beast.* Bantam 1712. VG+. B3d. $8.50

BROWN, Fredric. *Lights in the Sky Are Stars.* 1963. Bantam J 2578. 2nd prtg. SF. G. W2d. $6.00

BROWN, Fredric. *Lights in the Sky Are Stars.* 1954. Bantam 1285. 1st edn. SF. VG. M3d. $8.00

BROWN, Fredric. *Madball.* 1953. Dell 1st Edn 2E. PBO. c/gga. VG+. B6a #74. $59.00

BROWN, Fredric. *Madball.* 1953. Dell 1st Edn 2E. PBO. c/Griffith Foxley: gga. VG+. P6d. $20.00

BROWN, Fredric. *Madball.* 1953. Dell 1st Edn 2E. 1st edn. My. F. F2d. $40.00

BROWN, Fredric. *Madball.* 1963. Gold Medal S 1132. 1st prtg. My. NF. F2d. $20.00

BROWN, Fredric. *Madball.* Gold Medal 1132. VG. B3d. $7.00

BROWN, Fredric. *Martains, Go Home.* 1956. Bantam A 1546. 1st prtg. VG+. S1d. $11.00

BROWN, Fredric. *Martians, Go Home.* 1976. Ballantine 25314. 2nd edn. c/K Freas. SF. VG+. B5d. $6.50

BROWN, Fredric. *Martians, Go Home.* 1956. Bantam A 1546. 1st prtg. SF. NF. M1d. $15.00

BROWN, Fredric. *Mind Thing.* 1961. Bantam 2187. VG. B3d. $7.00

BROWN, Fredric. *Mind Thing.* 1961. Bantam 2187. 1st edn. SF. NF. F2d. $15.00

BROWN, Fredric. *Mostly Murder.* 1954. Pennant P 59. VG. P6d. $14.00

BROWN, Fredric. *Murder in Moonlight.* 1957. Bloodhound 1185. VG+. B3a. $55.00

BROWN, Fredric. *Murder Set to Music.* 1959. Saint My Library 120. PBO. VG. P6d. $8.00

BROWN, Fredric. *Murderers.* Bantam 2587. VG. B3d. $4.50

BROWN, Fredric. *Murderers.* 1963. Bantam 2587. 1st pb. NF. M1d. $20.00

BROWN, Fredric. *Night of the Jabberwock.* 1952. Bantam 990. 1st edn. PBO. c/Skemp. scarce. VG+. B6a #76. $55.00

BROWN, Fredric. *Nightmares & Geezenstacks.* Bantam J 2296. VG. G5d. $12.00

BROWN, Fredric. *Nightmares & Geezenstacks.* 1961. Bantam. 1st edn. NF. M1d. $30.00

BROWN, Fredric. *One for the Road.* 1959. Bantam 1990. c/Barye Phillips: gga. VG. P6d. $7.50

BROWN, Fredric. *Paradox Lost.* Berkley G 2656. VG+. B3d. $10.00

BROWN, Fredric. *Plot for Murder.* 1949. Bantam 735. 1st prtg. My. G+. R5d. $10.00

BROWN, Fredric. *Rogue in Space.* Bantam A 1701. 1st prtg. VG. S1d. $6.00

BROWN, Fredric. *Rogue in Space.* 1971. Bantam S 6763. 1st prtg. c/Lou Feck. SF. VG. P7d. $4.50

BROWN, Fredric. *Rogue in Space.* 1957. Bantam. 1st pb. F. M1d. $20.00

BROWN, Fredric. *Screaming Mimi.* 1950. Bantam 831. c/gga. VG. P6d. $12.00

BROWN, Fredric. *Space on My Hands.* 1952. Bantam 1077. c/Barye. VG+. B3d. $8.00

BROWN, Fredric. *Space on My Hands.* 1952. Bantam 1077. 1st pb. F. M1d. $15.00

BROWN, Fredric. *Star Shine.* Bantam 1423. VG. B3d. $6.00

BROWN, Fredric. *Star Shine.* 1956. Bantam 1423. 1st pb. F. M1d. $12.00

BROWN, Fredric. *Star Shine.* 1956. Bantam 1423. 1st prtg. SF. NF. F2d. $10.00

BROWN, Fredric. *What Mad Universe.* Bantam 10336. 1st prtg. F. S1d. $3.50

BROWN, Fredric. *What Mad Universe.* 1954. Bantam 1253. 1st prtg. SF. F. F2d. $25.00

BROWN, Fredric. *What Mad Universe.* 1954. Bantam 1253. 1st prtg. VG. S1d. $4.50

BROWN, Fredric. *What Mad Universe.* 1950. Bantam 835. 1st pb. VG. M1d. $15.00

BROWN, G. *Plot for Murder (Murder Can Be Fun).* Bantam 735. VG. B3d. $5.00

BROWN, Harry. *Gathering.* 1977. Ballantine 27386. 1st edn. TVTI. My. F. F2d. $10.00

BROWN, Harry. *Walk in the Sun.* Signet 1467. c/Barye. VG. B3d. $5.00

BROWN, Helen Gurley. *Sex & the Single Girl.* 1963. Cardinal GC 783. 1st prtg. VG. P7d. $3.50

BROWN, J.D. *Kings Go Forth.* 1958. Cardinal C 315. 1st prtg. VG. R5d. $2.50

BROWN, J.D. *Kings Go Forth.* Pan G 120. MTI. VG. B3d. $8.50

BROWN, J.D. *Stars in My Crown.* Pocket 645. VG+. B3d. $5.00

BROWN, Lyle. *Sports Quiz.* 1954. Pocket 996. Nfi. VG+. B4d. $2.50

BROWN, Rosel George. *Galactic Sibyl Sue Blue.* 1968. Berkley X 1503. c/Hoot. SF. VG. B5d. $4.00

BROWN, Rosel George. *Handful of Time.* 1963. Ballantine F 703. 1st edn. F. M1d. $10.00

BROWN, Wenzell. *Big Rumble.* 1955. Popular 685. JD. VG. P1d. $45.00

BROWN, Wenzell. *Dark Drums.* Popular 374. VG. B3d. $5.00

BROWN, Wenzell. *Gang Girl.* 1954. Avon 560. PBO. scarce. JD. VG. B6a #80. $36.50

BROWN, Wenzell. *Gang Girl.* 1954. Avon 560. 1st edn. My. F. F2d. $25.00

BROWN, Wenzell. *Golden Witch.* Monarch 460. VG. B3d. $4.50

BROWN, Wenzell. *Hoods Ride In.* 1959. Pyramid G 439. 1st edn. My. F. F2d. $30.00

BROWN, Wenzell. *Jailbait Jungle.* Belmont 90-265. scarce. JD. NF. B6a #76. $37.00

BROWN, Wenzell. *Jailbait Jungle.* 1962. Belmont 90-265. 1st edn. c/gga. scarce. My. F. F2d. $20.00

BROWN, Wenzell. *Jailbait Jungle.* 1962. Belmont 90-265. 1st prtg. My. VG. R5d. $6.00

BROWN, Wenzell. *Lonely Hearts Murder.* 1952. Signet 981. 1st prtg. c/gga. VG. G5d. $7.00

BROWN, Wenzell. *Monkey on My Back.* Popular 549. VG. B3d. $5.00

BROWN, Wenzell. *Murder Kick.* 1960. Gold Medal S 1013. My. NF. B6a #74. $45.25

BROWN, Wenzell. *Murder Kick.* 1960. Gold Medal 1013. PBO. F. B6d. $25.00

BROWN, Wenzell. *Naked Hours.* Popular 732. G+. G5d. $4.50

BROWN, Wenzell. *Possess & Conquer.* 1975. Warner 76-935. 1st edn. SF. F. F2d. $25.00

BROWN, Wenzell. *Possess & Conquer.* 1975. Warner 76-935. 1st prtg. VG. P7d. $5.00

BROWN, Wenzell. *Rum & Coco-Cola Murders.* 1960. Saint My Library 131. VG. P6d. $4.50

BROWN, Wenzell. *Run, Chico, Run.* 1953. Gold Medal 292. PBO. c/Barye. scarce. JD. NF. B6a #75. $48.50

BROWN, Wenzell. *Run, Chico, Run.* 1953. Gold Medal 292. PBO. JD. F. F2d. $25.00

BROWN, Wenzell. *Run, Chico, Run.* 1953. Gold Medal 292. PBO. VG. B6d. $18.00

BROWN, Wenzell. *Sherry.* 1964. Monarch 403. 1st edn. c/photo. My. F. F2d. $10.00

BROWN, Wenzell. *Witness to Death.* Saint My Library 119. PBO. VG. P6d. $4.50

BROWN, Will C. *Laredo Road.* 1959. Dell 1st Edn A 183. PBO. VG. M6d. $6.50

BROWN, Will C. *Man of the West.* Dell 986. MTI. c/Gross. VG. B3d. $4.50

BROWN, Will C. *Think Fast, Ranger!* Dell 1st Edn B 194. VG+. B3d. $4.50

BROWN, William F. *Abominable Showmen.* 1960. Signet S 1786. TVTI. VG. P1d. $10.00

BROWN & KUTTNER. *SF Adventures in Mutation.* Berkley F 1096. 1st pb. G+. M6d. $4.50

BROWN & REYNOLDS edts. *SF Carnival.* Bantam 1615. VG. B3d. $5.00

BROWN & REYNOLDS edts. *SF Carnival.* 1957. Bantam. 1st pb. F. M1d. $20.00

BROWNE, Eleanore. *Innocent Madame.* 1951. Lion 73. c/gga. Fa. VG. B4d. $7.50

BROWNE, Howard. *Thin Air.* Dell 894. VG+. B3d. $4.50

BROWNE, Robert. *New Atoms Bombshell.* 1980. Ballantine 28661. PBO. SF. NF. B6d. $3.00

BROWNING, Elizabeth. *Sonnets From the Portuguese.* 1958. Avon 251. Nfi. VG. B4d. $3.00

BROXON, Mildred. *Too Long a Sacrifice.* 1981. Dell 18603. PBO. Fa. NF. B6d. $3.00

BRUCE, Jean. *Last Quarter Hour.* 1965. Crest K 795. 1st Am edn. My. NF. F2d. $7.00

BRUCE, L. *How To Talk Dirty & Influence People.* Playboy 75184. VG. B3d. $5.00

BRUCE, Robert. *Face of Evil.* 1966. Midwood 32-629. Fa. F. B4d. $9.00

BRUCE, Robert. *Tina.* 1954. Lion 226. PBO. c/gga. VG. B3d. $8.00

BRUFF, N. *Manatee.* Pyramid 24. VG+. B3d. $6.00

BRUMMER/ROBERTS. *Listen! The Stars/ Rebellers.* Ace F 215. PBO. VG. B3d. $4.00

BRUNNER, John. *Age of Miracles.* 1973. Ace 01000. SF. VG. B5d. $3.00

BRUNNER, John. *Atlantic Abomination.* Ace 03300. SF. VG. B5d. $3.00

BRUNNER, John. *Avengers of Carrig.* 1969. Dell 00356. SF. F. W2d. $6.00

BRUNNER, John. *Bedlam Planet.* 1968. Ace G 709. 1st edn. F. P9d. $2.00

BRUNNER, John. *Bedlam Planet.* Ace 05301. PBO. c/J Jones. SF. VG+. B5d. $4.00

BRUNNER, John. *Black Is the Color.* 1969. Pyramid. 1st pb. F. M1d. $15.00

BRUNNER, John. *Book of John Brunner.* 1976. DAW 177. c/J Gaughan. SF. VG+. B5d. $4.00

BRUNNER, John. *Born Under Mars.* Ace G 664. 1st prtg. G+. S1d. $2.00

BRUNNER, John. *Born Under Mars.* 1973. Ace 07161. 2nd edn. SF. VG+. B5d. $4.00

BRUNNER, John. *Children of the Thunder.* 1989. Ballantine 31378. PBO. c/Whelan. SF. NF. B6d. $3.00

BRUNNER, John. *Conquer Chaos.* 1964. Ace F 277. 1st prtg. SF. VG. W2d. $4.50

BRUNNER, John. *Crucible of Time.* 1984. Ballantine 30235. SF. VG+. W2d. $3.50

BRUNNER, John. *Day of the Star Cities.* 1965. Ace F 361. NF. M1d. $8.00

BRUNNER, John. *Day of the Star Cities.* 1965. Ace F 361. 1st edn. SF. F. F2d. $12.50

BRUNNER, John. *Dramaturgies of Yan.* Ace 16668. SF. G+. W2d. $3.00

BRUNNER, John. *Dreaming Earth.* Pyramid F 829. VG. I1d. $7.00

BRUNNER, John. *Good Men Do Nothing.* Pyramid 2443. VG. B3d. $4.00

BRUNNER, John. *Infinitives of Go.* 1981. Ballantine 28497. 2nd prtg. SF. F. W2d. $3.25

BRUNNER, John. *Listen the Stars.* Ace F 215. VG+. I1d. $15.00

BRUNNER, John. *Long Result.* 1966. Ballantine U 2329. SF. G+. W2d. $3.25

BRUNNER, John. *Long Result.* 1966. Ballantine U 2329. 1st edn. VG. M1d. $5.00

BRUNNER, John. *Now Then!* 1968. Avon S 323. SF. F. W2d. $4.75

BRUNNER, John. *Now Then!* Mayflower 6500. VG. B3d. $6.00

BRUNNER, John. *Out of My Mind.* 1967. Ballantine. 1st edn. F. M1d. $6.00

BRUNNER, John. *Polymath.* 1974. DAW 85. c/V Difate. SF. VG+. B5d. $4.00

BRUNNER, John. *Productions of Time.* 1967. Signet P 3113. SF. VG+. B4d. $2.75

BRUNNER, John. *Quicksand.* 1969. Bantam S 4212. SF. VG. W2d. $4.00

BRUNNER, John. *Quicksand.* 1969. DAW UW 1245. SF. VG. W2d. $3.75

BRUNNER, John. *Repairmen of Cyclops.* 1965. Ace M 115. SF. VG+. B4d. $2.50

BRUNNER, John. *Sheep Look Up.* 1973. Ballantine 23612. 1st edn. NF. P9d. $2.00

BRUNNER, John. *Shockwave Rider.* 1976. Ballantine 24853. c/M Tinkelman. SF. VG+. B5d. $4.50

BRUNNER, John. *Squares of the City.* Ballantine U 6035. PBO. VG+. B3d. $5.50

BRUNNER, John. *Squares of the City.* 1965. Ballantine. 1st edn. F. M1d. $7.00

BRUNNER, John. *Stand on Zanzibar.* 1969. Ballantine 01713. SF. VG+. B4d. $5.00

BRUNNER, John. *Stand on Zanzibar.* 1974. Ballantine 24082. 5th edn. SF. VG+. B5d/W2d. $3.50

BRUNNER, John. *Stardroppers.* 1972. DAW 23. c/J Gaughan. SF. NF. B5d. $4.00

BRUNNER, John. *Stone That Never Came Down.* 1975. DAW UY 1150. 1st prtg. SF. VG. W2d. $3.50

BRUNNER, John. *Super Barbarians.* Ace D 547. NF. M1d. $8.00

BRUNNER, John. *Super Barbarians.* 1962. Ace D 547. 1st prtg. SF. VG. R5d. $4.50

BRUNNER, John. *Times Without Number.* 1969. Ace 81270. 2nd edn. F. P9d. $2.00

BRUNNER, John. *Timescoop.* 1969. Dell 8916. 1st prtg. SF. VG+. R5d. $2.75

BRUNNER, John. *To Conquer Chaos.* Ace F 277. NF. M1d. $10.00

BRUNNER, John. *Total Eclipse.* 1975. DAW 162. 1st edn. PBO. G. P9d. $1.00

BRUNNER, John. *Traveler in Black.* 1971. Ace 82210. SF. VG. W2d. $3.50

BRUNNER, John. *Wear the Butcher's Medal.* 1965. Pocket 50129. My. G+. B5d. $3.50

BRUNNER, John. *Web of Everywhere.* 1974. Bantam 8398. 1st edn. SF. F. F2d. $10.00

BRUNNER, John. *Whole Man.* 1964. Ballantine U 2219. 1st edn. NF. P9d. $6.00

BRUNNER, John. *World Swappers.* 1961. Ace G 649. 2nd edn. VG. P9d. $1.50

BRUNNER, John. *Wrong End of Time.* 1973. DAW 61. c/C Foss. SF. F. B5d. $5.00

BRUNNER/BRUNNER. *Astronauts Must Not Land/Space-Time Juggler.* Ace F 227. F. M1d. $8.00

BRUNNER/BRUNNER. *Castaways World/Rites of One.* 1963. Ace F 242. SF. F. M1d. $9.00

BRUNNER/BRUNNER. *Enigma From Tantalus/Repairmen of Cyclops.* Ace M 115. F. M1d. $10.00

BRUNNER/BULMER. *Meeting at Infinity/Beyond the Silver Sky.* 1961. Ace D 507. 1st edn. c/Emsh. F. M1d. $15.00

BRUNNER/CARTER. *Evil That Men Do/Purloined Planet.* 1969. Belmont B60-1010. SF. VG. B5d. $7.50

BRUNNER/CHANDLER. *Secret Agent of Terra/Rim of Space.* Ace F 133. F. M1d. $8.00

BRUNNER/CHANDLER. *Secret Agent of Terra/Rim of Space.* 1962. Ace F 133. PBO. c/E Emsh & E Valigursky. SF. VG+. B5d. $5.50

BRUNNER/DICK. *Skynappers/Vulcan's Hammer.* 1960. Ace D 457. 1st prtg. SF. VG. R5d. $17.50

BRUNNER/DICK. *Skynappers/Vulcan's Hammer.* 1976. Arrow 913300. SF. VG. P1d. $7.50

BRUNNER/DICK. *Skynappers/Vulcans Hammer.* 1960. Ace D 457. 1st prtg. G. S1d. $4.00

BRUNNER/DICK. *Slavers of Space/Dr Futurity.* 1960. Ace D 421. c/Emsh. VG+. B6d. $7.50

BRUNNER/DUNCAN. *Father of Lies/Mirror Image.* 1968. Belmont B 60-081. SF. VG. B5d. $4.00

BRUNNER/DUNCAN. *Father of Lies/Mirror Image.* 1968. Belmont B 60-081. 1st prtg. SF. G+. R5d. $2.50

BRUNNER/FOX. *Endless Shadow/Arsenal of Miracles.* Ace F 299. F. M1d. $10.00

BRUNNER/FOX. *Endless Shadow/Arsenal of Miracles.* Ace F 299. PBO. VG+. B3d. $6.00

BRUNNER/GRINNELL. *Atlantic Abomination/Martian Missile.* 1959. Ace D 465. 1st edn. F. M1d. $15.00

BRUNNER/GRINNELL. *Atlantic Abomination/Martian Missile.* Ace D 465. 1st edn. VG. I1d. $6.00

BRUNNER/GRINNELL. *Times Without Number/Destiny's Orbit.* 1962. Ace F 161. PBO. c/J Gaughan & E Valigursky. SF. VG. B5d. $4.50

BRUNNER/GRINNELL. *Times Without Number/Destiny's Orbit.* 1962. Ace F 161. SF. F. W2d. $12.50

BRUNNER/GRINNELL. *Times Without Number/Destiny's Orbit.* 1962. Ace F 161. 1st prtg. G+. S1d. $3.50

BRUNNER/GRINNELL. *100th Millenium/Edge of Time.* Ace D 362. c/Emsh. F. M1d. $15.00

BRUNNER/GRINNELL. *100th Millennium/Edge of Time.* Ace D 362. VG+. I1d. $5.00

BRUNNER/NOURSE. *Echo in the Skull/Rocket to Limbo.* Ace D 385. c/Emsh. F. M1d. $15.00

BRUNNER/NOURSE. *Echo in the Skull/Rocket to Limbo.* Ace D 385. PBO. VG. B3d. $4.50

BRUNNER/RACKHAM. *Planet of Your Own/ Beasts of Kohl.* Ace G 592. NF. M1d. $6.00

BRUNNER/RACKHAM. *Planet of Your Own/Beasts of Kohl.* Ace G 592. 1st prtg. G. S1d. $2.00

BRUNNER/ROBERTS. *Listen! The Stars!/ Rebellers.* Ace F 215. G. P9d/R5d. $2.00

BRUNNER/ROBERTS. *Listen! The Stars!/ Rebellers.* Ace F 215. NF. M1d. $6.00

BRUNNER/ROBERTS. *Listen! The Stars!/ Rebellers.* 1963. Ace F 215. PBO. c/E Emsh & J Gaughan. SF. VG. B5d. $4.50

BRUNNER/SHARKEY. *Sanctuary in the Sky/Secret Martians.* 1960. Ace D 471. 1st edn. F. M1d. $20.00

BRUNNER/SHARKEY. *Sanctuary in the Sky/Secret Martians.* 1960. Ace D 471. 1st prtg. PBO. c/gga. SF. VG. P7d. $6.00

BRUNNER/VAN VOGT. *World Swappers/ Seige of the Unseen.* 1959. Ace D 391. 1st edn. F. M1d. $15.00

BRUNNER/VAN VOGT. *World Swappers/ Siege of the Unseen.* 1959. Ace D 391. c/sgn. VG. B3d. $5.00

BRUNNER/WHITE. *Altar of Asconel/Android Avenger.* 1965. Ace M 123. SF. F. W2d. $8.50

BRUNNER/WHITE. *Altar on Asconel/ Android Avenger.* Ace M 123. PBO. VG+. B3d. $5.00

BRUSH, Katherine. *Bad Girl From Maine (Boy From Maine).* Avon 239. VG. B3d. $6.00

BRUSH, Katherine. *Free Woman.* Dell 10¢ 18. VG+. B3d. $30.00

BRUSH, Katherine. *Red-Headed Woman.* 1942. Avon. 1st pb. NF. M1d. $30.00

BRUSH, Katherine. *When She Was Bad.* 1948. Avon 154. c/gga. Fa. VG. B3d/I1d. $5.00

BRUSH, Katherine. *Young Man of Manhattan.* Avon 192. VG+. B3d. $5.00

BRYAN, Joseph. *Aircraft Carrier.* Ballantine 228. 2nd prtg. VG. B3d. $4.50

BRYAN, Walter. *Improbable Irish.* Ace 36990. Nfi. VG. B5d. $2.50

BRYANT, Ben. *Submarine Commander.* 1960. Ballantine F 447K. War. VG. B4d. $3.00

BRYANT, Matt. *Cue for Murder.* Berkley 333. VG. B3d. $4.00

BRYANT, Peter. *Red Alert.* 1959. Ace D 350. F. M1d. $10.00

BRYANT, Peter. *Red Alert.* 1959. Ace D 350. PBO. My. VG+. M3d. $7.50

BRYANT, Peter. *Red Alert.* 1959. Ace D 350. VG. B3d. $3.50

BRYANT, Peter. *Red Alert.* 1963. Ace F 210. SF. VG. B5d/I1d. $3.00

BUCHAN, John. *House of the Four Winds.* ANC 4. VG. G5d. $14.00

BUCHAN, John. *Mountain Meadow.* 1953. Bantam 1143. 2nd edn. Fa. VG. B4d. $2.00

BUCHAN, John. *Mountain Meadow.* 1946. Bantam 71. Fa. VG. B4d. $2.50

BUCHAN, John. *Prester John.* Pan 130. VG. B3d. $7.00

BUCHAN, John. *Prester John.* 1966. Pyramid X 1411. Fa. NF. B4d. $4.00

BUCHAN, John. *Three Hostages.* Bantam 31. VG+. B3d. $6.00

BUCHAN, John. *39 Steps.* Popular K 58. c/Teason. VG. B3d. $4.00

BUCHANAN, Jack. *MIA Hunter.* 1985. Jove 08068. My. VG. W2d. $3.00

BUCHWALD, Art. *Gift From the Boys.* 1959. Cardinal C 350. c/Bayre Philips: gga. Hu. VG+. B4d. $3.00

BUCK, Frank. *Wild Cargo.* 1966. Lancer 72-130. 1st pb. c/Gray Morrow. VG+. B6d. $7.00

BUCK, Pearl S. *Command the Morning.* 1960. Cardinal C 410. Fa. VG+. B4d. $2.00

BUCK, Pearl S. *East Wind: West Wind.* Pan G 445. VG+. B3d. $8.50

BUCK, Pearl S. *First Wife.* 1945. Avon Modern Story 23. Fi. G+. B5d. $2.50

BUCK, Pearl S. *Good Earth.* Pocket 11. 13th prtg. VG. B3d. $7.00

BUCK, Pearl S. *Hidden Flower.* 1954. Pocket 993. c/T Dunn. Fi. VG. B5d. $4.00

BUCK, Pearl S. *Journey for Life.* Dell 10¢ 8. VG+. B3d. $6.00

BUCK, Pearl S. *Letter From Peking.* 1958. Cardinal C 308. 1st prtg. c/Lee. VG. P7d. $3.50

BUCK, Pearl S. *Letter From Peking.* 1963. Cardinal GC 168. 1st prtg. VG+. P7d. $3.50

BUCK, Pearl S. *My Several Worlds.* 1956. Cardinal GC 35. 1st prtg. c/Binger. VG+. P7d. $4.00

BUCK, Pearl S. *Portrait of a Marriage.* 1961. Cardinal C 419. Fa. NF. B4d. $3.00

BUCK, Pearl S. *14 Stories.* 1963. Cardinal GC 163. VG. B4d. $2.00

BUCKINGHAM, Nancy. *Call of Glengarron.* 1968. Ace G 749. 1st prtg. My. VG. R5d. $1.75

BUCKNER, Robert. *Starfire.* 1960. Perma M 4185. 1st edn. F. M1d. $10.00

BUDRYS, Algis. *Amsirs & the Iron Thorn.* 1967. Gold Medal D 1852. SF. VG. B5d. $7.50

BUDRYS, Algis. *Amsirs & the Iron Thorn.* 1967. Gold Medal D 1852. 1st pb. NF. M1d. $10.00

BUDRYS, Algis. *Budrys' Inferno.* Berkley G 799. VG+. B3d. $4.50

BUDRYS, Algis. *Falling Torch.* 1964. Pyramid F 1028. NF. P9d. $1.50

BUDRYS, Algis. *Falling Torch.* 1962. Pyramid F 693. c/J Schoenherr. SF. NF. B5d. $5.00

BUDRYS, Algis. *Falling Torch.* 1959. Pyramid G 416. PBO. c/R Engle. SF. VG. B5d. $7.50

BUDRYS, Algis. *Falling Torch.* 1968. Pyramid X 1837. 4th edn. VG. P9d. $1.25

BUDRYS, Algis. *False Night.* 1954. Lion 230. c/sgn. VG+. B3d. $12.00

BUDRYS, Algis. *Man of Earth.* Ballantine 243. PBO. c/Powers: sgn. VG+. B3d. $8.00

BUDRYS, Algis. *Man of Earth.* 1958. Ballantine. PBO. NF. M1d. $12.00

BUDRYS, Algis. *Rogue Moon.* 1964. Gold Medal L 1474. 1st prtg. c/Powers. VG+. B3d/P7d/R5d/W2d. $5.00

BUDRYS, Algis. *Rogue Moon.* 1960. Gold Medal S 1057. 1st pb. F. M1d. $15.00

BUDRYS, Algis. *Some Will Not Die.* 1961. Regency 110. c/sgn. VG. B3d. $20.00

BUDRYS, Algis. *Unexpected Dimension.* 1960. Ballantine 388K. PBO. c/B Blanchard. SF. VG. B5d. $4.50

BUDRYS, Algis. *Unexpected Dimension.* 1960. Ballantine. 1st edn. F. M1d. $15.00

BUDRYS, Algis. *Who?* 1975. Ballantine 24569. 1st prtg. SF. VG. R5d. $1.75

BUDRYS, Algis. *Who?* 1958. Pyramid. 1st pb. NF. M1d. $15.00

BUEL, J.W. *Wild Bill Hickok: Gun Fighter.* 1946. Atomic 2. PBO. We. VG. B5d. $10.00

BUELL, John. *Pyx.* Crest 408. c/Barye. VG. B3d. $5.50

BULL, Lois. *Broadway Virgin.* 1949. Diversey Popular 1. 1st edn. PBO. rare. NF. B6a #80. $66.00

BULL, Lois. *Gold Diggers.* 1949. Novel Library 14. PBO. c/gga. very scarce. NF. B6a #74. $33.00

BULMER, H.K. *Encounter in Space.* Panther 29. VG. B3d. $8.00

BULMER, Kenneth. *Behold the Stars.* Priory 1145. SF. VG. B5d. $3.50

BULMER, Kenneth. *Cycle of Nemesis.* 1967. Ace G 680. SF. VG. B4d. $2.00

BULMER, Kenneth. *Hunters of Jundagai.* 1971. Ace 68310. 1st edn. SF. F. F2d. $14.00

BULMER, Kenneth. *Insane City.* 1971. Curtis 07122. 1st prtg. SF. G+. R5d. $1.50

BULMER, Kenneth. *Kandar.* 1969. PB Library 62-120. PBO. c/J Jones. SF. VG. B5d. $4.50

BULMER, Kenneth. *Roller Coaster World.* 1972. Ace 73438. 1st prtg. SF. VG+. W2d. $4.00

BULMER, Kenneth. *To Outrun Doomsday.* Ace G 625. F. M1d. $8.00

BULMER, Kenneth. *To Outrun Doomsday.* 1967. Ace G 625. 1st prtg. SF. VG. R5d. $2.75

BULMER, Kenneth. *Worlds for the Taking.* Ace F 396. 1st prtg. VG. S1d. $3.50

BULMER & SHRYACK. *Gauntlet.* 1977. Warner 89-470. 1st prtg. VG. R5d. $1.50

BULMER/CUMMINGS. *Secret of Zi/Beyond the Vanishing Point.* Ace D 331. c/Emsh. F. M1d. $15.00

BULMER/GLASBY. *Hunters of Jundagai/ Project Jove.* Ace 68310. PBO. c/K Freas. SF. VG+. B5d. $4.00

BULMER/GLASBY. *Hunters of Jundagai/ Project Jove.* 1971. Ace 68310. SF. F. W2d. $10.00

BULMER/HAMILTON. *Land Beyond the Map/Fugitive of the Stars.* Ace M 111. F. M1d. $10.00

BULMER/HAMILTON. *Land Beyond the Map/ Fugitive of the Stars.* Ace M 111. PBO. VG+. B3d. $4.50

BULMER/KOONTZ. *Star Venturers/Fall of the Dream Machine.* 1969. Ace 22600. 1st prtg. SF. VG+. R5d. $25.00

BULMER/LEIBER. *Million-Year Hunt/Ships to the Stars.* Ace F 285. NF. M1d. $8.00

BULMER/PURDOM. *Demons' World/I Want the Stars.* Ace F 289. F. M1d. $8.00

BULMER/PURDOM. *Demons' World/I Want the Stars.* Ace F 289. VG+. B3d. $4.50

BULMER/PURDOM. *Demons' World/I Want the Stars.* Ace F 289. 1st prtg. G+. S1d. $3.50

BULMER/RACKHAM. *Chariots of Ra/Earth-strings.* 1972. Ace 10293. PBO. SF. VG. B5d. $4.00

BULMER/RACKHAM. *Chariots of Ra/Earth-strings.* 1972. Ace 10293. 1st edn. SF. F. F2d. $14.00

BULMER/RACKHAM. *Electric Sword-Swal-lowers/Beyond Capella.* Ace 05595. SF. VG. B5d. $4.00

BULMER/REYNOLDS. *Behold the Stars/ Plan-etary Agent X.* Ace M 131. F. M1d. $9.00

BULMER/REYNOLDS. *Key to Venudine/ Mercenary From Tomorrow.* Ace H 65. 1st prtg. G+. S1d. $3.50

BULMER/SCHWARTZ. *Key to Irunium/Wander-ing Tellurian.* Ace H 20. 1st prtg. G+. S1d. $3.00

BULMER/ST. CLAIR. *Earth Gods Are Coming/ Games of Neith.* Ace D 453. G. P9d. $2.00

BULMER/ST. CLAIR. *Earth Gods Are Coming/ Games of Neith.* 1960. Ace D 453. VG+. I1d. $6.00

BULMER/ST. CLAIR. *Earth Gods Are Com-ing/Games of Neith.* 1960. Ace D 453. 1st edn. NF. M1d. $12.00

BULMER/STABLEFORD. *Wizards of Senchuria/ Cradle of the Sun.* Ace 12140. PBO. SF. NF. B5d. $5.00

BULMER/STABLEFORD. *Wizards of Senchuria/ Cradle of the Sun.* Ace 12140. 1st prtg. G+. S1d. $3.00

BULMER/SUTTON. *Ships of Durostorum/ Alton's Unguessable.* 1970. Ace 76095. PBO. c/J Gaughan & K Freas. SF. NF. B5d. $5.00

BUNCE, Frank. *So Young a Body.* Pocket 777. VG. B3d. $4.00

BUNTY, D. *Sex & the Swinging Secretary.* Barclay 7134. NF. B3d. $5.00

BUNYAN, Pat. *I Peddle Jazz.* Saber SA 16. reprint. NF. B6d. $15.00

BUNYAN, Pat. *I Peddle Jazz.* Saber SA 16. VG. B3d. $4.50

BUONANNO, J. *Godson.* Brandon House 6246. VG+. B3d. $5.00

BURCH, Ralph. *Lust in Space.* 1978. Trav-ellers 108. PBO. Ad/SF. VG+. B6d. $12.00

BURCHARDT/TRIMBLE. *Wildcatters/Man From Colorado.* Ace F 214. We. NF. B6d. $12.50

BURCHARDT/TRIMBLE. *Wildcatters/Man From Colorado.* 1963. Ace F 214. We. G+. B4d. $2.00

BURD, B. *Flesh Kick.* Candlelight 111. PBO. VG+. B3d. $4.00

BURGESS, A. *Small Woman.* Pan G 306. MTI. VG. B3d. $8.00

BURGESS, Ann Marie. *Girl Market.* 1963. Monarch 539. 1st edn. c/gga. F. F2d. $11.00

BURGESS, Anthony. *Clockwork Orange.* 1965. Ballantine U 5032. 1st edn. PBO. VG. P9d. $3.00

BURGESS, Anthony. *Little Wilson & Big God.* 1988. Penguin 10824. Nfi. VG. P1d. $12.50

BURGESS, Charles. *Other Woman.* 1960. Beacon B 362. 1st prtg. PBO. c/gga. VG. P7d. $7.50

BURGESS, L.W. edt. *Fifth Pan Book of Crosswords.* Pan G 568. 6th edn. VG+. B3d. $8.00

BURGESS, L.W. edt. *Fourth Pan Book of Crossword Puzzles.* Pan 01468. 10th prtg. VG+. B3d. $5.00

BURGESS, L.W. edt. *Pan Book of Cross-words #9.* Pan G 716. VG+. B3d. $8.00

BURGESS, L.W. edt. *Second Book of Cross-words.* Pan G 262. 10th prtg. VG+. B3d. $6.00

BURGESS, L.W. edt. *Sixth Pan Book of Cross-words.* Pan G 631. NF. G+. B5d. $3.50

BURGESS, M. *Where There's Smoke.* Mid-wood F 357. VG. I1d. $6.00

BURGESS, Michael. *Just This Once.* 1964. Midwood 32-420. 1st edn. c/leg art. NF. F2d. $7.00

BURKE, Fern. *Young Wife.* 1964. Beacon B 789X. PBO. c/A Rossi. Ad. VG+. B5d. $6.00

BURKE, J. *Corpse to Copenhagen.* Sexton Blake 385. NF. B3d. $8.50

BURKE, J. *Echoing Worlds.* Panther 103. VG. B3d. $6.00

BURKE, J. *Hard Days Night (Beatles).* Dell 0489. NF. I1d. $10.00

BURKE, J. *Hard Days Night (Beatles).* 1964. Dell 0489. 1st edn. c/photo. scarce. F. F2d. $25.00

BURKE, J. *Those Magnificent Men in Their Flying Machines.* 1965. Pocket 50189. 1st prtg. VG+. R5d. $3.50

BURKE, J.W. *Fraulein Lili Marlene.* 1956. Popular 766. 1st prtg. c/Kampen: gga. VG. P7d. $5.00

BURKE, J.W. *Of a Strange Woman.* 1955. Pyramid 164. 1st US edn. c/Lou Marchetti: gga. VG. P6d. $4.00

BURKE, James Lee. *Black Cherry Blues.* Avon 71204. NF. G5d. $6.50

BURKE, James Lee. *Heaven's Prisoners.* Pocket 67629. F. G5d. $6.00

BURKE, James Lee. *Two for Texas.* Pocket 44112. PBO. G+. M6d. $7.50

BURKE, John. *Moon Zero Two.* 1970. Signet P 4165. 1st prtg. SF. VG. W2d. $4.25

BURKE, John. *Strange Report.* 1970. Lancer 73219. TVTI. VG. P1d. $7.50

BURKE, Richard. *Frightened Pigeon.* Dell 204. 1st prtg. My. VG. R5d. $8.50

BURKE, Richard. *Frightened Pigeon.* 1947. Dell 204. 1st edn. PBO. c/Gerald Gregg. scarce. NF. B6a #75. $38.50

BURKE, Richard. *Here Lies the Body.* 1951. Popular 310. c/gga. My. VG. B4d. $7.00

BURKE, Richard. *Here Lies the Body.* 1951. Popular 310. VG+. B3a #24. $11.00

BURKE, Thomas. *Limehouse Nights.* Digit 486. c/Exotic. VG. B3a #24. $25.00

BURKE & GRACE. *Three Day Pass: To Kill.* Berkley G 164. c/Rader. VG+. B6a #77. $44.00

BURKS, Arthur J. *Great Mirror.* 1952. Gernal Swan NN. PBO. scarce. Fa. VG+. B6a #74. $67.25

BURLEY, W.J. *Charles & Elizabeth.* 1985. Walker 31066. c/O Pettingill. My. VG+. B5d. $4.00

BURLEY, W.J. *Death in a Salubrious Place.* 1984. Walker 30698. c/P Realo. My. NF. B5d. $5.00

BURLEY, W.J. *Death in Stanley Street.* 1984. Walker 30671. c/L Nargi. My. VG+. B5d. $4.00

BURLEY, W.J. *Death in Willow Pattern.* 1983. Walker 30256. c/A Berenzy: oriental. My. NF. B5d. $5.00

BURLEY, W.J. *To Kill a Cat.* 1983. Walker 30302. c/A Perkins. My. NF. B5d. $5.00

BURLEY, W.J. *Wycliffe & the School Girls.* 1984. Walker 30647. c/M Fresh. My. NF. B5d. $5.00

BURLINGAME, Roger. *Ben Franklin, 1st Mr American.* 1955. Signet K 321. Bio. VG+. B4d. $3.00

BURLINGAME, Roger. *Machines That Built America.* 1955. Signet KS 327. Nfi. VG+. B4d. $2.00

BURMAN, B.L. *Four Lives of Mundy Tolliver.* Bantam 1439. VG+. B3d. $4.00

BURNETT, Constance Buel. *Not Death But Love.* Pyramid Royal PC 34. biography of Elizabeth Barrett Browning. Nfi. G+. P1d. $2.50

BURNETT, H.S. *This Heart, This Hunter.* Popular 541. VG. B3d. $4.00

BURNETT, W.R. *Abilene Samson.* 1963. Pocket 7028. We. VG+. B5d. $4.00

BURNETT, W.R. *High Sierra.* 1950. Bantam 826. VG. I1d. $6.00

BURNETT, W.R. *High Sierra.* 1950. Bantam 826. 1st prtg. My. G+. R5d. $3.00

BURNETT, W.R. *High Sierra.* Murder My Monthly 40. VG. B3d. $10.00

BURNETT, W.R. *Little Caesar.* 1945. Avon 66. PBO. c/famous gangsters comic. scarce. VG. B6a #74. $45.00

BURNETT, W.R. *Little Caesar.* Bantam A 1871. G. G5d. $3.00

BURNETT, W.R. *Nobody Lives Forever.* Bantam 888. G+. G5d. $5.50

BURNETT, W.R. *Romelle.* Bantam 942. VG+. I1d. $4.00

BURNETT, W.R. *Sergeants 3.* 1962. Pocket 6150. MTI. c/Sinatra, Martin & Lawford: photo. VG. B4d. $3.00

BURNETT, W.R. *Stretch Dawson.* Gold Medal 106. VG. B3d. $7.00

BURNETT, W.R. *Underdog.* 1959. Corgi S 691. 1st pb. My. VG. B6d. $8.00

BURNETT, W.R. *Vanity Row.* Pennant P7. VG. B3d. $4.50

BURNETT, Whit & Hallie. *Things With Claws.* 1961. Ballantine 466K. PBO. SF. VG. B5d. $8.00

BURNETT, Whit & Hallie. *Things With Claws.* 1961. Ballantine 466K. 1st edn. F. M1d. $20.00

BURNETT, Whit & Hallie. *19 Tales of Terror.* 1957. Bantam A 1550. PBO. c/Steinbeck. Ho. VG. B6d. $9.00

BURNETT, Whit & Hallie. *19 Tales of Terror.* 1957. Bantam A 1550. 1st edn. F. M1d. $12.00

BURNETT, Whit. *Firsts of the Famous.* 1962. Ballantine F 598. Fi. VG. B5d. $3.50

BURNETT, Whit. *This Is My Funniest.* Perma M 3094. VG+. B3d. $5.00

BURNETT, Whit. *Time To Be Young (Anthology).* Armed Services 848. VG. B3d. $8.00

BURNS, Elizabeth. *Late Liz.* Popular 08187. 1st prtg. VG. R5d. $1.50

BURNS, J.H. *Cry of Children.* Bantam 1147. VG+. B3d. $5.00

BURNS, J.H. *Gallery.* Ace H 143. 2nd prtg. VG. B3d. $6.00

BURNS, K. *Grabber.* Pyramid 1111. VG+. B3d. $5.50

BURNS, Robert E. *I Am a Fugitive From a Chain Gang!* Arrow. VG. B3d. $8.00

BURNS, Robert E. *I Am a Fugitive From a Chain Gang!* 1952. Pyramid 45. 1st edn. PBO. MTI. c/H Barker. scarce. VG+. B6a #79. $33.00

BURNS, Vincent E. *Female Convict.* 1952. Pyramid 58. VG+. B3a #20. $10.75

BURROUGHS, Edgar Rice. *Apache Devil.* Ballantine U 2046. VG+. B3d. $5.00

BURROUGHS, Edgar Rice. *Apache Devil.* 1964. Ballantine U 2046. 1st edn. PBO. We. F. F2d. $15.00

BURROUGHS, Edgar Rice. *Apache Devil.* 1975. Ballantine 24605. 2nd edn. c/G & T Hilderbrandt. We. VG. B5d. $3.00

BURROUGHS, Edgar Rice. *At the Earth's Core.* Ace F 156. c/R Krenkel Jr. SF. VG+. B5d. $7.00

BURROUGHS, Edgar Rice. *At the Earth's Core.* Ace F 156. F. M1d. $15.00

BURROUGHS, Edgar Rice. *At the Earth's Core.* Ace F 156. VG. M6d/I1d. $5.00

BURROUGHS, Edgar Rice. *At the Earth's Core.* 1978. Ace 03326. SF. F. W2d. $3.75

BURROUGHS, Edgar Rice. *At the Earth's Core.* Ace 79851. SF. VG. W2d. $3.25

BURROUGHS, Edgar Rice. *Back to the Stone Age.* Ace F 245. F. M1d. $15.00

BURROUGHS, Edgar Rice. *Back to the Stone Age.* Ace F 245. VG+. I1d. $5.00

BURROUGHS, Edgar Rice. *Back to the Stone Age.* 1978. Ace 04636. 1st prtg. SF. VG. W2d. $3.25

BURROUGHS, Edgar Rice. *Beasts of Tarzan.* Ace F 203. c/F Frazetta. SF. G+. B5d. $3.50

BURROUGHS, Edgar Rice. *Beasts of Tarzan.* Ace F 203. F. M1d. $15.00

BURROUGHS, Edgar Rice. *Beasts of Tarzan.* Ace F 203. NF. M6d. $7.50

BURROUGHS, Edgar Rice. *Beasts of Tarzan.* 1963. Ballantine F 747. 1st edn. F. M1d. $12.00

BURROUGHS, Edgar Rice. *Beasts of Tarzan.* 1963. Ballantine F 747. 1st prtg. SF. VG+. W2d. $5.00

BURROUGHS, Edgar Rice. *Beasts of Tarzan.* 1969. Ballantine 01583. 3rd prtg. SF. F. W2d. $6.00

BURROUGHS, Edgar Rice. *Beasts of Tarzan.* 1972. Ballantine 02703. 4th prtg. SF. F. W2d. $3.75

BURROUGHS, Edgar Rice. *Beasts of Tarzan.* 1975. Ballantine 24161. 6th prtg. SF. VG. W2d. $3.50

BURROUGHS, Edgar Rice. *Beasts of Tarzan.* 1983. Ballantine 29513. 16th prtg. SF. VG. W2d. $3.00

BURROUGHS, Edgar Rice. *Beyond the Farthest Star.* 1964. Ace F 282. 1st edn. PBO. SF. F. F2d. $10.00

BURROUGHS, Edgar Rice. *Beyond the Farthest Star.* 1973. Ace 05652. 2nd prtg. Ad. VG. W2d. $3.50

BURROUGHS, Edgar Rice. *Beyond the Farthest Star.* 1964. Tandem NN. SF. VG+. B4d. $4.00

BURROUGHS, Edgar Rice. *Carson of Venus.* 1963. Ace F 247. 1st prtg. SF. G+. R5d. $2.25

BURROUGHS, Edgar Rice. *Carson of Venus.* Ace 09200. 3rd edn. VG. P9d. $1.50

BURROUGHS, Edgar Rice. *Carson of Venus.* 1979. Ace 09204. 1st prtg. SF. VG+. W2d. $3.50

BURROUGHS, Edgar Rice. *Cave Girl.* 1964. Ace F 258. 1st prtg. F. S1d. $7.00

BURROUGHS, Edgar Rice. *Cave Girl.* 1964. Ace F 258. 1st prtg. SF. F. F2d. $10.00

BURROUGHS, Edgar Rice. *Cave Girl.* 1973. Ace 09282. 3rd prtg. Ad. VG. W2d. $3.25

BURROUGHS, Edgar Rice. *Cave Girl.* Dell 320. 1st prtg. G. S1d. $3.50

BURROUGHS, Edgar Rice. *Cave Girl.* 1949. Dell 320. 1st edn. PBO. SF. G+. F2d. $15.00

BURROUGHS, Edgar Rice. *Cave Girl.* Dell 329. G. I1d. $7.00

BURROUGHS, Edgar Rice. *Cave Girl.* 1977. Tandem 18323. Ad. F. W2d. $6.00

BURROUGHS, Edgar Rice. *Chessmen of Mars.* 1962. Ace F 170. c/R Krenkel Jr. SF. G+. B5d. $3.50

BURROUGHS, Edgar Rice. *Chessmen of Mars.* 1962. Ace F 170. SF. VG. W2d. $7.50

BURROUGHS, Edgar Rice. *Chessmen of Mars.* 1962. Ace F 170. 1st edn. PBO. SF. F. F2d/M3d. $10.00

BURROUGHS, Edgar Rice. *Chessmen of Mars.* Ballantine F 776. 3rd edn. F. P9d. $3.50

BURROUGHS, Edgar Rice. *Chessmen of Mars.* 1973. Ballantine 23582. 4th prtg. SF. F. W2d. $3.75

BURROUGHS, Edgar Rice. *Chessmen of Mars.* 1981. Ballantine 27838. 13th prtg. SF. VG+. W2d. $3.00

BURROUGHS, Edgar Rice. *Chessmen of Mars.* 1963. Ballantine. 1st edn. F. M1d. $15.00

BURROUGHS, Edgar Rice. *Chessmen.* Ace F 170. F. M1d. $15.00

BURROUGHS, Edgar Rice. *Efficiency Expert.* Charter 18901. De/Cr. F. W2d. $4.50

BURROUGHS, Edgar Rice. *Escape on Venus.* Ace F 268. F. M1d. $15.00

BURROUGHS, Edgar Rice. *Escape on Venus.* Ace F 268. VG. B3d. $3.50

BURROUGHS, Edgar Rice. *Escape on Venus.* Ace 21564. SF. VG. W2d. $3.00

BURROUGHS, Edgar Rice. *Eternal Savage.* 1963. Ace F 234. NF. I1d. $6.00

BURROUGHS, Edgar Rice. *Eternal Savage.* 1963. Ace F 234. 1st edn. PBO. SF. F. F2d/M3d. $10.00

BURROUGHS, Edgar Rice. *Eternal Savage.* Ace 21801. 2nd edn. VG. P9d. $2.00

BURROUGHS, Edgar Rice. *Fighting Man of Mars.* Ace F 190. SF. VG. W2d. $7.50

BURROUGHS, Edgar Rice. *Fighting Man of Mars.* 1963. Ace F 190. 1st edn. PBO. SF. F. F2d. $10.00

BURROUGHS, Edgar Rice. *Fighting Man of Mars.* 1964. Ballantine U 2037. SF. VG. W2d. $4.50

BURROUGHS, Edgar Rice. *Fighting Man of Mars.* 1977. Ballantine 25825. 2nd prtg. SF. VG+. W2d. $3.55

BURROUGHS, Edgar Rice. *Girl From Farris'.* Charter 28903. De/Cr. F. W2d. $4.50

BURROUGHS, Edgar Rice. *Girl From Hollywood.* Ace 28911. We. VG. W2d. $3.75

BURROUGHS, Edgar Rice. *Gods of Mars.* 1963. Ballantine F 702. VG+. I1d. $4.00

BURROUGHS, Edgar Rice. *Gods of Mars.* 1963. Ballantine F 702. 1st edn. PBO. SF. F. F2d. $8.00

BURROUGHS, Edgar Rice. *Gods of Mars.* 1967. Ballantine U 2032. 3rd prtg. SF. VG. W2d. $3.75

BURROUGHS, Edgar Rice. *Gods of Mars.* 1973. Ballantine 23579. 6th prtg. SF. F. W2d. $4.25

BURROUGHS, Edgar Rice. *I Am a Barbarian.* Ace 35804. Ad. VG. W2d. $4.00

BURROUGHS, Edgar Rice. *John Carter of Mars.* 1982. Ballantine 27844. 13th prtg. SF. VG+. W2d. $3.00

BURROUGHS, Edgar Rice. *John Carter of Mars.* 1965. Ballantine. 1st edn. F. M1d. $15.00

BURROUGHS, Edgar Rice. *Jungle Tales of Tarzan.* Ace F 206. NF. M1d. $12.00

BURROUGHS, Edgar Rice. *Jungle Tales of Tarzan.* Ballantine F 750. VG+. I1d. $4.00

BURROUGHS, Edgar Rice. *Jungle Tales of Tarzan.* 1963. Ballantine. 1st edn. F. M1d. $12.00

BURROUGHS, Edgar Rice. *Lad & the Lion.* Ace 46870. Ad. G+. W2d. $2.50

BURROUGHS, Edgar Rice. *Lad & the Lion.* Ace 46870. SF. VG. B5d. $4.50

BURROUGHS, Edgar Rice. *Lad & the Lion.* 1964. Ballantine U 2048. VG. B3d. $5.00

BURROUGHS, Edgar Rice. *Lad & the Lion.* 1964. Ballantine U 2048. 1st prtg. F. S1d. $10.00

BURROUGHS, Edgar Rice. *Land of Hidden Men.* Ace F 232. NF. M1d. $12.00

BURROUGHS, Edgar Rice. *Land of Hidden Men.* Ace 47011. c/R Krenkel, Jr. SF. VG+. B5d. $5.00

BURROUGHS, Edgar Rice. *Land of Hidden Men.* 1978. Ace 47016. 1st prtg. Ad. VG+. W2d. $3.50

BURROUGHS, Edgar Rice. *Land of Terror.* Ace 46996. c/F Frazetta. SF. VG+. B5d/I1d. $5.00

BURROUGHS, Edgar Rice. *Land That Time Forgot.* 1963. Ace F 213. 1st edn. PBO. SF. F. F2d. $10.00

BURROUGHS, Edgar Rice. *Land That Time Forgot.* 1979. Ace 47025. 2nd prtg. SF. F. W2d. $4.75

BURROUGHS, Edgar Rice. *Llana of Gathol.* Ballantine F 762. VG. I1d. $4.00

BURROUGHS, Edgar Rice. *Llana of Gathol.* 1963. Ballantine 762. 1st edn. PBO. SF. F. F2d. $8.00

BURROUGHS, Edgar Rice. *Llana of Gothal.* 1964. Ballantine U 2040. 2nd prtg. SF. F. W2d. $5.00

BURROUGHS, Edgar Rice. *Llana of Gothal.* 1976. Ballantine 25829. 9th prtg. SF. VG. W2d. $3.25

BURROUGHS, Edgar Rice. *Lost Continent.* Ace F 235. F. M1d. $15.00

BURROUGHS, Edgar Rice. *Lost Continent.* Ace F 235. VG. I1d. $4.00

BURROUGHS, Edgar Rice. *Lost Continent.* Ace 49291. c/F Frazetta. SF. VG+. B5d. $3.50

BURROUGHS, Edgar Rice. *Lost on Venus.* 1963. Ace F 221. F. M1d. $18.00

BURROUGHS, Edgar Rice. *Lost on Venus.* 1963. Ace F 221. 1st prtg. SF. VG. R5d. $3.50

BURROUGHS, Edgar Rice. *Lost on Venus.* Ace 49506. SF. F. W2d. $5.00

BURROUGHS, Edgar Rice. *Mad King.* Ace 51401. Ad. F. W2d. $5.00

BURROUGHS, Edgar Rice. *Mad King.* Ace 51401. c/F Frazetta. SF. VG. B5d. $3.00

BURROUGHS, Edgar Rice. *Mastermind of Mars.* 1963. Ace F 181. c/R Krenkel Jr. SF. VG. B5d. $5.00

BURROUGHS, Edgar Rice. *Mastermind of Mars.* 1963. Ace F 181. 1st edn. PBO. SF. F. F2d. $10.00

BURROUGHS, Edgar Rice. *Mastermind of Mars.* Ballantine U 2036. VG+. I1d. $4.00

BURROUGHS, Edgar Rice. *Mastermind of Mars.* Ballantine U 2036. 1st prtg. VG. S1d. $3.00

BURROUGHS, Edgar Rice. *Mastermind of Mars.* 1973. Ballantine 23583. 4th prtg. SF. F. W2d. $3.75

BURROUGHS, Edgar Rice. *Mastermind of Mars.* 1982. Ballantine 27839. 12th prtg. SF. F. W2d. $3.25

BURROUGHS, Edgar Rice. *Mastermind of Mars.* 1984. Ballantine 33424. 15th prtg. SF. VG. W2d. $2.75

BURROUGHS, Edgar Rice. *Monster Men.* Ace F 182. 1st prtg. F. S1d. $7.00

BURROUGHS, Edgar Rice. *Monster Men.* Ace 53588. 1st prtg. SF. G+. R5d. $1.25

BURROUGHS, Edgar Rice. *Moon Maid.* Ace F 157. F. M1d. $15.00

BURROUGHS, Edgar Rice. *Moon Maid.* Ace G 745. SF. F. W2d. $5.25

BURROUGHS, Edgar Rice. *Moon Maid.* Ace 53701. SF. VG. W2d. $3.25

BURROUGHS, Edgar Rice. *Moon Men.* Ace F 159. F. M1d. $15.00

BURROUGHS, Edgar Rice. *Moon Men.* Ace F 159. G+. I1d. $3.00

BURROUGHS, Edgar Rice. *Moon Men.* Ace 53751. 4th edn. VG. P9d. $1.50

BURROUGHS, Edgar Rice. *Mucker.* 1974. Ace 54460. 1st prtg. Ad. VG. W2d. $4.00

BURROUGHS, Edgar Rice. *Mucker.* Ballantine U 6039. VG. I1d. $4.00

BURROUGHS, Edgar Rice. *Oakdale Affair.* Ace 60563. De/Cr. VG. W2d. $3.75

BURROUGHS, Edgar Rice. *Out of Time's Abyss.* Ace F 233. 1st prtg. F. S1d. $7.00

BURROUGHS, Edgar Rice. *Outlaw of Torn.* Ace A 25. VG. M1d. $10.00

BURROUGHS, Edgar Rice. *Pellucidar.* Ace F 158. c/R Krenkel Jr. SF. NF. B5d. $8.50

BURROUGHS, Edgar Rice. *Pellucidar.* 1972. Ace 65854. 2nd prtg. SF. VG+. W2d. $3.50

BURROUGHS, Edgar Rice. *People That Time Forgot.* Ace F 220. 1st prtg. F. S1d. $7.00

BURROUGHS, Edgar Rice. *People That Time Forgot.* 1973. Ace 65942. 3rd prtg. SF. F. W2d. $4.50

BURROUGHS, Edgar Rice. *Pirates of Venus.* Ace F 179. VG. I1d. $4.00

BURROUGHS, Edgar Rice. *Pirates of Venus.* Ace 66505. SF. F. W2d. $4.25

BURROUGHS, Edgar Rice. *Princess of Mars.* 1963. Ballantine F 701. 1st edn. PBO. SF. F. F2d. $8.00

BURROUGHS, Edgar Rice. *Princess of Mars.* 1963. Ballantine F 701. 1st prtg. SF. VG. M3d/W2d. $6.00

BURROUGHS, Edgar Rice. *Princess of Mars.* 1964. Ballantine U 2031. 2nd prtg. SF. G+. W2d. $3.25

BURROUGHS, Edgar Rice. *Princess of Mars.* 1973. Ballantine 23578. 6th prtg. SF. F. W2d. $3.75

BURROUGHS, Edgar Rice. *Princess of Mars.* 1977. Ballantine 27058. 12th prtg. SF. VG. W2d. $3.00

BURROUGHS, Edgar Rice. *Princess of Mars.* 1981. Ballantine 27834. 17th prtg. SF. F. W2d. $3.25

BURROUGHS, Edgar Rice. *Princess of Mars.* 1972. New English 1186. SF. VG. B5d. $5.00

BURROUGHS, Edgar Rice. *Return of Tarzan.* 1963. Ballantine F 746. VG. I1d. $4.00

BURROUGHS, Edgar Rice. *Return of Tarzan.* 1963. Ballantine F 746. 1st edn. F. M1d. $12.00

BURROUGHS, Edgar Rice. *Return of Tarzan.* 1967. Ballantine U 2002. 3rd edn. TVTI. VG. P1d. $6.00

BURROUGHS, Edgar Rice. *Return of Tarzan.* 1980. Ballantine 28996. 14th prtg. SF. VG. W2d. $3.00

BURROUGHS, Edgar Rice. *Return of Tarzan.* 1984. Ballantine 31575. 18th prtg. SF. VG+. W2d. $3.25

BURROUGHS, Edgar Rice. *Rider.* Ace 72280. c/F Frazetta. SF. VG. B5d. $5.00

BURROUGHS, Edgar Rice. *Savage Pellucidar.* Ace F 280. F. M1d. $15.00

BURROUGHS, Edgar Rice. *Savage Pellucidar.* Ace G 739. VG. M1d. $10.00

BURROUGHS, Edgar Rice. *Son of Tarzan.* 1963. Ace F 193. VG. M6d. $5.00

BURROUGHS, Edgar Rice. *Son of Tarzan.* 1963. Ace F 193. 1st edn. PBO. SF. F. F2d. $12.00

BURROUGHS, Edgar Rice. *Son of Tarzan.* 1963. Ballantine U 2004. 2nd prtg. SF. VG. W2d. $4.50

BURROUGHS, Edgar Rice. *Son of Tarzan.* 1969. Ballantine 01594. 3rd prtg. SF. F. W2d. $5.50

BURROUGHS, Edgar Rice. *Son of Tarzan.* 1972. Ballantine 02704. 4th prtg. SF. F. W2d. $4.00

BURROUGHS, Edgar Rice. *Son of Tarzan.* 1978. Ballantine 28130. 11th prtg. SF. F. W2d. $4.50

BURROUGHS, Edgar Rice. *Son of Tarzan.* 1984. Ballantine 29415. 18th prtg. SF. VG+. W2d. $3.00

BURROUGHS, Edgar Rice. *Swords of Mars.* 1963. Ballantine F 728. VG+. I1d. $4.00

BURROUGHS, Edgar Rice. *Swords of Mars.* 1963. Ballantine F 728. 1st edn. PBO. SF. F. F2d. $10.00

BURROUGHS, Edgar Rice. *Swords of Mars.* 1975. Ballantine 23585. 8th prtg. SF. VG+. W2d. $4.00

BURROUGHS, Edgar Rice. *Swords of Mars.* 1977. Ballantine 27546. 10th prtg. SF. F. W2d. $4.00

BURROUGHS, Edgar Rice. *Swords of Mars.* 1982. Ballantine 27841. 15th prtg. SF. F. W2d. $3.50

BURROUGHS, Edgar Rice. *Synthetic Men of Mars.* Ballantine F 739. NF. I1d. $5.00

BURROUGHS, Edgar Rice. *Synthetic Men of Mars.* 1963. Ballantine F 739. SF. VG+. B4d. $4.00

BURROUGHS, Edgar Rice. *Synthetic Men of Mars.* 1964. Ballantine U 2039. 2nd prtg. SF. VG+. W2d. $4.50

BURROUGHS, Edgar Rice. *Synthetic Men of Mars.* 1973. Ballantine 23586. 6th prtg. SF. F. W2d. $3.75

BURROUGHS, Edgar Rice. *Synthetic Men of Mars.* 1978. Ballantine 27679. 19th prtg. SF. G. W2d. $2.25

BURROUGHS, Edgar Rice. *Synthetic Men of Mars.* 1981. Ballantine 27842. 13th prtg. SF. F. W2d. $3.00

BURROUGHS, Edgar Rice. *Tanar of Pellucidar.* Ace F 171. SF. VG+. B5d. $6.00

BURROUGHS, Edgar Rice. *Tanar of Pellucidar.* Ace F 171. VG. M6d. $5.00

BURROUGHS, Edgar Rice. *Tanar of Pellucidar.* Ace 79791. 4th edn. VG. P9d. $2.00

BURROUGHS, Edgar Rice. *Tanar.* Ace F 171. F. M1d. $15.00

BURROUGHS, Edgar Rice. *Tarzan, Lord of the Jungle.* 1963. Ballantine F 772. 1st edn. F. M1d. $12.00

BURROUGHS, Edgar Rice. *Tarzan, Lord of the Jungle.* 1963. Ballantine F 772. 1st prtg. SF. VG. W2d. $4.50

BURROUGHS, Edgar Rice. *Tarzan, Lord of the Jungle.* 1972. Ballantine 03009. 4th prtg. SF. VG. W2d. $3.25

BURROUGHS, Edgar Rice. *Tarzan, the Invincible.* 1974. Ballantine 21908. 3rd prtg. SF. F. W2d. $4.00

BURROUGHS, Edgar Rice. *Tarzan, the Invincible.* 1975. Ballantine 24484. 4th prtg. SF. VG. W2d. $3.25

BURROUGHS, Edgar Rice. *Tarzan & Forbidden City.* 1964. Ballantine U 2020. 1st prtg. F. F2d. $10.00

BURROUGHS, Edgar Rice. *Tarzan & Jewels of Opar.* Ace F 204. VG. M1d. $10.00

BURROUGHS, Edgar Rice. *Tarzan & the Ant Men.* 1963. Ballantine F 754. 1st edn. NF. M1d. $10.00

BURROUGHS, Edgar Rice. *Tarzan & the Ant Men.* 1963. Ballantine F 754. 1st prtg. SF. VG. W2d. $3.75

BURROUGHS, Edgar Rice. *Tarzan & the Ant Men.* 1962. Ballantine U 2010. 2nd prtg. SF. VG. W2d. $5.00

BURROUGHS, Edgar Rice. *Tarzan & the Ant Men.* 1972. Ballantine 03008. 4th prtg. SF. F. W2d. $4.75

BURROUGHS, Edgar Rice. *Tarzan & the Ant Men.* Four Square 186. 1st pb. reprint. VG+. B6d. $8.00

BURROUGHS, Edgar Rice. *Tarzan & the Castaways.* Ballantine U 2024. 1st edn. PBO. F. P9d. $3.00

BURROUGHS, Edgar Rice. *Tarzan & the Castaways.* 1974. Ballantine 23861. 2nd prtg. SF. F. W2d. $4.25

BURROUGHS, Edgar Rice. *Tarzan & the Castaways.* 1977. Ballantine 25964. 4th prtg. SF. F. W2d. $4.00

BURROUGHS, Edgar Rice. *Tarzan & the City of Gold.* Ace F 205. c/F Frazetta. SF. VG. B5d. $5.00

BURROUGHS, Edgar Rice. *Tarzan & the City of Gold.* Ballantine U 2016. F. I1d. $4.00

BURROUGHS, Edgar Rice. *Tarzan & the Forbidden City.* Ballantine U 2020. 1st edn. PBO. F. P9d. $2.50

BURROUGHS, Edgar Rice. *Tarzan & the Foreign Legion.* 1964. Ballantine U 2022. SF. VG+. B4d. $2.50

BURROUGHS, Edgar Rice. *Tarzan & the Foreign Legion.* 1974. Ballantine 23859. 2nd prtg. SF. VG. W2d. $3.50

BURROUGHS, Edgar Rice. *Tarzan & the Foreign Legion.* Ballantine 24978. 3rd prtg. NF. B3d. $4.00

BURROUGHS, Edgar Rice. *Tarzan & the Golden Lion.* 1963. Ballantine F 753. 1st pb. VG. B6d/I1d. $4.00

BURROUGHS, Edgar Rice. *Tarzan & the Golden Lion.* 1976. Ballantine 24168. 6th prtg. SF. F. W2d. $4.50

BURROUGHS, Edgar Rice. *Tarzan & the Golden Lion.* 1984. Ballantine 28998. 12th prtg. SF. VG. W2d. $3.00

BURROUGHS, Edgar Rice. *Tarzan & the Golden Lion.* 1963. Ballantine. 1st edn. F. M1d. $12.00

BURROUGHS, Edgar Rice. *Tarzan & the Jewels of Opar.* Ace F 204. c/F Frazetta. SF. G+. B5d. $3.50

BURROUGHS, Edgar Rice. *Tarzan & the Jewels of Opar.* Ace F 204. VG. M6d. $4.00

BURROUGHS, Edgar Rice. *Tarzan & the Jewels of Opar.* Ace F 204. VG+. I1d. $5.00

BURROUGHS, Edgar Rice. *Tarzan & the Jewels of Opar.* Ballantine F 749. VG. I1d. $4.00

BURROUGHS, Edgar Rice. *Tarzan & the Jewels of Opar.* 1969. Ballantine 01595. 3rd prtg. SF. F. W2d. $4.75

BURROUGHS, Edgar Rice. *Tarzan & the Jewels of Opar.* 1984. Ballantine 32161. 15th prtg. SF. F. W2d. $3.25

BURROUGHS, Edgar Rice. *Tarzan & the Leopard Men.* Ballantine U 2018. VG+. I1d. $3.50

BURROUGHS, Edgar Rice. *Tarzan & the Leopard Men.* 1964. Ballantine U 2018. 1st prtg. F. F2d. $10.00

BURROUGHS, Edgar Rice. *Tarzan & the Leopard Men.* 1975. Ballantine 24488. 4th prtg. SF. F. W2d. $3.75

BURROUGHS, Edgar Rice. *Tarzan & the Leopard Men.* 1961. Four Square 380. 1st pb. VG+. B6d. $12.50

BURROUGHS, Edgar Rice. *Tarzan & the Leopard Men.* 1967. New English 1132. 3rd edn. TVTI. VG. P1d. $6.00

BURROUGHS, Edgar Rice. *Tarzan & the Lion Man.* 1963. Ace F 212. c/Frazetta. SF. VG+. M3d. $9.00

BURROUGHS, Edgar Rice. *Tarzan & the Lion Man.* Ballantine U 2017. NF. I1d. $3.50

BURROUGHS, Edgar Rice. *Tarzan & the Lion Man.* 1974. Ballantine 21911. 3rd prtg. SF. VG. W2d. $3.50

BURROUGHS, Edgar Rice. *Tarzan & the Lion Man.* 1965. Four Square 1253. 1st pb. VG+. B6d. $12.50

BURROUGHS, Edgar Rice. *Tarzan & the Lost Empire.* 1962. Ace F 169. c/F Frazetta. SF. VG. B5d. $5.00

BURROUGHS, Edgar Rice. *Tarzan & the Lost Empire.* 1962. Ace F 169. SF. NF. M3d. $10.00

BURROUGHS, Edgar Rice. *Tarzan & the Lost Empire.* 1962. Ace F 169. 1st edn. PBO. SF. F. F2d. $15.00

BURROUGHS, Edgar Rice. *Tarzan & the Lost Empire.* Ballantine F 777. NF. I1d. $5.00

BURROUGHS, Edgar Rice. *Tarzan & the Lost Empire.* Ballantine F 777. VG. B3d. $4.00

BURROUGHS, Edgar Rice. *Tarzan & the Lost Empire.* 1963. Ballantine F 777. SF. VG+. B4d. $3.25

BURROUGHS, Edgar Rice. *Tarzan & the Lost Empire.* 1972. Ballantine 03010. 1st prtg. SF. VG. W2d. $3.50

BURROUGHS, Edgar Rice. *Tarzan & the Lost Empire.* 1972. Ballantine 03010. 3rd prtg. SF. F. W2d. $5.00

BURROUGHS, Edgar Rice. *Tarzan & the Lost Empire.* 1974. Ballantine 23010. 5th prtg. SF. VG. W2d. $3.75

BURROUGHS, Edgar Rice. *Tarzan & the Lost Empire.* 1951. Dell 536. SF. VG. W2d. $20.00

BURROUGHS, Edgar Rice. *Tarzan & the Lost Empire.* 1951. Dell 536. 1st pb edn. F. F2d. $35.00

BURROUGHS, Edgar Rice. *Tarzan & the Madman.* 1965. Ballantine U 2023. 1st prtg. F. F2d. $10.00

BURROUGHS, Edgar Rice. *Tarzan & the Madman.* 1965. Ballantine U 2023. 1st prtg. VG+. P7d. $4.50

BURROUGHS, Edgar Rice. *Tarzan & the Madman.* 1974. Ballantine 23860. 2nd prtg. SF. VG+. W2d. $4.00

BURROUGHS, Edgar Rice. *Tarzan at the Earth's Core.* Ace F 180. 1st edn. PBO. VG. P9d. $2.00

BURROUGHS, Edgar Rice. *Tarzan at the Earth's Core.* 1963. Ace F 180. 1st edn. PBO. SF. F. F2d/M1d. $15.00

BURROUGHS, Edgar Rice. *Tarzan at the Earth's Core.* 1963. Ace F 180. 1st prtg. VG. S1d. $4.00

BURROUGHS, Edgar Rice. *Tarzan at the Earth's Core.* Ace G 736. 3rd edn. VG. P9d. $1.50

BURROUGHS, Edgar Rice. *Tarzan at the Earth's Core.* Ace 79851. SF. F. W2d. $4.50

BURROUGHS, Edgar Rice. *Tarzan at the Earth's Core.* Ballantine U 2013. 4th edn. F. P9d. $1.50

BURROUGHS, Edgar Rice. *Tarzan at the Earth's Core.* 1964. Ballantine U 2013. 1st prtg SF. VG+. W2d. $4.50

BURROUGHS, Edgar Rice. *Tarzan at the Earth's Core.* 1974. Ballantine 21907. 4th prtg. SF. F. W2d. $4.00

BURROUGHS, Edgar Rice. *Tarzan Invincible.* Ace F 189. NF. M1d. $12.00

BURROUGHS, Edgar Rice. *Tarzan of the Apes.* 1963. Ballantine F 745. 1st edn. NF. M1d. $10.00

BURROUGHS, Edgar Rice. *Tarzan of the Apes.* 1963. Ballantine F 745. 1st prtg. SF. VG. W2d. $4.50

BURROUGHS, Edgar Rice. *Tarzan of the Apes.* 1966. Ballantine U 2001. 3rd edn. TVTI. VG. P1d. $6.00

BURROUGHS, Edgar Rice. *Tarzan the Invincible.* Ace F 189. c/F Frazetta. SF. VG. B5d. $6.00

BURROUGHS, Edgar Rice. *Tarzan the Invincible.* Ballantine U 2014. 3rd edn. F. P9d. $4.00

BURROUGHS, Edgar Rice. *Tarzan the Invincible.* 1964. Ballantine U 2014. 1st prtg. F. F2d. $10.00

BURROUGHS, Edgar Rice. *Tarzan the Invincible.* 1958. Pinnacle NN. VG. B3d. $9.00

BURROUGHS, Edgar Rice. *Tarzan the Magnificent.* 1964. Ballantine U 2021. SF. VG. B3d/B4d. $2.00

BURROUGHS, Edgar Rice. *Tarzan the Magnificent.* 1964. Ballantine U 2021. VG+. I1d. $3.00

BURROUGHS, Edgar Rice. *Tarzan the Magnificent.* 1964. Ballantine U 2021. 1st prtg. F. F2d. $10.00

BURROUGHS, Edgar Rice. *Tarzan the Terrible.* Ballantine F 752. NF. I1d. $5.00

BURROUGHS, Edgar Rice. *Tarzan the Terrible.* 1963. Ballantine U 2008. 2nd prtg. SF. F. W2d. $5.00

BURROUGHS, Edgar Rice. *Tarzan the Terrible.* 1972. Ballantine 03006. 4th prtg. SF. VG. W2d. $3.00

BURROUGHS, Edgar Rice. *Tarzan the Terrible.* 1976. Ballantine 24167. 6th prtg. SF. VG+. W2d. $3.50

BURROUGHS, Edgar Rice. *Tarzan the Untamed.* 1963. Ballantine F 751. 1st edn. NF. M1d. $10.00

BURROUGHS, Edgar Rice. *Tarzan the Untamed.* 1963. Ballantine F 751. 1st prtg. SF. VG. W2d. $4.50

BURROUGHS, Edgar Rice. *Tarzan Triumphant.* Ace F 194. c/R Krenkel Jr. SF. VG. B5d. $5.00

BURROUGHS, Edgar Rice. *Tarzan Triumphant.* Ace F 194. F. M1d. $15.00

BURROUGHS, Edgar Rice. *Tarzan Triumphant.* Ballantine U 2015. 3rd edn. F. P9d. $3.00

BURROUGHS, Edgar Rice. *Tarzan Triumphant.* 1974. Ballantine 21909. 3rd prtg. SF. F. W2d. $4.00

BURROUGHS, Edgar Rice. *Tarzan Triumphant.* 1975. Ballantine 24485. 4th prtg. SF. F. W2d. $4.00

BURROUGHS, Edgar Rice. *Tarzan's Quest.* 1964. Ballantine U 2019. 1st edn. VC. M1d. $8.00

BURROUGHS, Edgar Rice. *Tarzan's Quest.* 1964. Ballantine U 2019. 1st prtg. F. F2d. $10.00

BURROUGHS, Edgar Rice. *Tarzan's Quest.* 1980. Ballantine 29562. 6th prtg. SF. VG. W2d. $3.25

BURROUGHS, Edgar Rice. *Thuvia, Maid of Mars.* Ace F 168. c/R Krenkel Jr. SF. VG. B5d. $4.50

BURROUGHS, Edgar Rice. *Thuvia, Maid of Mars.* Ace F 168. VG. M6d. $5.00

BURROUGHS, Edgar Rice. *Thuvia, Maid of Mars.* Ace F 168. 1st edn. PBO. G. P9d. $1.25

BURROUGHS, Edgar Rice. *Thuvia, Maid of Mars.* 1975. Ballantine 23581. 7th prtg. SF. VG. W2d. $3.25

BURROUGHS, Edgar Rice. *Thuvia, Maid of Mars.* 1982. Ballantine 27837. 15th prtg. SF. F. W2d. $4.50

BURROUGHS, Edgar Rice. *Thuvia, Maid of Mars.* 1963. Ballantine. 1st edn. NF. M1d. $12.00

BURROUGHS, Edgar Rice. *War Chief.* 1964. Ballantine U 2045. 1st edn. PBO. We. F. F2d. $15.00

BURROUGHS, Edgar Rice. *War Chief.* 1973. Ballantine 03082. 2nd prtg. We. VG+. W2d. $4.00

BURROUGHS, Edgar Rice. *Warlord of Mars.* 1963. Ballantine F 711. SF. NF. M3d. $5.00

BURROUGHS, Edgar Rice. *Warlord of Mars.* 1963. Ballantine F 711. SF. VG+. B4d. $4.00

BURROUGHS, Edgar Rice. *Warlord of Mars.* 1967. Ballantine U 2033. 4th prtg. SF. VG. W2d. $4.00

BURROUGHS, Edgar Rice. *Warlord of Mars.* 1973. Ballantine 23580. 7th prtg. SF. VG+. W2d. $3.75

BURROUGHS, Edgar Rice. *Warlord of Mars.* 1977. Ballantine 27059. 11th prtg. SF. F. W2d. $4.00

BURROUGHS, Edgar Rice. *Warlord of Mars.* 1981. Ballantine 27836. 17th prtg. SF. F. W2d. $3.50

BURROUGHS, Edgar Rice. *Warlord of Mars.* Four Square 367. G+. B3d. $4.50

BURROUGHS, Edgar Rice. *Wizard of Venus.* Ace 90190. c/R Krekel Jr. SF. VG+. B5d. $6.50

BURROUGHS, William. *Junkie.* 1967. Ace K 202. JD. VG. P1d. $10.00

BURROUGHS, William. *Junkie.* Ace 41841. VG. I1d. $5.00

BURROUGHS/HELBRANT. *Junkie/Narcotic Agent.* 1953. Ace D 15. 1st edn. scarce. G. F2d. $60.00

BURT, K.N. *Lady In the Tower.* Dell 191. VG. B3d. $6.00

BURTON, Edward. *Mouth Job.* 1982. Aquarius AP 1-128. c/photo. Ad. VG. B5d. $4.50

BURTON, Richard. *Erotic Traveler.* 1968. Berkley S 1509. 1st prtg. VG+. P7d. $5.00

BURTON, S.N. *Brutal Passions* 1965. Bell-Ringer 510. 1st edn. c/gga. My. F. F2d. $12.00

BUSBEE, J. Jr. *Son of Egypt.* Avon T 64. VG+. B3d. $5.00

BUSBY, F.M. *All These Earths.* 1985. Bantam. 1st pb. F. M1d. $6.00

BUSCH, F. *Drams of the Scharhorst.* Panther 686. VG. B3d. $7.00

BUSCH, F. *Holocaust at Sea.* Berkley G 115. NF. B3d. $4.50

BUSCH, Niven. *Duel in the Sun.* 1947. Popular 102. 4th prtg. G+. R5d. $1.50

BUSCH, Niven. *Hate Merchant.* Bantam 1204. VG+. B3d. $4.00

BUSCH, Niven. *San Franciscans.* 1963. Dell 7607. 1st prtg. G+. R5d. $1.50

BUSHNELL, O.A. *Peril in Paradise.* Ace K 114. c/gga. VG+. B3d. $4.50

BUSHYAGER, Linda E. *Spellstone of Shaltus.* 1980. Dell 18274. 1st edn. SF. F. F2d. $9.00

BUSHYAGER, Linda E. *Spellstone of Shaltus.* 1980. Dell 18274. 1st prtg. VG. S1d. $3.00

BUTLER, Gerald. *Blow Hot, Blow Cold.* Dell 726. VG. G5d. $6.50

BUTLER, Gerald. *Kiss the Blood Off My Hands.* Dell 197. c/G Gregg. My. VG. B5d. $7.50

BUTLER, Gerald. *Slippery Hitch.* Dell 511. c/R Stanley. My. G+. B5d/R5d. $2.50

BUTLER, Gerald. *Unafraid.* 1948. Dell 242. MTI. c/Lancaster & Fontaine: photo. VG. B4d. $4.00

BUTLER, Ivan. *Horror in the Cinema.* 1971. PB Library 66-627. Nfi. VG. P1d. $5.00

BUTLER, Octavia. *Dawn.* 1988. Questar 20518. F. P9d. $2.50

BUTLER, Octavia. *Pattern Master.* Avon 41806. 1st edn. PBO. F. P9d. $2.50

BUTLER, Samuel. *Way of All Flesh.* 1940. Pocket. NF. M1d. $8.00

BUTLER, Samuel. *Way of All Flesh.* 1960. Premier D 94. Fi. VG. B5d. $2.50

BUTLER, Samuel. *Way of All Flesh.* 1959. Washington Square W 561. Fi. VG. B5d. $2.50

BUTLER & BRADFORD. *Dunkirk.* Arrow 392. c/Stuka. VG. B3d. $6.00

BUTTERWORTH, M. *Edge of the Infinite.* 1977. Warner 88346. 1st prtg. TVTI. Space: 1999 #6. SF. VG. W2d. $5.00

BYRD, R.E. *Alone.* Ace H 179. VG. B3d. $6.00

BYRNE, Donn. *Crusade.* Avon G 1140. VG+. B3d. $4.50

BYRNE, Donn. *Messer Marco Polo.* Signet 611. VG+. B3d. $5.00

BYRNE, Donn. *Messer Marco Polo.* 1961. Washington Square W 176. Fi. VG. B5d. $2.50

BYRNE & FABIAN. *Groupie.* 1970. Bantam N 5244. c/Jim Bama. VG. P6d. $2.50

BYRON, James. *Take Only As Directed.* Penguin C 2126. VG. G5d. $5.50

BYRON, James. *TNT for Two.* 1956. Ace D 197. PBO. c/Barton. F. B6a #74. $53.50

BYRON, James. *TNT for Two.* 1956. Ace D 197. PBO. c/Barton. VG+. B6d. $25.00

CABELL, James Branch. *Cream of the Jest.* 1971. Ballantine. 1st edn. Ad/Fa. F. M1d. $15.00

CABELL, James Branch. *Figures of Earth.* 1969. Ballantine 01763. Fa. VG. P1d. $7.50

CABELL, James Branch. *Figures of Earth.* 1969. Ballantine. 1st edn. Ad/Fa. F. M1d. $15.00

CABELL, James Branch. *High Place.* 1970. Ballantine 01855. Fa. VG. P1d. $7.50

CABELL, James Branch. *High Place.* 1970. Ballantine. 1st edn. Ad/Fa. NF. M1d. $12.00

CABELL, James Branch. *Jurgen.* Avon VS 7. SF. VG. B5d. $5.00

CABELL, James Branch. *Jurgen.* 1946. Penguin (US) 601. Fa. F. P1d. $25.00

CABELL, James Branch. *Silver Stallion.* 1969. Ballantine 01678. Fa. F. P1d. $10.00

CABELL, James Branch. *Silver Stallion.* 1969. Ballantine 01678. 1st prtg. SF. VG+. R5d. $8.00

CABELL, James Branch. *Something About Eve.* 1971. Ballantine. 1st edn. Ad/Fa. NF. M1d. $12.00

CABOT, Isabel. *Nurse Craig.* 1961. Ace D 532. 1st prtg. c/Koenig: gga. VG. P7d. $3.50

CAESER, M. *Mark of the Hunter.* Popular 614. VG. B3d. $4.00

CAIDIN, Martin. *Almost Midnight.* 1974. Bantam T 7227. My. VG+. P1d. $4.50

CAIDIN, Martin. *Boeing 707.* Ballantine 322. PBO. VG+. B3d. $5.00

CAIDIN, Martin. *Cyborg.* 1972. Warner 66986. SF. F. W2d. $5.00

CAIDIN, Martin. *Exit Earth.* 1987. Baen 65630. 1st prtg. PBO. VG+. P7d. $5.50

CAIDIN, Martin. *Final Countdown.* 1980. Bantam 12155. 1st edn. SF. F. F2d. $8.00

CAIDIN, Martin. *Four Came Back.* 1970. Bantam N 4870. SF. VG. P1d. $4.50

CAIDIN, Martin. *Last Fathom.* 1974. Pinnacle 230483. SF/My. VG+. P1d. $4.50

CAIDIN, Martin. *Man Into Space.* 1961. Pyramid PR 35. Nfi. VG. B4d. $6.00

CAIDIN, Martin. *Marooned.* 1969. Bantam N 5206. SF. F. P1d. $10.00

CAIDIN, Martin. *Operation Nuke.* 1974. Warner 76-061. SF/My. VG. P1d. $6.00

CAIDIN, Martin. *Star Bright.* 1980. Bantam 12621. PBO. SF. NF. B6d. $3.00

CAIDIN, Martin. *Three Corners to Nowhere.* 1975. Bantam X 2040. SF/My. VG+. P1d. $4.50

CAIDIN, Martin. *Torch to the Enemy.* 1960. Ballantine F 425K. PBO. c/E Valigursky. NF. VG. B5d. $3.50

CAIDIN & SAKAI. *Samurai!* 1958. Ballantine F 248. SF. VG. P1d. $7.50

CAILLOU, Alan. *Khartoum.* 1966. Signet P 2941. MTI. c/gga. VG+. B4d. $2.25

CAILLOU, Alan. *Marseilles.* 1964. Cardinal 35006. My. VG. B5d. $2.50

CAILLOU, Alan. *Swamp War.* 1973. Pinnacle 164. PBO. NF. B6d. $6.00

CAIN, James M. *Butterfly.* 1949. Signet 720. c/R Schulz. My. G+. B5d. $4.00

CAIN, James M. *Butterfly.* 1949. Signet 720. 1st pb. c/Schulz. VG. B6d. $7.50

CAIN, James M. *Career in C Major & Other Stories.* 1945. Avon Modern Story 22. PBO. scarce. VG+. B6a. $67.25

CAIN, James M. *Double Indemnity.* 1943. Avon Murder My 16. PBO. scarce. VG. B6a #80. $53.50

CAIN, James M. *Double Indemnity.* Avon 137. VG. B3d. $5.00

CAIN, James M. *Double Indemnity.* Avon 60. c/Paul Stahr. rare. NF. B6a #75. $101.00

CAIN, James M. *Double Indemnity.* Avon 60. VG. B6d. $30.00

CAIN, James M. *Embezzler.* Avon 99. scarce. VG+. B6a #79. $67.25

CAIN, James M. *Embezzler.* 1946. Avon 99. 1st prtg. My. G+. R5d. $6.00

CAIN, James M. *Everybody Does It.* 1949. Signet 759. 1st prtg. VG+. R5d. $10.00

CAIN, James M. *Galatea.* 1954. Signet 1152. 1st pb. c/Zuckerberg. VG+. B6d. $16.50

CAIN, James M. *Love's Lovely Counerfeit.* Avon 421. NF. G5d. $9.00

CAIN, James M. *Love's Lovely Counterfeit.* 1947. Avon Murder My 44. VG+. B3a #21. $35.20

CAIN, James M. *Love's Lovely Counterfeit.* Avon 161. VG. B3d. $4.00

CAIN, James M. *Mildred Pierce.* Signet 591. VG+. B3d. $6.50

CAIN, James M. *Past All Dishonor.* 1948. Signet 680. 4th edn. My. VG. B5d. $3.00

CAIN, James M. *Postman Always Rings Twice.* Armed Services 1058. VG. B3a #24. $11.00

CAIN, James M. *Postman Always Rings Twice.* Pocket 443. G+. G5d. $5.00

CAIN, James M. *Root of His Evil.* 1952. Avon 455. 1st edn. PBO. VG+. B6a #79. $55.00

CAIN, James M. *Serenade.* 1947. Penguin 621. c/Jonas: gga. G+. P6d. $1.50

CAIN, James M. *Shameless (Root of His Evil).* Avon T 285. NF. G5d. $8.50

CAIN, James M. *Sinful Woman.* 1947. Avon Monthly Novel 1. PBO. VG. B6a #74. $73.00

CAIN, James M. *Sinful Woman.* Avon 174. VG. B3d. $4.50

CAIN, James M. *Sinful Woman.* 1989. Black Lizard NN. c/J Kirwan. My. F. B5d. $8.00

CAIN, Paul. *Fast One.* Avon 496. VG. B6d. $16.50

CALDECOTT, Moyra. *Shadow on the Stones.* 1980. Popular 04502. Fa. VG. P1d. $3.50

CALDER, Robert. *Dogs.* 1977. Dell 2102. Ho. VG+. P1d. $5.50

CALDER-MARSHALL, Arthur. *Scarlet Boy.* 1962. Corgi SN 1161. Ho. VG+. P1d. $12.00

CALDWELL, Eeskine. *Courting of Susie Brown.* Pan G 190. VG. B3d. $6.00

CALDWELL, Eeskine. *Gretta.* Pan G 219. VG. B3d. $6.00

CALDWELL, Erskine. *Bastard.* 1953. Novel Selections 51. VG. I1d. $6.00

CALDWELL, Erskine. *Claudelle English.* 1965. MacFadden 50-253. c/J Thurston. Fi. VG. B5d. $2.50

CALDWELL, Erskine. *Claudelle English.* Signet 1778. VG+. B3d. $5.00

CALDWELL, Erskine. *Claudelle.* Pan G 375. MTI. VG+. B3d. $10.00

CALDWELL, Erskine. *Complete Stories of Erskine Caldwell.* 1955. Signet D 1199. Fa. VG. B4d. $4.00

CALDWELL, Erskine. *Courting of Susie Brown.* 1965. MacFadden 50-237. c/Karol. Fi. VG+. B5d. $3.50

CALDWELL, Erskine. *Courting of Susie Brown.* 1953. Signet 1016. c/J Avati. Fi. G+. B5d. $3.00

CALDWELL, Erskine. *Episode in Palmetto.* 1953. Signet 983. 1st prtg. c/Avati: gga. VG. P7d. $5.00

CALDWELL, Erskine. *Georgia Boy.* Avon 134. VG. B3d. $4.50

CALDWELL, Erskine. *Georgia Boy.* Short-story 30. VG. B3d. $4.00

CALDWELL, Erskine. *Georgia Boy.* 1950. Signet 760. c/J Avati. Fi. VG+. B5d. $5.50

CALDWELL, Erskine. *God's Little Acre.* Pan G 148. MTI. VG+. B3d. $8.00

CALDWELL, Erskine. *Gretta.* 1956. Signet 1342. 1st pb. c/Avati: gga. VG+. B3d. $4.50

CALDWELL, Erskine. *House in the Upands.* 1964. MacFadden 50-227. c/B Phillips. Fi. VG+. B5d. $3.50

CALDWELL, Erskine. *In Search of Bisco.* 1966. Pocket 75117. Nfi. VG. B5d. $3.50

CALDWELL, Erskine. *Journeyman.* 1947. Penguin 646. 1st prtg. c/Jonas: gga. VG. P7d. $4.00

CALDWELL, Erskine. *Kneel to the Rising Sun.* Signet 869. c/Avati. VG. B3d. $5.00

CALDWELL, Erskine. *Lamp for Nightfall.* Pan G 350. VG. B3d. $5.00

CALDWELL, Erskine. *Lamp for Nightfall.* 1954. Signet 1091. c/Avati: gga. Fa. F. B4d. $15.00

CALDWELL, Erskine. *Lamp for Nightfall.* 1954. Signet 1091. c/Avati: gga. Fa. VG. B4d. $2.00

CALDWELL, Erskine. *Love & Money.* Signet 1272. VG+. B3d. $4.00

CALDWELL, Erskine. *Love & Money.* 1956. Signet 1272. c/J Avati. Fi. G+. B5d. $2.50

CALDWELL, Erskine. *Midsummer Passion.* 1948. Avon 177. c/gga. Fa. VG+. B4d. $14.00

CALDWELL, Erskine. *Midsummer Passion.* 1948. Avon 177. c/A Cantor. Fi. G+. B5d. $3.00

CALDWELL, Erskine. *Place Called Estherville.* Pan G 149. c/gga. VG+. B3d. $8.00

CALDWELL, Erskine. *Place Called Estherville.* 1952. Signet 918. c/J Avati. Fi. VG. B5d. $3.50

CALDWELL, Erskine. *Poor Fool.* Novel Selections 52. Fi. VG. B5d. $5.00

CALDWELL, Erskine. *Southways.* 1952. Signet 933. c/Avati: gga. Fa. VG. B4d/B5d. $4.00

CALDWELL, Erskine. *Sure Hand of God.* 1949. Signet 732. c/J Avati. Fi. G+. B5d. $3.00

CALDWELL, Erskine. *Swell-Looking Girl.* 1950. Signet 818. c/J Avati. Fi. VG. B5d. $4.00

CALDWELL, Erskine. *Tobacco Road.* 1959. Pan G 159. 3rd prtg. VG. B3d. $7.00

CALDWELL, Erskine. *Tragic Ground.* 1958. Signet 661. c/R Jonas. Fi. VG+. B5d. $5.50

CALDWELL, Erskine. *We Are the Living.* MacFadden 60-223. VG+. B3d. $4.00

CALDWELL, Erskine. *We Are the Living.* Pan G 514. VG. B3d. $5.50

CALDWELL, Erskine. *We Are the Living.* 1954. Signet 1136. c/J Avati. Fi. VG+. B5d. $5.00

CALDWELL, Erskine. *When You Think of Me.* 1960. Signet S 1839. c/gga. Fa. VG+. B4d. $2.75

CALDWELL, Erskine. *Woman in the House.* 1949. Signet 705. c/gga. Fa. VG. B4d. $3.00

CALDWELL, Erskine. *22 Great Modern Stories.* 1944. Avon Modern Story 14. Fi. VG. B5d. $4.00

CALDWELL, G. *Suburban Sex.* Bedside 1252. VG+. B3d. $6.00

CALDWELL, Jay Thomas. *Me an' You.* 1954. Lion 220. 1st edn. F. F2d. $22.00

CALDWELL, Taylor. *Dialogues With The Devil.* 1968. Crest T 1152. Ho. F. P1d. $12.50

CALDWELL, Taylor. *Maggie: Her Marriage.* Gold Medal 288. VG. B3d. $4.00

CALDWELL, Taylor. *This Side of Innocence.* 1950. Bantam Giants A 760. VG. P6d. $3.50

CALDWELL, Taylor. *Turnbulls.* 1963. Pyramid T 810. 1st pb. c/Binger. NF. B6d. $12.50

CALDWELL, Taylor. *Turnbulls.* Pyramid 1615. VG+. B3d. $4.50

CALDWELL, Taylor. *Your Sins & Mine.* Gold Medal 156. VG. B3d. $6.00

CALET, Henry. *Paris, My Love (Monsieur (Paul).* Berkley G 20. VG. B3d. $4.50

CALEY, Henri. *Young Man of Paris.* 1956. Berkley G 28. 1st edn. PBO. c/Victor Kalin: gga. NF. B6a #76. $28.00

CALIN, Harold. *Combat: Men Not Heroes.* 1963. Lancer 70-060. 1st prtg. TVTI. G+. R5d. $2.25

CALIN, Harold. *Kings of the Sun.* 1963. Lancer 70-062. MTI. c/Yul Brynner. VG+. B4d. $9.00

CALIN, Harold. *Search & Kill.* Belmont 50-743. PBO. VG. B3d. $4.00

CALITRI, Charles. *Rickey.* 1953. Popular 503. JD. F. P1d. $25.50

CALLAHAN, J. *Texas Fury.* Dell 677. VG. B3d. $4.50

CALLAHAN/PATTERSON. *Prairie Terror/ Rawhide Breed.* Ace D 252. VG. B3d. $5.00

CALMER, Ned. *Strange Land.* Signet D 1355. reprint. NF. B6d. $10.00

CALMER, Ned. *Strange Land.* Signet 851. c/Avati. VG. B3d. $4.50

CALVANO, Tony. *Gigolo.* Idle Hours 414. VG. B3d. $5.00

CALVANO, Tony. *Gutter Gang.* 1962. Midnight Reader 467. PBO. scarce. JD. VG+. B6a #79. $33.00

CALVANO, Tony. *Love Nest.* 1961. Nightstand NB 1711. PBO. Ad. VG. B5d. $4.00

CALVANO, Tony. *Lust Mob.* Ember Book EB 924. VG+. B3d. $5.00

CALVANO, Tony. *Night Train to Sodom.* Ember Lib 304. VG. B3d. $7.00

CALVANO, Tony. *Satin Vise.* Ember Book EB 948. VG. B3d. $4.00

CALVANO, Tony. *Sinner's Ballad.* 1966. Leisure 1161. PBO. NF. B6d. $15.00

CALVANO, Tony. *Sinning Season.* 1961. Nightstand NB 1561. Ad. VG. B5d. $4.50

CALVANO, Tony. *Skid Row Sinners.* 1963. Nightstand 1646. PBO. scarce. JD. VG+. B6a #79. $54.00

CALVIN, T. *Call Boy.* Ember Book EB 907. VG. B3d. $4.00

CALVINO, Italo. *Castle of Crossed Destinies.* 1978. Picador 25586. Fa. VG. P1d. $7.50

CAMERER, David M. *Damned Wear Wings.* 1959. Crest S 280. 1st prtg. VG+. P7d. $5.00

CAMERON, Bruce. *Sins of Maria.* 1959. Popular G 373. 1st prtg. c/De Soto: gga. VG. P7d. $4.00

CAMERON, Don. *While for a Shroud.* 1948. Bleak House 22. 1st prtg. VG. P7d. $10.00

CAMERON, Donald Clough. *Dig Another Grave.* Handi-Book 86. G+. G5d. $5.00

CAMERON, Ian. *Island at the Top of the World.* Avon 20966. 4th edn. SF. VG. P1d. $3.00

CAMERON, Ian. *Lost Ones.* 1970. Avon V 2327. SF. VG. P1d. $5.00

CAMERON, Lou. *Angel's Flight.* 1960. Gold Medal 1047. 1st edn. c/gga. F. F2d. $15.00

CAMERON, Lou. *Big Red Ball.* Gold Medal 1114. VG+. B3d. $5.00

CAMERON, Lou. *Black Camp.* 1963. Gold Medal 1286. 1st edn. My. F. F2d. $9.00

CAMERON, Lou. *Cybernia.* 1972. Gold Medal T 2593. SF. VG. P1d. $4.00

CAMERON, Lou. *Good Guy.* 1968. Lancer 74-960. PBO. My. VG. B6d. $9.00

CAMERON, Lou. *Good Guy.* 1968. Lancer 74-960. 1st edn. SF. F. F2d. $15.00

CAMERON, Lou. *Green Fields of Hell.* 1964. Gold Medal K 1493. We. VG+. B4d. $2.75

CAMERON, Lou. *None But the Brave.* 1965. Gold Medal K 1511. MTI. c/Frank Sinatra: photo. VG+. B4d. $4.00

CAMERON, Lou. *Outsider.* 1969. Popular 60-2373. TVTI. c/Darren McGavin: photo. VG+. B4d. $2.50

CAMERON, Lou. *Sky Divers.* 1962. Gold Medal 1183. VG. B3d. $4.00

CAMERON, Lou. *Tipping Point.* 1971. Lancer 75-169. 1st edn. c/Negro photo. My. F. F2d. $15.00

CAMERON, Owen. *Catch a Tiger.* 1954. Bantam 1195. 1st prtg. My. G. R5d. $1.00

CAMERON, Owen. *Demon Stirs.* 1958. Dell 983. 1st prtg. My. G+. R5d. $2.25

CAMERON, Owen. *Mountains Have No Shadow.* Bantam 1101. VG. B3d. $5.00

CAMERON. *Death at Her Elbow.* Green Dragon 20. VG. B3d. $5.00

CAMISSO, Gionanni. *Loves of the Orient.* 1965. Brown 899. VG. B3d. $6.50

CAMP, Joe. *Oh Heavenly Dog.* 1980. Scholastic 31400. 1st prtg. VG+. R5d. $1.75

CAMP, L. *Experiment.* Beacon 942. VG+. B3d. $6.00

CAMPBELL, Angus edt. *Scottish Tales of Terror.* 1972. Fontana 2922. Ho. VG. P1d. $5.00

CAMPBELL, E.S. *Chorus of Cuties.* 1951. Avon 499. VG+. I1d. $9.00

CAMPBELL, E.S. *Cuties.* 1945. Avon NN. PBO. rare. NF. B6a #76. $266.25

CAMPBELL, John W. *Analog #1.* 1964. PB Library 52-293. VG. P1d. $6.00

CAMPBELL, John W. *Analog #2.* 1965. PB Library 52-509. VG. P1d. $5.50

CAMPBELL, John W. *Analog #6.* 1969. Pocket 75357. VG. W2d. $4.00

CAMPBELL, John W. *Analog #7.* 1970. Belmont 52032. VG. W2d. $4.00

CAMPBELL, John W. *Astounding SF Anthology.* Berkley G 41. PBO. SF. G+. B5d. $2.50

CAMPBELL, John W. *Astounding SF Anthology.* Berkley G 41. VG. P1d. $8.00

CAMPBELL, John W. *Astounding Tales of Space & Time.* 1957. Berkley G 47. F. P1d. $15.00

CAMPBELL, John W. *Astounding Tales of Space & Time.* 1957. Berkley G 47. 1st prtg. G+. R5d. $2.50

CAMPBELL, John W. *Best of John W Campbell.* 1976. Ballantine 24960. c/H Van Dongen. SF. VG+. B5d. $6.00

CAMPBELL, John W. *Black Star Passes.* 1965. Ace F 346. SF. VG. P1d. $5.50

CAMPBELL, John W. *Black Star Passes.* 1972. Ace 06701. 2nd prtg. SF. G+. W2d. $3.00

CAMPBELL, John W. *Counter Commandment.* 1970. Curtis 07067. SF. VG+. P1d. $5.00

CAMPBELL, John W. *Invaders From the Infinite.* Ace M 154. F. M1d. $8.00

CAMPBELL, John W. *Islands of Space.* 1966. Ace M 143. SF. VG. P1d. $5.50

CAMPBELL, John W. *Mightiest Machine.* 1965. Ace F 364. SF. VG+. M3d. $6.00

CAMPBELL, John W. *Moon Is Hell.* 1973. Ace 53870. SF. VG+. B5d/P1d. $3.50

CAMPBELL, John W. *Who Goes There?* 1955. Dell D 150. SF. VG+. P1d. $15.00

CAMPBELL, Karen. *Suddenly in the Air.* Popular 02583. My. G. W2d. $2.25

CAMPBELL, Marilyn. *Come Into My Parlor.* Zebra 3933. c/sgn. NF. G5d. $5.00

CAMPBELL, Ramsey. *Cold Print.* 1987. TOR S 1660. 1st edn. PBO. F. P9d. $3.50

CAMPBELL, Ramsey. *Face That Must Die.* 1979. Star. 1st pb. F. M1d. $10.00

CAMPBELL, Ramsey. *Influence.* 1989. TOR 51638. 1st prtg. SF. VG+. W2d. $3.25

CAMPBELL, Ramsey. *New Terror I.* 1980. Pan. 1st pb. F. M1d. $5.00

CAMPBELL & BEDFORD. *You & Your Future Job.* Armed Services 1081. Nfi. VG. B5d. $4.00

CAMPBELL & MCLEAN. *Martha Logan's Meat Cookbook.* Pocket 852. 3rd prtg. VG+. B3d. $4.00

CAMPBELL & MCLEAN. *Meat & Poultry Cook Book.* 1969. Pocket 75343. 14th edn. Nfi. VG+. B5d. $3.50

CAMPBELL/CAMPBELL. *Ultimate Weapon/Planeteers.* 1966. Ace G 585. SF. F. P1d. $13.50

CAMRA, Ross. *Assault!* 1962. Epic 144. 1st edn. SF. F. F2d. $15.00

CANARY, Glenn. *Damned & the Innocent.* 1964. Monarch 486. Ad. VG+. B5d. $6.50

CANBY, Henry Seidel. *Walt Whitman.* Armed Servies K 22. Nfi. G+. B5d. $3.00

CANNAN, Joanna. *Taste of Murder (Poisonous Relations).* Dell 596. G+. G5d. $3.75

CANNING, John edt. *50 Great Horror Stories.* 1976. Bantam Y 2851. 5th edn. Nfi. F. P1d. $4.00

CANNING, John edt. *50 True Tales of Terror.* 1973. Bantam TP 7755. Nfi. G+. P1d. $3.00

CANNING, Victor. *Bird of Prey.* 1953. Bantam 1177. 1st pb. My. NF. B6d. $16.50

CANNING, Victor. *Bird of Prey.* 1953. Bantam 1177. 1st prtg. My. G+. R5d. $2.50

CANNING, Victor. *Burden of Proof.* Berkley F 881. VG+. G5d. $4.50

CANNING, Victor. *Chasm.* Bantam 313. VG+. B3d. $5.00

CANNING, Victor. *Chasm.* 1949. Bantam 313. Fa. NF. B4d. $12.50

CANNING, Victor. *Forest of Eyes.* 1951. Bantam A 948. 1st prtg. My. VG+. R5d. $5.00

CANNING, Victor. *Golden Salamander.* 1950. Bantam 834. 1st prtg. My. VG. R5d. $4.00

CANNING, Victor. *Handful of Silver.* 1964. Berkley F 889. 1st prtg. My. VG. R5d. $3.25

CANNING, Victor. *House of the Seven Flies.* 1963. Berkley F 730. 1st pb. My. NF. B6d. $12.50

CANNING, Victor. *Limbo Line.* 1965. Berkley F 1085. My. VG+. B4d. $6.00

CANNING, Victor. *Man From the Turkish Slave.* 1963. Berkley F 746. My. VG+. B5d. $5.00

CANNING, Victor. *Panther's Moon.* Bantam 734. 1st prtg. My. G+. R5d. $3.00

CANNING, Victor. *Panther's Moon.* Harlequin 41. VG. B3d. $6.00

CANNING, Victor. *Scorpio Letters.* 1966. Avon S 204. 1st prtg. My. VG+. R5d. $2.50

CANNON, Frank. *Forced Nympho.* 1962. Novel Book 6035. PBO. c/photo. Ad. NF. B5d. $7.00

CANNON, L.G. *Look to the Mountain.* Bantam 933. VG+. B3d. $5.00

CANTRELL, Wade B. *Brand of Cain.* 1955. Pyramid 173. PBO. VG. P6d. $4.00

CANTWELL, John. *Awakening.* 1960. Hillman 156. Fi. VG+. B5d. $5.50

CAPEK, Karel. *War With the Newts.* 1955. Bantam 1292. 1st prtg. SF. VG. R5d. $5.25

CAPEK, Karel. *War With the Newts.* 1967. Berkley S 1404. 1st prtg. SF. VG. R5d. $2.25

CAPON, Paul. *Brother Cain.* 1946. Guild S 217. Fi. VG. P1d. $10.50

CAPONEGRO, C. *Breeze Horror.* 1988. Onyx 40075. 1st prtg. SF. VG. W2d. $3.00

CAPOTE, Truman. *Breakfast at Tiffany's.* Signet D 1727. MTI. VG. M6d. $6.50

CAPOTE, Truman. *Grass Harp.* 1953. Signet 1020. 1st pb. c/Zuckerberg. VG. B6d. $6.00

CAPOTE, Truman. *Other Voices Other Rooms.* 1949. Signet 700. c/Jonas. Fa. VG+. B4d. $16.00

CAPOTE/CAPOTE. *Grass Harp/Tree of Night.* 1956. Signet S 1333. Fi. G+. B5d. $3.00

CAPP, Al. *Life & Times of the Shmoo.* 1949. Pocket 621. Fa. G+. P1d. $15.00

CAPPELLI, Mario. *Scramble!* 1962. Ace F 132. PBO. c/V Tossey. Fi. VG. B5d. $4.50

CAPPS, Carroll M. *Secret of the Sunless World.* 1969. Dell 7663. SF. F. P1d. $6.00

CAPRIO, F.S. *Modern Woman's Guide to Sexual Maturity.* 1971. Black Cat B 327-Z. Nfi. Nf. B5d. $5.00

CAPRIO, F.S. *Psychiatrist Talks About Sex.* Belmont 92-529. PBO. VG. B3d. $4.50

CARBERRY, Russ. *Shutterbug Caper.* 1967. PEC AN 06. PBO. My. VG. B6d. $5.00

CARCO, Francis. *Frenzy.* 1960. Berkley G 474. 1st edn. c/gga. My. F. F2d. $12.50

CARCO, Francis. *Infamy.* 1958. Berkley G 140. 1st US edn. c/gga. F. F2d. $15.00

CARCO, Francis. *Perversity.* Avon 401. VG+. B3d. $7.00

CARCO, Francis. *Perversity.* 1956. Berkley G 33. 1st pb edn. c/gga. F. F2d. $15.00

CARCO, Francis. *Perversity.* 1987. Black Lizard NN. c/J Kirwan. My. F. B5d. $8.00

CARCO, Francis. *Rue Pigalle.* Avon 555. VG. B3d. $4.50

CARCO, Francis. *Street of the Lost.* 1960. Berkley D 2031. 1st US edn. c/gga. My. F. F2d. $12.50

CARD, Orson Scott. *Abyss.* Pocket 67625. 2nd edn. SF. VG. P1d. $4.00

CARD, Orson Scott. *Capital.* Ace 09136. 1st prtg. VG. S1d. $3.00

CARD, Orson Scott. *Ender's Game.* 1986. TOR 53253. SF. VG. P1d. $5.00

CARD, Orson Scott. *Song Master.* 1987. TOR 53255. 1st pb. c/Nolan. SF. NF. B6d. $3.00

CARDER, Michael. *Cimarron Crossing.* 1952. Bantam 1057. We. VG+. B4d. $3.00

CAREN, Ellen. *Mirabelle: Woman of Passion!* 1949. Novel Library 22. c/gga. VG. P6d. $10.00

CAREW, S.C. *Hot Stick Man.* Brandon House 6078. VG. B3d. $4.00

CAREY, Michael. *Vice Net.* 1958. Avon 809. PBO. My. NF. B6d. $12.50

CAREY, Michael. *Vice-Squad Cop.* Avon F 176. reprint. My. VG. B6d. $5.00

CAREY, Michael. *Vice-Squad Cop.* 1957. Avon 763. PBO. c/Nappi: gga. VG. B6d. $7.50

CAREY, Webster. *Part 2 Walking Tall.* 1975. Bantam T 2331. 1st prtg. MTI. My. VG+. R5d. $2.50

CARGOE, Richard. *Back of the Tiger.* 1961. Belmont 242. 1st edn. My. F. F2d. $12.00

CARGOE, Richard. *Back of the Tiger.* 1961. Belmont 242. 1st prtg. VG. B3d/P7d. $5.00

CARGOE, Richard. *Maharajah.* 1952. Popular 451. c/gga. Fa. VG+. B4d. $7.50

CARL, Lillian Stewart. *Shadow Dancers.* 1987. Ace. 1st pb. F. M1d. $4.00

CARLETON, Marjorie. *One Night of Terror.* 1960. Berkley G 411. c/H Bennett. My. VG+. B5d. $5.50

CARLIN, Gage. *Stud To Swap.* 1970. Companion 647. PBO. c/gga. NF. B6a #76. $40.00

CARLINO, Lewis John. *Mechanic.* 1972. Signet Q 5338. 1st prtg. G+. R5d. $1.25

CARLINSK & GOODGOLD. *Compleat Beatles Quiz Book.* Warner. VG. B3d. $5.00

CARLINSKY & GOODGOLD. *World's Greatest Monster Quiz.* Berkley Z 2963. 2nd edn. Nfi. VG. P1d. $3.00

CARLISIE & LATHAM. *Miracles Ahead!* Armed Services 1140. Nfi. VG. B5d. $4.00

CARLISLE, E. *Quick Change.* After Hours 142. c/3lanton. VG. B3d. $6.00

CARLOVA, John. *Adam & Evil.* 1958. Berkley G 167. PBO. Fi. G+. B5d. $3.00

CARLSEN, Chris. *Bull Chief.* 1977. Sphere 4632. Fa. VG. P1d. $4.00

CARMICHAEL, K.C. *Snake & the Womb.* Brandon House 2050. VG+. B3d. $5.00

CARNEGIE, Dale. *How To Win Friends & Influence People.* 1940. Pocket 68. 3rd edn. c/photo. Nfi. VG. B5d. $3.00

CARNEGIE, Dale. *Unknown Lincoln.* 1952. Pocket 891. c/W Smith. Nfi. VG. B5d. $4.00

CARNEGIE COMMISSION. *Public Television: Program for Action.* 1967. Bantam PZ 3552. 1st prtg. VG. R5d. $1.75

CARNELL, John. *Lambda I.* 1964. Berkley F 883. SF. F. P1d. $12.00

CARNELL, John. *New Writings in SF #1.* 1966. Bantam F 3245. SF. VG. P1d. $5.50

CARNELL, John. *New Writings in SF #2.* 1966. Bantam F 3379. SF. VG+. P1d. $8.00

CARNELL, John. *New Writings in SF #3.* 1967. Bantam F 3380. SF. F. P1d. $10.00

CARNELL, John. *Weird Shadows From Beyond.* 1968. Avon S 345. SF. VG+. B4d. $3.00

CARNELL, John. *Weird Shadows From Beyond.* 1969. Avon S 345. 1st US edn. Ho. NF. B6d. $15.00

CARNEY, Robert H. *Anything Goes.* 1961. Newsstand 169. 1st edn. F. F2d. $13.00

CARPENTER, Elmer J. *Moonspin.* 1967. Flagship 715. SF. F. P1d. $10.00

CARPENTER, Elmer J. *Moonspin.* 1967. Flagship 715. 1st prtg. SF. G+. R5d. $2.75

CARPENTER, Jay. *Youngest Harlot.* 1960. Newsstand 130. PBO. scarce. JD. VG+. B6a #79. $44.00

CARPENTER, John. *Signal Guns at Sunup.* 1951. Pocket 834. c/H Geisen. We. VG+. B5d. $5.50

CARPOZI, George Jr. *Jackie & Ari: For Love or Money?* 1968. Lancer 74-985. 1st prtg. PBO. VG. P7d. $4.00

CARPOZI, George Jr. *Marilyn Monroe: Her Own Story.* 1961. Belmont L 508. PBO. c/Monroe: photo. rare. VG+. B6a #77. $90.75

CARPOZI, George Jr. *Sunstrike.* 1978. Pinnacle 40-365. SF. VG. P1d. $3.50

CARR, H. *Carnal Kiss.* Brandon House 6233. NF. B3d. $4.50

CARR, H. *Making of a Teen-Age Call Boy.* Barclay 7311. c/photo. VG+. B3d. $4.00

CARR, Ian edt. *1980 Comics Annual.* 1979. Potlatch 19. SF. F. P1d. $10.00

CARR, Jay. *Motel Wives.* 1963. Beacon B 605F. c/gga. Fa. F. B4d. $12.00

CARR, Jay. *She Wolves.* 1963. Beacon B 575F. PBO. c/gga. VG. P6d. $3.00

CARR, Jay. *Surburban Lovers.* 1962. Monarch 288. Ad. VG+. B5d. $6.50

CARR, Jay. *Weekend.* 1961. Beacon B 431Y. PBO. c/Darcy. Ad. VG+. B5d. $8.00

CARR, John Dickson. *Arabian Nights Murder.* 1943. Hillman Detective 1. G+. P6d. $6.50

CARR, John Dickson. *Below Suspicion.* Bantam 1119. G+. G5d. $6.50

CARR, John Dickson. *Blind Barber.* Berkley G 80. c/Kimmel: gga. NF. B6a #76. $33.00

CARR, John Dickson. *Blind Barber.* 1957. Berkley G 80. 1st prtg. c/Lu Kimmel: gga. VG+. P7d. $9.00

CARR, John Dickson. *Bride of Newgate.* Avon T 391. VG+. I1d. $5.00

CARR, John Dickson. *Bride of Newgate.* 1952. Avon 476. c/gga. Fa. VG. B4d. $8.00

CARR, John Dickson. *Bride of Newgate.* 1952. Avon 476. 1st prtg. My. F. F2d. $10.00

CARR, John Dickson. *Burning Court.* 1973. Award AN 1199. SF/My. G+. P1d. $3.00

CARR, John Dickson. *Burning Court.* 1954. Bantam 1207. 1st prtg. My. VG. R5d. $3.50

CARR, John Dickson. *Burning Court.* 1944. Popular 28. 1st prtg. My. VG+. F2d. $11.00

CARR, John Dickson. *Captain Cut-Throat.* Bantam 1472. VG. B3d. $4.00

CARR, John Dickson. *Case of the Constant Suicides.* Berkley G 60. 1st prtg. My. VG. B3d/R5d. $5.25

CARR, John Dickson. *Case of the Constant Suicides.* 1945. Dell 91. VG. I1d. $12.00

CARR, John Dickson. *Castle Skull.* 1960. Berkley G 412. 1st prtg. My. G+. R5d. $3.50

CARR, John Dickson. *Castle Skull.* 1947. Pocket 448. 1st prtg. VG+. P7d. $9.00

CARR, John Dickson. *Corpse in the Wax Works.* Dell 775. VG. I1d. $4.00

CARR, John Dickson. *Corpse in the Wax Works.* 1954. Dell 775. 1st prtg. c/Richard Powers. NF. P7d. $10.00

CARR, John Dickson. *Crooked Hinge.* 1944. Popular 19. 1st pb. My. G+. B6d. $7.50

CARR, John Dickson. *Dead Man's Knock.* 1960. Bantam A 2106. 1st prtg. My. G+. R5d. $1.25

CARR, John Dickson. *Death Turns the Tables.* 1945. Pocket 350. G. P6d. $1.50

CARR, John Dickson. *Death Watch.* Berkley G 101. 1st prtg. My. VG+. R5d. $8.00

CARR, John Dickson. *Death Watch.* 1945. Bestseller B 78. VG. F2d. $6.00

CARR, John Dickson. *Death Watch.* Dell 564. c/G Mayers. My. VG. B5d. $5.00

CARR, John Dickson. *Devil in Velvet.* 1952. Bantam A 1009. 1st prtg. My. VG. R5d. $6.75

CARR, John Dickson. *Eight of Swords.* 1957. Berkley G 48. 1st prtg. c/Maguire: gga. VG+. P7d. $9.00

CARR, John Dickson. *Eight of Swords.* 1971. Harrow HW 7009. My. NF. B5d. $4.50

CARR, John Dickson. *Eight of Swords.* Pan G 487. VG. B3d. $8.50

CARR, John Dickson. *Emperor's Snuff-Box.* Pocket 372. F. I1d. $10.00

CARR, John Dickson. *Fire, Burn.* 1959. Bantam A 1847. 1st pb. Fa/My. NF. B6d. $16.50

CARR, John Dickson. *Four False Weapons.* 1957. Berkley G 91. c/Maguire. My. VG. G5d. $8.00

CARR, John Dickson. *Four False Weapons.* Detective 40. VG. B3d. $5.00

CARR, John Dickson. *Hag's Nook.* 1958. Berkley G 129. 1st prtg. c/Maguire: gga. NF. P7d. $10.00

CARR, John Dickson. *Hag's Nook.* Dell 537. c/R Stanley. My. VG. B5d. $6.00

CARR, John Dickson. *He Who Whispers.* 1957. Bantam 1684. 1st prtg. My. G+. R5d. $1.50

CARR, John Dickson. *He Who Whispers.* 1951. Bantam 896. c/gga. My. VG. B4d. $5.00

CARR, John Dickson. *In Spite of Thunder.* 1961. Bantam A 2267. 1st prtg. My. VG+. R5d. $3.00

CARR, John Dickson. *It Walks by Night.* 1954. Avon 621. 1st prtg. My. F. F2d. $10.00

CARR, John Dickson. *Let's Make Mary.* Hillman 1. 3rd prtg. VG. B3d. $4.50

CARR, John Dickson. *Lost Gallows.* 1965. Berkley F 1130. 1st prtg. My. VG+. R5d. $4.00

CARR, John Dickson. *Lost Gallows.* Pocket 436. NF. I1d. $10.00

CARR, John Dickson. *Love Seekers.* Beacon 632. VG+. B3d. $7.00

CARR, John Dickson. *Mad Hatter Mystery.* 1953. Dell 706. VG. B3d/I1d. $5.00

CARR, John Dickson. *Man Who Could Not Shudder.* Bantam 365. VG+. B3d. $8.00

CARR, John Dickson. *Man Who Could Not Shudder.* 1949. Bantam 365. 1st prtg. c/gga. NF. P7d. $12.50

CARR, John Dickson. *My Father's Wife.* Monarch 221. PBO. c/De Soto. VG. B3d. $6.00

CARR, John Dickson. *Poison in Jest.* 1957. Berkley G 72. c/Maguire. VG+. P6d. $6.00

CARR, John Dickson. *Poison in Jest.* 1957. Berkley G 72. 1st prtg. My. G+. R5d. $3.50

CARR, John Dickson. *Poison in Jest.* Popular 349. c/Belarski: gga. NF. B6a #75. $42.00

CARR, John Dickson. *Poison in Jest.* Popular 349. VG. B3d. $9.00

CARR, John Dickson. *Problem of the Green Capsule.* 1947. Bantam 101. c/photo. My. VG. B5d. $6.50

CARR, John Dickson. *Problem of the Green Capsule.* 1947. Bantam 101. 1st prtg. My. F. F2d. $10.00

CARR, John Dickson. *Problem of the Wire Cage.* 1964. Bantam F 2877. 2nd prtg. My. G. W2d. $2.50

CARR, John Dickson. *Problem of the Wire Cage.* 1948. Bantam 304. c/G Fullington. My. G+. B5d. $3.50

CARR, John Dickson. *Problem of the Wire Cage.* 1970. Berkley S 1907. 1st prtg. My. VG. R5d. $1.75

CARR, John Dickson. *Punch & Judy Murders.* 1964. Berkley F 902. 1st prtg. My. F. F2d. $7.50

CARR, John Dickson. *Sleeping Sphinx.* 1947. Armed Services 1280. PBO. rare upright edn. VG+. B6a #74. $81.00

CARR, John Dickson. *Sleeping Sphinx.* 1958. Bantam A 1849. 1st edn. My. VG+. R5d. $2.25

CARR, John Dickson. *Sleeping Sphinx.* 1952. Bantam 996. 1st prtg. My. VG. B3d/R5d. $6.75

CARR, John Dickson. *Three Coffins.* 1949. Popular 174. 1st prtg. My. F. F2d. $10.00

CARR, John Dickson. *Till Death Do Us Part.* 1957. Bantam 1683. 2nd prtg. My. VG. R5d. $1.50

CARR, John Dickson. *Till Death Do Us Part.* 1950. Bantam 793. My. VG. B3d. $3.25

CARR, John Dickson. *Till Death Do Us Part.* 1950. Bantam 793. 1st prtg. My. F. F2d. $10.00

CARR, John Dickson. *To Wake the Dead.* Berkley G 42. 1st prtg. My. G. R5d. $2.00

CARR, John Dickson. *To Wake the Dead.* Dell 635. VG. I1d. $5.00

CARR, John Dickson. *To Wake the Dead.* Popular 10. VG. B3d. $6.00

CARR, John Dickson. *To Wake the Dead.* 1943. Popular 10. 1st edn. PBO. c/Hoffman. VG+. B6a #79. $59.00

CARR, John Dickson. *Witch of the Low Tide.* 1963. Bantam J2559. My. VG+. B5d. $4.00

CARR, John F. *Ophidian Conspiracy.* 1976. Major 3055. SF. VG. P1d. $3.50

CARR, John L. *Leigh Brackett: American Writer.* 1986. Drumm 22. Nfi. VG. P1d. $3.00

CARR, Robert Spencer. *Beyond Infinity.* 1954. Dell 781. c/Powers. SF. VG+. B5d/M3d. $7.00

CARR, Robert Spencer. *Beyond Infinity.* 1954. Dell 781. SF. F. P1d. $17.00

CARR, Terry edt. *Best SF of the Year #8.* 1979. Ballantine 28083. SF. VG+. B5d. $3.50

CARR, Terry edt. *Best SF of the Year.* 1972. Ballantine 02671. SF. VG. P1d. $4.00

CARR, Terry edt. *Fantasy Annual IV.* 1981. Timescape. 1st edn. F. M1d. $5.00

CARR, Terry edt. *New Worlds of Fantasy #2.* 1970. Ace S 7271. 1st edn. PBO. VG. P9d. $1.25

CARR, Terry edt. *New Worlds of Fantasy.* 1967. Ace A 12. 1st edn. PBO. VG. P9d. $1.50

CARR, Terry edt. *On Our Way to the Future.* 1970. Ace 62940. 1st edn. SF. F. F2d. $7.50

CARR, Terry edt. *Others.* 1969. Gold Medal R 2044. 1st prtg. SF. VG. R5d. $3.25

CARR, Terry edt. *Universe #1.* 1971. Ace 84600. SF. VG. P1d. $4.00

CARR, Terry edt. *Universe #4.* Popular 00290. 1st prtg. G. S1d. $1.50

CARR, Terry edt. *Universe #5.* 1976. Popular 00353. SF. F. P1d. $5.00

CARR, W.H.A. *Hollywood Tragedy.* Lancer 72-639. VG+. B3d. $6.00

CARR, W.H.A. *JFK, a Complete Biography 1917-1963.* 1964. Lancer 72-621. 1st prtg. VG. P7d. $4.00

CARR, W.H.A. *JFK, an Informal Biography.* Lancer 72-621. PBO. VG+. B3d. $4.50

CARR, W.H.A. *What Is Jack Paar Really Like?* 1962. Lancer 70-005 PBO. TVTI. c/J Parr photo. NF. VG. B5d. $45.00

CARR & DOYLE. *(New) Exploits of Sherlock Holmes.* 1956. Ace D 181. c/Vorn Tossey. VG. P6d. $4.00

CARR/WILLIAMS. *Warlord of Kor/Star Wasps.* Ace F 177. F. M1d. $15.00

CARR/WILLIAMS. *Warlord of Kor/Star Wasps.* 1963. Ace F 177. PBO. SF. NF. B5d. $7.50

CARRELL & MACDONALD. *Sweet & Deadly.* 1959. Zenith 29. 1st edn. c/gga. F. F2d. $8.00

CARRIER, Warren. *Hell of a Murder.* 1958. Avon T 283. 1st pb. c/Kalin: gga. My. VG. B6d. $7.50

CARRIGAN & CARRIGAN. *Siren Stars.* 1971. Pyramid T 2446. SF. F. P1d. $5.00

CARROLL, Ann. *Summer of Sex.* 1964. Saber SA 46. Ad. G+. B5d. $3.00

CARROLL, Jona. *Land of Laughs.* 1983. Ace 46987. 1st prtg. SF. VG+. W2d. $3.50

CARROLL, Joy. *Satan's Bell.* 1976. Pocket 80678. Ho. G+. P1d. $3.00

CARROLL, Lewis. *Alice in Wonderland.* 1961. Everyman 1836. Fa. F. P1d. $13.00

CARROLL, Thomas D. *Grounds for Murder.* Lancer 73-539. PBO. VG. M6d. $4.00

CARRUTHERS, Margaret. *His Best Friend's Wife.* 1961. Beacon 402. PBO. c/gga. VG+. B6d. $15.00

CARSE, Robert. *Devil's Spawn.* Dell 1st Edn 95. PBO. c/M Hooks. My. VG. B5d. $4.50

CARSE, Robert. *Drums of Empire.* Popular G 357. VG+. B3d. $4.50

CARSE, Robert. *End to Innocence.* 1959. Monarch 129. c/gga. Fa. VG. B4d. $6.00

CARSE, Robert. *Fabulous Buccaneer.* Dell 1st Edn B 109. VG+. B3d. $4.50

CARSE, Robert. *From the Sea & the Jungle.* Popular G 102. VG+. B3d. $5.00

CARSE, Robert. *From the Sea & the Jungle.* 1952. Popular G 102. c/gga. Fa. VG. B4d. $4.00

CARSON, Dave. *Woman Hater.* 1960. Midwood 32. PBO. c/Rader: gga. VG. B6d. $12.50

CARSON, Johnny. *Happiness Is a Dry Martini.* 1968. Crest T 1217. 1st prtg. VG. R5d. $3.00

CARSON, Robert. *Bride Saw Red.* 1948. Bantam 307. Fa. VG+. B4d. $5.00

CARSON, Robert. *Stranger in Our Midst.* 1953. Popular 496. c/gga. Fa. VG+. B4d. $7.50

CARTER, Alex. *Change Partners.* Beacon 568. VG+. B3d. $6.00

CARTER, Alex. *Free Lovers.* 1963. Beacon B 629F. PBO. Ad. VG+. B5d. $5.50

CARTER, Alex. *Love Too Soon.* Beacon 961. PBO. VG+. B3d. $6.50

CARTER, Angela. *Heroes & Villains.* 1972. Pocket. 1st pb. F. M1d. $10.00

CARTER, Angela. *Love.* 1972. Panther 03645. Fi. VG. P1d. $7.50

CARTER, Carmen. *Children of Hamlin.* Pocket 73555. 2nd edn. SF. VG. P1d. $4.00

CARTER, Diana. *Mind Out.* 1973. Pinnacle 00220. Ho. F. P1d. $10.00

CARTER, Dyson. *Night of Flame.* 1946. White Circle 256. Fi. G+. B5d. $4.00

CARTER, Lin. *As the Green Star Rises.* 1975. DAW UY 1156. SF. VG. P1d. $3.50

CARTER, Lin. *As the Green Star Rises.* 1975. DAW 138. 1st edn. SF. F. F2d. $8.00

CARTER, Lin. *Barbarian of World's End.* 1977. DAW UW 1300. SF. VG. W2d. $3.25

CARTER, Lin. *Beyond the Gates of Dream.* 1969. Belmont B60-1032. Fa. VG. P1d. $4.50

CARTER, Lin. *Beyond the Gates of Dream.* 1969. Belmont. 1st pb. F. M1d. $8.00

CARTER, Lin. *Beyond the Gates of Dream.* Leisure 5190K. SF. F. W2d. $4.25

CARTER, Lin. *Black Legion of Callisto.* 1972. Dell 0925. SF. VG+. P1d. $4.50

CARTER, Lin. *Black Legion of Callisto.* Orbit 7825. SF. VG. B5d. $5.00

CARTER, Lin. *Black Star.* 1973. Dell 0932. 1st edn. SF. F. F2d. $10.00

CARTER, Lin. *By the Light of the Green Star.* 1974. DAW UQ 1120. SF. F. P1d. $7.50

CARTER, Lin. *City Outside the World.* 1977. Berkley 03549. SF. VG. P1d. $3.50

CARTER, Lin. *Discoveries in Fantasy.* Ballantine 02546. PBO. Ad/Fa. VG+. B3d. $7.00

CARTER, Lin. *Discoveries in Fantasy.* 1972. Ballantine 02546. 1st edn. F. F2d. $13.00

CARTER, Lin. *Dragons, Elves, & Heroes.* Ballantine 01731. PBO. VG+. B3d. $6.00

CARTER, Lin. *Dragons, Elves, & Heroes.* 1969. Ballantine. 1st edn. Ad/Fa. G+. M1d. $4.00

CARTER, Lin. *Enchantress of World's End.* 1975. DAW UY 1172. SF. F. W2d. $5.75

CARTER, Lin. *Flashing Swords #1.* Dell 2640. G. P9d. $1.25

CARTER, Lin. *Flashing Swords #1.* 1973. Dell. 1st pb. F. M1d. $7.00

CARTER, Lin. *Flashing Swords #2.* 1974. Dell. 1st pb. F. M1d. $8.00

CARTER, Lin. *Flashing Swords #3.* 1976. Dell 2579. SF. VG+. P1d. $4.50

CARTER, Lin. *Flashing Swords #3.* 1976. Dell 2579. 1st edn. F. M1d. $8.00

CARTER, Lin. *Flashing Swords #5.* 1981. Dell. 1st pb. F. M1d. $8.00

CARTER, Lin. *Giant of World's End.* 1969. Belmont B 50-853. 1st edn. c/Jeff Jones. SF. F. F2d. $14.00

CARTER, Lin. *Golden Cities, Far.* Ballantine 02045. PBO. Ad/Fa. VG. B3d. $6.00

CARTER, Lin. *Golden Cities, Far.* 1970. Ballantine. 1st edn. Ad/Fa. NF. M1d. $12.00

CARTER, Lin. *Great Short Novels of Adult Fantasy I.* 1972. Ballantine. 1st edn. Ad/Fa. F. M1d. $15.00

CARTER, Lin. *Great Short Novels of Adult Fantasy VII.* 1973. Ballantine 03162. SF. VG. W2d. $6.50

CARTER, Lin. *Hurok of the Stone Age.* 1981. DAW 423. 1st edn. VG. P9d. $1.50

CARTER, Lin. *Imaginary Worlds.* 1973. Ballantine. 1st edn. Ad/Fa. F. M1d. $15.00

CARTER, Lin. *Immortal of Worlds's End.* 1976. DAW UY 1254. SF. VG. P1d. $3.50

CARTER, Lin. *In the Green Star's Glow.* 1976. DAW 180. 1st edn. SF. F. F2d. $8.00

CARTER, Lin. *Jandar of Callisto.* 1972. Dell 4182. SF. F. P1d. $5.00

CARTER, Lin. *Journey to the Underground World.* 1979. DAW UE 1499. SF. F. P1d. $5.00

CARTER, Lin. *Lankar of Callisto.* Dell 4648. 1st prtg. VG+. S1d. $3.50

CARTER, Lin. *Lankar of Callisto.* 1975. Dell 4648. SF. F. W2d. $5.75

CARTER, Lin. *Lost World of Time.* 1969. Signet 4068. 1st edn. SF. F. F2d/M1d. $10.00

CARTER, Lin. *Lovecraft: A Look Behind the 'Cthulhu Mythos.'* 1972. Ballantine 02427. SF. F. W2d. $9.50

CARTER, Lin. *Mad Empress of Callisto.* 1975. Dell 6143. SF. F. P1d. $5.00

CARTER, Lin. *Magic of Atlantis.* 1970. Lancer 74699. F. P9d. $3.00

CARTER, Lin. *Man Who Loved Mars.* 1973. Gold Medal T 2690. SF. VG. B5d/P1d. $3.50

CARTER, Lin. *Man Without a Planet.* 1966. Ace G 606. 1st edn. SF. NF. F2d. $8.00

CARTER, Lin. *Mind Wizards of Callisto.* 1975. Dell 5600. SF. F. P1d/W2d. $5.00

CARTER, Lin. *New Worlds for Old.* Ballantine 02365. VG+. B3d. $8.00

CARTER, Lin. *New Worlds for Old.* 1971. Ballantine. 1st edn. Ad/Fa. NF. M1d. $12.00

CARTER, Lin. *Outworlder.* 1971. Lancer 74-722. 1st edn. SF. F. F2d. $15.00

CARTER, Lin. *Pirate of World's End.* DAW 310. PBO. VG+. B3d. $4.50

CARTER, Lin. *Renegade of Callisto.* 1978. Dell 14377. SF. VG. W2d. $4.25

CARTER, Lin. *Sky Pirates of Callisto.* 1974. Dell 8050. 3rd prtg. SF. F. W2d. $6.50

CARTER, Lin. *Star Magicians.* 1966. Ace G 588. 1st edn. SF. F. F2d. $10.00

CARTER, Lin. *Star Rogue.* 1970. Lancer 74-649. 1st edn. SF. F. F2d. $8.00

CARTER, Lin. *Star Rogue.* 1970. Lancer 74649. SF. VG. W2d. $4.75

CARTER, Lin. *Thongor & the Dragon City.* 1970. Berkley. 1st pb. F. M1d. $8.00

CARTER, Lin. *Thongor & the Wizard of Lemuria.* 1976. Berkley N 3042. SF. VG. W2d. $3.75

CARTER, Lin. *Thongor & the Wizard of Lemuria.* 1969. Berkley X 1777. Fa. F. M1d/P1d. $10.00

CARTER, Lin. *Thongor Against the Gods.* 1967. PB Library 52-586. Fa. VG+. P1d. $7.50

CARTER, Lin. *Thongor Against the Gods.* 1967. PB Library 52-586. 1st edn. c/Frazetta. SF. F. F2d. $15.00

CARTER, Lin. *Thongor Against the Gods.* 1979. Warner 94178. 2nd prtg. SF. VG+. W2d. $4.25

CARTER, Lin. *Thongor at the End of Time.* 1968. PB Library 53-780. Fa. F. P1d. $10.00

CARTER, Lin. *Thongor Fights the Pirates of Tarakus.* 1970. Berkley 1861. 1st edn. SF. F. F2d/M1d. $10.00

CARTER, Lin. *Thongor in the City of Magicians.* 1968. PB Library 53-665. Fa. F. P1d/M1d. $10.00

CARTER, Lin. *Thongor of Lemuria.* 1966. Ace F 383. 1st edn. SF. F. F2d. $10.00

CARTER, Lin. *Time War.* 1974. Dell 8625. 1st edn. SF. F. F2d. $15.00

CARTER, Lin. *Tolkien: A Look Behind the Lord of the Rings.* 1974. Ballantine 21550. 8th edn. Nfi. VG. P1d. $3.25

CARTER, Lin. *Tower at the Edge of Time.* 1967. Belmont B 50-804. VG+. B3d. $4.50

CARTER, Lin. *Tower at the Edge of Time.* 1967. Belmont B 50-804. 1st pb. F. M1d. $10.00

CARTER, Lin. *Tower at the Edge of Time.* 1972. Belmont. SF. VG. W2d. $4.00

CARTER, Lin. *Under the Green Star.* 1972. DAW 30. 1st edn. SF. F. F2d/M1d. $8.00

CARTER, Lin. *Valley Where Time Stood Still.* 1976. Popular 00344. SF. VG. B5d. $3.00

CARTER, Lin. *Warrior of World's End.* 1974. DAW UY 1321. SF. VG+. W2d. $4.25

CARTER, Lin. *Warriors & Wizards.* 1976. Dell 2579. 1st prtg. SF. G+. R5d. $1.25

CARTER, Lin. *Weird Tales.* Zebra 8217. 2nd edn. F. P9d. $2.00

CARTER, Lin. *When the Green Star Calls.* 1973. DAW UQ 1062. SF. F. W2d. $6.50

CARTER, Lin. *When The Green Star Calls.* DAW 62. VG+. I1d. $4.00

CARTER, Lin. *Wizard of Lemuria.* 1965. Ace F 326. SF. VG+. P1d. $8.00

CARTER, Lin. *Wizard of Lemuria.* 1965. Ace F 326. 1st edn. SF. F. F2d. $15.00

CARTER, Lin. *Wizard of Lemuria.* 1973. Tandem 12386. 2nd prtg. SF. F. W2d. $4.50

CARTER, Lin. *Wizard of Zao.* 1978. DAW UE 1383. SF. VG. W2d. $3.25

CARTER, Lin. *Wizard of Zao.* 1978. DAW 293. 1st prtg. VG. S1d. $3.00

CARTER, Lin. *Year's Best Fantasy & SF #2.* 1976. DAW UY 1248. SF. VG+. W2d. $4.00

CARTER, Lin. *Year's Best Fantasy Stories #1.* 1975. DAW 166. NF. B3d. $4.50

CARTER, Lin. *Year's Best Fantasy Stories #2.* 1976. DAW 205. 1st prtg. F. S1d. $3.50

CARTER, Lin. *Ylana of Callisto.* 1977. Dell 14244. 1st prtg. PBO. c/gga. VG+. P7d. $4.50

CARTER, Lin. *Young Magicians.* 1969. Ballantine. 1st edn. Ad/Fa. F. M1d. $15.00

CARTER, Lin. *Zanthodon.* DAW 391. 1st prtg. VG. S1d. $3.00

CARTER, M.L. *Curse of the Undead.* 1970. Gold Medal T 2276. 1st prtg. SF. G+. R5d. $2.50

CARTER, M.L. *Demon Lovers & Strange Seductions.* 1972. Gold Medal T 2516. Ho. VG. P1d. $5.00

CARTER, Mary. *Fortune in Dimes.* 1963. Cardinal GC 214. 1st prtg. VG+. B3d/P7d. $4.00

CARTER, Mary. *My Years With Edgar Cayce.* 1974. Warner 76-456. Nfi. VG. P1d. $3.50

CARTER, Nicholas. *Cornered at Last.* New Magnet 1314. G. G5d. $12.00

CARTER, Nicholas. *Death Has Green Eyes!* Vital Book. c/skull. VG. B3d. $7.00

CARTER, Nicholas. *Rajah's Ruby.* New Magnet 1244. G. G5d. $12.00

CARTER, Nick. *#186-Zero-Hour Strike Force.* 1984. Charter 95935. My. F. W2d. $3.00

CARTER, Nick. *Amazon.* 1969. Award A 441X. 1st prtg. My. VG+. R5d. $3.00

CARTER, Nick. *Amsterdam.* 1968. Award A 366X. 1st prtg. My. VG. R5d. $1.75

CARTER, Nick. *Berlin.* 1969. Award A 455X. 1st prtg. My. VG. R5d. $1.50

CARTER, Nick. *Berlin.* 1969. Award A 455X. 2nd prtg. My. F. W2d. $4.00

CARTER, Nick. *Bullet for Fidel.* 1965. Award A 130. 1st prtg. My. VG+. R5d. $2.25

CARTER, Nick. *Casbah Killers.* 1969. Award A 560X. 1st prtg. My. VG+. R5d. $3.00

CARTER, Nick. *Checkmate in Rio.* 1964. Award A 110F. 1st prtg. My. VG+. R5d. $2.25

CARTER, Nick. *China Doll.* 1964. Award A 105F. 1st prtg. My. VG. R5d. $1.50

CARTER, Nick. *Chinese Paymaster.* 1967. Award A 239X. 1st prtg. My. VG+. R5d. $3.00

CARTER, Nick. *Cobra Kill.* 1969. Award A 495X. 1st prtg. My. F. R5d. $4.00

CARTER, Nick. *Danger Key.* 1966. Award A 183F. 1st prtg. My. VG. R5d. $1.75

CARTER, Nick. *Dead Men.* 1948. Atlas Digest 1. PBO. scarcest book in series. VG+. B6a #74. $27.00

CARTER, Nick. *Death Strain.* 1970. Award A 7035. 1st prtg. My. VG. W2d. $3.50

CARTER, Nick. *Devil's Cockpit.* 1968. Award A 238X. 2nd prtg. My. VG+. R5d. $1.25

CARTER, Nick. *Double Identity.* 1967. Award A 229X. 1st prtg. My. VG. R5d. $1.75

CARTER, Nick. *Dragon Flame.* 1966. Award A 173F. 1st prtg. My. VG. R5d. $1.75

CARTER, Nick. *Filthy Five.* 1967. Award A 276X. 1st prtg. My. VG+. R5d. $3.00

CARTER, Nick. *Golden Serpent.* 1967. Award A 216F. 1st prtg. My. VG+. R5d. $2.25

CARTER, Nick. *Hanoi.* 1966. Award A 182F. 1st prtg. My. VG. R5d. $1.75

CARTER, Nick. *Human Time Bomb.* 1969. Award A 456X. 1st prtg. My. VG+. R5d. $3.00

CARTER, Nick. *Istanbul.* 1965. Award A 157F. 1st prtg. My. VG+. R5d. $2.25

CARTER, Nick. *Judas Spy.* 1975. Award AQ 1501. 4th prtg. My. G+. W2d. $2.75

CARTER, Nick. *Living Death.* 1969. Award A 496X. 1st prtg. My. VG+. R5d. $2.25

CARTER, Nick. *Macao.* 1968. Award A 294X. 1st prtg. My. VG+. R5d. $2.25

CARTER, Nick. *Mind Killers.* 1970. Award A 655X. 1st prtg. My. F. W2d. $3.50

CARTER, Nick. *Mind Poisoners.* 1966. Award A 198F. 1st prtg. My. VG+. R5d. $2.25

CARTER, Nick. *Mission to Venice.* 1967. Award A 228X. 1st prtg. My. VG+. R5d. $2.25

CARTER, Nick. *Operation Che Guevara.* 1969. Award A 509X. 1st prtg. My. F. R5d. $4.00

CARTER, Nick. *Operation Moon Rocket.* 1968. Award A 295X. 1st prtg. My. VG. R5d. $1.75

CARTER, Nick. *Operation Moon Rocket.* 1970. Award A 295X. 3rd prtg. My. VG+. W2d. $4.25

CARTER, Nick. *Operation Snake.* 1969. Award A 559X. 1st prtg. My. VG+. R5d. $3.00

CARTER, Nick. *Operation Starvation.* 1966. Award A 197F. 1st prtg. My. VG+. R5d. $2.25

CARTER, Nick. *Our Agent in Rome Is Missing.* 1973. Award AN 1160. 1st prtg. My. VG. R5d. $1.25

CARTER, Nick. *Peking & the Tulip Affair.* 1969. Award A 424X. 1st prtg. My. F. R5d. $4.00

CARTER, Nick. *Red Guard.* 1969. Award A 261X. 2nd prtg. My. VG+. R5d. $1.50

CARTER, Nick. *Red Guard.* 1970. Award A 754S. 3rd prtg. My. VG. W2d. $3.25

CARTER, Nick. *Red Rays.* 1969. Award A 423X. 1st prtg. My. VG+. R5d. $3.00

CARTER, Nick. *Rhodesia.* 1968. Award A 409X. 1st prtg. My. VG+. R5d. $3.00

CARTER, Nick. *Safari for Spies.* 1965. Award A 114F. 2nd prtg. My. VG+. R5d. $1.25

CARTER, Nick. *Satan Trap.* 1979. Charter 75035. My. VG. W2d. $3.00

CARTER, Nick. *Sea Trap.* 1969. Award A 442X. 1st prtg. My. VG+. R5d. $3.00

CARTER, Nick. *Seven Against Greece.* 1967. Award A 247X. 1st prtg. My. VG+. R5d. $2.25

CARTER, Nick. *Terrible Ones.* 1966. Award A 172F. 1st prtg. My. VG. R5d. $1.75

CARTER, Nick. *Triple Cross.* Charter 82407. My. VC. W2d. $3.00

CARTER, Nick. *Weapon of Night.* 1967. Award A 215. 1st prtg. My. VG. W2d. $3.50

CARTER, Nick. *13th Spy.* 1965. Award A 139F. 1st prtg. My. VG+. R5d. $2.25

CARTER, Nick. *14 Seconds to Hell.* 1968. Award A 376X. 1st prtg. My. VG+. R5d. $2.25

CARTER, R. *Shadows of Lust.* Croydon 14. NF. I1d. $10.00

CARTER, Ralph. *Shadows of Lust.* 1949. Croyden 14. VG+. B3a. #22. $8.50

CARTER, Ross S. *Those Devils in Baggy Pants.* 1952. Signet 972. War. VG. B4d/B5d. $4.00

CARTER & DE CAMP. *Conan of Aquilonia.* Ace 11640. 2nd edn. SF. VG+. B5d. $3.50

CARTER & DE CAMP. *Conan of Aquilonia.* 1977. Ace 11682. Fa. F. P1d. $5.00

CARTER & DE CAMP. *Conan of the Isles.* 1968. Lancer 73-800. 1st edn. SF. F. F2d. $10.00

CARTER & DE CAMP. *Conan of the Isles.* 1970. Lancer 75-136. 1st prtg. SF. VG+. R5d. $6.00

CARTER & DE CAMP. *Conan the Barbarian.* 1982. Bantam 22544. 1st prtg. MTI. SF. VG+. R5d. $2.00

CARTER & GOLDSMITH. *Sailing Ships & Sailing Craft.* 1971. Bantam R 6816. c/photos. Nfi. VG+. B5d. $5.00

CARTER & GRINNELL/HIGH. *Destination: Saturn/Invader on My Back.* 1968. Ace H 85. PBO. c/Freas. VG+. B3d. $5.00

CARTER & HOWARD. *Conan.* Ace 11630. 5th prtg. SF. VG. W2d. $3.50

CARTER & HOWARD. *King Kull.* 1967. Lancer 73-650. NF. M1d. $12.00

CARTER & HOWARD. *King Kull.* 1967. Lancer 73-650. 1st edn. c/Roy Krenkel: gga. SF. F. F2d. $20.00

CARTER/LONG. *Thief of Thoth/And Others Shall Be Born.* 1968. Belmont B 50-809. SF. F. P1d/W2d. $12.50

CARTER/LONG. *Thief of Thoth/And Others Shall Be Born.* 1968. Belmont B 50-809. SF. G+. B5d/R5d. $3.50

CARTER/NEVILLE. *Flame of Iridar/Peril of the Starmen.* 1967. Belmont B 50-759. 1st pb. F. M1d. $15.00

CARTER/NEVILLE. *Flame of Iridar/Peril of the Starmen.* 1967. Belmont B50-759. PBO. SF. G+. B5d/S1d. $3.50

CARTER/RACKHAM. *Man Without a Planet/Time to Live.* Ace G 606. NF. M1d. $8.00

CARTER/SMITH. *Tower of the Medusa/Kar Kaballa.* Ace 42900. PBO. c/K Freas. SF. VG. B5d. $3.00

CARTER/SMITH. *Tower of the Medusa/Kar Kaballa.* Ace 42900. 1st prtg. G. S1d. $2.00

CARUSO, Dorothy. *Enrico Caruso: His Life & Death.* Armed Services 1070. Nfi. VG. B5d. $5.00

CARUSO & GARDNER. *World's Greatest Athlete.* 1973. Gold Medal T 2725. 1st prtg. VG. R5d. $1.50

CARVER, J. *Fair Young Wives.* Beacon 911. VG+. B3d. $6.50

CARVER, Jeffrey. *Down the Stream of Stars.* 1990. Bantam 28302. 1st edn. SF. F. F2d. $5.00

CARVER, Jeffrey. *Panglor.* 1980. Dell 17310. 1st edn. SF. F. F2d. $8.00

CARVER, Jeffrey. *Seas of Ernathe.* 1976. Laser 34. 1st edn. SF. F. F2d. $5.00

CARVER, John. *Sex Twist.* 1962. Beacon B 559F. PBO. Ad. NF. B5d. $6.50

CARVER, John. *Shame of Jenny.* 1963. Beacon B647F. PBO. Ad. F. B5d. $8.50

CARY, Joyce. *Herself Surprised.* Dell D 153. VG. B3d. $4.50

CASANOVA. *Casanova's Memoirs.* Hillman 3. VG. B3d. $4.00

CASANOVA. *Many Loves of Casanova.* 1961. Holloway 103 & 104. VG+. B3a #21. $21.51

CASE, David. *Fengriffen.* 1972. Lancer 75312. Ho. G+. P1d. $3.50

CASE, David. *Wolf Tracks.* 1980. Belmont Tower 51485. 1st edn. scarce. De. F. F2d. $20.00

CASEWIT, Curtis. *Peace-Makers.* 1968. MacFadden 60321. SF. G+. W2d. $3.25

CASEY, R.J. *Such Interesting People.* Armed Services M 18. VG. B3d. $5.00

CASH & ALBRIGHT. *Seven Firefights in Vietnam.* Bantam 26875. VG+. B3d. $6.00

CASH/HOLT. *Beach Stud/Sex in the Sun.* Midwood 35-110. PBO. VG. M6d. $6.50

CASHMAN, John. *LDS Story.* 1966. Gold Medal D 1716. Drug. VG+. B4d. $10.00

CASPARY, Vera. *Bedelia.* 1960. Dell D 356. 1st prtg. My. NF. G5d. $5.00

CASPARY, Vera. *Bedelia.* Popular 111. MTI. VG+. B3d. $8.00

CASPARY, Vera. *Evvie.* 1961. Dell F 143. My: VG. B5d. $3.00

CASPARY, Vera. *Laura.* 1957. Dell D 188. VG+. B3d. $4.50

CASPARY, Vera. *Laura.* 1961. Dell F 163. c/Forte. My. VG. B5d. $3.00

CASPARY, Vera. *Stranger Than Truth.* 1953. Guild NN. VG. B3d. $8.00

CASSELL, L.J. *Teen Model.* Midwood 33-743. VG+. B3d. $5.50

CASSELLS, John. *Presenting Inspector Flagg.* 1957. Midnight Thriller 16. PBO. G+. B3d. $6.00

CASSIDAY, Bruce. *Gang Girls.* 1963. Monarch 372. 1st edn. c/Bingham: gga. JD. F. F2d. $15.00

CASSIDAY, Bruce. *Marcus Welby MD.* 1970. Ace 51938. 1st edn. TVTI. c/photo. F. F2d. $8.00

CASSIDAY, Bruce. *Rock a Cradle Empty.* 1970. Ace 51938. 1st prtg. VG. R5d. $2.00

CASSIDAY, Bruce. *While Murder Waits.* Graphic 145. PBO. VG+. B3d. $5.00

CASSIDAY, R.V. *Wound of Love.* 1956. Avon 710. 1st edn. My. F. F2d. $18.00

CASSIDAY/LINKLATER. *Brass Shroud/Odd Woman Out.* 1958. Ace D 285. PBO. c/Barton & Tossey. My. VG. B3d. $3.50

CASSIDY, George. *Bait.* 1962. Beacon B525F. PBO. Ad. G+. B5d. $3.50

CASSIDY, George. *Wanton Bride.* Bedside 1226. PBO. c/hairy fist. VG+. B3d. $5.00

CASSILL, R.V. *Buccaneer.* 1959. Avon T 293. MTI. VG+. B4d. $6.00

CASSILL, R.V. *Buccaneer.* 1959. Avon T 293. 1st edn. Hi. F. F2d. $12.00

CASSILL, R.V. *Buccaneer.* Panther 904. PBO. MTI. VG. B3d. $8.00

CASSILL, R.V. *Dormitory Women.* 1954. Lion 216. c/gga. Fa. VG+. B4d. $15.00

CASSILL, R.V. *Dormitory Women.* Signet 1646. VG. B3d. $4.00

CASSILL, R.V. *Hungering Shame.* 1956. Avon 686. PBO. VG+. B6d. $12.00

CASSILL, R.V. *Hungering Shame.* 1956. Avon 686. 1st edn. My. F. F2d. $15.00

CASSILL, R.V. *Naked Morning.* 1957. Avon T 173. 1st edn. c/gga. My. F. F2d. $15.00

CASSILL, R.V. *Tempest.* 1959. Gold Medal Giant D 852. MTI. c/photo. VG+. R5d. $8.00

CASSILL, R.V. *Wife Next Door.* 1963. Gold Medal K 1362. 2nd edn. Fi. VG. B5d. $3.50

CASSILL & PROTTER. *Left Bank of Desire.* Ace S 104. VG. B3d. $5.00

CASTLE, Frank. *Blood Moon.* Gold Medal 970. NF. B3d. $7.00

CASTLE, Frank. *Dakota Boomtown.* Gold Medal 344. VG. B3d. $6.00

CASTLE, Frank. *Dakota Boomtown.* 1958. Gold Medal 752. We. VG+. B4d. $4.00

CASTLE, Frank. *Hawaiian Eye.* 1962. Dell 1st Edn K 112. TVTI. My. VG. P6d. $3.50

CASTLE, Frank. *Lovely & Lethal.* 1957. Gold Medal 695. PBO. My. VG+. B6d. $12.00

CASTLE, Frank. *Nero.* Avon T 521. PBO. Fi. VG. B5d. $3.00

CASTLE, Jeffery. *Satellite E One.* 1958. Bantam A 1766. SF. VG. W2d. $4.50

CASTLE, Jeffrey Lloyd. *Satellite E One.* 1958. Bantam. 1st pb. F. M1d. $8.00

CASTLE, John. *Password Is Courage.* Ballantine 221. VG+. B3d. $5.50

CASTLE, Mort. *Strangers.* 1984. Leisure 02174. SF. G+. W2d. $3.00

CASTRO, J. *Satan Was My Pimp.* Playtime 660. VG+. B3d. $6.50

CASTRO, Joe. *Young Hoods.* 1959. Beacon 245. 1st prtg. PBO. c/gga. JD. VG+. P7d. $15.00

CATLIN, Ralph. *Good-By to Gunsmoke.* Dell 913. c/R Stanley. We. VG. B5d. $3.00

CATTO, Max. *Devil at Four O'Clock.* Pan G 434. 3rd prtg. MTI. c/Peff. VG. B3d. $7.50

CAULFIELD, M.F. *Black City.* 1954. Signet 1164. c/R Maguire. My. VG. B5d. $4.00

CAULFIELD, Max. *Bruce Lee Lives?* 1975. Dell 4518. 1st US edn. c/photo. F. F2d. $10.00

CAUSEY, James O. *Killer Take All!* 1957. Graphic 147. 1st prtg. PBO. c/Lange: gga. VG. P7d. $6.50

CAVE, Hugh B. *Cross on the Drum.* 1959. Ace K 107. 1st edn. PBO. VG+. B6d. $25.00

CAVE, Hugh B. *Legion of the Dead.* 1979. Avon 44669. Ho. G+. P1d. $3.00

CAVE, Hugh B. *Nebulon Horror.* 1980. Dell 16001. 1st edn. c/Boris. Ho. F. F2d. $13.00

CAVE, Peter. *Cybernauts.* 1977. Futura 7575. SF/My. G+. P1d. $5.00

CAVE, Peter. *House of Cards.* 1976. Futura 7472. SF/My. VG. P1d. $7.50

CAVENEY, Philip. *Sins of Rachel Ellis.* 1979. Berkley 04144. SF. VG+. W2d. $3.75

CAYCE, Edgar Evans. *Edgar Cayce on Atlantis.* 1968. PB Library 54-656. Nfi. G+. P1d. $3.50

CAYCE, Edgar Evans. *On Atlantis.* Warner 92689. Nfi. VG+. W2d. $5.00

CAYCE, Hugh Lynn edt. *Edgar Cayce Reader #2.* 1969. PB Library 64-086. Nfi. VG. P1d. $4.50

CAYCE, Hugh Lynn edt. *Edgar Cayce Reader.* 1969. PB Library 64-037. Nfi. VG. P1d. $4.50

CELLINI, Benvenuto. *Cellini.* 1953. Pyramid 100. Bio. NF. B4d. $14.00

CELLINI, Benvenuto. *Cellini.* 1953. Pyramid 100. PBO. c/gga. VG. P6d. $6.00

CERF, B.A. edt. *Good for a Laugh.* Bantam 1231. VG+. B3d. $3.00

CERF, B.A. edt. *Laughter, Incorporated.* Bantam 1010. VG+. B3d. $4.50

CERF, B.A. edt. *Life of the Party.* 1958. Bantam A 1732. Hu. NF. B4d. $3.00

CERF, B.A. edt. *Pocket Book of Cartoons.* Pocket 233. VG. B3d. $.35

CERF, B.A. edt. *Pocket Book of Jokes.* 1945. Pocket 294. 1st prtg. VG. P7d. $5.00

CERF, B.A. edt. *Pocket Book of Modern American Plays.* 1942. Pocket 145. Nfi. VG. B5d. $6.00

CERF, B.A. edt. *Unexpected.* 1948. Bantam 502. NF. I1d. $8.00

CERRA, Gerda Ann. *Darker Heritage.* 1972. Lancer 75294. 2nd edn. VG. M6d. $6.50

CHABER, M.E. *Day It Rained Diamonds.* 1969. PB Library 63-231. My. VG+. B4d. $4.00

CHABER, M.E. *Lady Came To Kill.* Pocket 1240. VG. G5d. $5.50

CHABER, M.E. *So Dead the Rose.* 1960. Pocket 1274. c/J Allison. My. VG. B5d. $4.00

CHABER, M.E. *Splintered Man.* Perma M 3080. VG. B3d. $4.00

CHADWICK, Joseph. *Double Cross.* 1952. Gold Medal 245. We. VG. P6d. $3.50

CHADWICK, Joseph. *Golden Frame.* 1955. Gold Medal 493. 1st prtg. PBO. Cr. VG. P6d. $3.50

CHADWICK, Joseph. *Gunsmoke Reckoning.* Gold Medal 149. VG+. I1d. $8.00

CHADWICK, Joseph. *Man Chase.* 1961. Beacon 386. PBO. c/gga. VG+. B6d. $15.00

CHADWICK, Joseph. *No Land Is Free.* Avon F 162. We. VG. B5d. $2.50

CHADWICK, Joseph. *Rebel Raider.* 1954. Gold Medal 442. PBO. c/Ross. We. NF. B6d. $12.50

CHADWICK, Joseph. *Savage Breed.* 1959. Gold Medal 857. We. VG. P6d. $1.75

CHAFFIN, James. *Wolfer.* 1972. Belmont B 50-209. PBO. We. VG+. B6d. $6.00

CHALKER, Jack L. *And the Devil Will Drag You Under.* 1982. Ballantine 30504. 2nd prtg. SF. VG. W2d. $2.75

CHALKER, Jack L. *And the Devil Will Drag You Under.* 1979. Ballantine 27926. Fa. VG. P1d. $3.50

CHALKER, Jack L. *Cerberus: A Wolf in the Fold.* 1982. Ballantine 29371. SF. F. W2d. $3.75

CHALKER, Jack L. *Charon: A Dragon at the Gate.* 1982. Ballantine 29370. SF. VG+. W2d. $3.25

CHALKER, Jack L. *Demons of the Dancing Gods.* 1984. Ballantine 30893. SF. F. W2d. $3.50

CHALKER, Jack L. *Jungle of Stars.* 1976. Ballantine 25457. SF. F. P1d. $5.00

CHALKER, Jack L. *Jungle of Stars.* 1976. Ballantine 25457. 1st prtg. SF. VG+. R5d. $3.00

CHALKER, Jack L. *Lilith: A Snake In the Grass.* 1981. Ballantine 29369. SF. VG. W2d. $3.00

CHALKER, Jack L. *Lords of the Middle Dark.* 1986. Ballantine 32560. SF. G+. W2d. $2.75

CHALKER, Jack L. *Medusa: A Tiger by the Tail.* Ballantine 29372. SF. F. W2d. $4.25

CHALKER, Jack L. *Quest for the Well of Souls.* 1978. Ballantine 27702. SF. VG. W2d. $4.00

CHALKER, Jack L. *War of Shadow.* 1979. Ace 87195. SF. F. P1d. $6.00

CHALKER, Jack L. *Web of the Chozen.* 1978. Ballantine 27376. SF. VG+. P1d. $4.50

CHALLIS, George. *Bait & the Trap.* 1963. Ace G 527. Fa. VG. B4d. $2.00

CHALLON, David. *Suburban Affair.* 1960. Bedtime 961. Ad. VG. B5d. $5.00

CHALLON, David. *Thirst for Love.* Bedside 821. VG+. B3d. $5.50

CHAMBERLAIN, Anne. *Tall Dark Man.* 1963. Dell 8471. 1st prtg. c/Kalin. VG. P7d. $3.50

CHAMBERLAIN, Anne. *Tall Dark Man.* 1957. Dell 925. My. VG+. B4d. $4.00

CHAMBERLAIN, William. *Forced March at Loon Creek.* Ballantine U 1047. PBO. VG+. B3d. $5.00

CHAMBERS, A. edt. *Bumper Book of Ghost Stories.* 1976. Pan 25021. Ho. VG. P1d. $4.00

CHAMBERS, Dana. *Blonde Died First.* 1944. Handi-Book 22. 1st edn. PBO. scarce. VG+. B6a. $35.00

CHAMBERS, Dana. *Darling, This Is Death.* 1946. Handi-Book 51. 1st edn. PBO. scarce. VG+. B6a #77. $51.00

CHAMBERS, Dana. *Death Against Venus.* 1946. Handi-Book 57. VG+. I1d. $12.00

CHAMBERS, Dana. *Frightened Man.* 1944. Handi Book 28. 1st edn. PBO. rare. NF. B6a #75. $44.00

CHAMBERS, Dana. *Last Secret.* 1945. Handi-Book 34. SF. G+. P1d. $15.00

CHAMBERS, Dana. *She'll Be Dead.* Popular 238. VG+. I1d. $12.00

CHAMBERS, Dana. *Some Day I'll Kill.* 1949. Popular 177. 1st pb. My. VG. I1d. $12.00

CHAMBERS, Peter. *Armchair in Hell.* 1949. Dell 316. VG. P6d. $3.50

CHAMBERS, Peter. *Bullets to Baghdad.* Sexton Blake 450. VG. B3d. $7.50

CHAMBERS, Robert W. *King in Yellow.* 1965. Ace M 132. Ho. VG. P1d. $10.00

CHAMBERS, Whitman. *Come-On.* 1953. Pyramid 74. 1st pb. VG. B6d. $9.00

CHAMBERS, Whitman. *Dead Men Leave No Fingerprints.* Detective 28. VG. B3d. $4.50

CHAMBERS, Whitman. *In Savage Surrender.* Monarch 139. PBO. VG+. B3d. $6.00

CHAMBERS, Whitman. *Manhandled.* 1960. Monarch 156. Ad. VG. B5d. $6.00

CHAMBERS, Whitman. *Murder for a Wanton.* Detective 22. VG+. B3d. $5.00

CHAMBERS, Whitman. *Season for Love.* 1959. Monarch 122. 1st edn. c/Maguire: gga. F. F2d. $20.00

CHAMBLISS, W.C. *Boomerang!* 1945. Bantam 156. VG+. B3a. $25.80

CHANDLER, A. Bertram. *Alternate Maritans.* Ace M 129. PBO. VG+. B3d. $5.00

CHANDLER, A. Bertram. *Anarch Lords.* 1981. DAW 449. 1st edn. F. P9d. $2.00

CHANDLER, A. Bertram. *Big Black Mark.* 1975. DAW 139. 1st edn. F. P9d. $3.50

CHANDLER, A. Bertram. *Broken Cycle.* 1979. DAW UE 1496. SF. F. P1d. $6.00

CHANDLER, A. Bertram. *Broken Cycle.* 1979. DAW 360. 1st edn. NF. P9d. $2.00

CHANDLER, A. Bertram. *Coils of Time.* Bridbooks NN. 1st prtg. SF. VG. R5d. $2.75

CHANDLER, A. Bertram. *Coils of Time.* Priory 1058. SF. VG. P1d. $3.50

CHANDLER, A. Bertram. *Empress From Outer Space.* Ace M 129. VG+. B3d. $5.00

CHANDLER, A. Bertram. *Far Traveler.* 1979. DAW UW 1444. SF. F. P1d. $5.00

CHANDLER, A. Bertram. *Hamelin Plague.* 1963. Monarch 390. SF. VG+. P1d. $10.00

CHANDLER, A. Bertram. *Matilda's Stepchildren.* 1983. DAW UE 1845. SF. F. W2d. $5.25

CHANDLER, A. Bertram. *Rim of Space.* Bridbooks NN. 1st prtg. SF. VG. R5d. $3.50

CHANDLER, A. Bertram. *Rim of Space.* Priory 1057. SF. VG. P1d. $3.50

CHANDLER, A. Bertram. *Spartan Planet.* 1969. Dell 8174. SF. F. P1d. $6.00

CHANDLER, A. Bertram. *Spartan Planet.* 1969. Dell 8174. 1st prtg. VG. S1d. $3.50

CHANDLER, A. Bertram. *Star Courier.* 1977. DAW UY 1292. SF. F. P1d. $6.00

CHANDLER, A. Bertram. *To Keep the Ship.* 1978. DAW 295. 1st edn. SF. F. F2d. $10.00

CHANDLER, Evan. *Dying Light.* 1979. Signet J 8465. Ho. VG. P1d. $4.00

CHANDLER, Raymond. *Big Sleep.* Avon 38. c/Paul Stahr. VG. B6a #75. $91.00

CHANDLER, Raymond. *Big Sleep.* Avon 38. rare. VG. B6d. $225.00

CHANDLER, Raymond. *Farewell, My Lovely Little Sister.* Pocket 750. G. G5d. $5.50

CHANDLER, Raymond. *Finger Man & Others.* 1946. Avon Murder My 43. G+. B3a #20. $26.65

CHANDLER, Raymond. *Finger Man.* Ace H 309. rare UK edn. VG. B6a #77. $125.00

CHANDLER, Raymond. *Finger Man.* 1946. Avon Murder My 43. PBO. VG. B6d. $125.00

CHANDLER, Raymond. *Finger Man.* Avon 219. VG. B6d. $60.00

CHANDLER, Raymond. *Five Sinister Characters.* 1945. Avon Murder My 28. PBO. extremely scarce. VG+. B6a #79. $137.50

CHANDLER, Raymond. *High Window.* 1955. Pocket 2320. 3rd edn. c/gga. My. VG. B4d. $3.00

CHANDLER, Raymond. *High Window.* Pocket 320. G. G5d. $4.50

CHANDLER, Raymond. *High Window.* 1945. Pocket 320. c/E McKnight. VG. P6d. $15.00

CHANDLER, Raymond. *High Window.* 1945. Pocket 320. VG+. B3a #21. $16.20

CHANDLER, Raymond. *High Window.* Vintage V 141. My. F. W2d. $4.00

CHANDLER, Raymond. *Lady in the Lake.* 1959. Cardinal C 344. My. VG. B3d. $4.00

CHANDLER, Raymond. *Little Sister.* 1976. Ballantine 25727. 3rd prtg. My. F. W2d. $4.25

CHANDLER, Raymond. *Little Sister.* Pocket 750. G. G5d. $5.50

CHANDLER, Raymond. *Little Sister.* 1950. Pocket 750. 1st pb. My. VG. B6d. $18.00

CHANDLER, Raymond. *Long Goodbye.* Ballantine 02396. MTI. VG. M6d. $4.00

CHANDLER, Raymond. *Long Goodbye.* Pocket 1044. NF. G5d. $25.00

CHANDLER, Raymond. *Pearls Are a Nuisance.* 1953. Hamish-Hamilton NN. 1st prtg. VG. B3a #20. $44.00

CHANDLER, Raymond. *Pick-up on Noon Street.* Ace H 308. rare UK edn. VG. B6d. $125.00

CHANDLER, Raymond. *Pick-up on Noon Street.* 1977. Ballantine 25634. 3rd prtg. My. F. W2d. $4.25

CHANDLER, Raymond. *Playback.* 1977. Ballantine 27511. 2nd prtg. My. F. W2d. $4.25

CHANDLER, Raymond. *Playback.* 1980. Ballantine 28857. 4th prtg. My. VG+. R5d. $1.50

CHANDLER, Raymond. *Playback.* 1960. Cardinal C 375. 1st prtg. c/Ross: gga. VG. P7d. $9.00

CHANDLER, Raymond. *Simple Art of Murder.* 1964. Pocket 50086. 3rd edn. My. G+. B5d. $3.50

CHANDLER, Raymond. *Simple Art of Murder.* 1952. Pocket 916. 1st prtg. c/Meyers: gga. VG. P7d. $20.00

CHANDLER, Raymond. *Smart-Aleck Kill.* 1953. Hamish-Hamilton NN. PBO. VG. B6a #74. $220.00

CHANDLER, Raymond. *Smart-Aleck Kill.* 1953. Hamish-Hamilton NN. 1st prtg thus. VG+. B3a #22. $114.35

CHANDLER, Raymond. *Smart-Aleck Kill.* 1953. Hamish-Hamilton NN. 1st prtg. VG+. B3a #20. $73.85

CHANDLER, Raymond. *Trouble Is My Business.* Pocket 823. G+. G5d. $20.00

CHANDLER, Raymond. *5 Murderers.* 1944. Avon 63. VG. I1d. $40.00

CHANDLER & PARKER. *Poodle Springs.* 1990. Berkley 12343. 1st prtg. My. F. W2d. $4.50

CHANDLER. *Wild Horse Valley.* 1950s. Sierra 493. PBO. VG+. B6d. $7.50

CHANDLER/CHANDLER. *Alternate Martians/Empress of Outer Space.* Ace M 129. F. M1d. $10.00

CHANDLER/CHANDLER. *Alternate Martians/Empress of Outer Space.* 1965. Ace M 129. SF. VG+. B4d. $2.75

CHANDLER/CHANDLER. *Alternate Orbits/Dark Dimensions.* 1971. Ace 13783. SF. VG. P1d. $5.00

CHANDLER/CHANDLER. *Beyond the Galactic Rim/Ship From Outside.* 1963. Ace F 237. F. M1d. $12.00

CHANDLER/CHANDLER. *Beyond the Galactic/Ship From Outside.* 1963. Ace F 237. SF. VG+. B4d. $4.00

CHANDLER/CHANDLER. *Coil of Time/Into the Alternate Universe.* 1964. Ace M 107. 1st edn. SF. F. F2d. $12.00

CHANDLER/CHANDLER. *Coils of Time/Into the Alternate Universe.* Ace 114512. c/Rucker. SF. VG. B5d. $3.00

CHANDLER/CHANDLER. *Coils of Time/Into the Alternate Universe.* 1972. Ace 114512. F. P9d. $3.50

CHANDLER/CHANDLER. *Gateway to Never/Inheritors.* 1978. Ace 37063. SF. VG+. P1d. $5.50

CHANDLER/HIGH. *Contraband From Outerspace/Reality Forbidden.* 1967. Ace G 609. PBO. c/Freas: sgn. VG+. B3d. $7.00

CHANDLER/JANIFER. *Rim Gods/The High Hex.* 1969. Ace 72400. SF. VG. P1d. $5.50

CHANDLER/LORY. *Hard Way Up/Veiled World.* 1972. Ace 31755. PBO. c/K Freas. SF. VG+. B5d. $4.00

CHANDLER/PETAJA. *Space Mercenaries/Caves of Mars.* Ace M 133. PBO. c/sgn. VG+. B3d. $6.50

CHANDLER/PETAJA. *Space Mercenaries/Caves of Mars.* 1965. Ace M 133. 1st edn. c/Petaja: sgn. SF. F. F2d. $15.00

CHANDLER/REYNOLDS. *Nebula Alert/The Rival Rigellians.* 1967. Ace G 632. SF. F. P1d. $12.50

CHANDLER/RICHMOND. *Road to the Rim/Lost Millenium.* 1967. Ace H 29. 1st edn. SF. F. F2d. $10.00

CHANDLER/SIMAK. *Bring Back Yesterday/Trouble With Tycho.* 1961. Ace D 517. VG+. I1d. $7.00

CHANDLER/SIMAK. *Bring Back Yesterday/Trouble With Tycho.* 1961. Ace D 517. 1st edn. F. M1d. $15.00

CHANDLER/SIMAK. *Bring Back Yesterday/Trouble With Tycho.* 1961. Ace D 517. 1st prtg. SF. G. R5d. $2.00

CHANT, Joy. *High Kings.* 1985. Bantam. 1st pb. F. M1d. $5.00

CHANT, Joy. *Red Moons, Black Mountain.* 1971. Ballantine 02178. 1st edn. Ad/Fa. NF. M1d. $12.00

CHAPLIN, J.P. *Rumor Fear & the Madness of Crowds.* 1959. Ballantine 347K. PBO. NF. VG+. B5d. $5.50

CHAPMAN, Maristan. *Rogue's March.* Avon T 231. VG+. B3d. $4.50

CHAPMAN, Vera. *Blaedud the Birdman.* 1980. Avon 45070. Fa. VG+. P1d. $4.50

CHAPMAN, Vera. *King Arthur's Daughter.* 1978. Avon 38398. 1st prtg. SF. VG+. R5d. $1.75

CHARBONNEAU, Louis. *Barrier World.* 1970. Lancer 74687. SF. VG. P1d. $4.50

CHARBONNEAU, Louis. *Corpus Earthling.* 1960. Zenith ZB 40. 1st edn. F. M1d. $10.00

CHARBONNEAU, Louis. *Down to Earth.* 1967. Bantam 3442. 1st edn. SF. F. F2d. $12.00

CHARBONNEAU, Louis. *No Place on Earth.* 1959. Crest S 342. 1st pb. F. M1d. $12.00

CHARBONNEAU, Louis. *Psychedelic-40.* 1965. Bantam F 2929. SF. VG+. P1d. $8.00

CHARBONNEAU, Louis. *Sensitives.* 1968. Bantam H 3759. SF. VG+. P1d. $7.50

CHARBONNEAU, Louis. *Sentinel Stars.* 1963. Bantam J2686. SF. NF. B5d. $4.00

CHARBONNEAU, Louis. *Time of Desire.* 1960. Pyramid G 509. Fi. G+. P1d. $5.00

CHARBONNEAU, Louis. *Way Out.* 1967. Banner B 50-101. My. VG. P1d. $7.50

CHARKIN, Paul. *Living Gem.* 1963. Digit R 782. SF. G+. P1d. $4.50

CHARLES, B. *Mouth Trick.* Barclay 7738. VG+. B3d. $4.50

CHARLES, Neil. *Land of Esa.* 1952. Curtis NN. PBO. c/gga. scarce. SF. VG+. B6a #79. $55.00

CHARLES, Robert. *Clash of Hawks.* 1975. Pinnacle 20686. SF/My. VC. P1d. $3.50

CHARLES, Robert. *Cobra Strike.* 1980. Pinnacle 40089. 1st prtg. My. VG+. W2d. $3.50

CHARNAS, S.M. *Motherlines.* 1979. Berkley 04157. 1st pb. NF. B6d. $3.00

CHARNAS, Suzy. *Walk to the End of the World.* 1977. Ballantine 25661. 3rd prtg. SF. G. W2d. $2.25

CHARNAS, Suzy. *Walk to the End of the World.* 1978. Berkley 04239. SF. G. W2d. $2.50

CHARNWOOD, Lord. *Abraham Lincoln.* 1941. Pocket 19. 18th edn. Nfi. VG. B5d. $3.00

CHARROUX, Robert. *Forgotten Worlds.* 1973. Popular 00190. Nfi. VG. P1d. $4.00

CHARROUX, Robert. *Mysteries of the Andes.* 1977. Avon 33779. Nfi. VG. P1d. $3.50

CHARROUX, Robert. *One-Hundred Thousand Years of Man's Unknown History.* 1971. Berkley N 1964. Nfi. VG. P1d. $4.00

CHARTERIS, Leslie *Saint & Mr Teal.* Avon 629. My. VG. B5d. $5.00

CHARTERIS, Leslie. *Alias the Saint.* Avon 818. My. VG+. B5d. $6.00

CHARTERIS, Leslie. *Alias the Saint.* Bonded 5. VG+. B3d. $7.00

CHARTERIS, Leslie. *Alias the Saint.* Saint Novel K 110. 2nd edn. c/Roger Moore. My. VG. B4d. $6.00

CHARTERIS, Leslie. *Avenging Saint.* Avon 147. VG. B3d. $6.00

CHARTERIS, Leslie. *Avenging Saint.* 1953. Avon 518. 1st prtg. c/gga. VG. P7d. $6.00

CHARTERIS, Leslie. *Avenging Saint.* Saint Novel K 104. 1st prtg. TVTI. VG. R5d. $6.75

CHARTERIS, Leslie. *Brighter Buccaneer.* 1970. Pan O2412. 4th edn. My. G+. B5d. $3.00

CHARTERIS, Leslie. *Brighter Buccaneer.* Saint Novel K 112. TVTI. c/R Moore. My. G+. B5d. $4.00

CHARTERIS, Leslie. *Concerning the Saint.* 1958. Avon 834. c/gga. My. VG. B4d. $4.00

CHARTERIS, Leslie. *Death Stops at a Tourist Camp.* Saint My Library. C. C5d. $7.50

CHARTERIS, Leslie. *Enter the Saint.* 1980. Charter 20727. My. G+. W2d. $3.00

CHARTERIS, Leslie. *Enter the Saint.* 1963. Pan G 615. 1st pb. My. VG+. B5d. $6.00

CHARTERIS, Leslie. *Enter the Saint.* 1966. Pan X 437. My. VG. B5d. $4.00

CHARTERIS, Leslie. *Enter the Saint.* Pocket 257. VG. B3d. $4.00

CHARTERIS, Leslie. *Featuring the Saint.* Avon 803. My. G+. B5d. $3.00

CHARTERIS, Leslie. *Featuring the Saint.* 1964. Hodder 140. My. C+. B5d. $4.00

CHARTERIS, Leslie. *Featuring the Saint.* Saint Novel K 109. TVTI. c/Roger Moore. My. VG. B5d. $6.50

CHARTERIS, Leslie. *Paging the Saint.* Bonded 7. VG. B3d. $4.00

CHARTERIS, Leslie. *Saint & Mr Teal.* Pan G 217. 1st pb. reprint. My. VG+. B6d. $6.00

CHARTERIS, Leslie. *Saint & Mr Teal.* Saint Novel K 114. PBO. TVTI. c/Roger Moore. VG. P6d. $3.50

CHARTERIS, Leslie. *Saint & the Ace of Knaves.* 1955. Avon 663. 1st prtg. c/gga. VG. P7d. $6.00

CHARTERIS, Leslie. *Saint & the Fiction Makers.* 1968. Curtis 501-07199-075. TVTI. VG. P6d. $3.00

CHARTERIS, Leslie. *Saint & the Last Hero.* Avon 544. My. G+. W2d. $4.50

CHARTERIS, Leslie. *Saint Around the World.* Perma M 3103. NF. B3d. $5.00

CHARTERIS, Leslie. *Saint Around the World.* 1958. Perma M 3103. c/J Meese. My. VG. B5d. $4.00

CHARTERIS, Leslie. *Saint at the Thieves' Picnic.* 1951. Avon 347. VG. B3d. $6.00

CHARTERIS, Leslie. *Saint at the Thieves' Picnic.* Avon 440. VG. B3d. $5.00

CHARTERIS, Leslie. *Saint Cleans Up.* Avon 848. My. VG+. B5d. $5.50

CHARTERIS, Leslie. *Saint Closes the Case.* Saint Novel K 103. PBO. TVTI. c/Roger Moore. VG. P6d. $3.00

CHARTERIS, Leslie. *Saint Errant.* 1954. Avon 588. 1st prtg. c/gga. VG+. P7d. $7.50

CHARTERIS, Leslie. *Saint Goes On.* Avon 34. VG. B3d. $5.00

CHARTERIS, Leslie. *Saint Goes On.* 1966. Mac-Fadden 60-265. 1st prtg. VG. P7d. $4.00

CHARTERIS, Leslie. *Saint Goes West.* 1948. Avon 130. VG. B3d. $6.00

CHARTERIS, Leslie. *Saint Goes West.* Avon 420. VG. B3d. $5.00

CHARTERIS, Leslie. *Saint in Action.* Avon 463. VG. B3d. $7.00

CHARTERIS, Leslie. *Saint in England.* Avon T 250. VG+. B3d. $4.50

CHARTERIS, Leslie. *Saint in Europe.* 1954. Avon 611. c/gga. My. G+. B4d. $2.00

CHARTERIS, Leslie. *Saint in Miami.* 1942. Th Novel Classic 16. 1st pb. My. VG. B6d. $6.00

CHARTERIS, Leslie. *Saint in New York.* Avon 321. VG+. B3d. $8.00

CHARTERIS, Leslie. *Saint in New York.* Avon 44. VG. B3d. $6.00

CHARTERIS, Leslie. *Saint Intervenes.* Avon 71. VG. B3d. $6.00

CHARTERIS, Leslie. *Saint Meets His Match.* Bonded 14. VG+. B3d. $7.00

CHARTERIS, Leslie. *Saint Meets His Match.* Saint Novel K 108. TVTI. c/R Moore. My. G+. B5d. $4.00

CHARTERIS, Leslie. *Saint on Guard.* Avon 827. VC. B3d. $3.50

CHARTERIS, Leslie. *Saint on Guard.* 1968. Hodder 1124. 5th edn. My. VG. B5d. $4.00

CHARTERIS, Leslie. *Saint on the Spanish Main.* 1965. Pan X 436. 5th edn. My. VG+. B5d. $5.00

CHARTERIS, Leslie. *Saint on TV.* 1967. Curtis 07200. My. VG+. B4d. $7.00

CHARTERIS, Leslie. *Saint on TV.* Pan O2590. My. VG. B5d. $4.00

CHARTERIS, Leslie. *Saint Overboard.* 1943. Popular NN 1. 1st edn. PBO. c/Hoffman. scarce. VG. B6a. $55.00

CHARTERIS, Leslie. *Saint Sees It Through.* Avon 341. VG. B3d. $5.00

CHARTERIS, Leslie. *Saint Sees It Through.* 1955. Avon 619. My. G+. B4d. $2.00

CHARTERIS, Leslie. *Saint Sees It Through.* 1967. Hodder 68. 2nd edn. My. VG. B5d. $4.00

CHARTERIS, Leslie. *Saint Sees It Through.* Pan G 438. VG. B3d. $6.00

CHARTERIS, Leslie. *Saint Sees It Through.* Saint Novel K 102. c/Moore & Eaton: photo. My. VG. B4d. $6.00

CHARTERIS, Leslie. *Saint Steps In.* Saint Novel K 101. 2nd edn. My. VG+. B4d. $6.00

CHARTERIS, Leslie. *Saint to the Rescue.* 1961. Perma M 4196. My. VG+. B4d. $5.00

CHARTERIS, Leslie. *Saint Vs Scotland Yard.* Saint Novel K 113. PBO. TVTI. c/Roger Moore. VG. P6d. $3.00

CHARTERIS, Leslie. *Saint's Choice Volume 1.* Bonded 4. VG. B3d. $5.50

CHARTERIS, Leslie. *Saint's Choice Volume 2.* Bonded 6. VG. B3d. $4.50

CHARTERIS, Leslie. *Senor Saint.* 1971. Pan NN. 4th edn. My. G+. B5d. $3.00

CHARTERIS, Leslie. *Senor Saint.* 1960. Pocket 6004. My. VG+. B5d. $4.00

CHARTERIS, Leslie. *Stairway to Murder.* Saint My Library. VG. G5d. $10.00

CHARTERIS, Leslie. *Thanks to the Saint.* Pocket 1233. NF. B3d. $4.00

CHARTERIS, Leslie. *Trust the Saint.* 1966. MacFadden 60-253. 1st prtg. VG. P7d. $4.00

CHASE, Allan. *Shadow of a Hero.* 1951. Popular 335. My. VG+. B4d. $12.00

CHASE, Allan. *Wife Traders.* 1974. Liverpool TNS 595. Ad. VG+. B5d. $4.50

CHASE, Borden. *Lone Star.* 1952. Gold Medal 236. PBO. c/Barye. We. VG+. B6d. $10.00

CHASE, Borden. *Red River.* 1948. Bantam 205. 1st edn. PBO. MTI. c/John Wayne: photo. scarce. F. F2d. $25.00

CHASE, Bordon. *Red River.* 1948. Bantam 205. MTI. NF. B4d. $15.00

CHASE, Glen. *All New Cherry Delight: Where the Action Is.* 1977. Leisure 0-8439-0495-X. PBO. VG. P6d. $4.00

CHASE, Glen. *Greek Fire.* 1977. Leisure 462DK. SF/My. VG. P1d. $5.00

CHASE, Glen. *Made in Japan.* 1974. Leisure 423ZK. PBO. VG. P6d. $3.00

CHASE, Ilka. *In Bed We Cry.* 1947. Avon 140. Fi. B5d. $5.00

CHASE, James Hadley. *Cade.* Pocket 75736. NF. G5d. $3.75

CHASE, James Hadley. *Case of the Strangled Starlet.* 1958. Signet 1586. c/Robert Schulz: gga. VG. P6d. $3.50

CHASE, James Hadley. *Dead Ringer.* Ace 14150. My. NF. B5d. $6.00

CHASE, James Hadley. *Double Shuffle.* Signet 1112. 1st US edn. My. VG. B6d. $6.00

CHASE, James Hadley. *I Would Rather Stay Poor.* 1974. Pocket 77773. c/photo. My. VG. P6d. $3.00

CHASE, James Hadley. *Marijuana Mob.* 1952. Eton 116. 1st edn. PBO. scarce. My. VG. B6a. $55.00

CHASE, James Hadley. *Too Dangerous To Be Free.* 1952. Avon A 436. My. G+. B5d. $5.00

CHASE, James Hadley. *Twelve Chinks & a Woman.* Avon Monthly Novel NN. extremely scarce. VG. B6a #79. $43.00

CHASE, James Hadley. *Twelve Chinks & a Woman.* Avon 485. VG. I1d. $12.00

CHASE, James Hadley. *Twelve Chinks & a Woman.* Harlequin 160. rare. VG+. B6a #79. $95.00

CHASE, James Hadley. *Twelve Chinks & a Woman.* 1960. Novel Library 37. VG. B3a #24. $15.00

CHASE, James Hadley. *World in My Pocket.* 1962. Popular K 10. MTI. c/Rod Steiger: photo. VG. B4d. $3.00

CHASE, James Hadley. *You Never Know With Women.* Harlequin 206. VG. I1d. $20.00

CHASE, Mary Ellen. *Abby Aldrich Rockefeller.* 1966. Avon AAR 1. Nfi. VG. B5d. $2.50

CHASE, Mary Ellen. *Goodly Heritage.* 1945. Avon 73. 1st pb. VG. B6d. $7.50

CHASE, Nicholas. *Locksley.* 1984. Penguin. 1st pb. F. M1d. $4.00

CHASE, Robert R. *Game of Fox & Lion.* 1986. Ballantine. 1st edn. F. M1d. $5.00

CHATTERTON, Ruth. *Homeward Borne.* 1951. Pocket 830. c/A Sarnoff. Fi. NF. I1d. $5.00

CHAYEFSKI & HEDRIN. *Network.* 1976. Pocket 80767. 1st prtg. MTI. VG+. R5d. $2.25

CHAYEFSKY, Paddy. *Batchelor Party.* 1957. Signet S 1385. MTI. VG+. B4d. $6.00

CHEETHAM, Anthony edt. *Science Against Man.* 1970. Avon V 2374. SF. VG. P1d. $4.50

CHEEVER, John. *Enormous Radio.* 1958. Berkley G 119. SF. G+. P1d. $5.50

CHERRYH, C.J. *Brothers of Earth.* 1976. DAW UW 1257. SF. VG. P1d. $3.50

CHERRYH, C.J. *Chanur's Venture.* 1985. DAW 609. NF. P9d. $2.00

CHERRYH, C.J. *Cuckoo's Egg.* 1985. DAW 646. F. P9d. $3.00

CHERRYH, C.J. *Exile's Gate.* 1988. DAW. 1st edn. F. M1d. $7.00

CHERRYH, C.J. *Faded Sun: Kesrith.* 1978. DAW 300. 1st edn. VG. P9d. $1.50

CHERRYH, C.J. *Faded Sun: Shon'Jir.* 1979. DAW UJ 1453. SF. F. P1d. $6.00

CHERRYH, C.J. *Fires of Azeroth.* 1979. DAW UJ 1466. SF. G+. P1d. $2.75

CHERRYH, C.J. *Gate of Ivrel.* 1977. Orbit 7945. SF. VG. P1d. $4.00

CHERRYH, C.J. *Hestia.* 1979. DAW UJ 1488. SF. VG. P1d. $3.50

CHERRYH, C.J. *Hestia.* 1979. DAW 354. VG. P9d. $1.50

CHERRYH, C.J. *Legions of Hell.* 1987. Baen 65653. 1st prtg. SF. VG+. W2d. $3.50

CHERRYH, C.J. *Port Eternity.* 1982. DAW 500. F. P9d. $3.00

CHERRYH, C.J. *Pride of Chanur.* 1982. DAW 464. NF. P9d. $2.50

CHERRYH, C.J. *Voyager in Night.* 1984. DAW 573. G. P9d. $1.00

CHERRYH, C.J. *Wave Without a Shore.* 1981. DAW 444. SF. VG. B5d. $3.00

CHERRYH, C.J. *Well of Shiuan.* 1978. DAW UJ 1371. SF. VG. P1d. $3.50

CHESBRO, George C. *Affair of Sorcerers.* 1979. Signet E 9243. SF/My. VG. P1d. $4.00

CHESBRO, George C. *City of Whispering Stone.* 1979. Signet J 8812. SF/My. VG. P1d. $5.00

CHESBRO, George C. *Shadow of a Broken Man.* 1978. Signet J 8114. SF/My. G+. P1d. $2.75

CHESIRE, G. *Thunder on Mountain.* Curtis 6020. VG+. B3d. $4.50

CHESSER, Eustace. *Love Without Fear.* 1957. Signet 751. NF. VG+. B5d. $4.00

CHESSER, Eustace. *Unmarried Love.* 1966. Pocket 75151. Nfi. VG. B5d. $2.50

CHESSMAN, Caryl. *Cell 2455, Death Row.* Perma M 4063. VG+. B3d. $5.50

CHESSMAN, Caryl. *Kid Was a Killer.* 1960. Gold Medal 1002. 1st edn. F. F2d. $10.00

CHESSMAN, Caryl. *Kid Was a Killer.* Gold Medal 463. VG. B3d. $7.00

CHESTER, G. *Mystery of Double Burglary.* Sexton Blake 128. VG. B3d. $10.00

CHESTER, William L. *Hawk of the Wilderness.* 1966. Ace G 586. 1st pb. SF. NF. B6d. $9.00

CHESTER, William L. *Kioga of the Wilderness.* 1976. DAW UW 1253. SF. G+. P1d. $2.75

CHESTER, William L. *One Against a Wilderness.* 1977. DAW 228. 1st edn. SF. F. F2d. $12.00

CHESTERTON, G.K. *Adventures of Father Brown.* 1961. Dell F 133. 1st prtg. My. VG. R5d. $2.75

CHESTERTON, G.K. *Amazing Adventures of Father Brown.* Dell 819. c/D Gillon. My. VG. B5d. $4.00

CHESTERTON, G.K. *Man Who Was Thursday.* 1971. Ballantine 02305. Fa. F. P1d. $75.00

CHESTERTON, G.K. *Man Who Was Thursday.* 1938. Penguin 95. 4th edn. dust jacket. Fa. VG. P1d. $22.50

CHESTERTON, G.K. *Pocket Book of Father Brown.* 1943. Pocket 236. 1st prtg. PBO. VG. P7d. $9.00

CHESTERTON, G.K. *Secret of Father Brown & Other Stories.* Popular 153. VG. B3d. $4.50

CHESTERTON, G.K. *Ten Adventures of Father Brown.* Dell F 133. VG+. G5d. $4.50

CHESTNUT, Robert. *Syndicate.* 1960. Newsstand 513. Ad. VG B5d. $4.00

CHETWYND-HAYES, R. *Dominique.* 1979. Belmont Tower 51345. Ho. VG. P1d. $4.50

CHETWYND-HAYES, R. *Gaslight Tales of Terror.* 1976. Fontana 4149. Ho. VG. P1d. $4.50

CHETWYND-HAYES, R. *Monster Club.* 1976. New English 25586. Ho. VG. P1d. $7.50

CHETWYND-HAYES, R. *Tales of Terror From Outer Space.* 1976. Fontana 3960. Ho. VG. P1d. $4.50

CHEVALLIER, Gabriel. *Scandals of Clochmerle.* 1948. Bantam 141. 1st prtg. c/Kautman: gga. Fa. VG+. B4d/P7d. $5.00

CHEYNEY, Peter. *Calling Mr Callaghan.* Four Square 637. VG+. B3d. $6.00

CHEYNEY, Peter. *Case of the Dark Hero.* Avon 734. My. VG. B5d. $4.00

CHEYNEY, Peter. *Cocktails & the Killer.* Avon 797. VG. G5d. $5.00

CHEYNEY, Peter. *Cocktails & the Killer.* 1957. Avon 797. 1st pb. My. NF. B6d. $12.50

CHEYNEY, Peter. *Dames Don't Care.* Pan G 352. VG. B3d. $7.50

CHEYNEY, Peter. *Dark Interlude.* Bantam 730. VG. I1d. $5.00

CHEYNEY, Peter. *Dark Street Murders.* Avon 764. 1st prtg. My. G+. R5d. $2.75

CHEYNEY, Peter. *Dark Street Murders.* 1946. Avon 93. 1st prtg. My. VG. R5d. $9.00

CHEYNEY, Peter. *Double Sin.* Pocket 6144. G. G5d. $3.50

CHEYNEY, Peter. *Farewell to the Admiral.* Avon 30 Digest 45. My. VG+. B4d. $9.00

CHEYNEY, Peter. *G-Man at the Yard.* Four Square 658. VG+. B3d. $7.00

CHEYNEY, Peter. *Hickory Dickory Death.* Pocket 1151. VG+. G5d. $3.00

CHEYNEY, Peter. *I'll Bring Her Back.* Eton 115. VG+. B3d. $6.50

CHEYNEY, Peter. *London Spy Murders.* 1944. Avon 49. My. VG. B3d. $7.50

CHEYNEY, Peter. *London Spy Murders.* 1944. Avon 49. 1st pb. My. VG+. B6d. $12.50

CHEYNEY, Peter. *Man Nobody Saw.* 1956. Avon 712. c/E Kinstler. My. VG. B5d. $5.00

CHEYNEY, Peter. *Mister Caution Mister Callaghan.* Fontana. VG. G5d. $3.00

CHEYNEY, Peter. *Poison Ivy.* Fontana 375. VG+. B3d. $7.50

CHEYNEY, Peter. *Set-Up for Murder.* 1950. Pyramid 16. 1st pb. My. VG. B6d. $7.50

CHEYNEY, Peter. *Sinister Errand.* 1947. Avon 114. 1st prtg. My. VG. R5d. $9.00

CHEYNEY, Peter. *Sinister Murders.* Avon 776. VG. G5d. $5.00

CHEYNEY, Peter. *Sparkling Cyanide.* White Circle 179C. VG. G5d. $6.50

CHEYNEY, Peter. *Stars Are Dark.* Pan 40. VG+. B3d. $6.00

CHEYNEY, Peter. *Sweetheart of the Razors.* 1958. Ace H 226. VG. B3d. $8.50

CHEYNEY, Peter. *Terrible Night.* Avon T 365. VG+. G5d. $4.00

CHEYNEY, Peter. *Try Anything Twice.* Fontana 325. VG. B3d. $5.00

CHICHESTER, F. edt. *Along the Clipper Way.* 1966. Pan T 40. NF. B3d. $8.50

CHIDSEY, D.B. *Buccaneer's Blade.* 1959. Ace D 410. 1st edn. SF. F. F2d. $13.00

CHIDSEY, D.B. *Captain Adam.* Avon T 81. VG. B3d. $3.50

CHIDSEY, D.B. *Captain Bashful.* Graphic G 214. VG+. B3d. $5.50

CHIDSEY, D.B. *Captain Crossbones.* Ace D 318. VG+. B3d. $5.00

CHIDSEY, D.B. *Flaming Island.* 1959. Ace D 394. 1st edn. SF. NF. F2d. $12.00

CHIDSEY, D.B. *His Majesty's Highwayman.* Perma M 4029. VG. B3d. $4.00

CHIDSEY, D.B. *Pipes Are Calling.* Ace D 364. VG. B6d. $4.00

CHIDSEY, D.B. *Singapore Passage.* Dell 1st Edn 107. VG. B3d. $4.00

CHILD, Lincoln. *Tales of the Dark #2.* 1987. St Martins 90769. VG. P9d. $1.50

CHILD, Lincoln. *Tales of the Dark #3.* 1988. St Martins 90539. VG. P9d. $1.50

CHILSON, Robert. *As the Curtain Falls.* 1974. DAW 98. PBO. c/H Ulrich & U Oster-Walder. SF. VG. B5d. $3.00

CHILSON, Robert. *Star-Crowned Kings.* 1975. DAW UY 1190. SF. VG. P1d. $3.50

CHILTON, Charles. *Journey Into Space.* 1958. Pan 437. SF. G+. B5d. $7.50

CHILTON, Charles. *Red Planet.* 1960. Pan G 274. from the BBC radio serial. SF. VG. P1d. $7.50

CHILTON, Charles. *World in Peril.* 1962. Pan G 579. from the BBC radio serial. SF. VG. P1d. $7.50

CHINNOCK, Frank W. *Quiz Show Quiz Book.* 1977. Berkley 03542. TVTI. F. P1d. $8.50

CHRISTOPHER, John. *No Blade of Grass.* 1967. Avon S 288. SF. VG+. B4d. $3.00

CHITTENDEN, F.A. *Strange Welcome.* Boardman 165. c/McLoughlin. VG. B3d. $8.00

CHOISY, Maryse. *Month Among the Girls.* 1960. Pyramid G 557. c/photo. Fi. VG. B5d. $4.00

CHORON, S. *National Lampoon's.* 1982. Dell 16717. 1st prtg. VG. R5d. $1.50

CHRISTIAN, James L. edt. *Extraterrestrial Intelligence.* Prometheus 064. 2nd edn. Nfi. VG. P1d. $6.00

CHRISTIAN, Kit. *Death & Bitters.* 1944. De Novel Classic 36. 1st pb. My. VG. B6d. $7.00

CHRISTIAN, Paula. *Edge of Twilight.* 1978. Timely Books 931328-00-4. 1st edn. PBO. c/sgn. F. F2d. $15.00

CHRISTIE, Agatha. *ABC Murders.* 1941. Pocket 88. 1st edn. PBO. scarce. NF. B6a #75. $53.50

CHRISTIE, Agatha. *ABC Murders.* 1941. Pocket 88. 1st prtg. My. NF. F2d. $20.00

CHRISTIE, Agatha. *Agatha Christie, an Autobiography.* 1978. Ballantine 27646. 1st prtg. VG. P7d. $3.50

CHRISTIE, Agatha. *Appointment With Death.* 1944. Bestseller B 58. F. F2d. $7.00

CHRISTIE, Agatha. *Appointment With Death*. 1958. Dell D 236. 1st prtg. My. VG. R5d. $2.50

CHRISTIE, Agatha. *Big Four*. 1964. Avon G 1223. My. VG+. B4d. $3.50

CHRISTIE, Agatha. *Big Four*. 1950. Avon 245. 1st prtg. My. G. R5d. $2.50

CHRISTIE, Agatha. *Big Four*. Avon 3. G+. B3d. $4.00

CHRISTIE, Agatha. *Big Four*. 1956. Avon 690. 1st prtg. c/Kinstler: gga. G+. P7d. $4.00

CHRISTIE, Agatha. *Body in the Library*. Pocket 341. VG+. B3d/I1d. $6.00

CHRISTIE, Agatha. *Boomerang Clue*. Dell 46. 1st prtg. My. VG. R5d. $11.00

CHRISTIE, Agatha. *Boomerang Clue*. 1944. Dell 46. NF. F2d. $15.00

CHRISTIE, Agatha. *Boomerang Clue*. Dell 664. VG. I1d. $3.00

CHRISTIE, Agatha. *Cards on the Table*. Dell 293. VG. B3d. $5.00

CHRISTIE, Agatha. *Caribbean Mystery*. Pocket 50449. VG. B3d. $4.00

CHRISTIE, Agatha. *Case of the Moving Finger*. Avon 636. c/gga. F. F2d. $6.00

CHRISTIE, Agatha. *Crooked House*. Pocket 753. VG+. B3d. $5.00

CHRISTIE, Agatha. *Dead Man's Folly*. 1961. Cardinal C 420. 1st prtg. My. VG+. R5d. $2.50

CHRISTIE, Agatha. *Dead Man's Mirror*. 1958. Dell D 235. 1st prtg. My. VG. R5d. $2.50

CHRISTIE, Agatha. *Death Comes As the End*. 1959. Cardinal C 335. 1st prtg. My. VG+. R5d. $2.50

CHRISTIE, Agatha. *Death in the Air*. 1951. Avon 379. 1st prtg. c/Hilbert: gga. G+. P7d. $5.00

CHRISTIE, Agatha. *Death in the Air*. Avon 658. VG. B3d. $4.00

CHRISTIE, Agatha. *Death in the Air*. Avon 89. VG. B3d. $6.50

CHRISTIE, Agatha. *Death in the Air*. 1943. Jonathan Press My J 10. F. F2d. $5.00

CHRISTIE, Agatha. *Death on the Nile*. Avon T 149. reprint. VG. B6d. $7.00

CHRISTIE, Agatha. *Death on the Nile*. Avon T 401. My. VG. B5d. $3.00

CHRISTIE, Agatha. *Death on the Nile*. Avon 46. VG. I1d. $10.00

CHRISTIE, Agatha. *Death on the Nile*. 1944. Avon 46. 1st prtg. My. NF. F2d. $20.00

CHRISTIE, Agatha. *Double Sin*. 1964. Dell 2144. 1st prtg. My. VG. R5d. $1.75

CHRISTIE, Agatha. *Double Sin*. Pocket 6144. VG. B3d. $3.50

CHRISTIE, Agatha. *Easy To Kill*. 1945. Pocket 319. 1st prtg. My. F. F2d. $15.00

CHRISTIE, Agatha. *Easy To Kill*. 1965. Pocket 50441. My. VG+. B5d. $3.50

CHRISTIE, Agatha. *Funerals Are Fatal*. 1961. Cardinal C 421. 1st prtg. My. VG. R5d. $1.75

CHRISTIE, Agatha. *Funerals Are Fatal*. Pocket 1003. 4th prtg. VG+. B3d. $4.50

CHRISTIE, Agatha. *Hickory Dickory Death*. 1961. Cardinal C 422. 1st prtg. My. VG. R5d. $2.00

CHRISTIE, Agatha. *Hickory Dickory Death*. Pocket 1151. VG+. G5d. $3.50

CHRISTIE, Agatha. *Holiday for Murder*. 1947. Avon 124. VG. B3d. $6.00

CHRISTIE, Agatha. *Holiday for Murder*. 1947. Avon 124. 1st prtg. My. F. F2d. $18.00

CHRISTIE, Agatha. *Hollow*. 1948. Pocket 485. My. VG+. B4d. $9.00

CHRISTIE, Agatha. *Labors of Hercules*. 1959. Dell D 305. 1st prtg. My. VG. R5d. $2.50

CHRISTIE, Agatha. *Labors of Hercules*. 1964. Dell 4620. 1st prtg. My. VG. R5d. $1.75

CHRISTIE, Agatha. *Labors of Hercules*. Dell 491. VG. B3d. $4.00

CHRISTIE, Agatha. *Man in the Brown Suit*. 1949. Dell 319. 1st prtg. My. F. F2d. $10.00

CHRISTIE, Agatha. *Man in the Brown Suit*. Harlequin 337. VG. B3d. $7.50

CHRISTIE, Agatha. *Man in the Brown Suit*. 1955. Harlequin 337. VG. B3a #21. $12.00

CHRISTIE, Agatha. *Mr Parker Pyne, Detective*. Dell R 109. reprint. VG+. B3d. $4.50

CHRISTIE, Agatha. *Mr Parker Pyne, Detective*. Dell 961. VG. B3d. $4.00

CHRISTIE, Agatha. *Mrs McGinty's Dead*. 1953. Pocket 956. c/R Shulz. My. VG. B5d/G5d/I1d. $5.00

CHRISTIE, Agatha. *Mrs McGinty's Dead*. 1953. Pocket 956. 1st prtg. My. F. F2d. $8.00

CHRISTIE, Agatha. *Murder After Hours*. Dell 753. c/G Foxley. My. VG. G5d. $3.00

CHRISTIE, Agatha. *Murder at Hazelmoor*. 1950. Dell 391. VG+. B3d. $7.00

CHRISTIE, Agatha. *Murder at Hazelmoor*. 1950. Dell 391. 1st pb. My. VG. B6d. $9.00

CHRISTIE, Agatha. *Murder at the Vicarage*. Dell R 106. reprint. VG+. B3d. $4.50

CHRISTIE, Agatha. *Murder at the Vicarage*. Dell 226. 1st prtg. My. VG+. R5d. $8.00

CHRISTIE, Agatha. *Murder in Mesopotamia*. 1947. Dell 145. 1st edn. PBO. c/Frederiksen. VG+. B6a #75. $33.00

CHRISTIE, Agatha. *Murder in Mesopotamia*. 1947. Dell 145. 1st edn. PBO. c/Frederiksen. VG+. B6d. $25.00

CHRISTIE, Agatha. *Murder in Mesopotamia*. Dell 805. VG. I1d. $5.00

CHRISTIE, Agatha. *Murder in Three Acts*. Avon 316. scarce. NF. B6a #76. $49.00

CHRISTIE, Agatha. *Murder in Three Acts*. Avon 316. VG+. B6d. $30.00

CHRISTIE, Agatha. *Murder in Three Acts*. Avon 61. VG. I1d. $20.00

CHRISTIE, Agatha. *Murder Is Announced*. 1951. Pocket 820. c/Frank McCarthy: gga. VG. P6d. $1.50

CHRISTIE, Agatha. *Murder of Roger Ackroyd*. Pocket 5. 5th prtg. VG. B3d. $6.00

CHRISTIE, Agatha. *Murder on the Links*. 1959. Dell D 288. My. VG+. B4d. $3.50

CHRISTIE, Agatha. *Murder on the Links*. 1950. Dell 454. 1st prtg. My. F. F2d. $15.00

CHRISTIE, Agatha. *Murder on the Links*. Harlequin 441. VG. B3d. $8.00

CHRISTIE, Agatha. *Murder With Mirrors*. 1954. Pocket 1021. c/A Sussman. My. VG. B5d. $5.00

CHRISTIE, Agatha. *Mysterious Affair at Styles*. 1951. Avon 312. c/gga. My. VG+. B3d. $5.50

CHRISTIE, Agatha. *Mysterious Affair at Styles*. 1945. Avon 75. VG. B6d. $6.00

CHRISTIE, Agatha. *Mysterious Affair at Styles*. 1959. Pan G 112. 5th edn. My. VG. B5d. $4.50

CHRISTIE, Agatha. *Mysterious Mr Quin*. Bestseller Library B 9. SF/My. VG. P1d. $20.00

CHRISTIE, Agatha. *Mysterious Mr Quin*. Dell 570. c/R Jones. My. VG. B5d. $4.00

CHRISTIE, Agatha. *Mystery of the Blue Train*. 1956. Pocket 2038. 15th edn. My. VG. B5d. $5.00

CHRISTIE, Agatha. *N or M?* 1947. Dell 187. VG+. I1d. $9.00

CHRISTIE, Agatha. *N or M?* 1947. Dell 187. 1st prtg. My. F. F2d. $15.00

CHRISTIE, Agatha. *N or M?* Dell 6254. VG+. B3d. $4.50

CHRISTIE, Agatha. *N or M?* 1944. Jonathan Press My J 13. F. F2d. $5.00

CHRISTIE, Agatha. *Ordeal by Innocence.* 1968. Pocket 50461. 3rd edn. My. VG+. B5d. $3.50

CHRISTIE, Agatha. *Overdose of Death.* 1964. Dell 6780. 1st prtg. My. G+. R5d. $1.00

CHRISTIE, Agatha. *Overdose of Death.* Dell 683. c/C Bobertz. My. G+. B5d. $2.50

CHRISTIE, Agatha. *Partners in Crime.* 1963. Dell 6848. 1st prtg. My. G+. R5d. $1.00

CHRISTIE, Agatha. *Patriotic Murders.* Pocket 249. VG. B3d. $5.00

CHRISTIE, Agatha. *Poirot Investigates.* Avon 716. 1st prtg. My. G+. R5d. $3.00

CHRISTIE, Agatha. *Poirot Investigates.* Bantam A 2320. 2nd prtg. My. VG. R5d. $1.00

CHRISTIE, Agatha. *Poirot Loses a Client.* Avon T 192. VG+. G5d. $5.00

CHRISTIE, Agatha. *Poirot Loses a Client.* 1945. Avon 70. My. G. B5d. $5.00

CHRISTIE, Agatha. *Regatta Mystery.* Avon T 220. VG+. B3d. $4.50

CHRISTIE, Agatha. *Regatta Mystery.* Avon 371. c/Johnson: gga. VG+. B6a #76. $31.00

CHRISTIE, Agatha. *Regatta Mystery.* 1951. Avon 371. 1st prtg. My. VG+. R5d. $9.00

CHRISTIE, Agatha. *Regatta Mystery.* 1964. Dell 7336. 1st prtg. My. VG. R6d. $1.75

CHRISTIE, Agatha. *Sad Cypress.* 1968. Dell D 217. 1st prtg. My. VG. R5d. $2.50

CHRISTIE, Agatha. *Sad Cypress.* Dell 172. VG. B3d. $4.50

CHRISTIE, Agatha. *Secret Adversary.* Avon T 210. 1st prtg. My. G. R5d. $1.00

CHRISTIE, Agatha. *Secret Adversary.* 1946. Avon 100. 1st prtg. My. F. F2d. $18.00

CHRISTIE, Agatha. *Secret Adversary.* 1944. Bestseller B 48. 1st prtg. My. F. F2d. $10.00

CHRISTIE, Agatha. *Secret of the Chimneys.* 1959. Dell D 262. 1st prtg. My. VG+. R5d. $4.00

CHRISTIE, Agatha. *Secret of the Chimneys.* 1964. Dell 7708. 1st prtg. My. VG+. R5d. $2.00

CHRISTIE, Agatha. *Secret of the Chimneys.* Harlequin 377. VG. B3d. $6.00

CHRISTIE, Agatha. *Seven Dials Mystery.* 1957. Avon T 167. My. G+. B4d. $2.00

CHRISTIE, Agatha. *Seven Dials Mystery.* 1964. Bantam F 2714. 1st prtg. My. VG. R5d. $1.75

CHRISTIE, Agatha. *There Is a Tide.* 1955. Dell 830. 1st prtg. My. VG+. R5d. $4.00

CHRISTIE, Agatha. *They Came to Baghdad.* 1960. Cardinal C 396. 1st prtg. VG. P7d. $3.50

CHRISTIE, Agatha. *Thirteen at Dinner.* 1944. Dell 60. NF. F2d. $15.00

CHRISTIE, Agatha. *Three Blind Mice.* Dell 633. c/M Ludlow. My. VG. B5d. $5.00

CHRISTIE, Agatha. *Three Blind Mice.* 1952. Dell 633. 1st pb. My. VG+. B6d. $12.50

CHRISTIE, Agatha. *Towards Zero.* Pocket 398. VG. B3d. $4.00

CHRISTIE, Agatha. *Tuesday Club Murders.* Avon T 245. VG+. B3d. $4.00

CHRISTIE, Agatha. *Tuesday Club Murders.* 1963. Dell 9136. 1st prtg. My. VG+. R5d. $2.50

CHRISTIE, Agatha. *Witness for the Prosecution.* Dell 855. 1st prtg. My. VG. R5d. $2.75

CHRISTIE, Agatha. *13 at Dinner.* 1961. Dell D 404. 1st prtg. My. G. R5d. $1.00

CHRISTOPHER, John. *Beyond the Burning Lands.* 1974. Collier 04238. SF. VG. P1d. $3.50

CHRISTOPHER, John. *Caves of Night.* 1968. Avon S 350. SF/My. VG. P1d. $5.00

CHRISTOPHER, John. *City of Gold & Lead.* 1970. Black Knight 04215. SF. VG. P1d. $4.50

CHRISTOPHER, John. *Death of Grass.* 1958. Penguin 1300. SF. VG. P1d. $7.50

CHRISTOPHER, John. *Guardians.* 1973. Puffin 579. SF. VG. P1d. $4.00

CHRISTOPHER, John. *Long Winter.* 1963. Crest D 612. SF. VG. B4d. $2.00

CHRISTOPHER, John. *Long Winter.* Gold Medal T 2323. VG. P9d. $1.50

CHRISTOPHER, John. *No Blade of Grass.* 1967. Avon S 288. SF. VG+. B5d. $3.50

CHRISTOPHER, John. *No Blade of Grass.* 1958. Pocket 1183. c/T Dunn. SF. G. B5d. $4.00

CHRISTOPHER, John. *Planet in Peril.* 1959. Avon T 371. 1st pb. NF. M1d. $9.00

CHRISTOPHER, John. *Planet in Peril.* 1959. Avon T 371. 1st prtg. SF. VG. R5d. $3.25

CHRISTOPHER, John. *Pool of Fire.* 1971. Black Knight 10398. SF. VG. P1d. $4.00

CHRISTOPHER, John. *Pool of Fire.* 1970. Collier. 1st pb. VG. M1d. $5.00

CHRISTOPHER, John. *Possessors.* 1966. Hodder 812. SF. VG+. P1d. $8.00

CHRISTOPHER, John. *Prince in Waiting.* 1974. Collier 04240. SF. VG+. P1d. $4.50

CHRISTOPHER, John. *Scent of White Poppies.* 1960. Avon T 463. c/gga. Fa. VG+. B4d. $4.00

CHRISTOPHER, John. *Sword of the Spirits.* 1976. Collier. 1st pb. F. M1d. $7.00

CHRISTOPHER, John. *Sword of the Spirits.* 1973. Puffin 630. SF. VG. P1d. $4.00

CHRISTOPHER, John. *Twenty-Second Century.* 1962. Lancer. 1st pb. NF. M1d. $8.00

CHRISTOPHER, John. *White Mountains.* 1974. Collier 04271. 4th edn. SF. VG. P1d. $3.25

CHRISTOPHER, John. *Year of the Comet.* 1978. Sphere 2303. SF. VG. P1d. $4.00

CHURCH, Ralph. *Mork & Mindy.* 1979. Pocket 82729. SF. VG. P1d. $5.00

CHURCHILL, Allen. *They Never Came Back.* 1963. Ace F 218. Nfi. G+. P1d. $4.50

CHURCHWARD, James. *Children of Mu.* 1968. PB Library 54-639. 2nd edn. Nfi. VG. B3d/P1d. $4.00

CHURCHWARD, James. *Cosmic Forces of Mu.* 1968. PB Library 54-678. Nfi. VG. P1d. $5.00

CHURCHWARD, James. *Lost Continent of Mu.* 1968. PB Library 54-616. Nfi. VG. B5d. $3.00

CHURCHWARD, John. *What Beck'ning Ghost?* 1977. New English 02972. Ho. VG. P1d. $4.00

CHUTE, B.J. *Greenwillow.* 1960. Dell D 385. Fa. VG. P1d. $7.00

CHUTE, Verne. *Flight of an Angel.* Dell 470. 1st prtg. My. VG. R5d. $3.50

CHUTE, Verne. *Sweet & Deadly.* 1952. Popular 443. My. VG. B4d. $4.00

CLAD, Noel. *Savage.* Ace H 426. VG+. B3d. $7.50

CLAD, Noel. *Savage.* 1959. Perma M 4152. c/gga. My. VG. B4d/G5d. $3.00

CLAGETT, John. *Captain Whitecap.* Popular G 169. VG+. B3d. $5.00

CLAGETT, John. *Cradle of the Sun.* 1959. Popular G 341. Hi. VG. P1d. $7.00

CLAGETT, John. *Cradle of the Sun.* Popular 566. VG+. B3d. $4.50

CLAGETT, John. *Run the River Gauntlet.* Ace D 296. VG. I1d. $5.00

CLAGETT, John. *US Navy in Action.* Monarch 350. VG. B3d. $4.50

CLAGETT, John. *World Unknown.* 1975. Popular 00275. SF. VG. P1d. $3.50

CLAIRE, Marvin. *Drowning Wire.* 1955. Phantom 649. PBO. VG+. B3a. $46.30

CLAIRE, Suzy. *Around the World With Suzy Claire.* 1966. PB Library 54-366. 1st edn. c/photo. F. F2d. $8.00

CLAIRE/OURSLER. *Drowning Wire/Departure Delayed.* Ace D 37. PBO. VG. B3d. $10.00

CLAIRE/OURSLER. *Drowning Wire/Departure Delayed.* 1953. Ace D 37. 1st prtg. My. G+. R5d. $7.50

CLAMAN, Julian. *Aging Boy.* 1967. MacFadden 75-145. 1st prtg. c/gga. VG. P7d. $4.00

CLANCY, Eugene. *Owlhoot Justice.* 1970. Curtis 6119. 1st pb. We. NF. B6d. $7.50

CLANCY, Tom. *Clear & Present Danger.* 1990. Berkley 12212. 1st prtg. My. VG. W2d. $4.50

CLARK, Curt. *Anarchaos.* 1967. Ace F 421. PBO. G+. M6d. $10.00

CLARK, Curt. *Anarchaos.* 1967. Ace F 421. SF. F. P1d. $15.00

CLARK, Curt. *Anarchaos.* 1967. Ace F 421. 1st edn. sgn. SF. F. F2d. $17.00

CLARK, Curt. *Anarchaos.* 1967. Ace F 421. 1st prtg. PBO. NF. P7d. $9.00

CLARK, Curt. *Anarchaos.* 1967. Ace F 421. 1st prtg. SF. VG. B3d/R5d. $6.00

CLARK, D. *Continental Affair.* Night Shadow Book NS 302. VG+. I1d. $5.00

CLARK, Dale. *Blonde, the Gangster & the Private Eye.* 1949. Murder My Monthly 47. 1st edn. PBO. c/Cantor. rare. VG+. B6a #77. $121.00

CLARK, Dale. *Mambo to Murder.* 1955. Ace D 109. PBO. c/gga. scarce. NF. B6a #75. $38.50

CLARK, Dale. *Mambo to Murder.* 1955. Ace D 109. PBO. VG+. B6d. $40.00

CLARK, Dorine. *Hell Cat.* 1959. Beacon 243. 1st prtg. PBO. VG+. P7d. $12.50

CLARK, Dorine. *Husband for Hire.* 1966. PAD MP 769. Ad. VG. B5d. $3.50

CLARK, Dorine. *Perilous Rapture.* PAD 770. VG+. B3d. $5.00

CLARK, Douglas. *Sick to Death.* 1983. Perennial P 676. c/hypo. My. NF. B5d. $6.00

CLARK, Ford. *Open Square.* Gold Medal 1220. VG+. B3d. $5.00

CLARK, Ford. *Wicked Walk on Every Side.* Gold Medal K 1532. PBO. Fi. VG. B5d. $5.50

CLARK, G. Glenwood. *Thomas Alva Edison.* Berkley G 270. Nfi. VG. B5d. $2.50

CLARK, George. *Neighbors' Kids.* 1955. Gold Medal 532. PBO. VG. B6d. $4.50

CLARK, John O.E. *Computers at Work.* 1973. Bantam R 6834. c/photos. Nfi. VG+. B5d. $5.50

CLARK, M.B. *Model Corpse.* Boardman NN MC. VG. B3d. $8.50

CLARK, Marguerite. *Why So Tired?* Crest 601. VG+. B3d. $4.50

CLARK, Mary C. *Where Are the Children?* 1976. Dell 09593. 18th prtg. SF. VG. W2d. $3.25

CLARK, W.V.T. *Ox-Bow Incident.* Signet 1470. 7th prtg. VG+. B3d. $4.50

CLARK, Walter. *Ox-Bow Incident.* Signet 1160. reprint. We. VG+. B6d. $7.50

CLARK/MACKLIN. *Run For the Money/Thin Edge of Mania.* 1956. Ace D 149. PBO. c/B Barton. My. G+. B5d. $6.00

CLARK/NOEL. *Mambo to Murder/I See Red.* Ace D 109. c/Barton: gga. My. G+. B6d. $4.50

CLARKE, Anne. *Soon She Must Die.* 1988. Charter 5573. 1st prtg. My. VG. W2d. $3.00

CLARKE, Arthur C. *Against the Fall of Night.* 1954. Perma S 310. VG. B3d. $4.00

CLARKE, Arthur C. *Against the Fall of Night.* 1954. Perma S 310. 1st pb. SF. F. M1d. $12.00

CLARKE, Arthur C. *Against the Fall of Night.* Pyramid F 754. 4th edn. G. P9d. $1.25

CLARKE, Arthur C. *Against the Fall of Night.* 1962. Pyramid F 754. 2nd edn. SF. VG. B5d. $3.50

CLARKE, Arthur C. *Against the Fall of Night.* Pyramid G 554. 3rd edn. G. P9d. $1.00

CLARKE, Arthur C. *Challenge of the Spaceship.* Ballantine F 528. NF. I1d. $6.00

CLARKE, Arthur C. *Childhood's End.* 1972. Ballantine 02750. 22nd prtg. SF. VG. W2d. $3.50

CLARKE, Arthur C. *Childhood's End.* 1953. Ballantine 33. SF. F. P1d. $35.00

CLARKE, Arthur C. *Childhood's End.* 1953. Ballantine 33. 1st edn. NF. M1d. $15.00

CLARKE, Arthur C. *City & the Stars.* 1957. Signet S 1464. SF. VG. P1d. $7.50

CLARKE, Arthur C. *City & the Stars.* 1957. Signet Y 6452. 7th prtg. SF. F. W2d. $4.75

CLARKE, Arthur C. *Deep Range.* 1958. Signet S 1583. SF. VG+. P1d. $11.00

CLARKE, Arthur C. *Dolphin Island.* 1968. Berkley F 1495. SF. VG. P1d. $5.00

CLARKE, Arthur C. *Earthlight.* 1969. Ballantine 01560. 5th prtg. SF. VG+. W2d. $3.75

CLARKE, Arthur C. *Earthlight.* 1957. Ballantine 249. 2nd edn. SF. VG. B5d. $4.00

CLARKE, Arthur C. *Earthlight.* 1955. Ballantine 97. SF. VG+. B4d. $5.00

CLARKE, Arthur C. *Earthlight.* 1955. Ballantine 97. 1st prtg. F. S1d. $10.00

CLARKE, Arthur C. *Earthlight.* 1963. Pan G 641. 2nd edn. SF. VG+. P1d. $7.50

CLARKE, Arthur C. *Expedition to Earth.* 1953. Ballantine 52. SF. VG. B4d. $4.00

CLARKE, Arthur C. *Expedition to Earth.* 1953. Ballantine 52. 1st edn. F. M1d. $15.00

CLARKE, Arthur C. *Exploration of Space.* 1954. Cardinal C 135. VG+. P1d. $12.50

CLARKE, Arthur C. *Exploration of Space.* 1966. Gold medal R 228. 3rd prtg. VG. W2d. $3.50

CLARKE, Arthur C. *Fall of Moondust.* 1963. Dell 2463. SF. VG+. P1d. $9.00

CLARKE, Arthur C. *Fountains of Paradise.* 1980. Ballantine 25356. 1st prtg. SF. VG+. W2d. $3.50

CLARKE, Arthur C. *Glide Path.* 1965. Dell 2919. SF. VG. P1d. $5.50

CLARKE, Arthur C. *Glide Path.* 1973. Signet AE 1529. SF. VG+. W2d. $3.75

CLARKE, Arthur C. *Imperial Earth.* 1976. Ballantine 25352. SF. F. P1d. $5.00

CLARKE, Arthur C. *Islands in the Sky.* 1960. Signet S 1769. c/P Lehr. SF. VG. B5d. $4.00

CLARKE, Arthur C. *Islands in the Sky.* 1960. Signet S 1769. SF. F. P1d. $14.00

CLARKE, Arthur C. *Lost Worlds of 2001.* 1972. Signet Y 4929. Nfi. VG+. P1d. $6.00

CLARKE, Arthur C. *Master of Space.* 1961. Lancer 72-610. c/O Leibman. SF. VG. B5d. $4.00

CLARKE, Arthur C. *Other Side of the Sky.* 1963. Corgi YS 1289. SF. VG. P1d. $6.00

CLARKE, Arthur C. *Other Side of the Sky.* 1959. Signet S 1729. SF. VG. B4d/I1d. $4.00

CLARKE, Arthur C. *Other Side of the Sky.* 1959. Signet S 1729. 1st pb. F. M1d. $12.00

CLARKE, Arthur C. *Prelude to Space.* 1976. Ballantine 25113. 3rd prtg. SF. F. W2d. $4.00

CLARKE, Arthur C. *Prelude to Space.* 1954. Ballantine 68. SF. VG. P1d. $8.50

CLARKE, Arthur C. *Profiles of the Future.* 1964. Bantam H 2734. Nfi. VG. B5d. $2.50

CLARKE, Arthur C. *Promise of Space.* 1970. Pyramid V 2157. Nfi. VG. P1d. $4.50

CLARKE, Arthur C. *Reach for Tomorrow.* Ballantine U 2110. 3rd edn. VG. P9d. $1.50

CLARKE, Arthur C. *Reach For Tomorrow.* Ballantine 135. PBO. c/Powers. VG. B3d/I1d. $6.00

CLARKE, Arthur C. *Reach for Tomorrow.* 1956. Ballantine 135. SF. F. P1d. $20.00

CLARKE, Arthur C. *Rendezvous With Rama.* 1974. Ballantine 24175. SF. F. P1d/W2d. $5.00

CLARKE, Arthur C. *Report on Planet Three.* 1973. Signet Y 5409. Nfi. VG. P1d. $3.50

CLARKE, Arthur C. *Sands of Mars.* 1964. Pan X 281. SF. G+. P1d. $4.50

CLARKE, Arthur C. *Sands of Mars.* Perma M 4149. 1st prtg. F. S1d. $7.00

CLARKE, Arthur C. *Sands of Mars.* 1954. Pocket 989. VG. I1d. $6.00

CLARKE, Arthur C. *Sands of Mars.* 1954. Pocket 989. 1st edn. PBO. F. F2d. $15.00

CLARKE, Arthur C. *Sands of Mars.* 1974. Signet AE 4790. 10th prtg. SF. VG. W2d. $3.25

CLARKE, Arthur C. *Songs of Distant Earth.* 1987. Ballantine 32240. SF. VG+. W2d. $4.75

CLARKE, Arthur C. *Tales From the White Hart.* Ballantine U 2113. 3rd prtg. VG+. B3d. $4.50

CLARKE, Arthur C. *Tales From the White Hart.* 1957. Ballantine 186. Fa. VG+. P1d. $15.00

CLARKE, Arthur C. *Tales From the White Hart.* 1961. Ballantine 539. 2nd edn. SF. VG+. B6d. $6.00

CLARKE, Arthur C. *Tales of Ten Worlds.* 1964. Dell 8467. SF. VG. P1d. $6.00

CLARKE, Arthur C. *Tales of Two Worlds.* 1954. Dell. 1st pb. F. M1d. $10.00

CLARKE, Arthur C. *Time Probe.* 1967. Dell 8925. 1st prtg. SF. VG. W2d. $4.00

CLARKE, Arthur C. *Treasure of the Great Reef.* 1966. Scholastic 767. Nfi. VG. P1d. $5.50

CLARKE, Arthur C. *Voices From the Sky.* 1967. Pyramid X 1686. SF. VG. B4d/P1d. $5.00

CLARKE, Arthur C. *Wind From the Sun.* 1973. Signet Q 5581. SF. VG. P1d. $3.50

CLARKE, Arthur C. *2001: A Space Odyssey.* 1968. Signet E 6625. 24th prtg. MTI. SF. F. W2d. $4.75

CLARKE, Arthur C. *2001: A Space Odyssey.* 1968. Signet Q 3580. SF. VG+. P1d. $7.50

CLARKE, Arthur C. *2001: A Space Odyssey.* 1982. Signet 15580. 40th prtg. MTI. SF. F. W2d. $4.25

CLARKE, Arthur C. *2010: Odyssey Two.* 1984. Ballantine 30306. 1st pb. c/Whelan. SF. NF. B6d. $3.00

CLARKE, Arthur C. *2061: Odyssey Three.* 1989. Ballantine 35879. 1st pb. c/Whelan. SF. NF. B6d. $3.00

CLARKE, Comer. *Eichmann: The Man & His Crimes.* 1960. Ballantine F 424K. Nfi. VG+. B4d. $4.00

CLARKE, D.H. *Alabam.* 1949. Avon 232. VG. B3d. $4.50

CLARKE, D.H. *Confidential.* 1950. Avon 253. 1st prtg. My. VG+. R5d. $8.00

CLARKE, D.H. *Housekeeper's Daughter.* 1951. Avon 336. c/gga. Fa. VG. B4d. $5.00

CLARKE, D.H. *Impatient Virgin.* Avon 530. VG. B3d. $4.00

CLARKE, D.H. *Joe & Jennie.* Berkley 331. VG+. B3d. $5.00

CLARKE, D.H. *Kelly.* 1946. Avon 116. 1st prtg. c/Don Milsop: gga. VG. P7d. $7.50

CLARKE, D.H. *Lady Ann.* 1946. Avon 105. c/gga. Fa. VG. I1d. $4.50

CLARKE, D.H. *Lady Named Lou.* Avon 483. VG+. B3d. $6.00

CLARKE, D.H. *Louis Beretti.* 1951. Avon 384. 1st prtg. My. VG+. R5d. $10.00

CLARKE, D.H. *Murderer's Holiday.* Avon 394. VG. I1d. $4.00

CLARKE, D.H. *Nina.* 1949. Avon 213. c/gga. Fa. VG+. B3d. $15.00

CLARKE, D.H. *Nina.* Avon 593. VG. I1d. $5.00

CLARKE, D.H. *Regenerate Lover.* 1948. Novel Library 8. Ad. G+. B5d. $11.50

CLARKE, D.H. *Story of John Bartel, Jr.* 1948. Avon 149. c/gga. Fa. VG. B4d. $5.00

CLARKE, D.H. *Tawny.* Avon 237. VG. I1d. $5.00

CLARKE, D.H. *That Mrs Renney.* Avon 431. VG. B3d. $5.00

CLARKE, J. Brian. *Expediter.* 1990. DAW UE 2409. SF. VG. P1d. $3.50

CLARKE, John. *Lolita Lovers.* 1962. Monarch 250. PBO. c/De Soto. scarce. JD. VG+. B6a #80. $49.50

CLARKE & HYAMS. *Odyssey File.* 1985. Ballantine 32108. 1st edn. c/photos. SF. F. F2d. $9.00

CLARKE & PROCTOR edt. *SF Hall of Fame Volume 3.* 1982. Avon 79335. SF. VG. P1d. $4.00

CLASON, Clyde B. *Green Shiver.* Popular 50. VG. B3d. $5.00

CLAUSSEN, W.E. *El Paso.* Lion 55. VG. B3d. $4.50

CLAUSSEN, W.E. *Rebel's Roundup.* Avon 495. VG. M6d. $4.50

CLAY, Matthew. *French Alley.* 1960. Zenith 38. 1st pb edn. c/gga. F. F2d. $20.00

CLAY, Paul. *Housewarming.* Beacon 958. VG. B3d. $5.00

CLAYFORD, James. *Divorce Bait!* 1949. Exotic Digest 3. PBO. c/George Gross: gga. VG+. B6a #77. $82.50

CLAYFORD, James. *Lure for Love.* 1949. Quarter Book 28. PBO. c/George Gross: gga. VG+. B6a #74. $82.50

CLAYFORD, James. *Man Crazy.* 1951. Exotic Novel 15. PBO. c/Nappi: gga. VG. B6a #80. $78.00

CLAYFORD, James. *Man Crazy.* 1951. Exotic Novel 15. 1st edn. PBO. c/gga. scarce. VG. B6a #76. $68.25

CLAYTON, G. *Sin Family Robinson.* Barclay 7266. VG+. B3d. $5.00

CLAYTON, Henry C. *Frustration.* 1949. News Stand Library 12A. Fi. VG. B3d. $6.00

CLAYTON, Jo. *Blue Magic.* 1988. DAW UE 2270. Fa. VG. P1d. $3.50

CLAYTON, Jo. *Deadem From the Stars.* 1977. DAW UW 1293. SF. F. P1d. $5.00

CLAYTON, Jo. *Drinker of Souls.* 1986. DAW 668. 1st edn. VG. P9d. $1.50

CLAYTON, Jo. *Irsud.* DAW UE 1640. 4th edn. SF. VG. P1d. $3.00

CLAYTON, Jo. *Moongather.* 1982. DAW UE 1729. 2nd edn. SF. VG. P1d. $3.00

CLAYTON, Jo. *Moonscatter (Duel of Sorcery #2).* 1983. DAW UE 1798. 1st prtg. SF. VG+. W2d. $4.00

CLAYTON, Jo. *Nowhere Hunt.* 1981. DAW UE 1665. SF. VG. P1d. $3.50

CLAYTON, Jo. *Star Hunters.* 1980. DAW 394. PBO. c/M Mariano. SF. VG. B5d. $3.00

CLAYTON, John Bell. *Wait Son, October Is Near.* 1954. Bantam A 1236. c/gga. Fa. VG+. B4d. $2.25

CLEARY, Beverly. *Beaver & Wally.* 1966. Berkley F 1333. VG+. P6d. $5.50

CLEARY, Beverly. *Here's Beaver!* 1961. Berkley G 497. PBO. TVTI. NF. B6d. $18.00

CLEARY, Beverly. *Here's Beaver!* 1961. Berkley G 497. TVTI. c/photo. VG. P6d. $4.50

CLEARY, Beverly. *Leave It to Beaver.* 1960. Berkley G 406. 1st prtg. TVTI. G+. R5d. $4.50

CLEARY, Jon. *Sundowners.* 1960. Pocket 6012. 1st prtg. VG. R5d. $2.50

CLEARY, Jon. *Sundowners.* 1953. Pocket 939. c/T Dunn. Fi. VG. B5d. $4.00

CLEARY, Jon. *You Can't See Around Corners.* 1953. Popular 497. Fa. VG+. B4d. $12.00

CLEAVER, Vera. *Nurses Dilemma.* 1967. Pyramid R 1713. Ro. NF. B4d. $4.00

CLEBERT, J.P. *Blockhouse.* Avon T 379. VG+. B3d. $4.00

CLEEVE, Brian. *Judas Goat.* 1969. Corgi 8147. 1st pb. My. VG+. B6d. $6.00

CLEEVE, Brian. *Night Winds.* Ballantine 62. NF. B3d. $5.00

CLELAND, John. *Daughter of Fanny Hill.* Brandon House. VG+. B3d. $7.00

CLELAND, John. *Memoirs of a Coxcomb.* Lancer 74-826. NF. B3d. $4.50

CLEMENS, Brian. *More Stories From Thriller.* 1975. Fontana 3784. TVTI. VG+. P1d. $12.50

CLEMENS, Brian. *Thriller.* 1975. Fontana 3888. 3rd edn. TVTI. VG. P1d. $7.50

CLEMENS & RANDOLPH. *Camp-Meeting Murders.* 1945. Prize Mystery 15. VG+. B3a #22. $19.80

CLEMENT, Hal. *Best of Hal Clement.* 1979. Ballantine 27689. SF. VG. P1d. $5.00

CLEMENT, Hal. *Close to Critical.* 1964. Ballantine U 2215. SF. F. W2d. $5.00

CLEMENT, Hal. *Close to Critical.* 1975. Ballantine 24508. 3rd edn. SF. VG. P1d. $3.25

CLEMENT, Hal. *Cycle of Fire.* 1957. Ballantine. 1st edn. VG. M1d. $8.00

CLEMENT, Hal. *From Outer Space.* Avon G 1168. 4th edn. G. P9d. $1.25

CLEMENT, Hal. *From Outer Space.* Avon T 175. 1st pb. VG. M1d. $6.00

CLEMENT, Hal. *Iceworld.* 1977. Ballantine 25805. SF. F. P1d. $5.00

CLEMENT, Hal. *Mission of Gravity.* 1978. Ballantine 27092. SF. G+. P1d. $2.75

CLEMENT, Hal. *Mission of Gravity.* Galaxy SF 33. VG+. B3d. $6.00

CLEMENT, Hal. *Mission of Gravity.* 1962. Pyramid F 786. 1st pb. F. M1d. $10.00

CLEMENT, Hal. *Natives of Space.* 1965. Ballantine U 2235. SF. VG+. P1d. $8.00

CLEMENT, Hal. *Needle.* 1976. Avon Equinox 28555. SF. VG. P1d. $5.00

CLEMENT, Hal. *Needle.* 1967. Avon S255. c/H Garrido. SF. VG. B5d. $3.50

CLEMENT, Hal. *Needle.* 1969. Lancer 74557. SF. VG+. W2d. $3.50

CLEMENT, Hal. *Nitrogen Fix.* 1981. Ace. 1st pb. F. M1d. $4.00

CLEMENT, Hal. *Ocean on Top.* 1973. DAW UQ 1057. SF. VG. P1d. $3.50

CLEMENT, Hal. *Still River.* 1989. Ballantine 32917. 1st pb. c/Don Dixon. SF. VG+. B6d. $3.00

CLEMENT, Hal. *Through the Eye of a Needle.* 1978. Ballantine 25850. SF. VG. P1d. $3.50

CLEMENT, Henry. *Dillinger.* 1971. Curtis 07296. MTI. c/sgn. VG+. P6d. $4.00

CLEMENT, Henry. *She Waits.* 1975. Popular 00283. Ho. VG. P1d. $5.00

CLEMENT, Henry. *Sugarland Express.* 1974. Popular 08276. PBO. MTI. c/Goldie Hawn: photo. VG. M6d. $5.00

CLEMENT, Henry. *Sugarland Express.* 1974. Popular 08276. 1st edn. c/Goldie Hawn: photo. My. F. F2d. $12.50

CLEMENTS, Calvin. *Satan Takes the Helm.* Gold Medal 252. c/Barye. VG. B3d. $5.00

CLEMENTS, Henry. *Slaughter.* Curtis 07263. PBO. MTI. c/Jim Brown. VG. M6d. $5.00

CLEMENTS, Mark. *Holiday Weekend.* 1965. Midwood 32-434. PBO. NF. B3d. $6.50

CLEMENTS, Mark. *Love or Lust.* 1964. Midwood F 354. PBO. VG+. B6d. $9.00

CLEMENTS, Mark. *Wayward Wife.* Midwood 32-466. PBO. VG. M6d. $5.00

CLENDENING, Logan. *Human Body.* 1943. Pocket 198. Nfi. VG. B5d. $5.00

CLERI, Mario. *Six Graves to Munich.* 1967. Banner B 50-112. 1st prtg. My. G+. R5d. $3.00

CLEVE, John. *Accursed Tower.* 1974. Dell-Grove 3444. Hi. VG+. P1d. $7.50

CLEVE, John. *Julanar the Lioness.* 1975. Dell-Grove 4731. sgn/inscr. Hi. VG. P1d. $15.00

CLEVELY, H. *Case of the Criminal's Daughter.* Sexton Blake 323. VG. B3d. $10.00

CLEVELY, H. *Case of the Legion Deserter.* Sexton Blake 349. VG+. B3d. $7.00

CLEWES, Howard. *Long Memory.* Dell 787. 1st prtg. My. VG. R5d. $3.25

CLIFFORD, Francis. *Hunting Ground.* Signet P 2989. G+. G5d. $2.75

CLIFFORD, Francis. *Naked Runner.* 1967. Signet P 3112. 1st prtg. VG. R5d. $2.00

CLIFT & JOHNSTON. *High Valley.* 1951. Pocket 818. c/C Mueller. Fi. VG. B5d. $4.00

CLIFTON, Bud. *Bad Girls.* 1958. Pyramid G 364. 1st edn. JD. F. F2d. $12.00

CLIFTON, Bud. *D for Delinquent.* 1958. Ace D 270. 1st edn. JD. VG. F2d. $15.00

CLIFTON, Bud. *Let Him Go Hang.* 1961. Ace D 501. 1st edn. My. F. F2d. $8.00

CLIFTON, Bud. *Power Gods.* 1959. Pyramid G 410. PBO. c/Marchetti. scarce. JD. VG+. B6a #79. $36.50

CLIFTON, Bud. *Power Gods.* 1959. Pyramid G 410. 1st edn. PBO. JD. F. F2d. $13.00

CLIFTON, G. *Happy Hunted.* Panther 512. VG+. B3d. $8.00

CLIFTON, James M.E. *Counterfeit General Montgomery.* Avon 692. c/photo. Nfi. VG. B5d. $4.50

CLIFTON, Mark. *Eight Keys to Eden.* Ballantine F 639. SF. VG. B5d. $3.50

CLIFTON, Mark. *Eight Keys to Eden.* 1962. Ballantine. 1st pb edn. NF. M1d. $7.00

CLIFTON, Mark. *Kane's Odyssey.* 1976. Laser 16. 1st edn. NF. P9d. $2.50

CLIFTON, Mark. *When They Came From Space.* 1963. MacFadden 40-105. 1st pb. F. M1d. $8.00

CLIFTON, Mark. *When They Come From Space.* 1963. MacFadden 40-105. 1st prtg. c/Powers. VG. P7d/P9d. $4.00

CLIFTON & RILEY. *Forever Machine.* Galaxy Novel 35. VG. B3d. $4.50

CLIFTON & RILEY. *Forever Machine.* 1958. Galaxy Novel 35. 1st pb edn. c/Wally Wood. F. F2d. $20.00

CLINGERMAN, Mildred. *Cupful of Space.* 1961. Ballantine 519K. PBO. c/R Powers. SF. VG. B3d/B5d. $4.50

CLINGERMAN, Mildred. *Cupful of Space.* 1961. Ballantine. 1st edn. F. M1d. $12.00

CLINTEN, Max. *Don't Make Me Kill!* Comyns NN. G+. B3d. $12.00

CLINTON, Jeff. *Kane's Odyssey.* Laser 16. c/Freas. VG+. B3d. $5.00

CLINTON, Jeff. *Kane's Odyssey.* 1976. Laser 16. 1st edn. SF. F. F2d. $12.00

CLINTON, Jeff. *Killer's Choice.* 1972. Berkley X 2156. We. VG. P1d. $4.00

CLINTON, Jeff. *Range Killer*. Berkley G 660. PBO. VG. B3d. $4.50

CLINTON, Jeff. *Wanted: Wildcat O'Shea*. 1966. Berkley F 1313. PBO. c/Gross. We. VG+. B6d. $9.00

CLINTON, Jeff. *Wildcat Against the House*. 1963. Berkley Y 803. PBO. c/Gross. We. VG. B6d. $8.00

CLINTON, Jeff. *Wildcat on the Loose*. 1967. Berkely F 1382. PBO. c/Gross. NF. B6d. $12.50

CLINTON, Mark. *Ways of Passion*. 1966. Spartan 142. PBO. NF. B6d. $12.50

CLIPPINGER, Frances. *Elinda*. 1952. Signet 951. c/R DeSoto. Fi. VG. B5d. $4.00

CLOETE, Stuart. *Congo Song*. Popular G 110. NF. B3d. $6.00

CLOETE, Stuart. *Curve & the Tusk*. MacFadden 95-144. VG+. B3d. $5.00

CLOETE, Stuart. *Curve & the Tusk*. 1954. Signet S 1078. 1st pb. c/Meese. VG. B6d. $7.00

CLORFENE & MARGOLIS. *Childs Garden of Grass*. 1975. Pocket 80150. 2nd edn. VG+. B4d. $3.00

CLOSTERMANN, Pierre. *Big Show*. Ballantine F261. c/photos. NF. VG. B5d. $4.00

CLOU, John. *Golden Blade*. 1955. Graphic G 209. 1st pb. NF. M1d. $8.00

CLOU, John. *Golden Blade*. 1955. Graphic G 209. 1st prtg. c/Maguire. VG+. B3d. $5.00

CLUBB, S. *Hot Blood of Youth*. Beacon 1043. VG+. B3d. $6.00

CLUBB, S. *Trap of Lesbos*. 1970. Softcover SCLS 95159. PBO. c/gga. VG. P6d. $4.00

CLUBB, S. *Young Lust*. Beacon 827. PBO. VG. B3d. $5.00

CLUGSTON/COLTON. *Twist the Knife Slowly/Big Fix*. 1952. Ace D 3. G. I1d. $8.00

CLUGSTON/COLTON. *Twist the Knife Slowly/Big Fix*. 1952. Ace D 3. PBO. VG. B3a #21. $35.00

COATES, edt. *Mutts, Mongrels, Mischief*. 1960. Pyramid PG 29. PBO. VG. B6d. $4.00

COATES, R.M. *Night So Dark*. Popular G 173. VG. B3d. $4.50

COATES, R.M. *Wisteria Cottage*. 1950. Dell 371. 1st pb. My. VG+. B6d. $12.00

COBB, Humphrey. *Paths of Glory*. 1958. Dell D 209. MTI. VG. B4d. $2.50

COBEAN, S. *Naked Eye*. Pocket 899. NF. I1d. $5.00

COBERLY, V.J. *By Passion Obsessed*. Monarch 206. PBO. VG+. B3d. $5.00

COBLENTZ, Stanton A. *Animal People*. 1970. Belmont B 75-2038. SF. F. P1d. $10.00

COBLENTZ, Stanton A. *Animal People*. UNI-Book. SF. G+. W2d. $2.50

COBLENTZ, Stanton A. *Hidden World*. Airmont SF 6. SF. VG+. B5d. $4.00

COBLENTZ, Stanton A. *Into Plutonian Depths*. 1950. Avon 281. PBO. scarce. NF. B6a #75. $110.00

COBLENTZ, Stanton A. *Into Plutonian Depths*. 1950. Avon 281. PBO. VG. B6d. $25.00

COBLENTZ, Stanton A. *Into Plutonium Depths*. 1950. Avon 281. PBO. VG+. B3a #24. $44.00

COBLENTZ, Stanton A. *Island People*. 1971. Belmont B 75-2180. SF. F. P1d. $5.00

COBLENTZ, Stanton A. *Moon People*. Belmont B 752024. 1st prtg. F. S1d. $4.00

COBURN, Walt. *Branded*. 1959. Avon 858. We. F. B4d. $10.00

COBURN, Walt. *La Jornada*. 1967. Avon G 1325. 1st US edn. We. F. F2d. $7.00

COBURN, Walt. *Mavericks*. 1950. Popular 250. c/J Dreary. We. VG+. P6d. $3.50

COBURN, Walt. *Ring-tailed Rannyhans*. Popular 290. VG+. I1d. $7.00

COBURN, Walt. *Sky-Pilot Cowboy*. 1948. Popular 166. 1st pb. We. VG. B6d. $5.00

COCHRAN, Hamilton. *Rogue's Holiday*. Dell D 144. VG+. B3d. $4.50

COCHRAN, Hamilton. *Windward Passage*. Ace D 251. VG+. B3d. $5.00

COCHRAN, Jeff. *Guns of Circle 8*. Avon 556. PBO. We. G+. B5d. $3.50

COCHRAN & MURPHY. *Grandmaste*. 1984. Pinnacle 42205. SF. VG+. W2d. $3.25

COCHRELL, B. *Rage in the Wind*. Popular 509. VG. B3d. $4.50

CODY, Al. *Big Corral*. 1960. Pyramid G 539. We. VG. B5d. $3.50

CODY, Al. *Empty Saddles*. 1948. Handi-Book 81. VG+. B3a #24. $17.70

CODY, Al. *Empty Saddles*. Harlequin 93. VG. B3d. $8.00

CODY, Al. *Forbidden River*. Berkley 353. VG. B3d. $3.50

CODY, Al. *Guns Blaze at Sundown*. Avon 426. VG. I1d. $5.00

CODY, Al. *Marshal of Deer Creek*. 1951. Avon 378. c/D J Doore. We. VG. B5d. $5.50

CODY, Al. *Montana Helltown*. 1958. Avon 810. We. VG+. B4d. $10.00

CODY, Al. *Outlaw Justice at Hangman's Coulee*. Avon 460. VG. B3d. $5.00

CODY, Al. *Outlaw Justice at Hangman's Coulee*. 1952. Avon 460. We. VG+. B4d. $7.00

CODY, Al. *Outpost Trail*. Berkley GD 2030. VG. B3d. $6.00

CODY, Al. *Red Man's Range*. 1957. Berkley 374. PBO. c/L Newquist. We. VG. B5d. $4.00

CODY, Al. *Whiplash War*. Avon 704. PBO. VG. B3d. $4.00

CODY, C.S. *Lie Like a Lady*. Ace S 108. VG. B3d. $5.00

CODY, C.S. *Lie Like a Lady*. 1955. Ace S 108. 1st edn. My. F. F2d. $18.00

CODY, C.S. *Witching Night*. 1953. Dell 670. Ho. VG. P1d. $10.50

CODY, C.S. *Witching Night*. Lancer 73-720. reprint. NF. B6d. $10.00

COE, C.F. *Pressure*. Signet 942. VG. B3d. $4.00

COFFEY, Brian. *Blood Risk*. 1975. Futura 7167. PBO. scarce. NF. B6a #74. $25.00

COFFEY, Frank. *Night Prayers*. 1986. Jove 8453. PBO. Ho. VG+. B6d. $3.00

COFFMAN, Virginia. *Beckoning*. 1965. Ace K 221. 1st prtg. My. G+. R5d. $1.50

COFFMAN, Virginia. *Chalet Diabolique*. 1971. Lancer 74773. SF/My. VG. P1d. $4.50

COFFMAN, Virginia. *Devil Vicar*. 1966. Ace K 234. Fa. VG+. B4d. $2.00

COFFMAN, Virginia. *Devil's Mistress*. 1970. Lancer 74645. SF/My. VG. P1d. $4.50

COFFMAN, Virginia. *From Satan, With Love*. 1971. Lancer 75254. SF/My. VG. P1d. $4.00

COFFMAN, Virginia. *Masque of Satan*. 1978. Pinnacle 40-139. SF/My. VG. P1d. $3.50

COFFMAN, Virginia. *Priestess of the Damned*. 1970. Lancer 74697. 1st edn. SF. F. F2d. $8.00

COFFMAN, Virginia. *Vampyre of Moura*. 1970. Ace 86021. Ho. VG. P1d. $6.00

COGSWELL, Theodore. *Third Eye*. 1968. Belmont B 50-840. 1st edn. F. M1d. $10.00

COGSWELL, Theodore. *Third Eye*. 1968. Belmont B50-840. PBO. c/R Brillhart. SF. VG. B5d. $4.00

COGSWELL, Theodore. *Wall Around the World*. Pyramid 703. VG. B3d. $4.00

COGSWELL, Theodore. *Wall Around the World.* 1962. Pyramid 703. F. M1d. $15.00

COGSWELL & SPANO. *Spock, Messiah!* 1976. Bantam 10159. SF. VG. P1d/W2d. $5.00

COHEN, Daniel. *Greatest Monsters in the World.* 1977. Arch 24812. 1st prtg. SF. VG. W2d. $3.75

COHEN, Daniel. *Supermonsters.* 1978. Arch 29907. Nfi. VG. P1d. $3.50

COHEN, Leonard. *Spice-Box of Earth.* 1968. Bantam N 3672. 1st prtg. VG+. P7d. $4.00

COHEN, Lester. *Sweepings.* 1957. Crest Giant S 190. c/gga. VG+. P6d. $2.00

COHEN, Octavus Roy. *Backstage Mystery.* Green 14. My. G+. B5d. $4.00

COHEN, Octavus Roy. *Corpse That Walked.* Gold Medal 138. VG. B3d. $3.50

COHEN, Octavus Roy. *Danger in Paradise.* Popular 144. VG. B3d. $4.50

COHEN, Octavus Roy. *Dangerous Lady.* Popular 264. c/Belarski. VG. B3d. $6.50

COHEN, Octavus Roy. *Don't Ever Love Me.* 1951. Popular 332. 1st edn. PBO. c/Belarski: gga. scarce. NF. B6a #80. $82.50

COHEN, Octavus Roy. *Intruder.* Graphic 125. 1st pb. G+. M6d. $7.50

COHEN, Octavus Roy. *Lost Lady.* 1951. Gold Medal 172. VG+. B3d. $6.50

COHEN, Octavus Roy. *Love Has No Alibi.* 1949. Popular 162. 1st prtg. c/Belarski: gga. VG+. P7d. $17.50

COHEN, Octavus Roy. *Murder in Season (Romance in Crimson).* Popular 74. VG. B3d. $5.00

COHEN, Octavus Roy. *Romance in the First Degree.* Popular 88. VG+. B3d. $7.00

COHEN, Octavus Roy. *Sound of Revelry.* Popular 46. G+. G5d. $7.50

COHEN, Octavus Roy. *Sound of Revelry.* 1945. Popular 46. 1st pb. c/Hoffman. My. VG. B6d. $9.00

COHEN, Octavus Roy. *There's Always Time To Die.* Popular 196. VG+. B3d. $10.00

COINS, Wally. *Whispers of Heavenly Death.* 1979. Manor 23152. SF. VG+. P1d. $4.50

COKER, Elizabeth Boaturignt. *La Belle.* 1960. Dell F 113. c/M Hooks. Fi. VG. B5d. $2.50

COLBY, C.B. *Strangely Enough!* 1965. Popular SP 296. Nfi. VG. P1d. $6.00

COLBY, C.B. *Strangely Enough!* 1971. Scholastic 438. 11th prtg. VG. W2d. $3.00

COLBY, R. *Captain Must Die.* Gold Medal 835. c/sgn. VG. B3d. $5.50

COLBY, R. *Faster She Runs.* 1963. Monarch 379. Ad. VG. B5d. $5.00

COLBY, R. *Kim.* Monarch 244. VG+. I1d. $6.00

COLBY, R. *Lament for Julie.* Monarch 196. PBO. c/sgn. VG. B3d. $5.00

COLBY, R. *Secret of the Second Door.* Gold Medal 855. VG+. B3d. $5.50

COLBY, R. *Star Trap.* 1960. Gold Medal 1043. 1st prtg. PBO. c/gga. F. G5d. $9.00

COLBY, R. *Star Trap.* Gold Medal 8. c/sgn. VG+. B3d. $8.00

COLBY/DUDLEY. *Quaking Widow/Deep End.* 1956. Ace D 195. c/sgn. VG. B3d. $6.00

COLBY/DUDLEY. *Quaking Widow/Deep End.* 1956. Ace D 195. My. VG. P6d. $4.50

COLBY/DUFF. *Murder Mistress/Dangerous To Know.* Ace D 361. c/sgn. VG. B3d. $7.50

COLBY/STERLING. *Kill Me a Fortune/Five Alarm Funeral.* 1961. Ace D 515. PBO. VG. M6d. $6.50

COLBY/TRIMBLE. *In a Vanishing Room/ Surfside Caper.* Ace D 505. PBO. c/Colby: inscr. VG. B3d. $8.00

COLE, Adrian. *Dream Lords #1: A Plague of Nightmares.* 1977. Zebra 89083. 2nd prtg. SF. VG. W2d. $4.00

COLE, Adrian. *Lord of Nightmares.* 1975. Zebra 148. Fa. G+. P1d. $3.00

COLE, Burt. *Funco File.* 1970. Avon N 313. SF. F. P1d. $6.00

COLE, Jackson. *Border Hell.* 1952. Pyramid 51. We. G+. B5d. $5.00

COLE, Jackson. *Massacre Canyon.* 1961. Pyramid G638. 2nd edn. c/C Doore. We. VG. B5d. $3.50

COLE, Jackson. *Texas Fists.* 1953. Pyramid 81. We. VG. B4d. $7.50

COLE, Jackson. *Texas Tornado.* Pyramid 108. NF. I1d. $19.00

COLE, Jackson. *Trigger Law.* 1952. Pyramid 66. PBO. c/H Barker. We. G+. B5d. $4.50

COLE, Jackson. *Two-Gun Devil.* 1955. Pyramid 171. We. VG. B5d. $5.00

COLE, S. *Strangest Game.* Brandon House 2080. VG+. B3d. $6.00

COLE & COLE. *Death of a Millionaire.* Collins NN. 2nd edn. VG. B3d. $8.00

COLE & MCKEE edt. *You Damn Men Are All Alike.* Gold Medal 1254. c/cartoons. NF. B3d. $5.00

COLEMAN, C. *Flamingo Terrace.* Leisure 694. VG. B3d. $4.50

COLEMAN, James Nelson. *Null-Frequency Impulser.* 1969. Berkley X 1660. PBO. SF. NF. B5d. $3.50

COLEMAN, James Nelson. *Seeker From the Stars.* 1967. Berkely X 1438. PBO. c/Powers. SF. VG+. B6d. $8.00

COLEMAN, James Nelson. *Seeker From the Stars.* 1967. Berkley X 1438. 1st prtg. SF. VG. W2d. $4.00

COLEMAN, Lonnie. *Hot Spell.* 1958. Avon T 214. MTI. c/Anthony Quinn & Shirley Booth: photo. VG+. B4d. $4.00

COLEMAN, Lonnie. *Hot Spell.* 1958. Avon T 214. 1st edn. c/photo. F. F2d. $18.00

COLEMAN, Mitchell. *Born To Be Bad.* 1964. Belmont L 92-590. 1st edn. c/gga. F. F2d. $10.00

COLERIDGE, John. *Martian Martyrs.* Columbia SF Classics 1. VG. B3a #22. $22.00

COLES, Manning. *Basle Express.* Berkley F 892. c/n Fujita. My. VG. B5d. $3.50

COLES, Manning. *Drink to Yesterday.* Bantam 76. VG. G5d. $3.50

COLES, Manning. *Drink to Yesterday.* 1964. Berkley F 872. My. F. B4d. $7.00

COLES, Manning. *Fifth Man.* 1964. Berkley F 880. My. VG+. B4d. $6.00

COLES, Manning. *House at Pluck's Gutter.* 1968. Pyramid X 1782. c/Darrell Greene. My. VG+. B4d. $3.00

COLES, Manning. *They Tell No Tales.* 1964. Berkley F 899. 1st pb. My. VG+. B6d. $9.00

COLES, Manning. *They Tell No Tales.* 1964. Berkley F 899. 1st prtg. My. G+. R5d. $2.25

COLES, Manning. *Toast to Tomorrow.* 1947. Bantam 118. 1st pb. VG+. B6d. $8.00

COLES, Manning. *Toast to Tomorrow.* 1964. Berkley F 873. c/photo. My. VG. B5d. $3.50

COLES, Manning. *Vengeance Man.* 1967. Pyramid X 1631. c/Darrell Greene. My. NF. B4d. $4.00

COLETTE, S. *Claudine.* 1959. Avon T 301. c/gga. Fa. VG+. B4d. $3.75

COLETTE, S. *Ecstasy.* Popular G 536. PBO. MTI. c/Hedy Lamarr. VG. M6d. $7.50

COLETTE, S. *Ecstasy.* 1961. Popular G 536. 1st edn. c/Hedy Lamarr. F. F2d. $10.00

COLETTE, S. *Mitsou.* 1958. Avon T 269. MTI. c/gga. VG. B4d. $2.75

COLLANS, D. *I Was a House Detective.* Pyramid G 644. VG. G5d. $3.00

COLLIER, Hames. *Hypocritical American.* 1964. MacFadden 50-218 c/Karol. NF. VG. B5d. $3.00

COLLIER, Jennifer. *Costume Party.* 1972. Liverpool TNS 525. Ad. VG. B5d. $3.50

COLLIER, Jim. *Cheers!* Avon T 487. VG+. B3d. $4.50

COLLIER, John. *Fancies & Goodnights.* 1957. Bantam F 1703. 1st prtg. SF. VG+. B3d. $6.00

COLLIER, John. *Fancies & Goodnights.* 1953. Bantam 1106. G+. P1d. $7.50

COLLIER, John. *Fancies & Goodnights.* 1953. Bantam 1106. VG+. B3a #20. $18.70

COLLIER, John. *Fancies & Goodnights.* 1953. Bantam 1106. 1st pb. F. M1d. $20.00

COLLIER, Max. *Diane.* 1963. Midwood F 319. PBO. NF. B6d. $15.00

COLLIER, Max. *Man Crazy.* 1965. Midwood 32-568. Fa. F. B4d. $9.00

COLLIER, Max. *Mark of a Man.* Midwood 263. PBO. VG. B3d. $4.50

COLLIER, Max. *Sure Thing.* Midwood 303. NF. B3d. $6.00

COLLIER, Max. *Test of Love.* 1966. Midwood 33-683. Ad. VG+. B5d. $5.50

COLLIER, Max. *Thorn of Evil.* 1962. Midwood 199. 1st edn. c/Rader: gga. F. F2d. $17.00

COLLIER, R. *Lovely & the Damned.* Ace H 189. c/Cheong-Sam. VG. B3d. $7.00

COLLINS, Charles M. edt. *Fright.* 1963. Avon G 1178. PBO. c/Lovecraft. F. P1d. $15.00

COLLINS, Charles M. edt. *Walk With the Beast.* 1969. Avon S 397. Ho. VG. P1d. $5.50

COLLINS, Clark. *Counterfeit Cad.* 1962. Intimate 708. Ad. VG+. B5d. $5.50

COLLINS, Hunt. *Proposition.* 1955. Pyramid 151. PBO. c/gga. scarce. NF. B6a #74. $88.00

COLLINS, Hunt. *Tomorrow & Tomorrow.* 1956. Pyramid G 214. SF. VG. P1d. $8.00

COLLINS, Hunt. *Tomorrow & Tomorrow.* 1956. Pyramid G 214. 1st edn. F. M1d. $20.00

COLLINS, Hunt. *Tomorrow & Tomorrow.* 1961. Pyramid G 654. SF. VG+. B4d. $5.00

COLLINS, Mary. *Dead Center.* 1946. Bantam 62. My. VG. B4d. $3.25

COLLINS, Mary. *Death Warmed Over.* Bantam 718. VG+. I1d. $5.00

COLLINS, Mary. *Dog Eat Dog.* 1951. Bantam 877. NF. G5d. $7.00

COLLINS, Mary. *Fog Comes.* Bantam 23. VG. B3d. $4.00

COLLINS, Mary. *Only the Good.* 1948. Bantam 147. 1st prtg. My. G+. R5d. $1.75

COLLINS, Mary. *Sister of Cain.* 1950. Bantam 787. 1st prtg. My. G+. R5d. $2.75

COLLINS, Michael. *Lukan War.* 1969. Belmont B 60-1023. SF. F. P1d. $6.00

COLLINS, Michael. *Lukan War.* 1969. Belmont B 60-1023. 1st prtg. SF. VG. R5d. $3.00

COLLINS, Norman. *Black Ivory.* Pocket 632. NF. I1d. $7.00

COLLINS, Wilkie. *Haunted Hotel & 25 Other Ghost Stories.* Avon 6. G+. I1d. $30.00

COLLINS, Wilkie. *Haunted Hotel & 25 Other Ghost Stories.* Avon 6. 1st pb. NF. M1d. $65.00

COLLINS, Wilkie. *Moonstone.* 1953. Pyramid G 88. 2nd edn. My. G+. B5d. $3.50

COLLINS, Wilkie. *Moonstone.* 1967. Pyramid X 1402. 6th prtg. SF. G+. W2d. $3.00

COLLISON, Wilson. *Diary of Death.* Novel Library 30. VG. I1d. $9.00

COLLODI, Carlo. *Adventures of Pinocchio.* 1966. Airmont CL 101. 1st prtg. SF. VG. R5d. $2.00

COLLODI, Carlo. *Pinocchio.* 1940. Pocket 18. 2nd prtg. VG+. B3d. $8.00

COLOHAN, Charles E. *Overnight Blonde.* 1949. Quarter Book 50. PBO. c/Rodewald: gga. VG+. B6a #74. $77.00

COLOMBO, Pat. *Throw Back the Little Ones.* Avon F 171. PBO. My. VG. B5d. $2.50

COLT, Clem. *Quick Trigger Country.* 1957. Signet 1403. c/Schulz: gga. We. VG. P6d. $2.00

COLT, Clem. *Strawberry Roan.* Dell 020. VG+. B3d. $4.50

COLTER, Elizabeth. *Gull Cove Murders.* 1945. De Novel Classic 41. 1st pb. My. VG. B6d. $7.00

COLTER, Elizabeth. *Outcast of Lazy S.* 1949. Handi-Book 95. We. VG+. P6d. $7.00

COLTON, James. *Lost on Twilight Road.* 1964. National NLG 100. Ad. VG. B5d. $4.50

COLTON/KARNEY. *Point of No Escape/Knock 'Em Dead.* 1955. Ace D 101. PBO. My. G. B5d. $3.50

COLVIN, I. *Flight 777.* Superior Books NN. MTI. VG+. B3d. $12.00

COMFORT, Will Livingston. *Apache.* Bantam 922. 1st pb. G+. M6d. $7.50

COMICS, E.C. *Vault of Horror.* Ballantine U 2107. 1st pb. G+. M6d. $7.50

COMMAGER, H.S. edt. *Pocket History of Second World War.* Pocket 338. VG+. B3d. $4.00

COMMAGER & NEVINS. *Pocket History of the United States.* 1951. Pocket 195. Nfi. VG. B5d. $4.50

COMPTON, D G. *Steel Crocodile.* Ace 78575. PBO. c/L & D Dillon. SF. VG. B5d. $4.00

COMPTON, D.G. *Chronociles.* 1970. Ace 10480. SF. VG+. P1d. $5.00

COMPTON, D.G. *Continuous Katherine Mortenhoe.* 1975. Arrow 911030. SF. F. P1d. $5.00

COMPTON, D.G. *Electric Crocodile.* 1973. Arrow 907290. SF. F. P1d. $5.00

COMPTON, D.G. *Farewell, Earth's Bliss.* 1971. Ace 22830. SF. VG+. P1d. $4.50

COMPTON, D.G. *Missionaries.* Ace 53570. SF. VG+. B5d. $4.00

COMPTON, D.G. *Missionaries.* 1972. Ace 53570. 1st edn. SF. F. F2d. $12.50

COMPTON, D.G. *Quality of Mercy.* 1970. Ace 69540. 1st edn. F P9d. $3.00

COMPTON, D.G. *Silent Multitude.* Ace 76385. SF. F. P9d. $3.00

COMPTON, D.G. *Steel Crocodile.* 1970. Ace 78575. SF. F. P1d. $6.00

COMPTON, D.G. *Synthajoy.* 1968. Ace H 86. SF. F. P1d. $10.00

COMPTON, D.G. *Synthajoy.* 1979. Berkley 04207. SF. VG. W2d. $3.25

COMPTON, D.G. *Unsleeping Eye.* 1980. Pocket 83077. 1st prtg. SF. F. W2d. $3.75

COMSTOCK, H.T. *Terry.* Bart House 18. VG. I1d. $6.00

CONANT, James Bryant. *Two Modes of Thought.* 1965. Pocket 75059. Nfi. VG+. B5d. $3.00

CONANT, Paul. *Dr Gatskill's Blue Shoes.* 1953. Dell 741. 1st prtg. c/Bobertz: gga. VG. P7d. $5.50

CONCANNON, W. *Happy Birthday, Eddie Newhouse.* Brandon House 1017. VG+. B3d. $6.00

CONDON, Richard. *Manchurian Candidate.* 1960. Signet T 1826. 1st prtg. VG. P7d. $5.00

CONEY, Michael G. *Friends Come in Boxes.* 1973. DAW 56. 1st edn. F. M1d. $9.00

CONEY, Michael G. *Friends Come in Boxes.* 1973. DAW 56. 1st prtg. PBO. c/Holmes. VG. P7d. $4.00

CONEY, Michael G. *Hero of Downways.* 1973. DAW 70. SF. VG+. P1d. $4.50

CONEY, Michael G. *Hero of Downways.* 1973. DAW 70. 1st edn. SF. F. F2d. $10.00

CONEY, Michael G. *Jaws That Bite, the Claws That Catch.* 1975. DAW. 1st edn. F. M1d. $9.00

CONEY, Michael G. *Mirror Image.* 1972. DAW. SF. VG. P1d. $4.00

CONEY, Michael G. *Monitor Found in Orbit.* 1974. DAW 120. PBO. c/K Freas. SF. VG. B5d. $3.00

CONEY, Michael G. *Monitor Found in Orbit.* 1974. DAW 120. 1st edn. F. M1d. $9.00

CONEY, Michael G. *Rax.* 1975. DAW. 1st pb. F. M1d. $7.00

CONEY, Michael G. *Syzygy.* 1975. Arrow 911020. SF. VG+. P1d. $4.50

CONGDON, Don edt. *Combat: Pacific Theater: WW II.* 1958. Dell 1st Edn C 108. 1st prtg. VG. P7d. $4.50

CONGDON, Don edt. *Combat: War With Germany: WW II.* Dell 1381. PBO. c/Schulz. VG+. B3d. $4.50

CONGDON, Don edt. *Stories for the Dead of Night.* 1957. Dell 1st Edn B 107. 1st edn. F. F2d. $9.00

CONGDON, Don edt. *Stories for the Dead of Night.* 1967. Dell 8295. Ho. VG. P1d. $6.50

CONGDON, M & D edts. *Alone by Night.* Ballantine 563. VG. B3d. $4.50

CONKLIN, Groff. *Another Part of the Galaxy.* 1966. Gold Medal D 1628. 1st prtg. SF. VG. R5d. $3.50

CONKLIN, Groff. *Big Book of SF.* Berkley F 975. 3rd edn. VG. P9d. $2.00

CONKLIN, Groff. *Big Book of SF.* 1957. Berkley G 53. 1st pb. F. M1d. $8.00

CONKLIN, Groff. *Big Book of SF.* 1957. Berkley G 53. 1st prtg. SF. G+. R5d. $2.50

CONKLIN, Groff. *BR-R-R!* 1959. Avon T 289. 1st edn. F. M1d. $15.00

CONKLIN, Groff. *Crossroads in Time.* 1953. Perma P 254. SF. G+. P1d. $6.00

CONKLIN, Groff. *Crossroads in Time.* 1953. Perma P 254. 1st pb. F. M1d. $10.00

CONKLIN, Groff. *Dimension 4.* 1964. Pyramid F 973. SF. VG+. B4d. $5.00

CONKLIN, Groff. *Elsewhere & Elsewhen.* 1968. Berkley S 1561. SF. VG. P1d. $5.00

CONKLIN, Groff. *Five-Odd.* 1964. Pyramid R 1056. SF. VG. B4d. $3.75

CONKLIN, Groff. *Giants Unleashed.* Tempo T 111. G. P9d. $1.00

CONKLIN, Groff. *Graveyard Reader.* 1958. Ballantine 257. PBO. SF. VG+. M3d. $10.00

CONKLIN, Groff. *Graveyard Reader.* 1958. Ballantine 257. 1st edn. F. M1d. $20.00

CONKLIN, Groff. *Great SF by Scientists.* 1962. Collier AS 218. SF. VG. P1d. $6.50

CONKLIN, Groff. *Great SF by Scientists.* 1962. Collier AS 218. 1st pb. F. M1d. $8.00

CONKLIN, Groff. *Great Short Novels.* 1954. Dell 1st Edn D 9. PBO. c/Powers. VG+. B6d. $9.00

CONKLIN, Groff. *Great Stories of Space Travel.* 1963. Tempo T 39. SF. VG+. P1d. $9.00

CONKLIN, Groff. *In the Grip of Terror.* 1951. Perma. 1st pb. F. M1d. $25.00

CONKLIN, Groff. *Invaders of Earth.* 1955. Pocket 1074. SF. VG. P1d. $8.00

CONKLIN, Groff. *Minds Unleashed.* 1970. Tempo 5361. SF. VG+. P1d. $5.00

CONKLIN, Groff. *Operation Future.* 1955. Perma M 4022. PBO. c/R Schulz. SF. VG. B5d. $5.00

CONKLIN, Groff. *Operation Future.* 1955. Perma M 4022. SF. F. M1d. $12.00

CONKLIN, Groff. *Operation Future.* 1955. Perma M 4022. VG+. I1d. $6.00

CONKLIN, Groff. *Possible Worlds of SF.* 1955. Berkley G 3. 1st pb. NF. M1d. $8.00

CONKLIN, Groff. *Possible Worlds of SF.* 1960. Berkley G 471. c/R Powers SF. VG. B5d. $3.00

CONKLIN, Groff. *Possible Worlds of SF.* 1960. Berkley G 471. G. P9d. $1.00

CONKLIN, Groff. *Possible Worlds of SF.* 1960. Berkley G 471. 1st prtg. SF. VG+. R5d. $4.00

CONKLIN, Groff. *Possible Worlds of SF.* 1968. Berkley X 1633. 5th edn. SF. NF. B5d. $4.00

CONKLIN, Groff. *Seven Come Infinity.* 1967. Coronet 02880. SF. F. P1d. $10.00

CONKLIN, Groff. *Seven Come Infinity.* 1966. Gold Medal. 1st pb. G+. M1d. $6.00

CONKLIN, Groff. *Seven Trips Through Time & Space.* 1973. Coronet 10866. 3rd edn. SF. VG. P1d. $4.00

CONKLIN, Groff. *Seven Trips Through Time & Space.* 1968. Gold Medal R 1924. 1st prtg. SF. VG. R5d. $5.50

CONKLIN, Groff. *SF Adventures in Mutation.* 1965. Berkley F 1096. SF. VG. P1d. $5.50

CONKLIN, Groff. *SF Oddities.* 1966. Berkley S 1311. SF. VG. P1d. $5.50

CONKLIN, Groff. *SF Omnibus.* 1956. Berkley G 31. 1st pb. F. M1d. $12.00

CONKLIN, Groff. *SF Omnibus.* Berkley 851. c/R Powers. SF. VG+. B3d. $4.50

CONKLIN, Groff. *SF Terror Tales.* 1955. Pocket Book 1045. NF. B3a #21. $4.70

CONKLIN, Groff. *SF Terror Tales.* 1955. Pocket 1045. PBO. c/Brown & Dick. VG+. B6d. $12.00

CONKLIN, Groff. *SF Terror Tales.* 1955. Pocket 1045. SF. VG. P1d. $8.00

CONKLIN, Groff. *SF Terror Tales.* 1955. Pocket. 1st pb. F. M1d. $20.00

CONKLIN, Groff. *SF Thinking Machines.* 1955. Bantam 1352. 1st pb. F. M1d. $12.00

CONKLIN, Groff. *SF Thinking Machines.* 1955. Bantam 1352. 1st pb. VG+. B6d. $7.50

CONKLIN, Groff. *Supernatural Reader.* 1962. Collier. 1st pb. VG. M1d. $6.00

CONKLIN, Groff. *Thinking Machines.* 1955. Bantam 1352. SF. G+. W2d. $4.50

CONKLIN, Groff. *Treasury of SF.* Berkley G 63. c/R Powers. SF. VG. B5d. $4.00

CONKLIN, Groff. *Twisted.* 1967. Belmont B 50-771. SF. VG. B3d/B5d. $4.00

CONKLIN, Groff. *Twisted.* 1962. Belmont. 1st edn. F. M1d. $12.00

CONKLIN, Groff. *Worlds of When.* 1962. Pyramid F 733. SF. F. P1d. $13.00

CONKLIN, Groff. *Worlds of When.* 1962. Pyramid F 733. VG. B3d. $4.00

CONKLIN, Groff. *10 Mysteries by EA Poe.* 1960. TAB T 210. 2nd edn. VG+. B4d. $3.00

CONKLIN, Groff. *12 Great Classics of SF.* Crest T 2749. 1st prtg. VG+. S1d. $4.00

CONKLIN, Groff. *12 Great Classics of SF.* 1963. Gold Medal D 1366. PBO. SF. VG. B5d. $4.00

CONKLIN, Groff. *12 Great Classics of SF.* 1963. Gold Medal D 1366. SF. VG. W2d. $4.50

CONKLIN, Groff. *13 Above the Night.* 1965. Dell 8741. NF. P9d. $2.00

CONKLIN, Groff. *13 Above the Night.* 1965. Dell 8741. SF. VG. P1d. $5.50

CONKLIN, Groff. *13 Great Stories of SF.* 1960. Gold Medal S 997. SF. F. P1d. $17.50

CONKLIN, Groff. *13 Great Stories of SF.* 1960. Gold Medal S 997. SF. VG+. B4d. $6.00

CONKLIN, Groff. *13 Great Stories of SF.* 1960. Gold Medal S 997. 1st prtg. SF. G+. R5d. $3.50

CONKLIN, Groff. *17 X Infinity.* 1963. Dell 7746. SF. VG+. B4d. $2.00

CONKLIN, Groff. *4 for the Future.* 1959. Pyramid G 434. 1st pb. VG. M1d. $8.00

CONKLIN, Groff. *5 Unearthly Visions.* 1965. Gold Medal 1549. 1st edn. SF. NF. F2d. $8.00

CONKLIN, Groff. *5 Unearthly Visions.* Gold Medal D 1868. SF. F. W2d. $5.00

CONKLIN, Groff. *6 Great Short Novels of SF.* Dell 1st Edn 9. VG+. B3d. $4.00

CONKLIN, Groff. *6 Great Short Novels of SF.* 1955. Dell 1st Edn 9. 1st pb. F. M1d. $10.00

CONKLIN, Groff. *6 Great Short SF Novels.* 1960. Dell 1st Edn C 111. SF. F. P1d. $15.00

CONKLIN, Groff. *6 Great Short SF Novels.* 1960. Dell 1st Edn C 111. SF. VG. W2d. $6.00

CONKLIN & FABRICANT edt. *Great SF About Doctors.* 1965. Collier 01895. 3rd edn. SF. VG. P1d. $4.50

CONNELL, Brian. *Return of the Tiger.* 1960. Digit R 524. 1st pb. VG+. B6d. $7.50

CONNELL, E.S. Jr. *Diary of a Rapist.* Dell 1920. VG+. B3d. $5.00

CONNELL, Edwin. *I Had To Kill Her.* 1966. Ballantine U 2327. 1st prtg. My. G+. R5d. $1.50

CONNELL, Vivian. *Bachelors Anonymous.* 1956. Lion LL 140. Fa. VG+. B4d. $10.00

CONNELL, Vivian. *Golden Sleep.* Signet 724. c/Avati. VG+. B3d. $6.50

CONNELL, Vivian. *Man of Parts.* Gold Medal 130. VG. B3d. $4.50

CONNER, Rearden. *Shake Hands With the Devil.* 1959. Crest S 301. 1st prtg. VG. R5d. $4.50

CONNOLLY, Paul. *So Fair, So Evil.* 1955. Gold Medal 500. 1st prtg. PBO. Cr. VG. P6d. $4.50

CONQUEST, Robert. *World of Difference.* 1964. Ballantine U 2213. SF. F. P1d. $12.00

CONRAD, Barnaby. *Dangerfield.* Lancer 72-640. VG. B3d. $4.00

CONRAD, Barnaby. *Innocent Villa.* Avon 537. Fi. VG. B5d. $4.50

CONRAD, Barnaby. *Matador.* Dell 714. c/S Borack. Fi. VG+. B5d. $4.00

CONRAD, Harold. *Battle at Apache Pass.* Avon 729. MTI. VG. B3d. $5.00

CONRAD, Joseph. *Heart of Darkness & the Secret Sharer.* 1950. Signet 834. VG. B3d. $6.00

CONRAD, Joseph. *Lord Jim.* 1965. Signet D 2641. MTI. c/O'Toole & Lavi; photo. VG+. B3d. $4.50

CONRAD, Joseph. *Outcast of the Islands.* 1959. Pyramid G 378. c/gga. Fa. VG+. B4d. $4.75

CONRAD, Joseph. *Secret Agent.* 1954. Anchor A 8. 1st prtg. My. VG. R5d. $2.50

CONRAD/PATTERSON. *Scottsboro Boy.* 1951. Bantam 920. VG+. B4d. $12.00

CONROY, Albert. *Chiselers.* Gold Medal 608. 2nd prtg. VG+. B3d. $5.50

CONROY, Albert. *Looters.* Crest 431. PBO. VG+. B3d. $5.50

CONROY, Albert. *Mr Lucky.* 1960. Dell B 165. 1st edn. TVTI. My. F. F2d. $15.00

CONROY, Albert. *Murder in Room.* 1958. Gold Medal 806. 1st prtg. PBO. VG. P6d. $3.00

CONROY, Albert. *Road's End.* 1952. Gold Medal 231. 1st prtg. PBO. c/Barye Phillips. VG. P6d. $3.00

CONROY, Albert. *Soldato #4: Murder Mission!* Lancer 75459. My. VG+. W2d. $3.25

CONROY, Jim. *Fever.* 1967. Midwood 33-766. Ad. G+. B5d. $3.00

CONROY, Rick. *Mission From Mars.* 1949. Panther NN. PBO. c/gga. SF. VG+. B6a #74. $50.00

CONROY, Rick. *Mission From Mars.* 1952. Panther NN. SF. VG. P1d. $25.00

CONSIDINE, Bob. *General Douglas MacArthur.* Gold Medal 1408. VG+. B3d. $5.00

CONSTABLE & TOLIVER. *Horrido!: Fighter Aces of Luftwaffe.* Ballantine 08197. VG+. B3d. $6.00

CONSTATIN-WEYER, M. *Half-Breed.* Harlequin 318. VG. B3d. $4.00

CONSTINER, M. *Outrage at Bearskin Forks.* 1966. Ace F 401. PBO. VG+. B3d. $4.50

CONTE, Rick. *Shame Run Wild.* 1964. Bell BB 101. Ad. G+. B5d. $3.00

CONTO, W.A. *Spy Who Came to Bed.* Merit 459. VG+. B3d. $5.00

CONVERSE, Jane. *Emergency Nurse.* 1962. Signet S 2079. Fa. VG+. B4d. $4.00

CONVERSE, Jane. *Nurse in Hollywood.* 1965. Signet G 2771. Fa. VG+. B4d. $2.75

CONVERTITO, Bill. *Rombella Shuttle.* 1977. Major 3160. SF. VG+. P1d. $4.50

CONWAY, G.R. *Midnight Dancers.* 1971. Ace 52975. SF. F. P1d. $5.00

CONWAY, G.R. *Midnight Dancers.* 1971. Ace 52975. 1st edn. SF. G. P9d. $1.00

CONWAY, G.R. *Mindship.* 1974. DAW 90. c/K Freas. SF. VG+. B5d. $4.00

CONWAY, John. *Texas Rangers.* 1963. Monarch MA 333. PBO. VG. B3d/P6d. $4.00

CONWAY, John. *Woman Breaker.* 1962. Monarch MA 327. c/gga. Nfi. VG. B4d. $6.00

CONWAY, R. *Naked & Monique.* Brandon House 3028. VG+. B3d. $6.00

CONWAY, Randall. *Nightmare.* 1957. Badger SN 10. PBO. c/Pollack. VG. B6a #77. $50.00

CONWAY, Roger. *Golden Nymph.* 1968. Lancer 74-951. c/photo. Fi. VG. B5d. $4.00

CONWAY, Troy. *Best-Laid Plans.* 1969. PB Library 63-050. PBO. c/Coxeman. VG+. B6d. $6.00

CONWAY, Troy. *Big Broad Jump.* 1969. PB Library 63-240. PBO. c/Coxeman. VG+. B6d. $6.00

CONWAY, Troy. *Big Freak-Out.* 1968. PB Library 53-615. SF/My. VG. P1d. $5.00

CONWAY, Troy. *Billion-Dollar Snatch.* 1968. PB Library 53-675. PBO. c/Coxeman. NF. B6d. $8.00

CONWAY, Troy. *Good Peace.* 1969. PB Library 63-141. PBO. c/Coxeman. NF. B6d. $8.00

CONWAY, Troy. *Horror in the Cinema.* 1971. PB Library 66-627. 1st pb. VG. B6d. $9.00

CONWAY, Troy. *I'd Rather Fight Than Swish.* 1969. PB Library 63-194. PBO. c/Coxeman. VG+. B6d. $6.00

CONWAY, Troy. *It's Getting Harder All the Time.* 1968. PB Library 53-725. SF/My. VG+. P1d. $7.50

CONWAY, Troy. *It's What's Up Front That Counts.* 1969. PB Library 63-069. PBO. c/Coxeman. NF. B6d. $8.00

CONWAY, Troy. *Just a Silly Millimeter.* 1969. PB Library 63-201. PBO. c/Coxeman. VG+. B6d. $6.00

CONWAY, Troy. *Keep It Up, Rod!* 1968. PB Library 53-775. PBO. c/Coxeman. NF. B6d. $8.00

CONWAY, Troy. *Man-Eater.* 1968. PB Library 63-005. PBO. c/Coxeman. NF. B6d. $8.00

CONWAY, Troy. *Penetrator.* 1971. PB Library 64-596. PBO. c/Coxeman. VG+. B6d. $6.00

CONWAY, Troy. *Suspense in the Cinema.* 1971. PB Library 66-683. 1st pb. VG. B6d. $9.00

CONWAY, Troy. *Wham! Bam! Thank You, Ma'am Affair.* 1968. PB Library 53-692. SF/My. G+. P1d. $3.50

CONWAY, Troy. *Whatever Goes Up.* 1969. PB Library 63-125. PBO. c/Coxeman. VG+. B6d. $6.00

COOK, Fred J. *Girl in the Death Cell.* 1953. Gold Medal 306. VG. P6d. $3.50

COOK, Fred J. *Girl in the Death Cell.* Gold Medal 68. c/Barye. VG. B3d. $7.50

COOK, Fred J. *Girl on the Lonely Beach.* Red Seal 56. VG. B3d. $8.00

COOK, Glen. *All Darkness Met.* 1984. Berkley 06541. 2nd edn. Fa. VG. P1d. $3.00

COOK, Glen. *Shadow of All Night Falling.* 1979. Berkley 04260. SF. VG. W2d. $3.50

COOK, Glen. *Swordbearer.* 1982. Pocket 83687. SF. VG. W2d. $3.50

COOK, Rick. *Limbo System.* 1989. Baen 69835. SF. VG+. W2d. $3.75

COOK, Robin. *Mutation.* 1990. Berkley 11965. 1st prtg. SF. VG. W2d. $3.00

COOK, Will. *Drifter.* 1969. Bantam F 3934. We. VG. B5d. $2.50

COOK, Will. *Frontier Feud.* 1954. Popular 596. 1st prtg. VG. P7d. $5.00

COOK, Will. *Outcast of Cripple Creek.* Gold Medal 394. VG. B3d. $6.00

COOK, Will. *We Burn Like Fire.* 1959. Monarch 130. PBO. c/gga. NF. B6a. $67.25

COOK, Will. *Wranglers.* Gold Medal 978. PBO. VG. M6d. $6.50

COOKE, D.C. *Fighting Indians of the West.* Popular EB 53. VG. B3d. $4.00

COOKE, Ronald J. *House on Craig Street.* 1949. News Stand Library 11A. My. G+. B5d. $3.50

COOLIDGE, Dane. *Fighting Men of the West.* Bantam 1043. VG+. B3d. $5.00

COOLIDGE, Dane. *Hell in Paradise Valley.* 1945. We Novel Classic 58. VG. P6d. $3.50

COOMBS, Charles. *Mystery of Satellite 7.* 1962. Tempo T 9. SF. VG. P1d. $6.50

COOMBS, Charles. *Survival in the Sky.* 1959. Badger Science 2. Nfi. G+. P1d. $10.00

COON, Gene L. *Devil in the Dark.* 1978. Bantam 12021. SF. F. W2d. $17.50

COON, Gene L. *Metamorphosis.* 1978. Bantam 11349. Fotonovel. SF. VG+. P1d. $12.50

COON, Horace. *43,000 Years Later.* 1958. Signet S 1534. PBO. SF. VG. B6d. $6.00

COON, Horace. *43,000 Years Later.* 1958. Signet S 1534. 1st edn. SF. F. F2d. $13.00

COON, Susan. *Cassilee.* 1980. Avon 75887. SF. VG. P1d. $3.50

COON, Susan. *Rahne.* 1980. Avon 75044. SF. F. P1d. $6.00

COON, W.A. *House of Lust.* Merit 514. PBO. VG. B3d. $4.50

COONEY, Michael. *Doomsday England.* 1968. Corgi 08032. SF/My. VG. P1d. $5.00

COONTS, Stephen. *Final Flight.* 1989. Dell 20447X. 1st prtg. My. VG+. W2d. $4.25

COOPER, Clarence L. *Weed.* 1961. Regency 109. PBO. c/WA Smith. G+. P6d. $6.00

COOPER, Clarence L. *Weed.* 1961. Regency 109. PBO. c/WA Smith. scarce. VG. B6a #79. $28.00

COOPER, Courtney Ryley. *Pioneers.* Dell 290. c/J Des Vignes. We. NF. B5d. $7.50

COOPER, Edmund. *All Fools' Day.* 1967. Hodder 02860. SF. F. P1d. $10.00

COOPER, Edmund. *Cloud Walker.* 1973. Ballantine 03209. 1st prtg. PBO. VG+. P7d. $4.00

COOPER, Edmund. *Deadly Image.* 1958. Ballantine 260. PBO. VG+. B3d. $5.00

COOPER, Edmund. *Deadly Image.* 1958. Ballantine 260. 1st edn. F. M1d. $12.00

COOPER, Edmund. *Double Phoenix.* 1971. Ballantine 02420. Fa. VG+. P1d. $10.00

COOPER, Edmund. *Far Sunset.* 1968. Berkley X 1607. SF. F. P1d. $10.00

COOPER, Edmund. *Far Sunset.* 1968. Berkley X 1607. SF. VG+. W2d. $4.25

COOPER, Edmund. *Five to Twelve.* 1969. Berkley X 1768. SF. VG. P1d. $4.50

COOPER, Edmund. *Gender Genocide.* 1972. Ace 27905. SF. F. P1d. $5.00

COOPER, Edmund. *News From Elsewhere.* 1969. Berkley X 1696. c/K Freas. SF. NF. B5d. $5.00

COOPER, Edmund. *Overman Culture.* 1973. Berkley 02421. SF. VG+. P1d. $4.50

COOPER, Edmund. *Seed of Light.* 1959. Ballantine 327K. PBO. SF. VG. B5d. $4.50

COOPER, Edmund. *Seed of Light.* 1959. Ballantine 327K. 1st edn. NF. M1d. $10.00

COOPER, Edmund. *Tenth Planet.* 1974. Berkley N 2711. SF. F. P1d. $5.00

COOPER, Edmund. *Tomorrow's Gift.* 1958. Ballantine 279. NF. I1d. $10.00

COOPER, Edmund. *Tomorrow's Gift.* 1958. Ballantine 279. 1st edn. F. M1d. $12.00

COOPER, Edmund. *Transit.* 1965. Four Square 1391. SF. F. P1d. $11.00

COOPER, Hughes. *Sexmax.* 1969. PB Library 64-174. PBO. SF. VG. B5d. $4.00

COOPER, Hughes. *Sexmax.* 1969. PB Library 64-174. 1st edn. F. M1d. $7.00

COOPER, Jefferson. *Bloody Sevens.* 1957. Perma M 3064. PBO. c/C Binger. Fi. VG+. B5d. $6.50

COOPER, Jefferson. *Captain Seadog.* Pocket 1237. PBO. VG+. B3d. $4.50

COOPER, Jefferson. *Swordsman.* 1957. Cardinal C 262. 1st prtg. c/James Meese: gga. VG+. P7d. $5.50

COOPER, John C. *Haunted Strangler.* 1959. Ace D 359. Ho. G+. P1d. $20.00

COOPER, Louise. *Book of Paradox.* 1975. Dell 3344. SF. F. M3d. $7.00

COOPER, Louise. *Inferno.* 1989. TOR 50246. 1st US edn. Fa. NF. B6d. $3.00

COOPER, Lynna. *Brittany Stones.* 1974. Beagle 26614. Go. G+. P1d. $3.00

COOPER, Morton. *Delinquent!* 1958. Avon T 247. JD. G+. P1d. $8.50

COOPER, Morton. *Flesh & Mr Rawlie.* Gold Medal 311. VG+. B3d. $7.00

COOPER, Morton. *French Maid.* 1954. Cameo Books 351. 2nd prtg. reprints #339. G. P6d. $1.00

COOPER, Morton. *Love Survey.* 1961. Avon T 535. 1st edn. My. F. F2d. $12.00

COOPER, Morton. *Private Life of a Strip-Tease Artist.* 1962. Belmont 91-253. PBO. c/Nappi: gga. NF. B6a #74. $48.50

COOPER, Morton. *Ungilded Lily.* 1958. Gold Medal S 812. c/Milton Charles: gga. VG. B3d. $5.00

COOPER, Morton. *Young & Wild.* 1958. Avon T 229. JD. VG+. B4d. $7.50

COOPER, Page. *Big Book of Horse Stories.* 1959. Berkley G 222. 1st pb. NF. B6d. $12.00

COOPER, Parley J. *Feminists.* 1971. Pinnacle P 014-N. SF. VG. P1d. $20.00

COOPER, S.H. edt. *Book of Crossword Puzzles.* MacFadden 50-411. PBO. VG. B3d. $4.00

COOPER, Saul. *All in a Night's Work.* 1961. Popular G 527. MTI. c/Shirley Maclaine. VG+. B3d. $5.00

COOPER, Saul. *My Geisha.* 1961. Dell First Edition K 106. MTI. VG+. B3d. $5.00

COOPER, Sonni. *Black Fire.* 1983. Pocket 83632. SF. F. P1d. $6.00

COOPER, Susan. *Dark Is Rising.* Atheneum A 51. Fa. VG. P1d. $7.50

COOPER, Susan. *Man in the Green Chevy.* 1991. World Wide 26071. My. F. B5d. $6.00

COOPER, Susan. *Mandrake.* 1966. Penguin 2491. SF. VG. P1d. $5.50

COOPER, Susan. *Seaward.* 1985. Puffin 1711. Fa. VG. P1d. $4.00

COOPER & GREEN. *Double Phoenix.* 1971. Ballantine 02420. VG+. B3d. $7.50

COOPER & GREEN. *Double Phoenix.* 1971. Ballantine 02420. 1st edn. Ad/Fa. F. M1d. $15.00

COOVER, Robert. *Public Burning.* 1978. Bantam 11828. Fi. VG+. B5d. $5.50

COPPEL, Alec. *Moment to Moment.* 1966. Gold Medal D 1616. 1st prtg. G+. R5d. $2.25

COPPEL, Alfred. *Dark December.* 1960. Gold Medal S 989. SF. F. P1d. $17.50

COPPEL, Alfred. *Dark December.* 1960. Gold Medal S 989. 1st edn. VG. M1d. $10.00

COPPEL, Alfred. *Hastings Conspiracy.* 1982. Pocket 42609. 1st prtg. My. F. W2d. $3.75

COPPEL, Alfred. *Hero Driver.* 1955. Pocket 1059. c/C Hulings. Fi. VG. B5d. $5.00

COPPEL, Alfred. *Night of Fire & Snow.* Crest 212. VG+. B3d. $6.00

COPPEL, Alfred. *Thirty-Four East.* Popular 08357. My. VG. W2d. $3.50

COPPER, Basil. *Dossier of Solar Pons.* Pinnacle 40-267. G+. G5d. $7.50

COPPER, Basil. *Further Adventures of Solar Pons.* Pinnacle 40-650. F. G5d. $15.00

COPPER, Basil. *Great White Space.* 1976. Manor 12400. Ho. F. P1d. $7.50

CORAL, King. *Jackie.* Bee Line 188. PBO. G+. M6d. $7.50

CORAL, King. *Sweet Cherry.* 1967. Bee Line 206. PBO. NF. B6d. $12.50

CORBETT, Guy. *Grip of Lust.* 1960. Newsstand U 128. Ad. C. B5d. $2.00

CORBIN, G. *Cosa Nostra Circus.* Nite Time 98. VG. B3d. $4.50

CORBIN, Gary. *Ringside Tarts.* 1962. Pillow 105. 1st edn. My. F. F2d. $12.00

CORBIN, Gary. *Ringside Tarts.* 1962. Pillow 501. VG. B3d. $5.00

CORBIN, Glenn. *Trouble on Big Cat.* 1954. Dell 1st Edn 25. PBO. c/Borack. We. VG. B5d. $4.50

CORD, Barry. *Last Chance at Devil's Canyon.* Ace D 400. VG. B3d. $6.50

CORD, Barry. *Maverick Gun.* Hillman 127. VG+. B3d. $3.50

CORD, Barry. *Slade.* 1961. Hillman 200. We. VG. B5d. $4.00

CORD/RINGOLD. *Hell in Paradise Valley/Night Hell's Corners Died.* 1972. Ace 32718. We. VG. B5d. $3.00

CORELLI, Marie. *Mighty Atom.* 1975. Sphere 2544. SF. VG. P1d. $5.00

CORES, Lucy. *Woman in Love.* 1952. Perma P 161. 1st pb. VG. B6d. $6.00

COREY, Frank. *By Blood Alone.* 1961. Berkley G 494. PBO. c/gga. My. VG+. B6d. $15.00

COREY, Paul. *Planet of the Blind.* 1969. PB Library 63-147. PBO. c/R Powers. SF. VG+. B5d. $4.00

CORGAN, Grant. *Swing Shift.* 1964. Midwood 384. 1st edn. c/gga. F. F2d. $10.00

CORLE, Edwin. *Apache Devil.* 1952. Pyramid 63. 1st pb. We. VG. B6d. $9.00

CORLE, Edwin. *Billy the Kid.* 1954. Bantam A 1246. We. VG. B4d. $3.25

CORLE, Edwin. *Burro Alley.* Pennant P 27. VG+. B3d. $6.50

CORLE, Edwin. *In Winter Light.* 1954. Pennant P 65. Fa. VG. B4d. $5.00

CORLE, Edwin. *Mojave, a Book of Stories.* Pennant P 6. G+. I1d. $4.00

CORLEY, C. *Faces in Secret.* PEC HES 101. NF. B3d. $6.00

CORLEY, C. *Lover Mourned.* PEC FL 24. VG. B3d. $4.50

CORLEY, Edwin. *Jesus Factor.* 1972. Mayflower 12098. SF. VG. P1d. $4.00

CORLEY, Edwin. *Sargasso.* 1978. Dell 17575. SF. VG. P1d. $3.50

CORLISS, Richard. *Greta Garbo.* 1974. Pyramid M 3480. 1st prtg. VG. R5d. $5.00

CORNE, M.E. *Death Is No Lady.* Black Knight 2. VG. B3d. $6.00

CORNE, M.E. *Jealousy Pulls the Trigger.* 1943. Double Action Do 3. 1st pb. VG. B6d. $12.50

CORNELL, James. *Monster of Loch Ness.* Scholastic 3726. Nfi. VG. W2d. $3.00

CORREY/LEINSTER. *Contraband Rocket/Forgotten Planet.* Ace D 146. VG. B3d. $4.00

CORT, David. *Calm Man.* 1954. Dell 1st Edn 34. PBO. c/G Erickson. Fi. VG. B5d/I1d. $4.00

CORWIN, Norman. *Selected Radio Plays.* Armed Service R 7. VG. B3d. $8.00

CORY, Desmond. *Johnny Fedora: High Requiem.* 1969. Award A 408X. 1st prtg. My. VG. W2d. $4.50

CORY, Desmond. *Shockwave.* 1965. Signet D 2693. My. VG+. B4d. $3.00

CORY, Howard L. *Sword of Lankor.* 1966. Ace F 373. 1st prtg. F. S1d. $5.00

CORY/DICK. *Mind Monsters/Unteleported Man.* 1966. Ace G 602. SF. F. P1d. $35.00

CORY/DICK. *Mind Monsters/Unteleported Man.* 1966. Ace G 602. SF. G+. P1d. $10.00

CORY/DICK. *Mind Monsters/Unteleported Man.* 1966. Ace G 602. SF. VG. P1d. $20.00

COSS, Rollin. *Private Life of Eleanor.* Chariot CB 104. F. G5d. $7.00

COSTA, Rolf. *Craving Clan.* 1964. Prize 102. PBO. NF. B6d. $12.50

COSTAIN, Thomas B. *Black Rose.* Armed Services 1082. Fi. VG. B5d. $4.00

COSTAIN, Thomas B. *Black Rose.* Bantam A 818. c/Maguire. VG+. B6d. $2.50

COSTIGAN, Lee. *Hard Sell.* 1964. Tower 44-429. TVTI. VG. P1d. $7.50

COTTO, Max. *Devil at 4 O'Clock.* 1961. Popular SP 99. 1st prtg. VG. R5d. $2.75

COTTON, Jerry. *In the Lion's Den.* Threestar 101. VG+. B3d. $4.50

COTTON, Will. *Night Was Made for Murder.* 1959. Avon T 306. 1st edn. c/gga. My. F. F2d. $13.00

COTTRELL, L. *Lost Cities.* Pan G 304. VG. B3d. $6.50

COTTRELL, L. *Lost Pharaohs.* Pan GP 54. VG+. I1d. $6.00

COTTRELL, L. *Wonders on Antiquity.* Pan X 190. VG. B3d. $7.50

COUGHLAN, Robert. *Private World of William Faulkner.* 1962. Avon G 1144. Nfi. VG. P1d. $4.50

COULSON, Juanita. *Legacy of Earth.* Ballantine 28180. SF. VG+. W2d. $3.75

COULSON, Juanita. *Secret of Seven Oaks.* 1972. Berkley S 2167. My. VG. P1d. $4.00

COULSON, Juanita. *Space Trap.* 1976. Laser 20. PBO. c/K Freas: sgn. SF. VG. B5d. $4.50

COULSON, Juanita. *Space Trap.* 1976. Laser 20. 1st edn. SF. F. F2d. $10.00

COULSON, Juanita. *Tomorrow's Heritage.* 1981. Ballantine 28178. SF. VG. W2d. $3.00

COULSON, Juanita. *Unto the Last Generation.* 1975. Laser 11. PBO. c/K Freas: sgn. SF. F. B5d. $8.00

COULSON, Juanita. *Unto the Last Generation.* 1975. Laser 11. 1st prtg. F. S1d. $4.00

COULSON & DEWEESE. *Gates of the Universe.* 1975. Laser 4. PBO. c/K Freas: sgn. SF. F. B5d. $8.00

COULSON & TUBB. *Singing Stone/Derai.* 1968. Ace H 77. 1st prtg. VG. S1d. $4.00

COULTER, Adam. *Debauchee.* 1963. France 56. 1st edn. F. F2d. $10.00

COULTER, Adam. *Four To Go-Go-Go!* Boudoir 1402. VG+. B3d. $6.00

COULTER, Adam. *Golden Lust.* 1962. France 26. 1st edn. c/gga. F. F2d. $10.00

COULTER, Adam. *Insatiable!* 1964. Novel Book 6N264. 1st edn. My. F. F2d. $20.00

COULTER, Adam. *Rape of Eden.* 1962. Fabian 158. 1st edn. My. F. F2d. $12.00

COULTER, Adam. *Savage Passions.* 1961. Novel Book 5051. 1st edn. De. F. F2d. $20.00

COULTER, Stephen. *Damned Shall Be Desire.* Avon G 1048. Fi. VG. B5d. $2.50

COUNSEL, Firth. *Juvenile Jungle.* 1958. Avon T 219. PBO. MTI. c/photo. scarce. JD. NF. B6a #74. $22.00

COURTNEY, Vincent. *Vampire Beat.* 1991. Pinnacle 521. Ho. VG. P1d. $4.50

COUSTEAU & DUGAN. *Living Sea.* 1964. Pocket 75008. Nfi. VG+. B5d. $3.50

COVER, Arthur Byron. *Autumn Angels.* Pyramid V 3787. 1st prtg. VG+. S1d. $4.00

COVER, Arthur Byron. *Autumn Angels.* 1975. Pyramid V 3787. SF. F. P1d. $7.50

COVER, Arthur Byron. *East Wind Coming.* Berkley 00394. VG. G5d. $15.00

COVER, Arthur Byron. *East Wind Coming.* 1979. Berkley 04439. SF/My. VG. P1d. $7.50

COVER, Arthur Byron. *Flash Gordon.* 1980. Jove 5848. 1st edn. MTI. c/photos. SF. F. F2d. $10.00

COVER, Arthur Byron. *Planetfall.* 1988. Avon 75384. SF. VG. W2d. $3.50

COVER, Arthur Byron. *Sound of Winter.* 1976. Pyramid V 4017. SF. F. P1d. $7.50

COVERT, Paul. *Escape to Nowhere.* 1977. Major 3127. PBO. My. VG+. B6d. $7.00

COVINGTON, Ursula. *Swapper's Market.* 1972. Liverpool TNS 545. Ad. VG. B5d. $3.50

COVINGTON, Ursula. *Swapping Teachers.* 1973. Liverpool TNS 552. Ad. VG. B5d. $3.50

COVINGTON, Ursula. *Tricked Into Swapping.* 1974. Liverpool TNS 574. Ad. NF. B5d. $5.50

COWARD, Noel. *Short Stories, Short Plays, & Songs.* 1955. Dell 1st Edn D 80. PBO. c/N Coward photo. NF. VG. B5d. $3.00

COWARD, Noel. *Star Quality.* Pan 257. VG. B3d. $7.50

COWARD, Noel. *Tonight at 8:30.* Avon 28. VG. B3d. $5.00

COWPER, Richard. *Clone.* 1974. Avon 20453. SF. F. P1d. $5.00

COWPER, Richard. *Kuldesak.* 1973. Quartet 31075. SF. VG+. P1d. $5.00

COWPER, Richard. *Profundis.* 1981. Pocket 83502. SF. F. P1d. $5.00

COWPER, Richard. *Time Out of Mind.* 1976. Orbit 31242. SF. V.G P1d. $4.25

COWPER, Richard. *Twilight of Briareus.* DAW 158. 1st prtg. VG. S1d. $2.50

COX, I. *Cock-Sure Reporter.* Brandon House 6498. NF. B3d. $4.50

COX, Joan. *Mind Song.* 1979. Avon 43638. SF. VG. W2d. $3.50

COX, Joan. *Star Web.* 1980. Avon 75697. SF. VG. W2d. $3.25

COX, Sidney. *Swinger of Birches: Robert Frost.* 1961. Collier AS 124. Nfi. F. P1d. $10.00

COX, T. *Weekend.* Midwood 92. VG. B3d. $5.00

COX, William R. *Hell To Pay.* 1958. Signet 1555. 1st edn. JD. F. F2d. $25.00

COXE, G.H. *Alias the Dead.* Dell 377. VG+. B3d. $5.00

COXE, G.H. *Assignment in Guiana.* Dell 321. My. G+. B5d. $3.00

COXE, G.H. *Assignment in Guiana.* Dell 321. VG. B3d/I1d. $5.00

COXE, G.H. *Camera Clue.* 1944. Dell 27. F. F2d. $20.00

COXE, G.H. *Camera Clue.* 1944. Dell 27. 1st edn. PBO. c/Gerald Gregg. NF. B6a #75. $38.50

COXE, G.H. *Camera Clue.* Dell 453. c/R Stanley. My. VG. B5d. $5.00

COXE, G.H. *Charred Witness.* 1948. Dell 240. c/skull & burning hand. My. VG. B4d. $7.00

COXE, G.H. *Charred Witness.* 1948. Dell 240. G. G5d. $5.00

COXE, G.H. *Crimson Clue.* Perma M 3010. VG. B3d. $4.00

COXE, G.H. *Dangerous Legacy.* Dell 586. VG. G5d. $5.00

COXE, G.H. *Eye Witness.* Dell 902. VG. G5d. $5.00

COXE, G.H. *Fashioned for Murder.* Dell 678. My. G. W2d. $2.00

COXE, G.H. *Focus on Murder.* 1958. Dell 970. 1st prtg. My. VG. R5d. $2.75

COXE, G.H. *Four Frightened Women.* Dell 5. NF. F2d. $16.00

COXE, G.H. *Frightened Fiancee.* Dell 836. c/D Neiser. My. VG+. B5d. $4.00

COXE, G.H. *Glass Triangle.* Dell 522. VG. B3d. $4.50

COXE, G.H. *Groom Lay Dead.* Dell 502. 1st prtg. My. VG. R5d. $3.50

COXE, G.H. *Hollow Needle.* Dell 757. My. G+. W2d. $4.50

COXE, G.H. *Impetuous Mistress.* Dell D 421. VG+. G5d. $4.50

COXE, G.H. *Inland Passage.* Dell 799. VG. I1d. $4.00

COXE, G.H. *Jade Venus.* Dell 549. VG+. B3d. $5.00

COXE, G.H. *Lady Is Afraid.* Dell 147. c/G Gregg. My. G+. B5d. $5.00

COXE, G.H. *Mission of Fear.* 1965. Pyramid R 1206. My. NF. B4d. $5.00

COXE, G.H. *Murder For the Asking.* Dell 58. c/G Gregg. My. G+. B5d. $7.50

COXE, G.H. *Murder For the Asking.* 1944. Dell 58. PBO. c/Gerald Gregg. NF. B6a #74. $40.25

COXE, G.H. *Murder for Two.* Dell 276. My. NF. B5d. $10.00

COXE, G.H. *Murder for Two.* Dell 276. VG. B3d. $4.50

COXE, G.H. *Murder in Havana.* Dell 423. c/Barye. VG. B3d. $4.50

COXE, G.H. *Murder in Havana.* Dell 423. 1st prtg. My. G+. R5d. $3.00

COXE, G.H. *Murder on Their Minds.* Dell D 271. G. G5d. $3.50

COXE, G.H. *Murder With Pictures.* Dell 101. F. F2d. $15.00

COXE, G.H. *Murder With Pictures.* 1946. Dell 101. 1st prtg. My. VG. R5d. $8.00

COXE, G.H. *Murdock's Acid Test.* Dell 169. G+. G5d. $5.00

COXE, G.H. *Never Bet Your Life.* Dell 931. G+. G5d. $3.50

COXE, G.H. *No Time To Kill.* Dell 182. VG. B3d. $7.00

COXE, G.H. *No Time To Kill.* Dell 182. 1st prtg. My. G+. R5d. $5.50

COXE, G.H. *One Hour To Kill.* 1964. Pyramid R 1180. My. VG+. B4d. $4.00

COXE, G.H. *One Minute Past Eight.* 1960. Dell D 346. 1st prtg. My. VG. W2d. $5.00

COXE, G.H. *Silent Are the Dead.* Dell 225. c/G Gregg. My. G+. B5d. $5.00

COXE, G.H. *Silent Are the Dead.* Dell 225. VG. B3d. $8.00

COYNE, John. *Hobgoblin.* 1982. Berkley 05727. Ho. VG+. P1d. $5.50

COZZENS, James Gould. *Castaway.* Armed Services S 4. VG. B3d. $6.00

COZZENS, James Gould. *Castaway.* 1952. Bantam. 1st pb. F. M1d. $7.00

COZZENS, James Gould. *SS San Pedro.* Berkley 103. VG. B5d. $4.50

COZZENS, James Gould. *SS San Pedro.* 1955. Berkley 103. F. P1d. $16.00

COZZENS/COZZENS. *Castaway/SS San Pedro.* Modern Library P17. Fi. VG. B5d. $3.50

CRABB, Alfred Leland. *Dinner at Belmont.* 1952. Cardinal C 81. Fa. VG+. B4d. $2.00

CRACIUNAS, S. *Lost Footsteps.* Berkley G 747. VG+. B3d. $4.50

CRAIG, D.W. *Never Too Young.* 1965. Midwood 32-469. PBO. c/photo. Ad. VG. B5d. $4.00

CRAIG, D.W. *None But the Wicked.* 1963. Midwood F 249. Fa. VG+. B4d. $9.00

CRAIG, Jonathan. *Alley Girl.* 1954. Lion 206. PBO. c/gga. My. VG. B6d. $15.00

CRAIG, Jonathan. *Case of the Beautiful Body.* Gold Medal 702. c/Zuckerberg. VG. B3d. $4.00

CRAIG, Jonathan. *Case of the Brazen Beauty.* 1966. Gold Medal 1706. 1st edn. De. F. F2d. $10.00

CRAIG, Jonathan. *Case of the Laughing Virgin.* 1960. Gold Medal 1065. 1st edn. c/gga. De. F. F2d. $11.00

CRAIG, Jonathan. *Case of the Nervous Nude.* 1959. Gold Medal 872. 1st edn. c/gga. De. F. F2d. $10.00

CRAIG, Jonathan. *Case of the Nervous Nude.* Gold Medal 872. VG+. B3d. $4.50

CRAIG, Jonathan. *Case of the Petticoat Murder.* Gold medal 784. NF. G5d. $10.00

CRAIG, Jonathan. *Case of the Village Tramp.* 1959. Gold Medal 930. VG. P6d. $3.50

CRAIG, Jonathan. *Morgue for Venus.* 1956. Gold Medal 582. PBO. c/Barye. My. VG. B6d. $5.00

CRAIG, Jonathan. *Renegade Cop.* 1959. Berkley D 2015. 1st pb. c/Milo. My. NF. B6d. $15.00

CRAIG, Saxon. *Desert Lust.* 1968. Saber Book SA 132. PBO. c/gga. NF. B6a #76. $35.00

CRAIG & MCBAIN. *April Robin Murders.* Dell D 306. VG+. I1d. $5.00

CRANDALL, Edward. *White Violets.* 1965. PB Library 52-520. 1st pb. Go. NF. B6d. $6.00

CRANE, Frances. *Amethyst Spectacles.* Armed Services Q 17. NF. I1d. $8.00

CRANE, Frances. *Cinnamon Murder.* 1947. Bantam 130. 1st prtg. My. G. G5d. $4.50

CRANE, Frances. *Golden Box.* 1946. Popular 80. c/Hoffman. NF. B3a #21. $29.35

CRANE, Frances. *Golden Box.* 1946. Popular 80. 1st pb. c/Hoffman. My. VG. B6d/I1d. $12.50

CRANE, Frances. *Indigo Necklace Murders.* 1948. Bantam 312. My. VG+. B4d. $9.00

CRANE, Frances. *Murder on the Purple Water.* 1951. Bantam 874. c/Denver Gillen: gga. VG. B3d. $4.00

CRANE, Frances. *Yellow Violet.* 1947. Popular 108. 1st pb. My. VG. B6d. $12.50

CRANE, Frances. *13 White Tulips.* Penguin. VG. G5d. $8.50

CRANE, Robert. *Hero's Walk.* Ballantine 71. G+. I1d. $5.00

CRANE, Robert. *Hero's Walk.* 1954. Ballantine 71. SF. F. P1d. $20.00

CRANE, Robert. *Hero's Walk.* 1954. Ballantine 71. 1st prtg. PBO. VG. P7d/S1d. $7.50

CRANE, Stephen. *Illusion in Red & White.* 1962. Avon G 1139. 1st edn. F. F2d. $20.00

CRANE, Stephen. *Red Badge of Courage.* American Red Cross. VG. B3d. $8.00

CRANE, Stephen. *Red Badge of Courage.* Pocket 154. VG. B3d. $6.00

CRATER, Stella. *Empty Robe.* 1964. Dell 2346. Nfi. NF. B4d. $3.00

CRAWFORD, F. Marion. *Khaled.* 1971. Ballantine 02446. Fa. G+. P1d. $5.00

CRAWFORD, F. Marion. *Khaled.* 1971. Ballantine 02446. 1st edn. Ad/Fa. F. M1d. $15.00

CRAWFORD, John. *Dark Legion.* 1965. Badger SN 106. Ho. G+. P1d. $5.00

CRAWFORD, Oliver. *Blood on the Branches.* 1956. Ace S 141. PBO. c/gga. scarce. F. B6a #74. $63.00

CRAWFORD, Oliver. *Blood on the Branches.* 1956. Ace S 141. PBO. VG. B6d. $15.00

CRAWFORD, R. *Gang Girls.* 1963. Playtime 626. JD. F. P1d. $30.00

CRAWFORD, R. *Sex Playground.* Playtime 607. NF. B3d. $7.00

CRAWFORD & BAR-DAVID. *Galileo 7.* 1978. Bantam 12041. SF. VG+. P1d. $12.50

CRAWLEY, R. *Game of Sin.* Dragon Books 132. PBO. NF. B3d. $5.00

CRAY, E. *Pill Pushers.* Brandon House 1005. VG+. B3d. $6.00

CRAZE, Anthony. *Harvest Moon.* 1975. Orbit 7877. Ho. VG. P1d. $4.00

CREASEY, John. *Baron & the Missing Old Masters.* Lancer 74701. My. VG. W2d. $4.00

CREASEY, John. *Battle for Inspector West.* 1971. Lancer 74749. c/skull. My. VG+. B5d. $4.00

CREASEY, John. *Beauty for Inspector West.* Pan 383. 2nd prtg. VG. B3d. $5.50

CREASEY, John. *Beauty Queen Killer.* 1965. Berkley F 1095. 1st prtg. My. G+. R5d. $1.75

CREASEY, John. *Blight.* 1970. Hodder 12799. SF/My. VG. P1d. $4.50

CREASEY, John. *Blind Spot.* 1965. Berkley F 1052. My. VG+. B5d. $4.00

CREASEY, John. *Case of the Acid Throwers.* Avon 641. VG. B3d. $4.50

CREASEY, John. *Creepers.* 1954. Avon 563. 1st prtg. c/Al Rossi: gga. VG+. P7d. $7.50

CREASEY, John. *Dark Peril.* 1964. Arrow 779. SF/My. F. P1d. $12.00

CREASEY, John. *Death in Cold Print.* Lancer 74738. My. VG. W2d. $3.25

CREASEY, John. *Death of a Postman.* 1965. Berkley F 1167. 1st prtg. My. VG. R5d. $3.25

CREASEY, John. *Death of a Racehorse.* 1963. Berkley F 757. 1st pb. My. NF. B6d. $10.00

CREASEY, John. *Death of a Racehorse.* Lancer 74-767. reprint. My. NF. B6d. $7.50

CREASEY, John. *Depths.* 1974. Arrow 908680. SF/My. VG. P1d. $4.00

CREASEY, John. *Dissemblers.* 1968. Berkley X 1608. 1st prtg. My. G+. R5d. $1.00

CREASEY, John. *Figure in the Dusk.* Avon T 366. My. VG. B5d. $2.50

CREASEY, John. *Figure in the Dusk.* Avon 590. VG. I1d. $5.00

CREASEY, John. *Gelignite Gang.* 1959. Bantam 1884. 1st prtg. My. G+. R5d. $1.50

CREASEY, John. *Gun for Inspector West.* Hodder 246. VG. B3d. $6.50

CREASEY, John. *Hang the Little Man.* 1966. Berkley F 1280. c/V Kalin. My. VG+. B5d. $4.00

CREASEY, John. *Hit & Run.* 1961. Berkley G 552. c/V Kalin. My. VG. B5d. $3.00

CREASEY, John. *House of the Bears.* 1967. Arrow 1007. 2nd edn. SF/My. VG. P1d. $7.50

CREASEY, John. *Inspector West Alone.* Fontana 369. 2nd edn. VG. B3d. $6.00

CREASEY, John. *Inspector West at Bay.* Pan VG. G5d. $6.50

CREASEY, John. *Kill a Wicked Man.* Signet 1573. VG+. G5d. $3.75

CREASEY, John. *Leave It to the Toff.* 1965. Pyramid R 1121. My. F. W2d. $5.25

CREASEY, John. *Nest of Traitors.* 1973. Corgi 09162. 1st prtg. My. VG+. W2d. $4.25

CREASEY, John. *Plague of Silence.* 1973. Arrow 907520. SF/My. VG. P1d. $4.00

CREASEY, John. *Plague of Silence.* 1962. Hodder 542. SF/My. F. P1d. $13.00

CREASEY, John. *Plague of Silence.* Lancer 74602. SF. VG. W2d. $3.00

CREASEY, John. *Poison for the Toff.* Pyramid 1194. VG+. B3d. $4.00

CREASEY, John. *Policeman's Dread.* 1966. Berkley F 1202. 1st prtg. My. VG+. R5d. $4.00

CREASEY, John. *Policeman's Dread.* Pan X 391. VG. B3d. $5.00

CREASEY, John. *Rocket for the Toff.* 1964. Pyramid R 1085. 1st prtg. My. VG. W2d. $4.25

CREASEY, John. *Sleep.* 1971. Lancer 74759. SF/My. VG. P1d. $4.00

CREASEY, John. *Smog.* 1972. Award AN 1028. SF/My. VG. P1d. $4.00

CREASEY, John. *So Young, So Cold.* Dell 985. NF. G5d. $4.50

CREASEY, John. *Strike for Death.* Pan G 332. My. VG. B5d. $4.00

CREASEY, John. *Strike for Death.* Pan G 332. VG+. B3d. $7.00

CREASEY, John. *Terror Trap.* 1969. Popular 01537. My. VG+. B5d. $3.50

CREASEY, John. *Toff at the Fair.* Lancer 420053. My. F. W2d. $4.25

CREASEY, John. *Touch of Death.* 1960. Hodder 413. SF/My. VG+. P1d. $10.50

CREASEY, John. *Touch of Death.* 1971. Lancer 75237. My. VG. W2d. $3.25

CREASEY, John. *Traitor's Doom.* 1965. Arrow 853. SF/My. VG. P1d. $7.50

CREASEY, John. *Unbegotten.* 1975. Manor 12310. SF. VG. W2d. $3.50

CREIGHTON, John. *Destroying Angel.* 1956. Ace D 167. PBO. scarce. VG+. B6a. $34.25

CREIGHTON/MORRIS. *Dig Her a Grave/ Half Interest in Murder.* Ace D 425. PBO. B3d. $4.00

CREIGHTON/TRIMBLE. *Trial by Perjury/Smell of Trouble.* Ace D 321. VG. B3d. $4.50

CRICHTON, Michael. *Andromeda Strain.* 1970. Dell 0199. SF/My. VG. P1d. $4.50

CRICHTON, Michael. *Congo.* 1981. Avon 56176. SF/My. VG. P1d. $3.50

CRICHTON, Michael. *Sphere.* 1988. Ballantine 35314. 1st pb. SF. VG+. B6d. $3.00

CRICHTON, Michael. *Terminal Man.* 1973. Bantam X 7545. SF/My. VG. P1d. $3.50

CRICHTON, Michael. *Westworld.* 1974. Bantam Q 8441. SF. VG. P1d. $4.50

CRICHTON, Michael. *Westworld.* Bantam 9825. 2nd prtg. MTI. VG. B3d. $4.50

CRISP, Robert. *Gods Were Neutral.* 1961. Ballantine F 565. c/tanks. War. VG. B4d. $2.00

CRISPIN, A.C. *Time for Yesterday.* 1988. Pocket 60372-X. 1st edn. SF. F. F2d. $6.00

CRISPIN, A.C. *V.* 1984. Pinnacle 42237. SF. VG. W2d. $4.50

CRISPIN, A.C. *Yesterday's Son.* 1983. Pocket 47315. SF. F. W2d. $5.25

CRISPIN & MARSHALL. *Death Tide.* 1985. Pinnacle 42469. SF. VG. P1d. $4.50

CRISTABEL. *Cruachan & the Killane.* 1970. Curtis 07093. SF. VG. P1d. $4.50

CROCKETT, D. *Life of Davy Crockett.* 1955. Signet 1214. 2nd prtg. VG. B3d. $4.50

CROCKETT, Vivian. *Messalina.* 1955. Berkley G 14. c/R Nappi: gga. Fi. G+. V5d. $5.00

CROFT, F.W. *Tragedy in the Hollow.* Popular 18. VG. B3d. $5.00

CROFT-COOKE & HEAD. *Buffalo Bill.* Corgi 224. VG. B3d. $8.00

CROFTS, Freeman Wills. *Cask.* Penguin 575. VG. G5d. $5.00

CROFTS, Freeman Wills. *Cold-Blooded Murder.* 1947. Avon 126. 1st edn. PBO. VG. B6d. $18.00

CROFTS, Freeman Wills. *Sir John Magill's Last Journey.* Pocket 105. VG. B3d. $4.00

CROFTS, Freeman Wills. *Tragedy in the Hollow.* 1944. Popular 18. 1st pb. c/Hoffman. My. VG. B6d. $18.00

CROFTS, Freeman Wills. *Willful & Premeditated.* Avon 9. My. VG+. B6d. $18.00

CROHN, P. *How To Live With Your Heart.* Graphic G 204. VG. B3d. $4.00

CRONIN, A.J. *Spanish Gardener.* Bantam 1719. VG+. B3d. $4.50

CROSBY, Bing. *Call Me Lucky.* 1954. Cardinal C 146. Bio. VG+. B4d. $2.00

CROSS, Amanda. *Theban Mysteries.* 1973. PB Library 75-007. c/photo. My. VG. B5d. $4.00

CROSS, Beverley. *Nightwalkers.* Signet 1528. G+. G5d. $3.50

CROSS, Gene. *Nitty-Gritty Affair.* 1967. Ember Library 361. PBO. c/gga. VG+. B6a. $101.00

CROSS, James. *Dark Road.* 1960. Crest 366. VG. P6d. $2.00

CROSS, John Keir. *Other Passenger.* 1961. Ballantine 480K. PBO. c/R Powers. SF. VG+. B5d. $8.00

CROSS, Victor. *Blood Sport.* 1966. Award A 204XK. JD. F. P1d. $20.00

CROSS, Victor. *Blood Sport.* 1966. Award A 204XK. 1st prtg. PBO. c/gga. JD. VG. P7d. $5.00

CROSSEN, Kendall Foster. *Adventures in Tomorrow.* Belmont 75-215. VG+. B3d. $4.00

CROSSEN, Kendall Foster. *Year of Consent.* 1954. Dell 1st Edn 32. 1st edn. F. M1d. $10.00

CROSSEN, Kendell Foster. *Year of Consent.* 1954. Dell 1st Edn 32. PBO. c/R Powers. SF. VG. B3d/B5d. $5.00

CROSSMAN, R. edt. *God That Failed.* Bantam 963. VG+. B3d. $3.50

CROUSE, W.H. *Home Guide To Fix Your Bloody House.* Popular 323. VG. B3d. $4.00

CROW, C. *400 Million Customers.* Pocket 323. 1st prtg. NF. B3d. $5.00

CROWELL, A. *Body Abusers.* Barclay 7009. VG+. B3d. $4.50

CROWLEY, Aleister. *Confessions of Aleister Crowley.* 1971. Bantam Y 5820. 2nd edn. Nfi. VG. P1d. $5.00

CROWLEY, John. *Beasts.* 1978. Bantam 11102. SF. VG. P1d. $5.00

CROWLEY, John. *Engine Summer.* 1980. Bantam 13199. 1st prtg. SF. VG. R5d. $1.75

CROWLEY, Liz. *I Sell Love.* 1960. Monarch 508. c/gga. Nfi. F. B4d. $8.00

CROWLEY, Liz. *I Sell Love.* 1960. Monarch 508. PBO. scarce. NF. B6a #76. $27.50

CROWTHER, Bosley. *Hollywood Rajah.* 1961. Dell S 13. 1st prtg. Bio. VG+. R5d. $3.50

CROY, Homer. *Country Cured.* Armed Services L 21. G. G5d. $3.00

CROY, Homer. *Family Honeymoon.* Bantam 413. MTI. VG+. B3d. $5.00

CROY, Homer. *Last of the Great Outlaws.* 1958. Signet S 1495. 1st pb. VG. B6d. $7.00

CRUME, Vic. *Dr Syn, 'The Scarecrow.* 1975. Pyramid NN. MTI. VG. B4d. $2.75

CRUME, Vic. *Marked for Terror.* 1972. Curtis 06182. 1st prtg. My. VG. R5d. $1.75

CRUME, Vic. *Mystery in Dracula's Castle.* 1973. Scholastic 2443. My. VG. P1d. $4.50

CRUME, Vic. *Terror by Night.* 1971. Curtis 06148. 1st prtg. VG. R5d. $1.00

CRUME, Vic. *Unidentified Flying Oddball.* 1979. Scholastic 30061. 1st prtg. MTI. VG+. R5d. $1.75

CRUME, Vic. *Whiz Kid & the Carnival Caper.* 1975. Pyramid V 3948. TVTI. VG. B4d. $2.75

CRUMLEY, James. *Last Good Kiss.* Pocket 82813. VG. G5d. $4.50

CRUZ, Daniel. *Pipe Dream Finesse.* 1975. Ballantine 24436. 1st prtg. My. VG+. R5d. $2.00

CULBERTSON, Ely. *Contract Bridge for Everyone.* 1948. Signet 681. c/R Jonas. Nfi. VG. B5d. $3.50

CULBREATH & MARSHAK. *Fate of the Phoenix.* 1979. Bantam 12770. TVTI. Star Trek. SF. VG+. B5d. $5.50

CULBREATH & MARSHAK. *New Voyages.* Bantam 02719. 7th edn. TVTI. Star Trek. SF. NF. B5d. $5.00

CULBREATH & MARSHAK. *Price of the Phoenix.* Bantam 10978. NF. P9d. $1.75

CULLEN, Seamus. *Astra & Flondric.* 1979. Pocket 82256. SF. VG. W2d. $3.25

CULVER, Edward. *Playhouse of Passion.* 1960. Newsstand 510. 1st edn. c/gga. F. F2d. $13.00

CULVER, Edward. *She Had To Be Loved!* 1959. Newsstand U 117. Ad. VG+. B5d. $5.50

CULVER, Edward. *She Had To Be Loved!* Newsstand U 117. VG. B3d. $4.00

CULVER, Edward. *She Had To Be Loved!* 1959. Newsstand U 117. 1st edn. c/gga. F. F2d. $12.50

CULVER, Kathryn. *Sleepy Time Honey.* 1951. Rainbow Book 110. 1st edn. PBO. c/gga. VG+. B6a #80. $97.00

CUMMINGS, M.A. *Exile.* 1968. Flagship 864. SF. VG. P1d. $5.00

CUMMINGS, Ray. *Beyond the Stars.* 1963. Ace F 248. F. M1d. $10.00

CUMMINGS, Ray. *Beyond the Stars.* 1963. Ace F 248. SF. VG. P1d. $6.00

CUMMINGS, Ray. *Beyond the Vanishing Point.* Ace D 331. VG+. B3d. $5.00

CUMMINGS, Ray. *Brand New World.* 1964. Ace F 313. SF. VG+. W2d. $5.00

CUMMINGS, Ray. *Brand New World.* 1964. Ace F 313. 1st edn. SF. F. F2d. $8.00

CUMMINGS, Ray. *Brigands of the Moon.* 1958. Ace D 324. 1st edn. PBO. SF. NF. F2d. $8.00

CUMMINGS, Ray. *Exile of Time.* 1964. Ace F 343. 1st edn. PBO. SF. F. F2d. $8.00

CUMMINGS, Ray. *Exiles of Time.* 1964. Ace F 343. SF. VG+. W2d. $5.00

CUMMINGS, Ray. *Man Who Mastered Time.* 1956. Ace D 173. 1st edn. PBO. SF. VG. F2d. $12.00

CUMMINGS, Ray. *Princess of the Atom.* 1950. Avon Fantasy Novel 1. VG+. B3a #22. $22.50

CUMMINGS, Ray. *Princess of the Atom.* 1950. Avon Fantasy Novel 1. 1st edn. PBO. SF. NF. F2d. $30.00

CUMMINGS, Ray. *Shadow Girl.* 1962. Ace D 535. 1st edn. F. M1d. $15.00

CUMMINGS, Ray. *Shadow Girl.* 1962. Ace D 535. 1st edn. SF. F. F2d. $12.00

CUMMINGS, Ray. *Tama, Princess of Mercury.* 1966. Ace F 406. 1st edn. SF. F. F2d. $10.00

CUMMINGS, Ray. *Tama of the Light Country.* Ace F 363. VG. I1d. $4.00

CUMMINGS, Ray. *Tama of the Light Country.* 1965. Ace F 363. 1st edn. SF. F. F2d/M1d. $10.00

CUMMINGS/KELLEAM. *Man Who Mastered Time/Overlords From Space.* 1956. Ace D 173. PBO. c/E Valigursky. SF. VG+. B5d. $7.50

CUMMINGS/KELLEAM. *Man Who Mastered Time/Overlords From Space.* 1956. Ace D 173. SF. VG. P1d. $10.00

CUMMINGS/WOODCOTT. *Wandl the Invader/I Speak for Earth.* 1961. Ace D 497. SF. VG+. B4d. $5.00

CUMMINGS/WOODCOTT. *Wandl the Invader/I Speak for Earth.* 1961. Ace D 497. 1st edn. F. M1d. $15.00

CUNEO, Ernest. *Life With Fiorello.* 1960. Avon T 438. Bio. VG+. B4d. $4.00

CUNLIFFE, Marcus. *Literature of the US.* Pelican A 289. Nfi. G+. P1d. $3.00

CUNNINGHAM, A.B. *Affair at the Boat Landing.* De Novel Classic 30. VG. B3d. $4.00

CUNNINGHAM, A.B. *Death of a Wordly Woman.* 1950. Dell 365. VG. B3d. $4.50

CUNNINGHAM, A.B. *Death Visits the Apple Hole.* 1945. De Novel Classic 46. 1st pb. VG. B6d. $7.00

CUNNINGHAM, A.B. *Murder at Deer Lick.* 1942. Mystery Novel Month 35. 1st pb. VG+. B6d. $9.00

CUNNINGHAM, A.B. *Murder Before Midnight.* De Novel Classic 52. VG. M6d. $5.00

CUNNINGHAM, Eugene. *Border Guns.* Mayflower 0710. VG. B3d. $6.00

CUNNINGHAM, Eugene. *Buckaroo.* Popular 77. VG. B3d. $5.00

CUNNINGHAM, Eugene. *Gun Bulldogger.* Dell 776. VG. B3d. $4.00

CUNNINGHAM, Eugene. *Ranger Way.* Popular 148. VG. B3d. $6.00

CUNNINGHAM, Eugene. *Ranger Way.* Popular 148. VG+. I1d. $7.00

CUNNINGHAM, Eugene. *Red Range.* 1945. We Novel Classic 38. VG. P6d. $3.50

CUNNINGHAM, Eugene. *Riders of the Night.* 1947. Bantam 113. c/J Kelly. We. VG+. B5d. $4.00

CUNNINGHAM, Eugene. *Texas Sheriff.* Popular 375. VG. B3d. $5.00

CUNNINGHAM, Eugene. *Whistling Lead.* Signet 740. VG+. B3d. $7.00

CUNNINGHAM, Louis Arthur. *Sultry Love.* 1950. Archer NN. PBO. c/Reginald Heade: gga. NF. B6a #75. $36.50

CUNNINGHAM, Shirley edt. *Pocket Entertainer.* 1942. Pocket 165. c/J Thurber. Nfi. VG. B5d. $5.50

CUPPY, Will. *Great Bustard & Other People.* Armed Services P 7. VG. B3d. $5.00

CURIE, Eve. *Madame Curie.* 1959. Cardinal GC 57. c/L Gregori. NF. VG. B5d. $2.50

CURRAN, Robert. *Kennedy Women.* 1964. Lancer 74-827. 1st prtg. PBO. c/photo. VG. P7d. $4.00

CURRAN, Robert. *Writhing Tide.* 1967. Private Edition 422. PBO. VG+. B6d. $7.50

CURRAN, Ronald. *Witches, Wraiths & Warlocks.* 1971. Gold Medal M 517. SF. VG. W2d. $4.00

CURRY, Tom. *Famous Figures of the Old West.* 1965. Monarch 553. Nfi. VG. B4d. $4.00

CURRY, Tom. *Rio Kid Rides.* 1967. Curtis 502-06144-060. VG. P6d. $2.50

CURSON, S. *Lesbian Love Song.* Brandon House 609. VG+. B3d. $6.00

CURSON, S. *Passion Hill.* Brandon House 612. VG+. B3d. $5.00

CURTIN, Arthur. *Love Off-Limits.* 1956. Pyramid 176. 1st prtg. PBO. c/gga. VG+. P7d. $7.50

CURTIS, Brad. *Anatomy of a Mistress.* 1963. Midwood F 335. PBO. VG+. B6d. $12.50

CURTIS, Brad. *Female Female.* Midwood 33-670. PBO. VG. M6d. $8.50

CURTIS, Brad. *Jody.* 1966. Midwood 33-729. PBO. VG. B3d. $4.00

CURTIS, Brad. *Live & Let Live.* 1966. Midwood 32-598. Ad. VG+. B5d. $5.50

CURTIS, Brad. *Man-Tamer.* Midwood 385. NF. B3d. $6.00

CURTIS, Brad. *Private Property.* 1964. Midwood 32-425. Fa. VG+. B4d. $12.50

CURTIS, Charlotte. *First Lady.* 1962. Pyramid R 767. c/Jacqueline Kennedy. Bio. VG+. B4d. $3.75

CURTIS, Charlotte. *First Lady.* 1962. Pyramid R 767. 1st edn. c/photos. Bio. F. F2d. $10.00

CURTIS, J.L. *Dark Streets of Paris.* Popular 587. VG. B3d. $4.50

CURTIS, Paul. *Deadly Deceit.* 1961. Newsstand 178. 1st edn. c/gga. My. F. F2d. $12.50

CURTIS, Richard edt. *Future Tense.* 1968. Dell 2769. SF. VG. P1d. $5.00

CURTISS, Ursula. *Deadly Climate.* 1965. Ace G 565. 1st prtg. My. VG. R5d. $2.25

CURTISS, Ursula. *Deadly Climate.* 1955. Pocket 1077. c/J Meese. My. VG+. B5d. $6.50

CURTISS, Ursula. *Forbidden Garden.* Ace 88050. MTI. VG. B3d. $4.50

CURTISS, Ursula. *Iron Cobweb.* 1964. Ace G 549. 1st pb. My. VG. B6d. $3.00

CURTISS, Ursula. *Stairway.* Dell 8524. G+. G5d. $4.50

CURTISS, Ursula. *Widow's Web.* 1957. Pocket 1157. 1st pb. c/Meese. My. VG+. B6d. $12.00

CURWOOD, James Oliver. *River's End.* Harlequin 380. VG. B3d. $4.00

CURWOOD, James Oliver. *Steele of the Royal Mounted.* Pocket 362. G+. G5d. $2.50

CURWOOD, James Oliver. *Valley of Silent Men.* Harlequin 383. 2nd prtg. VG. B3d. $3.50

CUSHMAN, Dan. *Con Man.* 1960. Crest S 381. VG. P6d. $1.50

CUSHMAN, Dan. *Fastest Gun.* 1955. Dell 1st Edn 67. PBO. c/G Gross. We. G+. B5d. $2.50

CUSHMAN, Dan. *Jewel of the Java Sea.* Gold Medal 142. VG. B3d. $4.00

CUSHMAN, Dan. *Jewel of the Java Sea.* Red Seal 66. VG+. B3a. $16.00

CUSHMAN, Dan. *Naked Ebony.* 1958. Gold Medal S 828. c/Barye: gga. Fa. VG+. B4d. $8.00

CUSHMAN, Dan. *Opium Flower.* Bantam J 2553. VG. G5d. $3.50

CUSHMAN, Dan. *Port Orient.* 1955. Gold Medal 535. 1st prtg. PBO. c/Lu Kimmel: gga. Ad. VG. P6d. $4.50

CUSHMAN, Dan. *Savage Interlude.* 1952. Gold Medal 241. 1st edn. c/gga. My. F. F2d. $20.00

CUSSLER, Clive. *Night Probe!* 1984. Bantam 25676. 7th prtg. My. VG+. W2d. $3.00

CUSSLER, Clive. *Raise the Titanic!* 1977. Bantam 10888. SF/My. VG. P1d. $3.50

CUTHBERT, Clifton. *Joy Street.* Lion 54. VG+. B3d. $5.00

CUTHBERT, Clifton. *Shame of Mary Quinn.* Pyramid 28. VG. I1d. $6.00

CUTTER, John. *Talent for Revenge.* 1984. Signet 2799. 1st edn. My. F. F2d. $6.00

D'ALLARD, H. *Long Sword.* Avon G 1099. VG. B3d. $4.00

D'AMATO, Barbara. *Hands of Healing Murder.* Charter 31618. G+. G5d. $6.00

D'ANDORRA, V. *Champions of Love.* Holloway House 88-403. NF. B3d. $6.00

D'ORQUE, R. *Stranger in Town.* 1967. Unique Book 126. PBO. VG+. B3a #20. $6.00

DA DUE, Russell. *Hell-Bent With Jake.* 1952. Avon 457. c/Erickson. Fi. VG. B5d. $5.50

DA VINCI, Leonardo. *Deluge.* 1955. Lion 233. SF. VG. B4d/P1d. $15.00

DA VINCI, Leonardo. *Deluge.* 1955. Lion 233. 1st pb. F. M1d. $25.00

DACRUZ, Daniel. *Grotto of the Formigans.* 1980. Ballantine 29250. SF. VG+. P1d. $4.50

DAHL, Roald. *Kiss Kiss.* 1961. Dell F 128. SF/My. VG. P1d. $9.50

DAHL, Roald. *Someone Like You.* 1961. Dell F 139. SF/My. G+. P1d. $4.50

DAHL, Roald. *Wonderful Story of Henry Sugar.* 1979. Bantam Skylark 15051. 3rd edn. Fa. VG. P1d. $4.00

DAIN/TUBB. *Bane of Kanthos/Kalin.* 1969. Ace 42800. 1st prtg. SF. G+. R5d. $1.75

DALE, S. *Twilight Girls.* Gold Star 73. PBO. VG. B3d. $4.00

DALEY, Brian. *Doomfarers of Coramonde.* 1977. Dell Rey 25708. Fa. VG+. P1d. $4.50

DALEY, Brian. *Han Solo & the Lost Legacy.* 1980. Ballantine 28710. 2nd prtg. SF. F. W2d. $4.75

DALEY, Brian. *Han Solo at Stars' End.* 1979. Ballantine 28355. SF. VG. P1d. $5.00

DALEY, Brian. *Han Solo's Revenge.* 1980. Ballantine 29840. MTI. c/D Ellis & H Ford. SF. VG+. B5d. $3.50

DALEY, Brian. *Hans Solo & the Lost Legasy.* 1980. Ballantine 28710. SF. VG. W2d. $3.25

DALEY, Brian. *Star/Followers of Coramonde.* 1979. Ballantine 27495. Fa. F. P1d. $6.00

DALEY, Brian. *Tron.* 1982. Ballantine 30352. SF. VG. P1d. $3.50

DALMAS, John. *Fowler Formula.* 1970. Curtis 6034. 1st pb. My. NF. B6d. $9.00

DALMAS, John. *Regiment.* 1987. Baen 65626. SF. VG. W2d. $3.50

DALMAS, John. *Yngling.* 1971. Pyramid T 2466. 1st edn. VG. P9d. $1.50

DALMAS & MARTIN. *Touch the Stars: Emergence.* 1983. TOR 48-586. SF. VG. P1d. $3.50

DALRYMPLE, B. *Fundamentals of Fishing & Hunting.* Perma M 4136. PBO. VG. B3d. $4.50

DALY, Elizabeth. *Any Shape or Form.* Bantam 811. VG. B3d. $4.50

DALY, Elizabeth. *Book of the Crime.* Bestseller 199. My. G+. W2d. $10.00

DALY, Elizabeth. *Book of the Dead.* 1948. Bantam 353. c/E Grant. My. VG. B5d. $5.00

DALY, Elizabeth. *Book of the Dead.* 1947. Bestseller B 93. VG+. F2d. $6.00

DALY, Elizabeth. *Book of the Lion.* Berkley F 700. 1st prtg. My. VG. R5d. $3.25

DALY, Elizabeth. *Deadly Nightshade.* Bantam 78. VG+. B3d. $6.00

DALY, Elizabeth. *Deadly Nightshade.* 1963. Berkley F 759. 1st prtg. My. VG. R5d. $3.25

DALY, Elizabeth. *Evidence of Things Seen.* 1962. Berkley F 644. My. VG. B4d. $3.00

DALY, Elizabeth. *Murder Listens In (Arrow Pointing Nowhere).* Bantam 713. G+. G5d. $6.50

DALY, Elizabeth. *Nothing Can Rescue Me.* 1946. Bantam 53. 1st pb. My. VG. B6d. $6.00

DALY, Elizabeth. *Unexpected Night.* 1944. Superior M 639. My. VG. B4d. $3.00

DALY, Maureen. *My Favorite Mystery Stories.* 1968. Bantam HP 4238. 1st prtg. My. G+. R5d. $1.25

DALY, Maureen. *Perfect Hostess.* 1951. Pocket 751. Nfi. NF. B5d. $5.50

DAMAN, V.G. *I Learned About Women From Them.* Pyramid 903. VG+. B3d. $4.50

DAMMANN, Ernest. *Dark Hollay.* Fabian Z 147. PBO. VG. M6d. $6.00

DAMON, Damon. *Seduced!* Merit 508. PBO. VG. B3d. $5.00

DAMON, Ray. *Thrill Seeker.* Chariot 118. VG. B3d. $4.50

DANA, Richard Henry. *Two Years Before the Mast.* 1953. Pyramid 76. Fi. VG. B5d. $7.50

DANFORTH & HORAN. *Big City Crimes.* Perma M 4164. VG. B3d. $4.00

DANFORTH & HORAN. *DA's Man.* Perma M 4118. VG. G5d. $3.50

DANFORTH & HORAN. *DA's Man.* 1959. Perma M 4118. 1st pb. Cr. NF. B6d. $10.00

DANGLON, A. *Orgy Mob.* Twilight Reader 113. VG+. B3d. $4.00

DANIELS, Dorothy. *Diablo Manor.* 1971. PB Library 64-650. Fa. VG. B4d. $2.00

DANIELS, Dorothy. *Island of Evil.* 1970. PB Library 63-321. TVTI. VG. P1d. $7.50

DANIELS, Dorothy. *Libly Pond.* 1965. PB Library 52-883. PBO. Go. VG. B6d. $3.00

DANIELS, Dorothy. *Marble Leaf.* 1967. Lancer 73-699. 1st pb. Go. NF. B6d. $6.00

DANIELS, Dorothy. *Raxl, Voodoo Priestess.* 1970. PB Library 63-365. TVTI. VG+. P1d. $15.00

DANIELS, Dorothy. *Strange Paradise.* 1969. PB Library 63-259. TVTI. G+. P1d. $6.00

DANIELS, Dorothy. *Strange Paradise.* 1970. PB Library 63-321. 1st edn. TVTI. c/photo. scarce. Ho. F. F2d. $15.00

DANIELS, Harold R. *In His Blood.* 1955. Dell 1st Edn 73. 1st prtg. PBO. c/Borack: gga. VG+. P7d. $5.50

DANIELS, Harold R. *Snatch.* 1958. Dell 1st Edn A 170. c/Mitchell Hooks: gga. VG. P6d. $3.00

DANIELS, John S. *Smoke of the Gun.* 1958. Signet 1505. We. VG. B4d. $3.00

DANIELS, Les. *Black Castle.* 1979. Berkley 04198. SF. NF. M3d. $7.50

DANIELS, Les. *Silver Skull.* 1983. Ace 76687. Ho. VG+. P1d. $6.00

DANIELS, Mark. *Love's Final Act.* 1964. Saber Book SA 47. PBO. c/gga. VG+. B6a. $30.00

DANIELS, Max. *Offworld.* 1979. Pocket 81887. 1st edn. c/gga. Fa. F. F2d. $9.00

DANIELS, Max. *Passport to Terror.* 1960. Avon T 423. 1st edn. c/gga. My. F. F2d. $8.00

DANIELS, Norman. *Arrest & Trial.* 1963. Lancer 72-696. 1st edn. TVTI. c/Gazzara & Connors color photo. My. SF. F2d. $12.00

DANIELS, Norman. *Bedroom in Hell!* 1952. Rainbow 117. PBO. c/George Gross: gga. VG+. B6a #76. $77.00

DANIELS, Norman. *Ben Casey, a Rage for Justice.* 1962. Lancer 70-011. TVTI. VG+. B4d. $9.00

DANIELS, Norman. *Ben Casey: The Fire Within.* 1963. Lancer 70-045. 1st prtg. G+. R5d. $2.75

DANIELS, Norman. *Captive.* 1959. Avon T 370. PBO. c/gga. VG+. B6d. $9.00

DANIELS, Norman. *County Hospital Magnetic Man.* 1968. Berkley X 1637. Avengers #8. TVTI. VG. B3d/G5d. $5.00

DANIELS, Norman. *Deadly Game.* 1959. Avon 864. My. VG+. B4d. $8.00

DANIELS, Norman. *Detectives.* 1962. Lancer 71-316. TVTI. F. B4d. $8.00

DANIELS, Norman. *Dr Kildare's Finest Hour.* 1963. Lancer 70-032. TVTI. VG+. B3d. $4.00

DANIELS, Norman. *Dr Kildare's Secret Romance.* 1962. Lancer 70-007. TVTI. VG+. B3d. $4.00

DANIELS, Norman. *Killing in the Market.* 1967. Lancer 73-700. 1st edn. De. F. F2d. $10.00

DANIELS, Norman. *Lady for Sale.* 1960. Avon 868. 1st edn. c/gga. My. F. F2d. $16.50

DANIELS, Norman. *License To Kill.* 1972. Pyramid T 2849. 1st edn. My. F. F2d. $10.00

DANIELS, Norman. *Mausoleum Key.* Green Dragon 2. c/Hoffman. VG. B3d. $6.00

DANIELS, Norman. *Missing Witness.* 1964. Lancer 72-723. 1st edn. TVTI. c/Gazzara & Connors color photo. My. F. F2d. $15.00

DANIELS, Norman. *Missing Witness.* 1964. Lancer 72-723. 1st prtg. TVTI. VG+. R5d. $6.00

DANIELS, Norman. *Operation VC.* 1967. Pyramid R 1617. My. VG+. B4d. $2.50

DANIELS, Norman. *Overkill.* 1964. Pyramid R 1052. c/McGuire. My. VG+. B4d. $4.00

DANIELS, Norman. *Rat Patrol.* 1966. PB Library 53-387. TVTI. VG+. B4d. $7.50

DANIELS, Norman. *Some Die Running.* 1960. Avon 876. PBO. VG+. B6d. $8.00

DANIELS, Norman. *Spy Hunt.* 1960. Pyramid G 571. c/Victor Kalin. Fa. VG+. B4d. $4.00

DANIELS, Paul. *Backwoods Shack.* Magnet 312. VG. B3d. $4.50

DANIELS, Paul. *Pattern for Destruction.* 1963. Monarch 394. Ad. G+. B5d. $3.00

DANIELS, Paul. *Ruby.* 1963. Monarch 299. 1st edn. c/Bob Stanley: gga. F. F2d. $10.00

DANN, Jack. *Man Who Melted.* 1986. Bantam. 1st pb. F. M1d. $6.00

DANN & DOZOIS edt. *Mermaids!* 1986. Ace 52657. Fa. F. P1d. $5.00

DANNE, Max Hallan. *Premature Burial.* 1962. Lancer 71-313. Ho. VG. P1d. $10.00

DANTE. *Inferno.* 1954. Mentor MS 113. Fa. F. P1d. $17.00

DANTZ, William R. *Pulse.* 1990. Avon 75714. Ho. VG. P1d. $4.00

DARE, Will. *Web of Women.* 1963. Beacon 656. 1st edn. c/gga. F. F2d. $12.00

DARIEN, Kim. *Dark Rapture.* 1955. Ace S 117. 1st edn. My. F. F2d. $17.50

DARIEN, Kim. *Obsession.* 1961. Ace D 526. PBO. c/Elaine: gga. VG. B6d. $9.00

DARK, James. *Bamboo Bomb.* 1965. Signet D 2774. c/Barye: gga. My. VG+. B4d. $3.50

DARK, James. *Come Die With Me.* 1965. Signet D 2741. My. F. B4d. $3.00

DARK, James. *Hong Kong Incident.* 1966. Signet D 2935. My. VG. B4d. $2.00

DARK, James. *Horror Tales.* 1963. Horwitz 138. PBO. VG+. B6a #79. $82.50

DARK, James. *Invisibles.* 1969. Signet P 3956. Fa. VG+. B4d. $4.00

DARK, James. *Operation Scuba.* 1967. Signet P 3134. 1st edn. c/gga. Th. F. F2d/P1d. $10.00

DARLING, Lois & Louis. *Science of Life.* 1963. Bantam FP 26. Nfi. VG+. B5d. $3.00

DARLTON, Clark. *Attack From the Unseen.* 1974. Ace 66033. SF. NF. B5d. $5.50

DARLTON, Clark. *Blazing Sun.* 1976. Ace 66070. SF. F. P1d. $5.00

DARLTON, Clark. *Dead Live.* 1974. Ace 66031. SF. VG. P1d. $3.50

DARLTON, Clark. *Escape to Venus.* 1972. Ace 65984. SF. F. P1d. $5.00

DARLTON, Clark. *Giant's Partner.* 1973. Ace 66016. SF. VG+. B5d. $4.00

DARLTON, Clark. *Infinity Flight.* 1973. Ace 66007. SF. VG+. B5d. $4.00

DARLTON, Clark. *Mutants Vs Mutants.* 1972. Ace 65990. SF. NF. B5d. $4.00

DARLTON, Clark. *Plague of Oblivion.* 1973. Ace 66010. SF. F. B5d. $6.00

DARLTON, Clark. *Snowman in Flames.* 1973. Ace 66008. SF. NF. B5d. $5.50

DARLTON, Clark. *Thrall of Hypno.* 1972. Ace 65991. SF. VG+. B5d. $4.00

DARLTON, Clark. *Vagabond of Space.* 1976. Ace 66077. SF. VG. P1d. $10.00

DARLTON, Clark. *World Gone Mad.* 1973. Ace 66012. SF. F. B5d. $6.00

DARNAY, Arsen. *Hostage for Hinterland.* 1976. Ballantine 25306. SF. VG. W2d. $3.25

DARNAY, Arsen. *Siege of Faltara.* 1978. Ace 76341. SF. F. P1d. $6.00

DARROW, Whitney Jr. *Hold It, Florence.* 1954. Dell 786. Hu. VG. B4d. $2.00

DARVIN, Pierre. *Love Clinic.* 1963. Berkley 717. 1st edn. De. F. F2d. $12.50

DARWIN, Charles. *Voyage of the Beagle.* 1958. Bantam FC 11. 1st pb. NF. B6d. $7.50

DATLOW, Ellen edt. *Blood Is Not Enough.* 1990. Berkley 12178. Ho. VG. P1d. $4.00

DAUDET, Alphonse. *Sappho.* 1956. Avon 691. 1st prtg. c/gga. VG. P7d. $6.00

DAUGHERTY, Kermit. *Out of the Red Bush.* 1955. Signet 1202. c/gga. Fa. VG+. B4d. $10.00

DAVENPORT, Basil edt. *Deals With the Devil.* 1959. Ballantine 326K. VG. B4d. $4.00

DAVENPORT, Basil edt. *Great Escapes.* Cardinal C 118. VG. B3d. $4.00

DAVENPORT, Basil edt. *Invisible Men.* 1966. Bal-Hi U 2842. Ho. VG. P1d. $6.50

DAVENPORT, Basil edt. *Invisible Men.* 1960. Ballantine 401K. PBO. c/R Powers. SF. VG. B5d. $7.50

DAVENPORT, Basil edt. *Invisible Men.* 1960. Ballantine. 1st edn. F. M1d. $15.00

DAVENPORT, Basil edt. *SF Novel.* 1964. Advent. Nfi. F. P1d. $17.50

DAVENPORT, Basil edt. *Tales To Be Told in the Dark.* Ballantine 380K. NF. I1d. $12.00

DAVENPORT, Basil edt. *Tales To Be Told in the Dark.* 1960. Ballantine 380K. Ho. VG. P1d. $10.00

DAVENPORT, Gwen. *Belvedere.* 1949. Bantam 729. MTI. c/Casey Jones. VG. B4d. $2.75

DAVENPORT, Marcia. *My Brother's Keeper.* Cardinal C 224. VG+. B3d. $5.00

DAVENPORT, Marcia. *Valley of Decision.* Popular Z 21. 1st prtg. VG+. R5d. $3.00

DAVENTRY, Leonard. *Man of Double Deed.* 1967. Berkley X 1491. c/R Powers. SF. NF. B5d. $5.00

DAVENTRY, Leonard. *Reflections in a Mirage.* 1970. Curtis 07061. SF. F. P1d. $10.00

DAVENTRY, Leonard. *Ticking Is in Your Head.* 1970. Curtis 7065. 1st edn. PBO. NF. P9d. $2.00

DAVID, Jay. *Scarsdale Murder.* Leisure 08661. Nfi. VG+. W2d. $3.50

DAVID, Peter. *Return of Swamp Thing.* 1989. Jove 0-515-10113-3. PBO. MTI. c/photo. VG. P6d. $2.25

DAVIDOFF, Henry edt. *Pocket Book of Quotations.* 1942. Pocket 176. Nfi. VG. B5d. $5.00

DAVIDSON, A. *Pheonix & the Mirror*. Ace 66100. 1st prtg. F. S1d. $6.00

DAVIDSON, Angus. *Edward Lear*. 1950. Penguin 747. Nfi. VG. P1d. $10.00

DAVIDSON, Avram. *Best From Fantasy & SF 13th Series*. 1967. Ace H 26. SF. F. P1d. $10.00

DAVIDSON, Avram. *Best From Fantasy & SF*. 1967. Ace A 17. 14th series. PBO. G. P9d. $1.25

DAVIDSON, Avram. *Best From Fantasy SF*. 1967. Ace G 611. 12th series. F. S1d. $5.50

DAVIDSON, Avram. *Clash of Star-Kings*. Ace G 576. VG+. B3d. $5.00

DAVIDSON, Avram. *Crimes & Chaos*. 1962. Regency RB 308. Nfi. G+. P1d. $22.50

DAVIDSON, Avram. *Enemy of My Enemy*. 1966. Berkley. 1st edn. NF. I1d/M1d. $8.00

DAVIDSON, Avram. *Enquiries of Dr Ezzterlazy*. 1975. Warner 76981. G. P9d. $1.00

DAVIDSON, Avram. *Island Under the Earth*. 1969. Ace 37425. 1st edn. SF. VG. P9d. $2.00

DAVIDSON, Avram. *Masters of the Maze*. 1965. Pyramid R1208. PBO. c/J Schoenherr. SF. VG. B4d/B5d. $4.00

DAVIDSON, Avram. *Mutiny in Space*. 1964. Pyramid R 1069. PBO. c/J Schoenherr. SF. VG. B5d. $4.00

DAVIDSON, Avram. *Mutiny in Space*. 1964. Pyramid R 1069. 1st edn. F. M1d. $10.00

DAVIDSON, Avram. *Mutiny in Space*. Pyramid X 2070. 2nd edn. VG. P9d. $1.75

DAVIDSON, Avram. *Or All the Seas With Oysters*. 1962. Berkley F 639. PBO. c/R Powers. SF. G+. B5d. $4.00

DAVIDSON, Avram. *Or All the Seas With Oysters*. 1962. Berkley F 639. 1st edn. F. M1d. $8.00

DAVIDSON, Avram. *Rogue Dragon*. 1965. Ace F 353. F. M1d. $10.00

DAVIDSON, Avram. *Rogue Dragon*. 1965. Ace F 353. SF. VG+. P1d. $8.00

DAVIDSON, Avram. *Rork!* 1965. Berkley F 1146. SF. F. P1d. $11.00

DAVIDSON, Avram. *Ursus of Ultima Thule*. 1973. Avon 17657. SF. VG+. W2d. $4.00

DAVIDSON, Avram. *What Strange Stars & Skies*. 1965. Ace F 330. SF. F. P1d. $11.00

DAVIDSON, Bill. *Real & the Unreal*. Lancer 72-636. VG+. B3d. $5.00

DAVIDSON, David. *Hour of Truth*. Bantam 754. VG+. B3d. $4.00

DAVIDSON, David. *Night Is Mine*. Popular 510. VG+. B3d. $5.00

DAVIDSON, David. *Steeper Cliff*. 1950. Bantam 801. 1st prtg. My. VG. R5d. $3.25

DAVIDSON, John. *Blues for a Dead Lover*. 1962. Uptown 702. VG+. B3d. $6.50

DAVIDSON, John. *Tropic of Passion*. Epic 142. c/Nuetzel: sgn. VG. B3d. $6.00

DAVIDSON, John. *Woman Trap*. Uptown 705. VG+. B3d. $5.00

DAVIDSON, Lionel. *Night of Wenceslas*. Avon S 259. 1st pb. VG. M1d. $5.00

DAVIDSON, Michael. *Karma Machine*. Popular 00248. SF. VG+. B5d. $4.00

DAVIDSON & MOORE. *Joyleg*. Pyramid 805. c/Emsh. VG+. B3d. $6.00

DAVIDSON/LEGUIN. *Kar-Chee Reign/ Rocannon's World*. Ace G 574. VG+. B3d. $5.00

DAVIDSON/LEGUIN. *Kar-Chee Reign/Rocannon's World*. 1966. Ace G 574. F. M1d. $10.00

DAVIDSON/RACKHAM. *Clash of Star Kings/Danger From Vega*. Ace G 576. NF. M1d. $6.00

DAVIES, Fredric. *Cross Gold Affair*. Ace G 689. Man From Uncle #14. VG+. B3d. $4.50

DAVIES, Hunter. *Beatles*. 1969. Dell 0474. 1st US edn. Bio. VG. P6d. $7.00

DAVIES, L.P. *Dimension A*. 1972. Dell 1957. 1st prtg. SF. VG. R5d. $1.75

DAVIES, Valentine. *It Happens Every Spring*. 1950. Avon 249. Fa. VG. P1d. $10.00

DAVIES, Valentine. *Miracle on 34th Street*. 1952. Pocket 903. Fa. VG. P1d. $9.00

DAVIS, A.J. *Girl in Every Bush*. 1966. Vega Book 51. PBO. NF. B6d. $15.00

DAVIS, Burke. *Yorktown*. 1953. Cardinal C 123. 1st prtg. c/Tom Dunn: gga. VG+. P7d. $4.00

DAVIS, Clyde Brion. *Rebellion of Leo McGuire*. Armed Services 924. Fi. VG. B5d. $4.50

DAVIS, D. *Four in a Bed*. Playtime 752. VG+. B3d. $6.00

DAVIS, Don. *Two-Gun Rio Kid*. 1954. Pocket 1023. 1st pb. We. VG. B6d. $6.00

DAVIS, Dorothy Salisbury. *Gentle Murderer*. 1953. Bantam 1083. VG. B3d. $5.00

DAVIS, Dorothy Salisbury. *Gentle Murderer*. 1959. Dell D 286. VG. G5d. $3.50

DAVIS, Dorothy Salisbury. *Judas Cat*. Bantam 927. VG. B3d. $4.00

DAVIS, Dorothy Salisbury. *Town of Masks*. Dell 823. c/W George. My. VG. B5d. $3.00

DAVIS, Dorothy Salisbury. *Town of Masks*. Dell 823. 1st prtg. My. G+. R5d. $1.75

DAVIS, Eddie. *Laugh Yourself Well*. Popular 812. VG. B3d. $4.00

DAVIS, Eddie. *Stories for Stags*. 1956. Lion LL 95. PBO. VG+. B6d. $15.00

DAVIS, Franklin M. Jr. *Break-Through*. 1961. Monarch MA 306. PBO. c/photo. Nfi. VG. B3d/B5d. $4.50

DAVIS, Franklin M. Jr. *Kiss the Tiger*. 1961. Pyramid G 663. PBO. c/Asia: gga. My. VG+. B6d. $9.00

DAVIS, Franklin M. Jr. *Spearhead*. 1958. Perma M 3118. PBO. c/R Abbett. Fi. VG. B5d. $3.50

DAVIS, Fred L. *King of Sports*. 1966. PEC Giant G 1120. Ad. G+. B5d. $2.00

DAVIS, Frederick C. *Deadly Miss Ashley*. Pocket 804. VG+. G5d. $7.50

DAVIS, Fredrick C. *Let the Skeletons Rattle*. Hillman 78. VG. B3d. $4.50

DAVIS, Gerry. *Tenth Planet*. 1976. Target NN. 1st Cybermen Adventure. VG. M3d. $7.00

DAVIS, Gordon. *Counterfeit Kill*. Gold Medal 1348. VG+. B3d. $6.00

DAVIS, Gordon. *House Dick*. Gold Medal 1103. c/McGinnis. VG. B3d. $4.00

DAVIS, Gordon. *I Came To Kill*. 1953. Gold Medal 349. PBO. c/Meese. My. G+. B6d. $4.00

DAVIS, J. *Wild Spree*. Scorpion 101. NF. B3d. $5.00

DAVIS, J.P. *Love Against the Law*. 1966. Publishers Export 04. Nfi. VG+. P6d. $2.00

DAVIS, Jada M. *One for Hell*. 1952. Red Seal 24. 1st edn. Cr. F. F2d. $15.00

DAVIS, Jada M. *Outraged Sect*. 1956. Avon 713. PBO. VG. B6d. $7.50

DAVIS, Mac. *Great American Sports Humor*. Pocket 718. VG. B3d. $4.00

DAVIS, Maxine. *Woman's Medical Problems*. 1953. Pocket 957. c/photo. Nfi. VG+. B5d. $4.00

DAVIS, Mildred. *Room Upstairs*. Pocket 638. VG. G5d. $5.00

DAVIS, Norbert. *Dead Little Rich Girl* 1946. Handi-Book 40. G+. P6d. $4.00

DAVIS, Phil. *Dancer's Death*. 1981. Avon 76612. 1st prtg. My. VG. W2d. $3.00

DAVIS, Richard edt. *Year's Best Horror Stories II.* 1974. DAW. 1st edn. VG. M1d. $4.00

DAVIS, Richard edt. *Year's Best Horror Stories III.* 1975. DAW. 1st edn. VG. M1d. $4.00

DAVIS, Wesley Ford. *Time of the Panther.* 1959. Popular G 315. 1st pb. NF. B6d. $12.50

DAVIS & DAVIS. *Sins of the Flesh.* 1989. TOR 51679. Ho. F. P1d. $6.00

DAVIS/DAVIS. *High Heel Homicide/Night Drop.* 1961. Ace D 499. VG. B3d. $5.00

DAVIS/DAVIS. *They Buried a Man/Dark Place.* 1964. Ace G 543. My. VG+. B3d. $2.50

DAVIS/MILLER. *Why I Am So Beat/7-Day System for Gaining Self-Confidence.* 1955. Ace D 88. PBO. Nfi. VG. B5d. $4.50

DAVIS/WHITTINGTON. *Drag the Dark/You'll Die Next!* Ace D 63. PBO. VG. B3d. $17.50

DAVIS/WHITTINGTON. *Drag the Dark/You'll Die Next!* 1954. Ace D 63. PBO. My. G. B5d. $6.50

DAWN, Conrad. *Chartered Love.* 1960. Novel Book 3506. PBO. Ad. VG+. B3d. $6.00

DAWSON, Peter. *Bloody Gold.* 1963. Bantam 2585. 1st edn. Hi. F. F2d. $10.00

DAWSON, Peter. *Canyon Hell.* 1949. Lion 10. 3rd edn. c/Bob Stanley. G+. P6d. $2.00

DAWSON, Peter. *Crimson Horseshoe.* Bantam 94. VG+. B3d. $6.00

DAWSON, Peter. *Gunsmoke Graze.* Dell 352. VG+. I1d. $5.00

DAWSON, Peter. *Long Ride.* 1953. Pennant P 22. We. VG. B4d. $4.00

DAWSON, Peter. *Outlaw of Longbow.* Bantam 974. VG+. B3d. $4.00

DAWSON, Peter. *Stageline Feud.* 1948. Bantam 250. c/C Young. We. VG. B5d. $3.00

DAWSON, Peter. *Stageline Feud.* 1948. Bantam 250. 1st pb. We. NF. B6d. $10.00

DAWSON, Peter. *Stagline Feud.* Bantam 250. VG. B3d. $4.00

DAWSON, Peter. *Stirrup Boss.* 1951. Dell 490. 1st prtg. c/Stanley: gga. VG+. P7d. $7.50

DAY, Chon. *Brother Sebastian.* Pocket 1224. NF. B3d. $5.00

DAY, David. *Burroughs Bestiary.* 1978. New English 03442. Nfi. VG+. P1d. $15.00

DAY, Max. *In Bachelor Suburbia.* 1962. Beacon B 547F. PBO. c/R Schinella. Ad. VG+. B5d. $6.00

DAY, Max. *Resort.* 1960. Beacon 334. PBO. c/gga. NF. B6d. $22.50

DAY, Max. *Resort.* 1960. Beacon 334. 1st prtg. VG+. P7d. $9.00

DAY, Max. *So Nice, So Wild.* Stanley 68. PBO. VG. B3d. $4.50

DAYAN, Yael. *New Face in the Mirror.* 1960. Signet D 1832. We. VG+. B4d. $4.00

DE ALARCON, Pedro. *Miller & the Mayor's Wife.* 1949. Avon 199. c/Cantor. Fi. VG. P1d. $10.00

DE BALZAC, Honore. *Best of Balzac.* 1958. Crest S 220. Fi. G+. P1d. $5.50

DE BALZAC, Honore. *Best of Balzac.* Crest 220. VG+. B3d. $5.00

DE BALZAC, Honore. *Pere Goriot.* Pyramid 177. VG. B3d. $4.00

DE BALZAC, Honore. *Ten Droll Tales.* 1949. Hillman 12. Fi. VG. P1d. $10.00

DE BEKKER, J. *Keyhole Peeper.* Beacon 110. PBO. VG+. B3d. $6.00

DE BERG, Jean. *Image.* Black Cat B 307-N. Ad. Nf. B5d. $4.50

DE BIBIENA, Jean-Galli. *Amorous Philandre.* 1948. Avon 171. Ro. VG+. B4d. $6.00

DE BOLLENE, A. *Voyage to Eros.* Berkley G 615. PBO. VG+. B3d. $6.00

DE BOUT, Jacques. *Pierre's Woman.* 1954. Pyramid 133. PBO. c/Olson. NF. B6a #74. $75.00

DE BOUT, Jacques. *Pierre's Woman.* 1954. Pyramid 133. PBO. c/V Olson. Fi. G+. B5d. $4.00

DE CAMP, L. Sprague. *Ancient Engineers.* 1974. Ballantine 23783. Nfi. VG. P1d. $4.50

DE CAMP, L. Sprague. *Ancient Engineers.* 1980. Ballantine. 8th edn. VG. M1d. $3.00

DE CAMP, L. Sprague. *Best of LS De Camp.* 1978. Ballantine 25475. VG. P9d. $1.50

DE CAMP, L. Sprague. *Blade of Conan.* 1979. Ace 11670. Fa. F. P1d. $5.00

DE CAMP, L. Sprague. *Blade of Conan.* 1979. Ace. 1st edn. NF. M1d. $4.00

DE CAMP, L. Sprague. *Bran Mak Morn: Legion From the Shadows.* 1977. Zebra. F. M1d. $10.00

DE CAMP, L. Sprague. *Carnellian Cube.* 1967. Lancer. 1st pb. VG. M1d. $7.00

DE CAMP, L. Sprague. *Castle of Iron.* 1962. Pyramid F 722. 1st edn. PBO. SF. F. F2d. $8.00

DE CAMP, L. Sprague. *Clocks of Iraz.* 1971. Pyramid 2584. 1st edn. SF. F. F2d. $13.00

DE CAMP, L. Sprague. *Compleat Enchanter.* 1976. Ballantine 24638. Fa. F. P1d. $5.00

DE CAMP, L. Sprague. *Conan #5.* Lancer 75-137. c/Frazetta. VG+. I1d. $5.00

DE CAMP, L. Sprague. *Conan of Cimmeria.* 1969. Lancer. 1st pb. VG. M1d. $8.00

DE CAMP, L. Sprague. *Conan of the Isles.* 1968. Lancer 73-800. Fa. VG. P1d. $5.00

DE CAMP, L. Sprague. *Conan of the Isles.* 1968. Lancer 73-800. 1st pb. NF. M1d. $10.00

DE CAMP, L. Sprague. *Conan of the Isles.* Lancer 75136. SF. F. W2d. $5.00

DE CAMP, L. Sprague. *Conan of the Isles.* 1974. Sphere 4700. Fa. F. P1d. $6.00

DE CAMP, L. Sprague. *Conan the Avenger.* 1968. Lancer. 1st pb. F. M1d. $10.00

DE CAMP, L. Sprague. *Conan the Barbarian.* 1982. Bantam 22544. SF. VG. W2d. $3.50

DE CAMP, L. Sprague. *Conan the Buccaneer.* Ace 11676. SF. F. W2d. $4.50

DE CAMP, L. Sprague. *Conan the Buccaneer.* 1971. Lancer 75-181. 1st pb. F. M1d. $10.00

DE CAMP, L. Sprague. *Conan the Buccaneer.* 1971. Lancer 75-181. Fa. VG. P1d. $4.00

DE CAMP, L. Sprague. *Conan the Buccaneer.* 1976. Sphere 4712. 2nd edn. Fa. VG. P1d. $4.25

DE CAMP, L. Sprague. *Conan the Liberator.* 1979. Bantam 12706. Fa. F. P1d. $5.00

DE CAMP, L. Sprague. *Conan the Swordsman.* 1979. Sphere 2941. 2nd edn. Fa. F. P1d. $5.00

DE CAMP, L. Sprague. *Conan the Wanderer.* 1968. Lancer. 1st pb. F. M1d. $8.00

DE CAMP, L. Sprague. *Conan.* 1967. Lancer 73-685. 1st edn. F. M1d. $12.00

DE CAMP, L. Sprague. *Continent Makers.* 1971. Signet Q 4825. SF. F. P1d. $8.00

DE CAMP, L. Sprague. *Continent Makers.* 1971. Signet Q 4825. SF. VG+. W2d. $3.75

DE CAMP, L. Sprague. *Divide & Rule.* 1964. Lancer 72-768. SF. NF. B4d. $6.00

DE CAMP, L. Sprague. *Divide & Rule.* Lancer 72768. 1st prtg. G+. S1d. $4.00

DE CAMP, L. Sprague. *Dragon of Ishtar Gate.* 1968. Lancer 75-045. c/R Krenkel. Fi. G+. B5d. $3.00

DE CAMP, L. Sprague. *Dragon of the Ishtar Gate.* 1982. Donn 89865. SF. VG. W2d. $3.50

DE CAMP, L. Sprague. *Elephant for Aristotle.* Curtis 9059. 1st pb. VG. B6d/M1d. $5.00

DE CAMP, L. Sprague. *Engines.* 1969. Golden Press 7723. Nfi. VG. P1d. $5.00

DE CAMP, L. Sprague. *Fallible Fiend.* Signet Q 5370. 1st prtg. F. S1d. $4.00

DE CAMP, L. Sprague. *Fantastic Swordsmen.* 1967. Pyramid R 1621. Fa. VG. P1d. $6.00

DE CAMP, L. Sprague. *Fantastic Swordsmen.* 1967. Pyramid R 1621. 1st edn. SF. F. F2d. $20.00

DE CAMP, L. Sprague. *Fantastic Swordsmen.* Pyramid 1621. c/Bloch: sgn. VG+. B3d. $7.50

DE CAMP, L. Sprague. *Glory That Was.* 1971. PB Library 63-542. SF. VG. P1d. $4.00

DE CAMP, L. Sprague. *Glory That Was.* 1971. PB Library 63-542. 1st pb. F. M1d. $8.00

DE CAMP, L. Sprague. *Goblin Tower.* 1968. Pyramid T 1927. SF. VG+. B4d. $6.00

DE CAMP, L. Sprague. *Goblin Tower.* 1968. Pyramid T 1927. 1st edn. SF. F. F2d/P1d. $10.00

DE CAMP, L. Sprague. *Golden Wind.* 1970. Curtis 07091. Hi. VG+. P1d. $10.00

DE CAMP, L. Sprague. *Hostage of Zir.* 1978. Berkley 03870. SF. G+. W2d. $2.75

DE CAMP, L. Sprague. *Land of Unreason.* 1970. Ballantine 01814. Fa. F. P1d. $10.00

DE CAMP, L. Sprague. *Land of Unreason.* 1979. Dell 14736. SF. F. W2d. $4.25

DE CAMP, L. Sprague. *Lost Darkness Fall.* 1974. Ballantine 24139. SF. VG. B5d. $3.00

DE CAMP, L. Sprague. *Lest Darkness Fall.* 1955. Galaxy SF Novel 24. SF. VG. P1d. $20.00

DE CAMP, L. Sprague. *Lest Darkness Fall.* 1963. Pyramid F 817. SF. VG. P1d. $6.00

DE CAMP, L. Sprague. *Lest Darkness Fall.* 1963. Pyramid F 817. 1st pb. NF. M1d. $10.00

DE CAMP, L. Sprague. *Lost Continents: The Atlantis Theme.* 1975. Ballantine 24379. Nfi. VG. B5d. $7.50

DE CAMP, L. Sprague. *Lovecraft, a Biography.* 1976. Ballantine 25115. 1st edn. PBO. G. P9d. $1.25

DE CAMP, L. Sprague. *Million Cities.* 1963. Pyramid F 898. PBO. c/V Finlay. SF. VG+. B5d. $6.00

DE CAMP, L. Sprague. *Que No Caigan las Tinieblas.* 1968. Diana 89. Spanish text. SF. VG. P1d. $7.50

DE CAMP, L. Sprague. *Reluctant Shaman.* 1970. Pyramid T 2347. Fa. VG. P1d. $4.50

DE CAMP, L. Sprague. *Reluctant Shaman.* 1970. Pyramid 2347. 1st edn. SF. F. F2d. $15.00

DE CAMP, L. Sprague. *Road of Kings.* 1980. Bantam. NF. M1d. $4.00

DE CAMP, L. Sprague. *Rogue Queen.* 1965. Ace F 333. F. M1d. $10.00

DE CAMP, L. Sprague. *Rogue Queen.* 1965. Ace F 333. SF. VG+. M3d. $6.50

DE CAMP, L. Sprague. *Rogue Queen.* 1965. Ace F 333. VG. I1d. $4.00

DE CAMP, L. Sprague. *Rogue Queen.* 1965. Ace F 333. 1st prtg. G+. S1d. $3.75

DE CAMP, L. Sprague. *Rogue Queen.* 1952. Dell 600. PBO. SF. F. F2d. $25.00

DE CAMP, L. Sprague. *Rogue Queen.* 1952. Dell 600. SF. VG. P1d. $20.00

DE CAMP, L. Sprague. *Rogue Queen.* 1972. Signet Q 5256. SF. F. P1d. $5.00

DE CAMP, L. Sprague. *Rogue Queen.* 1972. Signet Q 5256. SF. VG+. B4d. $2.50

DE CAMP, L. Sprague. *Spell of Seven.* 1965. Pyramid R 1192. PBO. c/V Finlay. SF. G+. B5d. $5.00

DE CAMP, L. Sprague. *Spell of Seven.* 1965. Pyramid R 1192. VG. I1d. $9.00

DE CAMP, L. Sprague. *Spell of Seven.* 1965. Pyramid R 1192. 1st pb. NF. M1d. $10.00

DE CAMP, L. Sprague. *Spell of Seven.* Pyramid T 2133. 1st prtg. G+. S1d. $3.00

DE CAMP, L. Sprague. *Spell of Seven.* 1965. Pyramid 1192. 1st edn. c/Virgil Finlay. SF. F. F2d. $16.00

DE CAMP, L. Sprague. *Sprague De Camp's New Anthology.* 1953. Panther 92. SF. G+. P1d. $25.00

DE CAMP, L. Sprague. *Swords & Sorcery.* 1963. Pyramid R 950. Fa. F. P1d. $15.00

DE CAMP, L. Sprague. *Swords & Sorcery.* 1963. Pyramid R 950. 1st edn. c/De Camp: sgn. SF. F. F2d. $20.00

DE CAMP, L. Sprague. *Swords & Sorcery.* 1963. Pyramid R 950. 1st prtg. VG. S1d. $5.50

DE CAMP, L. Sprague. *Tower of Zanid.* 1963. Airmont SF 2. SF. VG. P1d. $6.00

DE CAMP, L. Sprague. *Tower of Zanid.* 1963. Airmont SF 2. 1st pb. NF. M1d. $10.00

DE CAMP, L. Sprague. *Tritonian Ring.* 1968. PB Library 53-618. Fa. F. P1d. $10.00

DE CAMP, L. Sprague. *Tritonian Ring.* 1968. PB Library 53-618. SF. VG+. B3d. $4.50

DE CAMP, L. Sprague. *Undying Wizard.* 1976. Zebra. 1st edn. F. M1d. $6.00

DE CAMP, L. Sprague. *Virgin & the Wheels.* 1976. Popular 00362. SF. F. W2d. $4.50

DE CAMP, L. Sprague. *Warlock & Warriors.* 1970. Berkley S 1944. 1st edn. PBO. SF. F. F2d. $10.00

DE CAMP, L. Sprague. *Warlocks & Warriors.* Berkley 1944. 1st prtg. G. S1d. $2.00

DE CAMP, L. Sprague. *Wheels of If.* 1970. Berkley. 1st pb. F. M1d. $7.00

DE CAMP & DE CAMP. *Citadels of Mystery.* 1973. Ballantine 03215. Nfi. VG. P1d. $4.00

DE CAMP & DE CAMP. *Hand of Zei/Search for Zei.* Ace F 249. 1st prtg. G. S1d. $2.00

DE CAMP & HOWARD. *Conan of Cimmeria.* 1969. Lancer 75-072. 1st edn. c/Frazetta. SF. F. F2d. $12.50

DE CAMP & HOWARD. *Conan the Adventurer.* 1966. Lancer 73-526. 1st prtg. SF. VG+. R5d. $4.00

DE CAMP & HOWARD. *Conan the Freebooter.* 1968. Lancer 74-963. 1st edn. SF. F. F2d. $12.50

DE CAMP & HOWARD. *Conan the Usurper.* 1967. Lancer 73 599. SF. VG+. W2d. $4.25

DE CAMP & HOWARD. *Conan the Warrior.* 1967. Lancer 73-549. 1st edn. c/Frazetta. SF. F. F2d. $10.00

DE CAMP & LORD. *Howard Collector.* 1979. Ace. 1st pb. F. M1d. $10.00

DE CAMP & MILLER. *Genus Homo.* 1961. Berkley 536. VG. B3d. $4.50

DE CAMP & MILLER. *Genus Homo.* 1961. Berkley 536. 1st pb. NF. M1d. $7.00

DE CAMP & OFFUT. *Sword of Skelos.* 1979. Bantam. 1st edn. NF. M1d. $5.00

DE CAMP & PRATT. *Carnelian Cube.* 1967. Lancer 73-662. 1st prtg. c/Freas: gga. VG. P7d. $5.00

DE CAMP & PRATT. *Castle of Iron.* Pyramid F 722. 1st prtg. F. S1d. $7.00

DE CAMP & PRATT. *Castle of Iron.* 1962. Pyramid F 722. c/E Emsh. SF. VG. B3d/B5d. $4.50

DE CAMP & PRATT. *Castle of Iron.* 1977. Pyramid. 1st pb. NF. M1d. $8.00

DE CAMP & PRATT. *Hand of Zei/Search for Zei.* 1963. Ace F 249. SF. F. W2d. $13.00

DE CAMP & PRATT. *Hand of Zei/Search for Zei.* 1963. Ace F 249. SF. VG. P1d. $7.50

DE CAMP & PRATT. *Incomplete Enchanter.* 1976. Ballantine. 1st edn. Ad/Fa. VG. M1d. $10.00

DE CAMP & PRATT. *Incomplete Enchanter.* 1962. Pyramid F 723. 1st edn. PBO. SF. F. F2d. $8.00

DE CAMP & PRATT. *Incomplete Enchanter.* 1962. Pyramid F 723. 2nd edn. c/E Emsh. SF. VG. B5d. $4.50

DE CAMP & PRATT. *Incomplete Enchanter.* 1960. Pyramid G 530. 1st pb. NF. M1d. $10.00

DE CAMP & PRATT. *Incomplete Enchanter.* 1960. Pyramid G 530. 1st prtg. VG. S1d. $6.00

DE CAMP/DE CAMP. *Hand of Zei/Search for Zei.* 1963. Ace F 249. NF. M1d. $9.00

DE CAMP/DE CAMP. *Hand of Zei/Search for Zei.* 1963. Ace F 249. 1st edn. PBO. SF. F. F2d. $10.00

DE CAMP/SIMAK. *Cosmic Manhunt/Ring Around the Sun.* Ace D 61. VG. P9d. $8.00

DE CAMP/SIMAK. *Cosmic Manhunt/Ring Around the Sun.* 1954. Ace D 61. 1st edn. F. M1d. $25.00

DE CAMP/SIMAK. *Cosmic Manhunt/Ring Around the Sun.* 1954. Ace D 61. 1st edn. SF. NF. F2d. $20.00

DE CARLO, Dan. *My Son the Teenager.* 1963. Belmont 91-288. 1st edn. F. F2d. $8.00

DE CHANCIE, John. *Castle for Rent!* 1989. Ace 09406. 1st edn. Fa. F. F2d. $6.00

DE FELITTA, Frank. *Entity.* 1979. Warner 85-589. Ho. VG. P1d. $4.00

DE FELITTA, Frank. *Sea Trial.* 1982. Avon 81414. 1st prtg. My. VG+. W2d. $3.00

DE FONTENAY, C.I. *Star.* 1975. DAW UY 1200 #167. SF. F. P1d. $5.00

DE FORD, Miriam Allen. *Overbury Affair.* 1962. Avon F 125. My. G. P1d. $3.00

DE FORD, Miriam Allen. *Real Bonnie & Clyde.* 1968. Ace H 63. Nfi. VG. P1d. $5.00

DE FORD, Miriam Allen. *Space, Time & Crime.* 1964. PB Library 52-502. SF. VG. P1d. $6.00

DE FORD, Miriam Allen. *Xenogenesis.* 1969. Ballantine 01546. SF. F. P1d. $10.00

DE FOREST, Barry. *Play Girl.* 1960. Beacon B 327. PBO. Ad. G+. B5d. $4.00

DE GOURMONT, Remy. *Physiology of Love.* Hillman 14. VG. B3d. $4.00

DE GRAEFF, Allen edt. *Human & Other Beings.* 1963. Collier AS 567. SF. VG. P1d. $6.00

DE HARTOG, Jan. *Key.* 1958. Pocket 2952. 4th prtg. VG. R5d. $1.50

DE HARTOG, Jan. *Little Ark.* 1955. Pocket 1042. c/T Dunn. Fi. VG. B5d. $4.00

DE HAZIR, E. *Livia.* Brandon House 6094. NF. B3d. $6.00

DE JOHN, P. *Make Me an Orgy.* Nite Time 110. NF. B3d. $6.00

DE KRUIF, Paul. *Hunger Fighters.* 1942. Pocket 155. Nfi. VG+. B5d. $5.50

DE KRUIF, Paul. *Male Hormone.* Perma P 12. NF. I1d. $4.00

DE KRUIF, Paul. *Men Against Death.* Armed Services 808. Nfi. G+. B5d. $3.50

DE KRUIF, Paul. *Microbe Hunters.* 1942. Pocket 49. 13th edn. Nfi. VG. B5d. $3.00

DE LA CROIX, Robert. *They Flew the Atlantic.* 1960. Monarch 166. Nfi. VG. B3d/B5d. $5.00

DE LA FFOREST, Roger. *Fate Control.* 1974. Berkley 02641. Nfi. VG. P1d. $3.50

DE LATTRE, Pierre. *Tales of a Dalai Lama.* 1973. Ballantine 03048. Fa. F. P1d. $7.50

DE LEEUW, Hendrik. *Sinful Cities of the Western World.* 1951. Pyramid 27. c/Meyer. VG. B3d. $4.00

DE LINT, Charles. *Wolf Moon.* 1988. Signet 451-AF5487. 1st edn. Ho. F. F2d. $7.00

DE LINT, Charles. *Yarrow.* 1986. Ace. 1st edn. F. M1d. $5.00

DE MARCO, Carl. *Suzanne.* Midwood 33-768. Ad. VG. B5d. $4.00

DE MARCO, Carl. *Woman on a String.* 1967. Midwood 33-808. PBO. Ad. VG+. B5d. $5.50

DE MARE, G. *Ruling Passion.* Crest 343. VG+. B3d. $4.50

DE MARIA, Robert. *Outbreak.* 1978. Jove Y 4433. SF/My. VG+. P1d. $4.50

DE MARINIS, Rick. *Scimitar.* 1978. Avon 37002. SF. VG+. P1d. $4.50

DE MAUPASSANT, Guy. *House of Madame Tellier.* Pyramid 202. VG. B3d. $4.50

DE MAUPASSANT, Guy. *House of Madame Tellier.* 1952. Pyramid 41. 1st prtg. c/Paul: gga. VG. P7d. $15.00

DE MAUPASSANT, Guy. *House of Madame Tellier.* World Dist 821. VG. B3d. $7.00

DE MAUPASSANT, Guy. *Mademoiselle Fifi.* 1952. Avon 459. c/Erickson: gga. VG. P6d. $5.00

DE MAUPASSANT, Guy. *Private Affairs of Bel Ami.* Avon 87. VG. I1d. $9.00

DE MAUPASSANT, Guy. *Yvette.* 1949. Avon 198. 1st edn. PBO. c/Barry Stephens: gga. NF. B6a #76. $45.00

DE MAUPASSANT, Guy. *Yvette.* 1949. Avon 198. 1st edn. PBO. VG+. B6d. $25.00

DE MEJO, O. *Diary of a Nun.* Pyramid 158. PBO. VG. B3d. $4.50

DE MEXICO, N.R. *Mariguana Girl.* Beacon 328. rare. JD. NF. B6a #80. $175.00

DE MEXICO, N.R. *Mariguana Girl.* Beacon 75124. scarce. NF. B6a #80. $82.50

DE MEXICO, N.R. *Mariguana Girl.* Stallion Book 204. scarce. VG. B6a #77. $82.50

DE MEXICO, N.R. *Mariguana Girl.* Uni-Book Digest 19. rare. VG. B6a #77. $110.00

DE MEXICO, N.R. *Private Chauffeur.* Beacon 313. VG. B3d. $5.00

DE MEYCLOW, Martha. *Starbreed.* 1970. Ballantine 01857. c/Savage. SF. VG+. B4d. $3.00

DE MEYER, John. *Bailey's Daughters.* 1952. Lion 102. PBO. c/gga. VG+. B6a #74. $36.50

DE MILLE, Nelson. *Ryker #3: The Terrorists.* 1974. Leisure 207ZK. 1st prtg. My. VG+. W2d. $3.50

DE PEREDA, Prudencio. *All the Girls We Loved.* 1955. Berkley 110. 1st pb. NF. B6d. $12.50

DE PEREDA, Prudencio. *All the Girls We Loved.* 1948. Signet 691. c/gga. Fa. VG+. B4d. $4.00

DE ROO, Edward. *Go, Man, Go!* 1959. Ace D 406. PBO. scarce. JD. F. B6a #74. $61.00

DE ROO, Edward. *Little Caesars.* 1961. Ace D 486. PBO. VG+. B3a #24. $30.00

DE ROO, Edward. *Rumble at the Housing Project.* 1960. Ace D 417. PBO. c/Marchetti. scarce. JD. VG+. B6a #77. $34.25

DE ROO, Edward. *Rumble at the Housing Project.* 1960. Ace D 417. PBO. JD. G+. P6d. $5.00

DE ROSSO, H.A. *End of the Gun.* 1955. Perma M 3014. PBO. c/T Ryan. We. VG. B5d. $4.00

DE ROSSO, H.A. *Tracks in the Sand.* Readers Choice 40. VG+. I1d. $8.00

DE ROSSO, H.A. *44.* Lion 129. NF. I1d. $14.00

DE SADE. *Bedroom Philosophers.* 1966. Lancer 74-850. 1st pb. VG+. B6d. $5.00

DE SAINT EXUPERY, Antoine. *Wind, Sand & Stars.* 1945. Bantam 14. Fa. NF. B4d. $7.50

DE SAINT EXUPERY, Antoine. *Wind, Sand & Stars.* 1945. Bantam 14. VG+. B3d. $5.00

DE STEIGUER, Walter. *Jewels for a Shroud.* Dell 614. 1st prtg. My. VG. R5d. $4.00

DE VET, Charles V. *Special Feature.* 1975. Avon 24562. SF. VG. P1d. $3.50

DE VET & MACLEAN/WILLIAMS. *Cosmic Checkmate/King of the Fourth Planet.* 1962. Ace F 149. PBO. c/E Valigursky. SF. VG. B5d. $4.50

DE VRIES, Marvin. *Frontier.* 1956. Ballantine 164. We. VG+. B4d. $8.00

DE VRIES, Peter. *Mackerel Plaza.* 1959. Signet S1648. c/B Phillips. Fi. VG. B5d. $3.00

DE VRIES, Peter. *Tunnel of Love.* Lion LL 34. VG+. B3d. $4.50

DE WEESE, Gene. *Jeremy Case.* 1976. Laser 72036. SF. V.G P1d. $5.00

DE WEESE, Jean. *Carnelian Cat.* 1975. Ballantine 24566. Go. VG. P1d. $3.50

DE WEESE, Jean. *Doll With Opal Eyes.* 1978. Popular 04197. Ho. G+. P1d. $3.00

DE WEESE, Jean. *Reimann Curse.* 1975. Beagle 26688. Go. VG. P1d. $3.50

DE WEESE, Jean. *Web of Guilt.* 1976. Ballantine 25258. Go. VG. P1d. $3.50

DE WITT, Jack. *Man in the Wilderness.* 1971. PB Library 65-765. PBO. MTI. NF. B6d. $7.50

DEAL, B.H. *Walk Through the Valley.* Popular G 222. VG+. B3d. $5.00

DEAN, A. *Screen Test.* Wee Hours 516. c/Bilbrew. NF. B3d. $11.00

DEAN, Abner. *What Am I Doing Here?* Signet 1382. VG+. B3d. $6.00

DEAN, Amber. *Devil Threw Dice.* 1956. Pocket 1090. c/L Marchetti. My. VG+. B5d. $5.50

DEAN, Amber. *Devil Threw Dice.* 1956. Pocket 1090. My. F. B4d. $8.00

DEAN, Amber. *Encounter With Evil.* 1962. Perma M 4254. 1st pbo. My. VG. B6d. $5.00

DEAN, Amber. *Something for the Birds.* 1961. Pocket 6069. My. VG+. B5d. $5.00

DEAN, B.J. *Schoolroom Stud.* 1969. Vega Book V 66. PBO. c/gga. NF. B6a. $33.00

DEAN, Dudley. *Broken Spur.* Gold Medal 511. PBO. G+. M6d. $5.00

DEAN, Dudley. *Gun the Man Down.* 1971. Gold Medal R 2388. We. VG+. B4d. $2.25

DEAN, Dudley. *Lawless Guns.* Gold Medal 882. VG. B3d. $4.00

DEAN, Dudley. *Lila My Lovely.* 1960. Gold Medal 1014. c/photo. VG. P6d. $3.00

DEAN, Dudley. *Man From Riondo.* 1966. Gold Medal K 1675. We. VG. B4d. $3.00

DEAN, Dudley. *Man From Riondo.* 1954. Gold Medal 436. PBO. We. VG+. B6d. $10.00

DEAN, Dudley. *Peril Is My Pay.* 1960. Gold Medal 1018. VG. P6d. $2.50

DEAN, Dudley. *Song of the Gun.* Gold Medal 925. 2nd prtg. VG+. B3d. $6.00

DEAN, Dudley. *Trail of the Hunter.* 1963. Berkley Y 824. We. VG+. B5d. $4.50

DEAN, J. *Hatred, Ridicule or Contempt.* Pan 362. VG+. B3d. $8.00

DEAN, Les. *Zorro, the Gay Blade.* 1981. Leisure 1007. 1st edn. c/photo. Av. F. F2d. $10.00

DEAN, Ralph. *Lingerie Limited.* 1960. Beacon 300. PBO. c/Gifford: gga. F. B6d. $25.00

DEAN, Ralph. *One Kind of Woman.* 1959. Beacon 251. 1st edn. c/bikini. F. F2d. $12.50

DEAN, Robert. *Murder by Marriage.* 1945. Bantam 6. My. VG+. B4d. $9.00

DEAN, Spencer. *Credit for a Murder.* Perma M 4276. G. G5d. $3.00

DEAN, Spencer. *Credit for a Murder.* 1963. Perma M 4276. 1st pbo. My. NF. B6d. $12.50

DEAN, Spencer. *Frightened Fingers.* Dell 893. c/W George. My. VG. B5d. $3.00

DEAN, Spencer. *Murder After a Fashion.* Pocket 6111. VG. G5d. $3.00

DEAN, Spencer. *Murder on Delivery.* Pocket 1220. G+. G5d. $3.25

DEAN, Spencer. *Murder on Delivery.* 1958. Pocket 1220. c/R Schultz. My. VG. B5d. $5.00

DEAN, Spencer. *Price Tag for Murder.* Pocket 6048. C+. C5d. $3.50

DEAN & WEISS. *Forbidden Thrills.* 1959. Bedtime Books 951. PBO. c/gga. VG. P6d. $4.50

DEAR, Ian. *Village of Blood.* 1975. New English 21343. Ho. VG. P1d. $7.50

DEARDEN, Warren. *Free Country.* 1971. Grove Press B 318Z. 1st prtg. VG+. P7d. $6.50

DEAREN, Patrick. *Starflight to Faroul.* 1980. Tower 51600. SF. F. W2d. $4.50

DEBOLT, Adriana. *Alien Within.* 1980. Carousel 70090. 1st prtg. SF. VG. R5d. $2.25

DEBOLT, Adriana. *Voyage of the Trigon.* 1981. Carousel 70097. 1st prtg. SF. VG. R5d. $2.50

DECKER, Jake. *Force #2: Death's Little Sister.* 1984. Pinnacle 42127. 1st prtg. My. VG. W2d. $3.00

DECKER/DUDLEY. *Devil's Punchbowl/Run If You Can.* Ace D 439. c/Maguire: gga. VG+. B6d. $18.00

DEE, Douglas. *Shared Wife.* 1964. Saber SA 71. Ad. VG. B5d. $4.00

DEE, Roger. *Let the Sky Fall.* 1957. Popular 819. Fi. VG. P1d. $7.50

DEE, Ron. *Brain Fever.* 1989. Pinnacle 55817. SF. F. W2d. $4.00

DEEDY, Ian. *Ride a Hot Mile.* Bee Line 107. NF. M6d. $12.50

DEEGAN, Jon J. *Exiles in Time.* 1952. Panther 117. SF. G+. P1d. $15.00

DEER, M.J. *Flames of Desire.* 1963. France F 66. SF. F. P1d. $20.00

DEFOE, Daniel. *Tales of Piracy, Crime & Ghosts.* 1945. Penguin. 1st pb. NF. M1d. $12.00

DEIGHTON, Len. *Funeral in Berlin.* 1966. Dell 2773. 1st prtg. My. VG+. W2d. $5.00

DEIGHTON, Len. *Ipscress File.* 1969. Crest T 1403. 1st prtg. VG. P7d. $4.00

DEIGHTON, Len. *SS-GB.* 1979. Panther 05002. SF/My. VG. P1d. $4.00

DEKKER, Carl. *Run for Your Life.* On-The-Spot My. VG. B3a #21. $19.80

DEKOBRA, Maurice. *Bedroom Eyes.* Avon Bedside Novel 4. c/Driben: gga. reprint. VG+. B6a #79. $66.00

DEKOBRA, Maurice. *Madonna of the Sleeping Cars.* Dell 256. VG+. B3d. $5.00

DEKOBRA, Maurice. *Street of Painted Lips.* Novel Library 9. VG. B3d. $15.00

DEKOBRA, Maurice. *Venus on Wheels.* Broadway 2. VG. B3d. $6.00

DEL MARTIA, Astron. *One Against Time.* 1970. PB Library 63-270. SF. NF. B5d. $5.50

DEL PIOMBO, A. *Boiler Maker.* Citadel NN. VG. B3d. $5.00

DELANEY, Joseph H. *In the Face of My Enemy.* 1985. Baen 55993. SF. VG. P1d. $3.50

DELANY, Samuel R. *Babel-17.* 1966. Ace F 388. 1st prtg. F. S1d. $8.00

DELANY, Samuel R. *Babel-17.* Ace 04591. c/J Podwil. SF. VG+. B4d/B5d. $4.00

DELANY, Samuel R. *Ballad of Beta 2.* Ace 04722. 2nd edn. F. P9d. $2.00

DELANY, Samuel R. *City of a Thousand Suns.* Ace F 322. NF. M1d. $12.00

DELANY, Samuel R. *City of a Thousand Suns.* Ace F 322. 1st prtg. VG+. S1d. $6.00

DELANY, Samuel R. *Driftglass.* 1971. Signet Q 4834. SF. VG. P1d. $5.00

DELANY, Samuel R. *Einstein Intersection.* 1967. Ace F 427. SF. F. P1d. $15.00

DELANY, Samuel R. *Einstein Intersection.* Ace 19681. 1st prtg. F. S1d. $3.50

DELANY, Samuel R. *Fall of the Towers.* Ace 22640. c/K Freas. SF. NF. B5d. $5.50

DELANY, Samuel R. *Fall of the Towers.* Ace 22640. SF. VG+. P1d. $4.50

DELANY, Samuel R. *Jewels of Aptor.* 1968. Ace G 706. SF. VG+. P1d. $7.50

DELANY, Samuel R. *Nova.* 1969. Bantam H 4738. SF. VG+. P1d. $5.00

DELANY, Samuel R. *Nova.* 1975. Bantam T 2243. 2nd prtg. SF. VG. W2d. $3.25

DELANY, Samuel R. *Out of the Dead City.* Ace 22643. SF. F. P1d. $5.00

DELANY, Samuel R. *Tales of Neveryon.* 1979. Bantam 12333. SF. F. M1d. $7.00

DELANY, Samuel R. *Towers of Toron.* Ace 81945. SF. VG. W2d. $3.00

DELANY, Samuel R. *Triton.* 1976. Bantam Y 2567. SF. F. P1d. $10.00

DELANY & HACKER. *Quark #1.* 1970. PB Library 66-480. SF. F. P1d. $25.00

DELANY & HACKER. *Quark #3.* 1971. PB Library 66-593. PBO. SF. VG+. B6d. $12.50

DELANY/PETAJA. *Ballad of Beta-2/Alpha Yes, Terra No!* 1965. Ace M 121. PBO. VG. B3d. $4.00

DELANY/PETAJA. *Ballad of Beta-2/Alpha Yes, Terra No!* 1965. Ace M 121. SF. F. W2d. $8.50

DELANY/PURDOM. *Empire Star/Tree Lord of Imeten.* Ace M 139. PBO. VG. B3d. $4.50

DELANY/PURDOM. *Empire Star/Tree Lord of Imeten.* 1966. Ace M 139. SF. F. W2d. $10.00

DELANY/WHITE. *Jewels of Aptor/Second Ending.* Ace F 173. F. M1d. $13.00

DELANY/WHITE. *Jewels of Aptor/Second Ending.* 1962. Ace F 173. SF. VG+. B5d. $9.50

DELANY/WILLIAMS. *Towers of Torin/Lunar Eye.* Ace F 261. PBO. VG. B3d. $5.00

DELANY/WILLIAMS. *Towers of Toron/Lunar Eye.* Ace F 261. NF. M1d. $10.00

DELANY/WILLIAMS. *Towers of Toron/Lunar Eye.* 1964. Ace F 261. SF. F. P1d. $15.00

DELANY/WOODCOTT. *Captives of the Flame/Psionic Menace.* 1963. Ace F 199. PBO. c/J Gaughan & E Emsh. SF. VG. B5d. $6.00

DELANY/WOODCOTT. *Captives of the Flame/Psionic Menace.* 1963. Ace F 199. SF. F. M1d. $20.00

DELISSER, H.G. *Psyche.* 1961. Baen. Hi. VG. P1d. $10.00

DELLA, Lew. *Ladies Sleep Alone.* 1951. Archer 72. F. I1d. $10.00

DELLA, Lew. *Ladies Sleep Alone.* 1951. Archer 72. VG+. B3a #20. $16.35

DELMAN, David. *Hard Sell.* 1959. Bantam A 1921. c/gga. Fa. VG. B4d. $2.00

DELMAR, Vina. *Bad Girl.* Avon 81. VG. B3d. $4.50

DELMAR, Vina. *Loose Ladies.* Avon 92. VG. B3d. $5.00

DELMAR, Vina. *Marriage Racket.* Avon 107. VG. B3d. $5.00

DELMAR, Vina. *New Orleans Lady.* Avon 209. VG. B3d. $5.00

DELMAR, Vina. *Restless Passion.* 1947. Avon 145. c/gga. Fa. VG. B3d/B4d. $5.00

DELMAR, Vina. *Strangers in Love.* Dell 10¢ 9. c/R Stanley. Fi. G+. B5d. $6.00

DELMAR, Vina. *Strangers in Love.* Dell 10¢ 9. VG+. B3d. $7.00

DELON, Eve. *Maid To Please.* 1967. Unique-Book UB 120. PBO. c/Ward. NF. B3a. $38.50

DEMARIS, Ovid. *Candyleg (Machine Gun McCain).* Gold Medal 2230. MTI. VG. B3d. $4.00

DEMARIS, Ovid. *Chip's Girls.* 1961. Beacon B 428B. PBO. Ad. G+. B5d. $3.50

DEMARIS, Ovid. *Dillinger Story.* 1961. Monarch 311. 1st edn. c/photo. Bio. F. F2d. $15.00

DEMARIS, Ovid. *Extortioners.* 1960. Gold Medal 960. 1st edn. c/gga. Cr. F. F2d. $10.00

DEMARIS, Ovid. *Hoods Take Over.* Gold Medal 680. c/Barye. VG. B3d. $5.00

DEMARIS, Ovid. *Lusting Drive.* 1958. Gold Medal 750. 1st edn. c/gga. My. F. F2d. $15.00

DEMARIS, Ovid. *Ride the Gold Mare.* 1957. Gold Medal 644. PBO. c/Barye. scrace drug book. VG+. B6a #77. $30.00

DEMARIS, Ovid. *Slasher.* 1959. Gold Medal 910. 1st edn. c/gga. My. F. F2d. $10.00

DEMING, Richard. *Big Jake.* 1971. PB Library 64-676. 1st prtg. VG+. R5d. $4.50

DEMING, Richard. *Death of a Pusher.* Pocket 35011. VG. G5d. $4.50

DEMING, Richard. *Fall Girl.* Zenith ZB 20. PBO. VG+. B3d. $7.00

DEMING, Richard. *Gallows in My Garden.* Dell 682. 1st prtg. My. VG. R5d. $4.50

DEMING, Richard. *Groovy Way To Die.* 1968. Pyramid X 1908. TVTI. c/photo. NF. B4d. $8.00

DEMING, Richard. *Hit.* 1970. Pyramid X 2214. 1st prtg. TVTI. VG. R5d. $4.50

DEMING, Richard. *She'll Hate Me Tomorrow.* 1963. Monarch 365. c/Lou Marchetti: gga. VG. P6d. $1.50

DEMING, Richard. *Spy-In.* 1969. Pyramid X 1986. TVTI. VG+. B4d. $4.00

DEMPSEY, David. *Flood.* Ballantine 143. PBO. VG. B3d. $4.00

DEMPSEY, Jack. *Dempsey.* 1960. Avon G 1068. 1st pb. VG. B6d. $4.00

DENAERDE, Stefan. *Amazing Spiderman.* 1978. Pocket 81444. PBO. F. B6d. $7.50

DENAERDE, Stefan. *Fantastic Four #1.* 1977. Pocket 81445. PBO. F. B6d. $7.50

DENAERDE, Stefan. *Operation Survival Earth.* 1977. Pocket 80840. SF. F. P1d. $5.00

DENBY, C. *Sophisticated Party.* Midwood 34-740. VG. B3d. $4.50

DENELLE, Shawna. *Obey the Rules.* 1967. Unique 132. c/Ward. NF. B3a #22. $18.15

DENHAM, Alice. *Ghost & Mrs Muir.* 1968. Popular 60-2348. Fa. G+. P1d. $5.00

DENNIS, Patrick. *Auntie Mame.* Pan G 183. 2nd prtg. MTI. VG. B3d. $8.50

DENNIS, Ralph. *Atlanta Deathwatch.* 1974. Popular 00572. 1st edn. De. F. F2d. $6.50

DENNIS, Robert C. *Sweat of Fear.* 1976. Ballantine 25148. SF/My. VG. P1d. $3.50

DENNIS, Robert E. *Sweat of Fear.* 1975. Arrow 91093. My. VG. W2d. $4.00

DENT, Lester. *Cry at Dusk.* 1952. Gold Medal 247. My. VG+. P1d. $20.00

DENT, Lester. *Cry at Dusk.* 1952. Gold Medal 247. 1st edn. c/Kenneth Robeson: sgn. My. F. F2d. $35.00

DENT, Roxanne. *Island of Fear.* 1973. Avon 15032. 1st edn. Ho. F. F2d. $10.00

DENTON, J. *Naked in Vegas.* Boudoir 1014. VG. B3d. $4.00

DENZER, Peter W. *I'm No Good.* 1956. Popular 744. JD. VG+. P1d. $18.00

DENZER, Peter W. *I'm No Good.* 1956. Popular 744. 1st edn. PBO. c/Johnson. scarce. JD. VG+. B6a #77. $33.00

DENZER, Peter W. *Practice of Passion.* Monarch 500. PBO. Ad. VG. B5d. $6.50

DERBY, Mark. *Afraid in the Dark.* 1953. Popular G 124. 1st pb. c/Malaya. VG. B6d. $4.50

DERBY, Mark. *Sun in the Hunter's Eyes.* 1959. Crest S 306. 1st prtg. My. VG+. R5d. $5.00

DERBY, Mark. *Womanhunt.* Ace D 458. VG. B3d. $4.00

DERBY, Mark. *Womanhunt.* 1960. Ace D 458. 1st pb. c/Malaya: gga. NF. B6d. $22.50

DERLERTH & LOVECRAFT. *Lurker at the Threshold.* 1971. Beagle 95058. 1st edn. PBO. F. F2d. $11.00

DERLETH, August. *Beachheads in Space.* 1957. Berkley G 77. SF. VG+. P1d. $11.00

DERLETH, August. *Beyond Time & Space.* Berkley G 104. VG. I1d. $3.00

DERLETH, August. *Beyond Time & Space.* 1958. Berkley G 104. SF. F. P1d. $15.00

DERLETH, August. *Mask of Cthulhu.* 1976. Ballantine. 2nd pb. VG. M1d. $4.00

DERLETH, August. *Mask of Cthulhu.* 1971. Beagle 95107. 1st edn. PBO. F. F2d. $10.00

DERLETH, August. *Not Long for This World.* 1961. Ballantine 542. Ho. VG. P1d. $8.00

DERLETH, August. *Other Side of the Moon.* 1959. Berkley G 249. SF. VG+. P1d. $10.50

DERLETH, August. *Outer Reaches.* Berkley G 116. 1st pb. VG. M6d. $3.50

DERLETH, August. *Outer Reaches.* 1958. Berkley G 116. SF. F. P1d. $15.00

DERLETH, August. *Outer Space.* Berkley G 116. VG+. I1d. $4.00

DERLETH, August. *Reminiscences of Solar Pons.* 1975. Pinnacle 0-523-00629-2. VG+. P6d. $3.25

DERLETH, August. *Someone in the Dark.* 1978. Jove 04738. SF. VG. W2d. $5.00

DERLETH, August. *Stories From Sleep No More.* 1967. Bantam H 3425. Ho. VG. P1d. $7.50

DERLETH, August. *Strange Ports of Call.* 1958. Berkley G 131. SF. F. P1d. $15.00

DERLETH, August. *Strange Ports of Call.* 1958. Berkley G 131. SF. VG. B5d. $4.00

DERLETH, August. *Tales of the Cthulhu Mythos.* 1974. Ballantine 23227. 3rd prtg. SF. G+. W2d. $3.75

DERLETH, August. *Time To Come.* 1958. Berkley G 189. 1st pb. F. M1d. $8.00

DERLETH, August. *Time To Come.* 1969. Pyramid T 2012. SF. F. W2d. $5.00

DERLETH, August. *Time To Come.* Tower 44-461. 1st prtg. G+. S1d. $3.00

DERLETH, August. *Trail of Cthulhu.* 1971. Beagle 95108. G+. M6d. $4.50

DERLETH, August. *Trail of Cthulhu.* 1971. Beagle 95108. SF. F. W2d. $12.00

DERLITH, August. *Trail of Cthulhu.* 1971. Beagle 95108. 1st pb. VG. M1d/P1d. $10.00

DERLETH, August. *Worlds of Tomorrow.* 1958. Berkley G 163. SF. VG. P1d. $7.50

DERLETH & LOVECRAFT. *Survivor & Others.* Ballantine. 1st pb edn. NF. M1d. $15.00

DERLITH & LOVECRAFT. *Lurker at the Threshold.* 1971. Beagle. VG. M1d. $4.00

DERN, Peggy. *Orchids for a Nurse.* 1963. Lancer 70-053. 1st pb. VG. B6d. $5.00

DERVAL, P. *Folies-Bergere.* Popular G 170. VG. B3d. $4.50

DES CARS, Guy. *Brute.* 1952. Pyramid G 69. 1st pb. c/gga. VG. B6d. $9.00

DES LIGNERIS, Francoise. *Fort Frederick.* 1960. Avon T 456. 1st US edn. PBO. VG. P6d. $4.50

DESMOND, Warren. *Night of Flame.* 1949. Signet 721. Fa. VG+. B4d. $3.50

DETIMMS, Graeme. *Split.* 1963. Digit R 807. SF. VG. P1d. $7.50

DEUTSCH, Ronald M. *Nuts Among the Berries.* 1961. Ballantine F 548. NF. VG. B5d. $3.50

DEUTSCHER, Isaac. *Great Contest.* 1961. Ballantine F 559. Nfi. NF. B5d. $5.50

DEUTSCHER, Isaac. *Great Contest.* 1961. Ballantine F 559. NFi. VG. B4d. $3.00

DEVANEY, John. *Baseball Life of Mickey Mantle.* 1969. Scholastic 1105. PBO. c/photo. VG. P6d. $4.50

DEVEREUX, James P.S. *Story of Wake Island.* Ace D 280. Nfi. VG. B5d. $3.50

DEVET & MACLEAN & WILLIAMS. *Cosmic Checkmate/King of the Fouth Planet.* Ace F 149. F. M1d. $9.00

DEVIGNY, Andre. *Man Escaped.* 1959. Berkley BG 254. Nfi. VG. B5d. $3.50

DEVLIN, Barry. *Make Sure I Win.* 1959. Beacon 255. 1st pb. c/gga. NF. B6d. $22.50

DEVLIN, Barry. *Night of the Lash.* Beacon 283. VG. B3d. $4.50

DEWEY, Thomas B. *Brave Bad Girls.* 1957. Perma M 3089. c/C Hulings. My. VG. B5d. $5.50

DEWEY, Thomas B. *Case of the Murdered Model.* 1955. Avon 626. VG. G5d. $6.00

DEWEY, Thomas B. *Case of the Murdered Model.* 1957. Avon 787. c/gga. My. VG+. B3d. $4.50

DEWEY, Thomas B. *Chased & the Unchaste.* 1960. Crest 360. 1st prtg. c/gga. VG. P7d. $5.00

DEWEY, Thomas B. *Don't Cry for Long.* Pocket 50223. VG. G5d. $5.50

DEWEY, Thomas B. *Draw the Curtain Close.* 1949. Signet 736. My. VG. B5d. $6.50

DEWEY, Thomas B. *Draw the Curtain Close.* 1949. Signet 736. NF. I1d. $10.00

DEWEY, Thomas B. *Every Bet's a Sure Thing.* Avon 564. VG. B3d. $5.00

DEWEY, Thomas B. *Girl in the Punchbowl.* Dell 2883. PBO. VG. B3d. $4.00

DEWEY, Thomas B. *Go, Honeylou.* 1962. Dell 1st Edn B 215. PBO. c/Kalin: gga. VG+. B6d. $12.50

DEWEY, Thomas B. *Golden Hooligan.* Dell 1st Edn B 207. NF. I1d. $6.00

DEWEY, Thomas B. *Handle With Fear.* Graphic 73. VG. B3d. $3.50

DEWEY, Thomas B. *How Hard To Kill.* Perma M 4291. VG+. I1d. $6.00

DEWEY, Thomas B. *Hunter at Large.* Pocket M 4277. G. G5d. $3.50

DEWEY, Thomas B. *Only on Tuesdays.* 1964. Dell 1st Edn 6680. PBO. c/Lesser. My. VG. B6d. $3.50

DEWEY, Thomas B. *Room for Murder.* 1950. Signet 814. 1st pb. My. VG. B6d. $9.00

DEWEY, Thomas B. *Sad Song Singing.* Pocket 35044. G. G5d. $3.00

DEWEY, Thomas B. *Season for Violence.* 1966. Gold Medal D 1676. PBO. My. G+. B6d. $3.50

DEWEY, Thomas B. *You've Got Him Cold.* 1959. Crest 323. 1st prtg. My. G+. R5d. $3.00

DEWEY. *Girl With the Sweet Plump Knees.* 1963. Dell 1st Edn 2917. PBO. My. VG. B6d. $2.75

DEXTER, John. *Anytime Amy.* 1966. Leisure 1178. PBO. c/gga. VG+. B6a #77. $73.00

DEXTER, John. *Community Wife.* 1969. Adult Book 467. PBO. c/gga. scarce. F. B6a #76. $49.00

DEXTER, John. *Flesh Hustler.* Sundown 539. NF. B3d. $7.00

DEXTER, John. *For Lust's Sake.* Companion 586. VG. B3d. $5.00

DEXTER, John. *Gay Ones.* Sundown Reader 605. PBO. VG+. B3d. $5.50

DEXTER, John. *Hay Ride to Hell.* 1966. Ember Library 320. PBO. c/Bonfils: gga. NF. B6a #76. $53.50

DEXTER, John. *Last-Chance Lust.* 1968. Adult Book 427. PBO. c/gga. NF. B6a #76. $33.00

DEXTER, John. *Lost House of Sin.* Ember Book EB 946. VG. B3d. $3.50

DEXTER, John. *Lust Dupe.* Idle Hour IH 425. VG+. I1d. $4.00

DEXTER, John. *Lust Lobby.* Ember Book EB 941. VG+. M6d. $9.50

DEXTER, John. *Mrs Brown's Body.* 1970. Candid Reader 1011. PBO. c/gga. NF. B6a #76. $36.50

DEXTER, John. *Narco Nympho.* 1967. Leisure 1197. PBO. c/gga. VG+. B6a #77. $150.00

DEXTER, John. *Sex Gambler.* Midnight MR 421. VG. B3d. $8.00

DEXTER, John. *Shame Tigers.* 1966. Ember Library 327. PBO. c/Biker: gga. VG+. B6a #79. $65.50

DEXTER, John. *Sin Festival.* 1961. Nightstand NB 1572. Ad. G+. B5d. $3.00

DEXTER, John. *Sin Song.* 1961. Nightstand NB 1562. Ad. G. B5d. $2.00

DEXTER, John. *Sin Stripper.* 1967. Adult Book 405. PBO. c/Bonfils. VG+. B6a #80. $63.50

DEXTER, John. *Sinners of Hwang.* 1965. Leisure 1106. PBO. rare. SF. VG+. B6a #79. $267.00

DEXTER, John. *Stripper!* 1960. Corinth Nightstand 1530. 1st edn. c/gga. F. F2d. $20.00

DEXTER, John. *Swap for the Birdie.* 1970. Companion 670. PBO. c/Bonfils: gga. F. B6a #76. $64.00

DEXTER, John. *Web of Lust.* 1965. Leisure LB 692. PBO. c/gga. VG. P6d. $5.00

DEXTER, William. *Children of the Void.* 1966. PB Library 52-357. SF. F. P1d. $11.00

DEXTER, William. *Children of the Void.* 1966. PB Library 52-357. SF. VG+. B5d. $6.50

DI DONATO, P. *Christ in Concrete.* Lion 18. VG. I1d. $5.00

DI LAMPEDUSA, Giuseppi. *Leopard.* 1961. Signet T 1960. 1st prtg. VG+. R5d. $5.00

DI PIRAJNO, A.D. *Cure for Serpents.* Pan GP 70. VG. I1d. $5.00

DIAMOND, Graham. *Dungeons of Kuba.* 1979. Playboy 16524. Fa. F. P1d. $5.00

DIAMOND, Graham. *Lady of the Haven.* 1978. Playboy 16477. Fa. VG. P1d. $3.50

DIAMOND, Graham. *Thief of Kalimar.* 1979. Gold Medal 1-4214. Fa. F. P1d. $5.00

DIAMOND/FLYNN. *Widow Maker/Deep Six.* 1961. Ace F 125. PBO. c/C Smith. My. VG. B5d. $5.00

DIBELL, Ansen. *Pursuit of the Screamer.* 1978. DAW UJ 1386. SF. VG+. P1d. $4.50

DIBELL, Anson. *Circle, Crescent, Star.* 1981. DAW. 1st edn. F. M1d. $6.00

DIBELL, Anson. *Summer Fair.* 1982. DAW. 1st edn. F. M1d. $6.00

DIBNER, Martin. *God for Tomorrow.* 1963. Lancer 72-652. My. NF. B5d. $5.50

DICK, Philip K. *Best of Philip K Dick.* 1977. Ballantine 25359. SF. VG. P1d. $7.50

DICK, Philip K. *Blade Runner (Do Androids Dream of Electric Sheep).* 1982. Ballantine 30129. SF. F. W2d. $6.00

DICK, Philip K. *Blade Runner.* 1982. Ballantine 30129. 1st prtg. MTI. SF. G+. R5d. $2.50

DICK, Philip K. *Book of PK Dick.* 1973. DAW 44. SF. VG+. B4d. $12.00

DICK, Philip K. *Clans of the Alphane Moon.* 1964. Ace F 309. SF. F. P1d. $20.00

DICK, Philip K. *Clans of the Alphane Moon.* 1964. Ace F 309. 1st prtg. SF. VG. B4d/R5d. $10.00

DICK, Philip K. *Confessions of a Crap Artist.* Pocket 44213. VG. M6d. $7.50

DICK, Philip K. *Crack in Space.* 1966. Ace F 377. PBO. VG+. B3a #21. $11.25

DICK, Philip K. *Crack in Space.* 1966. Ace F 377. PBO. VG+. B3d. $8.00

DICK, Philip K. *Deus Irea.* 1977. Dell 11838. SF. VG+. W2d. $7.50

DICK, Philip K. *Divine Invasion.* 1982. Pocket 44343. SF. VG. P1d. $7.50

DICK, Philip K. *Do Androids Dream of Electric Sheep?* 1969. Signet T 4758. 3rd prtg. SF. VG. W2d. $6.00

DICK, Philip K. *Dr Bloodmoney.* 1965. Ace F 337. SF. F. B4d. $22.00

DICK, Philip K. *Dr Bloodmoney.* 1965. Ace F 337. 1st prtg. VG. S1d. $11.00

DICK, Philip K. *Dr Bloodmoney.* 1990. C & G 88184. 2nd edn. SF. VG+. B4d. $4.00

DICK, Philip K. *Eye in the Sky.* 1957. Ace D 211. SF. VG. B4d. $17.50

DICK, Philip K. *Eye in the Sky.* 1957. Ace D 211. 1st prtg. SF. G+. B5d/R5d. $12.50

DICK, Philip K. *Eye in the Sky.* Ace H 39. 1st prtg. G+. S1d. $5.50

DICK, Philip K. *Eye in the Sky.* 1968. Ace H 39. SF. VG. B4d. $5.00

DICK, Philip K. *Eye in the Sky.* Ace 22387. SF. F. W2d. $7.50

DICK, Philip K. *Eye in the Sky.* 1971. Arrow 510. SF. VG+. P1d. $10.00

DICK, Philip K. *Eye in the Sky.* 1971. Arrow 510. 1st British edn. VG. B3d. $9.00

DICK, Philip K. *Game-Players of Titan.* 1963. Ace F 251. SF. F. B4d/P1d. $25.00

DICK, Philip K. *Game-Players of Titan.* 1963. Ace F 251. SF. VG+. B3d. $12.00

DICK, Philip K. *Game-Players of Titan.* Ace 27310. SF. VG. P1d. $7.50

DICK, Philip K. *Golden Man.* 1980. Berkley 04288. SF. V.G P1d. $6.00

DICK, Philip K. *Man in the High Castle.* 1974. Berkley D 3080. 3rd prtg. SF. VG+. W2d. $5.25

DICK, Philip K. *Man in the High Castle.* 1964. Popular SP 250. SF. VG. B4d. $16.00

DICK, Philip K. *Man in the High Castle.* 1968. Popular 60-2289. SF. VG. P1d. $10.00

DICK, Philip K. *Man Who Japed.* Ace 51910. SF. F. W2d. $10.00

DICK, Philip K. *Martian Time-Slip.* 1964. Ballantine U 2191. SF. F. P1d. $25.00

DICK, Philip K. *Martian Time-Slip.* 1964. Ballantine U 2191. SF. VG. W2d. $12.50

DICK, Philip K. *Martian Time-Slip.* Ballantine 25224. 2nd prtg. G+. S1d. $3.50

DICK, Philip K. *Maze of Death.* Bantam 10740. 1st prtg. VG. S1d. $7.00

DICK, Philip K. *Maze of Death.* DAW 533. VG. B3d. $5.00

DICK, Philip K. *Maze of Death.* 1971. PB Library 64-636. SF. VG. P1d. $10.00

DICK, Philip K. *Now Wait for Last Year.* 1968. MacFadden 60-352. SF. F. P1d. $20.00

DICK, Philip K. *Now Wait for Last Year.* 1968. MacFadden 60-352. SF. G+. W2d. $6.00

DICK, Philip K. *Our Friends From Frolix 8.* 1970. Ace 64400. SF. VG. P1d. $10.00

DICK, **Philip K.** *Penultimate Truth.* 1964. Belmont 92-603. SF. F. P1d. $25.00

DICK, **Philip K.** *Penultimate Truth.* 1964. Belmont 92-603. SF. VG+. B4d. $20.00

DICK, **Philip K.** *Penultimate Truth.* Dell 16926. SF. F. P1d. $12.50

DICK, **Philip K.** *Preserving Machine.* 1969. Ace 67800. SF. VG+. B4d. $10.00

DICK, **Philip K.** *Scanner Darkly.* Ballantine 26064. 3rd edn. G. P9d. $1.25

DICK, **Philip K.** *Simulacra.* 1964. Ace F 301. SF. G+. P1d/W2d. $7.50

DICK, **Philip K.** *Solar Lottery.* 1955. Ace D 103. PBO. scarce. VG+. B6a #74. $67.25

DICK, **Philip K.** *Solar Lottery.* 1959. Ace D 340. 2nd edn. SF. VG+. B4d. $6.00

DICK, **Philip K.** *Solar Lottery.* 1968. Ace G 718. VG+. S1d. $7.00

DICK, **Philip K.** *Solar Lottery.* 1968. Ace G 718. 3rd edn. G. P9d. $1.25

DICK, **Philip K.** *Solar Lottery.* Ace 77411. SF. VG. W2d. $10.00

DICK, **Philip K.** *Three Stigmata of Palmer Eldritch.* 1977. Bantam 10586. SF. VG. P1d. $7.50

DICK, **Philip K.** *Three Stigmata of Palmer Eldritch.* 1966. MacFadden 60-240. SF. VG. B3d. $5.00

DICK, **Philip K.** *Three Stigmata of Palmer Eldritch.* 1971. MacFadden 75-399. 2nd edn. SF. G+. M3d. $6.00

DICK, **Philip K.** *Time Out of Joint.* Belmont 51143. SF. VG+. B4d. $4.00

DICK, **Philip K.** *Time Out of Joint.* 1965. Belmont 92-618. SF. G+. M3d. $7.00

DICK, **Philip K.** *Time Out of Joint.* 1965. Belmont 92-618. SF. VG. P1d. $15.00

DICK, **Philip K.** *Time Out of Joint.* 1979. Dell 18860. SF. VG. W2d. $6.50

DICK, **Philip K.** *Transmigration of Timothy Archer.* Pocket 46751. PBO? VG. M6d. $5.00

DICK, **Philip K.** *Ubik.* 1970. Dell 9200. SF. VG. P1d/W2d. $10.00

DICK, **Philip K.** *Unteleported Man.* 1983. Berkley 06252. SF. VG. W2d. $7.00

DICK, **Philip K.** *Valis.* 1981. Bantam 14156. SF. G+. P1d. $4.50

DICK, **Philip K.** *Variable Man.* 1957. Ace D 261. PBO. c/E Emsh. SF. VG. B5d. $20.00

DICK, **Philip K.** *Vulcan's Hammer.* 1960. Ace D 457. SF. VG+. P1d. $30.00

DICK, **Philip K.** *We Can Build You.* DAW UQ 1014. 3rd edn. SF. VG. P1d. $6.00

DICK, **Philip K.** *We Can Build You.* 1972. DAW UY 1164. 4th edn. SF. VG+. B4d. $4.00

DICK, **Philip K.** *World Jones Made.* 1967. Ace F 429. c/Kelly Freas: sgn. SF. VG+. P1d. $20.00

DICK, **Philip K.** *World Jones Made.* 1967. Ace F 429. SF. VG. B3d. $6.00

DICK, **Philip K.** *Zap Gun.* 1978. Dell 19907. SF. VG. M1d. $6.00

DICK, **Philip K.** *Zap Gun.* 1967. Pyramid R 1569. SF. VG. P1d. $12.50

DICK & **NELSON.** *Ganymede Takeover.* 1967. Ace G 637. PBO. c/Jack Gaughan. VG. P6d. $6.00

DICK & **NELSON.** *Ganymede Takeover.* 1967. Ace G 637. SF. F. P1d. $25.00

DICK & **ZELAZNY.** *Deus Irae.* 1977. Dell 11838. SF. VG+. P1d. $7.50

DICK/DICK. *Dr Futurity/Unteleported Man.* 1972. Ace 15697. 2nd edn. c/skull. SF. G. B5d. $5.00

DICK/DICK. *Dr Futurity/Unteleported Man.* 1972. Ace 15697. 2nd edn. SF. VG+. B4d. $10.00

DICK/NORTH. *Cosmic Puppets/Sargasso of Space.* Ace D 249. c/Emsh. F. M1d. $30.00

DICK/NORTH. *Cosmic Puppets/Sargasso of Space.* 1957. Ace D 249. c/E Emsh. SF. G+. B5d. $12.50

DICK/NORTH. *Cosmic Puppets/Sargasso of Space.* 1957. Ace D 249. SF. VG. P1d. $25.00

DICK/ST. **CLAIR.** *World Jones Made/ Agent of the Unknown.* 1956. Ace D 150. SF. G+. P1d/W2d. $15.00

DICK/ST. **CLAIR.** *World Jones Made/ Agent of the Unknown.* 1956. Ace D 150. 1st prtg. SF. G+. R5d. $8.00

DICK/TUBB. *Man Who Japed/Space-Born.* 1956. Ace D 193. PBO. G. M6d. $5.00

DICK/TUBB. *Man Who Japed/Space-Born.* 1956. Ace D 193. PBO. VG. B3d. $15.00

DICKENS, **Bradford.** *Fornication Formula.* Adult Books AB 1519. PBO. VG. M6d. $6.50

DICKENS, **Charles.** *Christmas Carol.* Pocket 29. G+. B3d. $5.00

DICKENS, **Charles.** *Christmas Carol.* 1939. Pocket 29. Fa. VG. P1d. $20.00

DICKENS, **Charles.** *Tale of Two Cities.* Pocket 14. 7th prtg. VG. B3d. $6.00

DICKENS, **Charles.** *Tale of Two Cities.* 1939. Pocket 14. VG. B3a #20. $6.60

DICKENS, **Charles.** *Tale of Two Cities.* 1944. Quick Reader 119. VG. B3a #20. $16.05

DICKEY, **James.** *Alnilam.* 1988. Pinnacle 086. SF/My. VG. P1d. $4.50

DICKEY, **James.** *Deliverance.* 1971. Dell 1868. 1st prtg. MTI. VG+. R5d. $3.00

DICKEY, **James.** *Undead.* 1973. Pan 23797. Ho. G+. P1d. $5.00

DICKINSON, **Peter.** *Blue Hawk.* 1977. Ballantine 25759. 1st prtg. SF. G+. R5d. $1.50

DICKINSON, **Peter.** *Glass-Sided Ants' Nest.* 1981. Penguin 5864. My. VG. P1d. $4.00

DICKINSON, **Peter.** *King & Joker.* 1977. Avon 35006. My. VG. P1d. $3.50

DICKINSON, **Peter.** *Skin Deep.* 1970. Panther 02904. 2nd edn. My. VG. P1d. $5.00

DICKINSON, **Peter.** *Weather Monger.* 1974. DAW 104. 1st edn. PBO. F. M1d. $6.00

DICKINSON, **Susan edt.** *Ghostly Encounters.* 1973. Armada Lion C 611. Ho. G+. P1d. $3.50

DICKS, **Terrance.** *Auton Invasion.* 1974. Target 10313. SF. VG. P1d. $6.00

DICKS, **Terrance.** *Day of the Daleks.* 1979. Pinnacle 40-565. Dr Who #1. SF. VG. M3d/P1d. $5.00

DICKS, **Terrance.** *Day of the Daleks.* 1979. Pinnacle 40565. 1st prtg. Dr Who #1. SF. F. W2d. $6.00

DICKS, **Terrance.** *Doctor Who & the Android Invasion.* 1980. Pinnacle 40461. 1st prtg. SF. VG. W2d. $4.25

DICKS, **Terrance.** *Dr Who & the Talons of Weng-Chiang.* 1979. Pinnacle 40638. SF. VG. W2d. $5.00

DICKS, **Terrance.** *Face of Evil.* 1978. Target 20006. SF. VG. P1d. $5.00

DICKS, **Terrance.** *Genesis of the Daleks.* 1978. Target NN. SF. VG+. M3d. $5.00

DICKS, **Terrance.** *Giant Robot.* 1975. Target 10858. SF. VG. P1d. $6.00

DICKS, **Terrance.** *Image of the Fendahl.* 1979. Pinnacle 40-608. SF. VG. M3d. $5.00

DICKS, **Terrance.** *Invasion of Time.* 1984. Target 35. 4th prtg. SF. F. M3d. $4.00

DICKS, **Terrance.** *Keeper of Traken.* 1984. Target 37. 5th prtg. SF. NF. M3d. $4.00

DICKS, **Terrance.** *Loch Ness Monster.* 1979. Pinnacle 40-609. Dr Who #6. SF. F. P1d/W2d. $10.00

DICKS, Terrance. *Planet of the Daleks.* 1976. Target 11252. SF. VG. P1d. $5.00

DICKS, Terrance. *Revenge of the Cybermen.* 1976. Pinnacle 10997. SF. VG. P1d. $5.00

DICKSON, Carter. *And So To Murder.* Dell 175. 1st prtg. My. VG. R5d. $10.00

DICKSON, Carter. *And So To Murder.* 1947. Dell 175. VG+. B3a #24. $12.00

DICKSON, Carter. *Behind the Crimson Blind.* 1953. Dell 690. 1st prtg. c/Phillips: gga. VG+. P7d. $7.50

DICKSON, Carter. *Behind the Crimson Blind.* Pan G 340. VG+. B3d. $10.00

DICKSON, Carter. *Bowstring Murders.* 1959. Berkley G 214. c/R Maquire. My. VG+. I1d. $5.00

DICKSON, Carter. *Crossbow Murder.* 1964. Berkley F 870. My. VG. B5d. $4.50

DICKSON, Carter. *Curse of the Bronze Lamp.* 1967. Berkley X 1347. My. VG. B5d. $3.00

DICKSON, Carter. *Curse of the Bronze Lamp.* Pocket 568. VG. I1d. $6.50

DICKSON, Carter. *Death & the Gilded Man.* Pocket 478. G+. I1d. $4.00

DICKSON, Carter. *Death in Five Boxes.* 1964. Berkley F 879. My. VG. B5d. $3.50

DICKSON, Carter. *Death in Five Boxes.* 1946. Dell 108. NF. I1d. $20.00

DICKSON, Carter. *Death in Five Boxes.* 1946. Dell 108. VG. B3a #20. $8.00

DICKSON, Carter. *Death in Five Boxes.* 1946. Dell 108. VG+. B3d. $14.00

DICKSON, Carter. *Department of Queer Complaints.* Armed Services 1069. VG. B3a #20. $25.00

DICKSON, Carter. *Fear Is the Same.* 1959. Bantam A 2000. 1st prtg. My. VG+. R5d. $10.00

DICKSON, Carter. *Graveyard To Let.* 1968. Berkley X 1502. c/skull. My. VG. B5d. $3.00

DICKSON, Carter. *Graveyard To Let.* Dell 543. c/J Meese. VG. B3d. $4.50

DICKSON, Carter. *Judas Window.* Penguin 819. VG. G5d. $6.00

DICKSON, Carter. *Judas Window.* Pocket 231. G+. I1d. $9.00

DICKSON, Carter. *Night at the Mocking Widow.* 1969. Berkley X 1574. My. VG. B5d. $3.00

DICKSON, Carter. *Night at the Mocking Widow.* 1953. Dell 650. c/B Hilbert. My. G+. B5d. $3.00

DICKSON, Carter. *Night at the Mocking Widow.* 1953. Dell 650. 1st prtg. c/Hilbert: gga. VG. P7d. $6.50

DICKSON, Carter. *Plague Court Murders.* Avon NN 7. 1st prtg. My. VG. R5d. $12.50

DICKSON, Carter. *Punch & Judy Murders (The Magic Lantern Murders).* 1943. Pocket 219. VG. G5d. $9.00

DICKSON, Carter. *Punch & Judy Murders.* 1964. Berkley F 902. 1st prtg. My. VG+. R5d. $6.00

DICKSON, Carter. *Reader Is Warned.* Pocket 303. VG. B3d. $6.00

DICKSON, Carter. *Red Widow Murders.* Pocket 86. G. G5d. $7.00

DICKSON, Carter. *Scotland Yard: Department of Queer Complaints.* 1944. Dell 65. c/Gregg. scarce. VG+. B6a #77. $40.00

DICKSON, Carter. *Scotland Yard: Department of Queer Complaints.* 1944. Dell 65. VG. B3a #21. $17.70

DICKSON, Carter. *Seeing Is Believing.* 1966. Berkley F 1282. My. VG+. B5d. $4.00

DICKSON, Carter. *She Died a Lady.* Pocket 507. VG. G5d. $6.50

DICKSON, Carter. *Skeleton in the Clock.* Dell 481. c/R Stanley. My. G+. B5d. $3.50

DICKSON, Carter. *Ten Teacups (Peacock Feather Murders).* Penguin 817. G+. G5d. $9.00

DICKSON, Carter. *White Priory Murders.* 1963. Berkley F 847. My. VG+. B5d. $5.50

DICKSON, Carter. *White Priory Murders.* 1942. Pocket 156. VG. G5d. $11.00

DICKSON, Cary. *King's Women.* 1967. Bee Line 187. Ad. VG+. B5d. $10.00

DICKSON, Gordon R. *Alien Way.* 1965. Bantam F 2941. SF. F. P1d. $11.00

DICKSON, Gordon R. *Alien Way.* 1971. Warner 84552. SF. VG. W2d. $4.50

DICKSON, Gordon R. *Arcturus Landing.* 1988. TOR 53546. SF. F. W2d. $3.50

DICKSON, Gordon R. *Beginnings.* 1988. Baen 65429. PBO. SF. NF. B6d. $3.00

DICKSON, Gordon R. *Book of Gordon Dickson.* 1973. DAW 55. c/K Thole. SF. VG+. B5d. $4.00

DICKSON, Gordon R. *Dorsai Compaion.* 1986. Ace 16026. SF. VG. P1d. $5.00

DICKSON, Gordon R. *Dorsai!* 1982. Ace 16016. 4th prtg. SF. F. W2d. $4.00

DICKSON, Gordon R. *Dorsai!* 1976. DAW UE 1342. SF. F. W2d. $4.25

DICKSON, Gordon R. *Far Call.* 1978. Dell 12284. SF. F. P1d. $5.00

DICKSON, Gordon R. *Forever Man.* 1988. Ace 24713. c/J Gurney. SF. NF. B5d. $5.00

DICKSON, Gordon R. *Genetic General.* Ace F 426. 2nd edn. VG. P9d. $2.00

DICKSON, Gordon R. *Gordon R Dickson's SF Best.* 1978. Dell 13181. SF. F. P1d. $5.00

DICKSON, Gordon R. *Hour of the Horde.* 1971. Berkley S 1957. SF. VG. P1d. $4.00

DICKSON, Gordon R. *Hour of the Horde.* 1983. DAW 303. 1st edn. VG. P9d. $1.50

DICKSON, Gordon R. *Masters of Everon.* 1980. Ace 52115. 1st edn. c/sgn. SF. F. F2d. $20.00

DICKSON, Gordon R. *Masters of Everon.* 1980. Ace. SF. VG. W2d. $4.00

DICKSON, Gordon R. *Mission to Universe.* 1965. Berkley F 1147. SF. VG+. W2d. $5.00

DICKSON, Gordon R. *Mutants.* 1973. Collier 01954. SF. VG. P1d. $3.50

DICKSON, Gordon R. *Naked to the Stars.* 1977. DAW UW 1278 227. SF. F. P1d. $5.00

DICKSON, Gordon R. *Naked to the Stars.* 1961. Pyramid F682. PBO. c/E Emsh. SF. VG. B5d. $5.00

DICKSON, Gordon R. *Necromancer.* DAW 274. G. P9d. $1.00

DICKSON, Gordon R. *Necromancer.* 1979. Sphere 2976. SF. VG. P1d. $4.00

DICKSON, Gordon R. *No Room for Man.* 1963. MacFadden 50-179. SF. F. P1d. $12.00

DICKSON, Gordon R. *No Room for Man.* 1966. MacFadden 50-329. 2nd prtg. SF. VG. W2d. $4.00

DICKSON, Gordon R. *None But Man.* 1971. Pyramid T 2428. SF. F. P1d. $5.00

DICKSON, Gordon R. *Pritcher Mass.* 1973. DAW 69. SF. F. P1d. $5.00

DICKSON, Gordon R. *Pritcher Mass.* 1973. DAW 69. 1st prtg. c/Freas: gga. VG. P7d. $4.00

DICKSON, Gordon R. *Pro.* 1978. Ace 68023. SF. F. P1d. $5.00

DICKSON, Gordon R. *R-Master.* 1975. DAW 137. c/J Gaughan. SF. VG+. B5d. $5.00

DICKSON, Gordon R. *Secrets of the Deep.* 1985. Crit 931773. SF. F. W2d. $3.50

DICKSON, Gordon R. *Sleepwalker's World.* 1972. DAW UQ 1028 28. SF. F. P1d. $5.00

DICKSON, Gordon R. *Soldier, Ask Not.* 1980. Ace 77417. 1st edn. SF. VG. P1d. $3.50

DICKSON, Gordon R. *Soldier, Ask Not.* DAW 172. NF. B3d. $4.50

DICKSON, Gordon R. *Soldier, Ask Not.* 1967. Dell 1st Edn 8090. PBO. c/Lehr. SF. VG+. B6d. $3.50

DICKSON, Gordon R. *Space Swimmers.* 1979. Ace 77765. SF. G. W2d. $3.00

DICKSON, Gordon R. *Space Swimmers.* 1967. Berkley X 1371. PBO. NF. I1d. $6.00

DICKSON, Gordon R. *Space Swimmers.* 1967. Berkley X 1371. SF. F. P1d. $10.00

DICKSON, Gordon R. *Space Swimmers.* 1967. Berkley X 1371. SF. VG. B4d. $3.00

DICKSON, Gordon R. *Spacepaw.* 1976. Berkley Z 3083. SF. VG+. P1d. $4.50

DICKSON, Gordon R. *Spacial Delivery & Delusion World.* 1961. Ace F 119. 1st prtg. SF. R5d. $4.00

DICKSON, Gordon R. *Spirit of Dorsai.* 1979. Ace 77802. SF. F. P1d. $7.50

DICKSON, Gordon R. *Star Road.* 1974. DAW UY 1127 116. SF. VG. P1d. $3.50

DICKSON, Gordon R. *Tactics of Mistake.* DAW UQ 10099. NF. I1d. $5.00

DICKSON, Gordon R. *Tactics of Mistake.* DAW UQ 10099. sgn. SF. VG. P1d. $7.50

DICKSON, Gordon R. *Time Storm.* 1979. Bantam 12269. SF. VG+. P1d. $4.50

DICKSON, Gordon R. *Wolfling.* 1969. Dell 9633. SF. VG. P1d. $4.50

DICKSON, Peter. *Sinful Stones.* 1970. Ace 76721. My. VG. W2d. $3.00

DICKSON, R.C. *Sinners Don't Cry.* Period 102. VG+. B3d. $5.00

DICKSON/DICKSON. *Delusion World/Spacial Delivery.* 1961. Ace F 119. PBO. c/E Vallgursky. SF. VG+. B5d. $5.50

DICKSON/DICKSON. *Delusion World/Spacial Delivery.* 1961. Ace F 119. SF. F. P1d. $16.00

DICKSON/DICKSON. *Genetic General/Time To Teleport.* 1960. Ace D 449. F. M1d. $15.00

DICKSON/DICKSON. *Genetic General/Time To Teleport.* 1960. Ace D 449. SF. VG+. B4d. $6.00

DICKSON/NORTON. *Mankind on the Run/Crossroads of Time.* 1956. Ace D 164. F. M1d. $15.00

DICKSON/WILLIAMS. *Alien From Arcturus/Atom Curtain.* Ace D 139. F. M1d. $18.00

DICKSON/WILLIAMS. *Alien From Arcturus/Atom Curtain.* 1956. Ace D 139. PBO. SF. VG. B5d. $6.00

DIDION, Joan. *Play It As It Lays.* 1971. Bantam Q 6699. 1st prtg. VG+. P7d. $4.00

DIDONATO, Pietro. *Christ in Concrete.* 1950. Lion 18. Fa. VG. B4d. $6.00

DIEHL, W. *Sharkey's Machine.* 1981. Dell 18292. 1st prtg. VG+. R5d. $2.00

DIESPECKER, D. *Rebound.* Harlequin 234. VG+. B3d. $15.00

DIETRICH, Marlene. *Marlene Dietrich's ABC.* Avon G 1173. VG+. B3d. $5.00

DIETRICH, Robert. *Angel Eyes.* Dell 1st Edn B 203. c/Mc Ginnis. VG+. B3d. $4.50

DIETRICH, Robert. *Be My Victim.* 1956. Dell 1st Edn 106. PBO. c/Sussman. My. VG. B3d. $5.00

DIETRICH, Robert. *Curtains for a Lover.* Lancer 71-311. VG+. G5d. $4.00

DIETRICH, Robert. *End of a Stripper.* Dell A 197. 1st edn. c/gga. De. F. F2d. $13.00

DIETRICH, Robert. *End of a Stripper.* Dell A 197. PBO. c/Elliot: gga. My. VG. B6d. $7.50

DIETRICH, Robert. *One For the Road.* 1954. Pyramid 128. c/gga. Fa. VG+. B4d. $12.50

DIETRICH, Robert. *Steve Bentley's Calypso Caper.* Dell 1st Edn B 182. G+. G5d. $6.00

DIETZ, W.C. *Cluster Command.* 1989. Baen 69817. SF. F. W2d. $3.50

DIETZ, W.C. *McCade's Bounty.* 1990. Ace 52303. 1st edn. c/sgn. SF. F. F2d. $12.00

DIKES, M. *Sarabande for a Bitch.* Brandon House 3011. VG+. B3d. $5.00

DIKTY, T.E. edt. *5 Tales From Tomorrow.* 1963. Crest D 597. 2nd edn. SF. VG. P1d. $5.00

DIKTY, T.E. edt. *5 Tales From Tomorrow.* Crest S 197. VG+. I1d. $6.00

DIKTY, T.E. edt. *5 Tales From Tomorrow.* 1957. Crest S 197. SF. F. M1d/P1d. $15.00

DIKTY, T.E. edt. *5 Tales From Tomorrow.* 1957. Crest S 197. 1st prtg. SF. G+. R5d. $3.50

DIKTY, T.E. edt. *6 From Worlds Beyond.* 1958. Crest S 258. c/Bloch: sgn. VG. B3d. $6.50

DIKTY, T.E. edt. *6 From Worlds Beyond.* 1958. Crest S 258. SF. F. M1d/P1d. $15.00

DIKTY, T.E. edt. *6 From Worlds Beyond.* 1958. Crest S 258. 1st prtg. SF. VG. R5d. $4.00

DILLARD, J.M. *Bloodthirst.* Pocket 64489. F. P9d. $2.50

DILLARD, J.M. *Star Trek V: The Final Frontier.* 1989. Pocket 68008. 1st prtg. VG+. R5d. $3.00

DILLON, Jack. *Great Day for Dying.* 1968. Gold Medal D 1877. PBO. Ad. NF. B6d. $9.00

DILLON, Jack. *Spotted Horse.* 1957. Ballantine 194. PBO. We. VG+. B6d. $9.00

DIMAGGIO, Joe. *Baseball for Everyone.* 1949. Signet 719. 1st edn. PBO. scarce. VG. B6a #76. $44.50

DIMAGGIO, Joe. *Lucky To Be a Yankee.* Bantam 506. VG. B3d. $10.00

DIMNET, Ernest. *Art of Thinking.* 1942. Pocket 160. c/photo. Nfi. VG+. B5d. $6.00

DINESEN, Isak. *Seven Gothic Tales.* 1945. Armed Services 687. Fa. VG. P1d. $35.00

DINGWALL & LANDGON-DAVIES. *Unknown: Is It Nearer?* 1956. Signet KS 336. Nfi. VG. B4d. $1.75

DINNEEN, J.F. *Anatomy of a Crime.* 1956. Avon 701. 1st pb. Cr. VG. B6d. $7.50

DIOLE, P. *Sundersea Adventure.* Pan GP 29. VG+. B3d. $8.00

DIONE, R.L. *God Drives a Flying Saucer.* 1973. Bantam Q 7733. Nfi. VG. P1d. $3.50

DISCH, Thomas M. *Camp Concentration.* 1971. Avon V 2348. 1st edn. F. P9d. $2.50

DISCH, Thomas M. *Camp Concentration.* 1969. Panther 02846. SF. VG+. P1d. $7.50

DISCH, Thomas M. *Echo Round His Bones.* Berkley G 1349. c/sgn. VG+. B3d. $6.50

DISCH, Thomas M. *Genocides.* 1965. Berkley F 1170. PBO. SF. VG. B5d. $4.50

DISCH, Thomas M. *Genocides.* 1965. Berkley F 1170. SF. F. P1d. $16.00

DISCH, Thomas M. *MD.* 1992. Berkley 13261. Ho. VG. P1d. $5.00

DISCH, Thomas M. *One Hundred & Two H-Bombs.* Berkley G 2044. c/inscr. VG+. B3d. $8.00

DISCH, Thomas M. *Prisoner.* 1969. Ace 67900. TVTI. c/Patrick McGoohan: photo. VG+. B4d. $8.00

DISCH, Thomas M. *Puppies of Terra.* 1980. Pocket 82839. SF. F. P1d. $6.00

DISCH, Thomas M. *Ruins of Earth.* 1975. Arrow 909440. SF. VG. P1d. $5.00

DISCH/LE GUIN. *Mankind Under the Leash/Planet of Exile.* 1966. Ace G 597. F. M1d. $10.00

DISCH/LE GUIN. *Mankind Under the Leash/Planet of Exile.* 1966. Ace G 597. 1st prtg. SF. VG. B3d. $4.50

DISNEY, Doris Miles. *Family Skeleton.* 1946. My Novel Classic 98. 1st pb. VG. B6d. $4.00

DISNEY, Doris Miles. *Room for Murder.* MacFadden 60-392. VG. B3d. $3.50

DISNEY, Doris Miles. *Straw Man.* Dell 885. VG. G5d. $5.50

DISNEY, Doris Miles. *Who Rides a Tiger.* 1964. Ace K 197. 1st prtg. My. VG+. R5d. $2.50

DISNEY, Dorothy Cameron. *Balcony.* 1942. Pocket 152. My. G+. B5d. $5.00

DISNEY, Dorothy Cameron. *Crimson Friday.* Dell 137. VG+. B3d. $6.00

DISNEY, Dorothy Cameron. *Death in the Back Seat.* Dell 76. G. G5d. $6.50

DISNEY, Dorothy Cameron. *Explosion.* Bantam 761. VG. G5d. $6.50

DISNEY, Dorothy Cameron. *Golden Swan Murder.* Dell 15. VG. B3d. $5.00

DISNEY, Dorothy Cameron. *Hangman's Tree.* Ace K 189. F. G5d. $8.00

DISNEY, Dorothy Cameron. *Strawstack Murders.* Dell 62. G+. G5d. $8.00

DISNEY, Dorothy Cameron. *17th Letter.* Bantam 91. VG+. G5d. $6.00

DISNEY/DISNEY. *Mrs Meeker's Money/ Unappointed Rounds.* Ace G 529. VG+. G5d. $10.00

DISPALDO, A.R. *I Am Teresa.* Belmont 91-257. 2nd prtg. VG. B3d. $4.00

DIVONO, Sharman. *Pebbles & Bamm-Bamm: Man Planet X.* 1978. Ottenheimer. Fa. G+. P1d. $4.00

DIX & MILLHAUSER. *Hot Leather.* Bantam 554. VG+. B3d. $5.00

DIXON, Arnold. *Private Poll.* 1967. Wee Hours 539. PBO. NF. B3a #20. $15.40

DIXON, H. Vernor. *Cry Blood.* Gold Medal 564. c/Barye. VG. B3d. $4.00

DIXON, H. Vernor. *Deep Is the Pit.* 1952. Gold Medal G 212. PBO. c/Barye. VG+. B6d. $10.00

DIXON, H. Vernor. *Marriage Bed.* 1952. Red Seal 18. 1st edn. c/gga. F. F2d. $10.00

DIXON, H. Vernor. *Something for Nothing.* Bantam 875. VG+. B3d. $5.00

DIXON, H. Vernor. *To Hell Together.* 1959. Gold Medal S 922. 1st prtg. c/Barye: gga. VG. P7d. $5.00

DIXON, H. Vernor. *Too Rich To Die.* 1953. Gold Medal 285. 1st prtg. PBO. c/gga. VG. P7d. $7.50

DIXON, Lewis. *Wild Girl.* Cameo 335. 2nd edn. c/R Belarski. Fi. G+. B5d. $5.00

DIXON, Lewis. *Wild Girl.* 1954. Cameo 369. 3rd prtg. c/Belarski. VG+. B3a #21. $16.05

DIXON, P.L. *Complete Book of Surfing.* Ballantine U 6050. VG. B3d. $4.50

DIXON, P.L. *Men & Waves: Treasury of Surfing.* Ballantine U 6090. VG. B3d. $4.00

DIXON, Roger. *Noah II.* 1970. Ace 58250. SF. VG. P1d. $4.50

DOBERTY, Edward J. *Corpse Who Wouldn't Die.* Handi 49. VG. G5d. $12.50

DOBIE, J. Frank. *Coronado's Children.* 1953. Bantam A 1089. 1st prtg. VG. P7d. $4.50

DOBIE, J. Frank. *Mustangs.* 1954. Bantam A 1212. 1st pb. Nfi. VG. B6d. $6.00

DOCTOROW, E.L. *Welcome to Hard Times.* Signet 1959. c/Barye. VG+. B3d. $4.50

DODD, Carl. *For Whom the Belles Toil.* Bee Line 111. PBO. VG+. M6d. $9.50

DODD, Carl. *Of Vice & Men.* 1966. Bee Line 120 Ad. VG. B5d. $7.50

DODD, Carl. *Switch-Hitters.* Bee Line 103. VG+. B3d. $5.00

DODGE, David. *Bullets for the Bridegroom.* Popular 252. VG. B3d. $7.00

DODGE, David. *Death & Taxes.* 1948. Popular 168. 1st pb. c/Belarski. My. VG. B6d. $7.00

DODGE, David. *It Ain't Hay.* 1949. Dell 270. c/G Gregg. My. G. B5d. $5.00

DODGE, David. *It Ain't Hay.* 1949. Dell 270. VG. G5d. $14.00

DODGE, David. *Long Escape.* Dell 405. 1st prtg. My. G+. R5d. $3.50

DODGE, David. *Long Escape.* Penguin 100. VG. G5d. $5.50

DODGE, David. *Plunder of the Sun.* 1951. Dell 478. c/R Stanley. My. VG. B5d. $6.00

DODGE, David. *Red Tassel.* Dell 565. c/R Stanley. My. VG. B3d. $4.50

DODGE, David. *Shear the Black Sheep.* 1949. Popular 202. c/gga. VG+. P6d. $7.50

DODGE, David. *To Catch a Thief.* Dell 658. G+. G5d. $5.00

DODGE, Gil. *Flint.* 1957. Signet S 1414. We. VG+. Btd. $5.00

DODGE, Steve. *Shanghai Incident.* 1955. Gold Medal 456. 1st edn. dust jacket. My. VG. F2d. $8.00

DODGE. *All Died for Clementina.* 1950s. Cleveland 1574. PBO. We. NF. B6d. $10.00

DOERR, E. *Eden II.* 1974. Aquarius Press. 1st edn. F. M1d. $5.00

DOLAN, Mary. *Hannibal: Scourge of Imperial Rome.* Avon T 151. Fi. VG. B5d. $2.50

DOLAN, Mike. *Santana Morning.* 1970. Powell PP1008-N. SF. F. P1d. $10.00

DOLINSKY, Mike. *Mind One.* 1972. Dell 5648. SF. F. P1d. $5.00

DOLPH, Jack. *Murder Is Mutual.* 1950. Dell 419. VG. B3d. $4.00

DONAHUE, Jack. *Divorce American Style.* 1967. Popular 60-8048. 1st prtg. VG. R5d. $1.75

DONAHUE, Jack. *Someone To Hate.* 1962. Signet 2141. 1st edn. author's 1st book. My. F. F2d. $12.50

DONALDS, Richard. *Not Since Eve.* 1963. Midwood F 317. PBO. VG+. B6d. $15.00

DONALDS, Richard. *Toying With Passion.* Imperial 763. Ad. VG. B5d. $5.00

DONALDSON, Ssephen R. *Chronicles of Thomas Covenant the Unbeliever Book #3.* 1979. Ballantine 25718. 3rd prtg. SF. VG. W2d. $3.00

DONALDSON, Stephen R. *Mirror of Her Dreams.* 1987. Ballantine 34697. c/M Whelan. SF. VG+. B5d. $3.50

DONALDSON, Stephen R. *Mirror of His Dreams.* 1987. Ballantine. 1st pb. F. M1d. $5.00

DONALDSON, Stephen R. *Power That Preserves.* 1979. Ballantine 25718. Fa. VG+. P1d. $4.50

DONALDSON, Stephen R. *Wounded Land.* 1984. Ballantine 31042. 10th edn. Fa. F. P1d. $4.00

DONIS, Miles. *Fall of New York.* 1972. Lancer 78704. SF. F. P1d. $5.00

DONISTHORPE, G. *Loveliest of Friends.* Berkley 102. NF. I1d. $6.00

DONNELLY, Desmond. *Nearing Storm.* 1969. Arrow 181. SF/My. VG. P1d. $4.50

DONNER, Frank J. *Un-Americans.* 1961. Ballantine 510K. NF. VG. B5d. $3.50

DONNER, James. *That Motel Weekend.* 1964. Beacon B 782X. Ad. VG. B5d. $4.50

DONOHUE, H.E.F. *Conversations With Nelson Algren.* 1965. Berkley S 1134. Nfi. VG. B5d. $3.00

DONOHUE, P.S. *Dublin Affair.* 1989. Pinnacle 55817. My. VG. W2d. $4.00

DONOVAN, Curt. *Witch With Blue Eyes.* 1962. Beacon B504F. PBO. c/Darcy. Ad. VG+. B5d. $8.00

DONOVAN, John. *Eichman, Man of Slaughter.* 1960. Avon T 464. Nfi. VG+. B4d. $4.50

DONOVAN, Robert J. *PT 109.* 1964. Crest D 523. 3rd prtg. G+. R5d. $1.00

DOOLEY, Dennis. *Dashiell Hammett.* 1984. Ugar 6124. Nfi. VG. P1d. $8.00

DOOLEY, Thomas A. *Deliver Us From Evil.* 1961. Signet D 1992. Nfi. VG+. B4d. $4.00

DOOLEY, Thomas A. *Edge of Tomorrow.* Berkley G 272. c/photo. Nfi. VG. B5d. $3.50

DORER. *Return of the Eagle.* 1979. Manor 23267. PBO. SF. NF. B6d. $7.00

DORIAN, Elaine. *Double Trouble.* 1962. Beacon 548. 1st edn. c/gga. F. F2d. $15.00

DORIAN, Elaine. *Infidelity Game.* Beacon 499. VG+. B3d. $6.00

DORIAN, Elaine. *Love Now Pay Later.* 1961. Beacon B 449F. PBO. Ad. VG. B5d. $6.00

DORIAN, Elaine. *Sex Cure.* 1962. Beacon B 535F. PBO. Ad. G+. B5d. $3.00

DORIEN, Ray. *Call Dr Margaret.* Crest 511. VG. B3d. $4.00

DORNBERGER, W. *V-2.* Ballantine 273. VG. B3d. $4.00

DORS, Diana. *Behind Closed Dors.* 1979. Star. VG. B3d. $7.00

DORS, Diana. *For Adults Only.* 1978. Star NN. VG. B3d. $6.50

DORS, Diana. *Swingin' Dors.* World Dist 755. VG. B3d. $7.00

DORTORT, David. *Burial of the Fruit.* 1948. Avon 183. VG. B3d. $4.50

DORTORT, David. *Burial of the Fruit.* 1951. Avon 326. VG+. B3d. $6.00

DORTORT, David. *Burial of the Fruit.* Avon 541. Fi. G+. B5d. $3.00

DOS PASSOS, John. *Adventures of a Young Man.* Lion Library LL 42. VG. I1d. $4.00

DOSS, Helen. *Family Nobody Wanted.* 1960. Monarch 169. 1st edn. PBO. F. F2d. $8.00

DOSTOYEVSKY, F. *Brothers Karamazov.* 1958. Signet T 1488. MTI. c/Y Brynner & M Schell. Fi. VG. B5d. $3.50

DOSTOYEVSKY, F. *Crime & Punishment.* Avon G 1024. VG. B3d. $4.00

DOSTOYEVSKY, F. *Crime & Punishment.* Signet 733. c/Avati. VG. B3d. $4.50

DOUGALL, Bernard. *Singing Corpse.* Boardman NN SC. VG. B3d. $7.00

DOUGALL, Bernard. *Singing Corpse.* 1945. Pony 46. VG. I1d. $15.00

DOUGLAS, Bill. *Bloody Precinct.* Belmont 206. NF. B3d. $7.00

DOUGLAS, Carole Nelson. *Counterprobe.* 1990. TOR 53596. 1st prtg. SF. F W2d. $4.25

DOUGLAS, Carole Nelson. *Exiles of the Rynth.* 1984. Dell Rey 30836. 1st edn. SF. F. F2d. $7.00

DOUGLAS, Carole Nelson. *Fair Wind, Fiery Star.* 1981. Jove 6034. 1st edn. c/sgn/inscr. SF. F. F2d. $15.00

DOUGLAS, Dean. *Eleven Days of Barbara.* 1968. Publishers Export 1132. Ad. VG. B5d. $3.00

DOUGLAS, Gregory. *Nest.* Zebra 89083. SF. VG. W2d. $3.25

DOUGLAS, Henry Kyd. *I Rode With Stonewall.* 1961. Premier T 113. Nfi. VG. B5d. $2.50

DOUGLAS, Jack. *Adventures of Huckleberry Hashimoto.* 1965. Pocket 50195. Fi. VG. B5d. $3.00

DOUGLAS, Lloyd C. *Big Fisherman.* 1959. Cardinal GC 59. c/J Meese. Fi. VG. B5d. $2.50

DOUGLAS, Lloyd C. *Doctor Husdon's Secret Journal.* 1955. Pocket 1096. c/J Meese. Fi. VG. B5d. $3.00

DOUGLAS, Lloyd C. *Green Light.* Pocket 175. VG. B3d. $4.00

DOUGLAS, Lloyd C. *Invitalton To Live.* Dell 380. c/R Stanley. Nfi. VG+. B5d. $5.00

DOUGLAS, Lloyd C. *Invitation To Live.* Dell 380. G+. G5d. $2.50

DOUGLAS, Lloyd C. *Magnificent Obsession.* 1965. Pan X 148. 4th prtg. VG. B3d. $5.50

DOUGLAS, Lloyd C. *Robe.* 1958. Cardinal GC 53. 1st prtg. c/Tom Dunn. VG+. P7d. $4.00

DOUGLAS, Malcolm. *Prey by Night.* 1955. Gold Medal 477. 1st edn. author's 1st book. My. F. F2d. $15.00

DOUGLAS, Malcolm. *Pure Sweet Hell.* Gold Medal 972. 2nd edn. G+. M6d. $4.50

DOUGLAS, Malcolm. *Rain of Terror.* 1955. Gold Medal 539. 1st edn. My. F. F2d. $16.00

DOUGLAS, Malcolm. *Rain of Terror.* 1955. Gold Medal 539. c/James Meese: gga. Ad. VG. P6d. $5.00

DOUGLAS, Mike. *Mike Douglas: My Story.* 1979. Ballantine 28116. TVTI. VG. P1d. $4.00

DOUGLAS, William. *Savage Breed.* 1959. Newsstand 505. 1st edn. My. F. F2d. $10.00

DOUGLAS & KENT. *Death Song.* 1987. Leisure 2546. Ho. VG. P1d. $4.00

DOUGLASS, Donald M. *Many Brave Hearts.* 1960. Pocket 1273. c/H Bennett. My. VG. B5d. $4.00

DOUGLASS, Donald M. *Rebecca's Pride.* Pocket 1178. NF. I1d. $5.00

DOWD, Harrison. *Night Air.* 1952. Avon AT 52. 1st pb. c/Erickson. NF. B6d. $9.00

DOWDELL, D. *Border Nurse.* Ace D 576. VG. B3d. $3.50

DOWDELL, D. *Warlord of Chandor.* 1977. DAW UW 1315. Fa. F. P1d. $5.00

DOWDEY, Clifford. *Bugles Blow No More.* Perma P 159. VG. B3d. $4.00

DOWLING, T. *Coach: A Season With Lombardi.* Popular 00105. VG. B3d. $4.50

DOWNEY, Fairfax. *Indian Wars of the US Army.* 1964. Monarch 447. Nfi. VG+. B3d/B4d. $6.00

DOWNEY, Fairfax. *Indian-Fighting Army.* 1957. Bantam F 1661. Nfi. VG+. B4d. $3.00

DOWNING, Todd. *Cat Screams.* 1945. Popular 68. c/Hoffman. VG+. B3a #24. $14.55

DOWNING, Todd. *Cat Screams.* 1945. Popular 68. 1st pb. c/Hoffman. My. VG. B6d. $9.00

DOWST, Robert S. *Straight, Place & Show.* Armed Services 1090. Nfi. VG. B3d. $7.00

DOYLE, Arthur Conan. *Adventures of Sherlock Holmes.* 1966. Airmont CL 97. 1st prtg. My. VG. R5d. $2.00

DOYLE, Arthur Conan. *Casebook of Sherlock Holmes.* Pocket 670. VG. I1d. $5.00

DOYLE, Arthur Conan. *His Last Bow.* 1964. Berkley F 912. c/W Teason. My. VG+. B5d. $5.00

DOYLE, Arthur Conan. *Hound of the Baskervilles.* 1959. Dell D 302. 1st prtg. My. G+. R5d. $2.50

DOYLE, Arthur Conan. *Lost World.* 1965. Berkley F 1162. SF. F. S1d/W2d. $4.50

DOYLE, Arthur Conan. *Lost World.* 1965. Berkley F 1162. 1st prtg. SF. VG. R5d. $2.50

DOYLE, Arthur Conan. *Lost World.* 1953. Harlequin 238. SF. G+. P1d. $60.00

DOYLE, Arthur Conan. *Lost World.* 1953. Harlequin 238. SF. VG. P1d. $90.00

DOYLE, Arthur Conan. *Lost World.* 1953. Harlequin 238. VG. B3a #22. $58.60

DOYLE, Arthur Conan. *Lost World.* 1953. Harlequin 238. 1st edn. PBO. scarce. SF. VG+. B6a #79. $75.00

DOYLE, Arthur Conan. *Lost World.* 1949. Pan 100. 1st pb. SF. VG+. B6d. $12.50

DOYLE, Arthur Conan. *Lost World.* 1977. Pan 25108. SF. VG. P1d. $4.00

DOYLE, Arthur Conan. *Lost World.* 1954. Perma 279. SF. VG. P1d. $8.50

DOYLE, Arthur Conan. *Lost World.* 1954. Perma 279. 1st pb. NF. M1d. $12.00

DOYLE, Arthur Conan. *Lost World.* 1962. Pyramid F 713. 3rd prtg. SF. F. W2d. $6.00

DOYLE, Arthur Conan. *Lost World.* 1965. Pyramid F 713. 6th edn. SF. VG+. P1d. $7.00

DOYLE, Arthur Conan. *Lost World.* 1960. Pyramid G 514. MTI. c/T Beechan, C Rains, & J St John. SF. G+. B5d. $4.00

DOYLE, Arthur Conan. *Lost World.* 1958. Pyramid Royal PR 15. SF. G. P1d. $3.50

DOYLE, Arthur Conan. *Maracot Deep.* Modern Publishing. SF. VG. W2d. $3.75

DOYLE, Arthur Conan. *Memoirs of Sherlock Holmes.* 1949. Bantam 704. 1st pb. VG. M1d. $10.00

DOYLE, Arthur Conan. *Memoirs of Sherlock Holmes.* 1949. Bantam 704. 1st prtg. F. F2d. $12.50

DOYLE, Arthur Conan. *Poison Belt.* 1966. Berkley F 1203. SF. VG+. P1d. $10.00

DOYLE, Arthur Conan. *Return of Sherlock Holmes.* Pan 286. VG. B3d. $12.00

DOYLE, Arthur Conan. *Study in Scarlet & Sign of the Four.* 1963. Berkley F 798. 1st prtg. My. G. R5d. $1.00

DOYLE, Arthur Conan. *Tales of Terror & Mystery.* 1968. John Murray. 2nd edn. SF/My. VG. P1d. $6.00

DOYLE, Arthur Conan. *Valley of Fear.* Bantam 733. VG+. B3d. $8.00

DOYLE, Arthur Conan. *Valley of Fear.* 1950. Bantam. 1st pb. NF. M1d. $10.00

DOYLE, Arthur Conan. *Valley of Fear.* 1952. Pan 177. 2nd prtg. VG. B3d. $7.00

DOZOIS, Gardner. *Visible Man.* 1977. Berkley 03595. 1st edn. SF. F. F2d. $7.00

DRACHMAN, Theodore S. *Addicted to Murder.* 1960. Avon T 383. My. VG. P1d. $15.00

DRACHMAN/EDGLEY. *Cry Plague!/ Judas Goat.* 1953. Ace D 13. SF/My. VG. P1d. $100.00

DRAGO, Harry Sinclair. *Buckskin Empire.* 1953. Dell 660. c/R Stanley. We. VG. B5d. $3.00

DRAGO, Harry Sinclair. *Decision at Broken Butte.* 1956. Perma M 3068. PBO. c/Tom Ryan. We. NF. B6d. $15.00

DRAGO, Harry Sinclair. *Gun for Cantrell.* Belmont 235. VG+. B3d. $4.50

DRAGO, Harry Sinclair. *Showdown at Sunset.* Pocket 3115. PBO. VG. B3d. $4.00

DRAGO, Harry Sinclair. *Wild, Woolly & Wicked.* 1963. Pocket 7024. NF. VG+. B5d. $5.00

DRAGO, Harry Sinclair. *Women To Love.* 1949. Novel Library 16. VG+. I1d. $10.00

DRAKE, Alfred. *Anyone Can Win at Gin Rummy & Canasta.* 1949. Avon 218. VG. P6d. $2.00

DRAKE, Damon. *Seduced!* 1960. Merit Book 508. PBO. c/Sloan: gga. NF. B6a #75. $40.25

DRAKE, David. *Fleet.* 1988. Ace 24086. SF. VG+. W2d. $3.25

DRAKE, David. *Forlorn Hope.* 1984. TOR 53622-3. 1st edn. SF. F. F2d. $6.50

DRAKE, David. *Hammer's Slammers.* 1984. Ace 31595. 6th edn. SF. VG. P1d. $3.00

DRAKE, David. *Rank of Bronze.* 1986. Baen. 1st edn. NF. M1d. $4.00

DRAKE, H. *Sin for Breakfast.* Brandon House 3007. VG+. B3d. $6.00

DRAKE, H.B. *Slave Ship.* 1959. Beacon 217. 1st prtg. VG+. P7d. $15.00

DRAKE, W. Raymond. *Gods & Spacemen in Greece & Rome.* 1977. Signet W 7620. Nfi. VG. P1d. $3.50

DRAMER, George. *School for Girls.* 1958. Beacon 202. 1st prtg. VG+. P7d. $12.50

DRATLER, J.J. *Doctor Paradise.* Popular G 529. VG+. B3d. $4.50

DRATLER, J.J. *Doctor Paradise.* 1957. Popular 818. 1st edn. c/gga. My. F. F2d. $14.00

DRATLER, J.J. *Pitfall.* Bantam 710. VG+. B3d. $4.00

DRATLER, J.J. *Pitfall.* Popular 745. VG. B3d. $4.00

DREADSTONE, Carl. *Bride of Frankenstein.* 1977. Berkley 03414. Ho. VG. P1d. $7.50

DREADSTONE, Carl. *Werewolf of London.* 1977. Berkley 03413. Ho. G+. P1d. $5.00

DREW, Lincoln. *Die in the Saddle.* 1956. Perma 3063. We. VG. B4d. $4.00

DREW, Wayland. *Dragonslayer.* 1981. Ballantine 29694. MTI. c/photos. SF. VG+. B5d. $4.00

DREW, Wayland. *Willow.* 1988. Ballantine 35195. 2nd prtg. MTI. SF. F. W2d. $5.00

DREYFUSS, Ernst. *Unfrozen.* 1970. Tower T060-11. SF. VG. P1d. $4.50

DRISCOLL, Charles B. *Doubloons.* Pennant P 40. VG+. B3d. $4.50

DRIVER, J. *Bordello Base.* Intimate 729. VG+. B3d. $4.50

DRIVER, Steve. *Secret Captives.* 1980. Bizarre BB 182. VG+. P6d. $5.00

DROUGHT, James. *Gypsy Moths.* Crest 819. MTI. VG+. B3d. $5.00

DRUM, Chester. *Drum Beat-Berlin.* 1964. Gold Medal K 1420. c/gga. My. VG. B4d. $2.75

DRUMMOND, Ivor. *Jaws of the Watchdog.* 1973. MacMillan UK. 1st edn. TVTI. dust jacket. Th. F. F2d. $17.50

DRUMMOND, Ivor. *Priests of Abomination.* Pyramid 2962. NF. B3d. $9.00

DRUMMOND, Walter. *Philosopher of Evil.* 1962. Regency RB 301. PBO. c/Silverberg & Drummond: sgn. VG+. B3a #24. $22.00

DRUMMOND, William. *Gaslight.* 1966. PB Library 53-333. PBO. MTI. NF. B6d. $7.50

DRUON, Maurice. *Iron King.* Ace 37360. Fi. VG+. B5d. $4.00

DRURY, Allen. *Advise & Consent.* 1961. Cardinal GC 952. SF. VG. P1d. $6.50

DRURY, Allen. *Preserve & Protect.* 1970. Popular 125-73. SF. VG. P1d. $4.50

DRURY, Allen. *Shade of Difference.* 1972. Avon J 129. SF. VG. P1d. $4.00

DRYER, Bernard Victor. *Murder in Port Afrique.* 1956. Avon T 142. MTI. NF. B4d/B6d. $9.00

DRYER, Bernard Victor. *Port Afrique.* 1950. Avon 224. c/gga. VG+. P6d. $5.00

DU BOIS, Theodora. *Breaking Point.* 1961. Cardinal C 414. SF/My. VG. P1d. $6.50

DU BOIS, Theodora. *Case of the Perfumed Mouse.* 1946. Boardman NN. 1st pb. My. VG. B6d. $12.50

DU BOIS, Theodora. *Cavalier's Corpse.* Boardman 172. c/McLoughlin. VG. B3d. $12.00

DU BOIS, Theodora. *Death Sails in a Hight Wind.* Boardman NN DSHW. VG. B3d. $7.50

DU BOIS, Theodora. *House on the Strand.* Pan 25706. 7th edn. SF/My. VG. P1d. $4.00

DU BOIS, Theodora. *King's General.* 1950. Pocket 483. 3rd edn. Hi. VG. P1d. $8.00

DU BOIS, Theodora. *Rebecca.* 1945. Armed Services T 36. My. VG. P1d. $20.00

DU BOIS, Theodora. *Seeing Red.* Dell 860. VG. G5d. $3.50

DU BOIS, Theodora. *Shannon Terror.* 1964. Ace G 552. G+. G5d. $3.50

DU BOIS, Theodora. *Solution T-25.* 1970. Curtis 07076. SF. VG. P1d. $4.50

DU MAURIER, Daphne. *Breaking Point.* 1961. Cardinal C 414. 1st prtg. My. G+. R5d. $1.50

DU MAURIER, Daphne. *Jamaica Inn.* 1946. Pocket 403. VG. B3d. $4.50

DU MAURIER, Daphne. *Jamaica Inn.* 1946. Pocket 403. 1st prtg. c/Troop: gga. VG+. P7d. $6.00

DU MAURIER, Daphne. *King's General.* 1947. Pocket 483. 1st prtg. c/Kolada: gga. VG+. P7d. $5.50

DU MAURIER, Daphne. *Kiss Me Again, Stranger.* 1954. Cardinal C 168. 1st prtg. c/Dunn: gga. VG+. P7d. $4.00

DU MAURIER, Daphne. *Kiss Me Again, Stranger.* 1965. Pocket 50152. 3rd edn. SF. VG+. B5d. $3.50

DU MAURIER, Daphne. *Rebecca.* Pocket 205. VG. I1d. $4.00

DU MILIEU, P. *Bachelor's Guide To Women.* Hillman 195. VG. B3d. $3.50

DU SOE, Robert C. *Devil Thumbs a Ride.* 1949. Avon 208. c/A Cantor. Fi. G. B5d. $4.00

DUANE, Dane. *My Enemy, My Ally.* 1984. Pocket 50285. SF. VG+. W2d. $4.75

DUANE, Diane. *Door Into Fire.* 1979. Dell 11874. SF. F. P1d. $6.00

DUANE, Diane. *Wounded Sky (Star Trek).* 1983. Pocket 47389. 1st prtg. SF. VG. W2d. $4.50

DUANE & MORWOOD. *Romulan Way.* Pocket 63498. F. P9d. $2.00

DUBREIL, Linda. *Sunday Seducer.* 1970. Tower T 125-5. PBO. c/Jeff Jones. VG. P6d. $2.50

DUCHAMP, Laura. *Duet.* 1964. Midwood F 359. Ad. VG. P1d. $20.00

DUCHAMP, Laura. *Duet.* 1964. Midwood F 359. PBO. c/gga. scarce. VG+. B6a #80. $44.00

DUCHAMP, Laura. *Other Extreme.* 1964. Midwood 32-419. PBO. c/photo. VG. P6d. $4.00

DUCHAMP, Laura. *Time & Place.* 1965. Midwood 32-433. PBO. Ad. VG+. B5d. $8.00

DUERRENMATT, Friedrich. *Traps.* Ballantine F 679. Fi. VG+. B5d. $4.00

DUFF, Charles. *Handbook on Hanging.* 1956. Panther 577. PBO. c/Heade. scarce. VG+. B6a #74. $50.00

DUFF, James. *Some Die Young.* Graphic 139. VG. B3d. $5.00

DUFFIELD, A. *Grand Duchess.* Pan G 246. VG. B3d. $6.50

DUFFUS, R.L. *To-Morrow Never Comes.* 1946. Guild 21. Fi. G+. P1d. $7.50

DUFFY, Clinton T. *88 Men & 2 Women.* 1963. Perma M 5074. Nfi. VG+. B4d. $3.25

DUGGAN, Alfred. *Conscience of the King.* 1960. Ace K 129. Fa. VG+. B4d. $2.00

DUKE, Hal. *Duke.* 1950. Popular 219. 1st prtg. My. NF. F2d. $20.00

DUKE, Madelaine. *Claret, Sandwiches & Sin.* 1969. Curtis 06050. 1st prtg. SF. VG+. R5d. $2.50

DUKE, Will. *Fair Prey.* 1956. Graphic 142. PBO. c/sgn. NF. B6a #80. $36.50

DULACK, Tom. *Stigmata of Dr Constantine.* 1976. Bantam 02195. Ho. G+. P1d. $3.00

DUMAS, Alexandre. *Camille.* 1945. Quick Reader 149. VG+. B3a #20. $17.70

DUMAS, Alexandre. *Companions of Jehu.* Ace G 414. VG. B3d. $4.00

DUMAS, Alexandre. *Man in the Iron Mask.* 1950. Studio 109. Hi. VG. P1d. $30.00

DUMAS, Alexandre. *Three Musketeers Volume #1.* 1940. Pocket 36. VG. B3d. $10.00

DUMAS, Alexandre. *Three Musketeers Volume #2.* 1940. Pocket 37. VG. B3d. $7.50

DUNBAR, Paula. *Forced To Swap.* 1973. Liverpool TNS 562. Ad. VG+. B5d. $4.50

DUNCAN, David. *Beyond Eden.* 1955. Ballantine 102. SF. VG. B4d. $4.00

DUNCAN, David. *Beyond Eden.* 1955. Ballantine 102. 1st edn. F. M1d. $12.00

DUNCAN, David. *Dark Dominion.* 1954. Ballantine 56. PBO. VG+. B3d. $4.50

DUNCAN, David. *Dark Dominion.* 1954. Ballantine 56. 1st edn. F. M1d. $12.00

DUNCAN, David. *New Legions.* Sphere 31135. VG. B3d. $5.00

DUNCAN, David. *Occam's Razor.* 1957. Ballantine 230. PBO. c/R Powers. SF. VG. B5d. $6.00

DUNCAN, David. *Occam's Razor.* 1957. Ballantine 230. 1st edn. F. I1d. $12.00

DUNCAN, David. *Occam's Razor.* 1957. Ballantine 230. 1st prtg. SF. G+. R5d. $4.00

DUNCAN, David. *Shadow.* 1987. Ballantine. 1st edn. F. M1d. $5.00

DUNCAN, David. *Wives & Husbands.* 1953. Signet 1047. Fi. VG. P1d. $8.50

DUNCAN, David. *Worse Than Murder.* 1953. Pocket 985. 1st pb. c/gga. My. VG+. B6d. $15.00

DUNCAN, Harley. *West of Appomattox.* 1963. Perma M 5061. 1st prtg. VG. P7d. $4.00

DUNCAN, Lee. *Fidel Castro Assassinated.* 1961. Monarch MS 1. SF. VG. P1d. $10.00

DUNCAN, Peter. *Sweet Cheat.* Dell 1st Edn A 182. VG. B3d. $4.50

DUNCAN, Peter. *Telltale Tart.* 1961. Gold medal 1127. 1st edn. My. F. F2d. $15.00

DUNCAN, Thomas W. *Gus the Great.* Dell F 50. VG+. B3d. $5.00

DUNDY, Elaine. *Dud Avocado.* 1961. Signet D 1915. Fa. VG. B4d. $2.75

DUNHAM, D. *Zone of Violence.* Belmont 92-532. VG+. B3d. $4.00

DUNLAP, Katharine. *Encore for Love.* 1948. Bantam 412. c/gga. Ro. NF. B4d. $4.00

DUNMORE, Spencer. *Collision.* 1978. Zebra 326. Hi. VG. P1d. $3.50

DUNN, Bob. *Hospital Happy.* 1952. Avon 411. PBO. VG. B6d. $7.50

DUNN, Dorothy. *Murder's Web.* 1951. Pocket 806. 1st prtg. c/Hilbert. VG. P7d. $6.00

DUNN, Elizabeth. *Moonlight Voyage.* 1948. Bantam 450. Fa. G+. B4d. $2.00

DUNN, J. Allan. *Elimination Syndicate.* Thriller Novel 47. 2nd edn. G+. B3d. $8.00

DUNN, J. Allan. *Treasure of Atlantis.* 1970. Centaur NN 3. 1st prtg. SF. VG. P1d. $4.50

DUNN, N. *Up the Junction.* Ballantine U 5098. VG. B3d. $4.50

DUNN, Saul. *Cabal.* 1978. Corgi 10746. SF. VG. P1d. $4.00

DUNN, Saul. *Coming of Steeleye.* 1976. Coronet 20507. SF. VG+. P1d. $4.50

DUNN, Saul. *Evangelist.* 1979. Corgi 11047. SF. F. P1d. $5.00

DUNN, Saul. *Steeleye -- the Wideways.* 1976. Coronet 20790. SF. F. P1d. $5.00

DUNNING, John. *Looking for Ginger North.* Gold Medal 14317. VG. G5d. $17.50

DUNNING, Lawrence. *Keller's Bomb.* 1978. Avon 40873. 1st edn. My. F. F2d. $8.00

DUNSANY, Lord. *At the Edge of the World.* 1970. Ballantine 01879. 1st edn. Fa. NF. F2d. $7.00

DUNSANY, Lord. *Beyond the Fields We Know.* 1972. Ballantine 02599. Fa. VG. P1d. $7.50

DUNSANY, Lord. *Charwoman's Shadow.* 1973. Ballantine 03085. Fa. VG. P1d. $10.00

DUNSANY, Lord. *Charwoman's Shadow.* 1973. Ballantine 03085. SF. G. W2d. $4.00

DUNSANY, Lord. *Don Rodriquez.* 1971. Ballantine 02244. 1st prtg. SF. VG+. R5d. $8.00

DUNSANY, Lord. *Food of Death.* 1974. Newcastle F 102. PBO. c/D Menville. SF. VG. B5d. $5.00

DUNSANY, Lord. *Guerrilla.* 1945. Armed Services Q 14. Fi. VG. P1d. $35.00

DUNSANY, Lord. *King of Elfland's Daughter.* 1969. Ballantine 01628. Fa. G+. R5d. $5.00

DUNSANY, Lord. *King of Elfland's Daughter.* 1969. Ballantine 01628. Fa. VG. P1d. $7.50

DUNSANY, Lord. *Over the Hills & Far Away.* 1974. Ballantine 23886. Ad/Fa. VG+. P6d. $5.00

DUPERRAULT, Doug. *Bed of Fear.* 1959. Stanley SL 74. PBO. NF. B3a #22. $24.20

DUPERRAULT, Doug. *Confessions of a Dime-a-Dance Queen.* Quarter Books 96. c/gga. scarce. VG+. B6a #77. $70.00

DUPERRAULT, Doug. *Confessions of a Dime-a-Dance Queen.* 1951. Quarter Books 96. VG+. B3a #24. $36.95

DUPERRAULT, Doug. *Gang Mistress.* 1953. Croydon 34. PBO. VG. B3a #20. $18.15

DUPERRAULT, Doug. *Trailer Camp Woman.* Beacon 317. c/gga. reprint. VG+. B6d. $15.00

DUPEYRAT, A. *Mitsinari.* Beacon NN. c/photo. VG+. B3d. $7.00

DURAND, R. *Lady in a Cage.* Popular PC 1034. MTI. VG. B3d. $4.00

DURBRIDGE, Francis. *Time of Day.* 1961. Hodder 483. TVTI. VG. P1d. $10.00

DURNFORD. *Commando.* 1955. Kimber. 2nd prtg. VG. B3d. $6.00

DURRELL, Gerald M. *Bafut Beagles.* Ballantine 686. VG. B3d. $4.00

DURRELL, Gerald M. *Drunden Forest.* 1964. Berkley X 923. 1st pb. VG+. B6d. $7.50

DURRELL, Gerald M. *Overloaded Ark.* 1962. Ballantine F 621. 1st pb. VG+. B5d. $5.50

DURRELL, Lawrence *Balthazar.* 1961. Cardinal GC 99. Fi. VG+. B5d. $3.50

DURRELL, Lawrence. *Black Book.* 1962. Cardinal GC 769. Fa. VG+. B4d. $3.00

DURRELL, Lawrence. *Clea.* 1961. Cardinal GC 767. Fi. VG+. B5d. $3.50

DURRELL, Lawrence. *Nunquam.* 1971. Pocket 78072. SF. F. P1d. $5.00

DURRENMATT, F. *Judge & His Hangman.* Berkley G 190. VG+. B3d. $4.50

DURST, Paul. *Bloody River.* 1956. Lion Library LB 139. We. NF. B4d. $10.00

DURST, Paul. *Die, Damn You!* Lion 75. NF. I1d. $14.00

DURWOOD, Thomas edt. *Ariel, the Book of Fantasy.* 1977. Ballantine 27319. 2nd edn. SF. VG. P1d. $10.00

DURY, David. *Before I Wake.* 1968. Gold Medal T 1964. PBO. c/photo. NF. B6d. $7.00

DUSOE, Robert C. *Devil Thumbs a Ride.* 1949. Avon 208. 1st edn. PBO. c/Cantor. VG+. B6d. $15.00

DUTOURD, Jean. *Dog's Head.* Avon H 102. c/R Abbett. SF. VG. B5d. $3.50

DUTOURD, Jean. *Dog's Head.* 1954. Lion 196. 1st US edn. Fa. VG. B6d. $15.00

DVORKIN, David. *Children of Shiny Mountain.* 1977. Pocket 80954. SF. VG+. P1d. $4.50

DVORKIN, David. *Green God.* 1979. Pocket 82080. SF. F. P1d. $6.00

DWYER, K.R. *Dragonfly.* 1976. Ballantine 25140. My. VG. P1d. $20.00

DYE, Charles. *Prisoner in the Skull.* 1957. Corgi S 486. SF. VG. P1d. $10.00

DYE, Charles. *Prisoner in the Skull.* 1975. Major 3027. SF. VG. P1d. $3.50

DYER, Walter. *TV Tramps.* 1962. Midwood 186. PBO. c/Maguire: gga. VG+. B6a #79. $38.50

EAGLE, John. *Hoodlums.* Avon 546. VG+. I1d. $10.00

EAGLE, John. *Hoodlums.* Avon 735. 1st prtg. My. VG. R5d. $4.50

EARL, L. *River of Eyes.* Popular EB 48. VG+. B3d. $4.00

EARLL, Tony. *Mu Revealed.* 1970. PB Library 64-417. PBO. Nfi. VG+. B5d. $4.00

EARLL, Tony. *Mu Revealed.* 1972. PB Library 64-905. 2nd edn. Nfi. VG. P1d. $3.25

EAST, Michael. *Concubine.* 1958. Dell 1st Edn A 169. PBO. c/McGinnis; gga. VG. B6d. $7.50

EASTMAN, Elizabeth. *His Dead Wife.* 1950. Lion 44. 1st edn. PBO. c/gga. scarce. My. VG+. B6a #75. $27.50

EASTON, L. *Driven Flesh.* Ace S 119. VG. B3d. $6.00

EASTON, M. Coleman. *Fisherman's Curse.* 1987. Popular. 1st edn. F. M1d. $5.00

EASTWOOD, T. *Insatiable Co-Eds.* Barclay 7349. PBO. NF. B3d. $6.00

EATON, Evelyn. *Sea Is So Wide.* Harlequin 170. VG. B3d. $4.00

EATON, Frank. *Pistol Pete.* 1953. Signet 1050. 1st pb. We. NF. B3d. $6.00

EBERHART, Mignon G. *Alpine Condo Crossfire.* 1985. Warner 32855. 1st prtg. My. F. W2d. $3.50

EBERHART, Mignon G. *Another Man's Murder.* Dell D 259. VG. B3d. $4.00

EBERHART, Mignon G. *Chiffon Scarf.* Popular 60-2150. My. VG+. B5d. $3.50

EBERHART, Mignon G. *Danger In the Dark.* 1943. Popular NN (2). 1st pb. c/Hoffman. My. G. B6d. $6.00

EBERHART, Mignon G. *Dead Men's Plans.* Dell 767. VG. G5d. $5.00

EBERHART, Mignon G. *Deadly Is the Diamond.* Dell 10¢ 7. VG. B3d. $3.50

EBERHART, Mignon G. *Enemy in the House.* 1962. Popular K 53. My. VG+. B4d. $2.00

EBERHART, Mignon G. *Escape the Night.* Bantam 46. VG+. B3d. $6.00

EBERHART, Mignon G. *Fair Warning.* Century 19. VG. B3d. $6.00

EBERHART, Mignon G. *Hasty Wedding.* 1946. Popular 73. 1st pb. c/Hoffman. My. VG. B6d. $7.50

EBERHART, Mignon G. *House of Storm.* Bantam 885. VG. G5d/I1d. $4.00

EBERHART, Mignon G. *House on the Roof.* Popular 17. VG. B3d. $5.50

EBERHART, Mignon G. *Hunt With the Hounds.* Dell 546. 1st prtg. My. VG. I1d. $1.25

EBERHART, Mignon G. *Hunt With the Hounds.* 1963. Popular K 39. 1st pb. My. VG+. B6d. $6.00

EBERHART, Mignon G. *Man Missing.* Dell 877. c/W George. My. VG. B5d. $3.00

EBERHART, Mignon G. *Man Next Door.* Dell 161. c/G Gregg. My. G+. B5d. $5.00

EBERHART, Mignon G. *Never Look Back.* Dell 669. c/C Roberts. My. VG. B5d. $3.00

EBERHART, Mignon G. *Pattern of Murder.* 1948. Popular 167. 1st pb. c/Belarski. My. VG+. B6d. $16.50

EBERHART, Mignon G. *Postmark Murder.* 1957. Dell 955. 1st prtg. My. VG. R5d. $3.00

EBERHART, Mignon G. *Speak No Evil.* 1944. Dell 25. G. G5d. $7.00

EBERHART, Mignon G. *Speak No Evil.* 1944. Dell 25. 1st edn. PBO. c/Gregg. F. B6a #80. $75.00

EBERHART, Mignon G. *Speak No Evil.* Dell 628. VG. I1d. $3.00

EBERHART, Mignon G. *Speak No Evil.* Popular 01596. My. NF. B5d. $4.50

EBERHART, Mignon G. *Unidentified Woman.* 1948. Dell 213. My. VG. P6d. $3.50

EBERHART, Mignon G. *White Cockatoo.* Popular 01529. My. VG. W2d. $3.50

EBERHART, Mignon G. *White Dress.* Bantam 739. VG. B3d. $4.50

EBERHART, Mignon G. *Wings of Fear.* 1948. Bantam 137. 1st pb. My. VG+. B3d. $5.00

EBERHART, Mignon G. *With This Ring.* Dell 83. c/G Gregg. My. VG. B3d. $6.00

EBERHART, Mignon G. *With This Ring.* Popular 60-2128. My. NF. B5d. $4.00

EBERHART, Mignon G. *Wolf in Man's Clothing.* Dell 136. 1st edn. PBO. c/Gerald Gregg. scarce. NF. B6a #75. $38.50

EBERHART, Mignon G. *Wolf in Man's Clothing.* Dell 136. 1st edn. PBO. c/Gregg. VG+. B6d. $30.00

EBERHART. *Hunt With the Hounds.* 1951. Dell 546. 1st pb. c/Mayers. My. VG. B6d. $7.50

EBON, Martin. *Atlantis: The New Evidence.* 1977. Signet W 7371. Nfi. VG. P1d. $3.50

EBON, Martin. *Communicating With the Dead.* 1968. Signet P 3393. Nfi. VG. P1d. $5.00

EBON, Martin. *Exorcism: Fact Not Fiction.* 1974. Signet Y 5701. Nfi. VG. P1d. $3.50

EBON, Martin. *Psychic Scene.* 1974. Signet Y 5917. Nfi. VG. P1d. $3.50

EBON, Martin. *Riddle of the Bermuda Triangle.* 1975. Signet W 6637. Nfi. VG. P1d. $3.50

EBON, Martin. *Witchcraft Today.* Signet Q 5562. 4th edn. Nfi. VG. P1d. $3.00

EBY & FLEMING. *Velvet Fleece.* Dell 272. G. G5d. $4.00

ECHOLS. *Wildhorse Range.* 1963. MacFadden 40-127. 1st pb. c/Maguire. We. VG+. B6d. $6.00

ECHOLS/MANNING. *Double-Cross Brand/ Desperado Code.* Ace D 20. PBO. VG. B3d. $7.00

ECHOLS/WEST. *Gunsmoke Gold/Terror Rides the Range.* Ace D 8. G. I1d. $7.00

EDD, Karl. *Teen Tramp.* 1961. Beacon B 399. PBO. Ad. G+. B5d. $5.00

EDD, Karl. *Tenement Kid.* 1959. Newsstand U 122. JD. VG+. P1d. $25.00

EDDINGTON & HAYMES. *Errol & Me.* 1960. Signet D 1875. PBO. VG+. P6d. $2.50

EDDISON, E.R. *Fish Dinner in Memison.* 1968. Ballantine. 4th pb edn. NF. M1d. $3.00

EDDISON, E.R. *Mezentian Gate.* 1969. Ballantine. 1st US edn. NF. M1d. $8.00

EDDISON, E.R. *Mistress of Mistresses.* 1967. Ballantine U 7063. 1st pb. Fa. VG+. B6d. $8.00

EDDISON, E.R. *Worm Ouroboros.* Ballantine 24309. reprint. Fa. NF. B6d. $3.00

EDDY, Roger. *Bulls & the Bees.* 1957. Pocket 1164. VG+. B3d. $4.50

EDDY, Roger. *Bulls & the Bees.* 1957. Pocket 1164. 1st pb. NF. B6d. $9.00

EDELSON, Edward. *Great Monsters of the Movies.* 1974. Pocket Arch 29741. Nfi. VG. P1d. $3.50

EDELSON, Edward. *Great SF From the Movies.* 1976. Pocket Arch 29749. Nfi. VG. P1d. $3.50

EDELSON, Edward. *Great SF From the Movies.* 1976. Pocket Arch 29749. 1st prtg. F. S1d. $4.50

EDEN, Dorothy. *Crow Hollow.* 1966. Ace K 275. 1st prtg. My. G+. R5d. $1.50

EDEN, Dorothy. *Whistle for the Crows.* 1963. Ace K 184. 1st US edn. Go. NF. B6d. $6.00

EDGAR, Peter. *Cities of the Dead.* 1963. Digit R 796. SF. VG. P1d. $6.00

EDGE, Nelson. *Passion Fruit.* 1964. All Star 21. PBO. VG+. B6d. $8.00

EDGLEY/WEISS. *Tracked Down/Death Hitches a Ride.* Ace D 45. c/Barton: gga. My. VG. B6d. $12.50

EDMONDS, I.G. *Hollywood RIP.* 1963. Regency RB 320. 1st prtg. Nfi. G+. R5d. $9.00

EDMONDS, W.D. *Boyds of Black River.* Bantam 1254. VG. B3d. $4.50

EDMONDS, W.D. *Captive Women.* 1949. Bantam 708. c/gga. Fa. VG+. B4d. $3.50

EDMONDS, W.D. *Drums Along the Mohawk.* Armed Services E 149. VG. B3d. $5.50

EDMONDS, W.D. *Rome Haul.* Bantam 1099. VG. B3d. $4.00

EDMONDS, W.D. *Wedding Journey.* Dell 10¢ 6. NF. B3d. $9.00

EDMONDSON, G.C. *Aluminum Man.* 1975. Berkley N 2737. SF. VG. P1d. $3.50

EDMONDSON, G.C. *Blue Face.* 1972. DAW UQ 1017 17. SF. VG. P1d. $4.00

EDMONDSON, G.C. *Ship That Sailed the Time Stream.* 1978. Ace 76092. SF. VG+. P1d. $4.50

EDMONDSON, G.C. *To Sail the Century Sea.* 1981. Ace 81787. SF. F P1d. $5.00

EDMONDSON, Paul. *Little Revolution.* Crest 335. VG+. B3d. $4.50

EDMONDSON/EDMONDSON. *Stranger Than You Think/Ship That Sailed the Time Stream.* Ace M 109. PBO. F. M1d. $8.00

EDMONDSON/EDMONDSON. *Stranger Than You Think/Ship That Sailed the Time Stream.* Ace M 109. PBO. VG+. B3d. $4.50

EDMUND, Matty. *Anatomy of a Heel.* 1964. Beacon B 741X. c/gga. Fa. F. B4d. $14.00

EDMUNDSON, J. *Pan Book of Party Games.* 1962. Pan G 195. 6th prtg. VG. B3d. $6.00

EDSON, J.T. *Bunduki.* 1975. Corgi 09768. SF. VG. P1d. $4.00

EDSON, J.T. *Bunduki.* 1976. DAW UW 1243. 1st prtg. SF. F. W2d. $4.50

EDSON, J.T. *Bunduki.* 1976. DAW 201. c/M Whelan. SF. VG+. B5d. $6.00

EDSON, J.T. *Hell in the Palo Duro.* 1971. Corgi 08783. We. VG. P1d. $4.00

EDSON, J.T. *Quest for Bowie's Blade.* 1974. Corgi 09607. We. VG. P1d. $4.00

EDSON, J.T. *Rustlers.* 1966. Brown, Watson W 358. 2nd edn. We. VG. P1d. $4.50

EDSON, J.T. *To Arms! To Arms in Dixie!* 1972. Corgi 08971. We. VG. P1d. $4.00

EDWARDES, Allen. *Jewel in the Lotus.* Lancer 75-016. reprint. VG. B6d. $4.00

EDWARDS, Alexander. *Last of Sheila.* 1973. Warner 76-389. MTI. c/photo. VG+. B3d. $4.00

EDWARDS, Alexander. *Last of Sheila.* 1973. Warner 76-389. 1st edn. c/color photo. My. F. F2d. $9.00

EDWARDS, Alexander. *Star Is Born.* 1976. Warner 84-214. 1st prtg. VG. R5d. $1.75

EDWARDS, Anne. *Survivors.* 1969. Dell 8397. Ho. VG. P1d. $5.50

EDWARDS, Frank. *Flying Saucers: Here & Now!* 1968. Bantam S 3631. Nfi. VG. P1d. $5.00

EDWARDS, Frank. *Flying Saucers: Serious Business.* 1966. Bantam S 3378. 1st prtg. VG+. P7d. $4.00

EDWARDS, Frank. *Strange People.* Popular SP 225. VG. B3d. $4.50

EDWARDS, Frank. *Strange People.* 1965. Popular PC 1046. Nfi. VG. P1d. $6.00

EDWARDS, Frank. *Stranger Than Science.* 1962. Ace K 117. VG+. B3d. $5.00

EDWARDS, Frank. *Strangest of All.* Ace K 144. VG+. B3d. $5.00

EDWARDS, H. *Bottoms-Up Nieces.* Barclay 7486. c/photo. F. B3d. $4.50

EDWARDS, H. *Island of Love.* Gold Medal 1301. MTI. VG+. B3d. $5.00

EDWARDS, Norman. *Invasion From 2500.* 1964. Monarch 453. SF. G+. B5d. $5.00

EDWARDS, Norman. *Invasion From 2500.* 1964. Monarch 453. SF. VG+. P1d. $10.00

EDWARDS, Norman. *Invasion From 2500.* 1964. Monarch 453. 1st edn. F. M1d. $20.00

EDWARDS, Paul. *Deadly Cyborgs.* 1975. Pyramid N 3702. SF/My. VG. P1d. $3.50

EDWARDS, Samuel. *Devil's Prize.* Crest 259. NF. B3d. $6.00

EDWARDS & HOLDSTOCK. *Tour of the Universe.* 1980. Mayflower 8798. SF. VG. P1d. $15.00

EDWOOD, Roger. *Strange Gods.* Pocket 77754. 1st prtg. F. S1d. $5.50

EFFINGER, George Alec. *Man the Fugitive.* 1974. Award AN 1373. PBO. TVTI. NF. B3d. $4.50

EFFINGER, George Alec. *Those Gentle Voices.* 1976. Warner 86-113. SF. F. P1d. $7.50

EGLETON, Clive. *Piece of Resistance.* 1972. New English 010155. SF/My. VG+. P1d. $4.50

EHRLICH, Jack. *Court Martial.* 1959. Pyramid G 463. Fa. VG. B4d. $3.00

EHRLICH, Jack. *Cry Baby.* Dell 1st Edn B 227. NF. I1d. $5.00

EHRLICH, Jack. *Parole.* Dell 1st Edn B 154. VG. I1d. $5.00

EHRLICH, Jack. *Slow Burn.* Dell 1st Edn B 220. NF. I1d. $5.00

EHRLICH, Leonard. *God's Angry Man.* Armed Services 930. Fi. VG. B5d. $4.50

EHRLICH, Max. *Big Eye.* 1958. Bantam A 1860. SF. VG+. P1d. $11.00

EHRLICH, Max. *Big Eye.* 1950. Popular 273. c/Bergey. Fa. VG+. B4d. $12.50

EHRLICH, Max. *Big Eye.* 1950. Popular 273. G+. G5d. $7.00

EHRLICH, Max. *Big Eye.* 1950. Popular 273. NF. I1d. $20.00

EHRLICH, Max. *Big Eye.* 1950. Popular 273. SF. F. P1d. $25.00

EHRLICH, Max. *High Side.* Gold Medal 2207. c/Frazetta. VG. B3d. $6.50

EHRLICH, Max. *Savage Is Loose.* 1974. Bantam T 8518. 1st prtg. VG. R5d. $1.50

EHRLICH, Max. *Spin the Glass Web.* 1953. Bantam 1096. My. F. P1d. $17.00

EHRLICH, Max. *Spin the Glass Web.* 1953. Bantam 1096. VG+. B3d. $4.50

EIDEN & SABRE. *Glory Jumpers.* 1959. Monarch 140. 1st edn. c/gga. F. F2d. $15.00

EINSTEIN, Charles. *Bloody Spur.* 1953. Dell 1st Edn 5. PBO. c/P Marini. My. VG. B5d. $4.00

EINSTEIN, Charles. *Day New York Went Dry.* 1964. Gold Medal K 1446. PBO. SF. VG. B5d. $10.00

EINSTEIN, Charles. *Day New York Went Dry.* 1964. Gold Medal K 1446. SF. F. P1d. $15.00

EINSTEIN, Charles. *Day New York Went Dry.* 1964. Gold Medal K 1446. 1st prtg. SF. G+. R5d. $5.50

EINSTEIN, Charles. *No Time At All.* 1958. Dell D 224. TVTI. VG+. B4d. $3.00

EINSTEIN, Charles. *Wiretap!* Dell 1st Edn 76. VG. B3d/I1d. $4.00

EINSTEIN, Charles. *Wiretap!* 1955. Dell 1st Edn 76. 1st prtg. PBO. c/Schulz: gga. VG. P7d. $5.00

EISENBERG, Larry. *Best-Laid Schemes.* 1973. Collier 01977. SF. F. P1d. $5.00

EISINGER, Jo. *Walls Came Tumbling Down.* 1945. Handi-Book 36. 1st edn. PBO. rare. NF. B6a #75. $40.00

EISNER, Simon. *Naked Storm.* Lion LL 125. reprint. VG. B6d. $12.50

EISNER, Simon. *Naked Storm.* 1952. Lion 109. My. VG. P1d. $35.00

EISNER, Simon. *Star Jaws.* 1978. Baronet 044. Hu. VG. P1d. $4.00

EKLUND, Gordon. *All Times Possible.* 1974. DAW UQ 1117 108. SF. F. P1d. $5.00

EKLUND, Gordon. *Dance of the Apocalypse.* 1976. Laser 46. SF. VG+. P1d. $6.00

EKLUND, Gordon. *Dance of the Apocalypse.* 1976. Laser 46. 1st edn. SF. F. F2d. $13.00

EKLUND, Gordon. *Devil World.* 1979. Bantam 13297. SF. VG. B5d. $2.50

EKLUND, Gordon. *Eclipse of Dawn.* 1971. Ace 18630. SF. F. P1d. $5.00

EKLUND, Gordon. *Eclipse of Dawn.* 1971. Ace 18630. 1st edn. SF. VG. P9d. $1.50

EKLUND, Gordon. *Falling Toward Forever.* 1975. Laser 10. c/Freas. NF. B3d. $6.00

EKLUND, Gordon. *Falling Toward Forever.* 1975. Laser 10. PBO. c/K Freas. SF. VG. B5d. $4.00

EKLUND, Gordon. *Grayspace Beast.* 1977. Pocket 81390. SF. F. P1d. $5.00

EKLUND, Gordon. *Serving in Time.* 1975. Laser 6. PBO. c/K Freas. SF. NF. B5d. $6.50

EKLUND, Gordon. *Serving in Time.* 1975. Laser 6. SF. VG. I1d/W2d. $5.00

EKLUND, Gordon. *Starless World.* 1978. Bantam 12371. SF. F. P1d. $10.00

EKLUND, Gordon. *Trace of Dreams.* 1972. Ace 82070. SF. F. P1d. $5.00

EKLUND/WILSON. *Twilight River/The Tery.* 1979. Dell 11090. SF. VG+. P1d. $5.50

EKLUND/WILSON. *Twilight River/The Tery.* 1979. Dell 11090. 1st edn. SF. F. F2d. $15.00

ELAM, Richard M. *SF Stories.* 1964. Lantern Press 50096. SF. VG. P1d. $6.00

ELBERHART, M.G. *Deadly Is the Diamond.* 1951. Dell 10¢ 7. c/Bill Fleming: gga. VG+. P6d. $7.00

ELBERT, Joyce. *Martini on the Other Table.* 1963. Bantam J 2583. 1st prtg. PBO. VG. P7d. $3.50

ELDER, Joseph edt. *Farthest Reaches.* 1969. Pocket 75456. SF. VG. B5d. $3.00

ELDER, Michael. *Alien Earth.* 1971. Pinnacle P043-N. SF. VG. P1d. $4.00

ELDER, Michael. *Paradise Is Not Enough.* 1971. Pinnacle P034-N. SF. VG. P1d. $4.00

ELDRIDGE & VIERICK. *Salome.* 1954. Ace D 43. VG+. B3a #22. $19.80

ELDRIDGE & VIERICK. *Salome.* Ace D 43. G+. I1d. $8.00

ELEGANT, R.S. *Kind of Treason.* Avon S 273. VG. B3d. $4.50

ELGIN, Suzette. *At the Seventh Level.* 1972. DAW UQ 1010 10. SF. VG+. P1d. $4.50

ELGIN, Suzette. *Furthest.* Ace 25950. c/L & D Dillon. Ace SF Special. SF. VG. B5d. $5.00

ELGIN/TRIMBLE. *Communipaths/Noblest Experiment in the Galaxy.* 1970. Ace 11560. SF. VG. W2d. $8.00

ELGIN/TRIMBLE. *Communipaths/Noblest Experiment in the Galaxy.* 1970. Ace 11560. 1st edn. SF. F. F2d. $13.00

ELGIN/TRIMBLE. *Communipaths/Noblest Experiment In the Galaxy.* 1970. Ace 11560. 1st prtg. G. S1d. $2.25

ELIAS, Horace J. *Flash Gordon in the Sand World of Mongo.* 1976. King. SF. VG+. W2d. $3.00

ELIOT, Alexander. *Proud Youth.* 1955. Signet 1177. 1st pb. c/Hulings. VG+. B6d. $8.00

ELIOT, Dan. *Flesh Flames.* 1963. Ember Book EB 912. Ad. VG. P1d. $20.00

ELIOT, E.C. *Kemlo & the Space Lanes.* 1968. Merlin M 39. SF. VG. P1d. $5.00

ELIOT, T.S. *Murder in the Cathedral (A Play for Canterbury Festival).* Harvest House HB 72. My. VG+. W2d. $6.00

ELLIN, Stanley. *Big Night.* 1950. Lion 41. 1st pb. c/gga. My. VG. B6d. $16.50

ELLIN, Stanley. *Blessington Method.* Signet 2805. VG+. B3d. $4.00

ELLIN, Stanley. *Key to Nicholas Street.* Dell 763. G+. G5d. $3.50

ELLINGTON, Richard. *Exit for a Dame.* 1953. Pocket 941. c/D Ross. My. VG. B5d. $5.00

ELLINGTON, Richard. *It's a Crime.* Pocket 756. G+. G5d. $4.00

ELLINGTON, Richard. *Shoot the Works.* Pocket 624. VG. I1d. $5.00

ELLINGTON, Richard. *Stone Cold Dead.* Pocket 813. VG+. G5d. $6.00

ELLIOT & HOYLE. *For Andromeda.* Crest 1205. VG+. B3d. $5.00

ELLIOT & HOYLE. *For Andromeda.* Crest 773. F. B3d. $5.00

ELLIOTT, Ben. *Weekend Wife.* 1961. Beacon B423Y. PBO. Ad. VG. B5d. $6.00

ELLIOTT, Bruce. *Asylum Earth.* 1968. Belmont B50-819. PBO. SF. VG+. B5d. $5.50

ELLIOTT, Bruce. *One Is a Lonely Number.* 1952. Lion 100. PBO. c/Bergey. VG. B6d. $15.00

ELLIOTT, Bruce. *Woman.* 1961. Midwood 71. 1st edn. c/gga. My. F. F2d. $22.00

ELLIOTT, Charles. *Trial by Fire.* Popular G 254. VG+. B3d. $4.50

ELLIOTT, Don. *Alternate Wife.* Idle Hour IH 470. PBO. VG. M6d. $9.50

ELLIOTT, Don. *Convention Girl.* 1961. Nightstand NB 1547R. Ad. VG. P1d. $15.00

ELLIOTT, Don. *Diary of a Dyke.* 1967. Pleasure Reader 118. PBO. scarce. NF. B6a #75. $66.00

ELLIOTT, Don. *Expense Account Sinners.* 1961. Nightstand NB 1558. Ad. G+. B5d. $3.00

ELLIOTT, Don. *Game Susan Played.* Reed Nightstand 4042. VG. M6d. $9.50

ELLIOTT, Don. *Gang Girl.* 1959. Nightstand 1504. PBO. scarce. JD. VG+. B6a #79. $47.50

ELLIOTT, Don. *Gang Girl.* Reed Nightstand 3004. c/Silverberg. F. B6a #79. $101.00

ELLIOTT, Don. *Good Girl, Bad Girl.* Nightstand NB 17-51. PBO. VG. P6d. $4.00

ELLIOTT, Don. *Jungle Street.* Reed Nightstand 3024. NF. M6d. $8.50

ELLIOTT, Don. *Love Addict.* 1959. Nightstand 1501. PBO. c/Silverberg; sgn. VG+. B6a #80. $121.00

ELLIOTT, Don. *Love Addict.* Reed Nightstand 3001. c/Silverberg. NF. B6a #80. $125.00

ELLIOTT, Don. *Lust Cat.* 1966. Sundown Reader SR 589. Ad. VG+. P1d. $20.00

ELLIOTT, Don. *Lust Demon.* Sundown Reader SR 578. PBO. VG. M6d. $9.50

ELLIOTT, Don. *Lust Queen.* Midnight Reader MR 401R. VG. M6d. $9.50

ELLIOTT, Don. *Man Collector.* Reed Nightstand 3030. VG. M6d. $6.50

ELLIOTT, Don. *Naked Holiday.* Nightstand NB 1512 R. G+. M6d. $9.50

ELLIOTT, Don. *Nudie Packet.* 1965. Idle Hour IH 429. Ad. VG+. P1d. $20.00

ELLIOTT, Don. *Of Shame Reborn.* Nightstand NB 1741. VG. M6d. $7.50

ELLIOTT, Don. *Passion Patsy.* 1963. Midnight Reader MR 475. Ad. VG. P1d. $15.00

ELLIOTT, Don. *Passion Peeper.* Idle Hour IH 482. PBO. VG+. M6d. $15.00

ELLIOTT, Don. *Shame Scheme.* 1965. Nightstand NB 1729. Ad. F. P1d. $25.00

ELLIOTT, Don. *Sin Circuit.* 1964. Ember Book EB 936. Ad. F. P1d. $25.00

ELLIOTT, Don. *Sin Crazed.* Midnight Reader MR 469. PBO. VG. M6d. $6.50

ELLIOTT, Don. *Sin Spin.* Idle Hour IH 475. PBO. VG. M6d. $9.50

ELLIOTT, Don. *Sinful Ones.* Nightstand NB 1704. VG. M6d. $6.50

ELLIOTT, Don. *Streets of Sin.* 1961. Midnight Reader 406. PBO. c/gga. JD. VG+. B6a #79. $103.50

ELLIOTT, Don. *Summertime Affair.* Nightstand NB 1508. PBO. G+. M6d. $15.00

ELLIOTT, Don. *Those Who Lust.* 1967. Leisure 1191. PBO. c/Bonfils: gga. NF. B6a #76. $57.00

ELLIOTT, Don. *Untamed.* Reed Nightstand 4030. VG. M6d. $12.50

ELLIOTT, Don. *Virtuous Ones.* Idle Hour IH 506. PBO. VG. M6d. $9.50

ELLIOTT, Don. *Wanton Web.* Idle Hour IH 409. PBO. VG. M6d. $9.50

ELLIOTT, Don. *Woman Chaser.* 1961. Bedside 1201. PBO. VG+. B3d. $7.00

ELLIOTT, Don. *Young Wantons.* Sundown Reader SR 537. PBO. P6d. $3.50

ELLIOTT, John. *Dragon Feast.* 1970. Belmont B 95-2009. SF. VG. P1d. $4.50

ELLIOTT, John. *Dragon Feast.* 1976. Belmont. 1st edn. F. M1d. $7.00

ELLIOTT, Richard. *Sword of Allah.* 1984. Gold Medal. 1st edn. F. M1d. $4.00

ELLIOTT, William J. *Shipwreck Passion.* 1950. Harborough NN. PBO. rare. NF. B6a #80. $330.00

ELLIOTT/WHITTINGTON. *Valley of Savage Men/Brother Badman.* 1965. Ace M 126. We. G+. P1d. $7.00

ELLIS, A. *Love Pagoda.* Brandon House 931. 2nd prtg. NF. B3d. $6.00

ELLIS, Albert. *Sex Without Guilt.* 1959. Hillman 106. Nfi. VG. B5d. $4.00

ELLIS, Joan. *After Class.* 1964. Midwood F 360. Fa. VG+. B4d. $16.00

ELLIS, Joan. *Campus Jungle.* 1962. Midwood 182. PBO. c/Rader: gga. VG. B6d. $9.00

ELLIS, Joan. *Campus Jungle.* 1962. Midwood 182. 1st edn. c/Rader: gga. F. F2d. $21.00

ELLIS, Joan. *Campus Jungle.* 1965. Midwood 32-554. c/Rader: gga. F. F2d. $10.00

ELLIS, Joan. *Campus Kittens.* 1964. Midwood 32-417. PBO. c/Rader: gga. G+. P6d. $2.00

ELLIS, Joan. *Country Girl.* 1965. Midwood 32-579. Fa. F. B4d. $15.00

ELLIS, Joan. *Hold Me Tight.* Midwood F 279. G+. I1d. $4.00

ELLIS, Joan. *In the Shadows.* 1962. Midwood F 139. PBO. c/Maguire: gga. VG. B6d. $12.00

ELLIS, Joan. *Lana.* Midwood 54. PBO. c/Rader. VG. B3d. $4.00

ELLIS, Joan. *Mulatto.* 1961. Midwood F 113. VG. P6d. $3.50

ELLIS, Joan. *Once Too Often.* 1963. Midwood 257. VG. B3d. $3.50

ELLIS, Joan. *Pleasure Girl.* 1961. Midwood 76. PBO. c/Rader: gga. scarce. VG+. B6a #80. $48.50

ELLIS, R. *Model Maker.* Diamond Volume 102. c/photo. VG+. V3d. $4.50

ELLIS, R. *Sex Stud '70.* Barclay 7092. VG. B3d. $4.00

ELLIS, W.D. *Bounty Lands.* Dell D 71. c/buckskin shirt. NF. B3d. $5.00

ELLISON, Harlan. *Again, Dangerous Visions Volume #1.* 1973. Signet J 5672. c/sgn. SF. VG+. P1d. $20.00

ELLISON, Harlan. *Alone Against Tomorrow.* 1972. Collier 01978. SF. G+. P1d. $5.00

ELLISON, Harlan. *Approaching Oblivion.* Signet 6848 NF. B3d. $10.00

ELLISON, Harlan. *Beast That Shouted Love at the Heart of the World.* 1969. Avon V 2300. SF. VG. B3d. $5.00

ELLISON, Harlan. *Beast That Shouted Love at the Heart of the World.* 1969. Avon V 2300. 1st edn. c/sgn. SF. F. F2d. $30.00

ELLISON, Harlan. *Beast That Shouted Love at the Heart of the World.* 1969. Avon. 1st edn. NF. M1d. $15.00

ELLISON, Harlan. *Beast That Shouted Love at the Heart of the World.* 1974. Signet E 8590. 4th prtg. SF. G+. W2d. $7.50

ELLISON, Harlan. *Beast That Shouted Love at the Heart of the World.* 1974. Signet Y 5870. SF. G+. P1d. $10.00

ELLISON, Harlan. *City on the Edge of Forever.* 1977. Bantam 11345. Fotonovel. SF. F. P1d. $25.00

ELLISON, Harlan. *City on the Edge of Forever.* 1977. Bantam 11345. Fotonovel. SF. G+. P1d. $10.00

ELLISON, Harlan. *Dangerous Visions #1.* 1969. Berkley N 1686. SF. VG. P1d/P7d. $10.00

ELLISON, Harlan. *Dangerous Visions #3.* 1969. Berkley S 1714. SF. VG. B5d/P1d. $10.00

ELLISON, Harlan. *Deadly Streets.* 1958. Ace D 312. PBO. c/sgn. scarce. JD. VG. B6a #80. $194.00

ELLISON, Harlan. *Deadly Streets.* 1958. Ace D 312. PBO. c/sgn. VG. B3a #24. $90.75

ELLISON, Harlan. *Doomsman.* 1967. Belmont 779. 1st edn. SF. F. F2d. $35.00

ELLISON, Harlan. *Earthman, Go Home!* 1968. PB Library 53-727. 3rd edn. SF. F P1d. $20.00

ELLISON, Harlan. *Ellison in Wonderland.* 1962. PB Library 52-149. PBO. SF. VG. B6d. $9.00

ELLISON, Harlan. *Ellison in Wonderland.* 1962. PB Library 52-149. PBO. VG+. B3a #24. $15.40

ELLISON, Harlan. *Ellison in Wonderland.* 1962. PB Library 52-149. VG+. B3d. $15.00

ELLISON, Harlan. *Ellison in Wonderland.* 1962. PB Library 52-149. 1st edn. SF. F. F2d. $30.00

ELLISON, Harlan. *Ellison in Wonderland.* Signet 6041. VG+. B3d. $6.00

ELLISON, Harlan. *From the Land of Fear.* 1967. Belmont 069. 1st edn. SF. F. F2d. $14.00

ELLISON, Harlan. *From the Land of Fear.* Belmont 50750. VG+. B3d. $5.50

ELLISON, Harlan. *Gentleman Junkie.* 1975. Pyramid V 3933. My. VG. P1d. $15.00

ELLISON, Harlan. *Gentleman Junkie.* 1961. Regency RB 102. JD. F. P1d. $150.00

ELLISON, Harlan. *Gentleman Junkie.* 1961. Regency RB 102. My. F. P1d. $150.00

ELLISON, Harlan. *Gentlemen Junkie & Other Stories of the Hung-Up Generation.* 1961. Regency RB 101. 1st edn. JD. F. F2d. $170.00

ELLISON, Harlan. *Glass Teat.* 1983. Ace 28988. Nfi. VG. P1d. $20.00

ELLISON, Harlan. *Glass Teat.* 1970. Ace 29350. 1st edn. scarce. SF. NF. F2d. $25.00

ELLISON, Harlan. *I Have No Mouth & I Must Scream.* 1967. Pyramid X 1611. SF. VG. P1d. $17.50

ELLISON, Harlan. *I Have No Mouth & I Must Scream.* 1976. Pyramid 03521. 6th prtg. SF. VG. W2d. $6.00

ELLISON, Harlan. *Illustrated Harlan Ellison.* 1980. Ace. 1st pb. F. M1d. $15.00

ELLISON, Harlan. *Juvies.* 1961. Ace D 513. c/sgn. VG. B3a #24. $110.15

ELLISON, Harlan. *Juvies.* 1961. Ace D 513. PBO. rare. JD. VG. B6d. $250.00

ELLISON, Harlan. *Juvies.* 1961. Ace D 513. PBO. scarce. JD. VG. B6a #80. $176.00

ELLISON, Harlan. *Juvies.* 1961. Ace D 513. 1st edn. JD. G+. F2d. $200.00

ELLISON, Harlan. *Man With Nine Lives.* 1960. Ace D 413. PBO. c/Emsh. VG+. B6d. $45.00

ELLISON, Harlan. *Memos From Purgatory.* 1969. Powell PP 154. c/sgn. scarce. NF. B6a #80. $63.00

ELLISON, Harlan. *Memos From Purgatory.* 1969. Powell PP 154. JD. VG+. P1d. $100.00

ELLISON, Harlan. *Memos From Purgatory.* 1975. Pyramid V 3706. Bio. VG. B4d. $3.00

ELLISON, Harlan. *No Doors, No Windows.* 1975. Pyramid. 1st pb. F. M1d. $12.00

ELLISON, Harlan. *Other Glass Teat.* 1983. Ace 64274. Nfi. VG+. P1d. $20.00

ELLISON, Harlan. *Other Glass Teat.* Pyramid 03971. VG. B3d. $6.00

ELLISON, Harlan. *Over the Edge.* 1972. Belmont 505-50282-095. VG+. B6d. $6.50

ELLISON, Harlan. *Paingod & Other Delusions.* 1965. Pyramid R 1270. 1st edn. SF. F. F2d. $20.00

ELLISON, Harlan. *Paingod.* 1969. Pyramid X 1991. SF. VG. P1d. $12.50

ELLISON, Harlan. *Partners in Wonder.* Pyramid A 3801. 1st edn. VG+. I1d. $10.00

ELLISON, Harlan. *Phoenix Without Ashes.* Gold Medal M 3188. NF. I1d. $8.00

ELLISON, Harlan. *Phoenix Without Ashes.* 1975. Gold Medal M 3188. 1st prtg. SF. G+. R5d. $3.50

ELLISON, Harlan. *Phoenix Without Ashes.* 1975. Gold Medal 3188. 1st edn. SF. F. F2d. $15.00

ELLISON, Harlan. *Phoenix Without Ashes.* 1978. Savoy 003. SF. VG+. P1d. $20.00

ELLISON, Harlan. *Rockabilly.* 1961. Gold Medal S 1161. 1st edn. Ad. VG. F2d. $60.00

ELLISON, Harlan. *Rumble.* 1958. Pyramid G 352. PBO. rare. JD. VG. B6a #80. $50.00

ELLISON, Harlan. *Rumble.* 1958. Pyramid G 352. 1st edn. JD. VG. F2d. $75.00

ELLISON, Harlan. *Spider Kiss.* 1982. Ace 77793. JD. VG+. P1d. $20.00

ELLISON, Harlan. *Stalking the Nightmare.* 1984. Berkley 07169. SF. VG. P1d. $7.50

ELLISON, Harlan. *Web of the City (Rumble).* Pyramid 4061. 3rd new Canadian edn. VG. B3d. $4.50

ELLISON/ELLISON. *Touch of Infinity/Man With Nine Lives.* 1960. Ace D 413. 1st prtg. SF. VG. R5d. $25.00

ELLISON/ELLSION. *Touch of Infinity/Man With Nine Lives.* 1960. Ace D 413. 1st edn. SF. VG+. F2d. $40.00

ELLSBERG, Edward. *Far Shore.* Popular SP 86. VG+. B3d. $4.50

ELLSION, Ralph. *Invisible Man.* 1964. Signet T 1823. 6th prtg. SF. VG. W2d. $3.75

ELLSION, Ralph. *Invisible Man.* 1972. Vintage V 715. SF. G+. W2d. $4.50

ELLSION/HOFFMAN. *Doomsman/Telepower.* Belmont B 50-779. VG+. B3d. $8.00

ELLSION/HOFFMAN. *Doomsman/Telepower.* 1967. Belmont B50-779. 1st edn. scarce. SF. F. F2d. $35.00

ELLSON, Hal. *Duke.* 1959. Popular G 358. My. F. F2d. $8.00

ELLSON, Hal. *Duke.* 1950. Popular 219. JD. VG+. B4d. $25.00

ELLSON, Hal. *Golden Spike.* 1952. Ballantine 2. c/Maguire. VG+. B6a #79. $48.50

ELLSON, Hal. *I Take What I Want.* 1958. Midwood NN. PBO. NF. B3a. $52.50

ELLSON, Hal. *I'll Fix You.* Pedigree NN. VG+. B3d. $10.00

ELLSON, Hal. *I'll Fix You.* 1956. Popular 725. 1st edn. scarce. JD. F. F2d. $30.00

ELLSON, Hal. *Jailbait Street.* 1959. Monarch 137. 1st edn. JD. F. F2d. $20.00

ELLSON, Hal. *Jailbait Street.* 1963. Monarch 399. JD. F. B4d. $16.00

ELLSON, Hal. *Killer's Kiss.* 1959. Lillman 119. 1st edn. My. F. F2d. $12.00

ELLSON, Hal. *Knife.* 1961. Lancer 71-301. c/P Max. Fi. VG. B5d/I1d. $15.00

ELLSON, Hal. *Nest of Fear.* 1961. Ace D 522. JD. F. P1d. $40.00

ELLSON, Hal. *Nest of Fear.* 1961. Ace D 522. 1st edn. JD. VG. F2d. $10.00

ELLSON, Hal. *Nightmare Street.* 1964. Belmont 90-316. 1st edn. JD. VG. F2d. $10.00

ELLSON, Hal. *Rock.* 1955. Ballantine 103. JD. VG+. B4d. $18.00

ELLSON, Hal. *Rock.* 1955. Ballantine 103. PBO. VG+. B3a #22. $24.00

ELLSON, Hal. *Rock.* 1955. Ballantine 103. 1st edn. JD. F. F2d. $20.00

ELLSON, Hal. *Stairway to Nowhere.* 1959. Ballantine 319. 1st edn. scarce. JD. F. F2d. $35.00

ELLSON, Hal. *Summer Street.* 1953. Ballantine 27. 1st edn. JD. F. F2d. $16.00

ELLSON, Hal. *Tell Them Nothing.* 1956. Ballantine 129. JD. G+. P1d. $9.00

ELLSON, Hal. *This Is It.* 1956. Popular 776. PBO. c/Johnson. racial/JD. NF. B6a #74. $76.00

ELLSON, Hal. *This Is It.* 1956. Popular 776. VG+. B3a #22. $48.00

ELLSON, Hal. *Tomboy.* 1963. Bantam J 2509. Fi. VG. B5d. $3.00

ELLSON, Hal. *Tomboy.* 1951. Bantam 945. c/gga. JD. VG+. B4d. $6.00

ELLSON, Hal. *Tomboy.* 1951. Bantam 945. JD. F. P1d. $27.00

ELLSON, Hal. *Tomboy.* 1951. Bantam 945. NF. I1d. $12.00

ELLSWORTH, Henry. *College Male.* 1964. Monarch MB 548. c/photo. Nfi. VG. B5d. $4.00

ELMO, H.T. *Modern Casanova's Handbook.* 1955. Ace S 93. PBO. c/Wenzel. VG. B3d. $6.00

ELSTON, A.V. *Guns of the Cimarron.* Pocket 530. VG. B3d. $4.50

ELSTON, A.V. *Hit the Saddle.* Pocket 585. VG+. B3d. $5.00

ELSTON, A.V. *Lawless Border.* Berkley G 1274. VG+. B3d. $4.50

ELSTON, A.V. *Rio Grande Deadline.* Pocket 1254. VG+. B3d. $5.50

ELSTON, A.V. *Showdown.* 1956. Pocket 1103. c/S Borack. We. VG. B5d. $4.00

ELSTON, A.V. *Wagon Wheel Gap.* 1955. Pocket 1086. c/T Ryan. We. VG. B5d. $4.00

ELSTON, A.V. *Wyoming Manhunt.* 1960. Pocket 1278. We. VG. B5d. $4.00

ELWOOD, Muriel. *Heritage of the River.* Bantam 774. VG. B3d. $4.00

ELWOOD, Muriel. *Web of Destiny.* Bantam 1002. VG. B3d. $4.50

ELWOOD, Roger edt. *Alien Earth, et al.* 1969. MacFadden 75219. SF. VG. W2d. $5.50

ELWOOD, Roger edt. *Alien Worlds.* 1964. PB Library 52-320. SF. F. P1d. $12.50

ELWOOD, Roger edt. *Continuum 1.* 1975. Berkley N 2828. SF. VG. P1d/W2d. $10.00

ELWOOD, Roger edt. *Continuum 4.* 1976. Berkley N 3077. SF. VG. P1d. $3.50

ELWOOD, Roger edt. *Future City.* 1974. Pocket 77936. SF. VG. P1d. $10.00

ELWOOD, Roger edt. *Invasion of the Robots.* 1965. PB Library 52-519. SF. VG+. P1d. $8.00

ELWOOD, Roger edt. *Other Side of Tomorrow.* 1975. Pyramid V 3937. SF. VG. W2d. $3.50

ELWOOD, Roger edt. *Six SF Plays.* 1976. Pocket 48766. 1st prtg. SF. VG+. W2d. $4.00

ELWOOD, Roger edt. *Strange Gods.* 1974. Pocket 77754. SF. F. P1d. $5.00

ELWOOD, Roger edt. *Ten Tomorrows.* 1973. Gold Medal M 2820. SF. VG. P1d. $3.50

ELWOOD, Roger edt. *Ten Tomorrows.* 1973. Gold Medal M 2820. 1st prtg. SF. NF. I1d. $10.00

ELWOOD, Roger edt. *Visions of Tomorrow.* 1976. Pocket 80775. SF. VG+. P1d. $4.50

ELWOOD, Roger edt. *50-Meter Monsters & Other Horrors.* 1976. Arch 29794. Ho. G+. P1d. $3.00

ELWOOD & GHIDALIA. *Little Monsters.* MacFadden 75-282. VG. B3d. $4.00

ELWOOD & GHIDALIA. *Young Demons.* 1972. Avon V 2434. SF. VG. P1d. $4.00

ELWOOD & KIDD. *Wounded Planet.* 1974. Bantam Q 7789. SF. VG. P1d. $3.50

ELWOOD & MOSKOWIT. *Great Spy Novels & Stories.* 1965. Pyramid R 1219. My. VG. B5d. $3.50

ELY, David. *Trot.* 1964. Signet D 2447. My. VG. P1d. $6.00

EMENWEIN, Leslie. *High Gun.* 1961. Gold Medal S 1081. 2nd edn. reprint. We. VG. B4d. $2.50

EMENWEIN, Leslie. *Rampage West.* 1963. Monarch 375. We. F. B4d. $9.00

EMERICK, Lucille. *City Beyond.* 1953. Popular G 120. c/gga. Fa. G+. B4d. $3.00

EMERICK, Lucille. *Web of Evil.* Dell 479. c/R Stanley. My. VG. G5d. $6.00

EMERSON, Jill. *Enough of Sorrow.* 1965. Midwood 32-550. PBO. Ad. G+. B5d. $3.00

EMERSON, Jill. *Warm & Willing.* 1964. Midwood 32-402. PBO. c/photo. VG+. P6d. $4.00

EMERY, Carol. *Queer Affair.* Beacon 377. c/gga. reprint. NF. B6d. $18.00

ENDORE, Guy. *Detour at Night.* 1965. Award A 145F. 1st prtg. My. VG+. R5d. $3.00

ENDORE, Guy. *Furies in Her Body.* Avon 323. VG. B3d. $5.00

ENDORE, Guy. *Nightmare.* 1956. Dell D 183. My. VG. P1d. $8.00

ENDORE, Guy. *Werewolf of Paris.* Ace K 160. F. M1d. $10.00

ENDORE, Guy. *Werewolf of Paris.* 1951. Avon. 1st pb. NF. M1d. $25.00

ENDORE, Guy. *Werewolf of Paris.* 1941. Pocket 97. Ho. VG. P1d. $75.00

ENGLE, Eloise. *Countdown for Cindy.* 1964. Bantam J 2753. SF. F. P1d. $12.50

ENGLISH, A. *Resort Secretary.* Midwood 227. PBO. NF. B3d. $7.50

ENGSTRAND, Stuart. *Invaders.* Signet 890. NF. I1d. $5.00

ENGSTRAND, Stuart. *Invaders.* 1951. Signet 890. c/J Avati. Fi. VG. B5d. $3.50

ENGSTRAND, Stuart. *More Deaths Than One.* 1957. Signet S 1408. 1st pb. c/Avati. VG. B6d. $3.50

ENGSTRAND, Stuart. *Prince & the Showgirl.* 1957. Signet S 1409. PBO. MTI. c/Monroe. VG. B6d. $10.00

ENGSTRAND, Stuart. *Sling & the Arrow.* 1950. Signet 786. Fa. VG+. B4d. $12.00

ENGSTRAND, Stuart. *Son of the Giant.* 1950. Signet 826. c/J Avati. Fi. VG. B5d. $4.00

ENGSTRAND, Stuart. *They Sought for Paradise.* 1951. Signet 867. c/gga. Fa. VG. B4d. $4.00

ERICSON/SCOTT. *Darkess Within (Fallen Angel)/Shakedown.* Ace D 17. VG. B3d. $7.00

ERICSON/SCOTT. *Darkness Within/Shakedown.* 1957. Ace D 17. PBO. c/sgn. scarce. NF. B6a #80. $65.00

ERMINE, Will. *Iron Bronc.* 1957. Pocket 1134. WE. VG+. B4d. $4.00

ERMINE, Will. *Laramie Rides.* 1948. Signet 679. 1st pb. c/Jonas. We. VG+. B6d. $12.00

ERMINE, Will. *Last of the Longhorns.* Dell 378. VG. B3d. $4.00

ERMINE, Will. *Lobo Law.* Signet 685. VG+. B3d. $6.00

ERMINE, Will. *Outlaw on Horseback.* 1949. Dell 284. 1st pb. c/Meyers. We. VG. B6d. $6.00

ERMINE, Will. *Outlaw on Horseback.* 1953. Dell 653. 1st prtg. c/Stanley. VG. P7d. $5.50

ERMINE, Will. *Rustlers' Moon.* 1951. Pocket 761. c/F McCarthy. We. VG. B5d. $4.00

ERNENWEIN, Leslie. *Boss of Panamint.* 1948. Handi-Book Western 75. VG. B3a #21, $236.50

ERNENWEIN, Leslie. *Bullet Barricade.* Gold Medal 1839. VG. B3d. $4.00

ERNENWEIN, Leslie. *Bullet Barricade.* Gold Medal 464. VG. B3d. $5.00

ERNENWEIN, Leslie. *Bullet Breed.* 1947. Handi-Book Western 69. VG+. B3a. $28.60

ERNENWEIN, Leslie. *Faro Kid.* 1949. Handi-Book Western 83. VG. P6d. $6.00

ERNENWEIN, Leslie. *Give a Man a Gun.* 1953. Gold Medal 220. We. VG. P6d. $3.00

ERNENWEIN, Leslie. *Gun-Hung Men.* Lion LB 155. NF. B3d. $6.00

ERNENWEIN, Leslie. *Gunfighter's Return.* Gold Medal 329. reprint. We. VG. B6d. $6.00

ERNENWEIN, Leslie. *Gunhawk Harvest.* 1952. Signet 982. 1st pb. We. NF. B6d. $15.00

ERNENWEIN, Leslie. *High Gun.* Gold Medal 620. VG. B3d. $4.00

ERNENWEIN, Leslie. *Rampage West.* Monarch 375. PBO. VG+. B3d. $5.00

ERNENWEIN, Leslie. *Trigger Justice.* Signet 1340. 2nd prtg. VG+. B3d. $5.00

ERNENWEIN, Leslie. *Warrior Basin.* Avon T 478. VG. B3d. $4.00

ERNST, E.E. *Anatomy of a Swap.* Edka 119. VG+. B3d. $5.00

ERNST, Paul. *Bronze Mermaid.* Pennant P 41. VG. B3d. $4.50

ERNST, Paul. *Hangman's Hat.* Pocket 923. VG. G5d. $4.00

ERNST & LOTH. *American Sexual Behavior & the Kinsey Report.* 1948. Bantam 227. Nfi. VG. B5d. $3.00

ERNSTING & MAHR. *Invasion From Space.* 1970. Ace 65973. SF. VG. P1d. $4.50

ERSKINE, Dorothy. *Pink Hotel.* Crest 227. VG+. B3d. $5.00

ERSKINE, Dorothy. *Pink Hotel.* Crest 405. 2nd prtg. VG+. B3d. $5.00

ERSKINE, John. *Private Life of Helen of Troy.* 1946. Armed Services 994. Fa. G+. P1d. $7.50

ERSKINE, John. *Private Life of Helen of Troy.* 1956. Graphic G 216. Fa. VG. P1d. $8.00

ERSKINE, John. *Private Life of Helen of Troy.* 1948. Popular 147. Fa. VG+. B4d. $26.00

ERSKINE, John. *Private Life of Helen of Troy.* 1948. Popular 147. NF. I1d. $40.00

ERSKINE, Margaret. *Silver Ladies.* 1966. Ace K 270. 1st prtg. My. VG. R5d. $2.00

ERSKINE, Rosalind. *Passion Flower Hotel.* 1963. Cardinal GC 179. NF. VG+. B5d. $3.50

ERSKINE, Sylvia. *Young Nurse.* 1952. Cameo Digest 324. PBO. c/gga. VG+. B6a #77. $55.00

ERSKINE, Sylvia. *Young Nurse.* 1954. Cameo 340. VG+. B3a #24. $41.80

ERTZ, Susan. *Mary Hallam.* 1950. Bantam 789. Fi. VG. P1d. $9.50

ESHBACH, Lloyd Arthur. *Armlet of the Gods.* 1986. Ballantine 32463. 1st edn. SF. F. F2d. $8.00

ESHBACH, Lloyd Arthur. *Land Beyond the Gate.* 1984. Ballantine 31647. 1st edn. SF. F. F2d. $8.00

ESHBACH, Lloyd Arthur. *Of Worlds Beyond.* 1964. Advent. Nfi. VG+. P1d. $20.00

ESHBACH, Lloyd Arthur. *Of Worlds Beyond.* 1970. Advent. 2nd edn. Nfi. F. P1d. $15.00

ESTES, Rose. *Circus of Fear.* 1983. TSR 8510. Endless Quest #10. SF. F. W2d. $3.50

ESTES, Rose. *Dungeon of Dread.* 1983. TSR 8501. 5th prtg. Endless Quest SF. F. W2d. $3.50

ESTES, Rose. *Pillars of Pentagarn.* 1982. TSR 8503. 2nd prtg. Endless Quest. SF. VG. W2d. $3.00

ESTES, Rose. *Return to Brookmere.* 1983. TSR 52745. 5th prtg. Endless Quest #4. SF. VG. W2d. $3.00

ESTEVEN, John. *While Murder Waits.* Popular 343. NF. G5d. $12.50

ESTEY, Dale. *Lost Tale.* 1982. Ace 49525. Fa. VG+. P1d. $4.50

ESTEY, Norbert. *All My Sins.* Crest 133. VG. B3d. $4.50

ESTLEMAN, Loren D. *Sherlock Holmes Vs Dracula.* 1979. Penguin 5262. SF/My. VG. P1d. $7.50

ESTLEMAN, Loren D. *Wolfer.* Pocket 66144. We. G+. G5d. $10.00

ETCHISON, Dennis. *Darkside.* 1986. Charter 13819. F. P9d. $2.00

ETCHISON, Dennis. *Fog.* 1980. Bantam 13825. 1st edn. Ho. F. F2d. $10.00

ETCHISON, Dennis. *Masters of Darkness II.* 1988. TOR 51764. F. P9d. $3.00

ETHAN, John B. *Black Gold Murders.* 1960. Pocket 6013. My. VG. B5d. $3.00

ETHAN, John B. *Murder on Wall Street.* 1962. Pocket 6094. My. VG. B5d. $4.00

EUNSON, Robert. *Mig Alley.* Ace D 365. PBO. VG+. B3d. $5.00

EUSTACE & SAYERS. *Documents in the Case.* 1968. Avon V 2258. My. VG+. B5d. $4.00

EUSTIS, Helen. *Fool Killer.* Pocket 1079. NF. B3d. $6.00

EUSTIS, Helen. *Fool Killer.* 1964. Popular SP 261. 1st prtg. c/photo. VG. P7d. $4.50

EVANS, B. *Short History of English Literature.* 1951. Pelican A 72. 5th edn. Nfi. VG. P1d. $5.00

EVANS, Dean. *This Kill Is Mine.* 1956. Graphic 131. c/gga. My. NF. B4d. $6.00

EVANS, E. Everett. *Man of Many Minds.* 1959. Pyramid G 458. SF. VG+. P1d. $10.50

EVANS, Evan. *Montana Rides Again.* 1952. Signet 935. reprint. We. VG. B4d. $4.00

EVANS, Evan. *Montana Rides!* 1950. Signet 836. 2nd edn. We. VG. B5d. $3.50

EVANS, Evan. *Outlaw Valley.* Pennant P 38. VG+. B3d. $6.00

EVANS, Evan. *Rescue of Broken Arrow.* Bantam 211. VG+. B3d. $5.00

EVANS, Evan. *Rescue of Broken Arrow.* 1949. Bantam 211. c/C Doares. We. VG. B5d. $2.50

EVANS, Evan. *Song of the Whip.* 1953. Signet 1015. 2nd edn. We. VG. B4d. $1.25

EVANS, G. *Murder on Queer Street.* Brandon House 3044. VG+. B3d. $5.00

EVANS, Hodge. *Two Faces of Passion.* 1961. Beacon B443Y. PBO. c/R Johnson. Ad. VG+. B5d. $8.50

EVANS, John. *Lona.* 1952. Lion 94. VG+. B3a #24. $16.50

EVANS, John. *Lona.* 1952. Lion 94. 1st edn. PBO. c/Bergey: gga. scarce. VG+. B6a #79. $48.00

EVANS, John. *Love In the Shadows.* 1955. Avon T 104. 1st pb. VG+. B6d. $7.00

EVANS, Lesley. *Strange Are the Ways of Love.* 1959. Crest S 336. PBO. extremely scarce. VG+. B6a #77. $48.50

EVANS, M. *Rounders.* Bantam 2751. MTI. VG+. B3d. $5.00

EVANS, Peter. *Peter Sellers.* 1980. Signet E 9758. 1st prtg. Bio. VG. R5d. $2.00

EVANS, Robley. *JRR Tolkien.* 1972. Warner 68-988. Nfi. VG. P1d. $5.00

EVANS, Robley. *JRR Tolkien.* 1972. Warner 68-988. VG+. B3d. $6.00

EVARTS, Hal G. *Apache Agent.* Popular 651. VG. B3d. $4.00

EVARTS, Hal G. *Man From Yuma.* Popular G 232. VG+. B3d. $4.00

EVARTS, Hal G. *Settling of the Sage.* 1955. Perma M 3021. c/J Leone. We. VG. B5d. $3.50

EVARTS, Hal G. *Shortgrass.* Popular 279. VG. B3d. $4.00

EVARTS, Hal G. *Shortgrass.* 1950. Popular 279. 1st pb. c/Cherry. We. NF. B6d. $18.00

EVENS, Owen. *Chainlink.* Ballantine 670. c/M Crair. We. VG. B5d. $2.50

EVERARD, Katherine. *Cry Shame!* 1950. Pyramid 23. 1st pb. c/Bennett: gga. VG. B6d. $7.50

EVEREST & GUENTHE. *Fastest Man Alive.* 1959. Pyramid G 373. c/photo. NF. VG. B5d. $4.00

EVERETT, J. *Dark Yearning.* Magenta 320. VG+. B3d. $5.00

EVERETT, M.S. *Hygiene of Marriage.* 1951. Eton 103. Nfi. VG. P6d. $2.50

EVERETT, Peter. *Negatives.* 1968. Crest R 1139. 1st prtg. VG. P7d. $5.00

EVERETT, Wade. *Bullets for the Doctor.* 1965. Ballantine U 1032. We. VG+. B4d. $2.00

EVERETT, Wade. *Last Scout.* 1960. Ballantine 429K. We. VG+. B4d. $3.75

EVERETT, Wade. *Temporary Duty.* Ballantine 554. PBO. VG. B3d. $4.00

EVERETT, Wade. *Vengeance.* 1966. Ballantine U 2260. 1st edn. SF. F. F2d. $10.00

EVERHART, M.G. *Speak No Evil.* Dell 25. VG. B3d. $6.00

EVERHART, Roberta. *Third Paradise.* 1963. Saber SA 44. Ad. G+. B5d. $3.00

EVERHART, Roberta. *Wild Is the Fawn.* 1962. Paragon 156. PBO. VG+. B6d. $9.00

EVSLIN, Bernard. *Merchants of Venus.* 1964. Gold Medal D 1395. Fi. VG. B5d. $5.50

EWEN, David. *Leonard Bernstein.* 1961. Bantam F 2301. 1st prtg. c/photo. VG+. P7d. $4.00

EWERS, C.H. *Sidney Poitier: The Long Journey.* 1974. Signet T 5047. 1st prtg. Bio. VG. R5d. $1.75

EWING, Frederick R. *I, Libertine.* 1956. Ballantine 165. Hi. G+. P1d. $15.00

EWING, Frederick R. *I, Libertine.* 1956. Ballantine 165. 1st prtg. PBO. c/Kelly Freas: gga. scarce. VG. P7d. $17.50

EWING, Frederick R. *I, Libertine.* 1959. Panther 919. VG. B3d. $8.50

EWING, Fredrick R. *I, Libertine.* 1956. Ballantine 165. 1st edn. c/Kelly Freas. scarce. SF. F. F2d. $60.00

EWING, Fredrick R. *I, Libertine.* 1956. Ballantine 165. 1st edn. G+. M1d. $20.00

EXHOLS. *Barb Wire Showdown.* 1950. Readers Choice 10. 1st pb. We. VG. B6d. $6.00

EXLEY, Frederick. *Fan's Notes.* 1969. Ballantine 01705. 1st prtg. c/MacLean: gga. VG. P7d. $4.00

EYLES. *Marx Brothers.* 1971. PB Library 66-587. 1st pb. NF. B6d. $12.50

FABERT, Andre. *Pope Paul VI.* 1963. Monarch K 71. c/photo. Nfi. VG. B5d. $5.00

FABERT, Andre. *Pope Paul VI.* 1963. Monarch K 71. 1st edn. c/photo. F. F2d. $13.00

FABRICANT, Noah. *13 Famous Patients.* 1961. Pyramid R 649. Nfi. VG. P1d. $6.50

FADER, Daniel N. *Hooked on Books.* 1966. Berkley F 1276. PBO. c/photo. Nfi. VG. B5d. $3.50

FADIMAN, Clifton. *Any Number Can Play.* Avon G 1053. Nfi. VG. B5d. $2.50

FADIMAN, Clifton. *Lifetime Reading Plan.* 1961. Avon V 2034. Nfi. VG. P1d. $4.50

FADIMAN, Edwin Jr. *Who Will Watch the Watchers.* 1971. Pyramid V 2499. 1st prtg. NF. P7d. $5.00

FADIMAN, Edwin Jr. *21-Inch Screen.* 1960. Signet S 1716. Fi. VG. B5d. $4.00

FAGALY & SHORTEN. *More There Oughta Be a Law!* Graphic 109. VG+. B3d. $6.00

FAGALY & SHORTEN. *There Oughta Be a Law.* Midwood 4. VG+. B3d. $6.00

FAHERTY, Robert. *Big Old Sun.* 1952. Perma P 179. 1st prtg. c/gga. VG. P7d. $5.00

FAIR, A.A. *Bachelors Get Lonely.* 1963. Pocket 4604. My. VG. B5d. $3.00

FAIR, A.A. *Bats Fly at Dusk.* Dell 1st Edn D 348. c/McGinnis. reprint. My. VG+. B6d. $12.50

FAIR, A.A. *Bats Fly at Dusk.* 1948. Dell 254. VG+. B3d. $8.00

FAIR, A.A. *Bedrooms Have Windows.* 1966. Dell 0511. 1st prtg. c/Abbett: gga. VG. P7d. $4.00

FAIR, A.A. *Bedrooms Have Windows.* Dell 603. NF. I1d. $6.00

FAIR, A.A. *Bedrooms Have Windows.* Dell 603. 1st prtg. My. G. R5d. $1.50

FAIR, A.A. *Bigger They Come.* Pocket 228. VG. G5d. $4.00

FAIR, A.A. *Cats Prowl At Night.* Dell 315. G+. G5d. $5.00

FAIR, A.A. *Count of Nine.* Pocket 6124. VG. G5d. $5.00

FAIR, A.A. *Crows Can't Count.* 1950. Dell 472. 1st pb. c/Stanley. My. VG. B6d. $9.00

FAIR, A.A. *Crows Can't Count.* Dell 778. c/A Sussman. My. VG. B5d. $3.00

FAIR, A.A. *Cut Thin To Win.* Pocket 50412. VG. G5d. $3.50

FAIR, A.A. *Double or Quits.* Dell 160. VG+. B3d. $8.00

FAIR, A.A. *Double or Quits.* 1947. Dell 160. c/Gerald Gregg. scarce. NF. B6a #74. $42.50

FAIR, A.A. *Fish or Cut Bait.* 1966. Pocket 50410. 2nd edn. My. F. B5d. $6.00

FAIR, A.A. *Fools Die on Friday.* Dell R 105. c/McGinnis. reprint. VG+. B3d. $4.50

FAIR, A.A. *Fools Die on Friday.* Dell 542. G. G5d. $3.75

FAIR, A.A. *Give 'Em the Ax.* 1958. Dell 389. My. VG. B5d. $5.00

FAIR, A.A. *Gold Comes in Bricks.* 1961. Dell D 406. c/gga. My. VG. B4d. $2.00

FAIR, A.A. *Gold Comes in Bricks.* Dell 84. VG+. B3d. $8.00

FAIR, A.A. *Gold Comes in Bricks.* Dell 84. 1st prtg. My. G+. R5d. $6.00

FAIR, A.A. *Kept Women Can't Quit.* Pocket 4602. VG. G5d. $5.50

FAIR, A.A. *Kept Women Can't Quit.* 1965. Pocket 50406. 3rd edn. My. VG+. B5d. $3.50

FAIR, A.A. *Owls Don't Blink.* Dell 211. VG+. B3d. $6.50

FAIR, A.A. *Owls Don't Blink.* Dell 243. My. G+. B5d. $4.00

FAIR, A.A. *Pass the Gravy.* 1964. Pocket 45001. 3rd prtg. My. VG. W2d. $3.50

FAIR, A.A. *Pass the Gravy.* Pocket 4601. VG. B3d. $4.00

FAIR, A.A. *Shills Can't Cash Chips.* Pocket 4605. VG. G5d. $5.50

FAIR, A.A. *Some Slips Don't Show.* 1961. Pocket 6095. 1st pb. My. NF. B6d. $7.50

FAIR, A.A. *Some Women Won't Wait.* Dell 809. G+. G5d. $4.00

FAIR, A.A. *Spill the Jackpot.* 1946. Dell 109. 1st pb. c/Frederiksen. My. VG. B6d. $8.00

FAIR, A.A. *Spill the Jackpot.* 1952. Dell 619. 1st prtg. c/gga. VG+. P7d. $5.50

FAIR, A.A. *Top of the Heap.* 1959. Dell D 309. 1st prtg. My. VG. R5d. $2.75

FAIR, A.A. *Top of the Heap.* Dell 772. c/G Foxley. My. VG. B5d. $3.00

FAIR, A.A. *Traps Need Fresh Bait.* Pocket 50413. VG. G5d. $3.75

FAIR, A.A. *Try Anything Once.* 1964. Pocket 4607. My. VG. B4d. $3.00

FAIR, A.A. *Turn on the Heat.* Dell 59. VG. B3d. $8.00

FAIR, A.A. *Turn on the Heat.* Dell 620. G+. G5d. $4.00

FAIR, A.A. *Turn on the Heat.* 1958. New Dell Edition D 253. c/Bob Abbett. VG. P6d. $1.75

FAIR, A.A. *You Can Die Laughing.* 1964. Pocket 45004. 2nd prtg. My. G. W2d. $2.25

FAIR, A.A. *You Can Die Laughing.* Pocket 6062. VG. G5d. $5.00

FAIRBAIRN, Douglas. *Shoot.* 1976. Dell 8077. 1st prtg. G+. R5d. $1.25

FAIRCLOUGH, Peter edt. *Three Gothic Novels.* 1968. Penguin English EL 36. Ho. VG. P1d. $6.00

FAIRLIE, Gerald. *Bulldog Drummond on Dartmoor.* 1941. Th Novel Classic 2. 1st pb. VG. B6d. $3.00

FAIRLY, J.B. *Sex & the Coed.* Gold Star IL 740. VG. I1d. $4.00

FAIRMAN, Paul W. *Bridget Loves Bernie.* 1972. Lancer 74-795. 1st prtg. TVTI. G+. R5d. $2.50

FAIRMAN, Paul W. *City Under the Sea.* 1965. Pyramid R 1162. TVTI. VG. B4d. $6.00

FAIRMAN, Paul W. *Cover Girl.* 1969. MacFadden 75-286. Ad. F. P1d. $7.50

FAIRMAN, Paul W. *Frankenstein Wheel.* Popular Library 01544. VG. B3d. $5.00

FAIRMAN, Paul W. *Ghost of Graveyard Hill.* 1971. Curtis 06147. 1st prtg. G+. R5d. $1.50

FAIRMAN, Paul W. *Glass Ladder.* 1951. Harlequin 139. VG. B3d. $10.00

FAIRMAN, Paul W. *I, the Machine.* 1968. Lancer 73-735. PBO. c/Hoot. SF. VG+. B6d. $7.50

FAIRMAN, Paul W. *Junior Bonner.* 1972. Lancer 75-356. Hi. VG+. P1d. $4.50

FAIRMAN, Paul W. *Lancer.* 1968. Popular Library 60-2349. PBO. TVTI. c/photo. VG. P6d. $3.50

FAIRMAN, Paul W. *Montana Vixen.* 1952. Lion 113. 1st edn. PBO. c/gga. F. F2d. $17.50

FAIRMAN, Paul W. *Playboy.* 1970. MacFadden 75-296. Ad. VG+. P1d. $6.50

FAIRMAN, Paul W. *Search for a Dead Nympho.* 1967. Lancer 73-587. 1st edn. c/photo. My. F. F2d. $7.50

FAIRMAN, Paul W. *That Girl.* 1971. Popular 02588. TVTI. VG. P1d. $6.00

FAIRMAN, Paul W. *Whom the Gods Would Slay.* 1968. Belmont 849. 1st edn. c/Jeff Jones. SF. F. F2d. $12.50

FAIRMAN, Paul W. *World Grabbers.* 1964. Monarch 471. TVTI. VG. B4d/R5d. $8.00

FAIRMAN, Paul W. *World Grabbers.* 1964. Monarch 471. 1st edn. F. M1d. $20.00

FALK, Lee. *Assassins.* 1975. Avon 23283. SF/My. VG. P1d. $5.00

FALK, Lee. *Ghost Who Walks.* 1972. Avon V 2460. PBO. Phantom #1. c/G Wilson. SF. VG. B5d. $7.50

FALK, Lee. *Golden Circle.* Avon 14894. Phantom #5. F. G5d. $10.00

FALK, Lee. *Golden Circle.* Avon 14894. Phantom #5. VG+. G5d. $6.50

FALK, Lee. *Island of Dogs.* 1975. Avon. 1st edn. F. M1d. $10.00

FALK, Lee. *Killer's Town.* 1973. Avon 17731. SF/My. VG. P1d/M6d. $5.00

FALK, Lee. *Mysterious Ambassador.* 1973. Avon 15545. SF/My. F. P1d. $7.50

FALK, Lee. *Scorpio Menace.* 1972. Avon V 2481. Phantom. SF. F. W2d. $7.50

FALK, Lee. *Slave Market of Mucor.* 1972. Avon V 2470. Phantom. SF. F. W2d. $7.50

FALK, Lee. *Story of the Phantom.* 1972. Avon V 2460. SF/My. VG. P1d. $5.00

FALK, Lee. *Vampires & the Witch.* 1974. Avon 19406. SF/My. VG. P1d. $6.00

FALK, Lee. *Veiled Lady.* Avon 14490. Phantom #4. G+. G5d. $4.50

FALKIRK, Richard. *Blackstone.* 1974. Bantam Q 8258. Fa. F. B4d. $4.00

FALKNER, John. *Moonfleet.* Puffin 168. VG. B3d. $6.00

FALKNER, John. *Untrodden Streets of Time.* 1954. Panther 136. SF. G+. P1d. $15.00

FALL, Thomas. *Prettiest Girl in Town.* 1951. Signet 861. 2nd prtg. VG. B3d. $4.50

FALSTEIN, Louis. *Slaughter Street.* Lion LB 172. c/Maguire. reprint. My. NF. B6d. $20.00

FALSTEIN, Louis. *Slaughter Street.* 1953. Lion 151. PBO. c/Marchetti: gga. scarce. NF. B6a #75. $25.00

FALSTEIN, Louis. *Spring of Desire.* 1950. Monarch 112. Fa. VG+. B4d. $12.00

FANTE, John. *Ask the Dust.* 1954. Bantam 1194. c/Schaare. VG+. B3a #24. $15.00

FANTE, John. *Full of Life.* Bantam 1108. VG. B3d. $4.50

FANTE, John. *Full of Life.* Bantam 1574. MTI. VG. B3d. $5.00

FANTHORPE, R.L. *Neuron World.* Badger SN 108. VG. B3d. $9.00

FANTHORPE, R.L. *Space Fury.* 1963. Vega VSF 2. SF. VG. W2d. $6.00

FARBER, James. *Blood Island.* 1981. Pocket 83012. Ho. VG. P1d. $4.00

FARBER & JOSEPHS. *Teen-Age Party & Fun Quiz Book.* 1964. Lancer 72-770. 1st edn. F. F2d. $7.00

FARJEON, Jefferson. *Greenmask.* 1946. Dell 111. G+. G5d. $6.50

FARJEON, Jefferson. *Greenmask.* 1946. Dell 111. 1st edn. PBO. c/Gregg. VG+. B6d. $25.00

FARLEY, Ralph Milne. *Earthman on Venus.* Avon 285. NF. I1d. $75.00

FARLEY, Ralph Milne. *Earthman on Venus.* 1951. Avon 285. SF. F. P1d. $90.00

FARLEY, Ralph Milne. *Earthman on Venus.* 1951. Avon 285. 1st edn. PBO. VG. P9d. $20.00

FARLEY, Ralph Milne. *Radio Beasts.* 1964. Ace F 304. SF. F. M1d. $10.00

FARLEY, Ralph Milne. *Radio Beasts.* 1964. Ace F 304. 1st prtg. PBO. c/Emsh. VG. P7d. $5.00

FARLEY, Ralph Milne. *Radio Planet.* 1964. Ace F 312. SF. F. M1d. $10.00

FARLEY, Ralph Milne. *Radio Planet.* 1964. Ace F 312. 1st prtg. G+. S1d. $3.50

FARLEY, Ralph Milne. *Radio Planet.* 1965. Ace F 312. 1st prtg. PBO. c/Schoenherr. VG+. P7d. $5.50

FARLEY, Ralph Milne. *Radio Planet.* Ace 70320. SF. F. W2d. $4.00

FARMER, Arthur. *Nymph & the Satyr.* 1962. All Star AS 518. SF. VG+. P1d. $10.00

FARMER, Arthur. *Sin Ship.* Private Edition 300. VG+. B3d. $4.50

FARMER, Cindy. *Satan's Mistress.* 1968. Bee Line 338. PBO. NF. B6d. $8.00

FARMER, Philip Jose. *Adventure of the Peerless Peer.* Dell 0042. G+. G5d. $10.00

FARMER, Philip Jose. *Alley God.* Ballantine F 588. PBO. c/R Powers. SF. G+. B5d. $4.50

FARMER, Philip Jose. *Alley God.* 1962. Ballantine F 588. SF. F. P1d. $15.00

FARMER, Philip Jose. *Barnstormer in Oz.* 1982. Berkley 05641. SF. VG. P1d. $5.00

FARMER, Philip Jose. *Behind the Walls of Terra.* 1977. Ace 05357. c/B Vallejo. SF. VG+. B5d. $4.50

FARMER, Philip Jose. *Behind the Walls of Terra.* 1977. Ace 05357. SF. VG. W2d. $3.25

FARMER, Philip Jose. *Behind the Walls of Terra.* 1970. Ace 71135. SF. VG. P1d. $4.50

FARMER, Philip Jose. *Behind the Walls of Terra.* Berkley 7558. 1st prtg. VG+. S1d. $2.00

FARMER, Philip Jose. *Book of Philip Jose Farmer.* 1973. DAW UQ 1063 63. SF. F. P1d. $10.00

FARMER, Philip Jose. *Book of Philip Jose Farmer.* 1973. DAW 63. 1st edn. VG. P9d. $3.50

FARMER, Philip Jose. *Cache.* 1981. Doherty. 1st edn. F. M1d. $8.00

FARMER, Philip Jose. *Gates of Creation.* 1966. Ace F 412. 1st edn. SF. F. F2d. $10.00

FARMER, Philip Jose. *Celestial Blueprint.* Ace F 165. VG+. I1d. $6.00

FARMER, Philip Jose. *Dare.* 1965. Ballantine U 2193. PBO. VG+. B3d. $15.00

FARMER, Philip Jose. *Dare.* 1965. Ballantine 2193. 1st edn. SF. F. F2d/M1d. $20.00

FARMER, Philip Jose. *Dare.* 1979. Berkley 39536. SF. VG. W2d. $3.25

FARMER, Philip Jose. *Dark Design.* 1978. Berkley 03831. SF. VG. P1d. $3.50

FARMER, Philip Jose. *Doc Savage.* 1975. Bantam Q 8834. 1st edn. PBO. NF. P9d. $2.50

FARMER, Philip Jose. *Doc Savage: His Apocalyptic Life.* 1975. Bantam Q 8834. SF/My. VG. P1d. $5.00

FARMER, Philip Jose. *Doc Savage: His Apocalyptic Life.* 1975. Bantam. 1st pb. F. M1d. $10.00

FARMER, Philip Jose. *Doc Savage: His Apocalyptic Life.* 1981. Playboy 16854. 1st prtg. c/Ken Barr. VG. P7d. $5.00

FARMER, Philip Jose. *Down in the Black Gang.* 1971. Signet T 4805. SF. G+. W2d. $3.00

FARMER, Philip Jose. *Down in the Black Gang.* 1971. Signet T 4805. 1st pb. F. M1d. $10.00

FARMER, Philip Jose. *Fabulous Riverboat.* Berkley G 2808. 5th edn. VG+. B3d. $4.00

FARMER, Philip Jose. *Fabulous Riverboat.* 1973. Berkley 02329. SF. F. P1d. $5.00

FARMER, Philip Jose. *Father of the Stars.* 1981. TOR 48504. SF. G+. W2d. $2.75

FARMER, Philip Jose. *Feast Unknown.* 1980. Playboy BB 1027. 1st prtg. c/Enric: gga. VG. P7d. $3.50

FARMER, Philip Jose. *Feast Unknown.* Quartet. c/1st English edn. VG+. B3d. $10.00

FARMER, Philip Jose. *Fire & the Night.* 1962. Regency RB 118. Fi. F. P1d. $75.00

FARMER, Philip Jose. *Fire & the Night.* 1962. Regency RB 118. 1st edn. c/sgn. Av. F. F2d. $60.00

FARMER, Philip Jose. *Flesh.* 1960. Beacon 277. PBO. c/McConnel: sgn. SF. NF. B6a #75. $89.00

FARMER, Philip Jose. *Flesh.* 1960. Galaxy Beacon 277. SF. F. P1d. $75.00

FARMER, Philip Jose. *Flesh.* 1969. Signet. 1st edn. F. M1d. $5.00

FARMER, Philip Jose. *Flight to Opar.* 1976. DAW 197. 1st edn. SF. F. F2d. $12.00

FARMER, Philip Jose. *Flight to Opar.* 1976. DAW 197. 1st prtg. PBO. c/Krenkel. VG. P7d/S1d. $7.50

FARMER, Philip Jose. *Gate of Time.* 1966. Belmont B50-717. SF. F. P1d. $15.00

FARMER, Philip Jose. *Gate of Time.* 1966. Belmont 50-717. PBO. VG. B3d. $6.00

FARMER, Philip Jose. *Gates of Creation.* 1966. Ace F 412. SF. F. P1d. $11.00

FARMER, Philip Jose. *Gates of Creation.* 1966. Ace F 412. 1st edn. G. P9d. $2.00

FARMER, Philip Jose. *Gates of Creation.* Ace 27387. SF. VG. B5d. $5.00

FARMER, Philip Jose. *Gates of Creation.* Berkley 7193. 1st prtg. VG+. S1d. $2.00

FARMER, Philip Jose. *Green Odyssey.* 1967. Ballantine U 2345. SF. VG+. B4d. $2.00

FARMER, Philip Jose. *Green Odyssey.* 1957. Ballantine 210. PBO. c/R Powers. SF. VG. B5d. $16.50

FARMER, Philip Jose. *Hadon of Ancient Opar.* 1974. DAW UY 1107 100. SF. F. P1d/S1d. $7.50

FARMER, Philip Jose. *Hadon of Ancient Opar.* 1974. DAW UY 1107 100. SF. VG. W2d. $3.50

FARMER, Philip Jose. *Image of the Beast.* 1968. Essex House 0108. SF. VG. P1d. $175.00

FARMER, Philip Jose. *Image of the Beast.* 1976. Quartet. NF. M1d. $8.00

FARMER, Philip Jose. *Inside Outside.* Ballantine U 2192. VG. B3d. $5.00

FARMER, Philip Jose. *Inside Outside.* 1964. Ballantine U 2192. SF. F. M1d/P1d. $15.00

FARMER, Philip Jose. *Ironcastle.* 1976. DAW 187. 1st edn. SF. F. F2d. $12.00

FARMER, Philip Jose. *Ironcastle.* 1976. DAW 187. 1st prtg. VG+. S1d. $3.00

FARMER, Philip Jose. *Jesus on Mars.* 1979. Pinnacle 40-184. SF. VG. P1d. $4.00

FARMER, Philip Jose. *Lavalite World.* Ace 47420. PBO. c/B Vallejo. SF. VG+. B5d. $4.00

FARMER, Philip Jose. *Lavalite World.* 1977. Ace 47420. SF. F. P1d. $5.00

FARMER, Philip Jose. *Lavalite World.* 1977. Ace 47420. SF. VG. W2d. $3.50

FARMER, Philip Jose. *Lord Tyger.* 1972. Signet Q 5096. SF. F. P1d. $7.50

FARMER, Philip Jose. *Lovers.* 1980. Ballantine 28691. 1st prtg. c/Les Katz: gga. VG. P7d. $3.50

FARMER, Philip Jose. *Lovers.* 1961. Ballantine 507. PBO. VG. B3d. $8.00

FARMER, Philip Jose. *Lovers.* 1961. Ballantine 507. 1st edn. c/sgn. SF. F. F2d. $25.00

FARMER, Philip Jose. *Lovers.* 1961. Ballantine 507. 1st edn. NF. M1d. $20.00

FARMER, Philip Jose. *Lovers.* 1961. Ballantine 507K. SF. VG+. P1d. $15.00

FARMER, Philip Jose. *Magic Labyrinth.* 1981. Berkley 04854. SF. VG. P1d. $5.00

FARMER, Philip Jose. *Maker of Universes.* 1965. Ace F 367. F. M1d. $15.00

FARMER, Philip Jose. *Maker of Universes.* 1965. Ace F 367. SF. VG. P1d. $5.50

FARMER, Philip Jose. *Maker of Universes.* 1965. Ace F 367. 1st edn. c/sgn. SF. F. F2d. $25.00

FARMER, Philip Jose. *Maker of Universes.* 1965. Ace F 367. 1st prtg. PBO. c/Gaughan: gga. VG+. P7d. $9.00

FARMER, Philip Jose. *Maker of Universes.* Ace 51621. SF. VG. W2d. $3.75

FARMER, Philip Jose. *Night of Light.* 1966. Berkely 1248. VG. B3d. $6.00

FARMER, Philip Jose. *Night of Light.* 1966. Berkley 1248. SF. F. P1d. $12.50

FARMER, Philip Jose. *Night of Light.* 1972. Berkley S 2249. 2nd edn. VG. P9d. $1.50

FARMER, Philip Jose. *No Limits.* 1964. Ballantine. 1st edn. VG. M1d. $10.00

FARMER, Philip Jose. *Other Log of Phileas Fogg.* 1973. DAW UQ 1048 48. SF. F. P1d. $12.50

FARMER, Philip Jose. *Private Cosmos.* 1968. Ace G 724. SF. VG. P1d. $5.00

FARMER, Philip Jose. *Private Cosmos.* 1968. Ace G 724. 1st edn. SF. F. F2d/M1d. $15.00

FARMER, Philip Jose. *Private Cosmos.* 1970. Sphere 34517. SF. G+. P1d. $3.25

FARMER, Philip Jose. *Purple Book.* 1982. TOR 48-529. SF. VG. P1d. $3.50

FARMER, Philip Jose. *Riverworld & Other Stories.* 1979. Berkley 04208. SF. VG. P1d. $3.50

FARMER, Philip Jose. *Riverworld & Other Stories.* 1979. Berkley 04208. SF. VG+. W2d. $3.75

FARMER, Philip Jose. *Stone God Awakens.* 1970. Ace 78650. SF. VG. P1d. $4.50

FARMER, Philip Jose. *Stone God Awakens.* 1980. Ace 78654. 3rd prtg. SF. VG. W2d. $4.25

FARMER, Philip Jose. *Strange Relations.* Avon 41418. 3rd edn. SF. F. P1d. $4.00

FARMER, Philip Jose. *Strange Relations.* 1960. Ballantine 391K. 1st edn. NF. M1d. $15.00

FARMER, Philip Jose. *Strange Relations.* 1960. Ballantine 391K. 1st pb. VG. M6d. $9.50

FARMER, Philip Jose. *Tarzan Alive.* 1981. Playboy 16876. Fa. VG. P1d. $3.50

FARMER, Philip Jose. *Tarzan Alive.* Popular. 1st pb. NF. M1d. $10.00

FARMER, Philip Jose. *Time's Last Gift.* 1972. Ballantine 02468. SF. VG. P1d. $4.00

FARMER, Philip Jose. *Timestop!* 1970. Lancer 74616. c/Gene Szafran. SF. VG. B4d. $4.50

FARMER, Philip Jose. *Timestop!* 1970. Lancer 74616. SF. F. P1d. $6.00

FARMER, Philip Jose. *To Your Scattered Bodies Go.* 1971. Berkley S 2057. SF. VG. P1d. $4.00

FARMER, Philip Jose. *To Your Scattered Bodies Go.* 1971. Berkley S 2057. 1st prtg. G+. S1d. $3.00

FARMER, Philip Jose. *Tongues of the Moon.* 1978. Jove A 4595. SF. VG+. P1d. $4.50

FARMER, Philip Jose. *Tongues of the Moon.* 1964. Pyramid F 1055. PBO. c/E Emsh. SF. VG. B5d. $12.50

FARMER, Philip Jose. *Traitor to the Living.* 1973. Ballantine 23613. PBO. c/H Ulrich & U Osterwalder. SF. VG. B5d. $4.50

FARMER, Philip Jose. *Traitor to the Living.* 1973. Ballantine 23613. SF. F. P1d. $15.00

FARMER, Philip Jose. *Two Hawks From Earth.* 1979. Ace 83365. SF. VG. P1d. $3.50

FARMER, Philip Jose. *Venus on the Half-Shell.* 1975. Dell 6149. 1st edn. SF. F. F2d. $20.00

FARMER, Philip Jose. *Venus on the Half-Shell.* 1976. Dell. 5th edn. NF. M1d. $3.00

FARMER, Philip Jose. *Wind Whales of Ishmael.* 1971. Ace 89237. SF. F. P1d. $5.00

FARMER, Philip Jose. *Woman a Day.* 1960. Beacon 291. PBO. c/McConnel: sgn. SF. NF. B6a #75. $72.00

FARMER, Phillip Jose. *Flesh.* 1960. Beacon 277. VG. B3a #22. $40.00

FARMER/FARMER. *Cache From Outer Space/Celestial Blueprint.* 1962. Ace F 165. 1st prtg. PBO. VG+. P7d. $7.50

FARMER/FARMER. *Mad Goblin/Lord of the Trees.* 1970. Ace 51375. SF. VG. P1d. $7.50

FARR, John. *She-Shark.* Ace S 159. VG. B3d. $5.00

FARR/TRIMBLE. *Lady & the Snake/Nothing To Lose But My Life.* 1957. Ace D 235. My. VG. P1d. $10.00

FARRAR, Larston D. *Washington Lowdown.* 1956. Signet 1300. Nfi. VG. B4d. $3.00

FARRAR, Margaret edt. *Daily Puzzles Crosswords From the Times, Series 11.* 1965. Pocket 50158. Nfi. VG. B5d. $3.00

FARRAR, Stewart. *Twelve Maidens.* 1976. Arrow 912020. Ho. F. P1d. $6.00

FARRE, Rowena. *Seal Morning.* 1962. Ace K 146. 1st pb. VG. B6d. $5.00

FARRELL, Cliff. *California Passage.* Popular EB 98. VG+. B3d. $4.50

FARRELL, Cliff. *Follow the New Grass.* Bantam 1502. 1st pb. VG. M6d. $4.00

FARRELL, Henry. *Death on the 6th Day.* 1963. Avon G 1157. 1st pb. My/Ho. VG. B6d. $7.50

FARRELL, Henry. *Whatever Happened to Baby Jane?* 1960. Avon G 1146. 1st pb. MTI. VG. B6d. $7.50

FARRELL, James T. *Bernard Carr.* 1951. Signet S 893. c/Avati: gga. Fa. VG. B4d. $3.00

FARRELL, James T. *Dangerous Woman.* 1957. Signet S 1457. c/Avati: gga. VG+. B4d. $4.00

FARRELL, James T. *Father & Son.* 1953. Signet D 1066. 1st pb. c/Avati. VG+. B6d. $15.00

FARRELL, James T. *French Girls Are Vicious.* 1956. Signet 1349. Fi. VG. B5d. $4.00

FARRELL, James T. *French Girls Are Vicious.* 1956. Signet 1349. 1st edn. PBO. NF. F2d. $7.00

FARRELL, James T. *Gas-House McGinty.* Avon 290. NF. B3d. $8.00

FARRELL, James T. *Gas-House McGinty.* 1958. Crest S 200. 1st prtg. c/Barye: gga. VG+. P7d. $6.00

FARRELL, James T. *Looking 'Em Over.* Panther 1136. VG. B3d. $6.00

FARRELL, James T. *My Days of Anger.* 1954. Signet S 1118. 1st pb. c/Avati. VG. B6d. $9.00

FARRELL, James T. *Saturday Night.* 1952. Signet 831. c/Avati: gga. Fa. VG+. B3d. $5.50

FARRELL, James T. *This Man & This Woman.* Signet 1158. c/Avati. VG. B3d. $4.00

FARRELL, James T. *Yesterday's Love.* 1948. Avon 157. c/M Bouldin: gga. VG. P6d. $5.00

FARRELL, James T. *Yesterday's Love.* 1950. Avon 260. c/gga. VG+. B4d. $7.00

FARRELL, James T. *Yesterday's Love.* 1952. Avon 475. 4th edn. c/R Nappi. Fi. VG. B5d. $5.50

FARRELL, James T. *Young Lonigan.* Signet 643. c/Peng. VG. B3d. $6.00

FARRELL, James T. *Young Manhood of Studs Lonigan.* 1950. Signet 810. 1st prtg. c/Avati. VG. P7d. $6.00

FARRELL, M. *Fruit Town.* First Niter 112A. VG. B3d. $5.00

FARREN, Julian. *Train From Pittsburgh.* 1952. Popular 428. c/gga. Fa. VG. B4d. $4.00

FARREN, Mick. *Neural Atrocity.* 1977. Mayflower 12603. SF. G+. P1d. $5.00

FARREN, Mick. *Quest of the DNA Cowboys.* 1976. Mayflower 12448. SF. VG. P1d. $7.50

FARREN, Mick. *Texts of Festival.* 1975. Mayflower 12301. SF. VG. P1d. $6.00

FARRERE, Claude. *Black Opium.* 1958. Berkley G 120. Fa. VG+. P1d. $75.00

FARRERE, Claude. *Black Opium.* 1958. Berkley G 120. 1st edn. PBO. c/Bob Maguire: gga. VG. B6a #75. $56.00

FARRERE, Claude. *Black Opium.* 1958. Berkley G 120. 1st edn. PBO. c/Maguire: gga. VG. B6a #79. $71.50

FARRINGTON, Fielden. *Street of Brass.* 1961. Hillman 203. c/gga. F. F2d. $7.50

FARRINGTON, Robert. *Balboa.* Avon G 1149. VG. B3d. $4.00

FARRIS, John. *All Heads Turn When the Hunt Goes By.* 1977. Popular 04360. Ho. VG. P1d. $4.00

FARRIS, John. *Captors.* 1971. New English 2889. SF/My. VG. P1d. $4.00

FARRIS, John. *Corpse Next Door.* 1956. Graphic 138. c/gga. My. VG+. B4d. $8.00

FARRIS, John. *Corpse Next Door.* 1956. Graphic 138. 1st edn. Ho. F. F2d. $25.00

FARRIS, John. *Fury.* 1978. Popular 08620. SF. VC. W2d. $4.50

FARRIS, John. *Harrison High.* 1959. Dell F 90. c/Maquire. VG+. B3d. $5.50

FARRIS, John. *Harrison High.* 1965. Dell 3448. 1st prtg. c/Maguire: gga. VG. P7d. $4.00

FARRIS, John. *Sharp Practice.* 1976. Futura 7314. SF/My. VG. P1d. $4.00

FARRIS, John. *Trouble at Harrison High.* 1971. New English 00990. Fi. G. P1d. $2.00

FARRIS, John. *Trouble at Harrison High.* 1970. Pocket 75486. 1st edn. Ho. F. F2d. $10.00

FARRIS, John. *When Michael Calls.* 1969. Pocket 77112. 2nd edn. SF/My. VG. P1d. $3.50

FAST, Howard. *Citizen Tom Paine.* 1946. Bantam 30. Fa. VG+. B3d. $6.00

FAST, Howard. *Edge of Tomorrow.* 1961. Bantam A 2254. SF. VG. P1d. $6.50

FAST, Howard. *Edge of Tomorrow.* 1961. Bantam A 2254. 1st edn. F. M1d. $8.00

FAST, Howard. *Establishment.* 1980. Dell. advance reading copy. Hi. VG. P1d. $20.00

FAST, Howard. *Freedom Road.* 1946. Pocket 382. Hi. F. P1d. $21.00

FAST, Howard. *Last Frontier.* 1949. Avon 205. Hi. VG. P1d. $9.50

FAST, Howard. *Last Frontier.* 1949. Pocket 322. VG+. B3d. $5.00

FAST, Howard. *Mirage.* Crest 808. MTI. VG. B3d. $4.50

FAST, Howard. *My Glorious Brothers.* Panther 1123. VG. B3d. $8.00

FAST, Howard. *Patrick Henry & the Frigate's Keel.* Armed Services 787. VG+. B3d. $5.50

FAST, Howard. *Spartacus.* 1960. Bantam H 1985. Hi. VG. P1d. $7.00

FAST, Howard. *Touch of Infinity.* 1974. DAW 124. c/C Gross. SF. VG. B5d. $3.00

FAST, Howard. *Unvanquished.* 1967. Bantam S 3343. Hi. F. P1d. $10.00

FAST, Jonathan. *Mortal Gods.* 1979. Signet E 8573. SF. VG. P1d. $3.50

FAST, Jonathan. *Secrets of Synchronicity.* 1977. Signet W 7556. SF. VG. P1d. $3.50

FAST, Julius. *And Then Murder.* Hillman 126. VG. B3d. $4.50

FAST, Julius. *Beatles: The Real Story.* 1968. Berkley S 1653. Nfi. VG. P1d. $10.00

FAST, Julius. *League of Grey-Eyed Women.* 1971. Pyramid N 2574. SF. VG. P1d. $4.00

FAST, Julius. *Out of This World.* 1944. Signet 537. 4th prtg. c/Peng. VG. B3d. $4.50

FASTER, Gerald. *Virgin Barfly.* 1950. Quarter Book 57. 1st edn. PBO. c/George Gross: gga. VG+. B6a #77. $85.00

FATIMAN, Clifton. *Any Number Can Play.* Avon G 1053. Nfi. VG. B5d. $2.50

FAUCETT & RANDALL. *Lord of Cragsclaw.* 1989. Bantam 27462. Fa. F. P1d. $5.00

FAUCETTE, John. *Siege of Earth.* 1971. Belmont B95-2194. SF. F. P1d. $7.50

FAUCETTE, John. *Warriors of Terra.* 1970. Belmont B75-2002. SF. VG. P1d. $4.50

FAUCETTE & LISS. *Monkees.* Popular 50-8026. 1st edn. TVTI. c/photo. scarce. F. F2d. $15.00

FAUCETTE & LISS. *Monkees.* Popular 50-8026. TVTI. c/photos. VG+. B4d. $8.00

FAUCETTE/REYNOLDS. *Age of Ruin/Code Duello.* 1968. Ace H 103. 1st prtg. SF. VG. R5d. $2.25

FAULKNER, John. *Ain't Gonna Rain No More.* Gold Medal 927. PBO. c/Hooks. VG. M6d. $7.50

FAULKNER, John. *Cabin Road.* Gold Medal 178. VG. B3d. $3.50

FAULKNER, John. *Dollar Cotton.* Bantam 972. VG+. B3d. $7.00

FAULKNER, John. *Uncle Good's Weekend Party.* Gold Medal 1031. c/Barye. VG+. B3d. $7.00

FAULKNER, William. *Intruder in the Dust.* Signet 743. c/Avati. VG. B3d. $5.00

FAULKNER, William. *Knight's Gambit.* Signet 1315. 3rd prtg. VG. B3d. $4.00

FAULKNER, William. *Long Hot Summer.* 1958. Signet S 1501. MTI. VG+. B4d. $9.00

FAULKNER, William. *Mosquitoes.* Avon 12. G+. B3d. $5.00

FAULKNER, William. *Old Man.* 1948. Signet 692. c/R Jonas. Fi. VG. B3d. $6.00

FAULKNER, William. *Plyon.* 1951. Signet 863. Fi. VG. B5d. $4.00

FAULKNER, William. *Pylon.* 1958. Signet S 1485. 2nd edn. MTI. c/R Hudson & D Malone: photo. Fi. VG. B5d. $4.00

FAULKNER, William. *Sanctuary.* Signet 632. VG. B3d. $4.50

FAULKNER, William. *Soldiers' Pay.* 1952. Signet 887. 3rd edn. c/J Avati. Fi. VG+. B5d. $5.50

FAULKNER, William. *Sound & the Fury.* Four Square 113. 2nd prtg. MTI. VG. B3d. $6.00

FAULKNER, William. *Sound & the Fury.* 1959. Signet D 1628. MTI. c/Brynner & Woodward: photo. VG+. B4d. $3.00

FAULKNER, William. *Unvanquished.* Signet 977. VG+. I1d. $5.00

FAULKNER, William. *Wild Palms.* 1948. Penguin 659. 1st pb. VG+. B6d. $9.00

FAULKNER/FAULKNER. *Sanctuary/Requiem for a Nun.* 1954. Signet S 1079. c/Avati: gga. Fa. VG. B4d. $4.00

FAULKNER/FAULKNER. *Wild Palms/Old Man.* 1954. Signet S 1148. c/J Avati. Fi. VG. B5d. $4.00

FAURE, Raoul C. *Lady Godiva & Master Tom.* 1949. Bantam 469. c/gga. Fa. VG+. B4d. $5.00

FAY, Jerry. *Beverly Hillbillies.* 1965. Avon G 1250. 1st edn. TVTI. scarce. c/photo. F. F2d. $35.00

FAYE, Sheila. *Switch Partners.* 1963. Midwood F 344. PBO. VG+. B6d. $12.50

FEARING, Kenneth. *Big Clock.* 1949. Bantam 738. 1st prtg. My. G+. R5d. $2.25

FEARING, Kenneth. *Cry Killer (Dagger of the Mind).* Avon 823. G+. G5d. $5.50

FEARING, Kenneth. *Dagger of the Mind.* 1947. Bantam 93. My. VG+. B4d. $8.00

FEARN, John Russell. *Conquest of the Amazon.* 1976. Orbit 7858. SF. VG. P1d. $4.00

FEARN, John Russell. *Deathless Amazon.* 1955. Harlequin 320. VG+. B3a #22. $85.95

FEARN, John Russell. *Golden Amazon.* 1953. Harlequin 218. SF. VG. P1d. $150.00

FEARN, John Russell. *Golden Amazon.* 1953. Harlequin 218. 1st edn. PBO. c/Soik. scarce. SF. VG+. B6a #79. $110.00

FEARN, John Russell. *Golden Amazon's Truimph.* 1958. Harlequin 421. SF. VG. P1d. $150.00

FEARN, John Russell. *Golden Amazon's Truimph.* 1958. Harlequin 421. VG. B3a #21. $73.25

FEARN, John Russell. *Slaves of Ijax.* 1947. Kaner. c/Perl. SF. VG+. B3d. $6.00

FEDER & JOESTEN. *Luciano Story.* Popular G 155. VG. B3d. $4.00

FEDER & JOESTEN. *Luciano Story.* Popular G 417. reprint. VG. B6d. $5.00

FEDER & JOESTEN. *Luciano Story.* Popular SP 177. VG+. B3d. $5.00

FEDER & TURKUS. *Murder, Inc.* 1952. Perma P 187. 1st pb. Cr. VG. B6d. $5.00

FEDERBUSH, Arnold. *Man Who Lived in Inner Space.* 1975. Bantam Q 8794. SF. VG+. P1d. $4.50

FEHRENBACH, T.R. *Battle of Anzio.* 1962. Monarch MA 317. Nfi. VG. B5d. $4.00

FEHRENBACH, T.R. *US Marines in Action.* Monarch 319. VG. B3d. $4.50

FEIFFER, Jules. *Ackroyd.* Avon 39347. VG. G5d. $6.00

FEIFFER, Jules. *Harry, the Rat With Women.* 1964. Avon S 153. 1st pb. VG+. B6d. $7.50

FEIFFER, Jules. *Little Murders.* 1971. PB Library 64-521. MTI. c/photo. VG. P6d. $1.50

FEINMAN, Jeffrey. *Mysterious World of Agatha Christie.* 1975. Award AR 1489. Nfi. VG+. P1d. $4.50

FEINMAN, Jeffrey. *Mysterious World of Agatha Christie.* 1975. Award AR 1489. 1st prtg. Bio. VG. R5d. $2.50

FEINMAN, Jeffrey. *TV Superstars.* 1977. Xerox. TVTI. VG. P1d. $5.00

FEISEN, Henry. *Medic Mirth.* 1956. Ace S 152. PBO. c/H Williams. Nfi. VG. B5d. $8.00

FEISONG, Ruth. *Deadlock.* Dell 808. 1st pb. VG. M6d. $4.00

FEIST, Raymond. *Magician: Apprentice.* 1986. Bantam. 1st pb. F. M1d. $5.00

FELDMAN, Gene edt. *Beat Generation & Angry Young Men.* Panther 1075. VG. B3d. $6.00

FELDSTEIN, Albert. *Mad Sampler.* 1965. Signet D 2627. Hu. VG+. B4d. $3.00

FELDSTEIN, Albert. *Portable Mad.* Signet 4222. VG+. B3d. $5.00

FELLER, Bob. *Strike Out Story.* Bantam 501. VG. B3d. $5.00

FELSEN, Henry Gregor. *Hot Rod.* 1951. Bantam 923. NF. I1d. $5.00

FELSEN, Henry Gregor. *Hot Rod.* 1951. Bantam 923. 1st prtg. My. VG. R5d. $3.25

FELSEN, Henry Gregor. *Medic Mirth.* 1956. Ace S 152. PBO. c/H Williams. Nfi. VG. B5d. $8.00

FELSEN, Henry Gregor. *Road Rocket.* 1961. Bantam A 2315. JD. G+. P1d. $7.50

FELSEN, Henry Gregor. *Street Rod.* 1956. Bantam 1437. 1st prtg. VG. P7d. $4.00

FELSEN, Henry Gregor. *Two & the Town.* 1953. Pennant P20. Fi. VG. B5d. $5.00

FENADY, A.J. *Man With Bogart's Face.* Avon 36476. VG+. B3d. $4.50

FENISONG, Ruth. *Deadlock.* Dell 808. c/J McDermott. My. VG. B5d. $3.00

FENISONG, Ruth. *Death Is a Lovely Lady (Jenny Kissed Me).* Popular 173. VG+. G5d. $7.50

FENISONG, Ruth. *Death of the Party.* 1959. Zenith 17. 1st pb edn. F. F2d. $20.00

FENISONG/FENISONG. *But Not Forgotten/Schemers.* 1963. Ace G 508. My. VG. B4d. $2.50

FENTON, Charles. *Conduct Unbecoming.* 1954. Dell 1st Edn 19. PBO. c/Powell: gga. VG. B3d. $4.50

FENWICK, E.P. *Inconvenient Corpse.* 1946. Pony 62. G. P6d. $1.00

FERBER, Edna. *American Beauty.* Signet 650. VG+. B3d. $6.00

FERBER, Edna. *Giant.* 1962. Cardinal GC 144. Fa. NF. B4d. $3.25

FERBER, Edna. *Nobody's in Town.* Avon 51. VG. B3d. $5.00

FERBER, Edna. *Show Boat.* 1962. Cardinal GC 123. Fi. VG+. B5d. $3.50

FERBER, Edna. *They Brought Their Women.* 1944. Avon Murder My 19. Fi. G+. B5d. $2.50

FERBER, Edna. *They Brought Their Women.* Avon 19 Digest 49. Fa. VG+. B4d. $3.50

FERBER, Edna. *Trees Die at the Top.* Dell 10¢ 10. VG+. B3d. $6.00

FERGUSON, J.H. *Why Can't We Have a Baby?* Pyramid 256. VG. B3d. $4.00

FERGUSON, Margaret. *Sign of the Ram.* 1948. Bantam 158. MTI. c/S Peters: photo. Fi. VG. B5d. $4.00

FERGUSON, W.B.M. *Pilditch Puzzle.* 1946. Trophy Books 402. VG. B3a #20. $23.15

FERM, Betty. *False Idols.* 1975. Crest P 2453. Ho. VG+. P1d. $5.50

FERMAN, Edward L. edt. *Best From Fantasy & SF, 16th Series.* Ace 05455. SF. VG+. B5d. $4.00

FERMAN, Joseph W. edt. *No Limits.* 1964. Ballantine U 2220. SF. VG+. P1d. $9.00

FERNANDEZ-FLOREZ, Dario. *Dharma Bums.* 1959. Signet D 1718. VG. B4d. $10.00

FERNANDEZ-FLOREZ, Dario. *Lola, a Dark Mirror.* 1959. Signet D 1678. c/gga. Fa. VG. B4d. $2.50

FERRARS, E.X. *March Hare Murders.* 1950. Pocket 735. G+. G5d. $6.50

FERRARS, E.X. *March Hare Murders.* 1950. Pocket 735. 1st pb. My. VG+. B6d. $12.50

FERSEN, Nicholas. *Tombolo.* Popular EB 36. VG+. B3d. $4.50

FESSIER, Michael. *Fully Dressed & in His Right Mind.* Lion 214. VG. I1d. $15.00

FESSIER, Michael. *Fully Dressed & in His Right Mind.* 1954. Lion 214. 1st edn. PBO. c/gga. scarce. VG+. B6a #79. $44.00

FEUCHTWANGER, Lion. *Jew Suss.* 1951. Avon D 1001. VG. P6d. $6.00

FEUCHTWANGER, Lion. *Ugly Duchess.* 1951. Avon 313. c/gga. Fa. VG+. B4d. $13.00

FICKLING, G.G. *Blood & Honey.* 1961. Pyramid G 623. PBO. c/gga. B6a #74. $66.00

FICKLING, G.G. *Blood & Honey.* Pyramid R 1340. NF. I1d. $4.00

FICKLING, G.G. *Dig a Dead Doll.* 1960. Pyramid G 560. PBO. c/gga. NF. B6a #74. $44.00

FICKLING, G.G. *Dig a Dead Doll.* 1966. Pyramid R 1355. 2nd edn. TVTI. c/Anne Francis: photo. VG+. B4d. $3.00

FICKLING, G.G. *Girl on the Loose.* 1958. Pyramid G 366. c/gga. My. VG+. B4d. $9.00

FICKLING, G.G. *Girl on the Loose.* 1965. Pyramid R 1356. 2nd edn. TVTI. reprint. VG+. B4d. $3.25

FICKLING, G.G. *Girl on the Prowl.* 1959. Pyramid G 453. PBO. c/gga. NF. B6a #74. $44.00

FICKLING, G.G. *Girl on the Prowl.* 1965. Pyramid R 1339. 2nd prtg. G+. R5d. $1.25

FICKLING, G.G. *Gun for Honey.* 1965. Pyramid R 1167. 2nd edn. MTI. c/photo. VG+. B4d. $2.25

FICKLING, G.G. *Honey in the Flesh.* 1965. Pyramid R 1359. 3rd edn. TVTI. c/Anne Francis: photo. reprint. VG+. B4d. $4.00

FICKLING, G.G. *Kiss for a Killer.* 1960. Pyramid G 520. c/gga. NF. B6a #74. $44.00

FICKLING, G.G. *Naughty But Dead.* 1962. Belmont 91 252. PBO. My. VG. P6d. $2.25

FICKLING, G.G. *This Girl for Hire.* 1965. Pyramid R 1360. 5th prtg. TVTI. c/photo. My. VG. P6d. $4.00

FIELD, Medora. *Blood on Her Shoe.* 1949. Popular 201. VG+. I1d. $12.00

FIELD, Medora. *Blood on Her Shoe.* 1949. Popular 201. 1st edn. PBO. c/Belarski: gga. scarce. NF. B6a #75. $42.00

FIELD, Peter. *Coyote Gulch.* 1954. Pocket 990. 1st pb. c/Hulings. We. NF. B6d. $12.50

FIELD, Peter. *Dig the Spurs Deep.* 1964. Pocket 6231. We. VG. B5d. $3.00

FIELD, Peter. *Doctor Two-Guns.* 1954. Pocket 982. c/L Kimmel. We. VG. B5d. $3.50

FIELD, Peter. *End of the Trail.* 1952. Pocket 902. c/E Bergey. We. VG. B5d. $5.00

FIELD, Peter. *Guns From Powder Valley.* Bantam 68. VG. B3d. $4.50

FIELD, Peter. *Hell's Corner.* 1950. Bantam 775. We. VG. B4d. $2.75

FIELD, Peter. *Land Grabber.* 1949. Bantam 210. We. VG+. B4d. $6.00

FIELD, Peter. *Law Badge.* 1954. Pocket 1027. c/R Schultz. We. VG+. B5d. $5.50

FIELD, Peter. *Midnight Round-Up.* 1950. Pocket 711. c/R Brown. We. VG. B5d. $4.00

FIELD, Peter. *Outlaw of Castle Canyon.* 1965. Pocket 50197. We. VG+. B5d. $3.50

FIELD, Peter. *Outlaw of Eagle's Nest.* 1954. Pocket 1035. 1st pb. We. VG+. B6d. $10.00

FIELD, Peter. *Powder Valley Holdup.* 1962. Pocket 6116. We. VG+. B5d. $4.00

FIELD, Peter. *Powder Valley Pay-Off.* 1947. Bantam 104. We. VG. B5d. $3.00

FIELD, Peter. *Rawhide Rider.* 1966. Pocket 50236. We. VG+. B5d. $4.00

FIELD, Peter. *Ride for Trinidad!* 1964. Pocket 35001. We. VG+. B5d. $3.50

FIELD, Peter. *Smoking Iron.* Pocket 847. VG+. B3d. $4.50

FIELD. *Bedroom Panthers.* 1965. Playtime 716. PBO. NF. B6d. $20.00

FIELDING, William H. *Unpossessed.* 1951. Gold Medal 202. PBO. c/Kampen. VG. B6d. $7.50

FIELDING, William J. *Strange Superstitions & Magical.* 1966. PB Library 53-341. Nfi. VG. P1d. $5.50

FIELDS, Alonzo. *My 21 Years in the White House.* 1961. Crest D 492. Bio. NF. B4d. $3.00

FIELDS, Vin. *Highest Bidder.* 1965. Midwood 32-468. 1st edn. c/gga. VG+. F2d. $7.00

FIELDS, W.C. *Fields for President.* Dell 2525. NF. I1d. $6.00

FIENBURGH, W. *No Love for Johnnie.* Arrow 606. MTI. VG. B3d. $5.00

FIGGIS, Darrell. *Return of the Hero.* 1930. Boni-Books. Fa. G+. P1d. $15.00

FILLMORE, Paul. *Sex-Starved Debutante.* 1971. Bee Line 5064-T. Ad. NF. B5d. $10.00

FILS, C. *My Bachelor's Life.* Belmont 75-204. VG+. B3d. $5.00

FINCH, C. *Rainbow: Stormy Life of Judy Garland.* 1976. Ballantine 25173. 2nd prtg. Bio. VG. R5d. $2.50

FINCH, Sheila. *Infinite Web.* 1985. Bantam. 1st edn. F. M1d. $5.00

FINDLAY, D.K. *Northern Affair.* 1964. Popular 50069. Fa. VG. B4d. $1.25

FINDLEY, Ferguson. *My Old Man's Badge.* 1951. Popular 324. 1st edn. PBO. c/gga. scarce. NF. B6a #75. $44.00

FINDLEY, Ferguson. *Waterfront.* Popular 408. VG. B3d. $5.50

FINDLEY, Ferguson. *Waterfront.* 1952. Popular 408. 1st edn. PBO. c/gga. scarce. NF. B6a #80. $45.00

FINE, Benjamin. *1,000,000 Delinquents.* 1957. Signet D 1368. JD. VG+. P1d. $16.50

FINK, Harry Julian. *Major Dundee.* 1965. Gold Medal K 1519. MTI. c/Charlton Heston. VG+. B4d. $3.75

FINLAY, D.G. *Edge of Tomorrow.* 1979. Star 30407. SF. VG. P1d. $4.00

FINNEGAN, Robert. *Bandaged Nude.* Signet 1379. reprint. My. VG+. B6d. $12.00

FINNEGAN, Robert. *Bandaged Nude.* Signet 807. VG. G5d. $5.00

FINNEGAN, Robert. *Lying Ladies.* 1948. Bantam 351. c/gga. My. VG+. B4d. $7.00

FINNEGAN, Robert. *Many a Monster.* 1949. Bantam 363. c/gga. My. VG. B4d. $3.00

FINNEY, Charles G. *Circus of Dr Lao.* 1964. Bantam F 2755. 1st prtg. SF. G+. R5d. $1.75

FINNEY, Charles G. *Circus of Dr Lao.* 1964. Bantam F 2755. 1st prtg. VG+. S1d. $3.50

FINNEY, Charles G. *Ghosts of Manacle.* 1964. Pyramid R 1042. 1st edn. F. F2d. $20.00

FINNEY, Charles G. *Ghosts of Manacle.* 1964. Pyramid R 1042. 1st edn. VG. M1d. $15.00

FINNEY, Charles G. *Unholy City.* 1976. Panther 04305. VG+. B3d. $9.00

FINNEY, Charles G. *Unholy City.* 1968. Pyramid X 1818. SF. VG. B4d. $2.75

FINNEY, Charles G. *Unholy City.* 1968. Pyramid X 1818. VG+. B3d. $4.50

FINNEY, Jack. *Assault on a Queen.* 1960. Dell D 377. My. VG. P1d. $7.50

FINNEY, Jack. *Assault on a Queen.* 1966. Dell 0332. MTI. VG. B3d. $4.00

FINNEY, Jack. *Body Snatchers.* 1967. Dell 0674. SF. VG. W2d. $4.00

FINNEY, Jack. *Body Snatchers.* 1961. Dell 1st Edn B 204. 1st prtg. SF. VG. R5d. $4.50

FINNEY, Jack. *Body Snatchers.* 1955. Dell 1st Edn 42. PBO. c/McDermott. SF. VG. M1d. $30.00

FINNEY, Jack. *Body Snatchers.* 1955. Dell 1st Edn 42. SF. G+. M3d. $7.00

FINNEY, Jack. *Five Against the House.* 1955. Pocket 1078. c/G Erickson. Fi. G. B5d. $3.50

FINNEY, Jack. *Good Neighbor Sam.* 1964. Pocket 50012. MTI. c/Lemmon, Schneider & Robinson: photo. NF. B4d. $4.00

FINNEY, Jack. *House of Numbers.* 1957. Dell 1st Edn A 139. MTI. c/photo. F. B4d. $17.00

FINNEY, Jack. *House of Numbers.* 1957. Dell 1st Edn A 139. My. VG. P1d. $15.00

FINNEY, Jack. *House of Numbers.* 1957. Dell 1st Edn A 139. VG+. G5d. $6.50

FINNEY, Jack. *House of Numbers.* 1957. Dell 1st Edn A 139. 1st prtg. G+. R5d. $5.50

FINNEY, Jack. *Invasion of the Body Snatchers.* 1973. Award AN 1125. SF. VG. B3d. $4.50

FINNEY, Jack. *Night People.* 1978. Pocket 82156. Fi. VG. P1d. $5.00

FINNEY, Jack. *Third Level.* 1959. Dell D 274. 1st prtg. SF. G+. R5d. $3.00

FINNEY, Jack. *Third Level.* 1959. Dell 274. 1st prtg. NF. M1d. $8.00

FIORE & MCLUHAN. *War & Peace in the Global Village.* 1968. Bantam R 3845. 1st prtg. VG+. P7d. $5.00

FISCHER, Bruno. *Bleeding Scissors.* Bestseller B 106. My. G+. B5d. $4.00

FISCHER, Bruno. *Dead Men Grin.* Pyramid 22. VG. B3d. $12.50

FISCHER, Bruno. *Dead Men Grin.* 1950. Pyramid 22. 1st edn. PBO. rare. NF. B6a #76. $41.00

FISCHER, Bruno. *Evil Days.* Ballantine 24657. VG+. G5d. $3.50

FISCHER, Bruno. *Fast Buck.* Gold Medal 783. 2nd prtg. VG. B3d. $7.50

FISCHER, Bruno. *Fingered Man.* 1953. Ace D 27. 1st edn. PBO. c/Saunders. scarce. VG+. B6a #75. $68.25

FISCHER, Bruno. *Fingered Man.* 1953. Ace D 27. 1st edn. PBO. c/Saunders. VG. B6d. $15.00

FISCHER, Bruno. *Flesh Was Cold.* Signet 1474. c/Maguire. reprint. My. VG. B6d. $9.00

FISCHER, Bruno. *Flesh Was Cold.* Signet 833. G. I1d. $4.00

FISCHER, Bruno. *Fools Walk in.* 1951. Gold Medal 209. PBO. c/Barye. My. G. B6d. $3.50

FISCHER, Bruno. *Hornets' Nest.* 1945. Dell 79. 1st prtg. My. VG. R5d. $9.00

FISCHER, Bruno. *House of Flesh.* Gold Medal 123. 2nd edn. VG. I1d. $3.00

FISCHER, Bruno. *House of Flesh.* 1950. Gold Medal 123. 1st edn. My. F. F2d. $22.00

FISCHER, Bruno. *Knee-Deep in Death.* 1956. Gold Medal 591. PBO. My. VG. B6d. $9.00

FISCHER, Bruno. *Lady Kills.* 1951. Gold Medal 148. 1st prtg. PBO. VG. P6d. $9.00

FISCHER, Bruno. *Lady Kills.* 1958. Gold Medal 755. 3rd prtg. VG. B3d. $5.50

FISCHER, Bruno. *Pigskin Bag.* 1955. Dell 817. PBO. c/Bill George. scarce. NF. B6a #76. $48.50

FISCHER, Bruno. *Pigskin Bag.* 1955. Dell 817. VG. B3d. $6.00

FISCHER, Bruno. *Run for Your Life.* 1953. Gold Medal 343. PBO. VG. B6d. $15.00

FISCHER, Bruno. *Second-Hand Nude.* 1959. Gold Medal 928. 1st prtg. PBO. c/gga. VG. P7d. $7.50

FISCHER, Bruno. *Silent Dust.* 1951. Signet 51. c/Warren King: gga. G. P6d. $1.00

FISCHER, Bruno. *Silent Dust.* Signet 892. VG. B3d. $10.00

FISCHER, Bruno. *So Much Blood.* 1946. Golden Willow 52. 1st edn. PBO. scarce. VG+. B6a #76. $65.00

FISCHER, Bruno. *So Wicked My Love.* 1958. Gold Medal 753. 2nd prtg. PBO. c/photo. VG. P6d. $1.75

FISCHER, Bruno. *Spider Lily.* 1954. Dell 752. 1st edn. PBO. c/gga. F. F2d. $9.00

FISCHER, Bruno. *Spider Lily.* 1954. Dell 752. 1st prtg. c/Foxley: gga. VG. P7d. $5.50

FISCHER, Bruno. *Stairway to Death.* 1957. Pyramid G 270. 1st edn. PBO. c/Schaare. scarce. My. NF. B6a #75. $40.25

FISCHER, Bruno. *Stripped for Murder (Paper Circle).* Signet 988. VG. B3d. $3.50

FISCHER, Leonard. *Let Out the Beast.* 1950. Newsstand Library 18A. SF. F. P1d. $25.00

FISCHLER, S. *Hockey Stars of 1975.* Pyramid 3506. VG+. B3d. $5.00

FISH, Donald. *Airline Detective.* 1962. Fontana 749. TVTI. VG. P1d. $10.00

FISH, Robert L. *Murder League.* 1968. Ace 54710. My. G. W2d. $3.00

FISH, Robert L. *Shrunken Head.* Avon G 1266. G+. G5d. $4.00

FISH, Robert L. *Trials of O'Brien.* 1965. Signet D 2821. TVTI. c/Peter Falk: photo. VG+. B4d. $3.25

FISHER, Catherine. *Pan Book of Dogs.* Pan G 171. 1st pb. reprint. VG. B6d. $2.50

FISHER, Clay. *Brass Command.* 1965. Pocket 50199. We. VG+. B5d. $3.00

FISHER, Clay. *Crossing.* 1959. Cardinal C 373. 1st prtg. c/Raphael De Soto. VG. P7d. $4.00

FISHER, Clay. *Red Blizzard.* Pocket 927. VG+. I1d. $4.00

FISHER, Clay. *Tall Men.* Ballantine 59. PBO. NF. B3d. $8.00

FISHER, Clay. *War Bonnet.* Ballantine 11. VG+. B3d. $6.50

FISHER, James. *Great Brain Robbery.* Belmont 752072. 1st prtg G+. S1d. $3.50

FISHER, L. *Seduction on the Run.* 1959. Novel Book 3504. De. VG+. P1d. $10.50

FISHER, L. *Sunstop 8.* 1978. Dell 12662. 1st edn. SF. F. F2d. $12.50

FISHER, Steve. *Giveaway.* 1955. Bantam 1376. 1st pb. JD. VG. B6d. $10.00

FISHER, Steve. *Homicide Johnny.* 1950. Popular 229. 1st pb. c/Belarski. My. G+. B6d. $5.00

FISHER, Steve. *I Wake Up Screaming.* Handi-Book 27. G. G5d. $3.50

FISHER, Steve. *Night Before Murder.* 1951. Popular 317. 1st edn. PBO. c/Belarski: gga. VG+. B6a. $68.25

FISHER, Terry. *Odd Girl.* Midwood 61217. VG. M6d. $5.00

FISHER, Vardis. *Adam & the Serpent.* 1961. Pyramid R 677. 1st pb. NF. B6d. $15.00

FISHER, Vardis. *Adam & the Serpent.* 1961. Pyramid R 677. 1st prtg. c/Thurston. VG. P7d. $5.50

FISHER, Vardis. *Divine Passion.* 1963. Pyramid F 845. c/J Thurston. Fi. G+. B5d. $3.00

FISHER, Vardis. *Divine Passion.* Pyramid R 419. VG+. I1d. $15.00

FISHER, Vardis. *For Passion, for Heaven.* 1962. Pyramid T 746. Hi. VG. P1d. $6.50

FISHER, Vardis. *Goat for Azazel.* 1962. Pyramid X 705. c/G Forte. Fi. VG. B5d. $4.00

FISHER, Vardis. *Golden Rooms.* 1945. Armed Services 713. Fa. VG+. P1d. $35.00

FISHER, Vardis. *Golden Rooms.* 1960. Pyramid R 472. c/gga. Fa. VG. B4d. $4.00

FISHER, Vardis. *Golden Rooms.* 1962. Pyramid X 696. 2nd prtg. SF. VG. W2d. $4.00

FISHER, Vardis. *Great Confession.* 1962. Pyramid T 756. c/J Thurston. Fi. VG. B5d. $4.50

FISHER, Vardis. *In Tragic Life.* 1951. Cardinal C 3. Fi. VG. P1d. $9.00

FISHER, Vardis. *Intimations of Eve.* 1961. Pyramid R 657. Fa. F. P1d. $13.00

FISHER, Vardis. *Island of the Innocent.* 1961. Pyramid R 629. Hi. F. P1d. $13.00

FISHER, Vardis. *Jesus Came Again.* 1962. Pyramid X 716. c/J Thurston. Fi. VG+. B5d. $5.50

FISHER, Vardis. *Mothers.* 1960. Pyramid R 510. Fi. VG. P1d. $7.00

FISHER, Vardis. *Mountain Man.* 1967. Pocket 75211. Hi. F. P1d. $10.00

FISHER, Vardis. *My Holy Satan.* 1960. Pyramid R 546. Hi. VG+. P1d. $10.50

FISHER, Vardis. *No Villain Need Be.* 1955. Cardinal C 177. Fi. VG. P1d. $8.00

FISHER, Vardis. *Passions Spin the Plot.* 1952. Cardinal C 73. Fi. VG. P1d. $9.00

FISHER, Vardis. *Peace Like a River.* 1962. Pyramid X 777. Hi. VG+. P1d. $8.00

FISHER, Vardis. *Pemmican.* 1957. Cardinal C 253. 2nd edn. Hi. VG. P1d. $6.00

FISHER, Vardis. *Pemmican.* 1961. Pan X 02. Hi. F. P1d. $10.00

FISHER, Vardis. *Tale of Valor.* 1960. Cardinal GC 81. c/W George. Fi. VG. B5d. $3.00

FISHER, Vardis. *Valley of Vision.* 1961. Pyramid G 597. 2nd edn. c/V Kalin. Fi. G+. B5d. $4.50

FISHER, Vardis. *Wild Ones.* 1957. Pyramid G 310. c/gga. Fa. VG. B4d. $5.00

FISHER, Vardis. *Wild Ones.* 1952. Pyramid G 57. Hi. VG+. P1d. $13.50

FISHER & MC NAIR. *Black-Shirt (Mussolini).* Belmont L 520. VG. B3d. $3.50

FISHER/MCKNIGHT. *Fare Prey/Bikini Bombshell.* Ace D 387. PBO. VG. B3d. $5.50

FISK, Nicholas. *Flamers!* 1979. Knight 24028. SF. VG. P1d. $3.50

FITZGERALD, Arlene J. *Daredevil Nurse.* 1964. Pyramid K 1115. Fa. VG+. B4d. $3.00

FITZGERALD, Ed. *Kick-Off.* 1948. Bantam 504. Nfi. NF. B4d. $5.00

FITZGERALD, Ed. *Kick-Off!* 1948. Bantam 504. VG+. B3d. $5.00

FITZGERALD, F.S. *Great Gatsby.* Bantam 8. VG+. B3d. $5.00

FITZGERALD, F.S. *This Side of Paradise.* Dell D 140. VG. B3d. $4.00

FITZGERALD, Gregory edt. *Late Great Future.* 1976. Crest 2-3040. SF. F. P1d. $5.00

FITZGIBBON, Constantine. *Officers' Plot To Kill Hitler.* 1958. Avon T 222. Sf. VG+. P1d. $11.00

FITZGIBBON, Constantine. *Room for a Stranger.* 1955. Lion 232. My. VG+. P1d. $15.00

FITZGIBBON, Constantine. *When the Kissing Had To Stop.* 1961. Bantam F 2255. SF. F. M1d. $7.00

FIVELSON, Scott. *Guess What's Coming to Dinner?* 1983. Bantam 34047. SF. F. P1d. $5.00

FLACELIERE, Robert. *Literary History of Greece.* 1968. Mentor MW 868. Nfi. VG. P1d. $3.50

FLAGG, John. *Lady & the Cheetah.* 1951. Gold Medal 197. PBO. c/Barye: gga. My. VG+. B6d. $16.50

FLAGG, John. *Murder in Monaco.* Gold Medal 628. VG. B3d. $5.00

FLAGG, John. *Persian Cat.* 1950. Gold Medal 103. PBO. c/Downes: gga. NF. B6a #75. $61.00

FLAGG, John. *Persian Cat.* 1950. Gold Medal 103. PBO. VG. B6d. $16.50

FLAGG, John. *Woman of Cairo.* 1953. Gold Medal 282. PBO. c/gga. My. VG. B6d. $5.00

FLAIANO, Ennio. *Short Cut.* 1957. Signet S 1370. 5th edn. Fa. VG. B4d. $1.25

FLAIANO, Ennio. *Short Cut.* 1951. Signet 846. c/gga. Fa. VG. B4d. $4.00

FLAMMECHE, Pierre. *Silken Lure.* 1951. Archer 70. 1st US edn. c/gga. NF. B6a #75. $38.50

FLANAGAN, Richard. *Hunting Variety.* 1975. Popular 00315. Ho. G+. P1d. $3.00

FLANAGAN, Robert. *Maggot.* PB Library 66-741. 3rd edn. NF. B6d. $2.50

FLANDER, Ian. *Golden Girl.* 1965. Novel Book 7N765. 1st edn. scarce. Th. F. F2d. $30.00

FLANDERS, Eric. *Forever Children.* 1992. Zebra 3719. Ho. VG. P1d. $4.00

FLANNAGAN, Roy. *County Court.* Mercury 22. VG. G5d. $6.50

FLANNAGAN, Roy. *Luther.* Lion LB 94. reprint. VG. B6d. $9.00

FLANNERY, Sean. *Eagles Fly.* 1980. Charter 18016. 3rd prtg. My. F. W2d. $4.00

FLANNIGAN, J.A. *Vagabond Virgin.* 1960. Newsstand 518. 1st edn. c/gga. F. F2d. $15.00

FLAUBERT, Gustave. *Salambo.* 1966. Berkley F 1180. 4th prtg. VG. P6d. $1.50

FLAUBERT, Gustave. *Salambo.* Berkley G 5. VG. I1d. $5.00

FLAUBERT, Gustave. *Salambo.* 1962. New English 1002. Fi. VG. B5d. $4.50

FLEISCHER, Leonore. *Flatliners.* 1990. TOR 51188. 1st prtg. VG. R5d. $1.50

FLEISCHER, Leonore. *Lords of Fatbush.* 1977. Bantam 16036. 2nd prtg. MTI. JD. VG. R5d. $1.25

FLEISCHER, Leonore. *Lords of Flatbush.* Bantam 11138. MTI. VG. B3d. $5.00

FLEISCHER, Leonore. *Rose.* 1979. PB Library 82-996. PBO. MTI. c/Bette Midler. VG. B6d. $4.00

FLEISCHMAN, A.S. *Danger in Paradise.* 1953. Gold Medal 295. PBO. c/Barye. My. VG. B6d. $7.50

FLEISCHMAN, A.S. *Look Behind You, Lady.* Gold Medal 1364. 3rd prtg. VG+. B3d. $4.00

FLEISCHMAN, A.S. *Look Behind You Lady.* 1952. Gold Medal 223. VG+. B3d. $6.00

FLEISCHMAN, A.S. *Shanghai Flame.* Gold Medal 514. 3rd prtg. VG. B3d. $5.00

FLEISCHMAN, A.S. *Venetian Blonde.* Gold Medal 1367. c/gga. VG+. B3d. $6.50

FLEISCHMAN, Sid. *Bullwhip Griffin.* 1967. Avon S 263. MTI. VG+. B4d. $2.50

FLEISCHMAN/LEONARD. *Counterspy Express/Treachery in Trieste.* 1954. Ace D 57. PBO. VG. B3d. $5.50

FLEISHER, Siegel. *Down the Dark Street.* Popular 649. VG. B3d. $4.00

FLEMING, Ian. *Casino Royale.* 1960. Signet S 1762. 1st prtg. c/Barye: gga. VG. G5d/ P7d. $12.50

FLEMING, Ian. *Chitty Chitty Bang Bang.* 1969. Pan 02154. 3rd edn. Fa. VG. P1d. $5.00

FLEMING, Ian. *Diamonds Are Forever.* 1957. Perma M 3084. c/gga. My. VG. B4d. $15.00

FLEMING, Ian. *Diamonds Are Forever.* 1957. Perma M 3084. VG+. B3a #22. $40.90

FLEMING, Ian. *Diamonds Are Forever.* 1957. Perma M 3084. 1st edn. PBO. c/Bill Rose. scarce. VG+. B6a #79. $67.25

FLEMING, Ian. *Dr No.* Pan G 335. VG. B3d. $5.00

FLEMING, Ian. *Dr No.* 1964. Pan X 237. 14th prtg. MTI. VG. P6d. $5.00

FLEMING, Ian. *For Your Eyes Only.* 1961. Signet S 1948. 1st prtg. c/Barye: gga. VG. P7d. $12.50

FLEMING, Ian. *Live & Let Die.* 1956. Perma M 3048. c/J Meese: gga. My. G+. B5d. $12.50

FLEMING, Ian. *Man With the Golden Gun.* 1966. Signet P 2735. 1st prtg. VG. P7d/ W2d. $5.00

FLEMING, Ian. *Moonraker.* Signet P 2731. 23rd edn. VG. M6d. $3.00

FLEMING, Ian. *Moonraker.* Signet 1850. c/Barye. VG. B3d. $5.00

FLEMING, Ian. *On Her Majesty's Secret Service.* 1964. Signet D 2509. 4th prtg. My. VG. W2d. $3.50

FLEMING, Ian. *On Her Majesty's Secret Service.* Signet P 2732. 11th prtg. My. VG. W2d. $2.75

FLEMING, Ian. *Spy Who Loved Me.* Pan X 653. VG+. B3d. $10.00

FLEMING, Ian. *Spy Who Loved Me.* 1963. Signet D 2280. My. VG. B4d. $4.00

FLEMING, Ian. *Thrilling Cities.* 1965. Signet P 2694. Nfi. VG+. B4d. $3.00

FLEMING, Ian. *Thunderball.* 1962. Signet D 2126. My. VG+. B4d. $4.00

FLEMING, Ian. *Too Hot To Handle.* 1956. Perma M 3070. 1st edn. PBO. c/Marchetti. scarce. VG+. B6a #79. $67.25

FLEMING, Ian. *You Only Live Twice.* 1965. Signet P 2712. VG+. P6d. $3.50

FLEMING, Joan. *Chill & the Kill.* 1966. Ballantine U 5071. My. VG+. B4d. $3.25

FLEMING, Joan. *In the Red.* 1964. Lancer 72-711. 1st prtg. c/Goldberg: gga. VG. P7d. $5.00

FLEMING, Joan. *Maiden's Prayer.* 1968. Ballantine U 5075. c/skeleton hand holds a lily. My. VG+. B4d. $3.00

FLENDER, Harold. *Paris Blues.* 1961. Ballantine 551. 1st prtg. VG. R5d. $5.00

FLES, Barthold edt. *Post Fantasy Stories.* 1951. Avon 389. PBO. c/Kersh: gga. VG+. B6d. $12.50

FLES, Barthold edt. *Sat Evening Post Fantasy Stories.* 1951. Avon 389. Fa. F. P1d. $40.00

FLESCH, Rudolf. *Why Johnny Can't Read.* 1960. Popular PC 764. 1st prtg. VG+. P7d. $3.50

FLETCHER, Inglis. *Bennett's Welcome.* Perma P 171. VG+. B3d. $4.50

FLETCHER, J.S. *Pedigreed Murder Case.* Detective 2. VG. B3d. $4.00

FLETCHER & ULLMAN. *Night Man.* 1953. Bantam 1140. My. VG. P1d. $8.50

FLETCHER & ULLMAN. *Sorry, Wrong Number.* 1948. Bantam 356. MTI. NF. G5d. $7.00

FLETCHER & ULLMAN. *Sorry, Wrong Number.* 1948. Bantam 356. MTI. VG+. B3d. $4.50

FLETCHER & ULLMAN. *Sorry, Wrong Number.* 1948. Bantam 356. My. F. P1d. $20.00

FLETCHER & ULLMAN. *Sorry, Wrong Number.* 1948. Bantam 356. 1st prtg. MTI. My. G+. R5d. $3.00

FLEXNER, James Thomas. *Pocket History of American Painting.* 1950. Pocket 708. Nfi. VG. B5d. $5.50

FLINT, Homer E. *Devolutionist & the Emancipatrix.* 1965. Ace F 355. SF. F. P1d. $11.00

FLINT, Homer E. *Devolutionist & the Emancpatrix.* 1965. Ace F 355. VG. M1d. $6.00

FLINT, Homer E. *Lord of Death & Queen of Life.* Ace F 345. NF. M1d. $8.00

FLINT, J.B. *Lover Boy.* Stanley Library 71. PBO. VG. B3d. $5.00

FLINT, Kenneth C. *Champions of the Sidhe.* 1984. Bantam. 1st edn. F. M1d. $6.00

FLINT, Kenneth C. *Dark Druid.* 1987. Bantam. advance proof. publisher's letter laid in. Fa. F. P1d. $25.00

FLINT, Kenneth C. *Isle of Destiny.* 1988. Bantam. advance proof laid in. Fa. F. P1d. $25.00

FLINT, Kenneth C. *Master of the Sidhe.* 1985. Bantam. advance proof laid in. Fa. P1d. $20.00

FLINT, Kenneth C. *Master of the Sidhe.* 1985. Bantam. 1st edn. F. M1d. $6.00

FLINT, Kenneth C. *Storm Shield.* 1986. Bantam 26191. Fa. VG. P1d. $3.50

FLOHERTY, John J. *Inside the FBI.* Armed Services 1068. Nfi. VG. B5d. $4.50

FLOOD, Charles Bracelen. *Love Is a Bridge.* 1955. Signet D 1198. 1st pb. VG+. B6d. $9.00

FLOOD, Charles Bracelen. *More Lives Than One.* 1969. Avon V 2234. Fi. VG. P1d. $3.75

FLORA, Fletcher. *Desperate Asylum.* 1955. Lion LL 44. PBO. NF. B6d. $18.00

FLORA, Fletcher. *Hot-Shot.* 1956. Avon 693. 1st edn. My. F. F2d. $13.00

FLORA, Fletcher. *Leave Her to Hell!* Avon 839. VG+. G5d. $9.00

FLORA, Fletcher. *Let Me Kill You, Sweetheart!* 1958. Avon 811. 1st prtg. PBO. c/gga. VG+. P7d. $7.50

FLORA, Fletcher. *Most Likely To Love.* 1964. Monarch 426. c/gga. Fa. VG. B4d. $4.00

FLORA, Fletcher. *Seducer.* 1961. Monarch 217. PBO. c/De Soto. VG+. B3a #24. $16.65

FLORA, Fletcher. *Seducer.* 1961. Monarch 217. 1st edn. c/gga. My. F. F2d. $20.00

FLORA, Fletcher. *Skulldoggery.* 1967. Belmont B 50-738. PBO. My. NF. B6d. $9.00

FLORA, Fletcher. *Strange Sisters.* 1954. Lion 215. 1st edn. F. F2d. $25.00

FLORA, Fletcher. *Whispers of the Flesh.* 1958. Signet 1542. 1st edn. My. F. F2d. $20.00

FLOREN, Lee. *Gun Luck.* MacFadden 50-488. NF. B3d. $4.50

FLOREN, Lee. *Gun Slammer.* Lion 169. VG. I1d. $7.00

FLOREN, Lee. *Rifles on the Range.* MacFadden 50-375. VG+. B3d. $4.50

FLOREN, Lee. *Two-Gun Trail.* Star Books 17. c/Gross. VG. B3d. $8.00

FLOREN, Lee. *Wolf Dog Range.* MacFadden 40-132. VG+. B3d. $4.50

FLOREN/WHITTINGTON. *High Thunder/Trap For Sam Dodge.* 1961. Ace F 103. PBO. VG. B3d. $12.00

FLORESCU, Radu. *In Search of Frankenstein.* 1976. Warner 89-160. Nfi. VG. P1d. $4.00

FLYNN, Errol. *My Wicked, Wicked Ways.* 1961. Dell S 11. 1st prtg. Auto. VG. R5d. $2.50

FLYNN, J.M. *Drink With the Dead.* 1959. Ace D 379. PBO. c/Paul Rader: gga. NF. B6a #76. $61.00

FLYNN, J.M. *Hot Chariot.* Ace D 447. VG. B3d. $5.00

FLYNN, J.M. *One for the Death House.* 1961. Ace D 511. PBO. VG+. B6d. $27.50

FLYNN, J.M. *Warlock.* 1976. Pocket 80478. 1st prtg. SF. VG. W2d. $3.25

FLYNN, Jay. *Action Man.* Avon T 500. G. G5d. $3.00

FLYNN, Jay. *Body for McHugh.* 1960. Avon T 444. 1st edn. c/gga. De. F. F2d. $10.00

FLYNN, Jay. *Body for McHugh.* 1970. Manor 75378. 1st prtg. My. VG. W2d. $4.75

FLYNN, Jay. *Five Faces of Murder.* 1962. Avon F 156. My. VG+. B4d. $7.00

FLYNN, Jay. *It's Murder, McHugh.* 1960. Avon T 406. 1st edn. c/gga. My. F. F2d. $15.00

FLYNN, Jay. *McHugh.* Avon T 377. PBO. VG. B3d. $4.50

FLYNN, Jay. *Viva McHugh!* Avon T 466. PBO. VG+. B3d. $4.00

FLYNN, Jay. *Viva McHugh!* 1960. Avon T 466. 1st edn. My. F. F2d. $10.00

FLYNN, T.T. *Man From Laramie.* 1954. Dell 1st Edn 14. PBO. c/S Borack. We. VG. B5d. $4.00

FLYNN/MARTIN. *Girl From Las Vegas/To Have & To Kill.* 1961. Ace F 111. 1st edn. c/gga. My. F. F2d. $15.00

FLYNN/MCKNIGHT. *Hot Chariot/Kiss the Babe Goodbye.* 1960. Ace D 447. 1st edn. c/Maguire. VG. M1d. $10.00

FLYNN/MCKNIGHT. *One for the Death House/Drop Dead, Please.* Ace D 511. PBO. VG. B3d. $5.00

FLYNN/OLMSTEAD. *Ring Around a Rogue/Hot Diary.* Ace D 459. PBO. VG. B3d. $5.00

FODOR, Nandor. *Haunted Mind.* 1968. Signet T 3468. Nfi. VG. P1d. $5.00

FOGG, Charles. *Panic Button.* 1960. Ace D 438. Fi. VG+. P1d. $10.00

FOLDES, Yolanda. *Golden Earrings.* Dell 216. VG. B3d. $4.00

FOLEY, Charles. *Commando Extraordinary.* 1955. Ballantine 209. Fi. G+. P1d. $3.75

FOLEY, Rae. *Wake the Sleeping Wolf.* 1957. Bloodhound 189. VG. B3d. $9.00

FOLEY & BURNETT edt. *Best American Short Stories 1960.* Ballantine 473. VG+. B3d. $4.50

FOLEY & BURNETT edt. *Best American Short Stories 1962.* Ballantine S 695. Fi. VG. B5d. $3.50

FOLKES, M. *I'm Out of Pink.* Playboy 16173. VG+. B3d. $5.00

FOLLETT, Ken. *Key to Rebecca.* Signet AE 3509. 17th edn. Fi. VG. P1d. $4.00

FOLLETT, Ken. *Paper Money.* 1987. Signet AE 5002. 1st prtg. My. F. W2d. $3.25

FONG, C.K. *Year of the Ape.* 1975. Manor 12303. PBO. VG+. B6d. $5.00

FONG, C.K. *Year of the Cock.* 1975. Manor 12277. PBO. NF. B6d. $6.00

FONSTAD, Karen Wynn. *Atlas of Pern.* 1984. Ballantine 31434. Nfi. VG. P1d. $12.50

FONTANA, D.C. *Questor Tapes.* 1974. Ballantine 24236. SF. VG+. P1d. $10.00

FONTANA, D.C. *Vulcan's Glory.* Pocket 65667. F. P9d. $2.00

FONTENARY/TUBB. *Twice Upon a Time/ Mechanical Monarch.* 1958. Ace D 266. PBO. c/E Emsh. SF. G+. B5d. $4.00

FONTENAY, Charles. *Day the Ocean Overflowed.* 1964. Monarch 443. PBO. VG. M6d. $6.00

FONTENAY/MCINTOSH. *Rebels of the Red Planet/200 Years to Christmas.* 1961. Ace F 113. F. M1d. $15.00

FONTENAY/MCINTOSH. *Rebels of the Red Planet/200 Years to Christmas.* 1961. Ace F 113. PBO. c/E Valigursky. SF. VG+. B5d. $5.50

FONTENAY/TUBB. *Twice Upon a Time/ Mechanical Monarch.* 1958. Ace D 266. c/Emsh. F. M1d. $15.00

FONTENAY/TUBB. *Twice Upon a Time/ Mechanical Monarch.* 1958. Ace D 266. 1st prtg. PBO. c/Emsh: gga. SF. VG. P7d. $6.00

FOOTE, Horton. *Baby, the Rain Must Fall.* 1965. Popular SP 325. MTI. c/Remick & McQueen: photo. VG. B4d. $4.00

FOOTE, Horton. *Chase.* 1966. Signet P 2618. 1st prtg. VG+. R5d. $3.50

FOOTE, Shelby. *Love in a Dry Season.* 1952. Signet 970. c/gga. Fa. G+. B4d. $3.50

FOOTE, Shelby. *Night Before Chancellorsville.* 1957. Signet S 1415. Fi. VG. P1d. $4.50

FOOTE, Shelby. *Shiloh.* 1954. Signet 1104. Fi. VG. P1d. $5.50

FOOTNER, Hulbert. *Dark Ships.* 1944. Popular 38. 1st pb. c/Hoffman. My. VG. B6d. $9.00

FOOTNER, Hulbert. *Death of a Celebrity.* Hillman 52. VG. B3d. $4.50

FOOTNER, Hulbert. *Murder That Had Everything.* Dell 74. 1st pb. c/Gregg. My. VG. B6d. $9.00

FORAN, Tom. *Twisted Ones.* 1963. Beacon 644. NF. B3a #20. $19.80

FORBES, Colin. *Heights of Zervos.* 1972. Crest M 1670. Fi. G+. P1d. $3.00

FORBES, Colin. *Stone Leopard.* Crest 2-3129-1. 1st prtg. My. VG. R5d. $1.25

FORBES, Gordon. *Too Near the Sun.* 1955. Dell 1st Edn D56. PBO. c/R Maguire. Fi. VG. B5d. $3.50

FORBES, Kathryn. *Mama's Bank Account.* 1947. Bantam 135. MTI. c/Irene Dunn. VG+. B3d/B4d. $5.00

FORD, Bill. *Lt Robin Crusoe.* 1966. Tempo T 138. 1st prtg. MTI. G+. R5d. $2.25

FORD, Boris edt. *From Dryden to Johnson.* 1957. Pelican A 379. Nfi. G+. P1d. $4.50

FORD, D. *Incident at Muc Wa.* 1968. Pyramid T 1780. VG+. B3d. $5.00

FORD, Daniel. *Incident at Muc Wa.* 1968. Pyramid T 1780. Fi. VG. P1d. $3.25

FORD, Ed. *Can You Top This?* 1947. Bart 39. c/photo. Nfi. G. B5d. $2.50

FORD, Elizabeth. *Dangerous Holiday.* 1967. Ace K 293. 1st prtg. My. G+. R5d. $1.50

FORD, Hilary. *Bella on the Roof.* 1967. Banner B60-109. 1st prtg. My. VG. R5d. $3.50

FORD, J.D. *Lash of Lust!* 1964. Boudoir 0003. PBO. c/whip. Ad. G+. B5d. $5.50

FORD, Jean. *Mountain Woman.* 1953. Uni-Book 55. VG. B3d. $75.00

FORD, John M. *Final Reflection.* 1984. Pocket 47388. 1st edn. SF. F. F2d. $9.00

FORD, Leslie. *All for the Love of a Lady.* Bantam 359. VG. G5d. $5.00

FORD, Leslie. *Bahamas Murder Case.* Dell 689. 1st prtg. My. G+. R5d. $2.25

FORD, Leslie. *Clue of the Judas Tree.* Dell 61. VG+. B3d. $12.00

FORD, Leslie. *Date With Death.* Dell 547. VG. B3d. $5.00

FORD, Leslie. *Devil's Stronghold.* Dell 395. c/R Stanley. My. G+. B5d. $3.00

FORD, Leslie. *False to Any Man.* 1947. Bantam 80. My. VG+. B4d. $4.00

FORD, Leslie. *Girl From the Mimosa Club.* Popular 60-2173. My. NF. B5d. $4.00

FORD, Leslie. *Ill Met by Moonlight.* Dell 6. VG. B3d. $8.00

FORD, Leslie. *Ill Met by Moonlight.* 1943. Dell 6. VG+. B3a #21. $14.30

FORD, Leslie. *Murder With Southern Hospitality.* Dell 505. VG+. G5d. $6.00

FORD, Leslie. *Old Lover's Ghost.* Bantam 114. G+. G5d. $3.50

FORD, Leslie. *Old Lover's Ghost.* 1947. Bantam 114. c/L Kohn. My. VG. B5d. $4.50

FORD, Leslie. *Old Lover's Ghost.* 1947. Bantam 114. 1st pb. My. NF. B6d. $12.50

FORD, Leslie. *Philadelphia Murder Story.* Dell 354. VG+. G5d. $6.50

FORD, Leslie. *Road to Folly.* 1946. Bantam 42. 1st prtg. My. VG. R5d. $3.50

FORD, Leslie. *Siren in the Night.* 1948. Bantam 303. c/R Harris. My. VG. B5d. $4.00

FORD, Leslie. *Strangled Witness.* 1948. Popular 158. 1st pb. My. VG. B6d. $8.00

FORD, Leslie. *Woman in Black.* Dell 447. VG+. G5d. $9.00

FORD & HERSHFIELD. *Can You Top This?* Bart House 39. VG+. B3d. $7.00

FOREMAN, L.L. *Arrow in the Dust.* 1954. Dell First 11. PBO. c/R Stanley. We. VG. B5d. $4.00

FOREMAN, L.L. *Gunfire Men.* Dell 825. PBO. VG+. B3d. $4.50

FOREMAN, L.L. *Gunning for Trouble.* Popular 560. VG. B3d. $3.50

FOREMAN, L.L. *Mustang Trail.* 1966. Ace F 411. 1st pb. We. VG+. B6d. $8.00

FOREMAN, L.L. *Return of the Texan.* Ballantine 259. VG. B3d. $4.00

FOREMAN, L.L. *Road to San Jacinto.* 1951. Pocket 824. 1st edn. PBO. c/busty woman. F. F2d. $10.00

FOREMAN, L.L. *Rogue's Legacy.* Ace 73435. We. VG+. B5d. $4.00

FOREMAN, L.L. *Spanish Grant.* 1963. Ace D 570. 1st pb. We. VG+. B6d. $12.50

FOREMAN, L.L. *Woman of the Avalon.* 1955. Dell 1st Edn 57. PBO. c/S Borack. We. VG. B5d. $4.00

FOREMAN, Robert L. *Hot Half Hour.* Avon T 295. TVTI. VG. B3d. $4.00

FOREMAN, Robert L. *Hot Half Hour.* 1958. Avon T 295. 1st pb. c/photo. NF. B6d. $9.00

FOREMAN, Russell. *Long Pig.* 1959. Ace G 390. 1st pb. Ad. NF. B6d. $15.00

FOREST, Dael. *Barba the Slaver.* 1978. Ballantine 25670. Fi. NF. B5d. $8.50

FOREST, Dael. *Corissa, the Vestal Virgin #5: Slaves of the Empire.* 1978. Ballantine 25674. SF. F. W2d. $5.00

FOREST, Jean-Claude. *Barbarella.* 1968. Grove Press GS 2. SF. VG. P1d. $20.00

FORESTER, C.S. *Captain From Connecticut.* 1946. Bantam 40. Fa. NF. B4d. $9.00

FORESTER, C.S. *Death to the French.* 1977. Mayflower 12820. Fi. VG. P1d. $4.00

FORESTER, C.S. *Flying Colours.* 1950. Bantam 772. VG. P6d. $2.00

FORESTER, C.S. *General.* 1953. Bantam 1170. Fi. VG. P1d. $6.00

FORESTER, C.S. *Gun.* 1957. Bantam 1610. 1st prtg. VG+. R5d. $4.00

FORESTER, C.S. *Gun.* 1943. Infantry Journal. Fi. VG. P1d. $8.50

FORESTER, C.S. *Mr Midshipman Hornblower.* 1955. Bantam A 1305. Fa. VG+. B4d. $3.00

FORESTER, C.S. *Nightmare.* 1961. Dell F 158. Fi. VG+. B3d. $4.50

FORESTER, C.S. *Nightmare.* 1959. Pan. 1st pb. VG. M1d. $7.00

FORESTER, C.S. *Plain Murder.* 1954. Dell 1st Edn 30. 1st prtg. PBO. VG. P7d. $5.00

FORESTER, C.S. *Ship.* Bantam 1196. VG+. B3d. $5.00

FORESTER, C.S. *Sink the Bismark!* 1959. Bantam A 2060. MTI. VG+. B4d. $2.75

FORESTER, C.S. *Sky & the Forest.* 1963. Pyramid R 893. Fa. NF. B4d. $4.00

FORREST, David. *Last Blue Sea.* 1964. Ballantine U 5019. War. VG+. B4d. $2.00

FORREST, E.R. *Arizona's Dark & Bloody Ground.* Panther 543. VG. B3d. $10.00

FORREST, Norman. *Death Took a Greek God.* Detective 16. VG+. B3d. $7.00

FORREST, W. *Great Debauch.* Gold Medal 725. VG+. B3d. $5.00

FORREST, W. *Seed of Violence.* Crest 182. PBO. c/Barye. VG+. B3d. $5.50

FORRESTER, J.S. *Innocent Dark.* 1983. Dell 03852. Ho. G+. P1d. $3.00

FORRESTER, Larry. *Fly for Your Life.* 1959. Panther 964. Fi. VG. P1d. $6.00

FORRESTER, Larry. *Girl Called Fathom.* 1967. Gold Medal D 1843. c/Raquel Welch. VG+. B4d. $5.00

FORRESTER, Larry. *Girl Called Fathom.* 1967. Gold Medal D 1843. 1st US edn. MTI. SF. NF. B6d. $10.00

FORSTCHEN, William R. *Darkness Upon the Ice.* 1985. Ballantine 31682. SF. F. P1d. $5.00

FORSTER, Logan A. *Proud Land.* 1958. Bantam 1857. VG. B3d. $4.50

FORSTER, Margaret. *Georgy Girl.* 1966. Berkley X 1345. Fi. VG. B5d. $3.50

FORSYTH, Fredrick. *No Comebacks.* 1983. Corgi 12140. 4th prtg. My. F. W2d. $4.25

FORSYTH, Fredrick. *Odessa File.* 1974. Bantam 9838. 4th prtg. My. F. W2d. $4.00

FORT, Charles. *Book of the Damned.* 1962. Ace K 156. Nfi. VG. B4d. $2.25

FORT, Charles. *Lo!* 1964. Ace K 217. Nfi. VG+. B4d. $2.25

FORTUNE, J.I. *True Story of Bonnie & Clyde.* Signet 3437. 2nd edn. VG. B3d. $4.00

FORTUNE, J.I. *True Story of Bonnie & Clyde.* Signet 6333. VG+. B3d. $4.50

FOSDICK, Harry Emerson. *Great Time To Be Alive.* 1954. Pocket 980. c/C Skaggs. Nfi. NF. B5d. $5.50

FOSTER, Alan Dean. *Alien Nation.* 1988. Warner 35264. 1st prtg. MTI. SF. VG. W2d. $3.25

FOSTER, Alan Dean. *Black Hole.* 1979. Ballantine 28538. MTI. SF. VG. W2d. $4.25

FOSTER, Alan Dean. *Black Hole.* 1977. Ballantine 25507. SF. VG. W2d. $4.00

FOSTER, Alan Dean. *Blood Type.* 1977. Ballantine 25845. 2nd prtg. SF. VG. W2d. $3.00

FOSTER, Alan Dean. *Clash of the Titans.* 1981. Warner 93-675. 1st prtg. VG+. R5d. $2.00

FOSTER, Alan Dean. *Clash of the Titans.* 1981. Warner 93-675. SF. F. W2d. $4.50

FOSTER, Alan Dean. *Deluge Drivers.* Ballantine 33330. 1st prtg. G+. S1d. $2.50

FOSTER, Alan Dean. *Deluge Drivers.* 1987. Ballantine 33330. SF. VG+. B5d. $3.50

FOSTER, Alan Dean. *I Inside.* 1984. Warner 32027. SF. F. W2d. $4.25

FOSTER, Alan Dean. *Luana.* 1974. Ballantine 23793. PBO. MTI. c/F Frazetta. SF. G+. B5d. $8.00

FOSTER, Alan Dean. *Nor Crystal Tears.* Ballantine 29141. 1st prtg. VG. S1d. $2.50

FOSTER, Alan Dean. *Orphan Star.* 1977. Ballantine 25507. SF. VG. S1d. $2.50

FOSTER, Alan Dean. *Outland.* 1981. Warner 95-829-8. 1st prtg. VG+. R5d. $2.50

FOSTER, Alan Dean. *Paths of the Perambulator.* 1986. Warner 32679. SF. F. W2d. $3.50

FOSTER, Alan Dean. *Paths of the Perambulator.* 1986. Warner 32679. 1st prtg. VG+. S1d. $2.50

FOSTER, Alan Dean. *Splinter of the Mind's Eye.* 1978. Ballantine 26062. 3rd prtg. SF. VG. W2d. $3.50

FOSTER, Alan Dean. *Star Trek Log Five.* 1975. Ballantine 24532. 1st prtg. SF. VG+. R5d. $7.50

FOSTER, Alan Dean. *Star Trek Log Four.* 1975. Ballantine 24435. 1st prtg. VG+. R5d. $7.50

FOSTER, Alan Dean. *Star Trek Log One.* 1974. Ballantine 24014. 1st prtg. SF. G+. R5d. $2.50

FOSTER, Alan Dean. *Star Trek Log One.* 1975. Ballantine 24677. 9th prtg. SF. F. W2d. $7.50

FOSTER, Alan Dean. *Star Trek Log Six.* 1976. Ballantine 24655. SF. VG. W2d. $6.50

FOSTER, Alan Dean. *Star Trek Log Three.* 1975. Ballantine 24260. 1st prtg. VG+. R5d. $6.00

FOSTER, Alan Dean. *Star Trek Log Two.* 1974. Ballantine 24164. 2nd prtg. SF. VG. W2d. $7.00

FOSTER, Alan Dean. *Star Trek Log Two.* 1974. Ballantine 24184. 1st prtg. VG+. R5d. $6.00

FOSTER, Alan Dean. *Starman.* 1984. Warner 32598. 1st prtg. VG. R5d. $1.25

FOSTER, Alan Dean. *Tar-Aiym Krang.* 1972. Ballantine 02547. SF. VG+. M3d. $5.00

FOSTER, Alan Dean. *Tar-Aiym Krang.* Ballantine 24085. 2nd prtg. G+. S1d. $3.00

FOSTER, Alan Dean. *Time of Transference.* Warner 30009. 1st prtg. G+. S1d. $2.50

FOSTER, Alan Dean. *With Friends Like These.* 1977. Ballantine 25701. 1st prtg. SF. VG. R5d. $2.75

FOSTER, Bennett. *Barbed Wire.* 1948. Bantam 252. c/L Ross. We. VG. B5d. $3.00

FOSTER, Bennett. *Blackleg Range.* Bantam 725. VG. B3d. $4.00

FOSTER, Bennett. *Owl Hoot Trail.* 1950. Bantam 808. 1st pb. We. VG+. B6d. $8.00

FOSTER, Bennett. *Pay-Off at Ladron.* Ballantine 260. VG. B3d. $5.00

FOSTER, Bennett. *Rider of the Rifle Rock.* Bantam 841. VG. B3d. $4.50

FOSTER, Bennett. *Seven Slash Range.* 1950. Bantam 762. We. VG+. B4d. $3.00

FOSTER, John M. *Hell in the Heavens.* 1965. Ace G 507. Fi. VG. P1d. $3.75

FOSTER, John. *Dark Heritage.* 1955. Gold Medal 486. PBO. c/Meese. My. VG. B6d. $8.00

FOSTER, Joseph. *Cow Is Too Much Trouble in LA.* Signet 1072. VG+. B3d. $6.00

FOSTER, Joseph. *Danielle.* 1959. Beacon 262. 1st prtg. PBO. c/Milo: gga. VG+. P7d. $12.50

FOSTER, Joseph. *Street of the Barefoot Lovers.* Signet 1197. VG+. B3d. $4.50

FOSTER, M.A. *Day of the Klech.* 1979. DAW. 1st edn. F. M1d. $5.00

FOSTER, M.A. *Game Players of Zan.* 1977. DAW UJ 1287. SF. VG. W2d. $3.25

FOSTER, M.A. *Game Players of Zan.* 1977. DAW. 1st edn. F. M1d. $5.00

FOSTER, M.A. *Morphodite.* 1981. DAW. 1st edn. F. M1d. $5.00

FOSTER, M.A. *Warriors of Dawn.* 1975. DAW UW 1291. SF. VG. W2d. $3.50

FOSTER, Richard. *Bier for a Chaser.* 1959. Gold Medal 899. 1st edn. c/gga. De. F. F2d. $15.00

FOSTER, Richard. *Bier for a Chaser.* Gold Medal 899. VG. B3d. $4.00

FOSTER, Richard. *Girl From Easy Street.* 1955. Popular Eagle EB 32. JD. VG. P1d. $20.00

FOSTER, Richard. *Rest Must Die.* Gold Medal 853. VG+. B3d. $7.00

FOSTER, Richard. *Rest Must Die.* 1959. Gold Medal. 1st edn. F. M1d. $15.00

FOSTER, Richard. *Too Late for Mourning.* Gold Medal 995. VG. G5d. $7.00

FOSTER, Robert. *Complete Guide to Middle Earth.* 1979. Ballantine 27975. Nfi. F. B5d. $7.50

FOSTER, Robert. *Guide to Middle Earth.* 1974. Ballantine 24138. Nfi. VG+. P1d. $4.50

FOWLER, Gene. *Beau James.* 1957. Bantam A 1626. 1st prtg. G+. VG. R5d. $1.75

FOWLER, Gene. *Good Night, Sweet Prince.* 1947. Pocket 430. 1st prtg. Bio. VG+. R5d. $5.00

FOWLER, Gene. *Great Mouthpiece.* 1946. Bantam 32. Bio. VG+. B4d. $7.00

FOWLER, Gene. *Schnozzola.* Perma P 210. VG. I1d. $6.00

FOWLER, Gene. *Shoe the Wild Mare.* 1944. Avon 47. 1st pb. VG. B6d. $9.00

FOWLER, Gene. *Shoe the Wild Mare.* 1961. PB Library 52-123. Fi. VG. B5d. $3.00

FOWLER, Gene. *Shoe the Wild Mare.* Readers Choice 7. VG+. B3d. $8.00

FOWLER, Kenneth. *Range Bum.* Avon 871. PBO. VG. B3d. $5.00

FOWLER, Kenneth. *Summons to Silverhorn.* 1957. Gold Medal 713. PBO. We. NF. B6d. $12.50

FOWLES, John. *Collector.* 1965. Pan M 74. 1st pb. MTI. VG+. B6d. $7.50

FOX, Arthur. *Striptease Business.* 1963. Empso Ltd NN. VG. B3a #24. $57.20

FOX, Edward S. *Thus a Boy Becomes a Man.* 1963. Belmont 90-290. 1st edn. F. F2d. $8.50

FOX, G. *Earthquake: The Story of a Movie.* Signet 6264. MTI. c/photos. VG+. B3d. $4.50

FOX, Gardner F. *Borgia Blade.* 1953. Gold Medal 300. PBO. VG. B6d. $4.00

FOX, Gardner F. *City Under the Sea.* 1965. Pyramid R 1102. 1st edn. TVTI. SF. F. F2d. $10.00

FOX, Gardner F. *Conehead.* 1973. Ace 11658. 1st edn. SF. F. F2d. $10.00

FOX, Gardner F. *Conquering Prince.* 1957. Crest 166. 1st prtg. PBO. c/Binger: gga. VG. P7d. $6.00

FOX, Gardner F. *Conquering Prince.* Gold Medal 242. c/Binger. G+. B3d. $6.00

FOX, Gardner F. *Creole Woman.* Crest 304. PBO. VG. B3d. $6.00

FOX, Gardner F. *Curse of Quintana Roo.* 1972. Popular 01548. 1st edn. Ho. F. F2d. $15.00

FOX, Gardner F. *Easy Ride.* 1970. Belmont. 1st edn. My. F. F2d. $15.00

FOX, Gardner F. *Escape Across the Cosmos.* 1964. PB Library 52-273. 1st edn. NF. M1d. $10.00

FOX, Gardner F. *Five Weeks in a Balloon.* 1962. Pyramid 753. 1st edn. c/photo. Hi. F. F2d/M1d. $10.00

FOX, Gardner F. *Hunter Out of Time.* 1965. Ace F 354. SF. VG+. B4d. $5.00

FOX, Gardner F. *Hunter Out Time.* Ace F 354. NF. M1d. $10.00

FOX, Gardner F. *Iron Lover.* Avon T 341. PBO. VG+. B3d. $5.00

FOX, Gardner F. *Ivan the Terrible.* Avon T 498. PBO. Fi. G+. B5d. $3.00

FOX, Gardner F. *Ivan the Terrible.* 1961. Avon T 498. Fa. VG. B4d. $4.00

FOX, Gardner F. *Kothar, Barbarian Swordsman.* 1969. Belmont B 60-1003. VG+. B3d. $4.50

FOX, Gardner F. *Kothar, Barbarian Swordsman.* 1969. Belmont B60-1003. 1st prtg. SF. G. R5d. $1.25

FOX, Gardner F. *Kothar, Barbarian Swordsman.* 1969. Belmont. 1st edn. F. M1d. $12.00

FOX, Gardner F. *Kothar, Barbarian Swordsman.* 1973. Leisure 1465K. 2nd edn. F. P9d. $2.00

FOX, Gardner F. *Kothar & the Conjurer's Curse.* 1970. Belmont. 1st edn. F. M1d. $12.00

FOX, Gardner F. *Kothar & the Demon Queen.* 1969. Tower. 1st edn. F. M1d. $10.00

FOX, Gardner F. *Kothar & the Wizard Slayer.* 1970. Belmont. 1st edn. F. M1d. $12.00

FOX, Gardner F. *Kothar & the Wizard Slayer.* Uni-Book NN. 1st prtg. F. S1d. $3.00

FOX, Gardner F. *Kothar of the Magic Sword.* 1969. Belmont B60-1043. PBO. c/J Jones. SF. VG. B5d. $3.00

FOX, Gardner F. *Kyrik & the Lost Queen.* 1976. Leisure 420. 1st edn. SF. F. F2d. $15.00

FOX, Gardner F. *Lion of Lucca.* 1966. Avon V 2150. 1st prtg. c/George Gross: gga. VG. P7d. $4.00

FOX, Gardner F. *One Sword for Love.* 1953. Gold Medal 360. PBO. c/Geygan. VG. B6d. $8.00

FOX, Gardner F. *Queen of Sheba.* 1956. Gold Medal S 549. PBO. c/gga. VG. B6d. $9.00

FOX, Gardner F. *She Wouldn't Surrender.* 1960. Monarch 301. 1st edn. c/gga. F. F2d. $16.00

FOX, Gardner F. *Slave of the Roman Sword.* 1965. PB Library 54-800. 1st edn. Hi. F. F2d. $15.00

FOX, Gardner F. *Terror Over London.* Gold Medal 648. c/Hooks. VG. B3d. $8.00

FOX, Gardner F. *Terror Over London.* 1957. Gold Medal 648. PBO. c/Hooks. VG+. B6a #77. $20.00

FOX, Gardner F. *Thief of Llarn.* Ace F 399. NF. M1d. $8.00

FOX, Gardner F. *Thief of Llarn.* 1966. Ace F 399. 1st prtg. PBO. c/Morrow. VG. P7d. $5.00

FOX, Gardner F. *This Sword for Hire!* 1966. Popular 54-973. 1st edn. Hi. F. F2d. $8.00

FOX, Gardner F. *Tom Blood, Highwayman.* 1962. Avon G 1125. Fa. VG. B4d. $5.00

FOX, Gardner F. *Tom Blood, Highwayman.* 1962. Avon G 1125. PBO. TVTI. Bio. G+. P6d. $2.00

FOX, Gardner F. *Tom Blood, Highwayman.* 1962. Avon. 1st edn. F. M1d. $15.00

FOX, Gardner F. *Warrier of Llarn.* Ace F 307. 1st prtg. VG+. S1d. $4.00

FOX, Gardner F. *Warrior of Llarn.* Ace F 307. NF. M1d. $10.00

FOX, Gardner F. *Warrior of Llarn.* 1964. Ace F 307. SF. VG. W2d. $7.50

FOX, Gardner F. *Western Volume 1, #2.* 1957. Three-Book. PBO. VG+. B6d. $7.50

FOX, Gardner F. *Women of Kali.* 1954. Gold Medal 438. VG. B3d. $7.50

FOX, James M. *Death Commits Bigamy.* Dell 845. c/M Privatello. My. VG. B5d. $3.00

FOX, James M. *Death Commits Bigamy.* Graphic 14. G+. G5d. $3.25

FOX, James M. *Death Commits Bigamy.* 1949. Graphic 14. 1st prtg. VG. P7d. $5.00

FOX, James M. *Exiles.* 1971. Bantam N 5701. Fi. VG. P1d. $4.00

FOX, James M. *Fatal in Furs.* Dell 623. VG. G5d. $3.75

FOX, James M. *Free Ride.* 1957. Popular EB 82. G+. P6d. $1.00

FOX, James M. *Gentle Hangman.* Dell 526. 1st prtg. My. G+. R5d. $3.00

FOX, James M. *Inconvenient Bride.* Dell 463. G+. G5d. $4.00

FOX, James M. *Iron Virgin.* Dell 719. c/C Bobertz. My. VG. B5d. $3.00

FOX, James M. *Lady Regrets.* Dell 338. c/V Kalin. My. G+. B5d/I1d. $3.00

FOX, James M. *Lady Regrets.* Dell 338. VG. B3d. $4.00

FOX, James M. *Save Them for Violence.* 1959. Monarch 132. PBO. c/Lou Marchetti: gga. VG. B6a #77. $61.00

FOX, James M. *Save Them for Violence.* 1959. Monarch 132. 1st prtg. PBO. c/Maguire: gga. VG. P7d. $7.50

FOX, James M. *Scarlet Slippers.* Dell 685. c/J Meese. My. VG+. B5d. $4.50

FOX, James M. *Wheel Is Fixed.* Dell 573. VG. B3d. $4.50

FOX, James M. *Wheel Is Fixed.* 1982. World Wide 63022. 2nd prtg. My. F. W2d. $4.00

FOX, James M. *White Mischief.* 1984. Vintage 72366. 1st prtg. c/Gamarello: gga. VG. P7d. $4.00

FOX, Kenneth R. *Murder at Shirttail Flats.* 1968. Gold Medal 1971. 1st edn. My. F. F2d. $9.00

FOX, Norman A. *Badlands Beyond.* 1959. Dell 1002. c/R Stanley. We. NF. B5d. $5.00

FOX, Norman A. *Cactus Cavalier.* Dell 406. c/R Stanley. We. VG+. B5d. $6.00

FOX, Norman A. *Hard Pursued.* Dell D 432. VG+. B3d. $4.50

FOX, Norman A. *Longhorn Legion.* Dell 10¢ 12. VG+. B3d. $7.50

FOX, Norman A. *Rawhide Years.* Dell 831. c/R Stanley. We. VG. B5d. $3.00

FOX, Norman A. *Roughshod.* 1960. Dell 1014. c/J Leone. We. VG. B5d. $3.00

FOX, Norman A. *Shadow on the Range.* Dell 539. c/R Stanley. We. VG. B5d. $4.00

FOX, Norman A. *Shadow on the Range.* Dell 907. c/G Gross. We. G+. B5d. $2.50

FOX, Norman A. *Silent in the Saddle.* Dell 362. c/B Meyers. We. NF. B5d. $6.50

FOX, Norman A. *Silent in the Saddle.* Dell 362. VG. B3d. $4.00

FOX, Norman A. *Six-Gun Syndicate.* Pyramid 195. c/Engle. VG+. B3d. $5.00

FOX, Norman A. *Stranger From Arizona.* Dell 969. VG+. B3d. $4.00

FOX, Norman A. *Tall Man Riding.* Dell 980. VG+. B3d. $5.00

FOX, Norman A. *Thirsty Land.* Dell 864. c/R Stanley. We. VG+. B5d. $4.00

FOX, Norman A. *Trembling Hills.* Dell 8087. 1st pb. VG. M6d. $3.50

FOX, Paul. *Sailor Town.* 1950. Bantam 813. c/gga. Fa. VG. B4d. $2.75

FOX, Paula. *Desperate Characters.* 1971. Avon N 401. 1st pb. MTI. Ho. NF. B6d. $9.00

FOX, Richard. *Turncoat.* 1959. Beacon 233. 1st prtg. PBO. VG. P7d. $9.00

FOX, T. *That Girl on the River.* Popular EB 38. VG. B3d. $4.00

FOX, William Price. *Southern Fried.* 1966. Gold Medal D 1723. 1st prtg. c/Jack Davis. VG. P7d. $7.50

FOX/PERRY. *Devil's Saddle/Nightrider.* 1954. Ace D 72. We. VG. P6d. $7.50

FRAENKEL & MANVELL. *Dr Goebbels.* 1961. Pyramid R 587. NF. B3d. $6.00

FRAENKEL & MANVELL. *Dr Goebbels.* 1961. Pyramid R587. c/photo. Nfi. VG. B5d. $4.00

FRALEY, Oscar. *4 Against the Mob.* Popular G 512. VG. G5d. $5.50

FRAME, Bart. *Black Satin Jungle.* 1960. Zenith ZB 44. Fi. G+. B5d. $4.00

FRAME, Bart. *Sinful.* Avon T 277. VG+. B3d. $4.50

FRAME, Bart. *Sinful.* MacFadden 60-337. VG. M6d. $4.50

FRANCE, Anatole. *Red Lily.* 1957. Lion Library LL 170. Fa. NF. B4d. $12.50

FRANCE, Anatole. *Red Lily.* Pyramid G 417. reprint. NF. B6d. $12.00

FRANCE, Hector. *Musk, Hashish & Blood.* 1951. Avon 308. PBO. VG. B6d. $22.50

FRANCE, Hector. *Musk, Hashish & Blood.* 1969. Collectors Pub 21305. PBO. reprints. VG. P6d. $8.00

FRANCIS, Dick. *Odds Against.* Berkley 1350. VG. G5d. $3.50

FRANCIS, Dick. *Risk.* 1979. Pocket 68078. 10th prtg. My. VG+. W2d. $3.25

FRANCIS, Dorothy. *Two Against the Arctic.* 1976. Pyramid V 4026. TVTI. NF. B4d. $3.50

FRANCIS, Jean. *Fires of Lust.* Lancer 73-771. PBO. VG+. M6d. $5.00

FRANCIS, William. *Bury Me Not.* 1951. Boardman 106. VG. B3d. $8.00

FRANCIS, William. *Don't Dig Deeper.* Lion 123. G. G5d. $6.00

FRANCIS, William. *Don't Dig Deeper.* 1953. Lion 123. PBO. VG+. B3a #21. $20.00

FRANCIS, William. *IOU Murder.* 1951. Signet 865. 1st edn. PBO. c/gga. F. F2d. $8.00

FRANCIS, William. *Kill or Cure.* 1949. Signet 742. My. NF. B5d. $8.00

FRANK, Anne. *Diary of a Young Girl.* 1958. Cardinal C 317. Fi. VG. P1d. $6.00

FRANK, Anne. *Diary of a Young Girl.* 1955. Pan 307. 2nd prtg. VG. B3d. $8.00

FRANK, Martin M. *Diary of a DA.* 1961. Popular SP 80. My. VG. B4d. $2.00

FRANK, N. *Fortune's Bastard.* All Star 122. VG+. B3d. $5.00

FRANK, Pat. *Alas, Babylon.* 1960. Bantam F 2054. 1st prtg. VG. R5d. $2.00

FRANK, Pat. *Alas, Babylon.* 1964. Bantam HP 70. 16th prtg. SF. VG. W2d. $4.00

FRANK, Pat. *Hold Back the Night.* 1953. Bantam 1078. Fi. VC. P1d. $8.50

FRANK, William F. *Lover, Destroy Me!* 1963. Bedside 1249. c/gga. Fa. NF. B3d/B4d. $6.00

FRANK, Wolfgang. *German Raider Atlantis.* 1956. Ballantine 184. War. VG. B4d. $2.00

FRANK, Wolfgang. *Sea Wolves.* 1958. Ballantine F 258. 1st pb. VG+. B6d. $8.00

FRANK & ROGGE. *German Raider Atlantis.* 1957. Ballantine 184. Fi. VG. P1d. $5.00

FRANK & ROGGE. *Under 10 Flags.* 1960. Ballantine 395K. 5th edn. Fi. VG+. P1d. $7.50

FRANKE, Herbert W. *Mind Net.* 1974. DAW. 1st pb. F. M1d. $6.00

FRANKE, Herbert W. *Orchid Cage.* 1973. DAW 79. PBO. c/DiFate. SF. VG. B6d. $3.50

FRANKE, Herbert W. *Orchid Cage.* 1973. DAW 79. 1st edn. F. M1d. $6.00

FRANKLIN, D. *Playgirl's Stud.* PEC NL139. c/sgn. VG+. B3d. $8.00

FRANKLIN, F.K. *Combat Nurse.* 1956. Pocket 1147. Fi. F. P1d. $10.00

FRANKLIN, F.K. *To Love & Hate (Cleft in the Rock).* Popular 753. VG. B3d. $4.00

FRANKLIN, Jay. *Rat Race.* Galaxy Novel 10. VG. P9d. $4.50

FRANKLIN, Max. *Bounty Hunter.* 1977. Ballantine 25669. TVTI. VG. P1d. $5.00

FRANKLIN, Max. *Bounty Hunter.* 1977. Ballantine 25669. 1st prtg. TVTI. Starsky & Hutch #4. My. G+. R5d. $1.25

FRANKLIN, Max. *Death Ride.* 1976. Ballantine 23921. TVTI. VG. P1d. $5.00

FRANKLIN, Max. *Death Ride.* 1976. Ballantine 23921. 1st prtg. TVTI. Starsky & Hutch #3. My. VG. R5d. $1.75

FRANKLIN, Max. *Kill Huggy Bear.* 1976. Ballantine 25124. TVTI. VG. P1d. $5.00

FRANKLIN, Max. *Psychic.* 1977. Ballantine 25710. 1st prtg. TVTI. Starsky & Hutch #6. My. VG. R5d. $1.50

FRANKLIN, Max. *Terror on the Docks.* 1977. Ballantine 25709. TVTI. VG. P1d. $5.00

FRANKLIN, Max. *Terror on the Docks.* 1977. Ballantine 25709. 1st prtg. TVTI. Starsky & Hutch #5. My. VG. R5d. $1.75

FRANKLIN, Max. *Vegas.* 1978. Ballantine 28051. 1st prtg. TVTI. My. VG. R5d. $1.75

FRANSON, Robert. *Shadow of the Ship.* 1983. Ballantine 30688. SF. VG. W2d. $3.50

FRANZERO, C.M. *Cleopatra.* Panther 1402. 2nd prtg. VG. B3d. $7.50

FRASER, G.M. *Flashman.* Pan 02484. 2nd prtg. VG. B3d. $6.00

FRASER, Ian. *Frogman VC.* 1958. Beacon Books B 27. Fi. G+. P1d. $4.75

FRASER & YOUNG. *Puzzles Quizzes & Games.* 1947. Bantam 81. F. I1d. $7.00

FRAY, Al. *Come Back for More.* Dell 1st Edn A 161. G+. G5d. $3.00

FRAY, Al. *Come Back for More.* Dell 1st Edn A 161. VC. B3d. $4.50

FRAY, Al. *Dame's the Game.* Popular G 431. G+. G5d. $6.50

FRAY, Al. *Dice Spelled Murder.* Dell 1st Edn A 136. G+. G5d. $3.00

FRAYN, Michael. *Very Private World.* 1969. Dell 9303. SF. VG. W2d. $4.00

FRAZEE, Steve. *Alamo.* 1960. Avon T 446. 1st edn. c/photo. scarce in top condition. F. F2d. $15.00

FRAZEE, Steve. *Day To Die.* 1960. Avon T 458. PBO. TVTI. We. VG+. P6d. $2.50

FRAZEE, Steve. *Gold at Kansas Gulch.* Crest 261. VG. B3d. $4.00

FRAZEE, Steve. *Gunthrowers.* Lion LB 173. 2nd prtg. VG+. B3d. $5.00

FRAZEE, Steve. *Lawman's Feud.* 1953. Lion 150. PBO. We. VG. P6d. $6.00

FRAZEE, Steve. *Pistolman.* Lion 90. NF. I1d. $12.00

FRAZEE, Steve. *Spur to the Smoke.* 1954. Perma M 3003. We. G+. P6d. $1.25

FRAZEE, Steve. *Utah Hell Guns.* 1952. Lion 96. We. VG+. I1d. $12.00

FRAZEE, Steve. *Zorro.* 1968. Popular 2345. 1st edn. TVTI. c/photo. We. F. F2d. $7.50

FRAZER, Diane. *Date with Danger.* 1966. Pocket 50229. My. VG+. B5d. $5.00

FRAZER, Diane. *Special Case for Peggy Bruce, RN.* 1963. Perma M 4284. Fa. NF. B4d. $3.00

FRAZER, Robert Caine. *Hollywood Hoax.* Pocket 6064. NF. G5d. $6.50

FRAZER, Robert Caine. *Mark Kilby & the Miami Mob.* Pocket 6022. G. G5d. $4.00

FRAZER, Robert Caine. *Mark Kilby & the Secret Syndicate.* 1960. Pocket 6000. My. VG. B5d. $3.00

FRAZER, Robert Caine. *Mark Kilby Solves a Murder.* PB Library 1261. F. G5d. $10.00

FRAZER, Robert Caine. *Mark Kilby Solves a Murder.* 1959. Pocket 1261. My. VG+. B4d. $4.00

FRAZER, Robert Caine. *Mark Kilby Stands Alone.* 1962. Pocket 6138. 1st edn. De. F. F2d. $11.00

FRAZER, Robert Caine. *Mark Kilby Takes a Risk.* 1962. Pocket 6104. My. G+. B5d. $3.00

FREDERICKS, Diana. *Diana.* 1957. Berkley G 50. 1st edn. PBO. c/gga. NF. F2d. $15.00

FREDERICKS, E.J. *Cry Flood.* Ace D 370. VG. M1d. $6.00

FREDERICKS, Pierce G. *Great Adventure.* 1967. Ace K 151. Fi. VG. P1d. $4.00

FREDERICKS, Vic. *More for Doctors Only.* Pocket 6119. VG+. B3d. $5.00

FREE, Colin. *Soft Kill.* 1973. Berkley 2459. 1st edn. F. P9d. $2.00

FREE, Montague. *Pocket Book of Flower Gardening.* 1943. Pocket 200. PBO. VG+. B6d. $6.00

FREE, Montague. *Pocket Book of Flower Gardening.* 1943. Pocket 200. VG. B3d. $4.50

FREED & LANE. *Executive Action.* 1974. Dell 2348. 17th prtg. MTI. My. VG. W2d. $3.00

FREEDLAND, N. *Exotica in the Desert.* Brandon House 1162. VG+. B3d. $5.00

FREEDMAN, Nancy. *Joshua Son of None.* 1974. Dell 4344. 1st prtg. SF. VG+. W2d. $3.75

FREELING, Nicholas. *Because of the Cats.* 1965. Ballantine U 2131. c/skeleton. My. VG+. B4d. $4.00

FREELING, Nicholas. *Death in Amsterdam.* 1964. Ballantine U 2130. 1st pb. VG. M6d. $4.50

FREEMAN, A. *D'Arblay Mystery.* Pan 371. VG. B3d. $5.00

FREEMAN, R. Austin. *Dr Thorndyke's Discovery.* Avon 10. My. G+. B6d. $12.50

FREEMAN, R. Austin. *Mr Polton Explains.* Popular 70. VG. B3d. $4.50

FREEMAN, R. Austin. *Silent Witness.* 1942. Pocket 184. c/Hoffman. My. G+. B5d. $3.50

FREEMAN, R. Austin. *Stoneware Monkey.* 1943. Popular 11. My. VG. B4d. $20.00

FREEMAN, R. Austin. *Unconscious Witness.* 1947. Avon 122. c/gga. My. VG. B4d. $10.00

FREEMAN, R. Austin. *Unconscious Witness.* 1947. Avon 122. 1st edn. PBO. c/Dr Thorndyke. VG+. B6a #80. $61.00

FREEMAN, Walter. *All the Way Home.* 1955. Signet 1186. c/C Hulings. Fi. VG+. B5d. $4.50

FREEMAN, Walter. *Last Blitzkrieg.* 1959. Signet 1634. 1st prtg. MTI. c/Van Johnson. VG+. R5d. $5.00

FREEMAN & HULSE. *Children Who Kill.* 1962. Berkley F 654. 1st edn. My. F. F2d. $7.50

FREIDEN & RICHARDSON. *Fatal Decisions.* Berkley G 121. VG+. B3d. $4.50

FRENCH, Anthony. *Lyrics of Love.* 1967. Saber SA 947. Ad. VG+. B5d. $6.00

FRENCH, L. *Grimm's Ghost Stories.* White Circle 5778. SF. VG. W2d. $3.50

FREUCHEN, Peter. *Sea Tyrant.* 1953. Pyramid 98. 1st pb. VG. B6d. $5.00

FREUD, Sigmund. *General Intro to Psychoanalysis.* Perma P 202. VG+. B3d. $4.00

FREYER, Federic. *Case of the Black Hearse.* 1955. Avon 677. c/gga. My. VG+. B4d. $7.00

FRID, J. *Barnabas Collins: A Personal Picture Album.* 1969. PB Library 62-210. 1st prtg. VG+. R5d. $6.00

FRIDAY, B. *I Love You, Alice B Toklas!* 1968. Bantam 3919. 1st edn. c/Peter Sellers photo. F. F2d. $10.00

FRIED, Edrita. *On Love & Sexuality.* Black Cat B 321-Z. 5th edn. Nfi. VG+. B5d. $4.50

FRIEDBERG, Gertrude. *Revolving Box.* Ace H 58. 1st edn. PBO. SF. VG. P9d. $1.50

FRIEDMAN, B.H. *I Need To Love.* MacFadden 50-172. VG+. B3d. $6.00

FRIEDMAN, C.S. *In Conquest Born.* 1986. DAW 707. 1st edn. F. P9d. $2.50

FRIEDMAN, Favius. *Great Horror Movies.* 1974. Scholastic 2408. SF. VG+. W2d. $3.50

FRIEDMAN, M.J. *Fortune's Light.* 1991. Pocket 70836. Star Trek: The Next Generation #16. SF. VG. W2d. $4.00

FRIEDMAN, Mickey. *Fault Tree.* 1985. Ballantine 32198. c/skull. My. VG+. B5d. $3.50

FRIEDMAN, Philip. *Rage.* 1973. PB Library 76-133. PBO. MTI. NF. B6d. $7.50

FRIEDMAN, Stanley P. *Magnificent Kennedy Women.* Monarch MS 25. VG+. B3d. $4.50

FRIEDMAN, Stuart. *Bedside Corpse.* 1957. Lion LL 148. 1st pb. My. NF. B6d. $12.50

FRIEDMAN, Stuart. *Come-On Girl.* 1960. Belmont 214. 1st edn. c/gga. My. F. F2d. $15.00

FRIEDMAN, Stuart. *Damned Are the Meek.* 1964. Monarch 407. PBO. c/De Soto: gga. VG+. P6d. $5.50

FRIEDMAN, Stuart. *Irina.* 1963. Monarch 294. PBO. c/Tom Miller: gga. VG. P6d. $3.00

FRIEDMAN, Stuart. *Luscious Puritan.* 1964. Monarch 437. 1st prtg. PBO. c/Olson: gga. VG+. P7d. $6.00

FRIEDMAN, Stuart. *Nikki.* Monarch 125. 3rd prtg. c/Maguire. NF. I1d. $10.00

FRIEDMAN, Stuart. *Ravaged.* 1962. Monarch 257. PBO. c/Johnson: gga. scarce. JD. VG+. B6a #80. $38.50

FRIEDMAN, Stuart. *Revolt of Jill Braddock.* Monarch 144. PBO. VG+. B3d. $6.50

FRIEDMAN, Stuart. *Revolt of Jill Braddock.* 1963. Monarch 378. Ad. G+. B5d. $4.00

FRIEDMAN, Stuart. *Surgeons.* Monarch 272. VG. I1d. $5.00

FRIEDMAN, Stuart. *Trouble with Ava.* Monarch 491. PBO. VG. B3d. $4.50

FRIEDMAN, Stuart. *Woman & the Prowler.* 1957. Avon 773. 1st prtg. My. G+. R5d. $2.75

FRIEL, Arthur O. *Pathless Grail.* 1969. Centaur 1. c/J Jones. SF. VG. B5d/W2d. $4.50

FRIEL, Arthur O. *Tiger River.* 1971. Centaur 6. c/J Jones. SF. VG. B3d/B5d. $4.50

FRIEND, Ed. *Alvarez Kelly.* Gold Medal K 1732. PBO. MTI. We. VG. B5d. $3.00

FRIEND, Ed. *Coyote Gold.* 1969. Tempo 5302. High Chaparral. c/photo. VG. P6d. $5.00

FRIEND, Ed. *Green Hornet in the Infernal.* 1966. Dell 3231. TVTI. c/photo. VG. P6d. $4.50

FRIEND, Ed. *Scalphunters.* Gold Medal 1911. MTI. VG+. B3d. $4.50

FRIEND, O.J. *Range Doctor.* Handi 101. VG. B3d. $6.00

FRIEND, O.J. *Roundup.* Avon 299. VG. I1d. $5.00

FRIEND, O.J. *Roundup.* 1951. Avon 299. 1st edn. PBO. c/Bama. scarce. VG+. B6a #80. $48.50

FRIESNER, Esther. *Elf Defense.* 1988. Signet. 1st edn. VG. M1d. $3.00

FRIESNER, Esther. *Harlot's Ruse.* 1986. Popular 20208. 1st edn. Fa. F. F2d. $7.50

FRIESNER, Esther. *New York by Knight.* 1986. Signet 4496. 1st edn. Fa. F. F2d. $8.00

FRISCHAUER, Willi. *Goering.* 1960. Four Square 269. VG. B3d. $8.50

FRISCHAUER, Willi. *Rise & Fall of Hermann Goering.* 1960. Ballantine F 409K. Fi. VG+. P1d. $6.50

FRISCHAUER & JACKSON. *Navy's Here.* 1957. Pan GP 56. Fi. VG+. P1d. $7.00

FRITCH, Charles. *Crazy Mixed-Up Planet.* 1969. Powell. 1st edn. F. M1d. $20.00

FRITCH, Charles. *Horses' Asteroid.* 1970. Powell PP 1004. PBO. c/Bill Hughes. VG. P6d. $4.00

FRITCH, Charles. *Horses' Asteroid.* 1970. Powell PP 1004. 1st edn. F. M1d. $25.00

FRITCH/TRIMBLE. *Negative of a Nude/Til Death Do Us Part.* 1959. Ace D 367. PBO. My. VG. P6d. $6.50

FROME, David. *Eel Pie Murders.* 1943. Popular 9. VG. B3a #22. $11.00

FROME, David. *Eel Pie Murders.* 1943. Popular 9. VG. B3d. $7.00

FROME, David. *Hammersmith Murders.* Dell 36. 1st prtg. My. G+. R5d. $6.50

FROME, David. *Hammersmith Murders.* 1944. Dell 36. 1st edn. PBO. c/G Gregg. scarce. VG+. B6a. $49.00

FROME, David. *Man From Scotland Yard.* Pocket 153. G+. G5d. $5.00

FROME, David. *Mr Pinkerton Finds a Body.* Pocket 111. VG. B3d. $4.50

FROME, David. *Mr Pinkerton Grows a Beard.* Signet 541. c/Peng. VG. B3d. $6.00

FROME, David. *Mr Pinkerton Has the Clue.* 1944. Popular 26. 1st pb. My. VG. B6d. $9.00

FROST, Fredrick. *Spy Meets Spy.* Th Novel Classic 7. VG. B3d. $4.50

FUCHS, Daniel. *Summer in Williamsburg.* 1965. Berkley S 1066. Fi. VG+. B5d. $3.50

FULFORD, P. edt. *100 Best Cartoons.* Checker 12. VG. B3d. $10.00

FULLER, Blair. *Forbid Me Not.* 1957. Berkley G 103. VG. P6d. $4.50

FULLER, John G. *Incident at Exeter.* 1967. Berkley S 1354. 3rd prtg. SF. F. W2d. $4.50

FULLER, John G. *Interrupted Journey.* 1967. Dell 4068. 1st prtg. c/Allegro. VG. P7d. $4.00

FULLER, R. *All the Silent Voices.* Pocket 50056. PBO. TVTI. VG+. B3d. $5.00

FULLER, R. *Burke's Law.* Fontana 2019. 1st English edn. TVTI. VG. B3d. $5.00

FULLER, R. *Burke's Law.* Pocket 50030. NF. I1d. $6.00

FULLER, R. *Burke's Law: Who Killed Madcap Millicent?* 1964. Pocket 50030. 1st prtg. VG. R5d. $2.50

FULLER, Robert G. *Danger! Marines at Work!* Panther 1010. VG. B3d. $5.00

FULLER, Roger. *Eve of Judgement.* 1965. Pocket 50190. My. VG. B5d. $3.50

FULLER, Roger. *Facts of Life.* 1960. Perma M 4207. MTI. c/Lucille Ball & Bob Hope: photo. VG+. B4d. $3.00

FULLER, Roger. *Fear in a Desert Town.* 1964. Cardinal C 35012. 1st prtg. TVTI. My. VG. R5d. $2.50

FULLER, Roger. *On the Double.* 1961. Cardinal C 427. 1st prtg. MTI. My. G+. R5d. $1.50

FULLER, Roger. *Son of Flubber.* 1963. Perma M 4279. 1st prtg. G+. R5d. $2.50

FULLER, Roger. *Thrills of Peyton Place.* 1969. Pocket 75457. 1st edn. scarce. My. F. F2d. $15.00

FULLER, Roger. *Timeless Serpent.* 1965. Pocket 50161. Fi. VG+. B5d. $3.50

FULLER, Roger. *Who Killed Madcap Millicent?* 1964. Pocket 50030. MTI. c/Gene Barry. VG+. B4d. $3.00

FULLER, Samuel. *Crown of India.* 1966. Award A 180X. 1st prtg. My. G+. R5d. $1.25

FULLER, Timothy. *Harvard Has a Homicide.* Dell 54. VG. G5d. $15.00

FULLER, Timothy. *Keep Cool, Mr Jones.* Dell 594. VG. G5d. $4.00

FULLER, Timothy. *Reunion With Murder.* Popular 207. G+. G5d. $7.50

FULLER, Timothy. *This Is Murder, Mr Jones.* Popular 117. VG. B3d. $4.50

FULLER, Timothy. *Three Thirds of a Ghost.* Popular 81. VG. B3d. $4.50

FULLER, Timothy. *Three Thirds of a Ghost.* Popular 81. VG+. I1d. $12.00

FULLER, William. *Back Country.* 1954. Dell 1st Edn 8. 1st prtg. PBO. c/Borack: gga. VG. I1d/P7d. $5.00

FULLER, William. *Brad Dolan's Blonde Cargo.* 1957. Dell 1st Edn A 153. 1st prtg. PBO. c/Kalin: gga. VG. P7d. $5.00

FULLER, William. *Girl in the Frame.* 1957. Dell 1st Edn A 133. PBO. c/Vic Kalin. VG+. B3d. $4.50

FULLER, William. *Goat Island.* 1954. Dell 1st Edn 28. PBO. c/G Gross. My. VG. B5d. $5.00

FULLER, William. *Pace That Kills.* 1956. Dell 1st Edn 105. PBO. c/Hooks. My. VG. B6d. $4.50

FULLER, William. *Tight Squeeze.* 1959. Dell 1st Edn A 189. 1st prtg. PBO. c/Kalin: gga. VG. P7d. $5.00

FULLER & ROLFE. *Murder in the Glass Room.* 1948. Bantam 310. c/A Werner. My. VG. B3d/B5d. $4.50

FULLER & ROLFE. *Murder in the Glass Room.* 1948. Bantam 310. My. NF. B4d. $12.50

FULLERTON, Alexander. *No Man's Mistress.* 1957. Pan 433. Fi. G+. P1d. $3.50

FULTON, Jay. *Perverted Urge.* Merit 520. VG. B3d. $5.00

FULTON, W. *Ghetto Incest.* Barclay 7277. F. B3d. $4.00

FULTON, W. *Sex: The Blackmailer's Weapon.* Barclay 7419. NF. B3d. $5.00

FULTON, W. *Sorority Sex Freak.* Brandon House 6497. VG+. B3d. $4.50

FUNKE & BOOTH. *Actors Talk About Acting, Volume #1.* Avon V 2070. VG. B3d. $4.50

FUNNELL, Augustine. *Rebels of Merka.* 1976. Laser 48. 1st edn. VG. P9d. $1.50

FURIA, John Jr. *Singing Nun.* 1966. Popular 60-8015. MTI. c/Debbie Reynolds: photo. F. B4d. $4.00

FURLOUGH, J. *Pot of Honey.* Beacon 956. PBO. VG+. B3d. $6.00

FURLOUGH, J. *Vicious Virgin.* Brandon House 1140. NF. B3d. $7.00

FURMAN, A.L. *Mystery Companion.* Popular 130. VG. B3d. $5.00

FURMAN, A.L. *Outer Space Stories.* 1965. Lancer 50260. 1st prtg. SF. VG+. W2d. $4.00

FURMAN, A.L. *Outer Space Stories.* 1966. Lancer 50260. 2nd prtg. SF. G. W2d. $2.75

FURNEAUX, Robert. *World's Strangest Mysteries.* Ace K 163. F. M1d. $5.00

FYFE, H.B. *D-99.* 1962. Pyramid F 794. PBO. c/R Brillhart. SF. VG. B5d. $4.00

FYLNN, Jackson. *Duel at Dodge City.* 1974. Award AN 1328. PBO. TVTI. Gunsmoke #3. c/photo. VG. P6d. $2.00

G

GABREE, John. *World of Rock.* 1968. Gold Medal T2003. VG+. P6d. $6.50

GABY, Alex. *To End the Night.* 1953. Signet 1035. c/Cardiff. Fi. VG+. B5d. $5.50

GADDIS, Peggy. *Farmer's Woman.* 1954. Venus Digest 172. VG+. B6a #80. $77.00

GADDIS, Peggy. *Lust Seekers.* Belmont 92-605. NF. B3d. $5.00

GADDIS, Peggy. *Man-Crazy Nurse.* 1954. Croydon 90. PBO. G+. B6d. $3.75

GADDIS, Peggy. *Nurse Durand's Affair.* Belmont 244. VG. B3d. $4.00

GADDIS, Peggy. *One Wild Night!* 1951. Venus Digest 116. PBO. c/George Gross: gga. NF. B6a #80. $101.00

GADDIS, Peggy. *Roses in December.* 1967. MacFadden 50-385. 1st pb. NF. B6d. $6.00

GADDIS, Peggy. *Strangers in the Dark.* 1952. Carnival Books 905. 1st edn. PBO. c/George Gross: gga. G. P6d. $3.50

GADDIS, T.E. *Bird Man of Alcatraz.* 1962. Four Square 782. 3rd prtg. MTI. VG. B3d. $6.00

GAILLARD, Robert. *Marie of the Isles.* Popular G 139. VG+. B3d. $4.50

GAILLARD, Robert. *Marie of the Isles.* Popular SP 33. VG. B3d. $4.00

GAINES, Audrey. *Voodoo Goat.* Black Cat 21. My. G. B5d. $2.50

GAINES, Audrey. *While the Wind Howled.* 1944. Dell 51. 1st edn. PBO. c/G Gregg. scarce. NF. B6a #80. $65.00

GAINES, William M. *Bedside Mad.* Signet 1647. VG. B3d. $5.00

GAINES, William M. *Son of Mad.* 1963. Signet. G+. M1d. $5.00

GALANOY, Terry. *Tonight!* 1974. Warner 76-367. TVTI. VG. P1d. $6.00

GALEWITZ, Herb edt. *Snowflake & Shaky.* Gold Medal P 3428. Dick Tracy #2. VG. G5d. $3.50

GALLAGHER, Patricia. *Answer to Heaven.* Avon S 146. Fi. VG. B5d. $2.50

GALLAGHER, Patricia. *Fires of Brimstone.* 1966. Avon N 139. 1st prtg. c/Jim Bama: gga. VG. P7d. $4.00

GALLAGHER, Richard F. *Murder by Gemini.* 1971. Lancer 74-783. 1st edn. TVTI. c/photo. My. F. F2d. $7.00

GALLAGHER, Richard F. *Women Without Morals.* 1962. Avon G 1100. PBO. VG+. B6d. $9.00

GALLAGHER, Teresa. *Give Joy to My Youth.* 1966. Signet T 3002. Nfi. VG+. B4d. $1.25

GALLAND, Adolf. *First & the Last.* 1957. Ballantine F 193. 2nd edn. Fi. VG. P1d. $4.50

GALLERY, D.V. *Stand By-Y-Y To Start Engines.* PB Library 53-458. VG+. B3d. $4.50

GALLI DE BIBIENA, Jean. *Amorous Philandre.* 1948. Avon 171. c/B Stephens. SF. VG. B5d. $6.00

GALLICO, Paul. *Further Confessions of Story Writer.* Popular W 1125. VG+. B3d. $5.00

GALLICO, Paul. *Lonely.* Signet 1295. 2nd prtg. F. B3d. $5.00

GALLICO, Paul. *Lonely.* Signet 819. c/Barye. VG. B3d. $4.50

GALLICO, Paul. *Love of Seven Dolls.* Avon 760. c/date stamp top back. VG+. B3d. $5.00

GALLICO, Paul. *Love of Seven Dolls.* 1956. Avon 760. 1st prtg. c/gga. NF. P7d. $9.00

GALLICO, Paul. *Thief Is an Ugly Word.* Dell 10¢ 27. VG. B3d. $6.00

GALLICO, Paul. *Three Lives of Thomasina.* 1964. Popular SP 281. 1st prtg. VG. R5d. $2.25

GALLICO, Paul. *Trial by Terror.* Dell 717. c/W Brooks. My. VG. B5d. $3.00

GALLUN, Raymond Z. *Planet Strappers.* 1961. Pyramid G 658. SF. VG+. B4d. $6.00

GALLUN/KNOX. *Lest We Forget Thee, Earth/People Minus X.* Ace D 291. c/Emsh. VG. M1d. $9.00

GALOUYE, Daniel F. *Infinite Man.* 1973. Bantam N 7130. SF. NF. B5d. $4.00

GALOUYE, Daniel F. *Lords of the Psychon.* 1963. Bantam J 2555. SF. VG+. B5d. $3.50

GALOUYE, Daniel F. *Scourge of Screamers.* 1968. Bantam F 3585. 1st prtg. PBO. VG. P7d. $4.00

GALOUYE, Daniel F. *Simulacron-3.* 1964. Bantam J 2797. 1st prtg. SF. VG+. R5d. $3.00

GALSWORTHY, John. *Three Plays.* Pan 49. VG. B3d. $6.00

GALTON & SIMPSON. *Spy With a Cold Nose.* Arrow 930. MTI. VG. B3d. $6.50

GALUS, Henry S. *Impact of Women.* 1964. Monarch MB 549. 1st prtg. PBO. VG. B3d/P7d. $4.50

GAMOV, George. *Birth & Death of the Sun.* 1945. Pelican P 4. Nfi. G+. W2d. $5.00

GAMOV, George. *Planet Called Earth.* 1965. Bantam SP 114. SF. VG. W2d. $4.00

GANN, Ernest K. *High & the Mighty.* Perma M 4002. 2nd prtg. VG+. B3d. $4.00

GANN, Ernest K. *High & the Mighty.* Perma P 301. VG+. B3d. $5.00

GANN, Ernest K. *Island in the Sun.* 1953. Popular 516. Fa. VG+. B4d. $8.00

GANN, Ernest K. *Soldier of Fortune.* Perma M 4034. VG. B3d. $4.50

GANNETT, King. *Abnormal Cravings.* 1962. Novel Book 6052. Ad. G+. B5d. $3.00

GANNETT, Lewis. *I Saw It Happen.* 1942. Pocket 178. VG. B3d. $5.00

GANT, Matthew. *Queen Street.* 1963. Regency RB 315. JD. VG+. P1d. $20.00

GANT, Richard. *Ian Fleming: The Fantastic 007 Man.* 1967. Lancer 73-500. NF. VG. B5d. $4.50

GANT/TRIMBLE. *Never Say No To a Killer/ Stab in the Dark.* 1956. Ace D 157. My. VG. P1d. $10.00

GANTZ, Kenneth. *Not in Solitude.* 1961. Berkley Y 582. 1st pb. NF. M1d. $5.00

GARDEN, Nancy. *Vampires.* 1973. Lippincott LSC 17. 2nd prtg. SF. VG. M3d. $7.00

GARDEN, Nancy. *Vampires. Special Book Fair Edition.* 1979. Skyline 16245. 2nd prtg. Nfi. G. W2d. $5.00

GARDNER, Craig Shaw. *Back to the Future II.* 1989. Berkley 7191. MTI. SF. F. W2d. $4.25

GARDNER, Craig Shaw. *Back to the Future Part 2.* 1989. Berkley Special Edition. 1st prtg. VG+. R5d. $1.75

GARDNER, Craig Shaw. *Back to the Future Part 3.* 1990. Berkley Special Edition. 1st prtg. VG+. R5d. $2.00

GARDNER, Craig Shaw. *Batman.* Warner 35-487. c/Nicholson & Keaton: photo. NF. B3d. $4.00

GARDNER, Craig Shaw. *Difficulty With Dwarfs.* 1987. Ace 14779. SF. VG+. W2d. $3.25

GARDNER, Craig Shaw. *Excess of Enchantment.* 1988. Ace 22363-X. 1st edn. Fa. F. F2d. $7.00

GARDNER, Craig Shaw. *Malady of Magicks.* 1986. Ace 51661. 1st edn. c/sgn. SF. F. F2d. $15.00

GARDNER, Curtiss T. *Fatal Cast (Bones Don't Lie).* Graphic 83. VG+. B3d. $6.00

GARDNER, Dick. *Impossible.* 1962. Ballantine F 636. PBO. NF. VG. B5d. $3.50

GARDNER, Dick. *Impossible.* 1962. Ballantine F 636. 1st edn. NF. M1d. $7.00

GARDNER, Erle Stanley. *Case of the Angry Mourner.* 1955. Pocket 1092. G+. G5d. $6.50

GARDNER, Erle Stanley. *Case of the Backward Mule.* Pan 428. VG+. B3d. $8.50

GARDNER, Erle Stanley. *Case of the Backward Mule.* Pocket 6083. reprint. My. VG+. B6d. $5.00

GARDNER, Erle Stanley. *Case of the Backward Mule.* Pocket 855. VG+. I1d. $6.00

GARDNER, Erle Stanley. *Case of the Baited Hook.* Pocket 414. VG. B3d. $4.00

GARDNER, Erle Stanley. *Case of the Beautiful Beggar.* Pocket 50376. NF. G5d. $3.75

GARDNER, Erle Stanley. *Case of the Bigamous Spouse.* Pocket 4522. NF. G5d. $4.50

GARDNER, Erle Stanley. *Case of the Bigamous Spouse.* 1963. Pocket 4522. My. VG+. B5d. $4.00

GARDNER, Erle Stanley. *Case of the Black-Eyed Blonde.* Armed Services S 21. VG+. I1d. $10.00

GARDNER, Erle Stanley. *Case of the Black-Eyed Blonde.* 1962. Pocket 4502. My. NF. B5d. $4.50

GARDNER, Erle Stanley. *Case of the Borrowed Brunette.* 1959. Cardinal C 380. 1st prtg. c/Charles: gga. VG. P7d. $3.50

GARDNER, Erle Stanley. *Case of the Borrowed Brunette.* 1967. Pocket 50328. 12th edn. My. NF. B5d. $4.00

GARDNER, Erle Stanley. *Case of the Borrowed Brunette.* 1953. Pocket 856. 5th edn. My. VG. B5d. $3.00

GARDNER, Erle Stanley. *Case of the Buried Clock.* 1962. Pocket 4509. 9th edn. My. NF. B5d. $4.50

GARDNER, Erle Stanley. *Case of the Buried Clock.* 1962. Pocket 4509. 9th prtg. My. G+. W2d. $3.00

GARDNER, Erle Stanley. *Case of the Buried Clock.* Pocket 678. NF. I1d. $6.00

GARDNER, Erle Stanley. *Case of the Buried Clock.* Pocket 678. VG+. B3d. $4.50

GARDNER, Erle Stanley. *Case of the Calendar Girl.* 1964. Pocket 4529. 4th edn. My. NF. B5d. $4.50

GARDNER, Erle Stanley. *Case of the Calendar Girl.* 1961. Pocket 6040. My. VG. B5d. $3.00

GARDNER, Erle Stanley. *Case of the Cautious Coquette.* Pan GP 96. c/Peff. VG. B3d. $6.50

GARDNER, Erle Stanley. *Case of the Cautious Coquette.* 1963. Pocket 4527. 8th edn. My. NF. B5d. $4.50

GARDNER, Erle Stanley. *Case of the Counterfeit Eye.* 1942. Pocket 157. My. G+. B5d. $4.50

GARDNER, Erle Stanley. *Case of the Counterfeit Eye.* 1965. Pocket 50306. 26th edn. My. NF. B5d. $4.00

GARDNER, Erle Stanley. *Case of the Curious Bride.* 1967. Pocket 50305. My. VG+. B5d. $3.50

GARDNER, Erle Stanley. *Case of the Dangerous Dowager.* 1943. Pocket 252. 1st prtg. VG. P7d. $6.00

GARDNER, Erle Stanley. *Case of the Daring Decoy.* 1963. Pocket 4518. 5th edn. My. VG+. B5d. $3.50

GARDNER, Erle Stanley. *Case of the Daring Decoy.* 1960. Pocket 6001. My. VG. B5d. $3.00

GARDNER, Erle Stanley. *Case of the Daring Divorcee.* Pocket 50372. VG. G5d. $3.50

GARDNER, Erle Stanley. *Case of the Deadly Toy.* Pocket 6063. VG. G5d. $3.00

GARDNER, Erle Stanley. *Case of the Drowning Duck.* Pocket 643. G. G5d. $3.50

GARDNER, Erle Stanley. *Case of the Drowsy Mosquito.* Pocket 689. VG. I1d. $5.00

GARDNER, Erle Stanley. *Case of the Drowsy Mosquito.* 1969. Pocket 75523. 10th prtg. My. F. W2d. $4.25

GARDNER, Erle Stanley. *Case of the Dubious Bridegroom.* Pocket 976. G+. G5d. $3.50

GARDNER, Erle Stanley. *Case of the Duplicate Daughter.* 1962. Pocket 4504. My. VG. B5d. $3.00

GARDNER, Erle Stanley. *Case of the Duplicate Daughter.* 1962. Pocket 4504. My. VG+. B4d. $4.00

GARDNER, Erle Stanley. *Case of the Fabulous Fake.* 1971. Pocket 75581. My. NF. B5d. $3.50

GARDNER, Erle Stanley. *Case of the Fan-Dancer's Horse.* 1952. Pocket 886. c/gga. My. VG+. B4d. $6.00

GARDNER, Erle Stanley. *Case of the Fiery Fingers.* Pan G 224. c/Peff. VG+. B3d. $8.50

GARDNER, Erle Stanley. *Case of the Foot-Loose Doll.* 1960. Pocket 6016. My. VG+. B5d. $4.00

GARDNER, Erle Stanley. *Case of the Fugitive Nurse.* Pan G 555. 1st pb. reprint. My. VG+. B6d. $6.00

GARDNER, Erle Stanley. *Case of the Fugitive Nurse.* 1957. Pocket 1138. c/photo. My. VG+. B5d. $6.50

GARDNER, Erle Stanley. *Case of the Gilded Lily.* 1961. Pocket 6106. My. VG+. B4d. $3.00

GARDNER, Erle Stanley. *Case of the Glamorous Ghost.* 1957. Cardinal C 282. c/gga. My. VG. B4d. $2.50

GARDNER, Erle Stanley. *Case of the Glamorous Ghost.* Pan G 610. VG. B3d. $6.50

GARDNER, Erle Stanley. *Case of the Golddigger's Purse.* 1951. Pocket 812. c/photo. My. VG+. B5d. $6.50

GARDNER, Erle Stanley. *Case of the Grinning Gorilla.* Pocket 1121. G+. G5d. $3.00

GARDNER, Erle Stanley. *Case of the Grinning Gorilla.* 1966. Pocket 50340. 5th edn. My. VG+. B5d. $3.50

GARDNER, Erle Stanley. *Case of the Half-Wakened Wife.* Armed Services 1039. VG+. I1d. $10.00

GARDNER, Erle Stanley. *Case of the Half-Wakened Wife.* 1951. Pocket 832. c/photo. My. VG. B5d. $5.00

GARDNER, Erle Stanley. *Case of the Haunted Husband.* 1969. Pocket 55818. 24th prtg. My. VG+. W2d. $3.25

GARDNER, Erle Stanley. *Case of the Heiress.* 1952. Pocket 922. 1st prtg. c/Tossey: gga. VG+. P7d. $7.50

GARDNER, Erle Stanley. *Case of the Hesitant Hostess.* Pocket 1127. G+. G5d. $5.00

GARDNER, Erle Stanley. *Case of the Injured Parrot.* 1959. Cardinal C 379. c/gga. My. VG. B4d. $3.00

GARDNER, Erle Stanley. *Case of the Lame Canary.* 1943. Pocket 223. 1st pb. c/Hoffman. My. VG+. B6d. $12.00

GARDNER, Erle Stanley. *Case of the Lazy Lover.* 1952. Pocket 909. 1st prtg. c/Ross: gga. VG+. P7d. $7.50

GARDNER, Erle Stanley. *Case of the Lonely Heiress.* 1973. Pocket 77886. 10th prtg. My. G+. W2d. $2.75

GARDNER, Erle Stanley. *Case of the Lucky Legs.* 1967. Pocket 50303. My. NF. B5d. $4.00

GARDNER, Erle Stanley. *Case of the Lucky Loser.* Cardinal C 341. G+. G5d. $3.75

GARDNER, Erle Stanley. *Case of the Lucky Loser.* 1959. Cardinal C 341. 1st prtg. c/Green: gga. VG. P7d. $3.50

GARDNER, Erle Stanley. *Case of the Lucky Loser.* Pocket 4521. reprint. My. NF. B6d. $7.00

GARDNER, Erle Stanley. *Case of the Lucky Loser.* 1963. Pocket 4521. My. VG. B5d. $3.50

GARDNER, Erle Stanley. *Case of the Moth-Eaten Mink.* Pocket 1107. G. G5d. $3.50

GARDNER, Erle Stanley. *Case of the Mythical Monkeys.* Pocket 6082. VG. G5d. $3.00

GARDNER, Erle Stanley. *Case of the Negligent Nymph.* 1954. Pocket 1029. c/photo. My. VG. B5d. $5.00

GARDNER, Erle Stanley. *Case of the One-Eyed Witness.* 1954. Pocket 1041. 1st prtg. My. G+. W2d. $4.50

GARDNER, Erle Stanley. *Case of the Perjured Parrot.* Cardinal C 379. reprint. VG+. B6d. $5.00

GARDNER, Erle Stanley. *Case of the Perjured Parrot.* 1959. Cardinal C 379. 1st prtg. c/Grasso: gga. VG. P7d. $3.50

GARDNER, Erle Stanley. *Case of the Perjured Parrot.* Pocket 378. G. G5d. $3.00

GARDNER, Erle Stanley. *Case of the Perjured Parrot.* 1947. Pocket 378. 1st pb. My. VG+. B6d. $12.00

GARDNER, Erle Stanley. *Case of the Queenly Contestant.* 1968. Pocket 55878. 1st prtg. My. VG. W2d. $3.50

GARDNER, Erle Stanley. *Case of the Restless Redhead.* 1961. Pocket 6107. 2nd edn. My. NF. B5d. $5.00

GARDNER, Erle Stanley. *Case of the Rolling Bones.* Pocket 464. VG+. B3d. $5.00

GARDNER, Erle Stanley. *Case of the Runaway Corpse.* 1957. Cardinal C 281. My. VG. B4d. $2.50

GARDNER, Erle Stanley. *Case of the Screaming Woman.* 1963. Pocket 4523. 4th edn. My. VG+. B5d. $3.50

GARDNER, Erle Stanley. *Case of the Shapley Shadow.* 1963. Pocket 4507. My. F. B5d. $6.00

GARDNER, Erle Stanley. *Case of the Silent Partner.* 1962. Pocket 4506. 17th edn. My. VG+. B5d. $3.50

GARDNER, Erle Stanley. *Case of the Silent Partner.* Pocket 468. VG. B3d. $4.00

GARDNER, Erle Stanley. *Case of the Singing Skirt.* Pocket 6089. VG. B3d. $4.00

GARDNER, Erle Stanley. *Case of the Sleepwalker's Niece.* Pocket 277. VG+. B3d. $6.00

GARDNER, Erle Stanley. *Case of the Smoking Chimney.* Pocket 6014. reprint. My. VG+. B6d. $5.00

GARDNER, Erle Stanley. *Case of the Smoking Chimney.* Pocket 667. NF. G5d. $9.50

GARDNER, Erle Stanley. *Case of the Spurious Spinster.* Pocket 4515. VG. G5d. $3.50

GARDNER, Erle Stanley. *Case of the Stuttering Bishop.* 1943. Pocket 201. 1st pb. My. VG. B6d. $7.50

GARDNER, Erle Stanley. *Case of the Stuttering Bishop.* 1968. Pocket 55809. 30th prtg. My. VG. W2d. $3.50

GARDNER, Erle Stanley. *Case of the Stuttering Bishop.* 1960. Pocket 6007. 27th edn. My. NF. B5d. $3.50

GARDNER, Erle Stanley. *Case of the Sun Bather's Diary.* 1958. Cardinal C 268. My. VG. B4d. $1.50

GARDNER, Erle Stanley. *Case of the Turning Tide.* Pocket 544. VG. G5d. $6.00

GARDNER, Erle Stanley. *Case of the Vagabond Virgin.* 1953. Pocket 965. c/photo. My. VG+. B5d. $6.50

GARDNER, Erle Stanley. *Case of the Waylaid Wolf.* 1962. Pocket 4501. My. VG. B5d. $3.00

GARDNER, Erle Stanley. *Case of the Waylaid Wolf.* 1962. Pocket 4501. 3rd prtg. My. G+. W2d. $3.75

GARDNER, Erle Stanley. *Case of the Waylaid Wolf.* 1970. Pocket 75562. 10th prtg. My. G+. W2d. $2.75

GARDNER, Erle Stanley. *Case of Waylaid Wolf.* Pocket 4501. VG. G5d. $3.00

GARDNER, Erle Stanley. *Crows Can't Count.* Dell 1625. VG. B3d. $4.00

GARDNER, Erle Stanley. *DA Breaks a Seal.* Pocket 869. VG+. B3d. $5.00

GARDNER, Erle Stanley. *DA Breaks an Egg.* Pan G 281. c/Peff. VG+. B3d. $8.00

GARDNER, Erle Stanley. *DA Breaks an Egg.* 1955. Pocket 1052. 1st pb. My. NF. B6d. $15.00

GARDNER, Erle Stanley. *DA Calls a Turn.* Pocket 595. VG. G5d. $8.00

GARDNER, Erle Stanley. *DA Calls It Murder.* Pocket 263. G+. G5d. $5.00

GARDNER, Erle Stanley. *DA Cooks a Goose.* 1948. Pocket 561. 1st pb. My. VG. B6d. $7.50

GARDNER, Erle Stanley. *DA Draws a Circle.* 1946. Pocket 334. 1st prtg. VG+. P7d. $6.00

GARDNER, Erle Stanley. *DA Takes a Chance.* 1954. Pocket 1010. c/gga. My. VG. B4d/G5d. $5.00

GARDNER, Erle Stanley. *DA Takes a Chance.* 1954. Pocket 1010. 1st pb. My. VG+. B6d. $12.00

GARDNER, Erle Stanley. *Fan Dancers Horse.* Pocket 886. VG. I1d. $4.00

GARDNER, Erle Stanley. *Murder Up My Sleeve.* Pocket 368. 3rd edn. VG+. B3d. $4.50

GARDNER, Erle Stanley. *Perry Mason Case Book.* 1946. Pocket King. 1st edn. VG. F2d. $60.00

GARDNER, Erle Stanley. *This Is Murder.* Pocket 512. VG+. B3d. $5.00

GARDNER, H. *Who Is Harry Kellerman.?* 1971. Signet Y 4726. 1st prtg. VG. R5d. $1.75

GARDNER, Jeffrey. *Barbary Devil.* 1961. Pyramid G 643. PBO. c/R Johnson. Fi. VG+. B5d. $10.00

GARDNER, John. *Amber Nine.* Crest 1173. VG+. B3d. $4.00

GARDNER, John. *Brokenclaw.* 1991. Berkley 12721. 1st prtg. My. F. W2d. $4.75

GARDNER, John. *Liquidator.* 1965. Crest D 856. 1st prtg. VG+. P7d. $5.00

GARDNER, John. *Return of Moriarty.* Berkley T 3095. VG. G5d. $7.00

GARDNER, John. *Understride.* 1968. Crest D 1126. 1st prtg. VG. P7d. $4.00

GARDNER, Leland. *Vietnam Underside!* 1966. Publishers Export 3. 1st edn. F. F2d. $10.00

GARDNER, M. *Curse of Quintana Roo.* 1972. Popular 1548. PBO. Ho. NF. B6d. $15.00

GARDNER, Martin. *Fads & Fallacies.* 1960. Ballantine F 446K. 1st prtg. VG+. P7d. $7.00

GARDNER, Richard. *Mandrill.* 1975. Pocket 80047. PBO. c/Moll. SF. NF. B6d. $7.50

GARDNER, Richard. *Phoenix, of Megaron.* 1976. Pocket 80764. 1st US edn. TVTI. NF. B6d. $12.00

GARDNER, Richard. *Space Guardians.* 1975. Pocket 80198. 1st US edn. TVTI. VG+. B6d. $9.00

GARETH, Max. *Carnival Girl.* Chariot 113. VG+. B3d. $6.00

GARETH, Max. *Chita.* Midwood 43. VG. B3d. $4.50

GARFIELD, Brian Wynne. *Apache Canyon.* Ace F 324. PBO. VG. M6d. $4.50

GARFIELD, Brian Wynne. *Lawbringers.* 1964. Ace D 578. VG. B3d. $4.00

GARFIELD, Brian Wynne. *Vultures in the Sun.* 1964. Ace F 300. 1st pb. We. VG+. B6d. $9.00

GARFORTH, John. *Floating Game.* 1967. Berkley F 1410. 1st prtg. TVTI. VG+. R5d. $5.00

GARFORTH, John. *Passing of Gloria Munday.* 1967. Berkley F 1431. 1st prtg. VG+. R5d. $5.00

GARLAND, Bennett. *Brave Men.* 1962. Monarch 292. c/Bob Stanley: gga. VG. P6d. $3.75

GARLAND, Bennett. *High Storm.* 1963. Monarch 391. We. VG. B4d. $4.00

GARLAND, Bennett. *Last Outlaw.* 1964. Monarch 415. We. VG+. B4d. $5.00

GARLAND, George. *Apache Warpath.* Signet 1714. VG+. B3d. $4.50

GARLAND, Rodney. *Heart in Exile.* Lion LL 76. VG. B3d. $4.00

GARLAND, Rodney. *Troubled Midnight.* 1956. Lion LL 128. My. VG+. B4d. $10.00

GARNER, Alan. *Eliador.* Ace 20275. c/G Barr. SF. VG+. B5d. $4.00

GARNER, Alan. *Weirdstone of Brisingamon.* 1965. Ace G 570. SF. VG+. B4d. $5.00

GARNER, Leland. *Birds & Bees.* 1965. Private Edition 332. PBO. VG+. B6d. $7.50

GARNETT, David. *Lady Into Fox.* Armed Services P 1. VG+. B3a #21. $186.50

GARNETT, David. *Lady Into Fox.* Signet 615. c/Peng. VG. B3d. $6.00

GARNETT, David. *Lady Into Tiger.* 1946. Penguin. 1st pb. VG. M1d. $8.00

GARNETT, David. *Mirror in the Sky.* 1969. Berkley X 1743. SF. VG+. W2d. $4.25

GARNETT, David. *Starseekers.* 1971. Berkley S 1956. PBO. c/P Lehr. SF. VG+. B5d. $5.00

GARNETT, David. *Ways of Desire.* Popular G 435. NF. B3d. $5.00

GARNETT, Randall. *Lord Darcy Investigates.* 1981. Ace 49141. SF. F. W2d. $4.00

GARNETT, Roger. *Death in Piccadilly.* Streamline Thriller NN. 2nd edn. G+. B3d. $6.00

GARON & WILSON edt. *Erotica Exotica.* 1963. Belmont L 92-568. 1st prtg. PBO. VG+. P7d. $5.00

GARR, Hullen. *Garden of Eros.* 1968. Candid Reader 935. PBO. c/gga. NF. B6a. $48.50

GARRETT, James. *And Save Them for Pallbearers.* 1959. Bantam F 1920. Fi. VG+. P1d. $6.50

GARRETT, Randall. *Earth Invader.* Leisure 1059. 1st pb. SF. NF. B6d. $4.50

GARRETT, Randall. *Lord Darcy Investigates.* 1981. Ace. F. M1d. $7.00

GARRETT, Randall. *Steel of Raithskar.* Bantam 14607. 1st prtg. F. S1d. $4.00

GARRETT, Randall. *Too Many Magicians.* Curtis. 1st pb. VG. M1d. $10.00

GARRETT & HARRIS. *Pagan Passions.* 1959. Beacon 263. 1st prtg. PBO. c/Stanley: gga. VG+. P7d. $25.00

GARRIOCK, P.R. *Masters of Comic Book Art.* 1978. Images Graphiques 021. 1st edn. Nfi. F. P1d. $15.00

GARRISON, N. *Cocoa Butter.* Dominion 340. VG+. B3d. $4.00

GARRITY, D.A. *Kiss Off the Dead.* 1960. Gold Medal 948. 1st prtg. PBO. c/Abbett: gga. VG. P7d. $7.50

GARRITY, D.A. *Liam O'Flaherty: Selected Stories.* Signet 1553. VG. B3d. $4.00

GARRITY, Dave J. *Dragon Hunt.* 1967. Signet P 3203. c/gga. My. VG+. B4d. $2.25

GARTH, David. *Appointment With Danger.* 1948. Popular 136. 1st pb. My. VG+. B6d. $15.00

GARTH, David. *Challenge for Three.* Popular 84. VG. B3d. $4.50

GARTH, John. *Hill Man.* 1960. Pyramid G 534. c/L Marchetti. Fi. VG. B5d. $6.50

GARTH, John. *Hill Man.* 1954. Pyramid 112. PBO. c/J Paul. scarce. VG+. B6a #79. $45.00

GARTON, Ray. *Crucifax.* 1988. Pocket 62629. PBO. Ho. F. B6d. $15.00

GARTON, Ray. *Live Girls.* 1987. Pocket 62628. PBO. F. B6d. $20.00

GARTON, Ray. *Seductions.* 1984. Pinnacle 42309. 1st edn. scarce. Ho. F. F2d. $27.00

GARTON, Ray. *Warlock.* 1989. Avon 75712. PBO. MTI. Ho. F. B6d. $18.00

GARVE, Andrew. *By-Line for Murder.* Dell 765. G. G5d. $5.00

GARVE, Andrew. *Cuckoo Line Affair.* 1963. Lancer 72-677. 1st pb. My. NF. B6d. $9.00

GARVE, Andrew. *Hero for Leanda.* 1965. Lancer 72-783. c/gga. My. NF. B4d. $4.00

GARVE, Andrew. *Hole in the Ground.* Dell D 275. VG+. B3d. $4.00

GARVE, Andrew. *Megstone Plot.* 1958. Pyramid G 360. c/gga. Fa. VG. B4d. $5.00

GARVE, Andrew. *No Mask for Murder.* Dell 571. VG. G5d. $5.00

GARVE, Andrew. *No Tears for Hilda.* Dell 655. VG. G5d. $5.00

GARVE, Andrew. *No Tears for Hilda.* Lancer 72-739. VG. B3d. $4.00

GARVE, Andrew. *Sea Monks.* 1964. Lancer 72-759. 1st pb. My. VG. B6d. $5.00

GARY, Romain. *European Education.* 1961. Cardinal GC 106. Fi. VG. B5d/P7d. $3.50

GARY, Romain. *Lady L.* 1960. Cardinal C 369. 2nd prtg. VG+. R5d. $2.00

GARY, Romain. *Lady L.* 1966. Pocket 50187. 3rd prtg. VG. R5d. $1.25

GARY, Romain. *Talent Scout.* 1962. Pocket 6127. SF. VG. B5d. $3.50

GASH, Jonathan. *Judas Pair.* 1986. Arrow 00195. 1st prtg. My. F. W2d. $4.50

GASH, Jonathan. *Pearlhanger.* 1986. Penguin 08468. Lovejoy #9. My. F. W2d. $4.25

GASH, Jonathan. *Sleepers of Erin.* 1984. Haml 34300. 1st prtg. My. F. W2d. $4.50

GASH, Jonathan. *Tartan Sell.* 1987. Penguin 97457. Lovejoy #10. My. F. W2d. $4.25

GASH, Jonathan. *Vatican Rip.* 1986. Arrow 00225. 1st prtg. Lovejoy. My. F. W2d. $4.50

GASKELL, Jane. *Atlan.* 1970. PB Library 66-452. 2nd edn. SF. VG. B5d. $3.50

GASKELL, Jane. *Serpent.* 1968. PB Library 55-693. 1st US edn. c/Fracetta. SF. VG+. B6d. $15.00

GASSER, Henry. *How To Draw & Paint.* 1955. Dell 1st Edn F 54. PBO. c/H Gasser. NF. VG. B5d. $3.00

GAT, Dimitri. *Personal.* 1990. Pocket 67697. 1st edn. My. F. F2d. $10.00

GATES, Eleanor. *Wicked.* 1951. Uni-Book 4. 1st pb. VG. B6d. $6.00

GATES, G.P. *Airtime: Inside Story of CBS News.* 1979. Berkley 04190. 1st prtg. VG+. R5d. $2.50

GAULDEN, Ray. *Vengeful Men.* 1958. Perma M 3110. We. VG. B4d. $3.00

GAULDEN, Ray. *Wicked Women of Lobo Wells.* 1971. Belmont B 75-2122. 1st edn. My. F. F2d. $8.00

GAULDEN, Ray. *5-Card Stud (Glory Gulch).* Berkley G 1644. MTI. VG+. B3d. $5.00

GAULT, William Campbell. *Blood on the Boards*. Dell 835. c/sgn. VG. B3d. $6.00

GAULT, William Campbell. *Blood on the Boards*. 1955. Dell 835. 1st edn. PBO. c/Neiser. scarce. NF. B6a #76. $45.00

GAULT, William Campbell. *Blood on the Boards*. 1955. Dell 835. 1st edn. PBO. c/sgn. VG+. B6d. $45.00

GAULT, William Campbell. *Bloody Bokhara*. 1953. Dell 746. 1st pb. c/sgn. VG. B6d. $22.50

GAULT, William Campbell. *Come Die With Me*. Charter 11539. VG. M6d. $4.00

GAULT, William Campbell. *County Kill*. Charter 00017. 1st pb. VG. M6d. $5.00

GAULT, William Campbell. *Dead Seed*. Charter 14151. 1st pb. VG. M6d. $5.00

GAULT, William Campbell. *Death Out of Focus*. 1960. Dell 1012. 1st prtg. My. VG. R5d. $5.00

GAULT, William Campbell. *Don't Cry for Me*. 1953. Dell 672. 1st edn. PBO. c/James Meese. scarce. VG+. B6a #77. $77.00

GAULT, William Campbell. *End of a Call Girl*. 1958. Crest 248. PBO. c/sgn. scarce. VG. B6a #80. $37.00

GAULT, William Campbell. *Million-Dollar Tramp*. 1960. Crest 361. PBO. c/gga. VG. B6a #77. $34.50

GAULT, William Campbell. *Murder in the Raw*. 1957. Dell 926. c/sgn. VG. B3a #24. $10.00

GAULT, William Campbell. *Murder in the Raw*. 1957. Dell 926. 1st edn. PBO. c/Kalin. scarce. VG+. B6a #76. $44.00

GAULT, William Campbell. *Murder in the Raw*. 1957. Dell 926. 1st pb. G+. M6d. $9.50

GAULT, William Campbell. *Run, Killer, Run*. Dell 868. 1st edn. PBO. c/Borack. scarce. VG+. B6a #76. $45.00

GAULT, William Campbell. *Run, Killer, Run*. Dell 868. 1st edn. PBO. c/sgn. VG+. B6d. $45.00

GAULT, William Campbell. *Run, Killer, Run*. Dell 868. 1st pb. VG. M6d. $6.50

GAULT, William Campbell. *Square in the Middle*. 1957. Bantam 1602. 1st edn. PBO. c/sgn. scarce. VG+. B6a #80. $27.50

GAULT, William Campbell. *Sweet Blonde Trap*. Zenith 25. c/sgn: gga. rare. NF. B6a #80. $150.00

GAULT, William Campbell. *Sweet Wild Wench*. 1959. Crest 309. PBO. c/Gault: sgn. rare. NF. B6a #80. $67.25

GAULT, William Campbell. *Vein of Violence*. 1965. Award KA 125F. 1st prtg. VG. P7d. $7.50

GAULT, William Campbell. *Vein of Violence*. Charter 55773. VG. M6d. $3.50

GAUNTIER, Gene. *Sporting Lady*. 1954. Pyramid 113. c/gga. Fa. VG+. B4d. $9.00

GAVER & STANLEY. *There's Laughter in the Air!* Armed Services 967. VG. B3d. $7.00

GAY, Carmen. *Ripe for Love*. 1947. Prize 58. c/gga. VG. P6d. $6.50

GAYMAN, Ben. *By Sex Possessed*. 1966. Private Edition PE 363. Ad. VG+. B5d. $4.50

GAZEL, Stefan. *To Live & Kill*. Ballantine 339. PBO. VG+. B3d. $5.00

GAZZO, M.V. *Hatful of Rain*. 1957. Signet S 1412. 1st prtg. VG. R5d. $3.50

GEBLER, Ernest. *Plymouth Adventure*. 1952. Perma P 166. 1st pb. VG+. B6d. $9.00

GEDDES, D.P. *Franklin Delano Roosevelt -- Memorial*. Pocket 300. VG. B3d. $4.00

GEDDES, D.R. *Atomic Age Opens*. Pocket 340. 1st prtg. G+. S1d. $4.00

GEER, Andrew. *Canton Barrier*. 1957. Cardinal C 271. 1st prtg. My. G+. R5d. $1.50

GEER, Andrew. *Sea Chase*. 1949. Pocket 652. Fi. VG. P1d. $6.00

GEHMAN, Richard. *Driven*. Gold Medal 387. VG. B3d. $4.50

GEHMAN, Richard. *Each Life To Live*. 1952. Red Seal 8. 1st edn. F. F2d. $14.00

GEHMAN, Richard. *Murder in Paradise*. Signet S 1307. G+. G5d. $3.50

GEHMAN, Richard. *Sinatra & His Rat Pack*. 1961. Belmont L 514. PBO. VG+. B6d. $6.00

GEIS, Richard E. *Bedroom Blacklist*. Brandon House 1010. VG+. B3d. $10.00

GEIS, Richard E. *Eye at the Window*. Brandon House 1119. VG+. B3d. $10.00

GEIS, Richard E. *Girlsville*. 1963. France 35. 1st edn. De. F. F2d. $20.00

GEIS, Richard E. *Pleasure Lodge*. 1962. Midwood 223. 1st edn. F. F2d. $17.50

GEIS, Richard E. *Punishment*. 1967. Beacon 95215. 1st prtg. c/gga. SF. F. F2d. $8.00

GEIS, Richard E. *Saturday Night Party*. Beacon 582. VG. B3d. $5.00

GEIS, Richard E. *Saturday Night Party*. 1967. Beacon 95220. 1st prtg. c/gga. SF. F. F2d. $8.00

GEIS, Richard E. *Sex Kitten*. 1960. Newsstand 517. PBO. c/gga. VG. B6d. $5.00

GEIS, Richard E. *Sex Kitten*. 1960. Newsstand 517. 1st edn. c/gga. F. F2d. $20.00

GEIS, Richard E. *Slum Virgin*. 1963. Saber 30. 1st edn. c/gga. F. F2d. $20.00

GEIS/LAIRD. *Beatniks/Every Bed Is Narrow*. 1962. Dollar D 955. 1st edn. F. F2d. $12.50

GELLHORN, Martha. *Liana*. Popular 529. VG. B3d. $5.00

GELLHORN, Martha. *Wine of Astonishment*. Bantam 736. c/Avati. VG. B3d. $4.00

GELMAN, S. *Bob Cousy*. Sport 12. VG. B3d. $6.00

GENET, Jean. *Our Lady of the Flowers*. 1976. Black Cat B 389. Fi. VG. B5d. $10.00

GENTLE, Mary. *Golden Witchbreed*. 1983. Signet. 1st pb. F. M1d. $5.00

GEOGRAPHIA MAP CO., INC. *Perma Handy World Atlas*. 1950. Perma P 70. PBO. VG+. P6d. $3.00

GEORGE, Irving. *Madison Avenue Nympho*. 1962. Intimate 703. c/gga. Fa. VG+. B4d. $6.00

GEORGE, Peter. *Dr Stranglelove*. 1964. Bantam. 1st pb. VG. M1d. $10.00

GERARD, Francis. *Mark of the Moon*. 1953. Popular 544. VG. P6d. $6.00

GERNSBACK, Hugo. *Ralph 124C41+*. 1958. Crest 226. 1st edn. PBO. F. F2d/M1d. $15.00

GERROLD, David. *Alternities*. Dell 3195. 1st prtg. VG. S1d. $3.50

GERROLD, David. *Battle for the Planet of the Apes*. 1973. Award NN. MTI. SF. VG. W2d. $4.50

GERROLD, David. *Encounter at Farpoint*. 1987. Pocket 65241. 1st prtg. Star Trek: The Next Generation. SF. VG. W2d. $4.50

GERROLD, David. *Galactic Whirlpool*. 1980. Bantam 14242. SF. F. W2d. $5.00

GERROLD, David. *Moonstar Odyssey*. Signet W 7372. 1st prtg. G+. S1d. $4.00

GERROLD, David. *Protostars*. 1971. Ballantine 02393. SF. VG+. W2d. $4.50

GERROLD, David. *Protostars*. 1971. Ballantine 02393. 1st edn. SF. F. F2d. $18.00

GERROLD, David. *SF Emphasis #1*. 1974. Ballantine 23962. PBO. c/D Ellis. SF. VG. B5d. $3.00

GERROLD, David. *Trouble With Tribbles*. 1973. Ballantine 23402. SF. VG. W2d. $6.50

GERROLD, David. *Trouble With Tribbles.* 1973. Ballantine 23402. 1st prtg. SF. VG. R5d. $5.00

GERROLD, David. *World of Star Trek.* 1974. Ballantine 23403. 4th prtg. SF. VG. W2d. $6.00

GERROLD, David. *Yesterday's Children.* Dell 9780. 1st prtg. F. S1d. $5.00

GERROLD, David. *Yesterday's Children.* Popular 45361. 1st prtg. G. S1d. $2.50

GERROLD & NIVEN. *Flying Sorcerers.* 1971. Ballantine. 1st edn. F. M1d. $12.00

GERSON, Noel B. *Daughter of Eve.* 1959. Avon G 1041. c/gga. Fa. VG+. B4d. $5.00

GERSON, Noel B. *Highwayman.* Perma M 4070. F. B3d. $6.00

GERSON, Noel B. *Savage Cavalier.* 1952. Popular G 104. c/gga. Fa. VG+. B4d. $7.50

GERSON, Noel B. *Silver Lion.* 1958. Popular G 217. PBO. c/Hooks. VG+. B6d. $8.00

GERSON, Noel B. *Sword of Fortune.* Popular G 116. VG+. B3d. $4.50

GERWIN, W. *Beds I Lie On.* Uptown 704. VG. B3d. $4.50

GESTON, Mark S. *Affairs of Clio.* Chariot 181. PBO. VG+. B3d. $5.50

GESTON, Mark S. *Day Star.* 1972. DAW 6. PBO. c/G Barr. SF. VG. B5d/I1d. $3.00

GESTON, Mark S. *Out of the Mouth of the Dragon.* Ace 64460. SF. VG. W2d. $4.00

GESTON, Mark S. *Siege of Wonder.* 1977. DAW. 1st pb. F. M1d. $5.00

GHIDALIA, Vic. *Devil's Generation.* 1973. Lancer 75465. PBO. c/skull. SF. VG. B5d/M1d. $6.00

GHIDALIA, Vic. *Devil's Generation.* 1973. Lancer 75465. 1st prtg. F. S1d. $8.50

GHIDALIA, Vic. *Dracula's Guest & Other Stories.* 1972. Xerox F 394. SF. VG. W2d. $5.00

GHIDALIA, Vic. *Gooseflesh!* 1974. Berkley S 2732. c/ghoul. SF. VG+. B5d. $6.00

GHIDALIA, Vic. *Satan's Pets.* 1972. Manor 75-478. PBO. SF. VG. B6d. $6.00

GHIDALIA, Vic. *Wizards & Warlocks.* Manor 95-192. PBO. 1st edn. VG. B3d. $4.50

GHIDALIA & ELWOOD edt. *Beware More Beasts.* 1975. Manor 12276. PBO. SF. NF. B6d. $8.00

GHIDALIA & ELWOOD edt. *Venus Factor.* 1972. MacFadden 75-462. 1st edn. SF. F. F2d. $10.00

GIBBONS, Floyd. *Red Knight of Germany.* 1959. Bantam A 1919. Bio. VG. B4d. $2.75

GIBBS, Carlton. *Girl in a Cage.* 1962. Beacon B 537F. PBO. c/A Brule. Ad. G+. B5d/I1d. $4.00

GIBBS, Carlton. *Troubled Town.* 1962. Beacon B478F. PBO. Ad. VG. B5d. $6.00

GIBBS, Willa. *Fruit of Desire.* 1955. Lion LL 37. 1st pb. c/Maguire. VG. B6d. $5.00

GIBBS, Willa. *Seed of Mischief.* Perma P 280. VG+. B3d. $4.00

GIBRAN, Kahill. *Prophet.* Armed Services O 2. Nfi. VG. B5d. $5.00

GIBSON, G. *Enemy Coast Ahead.* Four Square 365. VG+. B3d. $8.00

GIBSON, Walter. *Anne Bonny, Pirate Queen.* 1962. Monarch 320. 1st edn. c/gga. scarce. F. F2d. $30.00

GIBSON, Walter. *Blonde for Murder.* 1948. Atlas 2. PBO. My. G+. B6d. $6.00

GIBSON, Walter. *Looks That Kill!* 1948. Atlas 5. c/Ames. scarce. VG. B6a #79. $40.25

GIBSON, Walter. *Magic Explained.* 1949. Perma 54. 1st edn. PBO. VG. F2d. $8.00

GIBSON, Walter. *Return of the Shadow.* Belmont 90-298. VG+. G5d. $10.00

GIBSON, Walter. *Rod Serling's Twilight Zone Revisited.* 1967. Tempo T 171. TVTI. VG. P1d. $7.50

GIBSON, Walter. *Stories From the Twilight Zone.* 1960. Bantam A 2046. TVTI. G+. P1d. $6.50

GIBSON, Walter. *Stories From the Twilight Zone.* 1965. Tempo T 89. 1st prtg. VG. R5d. $6.75

GIBSON & FITZGERALD. *I Always Wanted To Be Somebody.* 1960. Pyramid G 478. NF. VG. B5d. $4.50

GIBSON & PEPE. *From Ghetto to Glory.* Popular 751285. VG. B3d. $4.00

GIDDINGS, A.R. *River of Rogues.* Pocket 946. VG+. I1d. $5.00

GIES, Joseph. *Matter of Morals.* 1952. Popular 421. c/Barton: gga. Fa. VG+. B4d. $12.00

GIFFORD, D. *Karloff: Man, Monster, Movies.* Curtis. c/photo. $7.50

GIFFORD, Lee. *Pieces of the Game.* 1960. Gold Meda 1008. 1st edn. My. F. F2d. $6.00

GIFFORD, Lee. *Pieces of the Game.* 1960. Gold Medal 1008. VG+. B3d. $5.00

GIGON, Fernand. *Bomb.* 1960. Pyramid G 528. Fi. VG+. P1d. $6.50

GILBERT, Anthony. *After the Verdict.* 1964. Pyramid R 1041. My. VG+. B4d. $5.00

GILBERT, Anthony. *Death Against the Clock.* Pan G 524. c/Peff Strangulation. VG+. B3d. $7.00

GILBERT, Anthony. *Death at the Door.* 1947. Bantam 85. 1st pb. My. VG. B6d. $6.00

GILBERT, Anthony. *Death in the Blackout.* 1946. Bantam 51. VG+. G5d. $5.50

GILBERT, Anthony. *Death in the Blackout.* 1946. Bantam 51. 1st pb. My. NF. B6d. $12.50

GILBERT, Anthony. *Death Lifts the Latch.* Bantam 768. VG. B3d. $4.50

GILBERT, Anthony. *Death Takes a Redhead.* Arrow FDC 7 Digest 44. My. VG. B4d. $7.00

GILBERT, Anthony. *Incest Report.* Copley 142. VG+. B3d. $4.50

GILBERT, Anthony. *Innocent Bottle.* Bantam 851. VG+. B3d. $6.00

GILBERT, Anthony. *Murder Cheats the Bride.* 1948. Bantam 138. VG. B3d. $4.50

GILBERT, Anthony. *Murder Cheats the Bride.* 1948. Bantam 138. VG+. G5d. $6.50

GILBERT, Anthony. *Murder Cheats the Bride.* 1948. Bantam 138. 1st prtg. My. G+. R5d. $2.25

GILBERT, Anthony. *Question of Murder.* Pyramid R 1258. VG. G5d. $3.75

GILBERT, Anthony. *Woman In Red.* 1944. Handi Book 29. 1st edn. PBO. scarce. VG+. B6a #75. $42.50

GILBERT, Edwin. *Hard To Get.* 1952. Popular 469. c/gga. Fa. NF. B4d. $15.00

GILBERT, Elliott. *Too Much Woman.* 1961. Beacon B 419B. PBO. Ad. VG. B5d. $6.50

GILBERT, Michael. *Danger Within.* Dell 870. G+. G5d. $5.00

GILBERT, Michael. *Death Has Deep Roots.* Dell 744. 1st prtg. My. VG. R5d. $3.25

GILBERT, Michael. *Death Has Deep Roots.* Lancer 72-738. reprint. My. VG+. B6d. $7.50

GILBERT, Norma. *Pay for Play Girl.* 1966. Brandon House 957. c/Brandon. VG+. B3a #22. $20.00

GILBERT, Stephen. *Ratman's Notebooks.* 1970. Lancer 75-142. 1st pb. Ho. VG+. B6d. $12.50

GILBERT, Stephen. *Willard.* Lancer 75-189. 1st prtg. MTI. G+. R5d. $3.00

GILBERT, Stephen. *Willard.* 1971. Lancer 75-189. 1st prtg. MTI. SF. VG. R5d. $4.50

GILBERT, Stephen. *Willard.* Lancer 75-189. MTI. SF. G+. W2d. $3.25

GILBERT & SULLIVAN. *Best-Loved Operas.* 1950. Avon 228. PBO. Nfi. G+. B5d. $3.00

GILDEN, K.B. *Hurry Sundown.* 1966. Signet W 2860. 1st prtg. VG. R5d. $2.00

GILES, G.E. *Died Variously.* Black Cat 1. VG. B3d. $8.00

GILFORD, C.B. *Liquid Man.* 1969. Lancer 74-560. SF. VG+. B4d. $3.00

GILL, Brendan. *Day the Money Stopped.* 1958. Pocket 1199. c/C Hulings. Fi. VG+. B5d. $5.50

GILL, Elisabeth. *Wayward Nymph.* Zenith ZB 27. PBO. VG. B3d. $5.00

GILL, Elisabeth. *Young Sinner.* 1953. Cameo Digest 333. PBO. c/Pease: gga. scarce. VG. B6a #79. $71.25

GILL, Tom. *Firebrand.* 1946. Popular 119. We. NF. B4d. $8.00

GILL, Tom. *Gay Bandit of the Border.* 1949. Popular 190. c/gga. reprint. We. VG. P6d. $4.00

GILL, Tom. *Gentleman of the Jungle.* 1950. Dell 456. c/Robert Stanley: gga. Ad. VG. P6d. $3.00

GILL, Tom. *Guardians of the Desert.* 1948. Popular 142. 1st pb. We. VG. B6d. $9.00

GILLETTE, Paul J. *Cat O'Nine Tails.* 1971. Award 870. PBO. MTI. My. VG+. B6d. $6.00

GILLETTE, Paul J. *Play Misty for Me.* 1971. Award 907. 1st edn. My. F. F2d. $15.00

GILLIAN, Michael. *Warrant for a Wanton.* 1953. Pennant P 12. c/H Schaare. My. VG. B5d. $5.00

GILLIGAN, Edmund. *Gaunt Woman.* Dell 312. c/F Giles. Fi. VG. I1d. $4.00

GILLILAND, Alexis. *End of the Empire.* 1983. Ballantine 31334. SF. G+. W2d. $3.25

GILLILAND, Alexis. *Shadow Shaia.* 1990. Ballantine 36115. 1st edn. SF. F. F2d. $6.00

GILLON, Diana & Meir. *Unsleep.* 1962. Ballantine F 571. 1st prtg. VG. S1d. $7.00

GILLON, Diana & Meir. *Unsleep.* Four Square 811. VG. B3d. $6.00

GILLON, Philip. *Frail Barrier.* 1953. Signet 1026. c/Cardiff. Fi. VG. B5d. $4.00

GILMAN, Dorothy. *Mrs Pollifax on Safari.* 1977. Crest 23414. 1st prtg. My. F. W2d. $3.50

GILMAN, L. *Red Gate.* Ballantine 9. VG. B3d. $3.50

GILMAN, Robert C. *Rebel of Rhada.* Ace 71065. SF. VG+. W2d. $3.50

GILMAN, William. *Spy Trap.* 1944. Bart House 3. VG. B3d. $7.50

GILMAN, Wilson C. *Society Daughter.* Saber SA 6. VG+. B3d. $4.50

GILMORE, C. *Man in the Moonlight.* Berkley G 678. VG+. B3d. $4.50

GILMORE, George G. *Killer's Breed.* 1972. Pinnacle 00148. 1st edn. Hi. F. F2d. $8.00

GILMOUR, H.B. *Eyes of Laura Mars.* 1978. Bantam 2125. 1st edn. c/photo. My. F. F2d. $10.00

GILPATRIC, Guy. *French Summer.* 1948. Avon 180. c/gga. Fa. VG+. B4d. $10.00

GILPATRIC, Guy. *French Summer.* 1948. Avon 180. Fi. G. B5d. $3.00

GILPATRIC, Guy. *Mister Glencannon.* 1940. Pocket 87. Fi. G. B5d. $2.50

GINSBURG, Ralph. *Unhurried View of Erotica.* 1960. Ace K 119. Nfi. VG. B4d. $2.25

GIPE, George. *Gremlins.* 1984. Avon 89003. MTI. SF. F. W2d. $6.00

GIPE, George. *Gremlins.* 1972. Xerox F 394. MTI. SF. VG. W2d. $3.00

GIPSON, Fred. *Hound-Dog Man.* 1959. Perma M 4168. 1st prtg. G+. R5d. $3.50

GIPSON, Fred. *Old Yeller.* Pocket 1177. VG+. B3d. $4.50

GIRVAN, Helen. *Blue Treasure.* Pocket J 49. VG+. B3d. $5.50

GIVENS, Charles. *Big Mike.* 1953. Pyramid 104. PBO. c/Julian Paul. scarce in condition. NF. B6a #74. $42.00

GLADSON, Leslie. *Slaver.* 1968. Lancer 75-051. 1st edn. c/gga. SF. F. F2d. $10.00

GLANVILLE, B. *Along the Arno.* Ace H 276. VG. B3d. $5.00

GLASER, Alfred B. *Creature of Sin.* 1960. Newsstand U 145. 1st edn. De. F. F2d. $15.00

GLASER/LAND. *Platinum Blonde/Sporting Parlor.* 1962. Dollar D 952. 1st prtg. c/gga. F. F2d. $7.50

GLAY, George Albert. *Gina.* 1950. Readers Choice 3. 1st prtg. c/gga. VG+. P7d. $7.50

GLAY, George Albert. *Oath of Seven.* 1955. Ace S 102. PBO. c/gga. VG. B6d. $12.50

GLEMSER, Bernard. *Pleasure of His Company.* 1961. Bantam A 2162. 1st prtg. G. R5d. $1.00

GLENDINNING, Richard. *Retreat Into the Night.* Gold Medal 104. c/Barye. VG. B3d. $6.50

GLENDINNING, Richard. *Terror in the Sun.* 1952. Gold Medal 237. 1st edn. c/gga. F. F2d. $20.00

GLICK & BUCKHOLTZ. *Micro-Adventure.* 1984. Scholastic 33169. #5 Mind-Benders. SF. VG. W2d. $2.00

GLIDDEN, M.W. *Come Dwell With Death.* Black Knight 25. VG. B3d. $5.00

GLOAG, J. *In Camera.* Panther 555. c/Nazi. VG. B3d. $8.00

GLOVER, L.E. *Sex Life of the Modern Adult.* Belmont L 503. 2nd prtg. VG+. B3d. $5.00

GLUT, Donald F. *Spawn.* Laser 43. VG+. B3d. $5.00

GLUT, Donald F. *Star Wars: Empire Strikes Back.* 1980. Ballantine 28392. 1st prtg. MTI. SF. VG+. R5d. $2.50

GLUT, Donald F. *Star Wars: The Empire Strikes Back.* 1980. Ballantine 28392. MTI. SF. F. W2d. $4.75

GLUT, Donald F. *Star Wars: The Empire Strikes Back.* 1980. Sphere (BR). MTI. SF. W2d. $4.50

GLYNNE, A.A. *Border Bunch.* Badger BW 21. VG+. B3d. $8.00

GODDEN, Jon. *Seven Islands.* 1957. Pocket 1172. c/L Manso. Fi. NF. B5d. $6.00

GODDEN, Rumer. *Black Narcissus.* 1963. Dell 0573. 1st prtg. c/Abbett. VG. P7d. $4.00

GODWIN, Tom. *Space Barbarians.* 1964. Pyramid R 993. PBO. c/J Schoenherr. SF. VG+. B5d. $6.50

GODWIN, Tom. *Space Prison.* 1962. Pyramid F 774. 2nd edn. SF. VG. B5d. $6.50

GODWIN, Tom. *Space Prison.* 1960. Pyramid G 480. 1st pb. VG. M1d. $10.00

GOENEY, William M. *Power Play.* Avon T 407. My. VG. B5d. $2.50

GOFF, Georgena. *Black Dog.* 1971. Belmont B 75-2124. PBO. NF. B6d. $9.00

GOFF, Jerry M. Jr. *Eager Women.* 1963. Merit 651. PBO. c/Bonfils: gga. NF. B6a #75. $40.25

GOFF, Jerry M. Jr. *Sensual Ambitions.* Merit 414. VG. B3d. $4.50

GOFF, Jerry M. Jr. *Strange Loves.* Merit 618. PBO. VG+. B3d. $5.00

GOHIER, G. *Love in the Sun.* Berkley G 708. VG+. B3d. $6.00

GOINES, D. *Black Girl Lost.* Holloway House BH 441. VG+. B3d. $6.00

GOLD, H.L. *Bodyguard & 4 Other Short Novels.* 1962. Perma M 4252. 1st prtg. VG. S1d. $4.00

GOLD, H.L. *Mind Partner.* 1963. Perma M 4287. VG+. I1d. $4.00

GOLD, H.L. *Weird Ones.* 1962. Belmont L 92-541. 1st prtg. SF. G+. R5d. $4.50

GOLD, H.L. *Weird Ones.* 1962. Belmont. 1st edn. NF. M1d. $10.00

GOLD, H.L. *World That Couldn't Be.* 1961. Perma M 4197. NF. I1d. $5.00

GOLD, H.L. *World That Couldn't Be.* 1961. Perma M 4197. 1st pb. c/Matheson. SF. NF. B6d. $12.50

GOLD, H.L. *3rd Galaxy Reader.* Perma M 4172. VG. I1d. $5.00

GOLD, H.L. *3rd Galaxy Reader.* 1960. Perma M 4172. SF. F. W2d. $6.50

GOLD, H.L. *4th Galaxy Reader.* 1960. Perma M 4184. SF. VG+. B4d. $4.00

GOLD, H.L. *4th Galaxy Reader.* 1960. Perma M 4184. 1st prtg. F. S1d. $6.00

GOLD, H.L. *5 Galaxy Short Novels.* 1960. Perma M 4158. SF. VG. I1d/S1d. $3.00

GOLD, H.L. *5th Galaxy Reader.* 1963. Pocket 6163. SF. VG+. B5d. $4.50

GOLD, Herbert. *Room Clerk.* 1955. Signet D 1185. c/S Zuckerberg. My. VG. B5d. $4.00

GOLD, Herbert. *Salt.* 1964. Perma M 5081. VG+. B3d. $4.50

GOLD, Herbert. *Therefore Be Bold.* 1962. Lancer 70-002. Fi. VG. B5d. $4.00

GOLD, Herbert. *Wild Life.* 1957. Perma M 3073. Fa. VG. B4d. $2.75

GOLD, Michael. *Jews Without Money.* 1965. Avon VS 11. c/N Fasciano. Fi. VG. B5d. $3.00

GOLD, R.C. *All in the Game.* 1966. Midwood 33-667. Ad. VG. B5d. $4.00

GOLD, R.C. *For Lydia.* 1963. Beacon 566. 1st edn. c/gga. F. F2d. $15.00

GOLD, R.C. *Marriage Wreckers.* 1963. France 51. VG. P6d. $4.00

GOLDEN, Francis Leo. *For Doctors Only.* 1951. Pocket 796. 1st prtg. c/Quigley. VG. P7d. $5.00

GOLDEN, Francis Leo. *Jest What the Doctor Ordered.* Pocket 872. 3rd prtg. VG+. B3d. $4.50

GOLDEN, Francis Leo. *Laughter Is Legal.* 1953. Pocket 948. c/C Jones. Nfi. VG. B5d. $3.50

GOLDEN, Francis Leo. *Laughter Is Legal.* 1953. Pocket 948. c/gga. Hu. VG+. B4d. $4.00

GOLDEN, Francis Leo. *Tales for Salesmen.* 1954. Pocket 1013. c/C Jones. Nfi. VG. B5d/P7d. $5.00

GOLDIN, Stephen. *And Not Make Dreams Your Master.* 1981. Gold Medal 14410. SF. VG. W2d. $3.00

GOLDIN, Stephen. *Caravan.* 1975. Laser 8. PBO. c/K Freas. SF. F. B5d. $7.00

GOLDIN, Stephen. *Eternity Brigade.* 1980. Gold Medal 14336. SF. VG. W2d. $4.50

GOLDIN, Stephen. *Herds.* Laser 2. 1st prtg. VG. S1d. $4.00

GOLDIN, Stephen. *Herds.* 1975. Laser 2. PBO. c/K Freas. SF. NF. B3d/B5d. $6.00

GOLDIN, Stephen. *Mind Flight.* 1978. Gold Medal. 1st edn. VG. M1d. $4.00

GOLDIN, Stephen. *Scavenger Hunt.* 1976. Laser 25. VG. I1d. $5.00

GOLDIN, Stephen. *Scavenger Hunt.* 1976. Laser 25. 1st edn. SF. F. F2d. $10.00

GOLDING, Morton, J. *Night Mare.* 1970. Dell 06422. 1st prtg. c/Skurski. VG. P7d. $4.00

GOLDING, William. *Inheritors.* 1963. Cardinal GC 787. SF. VG. B5d. $2.50

GOLDING, William. *Sometime, Never.* 1957. Ballantine. 1st edn. F. M1d. $12.00

GOLDMAN, James. *They Might Be Giants.* 1970. Lancer 74740. 1st edn. scarce in top condition. My. F. F2d. $12.50

GOLDMAN, R.L. *Out on Bail.* Prize Mystery Novel 18. VG. B3d. $4.50

GOLDMAN, R.L. *Purple Shells.* Boardman 61. c/McLoughlin. G+. B3d. $5.00

GOLDMAN, William. *Dr Phibes Rises Again!* 1972. Award 1069 1st edn. c/photo. Ho. F. F2d. $20.00

GOLDMAN, William. *Great Waldo Pepper.* 1975. Dell 4631. 1st prtg. VG+. R5d. $2.00

GOLDMAN, William. *Magic.* 1979. Dell 15141. 5th prtg. SF. F. W2d. $3.25

GOLDMAN, William. *No Way To Treat a Lady.* 1968. Gold Medal D 1905. MTI. VG. B4d. $2.50

GOLDMAN, William. *Princess Bride.* 1974. Ballantine Special Edn. SF. F. W2d. $4.00

GOLDMAN, William. *Soldier in the Rain.* 1966. Bantam S 3265. 1st prtg. VG. P7d. $4.00

GOLDSMITH, J. *Return to Treasure Island.* 1986. Berkley 08873. 1st prtg. TVTI. VG+. R5d. $1.75

GOLDSTEIN & GOLDSTEIN. *TV Guide Quiz Book.* 1978. Bantam 11811. TVTI. VG. P1d. $5.00

GOLDSTON, Robert. *Satan's Disciples.* 1962. Ballantine F 581. PBO. c/gga. NF. B6a #74. $24.25

GOLDSTON, Robert. *Satan's Disciples.* 1962. Ballantine F 581. 1st edn. VG. M1d. $8.00

GOLDTHWAITE, Eaton K. *Date With Death.* 1947. Bantam 132. 1st prtg. c/Lannon: gga. VG. P7d. $4.00

GOLDTHWAITE, Eaton K. *Date With Death.* 1947. Bantam 132. 1st prtg. My. G+. R5d. $2.75

GOLDTHWAITE, Eaton K. *Scarecrow.* Dell 193. c/G Gregg. My. G+. B5d. $5.00

GOLDTHWAITE, Eaton K. *Scarecrow.* 1947. Dell 193. 1st edn. PBO. c/Gregg. VG+. B6d. $25.00

GOLDTHWAITE, Eaton K. *Sixpenny Dame.* 1954. Pennant P 49. My. VG. B5d. $5.00

GOLIGHTLY, Bonnie. *Breath of Scandal.* 1960. Avon T 474. MIT. NF. B4d. $5.00

GOLIGHTLY, Bonnie. *Integration of Maybelle Brown.* 1961. Belmont B 60-064. 1st edn. My. F. F2d. $14.00

GOLIGHTLY, Bonnie. *Wild One.* 1957. Avon T 194. PBO. c/gga. VG. B3d. $4.00

GONZALES, John. *Death for Mr Big.* Gold Medal 1100. 2nd prtg. c/Barye. VG. B3d. $4.00

GONZALES, John. *Death for Mr Big.* Gold Medal 204. VG. B3d. $4.00

GONZALES, John. *End of a JD.* 1962. Gold Medal 552. 1st pb. VG. B6d. $9.00

GOOCH, Mary S. *Amorous Dietitian.* Newsstand U 171. VG. B3d. $4.00

GOOCH, Mary S. *Cheating Woman.* 1960. Beacon 369. PBO. c/Rossi: gga. NF. B6d. $25.00

GOOCH, Mary S. *Lusting Breed.* 1958. Beacon 187. c/G Mayers. scarce. VG+. B6a #74. $46.75

GOOCH, Mary S. *Lusting Breed.* 1958. Beacon 187. 1st prtg. PBO. VG+. P7d. $12.50

GOOCH, Mary S. *Tainted Rosary.* 1960. Fabian Z 139. 1st prtg. c/gga. VG. P7d. $5.00

GOOD, Norris. *From Bed to Worse.* 1969. Candid Reader 963. PBO. c/gga. VG. B6a. $66.00

GOODEN, A.H. *Shadowed Trail.* Hillman 22. VG+. I1d. $10.00

GOODIN, Peggy. *Lie.* 1955. Signet 1179. Fa. VG+. B4d. $3.00

GOODIN, Peggy. *Mickey (Clementine).* Bantam 406. MTI. VG. B3d. $4.50

GOODIS, David. *Behold This Woman.* Bantam 407. VG. G5d. $25.00

GOODIS, David. *Black Friday.* Banner 63. G+. B3d. $6.00

GOODIS, David. *Black Friday.* 1954. Lion 224. PBO. VG+. B6a #79. $82.50

GOODIS, David. *Blonde on the Street Corner.* 1954. Lion 186. PBO. c/gga. extremely scarce. VG. B6a #77. $135.00

GOODIS, David. *Burglar.* 1953. Lion 124. PBO. extremely scarce. VG+. B6a #79. $110.00

GOODIS, David. *Cassidy's Girl.* Black Lizard. VG+. G5d. $6.00

GOODIS, David. *Cassidy's Girl.* Dell 1114. VG. M6d. $7.50

GOODIS, David. *Cassidy's Girl.* Gold Medal 189. 3rd edn. c/Kampen. VG+. B6d. $7.50

GOODIS, David. *Dark Passage.* 1988. Zebra 2417. 1st prtg. G+. R5d. $2.50

GOODIS, David. *Fire in the Flesh.* 1957. Gold Medal 691. PBO. c/Barye. VG+. B3a #21. $18.70

GOODIS, David. *Fire in the Flesh.* 1957. Gold Medal 691. PBO. c/Barye: gga. rare in condition. NF. B6a #74. $55.00

GOODIS, David. *Fire in the Flesh.* 1957. Gold Medal 691. PBO. VG+. B6d. $75.00

GOODIS, David. *Moon in the Gutter.* 1953. Gold Medal 348. PBO. G+. B6d. $12.50

GOODIS, David. *Night Squad.* 1961. Gold Medal 1083. VG+. B3a #22. $38.50

GOODIS, David. *Nightfall.* 1987. Black Lizard NN. c/J Kirwan. My. VG. B5d. $5.00

GOODIS, David. *Nightfall.* Lion LB 131. VG. B3d. $10.00

GOODIS, David. *Of Missing Persons.* 1951. Pocket 833. VG+. B3a #22. $33.00

GOODIS, David. *Of Tender Sin.* 1952. Gold Medal 226. PBO. c/gga. NF. B6a #74. $112.50

GOODIS, David. *Of Tender Sin.* 1952. Gold Medal 226. PBO. VG+. B6d. $90.00

GOODIS, David. *Shoot the Piano Player.* Black Cat BA 35. MTI. c/photo. My. G+. B5d. $10.00

GOODIS, David. *Shoot the Piano Player.* Black Lizard 88739. F. G5d. $5.00

GOODIS, David. *Shoot the Piano Player.* 1987. Black Lizard 88739. VG+. P6d. $2.50

GOODIS, David. *Somebody's Done For.* 1967. Banner B 60-111. 1st prtg. My. G. R5d. $8.00

GOODIS, David. *Street of No Return.* 1987. Black Lizard NN. c/J Kirwan. My. VG. B5d. $5.00

GOODIS, David. *Street of No Return.* 1954. Gold Medal 428. PBO. VG. B6d. $35.00

GOODIS, David. *Street of the Lost.* 1952. Gold Medal 256. 1st edn. My. G+. F2d. $25.00

GOODIS, David. *Street of the Lost.* 1957. Gold Medal 652. 1st prtg of this #/2nd edn of this title. F. F2d. $25.00

GOODMAN, Charles edt. *Hell's Brigade.* 1966. Lancer 73-516. Fi. F. P1d. $7.50

GOODMAN & LEWIN. *My Greatest Day in Football.* Bantam 715. VG. B3d. $5.00

GOODMAN & LEWIN. *New Ways to Greater Word Power.* 1955. Dell 1st Edn 43. PBO. NF. VG. B5d. $3.00

GORAN, L. *Harry Meyer's Capture.* Signet 3694. VG. B3d. $4.00

GORDEN, John. *Sin-Tangled Stud.* 1966. Royal Line 136. PBO. NF. B6d. $10.00

GORDIMER, Nadine. *Lying Days.* 1955. Signet 1237. 1st edn. PBO. c/Avati: gga. F. F2d. $8.00

GORDIMER, Nadine. *Soft Voice of the Serpent.* 1956. Signet S 1266. 1st prtg. VG. P7d. $5.00

GORDON, Alex. *Cipher.* 1966. Pyramid X 1483. MTI. My. VG. B5d. $2.50

GORDON, Anthony. *Sex Ladder.* Beacon 783. VG. B3d. $4.00

GORDON, Arthur. *One Man's Way.* 1964. Crest R 711. MTI. VG+. B4d. $2.00

GORDON, Arthur. *Reprisal.* 1951. Pocket 801. My. VG. B5d. $4.50

GORDON, Donald. *Flight of the Bat.* 1965. Lancer 73-442. 1st pb. VG. B6d. $4.50

GORDON, Gary. *Anatomy of Adultery.* 1964. Monarch 448. Nfi. VG+. B5d. $5.50

GORDON, Gary. *Anatomy of Rape.* Monarch K 70. PBO. VG+. B3d. $5.00

GORDON, Gary. *Rise & Fall of the Japanese Empire.* Monarch MS 4. PBO. VG. B3d. $4.50

GORDON, Gary. *Sex in Business.* 1964. Monarch 550. 1st edn. c/photo. F. F2d. $10.00

GORDON, Gary. *Sins of Our Cities.* 1962. Monarch MB 525. Nfi. VG. B5d. $5.50

GORDON, Gerald. *Dark Brother.* 1954. Pyramid G 129. 1st prtg. c/gga. VG. P7d. $7.50

GORDON, Ian. *After Innocence.* 1955. Dell 1st Edn 58. PBO. c/Maguire. VG. B6d. $7.50

GORDON, Ian. *Burden of Guilt.* Dell 727. c/S Borack. My. VG. B5d. $3.00

GORDON, Ian. *Deep Is My Desire (Whip Hand).* Popular 662. VG. B3d. $4.00

GORDON, Ian. *Night Thorn.* 1953. Popular 474. Black. VG+. B4d. $9.00

GORDON, Jane. *Mistress of Mount Fair.* 1965. Lancer 72-791. PBO. c/L Marchetti. My. VG+. B5d. $5.00

GORDON, Luther. *Immoral!* Quarter Books 29. VG+. B3d. $12.00

GORDON, Luther. *Shamed!* Quarter Books 67. VG. B3d. $12.00

GORDON, Luther. *Tempted!* 1949. Quarter Books 36. PBO. c/Rodewald: gga. VG+. B6a #74. $66.00

GORDON, Luther. *Wolf Trap Blonde.* 1949. Quarter Books 38. 1st edn. PBO. c/George Gross: gga. VG+. B6a #79. $90.00

GORDON, Noah. *Night Ward.* 1959. Signet 1660. c/Maguire: gga. Fa. VG+. B4d. $4.00

GORDON, Rex. *First on Mars.* Ace D 233. NF. M1d. $10.00

GORDON, Rex. *First on Mars.* 1957. Ace D 233. PBO. SF. VG. B5d. $5.00

GORDON, Rex. *First Through Time.* Ace F 174. F. M1d. $10.00

GORDON, Rex. *First Through Time.* 1962. Ace F 174. PBO. SF. VG+. B5d. $5.00

GORDON, Rex. *First to the Stars.* Ace D 405. F. M1d. $10.00

GORDON, Rex. *First to the Stars.* Ace D 405. PBO. VG+. B3d. $4.50

GORDON, Rex. *Paw of God.* 1967. Tandem T 107. VG. B3d. $6.00

GORDON, Rex. *She Posed for Death.* Avon 283. VG+. B3d. $6.00

GORDON, Rex. *Utopia Minus X.* Ace F 416. NF. M1d. $6.00

GORDON, Rex. *Yellow Fraction.* 1969. Ace 94350. 1st edn. NF. P9d. $2.00

GORDON, Russell. *She Posed for Death.* 1950. Avon 283. 1st prtg. My. VG. R5d. $8.00

GORDON, Stuart. *One-Eye.* 1973. DAW. 1st edn. NF. M1d. $4.00

GORDON, Stuart. *Three-Eyes.* 1975. DAW 171. 1st edn. F. P9d. $2.00

GORDON, Stuart. *Time Story.* 1973. DAW 47. c/J Kirby. SF. NF. B5d/W2d. $4.00

GORDON, William E. *Girl-Hungry.* 1952. Carnival Digest 908. 1st edn. PBO. c/Nappi. VG+. B6a #80. $73.00

GORDON, William E. *Girl-Hungry.* Carnival Digest 935. reprint. scarce. NF. B6a #80. $77.00

GORDON, William E. *Lovers Bewitched.* Carnival 903. VG. B3d. $10.00

GORDON. *Flight of the Bamboo Saucer.* 1967. Award 244. PBO. SF. NF. B6d. $7.50

GORDONS. *Case File: FBI.* Bantam 1273. VG+. G5d. $4.00

GORDONS. *Case of the Talking Bug.* 1956. Bantam 1455. 1st pb. My. VG. B6d. $7.00

GORDONS. *Murder Rides the Campaign Train.* 1956. Bantam 1475. My. VG+. B4d. $2.50

GORDONS. *That Darned Cat.* 1965. Bantam F 3084. 1st pb. MTI. NF. B6d. $9.00

GORDONS. *Tiger on My Back.* 1962. Bantam J 2491. 1st prtg. My. VG+. R5d. $2.75

GOREN, Charles H. *Fundamentals of Contact Bridge.* 1952. Perma P 184. Nfi. VG. B4d. $2.25

GORES, Joe. *Hammett.* 1976. Ballantine 25170. 1st pb edn. c/sgn. My. F. F2d. $17.50

GORES, Joe. *Hammett.* Perennial 631. MTI. c/sgn. VG+. B3d. $6.00

GORHAM, Charles. *Carlotta McBride.* 1960. Crest S 373. 1st prtg. c/gga. VG+. P7d. $5.00

GORHAM, Charles. *Future Mister Dolan.* 1949. Signet 752. JD. F. P1d. $28.50

GORHAM, Charles. *Future Mister Dolan.* 1949. Signet 752. 1st pb. c/Avati. VG+. B6d. $9.00

GORHAM, Charles. *Gilded Hearse.* Popular 593. VG. B3d. $4.50

GORHAM, Charles. *Gold of Their Bodies.* 1955. Signet D 1244. 1st prtg. c/gga. VG. P7d. $5.00

GORHAM, Charles. *Martha Crane.* Berkley G 83. VG. B3d. $4.00

GORHAM, Charles. *McCaffery.* 1962. Crest D 587. 1st prtg. My. G+. R5d. $1.50

GORHAM, Nicholas. *Cruise.* 1961. Popular G 559. 1st edn. My. F. F2d. $11.00

GORHAM, Nicholas. *Queen's Blade.* Ace D 342. VG. B3d. $4.00

GORKY, Maxim. *Autobiography, Book One; My Childhood.* 1950. Jaico NN. Nfi. G+. B5d. $3.00

GORMAN, M. *Love Is My Business.* Brandon House 1118. NF. B3d. $7.00

GOSCINNY, R. edt. *Cartoons the French Way.* Lion LL 38. VG+. B3d. $5.50

GOSLING, Paula. *Monkey Puzzle.* 1990. World Wide 26056. c/monkey. My. F. B5d. $6.00

GOTLIEB, Phyllis. *Sunburst.* 1964. Gold Medal K 1488. 1st pb. VG. M1d. $7.00

GOTSCHALK, Felix. *Growing Up in Tier 3000.* 1975. Ace 30420. 1st edn. SF. F. P9d. $2.00

GOTTLIEB & MARTIN. *Jerk.* 1979. Warner 92-523. 1st prtg. VG+. R5d. $2.50

GOTTSCHO, Samuel. *Pocket Guide to Wildflowers.* 1960. Washington Square W 630. Nfi. VG. B5d. $2.50

GOUDGE, Elisabeth. *Green Dolphin Street.* 1962. Lancer 74-806. 1st pb. Hi. VG+. B6d. $6.00

GOULART, Ron *Blood Wedding.* 1976. Warner 86-088. Vampirella #4. NF. B3a #21. $25.00

GOULART, Ron. *After Things Fall Apart.* 1970. Ace 00950. 1st edn. SF. F. P9d. $2.50

GOULART, Ron. *Big Bang.* 1982. DAW. 1st edn. F. M1d. $6.00

GOULART, Ron. *Black Death.* 1974. Warner 75-481. 1st edn. F. F2d. $9.00

GOULART, Ron. *Blood Countess.* 1975. Warner 75-783. 1st edn. F. F2d. $10.00

GOULART, Ron. *Blood Wedding.* Warner 86-088. Vampirella 4. VG. B3d. $8.00

GOULART, Ron. *Bloodstalk.* Warner 76-928. Vampirella. VG+. B3d. $10.00

GOULART, Ron. *Broke Down Engine & Other Stories.* 1972. Collier 02074. 1st prtg. SF. VG. R5d. $2.00

GOULART, Ron. *Calling Dr Patchwork.* 1978. DAW 283. 1st edn. F. M1d. $6.00

GOULART, Ron. *Challengers of the Unknown.* 1977. Dell 11337. 1st prtg. SF. VG. R5d. $2.00

GOULART, Ron. *Chameleon Corps.* 1973. Collier 2075. 1st pb. SF. VG+. B6d. $4.50

GOULART, Ron. *Curse of the Obelisk.* 1987. Avon 89858. 1st edn. SF. F. F2d. $8.00

GOULART, Ron. *Death Cell.* 1971. Beagle 95111. 1st prtg. SF. VG+. R5d. $3.25

GOULART, Ron. *Death Machine* 1975. Warner 75-770. 1st edn. F. F2d. $10.00

GOULART, Ron. *Death Walk.* 1976. Warner 76-390. Vamirella #3. NF. B3a #20. $15.70

GOULART, Ron. *Demon Island.* 1975. Warner 75-858. 1st edn. F. F2d. $7.00

GOULART, Ron. *Fire-Eater.* Ace 28860. c/R LaGrippo. SF. VG+. B5d. $4.50

GOULART, Ron. *Flux.* 1974. DAW 107. PBO. c/J Gaughan. SF. VG. B5d. $3.00

GOULART, Ron. *Flux.* 1974. DAW 107. 1st edn. F. M1d. $7.00

GOULART, Ron. *Green Killer.* 1974. Warner 75-394. 1st edn. F. F2d. $9.00

GOULART, Ron. *Hail, Hibbler.* 1980. DAW. 1st edn. F. M1d. $6.00

GOULART, Ron. *Hawkshaw.* 1972. Award 1202. PBO. SF. NF. B6d. $7.50

GOULART, Ron. *Hello, Lemuria, Hello.* 1979. DAW 331. 1st edn. VG. P9d. $1.50

GOULART, Ron. *Informal History of the Pulp Magazine.* 1973. Ace. 1st pb. NF. M1d. $10.00

GOULART, Ron. *Man From Atlantis.* 1974. Warner 75-609. 1st edn. F. F2d. $9.00

GOULART, Ron. *Nightwitch Devil.* 1974. Warner 75-672. 1st edn. F. F2d. $10.00

GOULART, Ron. *On Alien Wings.* 1975. Warner 76-929. Vampirella #2. NF. B3a #22. $13.35

GOULART, Ron. *On Alien Wings.* 1975. Warner 76-929. Vampirella #2. VG+. B3d. $10.00

GOULART, Ron. *Panchronicon Plot.* 1977. DAW 231. 1st edn. F. P9d. $2.00

GOULART, Ron. *Purple Zombie.* 1974. Warner 75-611. 1st edn. F. F2d. $10.00

GOULART, Ron. *Red Moon.* 1974. Warner 75-610. 1st edn. F. F2d. $7.00

GOULART, Ron. *Shaggy Planet.* Lancer 75420. 1st prtg. VG. S1d. $4.00

GOULART, Ron. *Spacehawk, Inc.* 1974. DAW 132. PBO. c/Arnold. SF. NF. B6d. $7.50

GOULART, Ron. *Suicide, Inc.* 1985. Berkley 07586. 1st prtg. SF. VG+. R5d. $2.00

GOULART, Ron. *Talent for the Invisable.* 1973. DAW 37. 1st edn. G. P9d. $1.25

GOULART, Ron. *Talent for the Invisible.* 1973. DAW 37. 1st edn. F. M1d. $7.00

GOULART, Ron. *Three Gold Crowns.* 1973. Warner 74-260. 1st edn. F. F2d. $10.00

GOULART, Ron. *Tin Angel.* 1973. DAW 80. PBO. c/J Gaughan. SF. VG+. B5d. $4.00

GOULART, Ron. *Tin Angel.* 1973. DAW 80. 1st edn. F. M1d. $7.00

GOULART, Ron. *Too Sweet To Die.* 1972. Ace 40590. PBO. My. NF. B6d. $5.00

GOULART, Ron. *Too Sweet To Die.* 1972. Ace 40590. 1st prtg. My. VG. R5d. $1.75

GOULART, Ron. *Upside Downside.* 1982. DAW. 1st edn. F. M1d. $6.00

GOULART, Ron. *What's Become of Screwloose.* 1973. DAW. 1st edn. F. M1d. $8.00

GOULART, Ron. *When the Waker Sleeps.* 1975. DAW. 1st edn. F. M1d. $7.00

GOULART, Ron. *Whiff of Madness.* 1978. DAW. 1st edn. F. M1d. $7.00

GOULART, Ron. *Wicked Cyborg.* 1978. DAW. 1st edn. F. M1d. $6.00

GOULART, Ron. *Wildsmith.* 1972. Ace 88872. SF. VG. W2d. $3.75

GOULART & HANE. *Star Hawks II.* 1981. Ace 17272. SF. VG. B5d. $3.50

GOULART & LARSON. *Long Patrol.* 1984. Berkley 07105. 1st edn. SF. F. F2d. $10.00

GOULART/GOULART. *Ghost Breaker/Clock Work's Pirates.* Ace 11182. NF. P9d. $3.00

GOULART/HAIBLUM. *Dr Scofflaw/Outworld.* 1979. Dent. 1st pb. F. M1d. $10.00

GOULD, Chester. *Pruneface.* 1975. Gold Medal P 3427. reprints. VG+. P6d. $3.00

GOULD, Elliot. *Whiffs.* 1975. Berkley N 2865. 1st prtg. VG. R5d. $1.75

GOULD, Lawrence. *Problems.* 1949. Avon 200. PBO. VG+. B6d. $35.00

GOW, Gordon. *Suspense in the Cinema.* 1971. PB Library. c/photo. VG. P6d. $4.00

GOWEN, Emmett. *Dark Moon of March.* Dell 572. c/V Kalin. Fi. VG. B5d. $4.00

GOWLAND, J.S. *Smoke Over Sikanaska.* Harlequin 455. VG+. B3d. $6.00

GRAAT, Heinrich. *Revenge of Increase Sewall.* 1969. Belmont B 751066. SF. F. W2d. $5.50

GRADY, James. *Six Days of the Condor.* 1975. Dell 7570. 1st prtg. VG. R5d. $1.75

GRADY, Tex. *High Mesa.* Popular 493. VG+. I1d. $5.00

GRAEME, G.A. *Evil Ear.* 1959. Newsstand 114. 1st edn. My. F. F2d. $12.00

GRAEME, G.A. *Peddlers.* Newsstand Library U 107. VG+. B3d. $4.50

GRAEME, G.A. *Peddlers.* 1959. Newsstand U 107. 1st edn. F. F2d. $15.00

GRAFTON, C.W. *Beyond a Reasonable Doubt.* Pocket 752. G+. G5d. $8.00

GRAFTON, C.W. *Rat Began To Gnaw the Rope.* Dell 180. 1st pb. c/Gregg. My. VG. B6d. $7.50

GRAFTON, C.W. *Rope Began To Hang the Butcher.* Dell 232. VG. B3d. $7.00

GRAFTON, Samuel. *Most Contagious Game.* 1956. Pocket 1102. c/T Dunn. My. VG. B5d. $4.00

GRAHAM, Winston. *Night Without Stars.* 1951. Perma P 128. 1st pb. My. VG. B6d. $7.50

GRAHAME, G.F. *Lotita.* Bee Line 114. NF. B3d. $6.00

GRANGE, Peter. *King Creole.* 1967. Arrow 005. VG. P6d. $2.50

GRANGER, K.R.G. *Ten Against Caesar.* Popular 505. NF. I1d. $6.00

GRANT, Charles L. *Curse.* 1977. Major 3150. 1st edn. scarce. Ho. VG+. F2d. $15.00

GRANT, Charles L. *Pet.* 1987. Doherty. 1st pb. F. M1d. $5.00

GRANT, Joan. *Castle Cloud.* 1966. Ace K 246. 1st prtg. My. VG+. R5d. $2.50

GRANT, Maxwell. *Black Master.* Pyramid N 3478. NF. G5d. $7.50

GRANT, Maxwell. *Black Master.* 1974. Pyramid N 3478. c/Steranko. Shadow #2. VG. P6d. $3.00

GRANT, Maxwell. *Cry Shadow!* Belmont 92-624. VG+. B3d. $5.00

GRANT, Maxwell. *Death Giver.* 1978. Jove V 4282. c/Steranko. Shadow #23. VG. G5d. $8.00

GRANT, Maxwell. *Death Tower.* Bantam H 4770. VG. G5d. $8.00

GRANT, Maxwell. *Death Tower.* 1969. Bantam. 1st pb. NF. M1d. $9.00

GRANT, Maxwell. *Destination: Moon.* 1967. Belmont B 50-737. PBO. Shadow. VG+. P6d. $10.00

GRANT, Maxwell. *Double Z #5.* Pyramid N 3700. G. G5d. $7.00

GRANT, Maxwell. *Eyes of the Shadow.* Bantam 4056. VG+. B3d. $5.00

GRANT, Maxwell. *Gangdom's Doom.* Bantam H 5413. VG. G5d. $8.00

GRANT, Maxwell. *Ghost Makers.* Bantam H 5329. G. G5d. $6.50

GRANT, Maxwell. *Grove of Doom.* 1969. Tempo. 1st pb. VG. M1d. $7.00

GRANT, Maxwell. *Hidden Death.* Bantam H 4884. VG. B5d. $8.00

GRANT, Maxwell. *Living Shadow.* 1969. Bantam H 4463. reprints. G+. P6d. $2.00

GRANT, Maxwell. *Living Shadow.* 1975. Pyramid N 3597. 2nd prtg. Shadow #1. My. VG. W2d. $5.00

GRANT, Maxwell. *Mark of the Shadow.* Belmont 50-683. VG+. B3d. $5.00

GRANT, Maxwell. *Mobsmen on the Spot.* 1974. Pyramid N 3554. c/Steranko. Shadow #3. NF. B3d. $5.00

GRANT, Maxwell. *Mobsmen on the Spot.* 1974. Pyramid N 3554. reprint. Shadow #3. VG. P6d. $3.50

GRANT, Maxwell. *Mox.* 1975. Pyramid N 3876. c/Steranko. Shadow #8. VG. P6d. $2.50

GRANT, Maxwell. *Night of the Shadow.* Belmont B 50-725. VG+. G5d. $9.00

GRANT, Maxwell. *Red Menace.* 1975. Pyramid N 3875. 1st prtg. c/Steranko. VG. P7d. $5.00

GRANT, Maxwell. *Return of the Shadow.* 1963. Belmont. 1st pb. F. M1d. $20.00

GRANT, Maxwell. *Roman Off Jewels.* 1975. Pyramid. 1st pb. G. M1d. $4.00

GRANT, Maxwell. *Shadow Laughs!* 1969. Bantam N 4688. 1st prtg. VG. P7d. $4.00

GRANT, Maxwell. *Shadow Strikes.* 1964. Belmont. 1st pb. NF. M1d. $15.00

GRANT, Maxwell. *Shadow.* 1975. Pyramid N 3875. My. VG+. B4d. $8.00

GRANT, Maxwell. *Shadow's Revenge.* Belmont 60-647. VG+. B3d. $5.00

GRANT, Maxwell. *Shadow's Shadow.* Pyramid V 4278. VG. G5d. $8.00

GRANT, Maxwell. *Silent Seven.* 1975. Pyramid N 3966. PBO. c/Steranko. Shadow #10. VG+. P6d. $4.00

GRANT, Ozro. *Bad 'Un.* 1954. Ace D 50. PBO. scarce. NF. B6a #75. $73.00

GRANT, Ozro. *Bad 'Un.* 1954. Ace D 50. PBO. VG+. B6d. $35.00

GRANT, Richard. *Man Bait.* 1951. Uni-Book 6. 1st pb. G+. B6d. $3.25

GRANT, Ursula. *Paint Her Scarlet.* 1966. Midwood 32-652. Ad. NF. B5d. $6.50

GRANTLAND, Keith. *Run From the Hunter.* 1960. Gold Medal 1062. 1st prtg. c/Barye: gga. VG+. P7d. $5.50

GRAU, Shirley Ann. *Black Prince.* 1956. Signet S 1318. Fi. VG+. B5d. $4.50

GRAU, Shirley Ann. *Hard Blue Sky.* Signet 1726. VG+. B3d. $5.00

GRAVES, Ralph. *Lost Eagles.* 1956. Cardinal C 225. 1st pb. c/Dunn. VG+. B6d. $6.00

GRAVES, Ralph. *Lost Eagles.* 1965. Pyramid T 1265. 1st pb. c/Meese. VG+. B6d. $6.00

GRAVES, Robert. *King Jesus.* 1961. Beacon Envoy 101. 1st pb edn. c/gga. F. F2d. $10.00

GRAVES, Robert. *They Hanged My Saintly Billy.* Avon G 1037. Fi. VG. B5d. $4.50

GRAY, Edwyn A. *Killing Time.* 1975. Pan 24285. Fi. VG. P1d. $3.00

GRAY, Eunice. *Steffi.* 1959. Beacon 216. 1st prtg. c/Micarelli: gga. NF. P7d. $12.50

GRAY, Harriet. *Bride of Violence.* Avon T 156. Fi. VG. B5d. $3.00

GRAY, Rod. *Beds to Mecca.* 1973. Belmont 50566. 1st prtg. My. VG. R5d. $5.00

GRAY, Rod. *Lady Killer.* 1975. Belmont 50838. 1st prtg. My. VG. R5d. $4.00

GRAY, Rod. *Lady Takes It All Off.* 1971. Belmont B 95-2114. 1st prtg. My. G+. R5d. $2.00

GRAY, Rod. *Laid in the Future.* Tower 095-1. VG. B3d. $4.00

GRAY & LIEBER. *Education of TC.* Armed Services 1060. MTI. Nfi. VG+. B5d. $5.50

GRAYSON, C. *Arena.* Panther 1334. VG. B3d. $7.50

GRAYSON, C. *New Stories for Men.* Perma P 122. 1st pb. c/Steinbeck. VG+. B6d. $10.00

GRAZIANO, Rocky. *Somebody Up There Likes Me.* 1956. Cardinal C 210. Nfi. VG. B4d. $2.00

GREELEY, Andrew. *Final Planet.* 1988. TOR 58338. SF. VG. W2d. $4.50

GREEN, Alan. *They Died Laughing.* 1953. Dell 701. c/R Powers. My. VG. B5d. $3.00

GREEN, Chalmers. *Scarlet Venus.* 1952. Gold Medal 246. c/gga. My. VG. B4d. $4.00

GREEN, F.L. *Odd Man Out.* 1947. Pocket 472. MTI. VG+. B4d. $6.00

GREEN, Gerald. *Lotus Eaters.* 1960. Cardinal GC 761. 1st prtg. VG. P7d. $3.50

GREEN, H. *Caught.* Berkley G 472. VG+. B3d. $6.00

GREEN, Joseph. *Conscience Interplanetary.* 1974. DAW. 1st edn. G+. M1d. $3.00

GREEN, Joseph. *Loafers in Refuge.* 1965. Ballantine U 2233. SF. G+. W2d. $3.25

GREEN, Joseph. *Loafers of Refuge.* 1965. Ballantine U 2233. 1st edn. F. M1d. $10.00

GREEN, Joseph. *Mind Behind the Eye.* 1972. DAW 2. 1st prtg. SF. VG. R5d. $2.50

GREEN, Julian. *Dark Journey.* Avon T 91. Fi. VG. B5d. $3.00

GREEN, Julian. *Moira.* 1953. Signet 998. Fi. VG. B5d. $4.00

GREEN, P. Dale. *Cult of the Cat.* 1970. Tower T 095-29. 1st pb. F. B6d. $5.00

GREEN, Roland. *Wandor's Ride.* 1973. Avon 16600. 1st prtg. SF. VG. R5d. $2.00

GREEN, Sharon. *Crystals of Mida.* 1982. DAW UE 1735. Jalav, Amazon Warrior #1. SF. F. W2d. $4.50

GREEN, Sharon. *Warrior Enchanted.* 1983. DAW 87997. SF. F. W2d. $4.00

GREEN, Sharon. *Warrior Rearmed.* 1984. DAW 560. 1st edn. SF. F. F2d. $7.00

GREEN, Sharon. *Warrior Within.* 1982. DAW. 1st edn. NF. M1d. $4.00

GREEN, Sharon. *Will of the Gods.* 1985. DAW 626. 1st edn. F. P9d. $2.50

GREEN, Simon R. *Hawk & Fisher: The God Killer.* 1991. Ace 29460. 1st edn. 3rd series. SF. F2d. $6.00

GREEN & LAURIE. *Show Biz.* 1953. Perma P 217S. Nfi. VG. B4d. $3.00

GREENBURG, Dan. *How To Be a Jewish Mother.* 1967. Signet T 3396. Hu. VG+. B4d. $2.25

GREENE, Graham. *Brighton Rock.* Bantam 315. VG. B3d/I1d. $5.00

GREENE, Graham. *Brighton Rock.* 1949. Bantam 315. My. F. B4d. $15.00

GREENE, Graham. *Brighton Rock.* 1949. Bantam 315. My. VG+. B4d. $9.00

GREENE, Graham. *Brighton Rock.* 1949. Bantam 315. VG. B3a #22. $54.75

GREENE, Graham. *Confidential Agent.* Armed Services 873. VG+. B3d. $7.50

GREENE, Graham. *England Made Me.* Pan 288. VG. B3d. $6.00

GREENE, Graham. *Heart of the Matter.* Bantam 1424. VG. B3d. $4.50

GREENE, Graham. *Human Factor.* 1979. Avon 41491. 1st prtg. My. F. W2d. $4.00

GREENE, Graham. *Man Within.* 1948. Bantam 355. NF. G5d. $5.50

GREENE, Graham. *Man Within.* 1948. Bantam 355. 1st prtg. My. VG. R5d. $4.00

GREENE, Graham. *Ministry of Fear.* Bantam F 2615. VG. M6d. $5.00

GREENE, Graham. *Ministry of Fear.* Signet 530. c/Peng. VG+. B3d. $9.00

GREENE, Graham. *Nineteen Stories.* Lion LL 31. VG. B3d. $4.00

GREENE, Graham. *Orient Express.* 1955. Bantam 1333. 1st prtg. My. VG. R5d. $2.25

GREENE, Graham. *Orient Express.* Livre De Poche 425. VG. M6d. $4.50

GREENE, Graham. *Our Man in Havana.* Bantam A 2018. VG. G5d. $3.25

GREENE, Graham. *Third Man.* 1968. Bantam H 3688. Fi. VG+. B5d. $3.00

GREENE, Graham. *Third Man.* 1950. Bantam 797. MTI. VG. B3d. $4.50

GREENE, Graham. *This Gun for Hire.* Superior M 652. G+. G5d. $5.00

GREENE, J. *Golden Platter.* Signet 2178. VG+. B3d. $5.00

GREENE, Laurence. *O'Mara.* 1953. Lion 182. 1st pb. VG. B6d. $12.50

GREENE, Ward. *Death in the Deep South.* Avon 266. VG. B3d. $6.00

GREENE, Ward. *Life & Loves of a Modern Mr Bluebeard.* 1949. Avon 190. c/gga. VG. P6d. $10.00

GREENFIELD, George. *This World Is Wide Enough.* 1966. Four Square 1639. Fi. G+. P1d. $2.75

GREENFIELD, Irving A. *Stars Will Judge.* 1974. Dell 8504. 1st edn. VG. P9d. $1.50

GREENFIELD, Irving A. *Waters of Death.* 1967. Lancer 73-672. PBO. c/Hoot. SF. NF. B5d. $6.00

GREENFIELD, Irving A. *Waters of Death.* 1967. Lancer 73-672. 1st prtg. SF. VG. R5d. $3.25

GREENFIELD, J. *Blume in Love.* 1973. Warner 76-405. 1st edn. c/color photo. F. F2d. $14.00

GREENHOOD, David. *Love in Dishevelment.* 1949. Signet 711. Fi. VG+. B5d. $5.50

GREENLEAF, William. *Tartarus Incident.* 1983. Ace 79846. SF. VG. W2d. $3.00

GREENO, E. *War on the Underworld.* Digit 494. VG. B3d. $6.00

GREENSHADE, Ted. *He Learned About Women.* 1949. News Stand Library 26A. Fi. VG. B5d. $5.50

GREENWALD, Harold. *Call Girl.* 1958. Ballantine F 280K. Nfi. VG+. B4d. $7.00

GREENWALD, Harold. *Great Cases in Psychoanalysis.* 1959. Ballantine F 333K. PBO. NF. VG+. B5d. $5.00

GREGAR, Martin. *Hell Cat!* Star Book 4. reprint. c/gga. scarce. VG. B6a #77. $53.50

GREGG, Maysie. *Ragamuffin.* John Long NN. 2nd edn. VG+. B3d. $9.00

GREGGSEN, Dale. *Sin & Sin Again.* 1966. Domino Books 82-113. PBO. c/photo. VG. P6d. $3.00

GREGOR, Manfred. *Bridge.* Avon T 532. 1st prtg. VG. R5d. $2.50

GREGOR, Manfred. *Town Without Pity.* Dell F 164. VG. G5d. $3.00

GREGOR, Paul. *Jump Into the Sun.* 1961. Berkley G 490. My. VG. B5d. $2.50

GREGORY, D. *Flesh Seller.* Pillow 107. c/gga. VG. B3d. $4.50

GREGORY, Dan. *Three Must Die!* Graphic 143. PBO. VG+. B3d/I1d. $6.00

GREGORY, David. *Man Minded.* 1963. Beacon B 573F. PBO. c/Victor Olsen: gga. VG. P6d. $2.50

GREGORY, Dick. *From the Back of the Bus.* Avon S 129. c/photo. Nfi. VG+. B5d. $4.00

GREGORY, Jackson. *Far Call.* Popular 313. NF. I1d. $9.00

GREGORY, Jackson. *Guardians of the Trail.* 1952. Popular 430. We. VG. B3d. $4.50

GREGORY, Jackson. *Man From Texas.* Popular 383. VG+. I1d. $7.00

GREGORY, Jackson. *Mystery at Spanish Hacienda.* Avon 13. c/skull. My. G. B5d. $12.50

GREGORY, Jackson. *Mystery at Spanish Hacienda.* Avon 13. VG+. B6d. $18.00

GREGORY, Jackson. *Secret Valley.* Popular 140. VG. B3d. $4.00

GREGORY, Jackson. *Silver Star.* 1956. Popular 160. 1st edn. PBO. F. F2d. $8.00

GREGORY, Jackson. *Sudden Bill Dorn.* 1950. Popular 226. c/gga. We. VG. B4d. $6.00

GREGORY, James. *David David David.* 1972. Curtis 06167. 1st edn. c/photo. Bio. F. F2d. $8.00

GREGORY, John. *Legacy of the Stars.* 1979. Leisure 634. PBO. SF. NF. B6d. $5.00

GREGORY, Paul. *Casting Couch.* 1962. Beacon B524F. PBO. Ad. VG. B5d. $6.00

GREGORY, Paul. *Naked Lens.* 1961. Beacon B459F. PBO. Ad. VG. B5d. $6.00

GREGORY & PRICE. *Visitor.* 1974. Piccolo 23477. 3rd edn. TVTI. VG. P1d. $5.00

GREIG, Maysie. *Candidate for Love.* Dell 239. c/G Gregg. Fi. VG. B5d. $4.00

GREIG, Maysie. *Cherry Blossom Love.* 1967. MacFadden 50-321. 1st pb. VG+. B6d. $5.00

GREIG, Maysie. *Doctor's Wife.* Pocket 463. NF. I1d. $4.00

GREIG, Maysie. *Reluctant Millionaire.* Dell 170. VG. B3d. $5.00

GREIG, Maysie. *Whispers in the Sun.* 1951. Dell 496. c/Robert Stanley. My. VG+. P6d. $3.50

GREIG, Maysie. *Yours Ever.* Dell 446. c/R Hilbert. Fi. VG. B5d. $3.00

GREPSE, George. *Sex U.* Private Edition PE 343. 2nd edn. Ad. VG+. B5d. $4.00

GRETZ, Will. *Stud's Pad.* Bow BB 103. Ad. VG+. B5d. $4.00

GREW, William. *Doubles in Death.* 1955. Perma M 3019. 1st pb. c/Schulz. My. VG. M6d. $6.50

GREW, William. *Murder Has Many Faces.* Graphic 105. VG. I1d. $5.00

GREY, Harry. *Portrait of a Mobster.* Signet 1572. VG+. B3d. $6.00

GREY, Harry. *Portrait of a Mobster.* Signet 1969. 2nd prtg. MTI. VG. B3d. $4.00

GREY, Zane. *Arizona Ames.* 1973. Pocket 75777. 1st pb. c/Duillo. We. VG+. B6d. $5.00

GREY, Zane. *Code of the West.* 1963. Cardinal C 440. We. VG. B4d. $2.00

GREY, Zane. *Code of the West.* 1962. Hodder 214. c/Heade. VG. B3d. $12.00

GREY, Zane. *Fighting Caravans.* 1958. Hodder NN. 1st pb. VG+. B6d. $12.50

GREY, Zane. *Fugitive Trail.* 1961. Cardinal C 441. 1st prtg. VG+. P7d. $5.00

GREY, Zane. *Last of the Plainsmen.* Pan 352. 2nd prtg. VG. B3d. $7.50

GREY, Zane. *Last of the Plainsmen.* 1953. Pennant P 2. We. VG. B4d. $4.00

GREY, Zane. *Rainbow Trail.* 1961. Cardinal C 430. 1st prtg. VG. P7d. $4.50

GREY, Zane. *Spirit of the Border.* 1952. Pocket 161. We. VG. B5d. $3.50

GREY, Zane. *Valley of Wild Horses.* 1959. Cardinal C 351. 1st prtg. c/Leone. VG. P7d. $4.50

GREY, Zane. *Wilderness Trek.* 1974. Pocket 75799. 6th edn. We. VG+. B5d. $3.50

GREY, Zane. *Wyoming.* 1961. Cardinal C 434. 1st prtg. VG. P7d. $4.50

GREYSON, M. *Pain.* Viceroy 373. VG. B3d. $4.00

GRIBBIN, John P. *Jupiter Effect.* 1976. Vintage 72221. 2nd prtg. SF. VG. W2d. $3.00

GRIDER, George. *War Fish.* Pyramid R 1045. reprint. VG+. B6d. $5.00

GRIERSON, Edward. *Crime of One's Own.* Berkley G 1681. VG. B3d. $4.00

GRIFF. *Silver Key.* Modern Fiction NN. G+. B3d. $8.00

GRIFF. *Trading With Bodies.* 1952. Modern Fiction NN. PBO. c/gga. scarce. VG. B6a #74. $30.25

GRIFFEN, Elizabeth L. *Shaggy Dog.* 1975. Scholastic 1111. 8th edn. TVTI. VG. P1d. $5.00

GRIFFIN, Russell. *Century's End.* 1981. Bantam 14525. SF. VG. W2d. $3.00

GRIFFIN, Russell. *Makeshift God.* 1982. Panther 05176. SF. F. B4d. $5.00

GRIFFITH, Maxwell. *Gadget Maker.* 1956. Cardinal. 1st pb. F. M1d. $5.00

GRIFFITH, Maxwell. *Port of Call.* 1953. Perma P 197. 1st pb. VG+. B6d. $9.00

GRIFFITHS, Bernard. *MacNamara's Band.* 1960. Kimber. Fi. VG. P1d. $7.50

GRILLET & ROBBE. *La Maison de Rendez-Vous.* Black Cat B 143. 2nd edn. c/gga. Fi. VG. B5d. $5.00

GRIMES, Lee. *Ax of Atlantis.* 1975. Warner 76704. SF. VG. W2d. $3.50

GRINNELL, David. *Across Time.* Ace G 728. SF. VG. W2d. $4.00

GRINNELL, David. *Edge of Time.* Ace M 162. F. M1d. $6.00

GRINNELL, David. *Edge of Time.* 1966. Ace M 162. SF. VG. B4d. $2.00

GRINNELL/SILVERBERG. *Across Time/ Invaders From Earth.* Ace D 286. c/Emsh. F. M1d. $15.00

GRINNELL/SILVERBERG. *Across Time/ Invaders From Earth.* 1958. Ace D 286. PBO. c/E Valigursky & E Emsh. SF. G+. B5d. $3.50

GRINNELL/TUBB. *To Venus! To Venus!/Jester at Scar.* Ace 81610. 1st prtg. VG. S1d. $3.50

GRINSTEAD, J.E. *Maverick Guns.* Harlequin 75. VG. B3d. $6.00

GRINSTEAD, J.E. *Raging Guns.* 1968. Belmont B 50-837. We. VG+. B5d. $4.00

GRINSTEAD, J.E. *Range King.* Handi-Book 115. VG. B3d. $6.00

GRINSTEAD, J.E. *When Texans Ride.* Handi-Book 123. VG+. I1d. $10.00

GRINSTEAD, J.E. *When Texans Ride.* Harlequin 119. VG. B3d. $5.50

GROH, Edwin. *Jackasses of Lost Causes.* 1964. Vega Book 36. PBO. NF. B6d. $15.00

GRONOWICZ, Antoni. *Hitler's Woman.* 1961. Belmont 219. Fi. VG+. P1d. $6.00

GROSS, Fred. *How To Work With Tools & Wood.* 1957. Cardinal C 260. Nfi. VG+. B4d. $2.00

GROSS, Fred. *How To Work With Tools & Wood.* 1955. Pocket 1057. c/photo. Nfi. VG+. B5d. $5.00

GROSSBACH, Robert. *Cheap Detective.* 1978. Warner 89557. 1st prtg. MTI. My. VG. W2d. $4.00

GROTTA-KURSKA, Daniel. *JRR Tolkien Architect of Middle Earth.* Warner 92-135. 4th edn. Nfi. VG. P1d. $4.00

GROVE, Fred. *Sun Dance.* 1957. Ballantine 251. We. VG+. B4d. $8.00

GROVE, Gene. *Inside the John Birch Society.* 1961. Gold Medal D 1141. Nfi. VG+. B4d. $3.00

GROVE, Walt. *Down.* Dell 1st Edn I1. VG+. I1d. $4.00

GROVE, Walt. *Hell-Bent for Danger.* 1950. Gold Medal 134. PBO. c/Barye. My. VG+. B6d. $12.50

GROVE, Walt. *Man Who Said No.* Gold Medal 120. VG. B3d. $4.00

GROVE, Walt. *Wings of Eagles.* 1957. Gold Medal 649. 1st edn. scarce. F. F2d. $20.00

GROVES, J.W. *Shellbreak.* 1970. PB Library 63-293. SF. VG. B4d. $3.00

GROVES, P. *Juvenile Lead.* Brandon House 3029. VG+. B3d. $5.00

GRUBB, Davis. *Fools' Parade.* Signet Q 4642. 4th edn. MTI. c/J Stewart. VG. M6d. $6.50

GRUBB, Davis. *Night of the Hunter.* 1955. Dell D 149. 1st prtg. VG. P7d. $4.50

GRUBB, Davis. *Twelve Tales of Suspense & Supernatural.* Crest 814. VG+. B3d. $5.00

GRUBB, Davis. *Watchman.* 1962. Crest D 578. 1st prtg. My. VG. R5d. $2.25

GRUBER, Frank. *Bitter Sage.* Bantam 1527. MTI. c/George Gross. reprint. VG+. B6d. $10.00

GRUBER, Frank. *Broken Lance.* Bantam 1198. VG. B3d. $4.50

GRUBER, Frank. *Broken Lance.* Superior NN. VG. B3d. $8.00

GRUBER, Frank. *Buffalo Box.* 1946. Bantam 50. VG. G5d. $6.00

GRUBER, Frank. *Fighting Man.* 1949. Bantam 212. 1st pb. c/Stanley. We. VG+. B3d. $6.50

GRUBER, Frank. *French Key Mystery.* 1942. Avon Monthly Mystery 4. c/G Tompkins & H Black. My. G. B5d. $3.50

GRUBER, Frank. *Gamecock Murders (Scarlet Feather).* Signet 753. G+. G5d. $3.50

GRUBER, Frank. *Gift Horse.* Bantam 2. VG+. B3d. $4.50

GRUBER, Frank. *Job of Murder.* 1950. Signet 827. G+. P6d. $2.75

GRUBER, Frank. *Job of Murder.* 1950. Signet 827. 1st edn. PBO. scarce. My. VG+. B6a #76. $34.25

GRUBER, Frank. *Job of Murder.* 1950. Signet 827. 1st pb. My. VG+. B6d. $15.00

GRUBER, Frank. *Laughing Fox.* Penguin 538. dust jacket. rare. NF. B6a #85. $85.00

GRUBER, Frank. *Leather Duke.* Murray Hill My NN. Fat edn. VG. B3a #20. $8.25

GRUBER, Frank. *Limping Goose.* Bantam 1488. G+. G5d. $3.50

GRUBER, Frank. *Limping Goose.* 1956. Bantam 1488. 1st pb. My. VG+. B6d. $10.00

GRUBER, Frank. *Lone Gunhawk.* Lion LB 117. reprint. VG+. B6d. $9.00

GRUBER, Frank. *Lone Gunhawk.* Lion LB 117. 2nd prtg. VG. B3d. $5.00

GRUBER, Frank. *Man From Missouri.* Popular G 499. VG+. B3d. $4.00

GRUBER, Frank. *Mighty Blockhead.* 1945. Bantam 144. VG. B3a. $50.10

GRUBER, Frank. *Mighty Blockhead.* Superior M 655. G+. G5d. $5.00

GRUBER, Frank. *Mood for Murder.* 1956. Graphic 119. 1st prtg. VG. I1d/P7d. $5.00

GRUBER, Frank. *Navy Colt.* Superior M 649. VG+. G5d. $5.00

GRUBER, Frank. *Outlaw.* Bantam 1934. VG. B3d. $5.00

GRUBER, Frank. *Silver Tombstone.* 1948. Signet 689. My. VG. B4d. $5.00

GRUBER, Frank. *Simon Lash Private Detective.* Penguin 562. NF. G5d. $15.00

GRUBER, Frank. *Swing Low, Swing Dead.* Belmont 92-568. G+. G5d. $3.00

GRUBER, Frank. *Tales of Wells Fargo.* 1958. Bantam 1726. 1st edn. TVTI. F. F2d. $15.00

GRUBER, Frank. *Tales of Wells Fargo.* 1958. Bantam 1726. 1st prtg. TVTI. G+. R5d. $3.50

GRUBER, Frank. *Talking Clock.* Signet 545. 2nd prtg. VG+. B3d. $7.00

GRUBER, Frank. *Whispering Master.* 1959. Signet 1636. c/gga. My. VG+. B4d. $4.00

GRUBER, Frank. *Whispering Master.* Signet 726. NF. I1d. $10.00

GRUBER, Frank. *Whispering Master.* 1949. Signet 726. 1st pb. My. VG. B6d. $6.00

GRUBER, Frank. *Yellow Overcoat.* 1949. Popular 188. 1st edn. PBO. c/Belarski. VG+. B6a #79. $49.25

GRUENBERG, S. *Your Child & You.* Gold Medal 112. VG. B3d. $6.00

GRUENBERG, S. *Your Child & You.* 1950. Gold Medal 112. 1st edn. c/photo. Nfi. F. F2d. $18.00

GUALT, O. *Passion Island.* Kozy Book 126. VG+. B3d. $5.50

GUARESCHI, Giovanni. *Little World of Don Camillo.* 1954. Pocket 1000. c/T Dunn. Fi. VG+. B5d. $5.00

GUBER, Peter. *Inside 'The Deep.'* 1977. Bantam 11136. 1st edn. c/photos. Ad. F. F2d. $15.00

GUENETTE, Robert. *Mysterious Monster.* 1975. S Sun 1548. SF. VG. W2d. $4.00

GUILD, Leo. *Bachelor's Joke Book.* 1953. Avon 513. PBO. VG+. B6d. $9.00

GUILD, Leo. *Girl Who Loved Black.* Holloway HH 173. PBO. VG. B3d. $5.00

GUILD, Leo. *Hollywood Screwballs.* Holloway HH 105. VG+. B3d. $6.00

GUILD, Leo. *Loves of Liberace.* Avon T 118. PBO. VG. B3d. $4.00

GUILD, Leo. *Seduction.* Avon Special NN. c/Driben. VG. B6d. $50.00

GUILD, Leo. *Seduction.* Avon Special NN. VG. B3a #21. $27.04

GUILD, Leo. *What Are the Odds?* 1960. Crest 369. TVTI. VG. P1d. $10.00

GUILD, Leo. *Zanuck: Hollywood's Last Tycoon.* Holloway House 88-409. c/photo. NF. B3d. $6.00

GUILD, Nicholas. *President's Man.* 1983. Pocket 46008. c/skull. My. NF. B5d. $5.00

GUILES, F.L. *Norma Jean: The Life of Marilyn Monroe.* Bantam Q 5499. 6th prtg. Bio. G+. R5d. $2.75

GUIN, Wymon. *Living Way Out.* 1967. Avon. 1st edn. F. M1d. $12.00

GUINN, William. *Death Lies Deep.* Gold Medal 503. PBO. VG. M6d. $5.00

GUINN, William. *Jazz Bum.* 1954. Lion 225. PBO. VG+. B6d. $16.50

GULICK, Bill. *Bend of the Snake.* 1951. Bantam 906. 1st pb. We. VG. B3d. $5.00

GULICK, Bill. *Drum Calls West.* 1953. Bantam 1094. 1st pb. We. VG+. B6d. $8.00

GULICK, Bill. *Hallelujah Trail.* 1965. Popular SP 388. MTI. F. B4d. $7.00

GULICK, Bill. *Land Beyond.* 1960. Signet S 1754. c/B Phillips. Fi. VG. B5d. $4.00

GULICK, Bill. *Moon-Eyed Appaloosa.* 1968. PB Library 52-673. 1st pb. c/Caras. We. VG+. B6d. $6.00

GUNN, James. *Deadlier Than the Male.* Chartered 18. VG. B3d. $5.00

GUNN, James. *Deadlier Than the Male.* Signet 1084. 2nd edn. VG+. B3d. $5.00

GUNN, James. *Deadlier Than the Male.* 1949. Signet 709. c/gga. My. VG. B4d. $3.50

GUNN, James. *Funny Side Up.* Dell 607. VG+. B3d. $5.00

GUNN, James. *Future Imperfect.* 1964. Bantam J 2717. SF. VG+. B5d. $3.50

GUNN, James. *Future Imperfect.* 1964. Bantam J 2717. 1st pb. F. M1d. $9.00

GUNN, James. *Immortals.* 1962. Bantam J 2484. 1st pb. VG. M1d. $5.00

GUNN, James. *Immortals.* 1962. Bantam J 2484. 1st prtg. SF. G+. R5d. $2.00

GUNN, James. *Joy Makers.* 1961. Bantam. 1st pb. F. M1d. $10.00

GUNN, James. *Station in Space.* 1958. Bantam. 1st pb. VG. M1d. $6.00

GUNN, James. *Witching Hour.* 1970. Dell 09605 1st edn. F. M1d. $9.00

GUNN, James. *Witching Hour.* 1970. Dell 09605. 1st prtg. PBO. VG. P7d. $4.00

GUNN, Tom. *Painted Post Gunplay.* 1954. Pocket 1002. c/R Schultz. We. G+. B5d. $4.00

GUNN, Victor. *Ironsides' Lone Hand.* 1943. White Circle 81. PBO. My. VG. P6d. $5.00

GUNN/SILVERBERG. *This Fortress World/ 13th Immortal.* Ace D 223. F. M1d. $18.00

GUNN/SILVERBERG. *This Fortress World/ 13th Immortal.* Ace D 223. VG. B3d. $4.50

GUNNARSSON, Thorarinn. *Revenge of the Valkyrie.* 1989. Ace 72359. 1st edn. SF. F. F2d. $6.00

GUNTHER, John. *Inside Europe Today.* 1962. Cardinal GC 605. Nfi. NF. B5d. $4.00

GURNEY, Gene. *Five Down & Glory.* 1961. Ballantine F 488K. Fi. VG+. P1d. $6.00

GURWELL, J.K. *Mass Murder in Houston.* Cordovan 72. VG+. B3d. $8.00

GUTHRIE, A.B. Jr. *These Thousand Hills.* Cardinal C 267. VG. B3d. $4.00

GUTTERIDGE, Lindsay. *Cold War in an English Garden.* 1973. Pocket 77623. 1st edn. PBO. F. P9d. $2.00

GUTTMACHER, Alan F. *Babies by Choice or by Chance.* 1961. Avon G 1065 Nfi. VG. B4d. $2.50

GUTTMACHER, Alan F. *Complete Book of Birth Control.* 1965. Ballantine U 2136. Nfi. VG+. B4d. $2.25

GWALTNEY, F.I. *Violators.* 1960. Crest Giant D 379. VG+. P6d. $2.00

GWALTNEY, F.I. *Whole Town Knew.* Popular 699. VG+. B3d. $6.00

GWINN, William. *Way With Women.* 1954. Lion 209. PBO. NF. B6d. $22.50

HAAS, Ben. *KKK.* 1965. Greenleaf GC 202. PBO. VG+. P6d. $4.00

HAASE, John. *Young Who Sin.* Avon T 251. VG+. I1d. $5.00

HAASE, John. *Young Who Sin.* 1958. Avon T 454. 1st edn. c/gga. My. F. F2d. $15.00

HABE, Hans. *Footloose Fraulein.* 1957. Beacon B 147. 1st prtg. c/gga. VG+. P7d. $12.50

HABER, Heinz. *Disney Story of Our Friend the Atom.* Dell 1st Edn B 104. VG+. B3d. $4.50

HACKETT, Paul. *Obscenity Trial.* 1964. Signet 2492. 1st edn. My. F. F2d. $12.00

HACKETT, Paul. *Palmeto Springs.* 1962. Signet D 2225. Fa. NF. B4d. $3.00

HACKNEY, Alan. *I'm All Right Jack.* 1960. Signet D 1876. 1st prtg. VG. R5d. $3.50

HADEN, Allen. *My Enemy, My Wife.* Dell 595. 1st prtg. My. VG+. R5d. $4.00

HADLEY, Arthur T. *Joy Wagon.* 1960. Berkley G 466. SF. VG. B5d. $3.00

HADLEY, Franklin. *Planet Big Zero.* 1964. Monarch 431. PBO. c/R Brillhart. SF. VG. B5d. $8.00

HADLEY, Franklin. *Planet Big Zero.* 1964. Monarch 431. 1st edn. F. M1d. $20.00

HADLEY. *Bunny Quest: Private Eyeful.* 1966. Bee Line 122. PBO. VG+. B6d. $9.00

HAGGARD, H. Rider. *Allan Quatermain.* Ballantine. NF. M1d. $8.00

HAGGARD, H. Rider. *Cleopatra.* 1963. Pocket 7025. 2nd edn. SF. VG. B5d. $3.50

HAGGARD, H. Rider. *King Solomon's Mines.* Armed Services 795. G+. I1d. $4.00

HAGGARD, H. Rider. *King Solomon's Mines.* Ballantine X 733. SF. VG. W2d. $4.75

HAGGARD, H. Rider. *King Solomon's Mines.* 1950. Dell. F. M1d. $30.00

HAGGARD, H. Rider. *King Solomon's Mines.* 1950. Dell 433. MTI. c/Granger & Kerr: photo. SF. VG. B5d. $12.50

HAGGARD, H. Rider. *King Solomon's Mines.* 1968. Lancer 13456. SF. F. W2d. $4.50

HAGGARD, H. Rider. *King Solomon's Mines.* 1952. Pan 163. 3rd edn. VG. B3d. $6.50

HAGGARD, H. Rider. *King Solomon's Mines.* 1965. Puffin 111. 5th prtg. SF. F. W2d. $5.00

HAGGARD, H. Rider. *People of the Mist.* 1974. Ballantine 23927. 2nd prtg. SF. VG+. R5d. $4.00

HAGGARD, H. Rider. *She.* 1962. Collins HS 13V. SF. VG+. W2d. $6.00

HAGGARD, H. Rider. *She.* 1949. Dell. F. M1d. $30.00

HAGGARD, H. Rider. *She.* 1965. Lancer 72-925. 1st prtg. c/color photo. scarce. F. F2d. $20.00

HAGGARD, H. Rider. *3 Adventure Novels.* 1951. Dover T 584. SF. F. W2d. $12.00

HAGGARD, Howard W. *Devils, Drugs & Doctors.* 1946. Pocket 379. 1st prtg. VG. P7d. $5.00

HAGGARD, William. *Antagonists.* Signet D 2720. G+. G5d. $3.50

HAGGARD, William. *High Wire.* Signet D 2519. G+. G5d. $5.00

HAGGARD, William. *Money Men.* 1985. Walker 31457. c/G Haas. My. VG+. B5d. $4.00

HAGGARD, William. *Unquiet Sleep.* Avon G 1197. c/V Kalin. My. VG. B5d. $3.00

HAGGARD'S, H. Rider. *She.* Dell 339. VG. I1d. $15.00

HAHN, Emily. *Miss Jill From Shangahai.* 1950. Avon 217. c/D Randall. Fi. VG. B3d. $4.50

HAHN, Emily. *With Naked Foot.* 1951. Bantam 858. c/gga. Fa. VG+. B4d. $7.00

HAHN, Steve. *Mindwipe!* 1976. Laser 51. 1st edn. SF. F. F2d. $15.00

HAIBLUM, Isadore. *Return.* 1973. Dell. 1st pb. G+. M1d. $2.00

HAIBLUM, Isidore. *Interworld.* 1977. Dell 12285. 1st edn. NF. P9d. $1.75

HAIBLUM, Isidore. *Out of Sync.* 1990. Ballantine 35501. 1st edn. SF. F. F2d. $5.00

HAIBLUM, Isidore. *Return.* 1973. Dell 7395. 1st edn. VG. P9d. $1.50

HAIBLUM, Isidore. *Transfer to Yesterday.* 1973. Ballantine 23418. SF. F. W2d. $4.75

HAINES, William Wister. *Command Decision.* 1959. Bantam A 1964. We. NF. B4d. $3.00

HAINES, William Wister. *Command Decision.* Pocket 571. F. G5d. $4.00

HAINES, William Wister. *High Tension.* Pocket 502. NF. I1d. $4.00

HAINING, Peter. *More Tales of Unknown Horror.* 1979. New English 4229. PBO. scarce. VG+. B6a #74. $24.25

HAINING, Peter. *Nightmare Reader.* 1976. Pan 24786. PBO. NF. B6a #74. $41.00

HALDEMAN, J.C. II. *Fall of Winter.* 1985. Baen 55947. SF. F. W2d. $3.75

HALDEMAN, Joe. *Mindbridge.* 1978. Avon 33605. 1 prtg. SF. VG. W2d. $3.00

HALDEMAN, Joe. *Planet of Judgement.* 1977. Bantam 11145. SF. F. W2d. $8.50

HALDEMAN, Joe. *Planet of Judgement.* 1977. Bantam 11145. 1st prtg. SF. VG+. R5d. $2.50

HALDEMAN, Joe. *World Without End (Star Trek).* 1979. Bantam 12583. SF. G+. W2d. $5.00

HALDEMAN, Linda. *Esbae: A Winter's Tale.* 1981. Avon. 1st edn. F. M1d. $3.00

HALE, Arlene. *Emergency for Nurse Selena.* 1966. Ace F 385. 1st prtg. c/gga. VG. P7d. $3.50

HALE, Arlene. *Nurse on Leave.* Ace F 352. PBO. VG+. B3d. $4.00

HALE, Arlene. *Nurse on the Beach.* 1967. Ace F 430. 1st prtg. c/gga. VG+. P7d. $4.00

HALE, Arlene. *Nurse on the Run.* 1965. Ace D 596. 1st prtg. PBO. c/gga. VG+. P7d. $4.00

HALE, Arlene. *Private Duty for Nurse Scott.* Ace F 399. VG+. B3d. $5.00

HALE, Arlene. *Symptoms of Love.* Ace D 580. VG. B3d. $5.00

HALE, Christopher. *Dead of Winter.* 1945. De Novel Classic 39. 1st pb. My. VG. B6d. $7.00

HALE, Christopher. *Hangman's Tie.* Boardman NN HT. VG. B3d. $7.00

HALE, Christopher. *Midsummer Nightmare.* Dell 150. VG+. B3d. $8.00

HALE, Christopher. *Murder on Display.* Boardman NN MOD. VG. B3d. $6.00

HALE, Christopher. *Rumor Hath It.* Boardman. VG. B3d. $10.00

HALE, Christopher. *Rumor Hath It.* De Novel Classic 51. VG. M6d. $4.00

HALE, Christopher. *Witch Wood.* Boardman NN WW. VG+. B3d. $9.00

HALE, Christopher. *Hangman's Tie.* 1946. Bart House 32. 1st prtg. My. VG. R5d. $5.25

HALE, Laura. *Sensual Woman.* 1961. Beacon 407. PBO. c/Marchetti: gga. VG. B6d. $9.00

HALES, Norman. *Spider in the Cup.* 1955. Signet 1173. c/gga. Fa. VG. B4d. $3.00

HALEVY, Julian. *Young Loves.* 1964. Dell 9856. 1st prtg. G+. R5d. $1.00

HALL, A. *Scars of Dracula.* Beagle 94071. MTI. VG. B3d. $4.00

HALL, Adam. *Sibling.* 1979. Playtime 16522. 1st prtg. SF. F. W2d. $4.00

HALL, Adam. *Tango Briefing.* Fontana 3909. NF. F. $4.50

HALL, Angus. *Late Boy Wonder.* 1969. Ace 47300. 1st US edn. c/gga. F. F2d. $10.00

HALL, Austin. *Blind Spot.* Ace G 547. 1st prtg. F. S1d. $4.50

HALL, Austin. *Spot of Life.* 1964. Ace F 318. 1st edn. VG. P9d. $2.00

HALL, Austin. *Spot of Life.* 1965. Ace F 318. SF. F. M1d. $7.00

HALL, Geoffrey Holiday. *End Is Known.* 1951. Pocket 776. c/P Kresse. My. VG+. B5d. $6.50

HALL, J.B. *Racers to the Sun.* Signet 2438. VG. B3d. $5.00

HALL, J.N. *Lost Island.* Armed Services P 5. VG+. B3d. $7.50

HALL, Oakley. *Corpus of Joe Bailey.* 1955. Perma M 4006. Fi. VG. B5d. $3.00

HALL, Oakley. *Mardios Beach.* 1956. Perma M 4042. c/T Dunn. Fi. VG. B5d. $3.00

HALL, Roger. *All My Pretty Ones.* 1961. Midwood 105. VG+. B3d. $6.50

HALL, Roger. *All My Pretty Ones.* 1961. Midwood 105. 1st edn. PBO. c/gga. F. F2d. $8.50

HALL & NORDHOFF. *Botany Bay.* 1964. Pyramid X 1091. 1st pb. c/McVicker. VG+. B6d. $7.50

HALL & NORDHOFF. *Dark River.* 1964. Pyramid R 998. c/gga. Fa. VG+. B4d. $3.75

HALL & NORDHOFF. *Falcons of France.* 1959. Monarch 141. Fi. G+. B5d. $3.00

HALL & NORDHOFF. *Men Against the Sea.* 1962. Cardinal C 458. 1st prtg. VG+. R5d. $2.50

HALL & NORDHOFF. *Pitcairn's Island.* 1962. Cardinal C 457. 3rd prtg. VG. R5d. $1.25

HALL & NORDHOFF. *Pitcairn's Island.* Pocket 457. VG+. B3d. $8.00

HALLAHAN, William H. *Monk.* 1983. Avon 64956. 1st prtg. SF. F. W2d. $3.75

HALLAHAN, William H. *Search for Joseph Tully.* 1977. Avon 33712. 1st prtg. SF. VG. W2d. $3.50

HALLAS, Richard. *You Play the Black & the Red Comes Up.* Dell 510. 1st prtg. My. VG+. R5d. $12.00

HALLERAN, E.E. *Colorado Creek.* Lion 134. VG. B3d. $4.00

HALLERAN, E.E. *Dark Raiders.* Gold Medal 1056. PBO. G+. M6d. $4.50

HALLERAN, E.E. *Gringo Gun.* Lancer 71-321. VG. B3d. $4.00

HALLERAN, E.E. *No Range Is Free.* Dell 616. c/R Stanley. We. VG. B5d. $2.50

HALLERAN, E.E. *Shadow of the Badlands.* Harlequin 61. VG. B3d. $5.00

HALLEY, J.P. *Baxter Trust.* 1989. Lynx 00404. My. VG. B5d. $3.00

HALLIBURTON, Richard. *Royal Road to Romance.* 1942. Pocket 147. Fi. VG. B5d. $5.00

HALLIDAY, Brett. *Before I Wake.* Dell 829. c/R Schulz. My. VG. B5d. $3.00

HALLIDAY, Brett. *Before I Wake.* Dell 829. VG+. G5d. $3.50

HALLIDAY, Brett. *Blonde Cried Murder.* Consul 1114. VG. B3d. $6.00

HALLIDAY, Brett. *Blonde Cried Murder.* 1963. Dell 0614. 1st prtg. c/McGinnis: gga. VG+. P7d. $4.50

HALLIDAY, Brett. *Blood on Biscayne Bay.* Dell D 342. c/McGinnis. VG. B3d. $4.00

HALLIDAY, Brett. *Blood on Biscayne Bay.* 1960. Dell D 342. 1st prtg. My. VG+. R5d. $3.25

HALLIDAY, Brett. *Blood on Biscayne Bay.* Dell 268. c/G Gregg. My. G. B5d. $2.50

HALLIDAY, Brett. *Blood on Biscayne Bay.* Dell 268. VG. B3d. $4.00

HALLIDAY, Brett. *Blood on Biscayne Bay.* Dell 268. 1st prtg. My. G+. R5d. $3.50

HALLIDAY, Brett. *Blood on the Black Market.* Dell 64. VG. B3d. $5.00

HALLIDAY, Brett. *Blood on the Stars.* Dell 385. c/R Stanley. My. VG. B5d/I1d. $5.00

HALLIDAY, Brett. *Blood on the Stars.* Dell 891. c/R Stanley. My. VG. B5d. $3.00

HALLIDAY, Brett. *Bodies Are Where You Find Them.* Dell 668. My. VG+. B5d. $5.50

HALLIDAY, Brett. *Bodies Are Where You Find Them.* 1966. Dell 668. VG. I1d/P7d/R5d. $4.00

HALLIDAY, Brett. *Bodies Are Where You Find Them.* De Novel Classic 31. G+. M6d. $3.50

HALLIDAY, Brett. *Bodies Are Where You Find Them.* Popular 192. 1st pb. c/Belarski. VG. B6d. $12.50

HALLIDAY, Brett. *Body Came Back.* 1964. Dell 0672. c/McGinnis. VG+. B3d. $4.50

HALLIDAY, Brett. *Call for Michael Shayne.* 1964. Dell 0972. 1st prtg. My. G+. R5d. $1.00

HALLIDAY, Brett. *Call for Michael Shayne.* Dell 428. 1st prtg. My. VG. R5d. $3.00

HALLIDAY, Brett. *Corpse Came Calling.* Dell 168. c/G Gregg. My. VG. B5d. $7.50

HALLIDAY, Brett. *Corpse Came Calling.* Dell 324. VG+. I1d. $5.00

HALLIDAY, Brett. *Corpse Came Calling.* Dell 324. 1st prtg. My. G+. R5d. $2.75

HALLIDAY, Brett. *Corpse Came Calling.* 1955. Dell 842. 1st prtg. c/Schulz: gga. VG. P7d. $5.50

HALLIDAY, Brett. *Corpse That Never Was.* 1964. Dell 1498. VG. B3d. $4.00

HALLIDAY, Brett. *Corpse That Never Was.* 1964. Dell 1498. 1st prtg. My. VG+. W2d. $6.00

HALLIDAY, Brett. *Counterfeit Wife.* 1949. Dell 280. c/G Gregg. My. NF. B5d. $10.00

HALLIDAY, Brett. *Counterfeit Wife.* 1949. Dell 280. VG+. B3d. $4.00

HALLIDAY, Brett. *Counterfeit Wife.* 1952. Dell 590. 1st prtg. c/Stanley: gga. VG. P7d. $5.50

HALLIDAY, Brett. *Dangerous Dames Selected by Mike Shayne.* Dell 1st Edn 77. NF. G5d. $6.50

HALLIDAY, Brett. *Dead Man's Diary & Dinner at Dupre's.* Dell 427. VG. I1d. $5.00

HALLIDAY, Brett. *Death Has Three Lives.* Dell 865. c/W George. My. VG+. B5d. $4.00

HALLIDAY, Brett. *Death Has Three Lives.* Dell 865. VG. G5d. $3.00

HALLIDAY, Brett. *Dividend on Death.* Dell 617. G+. G5d. $3.50

HALLIDAY, Brett. *Fit To Kill.* 1959. Dell D 314. 1st prtg. My. VG. R5d. $2.75

HALLIDAY, Brett. *Framed in Blood.* 1952. Dell 578. My. G+. W2d. $4.50

HALLIDAY, Brett. *Framed in Blood.* 1952. Dell 578. My. VG+. B4d. $10.00

HALLIDAY, Brett. *Framed in Blood.* 1957. Dell 958. VG. B3d. $4.00

HALLIDAY, Brett. *In a Deadly Vein.* Dell 4016. c/McGinnis. reprint. VG. B3d. $4.00

HALLIDAY, Brett. *In a Deadly Vein.* Dell 905. 1st prtg. My. VG. R5d. $2.50

HALLIDAY, Brett. *Killers From the Keys.* Dell 4476. VG. G5d. $4.50

HALLIDAY, Brett. *Marked for Murder.* 1948. Dell 222. 1st prtg. My. G+. I1d. $4.00

HALLIDAY, Brett. *Marked for Murder.* Dell 503. c/R Stanley. My. G+. B5d. $2.50

HALLIDAY, Brett. *Marked for Murder.* Dell 503. NF. 11d. $6.00

HALLIDAY, Brett. *Marked for Murder.* Dell 503. 1st prtg. My. VG. R5d. $4.50

HALLIDAY, Brett. *Michael Shayne's Long Chance.* Dell 325. VG+. 11d. $5.00

HALLIDAY, Brett. *Michael Shayne's Long Chance.* Dell 325. 1st prtg. My. G+. R5d. $3.50

HALLIDAY, Brett. *Michael Shayne's Long Chance.* Dell 5602. c/McGinnis. VG+. B3d. $4.00

HALLIDAY, Brett. *Michael Shayne's Long Chance.* Dell 866. VG. B3d. $4.00

HALLIDAY, Brett. *Mike Shayne's 50th Case.* 1965. Dell 5603. 1st prtg. c/McGinnis. VG. P7d. $3.50

HALLIDAY, Brett. *Mum's the Word for Murder.* Dell 743. c/B George. My. VG. B5d. $3.00

HALLIDAY, Brett. *Mum's the Word for Murder.* Dell 743. 1st prtg. My. G+. R5d. $1.75

HALLIDAY, Brett. *Murder & the Married Virgin.* Dell 128. c/G Gregg. My. G+. B5d. $5.00

HALLIDAY, Brett. *Murder & the Married Virgin.* Dell 323. G+. G5d. $5.50

HALLIDAY, Brett. *Murder & the Married Virgin.* Dell 323. VG+. B3d. $6.00

HALLIDAY, Brett. *Murder & the Married Virgin.* 1963. Dell 5932. 1st prtg. My. G+. R5d. $1.00

HALLIDAY, Brett. *Murder & the Married Virgin.* 1957. Dell 960. c/photo. My. VG. B5d. $3.00

HALLIDAY, Brett. *Murder by Proxy.* 1964. Mayflower 5949. 1st UK edn. VG. B3d. $7.50

HALLIDAY, Brett. *Murder in Haste.* Dell 5970. c/McGinnis. VG+. B3d. $4.50

HALLIDAY, Brett. *Murder Is My Business.* Dell 184. c/G Gregg. My. VG. B5d. $7.50

HALLIDAY, Brett. *Murder Is My Business.* Dell 184. G. G5d. $3.50

HALLIDAY, Brett. *Murder Is My Business.* Dell 184. 1st prtg. My. G+. R5d. $4.50

HALLIDAY, Brett. *Murder Is My Business.* 1949. Dell 326. My. VG. B4d. $4.00

HALLIDAY, Brett. *Murder Wears a Mummer's Mask.* Dell 388. G+. 11d. $3.00

HALLIDAY, Brett. *Never Kill a Client.* Dell 6300. VG+. G5d. $3.00

HALLIDAY, Brett. *One Night With Nora.* Dell 803. c/R Stanley. My. VG. B5d. $3.00

HALLIDAY, Brett. *Pay-Off in Blood.* 1963. Dell 1st Edn 6858. PBO. c/McGinnis. My. VG+. B6d. $6.00

HALLIDAY, Brett. *Private Practice of Michael Shayne.* 1943. Dell 23. 1st edn. PBO. NF. B6a #76. $53.00

HALLIDAY, Brett. *Private Practice of Michael Shayne.* 1940. Dell 429. My. G. W2d. $3.75

HALLIDAY, Brett. *She Woke to Darkness.* Dell 867. c/R Schulz. My. VG. B5d. $3.00

HALLIDAY, Brett. *She Woke to Darkness.* Dell 867. VG+. 11d. $6.00

HALLIDAY, Brett. *Shoot the Works.* Dell 988. VG+. B3d. $4.50

HALLIDAY, Brett. *Shoot the Works.* 1958. Dell 988. c/R Stanley. My. VG. B5d. $3.00

HALLIDAY, Brett. *Shoot To Kill.* Dell 7843. c/McGinnis. VG+. B3d. $4.50

HALLIDAY, Brett. *Stranger in Town.* 1961. Dell D 425. 1st prtg. My. VG+. R5d. $3.25

HALLIDAY, Brett. *Stranger in Town.* Dell 914. c/R Stanley. My. VG. B5d. $3.00

HALLIDAY, Brett. *Target: Mike Shayne.* Dell D 355. VG. G5d. $4.00

HALLIDAY, Brett. *Taste for Cognac.* Dell 10¢ 15. VG+. B3d. $7.00

HALLIDAY, Brett. *Taste for Violence.* 1950. Dell 426. c/gga. My. VG+. B4d. $5.00

HALLIDAY, Brett. *Taste for Violence.* 1950. Dell 426. c/R Stanley. My. VG. B5d. $4.00

HALLIDAY, Brett. *Taste for Violence.* 1950. Dell 426. G. 11d. $3.00

HALLIDAY, Brett. *Taste for Violence.* 1962. Dell 463. 1st prtg. c/McGinnis: gga. VG+. P7d. $4.50

HALLIDAY, Brett. *This Is It, Michael Shayne.* Dell 533. c/R Stanley. My. G+. B5d. $2.50

HALLIDAY, Brett. *This Is It, Michael Shayne.* 1957. Dell 957. c/R Stanley. My. VG. B5d. $3.00

HALLIDAY, Brett. *This Is It, Michael Shayne.* 1957. Dell 957. 1st prtg. My. VG+. R5d. $4.00

HALLIDAY, Brett. *Tickets for Death.* De Novel 21. VG+. B3d. $6.00

HALLIDAY, Brett. *Tickets for Death.* 1958. Dell 989. c/R Stanley. My. VG. B5d. $3.00

HALLIDAY, Brett. *Too Friendly, Too Dead.* 1964. Dell 1st Edn 8949. 1st pb. c/McGinnis. VG. B3d/B6d. $4.00

HALLIDAY, Brett. *Uncomplaining Corpses.* Dell 386. 1st prtg. My. VG. R5d. $4.50

HALLIDAY, Brett. *Uncomplaining Corpses.* Dell 9216. reprint. VG. B3d. $4.00

HALLIDAY, Brett. *Uncomplaining Corpses.* 1958. Dell 981. My. VG. B5d. $3.00

HALLIDAY, Brett. *Weep for a Blonde.* 1958. Dell 978. c/photo. My. VG+. B5d. $4.00

HALLIDAY, Brett. *What Really Happened.* Dell 768. 1st prtg. My. G+. R5d. $2.75

HALLIDAY, Brett. *What Really Happened.* 1954. Dell 768. My. VG+. B4d. $4.00

HALLIDAY, Brett. *When Dorinda Dances.* Dell D 359. c/McGinnis. VG+. B3d. $4.50

HALLIDAY, Brett. *When Dorinda Dances.* Dell 723. c/R Stanley. My. VG. B5d. $3.00

HALLIDAY, Brett. *You Killed Elizabeth.* Hillman 143. G+. B5d. $6.00

HALPER, Albert. *Atlantic Avenue.* Dell 1st Edn 94. VG. B3d. $4.00

HAM, Bob. *Overboard Book 2: The Wrath.* 1989. Bantam 27956-4. 1st edn. My. F. F2d. $7.00

HAM, Roswell G. Jr. *Gifted.* 1953. Avon 512. Fi. VG. B5d. $5.00

HAMBLY, Barbara. *Armies of Daylight.* 1983. Ballantine 29671. SF. F. W2d. $4.50

HAMBLY, Barbara. *Time of the Dark.* 1985. Ballantine 31965. 5th prtg. SF. F. W2d. $4.50

HAMBLY, Barbara. *Walls of Air.* 1983. Ballantine 29670. 3rd prtg. SF. F. W2d. $4.50

HAMBLY, Barbara. *Witches of Wenshar.* 1987. Ballantine 32934. PBO. VG+. B6d. $3.00

HAMES, J.W. *Support Your Local Gunfighter.* 1971. Popular 445-08159-075. c/Garner: photo. Av. F. F2d. $10.00

HAMILL, Ethel. *Runaway Nurse.* 1962. Ace D 554. 1st prtg. c/Nappi: gga. VG+. P7d. $4.00

HAMILL, Pete. *Dirty Laundry.* 1985. Golden Apple 19832. 1st prtg. My. F. W2d. $3.75

HAMILL, Pete. *Guns of Heaven.* 1985. Golden Apple 19833. 1st prtg. My. G+. W2d. $2.50

HAMILTON, Bruce. *Hanging Judge.* Hillman 15. VG. B3d. $5.00

HAMILTON, Donald. *Ambushers.* 1966. Gold Medal D 1618. My. VG+. B4d. $2.50

HAMILTON, Donald. *Ambushers.* 1963. Gold Medal K 1333. PBO. My. VG. B4d/B5d. $4.00

HAMILTON, Donald. *Ambushers.* 1963. Gold Medal T 2249. My. NF. B4d. $4.00

HAMILTON, Donald. *Assassins Have Starry Eyes.* Gold Medal L 1491. My. VG. B5d. $3.50

HAMILTON, Donald. *Assignment: Murder.* 1956. Dell 1st Edn A 123. 1st prtg. My. G+. W2d. $5.75

HAMILTON, Donald. *Betrayers*. 1966. Gold Medal D 1736. My. VG. B4d. $2.25

HAMILTON, Donald. *Betrayers*. Gold Medal T 2258. My. VG+. B5d. $4.00

HAMILTON, Donald. *Date With Darkness*. 1950. Dell 375. 1st prtg. My. VG. R5d. $8.50

HAMILTON, Donald. *Death of a Citizen*. 1966. Gold Medal D 1697. My. VG+. B4d. $3.00

HAMILTON, Donald. *Death of a Citizen*. Gold Medal K 1334. My. VG+. B5d. $4.50

HAMILTON, Donald. *Death of a Citizen*. Gold Medal 2901. VG+. B3d. $4.50

HAMILTON, Donald. *Death of a Citizen*. 1960. Gold Medal 957. PBO. VG. M6d. $5.00

HAMILTON, Donald. *Devastators*. Gold Medal D 1608. PBO. My. VG. B5d. $4.00

HAMILTON, Donald. *Devastators*. Gold Medal 2844. VG+. B3d. $4.00

HAMILTON, Donald. *Intimidators*. Gold Medal 2938. NF. B3d. $6.00

HAMILTON, Donald. *Line of Fire*. Gold Medal K 1480. My. G+. W2d. $2.75

HAMILTON, Donald. *Line of Fire*. Gold Medal K 1480. My. VG+. B5d. $4.50

HAMILTON, Donald. *Mad River*. Dell 1st Edn 91. VG. I1d. $4.00

HAMILTON, Donald. *Mad River*. 1956. Dell 1st Edn 91. PBO. c/George Gross. We. VG. B6d. $5.00

HAMILTON, Donald. *Matt Helm, the Interlopers*. 1969. Gold Medal M 2464. My. VG+. B4d. $2.00

HAMILTON, Donald. *Menacers*. Gold Medal D 1884. My. VG. B5d. $3.50

HAMILTON, Donald. *Menacers*. Gold Medal T 2199. Matt Helm #11. My. F. W2d. $3.50

HAMILTON, Donald. *Mona Intercept*. 1980. Gold Medal M 14374. 1st prtg. My. VG. W2d. $3.00

HAMILTON, Donald. *Murder Twice Told*. Gold Medal D 1623. My. VG. W2d. $3.75

HAMILTON, Donald. *Murder Twice Told*. Gold Medal R 2051. My. VG+. B5d. $4.00

HAMILTON, Donald. *Murderer's Row*. 1966. Gold Medal D 1687. MTI. c/photo. VG+. B4d. $3.25

HAMILTON, Donald. *Murderer's Row*. 1962. Gold Medal K 1391. My. VG+. B4d. $3.00

HAMILTON, Donald. *Murderer's Row*. Gold Medal S 1246. PBO. VG. M6d. $4.50

HAMILTON, Donald. *Night Walker*. Dell 1st Edn 27. VG+. I1d. $5.00

HAMILTON, Donald. *Night Walker*. Gold Medal K 1472. VG+. B3d/G5d. $5.00

HAMILTON, Donald. *On Guns & Hunting*. Gold Medal T 2289. 1st pb. VG. M6d. $7.50

HAMILTON, Donald. *Ravagers*. Gold Medal K 1452. PBO. NF. M6d. $7.50

HAMILTON, Donald. *Ravagers*. 1964. Gold Medal K 1452. My. VG. B4d. $4.00

HAMILTON, Donald. *Shadowers*. Gold Medal D 1602. My. VG. B5d. $3.50

HAMILTON, Donald. *Shadowers*. Gold Medal K 1386. PBO. NF. M6d. $7.50

HAMILTON, Donald. *Shadowers*. 1964. Gold Medal K 1386. PBO. My. VG. B5d. $5.00

HAMILTON, Donald. *Shadowers*. 1969. Gold Medal R 2085. My. VG+. B4d. $2.00

HAMILTON, Donald. *Silencers*. 1966. Gold Medal D 1641. MTI. c/Dean Martin: photo. VG. B4d. $2.25

HAMILTON, Donald. *Smoky Valley*. Dell 1st Edn 18. VG. B3d. $3.50

HAMILTON, Donald. *Steel Mirror*. Dell 473. VG+. I1d. $6.00

HAMILTON, Donald. *Steel Mirror*. 1948. Dell 473. 1st prtg. G. W2d. $2.75

HAMILTON, Donald. *Terminators*. Gold Medal 3214. VG+. B3d. $5.00

HAMILTON, Donald. *Texas Fever*. Gold Medal 1035. PBO. VG. M6d. $6.50

HAMILTON, Donald. *Wrecking Crew*. 1963. Gold Medal K 1335. 2nd edn. My. VG. B5d. $3.00

HAMILTON, Donald. *Wrecking Crew*. 1960. Gold Medal T 2263. My. NF. B4d. $2.75

HAMILTON, Donald. *Wrecking Crew*. 1960. Gold Medal 1025. VG+. G5d. $5.00

HAMILTON, Edmond. *Battle for the Stars*. 1967. PB Library 52-609. VG. P9d. $1.50

HAMILTON, Edmond. *Best of Leigh Brackett*. 1977. Ballantine 25954. 1st prtg. SF. VG. R5d. $2.50

HAMILTON, Edmond. *Beyond the Moon*. 1950. Signet. 1st pb. F. M1d. $15.00

HAMILTON, Edmond. *Calling Captain Future*. 1967. Popular 602421. SF. F. W2d. $8.00

HAMILTON, Edmond. *Captain Future & the Space Emperor*. 1967. Popular 602457. SF. VG. W2d. $7.50

HAMILTON, Edmond. *Captain Future's Challenge*. Popular 602430. SF. G+. W2d. $5.00

HAMILTON, Edmond. *City at World's End*. 1957. Crest S 184. 1st pb. NF. M1d. $10.00

HAMILTON, Edmond. *City at World's End*. 1961. Crest S 494. 3rd edn. F. P9d. $1.75

HAMILTON, Edmond. *City at World's End*. Crest 758. NF. B3d. $5.00

HAMILTON, Edmond. *City at World's End*. Galaxy SF 18. VG+. B3d. $6.00

HAMILTON, Edmond. *City at Worlds End*. 1957. Crest S 184. 1st prtg. G+. S1d. $3.00

HAMILTON, Edmond. *Closed Worlds*. 1968. Ace G 701. 1st edn. SF. F. F2d. $8.00

HAMILTON, Edmond. *Comet Kings*. Popular 602407. SF. F. W2d. $8.50

HAMILTON, Edmond. *Crashing Suns*. Ace F 319. 1st prtg. F. S1d. $5.00

HAMILTON, Edmond. *Doomstar*. 1966. Belmont B50-657. PBO. SF. VG. B5d. $5.50

HAMILTON, Edmond. *Galaxy Mission*. 1967. Popular 60-2437. SF. NF. B5d. $5.50

HAMILTON, Edmond. *Haunted Stars*. 1962. Pyramid F 698. c/V Kandinsky. SF. VG. B3d/B5d. $4.00

HAMILTON, Edmond. *Haunted Stars*. 1963. Pyramid F 698. 1st pb. NF. M1d. $8.00

HAMILTON, Edmond. *Magician of Mars*. 1968. Popular 602450. SF. VG. W2d. $7.50

HAMILTON, Edmond. *Outlaws of the Moon*. Popular 602399. 1st prtg. G+. S1d. $3.50

HAMILTON, Edmond. *Outside Universe*. Ace F 271. VG. M1d. $6.00

HAMILTON, Edmond. *Planets in Peril*. Popular 602416. VG+. B3d. $4.50

HAMILTON, Edmond. *Quest Beyond the Stars*. Popular. 1st edn. F. M1d. $12.00

HAMILTON, Edmond. *Return to the Stars*. Lancer 74612. SF. VG+. W2d. $5.00

HAMILTON, Edmond. *Star Kings*. PB Library 53-538. VG+. B3d. $4.50

HAMILTON, Edmond. *Star Kings*. PB Library 53-538. 3rd edn. F. P9d. $2.00

HAMILTON, Edmond. *Star Kings*. 1975. Warner 76842. 3rd prtg. SF. F. W2d. $4.50

HAMILTON, Edmond. *Star of Life*. 1959. Crest S 329. VG. I1d. $4.00

HAMILTON, Edmond. *Valley of Creation*. 1964. Lancer 72-721. 1st edn. F. M1d. $15.00

HAMILTON, Edmond. *Valley of Creation.* 1964. Lancer 72-721. 1st prtg. SF. VG. R5d. $5.50

HAMILTON, Edmond. *Weapon From Beyond.* 1967. Ace G 639. 1st prtg. Starwolf #1. G. S1d/W2d. $3.00

HAMILTON, Greg. *Any Man Will Do.* 1963. Midwood 273. 1st edn. c/Radar: gga. F. F2d. $20.00

HAMILTON, Greg. *Lady Awaits.* 1965. Midwood 32-512. Ad. VG. B5d. $4.00

HAMILTON, Greg. *Made To Order.* Midwood 298. PBO. c/Rader. VG. B3d. $4.00

HAMILTON, Greg. *Monica.* 1963. Midwood F 314. PBO. c/gga. NF. B6d. $22.50

HAMILTON, Greg. *Portrait in Flesh.* 1963. Midwood F 341. PBO. VG+. B6d. $12.50

HAMILTON, Greg. *So Eager To Please.* Midwood 33-669. Ad. VG. B5d. $4.50

HAMILTON, Greg. *Strange One.* 1965. Midwood 32-564. 1st edn. c/photo. F. F2d. $10.00

HAMILTON, K. *Young Doctor Glenn.* Harlequin 357. VG. B3d. $4.00

HAMILTON, W. *Gun Lobos.* Pyramid 1263. VG+. B3d. $4.50

HAMILTON, W. *Longhorn Brand.* Pyramid 1031. 2nd reissue. VG+. B3d. $4.50

HAMILTON, W. *Rimrock Renegade.* Pyramid 1047. 2nd prtg. VG+. B3d. $4.50

HAMILTON, W. *Sagebrush.* 1965. Pyramid F 1195. 1st pb. c/Lesser. We. VG+. B6d. $8.00

HAMILTON, W. *Trail's End.* Pyramid 1159. VG+. B3d. $5.00

HAMILTON/JORGENSON. *Sun Smasher/ Starhaven.* 1959. Ace D 351. F. M1d. $15.00

HAMILTON/JORGENSON. *Sun Smasher/ Starhaven.* 1959. Ace D 351. PBO. SF. VG. P6d. $4.50

HAMILTON/JORGENSON. *Sun Smasher/ Starhaven.* 1959. Ace D 351. VG+. I1d. $5.00

HAMILTON/ROCKLYNNE. *Yank at Valhalla/Sun Destroyers.* 1973. Ace 93900. SF. VG. W2d. $5.00

HAMLIN, Ken. *Guns of Revenge.* 1965. Monarch 555. c/A Leslie Ross. We. VG. P6d. $3.00

HAMMETT, Dashiell. *Adventures of Sam Spade & Other Stories.* 1944. Bestseller B 50. 1st edn. My. NF. F2d. $100.00

HAMMETT, Dashiell. *Blood Money.* 1951. Dell 486. c/gga. My. VG. B4d. $10.00

HAMMETT, Dashiell. *Blood Money.* 1944. Dell 53. My. VG. M1d/M3d. $40.00

HAMMETT, Dashiell. *Blood Money.* 1944. Dell 53. 1st prtg. My. F. F2d. $55.00

HAMMETT, Dashiell. *Continental Op.* 1946. Dell 129. My. VG. M3d. $25.00

HAMMETT, Dashiell. *Continental Op.* 1946. Dell 129. 1st edn. PBO. c/Gregg. rare. NF. B6a #76. $55.00

HAMMETT, Dashiell. *Continental Op.* 1946. Dell 129. 1st prtg. My. NF. F2d. $40.00

HAMMETT, Dashiell. *Creeping Siamese.* Dell 538. c/R Stanley. My. G. B5d. $5.00

HAMMETT, Dashiell. *Creeping Siamese.* 1951. Dell 538. 1st pb. VG. B6d. $15.00

HAMMETT, Dashiell. *Creeps by Night.* Belmont 230. VG+. B3d. $6.00

HAMMETT, Dashiell. *Creeps by Night.* 1961. Belmont 230. 1st pb. F. M1d. $20.00

HAMMETT, Dashiell. *Dain Curse.* 1968. Dell 1668. 1st prtg. VG+. P7d. $4.50

HAMMETT, Dashiell. *Dain Curse.* 1961. Perma M 4198. 1st prtg. My. F. F2d. $15.00

HAMMETT, Dashiell. *Dain Curse.* 1945. Pocket 295. 1st edn. PBO. VG. F2d. $20.00

HAMMETT, Dashiell. *Dead Yellow Women.* Dell 308. c/Gregg. VG. B6d. $32.50

HAMMETT, Dashiell. *Dead Yellow Women.* Dell 308. c/Gregg. VG+. B6a #77. $59.00

HAMMETT, Dashiell. *Glass Key.* 1961. Perma M 4199. 1st prtg. My. F. F2d. $12.00

HAMMETT, Dashiell. *Glass Key.* 1943. Pocket 211. 1st prtg. My. NF. F2d. $15.00

HAMMETT, Dashiell. *Hammett Homicides.* 1948. Dell 223. 1st edn. PBO. c/Gregg. rare. NF. B6a #76. $55.00

HAMMETT, Dashiell. *Hammett Homicides.* Dell 223. G+. B3d. $5.00

HAMMETT, Dashiell. *Hammett Homicides.* Dell 223. VG. I1d. $25.00

HAMMETT, Dashiell. *Maltese Falcon.* Pan 185. VG. B3d. $6.00

HAMMETT, Dashiell. *Maltese Falcon.* Perma M 3074. NF. B3d. $6.50

HAMMETT, Dashiell. *Maltese Falcon.* 1957. Perma M 3074. c/S Meltzoff. My. VG. B5d. $6.00

HAMMETT, Dashiell. *Maltese Falcon.* 1957. Perma M 3074. 1st prtg. My. F. F2d. $25.00

HAMMETT, Dashiell. *Maltese Falcon.* Pocket 268. G+. I1d. $50.00

HAMMETT, Dashiell. *Maltese Falcon.* 1946. Zephyr 19. 1st pb. VG. B6d. $18.00

HAMMETT, Dashiell. *Man Called Spade.* Dell 411. 1st prtg. G+. R5d. $6.00

HAMMETT, Dashiell. *Man Called Spade.* Dell 90. VG. G5d. $45.00

HAMMETT, Dashiell. *Man Called Spade.* 1945. Dell 90. My. G+. B4d. $7.50

HAMMETT, Dashiell. *Man Called Spade.* 1945. Dell 90. 1st pb edn. VG. F2d. $30.00

HAMMETT, Dashiell. *Nightmare Town.* Dell 379. c/R Stanley. My. G. B5d. $5.00

HAMMETT, Dashiell. *Red Brain.* 1961. Belmont 239. VG. B3d. $6.00

HAMMETT, Dashiell. *Red Brain.* 1961. Belmont 239. 1st pb. F. M1d. $25.00

HAMMETT, Dashiell. *Red Brain.* 1961. Belmont 239. 1st prtg. My. VG+. R5d. $10.00

HAMMETT, Dashiell. *Red Harvest.* 1956. Perma M 3043. 1st prtg. My. F. F2d. $15.00

HAMMETT, Dashiell. *Red Harvest.* 1943. Pocket 241. 1st prtg. c/Hoffman. VG+. P7d. $20.00

HAMMETT, Dashiell. *Red Harvest.* 1972. Vintage V 828. My. F. W2d. $4.25

HAMMETT, Dashiell. *Return of the Continental Op.* Dell 154. c/G Grogg. My. G. B5d. $5.00

HAMMETT, Dashiell. *Return of the Continental Op.* 1947. Dell 154. 1st prtg. My. NF. F2d. $40.00

HAMMETT, Dashiell. *Return of the Continental Op.* 1945. Jonathan J 17. 1st edn. My. VG+. F2d. $150.00

HAMMETT, Dashiell. *Thin Man.* Pocket 196. G+. G5d. $10.00

HAMMETT, Dashiell. *Thin Man.* 1942. Pocket 196. 1st pb. c/Hoffman. My. VG. I1d. $15.00

HAMMETT, Dashiell. *Thin Man.* 1942. Pocket 196. 1st prtg. My. NF. F2d. $20.00

HAMMETT, Dashiell. *Women in the Dark.* 1951. Jonathan J 59. VG. B3a #20. $26.40

HAMPTON, Stella. *Dark Quarters.* Fabian Z 117. VG+. B3d. $6.00

HAN, Suyln. *Many-Splendored Thing.* 1955. Signet D1183. c/S Zuckerberg. Nfi. VG. B5d. $3.50

HANCOCK, Lucy Agnes. *Doctor Kim.* 1948. Bantam 408. c/gga. Ro. NF. B4d. $4.00

HANCOCK, N. *Squaring the Circle.* 1977. Popular 04089. Circle of Light #4. SF. VG. W2d. $3.25

HAND, Arnold. *Willie Mays.* 1961. Sport Magazine 6. PBO. NF. B3a #22. $9.70

HANDLEY, Alan. *Terror in Times Square.* 1950. Pyramid 20. 1st US edn. PBO. c/Blickenstaff. VG+. B6a #79. $49.50

HANDLEY, Max. *Meanwhile.* 1985. Popular 20068. SF. F. W2d. $5.00

HANKINS, R.M. *Man From Wyoming.* Bantam 259. F. I1d. $7.00

HANKINS, R.M. *Man From Wyoming.* 1949. Bantam 259. c/R Stanley. We. NF. B5d. $5.00

HANKINS, R.M. *Rio Grande Kid.* 1949. Bantam 214. c/Saunders. We. VG. B3d. $5.00

HANLEY, G. *Consul at Sunset.* Pan 330. VG. B3d. $6.00

HANLEY, Gerald. *Gilligan's Last Elephant.* Crest 638. VG. B3d. $4.00

HANLEY, Gerald. *Last Safari.* 1968. Gold Medal D 1857. MTI. VG. B4d. $3.00

HANLEY, Jack. *Guy From Coney Island.* Avon 580. PBO. fi. G+. B5d. $5.50

HANLEY, Jack. *Let's Make Mary.* 1948. Hillman 1. Nfi. G+. B5d. $3.50

HANLEY, Jack. *Let's Make Mary.* 1948. Hillman 1. VG. M6d. $9.50

HANLEY, Jack. *Let's Make Mary.* Hillman 120. VG. B3d. $5.00

HANLEY, Jack. *Strip Street.* Berkley 261. VG. B3d. $4.00

HANLEY, Jack. *Tomcat in Tights.* 1951. Avon Monthly Novel 21. 1st edn. PBO. c/gga. scarce. VG. B6a #80. $48.50

HANLEY, Jack. *Very Private Secretary.* 1960. Beacon B 296. PBO. Ad. VG. B5d. $6.50

HANLEY, Jack. *Very Private Secretary.* 1960. Beacon 296. c/gga. scarce. NF. B6a #76. $33.00

HANLEY, Jack. *Violated One (City Streets).* MacFadden 60-386. VG. B3d. $4.50

HANLON, Edward S. *Great God Now.* 1968. PB Library 53-657. PBO. VG. P6d. $1.50

HANO, Arnold. *Marriage Italian Style.* 1965. Popular PC 1047. 1st prtg. VG+. R5d. $3.00

HANO, Arnold. *Western Roundup!* 1948. Bantam 256. PBO. c/C Young. We. VG. B5d. $4.50

HANO, Arnold. *Willie Mays, Say-Hey Kid.* 1961. Sport Magazine 6. PBO. VG+. B3d. $10.00

HANO, Arnold. *Willie Mays, Say-Hey Kid.* 1961. Sport Magazine 6. 1st edn. c/color photo. F. F2d. $20.00

HANSEN, Robert. *Walk a Wicked Mile.* 1956. Popular 774. 1st pb. My. VG+. B6d. $12.00

HANSER, Richard. *True Tales of Hitler's Reich.* 1962. Crest D 579. 1st prtg. PBO. VG+. P7d. $4.50

HANSON, Kitty. *Rebels in the Streets.* 1965. Tower 43-543. 1st edn. PBO. scarce. JD. F. B6a #80. $50.00

HARBINSON, W.A. *Genesis.* 1982. Dell 12832. 2nd prtg. SF. F. W2d. $4.00

HARBINSON, W.A. *Illustrated Elvis.* 1977. Tempo 36514. 1st prtg. Bio. G. R5d. $2.50

HARBINSON, W.A. *Revelation.* 1983. Dell 17216. 1st prtg. SF. VG. W2d. $3.25

HARBURG & SAIDY. *Finian's Rainbow.* 1968. Berkley 1624. 1st edn. F. F2d. $7.00

HARDIN, Dave. *Brandon's Empire.* 1953. Ballantine 57. We. VG+. B4d. $5.00

HARDIN, Peter. *Frightened Dove.* 1952. Bantam 1030. 1st pb. NF. B6d. $12.50

HARDIN, Peter. *Frightened Dove.* 1952. Bantam 1030. 1st prtg. My. G+. R5d. $2.75

HARDIN, Peter. *Hidden Grave.* Dell 922. c/D Gillon. My. VG. B5d. $3.00

HARDIN/LOMAX. *Hellbent for a Hangrope/ Ambush at Coffin.* Ace D 56. VG+. I1d. $10.00

HARDIN/WEST. *Paxman Feud/Showdown at Serano.* 1973. Ace 65501. 2nd edn. We. VG. B5d. $3.00

HARDIN/WYNNE. *Badge Shooters/Massacre Basin.* 1962. Ace F 144 We. VG+. B5d. $5.50

HARDING, Matt. *All Woman.* 1960. Beacon B 365. Ad. G. B5d. $2.50

HARDING, Matt. *Fly Girl.* 1961. Beacon B 433Y. PBO. c/Darcy. Ad. G+. B5d. $6.00

HARDING, Matt. *Fly Girl.* MacFadden 75-329. VG+. B3d. $4.50

HARDING, Matt. *Mattress Game.* 1961. Beacon B 400. PBO. Ad. VG+. B5d. $8.00

HARDING, Matt. *Men on Her Mind.* 1962. Beacon 480. 1st edn. c/gga. F. F2d. $15.00

HARDING, Matt. *Office Game.* Beacon B 447Y. PBO. VG. M6d. $4.50

HARDING, Matt. *They Couldn't Say No.* 1961. Beacon B 374. PBO. c/J Faragasso. Ad. VG. B5d. $6.00

HARDING, Max. *Young Widow.* 1960. Beacon 345. 1st prtg. PBO. c/Rossi: gga. NF. P7d. $12.50

HARDINGE, R. *Case of the African Hoodoo.* Sexton Blake 283. VG. B3d. $6.00

HARDINGE, R. *Case of the Secret Agent.* Sexton Blake 201. VG+. B3d. $6.00

HARDINGE, R. *Man From Chundking.* Sexton Blake 130. VG+. B3d. $12.00

HARDINGE, R. *Man With Five Enemies.* Sexton Blake 330. VG+. B3d. $7.00

HARDINGE, R. *Mystery of the Outlawed Black.* Sexton Blake 338. VG+. B3d. $8.50

HARDINGE, R. *Riddle of the Invisible Menace.* Sexton Blake 315. VG. B3d. $8.00

HARDINGE, R. *Tragedy of the Bromleights.* Sexton Blake 194. VG. B3d. $5.00

HARDINGE, R. *Victim of the Devil's Bowl.* Sexton Blake 325. VG. B3d. $10.00

HARDINGE, R. *Voyage of Fear.* Sexton Blake 308. VG+. B3d. $8.00

HARDINGE, R. *With Criminal Intent.* Sexton Blake 220. VG+. B3d. $7.00

HARDWICK, Michael. *Mr Bellamy's Story.* 1974. Sphere 4305. TVTI. VG. P1d. $6.00

HARDWICK, Mollie. *Mrs Bridges' Story.* 1975. Sphere 4303. TVTI. VG. P1d. $5.00

HARDWICK, Mollie. *Thomas & Sarah.* 1979. Sphere 0512. 2nd edn. TVTI. VG. P1d. $4.50

HARDWICK, Mollie. *War to End Wars.* 1975. Dell 5987. TVTI. VG. P1d. $5.00

HARDWICK, Mollie. *Years of Change.* 1974. Dell 6049. TVTI. VG+. P1d. $7.50

HARDWICK, Richard. *Hawk.* 1966. Belmont B 50-741. PBO. TVTI. VG. B6d. $3.00

HARDY, Lindsay. *Requiem for a Redhead.* 1954. Signet 1154. c/Erickson: gga. My. VG. B4d. $3.00

HARDY, Rene. *Place of Jackals.* Berkley G 23. VG+. B3d. $4.50

HARDY, S. *Man From Nowhere.* Gunfire 37. VG+. B3d. $5.50

HARDY, W.G. *Unfulfilled.* 1952. Popular 464. c/gga. Fa. VG+. B4d. $10.00

HARDY, William M. *Case of the Missing Coed (A Little Sin).* Dell D 360. G+. G5d. $3.00

HARDY, William M. *Lady Killer.* Dell 995. VG. G5d. $3.00

HARDY. *Secret of the 6th Magic.* 1984. Ballantine 30309. PBO. c/Rowena. VG+. B6d. $3.00

HARGROVE, Marion. *Girl He Left Behind.* 1956. Signet S 1364. MTI. Fi. VG+. B5d. $5.00

HARGROVE, Marion. *Something's Got To Give.* 1950. Popular 222. Fa. VG. B4d. $6.00

HARKEY, Dee. *Mean As Hell.* Signet 1196. c/McDermott. reprint. We. VG+. B6d. $8.00

HARKINS, P. *Touchdown Twins.* Pocket J 55. VG+. B3d. $5.00

HARKINS, S. *Oral Daughters.* Barclay 7136. VG+. B3d. $4.00

HARKINS & MARUYAMA. *Cultures Beyond the Earth.* 1975. Vintage V 602. 1st prtg. Nfi. VG+. W2d. $3.50

HARKNETT, Terry. *Crown-Bamboo Shoot-Out.* 1975. #71928. My. F. W2d. $4.25

HARLAND, Tom. *This Breed of Woman.* 1964. Beacon B 732X. c/gga. Fa. F. B4d. $14.00

HARLAND, Tom. *Torrid Widow.* 1963. Beacon B 616F. c/gga. Fa. VG+. B4d. $14.00

HARMON, J. *Celluloid Scandal.* Epic 109. VG+. B3d. $5.00

HARMON, J. *Drive-In Nympho.* Bee Line 266. VG. B3d. $5.00

HARMON, J. *Vixen Hollow.* Epic 104. VG. B3d. $5.00

HARMON, Jackson. *Night Spot.* 1966. Midwood 33-699. Ad. VG. B5d. $4.00

HARMON, Jackson. *Taste of Shame.* 1967. Midwood 32-795. Ad. VG+. B5d. $5.50

HARMON, Jim. *Great Radio Heroes.* 1967. Ace 30255. VG. P6d. $4.50

HARNESS, Charles L. *Ring of Ritornel.* Berkley 1630. VG+. B3d. $4.50

HARNESS, Charles L. *Rose.* 1969. Berkley X 1648. 1st US edn. SF. NF. B6d. $9.00

HARNESS, Charles L. *Rose.* Panther 2879. 1st pb. reprint. SF. NF. B6d. $3.50

HARNESS/WILLIAMSON. *Paradox Men/ Dome Around America.* Ace D 118. F. M1d. $20.00

HARNESS/WILLIAMSON. *Paradox Men/ Dome Around America.* 1955. Ace D 118. PBO. c/R Powers & E Valigursky. SF. G+. B5d. $7.00

HARPER, E.M. *Assassin.* 1960. Berkley D 2027. PBO. c/Copeland: gga. My. NF. B6d. $15.00

HARPER, Sydney. *Murder One.* Blueboy 80048. VG. G5d. $7.50

HARRAGAN, Steve. *Dope Doll.* 1953. Universal Giant 4. PBO. extremely scarce. VG. B6a #77. $63.50

HARRAGAN, Steve. *Dope Doll.* 1953. Universal Giant 4. VG. I1d. $20.00

HARRE, Everett. *Heavenly Sinner.* 1952. Pyramid G 64. 1st pb. c/Paul: gga. VG+. B6d. $15.00

HARREY, Gene. *Leg Art Virgin.* 1950. Quarter Book 74. PBO. c/George Gross. NF. B6a #74. $61.00

HARRID, John Benyon. *Secret People.* 1967. Lancer 72-155. c/F Frazetta. SF. VG. B5d. $4.00

HARRIMAN, P. *Niece & Uncle Incest.* Barclay 7473. c/photo. NF. B3d. $5.00

HARRINGTON, Len. *Savages Are Loose.* 1972. Venice VB 594. JD. VG+. P1d. $15.00

HARRIS, A.M. *Tall Man.* 1960. Pocket 1267. War. VG+. B4d. $4.00

HARRIS, Frank G. *My Wife & Lovers.* 1964. All Star AS 29. PBO. c/gga: photo. VG+. P6d. $5.50

HARRIS, Frank G. *Women of Beaver Mountain.* 1963. All Star 6. PBO. VG+. B6d. $8.00

HARRIS, J. *Old Trade of Killing.* Banner 60-101. VG. B3d. $5.00

HARRIS, J. *Sleeping Mountain.* Four Square 224. VG+. B3d. $7.00

HARRIS, John Benyon. *Secret People.* 1964. Lancer 72-701. 1st pb. VG. M1d. $10.00

HARRIS, Sara. *Skid Row USA.* 1961. Belmont 223. Nfi. VG. B5d. $4.00

HARRIS, Sydney. *To Cry Fear.* Digit D 175. NF. I1d. $5.00

HARRIS, Sydney. *Winners & Losers.* Argus 917. Nfi. VG. B5d. $2.50

HARRIS, Thomas. *Black Sunday.* Bantam T 4959. 1st pb. VG+. M6d. $4.50

HARRIS, Thomas. *Black Sunday.* 1976. Bantam Y 2100. 1st prtg. My. VG+. R5d. $2.50

HARRIS & MURTAGN. *Who Live in Shadow.* Belmont 205. Nfi. VG. B5d. $4.00

HARRISON, Chip. *Chip Harrison Scores Again.* 1971. Gold Medal 2421. PBO. scarce. VG. B6a #76. $61.00

HARRISON, Chip. *Chip Harrison Scores Again.* 1971. Gold Medal 2421. c/Elaine: gga. scarce. VG. P6d. $10.00

HARRISON, Chip. *Make Out With Murder.* 1974. Gold Medal M 3029. PBO. c/sgn. scarce. VG+. B6a #76. $67.25

HARRISON, Chip. *Make Out With Murder.* 1974. Gold Medal M 3029. 1st prtg. PBO. VG. P7d. $5.50

HARRISON, Chip. *No Score.* 1970. Gold Medal T 2285. PBO. scarce. VG. B6a #76. $61.00

HARRISON, Chip. *Topless Tulip Caper.* 1975. Gold Medal P 3274. PBO. c/Elaine. VG+. B6a #76. $61.00

HARRISON, G.B. *Introducing Shakespeare.* 1947. Pelican (US) P 14. Nfi. VG. P1d. $10.00

HARRISON, Harry. *Best SF: 1968.* 1969. Berkley 01742. SF. G. W2d. $3.00

HARRISON, Harry. *Bill, the Galactic Hero.* 1979. Avon 47183. 1st prtg. SF. F. W2d. $6.00

HARRISON, Harry. *Bill, the Galactic Hero.* 1966. Berkley F 1186. SF. VG. B3d/B5d. $4.50

HARRISON, Harry. *Captive Universe.* 1969. Berkley X 1725. c/P Lehr. SF. VG+. B5d. $4.00

HARRISON, Harry. *Captive Universe.* 1969. Berkley X 1725. 1st edn. SF. F. F2d. $12.00

HARRISON, Harry. *Captive Universe.* Berkley Z 3072. 2nd edn. SF. NF. B5d. $4.00

HARRISON, Harry. *Deathworld 3.* 1968. Dell 1849. 1st edn. VG. P9d. $1.50

HARRISON, Harry. *Make Room! Make Room!* 1967. Berkley X 1416. 1st pb. c/sgn. SF. VG. B6d. $12.50

HARRISON, Harry. *Make Room! Make Room!* 1967. Berkley 02390. MTI. SF. VG. W2d. $4.00

HARRISON, Harry. *Men From Pig & Robot.* 1978. Puffin 1004. 1st pb. SF. NF. B6d. $7.50

HARRISON, Harry. *Nova One.* 1971. Dell. 1st pb. VG. M1d. $5.00

HARRISON, Harry. *Outdated Man.* 1975. Dell 6661. 1st prtg. SF. VG+. R5d. $1.75

HARRISON, Harry. *Plague From Space.* 1968. Bantam F 3640. SF. VG. B5d. $3.00

HARRISON, Harry. *Planet of the Damned.* 1962. Bantam J 2316. SF. VG. W2d. $4.50

HARRISON, Harry. *Planet of the Damned.* 1962. Bantam 2316. 1st edn. SF. F. F2d/M1d. $20.00

HARRISON, Harry. *Stainless Steel Rat Is Born.* Bantam 24708. VG. G5d. $2.50

HARRISON, Harry. *Stainless Steel Rat Is Born.* 1985. Bantam. 1st edn. F. M1d. $7.00

HARRISON, Harry. *Stainless Steel Rat Saves the World.* 1973. Berkley 2475. 1st edn. PBO. F. P9d. $2.00

HARRISON, Harry. *Stainless Steel Rat.* 1961. Pyramid F 672. PBO. c/J Schoenherr. SF. VG. B5d. $8.00

HARRISON, Harry. *Stainless Steel Rat.* 1961. Pyramid F 672. 1st pb. F. M1d. $20.00

HARRISON, Harry. *Star-World.* 1984. Bantam. F. M1d. $8.00

HARRISON, Harry. *Technicolor Time Machine.* 1968. Berkley X 1640. c/S Kossin. SF. F. B5d. $6.00

HARRISON, Harry. *Two Tales & Eight Tomorrows.* 1968. Bantam. 1st edn. F. M1d. $10.00

HARRISON, Harry. *War With the Robots.* 1962. Pyramid F 771. c/John Schoenherr. SF. F. M1d. $12.00

HARRISON, Harry. *War With the Robots.* 1962. Pyramid F 771. PBO. c/J Schoenherr. SF. VG. B5d. $6.00

HARRISON, John. *Pastel City.* 1974. Ace 19711. 1st edn. VG. P9d. $1.50

HARRISON, M. *In the Footsteps of Sherlock Holmes.* 1976. Berkley U 3047. 1st prtg. PBO. Nfi. VG. R5d. $2.50

HARRISON, Tim. *Hot Summer.* Beacon B 485. NF. I1d. $10.00

HARRISON, Whit. *Any Woman He Wanted.* 1961. Beacon 392. 1st prtg. PBO. c/Micarelli: gga. VG. B3d/P7d. $15.00

HARRISON, Whit. *Army Girl.* PB Library 51-173. NF. B6a #75. $40.25

HARRISON, Whit. *Army Girl.* 1953. Venus 161. PBO. c/Belarski: gga. VG+. B6a #76. $72.50

HARRISON, Whit. *Army Girl.* Venus 194. c/Belarski: gga. VG+. B6a #76. $68.25

HARRISON, Whit. *Strip the Town Naked.* Beacon 350. VG. B3d. $7.50

HARRISON, William. *Rollerball.* 1975. Warner 76839. SF. VG. W2d. $4.50

HARRITY & MARTIN. *World War II: A Photographic Record of the War.* Gold Metal R 1565. Nfi. VG. B5d. $4.50

HARRY & OVERSREET. *What We Must Know About Communism.* 1960. Pocket 7000. Nfi. VG+. B4d. $2.50

HARSH, Alton. *Wicked Dreams of Paula Schultz.* Popular 60-8057. MTI. c/Somer & Crane. Fi. VG. B5d. $5.00

HART, Frances Noyes. *Bellamy Trial.* 1958. Dell D 233. 1st prtg. My. G+. R5d. $1.75

HART, Jack. *Gamble & Win.* 1963. Nite Time 91. 1st edn. F. F2d. $8.00

HART, Johnny. *BC Is Alive & Well!* Gold Medal 2117. VG+. B3d. $4.00

HART, Johnny. *Hurray for BC.* Gold Medal D 1904. c/J Hart: cartoons. Nfi. VG. B5d. $3.50

HART, Moss. *Winged Victory.* Avon 58. VG. B3d. $6.50

HART & KAUFMAN. *Man Who Came to Dinner.* 1942. Pocket 143. 1st prtg. VG. R5d. $7.00

HART & PARKER. *Charge!* 1978. Gold Medal 4046. 1st edn. F. F2d. $10.00

HART & PARKER. *Frammin' at the Jim Jam Frippin' in the Krotz!* 1974. Gold Medal M 3361. 1st edn. F. F2d. $8.00

HART & PARKER. *My Kingdom for a Horsie.* 1984. Gold Medal 12460. 1st end. F. F2d. $8.00

HART & PARKER. *Wizard's Back.* 1973. Gold Medal T 3040. c/J Hart: cartoons. Nfi. VG. B5d. $3.00

HARTE, Bret. *Outcasts of Poker Flat.* Avon 446. VG. I1d. $6.00

HARTKE & REDDING. *Inside the New Frontier.* 1962. MacFadden 50-153. PBO. c/photo. NF. VG+. B5d. $3.50

HARTLEY, L.P. *Facial Justice.* Curtis 07028. 1st prtg. SF. VG. R5d. $1.50

HARVESTER, Simon. *Chinese Hammer.* 1969. MacFadden 60-415. 1st prtg. NF. P7d. $5.00

HARVEY, Frank. *Air Force!* 1959. Ballantine 329K. SF. VG. B5d. $3.00

HARVEY, Gene. *City Streets.* Original Digest 744. c/DeSoto. reprint. scarce. VG+. B6a #77. $73.00

HARVEY, Gene. *Doctor's Nurse (Girl Named Joy).* Pyramid 1039. c/Nappi. VG+. B3d. $4.50

HARVEY, Gene. *Girl Called Joy.* 1951. Cameo Digest 309. PBO. c/George Gross: gga. VG+. B6a #77. $67.25

HARVEY, Gene. *Passion's Slave.* 1950. Exotic 6. VG. B3a #24. $52.00

HARVEY, J. *Women Who Swap Boys.* Impact 317. VG+. B3d. $4.50

HARVEY, James. *Game Is Sex.* Phantom 59. NF. B3d. $6.00

HARVEY, James. *Ladies' Masseur.* 1960. Midwood 50. PBO. c/gga. G. B6d. $3.00

HARVEY, James. *Lady Wrestler.* 1962. Midwood 193. PBO. c/Rader. NF. B3a #22. $28.00

HARVEY, James. *Mad About Women.* Flame 101. PBO. VG+. B3d. $4.00

HARVEY, James. *Stag Model.* 1960. Midwood 42. 1st edn. c/gga. My. F. F2d. $25.00

HARVEY, James. *Twilight Affair.* 1960. Midwood 59. PBO. c/Rader: gga. VG. B6d. $6.00

HARVEY, L. *Executive Bed.* Vega V 6. PBO. NF. B3d. $7.50

HARVEY, Stephen. *Joan Crawford.* 1974. Pyramid M 3417. 1st prtg. VG+. R5d. $6.00

HARVIN, Emily. *Madwoman?* 1951. Avon 276. 1st edn. PBO. VG. B6d. $18.00

HARWIN, Brian. *Home Is Upriver.* 1953. Signet 1063. Fa. VG+. B4d. $4.00

HASHIMOTO, M. *Sunk!* Avon T 246. VG+. B3d. $5.00

HASKELL, Frank. *Boarding House.* Cameo 348. 2nd edn. c/G Gross. Fi. VG+. B5d. $10.00

HASKELL, Frank. *Hotel Doctor.* Venus 184. c/gga. scarce. NF. B6a #76. $77.00

HASKELL, Frank. *Young Doctor.* Venus 191. c/Belarski: gga. scarce. NF. B6a #76. $72.25

HASKINS, James. *Witchcraft, Mysticism & Magic in the Black World.* 1976. Dell 8876. 1st prtg. VG+. P7d. $4.50

HASKINS, Robert. *Master of the Stars.* 1976. Laser 40. 1st edn. F. P9d. $2.00

HASKO, Marek. *8th Day of the Week.* 1959. Signet S 1706. 1st prtg. c/James Hill: gga. VG+. P7d. $5.50

HASLEY, Lucile. *Mouse Hunter.* 1963. All Saints AS 235. Nfi. VG+. B5d. $3.50

HASS, H. *Under the Red Sea.* Arrow 406. VG. B3d. $6.00

HASSEL, Sven. *Beast Regiment.* 1973. Bantam N 7748. 1st prtg. VG+. P7d. $4.00

HASSEL, Sven. *Gestapo.* 1972. Bantam N 7293. 1st prtg. PBO. VG+. P7d. $4.50

HASSELL, Max. *Prophets Without Honor.* 1971. Ace 68520. 1st edn. F. F2d. $7.50

HASTINGS, March. *Again & Again.* 1963. Midwood F 255. PBO. c/Bob Maguire. G+. P6d. $2.50

HASTINGS, March. *Anybody's Girl.* 1960. Midwood 37. PBO. c/Paul Rader: gga. VG+. B6a #77. $61.00

HASTINGS, March. *Circle of Sin.* 1958. Beacon 207. PBO. c/gga. VG+. B6d. $16.50

HASTINGS, March. *Crack-Up.* 1961. Newsstand U 152. Ad. VG. B5d. $6.00

HASTINGS, March. *Enraptured.* 1967. Midwood 33-798. Ad. G+. B5d. $3.50

HASTINGS, March. *Fear of Incest.* Newsstand Library U 116. NF. B3d. $7.00

HASTINGS, March. *Her Private Hell.* 1963. Midwood F 271. PBO. c/Rader: gga. VG. B6a #75. $87.50

HASTINGS, March. *Her Private Hell.* 1963. Midwood F 271. PBO. c/Rader: gga. VG+. B6a #79. $121.00

HASTINGS, March. *Man Who Came Back.* Panther 848. VG. B3d. $7.50

HASTINGS, March. *Obsessed.* Newsstand Library U 109. VG. B3d. $4.50

HASTINGS, March. *Obsessed.* 1959. Newsstand 109. 1st edn. F. F2d. $11.00

HASTINGS, March. *Soft Way.* 1963. Midwood F 240. c/Olson: gga. scarce in condition. VG+. B6a #74. $40.00

HASTINGS, March. *Unashamed.* 1960. Midwood 53. PBO. c/Rader. scarce. VG+. B6a #80. $55.00

HASTINGS, March. *Veil of Torment.* Newsstand Library U 118. VG+. B3d. $8.00

HASTINGS, March. *Whip of Desire.* Midwood 224. VG+. B3d. $5.00

HASTINGS, March. *3rd Theme.* Newsstand U 157. c/Bonfils. VG. M6d. $9.50

HASTINGS, March. *3rd Theme.* 1961. Newsstand U 157. Ad. G+. B5d. $4.00

HASTINGS, Phyllis. *Her French Husband.* 1956. Popular G 177. 1st prtg. c/gga. VG. P7d. $4.00

HASTINGS, Roderic. *Naked Tide.* Avon T 267. PBO. VG. B3d. $4.50

HASTINGS/JACKSON. *Design for Debauchery/Madam.* 1962. Dollar D 953. c/Bonfils. VG. B3a #22. $17.70

HASTY, J.E. *Some Mischief Still.* Gold Medal 648. VG. B3d. $7.00

HATCH, Alden. *Red Carpet for Mamie Eisenhower.* Popular G 164. VG+. B3d. $4.50

HATCH, Eric. *Crockett's Woman.* Gold Medal 176. VG. I1d. $5.00

HATCH, Eric. *Delinquent Ghost.* Bart 2. VG. B3d. $5.50

HATCH, Gerald. *Day the Earth Froze.* 1963. Monarch 354. SF. VG. B5d. $8.00

HATLO, Jimmy. *Newest Jimmy Hatlo Cartoon Book.* Avon 857. PBO. VG. B3d. $4.50

HATLO, Jimmy. *Office Hi-Jinks.* Avon T 501. PBO. c/J Hatlo: cartoons. Nfi. G+. B5d. $4.50

HATLO, Jimmy. *They'll Do It Every Time.* 1951. Avon 366. PBO. VG. B6d. $4.00

HATTEN, Homer. *Westport Landing.* Gold Medal 157. VG+. B3d. $6.00

HATTER, Amos. *Crossroads of Desire.* 1952. Cameo 312. PBO. VG+. B3a #24. $25.55

HATTER, Amos. *Lady With a Past.* 1951. Venus Digest 132. PBO. c/gga. scarce. VG. B6a #77. $61.00

HATTER, Amos. *Secret Affair.* 1951. Cameo Digest 308. PBO. c/gga. VG+. B6a #77. $61.00

HAUNT, Tom. *Wicked Wench.* 1964. Gaslight 111. PBO. NF. B6d. $9.00

HAUPT, E.A. *Seventeen Book of Young Living.* Popular G 522. 2nd prtg. VG. B3d. $5.00

HAUSER, G. *Be Happier, Be Healthier.* Crest 644. VG+. B3d. $4.00

HAVEMANN, Ernest. *Men, Women & Marriage.* 1963. Monarch MB 546. Nfi. NF. B5d. $6.00

HAVILAND, Monica. *Very Private Love.* 1964. Monarch 462. Fa. VG. B4d. $3.00

HAWK, A. *Mexican Standoff.* PB Library 63-335. NF. B3d. $6.00

HAWK, A. *Pecos Swap.* PB Library 63-182. NF. B3d. $6.00

HAWKESWORTH, John. *In My Lady's Chamber.* 1974. Dell 4166. TVTI. VG. P1d. $5.00

HAWKINS, Edward H. *Wellspring.* 1970. Apollo 101. 1st prtg. My. G+. R5d. $1.50

HAWKINS, Ward. *Kings Will Be Tyrants.* 1960. Crest S 393. 1st prtg. c/Mitchell Hooks: gga. VG+. P7d. $5.00

HAWKINS, Ward. *Torch of Fear.* 1987. Ballantine 33612. SF. VG+. W2d. $4.00

HAWKINS/PAYNE. *Violent City/This'll Slay You.* Ace D 289. VG. B3d. $4.50

HAWTHORNE, Nathaniel. *Celestrial Railroad, Etc.* 1963. Signet CT 401. 6th prtg. SF. G+. W2d. $3.00

HAWTHORNE, Nathaniel. *House of the Seven Gables.* 1954. Pocket PL 15. Fa. NF. B4d. $2.00

HAWTHORNE, Nathaniel. *Scarlet Letter.* Pocket 551. VG+. I1d. $4.00

HAWTHORNE, Nathaniel. *Wonder Book.* 1966. Airmont CL 118 Fi. NF. B5d. $4.00

HAYCOX, Ernest. *Adventurers.* Cardinal C 204. NF. B3d. $4.50

HAYCOX, Ernest. *Alder Gulch.* 1950. Dell 450. c/Bob Meyers. We. VG. P6d. $2.50

HAYCOX, Ernest. *Alder Gulch.* 1949. Dell 317. 1st pb. c/Meyers. We. VG+. B6d. $16.50

HAYCOX, Ernest. *Border Trumpet.* Pocket 301. 3rd edn. VG+. B3d. $5.00

HAYCOX, Ernest. *Bugles in the Afternoon.* Bantam 980. 5th prtg. VG+. B3d. $5.50

HAYCOX, Ernest. *By Rope & Lead.* Pocket 864. VG. B3d. $4.50

HAYCOX, Ernest. *Chaffee of Roaring Horse.* Popular G 237. reprint. We. VG+. B6d. $7.50

HAYCOX, Ernest. *Chaffee of Roaring Horse.* 1949. Popular 171. 1st pb. We. VG+. B6d. $12.00

HAYCOX, Ernest. *Dead Man Range.* Popular 831. VG. B3d. $3.50

HAYCOX, Ernest. *Deep West.* 1949. Pocket 594. 1st edn. PBO. F. F2d. $8.00

HAYCOX, Ernest. *Earthbrakers.* 1953. Cardinal C 97. 1st pb. We. VG+. B6d. $7.50

HAYCOX, Ernest. *Free Grass.* Popular 143. VG. B3d. $4.00

HAYCOX, Ernest. *Free Grass.* Popular 143. VG+. B3d. $6.00

HAYCOX, Ernest. *Head of the Mountain.* Popular G 351. VG+. B3d. $4.50

HAYCOX, Ernest. *Head of the Mountain.* 1952. Popular 442. We. VG+. B4d. $10.00

HAYCOX, Ernest. *Man in the Saddle.* Dell 120. VG. B3d. $5.00

HAYCOX, Ernest. *Man in the Saddle.* 1946. Dell 120. 1st pb. c/Gregg. We. NF. B6d. $20.00

HAYCOX, Ernest. *Murder on the Frontier.* Pocket 1011. VG+. B3d. $4.50

HAYCOX, Ernest. *Prairie Guns.* Pocket 1069. VG+. D3d. $5.00

HAYCOX, Ernest. *Rawhide Range.* Popular 460. VG+. B3d. $5.00

HAYCOX, Ernest. *Return of a Fighter.* 1956. Corgi T 193. 1st pb. We. VG+. B6d. $12.00

HAYCOX, Ernest. *Return of a Fighter.* 1958. Dell 975. c/G McConnell. We. VG+. B5d. $4.00

HAYCOX, Ernest. *Riders West.* Popular 271. VG. I1d. $5.00

HAYCOX, Ernest. *Riders West.* Popular 616. VG. I1d. $3.00

HAYCOX, Ernest. *Secret River.* Popular 700. VG. B3d. $4.50

HAYCOX, Ernest. *Silver Desert.* Popular 360. NF. I1d. $9.00

HAYCOX, Ernest. *Silver Desert.* 1951. Popular 360. c/gga. We. VG. B3d. $5.00

HAYCOX, Ernest. *Trouble Shooter*. 1954. Corgi T 72. 1st pb. We. VG+. B6d. $12.00

HAYCOX, Ernest. *Trouble Shooter*. 1952. Popular 450. We. VG+. B4d. $14.00

HAYCOX, Ernest. *Vengeance Trail*. Popular G 461. NF. B3d. $5.00

HAYCOX, Ernest. *Whispering Range*. Popular EB 4. VG. B3d. $5.00

HAYCOX, Ernest. *Wild Bunch*. 1949. Bantam 261. c/N Saunders. We. VG. B5d. $3.00

HAYES, Alfred. *All Thy Conquests*. Lion LL 68. reprint. VG. B6d. $3.50

HAYES, Alfred. *Girl on the Via Flaminia*. Pocket 666. NF. I1d. $4.00

HAYES, Bob. *Cheaters*. 1961. Novel Book 5044. PBO. Ad. VG. B5d. $35.00

HAYES, Douglas. *Kiss-Off*. Signet 949. VG. G5d. $3.00

HAYES, Helen. *Gift of Joy*. 1969. Crest T 1333. 1st prtg. Auto. VG. R5d. $1.50

HAYES, Joseph. *Desperate Hours*. Perma M 3007. F. G5d. $7.50

HAYES, Joseph. *Desperate Hours*. 1955. Perma M 3007. My. VG. B3d/B5d. $4.00

HAYES, Joseph. *Desperate Hours*. 1968. Pyramid X 1904. My. VG+. B4d. $3.00

HAYES, Joseph. *Hours After Midnight*. 1959. Bantam 1948. 1st pb. My. VG. B6d. $7.50

HAYES, Leal. *Harlequin House*. 1967. Ace G 612. 1st prtg. My. VG. R5d. $1.75

HAYES, R. *Black Desire*. Newsstand U 129. VG+. B3d. $6.00

HAYMES, N. *Errol & Me*. Signet 1875. PBO. VG+. B3d. $7.00

HAYWARD, Susan. *Ada Dallas*. 1961. Dell S 16. 1st prtg. VG. R5d. $2.50

HAZEL, Robert. *Lost Year*. 1954. Signet 1115. 1st pb. c/Zuckerberg. VG. B6d. $7.00

HEAD, Matthew. *Accomplice*. Dell 346. VG+. G5d. $7.00

HEAD, Matthew. *Cabinda Affair*. Dell 390. VG. G5d. $5.00

HEAD, Matthew. *Devil in the Bush*. 1947. Dell 158. 1st edn. PBO. c/Gerald Gregg. scarce. NF. B6a #75. $38.50

HEAD, Matthew. *Devil in the Bush*. Dell 158. 1st prtg. My. VG. R5d. $10.00

HEAD, Matthew. *Smell of Money*. 1948. Dell 219. 1st edn. PBO. c/Frederiksen. scarce. NF. B6a #75. $44.00

HEAD, Matthew. *Smell of Money*. Dell 219. VG+. B3d. $6.00

HEAD, Matthew. *Smell of Money*. 1948. Dell 219. 1st edn. PBO. c/Frederiksen. VG+. B6d. $35.00

HEALEY, Ben. *Waiting for a Tiger*. 1966. Lancer 73-518. 1st pb. NF. B6d. $7.00

HEALY, R.J. *New Tales of Space & Time*. 1952. Pocket 908. NF. I1d. $7.00

HEALY, R.J. *New Tales of Space & Time*. 1952. Pocket 908. 1st pb. F. M1d. $15.00

HEALY & MCCOMAS. *Adventures in Time & Space*. 1954. Pennant P 44. VG. I1d. $6.00

HEALY & MCCOMAS. *Adventures in Time & Space*. 1954. Pennant P 44. 1st pb. F. M1d. $12.00

HEALY & MCCOMAS. *More Adventures in Time & Space*. 1955. Bantam 1310. 1st prtg. SF. G+. R5d. $2.75

HEARD, Gerald. *Is Another World Watching?* 1953. Bantam 1079. 1st prtg. VG. P7d. $7.50

HEARD, H.F. *Doppelgangers*. 1966. Ace M 142. SF. VG. W2d. $4.00

HEARD, H.F. *Dopplegangers*. 1966. Ace M 142. SF. F. M1d. $7.50

HEARD, H.F. *Reply Paid*. 1944. Dell 44. VG. I1d. $12.00

HEARD, H.F. *Reply Paid*. 1944. Dell 44. 1st edn. PBO. c/Gregg. rare. F. B6a #80. $88.00

HEARD, H.F. *Reply Paid*. Lancer 72-754. c/Siegel. My. VG. B5d. $4.00

HEARD, H.F. *Taste for Honey*. Lancer 73-647. VG. B3d. $4.00

HEARD, H.F. *Taste for Murder*. Avon 625. reprint. NF. B6d. $12.50

HEARD, H.F. *Taste for Murder*. Avon 808. c/gga. F. F2d. $10.00

HEARD, H.F. *Taste for Murder*. Avon 808. My. VG+. B5d. $5.50

HEATH, Peter. *Assassins From Tomorrow*. 1967. Lancer 73631. SF. F. W2d. $5.00

HEATH, Peter. *Assassins From Tomorrow*. Lancer 73-631. 1st prtg. VG. S1d. $2.00

HEATH, Peter. *Men Who Die Twice*. 1968. Lancer 73-783. PBO. c/Q Weston. SF. VG+. B5d. $5.00

HEATH, Peter. *Mind Brothers*. 1967. Lancer 73-600. PBO. SF. NF. B5d. $5.50

HEATH, Sharon. *Jungle Nurse*. Ace F 359. PBO. VG. B3d. $4.00

HEATH, W.L. *Violent Saturday*. 1956. Bantam 1438. 1st prtg. My. VG. R5d. $2.50

HEATH, W.L. *Violent Saturday*. Black Lizard. NF. G5d. $4.50

HEATTER, Basil. *Act of Violence*. 1954. Lion 228. PBO. c/Leone. My. VG. B6d. $15.00

HEATTER, Basil. *Captain's Lady*. Popular 266. VG+. B3d. $6.00

HEATTER, Basil. *Captain's Lady*. 1950. Popular 266. 1st pb. c/Belarski. VG+. B6d. $16.50

HEATTER, Basil. *Dim View*. 1954. Popular 602. VG. P6d. $1.50

HEATTER, Basil. *Dim View*. 1948. Signet 668. Fi. VG+. B5d. $5.50

HEATTER, Basil. *Dim View*. 1948. Signet 668. 1st pb. NF. B6d. $8.00

HEBERDEN, M.V. *Murder Makes a Racket*. De Novel 48. VG. B3d. $5.00

HEBERDEN, M.V. *They Can't All Be Guilty*. Dell 401. VG. B3d. $4.50

HECHINGER & HECHINGER. *Teen-Age Tyranny*. 1964. Crest D 705. review slip laid in. JD. VG+. P1d. $25.00

HECHLER, Ken. *Bridge at Remagen*. Ballantine 234. PBO. VG+. B3d. $5.00

HECHT, Ben. *Child of the Century*. Signet 1212. VG+. B3d. $7.00

HECHT, Ben. *Count Bruga*. 1944. Quick Reader 117. VG+. B3a. $17.85

HECHT, Ben. *Hollywood Mystery*. Harlequin 32. G+. B3d. $4.50

HECHT, Ben. *Selected Ben Hecht*. Stortstory 11. VG+. B3d. $4.00

HECHT, Ben. *Selected Great Stories*. 1943. Avon Modern Story 11. Fi. G+. B5d. $2.50

HECKELMANN, Charles N. *Bullet Law*. 1957. Signet 1373. We. VG+. B5d. $4.50

HECKELMANN, Charles N. *Deputy Marshall*. Bantam 206. VG. B3d. $4.50

HECKELMANN, Charles N. *Fighting Ramrod*. 1952. Signet 965. We. VG. B4d. $3.00

HECKELMANN, Charles N. *Guns of Arizona*. Lion 34. VG. B3d. $4.00

HECKELMANN, Charles N. *Hard Man with a Gun*. Signet 1232. VG+. B3d. $4.50

HECKELMANN, Charles N. *Lawless Range*. 1946. Prize Western 21. 1st pb. VG. B6d. $8.00

HECKELMANN, Charles N. *Lawless Range*. Signet 694. VG. B3d. $5.00

HECKELMANN, Charles N. *Six-Gun Outcast*. Bantam 128. VG+. B3d. $5.50

HECKELMANN, Charles N. *Two-Bit Rancher*. Signet 842. VG+. B3d. $5.50

HEDDEN, W.T. *Other Room*. Bantam 463. VG+. B3d. $4.50

HEDRIN, S. *Network*. Pocket 80767. MTI. VG. B3d. $4.00

HEIMER, Mel. *Girl in Murder Flat*. 1955. Gold Medal 458. 1st prtg. PBO. c/photo. VG. P6d. $6.00

HEINLEIN, Robert A. *Assignment in Eternity*. 1954. Signet 1161. c/R Powers. SF. VG. B5d. $6.00

HEINLEIN, Robert A. *Assignment In Eternity*. 1954. Signet. 1st pb. F. M1d. $15.00

HEINLEIN, Robert A. *Between Planets*. Ace 05500. 3rd edn. F. P9d. $2.00

HEINLEIN, Robert A. *Between Planets*. 1981. Ballantine 30633. 5th prtg. SF. VG+. W2d. $3.50

HEINLEIN, Robert A. *Beyond This Horizon*. Signet S 1891. VG+. I1d. $4.00

HEINLEIN, Robert A. *Beyond This Horizon*. Signet T 4211. 8th prtg. SF. VG+. W2d. $3.25

HEINLEIN, Robert A. *Cat Who Walks Through Walls*. 1986. Berkley 09332. SF. VG+. W2d. $3.75

HEINLEIN, Robert A. *Day After Tomorrow*. Signet S 1677. reprint. SF. VG. B6d. $3.75

HEINLEIN, Robert A. *Day After Tomorrow*. 1951. Signet 882. SF. VG. B5d. $6.50

HEINLEIN, Robert A. *Day After Tomorrow*. 1951. Signet 882. 1st pb. NF. M1d. $10.00

HEINLEIN, Robert A. *Door Into Summer*. Signet D 2443. 4th prtg. SF. VG. W2d. $3.00

HEINLEIN, Robert A. *Door Into Summer*. 1959. Signet S 1639. 1st pb. VG. M1d. $6.00

HEINLEIN, Robert A. *Double Star*. 1957. Signet E 8905. 1st pb. F. M1d. $12.00

HEINLEIN, Robert A. *Double Star*. 1957. Signet S 1444. c/R Powers. SF. VG. B5d. $5.00

HEINLEIN, Robert A. *Farmer in the Sky*. 1975. Ballantine 24375. 2nd prtg. SF. F. W2d. $4.25

HEINLEIN, Robert A. *Farnham's Freehold*. Signet T 2704. NF. I1d. $5.00

HEINLEIN, Robert A. *Friday*. 1983. Ballantine 30988. c/M Whelan. SF. NF. B5d. $4.50

HEINLEIN, Robert A. *Friday*. 1983. Ballantine 30988. SF. VG. W2d. $3.25

HEINLEIN, Robert A. *Glory Road*. 1969. Avon V 2202. F. P9d. $2.00

HEINLEIN, Robert A. *Green Hills of Earth*. Signet S 1537. VG+. I1d. $5.00

HEINLEIN, Robert A. *Green Hills of Earth*. Signet T 3193. 7th prtg. SF. F. W2d. $3.75

HEINLEIN, Robert A. *Green Hills of Earth*. 1952. Signet 943. 1st pb. VG. M1d. $10.00

HEINLEIN, Robert A. *I Will Fear No Evil*. Berkley D 2321. 1st edn. PBO. G. P9d. $1.25

HEINLEIN, Robert A. *Man Who Sold the Moon*. 1951. Signet 8473 PBO. VG. M1d. $10.00

HEINLEIN, Robert A. *Menace From Earth*. 1962. Signet. 1st pb. NF. M1d. $10.00

HEINLEIN, Robert A. *Methesaleh's Children*. 1960. Signet S 1752. 1st pb. VG. M1d. $8.00

HEINLEIN, Robert A. *Methuselah's Children*. Signet D 2651. 3rd prtg. SF. G+. W2d. $3.00

HEINLEIN, Robert A. *Moon Is a Harsh Mistress*. 1968. Berkley N 1601. 1st prtg. SF. VG. R5d. $2.50

HEINLEIN, Robert A. *Orphans of the Sky*. Signet D 2816. 1st prtg. VG+. S1d. $6.00

HEINLEIN, Robert A. *Past Through Tomorrow*. 1986. Berkley 09350. SF. VG. W2d. $2.75

HEINLEIN, Robert A. *Podkayne of Mars*. 1966. Avon G 1211. 3rd prtg. SF. VG. R5d. $1.00

HEINLEIN, Robert A. *Podkayne of Mars*. 1970. Berkley S 1791. SF. VG. W2d. $3.25

HEINLEIN, Robert A. *Puppet Masters*. Signet S 1544. VG+. I1d. $5.00

HEINLEIN, Robert A. *Puppet Masters*. Signet W 7339. 18th prtg. SF. VG. W2d. $3.00

HEINLEIN, Robert A. *Puppet Masters*. 1952. Signet 980. 1st edn. PBO. G. P9d. $1.25

HEINLEIN, Robert A. *Red Planet*. Ace 71140. 2nd edn. SF. VG+. B4d. $3.00

HEINLEIN, Robert A. *Red Planet*. Ballantine 26069. SF. F. W2d. $3.75

HEINLEIN, Robert A. *Revolt in 2100*. Signet P 3563. 4th prtg. SF. VG. W2d. $3.25

HEINLEIN, Robert A. *Revolt in 2100*. 1955. Signet 1194. SF. VG. B5d. $5.00

HEINLEIN, Robert A. *Rocket Ship Galileo*. Ace 73330. c/S Savage. SF. G+. B5d. $3.00

HEINLEIN, Robert A. *Rolling Stones*. Ballantine 26067. 1st prtg. VG. S1d. $2.50

HEINLEIN, Robert A. *Space Cadet*. Ace 77730. c/Savage. SF. VG. B5d. $4.00

HEINLEIN, Robert A. *Space Family Stone*. 1971. New English 2839. SF. G+. W2d. $2.75

HEINLEIN, Robert A. *Star Beast*. Ace 78000. c/S Savage. SF. VG. B5d. $5.50

HEINLEIN, Robert A. *Star Beast*. 1977. Ballantine 26066. SF. F. W2d. $3.50

HEINLEIN, Robert A. *Starman Jones*. 1975. Ballantine 24354. 2nd prtg. SF. F. W2d. $3.50

HEINLEIN, Robert A. *Starship Troopers*. Berkley S 1560. SF. VG. W2d. $4.75

HEINLEIN, Robert A. *Stranger in a Strange Land*. Avon V 2056. SF. VG. B5d. $12.50

HEINLEIN, Robert A. *Stranger in a Strange Land*. 1955. Berkley 04688. 55th prtg. SF. VG. W2d. $3.00

HEINLEIN, Robert A. *Time Enough for Love*. 1974. Berkley. 1st pb. F. M1d. $8.00

HEINLEIN, Robert A. *Tomorrow, the Stars*. Signet 1044. VG+. B3d. $5.00

HEINLEIN, Robert A. *Tomorrow, the Stars*. 1953. Signet 1044. 1st pb. F. M1d. $15.00

HEINLEIN, Robert A. *Tunnel in the Sky*. Ace 82660. 1st prtg. VG. S1d. $3.00

HEINLEIN, Robert A. *Tunnel in the Sky*. 1977. Ballantine 26065. SF. F. W2d. $3.50

HEINLEIN, Robert A. *Universe*. Dell 10¢ 36. VG. I1d. $30.00

HEINLEIN, Robert A. *Universe*. 1951. Dell 10¢ 36. PBO. c/Stanley Foxley: scarce. NF. B6a #74. $110.00

HEINLEIN, Robert A. *Universe*. 1951. Dell 10¢ 36. PBO. c/Stanley. SF. F. B6a #79. $133.25

HEINLEIN, Robert A. *Universe*. 1951. Dell 10¢ 36. PBO. VG+. B3a #20. $43.10

HEINLEIN, Robert A. *Universe*. 1951. Dell 10¢ 36. VG+. B3a #22. $47.45

HEINLEIN, Robert A. *Unpleasant Profession of Jonathan Hoag*. 1976. Berkley. 1st pb. VG. M1d. $6.00

HEINLEIN, Robert A. *Waldo & Magic Inc*. 1970. Signet T 4142. SF. VG. W2d. $3.25

HEINLEIN, Robert A. *Worlds of Robert A Heinlein*. Ace F 375. F. M1d. $8.00

HEINLEIN, Robert A. *Worlds of Robert A Heinlein*. 1966. Ace 91501. reprints Ace F375. SF. VG+. B4d. $2.50

HEINLEIN, Robert A. *6 X H (6 Stories by Heinlein)*. 1963. Pyramid F 910. SF. VG. W2d. $3.75

HEINLEIN, Robert A. *6 X H (6 Stories by Heinlein).* Pyramid G 642. NF. I1d. $6.00

HEINRICH, Willi. *Rape of Honor.* 1962. Perma M 4247. c/gga. Fa. VG+. B4d. $4.00

HEINRICH, Willi. *Willing Flesh.* Corgi Books 468. 2nd edn. c/soldier. VG. B3d. $6.00

HELBRANT/LEE. *Narcotic Agent/Junkie.* 1953. Ace D 15. JD. VG. P1d. $200.00

HELD, Peter. *Take My Face.* Pyramid 327. c/sgn. VG. B3d. $35.00

HELLER, Deane & David. *Berlin Crisis.* 1961. Monarch MS 2. Nfi. VG+. B5d. $5.00

HELLER, Deane & David. *Jacqueline Kennedy.* 1961. Monarch K 54. PBO. c/photo. Nfi. VG. B5d. $5.00

HELLER, Deane & David. *Jacqueline Kennedy.* 1963. Monarch MS 23. c/photo. Nfi. VG+. B4d. $4.00

HELLER, Deane & David. *Kennedy Cabinet.* 1961. Monarch MA 312. Nfi. VG+. B4d. $3.00

HELLER, J. edt. *More Sex-Clusive.* Belmont 91-247. c/cartoons. VG. B3d. $4.00

HELLER, Joseph. *We Bombed in New Haven.* 1970. Dell 09435. 1st prtg. VG+. P7d. $4.50

HELLER, Mike. *So I'm a Heel.* 1957. Gold Medal 664. PBO. c/Barye. My. G+. B6d. $3.50

HELLER, Richard H. *Who's Who in TV.* 1967. Dell 9456. TVTI. G+. P1d. $5.00

HELLMAN, Lillian. *Pentimento.* Signet J 6091. 3rd edn. Nfi. G+. P1d. $2.00

HELSETH, H.E. *Chair for Martin Rome.* 1948. Pocket 484. VG. B3d. $4.00

HELSETH, H.E. *This Man Dawson.* 1962. Signet 2109. 1st edn. TVTI. Cr. F. F2d. $16.00

HELY, Elizabeth. *I'll Be Judge, I'll Be Jury.* 1962. Dell R 108. My. VG. B4d. $2.00

HEMENWAY, Robert. *Sandpiper.* 1965. Pocket 50175. MTI. VG+. B4d/R5d. $3.00

HEMINGWAY, Ernest. *Education of a French Model.* Belmont L 525. VG. B3d. $4.50

HEMINGWAY, Ernest. *Farewell to Arms.* Bantam 467. VG. B3d. $5.00

HEMINGWAY, Ernest. *For Whom the Bell Tolls.* Bantam 883. VG. B3d. $4.50

HEMINGWAY, Ernest. *Green Hills of Africa.* 1956. Perma M 3056. 2nd edn. c/R Schulz. Fi. VG. B5d. $5.00

HEMINGWAY, Ernest. *Sun Also Rises.* Bantam 717. NF. I1d. $10.00

HEMPSTONE, S. *Tract of Time.* Crest 964. VG. B3d. $4.50

HENDERSON, George Wylie. *Jule: Alabama Boy in Harlem.* 1954. Avon 577. c/gga. VG+. P6d. $7.50

HENDERSON, J.Y. *Circus Doctor.* 1952. Bantam 992. 1st prtg. VG. B3d/P7d. $4.50

HENDERSON, James Leal. *Whirlpool.* 1952. Popular 399. c/gga. Fa. VG+. B4d. $7.50

HENDERSON, Zenna. *Anything Box.* 1969. Avon V 2264. 1st pb. F. M1d. $10.00

HENDERSON, Zenna. *Anything Box.* 1969. Avon V 2264. 1st pb. SF. VG. B6d. $6.00

HENDERSON, Zenna. *Holding Wonder.* 1972. Avon N 445. 1st pb. NF. M1d. $7.00

HENDERSON, Zenna. *Holding Wonder.* 1972. Avon N 445. 1st prtg. SF. G+. W2d. $4.00

HENDERSON, Zenna. *Pilgrimage: Book of the People.* Avon G 1185. SF. VG. B5d. $4.00

HENDERSON, Zenna. *Pilgrimage: Book of the People.* Avon G 1185. 1st pb. SF. F. M1d. $13.00

HENDRICK, Richard P. *Cry of the Deep.* 1989. Zebra 02594. SF. VG+. B5d. $5.00

HENDRICKS, G.D. *Bad Man of the West.* Ace G 500. VG+. B3d. $5.50

HENDRICKSON, Walter. *Class G-Zero.* 1976. Major 3110. 1st edn. F. P9d. $2.00

HENDRYX, James B. *Blood of the North.* 1946. Pony 66. We. VG. B4d. $7.50

HENDRYX, James B. *Edges of Beyond.* Popular 314. VG+. I1d. $8.00

HENNEBERG, N.C. *Green Gods.* 1980. DAW 387. c/D Maitz. SF. VG+. B5d. $5.00

HENNING, W.E. *Heller.* Bantam 1708. VG+. B3d. $4.00

HENRY, L.C. edt. *Best Quotations for All Occasions.* Perma P 3. VG. B3d. $4.00

HENRY, O.; see O. Henry.

HENRY, Will. *Who Rides With Wyatt.* Bantam 1411. VG. B3d. $4.00

HENSLEY, J.L. *Black Roads.* 1976. Laser 17. PBO. c/K Freas. SF. VG+. B5d. $5.50

HENSLEY, J.L. *Color of Hate.* 1960. Ace D 452. PBO. c/Copeland. VG. B6d. $25.00

HENSTEL, Diana. *Friend.* 1985. Bantam 25315. SF. F. W2d. $3.75

HEPBURN, Andrew. *Letter of Marque.* 1959. Ace G 440. c/gga. Fa. VG+. B4d. $5.00

HEPPENSTALL, R. *Blaze of Noon.* Berkley G 204. VG. B3d. $5.00

HERBER, William. *Live Bait for Murder.* 1957. Bantam 1589. My. VG. B4d. $2.00

HERBERT, Frank. *Book of Frank Herbert.* 1973. DAW 39. 1st prtg. SF. VG. B3d. $4.00

HERBERT, Frank. *Children of Dune.* 1977. Berkley 03310. SF. VG. W2d. $3.25

HERBERT, Frank. *Destination: Void.* 1966. Berkley F 1249. PBO. c/Hoot. SF. VG. B5d. $4.50

HERBERT, Frank. *Destination: Void.* 1966. Berkley F 1249. 1st pb. F. M1d. $7.00

HERBERT, Frank. *Direct Descent.* Ace 14903. 1st prtg. VG+. S1d. $3.00

HERBERT, Frank. *Dosadi Experiment.* 1978. Berkley 03834. 5th prtg. SF. VG. W2d. $3.25

HERBERT, Frank. *Dragon in the Sea.* 1970. Avon V 2330. NF. P9d. $2.00

HERBERT, Frank. *Dune.* Ace N 3. NF. M1d. $15.00

HERBERT, Frank. *Eyes of Heisenberg.* 1966. Berkley F 1283. 1st edn. VG+. B3d. $6.00

HERBERT, Frank. *Eyes of Heisenberg.* 1970. Berkley N 2810. 9th prtg. SF. VG. W2d. $3.25

HERBERT, Frank. *God Emperor of Dune.* 1983. Berkley 06233. SF. VG. W2d. $4.00

HERBERT, Frank. *Green Brain.* Ace F 379. F. M1d. $8.00

HERBERT, Frank. *Green Brain.* Ace F 379. VG. I1d. $3.00

HERBERT, Frank. *Green Brain.* Ace 30261. c/G McConnell. SF. VG. B5d. $3.00

HERBERT, Frank. *Green Brain.* Ace 30261. 1st prtg. F. S1d. $4.00

HERBERT, Frank. *Green Brain.* Berkley 7676. 1st prtg. G+. S1d. $3.50

HERBERT, Frank. *Jesus Incident.* 1984. Berkley 07467. 11th prtg. SF. F. W2d. $3.50

HERBERT, Frank. *Santaroga Barrier.* 1968. Berkley S 1615. 7th prtg. SF. VG. W2d. $3.75

HERBERT, Frank. *Soul Catcher.* 1979. Berkley 04250. SF. VG. W2d. $3.75

HERBERT, Frank. *Under Pressure.* 1981. Ballantine 29859. 7th prtg. SF. F. W2d. $3.75

HERBERT, Frank. *21st-Century Sub.* 1961. Avon G 1092. c/A Sussman. SF. VG+. B5d. $3.50

HERBERT, Frank. *21st-Century Sub.* Avon T 146. 1st pb. F. M1d. $10.00

HERBERT, Frank. *21st-Century Sub.* 1956. Avon T 146. c/A Sussman. SF. VG. B5d. $3.50

HERBERT, James. *Magic Cottage.* 1988. ONYX 40106. 1st pb. Ho. NF. B6d. $3.00

HERBERT & HERBERT. *Man of Two Worlds.* 1987. Ace 51857. SF. VG. W2d. $3.25

HERIOTT, R. *Temptation.* Berkley 323. VG. B3d. $4.00

HERMANN, Walter. *Operation Intrigue.* 1956. Avon 706. Fa. VG+. B4d. $4.00

HERNDON, Booton. *Humor of JFK.* 1964. Gold Medal D 1514. Bio. F. B4d. $8.00

HERNDON, Booton. *Humor of JFK.* 1964. Gold Medal D 1514. VG+. B3d. $4.50

HERODOTUS. *Struggle for Greece.* 1962. Premier D 165. Nfi. VG. B5d. $2.50

HERON, Joseph. *Agreement To Love.* Newsstand U 126. VG. B3d. $4.50

HERON, Joseph. *So Strange Our Love.* 1961. Newsstand U 159. Ad. G+. B5d. $3.00

HERON, Joseph. *So Strange Our Love.* 1961. Newsstand U 159. 1st edn. c/gga. F. F2d. $14.00

HERON, K. *Colony of Sinners.* Playtime 601. PBO. VG. B3d. $4.00

HERRIES, Norman. *Death Has Two Faces.* 1955. Ace S 97. PBO. My. VG+. I1d. $7.00

HERRIES/JONES. *Prowl Cop/My Private Hangman.* Ace D 147. VG. B3d. $4.50

HERRINGTON, Lee. *Carry My Coffin Slowly.* 1952. Dell 641. 1st prtg. c/Marini. VG. P7d. $5.50

HERRIOT, J. *If Only They Could Talk.* Pan 23783. VG. B3d. $6.00

HERSEY, John. *Bell for Adano.* Bantam 45. VG+. B3d. $5.00

HERSEY, John. *Into the Valley.* 1943. Pocket 225. 1st pb. VG. I1d/M6d. $4.00

HERSEY, John. *Marmot Drive.* 1965. Popular SP 371. 1st pb. c/Marchetti. VG. B6d. $5.00

HERSEY, John. *Single Pebble.* Bantam 2182. VG+. B3d. $4.00

HERSEY, John. *South of Cancer.* 1947. Dell 10¢ 25. Fa. VG+. B4d. $12.00

HERSEY, John. *Wall.* 1953. Cardinal GC 12. 1st prtg. c/Ismar David. VG. P7d. $3.50

HERSHFIELD, Harry. *Book of Jokes (Now I'll Tell One).* Avon 65. VG. B3d. $6.00

HERSHFIELD, Harry. *Harry Hershfield Joke Book.* Ballantine U 2200. PBO. VG. B3d. $4.00

HERSHFIELD, Harry. *Sin of Harold Diddle-bock.* 1947. Bart 102. MTI. c/photo. Fi. G. B5d. $7.50

HERVEY, Michael. *Better Luck Next Crime.* Forsyte Press NN. VG. B3d. $12.00

HERZ, Peggy. *TV '74.* 1973. Scholastic 2592. 1st prtg. G+. R5d. $1.00

HERZ, Peggy. *TV Close-Ups.* 1975. Scholastic 3028. TVTI. VG. P1d. $5.00

HERZ, Peggy. *TV Talk 3.* 1977. Scholastic 3977. TVTI. VG. P1d. $4.50

HERZBERG, Max. *This Is America.* Pocket 730. PBO. VG+. B3d. $4.00

HERZOG, Arthur. *Earthbound.* Signet E 7255. 1st prtg. VG. S1d. $3.50

HERZOG, Arthur. *Swarm.* Signet E 8079. 11th prtg. VG+. R5d. $1.50

HETH, Edward Harris. *Big Bet.* Bantam 553. VG. B3d. $4.00

HEUMAN, William. *Gunhand From Texas.* Avon 569. PBO. We G+. B5d. $3.00

HEUMAN, William. *Guns at Broken Bow.* 1950. Gold Medal 131. VG. B3d. $4.00

HEUMAN, William. *Guns at Broken Bow.* 1950. Gold Medal 131. 1st edn. Av. F. F2d. $12.00

HEUMAN, William. *Heller From Texas.* Gold Medal 1536. VG+. B3d. $4.50

HEUMAN, William. *Heller From Texas.* 1957. Gold Medal 681. 1st prtg. PBO. c/Lu Kimmel. We. VG. P6d. $3.75

HEUMAN, William. *Keelboats North.* 1953. Gold Medal 310. PBO. c/Pioneer. VG. B6d. $7.00

HEUMAN, William. *Roll the Wagons.* 1951. Gold Medal 146. PBO. c/Getti. We. NF. B6d. $15.00

HEUMAN, William. *Stagecoach West.* 1957. Gold Medal 705. PBO. We. VG. B6d. $6.00

HEUMAN, William. *Wagon Train West.* Gold Medal 842. VG. B3d. $4.50

HEYER, Georgette. *Blunt Instrument.* Panther 1282. 1st pb. reprint. My. VG. B6d. $3.50

HEYER, Georgette. *Unfinished Clue.* 1979. Bantam 11442. 4th prtg. My. F. W2d. $3.50

HEYERDAHL, Thor. *Aku-Aku.* 1960. Cardinal GC 758. c/photos. Nfi. VG. B5d. $3.00

HEYERDAHL, Thor. *Kon-Tiki.* 1956. Perma M 4062. Nfi. VG. B4d. $3.00

HEYES, Douglas. *Kiss-Off.* 1956. Signet 1329. 2nd edn. My. VG. B5d. $3.50

HEYMAN, Evan Lee. *Cain's Hundred.* Popular PC 1010. TVTI. VG. B3d. $4.50

HEYMAN, Evan Lee. *Not With My Wife You Don't.* 1966. Popular 60-2143. 1st prtg. G+. R5d. $1.50

HEYMAN, Evan Lee. *Thomas Crown Affair.* 1968. Avon S 354. MTI. c/Steve McQueen & Fay Dunaway: photo. VG. B4d. $2.00

HEYWARD, Louis M. *My Son, the Doctor.* 1963. Perma M 4290. Hu. VG+. B4d. $3.00

HEYWOOD, Victor. *Prison Planet.* 1974. Papillon OSF 503. SF. VG. W2d. $4.25

HIBBELER, R. *Upstairs at Everleigh Club.* Volitant. VG+. B3d. $4.50

HIBBS, Ben edt. *Great Stories From Saturday Evening Post.* 1947. Bantam 116. c/S Donhanq. Fi. VG+. B5d. $6.50

HIBBS, Ben edt. *Great Stories From Saturday Evening Post.* 1948. Bantam 555. Fa. VG. B4d. $3.00

HICKMAN, Robert edt. *3rd Fontana Book of Great Ghost Stories.* 1971. Beagle 95156. SF. VG. B5d. $5.00

HICKOK, Will. *Restless Gun.* 1958. Signet 1541. 1st prtg. TVTI. VG. R5d. $5.25

HICKOK, Will. *Web of Gunsmoke.* Signet 1242. VG. B3d. $4.50

HIGGINS, George V. *City on a Hill.* 1977. Coronet 21786. 1st prtg. My. VG. R5d. $2.00

HIGGINS, H.Q. *Trailer Court Tramps.* Raven 704. VG. B3d. $4.00

HIGGINS, Jack. *Exocet.* 1984. Signet AE 3044. 1st prtg. My. F. W2d. $3.75

HIGGINS, Jack. *Season in Hell.* 1990. Pocket 69271. 1st prtg. My. VG. W2d. $3.25

HIGH, Philip E. *Prodigal Sun.* Ace F 255. VG. M1d. $6.00

HIGH, Philip E. *Twin Planets.* 1967. PB Library 52-392. PBO. SF. VG. B5d. $3.50

HIGH/LEINSTER. *Mad Metropolis/Space Captain.* Ace M 135. F. M1d. $8.00

HIGH/LEINSTER. *No Truce With Terra/Duplicators.* Ace F 275. F. F2d/M1d. $9.00

HIGH/RACKHAM. *These Savage Futurians/Double Invaders.* 1967. Ace G 623. SF. VG. W2d. $10.00

HIGH/TRIMBLE. *Time Mercenaries/Anthropol.* 1968. Ace H 59. SF. VG. W2d. $8.50

HIGHAM, Charles. *Curse of Dracula.* 1962. Horwitz 111. PBO. rare. VG+. B6a #79. $73.00

HIGHAM, Charles. *Hollywood Cameramen.* 1970. Indiana Univ 14. c/photos. NF. B3d. $7.00

HIGHAM, Charles. *Nightmare Stories.* 1962. Horwitz 117. PBO. c/Poe. VG+. B6a #79. $73.00

HIGHAM, Charles. *Spine-Tingling Tales.* 1962. Horwitz 98. PBO. rare. VG+. B6a #79. $82.50

HIGHAM, Charles. *Tales of Horror.* 1962. Horwitz 104. PBO. c/Poe. VG+. B6a #79. $73.00

HIGHAM, Charles. *Tales of Terror.* 1961. Horwitz 93. PBO. c/Poe. rare. VG+. B6a #79. $82.50

HIGHAM, Charles. *Weird.* 1961. Horwitz 82. PBO. c/Poe. rare. VG+. B6a #79. $85.00

HIGHES, Zach. *Legend of Miaree.* 1974. Ballantine 23888. PBO. c/G Szafran. SF. VG. B5d. $3.00

HIGHMORE, Jane. *Big City Nurse.* 1961. Perma M 4208. Fa. NF. B4d. $4.00

HIGHSMITH, David. *Step Down to Darkness.* 1961. Midwood F 90. PBO. VG. B3d. $3.50

HIGHSMITH, Patricia. *Cry of the Owl.* 1979. MacFadden 75-334. 1st pb. My. NF. B6d. $10.00

HIGHSMITH, Patricia. *Lament for a Lover.* Popular Eagle EB 58. G+. G5d. $4.50

HIGHSMITH, Patricia. *Strangers on a Train.* 1951. Bantam 905. 1st pb. My. VG+. B6d. $12.50

HIGHWATER, Helen. *Luscious Lesbian.* 1966. All Star AS79. PBO. Ad. G+. B5d. $3.00

HIGMAN, Dennis J. *Pranks.* 1989. Leisure 02526. SF. G+. W2d. $2.50

HIKEN, Nat. *Sergeant Bilko.* 1957. Ballantine 229. PBO. TVTI. c/P Silvers: photo. NF. G+. B5d. $5.00

HILDICK. *Daring Young Men.* 1969. Berkley S 1699. 1st prtg. VG+. R5d. $3.00

HILL, David C. & Albert F. *Deadly Mission.* 1977. Avon 32466. SF. G. W2d. $3.00

HILL, John. *ABC of Espionage.* 1966. Signet D 3045. TVTI. c/photo. F. B4d. $4.00

HILL, John. *Heartbeeps.* 1981. Jove O6183. SF. NF. B5d. $8.50

HILL, John. *Heartbeeps.* 1981. Jove 06183. 1st prtg. MTI. SF. VG. R5d. $2.25

HILL, K. *Case of the Absent Corpse.* Hillman 74. VG. B3d. $4.50

HILL, Kendall. *Female & Fatal.* France 36. VG+. B3d. $5.00

HILL, Kendall. *Female & Fatal.* 1963. France 36. 1st edn. c/gga. My. F. F2d. $15.00

HILL, P. *Portrait of a Sadist.* Avon T 514. VG+. B3d. $5.50

HILL, Weldon. *Onionhead.* 1958. Popular SP 13. 1st pb. c/Hooks. VG. B6d. $7.00

HILLARY, R. *Falling Through Space.* Dell D 244. VG+. B3d. $4.50

HILLER, B.B. *Big.* 1988. Ballantine 35488. 1st prtg. MTI. SF. F. W2d. $4.25

HILLER, B.B. *Ghostbusters II.* 1989. Dell 20023. 1st prtg. MTI. SF. VG+. R5d. $1.75

HILLER, B.B. *Ghostbusters.* 1989. Dell 40237. 1st prtg. VG+. R5d. $1.75

HILLERMAN, Tony. *Fly on the Wall.* Dell 2626. VG+. G5d. $6.50

HILTON, Francis W. *Skyline Riders.* Dell 250. c/E Sherwan. We. G+. B5d. $4.00

HILTON, James. *Catherine Herself.* 1946. Avon 79. Fa. G+. B4d. $4.00

HILTON, James. *Goodbye, Mr Chips.* 1957. Bantam A 1636. 1st prtg. VG. P7d. $3.50

HILTON, James. *Ill Wind.* 1951. Avon 325. c/gga. Fa. VG. B4d/B6d. $5.00

HILTON, James. *Ill Wind.* Avon 4. scarce. NF. B6d. $25.00

HILTON, James. *Lost Horizon.* 1942. Pocket 1. 21st edn. c/L Steinberg. SF. VG. B5d. $4.00

HILTON, James. *Lost Horizon.* 1961. Pocket 6100. 47th edn. S. VG+. B5d. $3.50

HILTON, James. *Nothing So Strange.* 1951. Avon 381. My. VG. B4d. $5.00

HILTON, James. *Rage in Heaven.* 1943. Avon 39. VG. I1d. $9.00

HILTON, James. *Rage in Heaven.* 1943. Avon 39. 1st prtg. c/Gonzales: gga. NF. P7d. $20.00

HILTON, James. *That French Girl.* Crest 424. NF. B3d. $6.00

HILTON, James. *Three Loves Had Margaret.* Avon 223. 1st prtg. c/gga. VG. P7d. $7.50

HILTON, James. *Was It Murder?* 1946. Bantam 29. My. VG+. B4d. $9.00

HILTON, James. *We Are Not Alone.* 1950. Avon 301. c/gga. Fa. VG+. B4d. $4.00

HILTON, James. *We Are Not Alone.* 1941. Pocket 118. MTI. c/P Muni. Fi. VG. B5d. $5.00

HILTON, James. *Without Armor.* 1941. Pocket 136. Fi. VG. B5d. $5.00

HILTON, James. *Without Armor.* 1964. Pyramid R 956. Fa. VG+. B4d. $3.00

HILTON, Joseph. *Angels in the Gutter.* 1959. Gold Medal S 913. JD. VG+. P1d. $19.50

HILTON, Joseph. *Angels in the Gutter.* 1955. Gold Medal 475. PBO. VG. B6d. $18.00

HILTON, Joseph. *City Jungle.* Brandon 994. reprint. JD. NF. B6d. $18.00

HILTON, Joseph. *Cry Baby Killer.* 1958. Avon T 230. JD. F. P1d. $22.50

HILTON, Joseph. *That French Girl.* Gold Medal 278. PBO. VG. M6d. $9.50

HILTON, T.H. *Holiday Cruise for Swappers.* Barclay 7304. c/photo. NF. B3d. $4.00

HILTON, T.H. *Swap Neighbors.* Barclay 7308. NF. B3d. $4.00

HIMES, Chester B. *Big Gold Dream.* Avon T 384. G. G5d. $4.00

HIMES, Chester B. *Cotton Comes to Harlem.* Dell 1513. 2nd edn. VG+. G5d. $4.50

HIMES, Chester B. *Cotton Comes to Harlem.* 1967. Panther 2197. 1st pb. My. VG+. B6d. $15.00

HIMES, Chester B. *For Love of Imabelle.* Dell 2697. G+. M6d. $9.50

HIMES, Chester B. *For Love of Imabelle.* Gold Medal 717. VG. B3d. $5.00

HIMES, Chester B. *If He Hollers Let Him Go.* Berkley G 139. c/Nappi. VG. B6a #80. $33.00

HIMES, Chester B. *If He Hollers Let Him Go.* 1949. Signet 756. c/Avati. VG+. B3a #24. $16.20

HIMES, Chester B. *If He Hollers Let Him Go.* 1949. Signet 756. NF. I1d. $15.00

HIMES, Chester B. *If He Hollers Let Him Go.* 1949. Signet 756. VG+. B4d. $14.00

HIMES, Chester B. *If He Hollers Let Him Go.* 1949. Signet 756. 1st edn. PBO. c/Avati. VG. B6a #75. $55.00

HIMES, Chester B. *Rage in Harlem (For Love of Imabelle).* Avon G 1244. VG+. B3d. $6.00

HIMMEL, Richard. *Chinese Keyhole.* 1951. Gold Medal 143. VG+. G5d/I1d. $9.00

HIMMEL, Richard. *Chinese Keyhole.* Gold Medal 543. 4th prtg. VG. B3d. $4.50

HIMMEL, Richard. *Cry of the Flesh.* 1955. Gold Medal 488. c/gga. Fa. VG. B4d. $3.75

HIMMEL, Richard. *I Have Gloria Kirby.* Gold Medal 179. G+. G5d. $4.50

HIMMEL, Richard. *I'll Find You.* 1950. Gold Medal 104. PBO. G+. M6d. $8.50

HIMMEL, Richard. *I'll Find You.* 1950. Gold Medal 104. 1st edn. c/gga. scarce top condition. F. F2d. $25.00

HIMMEL, Richard. *I'll Find You.* Gold Medal 256. VG. B3d. $6.00

HIMMEL, Richard. *Rich & the Damned.* 1958. Gold Medal S 735. 1st prtg. PBO. c/Darcy: gga. VG+. P7d. $9.00

HIMMEL, Richard. *Sharp Edge.* Gold Medal 234. VG. B3d. $4.00

HIMMEL, Richard. *Soul of Passion.* 1950. Stork Book 4. PBO. c/Rodewald: gga. scarest of series. VG+. B6a #74. $61.00

HIMMEL, Richard. *Two Deaths Must Die.* Gold Medal 800. 2nd prtg. VG. B3d. $4.50

HINCHCLIFFE, Philip. *Doctor Who & the Seeds of Doom.* 1980. Pinnacle 41620. 1st prtg. SF. VG+. W2d. $5.25

HINCHCLIFFE, Philip. *Masque of Mandragora.* 1979. Pinnacle 40-640. SF. VG+. M3d. $6.00

HINE, Al. *Unsinkable Molly Brown.* 1964. Gold Medal K 1433. PBO. MTI. c/D Reynolds. Fi. VG+. B5d. $5.00

HINE. *Beatles in 'Help.'* 1965. Dell 0486. 1st edn. c/photo. scarce. F. F2d. $35.00

HINKEMEYER, Michael T. *Dark Below.* 1975. Gold Medal M 3154. 1st prtg. SF. VG. R5d. $1.75

HINKLE, Thomas C. *Black Storm.* 1964. Scholastic 54. 8th edn. We. F. B4d. $3.00

HIRSCH, E.W. *Modern Sex Life.* Perma P 21. VG. B3d. $4.50

HIRSCH, E.W. *Modern Sex Life.* 1957. Signet S 1463. Nfi. NF. B4d. $3.00

HIRSCH, Phil. *By the She.* 1963. Pyramid F 861. PBO. c/Wenzel. NF. B6a #76. $25.00

HIRSCH, Phil. *Come on a My House.* 1965. Pyramid R 1175. PBO. c/P Wyma: cartoons. Nfi. VG. B5d. $4.00

HIRSCH, Phil. *Cop.* 1967. Pyramid X 1696. c/Lembit Rauk. Nfi. NF. B4d. $5.00

HIRSCH, Phil. *Hollywood Uncensored.* 1965. Pyramid R 1135. c/photo. VG. P6d. $2.00

HIRSCH, Phil. *Killer Subs.* 1965. Pyramid R 1120. Fi. VG. B5d. $3.00

HIRSCH, Phil. *Mister & Mistress.* 1963. Pyramid F 914. PBO. c/Wenzel. NF. B6a. $25.00

HIRSCH, Phil. *She Drives 'Em Crazy.* 1963. Pyramid F 890. 1st edn. F. F2d. $12.00

HIRSCH, Phil. *Too Funny for Words.* Pyramid 2376. VG. B3d. $5.50

HIRSCH, Phil. *Two on the Isle.* 1964. Pyramid F 1044. PBO. c/Wenzel. scarce. VG+. B6a #76. $25.00

HIRSCH, Phil. *Vietnam Combat.* Pyramid 1654. VG+. B3d. $5.00

HIRSCH, Phil. *Young Toughs.* 1970. Pyramid T 2302. JD. VG. P1d. $15.00

HIRSCH & HYMOFF. *Kennedy Courage.* 1965. Pyramid X 1238. Nfi. VG. B5d. $3.50

HIRSCHFELD, Burt. *Alex in Wonderland.* 1970. Lancer 74-706. PBO. MTI. VG+. B3d. $4.50

HIRSCHFELD, Burt. *Aspen.* 1976. Bantam Y 2491. 1st prtg. VG+. P7d. $4.00

HIRSCHFELD, Burt. *Bonnie & Clyde.* 1967. Lancer 73-684. 1st prtg. VG+. R5d. $6.00

HIRSCHFELD, Burt. *General Hospital.* 1963. Lancer 70-055. TVTI. VG+. B4d. $7.00

HIRSCHFELD, Burt. *General Hospital: Emergency Entrance.* 1965. Lancer 72-917. 1st edn. TVTI. F. F2d. $12.50

HIRSCHFELD, Burt. *Mercenary.* 1969. Lancer 73 884. 1st prtg. VG+. R5d. $4.50

HIRSCHFELD, Burt. *Women of Dallas.* 1981. Bantam 14497. 1st prtg. TVTI. VG. R5d. $1.25

HISTER, William W. *High Tension.* 1948. Pocket 502. Fa. VG+. B4d. $5.00

HITCHCOCK, Alfred. *Bar the Doors.* 1962. Dell F 166. 1st prtg. My. G+. R5d. $1.50

HITCHCOCK, Alfred. *Bar the Doors.* 1946. Dell 143. VG. B3d/I1d. $9.00

HITCHCOCK, Alfred. *Bar the Doors.* 1946. Dell 143. 1st prtg. PBO. c/Gregg. NF. P7d. $17.50

HITCHCOCK, Alfred. *Fear & Trembling.* 1948. Dell. 1st edn. NF. M1d. $20.00

HITCHCOCK, Alfred. *Fear & Trembling.* 1963. Dell 2495. 1st prtg. My. G+. R5d. $1.50

HITCHCOCK, Alfred. *Fear & Trembling.* Dell 264. VG. I1d. $12.00

HITCHCOCK, Alfred. *Hangman's Dozen.* 1962. Dell 3428. 1st prtg. My. G. R5d. $1.25

HITCHCOCK, Alfred. *Hitchcock Presents Stories Wouldn't Let Me Do on TV.* Pan X 71. 6th prtg. c/Bloch: sgn. VG. B3d. $6.50

HITCHCOCK, Alfred. *Hold Your Breath.* 1953. Dell. F. M1d. $25.00

HITCHCOCK, Alfred. *Let It All Bleed Out.* 1973. Dell 4755. 1st prtg. My. G+. W2d. $2.75

HITCHCOCK, Alfred. *More Favorites in Suspense.* Dell 3620. VG. I1d. $4.00

HITCHCOCK, Alfred. *More Stories for Late at Night.* Dell 5815. VG+. I1d. $5.00

HITCHCOCK, Alfred. *More Stories My Mother Never Told Me.* 1965. Dell 5816. 1st prtg. My. VG. W2d. $4.00

HITCHCOCK, Alfred. *Once Upon a Dreadful Time.* Dell 6622. VG. B3d. $4.00

HITCHCOCK, Alfred. *Rolling Stones.* 1971. Dell 7507. 1st prtg. My. VG. W2d. $3.75

HITCHCOCK, Alfred. *Rope.* Dell 262. MTI. G+. G5d. $10.00

HITCHCOCK, Alfred. *Rope.* 1948. Dell 262. MTI. VG. B4d. $15.00

HITCHCOCK, Alfred. *Solve-Them-Yourself Mystery #3.* 1986. Rand 88240. 4th prtg. My. VG. W2d. $3.75

HITCHCOCK, Alfred. *Suspense.* Dell 92. G+. I1d. $6.00

HITCHCOCK, Alfred. *Suspense.* 1945. Dell 92. 1st edn. very scarce in sharp condition. F. F2d. $45.00

HITCHCOCK, Alfred. *Suspense.* 1945. Dell 92. 1st edn. VG. M1d. $40.00

HITCHCOCK, Alfred. *12 Stories for Late at Night.* Dell 9178. VG+. I1d. $4.00

HITCHENS, Bert. *End of the Line.* Pocket 1230. NF. I1d. $5.00

HITCHENS, Dolores. *Bank With the Bamboo Door.* Lancer 73-778. reprint. My. VG. B6d. $6.00

HITCHENS, Dolores. *FOB Murder.* 1956. Perma M 3051. 1st pb. c/Schulz. My. VG+. B6d. $12.50

HITCHENS, Dolores. *Footsteps in the Night.* 1962. Perma M 4261. My. VG+. B4d. $3.00

HITCHENS, Dolores. *Stairway to an Empty Room.* Dell 659. G+. G5d. $3.75

HITCHENS, Dolores. *Widows Won't Wait.* 1954. Dell 779. My. VG. B4d. $3.00

HITCHENS & HITCHENS. *Man Who Followed Women.* Perma M 4220. G. G5d. $3.00

HITCHENS & HITCHENS. *One-Way Ticket.* 1958. Perma M 3100. c/J Meese. My. VG+. B5d. $6.00

HITCHMAN, Janet. *Such a Strange Lady.* 1976. New English 26574. Nfi. VG. P1d. $4.00

HITT, Orrie. *Add Flesh to the Fire.* 1959. Beacon 227. 1st prtg. PBO. VG+. P7d. $12.50

HITT, Orrie. *Affair With Lucy.* 1959. Midwood 10. PBO. c/Harry Barton: gga. extremely scarce. F. B6a #74. $58.50

HITT, Orrie. *Bold Affair.* Kozy Book 151. NF. B3d. $10.00

HITT, Orrie. *Campus Tramp.* Kozy Book 152. VG+. B3d. $8.00

HITT, Orrie. *Campus Tramp.* 1962. Kozy Book 152. c/gga. NF. F2d. $12.50

HITT, Orrie. *Cheat.* 1958. Beacon 206. 1st prtg. PBO. c/photo. VG+. P7d. $9.00

HITT, Orrie. *Dark Passion.* 1961. Kozy Book 128. PBO. VG. B6d. $3.50

HITT, Orrie. *Den of Eroticism.* 1964. Novel Book 6N282. 1st edn. c/photo. F. F2d. $20.00

HITT, Orrie. *Dial M for Man.* 1962. Beacon 465. 1st edn. c/gga. F. F2d. $14.00

HITT, Orrie. *Diploma Dolls.* 1961. Kozy Book 121. 1st edn. c/gga. F. F2d. $12.00

HITT, Orrie. *Dirt Farm.* 1961. Beacon 415. 1st edn. c/gga. F. F2d. $20.00

HITT, Orrie. *Dirt Farm.* Beacon 75128. VG. B3d. $5.00

HITT, Orrie. *Dolls & Dues.* 1957. Beacon 151. PBO. c/Popp: gga. NF. B6d. $25.00

HITT, Orrie. *Ellie's Shack.* 1958. Beacon 159. 1st prtg. PBO. VG+. P7d. $12.50

HITT, Orrie. *Ex-Virgin.* 1959. Beacon 267. PBO. c/gga. scarce. NF. B6a #74. $110.00

HITT, Orrie. *Girls' Dormitory.* Beacon B 191. VG+. I1d. $10.00

HITT, Orrie. *Hot Cargo.* 1958. Beacon 203. 1st prtg. VG. P7d. $9.00

HITT, Orrie. *Hotel Hostess.* 1960. Kozy Book 99. 1st pb edn. F. F2d. $25.00

HITT, Orrie. *I Need a Man!* 1962. Novel Book 6097. 1st edn. F. F2d. $20.00

HITT, Orrie. *I'll Call Every Monday.* 1954. Avon 554. c/gga. Fa. VG. B4d. $6.00

HITT, Orrie. *Ladies' Man.* 1961. Beacon B 395. c/photo. VG. P6d. $5.00

HITT, Orrie. *Libby Sin.* 1962. Chariot 1617. 1st edn. c/gga. NF. F2d. $10.00

HITT, Orrie. *Love Seekers.* 1964. Novel Book 6N256. 1st edn. F. F2d. $20.00

HITT, Orrie. *Love Slave.* Kozy Book 169. VG. B3d. $4.00

HITT, Orrie. *Mail Order Sex.* Midwood 150. VG+. B3d. $9.00

HITT, Orrie. *Man's Nurse.* Chariot 187. PBO. VG. B3d. $5.00

HITT, Orrie. *Married Mistress.* Midwood 115. c/gga. scarce. NF. B6a #76. $49.00

HITT, Orrie. *More! More! More!* 1964. Novel Book 6N252. 1st edn. c/gga. F. F2d. $12.50

HITT, Orrie. *Motel Girls.* 1960. Beacon 314. 1st prtg. VG+. P7d. $12.50

HITT, Orrie. *Nudist Camp.* 1959. Beacon 212. 1st prtg. NF. P7d. $15.00

HITT, Orrie. *Party Doll.* Chariot 167. PBO. VG. B3d. $7.00

HITT, Orrie. *Passion Street.* Chariot 1619. PBO. VG. B3d. $4.00

HITT, Orrie. *Private Club.* 1959. Beacon 232. PBO. c/Al Rossi: gga. VG+. B6a #76. $25.00

HITT, Orrie. *Private Club.* 1959. Beacon 232. 1st prtg. VG+. P7d. $12.50

HITT, Orrie. *Prowl by Night.* 1961. Beacon 401. 1st prtg. PBO. c/Peeper: gga. VG. P7d. $9.00

HITT, Orrie. *Rotten to the Core.* 1958. Beacon 209. 1st prtg. PBO. VG+. P7d. $12.50

HITT, Orrie. *Shabby Street.* 1954. Beacon 104. 1st edn. My. NF. F2d. $10.00

HITT, Orrie. *Shabby Street.* 1958. Beacon 194. 1st prtg. c/Walter Popp: gga. VG. P7d. $9.00

HITT, Orrie. *She Got What She Wanted.* Beacon 195. c/gga. VG+. B6d. $18.00

HITT, Orrie. *Sheba.* 1959. Beacon 211. 1st prtg. PBO. VG+. P7d. $12.50

HITT, Orrie. *Shocking Mistress!* 1961. Novel Book 6006. 1st edn. F. F2d. $20.00

HITT, Orrie. *Sin Doll.* 1959. Beacon 254. PBO. c/Milo: gga. NF. B6d. $22.50

HITT, Orrie. *Sins of Flesh.* 1960. Kozy Book 94. 1st pb edn. F. F2d. $25.00

HITT, Orrie. *Strip Alley.* Kozy Book 180. VG+. B3d. $10.00

HITT, Orrie. *Suburban Interlude.* Kozy 108. VG. B3d. $4.50

HITT, Orrie. *Sucker.* 1957. Beacon 132. PBO. c/Warren King: gga. VG. B6d. $10.00

HITT, Orrie. *Sucker.* 1957. Beacon 132. 1st prtg. c/Warren King: gga. G+. P7d. $5.00

HITT, Orrie. *Sucker.* Beacon 370. c/Warren King: gga. reprint. NF. B6d. $16.50

HITT, Orrie. *Summer Romance.* 1959. Midwood 16. PBO. c/Harry Barton: gga. scarce. NF. B6a #74. $68.25

HITT, Orrie. *Tavern.* 1966. Beacon 987. 1st edn. F. F2d. $20.00

HITT, Orrie. *Tavern.* 1966. Softcover Library B 897X. VG. P6d. $3.50

HITT, Orrie. *Teaser.* 1957. Beacon 158. 1st pb. c/photo. VG+. B6d. $15.00

HITT, Orrie. *Teaser.* 1957. Beacon 158. 1st prtg. c/photo. VG+. P7d. $9.00

HITT, Orrie. *Tell Them Anything.* 1960. Beacon 325. PBO. c/Milo: gga. scarce. NF. B6a #76. $25.00

HITT, Orrie. *Too Hot To Handle.* 1959. Beacon 250. 1st prtg. PBO. G+. P7d. $5.00

HITT, Orrie. *Torrid Teens.* 1960. Beacon 294. 1st prtg. PBO. VG+. P7d. $15.00

HITT, Orrie. *Trapped.* 1958. Beacon 186. 1st prtg. VG+. P7d. $9.00

HITT, Orrie. *Unfaithful Wives.* 1956. Beacon 126. PBO. c/Safran: gga. VG. B6d. $9.00

HITT, Orrie. *Unfaithful Wives.* 1956. Beacon 126. 1st prtg. PBO. VG+. P7d. $12.50

HITT, Orrie. *Unfaithful Wives.* 1961. Beacon 378. 1st prtg. F. F2d. $12.50

HITT, Orrie. *Violent Sinners.* Kozy Book 164. VG+. B3d. $9.00

HITT, Orrie. *Widow.* 1959. Beacon 222. 1st prtg. PBO. VG+. P7d. $12.50

HITT, Orrie. *Wild Oats.* 1958. Beacon B 169. 1st prtg. PBO. c/gga. VG+. P7d. $15.00

HITT, Orrie. *Woman Hunt.* 1958. Beacon 197. PBO. c/George Gross: gga. NF. B6d. $30.00

HIX, Elsie. *Strange As It Seems.* 1955. Bantam 1334. 1st prtg. VG+. P7d. $4.50

HOBART, A.T. *Oil for the Lamps of China.* Bantam 20. VG+. B3d. $6.50

HOBART, A.T. *Oil for the Lamps of China.* Pyramid 848. VG. B3d. $4.50

HOBART, A.T. *This Earth Is Mine.* 1958. Dell F80. MTI. c/V Kalin, R Hudson & J Simmons. Fi. VG. B5d. $2.50

HOBSON, Burton. *Coins & Coin Collecting.* 1965. Gold Medal D 1554. 1st prtg. VG. P7d. $4.50

HOCH, Edward. *Shattered Raven.* 1969. Lancer 74-525. PBO. My. VG. B6d. $5.00

HOCH, Edward. *Transvection Machine.* 1973. Pocket 77640. 1st edn. F. P9d. $2.50

HOCHHUTH, Rolf. *Soldiers.* 1968. Black Cat B 200. c/play: photo. Nfi. F. B5d. $10.00

HOCHSTEIN, Peter. *Blue Alice.* 1972. Dell 0733. 1st edn. c/photo. F. F2d. $10.00

HODGES, Carl G. *Murder by the Pack.* 1953. Ace D 33. PBO. c/Saunders. VG+. B6d. $30.00

HODGSON, William Hope. *Boats of the Glen Carrig.* Ballantine 02145. VG+. B3d. $10.00

HODGSON, William Hope. *Ghost Pirages.* Sphere 33. 1st prtg. NF. S1d. $6.00

HODGSON, William Hope. *House on the Borderland.* 1962. Ace D 553. SF. G+. M3d. $4.00

HODGSON, William Hope. *House on the Borderland.* 1962. Ace D 553. 1st pb. SF. NF. B6d. $22.50

HODGSON, William Hope. *House on the Borderland.* 1962. Ace D 553. 1st prtg. SF. VG. R5d. $7.00

HODGSON, William Hope. *House on the Borderland.* 1983. Carroll & Graf. 1st edn. G+. M1d. $4.00

HODGSON, William Hope. *House on the Borderland.* Freeway 2038. 1st prtg. F. S1d. $2.50

HODGSON, William Hope. *House on the Borderland.* 1972. Panther 02682. 2nd edn. SF. VG+. B5d. $7.50

HODGSON, William Hope. *Nightland, Volume #1 & #2.* 1972. Ballantine 02670. 1st edn. Ad/Fa. G+. M1d. $15.00

HODGSON, William Hope. *Nightland, Volume #2.* 1972. Ballantine 02670. 1st prtg. SF. G+. R5d. $4.00

HOEHLING, A.A. *They Sailed Into Oblivion.* 1960. Ace K 115. Nfi. VG+. B4d. $2.00

HOFFENBERG, Mason. *Sin for Breakfast.* 1967. Traveller Companion 210. 1st edn. F. F2d. $10.00

HOFFER, Eric. *True Believer.* 1958. Mentor MD 228. NF. F. B4d. $4.00

HOFFMAN, Lee. *Always the Black Knight.* 1970. Avon S417. PBO. SF. VG+. B5d. $4.00

HOFFMAN, Lee. *Return to Broken Crossing.* Ace 71720. We. VG+. B5d. $4.00

HOFFMAN & BISHOP. *Girl in Poison Cottage.* Gold Medal 267. c/Barye. VG. B3d. $8.50

HOFFMANN, D. *Beatle Book.* Lancer 72-732. VG+. I1d. $12.00

HOGAN, James P. *Genesis Machine.* 1978. Ballantine 27231. 1st prtg. SF. VG+. R5d. $3.00

HOGAN, James P. *Gentle Giants of Ganymede.* 1982. Ballantine. F. M1d. $5.00

HOGAN, James P. *Proteus Operation.* 1986. Bantam 25698. SF. VG+. W2d. $4.25

HOGAN, Ray. *Life & Death of Clay Allison.* 1961. Signet 2010. 1st edn. SF. F. F2d. $10.00

HOGAN, Ray. *Raider's Revenge.* 1960. Pyramid G 498. We. NF. B4d. $6.00

HOGAN, Ray. *Stranger in Apache Basin.* 1963. Avon F 178. We. VG+. B4d. $2.75

HOGAN, Ray. *Wolver.* 1967. Ace M 163. PBO. We. NF. B6d. $15.00

HOGAN, Robert J. *Ace of the White Death.* 1970. Berkley. 1st pb. F. M1d. $15.00

HOGAN, Robert J. *Bat Staffel.* Berkley G 1734. VG. B3d. $4.50

HOGAN, Robert J. *Bat Staffel.* 1969. Berkley. 1st pb. NF. M1d. $12.00

HOGAN, Robert J. *Bombs From the Murder Wolves.* 1971. Berkley. 1st pb. F. M1d. $15.00

HOGAN, Robert J. *Challenge of Smoke Wade.* 1952. Avon 454. 1st pb. We. VG+. B6d. $12.00

HOGAN, Robert J. *Flight From the Grave.* 1971. Berkley. 1st pb. VG. M1d. $10.00

HOGAN, Robert J. *Mark of the Vulture.* 1972. Berkley. 1st pb. NF. M1d. $10.00

HOGAN, Robert J. *Marshal Without a Badge.* Gold Medal 432. VG. B3d. $5.00

HOGAN, Robert J. *Mosby's Last Ride.* MacFadden 50-296. PBO. VG+. B3d. $4.50

HOGAN, Robert J. *Outlaw Marshal.* Gold Medal 402. VG. B3d. $7.00

HOGAN, Robert J. *Purple Aces.* 1970. Berkley X 1746. c/Steranko. PBO. VG. P6d. $3.00

HOGAN, Robert J. *Purple Aces.* 1970. Berkley X 1746. 1st pb. F. M1d. $12.00

HOGAN, Robert J. *Raider's Revenge.* Pyramid 498. c/Schaare. VG+. B3d. $4.50

HOGAN, Robert J. *Rebel Ghost.* MacFadden 50-196. PBO. VG+. B3d. $5.00

HOGAN, Robert J. *Roaring Guns at Apache Landing.* Avon 469. VG. B3d. $5.00

HOGAN, Robert J. *Scourge of the Steel Mask.* 1985. Dimedia. 1st pb. F. M1d. $6.00

HOGAN, Robert J. *Shotgunner.* Avon T 411. VG. B3d. $4.50

HOGAN, Robert J. *Texas Lawman.* Lancer 72-161. VG+. B3d. $4.00

HOGAN, Robert J. *Trackers.* Signet 2425. VG+. B3d. $5.00

HOGAN, Robert J. *Wanted: Smoke Wade.* Avon T 542. VG. B3d. $4.00

HOGAN/JAKES. *Friendless One/Wear a Fast Gun.* Ace D 220. VG. B3d. $3.50

HOGAN/PATTERSON. *Trouble at Hang dog/Hoodoo Guns.* Ace M 102. We. VG. B6d. $7.00

HOGAN/WEST. *Side Me With Sixes/ Ridgerunner.* 1960. Ace D 450. PBO. VG. B3d. $4.00

HOGARTH, Emmett. *Death by Remote Control.* Detective 3. VG. B3d. $5.50

HOKE, N.W. *Double Entendre.* Pocket 1160. PBO. VG+. B3d. $6.00

HOLDEN, Larry. *Hide-Out.* 1953. Eton 132. PBO. scarce. NF. B6a. $42.00

HOLDEN, Richard. *Snow Fury.* 1956. Perma M 3034. 1st pb. c/Meese. SF. VG. B6d. $7.50

HOLDER, William. *Case of the Dead Divorcee.* 1958. Signet 1539. c/gga. My. VG+. B4d. $3.50

HOLDING & HOLDING. *Trial by Murder.* Thrill Novel Classic 17. VG. B3d. $4.50

HOLDING/HOLDING. *Blank Wall/Girl Who Had To Die.* Ace G 512. VG. G5d. $3.50

HOLDING/HOLDING. *Death Wish.* 1949. Popular 189. 1st pb. c/Belarski. My. VG. B3d. $4.00

HOLDING/HOLDING. *Kill Joy/Speak of the Devil.* 1963. Ace G 534. My. VG. B4d. $2.75

HOLDING/HOLDING. *Lady Killer.* 1950. Harlequin 60. 1st edn. PBO. scarce. My. VG+. B6a #75. $40.25

HOLDING/HOLDING. *Murder Is a Kill-Joy.* Dell 103. VG. B3d. $6.00

HOLDING/HOLDING. *Net of Cobwebs.* 1946. Bantam 26. My. VG. B4d. $3.75

HOLDING/HOLDING. *Net of Cobwebs/ Unfinished Crime.* 1963. Ace G 530. 1st prtg. c/Schinella. VG. P7d. $3.50

HOLDING/HOLDING. *Obstinate Murderer/Old Battle Axe.* Ace G 519. VG. G5d. $5.00

HOLDING/HOLDING. *Widow's Mite/Who's Afraid?* Ace G 524. VG. G5d. $3.00

HOLLAND, Cecelia. *Kings in Winter.* 1969. Pocket 75380. Fi. VG+. B5d. $3.50

HOLLAND, D. *Sin Town.* 1962. Bedside BB 1233. Ad. G+. B5d. $3.50

HOLLAND, D. *Wild Ones.* Playtime 618. VG+. B3d. $4.50

HOLLAND, Marty. *Blonde Baggage.* 1950. Novel Library 45. c/gga. VG. P6d. $17.00

HOLLAND, Marty. *Her Private Passions.* 1948. Avon 181. c/gga. Fa. G+. B4d. $2.50

HOLLANDER, Xaviera. *Xaviera.* 1973. PB Library 78-278. c/X Hollander photo. Nfi. VG+. B5d. $7.50

HOLLIDAY, Don. *Any Bed for Myra.* 1963. Nightstand NB 1722. Ad. VG. B5d. $4.00

HOLLIDAY, Don. *Blow the Man Down-Camp.* Late-Hour Library LL 763. PBO. NF. M6d. $20.00

HOLLIDAY, Don. *Carnal Code.* Ember Book EB 933. VG+. B3d. $5.00

HOLLIDAY, Don. *Holiday Gay.* Companion 545. VG+. B3d. $5.00

HOLLIDAY, Don. *Lust Knot.* Sundown Reader SR 507. VG+. l1d. $4.00

HOLLIDAY, Don. *Lust Lodge.* 1962. Nightstand NB 1621. Ad. VG+. B5d. $6.00

HOLLIDAY, Don. *Sin Brothers.* 1965. Nightstand NB 1737. Ad. G+. B5d. $3.00

HOLLIDAY, Don. *Sins of Martha Leslie.* Midwood 39. PBO. c/Rader. G+. M6d. $9.50

HOLLIDAY, Don. *Sins of Martha Leslie.* 1960. Midwood 39. PBO. c/Rader: gga. scarce. VG+. B6a #80. $53.50

HOLLIDAY, Don. *Stud.* 1960. Nightstand NB 1532 Ad. G+. B5d. $3.00

HOLLIDAY, Don. *Sun Sinners.* Idle Hours 417. c/gga. VG. B3d. $4.00

HOLLO, J.D. *Snap Back From Your Heart Attack.* Brandon House 1078. VG. B3d. $6.00

HOLLOWAY, E.H. *Cobweb House.* Dell 133. VG+. B3d. $6.00

HOLLY, J.H. *Assassination Affair.* 1967. Ace G 636. 1st prtg. My. G+. R5d. $1.75

HOLLY, J.H. *Encounter.* 1962. Monarch 240. SF. NF. B5d. $12.50

HOLLY, J.H. *Encounter.* 1962. Monarch 240. SF. VG. B4d. $6.00

HOLLY, J.H. *Encounter.* 1962. Monarch 240. 1st pb. F. M1d. $15.00

HOLLY, J.H. *Flying Eyes.* 1962. Monarch 260. 1st edn. F. M1d. $20.00

HOLLY, J.H. *Flying Eyes.* 1962. Monarch 260. 1st prtg. G+. l1d/S1d. $4.00

HOLLY, J.H. *Green Planet.* 1961. Monarch 213. SF. VG. B5d. $8.00

HOLLY, J.H. *Green Planet.* 1961. Monarch 213. SF. VG+. B4d. $10.00

HOLLY, J.H. *Green Planet.* 1961. Monarch 213. 1st edn. PBO. G. P9d. $2.00

HOLLY, J.H. *Green Planet.* 1961. Monarch 213. 1st pb. F. M1d. $20.00

HOLLY, J.H. *Keeper.* 1976. Laser 72022. SF. VG. l1d/W2d. $5.00

HOLLY, J.H. *Mind Traders.* MacFadden 60291. 1st prtg. G+. S1d. $2.50

HOLLY, J.H. *Mind Traders.* 1967. MacFadden 60291. SF. VG. W2d. $4.00

HOLLY, J.H. *Running Man.* Monarch 342. VG. l1d. $6.00

HOLLY, J.H. *Running Man.* 1963. Monarch 342. SF. VG+. B5d. $10.00

HOLLY, J.H. *Running Man.* 1963. Monarch 342. 1st edn. F. M1d. $20.00

HOLLY, J.H. *Sheperd.* 1977. Laser 55. 1st edn. very scarce. SF. F. F2d. $40.00

HOLLY, J.H. *Time Twisters.* 1964. Avon G 1231. 1st prtg. SF. VG+. R5d. $4.00

HOLLY, Joan Hunter. *Assassination Affair.* Ace G 636. Man From UNCLE #10. G+. G5d. $3.00

HOLMAN, Hugh. *Another Man's Poison.* 1949. Signet 718. My. VG. B5d. $5.00

HOLMAN, Hugh. *Slay the Murderers.* 1948. Signet 684. 1st edn. PBO. De. F. F2d. $6.00

HOLMES, Clellon. *Go.* 1957. Ace D 238. 1st edn. PBO. VG. B6d. $22.50

HOLMES, David. *Night Nurse.* 1960. Pyramid G 493. c/McGuire: gga. Fa. VG. B4d. $4.00

HOLMES, David. *Velvet Ape.* Perma M 3122. VG. G5d. $3.00

HOLMES, Geoffrey. *Case of the Mexican Knife.* Bantam 309. G. G5d. $5.50

HOLMES, Geoffrey. *Case of the Unhappy Angels (Six Silver Handles).* Bantam 779. VG. G5d. $9.00

HOLMES, Geoffrey. *Doctor Died at Dusk.* Dell 14. G+. B3d. $5.00

HOLMES, Geoffrey. *Doctor Died at Dusk.* 1943. Dell 14. 1st edn. PBO. c/Strohmer. rare. F. B6a #80. $75.00

HOLMES, Geoffrey. *Finders Keepers.* 1947. Bantam 89. 1st pb. My. NF. B6d. $12.50

HOLMES, Geoffrey. *Man Who Murdered Goliath.* Dell 86. G+. B3d. $4.00

HOLMES, Geoffrey. *No Hands on the Clock.* Bantam 52. 2nd prtg. VG. B3d. $5.00

HOLMES, Geoffrey. *No Hands on the Clock.* 1946. Bantam 52. My. VG+. B4d. $7.50

HOLMES, Geoffrey. *Stiffs Don't Vote.* 1947. Bantam 117. VG. B3d. $4.50

HOLMES, Geoffrey. *Then There Were Three.* Bantam 12. VG. G5d. $7.50

HOLMES, H.H. *Rocket to the Morgue.* 1942. Phantom Mystery 1. PBO. c/Shayn: sgn. VG. P6d. $55.00

HOLMES, H.H. *Rocket to the Morgue.* 1942. Phantom Mystery 1. PBO. scarce. VG. B6a #79. $78.75

HOLMES, H.H. *Rocket to the Morgue.* 1942. Phantom Mystery 1. scarce. VG. l1d. $55.00

HOLMES, John Clellon. *Get Home Free.* 1966. MacFadden 75-112. 1st edn. PBO. c/Meese: gga. NF. B6a #76. $33.00

HOLMES, L.P. *Apache Desert.* Pennant P 13. VG+. B3d. $6.00

HOLMES, L.P. *Bloody Saddles.* 1950. Readers Choice 18. 1st pb. We. VG. B6d. $7.50

HOLMES, L.P. *Desert Rails.* 1950. Pocket 675. 1st edn. PBO. F. F2d. $6.00

HOLMES, L.P. *Gunman's Creed.* 1957. Graphic 144. We. VG. B5d. $3.50

HOLMES, L.P. *Gunman's Greed.* Graphic 77. VG. B3d. $4.50

HOLMES, L.P. *Plunderers.* 1958. Bantam 1822. 1st pb. We. VG+. B6d. $9.00

HOLMES, L.P. *Range Pirate.* 1950. Bantam 823. We. VG. B4d. $3.00

HOLMES, L.P. *Somewhere They Die.* 1956. Bantam 1514. 1st pb. WE. NF. B6d. $10.00

HOLMES, P. *Sheppard Murder Case.* Bantam 2439. VG. B3d. $4.00

HOLMES, Rick. *Child-Woman.* 1965. Monarch 563. 1st prtg. PBO. c/De Soto: gga. VG. P7d. $8.50

HOLMES, Rick. *New Widow.* 1963. Beacon B620. PBO. Ad. VG. B5d. $5.00

HOLMES, Rick. *Tropic of Cleo.* 1962. Monarch 262. PBO. c/Ray Johnson: gga. VG+. P6d. $7.50

HOLT, E. *World at War.* Panther 878. VG. B3d. $7.50

HOLT, Tex. *Dark Canyon*. Handi-Book 136. c/Saunders. G+. I1d. $6.00

HOLTON, Leonard. *Secret of the Doubting Saint*. Dell 7713. G. G5d. $4.00

HOMER. *Odyssey*. Signet 613. VG+. B3d. $7.50

HONIG, Donald. *No Song To Sing*. 1963. MacFadden 50-164. JD. VG. P1d. $9.00

HOOD, Margaret Page. *Murders on Fox Island*. 1960. Dell 1st Edn D 365. 1st pb. My. VG+. B6d. $12.00

HOOD, Margaret Page. *Silent Women*. Dell 880. G+. G5d. $5.00

HOOKER, Richard. *M*A*S*H Goes to Maine*. 1973. Pocket 78254. 1st prtg. TVTI. VG+. R5d. $2.00

HOOKER & BUTTERWORTH. *M*A*S*H Goes to Las Vegas*. 1976. Pocket 80265. 1st prtg. VG. R5d. $1.25

HOOKER & BUTTERWORTH. *M*A*S*H Goes to New Orleans*. 1975. Pocket 78490. 1st prtg. VG. R5d. $1.25

HOOKER & BUTTERWORTH. *M*A*S*H Goes to Paris*. 1975. Pocket 78491. 1st prtg. TVTI. VG+. B4d. $3.00

HOOVER, P.A. *Backwater Woman*. 1957. Ace S 219. PBO. Fi. VG. B5d. $5.50

HOOVER, P.A. *Riverboat Girl*. 1956. Ace S 168. PBO. VG. B6d. $15.00

HOPE, Anthony. *Prisoner of Zenda*. 1946. Bantam 33. Fa. F. I1d. $6.00

HOPE, Anthony. *Prisoner of Zenda*. Pyramid 595. VG+. B3d. $4.00

HOPE, Edward. *She Loves Me Not*. Bantam 66. VG. B3d. $5.00

HOPE, S. *Case of Monta Grandee Diamonds*. Sexton Blake 103. VG+. B3d. $12.00

HOPKINS, Tom J. *Dead Man's Range*. 1948. Bantam 208. We. VG+. B4d. $7.00

HOPKINS, Tom J. *Horsethief Crossing*. 1955. Perma M 3308. 1st pb. We. VG. B6d. $7.50

HOPKINS, Tom J. *Trouble in Tombstone*. 1953. Signet 989. 1st pb. We. NF. B6d. $15.00

HOPLEY, George. *Fright*. 1952. Popular 424. PBO. c/Belarski. VG+. B6a #74. $172.00

HOPLEY, George. *Fright*. 1952. Popular 424. 1st edn. PBO. c/Belarski: gga. rare. VG+. B6a #79. $145.00

HOPLEY, George. *Night Has 1000 Eyes*. Dell 679. 1st prtg. My. VG. R5d. $17.50

HOPLEY, George. *Night Has 1000 Eyes*. 1953. Dell 679. PBO. c/Shoemaker. VG+. B6a #74. $61.00

HOPSON, William. *Apache Greed*. Lion 195. VG. B3d. $4.00

HOPSON, William. *Arizona Round-Up*. Western Novel Monthly 3. VG. B3d. $8.00

HOPSON, William. *Cry Viva!* MacFadden 50-386. VG+. B3d. $4.50

HOPSON, William. *Desperado*. Century 118. VG. B3d. $7.00

HOPSON, William. *Gringo Bandit*. 1952. Avon 414. 1st pb. Wd. NF. B6d. $15.00

HOPSON, William. *Gunfire at Salt Creek*. 1966. Gold Medal K 1715. We. VG+. B4d. $2.75

HOPSON, William. *Gunfire at Salt Fork*. 1966. Gold Medal S 1265. We. VG. B4d. $2.00

HOPSON, William. *Hangtree Range*. 1957. Lion LB 156. 1st pb. We. VG. B6d. $8.00

HOPSON, William. *Hell's Horseman*. Lancer 70-071. reprint. We. NF. B6d. $9.00

HOPSON, William. *Hell's Horseman*. Lancer 70-071. VG+. B3d. $5.00

HOPSON, William. *Ranch Cat*. 1951. Lion 66. c/Mitchell Hooks: sgn. VG. B3a #21. $16.50

HOPSON, William. *Ranch Cat*. 1951. Lion 66. 1st pb. c/Hooks: gga. We. VG. B6d. $15.00

HOPSON, William. *Vegas, Gunman Marshal*. Avon 687. c/Kenyon. We. VG+. B5d. $6.00

HOPSON, William. *Vegas, Gunman Marshal*. Avon 875. We. VG. B5d. $4.50

HOPSON, William. *Yucca City Outlaw*. 1951. Handi-Book 137. c/Norman Saunders. We. VG+. P6d. $4.50

HOPSON & O'CONNER. *Mexico After Dark*. 1968. MacFadden NN. VG. B3d. $7.50

HOPSON/FLOREN. *Backlash at Cajon Pass/Riders in the Night*. Ace D 272. VG. B3d. $4.50

HOPSON/LUTZ. *Winter Drive/Wild Quarry*. Ace D 492. PBO. VG. B3d. $4.00

HOPSON/O'CONNOR. *Mexico After Dark*. MacFadden 50-222. VG. B3d. $4.00

HOPSON/TOPKINS. *Bullet: Brand Empire/Deadwood*. Ace D 68. PBO. We. G+. P6d. $3.00

HOPWOOD & RINEHART. *Bat*. 1965. Dell 0465. 1st prtg. c/Kalin. VG. P7d. $4.00

HOPWOOD & RINEHART. *Bat*. 1948. Dell 241. 1st pb. c/Gregg. My. VG+. B6d. $22.50

HOPWOOD & RINEHART. *Bat*. Dell 652. VG. I1d. $3.00

HORAN, James D. *Desperate Men*. 1951. Avon 330. Bio. NF. B4d. $15.00

HORAN, James D. *Wild Bunch*. 1958. Signet S 1557. We. VG. B5d. $4.50

HORGAN, Paul. *Peach Stone*. 1971. PB Library 66-550. 1st pb. NF. B6d. $9.00

HORNBLOW, Leonora. *Love-Seekers*. 1958. Signet D 1548. Fa. VG. B4d. $2.75

HORNE, A. *Bar Broad*. Playtime 669. VG+. B3d. $6.00

HORNER, Lance. *Rogue Roman*. 1968. Gold Medal T 1978. Fa. VG+. B4d. $3.00

HORNER & ONSTOTT. *Child of the Sun*. Gold Medal 2633. VG. B3d. $5.50

HORNER & ONSTOTT. *Tattooed Rood*. 1965. Crest T 809. 1st prtg. VG. P7d. $4.00

HORNUNG, E.W. *Shadow of the Rope*. Lancer 73-496. NF. B3d. $4.50

HOROWITZ, Anthony. *Silver Citadel*. 1986. Berkley 08890. 1st edn. Ho. F. F2d. $8.00

HORWITZ, Julius. *Can I Get There by Candlelight*. 1965. Bantam S 2911. Nfl. VG. B5d. $2.50

HOSKINS, Robert. *Future Now*. 1977. Crest 23227. SF. F. W2d. $12.50

HOSKINS, Robert. *Infinity Two*. 1971. Lancer. 1st edn. F. M1d. $5.00

HOSKINS, Robert. *Swords Against Tomorrow*. Signet T 4327. 1st prtg. VG. S1d. $4.00

HOSSENT, Harry. *Fear Business*. 1968. Arrow 042. 1st prtg. My. G+. R5d. $1.50

HOTTER, Amos. *Waterfront Girl*. 1953. Original Novel 730 PBO. c/Gross: gga. scarce. NF. B6a #76. $82.50

HOUGH, Emerson. *Covered Wagon*. Pocket 410. G+. G5d. $2.50

HOUGH, Emerson. *North of 36*. 1961. Pocket 6070. c/skull. We. VG+. B5d. $5.00

HOUGH, Richard. *Fleet That Had To Die*. 1960. Ballantine 451K. War. VG. B4d. $3.00

HOUGHTON, Claude. *Passing of Third Floor Back*. Reader's Library NN. 2nd edn. VG. B3d. $8.00

HOUGRON, Jean. *Trapped (A Question of Character)*. Dell 1006. VG. G5d. $3.50

HOUSE, Brant. *Cartoon Annual #3*. Ace S 275. VG. B3d. $6.00

HOUSE, Brant. *Cartoon Annual #3*. 1958. Ace S 275. VG+. B3a #20. $14.30

HOUSE, Brant. *From Eve.* 1958. Ace D 307. PBO. VG. B6d. $10.00

HOUSE, Brant. *Goofed!* 1956. Ace S 188. VG+. B3a #20. $18.70

HOUSE, Brant. *Greatest Quarterbacks.* Short 10. VG. B3d. $5.00

HOUSE, Brant. *Lincoln's Wit.* Ace D 268. VG. B3d. $4.00

HOUSE, Brant. *Little Monsters.* 1956. Ace S 145. PBO. scarce. NF. B6a #76. $43.00

HOUSE, Brant. *Love & Hisses.* 1956. Ace S 165. PBO. VG+. B6a #79. $82.50

HOUSE, Brant. *Secret Agent X: Mandarin's Fan.* 1966. Corinth CR130. VG+. B3a #21. $4.25

HOUSE, Brant. *Squelches.* 1956. Ace S 179. Hu. VG. B4d. $6.00

HOUSE, Brant. *Squelches.* 1956. Ace S 179. PBO. VG+. B6d. $15.00

HOUSE, Brant. *Strange Powers of Unusual People.* Ace K 176. F. M1d. $7.00

HOUSE, Brant. *Violent Ones.* 1958. Ace D 323. VG. B3a #21. $46.20

HOUSEHOLD, Geoffrey. *Fellow Passenger.* 1963. Pyramid R944. c/R Maguire. My. VG. B5d. $4.00

HOUSEHOLD, Geoffrey. *Fog Comes.* 1946. Bantam 23. 1st pb. My. NF. B6d. $12.50

HOUSEHOLD, Geoffrey. *Rogue Male.* 1945. Bantam 9. 1st pb. My. VG+. B6d. $9.00

HOUSEHOLD, Geoffrey. *Rough Shoot.* 1953. Bantam 1019. 1st prtg. My. G+. R5d. $2.25

HOUSEHOLD, Geoffrey. *Spanish Cave.* 1948. Comet 12. SF. G+. M3d. $5.00

HOUSEHOLD, Geoffrey. *Time To Kill.* 1954. Corgi 11. VG. B3d/G5d. $5.50

HOUSEHOLD, Geoffrey. *Time To Kill.* 1964. Pyramid R 979. c/R Maguire. My. VG. B5d. $3.50

HOUSMAN, A.E. *Shropshire Lad.* 1950. Avon 246. Nfi. G+. B5d. $7.50

HOUSTON, David. *Swamp Thing.* TOR 48039. 1st prtg. VG. S1d. $2.00

HOUSTON, David. *Tales of Tomorrow #1.* Leisure 928. 1st prtg. VG. S1d. $3.50

HOUSTON, David. *Wing Master.* 1981. Leisure 945. PBO. SF. NF. B6d. $5.00

HOUSTON/LOOMIS. *Open All Night/ Marina Street Girls.* 1953. Ace D 35. PBO. c/V Olson. Fi. G. B5d. $3.50

HOWARD, Hayden. *Eskimo Invasion.* 1967. Ballantine. 1st edn. NF. M1d. $8.00

HOWARD, Ivan. *Escape to Earth.* 1963. Belmont 92-571. SF. F. W2d. $5.75

HOWARD, Ivan. *Novelets of SF.* Belmont 50-770. VG. B3d. $4.00

HOWARD, Ivan. *Novelets of SF.* Belmont 92-567. VG+. B3d. $4.50

HOWARD, Ivan. *Rare SF.* 1963. Belmont L 92-557. 1st edn. F. M1d. $15.00

HOWARD, Ivan. *Rare SF.* 1963. Belmont L 92-557. 1st prtg. SF. G+. R5d. $2.75

HOWARD, Ivan. *Rare SF.* 1963. Belmont L 92-557. 1st prtg. VG. S1d. $4.00

HOWARD, Ivan. *Things.* 1964. Belmont L 92-582. 1st edn. F. P9d. $2.00

HOWARD, Ivan. *6 & the Silent Scream.* 1963. Belmont L 92-564. c/Maguire. NF. I1d/M1d. $10.00

HOWARD, Ivan. *6 & the Silent Scream.* Belmont 92-564. PBO. VG. B3d. $4.50

HOWARD, L. *Blind Date.* Corgi 462. VG+. B3d. $8.00

HOWARD, Mel. *Call Me Anytime.* 1966. Midwood 34-726. Ad. VG. B5d. $4.00

HOWARD, Peter. *Sex & the Oriental.* 1965. Gold Star IL 7-67. PBO. VG+. B3a. $11.00

HOWARD, Robert E. *Almuric.* 1964. Ace F 305. 1st edn. SF. F. F2d. $25.00

HOWARD, Robert E. *Almuric.* 1977. Berkley 03483. SF. F. W2d. $7.00

HOWARD, Robert E. *Black Canaan.* 1978. Berkley 03711. c/poster. SF. VG. B5d. $3.00

HOWARD, Robert E. *Black Canaan.* 1978. Berkley 03711. SF. F. W2d. $8.50

HOWARD, Robert E. *Black Vulmea's Vengeance.* 1979. Berkley 04296. SF. VG. W2d. $6.00

HOWARD, Robert E. *Black Vulmea's Vengeance.* 1977. Zebra 89083. SF. F W2d. $7.50

HOWARD, Robert E. *Bran Mak Morn.* 1969. Dell 0774. 1st edn. SF. F. F2d/M1d. $15.00

HOWARD, Robert E. *Breckinridge Elkins.* 1975. Zebra 132. c/J Jones. Fi. VG. B5d. $4.00

HOWARD, Robert E. *Conan of Cimmeria.* Ace 11631. SF. F. W2d. $4.75

HOWARD, Robert E. *Conan of Cimmeria.* Ace 11631. 3rd edn. SF. VG+. B5d. $3.50

HOWARD, Robert E. *Conan of Cimmeria.* 1969. Lancer 75-072. 1st edn. SF. F. F2d. $15.00

HOWARD, Robert E. *Conan of the Isles.* 1968. Lancer 73-800. 1st edn. SF. F. F2d. $10.00

HOWARD, Robert E. *Conan the Adventurer.* Ace 11675. SF. F. W2d. $4.50

HOWARD, Robert E. *Conan the Adventurer.* Lancer 73-526. 1st prtg. G. S1d. $2.50

HOWARD, Robert E. *Conan the Adventurer.* 1966. Lancer 73-526. SF. VG. W2d. $5.00

HOWARD, Robert E. *Conan the Adventurer.* 1966. Lancer 73-526. 1st edn. c/Frazetta. SF. F. F2d. $13.00

HOWARD, Robert E. *Conan the Avenger.* 1968. Lancer 73-780. c/Frazetta. SF. VG+. M3d. $5.00

HOWARD, Robert E. *Conan the Avenger.* 1968. Lancer 73-780. 1st edn. SF. F. F2d. $10.00

HOWARD, Robert E. *Conan the Buccaneer.* 1971. Lancer 75-181. 1st edn. SF. F. F2d. $10.00

HOWARD, Robert E. *Conan the Conqueror.* 1953. Ace D 36. VG. I1d. $30.00

HOWARD, Robert E. *Conan the Conqueror.* 1953. Ace D 36. 1st edn. PBO. c/Saunders. NF. B6a #75. $82.50

HOWARD, Robert E. *Conan the Conqueror.* 1953. Ace D 36. 1st edn. PBO. c/Saunders. VG+. B6d. $45.00

HOWARD, Robert E. *Conan the Conqueror.* 1953. Ace D 36. 1st edn. PBO. SF. G. F2d. $25.00

HOWARD, Robert E. *Conan the Conqueror.* Ace 11679. SF. VG+. W2d. $4.00

HOWARD, Robert E. *Conan the Conqueror.* 1967. Lancer 73-572. c/F Frazetta. SF. VG. B5d. $5.00

HOWARD, Robert E. *Conan the Conqueror.* 1967. Lancer 73-572. 1st pb. NF. M1d. $8.00

HOWARD, Robert E. *Conan the Conqueror.* 1970. Lancer 75-137. 1st prtg. SF. G+. R5d. $3.00

HOWARD, Robert E. *Conan the Flame Knife.* Ace 11666. 1st prtg. G+. S1d. $2.00

HOWARD, Robert E. *Conan the Freebooter.* Ace 11632. SF. F. W2d. $4.75

HOWARD, Robert E. *Conan the Freebooter.* 1968. Lancer 74-963. 1st edn. SF. F. F2d. $10.00

HOWARD, Robert E. *Conan the Usurper.* 1967. Lancer 73-599. 1st edn. c/DeCamp: sgn. SF. F. F2d. $20.00

HOWARD, Robert E. *Conan the Usurper.* 1967. Lancer 73-599. 1st edn. c/Frazetta. SF. F. F2d/M1d. $12.50

HOWARD, Robert E. *Conan the Wanderer.* 1980. Ace 11633. SF. VG. W2d. $3.50

HOWARD, Robert E. *Conan the Wanderer.* 1968. Lancer 74-976. 1st edn. c/DeCamp: sgn. SF. F. F2d. $20.00

HOWARD, Robert E. *Conan the Warrior.* Ace 11677. SF. F. W2d. $5.00

HOWARD, Robert E. *Conan the Warrior.* 1967. Lancer 73-549. 1st edn. SF. F. F2d. $10.00

HOWARD, Robert E. *Conan the Warrior.* 1967. Lancer 73-549. 1st prtg. SF. VG. R5d. $4.50

HOWARD, Robert E. *Conan.* Ace 11630. SF. F. W2d. $5.00

HOWARD, Robert E. *Conan.* Ace 11671. SF. VG. B5d. $4.00

HOWARD, Robert E. *Conan.* 1967. Lancer 73-685. 1st edn. SF. F. F2d. $10.00

HOWARD, Robert E. *Conan.* 1975. Sphere 4709. 2nd prtg. SF. VG. W2d. $5.00

HOWARD, Robert E. *Conan: People of the Black Circle.* 1977. Berkley 03609. SF. F. W2d. $8.50

HOWARD, Robert E. *Conan: Red Nails.* 1977. Berkley 03610. SF. VG. W2d. $5.00

HOWARD, Robert E. *Conan: The Hour of the Dragon.* 1977. Berkley 03608. SF. F. W2d. $4.75

HOWARD, Robert E. *Conan: The Treasure of Tranicos.* 1980. Ace 82245. SF. VG+. W2d. $5.00

HOWARD, Robert E. *Dark Man.* Lancer 75265. SF. G+. W2d. $4.50

HOWARD, Robert E. *Garden of Fear.* Crawford. VG+. B3d. $8.00

HOWARD, Robert E. *Gent From Bear Creek.* 1975. Zebra. 1st pb. VG. M1d. $5.00

HOWARD, Robert E. *Gods of Bal-Sagoth.* 1979. Ace 29525. SF. VG. W2d. $6.00

HOWARD, Robert E. *Grey God Passes.* 1975. Miller. 1st edn. c/Walt Simonson: sgn. SF. F. F2d. $25.00

HOWARD, Robert E. *Hand of Kane.* 1970. Centaur 4. c/J Jones. SF. VG+. B5d. $6.00

HOWARD, Robert E. *Incredible Adventures of Dennis Dorgan.* 1975. Zebra. 1st pb. F. M1d. $8.00

HOWARD, Robert E. *Last Ride.* 1978. Berkley 03754. We. F. W2d. $8.00

HOWARD, Robert E. *Lost Valley of Iskander.* 1976. Zebra 157. SF. G. W2d. $2.50

HOWARD, Robert E. *Lost Valley of Iskander.* 1976. Zebra 157. 1st pb. F. M1d. $8.00

HOWARD, Robert E. *Moon of Skulls.* 1969. Centaur 2. c/J Jones. SF. NF. B5d. $7.00

HOWARD, Robert E. *Pigeons From Hell.* 1979. Ace 66320. SF. VG+. W2d. $6.50

HOWARD, Robert E. *Pigeons From Hell.* Zebra 189. c/Jones. VG+. B3d. $5.50

HOWARD, Robert E. *Pigeons From Hell.* 1976. Zebra 189. PBO. c/Jeff Jones. F. B6d. $12.50

HOWARD, Robert E. *Road to Azrad.* 1980. Bantam 13326. SF. VG+. W2d. $6.50

HOWARD, Robert E. *Skulls In the Stars.* 1978. Bantam 12031. SF. G. W2d. $4.25

HOWARD, Robert E. *Solomon Kane.* 1971. Centaur 5. c/J Jones. SF. F. B5d. $9.00

HOWARD, Robert E. *Son of the White Wolf.* 1978. Berkley 03710. SF. F. W2d. $7.50

HOWARD, Robert E. *Sowers of Thunder.* 1979. Ace 77620. SF. F. W2d. $6.50

HOWARD, Robert E. *Sowers of Thunder.* 1975. Zebra 113. SF. VG. W2d. $6.25

HOWARD, Robert E. *Sword Woman.* 1977. Zebra 261. 1st pb. F. M1d. $8.00

HOWARD, Robert E. *Swords Against Darkness.* 1977. Zebra 89083. SF. F. W2d. $7.50

HOWARD, Robert E. *Swords of Shahrazar.* 1978. Berkley 03709. SF. VG. W2d. $7.50

HOWARD, Robert E. *Three-Bladed Doom.* 1987. Ace 80781. 2nd prtg. SF. VG. W2d. $6.25

HOWARD, Robert E. *Three-Headed Doom.* 1977. Ace. 1st pb. F. M1d. $6.00

HOWARD, Robert E. *Tigers of the Sea.* 1977. Zebra 89083. 5th prtg. SF. VG. B3d/W2d. $4.50

HOWARD, Robert E. *Vultures of Whapeton.* 1975. Zebra 09083. SF. G+. W2d. $6.00

HOWARD, Robert E. *Vultures of Whapeton.* 1975. Zebra 144. 1st pb. c/J Jones. VG+. B6d. $7.50

HOWARD, Robert E. *Wolfhead.* Lancer 75-299. 1st prtg. F. S1d. $6.50

HOWARD, Robert E. *Wolfshead.* 1968. Lancer 73-721. 1st edn. SF. F. F2d. $15.00

HOWARD, Robert E. *Worms of the Earth.* 1979. Ace 91770. SF. VG. W2d. $6.00

HOWARD, Robert E. *Worms of the Earth.* Zebra 124. c/Jones. VG+. B3d. $5.00

HOWARD, Robert E. *Worms of the Earth.* 1977. Zebra 234. 4th prtg. SF. G. W2d. $4.00

HOWARD, Vechel. *Murder on Her Mind.* Gold Medal 1955. 878. 1st edn. De. F. F2d. $15.00

HOWARD, Vechel. *Murder on Her Mind.* Gold Medal 878. G+. G5d. $3.50

HOWARD, Vechel. *Murder With Love.* Gold Medal 854. G+. G5d. $3.50

HOWARD, Vechel. *Murder With Love.* 1959. Gold Medal 854. 1st prtg. PBO. c/gga. VG+. P7d. $9.00

HOWARD, Vechel. *Stage to Painted Creek.* 1959. Gold Medal 943. 1st prtg. PBO. We. VG. P6d. $2.50

HOWARD, Vechel. *Tall in the West.* Gold Medal 789. VG. B3d. $5.00

HOWARD & NYBERG. *Conan the Avenger.* Lancer 75-149. SF. VG+. W2d. $4.75

HOWE, Cliff. *Lovers & Libertines.* 1958. Ace D 271. PBO. VG. P6d. $3.00

HOWE, Cliff. *Scoundrels, Fiends & Human Monsters.* 1958. Ace D 282. PBO. Nfi. G+. B5d. $2.50

HOWE, Cliff. *Scoundrels, Fiends & Human Mosters.* Ace D 282. VG. B3d. $4.00

HOWE, Margaret. *Special Nurse.* 1958. Bantam 1711. Fa. VG+. B4d. $2.00

HOWE, Quincy edt. *Pocket Book of the War.* 1941. Pocket 127. PBO. c/Silten. Nfi. VG. B5d. $5.50

HOWIE, E. *No Face to Murder.* Boardman NN. VG+. B3d. $8.00

HOYER, N. *Man Into Women.* Popular 100. VG. I1d. $4.00

HOYLE, Fred. *Black Cloud.* 1959. Signet 1673. 1st edn. PBO. F. M1d. $10.00

HOYLE, Fred. *Fifth Planet.* Gold Medal M 2873. SF. VG. W2d. $3.50

HOYLE, Fred. *Fifth Planet.* Gold Medal T 2243. 1st prtg. VG+. S1d. $4.00

HOYLE, Fred. *October the First Is Too Late.* Crest 1155. VG+. B3d. $5.00

HOYLE, Fred. *Ossian's Ride.* 1961. Berkley G 495. SF. VG. B3d/I1d/R5d. $4.00

HOYLE, Fred. *Ossian's Ride.* 1961. Berkley G 495. 1st pb. F. M1d. $10.00

HOYLE, Fred. *Ossian's Ride.* 1961. Berkley G 495. 1st prtg. G. S1d. $2.00

HOYLE, Fred. *Ossian's Ride.* 1968. Berkley X 1506. 1st prtg. SF. G+. R5d. $1.50

HOYLE, Fred. *Rockets to Ursa Major.* 1971. Crest T 1648. SF. G+. W2d. $3.00

HOYLE, Trevor. *This Sentient Earth.* 1979. Zebra 473. PBO. SF. F. B6d. $7.00

HUBBARD, L. Ron. *Dianetics.* 1982. Bridg 88404. SF. F. W2d. $4.75

HUBBARD, L. Ron. *Fear/Typewriter in the Sky.* 1977. Popular 04006. SF. G+. B5d. $8.00

HUBBARD, L. Ron. *Ole Doc Methuselah.* 1972. DAW 20. 1st prtg. VG. P7d. $7.50

HUBBARD, L. Ron. *Presents Writers of the Future.* 1986. Volumes I & II. F. M1d. $10.00

HUBBARD, L. Ron. *Return to Tomorrow.* 1954. Ace S 66. VG. B3a #22. $11.00

HUBBARD, L. Ron. *Return to Tomorrow.* 1957. Panther 697. 1st pb. SF. VG. B6d. $12.50

HUBBARD, L. Ron. *Seven Steps to the Arbiter.* 1975. Major 3018. SF. G+. W2d. $3.50

HUBBARD, L. Ron. *Slaves of Sleep.* 1979. Dell 17646. SF. VG. W2d. $5.00

HUBBARD, L. Ron. *Slaves of Sleep.* 1967. Lancer 73-573. c/K Freas. SF. VG. B5d. $10.00

HUBBARD, P.M. *Flush As May.* Ballantine U 2217. VG+. B3d. $4.00

HUBBELL, Ned. *Adventures of Creighton Holmes.* Popular 04350. VG. G5d. $8.00

HUBBELL, Ned. *Adventures of Creighton Holmes.* 1979. Popular 04350. 1st edn. scarce. My. F. F2d. $20.00

HUBLER, R.G. *Brass God.* Popular 594. VG+. B3d. $5.00

HUBLER, R.G. *Walk Into Hell.* 1963. Popular SP 229. 1st prtg. c/Hooks. VG+. P7d. $4.00

HUDIBURG, Edward. *Killers' Game.* 1956. Lion LB 137. PBO. c/Schaare. My. VG. B3d. $4.00

HUDSON, Dean. *Flesh Sisters.* Idle Hour IH 427. VG+. I1d. $5.00

HUDSON, Dean. *Hasbeen.* Leisure LB 1107. PBO. VG. M6d. $9.50

HUDSON, Dean. *Honeysuckle Rose.* 1966. Ember Library 342. PBO. c/gga. VG+. B6a #79. $101.00

HUDSON, Dean. *Shame Takers.* Leisure LB 1145. PBO. VG. M6d. $5.00

HUDSON, Dean. *Sin Sheet.* 1963. Nightstand NB 1642. Ad. NF. B5d. $65.00

HUDSON, Dean. *Twisted Tulips.* 1966. Leisure 1181. PBO. c/gga. rare. Ad/SF. F. B6a #74. $212.50

HUDSON, Edward S. *Alien Death Fleet.* 1989. Page 00688. SF. F. W2d. $3.75

HUDSON, J. *Love Cult.* 1961. Pike 205. VG+. B3a #20. $11.90

HUDSON, J. *Love Cult.* Pike 205. c/Hudson & Smith: sgn. VG. B3d. $6.50

HUDSON, Peggy. *Television Scene.* 1972. Scholastic 2109. TVTI. VG. P1d. $5.00

HUDSON, Peggy. *TV 70.* 1969. Scholastic 1495. TVTI. VG. P1d. $7.50

HUDSON, T. *Small-Town Swingers.* Barclay 7337. c/photo. F. B3d. $5.00

HUDSON, Virginia Cary. *O Ye Jigs & Juleps!* 1963. MacFadden 60-131. 1st prtg. c/Kuksin. VG. P7d. $4.00

HUDSON, W.H. *Green Mansions.* 1965. Airmont CL 87. Fa. VG+. B4d. $2.00

HUDSON, W.H. *Green Mansions.* 1959. Bantam F 1878. 1st prtg. G+. R5d. $1.25

HUDSON, W.H. *Green Mansions.* 1946. Bantam 63. Ro. VG. B4d. $5.00

HUDSON, W.H. *Green Mansions.* 1939. Pocket 16. SF. VG. B5d. $15.00

HUEBNER, Fredrick D. *Black Rose.* 1987. Gold Medal 13225. 1st edn. De. F. F2d. $7.00

HUEBNER, Fredrick D. *Judgment by Fire.* 1988. Gold Medal 13421. 1st edn. Th. F. F2d. $7.00

HUESTON, Ethel. *Calamity Jane of Deadwood Gulch.* 1951. Avon 362. c/R Johnson. We. G. B5d. $4.50

HUESTON, Ethel. *Calamity Jane of Deadwood Gulch.* 1951. Avon 362. 1st pb. F. M1d. $25.00

HUFF, Darrell & Frances. *How To Lower Your Food Bills.* 1963. MacFadden 50-168. NF. VG. B5d. $3.00

HUFF, Darrell. *Score.* 1965. Ballantine U 5043. Nfi. VG+. B4d. $2.00

HUFF, Theodore. *Charlie Chaplin.* 1964. Pyramid T 1095. 2nd prtg. Bio. VG. R5d. $2.25

HUFFAKER, C. *Guns of Rio Conchos.* Gold Medal 1459. VG. B3d. $4.00

HUFFAKER, C. *Guns of Rio Conchos.* Gold Medal 733. VG+. B3d. $5.00

HUFFAKER, C. *Rider From Thunder Mountain.* Crest 193. PBO. VG+. B3d. $4.50

HUGGINS, Roy. *Double Take.* 1948. Pocket 524. De. VG. P6d. $3.00

HUGGINS, Roy. *Lovely Lady, Pity Me.* 1951. Avon 282. c/gga: photos. VG. P6d. $8.00

HUGGINS, Roy. *Sunset Strip.* 1959. Dell 1st Edn A 176. 3rd prtg. TVTI. VG. R5d. $1.75

HUGGINS, Roy. *77 Sunset Strip.* 1959. Dell 1st Edn A 176. 1st prtg. PBO. c/Bob McGinnis: gga. VG+. P7d. $6.50

HUGHES, Dorothy B. *Bamboo Blonde.* Pocket 394. VG. B3d. $4.50

HUGHES, Dorothy B. *Blackbirder.* 1947. Dell 149. 1st pb. c/Gregg. My. VG+. B6d. $16.50

HUGHES, Dorothy B. *Candy Kid.* Pocket 845. G+. G5d. $3.25

HUGHES, Dorothy B. *Candy Kid.* Pocket 845. VG. B3d. $4.00

HUGHES, Dorothy B. *Cross-Eyed Bear Murders.* Dell 48. G+. I1d. $4.00

HUGHES, Dorothy B. *Cross-Eyed Bear Murders.* 1944. Dell 48. VG. B3a #20. $10.00

HUGHES, Dorothy B. *Delicate Ape.* 1946. Pocket 422. 1st pb. My. VG+. B6d. $12.50

HUGHES, Dorothy B. *Dread Journey.* Pocket 454. 1st pb. VG. M6d. $4.00

HUGHES, Dorothy B. *Dread Journey.* 1947. Pocket 454. 1st pb. My. NF. B6d. $16.50

HUGHES, Dorothy B. *Expendable Man.* 1964. Avon S 161. 1st pb. My. NF. B6d. $8.00

HUGHES, Dorothy B. *Fallen Sparrow.* Dell 31. VG. B3d. $6.50

HUGHES, Dorothy B. *In a Lonely Place.* 1979. Bantam 12114. 1st prtg. c/Bogart. My. VG. W2d. $4.00

HUGHES, Dorothy B. *Johnnie.* Bonded 11. G+. G5d. $7.00

HUGHES, Dorothy B. *Ride the Pink Horse.* Dell D 225. NF. B3d. $4.50

HUGHES, Dorothy B. *Ride the Pink Horse.* Dell 210. G. G5d. $3.00

HUGHES, Dorothy B. *Ride the Pink Horse.* 1946. Dell 210. 1st pb. c/Gregg. My. VG. B6d. $7.00

HUGHES, Dorothy B. *Ride the Pink Horse.* 1988. Penguin CC 10386. 1st prtg. My. F. W2d. $4.50

HUGHES, Dorothy B. *So Blue Marble.* Dell 100. VG. G5d. $10.00

HUGHES, Dorothy B. *So Blue Marble.* Dell 100. 1st prtg. My. G+. R5d. $7.50

HUGHES, Helen MacBill edt. *Fantastic Lodge.* 1964. Monarch 459. c/photo: Ad. VG. B5d. $7.50

HUGHES, Richard. *High Wind in Jamaica.* Four Square 60. VG. B3d. $6.00

HUGHES, Richard. *High Wind in Jamaica.* 1965. Signet P 2648. 1st prtg. VG+. R5d. $3.00

HUGHES, Robert D. *Prophet of Lamath.* 1979. Ballantine 28211. 1st prtg. SF. VG+. W2d. $4.25

HUGHES, Robert D. *Wizard in Waiting.* 1982. Ballantine 28574. 1st prtg. SF. VG+. W2d. $3.50

HUGHES, Zach. *Killbird.* 1980. Signet 9263. PBO. SF. NF. B6d. $3.00

HUGHES, Zach. *Seed of the Gods.* 1974. Berkley O2642. c/V DiFate. SF. VG+. B5d. $3.50

HUGHES, Zach. *Stork Factor.* 1975. Berkley N 2781. 1st prtg. SF. VG. R5d. $1.50

HUGHES, Zach. *Tiger in the Stars.* 1976. Laser 72049. SF. F. W2d. $6.00

HUGO, Victor. *Hunchback of Notre Dame.* 1957. Avon T 190. MTI. VG. B4d. $7.00

HUGO, Victor. *Hunchback of Notre Dame.* 1956. Bantam F 1526. Fa. VG. B4d. $2.75

HUIE, William Bradford. *Americanization of Emily.* Signet S 1825. VG. I1d. $4.00

HUIE, William Bradford. *Execution of Private Slovik.* 1954. Signet I 1113. Nti. VG. B3d. $4.00

HUIE, William Bradford. *Mud on the Stars.* 1955. Signet S1162. c/C Hulings. Fi. VG. B3d/B5d. $4.00

HUIE, William Bradford. *Revolt of Mamie Stover.* Signet 959. VC. B3d. $4.50

HULBURD, David. *H Is For Heroin.* 1953. Popular 495. JD. VG. P1d. $17.50

HULBURD, David. *H Is for Heroin.* 1953. Popular 495. 1st edn. PBO. c/DeSoto. VG+. B6a #79. $50.00

HULKE, Malcolm. *Dinosaur Invasion.* 1984. Pinnacle 42498. 5th prtg. Doctor Who #3. SF. F. W2d. $5.00

HULL, E.M. *Sheik.* Dell 1174. 2nd edn. MTI. c/Valentino & Parker: photo. My. G+. B5d. $6.00

HULL, E.M. *Sons of the Sheik.* Dell 279. c/F Giles. F. VG. B5d. $5.00

HULL, Richard. *Murder of My Aunt.* Pocket 381. VG+. G5d. $8.50

HULL, Richard. *My Own Murderer.* Signet 526. c/Peng. VG. B3d. $6.00

HULL & VAN VOGT. *Planets for Sale.* 1965. Book Co of America 14. c/Van Vogt: sgn. VG+. B3d. $7.50

HULL & VAN VOGT. *Planets for Sale.* 1965. Book Co of America 14. 1st edn. PBO. G. P9d. $1.25

HULME, Kathryn. *Nun's Story.* 1958. Cardinal GC 54. 1st prtg. VG. R5d. $1.75

HULME, Kathryn. *Nun's Story.* 1960. Great Pan G 291. 4th prtg. VG. R5d. $2.00

HUME, Doris. *Sin of Susan Slade.* 1961. Dell 1st Edn K 104. 1st prtg. G+. R5d. $2.25

HUMPHRIES, A. *Lady Doctor.* Popular K 69. VG. B3d. $4.00

HUMPHRIES, R. *New Poems by American Poets.* Ballantine 39. PBO. VG+. B3d. $5.00

HUNEKER, James. *Painted Veils.* Avon T 260. VG+. B3d. $4.50

HUNEKER, James. *Painted Veils.* 1973. Avon T 71. VG+. B3d. $6.00

HUNT, Gill. *Galactic Storm.* Curtis Warren. NF. B3a. $44.00

HUNT, Howard. *Dark Encounter.* Signet 768. VG. I1d. $3.00

HUNT, Howard. *Lovers Are Losers.* 1953. Gold Medal 297. c/gga. Fa. VG. B4d. $4.00

HUNT, Howard. *On Hazardous Duty.* 1965. Signet 2684. 1st edn. De. F. F2d. $14.00

HUNT, Howard. *Violent Ones.* 1958. Gold Medal 738. 1st prtg. c/gga. VG+. P7d. $6.00

HUNT, Howard. *Where Murder Waits.* 1973. Gold Medal M 2857. My. VG+. B5d. $5.00

HUNT, Howard. *Whisper Her Name.* 1952. Gold Medal 268. PBO. My. NF. B6d. $16.50

HUNT, Howard. *Whisper Her Name.* 1952. Gold Medal 268. 1st prtg. PBO. c/gga. VG. P7d. $7.50

HUNT, Kyle. *Kill a Wicked Man.* 1958. Signet 1573. My. VG. B5d. $4.00

HUNT, Kyle. *Kill Once, Kill Twice.* 1957. Signet 1472. 1st prtg. c/Maguire: gga. VG. P7d. $5.00

HUNT, Kyle. *Kill Once, Kill Twice.* 1957. Signet 1472. 1st edn. PBO. c/Maguire: gga. F. F2d. $8.00

HUNT, Morton M. *Mental Hospital.* 1952. Pyramid R 762. Nfi. F. B4d. $5.00

HUNTER, A.A. *Courage in Both Hands.* Ballantine 645. c/inscr. VG. B3d. $5.00

HUNTER, Alan B. *Gently Go Man.* 1963. Pan G 612. 1st pb. JD. My. VG+. B6d. $15.00

HUNTER, Edward. *Brainwashing.* 1961. Pyramid R612. c/M Crair. Fi. VG+. B5d. $5.50

HUNTER, Evan *Evil Sleep.* 1952. Falcon 41. 1st edn. scarce. My. F. F2d. $155.00

HUNTER, Evan. *Blackboard Jungle.* 1976. Avon 31260. JD. VG. P1d. $5.00

HUNTER, Evan. *Blackboard Jungle.* 1955. Cardinal C 187. 1st prtg. MTI. My. G. R5d. $1.25

HUNTER, Evan. *Blackboard Jungle.* 1966. Dell 0579. JD. VG. P1d. $8.00

HUNTER, Evan. *Don't Crowd Me.* 1953. Popular 478. PBO. c/Popp. My. VG. B6d. $7.50

HUNTER, Evan. *I Like 'Em Tough.* 1958. Gold Medal 743. 1st edn. My. NF. F2d. $15.00

HUNTER, Evan. *Jungle Kids.* 1967. Dell 4331. JD. VG. P1d. $10.00

HUNTER, Evan. *Jungle Kids.* Pocket 1126. VG+. B3d. $7.50

HUNTER, Evan. *Jungle Kids.* 1956. Pocket 1126. PBO. c/Tom Dunn. JD. VG. P6d. $6.00

HUNTER, Evan. *Jungle Kids.* 1956. Pocket 1126. 1st edn. scarce. JD. F. F2d. $30.00

HUNTER, Evan. *Killer's Wedge.* 1959. Perma M 4150. 1st edn. My. F. F2d. $14.00

HUNTER, Evan. *Matter of Conviction.* 1960. Cardinal GC 94. MTI. c/Burt Lancaster: photo. VG. B4d. $2.00

HUNTER, Evan. *Mothers & Daughters.* 1962. Cardinal GC 606. 1st prtg. c/Hill: gga. VG. P7d. $4.00

HUNTER, Evan. *Murder in the Navy.* 1955. Gold Medal 507. 1st edn. scarce. My. F. F2d. $30.00

HUNTER, Evan. *Pusher.* 1956. Perma 3062. 1st edn. My. F. F2d. $15.00

HUNTER, Evan. *So Nude, So Dead.* 1956. Crest 139. 1st edn. PBO. My. F. F2d. $20.00

HUNTER, Evan. *Spiked Heel.* 1957. Crest 178. 1st pb edn. c/gga. F. F2d. $12.00

HUNTER, Evan. *Tomorrow & Tomorrow.* 1956. Pyramid G 214. 1st edn. PBO. SF. F. F2d. $15.00

HUNTER, Evan. *Vanishing Ladies.* 1957. Perma M 3097. 1st edn. My. NF. F2d. $20.00

HUNTER, Georgiana. *Girl on the Couch.* 1956. Pyramid 200. PBO. c/photo. Fi. VG. B5d. $5.00

HUNTER, J. *Case of Defaulting Sailor.* Sexton Blake 118. VG+. B3d. $9.00

HUNTER, J. *Case of the Stolen Ransom.* Sexton Blake 320. VG. B3d. $5.00

HUNTER, J.A. *Hunter.* 1955. Bantam A 1391. 1st pb. VG. B6d. $5.00

HUNTER, Jack D. *One of Us Works for Them.* 1968. Bantam S 3633. 1st prtg. My. VG+. R5d. $2.25

HUNTER, John. *Ride the Wind South.* 1957. Perma M 3092. PBO. c/T Ryan. We. VG+. B5d. $4.50

HUNTER, Karen. *House of Love.* 1967. PB Library 54-563. 1st edn. c/gga. F. F2d. $8.00

HUNTER, Samuel. *Modern American Painting & Sculpture.* Dell LY 102. VG. B3d. $6.00

HUNTER, W. *Man on the Make.* Playtime 649. VG+. B3d. $5.00

HUNTINGTON, Charlie. *Nightmare on Vega 3.* 1972. Award A 51045. 1st edn. NF. P9d. $2.00

HUNTLEY, Tim. *One More on Me.* 1980. DAW. 1st edn. F. M1d. $5.00

HURLEY, Richard J edt. *Beyond Belief.* 1969. Scholastic 573. SF. VG+. B5d. $3.00

HURST, Fannie. *Back Street.* 1961. Perma M 5037. 1st prtg. VG. R5d. $2.25

HURST, Fannie. *Imitation of Life.* 1959. Perma M 4124. 1st prtg. VG. R5d. $3.25

HURST, Fannie. *Lummox.* 1946. Popular 101. 1st prtg. VG+. P7d. $9.00

HURST, Fannie. *Name Is Mary.* Dell 10¢ 14. VG+. B3d. $7.00

HURWOOD, B.J. *Eerie Tales of Terror & Dread.* 1973. Scholastic 2327. SF. F. W2d. $4.25

HURWOOD, B.J. *Invisibles.* 1971. Gold Medal T 2449. SF. VG. W2d. $3.75

HURWOOD, B.J. *Mind Master.* 1973. Gold Medal T 2670. SF. VG+. B5d. $4.00

HURWOOD, B.J. *Monstrous Undead.* 1969. Lancer 75-085. Nfi. VG. B5d. $7.50

HURWOOD, B.J. *Strange Lives.* 1966. Popular 50453. Nfi. VG. W2d. $4.00

HURWOOD, B.J. *Strange Talents.* 1967. Ace H 276. Nfi. VG. W2d. $4.00

HURWOOD, B.J. *Strange Talents.* 1967. Ace K 276. 1st edn. F. F2d. $6.00

HURWOOD, B.J. *Terror by Night.* Lancer 72-656. VG. B3d. $4.00

HURWOOD, B.J. *Terror by Night.* 1963. Lancer 72-656. 1st edn. F. M1d. $7.00

HURWOOD, B.J. *Vampires, Werewolves & Other Demons.* 1975. Scholastic 1976. 2nd edn. Nfi. VG+. B5d. $3.50

HUTCHINS, Maude. *Diary of Love.* Pyramid 130. VG. B3d. $4.00

HUTCHINS, Maude. *Diary of Love.* 1952. Pyramid 49. Fa. VG+. B4d. $7.50

HUTCHINS, Maude. *Honey on the Moon.* 1965. Pocket 50111. Fi. VG+. B5d. $4.00

HUTCHINSON, A.S.M. *If Winter Comes.* 1947. Pocket 486. MTI. VG+. B4d. $7.00

HUTCHINSON, A.S.M. *If Winter Comes.* 1947. Pocket 486. 1st prtg. G+. R5d. $3.00

HUTTON, Denise. *Nymphomaniac.* 1973. Cameo CC 157. Ad. G+. B5d. $4.50

HUXLEY, Aldous. *After Many a Summer Dies the Swan.* 1952. Avon AT 435. SF. NF. B5d. $14.00

HUXLEY, Aldous. *After Many a Summer Dies the Swan.* 1954. Avon T 75. 2nd edn. SF. VG. B5d. $3.50

HUXLEY, Aldous. *After the Fireworks.* 1957. Avon T 160. Fa. VG. B4d. $2.25

HUXLEY, Aldous. *Antic Hay.* 1953. Bantam 1142. Fa. VG. B4d. $3.00

HUXLEY, Aldous. *Ape & Essence.* 1958. Bantam A 1793. 1st pb. SF. VG. B6d. $6.00

HUXLEY, Aldous. *Brave New World.* 1952. Bantam A 1071. 1st pb. c/Binger. SF. VG. M1d. $10.00

HUXLEY, Aldous. *Crome Yellow.* 1954. Bantam A 1260. Fa. VG. B4d. $4.00

HUXLEY, Aldous. *Genius & the Goddess.* 1963. Bantam F 2670. 3rd edn. Fi. VG+. B5d. $3.50

HUXLEY, Aldous. *Point Counter Point.* Avon G 1020. VG. B3d. $6.00

HUXLEY, Aldous. *Those Barren Leaves.* 1957. Avon G 1027. Fa. VG. B4d. $2.75

HUXLEY, Aldous. *Time Must Have a Stop.* 1948. Berkley BG 66. c/R Maguire. SF. G+. B5d. $4.00

HUXLEY, Elspeth. *African Poison Murders.* Popular 100. NF. I1d. $12.00

HUXLEY, Elspeth. *Murder on Safari.* 1990. Penguin 11296. 1st prtg. My. F. W2d. $4.25

HUXLEY, L.A. *You Are Not the Target.* Crest 815. VG+. B3d. $4.50

HYDE, H. Montgomery. *History of Pornography.* 1966. Dell 3611. 1st prtg. VG+. P7d. $4.50

HYDE, H. Montgomery. *Room 3603.* Dell 7590. G+. G5d. $3.50

HYE, Celia. *I Made My Bed.* 1958. Beacon 188. PBO. c/photo. scarce. JD. VG+. B6a #79. $75.00

HYE, Celia. *I Made My Bed.* 1958. Beacon 188. PBO. c/photo: scarce. JD. NF. B6a #74. $88.00

HYMAN, Mac. *No Time for Sergeants.* 1956. Signet S 1285. MTI. VG+. B4d. $4.00

HYMAN, Mac. *No Time For Sergeants.* 1956. Signet S 1285. 1st pb. NF. B6d. $8.00

HYND, Alan. *Case of the Burning Bride.* Avon 604. G. G5d. $2.50

HYND, Alan. *Pinkerton Case Book.* Signet 667. c/Jonas. VG. B3d. $5.50

HYND, Alan. *Public Enemies.* 1949. Gold Medal 101. PBO. VG. B6d. $12.50

HYND, Alan. *Violence in the Night.* 1955. Gold Medal 473. 1st edn. c/gga. My. F. F2d. $15.00

HYND, Noel. *Revenge.* 1978. Dell 17442. 1st prtg. My. VG. W2d. $3.00

HYNE, Cutcliffe. *Lost Continent.* 1972. Ballantine O 2502. 1st edn. NF. M1d. $10.00

HYNE, Cutcliffe. *Lost Continent.* 1972. Ballantine 02502. 1st prtg. SF. G. R5d. $1.50

HYTES, Jason. *Never Enough.* 1963. Midwood F 237. PBO. c/Rader: gga. NF. B6a #80. $61.00

HYTES, Jason. *Never Enough.* 1967. Midwood 34-7830. Ad. NF. B5d. $6.00

HYTES, Jason. *One Last Fling.* Midwood F 368. reprint. F. B6d. $15.00

HYTES, Jason. *One-Way Ticket.* Midwood 195. PBO. VG. B3d. $4.50

HYTES, Jason. *Over-Exposed.* 1962. Midwood F 207. PBO. c/Rader: gga. scarce. VG+. B6a #80. $42.50

HYTES, Jason. *Over-Exposed.* Midwood 207. PBO. c/Rader. VG+. B3d. $6.00

HYTES, Jason. *Over-Exposed.* Midwood 32-555. G+. G5d. $5.00

HYTES, Jason. *Secret Session (Doctor & the Dyke).* Midwood 32-527. 2nd prtg. VG. B3d. $5.00

HYTES, Jason. *Street Walker.* Midwood F 375. PBO. G+. M6d. $6.50

HYTES, Jason. *Time of Torment.* Midwood 302. VG. B3d. $4.00

HYTES, Jason. *Twice With Julie.* Midwood 188. PBO. VG+. B3d. $10.00

HYTES, Jason. *Twice With Julie.* 1962. Midwood 188. PBO. c/Maguire. NF. B3a #24. $27.50

HYTES, Jason. *Wait Your Turn.* 1962. Midwood F 216. PBO. c/gga. VG+. B6d. $16.50

HYTES, Jason. *Wild Week.* 1963. Midwood D 231. PBO. c/Rader. rare. VG+. B6a #77. $105.00

HYTES/KEMP. *Immoral/Forbidden.* 1964. Midwood S 338. PBO. VG+. B6d. $15.00

HYTES/KEMP. *Perfumed/Pampered.* 1963. Midwood S 277. PBO. scarce. VG+. B6a #75. $82.50

IAMS, Jack. *Body Missed the Boat.* Dell 274. VG. B3d. $4.00

IAMS, Jack. *Death Draws the Line.* Dell 457. 1st pb. VG. B3d/M6d. $5.00

IAMS, Jack. *Do Not Murder Before Christmas.* Dell 514. VG. I1d. $5.00

IAMS, Jack. *Girl Meets Body.* Dell 384. VG+. G5d. $9.00

IAMS, Jack. *Love & the Countess to Boot.* Dell 139. VG. G5d. $4.50

IAMS, Jack. *Shot of Murder.* 1953. Dell 722. My. VG. G5d. $5.00

IAMS, Jack. *Shot of Murder.* 1953. Dell 722. 1st prtg. c/gga. VG+. P7d. $7.50

IAMS, Jack. *Slight Case of Scandal.* 1950. Lion 46. c/Van Kaufman: gga. G+. P6d. $2.50

IAMS, Jack. *What Rhymes With Murder?* Dell 631. G+. G5d. $7.00

IANNUZZI, J.N. *What's Happening.* PB Library 53261. VG. I1d. $6.00

IBANEZ, Vincente Blasco. *Blood & Sand.* 1951. Dell 500. 1st prtg. c/gga. VG+. P7d. $7.50

IBANEZ, Vincente Blasco. *Four Horsemen of the Apocalypse.* 1961. Dell S 23. 1st prtg. VG. R5d. $2.50

IDELL, Albert. *This Woman.* Gold Medal 1479. c/Barye. VG. B3d. $4.50

IDELL, Albert. *This Woman.* Gold Medal 953. 2nd prtg. c/Barye. VG+. B3d. $5.00

IDELL, Albert. *This Woman.* 1952. Red Seal 9. 1st edn. c/gga. F. F2d. $15.00

ILES, Frances. *Before the Fact.* 1958. Dell D 215. 1st prtg. My. G. R5d. $1.00

ILES, Frances. *Before the Fact.* 1947. Pocket 419. MTI. VG. P6d. $3.00

ILES, Frances. *Malice Aforethought.* Pan 46. VG. B3d. $10.00

ILES, Francis. *Malice Aforethought.* Pocket 432. G. G5d. $3.75

ILES, Francis. *Malice Aforethought.* 1947. Pocket 432. 1st pb. My. VG+. B6d. $12.50

ILTON, Paul. *Secret of Mary Magdalene.* 1956. Signet 1301. PBO. c/J Avati. Fi. VG. B5d. $5.50

ING, Dean. *Soft Targets.* 1986. Ace 77407. 2nd prtg. SF. F. W2d. $3.25

INGE, William. *Bus Stop.* Bantam 1518. 3rd prtg. VG. R5d. $4.00

INGE, William. *Dark at the Top of the Stars.* 1960. Bantam A 2164. MTI. VG. G5d/R5d. $2.50

INGE, William. *Picnic.* Bantam 1457. MTI. VG. B3d. $3.50

INGERSOLL, Ralph. *Great Ones.* Popular 248. VG. B3d. $5.00

INGERSOLL, Ralph. *Wine of Violence.* 1952. Popular 401. c/George Rozen: gga. VG. P6d. $3.00

INGLES, James W. *Woman of Samaria.* Popular 299. VG. B3d. $6.00

INGLES, James W. *Woman of Samaria.* 1950. Popular 299. 1st edn. PBO. c/gga. F2d. $50.00

INGRID, Charles. *Return Fire.* 1989. DAW 88677. Sand War #5. SF. F. W2d. $4.25

INNES, Hammond. *Air Bridge.* Bantam 1125. VG. G5d. $4.50

INNES, Hammond. *Angry Mountain.* Ballantine F 642. Fi. VG. B5d. $3.50

INNES, Hammond. *Blue Ice.* 1962. Ballantie 615. 1st prtg. My. VG+. R5d. $5.00

INNES, Hammond. *Campbell's Kingdom.* 1956. Bantam 1516. 1st prtg. My. VG. R5d. $2.00

INNES, Hammond. *Doomed Oasis.* 1963. Dell 1st Edn 2133. 1st pb. VG+. B6d. $3.50

INNES, Hammond. *Fire in the Snow.* 1949. Bantam 364. o/R Doares. My. G. B5d. $3.00

INNES, Hammond. *Gale Warning.* Ballantine F 614. Fi. VG. B5d. $3.50

INNES, Hammond. *Gale Warning.* Bantam 741. VG. B3d. $4.00

INNES, Hammond. *Land God Gave to Cain.* 1970. Avon V 2371. 1st prtg. My. VG. R5d. $1.50

INNES, Hammond. *Trojan Horse.* Pan 335. NF. B3d. $8.00

INNES, Michael. *Appleby on Ararat.* 1964. Berkley F 947. My. VG. B5d. $4.00

INNES, Michael. *Bloody Wood.* 1967. Berkley X 1415. 1st pb. My. VG+. B6d. $9.00

INNES, Michael. *Bloody Wood.* 1986. Perennial P 811. 1st prtg. My. VG+. W2d. $3.50

INNES, Michael. *Case of the Journeying Boy.* 1950. Pocket 741. My. VG. B5d. $5.00

INNES, Michael. *Crabtree Affair.* 1963. Berkley F 820. 1st pb. My. NF. B6d. $12.50

INNES, Michael. *Daffodil Affair.* 1964. Berkley F 925. 1st pb. My. VG+. B6d. $9.00

INNES, Michael. *Death by Moonlight.* Avon 752. My. VG. B5d. $4.00

INNES, Michael. *Hare Sitting Up.* 1964. Berkley F 958. 1st pb. My. VG. B6d. $7.00

INNES, Michael. *Long Farewell.* 1963. Berkley F 821. 1st pb. My. VG+. B6d. $9.00

INNES, Michael. *Man From the Sea.* 1964. Avon G 1247. 1st prtg. VG+. P7d. $4.00

INNES, Michael. *Murder Is an Art.* 1959. Avon T 351. My. VG. B5d. $3.00

INNES, Michael. *Night of Errors.* 1963. Berkley F 833. 1st pb. My. NF. B6d. $12.50

INNES, Michael. *One Man Show.* 1983. Perennial P 672. c/I Freeman. My. VG+. B5d. $4.00

INNES, Michael. *Silence Observed.* 1964. Berkley F 915. 1st prtg. My. G+. R5d. $2.25

INOGUCHI, R. *Divine Wind.* Four Square 303. c/Jap pilot. NF. B3d. $9.00

IRISH, William. *After-Dinner Story.* Armed Services S20. VG+. B3a #20. $48.40

IRISH, William. *And So to Death.* Jonathan J 31. VG. G5d. $25.00

IRISH, William. *Borrowed Crime.* 1946. Avon Murder My 42. PBO. extremely scarce. VG+. B6a #77. $242.00

IRISH, William. *Borrowed Crime.* 1946. Avon Murder My 42. PBO. My. G+. D5d. $35.00

IRISH, William. *Borrowed Crime.* Murder My Monthly 42. NF. C5d. $90.00

IRISH, William. *Dancing Detective.* 1951. Popular 309. 1st edn. PBO. c/Belarski. scarce. VG+. B6a #80. $121.50

IRISH, William. *Dancing Detective.* 1951. Popular 309. 1st edn. PBO. c/Belarski: gga. VG+. B6a #75. $48.50

IRISH, William. *Dead Man Blues.* Mercury Mystery 135. VG. G5d. $20.00

IRISH, William. *Dead Man Blues.* 1947. Mercury Mystery 135. PBO. scarce. VG+. B6a #80. $49.50

IRISH, William. *Deadline at Dawn.* 1949. Graphic 16. 1st edn. PBO. extremely scarce. B6a #77. $55.00

IRISH, William. *Deadly Night Call.* Graphic 81. G+. I1d. $4.00

IRISH, William. *Deadly Night Call.* 1954. Graphic 81. c/gga. reprints Graphic 31. My. VG+. B4d. $16.00

IRISH, William. *I Married a Dead Man.* 1949. Avon 220. 1st edn. PBO. rare. VG+. B6a #80. $97.00

IRISH, William. *I Wouldn't Be in Your Shoes.* Mercury 82. G. G5d. $17.50

IRISH, William. *If I Should Die Before I Wake.* 1946. Avon 104. VG. B3a #20. $25.55

IRISH, William. *If I Should Die Before I Wake.* 1946. Avon 104. VG. B3d/B6d. $15.00

IRISH, William. *Marihuana.* 1951. Dell 10¢ 11. PBO. c/Fleming. rare. My. VG+. B6a #75. $182.50

IRISH, William. *Marihuana.* 1951. Dell 10¢ 11. PBO. VG. B6d. $150.00

IRISH, William. *Mystery Storyteller.* 1946. Avon 86. PBO. VG. B6d. $16.50

IRISH, William. *Night Has a 1000 Eyes.* 1953. Del 679. VG. l1d. $25.00

IRISH, William. *Night Has a 1000 Eyes.* 1953. Dell 679. c/T Shoemaker. My. G+. B5d. $15.00

IRISH, William. *Nightmare.* Readers Choice 12. G+. B3d. $4.50

IRISH, William. *Nightmare.* Readers Choice 12. VG. l1d. $15.00

IRISH, William. *Nightmare.* 1950. Readers Choice 12. VG+. B3a #22. $46.20

IRISH, William. *Phantom Lady.* 1957. Dell D 207. 1st prtg. My. VG+. R5d. $6.00

IRISH, William. *Phantom Lady.* Graphic 108. VG. l1d. $8.00

IRISH, William. *Phantom Lady.* 1944. Pocket 253. 1st prtg. c/Manso. VG. P7d. $15.00

IRISH, William. *Six Nights of Mystery.* Popular 258. G+. G5d. $30.00

IRISH, William. *Six Nights of Mystery.* 1950. Popular 258. VG. B3a #22. $30.80

IRISH, William. *Six Times Death.* Popular 137. rare. VG+. B6a #79. $122.50

IRISH, William. *Six Times Death.* 1948. Popular 137. VG+. B3a #24. $22.00

IRISH, William. *Waltz Into Darkness.* 1954. Ace D 40. 1st edn. PBO. scarce. NF. B6a #76. $101.00

IRISH, William. *You'll Never See Me Again.* 1951. Dell 10¢ 26. PBO. c/Stanley. scarce. NF. B6a #75. $75.00

IRISH, William. *You'll Never See Me Again.* 1951. Dell 10¢ 26. PBO. VG+. B3a #20. $58.25

IRISH, William. *You'll Never See Me Again.* 1951. Dell 10¢ 26. VG. B3a #21. $52.25

IRVING, Alexander. *Bitter Ending.* 1949. Dell 289. c/F Kenwood Giles. My. VG. B3d. $6.00

IRVING, Clifford. *Losers.* 1959. Popular G 311. c/gga. JD. VG+. B4d. $7.00

IRWIN, Amy. *Gay Way.* 1965. Brandon 727. VG+. B3a #21. $19.00

IRWIN, Amy. *Paula's Girls.* 1965. Brandon 724. c/Brandon. VG+. B3a #24. $16.50

IRWIN, I.H. *Woman Swore Revenge.* Boardman 90. VG. B3d. $15.00

IRWIN, T.D. *Collusion.* Hillman 18. VG. B3d. $5.00

IRWIN & LOVE. *Best of Star Trek #12.* Signet AE 4935. F. P9d. $2.50

IRWIN & LOVE. *Best of Star Trek #13.* Signet AE 5325. F. P9d. $2.50

ISHERWOOD, Christopher. *Goodbye to Berlin.* Signet 1252. MTI. 2nd prtg. VG. B3d. $6.00

ISHERWOOD, Christopher. *Goodbye to Berlin.* 1952. Signet 937. 1st prtg. c/Avati: gga. VG. P7d. $5.00

ISHERWOOD, Christopher. *Last of Mr Norris.* 1952. Avon 448. Fi. G+. B5d. $3.00

ISHERWOOD, Christopher. *Last of Mr Norris.* Berkley G 153. c/Maguire. VG+. l1d. $7.00

ISRAEL, C.E. *Mark.* Pan G 346. MTI. VG+. B3d. $10.00

ISYURHASH & RUSOFF. *Gourmet Guide to Grass.* 1974. Pinnacle 0230463. 1st prtg. c/photo. VG+. P7d. $5.00

IVERSEN, W. *Pious Pornographers.* Mac-Fadden 60-195. VG+. B3d. $4.50

IVES, Morgan. *Spare Her Heaven.* 1963. Monarch 325. PBO. Ad. G+. B5d. $27.50

JACKSON, Charles. *Cheat.* Belmont L 505. PBO. NF. B3d. $5.00

JACKSON, Charles. *Earthly Creatures.* 1953. Ballantine 36. PBO. c/Maguire. VG+. B6d. $10.00

JACKSON, Charles. *Fall of Valor.* 1949. Signet 715. Fa. VG+. B4d. $12.50

JACKSON, Charles. *Lost Weekend.* 1948. Signet 683. c/Ray Milland. Fa. VG+. B4d. $16.00

JACKSON, Charles. *Outer Edges.* 1950. Signet 781. c/Avati. My. VG. B4d. $3.00

JACKSON, Charles. *Sunnier Side.* Dell 504. c/G Meyers. Fi. G+. B5d. $3.00

JACKSON, Charles. *Thread of Evil.* 1957. Lion LL 105. 1st prtg. c/Marchetti. VG. P7d. $5.00

JACKSON, Charles. *Thread of Evil.* 1957. Lion LL 143. NF. B4d. $12.50

JACKSON, Delmar. *Night Is My Undoing.* 1954. Popular 599. c/gga. Fa. VG. B3d. $4.00

JACKSON, Felix. *Strange Affair.* Popular G 281. VG. B3d. $4.50

JACKSON, Giles. *Court of Shadows.* 1944. Handi-Book 25. 1st edn. PBO. rare. NF. B6a #75. $40.00

JACKSON, Joseph. *San Francisco Murders.* 1948. Bantam 354. 1st pb. Cr. VG+. B6d. $9.00

JACKSON, L. *Case of Discharged Policeman.* Sexton Blake 195. VG. B3d. $8.50

JACKSON, L. *Case of Night Lorry Driver.* Sexton Blake 126. VG. B3d. $8.00

JACKSON, L. *Case of the Fatal Souvenir.* Sexton Blake 119. VG+. B3d. $9.00

JACKSON, L. *Crime on the Cliff.* Sexton Blake 136. VG. B3d. $10.00

JACKSON, L. *Trail of Five Red Herrings.* Sexton Blake 101. VG. B3d. $14.00

JACKSON, Norman. *Fanny for Free.* 1969. Lancer 73-828. c/gga. Fa. NF. B4d. $6.00

JACKSON, R. *Fighter Aces of WW2.* 1978. Corgi 10783. c/Knight. NF. B3d. $7.50

JACKSON, Shirley. *Bird's Nest.* Ace 06235. Fi. VG. B5d. $3.00

JACKSON, Shirley. *Hangsaman.* 1976. Popular 03117. c/noose. Fi. VG. B5d. $4.00

JACKSON, Shirley. *Haunting of Hill House.* Popular 75-8107. 1st prtg. G+. R5d. $1.50

JACKSON, Shirley. *Life Among the Savages.* 1955. Perma M 3004. 1st pb. NF. B6d. $12.00

JACKSON, Shirley. *Life Among the Savages.* 1955. Perma M 3004. 1st prtg. VG. B3d/P7d. $5.00

JACKSON, Shirley. *Lizzie.* 1957. Signet. 1st pb. VG. M1d. $10.00

JACKSON, Shirley. *Lottery.* 1950. Lion 14. VG. B3a #20. $33.75

JACKSON, Shirley. *Road Through the Wall.* 1950. Lion 36. 1st pb. VG. B6d. $9.00

JACKSON, Shirley. *Sundial.* 1962. Ace K 166. SF. VG+. B4d. $3.00

JACKSON, Shirley. *We Have Always Lived in the Castle.* Popular 60-2137. SF. VG. B5d. $3.50

JACKSON, Shirley. *We Have Always Lived in the Castle.* Popular 75-8106. 1st pb. F. M1d. $8.00

JACKSON, W. *Cavern of Rage.* Newsstand U 143. 2nd prtg. NF. B3d. $7.00

JACKSON, Warner. *Lust for Youth.* 1960. Newsstand 519. VG+. B3d. $5.00

JACKSON, Warner. *Lust for Youth.* 1960. Newsstand 519. 1st edn. F. F2d. $13.50

JACKSON & OFFORD. *Girl in the Belfry.* 1957. Gold Medal S 688. c/Richard Powers. SF. VG. P6d. $6.00

JACOBI, Carl. *Revelations in Black.* 1979. Jove Y 4744. 1st prtg. SF. VG. R5d. $2.00

JACOBS, Bruce. *Baseball Stars of 1954.* 1954. Lion 194. PBO. scarce. VG. B6a #80. $82.50

JACOBS, Bruce. *Baseball Stars of 1957.* 1957. Lion Library 150. PBO. rare. NF. B6a #80. $115.00

JACOBS, Bruce. *Depraved Sex Circus.* Bentley 187. NF. B3d. $4.00

JACOBS, Bruce. *Korea's Heroes.* 1953. Lion 172. Nfi. VG. B4d. $6.00

JACOBS, Edward R. *Gay Boy.* Nite Time 123. PBO. Ad. VG. B5d. $7.50

JACOBS & CLARKE. *Mad's Believe It or Nuts!* Warner 31-475. VG+. B3d. $4.00

JACQUIN, Lee. *Wife & the Wolf.* Knickerbocker NN. VG. B3d. $4.00

JADE, George. *Wolf Woman.* 1963. Boudoir 1043. PBO. My. VG. B6d. $6.00

JAEDIKER, Kermit. *Hero's Lust.* 1953. Lion 156. PBO. c/Marchetti: gga. scarce. NF. B6a #75. $44.00

JAEDIKER, Kermit. *Tall, Dark & Dead.* Lion 51. G. G5d. $5.00

JAEDIKER, Kermit. *Tall, Dark & Dead.* 1951. Lion 51. c/Maguire. NF. B3a #21. $30.00

JAHN, Michael. *Switch.* 1976. Star 39881. TVTI. VG. P1d. $5.00

JAHN, Mike. *Secret of Bigfoot Pass.* 1976. Berkley Z 3307. 1st prtg. TVTI. SF. VG. R5d. $1.75

JAHN, Mike. *Switch.* 1976. Berkley Z 3082. 1st prtg. TVTI. VG. R5d. $1.75

JAHN, Mike. *Wine, Women & War.* 1975. Warner 76-833. 1st prtg. VG. R5d. $1.50

JAKES, John. *Arena.* 1963. Ace G 520. 1st edn. HA. F. F2d. $12.00

JAKES, John. *Asylum World.* PB Library 63-236. PBO. VG+. B3d. $7.50

JAKES, John. *Black in Time.* PB Library 63-426. PBO. VG. B3d. $4.50

JAKES, John. *Brak the Barbarian Versus the Mark of the Demons.* 1969. PB Library 63-104. PBO. SF. VG. B5d. $3.50

JAKES, John. *Brak the Barbarian Versus the Mask of the Demons.* 1969. PB Library 63-184. 1st edn. F. M1d. $12.00

JAKES, John. *Brak the Barbarian Versus the Sorceress.* 1969. PB Library 63-089. SF. VG+. W2d. $4.50

JAKES, John. *Brak the Barbarian Versus the Sorceress.* 1969. PB Library 63-089. 1st edn. F. M1d. $12.00

JAKES, John. *Brak the Barbarian.* 1968. Avon S 363. 1st edn. F. M1d. $12.00

JAKES, John. *Brak the Barbarian.* 1968. Avon S 363. 1st prtg. SF. VG. R5d. $3.50

JAKES, John. *Brak the Barbarian.* Tower 51650. SF. G+. W2d. $3.00

JAKES, John. *Conquest of Planet of the Apes.* 1974. Award 1241. PBO. MTI. VG+. B6d. $5.00

JAKES, John. *Defiled Sister.* Period 103. VG. B3d. $4.00

JAKES, John. *I, Barbarian.* 1959. Avon T 375. 1st edn. HA. F. F2d. $20.00

JAKES, John. *Johnny Havoc & the Doll Who Had It.* 1963. Belmont 289. 1st edn. De. VG. F2d. $12.00

JAKES, John. *Johnny Havoc Meets Zelda.* 1962. Belmont 90-261. 1st edn. My. F. F2d. $20.00

JAKES, John. *Johnny Havoc Meets Zelda.* 1962. Belmont 90-261. 1st edn. VG. M1d. $10.00

JAKES, John. *Johnny Havoc.* 1960. Belmont 204. 1st edn. My. F. F2d. $20.00

JAKES, John. *Last Magician.* 1969. Signet T 3988. SF. VG. W2d. $4.00

JAKES, John. *Master of the Dark Gate.* 1970. Lancer 75-113. 1st edn. SF. VG. F2d. $20.00

JAKES, John. *Mention My Name in Atlantis.* 1972. DAW 25. 1st prtg. SF. VG. R5d. $6.00

JAKES, John. *Planet Wizard.* Ace 67060. PBO. c/Jones. NF. B3d. $6.00

JAKES, John. *Planet Wizard.* 1969. Ace 67060. PBO. c/J Jones. SF. VG+. B5d. $4.00

JAKES, John. *Planet Wizard.* 1969. Ace 67060. 1st edn. c/Jeff Jones. SF. F. F2d. $12.50

JAKES, John. *Planet Wizard.* 1977. Ace 67061. 2nd prtg. SF. F. W2d. $3.75

JAKES, John. *Seventh Man.* 1981. TOR 48018. 1st pb. My. NF. B6d. $3.00

JAKES, John. *Sir Scoundrel.* 1962. Ace F 146. 1st edn. HA. F. F2d. $12.00

JAKES, John. *Six-Gun Planet.* 1970. PB Library 63-313. PBO. c/R Powers & LaZorg. SF. VG. B5d. $4.50

JAKES, John. *Strike the Black Flag.* 1961. Ace D 523. 1st edn. HA. VG. F2d. $8.00

JAKES, John. *Tonight We Steal the Stars.* 1969. Ace 81680. 1st edn. SF. F. F2d. $10.00

JAKES, John. *Veils of Salome.* 1962. Avon F 123. 1st edn. HA. F. F2d. $25.00

JAKES, John. *When the Star Kings Die.* 1967. Ace G 656. PBO. VG. M1d/M6d. $5.00

JAKES, John. *When the Star Kings Die.* 1967. Ace G 656. 1st edn. SF. F. F2d. $12.00

JAKES, John. *When the Star Kings Die.* 1967. Ace G 656. 1st prtg. SF. G+. R5d. $2.50

JAKES, John. *Witch of the Dark Gate.* Lancer 75-415. SF. VG. W2d. $5.00

JAKES, John. *Witch of the Dark Gate.* 1972. Lancer 75415. 1st edn. SF. F. F2d. $10.00

JAKES/JANIFER & TREIBICH. *Tonight We Steal the Stars/Wagered World.* 1969. Ace 81680. PBO. c/J Gaughn & K Freas. SF. NF. B5d. $6.00

JAKES/JANIFER & TREIBICH. *Tonight We Steal the Stars/Wagered World.* 1969. Ace 81680. 1st prtg. SF. G+. R5d. $2.00

JAKES/MUNDT. *Gonzaga's Women/Affair in Araby.* Royal Books Giant 22. VG. I1d. $15.00

JAKES/WALLACE. *Night for Treason/Three Times a Victim.* 1957. Ace D 209. VG. B3d. $4.00

JAKES/WALLACE. *Night for Treason/Three Times a Victim.* 1957. Ace D 209. 1st edn. PBO. My. NF. F2d. $11.00

JAMES, Al. *Halfbreed.* Midwood 133. PBO. VG. B3d. $5.50

JAMES, Al. *Lover.* Midwood 111. VG. B3d. $4.00

JAMES, Al. *Potent Stuff.* 1961. Novel Book 5048. PBO. c/photo. Ad. VG. B5d. $35.00

JAMES, Al. *Running Girls.* Beacon B 406. NF. I1d. $10.00

JAMES, Al. *Running Girls.* 1961. Beacon B 406. PBO. Ad. VG. B5d. $5.50

JAMES, Barbara. *Beauty That Must Die.* 1967. Ace G 684. 1st prtg. My. VG. R5d. $1.75

JAMES, Don. *Dark Hunger.* 1958. Monarch 101. c/gga. Fa. VG+. B4d. $6.00

JAMES, Don. *Girls & Gangs.* 1963. Monarch MB 534. JD. VG. P1d. $35.00

JAMES, Don. *Key Game.* 1962. Monarch 237. PBO. c/H Schaare. Ad. VG+. B5d. $9.00

JAMES, Don. *Pitchmen.* Monarch 358. PBO. NF. B3d. $6.00

JAMES, Don. *Power of Marital Love.* 1960. Monarch MB 506. c/gga. Nfi. F. B4d. $15.00

JAMES, J. *Nympho Nurse.* Gold Star 75. VG. B3d. $4.00

JAMES, J. *Wild Flesh.* Private Edition 310. VG+. B3d. $5.00

JAMES, Laurence. *War on Aleph.* 1974. Zebra 0035. 1st edn. SF. F. F2d. $10.00

JAMES, Leigh. *Push-Button Spy.* Manor 15163. 1st pb. VG. M6d. $4.00

JAMES, M.E. Clifton. *Conterfeit General Montgomery.* Avon 692. c/photo. Nfi. VG. B5d. $4.50

JAMES, M.R. *More Ghost Stories of an Antiquary.* 1955. Pan 359. VG. B3d. $7.50

JAMES, Marquis. *Raven.* 1962. PB Library 54-144. 1st pb. c/Sam Houston. Bio. VG+. B6d. $7.50

JAMES, Neal. *Cheater's Paradise.* Beacon B 661F. VG. M6d. $8.50

JAMES, Roger. *Dangerous Dames.* Bee Line 165. PBO. VG+. M6d. $9.50

JAMES, Roger. *High Price of Loving.* 1967. Bee Line 191. PBO. VG+. M6d. $9.50

JAMES, Roger. *High Price of Loving.* 1967. Bee Line 191. 1st edn. My. F. F2d. $15.00

JAMES, Roger. *Office Tramp.* 1967. Bee Line 280. Ad. G+. B5d. $5.00

JAMES, Stuart. *Bucks County Report.* 1961. Midwood F 77. PBO. NF. B6d. $18.00

JAMES, Stuart. *Jack the Ripper.* 1960. Monarch 143. PBO. MTI. c/Johnson: gga. rare. VG+. B6a #79. $72.50

JAMES, Stuart. *Stranglers.* 1960. Monarch MM 601. MTI. VG+. B4d. $14.00

JAMES, Viola. *Honeymoon Swappers.* 1973. Liverpool TNS 561. Ad. VG. B5d. $3.50

JAMES, Walter S. *Dust Devil.* Dell D 418. 1st pb? c/Stanley. VG. M6d. $4.50

JAMES, William. *Psychology.* 1963. Premier NN 194. Nfi. VG+. B5d. $4.00

JAMES/JAMES. *Turn of the Screw/Daisy Miller.* 1954. Dell 800. F. F2d. $7.50

JAMES/JAMES. *Turn of the Screw/Daisy Miller.* 1954. Dell 800. VG+. B4d. $4.00

JAMES/JAMES. *Turn of the Screw/Daisy Miller.* 1970. Dell 9154. 22nd prtg. SF. VG. W2d. $4.00

JAMESON, Leland. *Attack!* Ace S 262. c/E Emsh. Fi/VG+. B5d. $5.50

JAMESON, Malcolm. *Atomic Bomb.* 1945. Bonded 10A. VG. B3a #21. $32.00

JAMESON, Malcolm. *Tarnished Utopia.* Galaxy SF 27. VG+. B3d. $6.00

JAMIESON, Leland. *Attack.* 1957. Ace S 262. War. VG. B3d. $4.00

JANEWAY, Elizabeth. *Walsh Girls.* 1946. Pocket 393. Fa. VG. B4d. $3.00

JANIFER, Laurence M. *Bloodworld.* 1968. Lancer 73-752. 1st prtg. SF. VG. R5d. $4.50

JANIFER, Laurence M. *Bloodworld.* Lodestone B 5016. SF. NF. B5d. $7.00

JANIFER, Laurence M. *Impossible?* Belmont 50-810. VG+. B3d. $4.50

JANIFER, Laurence M. *Impossible?* 1968. Belmont 50-810. 1st edn. F. M1d. $10.00

JANIFER, Laurence M. *Piece of Martin Cann.* 1968. Belmont B 50-811. 1st prtg. SF. VG. R5d. $5.50

JANIFER, Laurence M. *Power.* 1974. Dell 1st Edition 8527. 1st edn. SF. F. F2d. $10.00

JANIFER, Laurence M. *Slave Planet.* 1963. Pyramid F 840. PBO. c/J Gaughan. SF. VG. B5d. $6.00

JANIFER, Laurence M. *Wonder War.* 1964. Pyramid F 963. PBO. c/E Emsh. SF. VG. B5d. $6.50

JANIFER, Laurence M. *Wonder War.* 1964. Pyramid F 963. 1st edn. F. M1d. $20.00

JANIFER, Laurence M. *You Can't Escape.* 1967. Lancer 73-611. 1st edn. My. F. F2d. $13.00

JANIFER, Laurence M. *You Sane Men.* 1965. Lancer 72-789. SF. VG. B5d. $5.50

JANIFER, Laurence M. *You Sane Men.* 1965. Lancer 72-789. 1st edn. F. M1d. $10.00

JANNEY, Russell. *Miracle of the Bells.* Dell 474. c/R Munsell. SF. VG. B5d. $4.00

JANSON, Hank. *Amorous Captive Volume #1.* 1958. Alexander Moring. PBO. c/gga. scarce British. VG+. B6a #74. $49.50

JANSON, Hank. *Amorous Captive Volume #2.* 1959. Alexander Moring. PBO. c/gga. scarce British. NF. B6a #74. $44.00

JANSON, Hank. *Amorous Captive Volume #3.* 1959. Alexander Moring. PBO. c/gga. VG. B6a #74. $49.50

JANSON, Hank. *Avenging Nymph.* Alexander Moring NN. VG. B3d. $7.00

JANSON, Hank. *Brazen Seductress.* 1963. Gold Star 13. 1st US edn. c/Maguire: gga. NF. B6a #75. $40.00

JANSON, Hank. *Broads Don't Scare Easy.* New Fiction NN. VG. B3d. $10.00

JANSON, Hank. *Catch Me a Renegade.* 1965. Compact 290. VG. B3d. $7.00

JANSON, Hank. *Desert Fury.* 1956. Alexander Moring NN. PBO. c/Heade: gga. VG+. B6a #76. $40.25

JANSON, Hank. *Desert Fury.* 1953. Gaywood Press NN. PBO. c/Heade: gga. scarce. VG. B6a #76. $51.75

JANSON, Hank. *Desert Fury.* New Fiction NN. VG. B3d. $15.00

JANSON, Hank. *Don't Cry Now.* 1957. Alexander Moring NN. c/gga. scarce. VG+. B6a #79. $67.25

JANSON, Hank. *Escape.* 1957. Alex Moring NN. 3rd prtg. VG. B3d. $8.00

JANSON, Hank. *Escape.* 1955. Alexander Moring NN. PBO. c/Heade: gga. VG+. B6a #76. $50.00

JANSON, Hank. *Expectant Nymph.* 1964. Gold Star 32. 1st US edn. c/Maguire: gga. NF. B6a #75. $44.00

JANSON, Hank. *Flight From Fear.* 1956. Alexander Moring NN. PBO. c/Heade: gga. scarce. NF. B6a #76. $55.00

JANSON, Hank. *Hell's Angel.* 1959. Alexander Moring NN. PBO. c/gga. NF. B6a #74. $44.00

JANSON, Hank. *Hellcat.* 1956. Alexander Moring NN. PBO. c/Heade: gga. scarce. VG+. B6a #76. $48.50

JANSON, Hank. *Lady, Mind That Corpse.* 1949. Checker 10. c/gga. VG. B6a #79. $101.00

JANSON, Hank. *One Man in His Time.* New Fiction NN. c/Heade. VG. B3d. $9.00

JANSON, Hank. *Passionate Playmates.* 1964. Gold Star 18. c/Maguire: gga. VG+. B6a #77. $34.25

JANSON, Hank. *Persian Pride.* 1956. Alexander Moring NN. PBO. c/Heade: gga. NF. B6a #76. $42.50

JANSON, Hank. *Pursuit.* New Fiction NN. c/Meade. VG+. B3a #22. $14.70

JANSON, Hank. *Sinister Rapture.* Alexander Moring. VG. B3d. $7.00

JANSON, Hank. *Smart Girls Don't Talk.* 1949. Caywood Press NN. PBO. c/gga. scarce. VG. B6a #77. $71.50

JANSON, Hank. *Strange Destiny.* 1956. Alexander Moring NN. PBO. c/Heade: gga. VG+. B6a #76. $55.00

JANSON, Hank. *Sweet Fury.* 1955. Alexander Moring NN. PBO. c/Heade: gga. VG+. B6a #76. $35.00

JANSON, Hank. *Sweetheart, Here's Your Grave.* 1949. S Francis NN. VG. B3a #24. $22.00

JANSON, Hank. *Tomorrow & a Day.* 1955. Alexander Moring NN. PBO. c/Heade: gga. scarce. SF. NF. B6a #76. $50.00

JANSON, Hank. *Torrid Temptress.* 1956. Alexander Moring NN. PBO. c/Heade: gga. scarce. NF. B6a #76. $44.00

JANSON, Hank. *Untamed.* 1955. Alexander Moring NN. PBO. c/Heade: gga. VG+. B6a #76. $37.00

JANSON, Hank. *Wild Girl.* 1959. Alexander Moring NN. PBO. c/Heade: gga. scarce. VG+. B6a #76. $48.50

JANTZEN, F. *Berlin Bed.* Europa 1101. c/Neutzel. sgn. VG. B3d. $6.00

JANUARY, Steve. *Rusty Desmond.* 1954. Avon 553. JD. VG+. P1d. $19.00

JAPRISOT, Sebastien. *Trap for Cinderella.* 1965. Pocket 50145. My. VG. B5d. $4.00

JAPRISOT, Sebastien. *10:30 From Marseille.* 1965. Pocket 50085. My. VG. B5d. $3.00

JASON, Hank. *Pursuit.* New Fiction NN. 2nd edn. VG. B3d. $8.00

JASON, Stuart. *Kill Quick or Die.* 1970. Pinnacle PO 11N. c/gga. Fa. VG. B4d. $2.00

JASON, Stuart. *Kingblood.* 1969. PB Library 65-219. PBO. NF. B6d. $15.00

JASON, Stuart. *Love Pirate.* 1968. Bee Line 529. 1st edn. Cr. F. F2d. $12.50

JAVOR, F.A. *Rim-World Legacy.* 1967. Signet P 3183. SF. F. W2d. $5.50

JAVOR, F.A. *Rim-World Legacy.* Signet Q 5213. 1st prtg. F. S1d. $4.00

JAY, Charlotte. *Beat Not the Bones.* Avon T 376. NF. B3d. $4.00

JAY, Charlotte. *Beat Not the Bones.* 1952. Avon 623. My. NF. M3d. $8.00

JAY, Charlotte. *Fugitive Eye.* Avon 670. NF. I1d. $5.00

JAY, Charlotte. *Hank of Hair.* 1970. MacFadden 60443. 2nd prtg. My. VG+. W2d. $5.50

JAY, Charlotte. *Yellow Turban.* 1956. Avon 736. My. VG+. B4d. $6.00

JAY, Mel. *Orbit One.* Uni-Book. 1st prtg. NF. S1d. $2.00

JEFFERS, Albert. *Design for Dying.* Bleak House 12. VG. B3d. $12.00

JEFFREY, Adi-Ken. *Bermuda Triangle.* 1975. Warner 59961. 1st prtg. Nfi. F. W2d. $4.00

JEFFREY, B. *White Coolies.* Panther 738. VG+. B3d. $12.00

JEFFREYS, J.G. *Captain Bolton's Corpse.* 1986. Walker 31627. c/L Nargi. My. VG+. B5d. $4.00

JEFFRIES, Wendy. *That's Incredible! Volume #1.* 1980. Jove. TVTI. VG. P1d. $4.50

JEFFRIES, Wendy. *That's Incredible! Volume #4.* 1981. Jove 06171. TVTI. VG. P1d. $4.50

JEFFSON, J.O. *Second Experiment.* 1974. Crest 23005. SF. VG. W2d. $3.50

JELLETT & MARSH. *Nursing Home Murders.* 1965. Berkley F 1140. 1st prtg. G+. R5d. $2.25

JENKINS, Cecil. *Message From Sirius.* Bantam J 2552. 1st prtg. F. S1d. $4.00

JENKINS, Dorothy H. *Complete Book of Roses.* 1956. Bantam A 1418. PBO. VG+. B6d. $7.50

JENKINS, Elizabeth. *Harriet.* 1946. Bantam 64. 1st prtg. VG+. P7d. $5.00

JENKINS, Elizabeth. *Six Criminal Women.* 1958. Pan G 152. 1st pb. Cr. VG. B6d. $7.50

JENKINS, Geoffrey. *Disappearing Island.* Avon S 158. 1st prtg. My. VG+. R5d. $2.50

JENKINS, Geoffrey. *River of Diamonds.* 1966. Avon S 196. 1st pb. c/Borack. My. NF. B6d. $8.00

JENKINS, W.F. *Dallas.* 1950. Gold Medal 126. VG. B3d. $8.00

JENKINS, W.F. *Dallas.* 1950. Gold Medal 126. 1st edn. NF. I1d. $35.00

JENKINS, W.F. *Dallas.* Gold Medal 504. MTI. VG. B3d. $8.00

JENKINS, W.F. *Man Who Feared.* Hangman House 4. My. G. B5d. $5.00

JENKINS, W.F. *Son of the Flying Y.* Red Seal 74. VG. B3d. $8.00

JENNINGS, D.K. *And the Glory.* Badger RS 11. c/Asian nurse. G+. B3d. $7.00

JENNINGS, D.K. *Wayward Heart.* Badger RS 03. VG. I1d. $5.00

JENNINGS, Jan. *Vampyr.* 1981. TOR 48-010. SF. VG+. M3d. $6.00

JENNINGS, John. *Chronicle of the Calypso Clipper.* 1956. Perma M 3071. VG. B3d. $4.00

JENNINGS, John. *Golden Eagle.* Dell D 267. c/De Soto. VG+. B3d. $5.00

JENNINGS, John. *Rogue's Yarn.* 1955. Pocket 1047. 1st pb. c/Mayers. VG. B6d. $5.00

JENNINGS, John. *Sea Eagles.* 1951. Perma P 133. 1st pb. c/Tom Dunn. VG+. B6d. $9.00

JEPSON, Selwyn. *Killer by Proxy.* Bantam 803. VG+. B3d. $4.50

JEROME, Ace. *Fun & Games.* 1967. All Star AS 141. Ad. VG+. B5d. $5.00

JEROME, Owen Fox. *Corpse Awaits.* Handi-Book 58. VG. G5d. $5.00

JERVIS, Don. *Sugar Daddy's Diamond.* Bernardo NN. VG. B3d. $10.00

JESSUP, Richard. *Cheyenne Saturday.* Gold Medal 647. PBO. VG. M6d. $4.50

JESSUP, Richard. *Cincinnati Kid.* Dell 1279. VG. B3d. $4.50

JESSUP, Richard. *Cunning & the Haunted.* Gold Medal 440. VG. B3d. $6.00

JESSUP, Richard. *Deadly Duo.* 1959. Dell 1st Edition A 194. 1st prtg. PBO. c/Elliot: gga. NF. P7d. $7.50

JESSUP, Richard. *Night Boat to Paris.* 1956. Dell 1st Edition 92. PBO. c/George Ziel. VG+. P6d. $3.50

JESSUP, Richard. *Sabadilla.* Gold Medal 528. VG. B3d. $5.00

JETER, K.W. *Dreamfields.* 1976. Laser 33. 1st edn. scarce. SF. F. F2d. $20.00

JETER, K.W. *Mantis.* 1987. TOR 52009. SF. VG+. M3d. $7.50

JETER, K.W. *Morlock Night.* DAW 343. VG. B3d. $4.00

JETER, K.W. *Seeklight.* 1975. Laser 7. PBO. author's 1st book. c/K Freas. SF. VG. M3d. $11.00

JETER, K.W. *Seeklight.* 1975. Laser 7. SF. F. W2d. $16.50

JEWELL, Derek edt. *Alamein & the Desert War.* 1968. Ballatnine U 7093. War. VG+. B4d. $3.00

JOESTEN, Joachim. *Dope, Inc.* 1953. Avon 538. 1st edn. F. F2d. $30.00

JOESTEN, Joachim. *Vice, Inc.* 1954. Ace S 58. 1st edn. c/gga. F. F2d. $20.00

JOHN, Owen. *Dead on Time.* 1969. PB Library 63-189. 1st edn. c/photo. Th. F. F2d. $10.00

JOHNEN, Wilhelm. *Battling the Bombers.* Ace D 326. VG. B3d. $4.00

JOHNSON, B.B. *Black Is Beautiful.* 1973. PB Library 64-305. 1st edn. My. F. F2d. $8.00

JOHNSON, Dorothy. *Indian Country.* Ballantine 241. 2nd prtg. PBO. VG+. B3d. $4.50

JOHNSON, Dorothy. *Indian Country.* 1953. Ballantine 29. PBO. We. VG. B6d. $6.00

JOHNSON, Dorothy. *Indian Country.* 1962. Ballantine 610. 1st prtg. c/Mel Crair. VG+. P7d. $5.00

JOHNSON, Duff. *Racing Crazy.* Hamilton NN. VG. B3d. $6.00

JOHNSON, Eric W. *Our World Into Words.* 1977. Bantam 10892. Nfi. NF. B5d. $4.00

JOHNSON, George. *Eisenhower.* 1962. Monarch K-64. PBO. c/photo. Nfi. VG. B5d. $5.00

JOHNSON, George. *Eleanor Roosevelt.* 1962. Monarch K 61. Nfi. VG+. B4d. $4.00

JOHNSON, Grady. *Five Pennies.* 1959. Dell B 128. MTI. VG+. B4d. $7.00

JOHNSON, James. *Disaster & Shadow.* 1981. DAW. 1st edn. F. M1d. $5.00

JOHNSON, Ken. *Hounds of Dracula.* 1977. Signet 7739. 1st edn. Ho. F. F2d. $10.00

JOHNSON, Lyndon B. *Time for Action.* 1964. Cardinal GC 224. c/Lyndon B Johnson. Nfi. VG+. B4d. $2.50

JOHNSON, Robert S. *Thunderbolt.* 1959. Ballantine F 323K. War. VG. B4d. $3.00

JOHNSON, Ryerson. *Lady in Dread.* GM 459. VG. G5d. $5.00

JOHNSON, Ryerson. *Naked in the Streets.* Red Seal 10. G+. G5d. $3.00

JOHNSON, Victor H. *Bold Moment.* 1954. Pyramid 125. 1st pb. VG. B6d. $9.00

JOHNSON, Victor H. *Cry Torment.* 1955. Graphic 101. Fa. VG+. B4d. $4.00

JOHNSON, Victor H. *Cry Torment.* 1955. Graphic 101. G+. G5d. $3.00

JOHNSON & NOLAN. *Logan's Run.* 1976. Bantam 2517. c/Nolan: sgn. VG. B3d. $6.00

JOHNSON & NOLAN. *Logan's Run.* 1976. Bantam 2517. 1st edn. PBO. MTI. c/photos. SF. F. F2d. $10.00

JOHNSTON, Mary. *To Have & To Hold.* 1959. Cardinal C 322. 1st prtg. c/Fredman: gga. VG. P7d. $3.50

JOHNSTON, Stanley. *Queen of the Flat-Tops.* 1968. Ballantine 72125. 1st prtg. c/Valigursky. VG+. P7d. $4.00

JOHNSTON, Stanley. *Queen of the Flat-Tops.* Dell 37. VG. B3d. $10.00

JOHNSTON, William. *And Loving It.* 1967. Tempo T 159. 1st prtg. TVTI. VG. R5d. $5.50

JOHNSTON, William. *April Fools.* 1969. Popular 60-8086. 1st prtg. G+. R5d. $1.50

JOHNSTON, William. *Ben Casey.* 1962. Lancer 70-006. PBO. TVTI. c/V Edwards photo. Fi. VG. B5d. $5.00

JOHNSTON, William. *Ben Casey.* 1962. Lancer 70-006. TVTI. VG+. B4d. $7.50

JOHNSTON, William. *Ben Casey.* 1962. Lancer 70-006. 1st prtg. TVTI. G+. R5d. $2.75

JOHNSTON, William. *Bloop Box.* 1970. Lancer 73205. 1st edn. TVTI. F. F2d. $12.00

JOHNSTON, William. *Captain Nice.* Tempo. PBO. TVTI. VG+. B3d. $4.50

JOHNSTON, William. *Count Up Blast Down.* Lancer 73-872. TVTI. Brady Bunch #3. VG. B3d. $4.00

JOHNSTON, William. *Dick Tracy.* 1970. Tempo 5334. 1st prtg. My. VG+. W2d. $11.00

JOHNSTON, William. *Dr Starr in Crisis.* 1964. Monarch 442. Ro. VG+. B4d. $5.00

JOHNSTON, William. *Faces of Love.* Lancer 70-049. PBO. Dr Kildare. VG+. B3d. $4.00

JOHNSTON, William. *Faces of Love.* 1963. Lancer 70-049. 1st prtg. Dr Kildare. VG+. R5d. $5.00

JOHNSTON, William. *Fonzie Drops In.* 1974. Tempo 7452. 1st prtg. Happy Days #2. G+. R5d. $1.25

JOHNSTON, William. *Fonzie Superstar.* 1976. Tempo 12414. 1st prtg. VG. R5d. $1.75

JOHNSTON, William. *Get Smart Once Again!* 1966. Tempo T 121. 2nd prtg. TVTI. G+. R5d. $1.25

JOHNSTON, William. *Heart Has an Answer.* 1963. Lancer 70-043. TVTI. c/photo. Dr Kildare. VG+. B4d. $7.50

JOHNSTON, William. *Heart Has an Answer.* 1963. Lancer 70-043. 1st prtg. Dr Kildare. VG. R5d. $3.25

JOHNSTON, William. *Invaders.* 1975. Tempo 12267. 1st prtg. Happy Days. VG. R5d. $1.75

JOHNSTON, William. *Klute.* PB Library 64-639. c/Jane Fonda: photo. NF. B3d. $4.50

JOHNSTON, William. *Klute.* 1971. PB Library 64-639. MTI. VG+. B4d. $3.00

JOHNSTON, William. *Max Smart & the Ghastly Ghost Affair.* 1969. Tempo 5326. 1st prtg. VG. R5d. $4.50

JOHNSTON, William. *Max Smart & the Perilous Pellets.* 1966. Tempo T 140. PBO. TVTI. c/photo. VG+. P6d. $2.50

JOHNSTON, William. *Miracle at San Tanco.* Ace G 702. c/photo. Flying Nun. VG+. B3d. $5.00

JOHNSTON, William. *New Interns.* 1964. Bantam S 2841. 1st prtg. G+. R5d. $1.50

JOHNSTON, William. *Ready To Go Steady.* 1974. Tempo 5794. 1st prtg. Happy Days #1. G+. R5d. $1.50

JOHNSTON, William. *Save Her for Loving.* 1962. Monarch 275. PBO. c/Barton: gga. scarce. VG+. B6a #79. $42.00

JOHNSTON, William. *Sea Gold Incident.* 1970. Ace 95051. TVTI. VG. P1d. $6.00

JOHNSTON, William. *Sorry, Chief.* 1966. Tempo T 119. 1st prtg. My. VG+. W2d. $8.00

JOHNSTON, William. *Sweathog Newshawks.* 1976. Tempo 12407. 1st prtg. Welcome Back, Kotter #2. G+. R5d. $1.25

JOHNSTON, William. *Sweathog Trail.* 1976. Tempo 12406. 1st prtg. Welcome Back, Kotter #1. G+. R5d. $1.25

JOHNSTON, William. *Then Came Bronson.* 1969. Pyramid T 2106. TVTI. VG. P1d. $7.50

JOHNSTON, William. *What Ever Happened to Mavis Rooster.* 1970. Tempo 5339. 1st prtg. VG+. R5d. $4.00

JOHNSTON, William. *10-4 Sweathogs!* 1976. Tempo 12706. TVTI. VG. P1d. $5.00

JONES, D.F. *Colossus.* 1967. Berkley X 1455. SF. VG. W2d. $4.00

JONES, D.F. *Floating Zombie.* 1975. Berkley Z 2980. 1st prtg. SF. G+. R5d. $1.25

JONES, E.H. *Road to En-Dor.* Pan 364. VG+. B3d. $6.00

JONES, George. *Trap.* Graphic 106. G+. G5d. $4.00

JONES, George. *Twisted.* 1961. Beacon 373. 1st prtg. c/George Gross: gga. VG. P7d. $7.50

JONES, Guy & Constance. *Peabody's Mermaid.* 1948. Pocket. 1st pb. MTI. G+. M1d. $6.00

JONES, H. *Spanking: Sex or Sadism?* Brandon House 938. VG. B3d. $4.00

JONES, H. Bedford. *Malay Gold.* 1953. Harlequin 232. G+. B3d. $15.00

JONES, H. Spencer. *Life on Other Worlds.* 1949. Mentor. 1st pb. VG. M1d. $3.00

JONES, James. *From Here to Eternity.* 1953. Signet T 1075. Fi. VG. B5d. $4.00

JONES, James. *Merry Month of May.* 1972. Dell 05588. 1st prtg. VG. P7d. $4.00

JONES, James. *Some Came Running.* 1958. Signet T 1637. Fi. VG. B5d. $4.50

JONES, Ken. *FBI in Action.* 1957. Signet S 1476. PBO. Cr. VG+. B4d. $4.00

JONES, Madison. *I Walk the Line.* Popular 08144. 1st prtg. G+. R5d. $1.50

JONES, Nard. *Ride the Dark Storm.* 1955. Gold Medal 512. PBO. c/Maguire. My. VG. B6d. $9.00

JONES, Neil R. *Doomsday on Ajiat.* 1968. Ace G 719. SF. G+. W2d. $3.00

JONES, Neil R. *Non-Statistical Man.* Belmont L 92-588. 1st prtg. F. S1d. $4.50

JONES, Neil R. *Planet of Double Sun.* Ace F 420. F. M1d. $6.00

JONES, Neil R. *Planet of the Double Sun.* Ace F 420. 1st prtg. Professor Jameson #1. SF. F. W2d. $5.00

JONES, Neil R. *Planet of the Double Sun.* 1967. Ace F 420. SF. F. W2d. $4.75

JONES, Neil R. *Sunless World.* Ace G 631. Professor Jameson. SF. VG. W2d. $3.75

JONES, Neil R. *Sunless World.* 1967. Ace G 631. 1st edn. G. P9d. $1.25

JONES, Raymond F. *Alien.* 1966. Belmont B 50708. SF. F. W2d. $5.50

JONES, Raymond F. *Cybernetic Brains.* 1969. PB Library 63-063. SF. NF. B5d. $5.00

JONES, Raymond F. *Deviates.* Beacon 242. VG. B3d. $8.00

JONES, Raymond F. *King of Eolim.* 1975. Laser 12. PBO. c/K Freas. SF. NF. B3d/B5d. $6.00

JONES, Raymond F. *Man of Two Worlds.* 1963. Pyramid F 941. c/J Schoenherr. SF. NF. B5d. $6.00

JONES, Raymond F. *Non-Statistical Man.* 1968. Belmont B 50 820. 1st prtg. SF. VG. R5d. $3.00

JONES, Raymond F. *Non-Statistical Man.* 1968. Belmont B 50-820. 2nd prtg. NF. B3d. $4.50

JONES, Raymond F. *Non-Statistical Man.* 1964. Belmont L 92-588. SF. VG. W2d. $4.50

JONES, Raymond F. *Renegades of Time.* 1975. Laser 1. PBO. c/K Freas. SF. NF. B5d. $6.50

JONES, Raymond F. *Renegades of Time.* 1975. Laser 1. 1st edn. c/Freas. VG+. B3d. $5.00

JONES, Raymond F. *River & the Dream.* 1977. Laser 54. 1st edn. SF. F. F2d. $15.00

JONES, Raymond F. *Syn.* 1969. Belmont. 1st edn. VG. M1d. $6.00

JONES, Robert Page. *Heisters.* 1963. Monarch 396. PBO. c/L Marchetti. My. VG. B5d. $4.50

JONES, S.A. *Bedfellows & Other Strangers.* Barclay 7387. VG+. B3d. $4.00

JONES, S.A. *Thrill Circus.* Barclay 7371. PBO. NF. B3d. $5.00

JORDAN, Gail. *Made for Love.* Knickerbocker NN. VG+. B3d. $5.00

JORDAN, Gail. *Palm Beach Apartment.* 1949. Pyramid 15. 1st pb. c/Geygan. VG. B6d. $12.50

JORDAN, Robert. *Conan the Destroyer.* 1984. TOR 54238. 1st prtg. VG+. R5d. $2.50

JORDON, R.K. *Dawn Command.* Badger WW 97. VG+. B3d. $7.50

JORGENSEN, Ivar. *Rest in Agony.* 1963. Monarch 362. 1st edn. F. P9d. $3.00

JORGENSEN, Ivar. *Ten From Infinity.* 1963. Monarch 297. PBO. c/R Brillhart. SF. VG. B5d. $8.00

JORGENSEN, Ivar. *Ten From Infinity.* 1963. Monarch 297. 1st edn. F. M1d. $15.00

JORGENSEN, Ivar. *Whom the Gods Would Slay.* 1968. Belmont B 50-849. PBO. c/J Jones. SF. VG+. B5d. $5.00

JORGENSEN, Ivar. *Whom the Gods Would Slay.* 1968. Belmont B 50-849. 1st edn. F. M1d. $10.00

JOSCELYN, Archie. *Death in the Saddle.* 1946. We Novel Classic 70. 1st pb. VG. B6d. $6.00

JOSCELYN, Archie. *Gun Thunder Valley.* 1951. Star Book 13. PBO. c/Gross. We. G+. B6d. $3.50

JOSCELYN, Archie. *Gunhand's Pay.* 1957. Pyramid. c/M Crair. We. VG. B5d. $5.00

JOSEPH, Robert. *Berlin at Midnight.* Harlequin 137. G+. B3d. $4.00

JOSWICK & KEATING. *Combat Camera Man.* 1962. Pyramid R 800. War. NF. B4d. $5.00

JOYCE, Carlton. *Bachelor's Degree.* Beacon 188. VG. B3d. $9.00

JOYCE, Carlton. *Campus Scandal.* 1962. Beacon B 539F. c/gga. Fa. F. B4d. $12.00

JOYCE, Carlton. *Fraternity Row.* Monarch 366. PBO. NF. B3d. $8.00

JUDD, Cyril. *Outpost Mars.* 1954. Dell 760. c/R Powers. SF. VG+. B5d. $8.50

JUDD, Cyril. *Outpost Mars.* 1954. Dell 760. VG. I1d. $6.00

JUDD, Cyril. *Sin in Space.* Beacon 312. c/Stanley: gga. VG+. B6a #74. $55.00

JUDD, Cyril. *Sin in Space.* Beacon 312. VG+. I1d. $25.00

JUDD, Harrison. *Shadow of a Doubt?* 1961. Gold Medal S 1124. 1st prtg. PBO. VG. P7d. $5.00

JUDD, J. *Dawn of Doubt.* Brandon House 2064. VG. B3d. $4.50

JUDD/PIPER & MCGUIRE. *Gunner Cade/Crisis in 2140.* 1957. Ace D 227. 1st prtg. PBO. VG. P7d. $6.00

JULIAN, Peter. *Seventh Trumpet.* 1957. Lion LL 174. VG+. B3d. $5.00

JUNEAU, James. *Judy Garland.* 1974. Pyramid 3482. 1st edn. c/photos. Bio. F. F2d. $15.00

JUNGE, Werner. *African Jungle Doctor.* 1956. Panther 637. VG. B3d. $8.00

KAHLER, Jack. *Latex Lady.* 1964. Carousel 521. NF. B3a #24. $39.15

KAHLER, Jack. *Passion Sauce.* 1965. Satan Press 109. PBO. c/gga. NF. B6a #74. $60.00

KAHLER, Jack. *Sex Master.* Allstar AS 13. VG. B3d. $3.50

KAHN, James. *Indiana Jones & the Temple of Doom.* 1984. Ballantine 31457. 1st prtg. MTI. My. VG+. R5d. $2.50

KAHN, James. *Poltergeist.* 1982. Warner 30222. PBO. MTI. Ho. VG+. B6d. $3.00

KAHN, James. *Star Wars, Return of the Jedi.* 1983. Ballantine 30960. 1st edn. SF. F. F2d. $15.00

KAHN, James. *World Enough, & Time.* 1980. Ballantine 29247. PBO. SF. NF. B6d. $3.00

KAHN, Joan. *Some Things Fierce & Fatal.* 1975. Avon 24836. SF. VG. W2d. $5.50

KAHN, Lawrence H. *Tank Destroyers.* 1958. Pocket 1202. 1st pb. c/Dunn. VG. B6d. $7.00

KALMAN, Victor. *Guide to Natural Bowling.* Perma M 4147. 5th prtg. VG. B3d. $3.50

KALMAN, Victor. *Guide to Natural Bowling.* 1959. Perma M 4147. 1st prtg. PBO. VG+. P7d. $4.50

KALNEN, Ray. *Love Box.* 1967. Greenleaf GC 218. Fa. G+. B4d. $5.00

KAMAL, Ahmad. *High Pressure.* 1951. Bantam 716. 2nd prtg. My. G+. R5d. $1.00

KAMIN/RACKHAM. *Herod Men/Dark Planet.* 1971. Ace 13805. SF. VG. W2d. $5.00

KAMIN/RACKHAM. *Herod Men/Dark Planet.* 1971. Ace 13805. 1st edn. SF. F. F2d. $13.00

KAMIN/RICHMOND. *Earthrim/Phoenix Ship.* 1969. Ace 66160. PBO. c/P Koutrouboussis. SF. VG+. B5d. $4.00

KANDEL, A. *City for Conquest.* Harlequin 144. 2nd prtg. VG. B3d. $6.00

KANDEL & SAFRAN. *Nudeniks.* 1963. Belmont 574. 1st edn. F. F2d. $11.00

KANE, Abel. *Slaughter's Big Rip-Off.* 1973. Curtis 07320. 1st edn. c/Jim Brown photo. scarce. De. F. F2d. $15.00

KANE, Bob. *Batman.* Signet D 2939. VG. I1d. $6.00

KANE, Frank. *Bare Trap.* 1954. Dell 749. 1st prtg. c/Bobertz: gga. VG. M6d. $4.50

KANE, Frank. *Barely Seen.* Dell 0458. NF. I1d. $6.00

KANE, Frank. *Barely Seen.* 1964. Dell 0458. My. VG. B4d. $3.00

KANE, Frank. *Bullet Proof.* 1961. Dell D 451. 1st prtg. My. VG. B3d. $2.25

KANE, Frank. *Crime of Their Life.* Dell 1st Edn 1557. VG. B3d. $4.50

KANE, Frank. *Dead Rite.* Dell 1st Edn B 187. NF. I1d. $5.00

KANE, Frank. *Dead Weight.* 1953. Dell 665. NF. G5d. $6.00

KANE, Frank. *Dead Weight.* 1953. Dell 665. 1st edn. PBO. My. F. F2d. $10.00

KANE, Frank. *Due or Die.* Dell 1st Edn B 174. VG. G5d. $3.00

KANE, Frank. *Esprit de Corpse.* 1965. Dell 1st Edn 2409. F. I1d. $6.00

KANE, Frank. *Esprit de Corpse.* 1965. Dell 1st Edn 2409. PBO. c/Lesser. My. VG. B6d. $3.50

KANE, Frank. *Fatal Foursome.* 1958. Dell 973. c/V Kalin. My. VG+. B5d. $4.00

KANE, Frank. *Fatal Undertaking.* 1964. Dell 1st Edn 2489. PBO. c/Lesser. My. VG+. B6d. $4.50

KANE, Frank. *Final Curtain.* 1964. Dell 1st Edn 2522. PBO. c/Lesser. My. VG. B6d. $3.50

KANE, Frank. *Frank Kane's Stacked Deck.* 1961. Dell B 197. 1st edn. c/gga. De. F. F2d. $10.00

KANE, Frank. *Grave Danger.* Dell 886. c/V Kalin. My. VG. B5d. $3.50

KANE, Frank. *Green Light for Death.* Dell 918. c/V Kalin. My. VG. B5d. $4.00

KANE, Frank. *Green Light for Death.* Readers Choice 8. VG. B3d. $7.00

KANE, Frank. *Green Light for Death.* 1950. Readers Choice 8. 1st edn. PBO. c/gga. NF. B6a #76. $48.50

KANE, Frank. *Guilt-Edged Frame.* 1964. Dell 3289. 1st prtg. My. G+. W2d. $3.25

KANE, Frank. *Hearse Class Male.* Dell 3528. VG. G5d. $3.00

KANE, Frank. *Johnny Come Lately.* 1963. Dell 1st Edn 4243. PBO. c/Lesser. My. VG+. B6d. $4.50

KANE, Frank. *Johnny Come Lately.* 1963. Dell 1st Edn 4243. 1st edn. c/gga. De. F. F2d. $10.00

KANE, Frank. *Johnny Liddell's Morgue.* 1956. Dell A 117. 1st edn. De. F. F2d. $10.00

KANE, Frank. *Johnny Liddell's Morgue.* Dell 1st Edn A 117. NF. I1d. $6.00

KANE, Frank. *Jukebox King.* 1959. Dell 1st Edn B 137. 1st prtg. PBO. c/Elliot: gga. VG. P7d. $5.50

KANE, Frank. *Jukebox King.* 1959. Dell 1st Edn B 137. 1st edn. My. VG. F2d. $7.00

KANE, Frank. *Key Witness.* 1956. Dell 1st Edn A 126. c/Vic Kalin. JD. VG. P6d. $3.00

KANE, Frank. *Lineup.* 1959. Dell B 125. 1st edn. c/photo. My. F. F2d. $18.00

KANE, Frank. *Living End.* 1957. Dell 1st Edn A 142. 1st prtg. PBO. c/Kalin: gga. VG. P7d. $5.00

KANE, Frank. *Liz.* 1955. Beacon B 111. PBO. Ad. VG. B5d. $6.50

KANE, Frank. *Mourning After.* Mayflower 5848. 1st UK edn. VG+. B3d. $7.00

KANE, Frank. *Poisons Unknown.* 1960. Dell D 334. 1st prtg. My. G+. R5d. $2.25

KANE, Frank. *Poisons Unknown.* Dell 822. c/W George. My. VG. B5d. $3.00

KANE, Frank. *Poisons Unknown.* 1955. Dell 822. c/William George: gga. My. G+. B4d. $2.00

KANE, Frank. *Real Gone Guy.* 1958. Dell D 226. 1st prtg. c/Kalin: gga. VG. P7d. $4.00

KANE, Frank. *Real Gone Guy.* Dell 7267. reprint. VG. B3d. $4.00

KANE, Frank. *Red-Hot Ice.* Dell 901. VG. G5d/M6d. $5.00

KANE, Frank. *Ring-A-Ding-Ding.* Dell 1st Edn 7451. VG+. B3d. $4.50

KANE, Frank. *Ring-a-Ding-Dong.* 1963. Dell 1st Edn 7451. PBO. c/Lesser. My. VG+. B6d. $4.50

KANE, Frank. *Slay Ride.* 1959. Dell D 264. c/Victor Kane. My. VG. B4d. $3.00

KANE, Frank. *Time To Prey.* Dell 1st Edn B 159. VG. G5d. $5.50

KANE, Frank. *Time To Prey.* 1966. Dell 8924. 1st prtg. c/Livoti: gga. VG. B3d/P7d. $4.00

KANE, Frank. *Two To Tangle.* 1965. Dell 1st Edn 9213. PBO. c/Lesser. My. VG. B6d. $3.50

KANE, Henry. *Armchair in Hell.* 1949. Dell 316. c/Gregg: gga. VG. P6d. $3.75

KANE, Henry. *Case of the Murdered Madame.* 1955. Avon 646. 1st prtg. My. VG. B5d. $5.00

KANE, Henry. *Dead in Bed.* 1961. Lancer 71-304. 1st edn. De. F. F2d. $10.00

KANE, Henry. *Death for Sale.* 1957. Dell 1st Edn A 144. 1st edn. My. F. F2d. $10.00

KANE, Henry. *Death of a Flack.* 1961. Signet 1940. 1st edn. c/gga. De. F. F2d. $10.00

KANE, Henry. *Death on the Double.* 1957. Avon 761. PBO. My. VG. B5d. $6.00

KANE, Henry. *Dirty Gertie.* 1965. Belmont 92-623. 1st prtg. c/gga. NF. P7d. $9.00

KANE, Henry. *Edge of Panic.* Dell 535. VG. G5d. $5.00

KANE, Henry. *Edge of Panic.* 1958. Signet 1523. 1st prtg. F. F2d. $9.00

KANE, Henry. *Fistful of Death.* 1958. Avon T 276. PBO. c/gga. My. NF. I1d. $6.00

KANE, Henry. *Fistful of Death.* 1965. Signet D 2825. c/gga. My. F. B4d. $6.00

KANE, Henry. *Glow Job.* 1971. Lancer 75-158. 1st edn. De. NF. F2d. $12.00

KANE, Henry. *Halo for Nobody.* Dell 231. c/G Gregg. My. VG. B5d. $6.00

KANE, Henry. *Hang by Your Neck.* 1950. Dell 455. 1st pb edn. De. F. F2d. $7.00

KANE, Henry. *Hang by Your Neck.* 1958. Signet 1515. 1st edn. PBO. scarce. My. VG+. B6a #76. $21.00

KANE, Henry. *Kiss, Kiss, Kill, Kill.* 1970. Lancer 74-643. 1st edn. c/photo. De. F. F2d. $15.00

KANE, Henry. *Kisses of Death.* 1962. Belmont 90-259. 1st edn. scarce. De. F. F2d. $16.00

KANE, Henry. *Laughter Came Screaming.* 1954. Avon 572. PBO. My. NF. B6d. $22.50

KANE, Henry. *Martinis & Murder.* Avon T 460. 1st prtg. My. G+. R5d. $2.25

KANE, Henry. *Martinis & Murder.* Avon 745. VG. B3d. $5.00

KANE, Henry. *Murder of the Park Avenue Playgirl.* 1956. Avon 751. c/gga. My. VG. B4d/B5d. $4.00

KANE, Henry. *My Business Is Murder.* Avon 602. VG. B3d. $4.50

KANE, Henry. *My Darlin' Evangeline.* 1961. Dell 1st Edn B 198. VG+. I1d. $4.00

KANE, Henry. *My Darlin' Evangeline.* 1961. Dell 1st Edn B 198. 1st edn. My. F. F2d. $17.00

KANE, Henry. *Never Give a Millionaire an Even Break.* Lancer 70-048. VG. G5d. $3.00

KANE, Henry. *Nobody Loves a Loser.* 1963. Belmont 90-302. PBO. My. VG. B5d. $4.50

KANE, Henry. *Perfect Crime.* 1967. Belmont B 50-758. My. VG. B5d. $4.00

KANE, Henry. *Peter Gunn.* 1960. Dell B 155. TVTI. c/Craig Stevens: photo. VG+. B4d. $8.00

KANE, Henry. *Peter Gunn.* 1960. Dell 1st Edn B 155. 1st edn. TVTI. c/stamp inside. My. F. F2d. $10.00

KANE, Henry. *Private Eyeful.* 1959. Pyramid G 432. 1st edn. c/gga. De. F. F2d. $25.00

KANE, Henry. *Report for a Corpse.* Dell 330. VG. I1d. $5.00

KANE, Henry. *To Die or Not To Die.* 1974. Belmont 50691. 1st prtg. My. VG+. W2d. $3.75

KANE, Henry. *Too French & Too Deadly.* 1955. Avon 672. NF. G5d/I1d. $8.00

KANE, Henry. *Too French & Too Deadly.* 1955. Avon 672. 1st edn. De. F. F2d. $12.50

KANE, Henry. *Trinity in Violence.* 1955. Avon 618. 1st prtg. My. VG. R5d. $5.00

KANE, Henry. *Two Must Die.* 1963. Midwood F 330. PBO. My. VG+. B6d. $12.00

KANE, Henry. *Virility Factor.* 1972. PB Library 66-878. 1st pb. SF. NF. B6d. $10.00

KANE, Henry. *Who Killed Sweet Sue?* 1956. Avon 733. PBO. VG. B3d. $4.50

KANE, Henry. *Who Killed Sweet Sue?* 1965. Signet D 2575. 1st prtg. c/Barye: gga. VG+. P7d. $5.50

KANE, Henry. *Who Killed Sweet Sue?* 1965. Signet 2575. 1st revised edn. De. F. F2d. $10.00

KANE, J.M. *Perma Quiz Book.* Perma M 3039. 2nd prtg. PBO. VG. B3d. $5.00

KANE, Louis. *Lady Lust.* Bachelor Book 506. c/gga. F. F2d. $6.00

KANE, S. *Naked Obsession.* Headline 102. My. VG. B3d. $5.00

KANE, Sid. *Hot Tequila.* 1960. Headline 107. PBO. c/gga. scarce. NF. B6a #76. $91.00

KANE, V. *Treasure Hunt.* Middle America. NF. B3d. $4.50

KANE, William. *Lust Lashed.* Midnight Reader MR 490. VG+. I1d. $5.00

KANE, William. *Sexecutive.* Midnight Reader MR 443. VG+. I1d. $4.00

KANIN, Fay & Michael. *Teacher's Pet.* 1958. Bantam 1780. PBO. MTI. c/C Gable. VG. B6d. $4.00

KANIN, Garson. *Rat Race.* 1960. Cardinal C 401. PBO. MTI. VG+. B6d. $5.00

KANTO, P.M. *Beach Wife.* Brandon House 975. VG+. B3d. $5.00

KANTO, Peter. *License To Prowl.* Brandon House 1002. VG+. B3d. $5.00

KANTO, Peter. *Matinee in Three Scenes.* 1967. Brandon House 1060. Ad. VG. B5d. $5.50

KANTOE, M. *Long Remember.* Bantam 1008. VG. B3d. $4.50

KANTOR, Hal. *$1,000,000.00 Broad.* PAD 529. VG+. B3d. $5.00

KANTOR, MacKinlay. *Arouse & Beware.* Bantam 900. VG. B3d. $4.00

KANTOR, MacKinlay. *Don't Touch Me.* Bantam 1038. VG. B3d. $4.50

KANTOR, MacKinlay. *Gentle Annie.* Popular 183. c/Belarski. VG. B3d. $5.50

KANTOR, MacKinlay. *Gentle Annie.* 1949. Popular 183. c/Belarski. Fa. VG+. B4d. $8.00

KANTOR, MacKinlay. *Long Remember.* Pocket 135. VG. B3d. $4.00

KANTOR, MacKinlay. *One Wild Oat.* Gold Medal 122. VG. B3d. $4.00

KANTOR, MacKinley. *Midnight Lace.* 1950. Bantam 753. c/gga. Fa. VG. B4d. $3.25

KAPELNER, Alan. *Lonely Boy Blues.* Belmont 224. VG. B3d. $4.00

KAPELNER, Alan. *Lonely Boy Blues.* 1956. Lion LB 92. 1st pb. NF. B6d. $18.00

KAPLAN, Arthur edt. *Fine Art of Espionage.* 1967. Award A 209S. 1st prtg. My. VG. R5d. $1.50

KAPLAN, Edgar. *Italian System of Winning Bridge.* 1959. Signet KD 368. Nfi. VG. B4d. $2.00

KAPLAN, G. *Orality Girls.* Barclay 7068. NF. B3d. $6.00

KAPP, Colin. *Chaos Weapon.* 1977. Ballantine 27115. SF. VG. W2d. $3.25

KAPP, Colin. *Ion War.* 1978. Ace 37217. 1st edn. SF. F. F2d. $10.00

KAPP, Colin. *Transfinite Man.* 1964. Berkley F 974. PBO. SF. VG. B5d. $4.00

KAPP, Colin. *Wizard of Anharitte.* 1973. Award AN 1156. 1st prtg. SF. VG+. R5d. $2.50

KAPUSTA, Paul. *Avenging Eagle.* 1950s. Digit D 147. 1st pb. VG+. B6d. $8.00

KARIG, Walter. *Lower Than Angels.* 1952. Popular 419. c/De Soto: gga. Fa. VG+. B4d. $12.50

KARL, Don. *Wild Honey.* 1963. Midwood F 236. 1st prtg. PBO. c/Rader: gga. VG. P7d. $10.00

KARLOFF, Boris edt. *Boris Karloff Horror Anthology.* 1975. Everest. c/Bloch: sgn. NF. B3d. $9.00

KARLOFF, Boris edt. *Boris Karloff's Favorite Horror Stories.* 1965. Avon. 1st edn. NF. M1d. $10.00

KARLOVE, I.S. *Dreadful Hollow.* Dell 125. VG+. B3d. $7.00

KARNEY, Jack. *Cop.* 1952. Pocket 898. 1st prtg. c/Zuckerberg: gga. VG. P7d. $5.50

KARNEY, Jack. *Cry, Brother, Cry.* 1959. Popular G 304. JD. VG. P1d. $20.00

KARNEY, Jack. *Cry, Brother, Cry.* 1959. Popular G 304. 1st edn. c/gga. scarce. JD. F. F2d. $25.00

KARNEY, Jack. *Knock 'Em Dead.* 1955. Ace D 101. PBO. c/gga. VG+. B6a #40. $40.00

KARNEY, Jack. *Knock 'Em Dead.* 1955. Ace D 101. PBO. VG+. B6d. $40.00

KARNEY, Jack. *There Goes Shorty Higgins.* 1953. Pyramid 99. 1st pb. VG+. B6d. $12.50

KARNEY, Louis. *Devil's Lash.* Newsstand 506. VG+. B3d. $5.00

KARP, David. *Brotherhood of Velvet.* 1967. Banner B 50-113. 1st prtg. My. VG. R5d. $4.50

KARP, David. *Brotherhood of Velvet.* Lion 105. PBO. VG. B3d. $8.00

KARP, David. *Cry, Flesh.* 1953. Lion 132. 1st edn. My. F. F2d. $23.00

KARP, David. *Girl on Crown Street.* 1956. Lion LB 86. 2nd prtg. c/Robert Stanley. VG. P6d. $3.00

KARP, David. *Girl on Crown Street.* Lion LL 86. VG. G5d. $6.50

KARP, Marvin A. *Unhumans.* 1965. Popular SP 405. SF. G+. W2d. $4.50

KARR & KRAMER. *Teen-Age Gangs.* 1954. Popular 592. JD. VG+. B4d. $14.00

KARTA, Nat. *Too Good for the Poor.* Muir-Watson NN. VG. B3d. $12.00

KASTLE, Herbert D. *Bachelor Summer.* Avon T 355. PBO. c/photo. Fi. VG+. B5d. $4.00

KASTLE, Herbert D. *Bachelor Summer.* 1959. Avon T 355. 1st edn. c/photo. F. F2d. $16.00

KASTLE, Herbert D. *Hot Prowl.* Gold Medal 1591. NF. B3d. $5.50

KASTLE, Herbert D. *Reassembled Man.* 1964. Gold Medal L 1494. 1st prtg. F. S1d. $6.00

KASTLE, Herbert D. *Reassembled Man.* 1969. Gold Medal R 2041. 1st prtg. PBO. c/Frank Frazetta. SF. VG+. P6d. $3.50

KASTNER, Erich. *Missing Miniature.* Mercury 21. VG. G5d. $6.50

KATKOV, Norman. *Eagle at My Eyes.* 1950. Popular 251. 1st pb. c/gga. VG. B6d. $6.00

KAUFMAN, Lenard. *Jubal's Children.* 1951. Signet 896. Fi. VG. B5d. $4.00

KAUFMAN, Lenard. *Juvenile Deliquents.* 1955. Avon T 105. JD. VG+. P1d. $18.00

KAUFMAN, Maxine. *I Am Adam.* 1957. Pyramid R 289. c/M Crair. Fi. VC. B5d. $4.50

KAUFMAN, Sue. *Green Holly.* 1971. PB Library 65-769. 1st pb. NF. B6d. $6.00

KAUFMAN, William I. *Great Television Plays.* 1972. Dell 3207. 8th edn. TVTI. VG. P1d. $5.00

KAUFMAN & MORHEIM. *Isolation Booth.* Gold Medal 577. c/Hooks. VG. B3d. $6.00

KAUFMANN, Richard. *Heaven Pays No Dividends.* 1953. Signet S 1052. 1st prtg. c/Maguire: gga. VG. B3d. $4.00

KAVINOKY, Bernice. *Honey From a Dark Hive.* Popular G 487. c/Johnson. reprint. VG+. B6d. $9.00

KAVINOKY, Bernice. *We Burn Like Candles.* 1954. Popular 580. c/gga. Fa. VG+. B4d. $9.00

KAY, Cameron. *Thieves Fall Out.* 1953. Gold Medal 311. PBO. My. G+. B6d. $7.50

KAYE, H.R. *Dark Mansion.* Brandon House 3034. VG+. B3d. $5.00

KAYE, H.R. *Hitchhiker.* Brandon House 6007. VG+. B3d. $5.00

KAYE, H.R. *Maid.* Brandon House 3026. NF. B3d. $5.00

KAYE, M. edt. *Fiends & Creatures.* Popular 00289. c/Bloch: sgn. VG. B3d. $4.50

KAYE, Marvin. *Ghosts of Night & Morning.* 1987. Charter. 1st edn. F. M1d. $5.00

KAYE, Merlin. *Rape of the Red Witch.* 1980. Hustler 10-160. VG+. B3a #22. $27.50

KAYE, P.B. *Taffy.* Avon 377. VG. B3d. $5.00

KAYE, T. *It Had Been a Mild, Delicate Night.* Popular G 573. VG+. B3d. $4.50

KAZAN, Elia. *America America.* 1964. Popular M 2049. 1st prtg. VG+. R5d. $2.50

KEATING, E.P. *Good-Time Man.* 1949. Novel Library 13. Ad. G. B5d. $5.00

KEATING, E.P. *Hard-Boiled Mistress.* 1948. Magazine Village 7. VG. B3a #20. $23.00

KEATS, Charles. *Body of Love.* Berkley G 51. c/Maguire. VG+. B3a #22. $22.00

KEATS, Charles. *Body of Love.* 1957. Berkley G 51. PBO. c/Maguire: gga. VG+. B6a #76. $43.00

KEATS, John. *Crack in the Picture Window.* Ballantine 233. NF. VG. B5d. $5.00

KEEL, John A. *Fickle Finger of Fate.* 1966. Gold Medal D 1719. PBO. c/Jaffe. SF. VG. B5d/M6d. $12.50

KEEL, John A. *Strange Creatures From Time & Space.* Gold Medal T 2219. SF. G+. W2d. $3.25

KEENE, Day. *Acapulco.* Dell 0019. PBO. VG. B3d. $4.50

KEENE, Day. *Big Kiss-Off.* Berkley Diamond D 2003. c/Darcy: gga. scarce. NF. B6a #44. $44.00

KEENE, Day. *Big Kiss-Off.* 1954. Graphic 75. 1st edn. F. F2d. $18.00

KEENE, Day. *Big Kiss-Off.* 1954. Graphic 75. 1st prtg. PBO. c/Ross. VG+. P7d. $12.50

KEENE, Day. *Brimstone Bed.* 1960. Avon T 459. PBO. c/gga. scarce. VG+. B6a #77. $44.00

KEENE, Day. *Bring Him Back Dead.* Gold Medal 603. VG+. I1d. $10.00

KEENE, Day. *Chicago 11.* 1966. Dell 1198. 1st prtg. PBO. c/Abbett: gga. G+. P7d. $3.50

KEENE, Day. *Dead Dolls Don't Talk.* 1959. Crest 286. PBO. c/photo. scarce. VG. B6a #77. $67.25

KEENE, Day. *Dead Dolls Don't Talk.* 1959. Crest 286. 1st edn. My. F. F2d. $14.00

KEENE, Day. *Dead Man's Tide.* 1953. Graphic 60. 1st edn. My. VG. F2d. $12.00

KEENE, Day. *Death House Doll.* 1954. Ace D 41. 1st edn. PBO. scarce. VG+. B6a #77. $82.50

KEENE, Day. *Flight by Night.* 1956. Ace D 170. PBO. c/Barton. VG. B6d. $22.50

KEENE, Day. *Framed in Guilt.* 1966. MacFadden 60-234. 1st prtg. c/gga. VG. P7d. $4.50

KEENE, Day. *Home Is the Sailor.* 1952. Gold Medal 225. 1st edn. My. VG. F2d. $10.00

KEENE, Day. *Home Is the Sailor.* MacFadden 60-336. VG+. B3d. $8.00

KEENE, Day. *Homicidal Lady.* 1954. Graphic 87. PBO. c/gga. scarce. NF. B6a #75. $53.50

KEENE, Day. *Homicidal Lady.* 1954. Graphic 87. 1st edn. My. F. F2d. $25.00

KEENE, Day. *Homicidal Lady.* MacFadden 75-359. VG. B3d. $4.50

KEENE, Day. *Hunt the Killer.* 1951. Phantom Book 507. PBO. extremely scarce. VG. B6a #79. $42.50

KEENE, Day. *If the Coffin Fits.* Graphic 43. G. I1d. $5.00

KEENE, Day. *Joy House.* 1964. Consul Books 1329. VG. B3d. $8.00

KEENE, Day. *Joy House.* 1954. Lion 210. PBO. c/gga. My. VG. B6d. $25.00

KEENE, Day. *Joy House.* 1954. Lion 210. PBO. scarce. VG+. B6a #79. $67.25

KEENE, Day. *LA 46.* 1964. Dell 4606. PBO. VG+. B3d. $10.00

KEENE, Day. *Love Me & Die.* 1973. Manor 95287. 1st prtg. c/gga. VG. P7d. $4.00

KEENE, Day. *Miami 59.* 1965. Dell 5598. 1st prtg. c/Abbett: gga. G+. P7d. $3.50

KEENE, Day. *Moran's Woman.* MacFadden 50-358. VG. B3d. $7.50

KEENE, Day. *Moran's Woman.* 1959. Zenith 24. PBO. c/Nappi: gga. rare. VG. B6a #77. $82.50

KEENE, Day. *My Flesh Is Sweet.* 1951. Lion 68. PBO. c/gga. extremely scarce. VG+. B6a #77. $75.00

KEENE, Day. *Naked Fury.* Berkley Diamond D 2020. c/Milo. scarce. VG. B6a #80. $22.25

KEENE, Day. *Naked Fury.* 1952. Phantom Book 509. PBO. scarce. VG. B6a #80. $77.00

KEENE, Day. *Notorious.* 1954. Gold Medal 372. PBO. c/Carny. VG. B3a #22. $27.50

KEENE, Day. *Passion Murders.* Avon 684. PBO. c/gga. scarce. VG. B6a #77. $53.60

KEENE, Day. *Sleep With the Devil.* 1954. Lion 204. PBO. rare. NF. B6a #80. $67.25

KEENE, Day. *So Dead My Lovely.* 1959. Pyramid G 395. PBO. c/Maguire. VG+. B3a #20. $60.00

KEENE, Day. *Southern Daughter.* MacFadden 50-376. VG. B3d. $5.50

KEENE, Day. *Strange Witness.* Paladin NN. VG. B3a #20. $25.30

KEENE, Day. *There Was a Crooked Man.* 1954. Gold Medal 405. PBO. VG+. B3a #20. $59.00

KEENE, Day. *This Is Murder, Mr Herbert.* 1948. Avon 159. PBO. c/gga. scarce. VG+. B6a #75. $101.00

KEENE, Day. *To Kiss, or Kill.* 1951. Gold Medal 206. PBO. VG+. B6d. $45.00

KEENE, Day. *To Kiss, or Kill.* 1952. Gold Medal 206. 1st edn. My. VG. F2d. $20.00

KEENE, Day. *Too Black for Heaven.* MacFadden 50-399. VG. B3d. $6.50

KEENE, Day. *Too Black for Heaven.* 1959. Zenith ZB 31. PBO. VG. B3a #24. $38.50

KEENE, Day. *Too Black for Heaven.* 1959. Zenith 31. PBO. c/M Kunstler: gga. VG. B6a #77. $88.00

KEENE, Day. *Too Hot To Hold.* 1959. Gold Medal 931. PBO. My. VG. B6d. $10.00

KEENE, Day. *Too Hot To Hold.* 1959. Gold Medal 931. 1st edn. My. NF. F2d. $12.00

KEENE, Day. *Wake Up to Murder.* Avon 660. G+. G5d. $5.00

KEENE, Day. *Wake Up to Murder.* Avon 660. My. VG. B5d. $5.00

KEENE, Day. *Who Has Wilma Lathrop?* 1955. Gold Medal 494. PBO. c/Barye. scarce. VG+. B6a #79. $36.50

KEENE, Day. *World Without Women.* Gold Medal L 1504. 1st prtg. SF. G+. R5d. $2.00

KEENE, Day. *World Without Women.* 1960. Gold Medal S 975. 1st edn. SF. F. F2d. $15.00

KEENE, James. *Sixgun Wild.* 1960. Avon T 476. PBO. We. VG. P6d. $1.50

KEENE, James. *Texas Pistol.* Dell 930. VG. B3d. $4.50

KEENE, Nan. *Twice As Gay.* 1964. After Hours 109. c/Stanton. VG+. B3a #20. $16.20

KEENE/STUART. *Mrs Homicide/Dead Ahead.* 1953. Ace D 11. PBO. c/Saunders. VG. B6d. $35.00

KEENE/STUART. *Mrs Homicide/Dead Ahead.* 1953. Ace D 11. 1st edn. c/gga. My. F. F2d. $50.00

KEESING, Felix M. *Native Peoples of the Pacific.* 1945. Infantry NN. Nfi. NF. B4d. $6.00

KEITH, Alexander. *Love Gun.* 1970. Midwood M 125-55. Ad. VG+. B5d. $5.50

KEITH, Carlton. *Gem of a Murder.* Dell 1007. VG. G5d. $3.00

KEITH, Darielle. *Dark Union.* 1983. Dell 01694. PBO. Ho. VG+. B6d. $3.00

KEITH, William H. Jr. *Decision at Thunder Rift.* 1988. FASA 8601. 3rd prtg. SF. VG+. W2d. $3.75

KELLAND, Clarence B. *Arizona.* Ad Novel Classic 30. We. VG. P6d. $3.00

KELLAND, Clarence B. *Arizona.* Bantam 257. VG. B3d. $4.50

KELLAND, Clarence B. *Gold.* Hillman 16. VG. M6d. $8.50

KELLAND, Clarence B. *Great Mail Robbery.* 1952. Popular 432. c/Bergey: gga. My. VG+. B4d. $15.00

KELLAND, Clarence B. *Nameless Corpse.* Pyramid G 355. G. G5d. $5.50

KELLAND, Clarence B. *Sugarfoot!* 1948. Bantam 203. 1st prtg. c/Doares: gga. VG+. P7d. $5.00

KELLEAM, J.E. *Blackjack.* 1949. Bantam 700. c/CC Beall. VG. P6d. $2.25

KELLER, A. *Thunder at Harper's Ferry.* Ace D 395. VG. B3d. $5.00

KELLER, James. *Make Each Day Count.* Dell F 65. VG+. B3d. $4.50

KELLER, James. *Three Minutes a Day.* Perma P 105. VG. B3d. $4.50

KELLER, James. *You Can Change the World.* 1950. Signet 762. Nfi. VG+. B4d. $3.00

KELLER, Reamer. *Why the Long Puss?* 1956. Bantam 1460. PBO. VG+. B6d. $9.00

KELLEY, Leo P. *Coins of Murph.* 1971. Berkley S 2069. 1st prtg. SF. VG. R5d. $1.75

KELLEY, Leo P. *Counterfeits.* 1967. Belmont B 50-797. SF. VG. B5d/I1d. $4.00

KELLEY, Leo P. *Earth Tripper.* Gold Medal T 2719. 1st prtg. G+. S1d. $2.50

KELLEY, Leo P. *Mythmaster.* 1974. Coro 18832. SF. F. W2d. $5.00

KELLEY, Leo P. *Mythmaster.* 1973. Dell 6216. 1st prtg. SF. VG+. R5d. $2.25

KELLEY, Leo P. *Odyssey to Earthdeath.* 1968. Belmont B 60-085. 1st edn. SF. NF. F2d. $8.00

KELLEY, Leo P. *Time Rogue.* Lancer 74627. 1st prtg. VG+. S1d. $4.50

KELLEY & RYAN. *Mac Arthur: Man of Action.* 1951. Lion 67. VG. B3d. $5.00

KELLEY & WALLACE. *Witness.* Pocket 54595. MTI. VG. G5d. $3.00

KELLIER, Elizabeth. *Patient at Tonesbury Manor.* 1966. Ace M 145. Fa. VG. B4d. $2.00

KELLY, F.J. *Gates of Brass.* 1963. Monarch 296. My. VG. B5d. $7.50

KELLY, G. Lombard. *Sexual Feeling in Married Men & Women.* 1951. Pocket 825. Nfi. NF. B4d. $3.50

KELLY, G.R. *Teach Me To Love.* 1963. Beacon B 689X. PBO. Ad. VG. B5d. $4.50

KELLY, G.R. *Teach Me To Love.* 1963. Beacon B 689X. VG+. B3d. $6.00

KELLY, Karl. *Jazz Me Baby.* 1962. France 29. 1st edn. c/photo. My. F. F2d. $16.00

KELLY, Leo. *Coins of Murph.* 1971. Berkley 52069. 1st edn. VG. P9d. $1.50

KELLY, Walt. *Pogo for President.* 1964. Crest S 708. VG. P6d. $3.50

KELSEY, R. *Amorous Avenger.* Newsstand U 153. VG+. B3d. $5.50

KELSON/RABE. *Kill One, Kill Two/Cut of the Whip.* Ace D 297. VG. B3d. $25.00

KELSTON, Robert. *Murder's End.* 1956. Graphic 126. 1st prtg. PBO. c/Maguire: gga. VG. P7d. $7.50

KELTON, Elmer. *Buffalo Wagons.* 1956. Ballantine 187. PBO. We. VG. B6d. $8.00

KELTON, Elmer. *Buffalo Wagons.* Ballantine 535. We. VG. B5d. $4.00

KELTON, Elmer. *Donovan.* 1961. Ballantine 534. 1st edn. We. F. F2d. $11.00

KELTON, Elmer. *Horsehead Crossing.* 1963. Ballantine Y 735. PBO. We. NF. B6d. $12.50

KEMELMAN, Harry. *Tuesday the Rabbi Saw Red.* 1975. Crest Q 2336. 1st prtg. My. VG+. R5d. $2.00

KEMP, Kimberly. *Different.* 1963. Midwood F 331. PBO. Ad. NF. B6a #74. $64.25

KEMP, Kimberly. *Labor of Love.* 1964. Midwood 32-411. PBO. Ad. VG. B5d. $9.00

KEMP, Kimberly. *Lap of Luxury.* 1962.. Midwood 214. PBO. c/Rader. NF. B3a #20. $19.30

KEMP, Kimberly. *Party Time.* 1964. Midwood 32-426. PBO. c/Rader: gga. VG+. P6d. $4.50

KEMP, P. *No Colours or Crest.* Panther 1023. VG+. B3d. $7.00

KEMPER, William E. Jr. *Another Man's Hell.* 1962. Chicago PB House A 108. SF. G+. W2d. $8.00

KEMPTON, Edward. *Swamp Tease.* 1960. Avon T 387. PBO. c/Darcy: gga. Fi. VG. P6d. $2.50

KEMPTON, Edward. *Swamp Tease.* 1960. Avon T 387. 1st edn. c/gga. F. F2d. $20.00

KENDRICK, Baynard. *Blind Man's Bluff.* 1948. Dell 230. G+. P6d. $2.00

KENDRICK, Baynard. *Bright Victory.* Bantam 937. MTI. VG+. B3d. $4.50

KENDRICK, Baynard. *Death Knell.* Dell 273. 1st prtg. My. VG. R5d. $6.75

KENDRICK, Baynard. *Eleven of Diamonds.* Penguin 616. G+. G5d. $7.50

KENDRICK, Baynard. *Flames of Time.* 1951. Bantam A 902. 1st edn. PBO. c/gga. VG. B6a #79. $30.00

KENDRICK, Baynard. *Iron Spiders.* 1944. Dell 50. 1st edn. PBO. c/G Gregg. scarce. NF. B6a #80. $66.00

KENDRICK, Baynard. *Murder Made in Moscow.* Saint 122. VG+. B3d. $6.00

KENDRICK, Baynard. *Murder Who Wanted More.* Dell 10¢ 32. VG+. I1d. $12.00

KENDRICK, Baynard. *Odor of Violets.* 1947. Dell 162. 1st pb. c/Gregg. My. VG. B6d. $12.50

KENDRICK, Baynard. *Out of Control.* 1950. Dell 376. c/photo. My. VG+. P6d. $5.00

KENDRICK, Baynard. *Whistling Hangman.* 1946. Dell 113. 1st pb. c/Gregg. My. VG. B3d. $7.00

KENDRICKS, James. *Adulterers.* 1964. Monarch 425. Ad. NF. B5d. $9.00

KENDRICKS, James. *Sword of Casanova.* Monarch 111. VG+. B3d. $6.50

KENNAWAY, James. *Tunes of Glory.* 1961. Avon T 527. MTI. VG+. B4d. $4.00

KENNEALLEY, Thomas. *Chant of Jimmie Blacksmith.* 1975. Ballantine 23558. 1st prtg. My. VG. R5d. $1.50

KENNEDY, Burt. *7 Men From Now.* 1956. Berkley 361. 1st edn. c/photo. scarce esp in top condition. F. F2d. $15.00

KENNEDY, C.O. edt. *American Ballads.* Red Seal 22. VG. B3d. $5.00

KENNEDY, Donald. *So You Think You Know TV.* 1971. Ace 77680. TVTI. G+. P1d. $3.50

KENNEDY, George. *Murder on High.* 1984. Avon 88062. 1st prtg. My. F. W2d. $4.00

KENNEDY, George. *Murder on Location.* Avon 83857. VG. G5d. $3.00

KENNEDY, John F. *Strategy of Peace.* 1961. Popular PC 1002. 1st prtg. VG. P7d. $3.50

KENNEDY, M. *Constant Nymph.* Pan 229. VG. B3d. $5.50

KENNEDY, Mark. *Boy Gang.* 1955. Perma M 3006. 1st edn. PBO. c/art. F. F2d. $20.00

KENNEDY, Robert F. *To Seek a Newer World.* 1968. Bantam N 3844. 1st prtg. VG. P7d. $3.50

KENNERLEY, Juba. *Terror of the Leopard.* 1951. Avon 339. 1st US edn. F. F2d. $30.00

KENT, A. *Inclining to Crime.* Sexton Blake 364. VG+. B3d. $8.00

KENT, David. *Knife Is Silent.* Lion LL 91. VG+. I1d. $5.00

KENT, Justin. *Mavis.* 1960. Beacon 282. 1st pb. c/gga. NF. B6d. $22.50

KENT, Mona. *Mirror, Mirror on the Wall.* Popular 269. VG. B3d. $4.00

KENT, Nial. *Divided Path.* 1964. Pyramid X 452. 5th edn. c/H Schaare. Fi. VG. B5d. $5.00

KENT, Nial. *Divided Path.* 1951. Pyramid 32. Fa. VG+. B4d. $8.00

KENT, Richard. *Householder's Manual.* 1954. Signet K 312. Nfi. F. B4d. $4.00

KENT, Richard. *Householder's Manual.* 1954. Signet K 312. Nfi. VG+. B4d. $2.00

KENT, W.H.B. *Tenderfoot.* 1948. Bantam 202. 1st prtg. c/Doares. VG+. P7d. $5.00

KENTON, Maxwell. *Candy.* 1965. Brandon 721. Fa. NF. B4d. $8.00

KENTON, Maxwell. *Candy.* Lancer 74-841. 1st pb. VG. M6d. $5.00

KENYON, Larry. *Challenge at LeMans.* 1967. Avon G 1308. 1st edn. My. F. F2d. $10.00

KENYON, Larry. *Countdown at Monaco.* 1967. Avon G 1316. 1st edn. My. F. F2d. $10.00

KENYON, Michael. *May You Die in Ireland.* 1968. Crest R 1211. 1st prtg. My. G+. R5d. $1.25

KEOGH, Theodora. *Meg.* 1951. Signet 857. c/Avati. Fa. VG+. B4d. $5.00

KEOGH, Theodora. *Mistress.* 1959. Avon T 358. 1st edn. c/gga. My. F. F2d. $14.00

KEOGH, Theodora. *Tattooed Heart.* 1954. Signet 1100. c/Erickson: gga. Fa. VG. B4d. $3.50

KEON, Michael. *Durian Tree.* 1961. Perma M 4225. 1st pb. c/Johnson. VG+. B6d. $7.50

KERN, Gregory. *Beyond the Galactic Lens.* DAW 176. 1st prtg. VG. S1d. $2.50

KERN, Gregory. *Beyond the Galactic Lens.* 1975. DAW. 1st edn. F. M1d. $5.00

KERN, Gregory. *Ghosts of Epidoris.* 1975. DAW UQ 1159. Cap Kennedy #14. SF. VG. W2d. $4.00

KERN, Gregory. *Planet of Dread.* 1974. DAW UQ 1123. Cap Kennedy #10. SF. VG. W2d. $4.00

KEROUAC, Jack. *On the Road.* 1958. Signet D 1619. c/Barye Phillips. VG. P6d. $8.00

KEROUAC, Jack. *Subterraneans.* 1959. Avon T 302. 1st pb. VG+. B4d/B6d. $15.00

KEROUAC, Jack. *Subterraneans.* 1960. Avon T 390. Beat. VG. B4d. $6.00

KEROUAC, Jack. *Subterraneans.* 1959. Avon 302. 1st pb. G+. M1d. $10.00

KERR, Ben. *Blonde & Johnny Malloy.* Popular EB 104. PBO. c/gga. NF. B6a #75. $44.00

KERR, Ben. *Club 17.* 1957. Popular 803. PBO. c/gga. VG+. B6a #76. $44.00

KERR, Ben. *I Fear You Not.* 1956. Popular 763. PBO. VG. B6d. $7.50

KERR, Geoffrey. *Under the Influence.* 1961. Berkley. 1st pb. F. M1d. $8.00

KERR, J. *Please Don't Eat the Daisies.* Pan G 372. MTI. VG. B3d. $8.00

KERR, Jean. *Snake Has All the Lines.* Crest 514. VG+. B3d. $4.50

KERRIGAN, John. *Phoenix Assault.* 1980. Signet E 9522. 1st prtg. My. VG. W2d. $3.00

KERSH, Gerald. *Dead Look On.* Ace 171. 2nd prtg. VG. B3d. $9.00

KERSH, Gerald. *Night & the City.* 1950. Dell 374. MTI. c/photo. VG. P6d. $7.50

KERSH, Gerald. *Nightshade & Damnation.* 1968. Gold Medal 1887. 1st edn. VG. M1d. $15.00

KERSH, Gerald. *Nightshade & Damnation.* 1968. Gold Medal 1887. 1st edn. c/Dillons. My. F. F2d. $20.00

KERSH, Gerald. *On an Odd Note.* 1958. Ballantine 268. PBO. c/R Powers. SF. G+. B5d/R5d. $4.50

KERSH, Gerald. *On an Odd Note.* 1958. Ballantine 268. 1st edn. F. M1d. $20.00

KERSH, Gerald. *Prelude to a Certain Midnight.* 1952. Lion. 1st pb. VG. M1d. $25.00

KERSH, Gerald. *Secret Masters.* 1953. Ballantine 28. PBO. c/Powers. VG. P6d. $8.00

KERSH, Gerald. *Secret Masters.* 1953. Ballantine 28. 1st edn. F. M1d. $20.00

KESSEL, Joseph. *Man With the Miraculous Hands.* Dell F 182. VG. B3d. $4.00

KETCHAM, Hank. *Baby Sitter's Guide.* 1953. Pocket 1080. c/H Ketcham: cartoons. Nfi. VG. B5d. $5.00

KETCHAM, Hank. *Dennis the Menace Baby Sitter's Guide*. Pocket 1080. VG. B3d. $4.00

KETCHAM, Hank. *Dennis the Menace Rides Again*. Crest 467. 3rd prtg. VG+. B3d. $4.50

KETCHAM, Hank. *Dennis the Menace*. Pocket 1217. VG+. I1d. $4.00

KETCHAM, Hank. *Dennis the Menace: Teacher's Threat*. Crest 378. VG+. B3d. $4.50

KETCHAM, Hank. *Dennis the Menace: Teacher's Threat*. Gold Medal 2765. VG+. B3d. $5.00

KETCHAM, Hank. *In This Corner...Dennis the Menace*. 1959. Crest 298. 1st prtg. VG+. P7d. $6.00

KETCHAM, Hank. *Short & Snappy*. Crest D 1243. NF. I1d. $5.00

KETCHAM, Hank. *Wanted: Dennis the Menace*. Pocket 1153. VG+. I1d. $5.00

KETCHUM, Philip. *Apache Dawn*. Avon F 240. VG+. B3d. $4.00

KETCHUM, Philip. *Apache Dawn*. Avon T 467. PBO. VG+. B3d. $4.50

KETCHUM, Philip. *Big Gun*. Popular SP 267. VG+. B3d. $4.50

KETCHUM, Philip. *Dead Man's Trail*. Popular SP 254. NF. B3d. $5.00

KETCHUM, Philip. *Dead-Shot Kid*. Signet 1744. VG. B3d. $4.00

KETCHUM, Philip. *Death in the Library*. Dell 1. c/Strohmer. VG. B6d. $60.00

KETCHUM, Philip. *Elkhorn Feud*. Popular SP 256. reprint. We. VG+. B3d. $5.00

KETCHUM, Philip. *Elkhorn Feud*. Popular SP 256. VG+. B3d. $5.00

KETCHUM, Philip. *Feud at Forked River*. Gold Medal 374. VG+. B3d. $8.00

KETCHUM, Philip. *Good Night for Murder*. Dagger 22. VG. B3d. $5.00

KETCHUM, Philip. *Guns of the Barricade Bunch*. Popular 499. VG. B3d. $4.00

KETCHUM, Philip. *Gunsmoke Territory*. Hillman 137. PBO. VG. B3d. $4.50

KETCHUM, Philip. *Kill at Dusk*. Newsstand 144. VG. B3d. $6.50

KETCHUM, Philip. *Kill at Dusk*. Newstand 144. G+. G5d. $4.50

KETCHUM, Philip. *Man From Granite*. Ballantine U 2324. PBO. VG+. B3d. $4.00

KETCHUM, Philip. *Man From Granite*. 1967. Ballantine U 2334. PBO. We. NF. B6d. $10.00

KETCHUM, Philip. *Rattlesnake*. 1970. Ballantine 01904. We. VG+. B4d. $2.00

KETCHUM, Philip. *Renegade Range*. Monarch 256. PBO. VG+. B3d. $4.00

KETCHUM, Philip. *Six-Gun Maverick*. Popular 797. VG. B3d. $4.50

KETCHUM, Philip. *Texan on the Road*. Popular 472. NF. I1d. $6.00

KETCHUM, Philip. *Traitor Guns*. Avon F 126. PBO. VG. B3d. $4.00

KETCHUM, Philip. *Woman in Armour*. 1963. Avon G 1164. 1st edn. Ad. F. F2d. $14.00

KETCHUM/TRIMBLE. *Cougar Basin War/ Trouble Valley*. 1970. Ace 11785. We. VG+. B5d. $4.00

KETON, Elmer. *Shadow of a Star*. 1959. Ballantine 304K. 1st edn. Hi. F. F2d. $10.00

KEVEY, R.A. *Murder in Lima*. Avon 792. VG. B3d. $4.50

KEY, Alexander. *Escape to Witch Mountain*. 1973. Archer 42453. 16th prtg. MTI. SF. F. W2d. $4.00

KEY, Alexander. *Wrath & the Wind*. 1950. Popular 291. 1st edn. PBO. c/gga. F. F2d. $12.00

KEY, Alexander. *Wrath & the Wind*. 1954. Popular 608. c/gga. Fa. VG+. B4d. $10.00

KEY, Ted. *Cat From Outer Space*. 1978. Pocket 56054. 5th prtg. SF. G+. W2d. $2.50

KEY, Ted. *If You Like Hazel*. Bantam 1813. VG+. B3d. $5.00

KEY, Ted. *Phyllis*. Berkley 386. c/baseball. VG+. B3d. $4.00

KEYES, Frances Parkinson. *Career of David Noble*. Lancer 72-609. VG+. B3d. $5.00

KEYES, Frances Parkinson. *Chess Players*. Crest 553. VG. B3d. $4.00

KEYES, Frances Parkinson. *Crescent Carnival*. Dell 561. c/G Mayers. Fi. VG. B5d. $3.00

KEYES, Frances Parkinson. *Dinner at Antoine's*. 1950. Dell 443. c/Ric Grasso. Ro. G+. P6d. $1.50

KEYES, Frances Parkinson. *River Road*. Dell 692. c/G Foxley. Fi. VG. B5d. $3.00

KEYES, Frances Parkinson. *Station Wagon in Spain*. 1964. Avon S 154. Fa. VG+. B4d. $2.50

KEYES, Noel edt. *Contact*. 1965. PB Library. F. M1d. $7.00

KEYES, P. *Carol's Landing*. All Star 114. VG+. B3d. $4.50

KEYES, P. *Love Formula*. Brandon House 1141. VG+. B3d. $6.00

KEYHOE, Donald. *Flying Saucers Are Real*. 1950. Gold Medal 107. 1st edn. NF. M1d. $10.00

KEYHOE, Donald. *Flying Saucers Are Real*. 1950. Gold Medal 107. 1st prtg. PBO. VG. P7d. $5.50

KEYHOE, Donald. *Flying Saucers From Outer Space*. Perma 297. VG. I1d. $4.00

KEYHOE, Donald. *Platos Voladores de Otros Mundos*. 1955. Populibros NN. c/UFO. Nfi. VG. B5d. $10.00

KHAYYAM, Omar. *Rubaiyat*. 1941. Pocket 128. c/G Ross: poetry. Nfi. VG. B5d. $7.50

KIERAN, James. *Come Murder Me*. 1951. Gold Medal 150. 1st prtg. PBO. c/Barye: gga. VG+. P7d. $7.50

KILGORE, G. *Starlet Whore*. Brandon House 6500. F. B3d. $4.50

KILIAN, Crawford. *Eyas*. 1965. Bantam. F. M1d. $4.00

KILLEN, J. *Luftwaffe*. 1969. Sphere 52237. VG+. B3d. $8.00

KILRAIN, George. *Maverick With a Star*. 1953. Ace D 14. PBO. c/Saunders. VG+. B6d. $30.00

KILWORTH, Garry. *Genuine God*. 1982. Penguin. 1st pb. VG. M1d. $4.00

KIMBROUGH, Edward. *Night Fire*. 1954. Ace D 65. PBO. c/Barton: gga. F. B6a #74. $66.00

KIMBROUGH, Edward. *Night Fire*. 1954. Ace D 65. 1st edn. PBO. c/Barton. VG+. B6d. $30.00

KIMBROUGH & SKINNER. *Our Hearts Were Young & Gay*. Bantam 105. 2nd edn. c/Alajalov. Fi. VG+. B5d. $3.50

KIMBROUGH/OSBORNE. *Night Fire/Tornado*. 1954. Ace D 65. c/Barton: gga. VG. P6d. $6.00

KINDER, Gary. *Victim*. 1984. Dell 39306. 1st prtg. Nfi. F. W2d. $3.75

KING, Alan. *Anybody Owns His Own Home Deserves It*. Avon G 1160. VG+. B3d. $4.50

KING, Alan. *May This House Be Safe From Tigers*. Signet 1903. VG+. B3d. $5.00

KING, Bruce. *Demon Shield*. 1989. Lynx 55802. 1st edn. Ho. F. F2d. $10.00

KING, Dave. *Brutal Lust*. 1966. Publishers Export N 119. PBO. c/gga. NF. B6a #75. $30.25

KING, Dave. *Run, Lez, Run*. 1967. Publishers Export FL 10. PBO. NF. B6a #74. $82.50

KING, David. *In Desert Masquerade*. 1967. PB Library 53-411. TVTI. Rat Patrol #2. VG+. B4d. $6.00

KING, David. *In Desert Masquerade*. 1968. PB Library 53-696. PBO. TVTI. c/photo. Rat Patrol #6. Fi. VG+. B5d. $5.50

KING, David. *In Desert Masquerade*. 1968. PB Library 53-696. TVTI. Rat Patrol #6. F. B4d. $8.00

KING, G.A. *Six-Way Swap*. Beacon 1103. VG. B3d. $5.00

KING, H. *Partner's in Crime.* Sexton Blake 232. VG. B3d. $6.00

KING, M. *Only for Money.* Unique 146. c/Stanton. VG. B3d. $7.50

KING, Rufus. *Crime of Violence.* 1943. Popular NN 3. 1st edn. PBO. c/Hoffman. rare. VG+. B6a #80. $63.50

KING, Rufus. *Crime of Violence.* 1943. Popular NN 3. 1st pb. c/Hoffman. My. G+. B6d. $7.50

KING, Rufus. *Deadly Dove.* 1951. Popular 318. 1st edn. PBO. c/Belarski: gga. My. VG+. B6a #79. $38.50

KING, Rufus. *Deadly Dove.* 1951. Popular 318. 1st pb. c/Belarski. My. VG+. B6d. $18.00

KING, Rufus. *Design in Evil.* Popular 124. VG. B3d. $5.50

KING, Rufus. *Diagnosis: Murder.* Century 14. VG. B3d. $5.00

KING, Rufus. *Fatal Kiss Mystery.* Popular 43. VG. B3d. $6.00

KING, Rufus. *Holiday Homicide.* 1943. Dell 22. 1st edn. PBO. c/Gregg. rare. F. B6a #80. $82.50

KING, Rufus. *Murder by the Clock.* 1966. Collins 02194. 1st prtg. My. VG. W2d. $3.25

KING, Rufus. *Murder Challenges Valcour.* Dell 39. VG. B3d. $6.00

KING, Rufus. *Murder in the Willett Family.* 1945. Popular 55. c/Hoffman. VG+. B3a #22. $23.40

KING, Rufus. *Murder Masks Miami.* 1944. Popular 22. VG+. B3a #21. $26.05

KING, Rufus. *Murder on the Yacht.* 1945. Popular 67. 1st pb. c/Hoffman. My. VG. B3d. $5.00

KING, Rufus. *Murderer in This House.* Detective 38. VG. B3d. $5.00

KING, Rufus. *Secret Beyond the Door.* 1947. Bantam 120. MTI. c/D Atti, J Bennett & M Redgrave. My. VG. B5d. $5.00

KING, Rufus. *Secret Beyond the Door.* 1947. Bantam 120. MTI. c/gga. NF. B4d. $9.00

KING, Rufus. *Somewhere in This House.* 1950. Popular 276. 1st pb. c/Belarski. My. VG. B6d. $7.50

KING, Rufus. *Valcour Meets Murder.* Popular 13. G. G5d. $6.00

KING, Rufus. *Variety of Weapons.* 1946. Popular 97. 1st pb. My. VG. B3d. $10.00

KING, Stephen. *Bachman Books.* 1986. Signet AE 4736. SF. VG+. W2d. $7.50

KING, Stephen. *Carrie.* 1975. Signet J 7280. 16th prtg. SF. VG. W2d. $5.00

KING, Stephen. *Carrie.* Signet 451. 1st prtg. VG. S1d. $2.50

KING, Stephen. *Christine.* Signet AE 2837. G+. G5d. $4.00

KING, Stephen. *Cujo.* Signet AE 1729. NF. G5d. $6.00

KING, Stephen. *Danse Macabre.* 1982. Berkley 05345. Nfi. VG. P1d. $15.00

KING, Stephen. *Dead Zone.* 1980. Signet E 9338. SF. F. W2d. $6.00

KING, Stephen. *Eyes of the Dragon.* 1988. Signet AE 5125. 1st edn. PBO. VG. P9d. $2.00

KING, Stephen. *Firestarter.* 1981. Signet E 9964. 2nd prtg. SF. F. W2d. $5.00

KING, Stephen. *Misery.* 1988. Signet AE 5355. SF. F. W2d. $5.00

KING, Stephen. *Pet Sematary.* 1984. Signet AE 3237. 1st pb. VG. M1d. $5.00

KING, Stephen. *Rage.* 1977. Signet W 7645. 1st edn. VG. P9d. $35.00

KING, Stephen. *Salem's Lot.* 1976. Signet E 8000. 13th prtg. SF. F. W2d. $7.00

KING, Stephen. *Shining.* 1978. Signet E 7872. 1st prtg. SF. VG. W2d. $7.00

KING, Vincent. *Another End.* 1971. Ballantine 02109. SF. VG+. B4d. $3.00

KING, Vincent. *Light a Last Candle.* 1969. Ballantine 01654. 1st edn. G. P9d. $1.25

KING, W. *Strumpet.* Ember Book EB 903. VG. B3d. $4.50

KING & RICE. *Stairway to Murder.* Saint My Library 118. VG. M6d. $7.50

KING & STRAUB. *Talisman.* 1985. Berkley 08181. 1st prtg. SF. VG. R5d. $3.00

KING-HALL, Magdalen. *Wicked Lady Skelton.* Dell 640. c/H Bischoff. My. NF. B5d. $7.50

KING-HALL, Magdalen. *Wicked Lady Skelton.* 1949. Harlequin 11. 1st edn. PBO. c/Heal: gga. scarce. Fa. VG+. B6a #75. $44.00

KINGERY, Don. *Swamp Fire.* Popular 815. VG. B3d. $3.50

KINGSLEY, Michael J. *Black Man, White Man, Dead Man.* Ace 06610. My. VG. B5d. $4.50

KINNEMAN, L.R. *Dangerous Sex: Adultery.* Genell 115. NF. B3d. $5.00

KINSEY, Chet. *Kate.* 1959. Beacon 225. PBO. c/Barton: gga. VG+. B6d. $18.00

KIPLING, Rudyard. *Captains Couragous.* 1946. Bantam 58. Fa. VG+. B4d. $8.00

KIPLING, Rudyard. *Kim.* 1965. Airmont CL 75. Fa. VG+. B4d. $3.00

KIPLING, Rudyard. *2nd Jungle Book.* Pan X 719. 1st pb. MTI. reprint. VG. B6d. $5.00

KIPPAX & MORGAN. *Thunder of Stars.* 1970. Ballantine 01922. SF. VG+. B4d. $3.00

KIRBY, Mark. *Harling College.* 1961. Beacon 384. PBO. c/gga. NF. B6d. $25.00

KIRCH, A.M. edt. *Women.* Dell 1st Edn D 3. PBO. c/W Brooks. NF. VG. B5d. $4.00

KIRK, Philip. *Hydra Conspiracy.* 1979. Leisure 655. 1st edn. Th. F. F2d. $10.00

KIRK, Russell. *Old House of Fear.* 1962. Avon G 1134. PBO. scarce. Ho. NF. B6a #76. $24.25

KIRK, Russell. *Surley Sullen Bell.* 1964. PB Library. 1st pb. F. M1d. $8.00

KIRKBRIDE, Ronald. *Girl Named Tamiko.* 1967. Avon S 287. c/gga. Fa. VG+. B4d. $3.00

KIRST, Hans Hellmut. *Revolt of Gunner Asch.* 1964. Pyramid X 1036. 1st prtg. c/Greene: gga. VG. P7d. $4.00

KITCHIN, C.H. *You May Smoke.* Award 190. VG+. B3d. $4.50

KJELGAARD, Jim. *Big Red.* 1949. Comet 18. 1st pb. VG+. B6d. $7.00

KLEIN, Alexander. *Counterfeit Traitor.* 1962. Perma M 4122. 3rd prtg. VG+. R5d. $2.50

KLEIN, Alexander. *Counterfeit Traitor.* 1967. Pyramid T 1722. c/swastica. Nfi. NF. B4d. $4.00

KLEIN, Alexander. *Fabulous Rogues.* Ballantine 408K. F. I1d. $8.00

KLEIN, Alexander. *Grand Deception.* Ballantine 372K. NF. VG. B5d. $3.50

KLEIN, Ernst. *Blackmailer.* Avon 404. VG+. B3d. $6.00

KLEIN, Gerard. *Day Before Tomorrow.* 1972. DAW 11. 1st edn. VG+. I1d. $4.00

KLEIN, Gerard. *Mote in Time's Eye.* 1975. DAW 134. c/J Kirby. SF. VG. B5d. $3.50

KLEIN, Gerard. *Mote in Time's Eye.* 1975. DAW 134. 1st edn. SF. F. F2d. $7.50

KLEIN, Gerard. *Starmaster's Gambit.* 1973. DAW UE 1464. F. P9d. $2.00

KLEIN, Ted. *Ceremonies.* 1985. Bantam 25055. 1st edn. PBO. VG. P9d. $2.00

KLEINBAUM, N.H. *DARYL.* 1985. Berkley 08432. 1st prtg. MTI. SF. VG+. R5d. $2.00

KLIMO, V. *Hemingway & Jake.* Popular 00176. VG+. B3d. $4.50

KLINE, Otis Adelbert. *Jan in India.* 1974. Fictioneer 1. 1st edn. SF. F. F2d. $15.00

KLINE, Otis Adelbert. *Jan of the Jungle.* Ace F 400. VG+. B3d. $4.50

KLINE, Otis Adelbert. *Jan of the Jungle.* 1966. Ace F 400. 1st edn. PBO. SF. F. F2d/M1d. $10.00

KLINE, Otis Adelbert. *Man Who. Limped.* 1946. Chartered Digest 22. PBO. rarest. VG+. B6a #74. $150.00

KLINE, Otis Adelbert. *Maza of the Moon.* Ace F 321. VG. I1d. $3.00

KLINE, Otis Adelbert. *Maza of the Moon.* 1965. Ace F 321. 1st edn. PBO. SF. F. W2d. $12.00

KLINE, Otis Adelbert. *Outlaws of Mars.* 1961. Ace D 531. 1st edn. PBO. SF. F. F2d/M1d. $10.00

KLINE, Otis Adelbert. *Planet of Peril.* Ace F 211. c/R Krenkel Jr. SF. VG. B5d/I1d. $3.50

KLINE, Otis Adelbert. *Planet of Peril.* 1963. Ace F 211. 1st edn. PBO. SF. F. F2d. $9.00

KLINE, Otis Adelbert. *Port of Peril.* 1964. Ace F 294. 1st edn. PBO. SF. F. W2d. $12.00

KLINE, Otis Adelbert. *Prince of Peril.* Ace F 259. F. M1d. $10.00

KLINE, Otis Adelbert. *Prince of Peril.* 1964. Ace F 259. SF. NF. B4d. $6.00

KLINE, Otis Adelbert. *Swordsman of Mars.* 1961. Ace D 516. 1st edn. PBO. SF. F. F2d. $9.00

KLINE, Otis Adelbert. *Swordsman of Mars.* Ace G 692. SF. VG. W2d. $8.00

KLING, Ken. *How I Pick Winners.* Popular 181. VG. B3d. $4.00

KLINGER, Henry. *Murder Off Broadway.* 1962. Pocket M 4255. 1st edn. De. F. F2d. $10.00

KLOMER, M. *Lust Sinner.* Dragon Books 126. PBO. VG+. B3d. $5.50

KLUCKHOHN, Frank L. *America: Listen!* 1962. Monarch MS 3A. Nfi. VG+. B4d. $5.00

KLUCKHOHN, Frank L. *America: Listen!* 1962. Monarch MS 3A. PBO. c/photo. Nfi. VG. B5d. $4.00

KNEALE, Nigel. *Quatermass.* 1979. Arrow. 1st pb. VG. M1d. $6.00

KNIBBS, Henry Herbert. *Ridin' Kid From Power River.* Dell 399. c/R Stanley. We. VG. B5d. $4.00

KNIGHT, Adam. *Girl Running.* 1956. Signet 1347. c/gga. My. VG. B4d. $4.00

KNIGHT, Adam. *I'll Kill You Next!* 1956. Signet 1276. c/gga. My. VG+. B4d. $5.00

KNIGHT, Adam. *Kiss & Kill.* Signet 1139. VG. B3d. $4.00

KNIGHT, Adam. *Murder for Madame.* 1952. Signet 920. Fa. VG+. B4d. $9.00

KNIGHT, Adam. *Sunburned Corpse.* 1954. Signet 1103. 1st edn. PBO. c/Cozzarelli. scarce. VG+. B6a #79. $26.25

KNIGHT, Adam. *Triple Slay.* Signet 1724. G+. G5d. $3.00

KNIGHT, Adam. *Triple Slay.* Signet 1724. VG+. B3d. $5.00

KNIGHT, Billy. *Orgy Ship.* 1966. Red Light 103. 1st edn. c/gga. F. F2d. $12.50

KNIGHT, Clifford. *Affair of the Scarlet Crab.* 1945. Dell 75. c/Gerald Gregg. My. VG. P6d. $7.00

KNIGHT, Damon. *A for Anything.* 1972. Gold Medal T 2545. 1st prtg. SF. VG+. W2d. $3.75

KNIGHT, Damon. *Analogue Man.* 1962. Berkley. NF. M1d. $5.00

KNIGHT, Damon. *Beyond the Barrier.* 1965. MacFadden 50-234. SF. VG+. B4d. $3.75

KNIGHT, Damon. *Beyond the Barrier.* 1965. MacFadden 50-234. 1st pb. F. M1d. $7.00

KNIGHT, Damon. *Beyond the Barrier.* 1970. MacFadden 60-444. 4th edn. VG. P9d. $1.50

KNIGHT, Damon. *Century of SF.* 1963. Dell 1157. 1st edn. PBO. F. P9d. $2.50

KNIGHT, Damon. *Century of Short SF Novels.* 1965. Dell 1158. 1st edn. PBO. VG. P9d. $1.50

KNIGHT, Damon. *Cities of Wonder.* 1967. MacFadden 75-183. 1st edn. PBO. F. P9d. $2.50

KNIGHT, Damon. *CV.* 1986. TOR 54333. 1st pb. c/Tony Roberts. SF. F. B6d. $3.00

KNIGHT, Damon. *Dark Side.* 1965. Curtis 7029. 1st edn. PBO. NF. P9d. $2.00

KNIGHT, Damon. *Far Out.* 1962. Berkley F 616. 1st edn. PBO. F. M1d. $7.00

KNIGHT, Damon. *Final Flight.* 1963. Lancer. 72-145 1st edn. VG. M1d/R5d. $4.00

KNIGHT, Damon. *First Voyage.* 1981. Avon. 1st edn. NF. M1d. $4.00

KNIGHT, Damon. *For Anything.* 1965. Berkley F 1136. 2nd edn. F. P9d. $2.00

KNIGHT, Damon. *For Anything.* Four Square 382. 1st English edn. VG. B3d. $7.50

KNIGHT, Damon. *Hell's Pavement.* 1955. Lion LL 13. c/sgn. VG. B3d. $8.00

KNIGHT, Damon. *Hell's Pavement.* 1955. Lion LL 13. 1st edn. NF. I1d. $20.00

KNIGHT, Damon. *Hell's Pavement.* 1955. Lion LL 13. 1st edn. SF/Fa. F. F2d. $25.00

KNIGHT, Damon. *In Deep.* 1963. Berkley F 760. NF. B3d. $5.00

KNIGHT, Damon. *In Deep.* 1963. Berkley F 760. PBO. c/R Powers. SF. G+. B5d/R5d. $3.00

KNIGHT, Damon. *In Deep.* 1963. Berkley F 760. 1st pb. F. M1d. $8.00

KNIGHT, Damon. *In Search of Wonder.* 1968. Advent 1968. 2nd edn. Nfi. F. P1d. $15.00

KNIGHT, Damon. *Lot of Lolita.* Golden 803. NF. B3d. $4.50

KNIGHT, Damon. *Mind Switch.* 1965. Berkley F 1160. c/Hoot. SF. VG. B4d. $3.00

KNIGHT, Damon. *Nebula Award Stories.* 1969. Pocket 75275. 3rd prtg. SF. VG. W2d. $4.00

KNIGHT, Damon. *Now Begins Tomorrow.* 1969. Lancer 74-585. SF. VG. B5d. $4.00

KNIGHT, Damon. *Off Center & the Rithian Terror.* 1965. Ace M 113. 1st prtg. SF. G+. R5d. $1.75

KNIGHT, Damon. *Orbit #10.* 1972. Berkley N 2236. SF. VG. B5d. $3.00

KNIGHT, Damon. *Orbit #11.* 1973. Berkley 2316. 1st edn. PBO. F. P9d. $2.00

KNIGHT, Damon. *Orbit #13.* 1974. Berkley N 2698. 1st edn. PBO. F. P9d. $2.00

KNIGHT, Damon. *Orbit #2.* 1967. Berkley S 1448. c/P Lehr. SF. VG. B5d. $3.00

KNIGHT, Damon. *Orbit #3.* 1968. Berkley S 1608. 1st prtg. SF. G+. R5d. $1.50

KNIGHT, Damon. *Orbit #4.* 1969. Berkley S 1724. c/P Lehr. SF. VG+. B5d. $4.00

KNIGHT, Damon. *Orbit #4.* 1969. Berkley X 1724. c/P Lehr. SF. VG+. B5d. $4.00

KNIGHT, Damon. *Orbit #5.* 1969. Berkley S 1778. c/P Lehr. SF. VG. B5d. $3.00

KNIGHT, Damon. *Orbit #6.* 1970. Berkley S 1848. 1st prtg. SF. VG. R5d. $2.50

KNIGHT, Damon. *People Maker.* 1959. Zenith ZB 14. 1st edn. F. M1d. $20.00

KNIGHT, Damon. *People Maker.* 1959. Zenith ZB 14. PBO. SF. G+. B5d. $4.50

KNIGHT, Damon. *Tomorrow X4.* 1964. Gold Medal D 1428. SF. VG. B4d. $4.00

KNIGHT, Damon. *Tomorrow X4.* 1964. Gold Medal D 1428. 1st prtg. F. S1d. $7.00

KNIGHT, Damon. *Turning On.* Ace G 677. 1st prtg. VG+. S1d. $3.00

KNIGHT, Damon. *Worlds To Come.* Gold Medal R 1942. 1st edn. PBO. NF. P9d. $2.00

KNIGHT, Damon. *Worlds To Come.* Gold Medal R 1942. 1st prtg. SF. G+. R5d. $1.50

KNIGHT, Damon. *13 French SF Stories.* 1965. Bantam. 1st edn. F. M1d. $5.00

KNIGHT, David. *Dragnet Case #561.* Pocket 1120. TVTI. G+. G5d. $3.50

KNIGHT, David. *Pattern for Murder.* Graphic 48. VG. G5d. $6.00

KNIGHT, E.F. *Cruise of the Alerte.* Panther 599. VG. B3d. $5.50

KNIGHT, M. *Malignant Metaphysical Menace.* 1968. Award A 369X. 1st prtg. PBO. VG. P7d. $5.00

KNIGHT, Malcolm. *Kiss of Death.* 1960. Merit Books 501. PBO. c/Sloan. VG. P6d. $3.00

KNIGHT, Mallory T. *Dozen Deadly Dragons of Joy.* Award A 212X. PBO. Tomcat. VG. M6d. $5.00

KNIGHT, Mallory T. *Million Missing Maidens.* Award A 237X. PBO. Tomcat #2. G+. M6d. $5.00

KNIGHT, Mullory T. *Peking Pornographer.* 1969. Award 539. PBO. Tomcat #8. VG+. B6d. $7.00

KNIGHT, S. *RX for Passion.* Galaxy 809. VG+. B3d. $5.00

KNIGHT/KNIGHT. *Off Center/Rithian Terror.* Ace M 113. F. M1d. $7.00

KNIGHT/SMITH. *Masters of Evolution/Fire in the Heavens.* Ace D 375. c/Emsh. VG. M1d. $8.00

KNIGHT/WALLIS. *Sun Saboteurs/Light of Lilith.* 1961. Ace F 108. F. M1d. $10.00

KNIGHT/WALLIS. *Sun Saboteurs/Light of Lilith.* 1961. Ace F 108. PBO. c/E Valigursky & E Emsh. SF. VG. B5d. $4.50

KNOX/LESSER. *Plot Against Earth/Recruit for Andromeda.* Ace D 358. F. M1d. $15.00

KNOX/LESSER. *Plot Against Earth/Recruit for Andromeda.* Ace D 358. VG. I1d. $5.00

KNOX/VAN VOGT. *One of Our Asteroids Is Missing/Twisted Men.* Ace F 253. F. P9d. $8.00

KNOX/VAN VOGT. *One of Our Asteroids Is Missing/Twisted Men.* Ace F 253. NF. M1d. $7.00

KNOX/VAN VOGT. *One of Our Asteroids Is Missing/Twisted Men.* 1964. Ace F 253. PBO. c/J Gaughan. SF. VG. M3d. $5.00

KOBER, Arthur. *My Dear Bella.* Bantam 35. VG+. B3d. $4.50

KOBY, Dale. *Sex by Appointment.* 1968. Saber SA 122. 1st edn. c/gga. F2d. $15.00

KOCH, Howard. *Panic Broadcast.* 1971. Avon N 408. Nfi. VG+. B5d. $5.50

KOENIG, H.P. *Doctor's Woman.* Avon 657. VG. B3d. $5.00

KOENIG, Walter. *Chekov's Enterprise.* 1980. Pocket 83286. 1st edn. Star Trek. SF. F. F2d. $10.00

KOESTLER, Arthur. *Darkness at Noon.* Signet 671. c/Peng: sgn. VG+. B3d. $6.50

KOESTLER, Arthur. *Darkness at Noon.* 1948. Signet 671. Fi. VG. B5d. $3.50

KOESTLER, Arthur. *Gladiators.* 1954. Graphic G 206. 1st prtg. c/gga. VG. P7d. $5.00

KOESTLER, Arthur. *Gladiators.* Graphic G 213. 2nd prtg. VG+. B3d. $5.50

KOFSKY, Frank. *Lenny Bruce.* 1974. Monad Press NN. 1st edn. c/photo. Bio. F. F2d. $15.00

KOGON, Eugen. *Theory & Practice of Hell.* Berkley S 888. 4th edn. c/photo. Nfi. VG+. B5d. $3.50

KOHNER, Frederick. *Gidget Goes Hawaiian.* 1961. Bantam A 2235. 1st prtg. G+. R5d. $1.50

KOLB, S. & J. *Treasury of Folk Songs.* Bantam 123. VG. B3d. $4.50

KOMROFF, Manuel. *Everyman's Bible.* 1953. Lion 167. Nfi. VG+. B3d. $5.00

KOMROFF, Manuel. *Gods & Demons.* 1954. Lion. 1st edn. VG. M1d. $10.00

KOMROFF, Manuel. *Life, the Loves, the Adventures of Omar Khayyam.* 1957. Signet 1377. Fi. VG. B5d. $4.00

KOMROFF, Manuel. *Travels of Marco Polo.* Armed Services H 236. VG. P6d. $4.50

KONINGSBERGER, Hans. *Affair.* 1959. Pyramid G 407. c/H Schaare. Fi. VG. B5d. $3.50

KONINGSBERGER, Hans. *Love & Hate in China.* 1967. Signet T 3154. Nfi. NF. B4d. $2.25

KONINGSBERGER, Hans. *Walk With Love & Death.* Popular 60-8101. 1st prtg. VG. R5d. $1.75

KOONTZ, Dean R. *After the Last Race.* 1975. Crest Q 2650. 1st prtg. c/gga. VG+. P7d. $10.00

KOONTZ, Dean R. *Beastchild.* Lancer 74-719. 1st prtg. G+. S1d. $7.50

KOONTZ, Dean R. *Beastchild.* 1970. Lancer 74-719. 1st prtg. SF. VG. R5d. $14.00

KOONTZ, Dean R. *Crimson Witch.* 1971. Curtis 7156. PBO. rare. SF. NF. B6a #75. $110.00

KOONTZ, Dean R. *Darker Heritage.* 1972. Lancer 75-294. 1st edn. Ho. F. F2d. $25.00

KOONTZ, Dean R. *Darkness in My Soul.* DAW 12. NF. I1d. $20.00

KOONTZ, Dean R. *Darkness in My Soul.* 1972. DAW 12. PBO. SF. VG. M3d. $15.00

KOONTZ, Dean R. *Darkness in My Soul.* 1972. DAW 12. 1st prtg. PBO. c/Gaughan. G+. P7d. $5.50

KOONTZ, Dean R. *Demon Seed.* 1973. Bantam N 7190. 1st prtg. G. S1d. $4.50

KOONTZ, Dean R. *Demon Seed.* 1973. Bantam N7190. 1st edn. NF. F2d. $15.00

KOONTZ, Dean R. *Eyes of Darkness.* 1981. Pocket 82784. 1st edn. scarce. SF. F. F2d. $10.00

KOONTZ, Dean R. *Fall of the Dream Machine.* 1969. Ace 22600. 1st edn. SF. NF. F2d. $15.00

KOONTZ, Dean R. *Fear That Man.* Ace 23140. PBO. G+. M6d. $5.00

KOONTZ, Dean R. *Funhouse.* 1980. Jove 5726. 1st edn. Ho. NF. F2d. $10.00

KOONTZ, Dean R. *Haunted Earth.* 1973. Lancer 75-445. PBO. VG. B3d. $5.00

KOONTZ, Dean R. *Haunted Earth.* 1973. Lancer 75-445. 1st edn. SF. F. F2d. $25.00

KOONTZ, Dean R. *House of Thunder.* 1982. Pocket 43266. 1st edn. Ho. NF. F2d. $20.00

KOONTZ, Dean R. *Long Sleep.* 1975. Popular 00325. 1st edn. SF. G. F2d. $10.00

KOONTZ, Dean R. *Mask.* 1988. Berkley 09777. SF. F. W2d. $4.00

KOONTZ, Dean R. *Mask.* 1981. Jove 5695. 1st edn. Ho. F. F2d. $20.00

KOONTZ, Dean R. *Nightmare Journey.* Berkley N 2923. 1st pb. G+. M6d. $8.50

KOONTZ, Dean R. *Star Quest.* 1968. Ace H 70. 1st edn. SF. NF. F2d. $15.00

KOONTZ, Dean R. *Starblood.* 1972. Lancer 75-306. PBO. SF. VG. M3d. $10.00

KOONTZ, Dean R. *Strangers.* 1986. Berkley 9217. 1st edn. PBO. NF. P9d. $2.50

KOONTZ, Dean R. *Vision.* 1978. Bantam 11898. 1st edn. PBO. VG. P9d. $1.50

KOONTZ, Dean R. *Voice of the Night.* 1991. Berkley 12816. 3rd edn. F. P9d. $2.50

KOONTZ, Dean R. *Warlock.* 1972. Lancer 75-386. SF. VG+. B4d. $22.00

KOONTZ, Dean R. *Watchers.* 1988. Berkley 10746. 9th prtg. SF. VG+. W2d. $4.75

KOONTZ, Dean R. *Werewolf Among Us.* 1973. Ballantine 3055. 1st edn. Ho. NF. F2d. $25.00

KOONTZ, Dean R. *Werewolf Among Us.* 1973. Ballantine 3055. 1st prtg. SF. VG. R5d. $20.00

KOONTZ, Leigh Nichols. *Eyes of Darkness.* Pocket 82784. PBO. VG. M6d. $6.50

KOONTZ, Leigh Nichols. *Shadowfires.* Avon 75216. PBO. VG. M6d. $3.50

KOONTZ, Owen West. *Funhouse.* Nelson Doubleday 3494. MTI. 1st edn. VG+. M6d. $8.50

KOONTZ/KOONTZ. *Dark of the Woods/Soft Come the Dragons.* 1970. Ace 13793. SF. NF. B4d. $22.00

KOONTZ/PETAJA. *Star Quest/Doom of the Green Planet*. 1968. Ace H 70. SF. VG+. B4d. $10.00

KOONTZ/TUBB. *Fear That Man/Toyman*. Ace 23140. c/J Gaughan & K Freas. SF. G+. $12.50

KORDEL, L. *Eat Your Troubles Away*. Belmont L 517. 8th prtg. VG. B3d. $4.00

KORNBLUTH, C.M. *Explorers*. Ballantine 708. 2nd edn. NF. B3d. $5.00

KORNBLUTH, C.M. *Explorers*. Ballantine 86. PBO. VG+. B3d. $5.50

KORNBLUTH, C.M. *Explorers*. 1954. Ballantine 86. PBO. SF. F. F2d. $10.00

KORNBLUTH, C.M. *Half*. 1953. Lion 135. 1st edn. Ad. F. F2d. $40.00

KORNBLUTH, C.M. *Man of Cold Rages*. 1958. Pyramid G 368. 1st edn. scarce. My. NF. F2d. $35.00

KORNBLUTH, C.M. *Marching Morons*. 1959. Ballantine 303K. PBO. c/photo. SF. G+. B5d. $3.50

KORNBLUTH, C.M. *Marching Morons*. 1959. Ballantine 303K. 1st edn. SF. F. F2d. $10.00

KORNBLUTH, C.M. *Mile Beyond the Moon*. MacFadden 40-100. VG+. B3d. $5.00

KORNBLUTH, C.M. *Mile Beyond the Moon*. MacFadden 40-100. 1st prtg. VG. S1d. $4.50

KORNBLUTH, C.M. *Mile Beyond the Moon*. 1962. MacFadden 40-100. PBO. NF. M1d. $10.00

KORNBLUTH, C.M. *Mile Beyond the Moon*. 1966. MacFadden 50-208. 2nd edn. SF. VG. B5d. $3.00

KORNBLUTH, C.M. *Syndic*. 1955. Bantam 1317. 1st edn. PBO. SF. F. F2d. $14.00

KORNBLUTH, C.M. *Syndic*. 1955. Bantam 1317. 1st prtg. VG+. P7d. $5.00

KORNBLUTH, C.M. *Syndic*. 1965. Berkley F 1032. SF. VG. B5d. $4.00

KORNBLUTH, C.M. *Takeoff*. 1953. Pennant P 15. c/Charles Binger. SF. VG. B3d/B4d. $4.00

KORNBLUTH, C.M. *Takeoff*. 1953. Pennant P 15. 1st pb. F. M1d. $20.00

KORNBLUTH, C.M. *Thirteen O'Clock*. 1970. Dell 8731. 1st edn. SF. F. F2d. $10.00

KORNBLUTH, C.M. *Wonder Effect*. 1962. Ballantine. 1st edn. F. M1d. $12.00

KORNBLUTH & POHL. *Gladiator-at-Law*. 1962. Ballantine F 570. 2nd edn. SF. VG. B5d. $4.00

KORNBLUTH & POHL. *Gladiator-at-Law*. 1955. Ballantine 107. PBO VG. I1d. $6.00

KORNBLUTH & POHL. *Presidential Year*. 1956. Ballantine 144. 1st edn. VG. M1d. $15.00

KORNBLUTH & POHL. *Wolfbane*. 1959. Ballantine 335K. PBO. c/R Powers. SF. VG. B5d. $5.00

KORNBLUTH & POHL. *Wolfbane*. 1976. Bantam. 1st edn. F. M1d. $5.00

KORNBLUTH & POHL. *Wonder Effect*. 1962. Ballantine F 638. VG. I1d. $4.00

KORNBLUTH & POHL. *Wonder Effect*. 1962. Ballantine F 638. 1st edn. NF. M1d. $8.00

KORNBLUTH & WILLIAMSON. *Starchild*. 1965. Ballantine U 2176. 1st edn. F. M1d. $6.00

KOSLOFF, Myron. *Dial P for Pleasure*. 1964. First Niter 110. 1st edn. F. F2d. $17.50

KOSLOFF, Myron. *Love Cult*. 1963. Nitey-Nite 100. 1st edn. c/gga. SF. F. F2d. $20.00

KOTEN, Bernard. *Low Calorie Cookbook*. 1960. Hillman 171. Nfi. VG+. B5d. $7.50

KOTZWINKLE, William. *ET, the Extraterrestrial*. 1982. BBC 05950. SF. F. W2d. $4.50

KOTZWINKLE, William. *Superman III*. 1983. Warner 30699. SF. F. W2d. $6.00

KOZIANKIN, Vlad. *SF Mazes*. Tempo 17028. Nfi. VG. W2d. $2.75

KOZLENKO, William. *Men & Women*. 1953. Lion 177. PBO. c/Steinbeck. VG. B6d. $12.50

KOZOL, Jonathan. *Fume of Poppies*. 1959. Bantam A 1986. 1st pb. VG+. B6d. $6.00

KRAMER, A. *Tropical Spitfire*. Carousel 524. VG. B3d. $4.00

KRAMER, Freda. *Glen Campbell Story*. 1970. Pyramid 2139. 1st edn. c/photo. Bio. F. F2d. $10.00

KRAMER, George. *School for Girls*. 1958. Beacon 202. 1st edn. PBO. c/gga. scarce. VG+. B6a #79. $50.00

KRAMER, Gerald. *Penthouse Party*. 1965. Midwood 32-467. PBO. c/Victor Olsen: gga. VG+. P6d. $3.50

KRAMER, Karl. *Common-Law Wife*. 1961. Midwood 75. VG. I1d. $6.00

KRAMER, Karl. *Common-Law Wife*. 1961. Midwood 75. 1st edn. c/Rader: gga. F. F2d. $17.00

KRAMER, Karl. *Flame Too Hot*. 1964. Monarch 490. 1st prtg. c/Barton: gga. VG. P7d. $5.00

KRAMER/MOORE. *Wrong Kind/Never Ask Why*. Midwood 34-491. VG+. B3d. $6.50

KRASNEY, Samuel A. *Death Cries in the Street*. 1956. Popular 749. 1st pb. My. VG. B6d. $7.00

KRASNEY, Samuel A. *Homicide West*. 1962. Pocket 6140. My. VG+. B4d. $3.00

KRASNEY, Samuel A. *Mania for Blondes*. 1960. Ace D 495. 1st edn. c/gga. My. F. F2d. $18.00

KRASNEY, Samuel A. *Mania For Blondes*. 1961. Ace D 495. PBO. c/Rader. VG+. B6a #77. $65.00

KRASNEY, Samuel A. *Morals Squad*. 1959. Ace D 336. 1st edn. My. NF. F2d. $13.00

KRASNEY, Samuel A. *Rapist*. 1959. Ace D 363. 1st edn. c/gga. My. NF. F2d. $15.00

KRAUSS, B. *Here's Hawaii*. Perma M 4215. VG+. B3d. $4.00

KRAVCHENDO, V. *I Chose Freedom*. Hillman 8. VG. B3d. $4.50

KREPPS, Robert W. *Big Gamble*. 1961. Gold Medal S 1101. 1st prtg. G+. R5d. $3.00

KREPPS, Robert W. *Big Gamble*. Gold Medal 1101. MTI. c/Bayre. VG. B3d. $5.00

KREPPS, Robert W. *Boy's Night Out*. Gold Medal 1211. MTI. VG+. B3d. $5.00

KREPPS, Robert W. *Courts of the Lion*. 1951. Bantam 894. VG. B3d. $5.50

KREPPS, Robert W. *Courts of the Lion*. 1951. Bantam 894. 1st edn. PBO. Av. NF. F2d. $7.50

KREPPS, Robert W. *Diamond Fever*. 1961. Dell F 174. c/R Abbett. Fi. VG. B5d. $2.50

KREPPS, Robert W. *El Cid*. 1961. Gold Medal D 1169. 1st prtg. VG. R5d. $3.50

KREPPS, Robert W. *Hour of the Gun*. Gold Medal D 1854. VG. B3d. $4.00

KREPPS, Robert W. *Hour of the Gun*. 1967. Gold Medal D 1854. PBO. MTI. We. NF. B6d. $10.00

KREPPS, Robert W. *Stagecoach*. 1967. Gold Medal K 1667. MTI. c/N Rockwell & A Bargaret. We. VG. B5d. $5.50

KREPPS, Robert W. *Taras Bulba*. 1962. Gold Medal S 1253. 1st prtg. VG. R5d. $3.50

KREPPS, Robert W. *Tell It on the Drums*. Dell D 156. VG+. B3d. $5.00

KRESS, Nancy. *Alien Night*. 1989. Avon 70706. SF. VG+. W2d. $3.75

KRICH, A.M. *Men*. Dell 1st Edn 15. VG+. B3d. $4.50

KRICH, A.M. *Women*. Dell 1st Edn 3. VG+. B3d. $4.50

KRIM, Seymour. *Manhattan*. Bantam 1201. VG. B3d. $4.00

KRISCH, Phil edt. *Mad Passion for Murder*. 1966. Pyramid R 1536. 1st prtg. c/gga. VG. P7d. $5.00

KROLL, Harry Harrison. *Cabin in the Cotton*. Dell 589. c/S Levine. Fi. G+. B5d. $3.00

KROLL, Harry Harrison. *Smoldering Fire*. 1955. Ace S 111. PBO. c/gga. VG. B3d. $4.00

KROLL, Harry Harrison. *Their Ancient Grudge*. Dell 435. c/V Kalin. F. G+. B5d. $3.00

KRONE, Chester. *World of the Dolphin*. 1972. Belmont 50223. PBO. NF. B6d. $4.50

KRUEGER, Terry. *Vectors*. 1984. Dell 19298. 1st edn. My. F. F2d. $10.00

KRUGER, Paul. *Bedroom Alibi*. 1961. Newsstand U 164. PBO. c/gga. VG. P6d. $2.00

KRUGER, Paul. *If the Shroud Fits*. 1970. PB Library 63-458. PBO. My. NF. B6d. $7.00

KRUGER, Paul. *Weave a Wicked Web*. 1969. PB Library 63-180. 1st pb. My. VG+. B6d. $7.50

KUBERT & MOORE. *Tales of the Green Berets*. 1966. Signet D 3001. c/Kubert. VG+. P6d. $5.00

KUBIS, P. *Ocean's Edge*. 1968. Avon S 338. 1st edn. c/gga. F. F2d. $10.00

KUBLY, H. *Varieties of Love*. Belmont L 501. VG+. B3d. $6.00

KULLINGER, J.L. *Sex Scene '70*. Barclay 7066. F. B3d. $6.00

KUPRIN, Alexandre. *Yama, the Hell Hole*. 1952. Pyramid G 50. c/gga. Fa. VG+. B4d. $9.00

KURLAND, Michael. *Infernal Device*. Signet J 8492. VG. G5d. $12.50

KURLAND, Michael. *Mission: Third Force*. 1967. Pyramid R 1578. 1st edn. My. NF. F2d. $10.00

KURLAND, Michael. *Plague of Spies*. 1969. Pyramid X 2098. c/F Kalan: gga. My. VG+. B4d. $3.00

KURLAND, Michael. *Pluribus*. Ace 67145. 1st pb. c/Boris. SF. NF. B6d. $3.00

KURNITZ, Harry. *Invasion of Privacy*. 1956. Perma M 3053. c/gga. My. NF. B4d. $5.00

KURTZ, Katherine. *Deryni Checkmate*. 1972. Ballantine. 1st edn. Ad/Fa. NF. M1d. $10.00

KURTZ, Katherine. *Deryni Rising*. 1970. Ballantine. 1st Ad/Fa. F. M1d. $12.00

KURTZ, Katherine. *King's Justice Volume #2*. Ballantine 33196. 1st pb. VG+. B6d. $3.00

KURTZMAN & ELDER. *Executive's Comic Book*. 1962. MacFadden. 1st edn. VG. M1d. $12.00

KUTTNER, Henry. *Ahead of Time*. Ballantine 30. PBO. VG. B3d. $4.50

KUTTNER, Henry. *Ahead of Time*. 1953. Ballantine 30. 1st edn. F. M1d. $15.00

KUTTNER, Henry. *Best of H Kuttner*. Ballantine 24415. 1st prtg. VG. S1d. $4.00

KUTTNER, Henry. *Bypass to Otherness*. 1961. Ballantine 497. c/Blanchard. VG. B3d. $4.00

KUTTNER, Henry. *Bypass to Otherness*. 1961. Ballantine 497. 1st edn. F. M1d. $12.00

KUTTNER, Henry. *Creature From Beyond Infinity*. 1968. Popular 60-2355. SF. VG+. B5d. $4.00

KUTTNER, Henry. *Creature From Beyond Infinity*. 1968. Popular 60-2355. 1st edn. c/Frazetta. SF. F. F2d. $13.00

KUTTNER, Henry. *Creature From Beyond Infinity*. 1968. Popular 60-2355. 1st edn. NF. M1d. $10.00

KUTTNER, Henry. *Dark World*. Ace F 327. F. M1d. $15.00

KUTTNER, Henry. *Dark World*. Ace F 327. SF. VG+. W2d. $7.50

KUTTNER, Henry. *Dark World*. Ace F 327. 1st edn. NF. I1d. $10.00

KUTTNER, Henry. *Destination: Infinity*. Avon T 276. VG. B3d. $4.00

KUTTNER, Henry. *Fury*. Lancer 75-413. SF. F. W2d. $5.25

KUTTNER, Henry. *Fury*. Lancer 75-413. 1st prtg. VG. S1d. $4.00

KUTTNER, Henry. *Man Drowning*. 1953. Bantam 1154. 1st prtg. My. G+. R5d. $5.50

KUTTNER, Henry. *Mask of Circe*. Ace 52075. c/R Pepper. SF. VG. B5d. $4.00

KUTTNER, Henry. *Murder of a Wife*. Perma M 4096. VG+. I1d. $18.00

KUTTNER, Henry. *Murder of Ann Avery*. 1956. Perma 3058. PBO. c/Jim Meese. VG. P6d. $10.00

KUTTNER, Henry. *Mutant*. Ballantine 724. VG+. B3d. $4.50

KUTTNER, Henry. *Return to Otherness*. 1962. Ballantine F 619. PBO. VG. B3d. $4.00

KUTTNER, Henry. *Time Axis*. Ace F 356. F. M1d. $15.00

KUTTNER, Henry. *Time Axis*. Ace F 356. PBO. VG+. B3d. $5.00

KUTTNER, Henry. *Well of the Worlds*. 1965. Ace F 344. PBO. F. M1d. $15.00

KUTTNER, Henry. *Well of the Worlds*. 1965. Ace F 344. 1st prtg. SF. G+. R5d. $2.75

KUTTNER & MOORE. *No Boundaries*. Ballantine 122. PBO. VG+. B3d/I1d. $8.00

KYLE, G. *Teen Deviate '70*. Barclay 7104. NF. B3d. $5.00

KYLE, Robert. *Ben Gates Is Hot*. 1964. Dell 0534. 1st prtg. c/Lesser: gga. VG+. P7d. $4.50

KYLE, Robert. *Crooked City*. Dell 1st Edn 17. VG. G5d. $4.00

KYLE, Robert. *Golden Urge*. Dell 1st Edn 36. VG+. G5d. $3.25

KYLE, Robert. *Golden Urge*. 1963. Gold Medal 1338. VG. B3d. $4.50

KYLE, Robert. *Golden Urge*. Gold Medal 715. VG. B3d. $6.00

KYLE, Robert. *Model for Murder*. Dell 1st Edn A 192. VG. G5d. $3.75

KYLE, Robert. *Model for Murder*. 1959. Dell 1st Edn A 192. PBO. c/McGinnis: gga. My. VG+. B6d. $9.00

KYLE, Robert. *Some Like It Cool*. Dell 1st Edn 8100. G+. G5d. $3.00

KYLE, Robert. *Tiger in the Night*. 1955. Dell 1st Edn 66. 1st prtg. PBO. c/Gross: gga. VG. P7d. $5.00

KYNE, Peter B. *Jim the Conqueror*. Dell 294. VG+. I1d. $6.00

KYNE, Peter B. *Money To Burn*. 1950. Dell 467. c/D Attie. Fi. G+. B5d. $2.50

L

L'AMOUR, Louis. *Broken Gun.* Bantam 3098. VG. B3d. $5.50

L'AMOUR, Louis. *Catlow.* Bantam J 2579. PBO. VG. M6d. $9.50

L'AMOUR, Louis. *Conagher.* 1969. Bantam H 4628. We. VG+. B4d. $4.00

L'AMOUR, Louis. *Heller With a Gun.* Gold Medal 2382. VG+. B3d. $4.50

L'AMOUR, Louis. *Heller With a Gun.* 1955. Gold Medal 478. PBO. c/Baumhofer. scarce. B6a #80. $36.50

L'AMOUR, Louis. *Hondo.* 1953. Gold Medal 347. PBO. MTI. scarce. VG. B6a #75. $88.00

L'AMOUR, Louis. *Jubal Sackett.* 1985. Bantam. 1st edn. dust jacket. Ad. F. F2d. $16.00

L'AMOUR, Louis. *Lando.* 1962. Bantam 2494. 1st edn. Hi. F. F2d. $12.00

L'AMOUR, Louis. *Last Stand at Papago Wells.* Gold Medal 2029. reprint. VG. B3d. $4.00

L'AMOUR, Louis. *Reilly's Luck.* 1970. Bantam H 5485. We. VG+. B4d. $3.00

L'AMOUR, Louis. *Tall Stranger.* 1957. Gold Medal 700. PBO. MTI. VG. B3a. $7.00

L'AURNAUD, D. *Sandra.* MC Pubs NN (Scottish). VG. B3a #20. $19.80

L'ENGLE, Madeleine. *Swiftly Tilting Planet.* 1979. Dell 90158. 3rd prtg. SF. F. W2d. $5.00

L'ENGLE, Madeleine. *Wrinkle in Time.* 1983. Dell 99805. 19th prtg. SF. VG+. W2d. $3.25

L'ENGLE, Madeleine. *Wrinkle in Time.* 1970. Dell. VG. M1d. $4.00

LA CAPRIA, Raffaele. *First Affair.* 1955. Signet 1223. c/Hulings: gga. Ro. VG+. B4d. $3.00

LA FARGE, Oliver. *Laughing Boy.* 1951. Pocket 764. Fi. VG. B5d. $4.00

LA FRANCE, Marston. *Miami Murder-Go-Round.* 1952. Pocket 896. c/M Kane. My. VG. B5d. $5.00

LA GUARDIA, R. *Wonderful World of TV Soap Operas.* 1974. Ballantine 24057. 1st prtg. VG. R5d. $2.00

LA MOUREUX, John. *French Way.* 1963. Midwood F 316. PBO. NF. B6d. $18.00

LA MURE, Pierre. *Moulin Rouge.* Pyramid 1329. VG+. B3d. $4.50

LA VANWAY, Ed. *Brad Rider.* 1961. Dell D 429. c/John Leone. We. VG. P6d. $1.00

LAAS, William. *IW Harper Hospitality Tour of the United States.* Popular Library 08129. Nfi. NF. B5d. $4.00

LABAN, L.E. *Shame: Confessions of a Woman.* Brandon House 3010. VG+. B3d. $6.00

LACY, Ed. *Big Bust.* 1969. Pyramid 2037. 1st edn. c/gga. Th. F. F2d. $15.00

LACY, Ed. *Double Trouble.* 1967. Lancer 72-162. My. NF. B4d. $4.00

LACY, Ed. *Enter Without Desire.* 1954. Avon 561. 1st edn. c/gga. F. F2d. $12.50

LACY, Ed. *Go for the Body.* Avon 566. VG. B3d. $4.50

LACY, Ed. *Men From the Boys.* 1957. Pocket 1152. 1st pb. c/Marchetti. My. VG. B6d. $8.00

LACY, Ed. *Shakedown for Murder.* 1958. Avon T 288. 1st prtg. My. VG. R5d. $4.50

LACY, Ed. *Sin in Their Blood.* 1952. Eton 111. PBO. scarce hardboiled. VG+. B6a #74. $55.00

LACY, Ed. *South Pacific Affair.* 1961. Belmont 220. Fi. VG. B5d. $4.50

LACY, Ed. *Strip for Violence.* 1953. Eton 123. PBO. c/great. scarce hardboiled. VG+. B6a #74. $38.50

LACY, Ed. *Visa to Death.* 1956. Perma M 3036. My. VG. B4d. $4.00

LADWICK, Monty. *Troubled Women.* Gaywood NN. VG+. B3a #21. $16.50

LAFFERTY, R.A. *Arrive at Easterwine.* 1973. Ballantine 03164. 1st edn. PBO. SF. F. F2d. $10.00

LAFFERTY, R.A. *Devil Is Dead.* 1971. Avon V 2406. 1st edn. F. P9d. $3.00

LAFFERTY, R.A. *Reefs of Earth.* 1968. Berkley X 1528. PBO. c/Powers. SF. VG+. M3d. $6.00

LAFLIN, Jack. *Reluctant Spy.* 1966. Belmont B 50-733. 1st prtg. My. VG. R5d. $3.50

LAFLIN, Jack. *Silent Kind of War.* 1965. Belmont 92-613. 1st prtg. My. VG. R5d. $4.00

LAFLIN, Jack. *Spy in White Gloves.* 1965. Belmont B 50-631. 1st prtg. My. VG+. R5d. $6.00

LAFLIN, Jack. *Spy Who Didn't.* 1966. Belmont B 50-691. 1st prtg. My. VG+. R5d. $5.00

LAGERKVIST, P. *Barabbas.* 1962. Bantam F 2417. 1st prtg. VG. R5d. $2.00

LAING, Alexander. *Clipper Ship Men.* Armed Services S 15. VG. B3d. $6.00

LAIRD, Charlton. *Miracle of Language.* 1957. Premier D 51. Nfi. VG+. B5d. $4.00

LAIT & MORTIMER. *Big City After Dark.* Dell 400. VG. B3d. $4.00

LAIT & MORTIMER. *New York: Confidential.* Dell D 101. VG. B3d. $4.00

LAIT & MORTIMER. *New York: Confidential!* Dell 1440. 2nd edn. c/R Stanley. Nfi. VG. B5d. $2.50

LAIT & MORTIMER. *New York: Confidential!* Dell 1534. 2nd edn. c/R Stanley. VG. B5d. $3.00

LAIT & MORTIMER. *Washington.* 1952. Dell D 108. Nfi. VG+. B4d. $3.00

LAKE, Barry. *Three for the Money.* 1960. Berkley D 2035. c/R Maquire. My. G+. B5d. $3.00

LAKE, David. *Gods of Xuma.* 1978. DAW UW 1360. 1st prtg. SF. F. W2d. $5.00

LAKE, David. *Gods of Xuma.* 1978. DAW 279 PBO. SF. VG+. B5d. $4.00

LAKE, David. *Right Hand of Dextra.* 1977. DAW. 1st edn. F. M1d. $6.00

LAKE, David. *Walkers on the Sky.* 1978. DAW. 1st edn. F. M1d. $6.00

LAKE, David. *Wildings of Westron.* 1977. DAW. 1st edn. F. M1d. $6.00

LAKE, Lester. *House of Lust.* 1964. All Star AS 30. PBO. c/gga: photo. VG+. P6d. $7.00

LAKE, Lester. *Love Kitten.* 1962. All Star 520. PBO. NF. B6d. $7.50

LAKE, Stuart N. *Wyatt Earp, Frontier Marshal.* 1952. Bantam A 986. We. VG. B4d. $4.00

LAKEIN, Alan. *It's About Time & It's About Time.* 1975. Bantam B 7647. c/photos. Nfi. NF. B5d. $6.50

LAKIN, Richard. *Body Fell on Berlin.* Detective 50. VG. B3d. $4.50

LAMB, Harold. *Alexander of Macedon.* Bantam 1353. VG+. B3d. $4.50

LAMB, Harold. *Babur the Tiger.* 1964. Bantam H 2852. Nfi. VG+. B5d. $2.50

LAMB, Harold. *Babur the Tiger.* 1964. Bantam H 2852. 1st pb. NF. M1d. $7.00

LAMB, Harold. *Genghis Khan, Emperor of All Men.* 1953. Bantam 1127. 1st pb. VG. M1d. $8.00

LAMB, Harold. *Suleiman the Magnificent.* Bantam 1234. NF. V3d. $6.00

LAMB, Hugh edt. *Taste of Fear.* 1977. Coronet. 1st pb. F. M1d. $5.00

LAMBERT, Alice. *Women Are Like That.* 1946. Dell 117. 1st pb. c/Gregg. Ro. VG. B6d. $6.00

LAMBERT, H. *3 Parts Evil.* Pike 211. c/Neutzel: sgn. VG+. B3d. $7.50

LAMBERT, W.J. *Stepchild Incest.* Barclay 7471. c/photo. VG+. B3d. $4.00

LAMES, Stuart. *Too Late Blues.* 1962. Lancer 71-309. MTI. c/photo. VG+. B4d. $7.50

LAMKIN, Speed. *Tiger in the Garden.* 1951. Signet 845. 1st pb. c/Hooks. VG. B6d. $7.00

LAMPARSKI, R. *Whatever Became of? Volume #2.* 1970. Ace 88076. 1st prtg. c/photo. Bio. VG+. R5d. $3.00

LAMPTON, Chris. *Cross of Empire.* Laser 72042. SF. VG. W2d. $4.25

LANCASTER, Bruce. *Bright to the Wanderer.* Perma P 266. VG+. B3d. $4.50

LANCASTER, Bruce. *Phantom Fortress.* 1952. Perma P 149. 1st pb. VG. B6d. $7.00

LANCASTER, Bruce. *Secret Road.* Perma M 3016. NF. B3d. $5.00

LANCASTER, Bruce. *Trumpet to Arms.* 1952. Perma P 176. VG+. B3d. $6.00

LANCASTER, Bruce. *Trumpet to Arms.* 1952. Perma P 176. 1st pb. c/Pease. NF. B6d. $12.50

LAND, Wanda. *Red House on Green Street.* 1960. Newsstand 514. Ad. VG. B5d. $4.00

LANDAU, V. *Around the Clock Sinners.* Globe 102. VG. B3d. $4.50

LANDIS, Arthur. *Camelot in Orbit.* DAW 315. 1st prtg. G+. S1d. $2.50

LANDIS, Arthur. *Camelot in Orbit.* 1978. DAW 315. 1st edn. F. M1d. $6.00

LANDIS, Arthur. *Home to Avalon.* DAW 505. 1st prtg. VG+. S1d. $2.00

LANDIS, Arthur. *Magick of Camelot.* 1981. DAW. 1st edn. F. M1d. $6.00

LANDIS, Arthur. *World Called Camelot.* 1976. DAW. 1st edn. F. M1d. $6.00

LANDOLF & NORTON. *I Prefer Murder.* 1956. Graphic 132. PBO. c/Saul Levine: gga. VG. P6d. $3.50

LANDOLF & NORTON. *I Prefer Murder.* 1956. Graphic 139. PBO. c/Saul Levine: gga. VG. P6d. $2.50

LANDON, Margaret. *Anna & the King of Siam.* 1961. Cardinal C 222. 6th prtg. G+. R5d. $.75

LANDSBOROUGH, Gordon. *Battle of the River Plate.* 1957. Panther 626. photos. NF. VG. B5d. $4.50

LANDSBURG, A. *In Search of Strange Phenomena.* 1977. Bantam 10855. 1st prtg. TVTI. G+. R5d. $1.25

LANE, Frank W. *Animal Wonder World.* 1957. Premier S 44. Nfi. VG. B5d. $2.50

LANE, John. *Maid of Thuro.* 1952. Curtis NN. PBO. c/gga. scarce. SF. VG+. B6a #79. $68.25

LANE, Sheldon edt. *For Bond Lovers Only.* 1965. Dell 2672. F. G5d. $7.00

LANE, W. *Red House on Green Street.* News Stand Library 514. VG. B3d. $4.50

LANG, B. *Crockett on the Loose.* Leisure 283. VG. B3d. $4.00

LANG, Simon. *All the Gods of Eisernon.* 1973. Avon 15339. 1st prtg. SF. G+. R5d. $1.25

LANG, Simon. *Elluvan Gift.* 1975. Avon 26518. 1st edn. F. P9d. $2.50

LANGDON, John. *Night in Manila.* 1954. Pyramid 136. PBO. c/gga. NF. B6a. $50.00

LANGDON-DAVIES, John. *Seeds of Life.* 1957. Signet KS 345. Nfi. VG+. B4d. $2.25

LANGE, John. *Odds On.* 1966. Signet P 3068. 1st prtg. PBO. c/photo. VG. P7d. $5.00

LANGHAM, James R. *Sing a Song of Homicide.* Popular Library 63. G+. G5d. $5.00

LANGLEY, A.L. *Lion Is in the Streets.* Bantam 815. VG+. B3d. $6.50

LANGLEY, N. *Cabbage Patch.* Barker Dragon 4. VG+. B3d. $6.00

LANGLEY, N. *Cage Me a Peacock.* Lion 63. VG. B3d. $5.00

LANHAM, Edwin. *Death in the Wind.* 1957. Perma M 3072. c/J Meese. My. VG. B5d. $5.50

LANHAM, Edwin. *Death in the Wind.* 1957. Perma M 3072. 1st pb. c/Meese. My. NF. B6d. $15.00

LANHAM, Edwin. *Double Jeopardy.* 1961. Perma M 4217. 1st pb. My. VG+. B4d. $4.00

LANHAM, Edwin. *Headlined for Murder.* 1948. Bantam 301. c/G Darling. My. G+. B5d. $3.00

LANHAM, Edwin. *Murder on My Street.* 1961. Pocket 6038. c/gga. My. VG+. B4d. $3.00

LANHAM, Edwin. *Politics Is Murder.* 1950. Bantam 746. 1st prtg. My. G. G5d. $3.50

LANNING, George. *Pedestal.* 1968. Avon S 376. SF. F. W2d. $6.00

LANSDALE, Joe R. *Drive-In 2.* 1989. Bantam 27905. 1st edn. c/sgn. SF. F. F2d. $20.00

LANSDALE, Joe R. *Drive-In.* 1988. Bantam 27481. 1st edn. c/sgn. Ho. F. F2d. $25.00

LANSDALE, Joe R. *Savage Season.* 1990. Bantam 28563. 1st edn. c/sgn. Th. F. F2d. $12.00

LANSING, Alfred. *Edurance.* Avon G 1050. Fi. VG. B5d. $2.50

LAREDO, Johnny. *Come & Get Me.* 1956. Popular Library 720. PBO. c/Johnson. scarce. JD. VG+. B6a #74. $67.25

LARIAR, Lawrence. *Day I Died.* 1953. Signet 1083. My. VG. B5d/G5d. $4.00

LARIAR, Lawrence. *Death Is Confidential.* 1959. Hillman 125. PBO. My. G+. P6d. $1.50

LARIAR, Lawrence. *Friday for Death.* 1951. Boardman 102. c/McLoughlin. VG. B3d. $8.00

LARIAR, Lawrence. *Frightened Eyes.* 1949. Handi-Book 92. 1st edn. PBO. scarce. VG+. B6a #77. $44.00

LARIAR, Lawrence. *Girl With the Frightened Eyes.* 1956. Avon 746. c/gga. My. VG. B4d. $5.00

LARIAR, Lawrence. *Girl With the Frightened Eyes.* 1956. Avon 746. 1st pb. My. G+. B6d. $3.00

LARIAR, Lawrence. *He Died Laughing.* Boardman NN. VG. B3d. $8.00

LARIAR, Lawrence. *Lady Chatterley's Daughter.* 1960. Popular Library PC 500. PBO. c/De Soto: gga. VG+. B6a #76. $25.25

LARIAR, Lawrence. *You Can't Catch Me.* 1952. Popular Library 448. 1st pb. My. VG+. B6d. $15.00

LARKIN, R.T. *For Godmother & Country.* 1972. Lancer 78 709. My. VG+. B5d. $4.00

LARKIN, R.T. *For Godmother & Country.* 1972. Lancer 78-709. PBO. NF. B6d. $7.00

LARKIN, R.T. *For Godmother & Country.* 1972. Lancer 78-709. 1st edn. My. F. F2d. $9.00

LARKIN, R.T. *Godmother.* Lancer 79-310. reprint. VG+. B6d. $5.00

LARKIN, R.T. *Honor Thy Godmother.* 1972. Lancer 78-703. PBO. VG+. B6d. $6.00

LARNER, Jeremy. *Answer.* 1969. Signet T 4075. 1st prtg. c/photo. VG+. P7d. $5.50

LARNER, Jeremy. *Drive, He Said.* 1971. Bantam N 6785. 1st prtg. VG. P7d. $4.00

LARRICK, Nancy. *Parent's Guide to Children's Reading.* 1958. Cardinal C 314. Nfi. G+. P1d. $3.75

LARRICK, Nancy. *Parent's Guide to Children's Reading.* 1964. Cardinal GC 218. Nfi. NF. B5d. $3.50

LARRIMORE, Lida. *Robin Hill.* 1946. Dell 119. 1st pb. c/Frederiksen. Ro. VG+. B3d. $5.00

LARSON, Glen A. *Battlestar Galactica: The Photostory.* 1979. Berkley 04139. 1st prtg. TVTI. VG. B4d/R5d. $5.00

LARSON, Glen A. *Tombs of Kobol.* 1979. Berkley 04267. Battlestar. SF. F. W2d. $5.50

LARSON, M.A. *Wanton Sinner.* Tuxedo 111. VG+. B3d. $4.50

LARSON & RESNICK. *Galactica Discovers Earth.* 1980. Berkley 4744. 1st edn. SF. F. F2d. $8.00

LARSON & THURSTON. *Battlestar Galactica.* 1978. Berkley 03958 TVTI. c/L Greene. SF. VG+. B5d. $5.00

LARSON & THURSTON. *Battlestar Galactica.* 1978. Berkley 03958. 1st prtg. TVTI. SF. VG+. R5d. $2.00

LARSON & THURSTON. *Cylon Death Machine.* 1979. Berkley 04080. Battlestar Galactica 2. SF. VG. B5d. $4.00

LASCH, S. *Torrid Women for the Young Boys.* Brandon House 6195. VG. B3d. $4.00

LASKI, Marghanita. *Victorian Chaise Longue.* 1960. Ballantine. 1st pb edn. F. M1d. $8.00

LASKY, J. *Cry the Lonely Flesh.* Popular Library 628. VG. B3d. $5.00

LASKY, J. *Naked in a Cactus Garden.* Popular Library SP 164. VG+. B3d. $5.00

LASLY, Walt. *Turn the Tigers.* 1956. Ballantine 173. PBO. VG+. B6d. $15.00

LATHAN, Emma. *Accounting for Murder.* Avon G 1292. 1st prtg. My. VG+. R5d. $3.25

LATIMER, Jonathan. *Dead Don't Care.* MacFadden 50-213. VG. B3d. $3.50

LATIMER, Jonathan. *Fifth Grave.* 1950. Popular Library 301. My. VG. B4d. $7.50

LATIMER, Jonathan. *Lady in the Morgue.* 1943. Pocket 246. My. VG. B4d. $5.00

LATIMER, Jonathan. *Murder in the Madhouse.* 1943. Popular Library 4. G+. F2d. $8.00

LATIMER, Jonathan. *Murder in the Madhouse.* 1943. Popular Library 4. 1st edn. PBO. c/Hoffman. scarce. VG+. B6a #75. $75.00

LATIMER, Jonathan. *Red Gardenias.* Century 34. VG. B3d. $5.00

LATIMER, Jonathan. *Sinners & Shrouds.* 1956. Pocket 1136. 1st pb. c/Meese. My. VG+. B6d. $12.50

LAUBENTHAL, Sanders. *Excalibur.* 1973. Ballantine. 1st edn. Ad/Fa. NF. M1d. $12.00

LAUMER, Keith. *Catastrophe Planet.* 1966. Berkley F 1273. 1st prtg. SF. VG. R5d. $5.00

LAUMER, Keith. *Dinosaur Beach.* DAW UQ 1021. NF. I1d. $4.00

LAUMER, Keith. *Dinosaur Beach.* DAW UQ 1021. SF. F. W2d. $5.00

LAUMER, Keith. *Enemies From Beyond.* 1967. Pyramid X 1689. TVTI. Invaders #2. VG+. B4d. $6.00

LAUMER, Keith. *Envoy to New Worlds.* Ace 20730. SF. VG+. B5d. $4.00

LAUMER, Keith. *Galactic Odyssey.* 1967. Berkley X 1447. 1st prtg. SF. VG. R5d. $5.00

LAUMER, Keith. *Glory Game.* Popular Library 00526. SF. VG+. B5d. $3.50

LAUMER, Keith. *Gold Bomb.* 1968. Berkley X 1592. Avengers #7. My. G+. W2d. $6.00

LAUMER, Keith. *Great Time Machine Hoax.* 1978. Ace 30256. SF. VG. W2d. $3.25

LAUMER, Keith. *Great Time Machine Hoax.* 1965. Pocket 50-158. 1st edn. F. M1d. $8.00

LAUMER, Keith. *Greylorn.* 1968. Berkley 1514. 1st edn. SF. F. F2d. $15.00

LAUMER, Keith. *Invaders.* 1967. Pyramid R 1664. SF. VG. W2d. $7.25

LAUMER, Keith. *Invaders.* 1967. Pyramid R 1664. 1st prtg. TVTI. G. R5d. $2.00

LAUMER, Keith. *It's a Mad, Mad, Mad Galaxy.* 1968. Berkley X 1641. PBO. c/Powers. SF. NF. B6d. $12.00

LAUMER, Keith. *It's a Mad, Mad, Mad Galaxy.* 1968. Berkley X 1641. 1st prtg. SF. G+. R5d. $2.75

LAUMER, Keith. *Monitors.* 1966. Berkley X 1340. PBO. c/R Powers. SF. NF. M1d. $7.00

LAUMER, Keith. *Night of Delusions.* 1974. Berkley N 2497. 1st prtg. SF. VG. R5d. $2.00

LAUMER, Keith. *Nine by Laumer.* 1969. Berkley X 1659. SF. VG+. B5d. $4.00

LAUMER, Keith. *Other Side of Time.* 1965. Berkley F 1129. VG. I1d. $5.00

LAUMER, Keith. *Other Side of Time.* 1965. Berkley F 1129. 1st prtg. SF. G+. R5d. $3.00

LAUMER, Keith. *Plague of Demons.* 1971. PB Library 64-595. c/skull. SF. VG+. B5d. $4.00

LAUMER, Keith. *Retief: Emissary to the Stars.* 1975. Dell 7425. SF. VG+. W2d. $3.75

LAUMER, Keith. *Star Colony.* 1983. Ace 78035. SF. VG. W2d. $3.25

LAUMER, Keith. *Star Treasure.* Berkley G 2025. VG. B3d. $4.50

LAUMER, Keith. *Time Bender.* 1966. Berkley F 1185. PBO. c/Powers. SF. NF. B6d. $10.00

LAUMER, Keith. *Time Bender.* 1966. Berkley F 1185. PBO. c/R Powers. SF. VG. B5d. $4.50

LAUMER, Keith. *Time Trap.* 1970. Berkley S 1871. c/R Powers. SF. VG. B5d. $3.00

LAUMER, Keith. *Timetracks.* 1972. Ballantine 02575. 1st edn. SF. F. F2d. $13.00

LAUMER, Keith. *Trace of Memory.* 1963. Berkley F 780. PBO. c/R Powers. SF. VG+. B5d. $5.50

LAUMER, Keith. *Trace of Memory.* 1963. Berkley F 780. 1st prtg. SF. G+. R5d. $3.00

LAUMER, Keith. *Trace of Memory.* 1972. PB Library 65-712. NF. B3d. $4.50

LAUMER, Keith. *Trace of Memory.* PB Library 66-712. 1st prtg. F. S1d. $5.00

LAUMER, Keith. *Undefeated.* 1974. Dell 9285. 1st prtg. SF. VG+. R5d. $2.50

LAUMER, Keith. *World Shuffler.* 1970. Berkley S 1895. 1st edn. PBO. VG. P9d. $1.50

LAUMER, Keith. *Worlds of the Imperium.* 1967. Ace M 165. 1st prtg. SF. VG. B3d. $4.50

LAUMER, Keith. *Worlds of the Imperium.* 1967. Ace M 165. 2nd edn. F. M1d. $6.00

LAUMER & DICKSON. *Planet Run.* 1968. Berkley X 1588. c/P Lehr. SF. VG+. B5d. $3.50

LAUMER/WILLIAMS. *Envoy to New Worlds/ Flight From Yesterday.* 1963. Ace F 223. F. M1d. $8.00

LAUMER/WILLIAMS. *Envoy to New Worlds/ Flight From Yesterday.* 1963. Ace F 223. PBO. c/E Emsh & J Gaughan. SF. NF. B5d. $7.00

LAUMER/WILLIAMS. *Envoy to New Worlds/ Flight From Yesterday.* 1963. Ace F 223. VG. P9d. $3.50

LAUREN, Bill. *Blonde Danger.* 1960. New Stand Library 522. 1st edn. F. F2d. $15.00

LAUREN, Bill. *Blonde Danger.* 1960. Newsstand 522. Ad. G+. B5d. $3.00

LAURENCE, Margaret. *Rachel, Rachel.* Popular Library 60-8076. 1st prtg. G+. R5d. $1.25

LAURENCE, S. *Georgia Hotel.* Pyramid 68. VG. B3d. $4.50

LAURENCE, W. *For Value Received.* Midwood 117. VG. I1d. $4.00

LAURIA, Frank. *Seth Papers.* 1979. Ballantine 27329. SF. VG. W2d. $3.25

LAURIE, J. Jr. *Off the Cuff.* Pocket 1100. PBO. VG+. B3d. $5.00

LAWN, M.D. *Passionate Orphan.* Brandon House 6496. NF. B3d. $7.00

LAWRENCE, Alfred. *Christmas Killing.* 1975. Star 39818. 1st prtg. Columbo. VG. R5d. $2.50

LAWRENCE, Alfred. *Columbo.* 1972. Popular Library 01524. TVTI. c/Peter Falk: photo. VG+. B4d. $4.00

LAWRENCE, Alfred. *Dean's Death.* 1975. Popular Library 00265. 1st prtg. Columbo #2. VG. R5d. $1.50

LAWRENCE, Ann. *Gin Wedding.* 1951. Intimate 8. 1st pb. VG. B6d. $9.00

LAWRENCE, D.H. *First Lady Chatterley.* 1956. Avon T 114. Fa. VG. B4d. $2.00

LAWRENCE, D.H. *First Lady Chatterley.* 1956. Avon T 114. NF. I1d. $4.00

LAWRENCE, D.H. *First Lady Chatterley.* Avon 238. VG. B3d. $4.00

LAWRENCE, D.H. *First Lady Chatterley.* 1958. Berkley BG 150. Fi. G+. B5d. $3.00

LAWRENCE, D.H. *Lady Chatterley's Lover.* Grove Press FG 5. 1st prtg. VG. P7d. $5.00

LAWRENCE, D.H. *Lady Chatterley's Lover.* 1946. Penguin 610. 1st prtg. c/Jonas: gga. VG. P7d. $6.00

LAWRENCE, D.H. *Love Among the Haystacks.* 1950. Avon 248. H. G+. B5d. $4.00

LAWRENCE, D.H. *Love Amongst the Haystacks.* 1952. Avon 423. c/gga. Fa. G+. B4d. $5.00

LAWRENCE, D.H. *Modern Lover.* 1958. Avon T 218. 1st prtg. c/gga. VG. P7d. $5.00

LAWRENCE, D.H. *Modern Lover.* Avon 296. VG. B3d. $6.00

LAWRENCE, D.H. *Shadow in the Rose Garden.* Belmont L 512. VG. B3d. $4.00

LAWRENCE, D.H. *Shadow in the Rose Garden.* Belmont L 512. 1st pb. VG+. B6d. $6.00

LAWRENCE, D.H. *Sons & Lovers.* 1953. Signet S 1039. 1st prtg. c/Avati: gga. VG. P7d. $6.00

LAWRENCE, D.H. *Thorn in the Flesh.* Berkley G 17. VG+. B3d. $5.00

LAWRENCE, D.H. *Trespasser.* Penguin 1480 Brit 60. Fa. NF. B4d. $4.00

LAWRENCE, D.H. *Virgin & the Gypsy & St Mawr.* Ace H 299. VG+. B3d. $8.00

LAWRENCE, D.H. *Virgin & the Gypsy.* 1952. Avon 449. Fi. VG. B5d. $5.50

LAWRENCE, D.H. *Virgin & the Gypsy.* 1946. Avon 98. 1st prtg. c/Stahr: gga. VG+. B3d. $6.00

LAWRENCE, D.H. *Virgin & the Gypsy.* Berkley G 52. c/Maguire. NF. I1d. $10.00

LAWRENCE, D.H. *Women in Love.* Ace 242. VG. B3d. $8.50

LAWRENCE, D.H. *Women Who Rode Away.* Berkley G 59. c/Maguire. NF. I1d. $18.00

LAWRENCE, Gil. *Fury With Legs.* 1962. Pyramid F 802. 3rd edn. Fi. VG+. B5d. $5.00

LAWRENCE, Gil. *Woman Racket.* 1959. Pyramid G 468. 1st edn. c/gga. scarce. Cr. F. F2d. $20.00

LAWRENCE, Hilda. *Blood Upon the Snow.* Pocket 336. G+. G5d. $6.00

LAWRENCE, Hilda. *Deadly Pavilion.* Pocket 492. VG. G5d. $4.50

LAWRENCE, Hilda. *Death of a Doll.* Pocket 540. VG. G5d. $6.50

LAWRENCE, Hilda. *House.* Avon PN 387. VG+. G5d. $4.50

LAWRENCE, Hilda. *Time To Die.* 1947. Pocket 439. 1st pb. My. VG+. B6d. $12.50

LAWRENCE, J.A. *Mudd's Angels.* 1978. Bantam 11802. Star Trek. SF. F. W2d. $6.50

LAWRENCE, J.A. *Mudd's Angels.* 1978. Bantam 11802. TVTI. Star Trek. SF. VG. B5d. $4.00

LAWRENCE, M. *I Like It Cool.* 1960. Popular Library G 488. PBO. c/beatnik. My. VG. B6d. $6.00

LAWRENCE. *Blondes Don't Have All the Fun.* PB Library 65-497. reprint. NF. B6d. $6.00

LAWRENCE/WEST. *With Blood in Their Eyes/Killer's Canyon.* Ace D 496. PBO. VG. B3d. $4.50

LAWSON, Don. *US in World War 1.* 1964. Scholastic 576. Nfi. VG+. B4d. $2.50

LAWSON, Larry. *Naked Spurs.* Pyramid 325. VG. B3d. $4.00

LAWTON, Harry. *Tell Them Willie Boy Is Here.* 1969. Award A 4525. PBO. MTI. c/photo. VG+. P6d. $3.00

LAYNE, James. *Fire in a Woman.* 1964. Beacon B 697X. PBO. Ad. VG. B5d. $5.00

LAYNE, James. *Lend My Your Wife.* 1961. Beacon B 413F. PBO. Ad. VG. B5d. $7.00

LAYNE, James. *Six-Weekers.* 1962. Beacon B 484. NF. B3d. $7.00

LAYNE, James. *Six-Weekers.* 1962. Beacon B 484F. PBO. c/Darcy. Ad. G+. B5d. $4.50

LE BLANC, Edward. *Buffalo Bill's Feather-Weight/Denver Dan Jr & the Renegade.* Gold Star IL7-44. We. VG. B5d. $3.50

LE BLANC, Edward. *Buffalo Bill's Spy Shadower.* Gold Star IL7-34. We. G+. B5d. $2.50

LE BLANC, Edward. *Young Wild West Running the Gauntlet/Dandy Dan of Deadwood.* Gold Star IL7-37. We. G+. B5d. $2.50

LE BLANC, G. *Way Out Rush of Passion.* Target. VG+. B3d. $4.50

LE BLANC, Maurice. *Wanton Venus.* 1948. Novel Library 5. VG. B3d/P6d. $7.50

LE CARRE, John. *Murder of Quality.* Popular Library 00494. My. VG+. B5d. $4.00

LE CARRE, John. *Murder of Quality.* Signet 2529. VG+. B3d. $4.00

LE CARRE, John. *Small Town in Germany.* 1970. Dell 8036. 4th prtg. My. VG+. W2d. $3.50

LE FANU, Joseph Sheridan. *Room in the Dragon Inn.* 1956. Avon 702. 1st prtg. VG. P7d. $6.00

LE FEBURE, Charles. *Blood Cults.* 1969. Ace 06715. PBO. Nfi. VG. B5d. $6.50

LE GUIN, Ursula K. *Beginning Place.* 1981. Bantam 14259. SF. VG. W2d. $3.75

LE GUIN, Ursula K. *City of Illusions.* 1967. Ace G 626. 1st edn. G. P9d. $2.00

LE GUIN, Ursula K. *City of Illusions.* Ace 10701. SF. F. W2d. $5.00

LE GUIN, Ursula K. *Compass Rose.* 1988. Bantam 23512. SF. VG. B5d. $3.50

LE GUIN, Ursula K. *Dispossessed.* 1975. Avon 57331. 11th prtg. SF. F. W2d. $3.25

LE GUIN, Ursula K. *Farthest Star.* 1975. Bantam. 1st pb. VG. M1d. $5.00

LE GUIN, Ursula K. *Interfaces.* 1980. Ace 37093. SF. VG. W2d. $3.75

LE GUIN, Ursula K. *Lathe of Heaven.* 1973. Avon 14530. 1st edn. PBO. VG. P9d. $1.50

LE GUIN, Ursula K. *Left Hand of Darkness.* Ace 47800. c/L & D Dillon: Ace SF Special. B5d. $7.50

LE GUIN, Ursula K. *Left Hand of Darkness.* 1981. Ace 47806. 21st prtg. SF. VG+. W2d. $3.25

LE GUIN, Ursula K. *Olcott, Anthony.* 1984. Bantam 24234. c/skull. My. VG+. B5d. $4.50

LE GUIN, Ursula K. *Planet of Exile.* Ace 66951. 2nd edn. NF. P9d. $2.00

LE GUIN, Ursula K. *Tombs of Atuan.* 1977. Bantam 11600. 11th prtg. SF. VG. W2d. $2.75

LE GUIN, Ursula K. *Wizard of Earthsea.* Ace 90075. 1st edn. PBO. SF. VG. P9d. $2.50

LE JEUNE, Anthony. *Death of a Pornographer.* 1967. Lancer 73-627. My. VG+. B5d. $5.50

LE MARCHAND, Elizabeth. *Death of an Old Girl*. 1970. Award A 704S. 1st prtg. My. G+. W2d. $2.75

LE MAY, Alan. *Cattle Kingdom*. Signet 1219. 2nd prtg. VG. B3d. $4.00

LE MAY, Alan. *Cattle Kingdom*. 1948. Signet 672. NF. I1d. $8.00

LE MAY, Alan. *Cattle Kingdom*. 1948. Signet 672. We. VG+. B5d. $5.00

LE MAY, Alan. *Hell for Breakfast*. 1947. Bantam 134. c/J Kelly. We. VG+. B3d. $5.00

LE MAY, Alan. *Painted Ponies*. Popular Library G 267. c/Ross. reprint. We. NF. B6d. $9.00

LE MAY, Alan. *Searchers*. Popular Library 60-2284. 1st prtg. VG. P7d. $3.50

LE MAY, Alan. *Thunder in the Dust*. Popular Library 161. VG. B3d. $5.00

LE MAY, Alan. *Unforgiven*. 1959. Crest S 244. 2nd prtg. G+. R5d. $1.00

LE MAY, Alan. *Wild Justice*. 1948. Bantam 253. We. VG+. B4d. $7.00

LE MAY, Alan. *Winter Range*. Popular Library 141. VG. I1d. $5.00

LEA, Tom. *Brave Bulls*. 1951. Pocket 771. 1st prtg. c/Shoyer. VG. P7d. $5.00

LEARY, Bill. *Graffiti*. 1970. Gold Medal D 2156. P6d. $2.50

LEARY, F. *Fire & Morning*. Ace G 352. VG+. B3d. $5.00

LEATHAM, H. *Sex for One*. Viceroy 219. VG+. B3d. $5.00

LEATHAM & JONES. *Seven Sexes of Eve*. Venice 322. VG+. B3d. $4.50

LECKIE, Robert. *Helment for My Pillow*. 1958. Bantam A 1826. 1st pb. VG+. B6d. $7.50

LEDEERMAN, Frank. *Tremor*. Kaye 00. SF. G+. B5d. $5.00

LEDERER, W.J. *Nation of Sheep*. Crest 545. VG+. B3d. $4.00

LEE, Bruce. *Legend of Bruce Lee*. 1974. Dell 4811. 1st edn. c/color photos. My. F. F2d. $10.00

LEE, C.Y. *Flower Drum Song*. 1961. Dell F 175. 1st prtg. VG+. R5d. $3.25

LEE, C.Y. *Flower Drum Song*. Pan G 334. VG+. B3d. $8.00

LEE, C.Y. *Virgin Market*. 1965. Dell 9344. 1st prtg. c/Barye: gga. VG. P7d. $3.50

LEE, D. *Play for Pay Studs*. Jade 101. VG+. B3d. $4.50

LEE, Don. *Matter of Adultery*. 1961. Newsstand Library 156. 1st edn. c/gga. My. F. F2d. $10.00

LEE, E. *Love Address*. Brandon House 1154. NF. B3d. $4.00

LEE, Edna. *Queen Bee*. 1950. Bantam 848. 1st pb. Th. VG+. B6d. $10.00

Lee, Gypsy Rose. *G-String Murders*. PB Library 425. VG. G5d. $7.50

LEE, Gypsy Rose. *Gypsy*. Dell D 307. VG. B3d. $4.00

LEE, Gypsy Rose. *Gypsy*. 1959. PAN X 40. VG+. B3a #20. $40.00

LEE, Gypsy Rose. *Mother Finds a Body*. 1944. Popular Library 37. 1st edn. PBO. c/Hoffman. scarce. VG+. B6a #80. $54.00

LEE, Gypsy Rose. *Mother Finds a Body*. Popular Library 547. c/Johnson. NF. B6a #80. $44.00

LEE, Howard. *Kung Fu #1*. 1973. PB Library 76-464. PBO. TVTI. F. B6d. $7.50

LEE, Howard. *Kung Fu #2*. 1973. PB Library 76-465. PBO. TVTI. F. B6d. $7.50

LEE, Howard. *Kung Fu #3*. 1973. PB Library 76-466. PBO. TVTI. F. B6d. $7.50

LEE, Howard. *Kung Fu #4*. 1974. PB Library 76-467. PBO. TVTI. NF. B6d. $7.00

LEE, J. *Career*. Dell 1st Edn B 148. MTI. VG. B3d. $4.00

LEE, M. *Lion House*. Crest 413. c/McGinnis. VG+. B3d. $5.00

LEE, Patrick. *Gundown at Golden Gate*. 1981. Pinnacle 192. 1st edn. Hi. F. F2d. $6.00

LEE, Patrick. *Kamikaze Justice*. 1981. Pinnacle 416. 1st edn. We. F. F2d. $6.00

LEE, Stan. *Amazing Spider Man*. 1966. Lancer 72-112. PBO. VG+. P6d. $6.00

LEE, Stan. *Battlestar Galactica*. 1978. Tempo. 1st edn. F. M1d. $10.00

LEE, Stan. *Mighty Thor!* 1966. Lancer 72-125. PBO. comics. SF. VG. B5d. $5.00

LEE, Stan. *World of Fire*. 1982. Marvel 02849. Star Wars #2. SF. VG+. B4d. $4.00

LEE, Tanith. *Days of Grass*. 1985. DAW 651. 1st edn. VG. P9d. $1.75

LEE, Tanith. *Death's Master*. DAW VE 1741. 3rd edn. VG. P9d. $1.50

LEE, Tanith. *Death's Master*. 1979. DAW 324. 1st edn. NF. P9d. $2.00

LEE, Tanith. *Delusion's Master*. DAW UE 2197. 5th edn. F. P9d. $1.50

LEE, Tanith. *Delusion's Master*. 1981. DAW 448. 1st edn. VG. P9d. $1.50

LEE, Tanith. *Kill the Dead*. 1980. DAW 401. PBO. c/Maitz. SF. VG+. B6d. $6.00

LEE, Tanith. *Night's Master*. DAW UE 2131. 3rd edn. NF. P9d. $2.50

LEE, Tanith. *Night's Master*. DAW 313. 1st prtg. VG. S1d. $2.50

LEE, Tanith. *Red As Blood*. 1983. DAW 513. 1st edn. F. P9d. $2.50

LEE, Tanith. *Silver Metal Lover*. 1982. DAW UE 1721. SF. VG. W2d. $3.25

LEE, Tanith. *Silver Metal Lover*. DAW 476. VG. P9d. $1.50

LEE, Tanith. *Storm Lord*. 1976. DAW UE 1233. SF. VG. W2d. $3.25

LEE, Tanith. *Storm Lord*. 1976. DAW 193. 1st prtg. PBO. c/D'Achille: gga. VG. P7d. $4.00

LEE, Tanith. *Vazkor, Son of Vazkor*. 1978. DAW 272. 1st edn. VG. P9d. $1.50

LEE, Ted. *Pleasure in Women*. Monarch 285. PBO. VG. B3d. $4.50

LEES, Hannah. *Women Will Be Doctors*. 1947. Bantam 115. Fi. VG+. B5d. $4.00

LEEUW, H. *Sinful Cities*. Pyramid 27. G+. I1d. $6.00

LEHMAN, Paul Evan. *Blood of the West*. Signet 1352. reprint. VG+. B6d. $8.00

LEHMAN, Paul Evan. *Blood of the West*. 1948. Signet 682. 1st pb. c/Jonas. We. VG+. B6d. $12.00

LEHMAN, Paul Evan. *Brother of the Kid*. 1951. Signet 849. We. VG. B5d. $4.00

LEHMAN, Paul Evan. *Bullets Don't Bluff*. 1954. Ace D 64. PBO. c/Saunders. VG+. B6d. $40.00

LEHMAN, Paul Evan. *Cold Trail*. MacFadden 35-122. VG. G5d. $2.50

LEHMAN, Paul Evan. *Colt '60*. MacFadden 35-133. 2nd prtg. VG+. B3d. $4.50

LEHMAN, Paul Evan. *Comedian*. 1957. Signet 1446. TVTI. c/M Rooney. Fi. VG. B5d. $4.00

LEHMAN, Paul Evan. *Cow Kingdom*. 1946. Handi-Book Western 1. VG. B3a #24. $16.50

LEHMAN, Paul Evan. *Faces in the Dust*. Graphic 100. 2nd prtg. PBO. VG+. B3d. $7.50

LEHMAN, Paul Evan. *Gun Whipped*. 1958. Avon 825. We. VG. B4d. $3.25

LEHMAN, Paul Evan. *Gunman*. Pyramid 194. VG+. I1d. $6.00

LEHMAN, Paul Evan. *Gunsmoke at Buffalo Basin.* 1959. Avon 843. 1st prtg. VG. P7d. $5.00

LEHMAN, Paul Evan. *Montana Man.* Signet 731. VG+. B3d. $5.50

LEHMAN, Paul Evan. *Montana Man.* 1949. Signet 731. We. NF. B5d. $6.50

LEHMAN, Paul Evan. *Range Justice.* PB Library 50-319. VG+. B3d. $4.00

LEHMAN, Paul Evan. *Range War at Keno.* PB Library 56-499. 2nd prtg. VG+. B3d. $4.50

LEHMAN, Paul Evan. *Redrock Gold.* Harlequin 358. VG. B3d. $6.00

LEHMAN, Paul Evan. *Sheep Killers.* 1951. Star Book 16. PBO. c/Gross. We. VG. B6d. $9.00

LEHMAN, Paul Evan. *Smoke of the Texan.* 1964. MacFadden 35-131. We. VG. B5d. $3.00

LEHMAN, Paul Evan. *Stagecoach to Hellfire Pass.* Belmont 50-746. VG+. B3d. $4.50

LEHMAN, Paul Evan. *Sweet Smell of Sucess.* 1957. Signet S 1413. MTI. c/B Lancaster & T Curtis. Fi. VG. B3d/B5dR5d. $4.00

LEHMAN, Paul Evan. *Texas Men.* 1951. Graphic 34. PBO. G+. P6d. $1.50

LEHMAN, Paul Evan. *Twisted Trail.* MacFadden 50-353. VG+. B3d. $4.50

LEHMAN, Paul Evan. *Valley of Hunted Men.* Pyramid 1112. VG. B3d. $4.50

LEHMAN, Paul Evan. *Valley of Hunted Men.* 1948. Signet 666. We. VG. B5d. $4.50

LEHMAN, Paul Evan. *Vengeance Valley.* 1950. Handi-Book 119. VG+. I1d. $15.00

LEHMAN, Paul Evan. *West of the Wolverine.* 1967. Belmont B 50-775. reprint. We. VG+. B6d. $5.00

LEHMANN, Rosamond. *Invitation to a the Waltz.* 1948. Signet 662. Fa. VG. B4d. $4.00

LEHRER, James. *Viva Max!* Popular Library 75-8111. 1st prtg. c/sgn. G+. R5d. $3.00

LEIBER, Fritz. *Big Time.* Ace G 627. SF. F. M3d. $5.00

LEIBER, Fritz. *Big Time.* Ace 06219. 1st prtg. VG. S1d. $4.00

LEIBER, Fritz. *Big Time.* 1972. Ace 06221. 3rd edn. SF. NF. B5d. $5.00

LEIBER, Fritz. *Big Time.* 1982. Ace 06223. SF. VG. W2d. $3.00

LEIBER, Fritz. *Book of Fritz Leiber.* DAW 87. NF. I1d. $6.00

LEIBER, Fritz. *Book of Fritz Leiber.* DAW 87. 1st prtg. VG. S1d. $2.50

LEIBER, Fritz. *Conjure Wife.* Award AN 1143. VG. M6d. $4.50

LEIBER, Fritz. *Conjure Wife.* 1962. Berkley F 621. 1st pb edn. MTI. scarce. SF. F. F2d. $30.00

LEIBER, Fritz. *Conjure Wife.* 1953. Lion 179. 1st edn. PBO. c/Maguire. scarce. VG+. B6a #79. $82.50

LEIBER, Fritz. *Conjure Wife.* 1953. Lion 179. PBO. c/Maguire: gga. VG. F2d. $27.00

LEIBER, Fritz. *Conjure Wife.* 1953. Lion 179. PBO. NF. M1d. $40.00

LEIBER, Fritz. *Destiny Times Three.* Galaxy SF 28. VG+. B3d. $6.00

LEIBER, Fritz. *Gather, Darkness!* Berkley G 679. c/Powers. VG+. B3d. $5.50

LEIBER, Fritz. *Gather, Darkness!* 1962. Berkley G 679. 1st pb edn. SF. F. F2d. $15.00

LEIBER, Fritz. *Green Millenium.* 1954. Lion LL 7. c/gga. G+. P6d. $2.00

LEIBER, Fritz. *Green Millenium.* 1954. Lion LL 7. 1st prtg. VG. S1d. $7.00

LEIBER, Fritz. *Green Millennium.* 1954. Lion LL 7. NF. I1d. $12.00

LEIBER, Fritz. *Green Millennium.* 1954. Lion LL 7. 1st pb edn. F. F2d. $15.00

LEIBER, Fritz. *Night of the Wolf.* 1966. Ballantine U 2254. 1st edn. SF. F. F2d. $25.00

LEIBER, Fritz. *Night of the Wolf.* 1966. Ballantine U 2254. 1st edn. VG. M1d. $12.00

LEIBER, Fritz. *Night's Black Agents.* 1977. Sphere. F. M1d. $6.00

LEIBER, Fritz. *Pail of Air.* 1964. Ballantine U 2216. SF. VG. W2d. $4.25

LEIBER, Fritz. *Shadows With Eyes.* 1962. Ballantine 577. PBO. Ho. VG. B6d. $9.00

LEIBER, Fritz. *Shadows With Eyes.* 1962. Ballantine 577. PBO. SF. G+. B5d. $5.00

LEIBER, Fritz. *Silver Eggheads.* 1961. Ballantine F 561. PBO. c/Powers. VG+. B6d. $9.00

LEIBER, Fritz. *Silver Eggheads.* 1961. Ballantine F 561. PBO. c/R Powers. SF. G+. B5d. $4.00

LEIBER, Fritz. *Silver Eggheads.* Ballantine 01634. 2nd edn. F. P9d. $2.00

LEIBER, Fritz. *Spector Is Haunting Texas.* 1971. Bantam. 1st pb. F. M1d. $8.00

LEIBER, Fritz. *Swords & Deviltry.* 1970. Ace 79170. 1st edn. sgn/inscr. SF. F. F2d. $20.00

LEIBER, Fritz. *Swords & Ice Magic.* 1979. Ace 79168. 2nd prtg. SF. VG. W2d. $3.00

LEIBER, Fritz. *Swords Against Death.* Ace 79150. c/Jones: sgn. VG+. B3d. $6.00

LEIBER, Fritz. *Swords Against Death.* 1970. Ace 79150. 1st edn. sgn. SF. F. F2d. $20.00

LEIBER, Fritz. *Swords Against Wizardry.* Ace H 73. NF. M1d. $6.00

LEIBER, Fritz. *Swords Against Wizardry.* Ace H 73. SF. F. W2d. $8.50

LEIBER, Fritz. *Swords in the Mist.* Ace H 90. F. M1d. $8.00

LEIBER, Fritz. *Swords in the Mist.* Ace H 90. 1st prtg. VG. S1d. $3.50

LEIBER, Fritz. *Swords of Lankhmar.* 1968. Ace H 38. F. M1d. $8.00

LEIBER, Fritz. *Swords of Lankhmar.* 1968. Ace H 38. PBO. SF. NF. M3d. $7.50

LEIBER, Fritz. *Swords of Lankhmar.* Ace 79221. SF. VG. W2d. $3.00

LEIBER, Fritz. *Tarzan & the Valley of Gold.* 1966. Ballantine U 6125. 1st edn. c/sgn. SF. F. F2d. $30.00

LEIBER, Fritz. *Tarzan & the Valley of Gold.* 1966. Ballantine U 6125. 1st prtg. MTI. SF. G+. R5d. $4.50

LEIBER, Fritz. *Tarzan & the Valley of Gold.* 1966. Ballantine U 6125. 1st prtg. SF. F. W2d. $12.00

LEIBER, Fritz. *Wanderer.* 1964. Ballantine U 6010. 1st edn. SF. F. F2d. $18.00

LEIBER, Fritz. *Wanderer.* 1964. Ballantine U 6010. 1st edn. VG. P9d. $3.00

LEIBER, Fritz. *You're All Alone.* Ace 95146. 1st prtg. VG. S1d. $2.50

LEIBER, Murray. *Land of the Giants.* 1968. Pyramid X 1846. PBO. TVTI. c/photo. SF. VG+. M3d. $8.00

LEIBER/LEIBER. *Big Time/Mind Spider & Other Stories.* 1961. Ace D 491. SF. VG+. B3d. $5.00

LEIBER/LEIBER. *Big Time/Mind Spider & Other Stories.* 1961. Ace D 491. 1st edn. NF. M1d. $12.00

LEIBER/LEIBER. *Green Millennium/Night Monsters.* 1969. Ace 30300. SF. VG+. W2d. $10.50

LEIBER/LEIBER. *Green Millennium/Night Monsters.* 1969. Ace 30300. 1st edn. c/Leiber. SF. F. F2d. $15.00

LEIBER/WILLIAMS. *Sinful Ones/Bulls, Blood & Passion.* 1955. Universal Giant 5. PBO. rare. NF. B6a #76. $48.50

LEIBER/WILLIAMS. *Sinful Ones/Bulls, Blood & Passion.* 1955. Universal Giant 5. VG+. I1d. $40.00

LEIGH, Randolph. *48M Tons to Eisenhower.* 1945. Infantry NN. Nfi. VG+. B4d. $4.00

LEIGH, S. *Chanling.* Ace 73127. 1st prtg. VG+. S1d. $2.50

LEIGH, Stephen. *Slow Fall to Dawn.* 1981. Bantam 14902. SF. NF. B5d. $5.00

LEIGHTON, F.S. *Patty Goes to Washington.* 1964. Ace F 278. PBO. TVTI. NF. B6d. $16.50

LEIGHTON, Lee. *Big Ugly.* Ballantine U 2301. PBO. VG. B3d. $4.00

LEIGHTON, Lee. *Hanging at Pulpit Rock.* Ballantine U 2302. PBO. VG. B3d. $4.00

LEIGHTON, Lee. *You'll Never Hang Me.* 1971. Ballantine 02370. c/Hantman. We. VG+. B4d. $2.25

LEINSTER, Murray. *Aliens.* 1960. Berkley G 410. 1st edn. NF. M1d. $10.00

LEINSTER, Murray. *Best of Murray Leinster.* 1978. Ballantine 25800. c/H Van Dongen. SF. VG+. B5d. $6.00

LEINSTER, Murray. *Black Galaxy.* Galaxy SF 20. VG+. B3d. $8.00

LEINSTER, Murray. *Checkpoint Lambda.* 1966. Berkley F 1263. PBO. c/R Powers. SF. VG. B5d. $4.50

LEINSTER, Murray. *Checkpoint Lambda.* 1966. Berkley F 1263. 1st edn. NF. M1d. $8.00

LEINSTER, Murray. *Creatures of the Abyss.* 1961. Berkley G 549. PBO. c/R Powers. SF. VG+. B5d. $5.50

LEINSTER, Murray. *Doctor to the Stars.* 1964. Pyramid F 987. SF. VG+. B4d. $4.00

LEINSTER, Murray. *Fight for Life.* 1949. Prize SF 10. PBO. VG. B6d. $15.00

LEINSTER, Murray. *Forgotten Planet.* 1956. Ace D 146. F. M1d. $18.00

LEINSTER, Murray. *Forgotten Planet.* 1956. Ace D 146. G. M1d. $4.00

LEINSTER, Murray. *Forgotten Planet.* 1956. Ace D 146. 1st edn. PBO. SF. VG. F2d. $10.00

LEINSTER, Murray. *Forgotten Planet.* Ace D 528. VG. M1d. $10.00

LEINSTER, Murray. *Four From Planet 5.* 1959. Gold Medal S 937. 1st edn. SF. F. F2d. $10.00

LEINSTER, Murray. *Four From Planet 5.* 1959. Gold Medal S 937. 1st prtg. VG+. S1d. $8.00

LEINSTER, Murray. *Four From Planet 5.* Gold Medal 1397. 2nd prtg. VG+. B3d. $4.50

LEINSTER, Murray. *Get Off My World!* 1966. Belmont. 1st pb. VG. M1d. $7.00

LEINSTER, Murray. *Greks Bring Gifts.* 1964. MacFadden 50-224. 1st edn. F. M1d. $10.00

LEINSTER, Murray. *Greks Bring Gifts.* 1975. Manor 95400. SF. F. W2d. $5.00

LEINSTER, Murray. *Hot Spot.* 1969. Pyramid X 1921. 1st edn. Land of the Giants #2. VG. M1d. $8.00

LEINSTER, Murray. *Invaders of Space.* 1964. Berkley F 1022. 1st prtg. SF. VG. R5d. $4.50

LEINSTER, Murray. *Land of the Giants.* Pyramid X 1846. 1st prtg. VG. I1d/S1d. $4.00

LEINSTER, Murray. *Land of the Giants.* 1968. Pyramid 1846. 1st edn. TVTI. SF. F. F2d. $9.00

LEINSTER, Murray. *Last Spaceship.* Galaxy SF 25. VG. B3d. $4.50

LEINSTER, Murray. *Men Into Space.* 1960. Berkley G 461. 1st edn. NF. M1d. $10.00

LEINSTER, Murray. *Men Into Space.* 1960. Berkley G 461. 1st prtg. TVTI. SF. VG. R5d. $4.00

LEINSTER, Murray. *Miner in the Sky.* 1967. Avon G 1310. SF. VG. W2d. $4.75

LEINSTER, Murray. *Monster From Earth's End.* 1959. Gold Medal S 832. 1st edn. SF. F. F2d/M1d. $15.00

LEINSTER, Murray. *Monster From Earth's End.* 1959. Gold Medal S 832. 1st prtg. SF. VG. R5d. $10.00

LEINSTER, Murray. *Monsters & Such.* 1959. Avon T 345. c/Kalin. SF. VG+. B3d. $4.50

LEINSTER, Murray. *Monsters & Such.* 1959. Avon T 345. 1st edn. F. M1d. $15.00

LEINSTER, Murray. *Monsters & Such.* 1959. Avon T 345. 1st edn. VG. P9d. $3.00

LEINSTER, Murray. *Operation Terror.* 1962. Berkley F 694. PBO. c/R Powers. SF. G+. B5d. $2.50

LEINSTER, Murray. *Operation Terror.* 1962. Berkley F 694. 1st edn. c/Powers. SF. F. F2d. $15.00

LEINSTER, Murray. *Operation Terror.* 1962. Berkley F 694. 1st prtg. SF. VG+. R5d. $5.00

LEINSTER, Murray. *Operation: Outer Space.* Signet S 1346. 3rd edn. G. P9d. $1.50

LEINSTER, Murray. *Operation: Outer Space.* 1957. Signet S 1346. c/R Schulz. SF. VG. B3d/B5d. $5.00

LEINSTER, Murray. *Operation: Outer Space.* 1957. Signet S 1346. 1st pb. F. M1d. $10.00

LEINSTER, Murray. *Other Side of Nowhere.* 1964. Berkley F 918. PBO. c/R Powers. SF. G+. B5d. $2.50

LEINSTER, Murray. *Other Side of Nowhere.* 1964. Berkley F 918. 1st edn. VG+. I1d. $10.00

LEINSTER, Murray. *Outlaw Deputy.* 1950. New Stand Library 133. G+. B3d. $7.00

LEINSTER, Murray. *Planet Explorer.* Avon T 202. 1st prtg. F. S1d. $6.50

LEINSTER, Murray. *Planet Explorer.* 1957. Avon T 202. SF. VG+. B5d. $4.50

LEINSTER, Murray. *Planet Explorer.* 1957. Avon T 202. 1st pb. NF. M1d. $8.00

LEINSTER, Murray. *Planet Explorer.* 1957. Avon T 202. 1st prtg. SF. VG. R5d. $2.50

LEINSTER, Murray. *SOS From Three Worlds.* 1967. Ace G 647. 1st edn. NF. P9d. $2.00

LEINSTER, Murray. *Space Platform.* 1965. Belmont 92-625. SF. VG+. B5d. $4.50

LEINSTER, Murray. *Space Platform.* 1965. Belmont 92-625. 1st prtg. SF. VG. R5d. $3.50

LEINSTER, Murray. *Space Platform.* 1953. Pocket 920. c/E Bergey. SF. G+. B5d. $5.00

LEINSTER, Murray. *Space Platform.* 1953. Pocket 920. 1st edn. PBO. SF. F. F2d. $8.00

LEINSTER, Murray. *Space Tug.* 1965. Belmont B 50-632. c/J Gaughan. SF. VG. B5d. $4.50

LEINSTER, Murray. *Space Tug.* 1968. Belmont B 50-846. 2nd edn. SF. VG+. B5d. $5.50

LEINSTER, Murray. *Space Tug.* 1954. Pocket 1037. 1st pb. F. M1d. $15.00

LEINSTER, Murray. *This World Is Taboo.* 1961. Ace D 525. 1st edn. SF. F. F2d. $8.00

LEINSTER, Murray. *Time Slip.* 1967. Pyramid R 1680. SF. VG+. W2d. $7.50

LEINSTER, Murray. *Time Slip.* 1967. Pyramid R 1680. 1st edn. TVTI. SF. F. F2d. $9.00

LEINSTER, Murray. *Time Slip.* 1967. Pyramid R 1680. 1st prtg. Time Tunnel #2. G+. R5d. $3.75

LEINSTER, Murray. *Time Tunnel.* 1966. Pyramid R 1043. 2nd prtg. SF. F. W2d. $7.50

LEINSTER, Murray. *Time Tunnel.* 1967. Pyramid R 1522. TVTI. VG+. P1d. $12.50

LEINSTER, Murray. *Twists in Time.* Avon T 389. NF. I1d. $5.00

LEINSTER, Murray. *Twists in Time.* Avon T 389. 1st pb. F. M1d. $12.00

LEINSTER, Murray. *Unknown Danger.* 1969. Pyramid 2105. 1st edn. TVTI. SF. F. F2d. $9.00

LEINSTER, Murray. *Wailing Asteroid.* 1960. Avon T 483. PBO. c/R Powers. SF. VG. B5d. $4.50

LEINSTER, Murray. *War With the Gizmos.* 1958. Gold Medal S 751. PBO. c/Powers. SF. VG+. B6d. $8.00

LEINSTER, Murray. *War With the Gizmos.* 1958. Gold Medal S 751. 1st edn. G. M1d. $3.00

LEINSTER, Murray. *War With the Gizmos.* 1958. Gold Medal S 751. 1st edn. SF. F. F2d. $12.00

LEINSTER/BELLAMY. *Brain Stealers/Atta.* Ace D 79. F. M1d. $22.00

LEINSTER/CORREY. *Forgotten Planet/Contraband Rocket: Correy.* Ace D 146. SF. VG. F2d. $10.00

LEINSTER/LEINSTER. *City on the Moon/Men on the Moon.* 1958. Ace D 277. 1st edn. PBO. SF. F. F2d. $10.00

LEINSTER/LEINSTER. *Pirates of Zan/Mutant Weapon.* 1959. Ace D 403. PBO. VG. B3d. $5.00

LEINSTER/LEINSTER. *Pirates of Zan/Mutant Weapon.* 1959. Ace D 403. 1st edn. c/Emsh. NF. M1d. $15.00

LEINSTER/VAN VOGT. *Gateway to Elsewhere/Weapon Shops of Isher.* 1954. Ace D 53. PBO. F. M1d. $25.00

LEINSTER/VAN VOGT. *Gateway to Elsewhere/Weapon Shops of Isher.* 1954. Ace D 53. PBO. SF. VG. B5d. $9.00

LEINSTER/VAN VOGT. *Other Side of Here/One Against Eternity.* Ace D 94. F. M1d. $20.00

LEINSTER/WOLLHEIM. *City on the Moon/Men on the Moon.* 1958. Ace D 277. c/Emsh. F. M1d. $15.00

LEINSTER/WOLLHEIM. *City on the Moon/Men on the Moon.* 1958. Ace D 277. PBO. c/E Emsh. SF. G+. B5d. $3.00

LEINSTER/WOLLHEIM. *City on the Moon/Men on the Moon.* 1958. Ace D 277. VG+. I1d. $6.00

LEINWAND, Gerald edt. *Crime & Juvenile Delinquency.* 1968. Pocket 77470. JD. VG+. P1d. $11.00

LEISY, J.F. edt. *Hootenanny Tonight.* Gold Medal 1457. VG. B3d. $5.00

LEITFRED, R.H. *Man Who Was Murdered Twice.* Green Dragon 21. VG. B3d. $4.00

LEITFRED, R.H. *Murder Is My Racket.* 1940s. Tech Mystery 2. 1st pb. VG+. B6d. $12.00

LEITHEAD, J. Edward. *Bloody Hoofs.* 1952. Ace D 2. PBO. c/Saunders. VG. B6d. $25.00

LEITHEAD, J. Edward. *Bronc Buckaroo.* 1952. Avon 486. We. G+. P6d. $3.00

LEITHEAD, J. Edward. *Bronc Buckeroo.* 1948. Avon 170. c/E Moore. We. VG. B5d. $7.50

LEITHEAD/WARD. *Lead-Slingers/Hanging Hills.* 1953. Ace D 18. PBO. c/N Saunders. We. VG. B5d. $10.00

LEM, Stanislaw. *Invincible.* Ace 37170. c/skull. Ace SF Special. SF. VG. B5d. $5.00

LEMANS, Jean. *Virgin's Bed.* 1963. Nitey-Nite N 101. VG+. B3a #22. $16.50

LENGEL, F. *Young Adam.* Greenleaf 204. c/Trocchi. VG+. B3d. $5.00

LENGYEL, Cornel. *Presidents of the USA: Profiles & Pictures.* 1961. Bantam GDQ 4. Nfi. NF. B5d. $4.50

LENNOX, Susan. *Doctor's Choice.* 1961. Monarch 208. Ro. VG+. B4d. $7.00

LEOKUM, Arkady. *Please Send Me Absolutely Free!* 1951. Popular Library 366. c/gga. Fa. VG+. B4d. $7.50

LEONARD, Burgess. *Thoroughbred & the Tramp.* Ace D 374. VG+. B3d. $6.50

LEONARD, Elmore. *Bandits.* Warner 30130. VG. G5d. $3.00

LEONARD, Elmore. *Big Bounce.* 1969. Gold Medal R 2079. PBO. MTI. My. G+. B5d. $9.00

LEONARD, Elmore. *Bounty Hunters.* Bantam 13295. G+. M6d. $4.00

LEONARD, Elmore. *Last Stand at Saber River.* Dell 1st Edn A 184. PBO. G+. M6d. $9.50

LEONARD, Elmore. *Law at Randado.* 1955. Dell 863. PBO. c/Gross. VG. B6d. $18.00

LEONARD, Elmore. *Mr Majestyk.* 1974. Dell 5887. Fa. VG+. B4d. $5.00

LEONARD, Elmore. *Mr Majestyk.* 1974. Dell 5887. 1st prtg. C1. R5d. $2.50

LEONARD, Elmore. *Swag.* 1984. Penguin. 1st pb. F. M1d. $6.00

LEONARD, J.N. *Flight Into Space.* 1954. Signet 317. 1st pb. F. M1d. $5.00

LEOPOLD, Jules. *Check Your Wits.* Popular Library 315. VG. B3d. $4.50

LEOURLER, Christian. *Mountains of the Sun.* 1974. Berkley O2570. SF. NF. B5d. $4.50

LERANGIS, Peter. *In Search of a Shark.* 1987. Scholastic 40338. Explorer #3. SF. VG. W2d. $3.00

LERNER, Alan Jay. *My Fair Lady.* 1958. Signet S 1551. 1st prtg. VG+. R5d. $5.00

LEROUX, Gaston. *Phantom of the Opera.* Dell 24. 1st pb. G. M1d. $10.00

LEROUX, Gaston. *Phantom of the Opera.* 1944. Dell 24. VG. B3a #20. $18.70

LEROUX, Gaston. *Phantom of the Opera.* 1962. Popular Library PC 1020. MTI. c/Phantom & Heather: photo. VG+. B4d. $5.00

LESCROART, John T. *Rasputin's Revenge.* Leisure 2671. VG+. G5d. $7.50

LESLIE, A.S. *Stranger in Boots.* Pyramid 44. VG. I1d. $7.00

LESLIE, A.S. *Tombstone Trail.* Pyramid 36. VG. I1d. $7.00

LESLIE, Bill. *Violator.* 1962. France 6. 1st edn. c/gga. My. F. F2d. $12.00

LESLIE, Peter. *Divine Dames Affair.* 1967. Ace G 617. 1st prtg. My. G+. R5d. $2.25

LESLIE, Peter. *Diving Dames.* Ace G 617. Man From Uncle #9. VG. B3d. $4.00

LESLIE, Peter. *Hell for Tomorrow.* 1966. MacFadden 50-280. 1st prtg. G+. R5d. $2.00

LESLIE, Peter. *Radioactive Camel Affair.* Ace G 600. Man From UNCLE #7. NF. G5d. $6.00

LESLIE, S. *Stranger in Boots.* Pyramid 44. VG. B3d. $4.00

LESLIE, Warren. *Best Thing That Ever Happened.* 1953. Signet S 1070. c/Avati: gga. Fa. VG. B4d. $2.75

LESSER, Milton. *Jeopardy Is My Job.* 1962. Gold Medal 1214. 1st edn. Th. F. F2d. $14.00

LESSER, Milton. *Peril Is My Pay.* 1960. Gold Medal 1018. 1st edn. Th. F. F2d. $18.00

LESSER, Milton. *Secret of the Black Planet.* Belmont 01054. SF. G+. W2d. $3.50

LESSER, Milton. *Secret of the Black Planet.* Belmont. 1st edn. VG. M1d. $8.00

LESTER, Teri. *Episode in Rome.* 1967. Signet D 3201. Ro. VG+. B4d. $2.75

LEVERIDGE, Ralph. *Walk on the Water.* Signet 940. VG. B3d. $4.00

LEVEY, Robert A. *Murder in Lima.* 1957. Avon 792. My. VG+. B4d. $5.00

LEVEY, Robert A. *Murder in Lima.* 1957. Avon 792. PBO. c/A Sussman. My. G+. B5d. $3.00

LEVI, Carlo. *Christ Stopped at Eboli.* 1965. Pocket 75053. Fi. VG. B5d. $3.00

LEVIE, Rex Dean. *Insect Warriors.* 1965. Ace F 334. PBO. F. M1d. $8.00

LEVIE, Rex Dean. *Insect Warriors.* 1965. Ace F 334. 1st prtg. SF. VG. R5d. $3.25

LEVIN, Dan. *Mask of Glory.* Popular Library G 103. VG. B3d. $4.00

LEVIN, Ira. *Kiss Before Dying.* 1954. Signet 1147. My. VG. B3d/B5d. $4.50

LEVIN, Ira. *Rosemary's Baby.* 1968. Dell 7509. 2nd prtg. MTl. SF. VG. R5d. $1.50

LEVIN, Ira. *Stepford Wives.* 1973. Crest P 1876. 1st prtg. SF. VG+. R5d. $2.00

LEVIN, Ira. *This Perfect Day.* 1976. Pan 02657. 3rd prtg. SF. VG. W2d. $4.50

LEVIN, Meyer. *Young Lovers.* Signet 911. VG+. B3d. $5.00

LEVINREW, Will. *Wheel Chair Corpse.* 1945. Bart 14. My. G+. B5d. $4.50

LEWIN, Michael Z. *Outside In.* 1980. Knopf. 1st edn. dust jacket. De. F. F2d. $17.50

LEWINSOHN, Richard. *Science, Prophecy & Prediction.* 1962. Premier T 168. Nfi. VG. B5d. $2.50

LEWIS, C.S. *Hideous Strength.* 1977. MacFadden 86920. 19th prtg. SF. VG. W2d. $3.25

LEWIS, C.S. *Last Battle.* 1976. Collins 04421. 15th prtg. Chronicals of Narnia Book #7. SF. F. W2d. $4.75

LEWIS, C.S. *Lion the Witch & the Wardrobe.* 1976. Collins 04422. 18th prtg. Chronicals of Narnia Book #1. SF. F. W2d. $4.25

LEWIS, C.S. *Magician's Nephew.* 1976. Collins 04423. 16th prtg. Chronicals of Narnia Book #6. SF. F. W2d. $4.75

LEWIS, C.S. *Out of Silent the Planet.* 1949. Avon 195. 1st pb. VG. M1d. $30.00

LEWIS, C.S. *Out of the Silent Planet.* Avon T 410. 3rd edn. NF. P9d. $2.00

LEWIS, C.S. *Out of the Silent Planet.* 1949. Avon 195. c/A Cantor. SF. G. B5d. $5.00

LEWIS, C.S. *Perelandra.* 1957. Avon T 157. 1st prtg. SF. G+. R5d. $1.75

LEWIS, C.S. *Perelandra.* 1950. Avon 277. NF. I1d. $25.00

LEWIS, C.S. *Perelandra.* 1950. Avon 277. VG. B3d. $15.00

LEWIS, C.S. *Perelandra.* 1950. Avon 277. VG+. B3a #24. $8.05

LEWIS, C.S. *Perelandra.* 1965. MacFadden 86900. 24th prtg. SF. VG. W2d. $3.25

LEWIS, C.S. *Prince Caspian.* 1976. Collins 04424. 16th prtg. Chronicals of Narnia Book #2. SF. F. W2d. $4.25

LEWIS, C.S. *Silver Chair.* 1970. Collins 44250. 31st prtg. Chronicals of Narnia Book #4. SF. F. W2d. $4.25

LEWIS, C.S. *That Hideous Strength.* Pan 321. VG. B3d. $6.50

LEWIS, C.S. *Tortured Planet.* Avon T 211. SF. VG. B5d. $3.50

LEWIS, C.S. *Tortured Planet.* 1957. Avon T 211. 1st pb. F. M1d. $10.00

LEWIS, C.S. *Tortured Planet.* 1957. Avon T 211. 1st prtg. SF. G+. R5d. $2.00

LEWIS, C.S. *Voyage of the Dawn Treader.* 1976. Collins 04426. 16th prtg. Chronicals of Narnia Book #3. SF. VG+. W2d. $3.75

LEWIS, Claude. *Adam Clayton Powell.* Gold Medal 1361. PBO. VG+. B3d. $8.00

LEWIS, E. edt. *Trader Horn.* Pan 36. VG+. B3d. $8.00

LEWIS, H.C. *Silver Dark.* Pyramid 383. VG+. B3d. $6.00

LEWIS, J. *Official Liquor & Wine Buying Guide.* Holloway House BH 439. VG+. B3d. $4.50

LEWIS, Jack. *Blood Money.* 1960. Headline 108. c/gga. Fa. G+. B4d. $4.00

LEWIS, Jack. *Nymph Bait!* 1960. Merit 655. 1st edn. De. F. F2d. $20.00

LEWIS, L. *Murder Among Friends.* Bart House 36. VG+. B3d. $8.00

LEWIS, Lange. *Meat for Murder.* Dell 135. 1st prtg. My. G+. R5d. $5.50

LEWIS, Sinclair. *Babbitt.* 1946. Bantam 22. dust jacket. VG+. B3a #24. $39.95

LEWIS, Sinclair. *Babbitt.* 1946. Bantam 22. Fa. VG+. B4d. $6.00

LEWIS, Sinclair. *Cass Timberlane.* Bantam 893. c/Zuckerberg. VG+. B3d. $4.50

LEWIS, Sinclair. *Elmer Gantry.* Avon 1. VG. B3d. $10.00

LEWIS, Sinclair. *Ghost Patrol.* 1946. Avon 74. VG. B4d/I1d. $10.00

LEWIS, Sinclair. *It Can't Happen Here.* Dell S 19. VG. B3d. $4.00

LEWIS, Sinclair. *Kingsblood Royal.* 1949. Bantam 705. 2nd edn. c/Avati. VG+. B4d. $5.00

LEWIS, Sinclair. *Man From Main Street.* 1963. Cardinal GC 610. Nfi. VG+. B5d. $3.50

LEWIS, Sinclair. *World So Wide.* 1956. Lion LL 113. 1st pb. c/Borack. VG. B6d. $5.00

LEWIS, Sinclair. *World So Wide.* 1961. Pyramid G 596. Fa. VG. B4d. $2.75

LEWIS, Sinclair. *7 Sinclair Lewis Short Stories.* Shortstory 6. VG. B3d. $4.00

LEWIS & MARTIN. *Naked Eye.* Pocket 770. VG+. G5d. $7.00

LEWISOHN, Ludwig. *Don Juan.* Avon 221. VG. B3d. $4.00

LEWISOHN, Ludwig. *For Ever Wilt Thou Love.* 1949. Signet 749. c/gga. Fa. VG. B4d. $15.00

LEWISOHN, Ludwig. *In a Summer Season.* 1957. Signet 1397. Fi. VG. B5d. $4.00

LEWISOHN, Ludwig. *Sins of Joy Munson.* Lion LL 60. c/gga. reprint. VG. B6d. $7.50

LEWISOHN, Ludwig. *Vehement Flame.* 1949. Signet 702. Fi. G+. B5d. $3.00

LEWTON, Val. *No Bed of Her Own.* 1950. Novel Library 39. VG. B3a #22. $11.00

LEY, Willy. *On Earth & in the Sky.* Ace 24851. 1st prtg. F. S1d. $3.00

LEY, Willy. *Satellites, Rockets & Outer Space.* 1958. Signet KS 360. My. VG+. M3d. $7.00

LIBBY, Patricia. *Hollywood Nurse.* 1962. Ace D 552. 1st prtg. VG+. P7d. $4.00

LIBBY, Patricia. *Winged Victory for Nurse Kerry.* Ace D 599. VG. B3d. $4.00

LICATA, T. edt. *Great SF.* 1965. Three Star 102. c/Brown & Bradbury. VG+. B3d. $4.50

LICHTENBERG, J. *Star Trek Lives!* 1975. Bantam Y 2151. 3rd prtg. SF. VG. W2d. $6.00

LIEBERMAN, Rosalie. *Man Who Sold Christmas.* 1963. All Saints AS 234. SF. VG. B5d. $3.00

LIEBERS, Arthur. *Wit's End.* 1963. Tempo T 23. 1st prtg. c/Goff. VG. P7d. $4.00

LIEBERSON, Will & Martin edt. *College Parodies.* 1961. Ballantine S 541. 1st edn. VG+. F2d. $7.00

LIEBLING, A.J. *Press.* 1961. Ballantine 530. PBO. NF. B3d. $5.00

LIEBLING, A.J. *Sweet Science.* Black Cat 44. VG. B3d. $5.00

LIEF, Evelyn. *Amazing Spiderman #1.* 1980. Pocket 83489. PBO. F. B6d. $7.50

LIEF, Evelyn. *Clone Rebellion.* 1980. Pocket 83156. PBO. SF. NF. B6d. $7.50

LINDBERGH, Anne Morrow. *Gift From the Sea.* 1957. Signet S 1367. c/Mrs Lindbergh; photo. Nfi. VG+. B4d. $8.00

LINDEN, Millicent. *Tensions in Repose.* 1966. Gold Medal D 1614. Nfi. VG+. B4d. $3.00

LINDER, D. Barry. *Half Past Sex.* Greenleaf Classic GC 417. VG. M6d. $6.50

LINDER, Robert. *Must You Conform?* Black Cat BB 6. 2nd edn. c/gga. Nfi. VG+. B5d. $5.50

LINDHOLM, Megan. *Limbreth Gate.* 1984. Ace 48358. PBO. SF. NF. B6d. $3.00

LINDOP, Audrey E. *Bandit & the Priest.* 1954. Cardinal C 149. 1st prtg. My. G+. R5d. $1.75

LINDSAY, David. *Voyage to Arcturus.* 1973. Ballantine. 3rd edn. Ad/Fa. VG. M1d. $4.00

LINDSAY, Norman. *Age of Consent.* 1959. Cardinal C 383. Fa. VG+. B4d. $2.00

LINDSAY, Norman. *Cautious Amorist.* 1947. Bantam 100. c/V Kaufman. Fi. VG. B5d. $3.50

LINDSAY, P. *As Good As Married.* Quarter 48. c/Gross. VG. B3d. $10.00

LINDSAY, Perry. *Passionate Virgin.* 1949. Pyramid 11. 1st pb. VG+. B6d. $18.00

LINDSAY, Perry. *Unashamed.* 1947. Century 85. c/Malcolm Smith. VG. P6d. $5.00

LINDSAY, Philip. *Sir Naked Blade.* Avon T 136. Fi. VG. B5d. $3.00

LINDSAY, Philip. *To Love by Candlelight.* Avon T 122. VG. B3d. $4.50

LINDSAY, Vachel. *Daniel Jazz.* Armed Services 901. VG. B3d. $5.00

LINGEMAN & NAVASKY. *Monocle Peep Show.* Bantam 2994. VG. B3d. $5.00

LINK, Henry C. *Return to Religion.* 1943. Pocket 183. Nfi. VG. B5d. $4.00

LINKLETTER, Art. *Child's Garden of Misinformation.* 1968. Gold Medal D 1953. 1st prtg. VG+. P7d. $4.50

LINKLETTER, Art. *People Are Funny.* 1960. Cardinal C 384. 1st prtg. TVTI. VG+. R5d. $3.50

LINKLETTER, E. *Flying High.* Fitz Pubs 3001. VG+. B3d. $4.00

LINN, Ed. *Ted Williams: The Eternal Kid.* 1961. Sport Magazine 3. PBO. c/photo. Bio. VG. P6d. $3.00

LINSCOTT, R.N. edt. *Comic Relief.* Armed Services 1076. Nfi. G+. B5d. $3.00

LINSCOTT, R.N. edt. *Omnibus of American Humor.* Popular Library 170. VG. B3d. $4.00

LINTON, Duke. *Killer Bait.* Scion NN. VG+. B3a #20. $29.00

LIONEL, Robert. *Time Echo.* 1964. Uni-Book NN. SF. VG. B4d. $2.00

LIPMAN, Clayre & Michel. *House of Evil.* 1954. Lion 231. 1st edn. scarce. My. F. F2d. $22.50

LIPSKY, E. *Hoodlum.* Lion 161. VG. I1d. $15.00

LISTON, Jack. *Man Bait.* 1960. Dell 1st Edn B 158. c/Bob Maguire: gga. Cr. VG. P6d. $3.00

LISTON, Jack. *Man Bait.* 1960. Dell 1st Edn 60. c/Bob Maguire: gga. VG. P6d. $2.50

LITHGOW, M. *Mach One.* Panther 519. VG. B3d. $6.50

LITTEN, F.N. *Kingdom of Flying Men.* Pocket J 51. NF. B3d. $5.50

LITTLE, C. *Sound of Trumpets.* Monarch 493. VG+. B3d. $5.00

LITTLE, C. & G. *Black Shrouds.* Popular Library 112. VG. B3d. $6.00

LITTLE, C. & G. *Black-Headed Pins.* Popular Library 83. VG+. B3d. $10.00

LITTLE, C. & G. *Black-Headed Pins.* 1946. Popular Library 83. VG+. B3a #21. $7.40

LITTLE, C. & G. *Great Black Kanba.* Dell 181. c/G Gregg. My. VG. B5d. $8.50

LITVINOFF, Emanuel. *Lost Europeans.* 1960. Pyramid G 559. c/swastika. Fi. G+. B5d. $2.50

LITVINOFF, Emanuel. *Lost Europeans.* 1960. Pyramid G 559. VG+. B3d. $4.50

LIVINGSTON, Armstrong. *Magic for Murder.* Cavalcade Book. 2nd prtg. VG+. B3d. $7.50

LIVINGSTON, Harold. *Climacticon.* 1960. Ballantine 406K. 1st edn. F. M1d. $13.00

LIVINGSTON, Harold. *Climacticon.* 1960. Ballantine 406K. 1st prtg. VG. S1d. $4.50

LLES, Francis. *Before the Fact.* 1947. Pocket 419. MTI. VG+. B4d. $9.00

LLEWELLYN, Edward. *Bright Companion.* 1980. DAW. 1st edn. F. M1d. $5.00

LLEWELLYN, Edward. *Fugitive in Transit.* 1985. DAW 614. 1st edn. VG. P9d. $2.00

LLOYD, D.D. *Sirens Let Him Go.* Popular Library SP 184. VG+. B3d. $4.50

LOCKE, C.O. *Hell Bent Kid.* Popular Library G 225. MTI. VG. B3d. $4.00

LOCKE, C.O. *Hell Bent Kid.* Popular Library K 62. VG+. B3d. $4.50

LOCKE, C.O. *Last Princess.* 1954. Popular Library 622. c/gga. Fa. NF. B4d. $12.00

LOCKLEY. *Pan Book of Cage Birds.* 1961. Pan G 452. 1st pb. VG+. B6d. $5.00

LOCKRIDGE & LOCKRIDGE. *Death Has a Small Voice.* Avon T 422. VG. B3d. $4.00

LOCKRIDGE & LOCKRIDGE. *Death of a Tall Man.* 1949. Dell 322. 1st prtg. NF. P7d. $12.50

LOCKRIDGE & LOCKRIDGE. *Death on the Aisle.* Armed Services 747. NF. I1d. $12.00

LOCKRIDGE & LOCKRIDGE. *Death on the Aisle.* Pocket 411. VG+. B3d. $5.00

LOCKRIDGE & LOCKRIDGE. *Death Takes a Bow.* 1948. Avon 131. My. VG. B5d. $8.00

LOCKRIDGE & LOCKRIDGE. *Dishonest Murderer.* 1951. Avon 369. c/Bob Hilbert. My. VG. B5d. $8.00

LOCKRIDGE & LOCKRIDGE. *Hanged for a Sheep.* 1948. Bantam 305. c/G Fullington. My. VG. B5d. $5.00

LOCKRIDGE & LOCKRIDGE. *Hanged for a Sheep.* 1948. Bantam 305. My. NF. B4d. $12.50

LOCKRIDGE & LOCKRIDGE. *Killing the Goose.* Avon 142. VG+. I1d. $8.00

LOCKRIDGE & LOCKRIDGE. *Long Skeleton.* Pyramid R 824. G+. G5d. $5.50

LOCKRIDGE & LOCKRIDGE. *Murder Comes First.* 1952. Avon 434. c/Leone. Fi. G. B5d/G5d. $5.00

LOCKRIDGE & LOCKRIDGE. *Murder in a Hurry.* Avon 484. G+. G5d. $5.00

LOCKRIDGE & LOCKRIDGE. *Murder Is Served.* 1951. Avon 363. 1st pb. My. VG+. B6d. $16.50

LOCKRIDGE & LOCKRIDGE. *Norths Meet Murder.* 1942. Pocket 166. 1st edn. PBO. scarce. My. NF. B6a #75. $44.50

LOCKRIDGE & LOCKRIDGE. *Pinch of Poison.* Pocket 346. G. G5d. $7.50

LOCKRIDGE & LOCKRIDGE. *Stand Up & Die.* 1954. Graphic 82. c/Saul Levine. VG. P6d. $3.25

LOCKRIDGE/LOCKRIDGE. *Mr & Mrs North/ Poisoned Playboy.* 1957. Avon 766. 1st pb. VG. B6d. $4.00

LOCKWOOD, Mary. *Accessory.* 1970. Dell 0191. 1st prtg. My. G+. W2d. $3.25

LOFTS, Norah. *Town House.* 1961. Cardinal GC 763. 1st prtg. VG. P7d. $3.50

LOGAN, Ford. *Fire in the Desert.* Ballantine 666. We. VG. B5d. $3.50

LOGSDON, Syd. *Jandrax.* 1979. Ballantine 28185. SF. NF. B5d. $5.50

LOHNDORFF, Ernst. *Forest of Fear.* 1957. Corgi 490. Ad. VG. B3d. $8.50

LOMAS, Bliss. *Fight for the Sweetwater.* 1951. Pocket 768. c/W Shoyer. We. VG+. B5d. $5.50

LOMAX, Bliss. *Colt Comrade.* Pocket 809. VG. B3d. $4.50

LOMAX, Bliss. *Guns Along the Yellowstone.* 1953. Dell 724. 1st prtg. c/Borack: gga. VG+. P7d. $6.50

LOMAX, Bliss. *Gunsmoke & Trail Dust.* Dell 271. c/B Meyers. We. NF. B5d. $8.00

LOMAX, Bliss. *Gunsmoke & Trail Dust.* Dell 271. VG+. B3d. $6.00

LOMAX, Bliss. *It Happened at Thunder River.* Avon 849. VG. B3d. $4.50

LOMAX, Bliss. *Last Call for a Gunfighter.* 1960. Dell 1010. c/J Leone. We. VG. B5d. $3.00

LOMAX, Bliss. *Leather Burners.* Century 54. VG. B3d. $7.00

LOMAX, Bliss. *Riders of the Buffalo Grass.* Dell 801. c/R Stanley. We. VG+. B5d. $4.00

LOMAX, Bliss. *Rusty Guns.* 1949. Hillman 33. VG+. B3a. $10.90

LOMAX, Bliss. *Secret of the Wastelands.* Dell 967. c/Gross. VG. B3d. $4.50

LOMAX, Bliss. *Secret of the Wastelands.* 1958. Dell 967. c/G Gross. We. G+. B5d. $2.50

LOMAX, Bliss. *Stagebrush Bandit.* 1957. Dell 942. c/G Gross. We. VG. B5d. $3.00

LOMAX/MAYO. *Outlaw River/Showdown at Yellow Butte.* 1953. Ace D 38. PBO. VG+. B3a #24. $27.50

LOMBARDI, Vince. *Run to Daylight!* 1968. Tempo T 188. Nfi. VG. B4d. $2.00

LONDON, Jack. *Best Short Stories.* 1962. Premier D 180. Fi. VG+. B5d. $4.00

LONDON, Jack. *Call of the Wild.* Pocket 593. VG. B3d. $5.00

LONDON, Jack. *Martin Eden.* Sigent 587. VG+. B3d. $5.00

LONDON, Jack. *People of the Abyss.* Panther 1595. VG. B3d. $6.00

LONDON, Jack. *Seed of McCoy.* 1956. Pyramid G 180. Fa. G+. B4d. $8.00

LONDON, Jack. *South Sea Tales.* 1952. Lion 92. G. P6d. $2.00

LONDON, Jack. *South Sea Tales.* 1952. Lion 92. 1st edn. PBO. c/gga. scarce. VG+. B6a #79. $56.25

LONDON, Jack. *White Fang.* Airmont CL 36. VG+. B6d. $2.50

LONG, D. *Case of Lord Greyburn's Son.* Sexton Blake 133. VG. B3d. $8.00

LONG, Frank Belknap. *Androids.* 1969. Tower. 1st edn. VG. M1d. $7.00

LONG, Frank Belknap. *Day of the Robot.* 1963. Belmont 90-277. 1st prtg. SF. VG. R5d. $5.00

LONG, Frank Belknap. *Hounds of Tindalos.* 1963. Belmont 92-569. 1st pb. F. M1d. $20.00

LONG, Frank Belknap. *It Was the Day of the Robot.* 1963. Belmont 90-277. PBO. SF. VG. B5d. $5.50

LONG, Frank Belknap. *It Was the Day of the Robot.* 1963. Belmont 90-277. 1st edn. scarce. SF. F. F2d. $25.00

LONG, Frank Belknap. *John Carstairs.* 1952. Fantasy Book 400. PBO. c/R Turner. scarce. NF. B6a #74. $75.00

LONG, Frank Belknap. *Journey Into Darkness.* 1967. Belmont B 50-757. 1st prtg. SF. VG. R5d. $4.50

LONG, Frank Belknap. *Lest Earth Be Conquered.* 1966. Belmont B 50-726. SF. VG. B5d. $4.50

LONG, Frank Belknap. *Lest Earth Be Conquered.* 1966. Belmont B 50-726. 1st edn. F. M1d. $10.00

LONG, Frank Belknap. *Mars Is My Destination.* 1962. Pyramid F 742. PBO. c/J Schoenherr. SF. VG. B5d. $4.50

LONG, Frank Belknap. *Mars Is My Destination.* 1962. Pyramid F 742. SF. G+. W2d. $4.00

LONG, Frank Belknap. *Mars Is My Destination.* 1962. Pyramid F 742. 1st edn. NF. M1d. $12.00

LONG, Frank Belknap. *Monster From Out of Time.* Popular Library 02474. c/F Frazetta. SF. VG. B5d. $6.00

LONG, Frank Belknap. *Night of the Wolf.* 1972. Popular Library 1562. PBO. Ho. NF. B6d. $15.00

LONG, Frank Belknap. *Night of the Wolf.* 1972. Popular Library 1562. SF. G. W2d. $3.00

LONG, Frank Belknap. *Odd SF.* Belmont L 92600. 1st prtg. NF. S1d. $6.50

LONG, Frank Belknap. *Space Station #1.* Ace D 544. NF. M1d. $8.00

LONG, Frank Belknap. *Space Station #1.* Ace D 544. VG+. I1d. $5.00

LONG, Frank Belknap. *Survival World.* 1971. Lancer 74-750. SF. VG. B5d. $3.50

LONG, Frank Belknap. *This Strange Tomorrow.* 1966. Belmont B 50-663. SF. VG. B5d. $5.00

LONG, Frank Belknap. *This Strange Tomorrow.* 1966. Belmont B 50-663. 1st prtg. SF. VG+. R5d. $7.00

LONG, Frank Belknap. *Woman From Another Planet.* Chariot CB 123. VG+. B3a #21. $15.00

LONG, Frank Belknap. *Woman From Another Planet.* Chariot CB 123. 1st edn. NF. M1d. $15.00

LONG, Lydia. *Shape of Fear.* 1971. Beagle. 1st edn. F. M1d. $10.00

LONG, Manning. *Bury the Hatchet.* 1953. Pocket 85. VG. B3d. $5.50

LONG, Richard B. *Swapper.* 1970. Adult Book 1524. PBO. c/Bonfils. NF. B6a #76. $59.00

LONG/VAN VOGT. *Space Station #1/Empire of the Atom.* Ace D 242. F. M1d. $12.00

LONG/VAN VOGT. *Space Station #1/Empire of the Atom.* 1957. Ace D 242. PBO. c/E Emsh & E Valigursky. SF. G+. B5d. $5.00

LONGBAUGH, Harry. *No Way To Treat a Lady.* 1964. Gold Medal 1384. 1st edn. scarce. My. F. F2d. $35.00

LONGBAUGH, Harry. *No Way To Treat a Lady.* 1964. Gold Medal K 1384. 1st prtg. PBO. c/gga. VG+. P7d. $7.50

LONGMAN, Marlene. *Lesbian Love.* 1965. Nightstand NB 1523. PBO. VG. P6d. $12.00

LONGO. *Family on Vendetta Street.* Curtis 7074. 1st pb. NF. B6d. $6.00

LONGSTREET, Stephen & Ethel. *Geisha.* 1969. MacFadden 75-218. 1st prtg. c/gga. VG. P7d. $4.00

LONGSTREET, Stephen & Ethel. *Geisha.* Popular Library G 501. c/gga. VG. B3d. $4.50

LONGSTREET, Stephen. *Beach House.* 1961. Popular Library SP 101. 1st prtg. c/gga. VG. P7d. $4.00

LONGSTREET, Stephen. *Crystal Girl.* Novel Library 34. VG+. I1d. $15.00

LONGSTREET, Stephen. *Lion at Morning.* Ace D 210. VG. B3d. $5.00

LONGSTREET, Stephen. *Living High.* Gold Medal 1205. VG. B3d. $5.50

LONGSTREET, Stephen. *Promoters.* 1958. Cardinal C 290. Fa. VG. B4d. $2.00

LONGSTREET, Stephen. *Two Beds for Roxane.* 1952. Avon 406. Fi. G+. B5d. $4.00

LONGSTREET, Stephen. *Wild Harvest.* Gold Medal 1068. VG. B3d. $4.50

LOOMIS, David. *Try for Elegance.* Popular Library G 502. VG. B3d. $4.50

LOOMIS, Frederic. *Consultation Room.* 1949. Pocket 654. Nfi. VG+. B4d. $4.00

LOOMIS, Noel. *Above the Palo Duro.* Gold Medal 865. VG. B3d. $5.00

LOOMIS, Noel. *Buscadero.* 1956. Bantam 1515. We. VG+. B4d. $2.00

LOOMIS, Noel. *Cheyenne War Cry.* 1959. Avon T 368. 1st edn. Hi. F. F2d. $10.00

LOOMIS, Noel. *City of Glass.* 1955. Double Action SF NN. PBO. c/Emsh. VG. B6d. $15.00

LOOMIS, Noel. *Have Gun, Will Travel.* 1960. Dell B 156. TVTI. c/Robert Stanley. VG. B4d. $7.50

LOOMIS, Noel. *Johnny Concho.* Gold Medal S 587. PBO. MTI. c/Frank Sinatra. VG. M6d. $8.50

LOOMIS, Noel. *North to Texas.* 1955. Ballantine 125. We. VG+. B4d. $8.00

LOOMIS, Noel. *Rim of the Caprock.* Bantam 1132. VG+. B3d. $5.00

LOOMIS, Noel. *West to the Sun.* Gold Medal 167. VG. B3d. $5.00

LOOMIS, Rae. *Luisita.* 1954. Ace S 70. PBO. c/Maguire. G+. B6d. $10.00

LOOMIS, Rae. *Luisita.* 1954. Ace S 70. PBO. c/Maguire: gga. NF. B6a #76. $44.00

LOOMIS, Rae. *Marina Street Girls.* 1953. Ace D 35. PBO. c/Olson. VG. B6d. $15.00

LORAC, E.C.R. *Checkmate to Murder.* 1946. Bart House 22. VG. P6d. $5.00

LORAINE, Philip. *And to My Beloved Husband.* Pocket 912. VG+. B3d. $5.00

LORAINE, Philip. *Angel of Death.* Ace 02276. My. VG+. B4d. $2.00

LORD, James. *Loving & the Lose.* 1957. Crest Giant S 175. VG. P6d. $1.50

LORD, Jeffery. *Blade.* 1973. Pinnacle 202. 1st edn. F. P9d. $2.00

LORD, Jeffrey. *Bronze Ape.* 1969. Mac-Fadden. 1st edn. F. M1d. $10.00

LORD, Jeffrey. *Bronze Axe.* 1974. Pinnacle 210201. 3rd prtg. Blade #1. SF. VG+. W2d. $3.50

LORD, Jeffrey. *Dimensions of Dreams.* 1974. Pinnacle 00474. SF. VG+. W2d. $4.00

LORD, Jeffrey. *Jado Warrior.* 1969. Mac Fadden. 1st edn. NF. M1d. $8.00

LORD, Jeffrey. *Jade Warrior.* 1974. Pinnacle 220593. 3rd prtg. Blade #1. SF. VG. W2d. $3.25

LORD, Jeffrey. *Jeb.* 1970. PB Library 65-157. PBO. NF. B6d. $15.00

LORD, Jeffrey. *Looters of Tharn.* 1976. Pinnacle 220855. Blade #19. SF. F. W2d. $4.50

LORD, Jeffrey. *Pearl of Patmos.* 1973. Pinnacle. 1st edn. F. M1d. $7.00

LORD, Sheldon. *April North.* Beacon 456. VG. B3d. $4.50

LORD, Sheldon. *Barrow Street.* Midwood F 103. reprint. VG. B6d. $12.50

LORD, Sheldon. *Born To Be Bad.* 1959. Midwood 14. PBO. c/Rader: gga. rare. NF. B6a #80. $44.00

LORD, Sheldon. *Pads Are for Passion.* 1961. Beacon B 387. PBO. Ad. VG+. B5d. $8.50

LORD, Sheldon. *Sex Is a Woman.* Signal City B 704X. Ad. VG. B5d. $5.00

LORD, Sheldon. *21 Gay Street.* Midwood 33854. NF. I1d. $8.00

LORD, Sheldon. *21 Gay Street.* 1960. Midwood 55. PBO. c/gga. VG+. B6a #74. $30.00

LORD, William edt. *Perma Treasury of Love Poems.* 1950. Perma P 91. PBO. VG. P6d. $3.50

LORD & MARSHALL. *Girl Called Honey.* 1960. Midwood 41. PBO. VG. B6d. $7.50

LORD & MARSHALL. *So Willing.* 1960. Midwood 48. PBO. c/gga. scarce. NF. B6a #80. $93.50

LORENZ, Frederick. *Night Never Ends.* 1954. Lion 193. PBO. c/Hulings. VG+. B6d. $22.50

LORENZ, Frederick. *Rage at Sea.* Lion LB 165. 2nd prtg. VG+. B3d. $5.50

LORENZ, Frederick. *Rage at Sea.* 1957. Lion LB 165. Fa. NF. B4d. $15.00

LORENZ, Konrad. *King Soloman's Ring.* Pan GP 61. 1st pb. reprint. FA. VG+. B6d. $6.00

LORRAINE, L. *Commuter Widow.* Beacon 477. VG. B3d. $4.50

LORRAINE, Louis. *Blonde Dynamite.* Beacon B 458F. G+. M6d. $6.50

LORY, Robert. *Challenge to Dracula.* 1975. Pinnacle 220711. PBO. Ho. VG+. M3d. $7.00

LORY, Robert. *Dracula Returns.* 1973. Pinnacle 00184. SF. VG. W2d. $7.50

LORY, Robert. *Dracula's Disciple.* 1975. Pinnacle 220581. 1st prtg. PBO. VG. P7d. $4.00

LORY, Robert. *Drums of Dracula.* 1974. Pinnacle 00322. PBO. Ho. VG. M3d. $5.00

LORY, Robert. *Drums of Dracula.* 1974. Pinnacle 00322. SF. F. W2d. $9.00

LORY, Robert. *Hand of Dracula!* 1973. Pinnacle 00200. PBO. Ho. VG. M3d. $7.00

LORY, Robert. *Harvest of Hoodwinks/Masters of the Lamp.* Ace 52810. PBO. SF. NF. B5d. $5.50

LORY, Robert. *Master of the Etrax.* 1970. Dell 05523. SF. VG. W2d. $4.00

LORY, Robert. *Witching of Dracula.* 1974. Pinnacle 21-398. PBO. Ho. VG. M3d. $5.00

LORY/REYNOLDS. *Eyes of Bolsk/Space Barbarians.* Ace 77710. PBO. c/J Gaughn & K Freas. SF. VG. B5d. $3.00

LOTH, David. *Erotic in Literature.* 1962. MacFadden 60-109. 1st prtg. VG+. P7d. $4.50

LOTH, David. *Gold Brick Cassie.* 1954. Gold Medal 364. PBO. VG. B6d. $7.50

LOTT, Arnold. *Most Dangerous Sea.* Ballantine F 440K. NF. VG+. B5d. $5.00

LOTTMAN, E. *Greek Tycoon.* 1978. Warner 82-712. 1st prtg. VG+. R5d. $2.00

LOUIS, J. *Devils' Cult.* Headline 103. VG+. B3d. $5.00

LOUIS, Ort. *I Know the Score.* 1962. Midwood 144. PBO. VG. B3d. $5.00

LOUIS, Ort. *I Know the Score.* 1962. Midwood 144. 1st edn. F. F2d. $16.00

LOUIS, Ort. *Pleasure & the Pain.* 1963. Midwood 241. 1st edn. F. F2d. $13.50

LOUPOO. *Bamboo Doll.* 1966. Bee Line 163. PBO. c/Korea. VG. B6d. $6.00

LOUYS, Pierre. *Aphrodite.* Avon 113. VG+. B3d. $7.00

LOUYS, Pierre. *Aphrodite.* 1946. Avon 113. Fa. VG. B4d/I1d. $5.00

LOUYS, Pierre. *Aphrodite.* Avon 257. c/gga. scarce. Fa. VG+. B6a #76. $42.50

LOUYS, Pierre. *Aphrodite.* Avon 257. VG. B3d. $5.00

LOUYS, Pierre. *Aphrodite.* 1959. Berkley G 283. Fi. VG. B5d. $4.50

LOUYS, Pierre. *Woman & the Puppet.* 1947. Avon 135. c/gga. VG. B4d/P6d. $3.00

LOUYS, Pierre. *Woman & the Puppet.* 1951. Avon 358. 1st prtg. c/gga. VG+. P7d. $9.00

LOVE, Jack. *Sex Symbol.* 1966. Publishers Export N 118. PBO. c/gga. NF. B6a #75. $30.25

LOVECRAFT, H.P. *At the Mountain of Madness.* 1973. Ballantine 03225. 3rd prtg. SF. F. W2d. $9.00

LOVECRAFT, H.P. *Case of Charles Dexter Ward.* 1976. Ballantine 24118. 2nd prtg. SF. F. M1d. $6.00

LOVECRAFT, H.P. *Case of Charles Dexter Ward.* Beagle 95123. VG. M6d. $7.50

LOVECRAFT, H.P. *Case of Charles Dexter Ward.* 1965. Belmont 92-617. 1st pb. G. M1d. $5.00

LOVECRAFT, H.P. *Case of Charles Dexter Ward.* 1965. Belmont 92-617. 1st prtg. SF. VG+. W2d. $13.50

LOVECRAFT, H.P. *Colour Out of Space.* 1978. Jove M 4512. VG+. B4d. $6.00

LOVECRAFT, H.P. *Colour Out of Space.* 1964. Lancer 73-425. 1st pb. VG. M1d. $15.00

LOVECRAFT, H.P. *Colour Out of Space.* 1969. Lancer 74-501. SF. VG. R5d. $3.50

LOVECRAFT, H.P. *Cry Horror.* 1958. Avon T 284. VG+. B3d. $5.50

LOVECRAFT, H.P. *Cry Horror.* 1958. Avon T 284. 1st prtg. SF. G+. R5d. $3.00

LOVECRAFT, H.P. *Doom That Came to Sarnath.* 1971. Ballantine 02146. SF. F. W2d. $12.50

LOVECRAFT, H.P. *Dream-Quest of Unknown Kadath.* Ballantine 01923. VG+. B3d. $5.00

LOVECRAFT, H.P. *Dream-Quest of Unknown Kadath.* 1974. Ballantine 24048. 4th prtg. SF. F. W2d. $12.00

LOVECRAFT, H.P. *Dream-Quest of Unknown Kadath.* 1974. Ballantine 24048. 4th prtg. VG. B3d. $4.00

LOVECRAFT, H.P. *Dunwich Horror & Others.* 1978. Jove M 4511. 1st prtg. SF. VG+. B5d/R5d. $3.00

LOVECRAFT, H.P. *Dunwich Horror.* 1945. Bart House 12. PBO. scarce. VG+. B6a #75. $90.75

LOVECRAFT, H.P. *Dunwich Horror.* 1945. Bart House 12. 1st edn. VG. B6d/P9d. $25.00

LOVECRAFT, H.P. *Dunwich Horror.* Lancer 72-702. VG. M6d. $7.50

LOVECRAFT, H.P. *Dunwich Horror.* 1963. Lancer 72-702. 1st pb. F. M1d. $15.00

LOVECRAFT, H.P. *Dunwich Horror.* Lancer 75-247. SF. VG+. W2d. $9.50

LOVECRAFT, H.P. *Horror in the Museum.* 1976. Ballantine 25094. 1st prtg. SF. VG+. R5d. $4.00

LOVECRAFT, H.P. *Lurking Fear.* 1947. Avon. 1st pb. VG. M1d. $40.00

LOVECRAFT, H.P. *Lurking Fear.* 1975. Ballantine 24690. 6th prtg. SF. G+. W2d. $6.50

LOVECRAFT, H.P. *Shadow Over Innsmouth.* 1971. Scholastic 1934. SF. F. W2d. $12.50

LOVECRAFT, H.P. *Shuttered Room.* 1973. Ballantine 03229. 2nd prtg. SF. F. W2d. $10.00

LOVECRAFT, H.P. *Shuttered Room.* 1973. Ballantine. 2nd pb edn. VG. M1d. $4.00

LOVECRAFT, H.P. *Survivor & Others.* 1971. Ballantine 02148. 2nd prtg. SF. F. W2d. $12.00

LOVECRAFT, H.P. *Tales of the Cthulhu Mythos VI.* 1971. Beagle 95080. SF. F. W2d. $10.50

LOVECRAFT, H.P. *Tomb & Other Tales.* 1975. Ballantine 24689. SF. VG. W2d. $7.50

LOVECRAFT, H.P. *Tomb & Other Tales.* 1971. Beagle 95032. 2nd prtg. SF. VG. W2d. $9.00

LOVECRAFT, H.P. *Weird Shadow Over Innsmouth.* 1944. Bart House 4. PBO. scarce. VG+. B6a #75. $90.75

LOVECRAFT, H.P. *Weird Shadow Over Innsmouth.* 1944. Bart House 4. SF. VG. W2d. $60.00

LOVECRAFT, H.P. *Weird Shadow Over Innsmouth.* 1944. Bart House 4. VG. B3a #21. $20.90

LOVEJOY, Jack. *Star Gods.* 1978. Major 3230. PBO. SF. NF. B6d. $8.00

LOVEJOY, Jack. *Vision of Beasts.* 1984. TOR 54500. PBO. SF. NF. B6d. $3.00

LOVELACE, D.W. *King Kong.* 1976. Ace 44470. MTI. c/F Frazetta. SF. G+. B5d. $3.00

LOVELACE, D.W. *King Kong.* 1965. Bantam 3093. 1st edn. PBO. MTI. NF. F2d. $15.00

LOVELACE, D.W. *King Kong.* Tempo 12786. SF. VG+. W2d. $3.75

LOVELACE, Leland. *Lost Mines & Hidden Treasure.* Ace G 474. VG. B3d. $5.00

LOVELL/MCKNIGHT. *Rage To Kill/Downwind.* Ace D 217. VG. B3d. $5.00

LOVERIDGE, Arthur. *Reptiles of the Pacific.* 1944. Infantry NN. Nfi. VG+. B4d. $4.00

LOW, Gardner. *Invitation To Kill.* Prize 17. VG. B3d. $7.00

LOW, Glenn. *Backhill Sinners.* Novel Book 5004. NF. B3d. $10.00

LOW, Glenn. *Barn.* 1961. Beacon B 438Y. PBO. Ad. G+. B5d. $4.00

LOW, Glenn. *Perverted Passions.* 1960. Novel Book 5018. PBO. Ad. VG. B5d. $4.00

LOW, Glenn. *Reckless Virgin.* 1961. Beacon B 420. c/gga. Fa. NF. B4d. $10.00

LOW, Glenn. *Reckless Virgin.* 1965. Beacon B 817X. Fa. VG+. B4d. $12.00

LOWELL, Juliet. *Dear Sir.* 1951. Avon 318. 1st prtg. c/Carl Rose. VG. B3d/P7d. $7.50

LOWENKOPF. *Love of the Lion.* 1962. Kozy 149. PBO. VG+. B6d. $7.50

LOWNDES, G. *Eveline.* Brandon House 3027. NF. B3d. $7.00

LOWNDES, R.A. *Best of James Blish.* Ballantine 2560. 1st prtg. G+. S1d. $2.00

LOWRY, Robert. *Big Cage.* Popular Library G 105. c/De Soto. VG+. B3d. $6.00

LOWRY, Robert. *Casualty.* 1951. Popular Library 387. 1st pb. VG+. B6d. $15.00

LOWRY, Robert. *Find Me in Fire.* Popular Library G 395. VG+. B3d. $4.50

LOWRY, Robert. *Find Me in Fire.* 1950. Popular Library 244. 1st edn. PBO. c/Bergey: gga. VG+. B6a #80. $67.25

LOWRY, Robert. *That Kind of Woman.* 1959. Pyramid G 430. PBO. MTI. c/S Loren & T Hunter: photos. Fi. VG. B5d. $7.00

LOWRY, Robert. *This Is My Night.* Popular Library 675. VG. B3d. $3.50

LOWRY, Robert. *Wolf That Fed Us.* Popular Library 295. VG. B3d. $5.00

LOWRY, Robert. *Wolf That Fed Us.* 1950. Popular Library 295. c/gga. Fa. VG+. B4d. $8.00

LUCAS, Bob. *Naked in Hollywood.* 1962. Lancer 70-009. Fi. VG. B5d. $4.00

LUCAS, Cary. *Unfinished Business.* Dell 366. 1st prtg. My. G. R5d. $2.00

LUCAS, Cary. *Unfinished Business.* 1950. Dell 366. c/gga. My. VG. P6d. $5.00

LUCAS, Curtis. *Forbidden Fruit.* 1958. Beacon B 173. 1st prtg. c/gga. VG. P7d. $10.00

LUCAS, George. *Star Wars.* 1977. Ballantine 26079. 7th prtg. MTI. SF. VG. W2d. $3.50

LUCAS, Mark. *Sex Racket.* 1966. Saber Tropic 928. 1st edn. c/gga. My. F. F2d. $15.00

LUCAS, Rick. *Convention Girl.* 1959. Beacon 279. 1st prtg. VG. P7d. $9.00

LUCAS, Rick. *Hucksters' Women.* Beacon B 309. Ad. VG. B5d. $6.00

LUCAS, Rick. *Restless Women.* 1960. Beacon B 303. PBO. Ad. VG. B5d. $6.00

LUCCHESI, Aldo. *Feast of the Jackals.* 1972. Lancer 31-006. PBO. VG+. B6d. $9.00

LUCCHESI, Aldo. *Strange Breed.* Midwood F 252. reprint. VG. B6d. $12.50

LUCE & SEGA. *Sleep.* 1967. Lancer 74-874. Nfi. VG+. B5d. $5.00

LUDLUM, Robert. *Aquitaine Progression.* 1985. Bantam 24900. 1st prtg. My. VG+. W2d. $3.50

LUDLUM, Robert. *Matarese Circle.* 1980. Bantam 13098. My. VG+. W2d. $3.50

LUDLUM, Robert. *Parsifal Mosaic.* 1983. Bantam 23021. 5th prtg. My. VG+. W2d. $3.25

LUDLUM, Stuart D. *Willie & the Yank.* 1967. Scholastic 989. TVTI. VG. P1d. $7.50

LUEDDECKE, W.J. *Morituri.* 1965. Gold Medal D 1562. MTI. VG+. B4d. $4.00

LUIGI, Belli. *Master-Mind Menace.* 1950. World Fantasy NN. PBO. c/classic. SF. NF. B6a #74. $75.00

LUKE, Thomas. *Hell Candidate.* 1980. Pocket 81769. SF. VG+. W2d. $4.00

LUMBARD, C.G. *Kiss the Night Away.* 1955. Popular Library 640. c/gga. Fa. VG+. B4d. $9.00

LUMLEY, Brian. *Clock of Dreams.* 1978. Jove 4489. 1st edn. SF. F. F2d. $20.00

LUMLEY, Brian. *Transition of Titus Crow.* 1975. DAW 151. 1st edn. Ho. NF. F2d. $10.00

LUNDWALL, Sam J. *Alice's World.* 1975. Arrow UK 910030. 1st edn. SF. NF. F2d. $8.00

LUNDWALL, Sam J. *Bernhard the Conqueror.* 1973. DAW 58. PBO. c/T Kirk. SF. VG+. B5d. $3.50

LUNDWALL, Sam J. *Bernhard the Conqueror.* 1973. DAW 58. 1st edn. F. M1d. $6.00

LUNDWALL, Sam J. *SF: What It's All About.* Ace 75440. c/D Ellis. Nfi. VG. B5d. $4.50

LUNDWALL, Sam J. *2018 AD or the King Kong Blues.* 1975. DAW 142. c/J Kirby. SF. VG+. B5d. $5.00

LUNDWALL, Sam J. *2018 AD or the King Kong Blues.* 1975. DAW 142. 1st edn. F. M1d. $6.00

LUNDWALL/LUNDWALL. *Alice's World/No Time for Heroes.* 1971. Ace 58880. PBO. c/J Kirby. SF. F. B5d. $7.00

LUNGS, Kai. *Golden Hours.* Ballantine 02574. 1st prtg. F. S1d. $9.00

LUPOFF, Richard A. *Buck Rogers in the 25th Century.* 1978. Dell 10843. 1st edn. SF. F. F2d. $15.00

LUPOFF, Richard A. *Comic Book Killer.* 1989. Bantam 27781. 1st prtg. My. VG. R5d. $1.75

LUPOFF, Richard A. *Crack in the Sky.* 1976. Dell 5419. 1st prtg. SF. VG+. R5d. $2.00

LUPOFF, Richard A. *Edgar Rice Burroughs, Master of Adventure.* Ace N 6. F. M1d. $15.00

LUPOFF, Richard A. *Edgar Rice Burroughs, Master of Adventure.* 1968. Ace N 6. Nfi. VG. P1d. $5.00

LUPOFF, Richard A. *Edgar Rice Burroughs, Master of Adventure.* Ace 18771. Ad. VG+. W2d. $5.00

LUPOFF, Richard A. *Into the Aether.* 1974. Dell 3830. 1st edn. c/Frazetta: sgn. scarce. SF. F. F2d. $15.00

LUPOFF, Richard A. *One Million Centuries.* 1967. Lancer 74-892. 1st edn. NF. P9d. $2.00

LUPOFF, Richard A. *Sandworld.* 1976. Berkley 23116. 1st edn. NF. P9d. $1.75

LUPOFF, Richard A. *Space War Blues.* 1978. Dell 16292. 1st edn. VG. P9d. $1.50

LUPOFF, Richard A. *Sun's End.* 1984. Berkley 07022. SF. 'G. W2d. $3.00

LUPTON, Leonard. *Murder Without Tears.* Graphic 149. PBO. VG. B3d. $5.00

LURIE, Alison. *Imaginary Friends.* 1968. Avon N 191. 1st pb. SF. NF. B6d. $9.00

LURMANN, V.C. *Anatomy of the Co-Ed.* Chariot 206. VG+. B3d. $4.50

LURTON, Douglas E. *Make the Most of Your Life.* Armed Services 1032. Nfi. VG+. B5d. $4.00

LUSTGARTEN, Edgar. *Blonde Iscariot.* Avon 179. G+. G5d. $8.00

LUSTGARTEN, Edgar. *One More Unfortunate.* 1949. Bantam 360. c/B Safran. My. VG. B5d. $4.00

LUSTGARTEN, Edgar. *Verdict in Dispute.* Bantam 861. NF. B3d. $6.00

LUSTGARTEN, Edgar. *Verdict in Dispute.* Bantam 861. VG. G5d. $5.00

LUSTGARTEN, Edgar. *Woman in the Case.* Pan G 117. VG. B3d. $7.00

LUTZ, E.H.G. *Miracles of Modern Medicine.* Ace K 157. VG+. B3d. $5.00

LUTZ, Giles A. *Blood Feud.* 1974. Gold Medal T 2927. We. VG+. B4d. $3.00

LUTZ, Giles A. *Outcast Gun.* Gold Medal 1615. VG+. B3d. $4.00

LUTZ, Giles A. *Relentless Gun.* Gold Medal K 1538. NF. I1d. $4.50

LUTZ, Giles A. *Stranger in My Bed.* 1960. Beacon B 353. PBO. Ad. VG+. B5d. $8.00

LUTZ, Giles A. *Stranger in My Bed.* 1960. Beacon 353. 1st edn. c/gga. F. F2d. $12.50

LUTZ, Giles A. *To Hell & Texas.* 1965. Gold Medal K 1542. 1st prtg. VG. I1d/P7d. $4.00

LUTZ, Giles A. *To Hell & Texas.* Gold Medal 1148. 2nd prtg. VG+. B3d. $4.50

LUTZ, Giles A. *To Hell & Texas.* 1956. Gold Medal 548. We. VG+. B3d. $7.50

LUTZ, John. *Truth of the Matter.* BL 88739. G+. G5d. $6.50

LYLE, John H. *Dry & Lawless Years.* 1961. Dell F 162. c/V Kalin. NF. VG+. $3.50

LYMINGTON, John. *Froomb!* 1967. MacFadden 60-287. 1st prtg. VG. P7d. $4.50

LYMINGTON, John. *Froomb!* 1970. MacFadden 75-355. 4th edn. NF. P9d. $1.75

LYMINGTON, John. *Giant Stumbles.* 1961. Corgi. 1st pb. NF. M1d. $5.00

LYMINGTON, John. *Grey Ones.* 1969. MacFadden G 0461. 1st edn. F. P9d. $2.00

LYMINGTON, John. *Sleep Eaters.* 1969. MacFadden 75224. 1st edn. NF. P9d. $2.00

LYNCH, Dan. *Four-Time Loser.* Gold Medal 1240. VG. B3d. $4.00

LYNCH, Jennifer. *Secret Diary of Laura Palmer.* 1990. Pocket 73590. TVTI. VG. P1d. $7.50

LYNCH, Miriam. *Moon of Darkness.* 1969. Belmont B 50-856. 1st prtg. My. G+. R5d. $1.75

LYNCH/MINTON. *Amber Twilight/Portrait of Terror.* 1967. Belmont B 60-066. 1st prtg. My. G+. R5d. $1.50

LYNDON & SANGSTER. *Man Who Could Cheat Death.* 1959. Avon T 362. PBO. MTI. c/C Lee. SF. VG. B5d. $5.50

LYNDON & Sangster. *Man Who Could Cheat Death.* 1959. Avon T 362. 1st pb. F. M1d. $20.00

LYNDS, Dennis. *Crossfire.* 1975. Pocket 80241. 1st prtg. TVTI. SWAT #1. VG. R5d. $1.75

LYNN, E.A. *Different Light.* Berkley 04824. c/sgn. VG+. B3d. $5.00

LYNN, E.A. *Northern Girl.* 1981. Berkley 04725. Chronicles of Tornor Book #3. SF. VG. W2d. $3.25

LYNN, E.A. *Sardonyx Net.* 1987. Berkley. 1st pb. F. M1d. $5.00

LYNN, E.A. *Watchtower.* 1980. Berkley 04725. Chronicles of Tornor Book #1. SF. VG. W2d. $3.25

LYNN, Jack. *Shockingest Seductions!* 1964. Novel Book 6N 263. 1st edn. De. F. F2d. $25.00

LYON, Dana. *Lost One & the Frightened Child.* 1963. Ace G 535. 1st prtg. My. VG+. R5d. $3.25

LYON, Dana. *Tentacles & Spin the Web.* 1963. Ace G 525. 1st prtg. My. VG. R5d. $2.75

LYON, Dana. *Trusting Victim.* Ace G 545. VG. G5d. $5.00

LYON, Winston. *Bat Man Vs Three Villians of Doom.* 1966. Signet D 2940. SF. VG. W2d. $7.00

LYON, Winston. *Batman Vs Three Villains of Doom.* 1966. Signet D 2940. 1st prtg. TVTI. G+. R5d. $3.00

LYON, Winston. *Criminal Court.* Pocket 50313. VG. G5d. $3.50

LYONS, Arthur. *Dead Are Discreet.* Ballantine 24974. G+. G5d. $4.00

LYONS & NOGUCHI. *Physical Evidence.* 1990. Jove 10453. My. F. P1d. $5.00

LYSENKO, G.C. *Rasputin, the Sex-Mad Monk.* 1966. Viceroy 204. 1st edn. F. F2d. $12.50

LYSENKO, G.C. *Rasputin: Sex & Monk.* Challenge 204. NF. B3d. $6.00

M'INTUXH, J.T. *World Out of Mind.* Perma M 3027. 1st prtg. VG. S1d. $4.50

MACAPP, C.C. *Bumsider.* 1972. Lancer 75-421. SF. G+. W2d. $2.75

MACAPP, C.C. *Bumsider.* 1972. Lancer 75-421. 1st edn. VG. M1d. $4.00

MACAPP, C.C. *Omha Abides.* 1968. PB Library 52-649. 1st edn. F. M1d. $6.00

MACAPP, C.C. *Recall Not Earth.* 1970. Dell 7281. SF. VG+. W2d. $5.00

MACAPP, C.C. *Subb.* 1971. PB Library 64-532. PBO. SF. VG+. B5d. $4.50

MACARTHUR, Douglas. *Reminiscences.* 1965. Crest M 850. 1st prtg. c/photo. VG. P7d. $4.00

MACAVOY, R.A. *Book of Kells.* 1985. Bantam 25260. 1st prtg. SF. VG+. W2d. $3.50

MACBRIAN, James. *Revolt of Abbe Lee.* 1964. Monarch 429. VG+. B5 $6.50

MACBRIAN, James. *Revolt of Abbe Lee.* 1964. Monarch 429. 1st edn. c/gga. F. F2d. $12.50

MACBRIAN, James. *Roz.* 1963. Monarch 382. PBO. c/Stanley Borack: gga. VG. P6d. $2.00

MACCAMMON, Robert R. *Bethany's Sin.* Avon 47712. G+. M6d. $6.50

MACCAMMON, Robert R. *Mine.* 1990. Pocket. 1st edn. dust jacket. Ho. F. F2d. $22.00

MACCORMAC, John. *This Time for Keeps.* Dell 32. VG. B3d. $6.00

MACDONALD, Fred. *Illicit Bed.* 1963. France 62. 1st edn. F. F2d. $11.00

MACDONALD, George. *Lilith.* 1973. Ballantine. 2nd edn. Ad/Fa. NF. M1d. $5.00

MACDONALD, George. *Phantasies.* 1970. Ballantine 01902. 1st edn. Ad/Fa. NF. M1d. $12.00

MACDONALD, George. *Phantastes.* 1970. Ballantine 01902. c/Gervasio Gellardo. SF. VG. M3d. $6.00

MACDONALD, J.D. *Contrary Pleasure.* Popular697. VG. B3d. $6.00

MACDONALD, John D. *All These Condemned.* Gold Medal K1547. c/photo. My. VG+. B5d. $7.50

MACDONALD, John D. *All These Condemned.* Gold Medal T 2590. My. VG+. W2d. $5.00

MACDONALD, John D. *April Evil.* 1960. Dell 1st Edn B 146. 1st prtg. c/McGinnis: gga. G+. P7d. $5.00

MACDONALD, John D. *April Evil.* 1956. Dell 85. 1st edn. scarce. My. F. F2d. $50.00

MACDONALD, John D. *April Evil.* Gold Medal D 1579. My. F. W2d. $12.00

MACDONALD, John D. *Area of Suspicion.* 1954. Dell 1st Edn 12. PBO. c/Borack. VG+. B6d. $60.00

MACDONALD, John D. *Area of Suspicion.* 1954. Dell 1st Edn 12. VG. I1d. $30.00

MACDONALD, John D. *Area of Suspicion.* 1954. Dell 1st Edn 12. 1st edn. My. G+. $12.00

MACDONALD, John D. *Area of Suspicion.* Gold Medal R 1809. c/B Phillips. My. VG. B5d. $6.00

MACDONALD, John D. *Ballroom of the Skies.* 1968. Gold Medal R 1993. My. VG. B4d. $9.00

MACDONALD, John D. *Ballroom of the Skies.* 1968. Gold Medal R 1993. SF. NF. B4d. $22.00

MACDONALD, John D. *Ballroom of the Skies.* Gold Medal T 2380. 1st prtg. VG. S1d. $4.00

MACDONALD, John D. *Beach Girls.* Gold Medal S 907. VG+. I1d. $20.00

MACDONALD, John D. *Beach Girls.* Gold Medal T 2604. My. VG+. B5d. $7.50

MACDONALD, John D. *Border Town Girl.* Popular 750. PBO. rarest. VG+. B6a #79. $88.00

MACDONALD, John D. *Brass Cupcake.* 1950. Gold Medal 124. c/Barye. VG. B3a #21. $32.35

MACDONALD, John D. *Brass Cupcake.* 1950. Gold Medal 124. PBO. VG. B5d. $50.00

MACDONALD, John D. *Brass Cupcake.* 1950. Gold Medal 124. 1st prtg. PBO. G. P6d. $3.50

MACDONALD, John D. *Brass Cupcake.* Gold Medal 1566. reprint. VG+. B3d. $7.50

MACDONALD, John D. *Brass Cupcake.* Gold Medal 482. c/Barye. reprint. VG+. B6d. $9.00

MACDONALD, John D. *Bright Orange for the Shroud.* 1965. Gold Medal D 1573. My. VG+. B4d. $22.00

MACDONALD, John D. *Bright Orange for the Shroud.* 1969. Gold Medal T 2134. 1st prtg. VG. P7d. $5.00

MACDONALD, John D. *Bullet for Cinderella.* 1955. Dell 1st Edn 62. PBO. c/G Gross. scarce. VG+. B6a #80. $77.00

MACDONALD, John D. *Bullet for Cinderella.* 1955. Dell 1st Edn 62. PBO. c/George Gross. scarce. VG+. B6a #75. $48.50

MACDONALD, John D. *Cancel All Our Vows.* 1959. Signet 1665. 1st edn. PBO. My. F. F2d. $20.00

MACDONALD, John D. *Cinnamon Skin.* 1983. Gold Medal 12505. My. VG. B5d. $3.00

MACDONALD, John D. *Clemmie.* Gold Medal M 2456. My. VG+. B5d. $7.50

MACDONALD, John D. *Clemmie.* Gold Medal R 1723. My. VG. M1d. $3.75

MACDONALD, John D. *Clemmie.* Gold Medal S 777. VG. I1d. $15.00

MACDONALD, John D. *Clemmie.* 1958. Gold Medal 777. 1st edn. c/gga. scarce in top condition. My. F. F2d. $35.00

MACDONALD, John D. *Crossroads.* Gold Medal R 2005. My. VG. B5d. $4.50

MACDONALD, John D. *Crossroads.* 1965. PAN G 696. VG+. B3a #20. $22.30

MACDONALD, John D. *Cry Hard, Cry Fast.* Gold Medal D 1739. My. VG. B5d. $3.50

MACDONALD, John D. *Cry Hard, Cry Fast.* 1969. Gold Medal R 2046. 2nd prtg. My. G+. W2d. $3.50

MACDONALD, John D. *Cry Hard, Cry Fast.* PopularG 271. reprint. My. VG. B6d. $9.00

MACDONALD, John D. *Damned.* Gold Medal D 1767. My. G+. W2d. $2.25

MACDONALD, John D. *Damned.* Gold Medal D 1767. My. VG+. B5d. $6.00

MACDONALD, John D. *Damned.* 1969. Gold Medal R 2052. 9th edn. My. NF. M3d. $6.00

MACDONALD, John D. *Damned.* 1952. Gold Medal 240. VG. B3a #20. $28.15

MACDONALD, John D. *Damned.* 1952. Gold Medal 240. VG. I1d. $20.00

MACDONALD, John D. *Darker Than Amber.* 1966. Gold Medal D 1674. My. VG+. B4d. $22.00

MACDONALD, John D. *Darker Than Amber.* 1968. Gold Medal M 2825. 11th edn. My. VG+. B4d. $3.00

MACDONALD, John D. *Darker Than Amber.* 1968. Gold Medal R 1957. My. VG. B4d. $3.00

MACDONALD, John D. *Darker Than Amber.* 1966. Gold Medal T 2519. 8th edn. My. VG. B4d. $3.00

MACDONALD, John D. *Dead Low Tide.* Gold Medal P 3523. My. VG. B5d. $5.00

MACDONALD, John D. *Dead Low Tide.* Gold Medal T 2432. My. F. W2d. $6.00

MACDONALD, John D. *Dead Low Tide.* 1953. Gold Medal 298. PBO. c/Barye. My. VG. B6d. $12.50

MACDONALD, John D. *Deadly Shade of Gold.* 1965. Gold Medal D 1499. My. NF. B4d. $15.00

MACDONALD, John D. *Deadly Welcome.* 1959. Dell 1st Edn B 127. c/Bob McGinnis. VG. P6d. $14.00

MACDONALD, John D. *Death Trap.* Gold Medal M 2993. My. VG+. B5d. $5.50

MACDONALD, John D. *Deceivers.* 1965. Gold Medal D 1563. 1st prtg. VG. P7d. $5.00

MACDONALD, John D. *Deep Blue Good-By.* 1964. Gold Medal K 1405. My. VG+. B4d. $30.00

MACDONALD, John D. *Deep Blue Good-By.* 1964. Gold Medal K 1405. 1st prtg. PBO. c/Lesser: gga. VG. P7d. $15.00

MACDONALD, John D. *Deep Blue Good-By.* 1968. Gold Medal R 2025. My. G+. B4d. $4.00

MACDONALD, John D. *Dreadful Lemon Sky.* 1975. Gold Medal Q 3285. C+. C5d. $3.00

MACDONALD, John D. *Dreadful Lemon Sky.* 1975. Gold Medal Q 3285. My. VG+. B4d. $12.00

MACDONALD, John D. *Dress Her in Indigo.* 1969. Gold Medal T 2127. My. NF. B4d. $20.00

MACDONALD, John D. *Dress Her in Indigo.* Pan 02009. VG. B3d. $9.00

MACDONALD, John D. *Drowner.* Gold Medal D 1599. My. G+. W2d. $5.00

MACDONALD, John D. *Drowner.* 1963. Gold Medal 1302. 1st edn. My. G+. F2d. $17.00

MACDONALD, John D. *Drowner.* 1980. Lancer 04360. VG. B3d. $7.50

MACDONALD, John D. *Empty Copper Sea.* Gold Medal 14149. My. VG. W2d. $3.75

MACDONALD, John D. *Empty Copper Sea.* Gold Medal 4149. VG. G5d. $3.50

MACDONALD, John D. *Empty Trap.* Gold Medal P 3380. My. G+. B5d. $3.00

MACDONALD, John D. *End of the Night.* Gold Medal R 1969. My. F. W2d. $5.00

MACDONALD, John D. *End of the Tiger.* 1969. Gold Medal R 2106. 2nd prtg. My. VG. W2d. $3.75

MACDONALD, John D. *Executioners.* Gold Medal R 2055. My. VG. B5d. $4.50

MACDONALD, John D. *Free Fall in Crimson.* 1981. Gold Medal 4441. My. VG. B4d. $6.00

MACDONALD, John D. *Girl, the Gold Watch, & Everything.* Gold Medal T 2259. SF. VG. B5d. $4.50

MACDONALD, John D. *Girl, the Gold Watch, & Everything.* 1962. Gold Medal T 2259. 5th edn. SF. NF. M3d. $10.00

MACDONALD, John D. *Girl, the Gold Watch & Everything.* Gold Medal K 1513. SF. VG+. W2d. $6.00

MACDONALD, John D. *Girl, the Gold Watch & Everything.* Gold Medal M 2859. SF. VG+. W2d. $5.00

MACDONALD, John D. *Girl in the Plain Brown Wrapper.* 1968. Gold Medal M 2430. My. VG+. B4d. $5.00

MACDONALD, John D. *Girl in the Plain Brown Wrapper.* Gold Medal P 3010. My. VG+. B5d. $7.50

MACDONALD, John D. *Girl in the Plain Brown Wrapper.* 1968. Gold Medal T 2023. My. VG. B4d. $15.00

MACDONALD, John D. *I Could Go on Singing.* 1963. Gold Medal K 1291. PBO. MTI. rare. NF. B6a #75. $55.00

MACDONALD, John D. *Judge Me Not.* Gold Medal D 1580. My. VG. W2d. $7.00

MACDONALD, John D. *Judge Me Not.* 1951. Gold Medal M 3111. 10th edn. My. NF. B4d. $3.00

MACDONALD, John D. *Judge Me Not.* 1951. Gold Medal 186. PBO. VG. B6d. $25.00

MACDONALD, John D. *Judge Me Not.* 1951. Gold Medal 186. PBO. VG+. B3a #21. $36.30

MACDONALD, John D. *Key to the Suite.* 1962. Gold Medal K 1496. 2nd edn. My. VG+. B4d. $3.00

MACDONALD, John D. *Key to the Suite.* 1962. Gold Medal S 1198. My. NF. B4d. $15.00

MACDONALD, John D. *Last One Left.* 1968. Crest T 1085. 2nd edn. Fa. VG+. B4d. $3.00

MACDONALD, John D. *Long Lavender Look.* 1970. Gold Medal M 2325. My. F. W2d. $5.25

MACDONALD, John D. *Long Lavender Look.* 1970. Gold Medal M 2325. My. VG. B4d. $3.00

MACDONALD, John D. *Man of Affairs.* 1957. Dell 1st Edn B 112. My. VG+. B4d. $40.00

MACDONALD, John D. *Man of Affairs.* 1957. Dell 1st Edn B 112. 1st prtg. PBO. c/Kalin. G+. P7d. $9.00

MACDONALD, John D. *Man of Affairs.* 1957. Gold Medal D 1552. My. G+. B4d. $3.00

MACDONALD, John D. *Man of Affairs.* 1967. Gold Medal D 1866. 2nd prtg. My. G+. W2d. $4.00

MACDONALD, John D. *Man of Affairs.* Gold Medal M 2849. My. VG+. B5d. $7.50

MACDONALD, John D. *Meet Me at the Morgue.* Pocket 1020. 3rd prtg. VG+. B3d. $5.00

MACDONALD, John D. *Murder in the Wind.* 1956. Gold Medal R 1954. 3rd edn. My. VG+. B4d. $3.00

MACDONALD, John D. *Neon Jungle.* Gold Medal R 1979. My. VG. B5d. $5.00

MACDONALD, John D. *Neon Jungle.* 1953. Gold Medal 323. PBO. VG. B6d. $45.00

MACDONALD, John D. *Nightmare in Pink.* Gold Medal D 1682. c/R Lesser. My. VG. B5d. $5.00

MACDONALD, John D. *Nightmare in Pink.* 1964. Gold Medal K 1406. 2nd edn. My. F. B4d. $18.00

MACDONALD, John D. *On the Run.* 1963. Gold Medal K 1292. My. G+. B4d. $18.00

MACDONALD, John D. *On the Run.* Gold Medal 1587. 2nd prtg. NF. B3d. $5.00

MACDONALD, John D. *One Fearful Yellow Eye.* 1966. Gold Medal D 1848. My. VG+. B4d. $18.00

MACDONALD, John D. *One Fearful Yellow Eye.* Gold Medal T 2135. My. F. W2d. $4.75

MACDONALD, John D. *One Fearful Yellow Eye.* 1966. Gold Medal 1750. 1st edn. My. F. F2d. $15.00

MACDONALD, John D. *One Monday We Killed Them All.* Gold Medal K 1451. c/B Johnson. My. G+. B5d. $4.00

MACDONALD, John D. *One Monday We Killed Them All.* 1961. Gold Medal S 1177. Fa. G+. B4d. $14.00

MACDONALD, John D. *One Monday We Killed Them All.* 1961. Gold Medal S 1177. VG. I1d. $20.00

MACDONALD, John D. *One Monday We Killed Them All.* Gold Medal T 2602. My. VG+. B5d. $7.50

MACDONALD, John D. *Only Girl in the Game.* Gold Medal R 2010. My. VG. W2d. $4.50

MACDONALD, John D. *Only Girl in the Game.* 1960. Gold Medal S 1015. My. VG+. B4d. $24.00

MACDONALD, John D. *Only Girl in the Game.* 1960. Gold Medal S 1015. 1st prtg. PBO. VG. P7d. $17.50

MACDONALD, John D. *Other Times, Other Worlds.* Gold Medal 14037. SF. VG. W2d. $3.50

MACDONALD, John D. *Pale Gray for Guilt.* 1968. Gold Medal D 1893. G+. G5d. $3.50

MACDONALD, John D. *Pale Gray for Guilt.* 1968. Gold Medal D 1893. My. VG+. B4d. $20.00

MACDONALD, John D. *Pale Gray for Guilt.* 1968. Gold Medal P 3134. My. VG+. B4d. $3.00

MACDONALD, John D. *Pale Gray for Guilt.* 1968. Gold Medal R 1970. My. VG. B4d. $15.00

MACDONALD, John D. *Planet of the Dreamers.* 1962. Corgi SS 1143. 1st pb. SF. VG. B6d. $9.00

MACDONALD, John D. *Planet of the Dreamers.* 1953. Pocket 943. c/R Dunham. SF. VG. B5d. $9.00

MACDONALD, John D. *Planet of the Dreamers.* 1953. Pocket 943. 1st pb edn. F. M1d. $20.00

MACDONALD, John D. *Planet of the Dreamers.* 1953. Pocket 943. 1st prtg. c/Dunham. G+. G5d/P7d. $5.00

MACDONALD, John D. *Please Write for Details.* 1960. Crest 359. c/Hooks. VG. B3d. $5.50

MACDONALD, John D. *Please Write for Details.* 1960. Crest 359. 1st edn. PBO. My. F. F2d. $15.00

MACDONALD, John D. *Please Write for Details.* 1959. Gold Medal R 1649. Fa. VG+. B4d. $5.00

MACDONALD, John D. *Price of Murder.* Gold Medal M 2850. My. VG. B5d. $3.50

MACDONALD, John D. *Purple Place for Dying.* 1964. Gold Medal K 1417. My. F. B4d. $20.00

MACDONALD, John D. *Purple Place for Dying.* 1964. Gold Medal K 1417. PBO. c/R Lesser. My. G+. B5d. $9.00

MACDONALD, John D. *Purple Place for Dying.* 1964. Gold Medal K 1417. 1st prtg. PBO. c/Lesser: gga. VG. P7d. $15.00

MACDONALD, John D. *Quick Red Fox.* 1964. Gold Medal K 1464. My. F. B4d. $30.00

MACDONALD, John D. *Quick Red Fox.* 1964. Gold Medal K 1464. My. G+. B4d. $8.00

MACDONALD, John D. *Quick Red Fox.* 1964. Gold Medal K 1464. My. VG. B4d. $15.00

MACDONALD, John D. *Quick Red Fox.* 1964. Gold Medal M 2828. reprint. VG. B3d. $4.00

MACDONALD, John D. *Quick Red Fox.* 1964. Gold Medal M 2828. 7th edn. My. G+. B4d. $3.00

MACDONALD, John D. *Quick Red Fox.* Gold Medal T 2272. My. VG+. W2d. $4.50

MACDONALD, John D. *Quick Red Fox.* 1964. Gold Medal 1610. 1st edn. My. VG. F2d. $10.00

MACDONALD, John D. *Scarlet Ruse.* 1973. Gold Medal P 2744. My. VG+. B4d. $18.00

MACDONALD, John D. *Scarlet Ruse.* 1973. Gold Medal Q 3222. My. VG+. B4d. $3.00

MACDONALD, John D. *Slam the Big Door.* Gold Medal D 1606. My. G+. W2d. $3.00

MACDONALD, John D. *Slam the Big Door.* 1963. Gold Medal S 1354. 2nd edn. My. VG. B4d. $3.00

MACDONALD, John D. *Slam the Big Door.* 1960. Gold Medal S 961. My. G+. B4d. $15.00

MACDONALD, John D. *Slam the Big Door.* 1960. Gold Medal S 961. PBO. c/gga. scarce. NF. B6a #74. $62.00

MACDONALD, John D. *Slam the Big Door.* 1960. Gold Medal 961. 1st edn. My. F. F2d. $30.00

MACDONALD, John D. *Soft Touch.* 1958. Dell 1st Edn B 121. PBO. c/Kalin. My. VG. B6d. $18.00

MACDONALD, John D. *Soft Touch.* 1958. Dell 1st Edn B 121. 1st edn. My. F. F2d. $28.00

MACDONALD, John D. *Soft Touch.* Dell 1st Edn K 116. c/McGinnis. VG. B3d. $5.00

MACDONALD, John D. *Tan & Sandy Silence.* 1972. Gold Medal M 2513. My. G+. B4d. $3.00

MACDONALD, John D. *Tan & Sandy Silence.* 1972. Gold Medal M 2513. My. VG. G5d. $6.50

MACDONALD, John D. *Tan & Sandy Silence.* 1972. Gold Medal M 2513. 1st edn. My. F. F2d. $15.00

MACDONALD, John D. *Turquoise Lament.* 1974. Gold Medal P 2810. My. VG+. B4d. $25.00

MACDONALD, John D. *Weep for Me.* 1951. Gold Medal 200. 1st edn. c/gga. My. VG. F2d. $12.50

MACDONALD, John D. *Wine of the Dreamers.* Crest T 2400. 1st prtg. VG. S1d. $3.00

MACDONALD, John D. *Wine of the Dreamers.* Gold Medal P 3263. SF. F. W2d. $5.00

MACDONALD, John D. *Wine of the Dreamers.* 1968. Gold Medal R 1994. My. VG. B4d/M3d. $6.00

MACDONALD, John D. *Wine of the Dreamers.* 1968. Gold Medal R 1994. SF. G+. G5d. $4.50

MACDONALD, John D. *Wine of the Dreamers.* Gold Medal T 2400. SF. VG. B5d. $5.00

MACDONALD, John D. *You Live Once.* Gold Medal T 2314. My. VG. B5d. $5.50

MACDONALD, John Ross. *Barbarous Coast.* 1957. Bantam 1613. VG. P6d. $5.50

MACDONALD, John Ross. *Barbarous Coast.* 1957. Bantam 1613. 1st prtg. My. G+. R5d. $5.00

MACDONALD, John Ross. *Blue City.* 1968. Bantam F 3867. 1st prtg. My. G+. R5d. $.75

MACDONALD, John Ross. *Find a Victim.* Bantam 1360. 1st pb. c/Hooks. G+. M6d. $7.50

MACDONALD, John Ross. *Galton Case.* 1983. Bantam 22621. 16th prtg. My. VG+. W2d. $3.25

MACDONALD, John Ross. *Harper.* Pocket 50218. 4th edn. MTI. c/Paul Newman. VG. M6d. $6.50

MACDONALD, John Ross. *Harper.* 1966. Pocket 50218. 4th prtg. G+. R5d. $1.25

MACDONALD, John Ross. *Meet Me at the Morgue.* 1954. Pocket 1020. c/C Hulings My. G+. B5d. $5.50

MACDONALD, John Ross. *Meet Me at the Morgue.* 1954. Pocket 1020. 1st pb. My. NF. B6d. $22.50

MACDONALD, John Ross. *Name Is Archer.* 1955. Bantam 1295. PBO. c/Hooks. NF. B6a #76. $77.00

MACDONALD, John Ross. *Three Roads.* 1960. Bantam A 2096. c/gga. My. VG. B4d. $4.00

MACDONALD, John Ross. *Trouble Follows Me.* 1972. Bantam N 7189. 1st prtg. My. VG. R5d. $2.75

MACDONALD, John Ross. *Way Some People Die.* 1977. Bantam 10987 8th prtg. My. VG+. W2d. $3.25

MACDONALD, John Ross. *Way Some People Die.* 1952. Pocket 907. 1st prtg. My. G+. W2d. $5.00

MACDONALD, Philip. *Death & Chicanery.* PopularSP 248. VG+. B3d. $4.00

MACDONALD, Philip. *Harbour.* 1946. Bonded Mystery 13. G+. I1d. $6.00

MACDONALD, Philip. *List of Adrian Messenger.* Bantam 2186. VG+. B3d. $4.50

MACDONALD, Philip. *Mystery of the Dead Police.* Dell D 247. VG+. B3d. $4.00

MACDONALD, Philip. *Warrant for X.* 1957. Dell D 194. c/Bogart. My. VG. B4d. $3.00

MACDONALD, Philip. *Warrant for X.* Pocket 328. VG. B3d. $6.00

MACDONALD, William Colt. *Action at Arcanum.* Avon T 409. We. VG. B5d. $3.00

MACDONALD, William Colt. *Black Sombrero.* Signet 698. VG+. B3d. $6.00

MACDONALD, William Colt. *Cow Thief.* 1953. Pyramid 101. We. VG+. B4d. $3.75

MACDONALD, William Colt. *Dead Man's Gold.* 1950. Signet 835. c/L Ross. We. NF. B5d. $6.00

MACDONALD, William Colt. *Fighting Kid From Eldorado.* 1955. Avon 678. We. VG+. B4d. $3.25

MACDONALD, William Colt. *Gunsight Range.* 1951. Signet 880. VG. B3d. $5.00

MACDONALD, William Colt. *Law & Order, Unlimited.* Signet 1168. 1st pb. We. NF. B6d. $15.00

MACDONALD, William Colt. *Mad Marshal.* 1958. Pyramid G 363. We. VG+. B4d. $5.00

MACDONALD, William Colt. *Mesquiteer Mavericks.* Avon 491. VG. B3d. $5.00

MACDONALD, William Colt. *Rebel Ranger.* 1954. Avon 579. We. VG. B4d. $4.00

MACDONALD, William Colt. *Red Rider of Smoky Range.* Hillman 19. VG. B3d. $6.00

MACDONALD, William Colt. *Roaring Lead.* 1974. Avon 20198. 1st pb. We. VG+. B6d. $5.00

MACDONALD, William Colt. *Roaring Lead.* 1945. Century 61. 1st edn. PBO. F. F2d. $15.00

MACDONALD, William Colt. *Shadow Rider.* Signet 792. VG. B3d. $5.00

MACDONALD, William Colt. *Shadow Rider.* 1950. Signet 792. c/L Ross. We. VG. B5d. $4.00

MACDONALD, William Colt. *Showdown Trail.* Pyramid 95. NF. I1d. $12.00

MACDONALD, William Colt. *Showdown Trail.* 1953. Pyramid 95. We. VG. B4d. $5.00

MACDONALD, William Colt. *Singing Scorpion.* Graphic 50. VG+. I1d. $6.00

MACDONALD, William Colt. *Six-Shooter Showdown.* Signet 764. VG+. B3d. $7.00

MACDONALD, William Colt. *Six-Shooter Showdown.* 1950. Signet 764. We. VG. B5d. $4.00

MACDONALD, William Colt. *Spanish Pesos.* Avon T 443. VG. B3d. $4.00

MACDONALD, William Colt. *Three-Notch Cameron.* Avon 536. We. VG. B5d. $4.50

MACDONALD, William Colt. *Three-Notch Cameron.* 1953. Avon 536. We. VG+. B4d. $6.00

MACDONALD, William Colt. *Two-Gun Deputy.* 1954. Pyramid 115. c/C Doore. We. G+. B5d. $4.00

MACDONALD, William Colt. *Wheels in the Dust.* Hillman 31. VG. B3d. $5.00

MACDONALD, William Colt. *Wildcat Range.* Berkley Y 1006. reprint. We. VG+. B6d. $9.00

MACDONNELL, J.E. *Frogman!* 1960. Pyramid G 473. 1st US edn. c/Mel Crair. NF. B6d. $12.50

MACE, Merlda. *Headlong for Murder.* 1945. Black Cat 15. G+. M6d. $9.50

MACGREGOR, James. *When the Ship Sank.* Ace D 460. VG+. B3d. $4.50

MACGREGOR, Rob. *Indiana Jones & the Last Crusade.* 1989. Ballantine 36161. 1st prtg. MTI. My. vG. R5d. $2.00

MACHAUG, WILLIAM. *Smart Guy.* 1951. Popular 340. c/gga. My. VG+. B4d. $7.50

MACHEN, Arthur. *Three Impostors.* 1972. Ballantine 2643. SF. VG+. M3d. $10.00

MACHLIN, Milt. *Private Holl of Hemingway.* 1962. PB Library 52-128. Nfi. G+. P1d. $3.00

MACINNES, Helen. *Above Suspicion.* 1942. Pocket 186. c/Troop. My. VG. B5d. $6.00

MACINNES, Helen. *Neither Five Nor Three.* Crest M 1310. 1st prtg. VG. R5d. $1.50

MACINNES, Helen. *Neither Five Nor Three.* 1952. Popular 453. c/gga. Fa. VG+. B4d. $7.00

MACINNES, Helen. *While We Still Live.* Crest 748. VG. B3d. $4.00

MACINTYRE, Donald. *U-Boat Killer.* 1957. Avon T 205. War. VG. B4d. $2.00

MACK & SPRISSLER. *Spectre Bullet & the Avenging Note.* Stellar 17. SF. F. W2d. $40.00

MACKELWORTH, R.W. *Diabols.* 1969. PB Library 63-110. SF. VG+. B5d. $4.00

MACKENDRICK. *Passion for Honor.* 1977. Leisure 467. PBO. NF. B6d. $7.50

MACKENROTH, Nancy. *Trees of Zharka.* 1975. Popular 639. SF. NF. B5d. $4.50

MACKENROTH, Nancy. *Trees of Zharka.* 1975. Popular 639. 1st edn. VG. P9d. $1.50

MACKENZIE, Donald. *Gentlemen at Crime.* Corgi 547. VG. B3d. $9.00

MACKENZIE, Donald. *I, Spy.* 1963. Avon G 1214. Fa. VG+. B4d. $3.00

MACKEY, Joe. *Cruel City.* Belmont 207. PBO. VG. B3d. $4.00

MACKINNON, Allan. *House of Darkness.* Dell 237. 1st prtg. My. VG+. R5d. $8.00

MACKLIN, John. *Dwellers in the Darkness.* Ace H 94. 1st prtg. VG. S1d. $3.00

MACKLIN, John. *Out of This World.* 1972. Ace 64475. Nfi. VG+. B5d. $4.00

MACKLIN, Mark. *Thin Edge of Mania.* 1956. Ace D 149. PBO. scarce. F. B6a #74. $61.00

MACKLIN, Mark. *Thin Edge of Mania.* 1956. Ace D 149. PBO. VG+. B6d. $30.00

MACLANE, Kirby. *For Women Only.* 1969. Softcover S 75130. PBO. c/Victor Kalin: gga. VG. P6d. $4.00

MACLEAN, Alistair. *Athabasca.* 1981. Fontana C 16457. My. VG+. W2d. $4.00

MACLEAN, Alistair. *Black Shrike.* 1970. Gold Medal M 2340. My. VG+. B5d. $5.00

MACLEAN, Alistair. *Broken Toy.* Sexton Blake 362. VG+. B3d. $8.00

MACLEAN, Alistair. *Canvas Jungle.* Sexton Blake 370. VG. B3d. $7.00

MACLEAN, Alistair. *Cross of Gold Affair.* Ace G 689. Man From UNCLE #14. VG+. G5d. $5.00

MACLEAN, Alistair. *Dark Frontier.* Sexton Blake 368. VG+. B3d. $8.00

MACLEAN, Alistair. *Deadline for Danger.* Sexton Blake 380. VG+. B3d. $7.50

MACLEAN, Alistair. *Fear Is the Key.* Gold Medal P 3004. My. NF. B5d. $5.00

MACLEAN, Alistair. *Goodbye California.* 1979. Crest 20302. SF. F. W2d. $4.00

MACLEAN, Alistair. *Guns of Navarone.* Perma M 4089. 3rd prtg. MTI. VG. B3d. $4.00

MACLEAN, Alistair. *Ice Station Zebra.* 1974. Fontana L 11838. 15th prtg. My. VG. W2d. $3.75

MACLEAN, Alistair. *Mind-Twisters Affair.* Ace G 663. Man From UNCLE #12. VG+. G5d. $5.00

MACLEAN, Alistair. *Night Beat.* Sexton Blake 365. VG+. B3d. $9.00

MACLEAN, Alistair. *Puppet on a Chain.* 1970. Crest M 1482. My. VG. W2d. $4.00

MACLEAN, Alistair. *River of Death.* 1983. Crest 20058-2. 1st prtg. My. VG+. R5d. $2.00

MACLEAN, Alistair. *Satan Bug.* Gold Medal Q 3439. My. VG. W2d. $3.25

MACLEAN, Alistair. *Seawitch.* 1977. Crest 23597. 1st prtg. My. VG. W2d. $3.00

MACLEAN, Alistair. *South by Java Head.* Gold Medal M 2924. My. VG+. B5d. $4.00

MACLEAN, Katherine. *Diploids.* 1962. Avon G 1143. 1st prtg. SF. VG. R5d. $4.50

MACLEAN, Katherine. *Diploids.* 1962. Avon. 1st edn. F. M1d. $8.00

MACLEAN, Robinson. *Baited Blonde.* Dell 508. c/R Stanley. My. VG. B5d. $4.00

MACLEISH, Rod. *Prince Ombra.* TOR 54550. SF. VG. W2d. $3.00

MACLEOD, Robert. *Muleskinner.* 1967. Gold Medal D 1786. PBO. We. VG+. B6d. $9.00

MACLEOD, William. *Beyond the Rio Grande.* 1951. Popular359. VG. P6d. $2.25

MACLEOD. *Withdrawing Room.* 1981. Avon 56473. 1st prtg. My. VG. W2d. $2.75

MACNEIL, Neil. *Mexican Slay Ride.* 1962. Gold Medal S 1182. c/gga. My. VG. B4d. $5.00

MACNEIL, Neil. *Spy Catchers.* 1966. Gold Medal D 1658. My. VG+. B4d. $4.00

MACNEIL, Neil. *Third on a Seesaw.* Gold Medal 476. VG+. B3d. $8.00

MACNEIL, Neil. *Two Guns for Hire.* Gold Medal S 898. G+. G5d. $5.00

MACNEIL, Neil. *Two Guns for Hire.* Gold Medal 1484. VG+. B3d. $4.50

MACPHERSON, Michael. *Abducted.* 1968. Essex 0105. PBO. VG. B6d. $15.00

MACRAUCH, Earl. *New York, New York.* 1977. Pocket 80850. 1st edn. MTI. c/photo. F. F2d. $8.00

MACTYRE, Paul. *Doomsday, 1999.* 1963. Ace F 201. NF. M1d. $6.00

MACTYRE, Paul. *Doomsday, 1999.* 1963. Ace F 201. 1st edn. SF. F. F2d. $11.00

MACY, L. *Lovemaster.* Beacon 1033. VG+. B3d. $8.00

MADDEN, N.C. *Real Howard Hughes Story.* 1976. Manor 15197. 1st prtg. Bio. VG. R5d. $1.50

MADDOCK, Larry. *Emerald Elephant.* 1967. Ace G 644. Agent of TERRA #3. SF. F. W2d. $5.00

MADDOCK, Larry. *Flying Saucer Gambit.* 1966. Ace G 605. Agent of TERRA #1. SF. F. W2d. $5.00

MADDOCK, Larry. *Golden Goddess Gambit.* 1967. Ace G 620. Agent of TERRA #2. SF. VG. W2d. $4.00

MADDOCK, Larry. *Time Trap Gambit.* 1967. Ace 01043. 1st edn. F. P9d. $1.75

MADDOX, Brenda. *Who's Afraid of Elizabeth Taylor?* 1978. Jove O4583. NF. VG. B5d. $3.00

MADIGAN, Kip. *Incest for Rene.* Fabian Z 107. 4th prtg. VG. B3d. $4.00

MADISON, Russ. *Victory Among the Insane.* 1970. Grove Press B 274. 1st prtg. VG+. P7d. $7.50

MAGEE, Martin. *Virginity.* 1963. Monarch MB 545. Nfi. F. B4d. $9.00

MAGEE, Martin. *Virginity.* 1963. Monarch MB 545. Nfi. G+. B5d. $3.00

MAGER, Sylvia K. *Complete Guide to Home Sewing.* 1952. Pocket 890. c/Ernest Chiriaka: gga. VG+. P6d. $4.00

MAGGIN, Elliot S. *Superman: Last Son of Krypton.* 1978. Warner 82219. 4th prtg. SF. VG. W2d. $3.75

MAHAN, P.W. *Doctor, You've Got To Be Kidding.* 1966. Avon S 240. 1st prtg. VG. R5d. $1.75

MAHANNAH, Floyd. *Broken Angel.* 1958. Pocket 1231. 1st pb. My. NF. B6d. $15.00

MAHANNAH, Floyd. *Broken Body.* 1952. Signet 957. 1st pb. My. VG. B6d. $5.00

MAHANNAH, Floyd. *Golden Widow.* 1957. Perma M 3087. c/C Hulings. My. VG. B5d. $4.00

MAHANNAH, Floyd. *No Luck for a Lady.* 1951. Signet 879. 1st pb. My. VG. B6d. $12.00

MAHR, Kurt. *Beware the Microbots.* 1973. Ace 66018. Perry Rhodan #35. SF. F. B5d. $6.00

MAHR, Kurt. *Ghosts of Gol.* Ace 65979. Perrt Rhodan. SF. VG. W2d. $3.50

MAHR, Kurt. *Peril on Ice Planet.* 1973. Ace 66006. Perry Rhodan #23. SF. F. B5d. $6.00

MAHR, Kurt. *Planet of the Dying Sun.* 1972. Ace 65980. Perry Rhodan #11. SF. VG+. B5d. $4.00

MAHR, Kurt. *To Arkon!* 1973. Ace 66013. Perry Rhodan #30. SF. VG+. B5d. $5.00

MAHR, Kurt. *Venus Trap.* 1972. Ace 65987. Perry Rhodan #17. SF. NF. B5d. $5.00

MAHR & SCHEER. *Radiant Dome.* 1969. Ace 65971. Perry Rhodan #2. SF. VG+. B5d. $4.00

MAIER, William. *Pleasure Island.* 1950. Bantam 785. Fa. VG. B4d. $2.25

MAILER, Norman. *Advertisements for Myself.* 1966. Berkley N 1200. Nfi. VG. B5d. $4.00

MAILER, Norman. *Advertisements for Myself.* 1961. Signet T 1889. 1st prtg. VG. P7d. $5.00

MAILER, Norman. *American Dream.* Dell 0129. VG+. B3d. $7.00

MAILER, Norman. *Barbary Shore.* Ace H 182. VG. B3d. $8.00

MAILER, Norman. *Barbary Shore.* 1953. Signet 1019. c/S Zuckerberg. Fi. VG. B4d/B5d. $4.00

MAILER, Norman. *Marilyn.* 1975. Warner 71-850. 2nd prtg. Bio. G+. R5d. $3.50

MAILER, Norman. *Miami & the Siege of Chicago.* 1968. Signet Q 3785. 1st prtg. VG. P7d. $4.50

MAINE, Charles Eric. *BEAST.* 1967. Ballantine U 6092. 1st US edn. VG+. P7d. $5.00

MAINE, Charles Eric. *Fire Past the Future.* 1959. Ballantine. 1st edn. F. M1d. $9.00

MAINE, Charles Eric. *He Owned the World.* Avon T 524. VG+. B3d/I1d. $4.00

MAINE, Charles Eric. *He Owned the World.* Avon T 524. 1st pb edn. F. M1d. $10.00

MAINE, Charles Eric. *High Vacuum.* 1957. Ballantine 218. PBO. c/R Powers. SF. VG. B5d. $6.00

MAINE, Charles Eric. *High Vacuum.* 1957. Ballantine 218. 1st edn. SF. F. F2d. $12.00

MAINE, Charles Eric. *Spaceways.* Pan 297. VG+. B3d. $8.00

MAINE, Charles Eric. *Survival Margin.* 1968. Gold Medal R 1918. 1st prtg. SF. VG. R5d. $3.25

MAINE, Charles Eric. *Survival Margin.* Gold Medal 1918. VG+. B3d. $4.50

MAINE, Charles Eric. *Tide Went Out.* 1959. Ballantine 290K. PBO. c/R Powers. SF. VG. B5d. $6.00

MAINE, Charles Eric. *Tide Went Out.* 1959. Ballantine. 1st edn. F. M1d. $10.00

MAINE, Charles Eric. *Timeliner.* 1956. Bantam A 1470. 1st prtg. SF. VG. R5d. $3.00

MAINE, Charles Eric. *Timeliner.* 1956. Bantam. 1st pb edn. F. M1d. $10.00

MAINE, Charles Eric. *Timeliner.* Corgi S 554. 1st prtg. G+. S1d. $3.50

MAINE, Charles Eric. *World Without Men.* Ace D 274. F. M1d. $20.00

MAINE, Charles Eric. *World Without Men.* Ace D 274. VG. B3d. $5.00

MAINE, Charles Eric. *World Without Men.* 1958. Ace D 274. PBO. c/E Emsh. SF. G. B5d. $7.50

MAINE, Charles Eric. *World Without Men.* 1958. Ace D 274. VG+. I1d. $40.00

MAINE, Harold. *If a Man Be Mad.* 1952. Perma P 156. 1st pb. c/Tom Dunn. VG. B6d. $7.00

MAIR, George B. *Day Khruschev Panicked.* 1963. MacFadden 50-183. c/S Borack. SF. VG. B5d. $5.50

MAIR, George B. *Miss Turquoise.* 1968. Berkley X 1605. 1st prtg. My. G+. R5d. $1.50

MAJORS, S. *Druid Stone.* PB Library 52-488. VG+. B3d. $5.00

MAKOW, Henry. *Ask Henry.* 1963. Ace F 219. scarce. VG. B3d. $5.00

MALACHY, Frank. *Hot Town.* 1956. Perma 3059. c/T Ryan. We. VG+. B5d. $12.50

MALAMUD, Bernard. *Assistant.* 1958. Signet S 1514. Fi. VG. B5d. $4.50

MALCOLM, Donald. *Unknown Shore.* 1976. Laser 19. PBO. c/K Freas. SF. VG+. B5d/ I1d. $5.00

MALCOLM-SMITH, George. *Mugs, Molls & Dr Harvey.* Graphic 104. VG. B3d. $4.00

MALLAN, Lloyd. *Secrets of Space Flight.* 1956. Gold Medal 298. 1st edn. F. F2d. $20.00

MALLEY, Louis. *Horns for the Devil.* 1952. Pocket 894. 1st pb. c/Mafia. NF. B6d. $12.00

MALLEY, Louis. *Love Mill.* Belmont 243. PBO. VG+. B3d. $5.00

MALLEY, Louis. *Stool Pigeon.* Avon 551. VG. B3d/G5d. $5.50

MALLEY, Louis. *Tiger in the Streets.* 1957. Ace D 257. JD. VG+. P1d. $45.00

MALLEY, Louis. *Tiger in the Streets.* 1957. Ace D 257. PBO. c/Tossey. JD. VG. B6d. $35.00

MALLEY, Louis. *Tiger in the Streets.* 1957. Ace D 257. PBO. c/Tossey. scarce. JD. VG. B6a #76. $42.00

MALLEY, Terence. *Richard Brautigan.* 1972. Warner 68-942. Nfi. VG. P1d. $5.00

MALLOY, Fred. *Infidelity.* Beacon 310. VG. B3d. $4.50

MALLOY, Fred. *Infidelity.* 1960. Beacon 310. PBO. c/Darcy: gga. NF. B6d. $25.00

MALLOY, Fred. *Lita.* 1959. Beacon B 235. VG. B3d. $5.00

MALLOY, Fred. *Rooming House.* 1954. Beacon 103. 1st edn. c/gga. scarce. F. F2d. $25.00

MALLOY, Fred. *Rooming House.* 1958. Beacon 185. 1st prtg. VG+. P7d. $9.00

MALLOY, Fred. *Strumpet's Seed.* 1959. Beacon 218. 1st prtg. VG+. P7d. $9.00

MALLOY, Fred. *Wicked Woman.* 1958. Berkley G 185. 1st edn. PBO. c/gga. VG+. B6a #77. $42.50

MALLOY, Fred. *Wild Hunger.* 1958. Beacon 171. 1st prtg. VG+. P7d. $12.50

MALONE, Dorothy. *Cookbook for Beginners.* Ace D 32. VG. P6d. $4.50

MALZBERG, Barry N. *Beyond Apollo.* 1975. Orbit 7872. SF. VG. B5d. $3.50

MALZBERG, Barry N. *Beyond Apollo.* Pocket 77687. 1st prtg. VG. S1d. $2.50

MALZBERG, Barry N. *Day of the Burning.* 1974. Ace 13902. 1st prtg. VG. S1d/W2d. $4.50

MALZBERG, Barry N. *Falling Astronauts.* Ace 22690. 1st prtg. G+. S1d. $3.50

MALZBERG, Barry N. *Galaxies.* Pyramid V 3734. 1st prtg. G. S1d. $2.50

MALZBERG, Barry N. *Gamesman.* Pocket 80174. 1st prtg. VG+. S1d. $4.00

MALZBERG, Barry N. *Herovit's World.* Pocket 77753. 1st prtg. VG. S1d. $3.50

MALZBERG, Barry N. *Many Worlds of Barry Malzberg.* 1975. Popular 298. SF. VG. B5d. $4.00

MALZBERG, Barry N. *Men Inside.* 1973. Lancer 75-486. 1st edn. F. M1d. $7.00

MALZBERG, Barry N. *Men Inside.* 1973. Lancer 75-486. PBO. SF. VG. B5d. $4.00

MALZBERG, Barry N. *Men Inside.* Lancer 75-486. 1st prtg. G. S1d. $2.00

MALZBERG, Barry N. *On a Planet Alien.* Pocket 77-766. 1st prtg. G. S1d. $2.00

MALZBERG, Barry N. *Overlay.* 1972. Lancer 75-345. SF. VG+. B4d. $4.00

MALZBERG, Barry N. *Phase IV.* Pocket 77-710. 5th prtg. SF. G+. W2d. $2.75

MALZBERG, Barry N. *Scop.* Pyramid V 3895. 1st prtg. G. S1d. $2.00

MALZBERG, Barry N. *Tactics of Conquest.* Pyramid N 3330. 1st prtg. VG+. S1d. $3.50

MALZBERG, Barry N. *Tactics of Conquest.* 1974. Pyramid 3330. 1st edn. SF. F. F2d. $10.00

MANCERON, Genevieve. *Deadlier Sex.* 1961. Dell D 417. 1st prtg. My. VG. R5d. $2.25

MANCHESTER, W. *Portrait of a President.* MacFadden 60-162. VG+. B3d. $4.50

MANCHESTER, William. *Cairo Intrigue.* 1959. Pocket 1252. c/J Meese. My. VG. B5d. $4.00

MANDEL, George. *Beatville USA.* 1961. Avon T 489. VG+. B4d. $9.00

MANFRED, Frederick F. *Lord Grizzly.* 1955. Cardinal C 192. 1st pb. c/Hulings. VG+. B6d. $6.00

MANKIEWICZ, Don M. *Trial.* 1956. Dell D 160. 1st prtg. My. G+. R5d. $1.75

MANKOWITZ, Wolf. *Cockatrice.* 1964. Perma M 5096. Fa. VG+. B4d. $3.00

MANKOWITZ, Wolf. *Old Soldiers Never Die.* 1958. Signet 1471. Fi. VG+. B5d. $4.50

MANN, Abby. *Judgment at Nuremberg.* 1961. Signet D 2025. 1st prtg. VG+. R5d. $6.00

MANN, Arthur. *Jackie Robinson Story.* 1950. FJ Low Co NN. MTI. G+. B3a. $42.35

MANN, E.B. *Stampede.* Dell 333. We. VG. B5d. $4.00

MANN, E.B. *Troubled Range.* Pocket 1022. VG+. B3d. $4.00

MANN, May. *Private Elvis.* 1977. Pocket 81884. 2nd prtg. Bio. VG. R5d. $5.00

MANN, Richard. *Elvis.* 1977. Bible Voice NN. 1st prtg. Bio. VG. R5d. $10.00

MANN, Thomas. *Confessions of Felix Krull, Confidence Man.* 1957. Signet D 1411. Fi. VG. B5d. $4.00

MANN/MANN. *Gunlick by Request/Luck Rides With the Fastest Gun.* Belmont 50-630. NF. B3d. $4.50

MANNERS, Dorine. *Sin Street (Scarlet Patrol).* Pyramid 249. VG. B3d. $4.00

MANNERS, Dorine. *Sin Street.* 1950. Pyramid 21. 1st edn. PBO. c/gga. F. F2d. $15.00

MANNERS, Margaret. *Love of Life.* 1961. Dell 1st Edn B 183. 1st prtg. TVTI. G+. R5d. $1.75

MANNERS, William. *Wharf Girl.* 1954. Lion 219. PBO. scarce. NF. B6a #76. $40.25

MANNERS. *Barking Cat Case.* 1963. Collier 59. PBO. My. NF. B6d. $6.00

MANNES, Marya. *Message From a Stranger.* Dell 515. c/R Stanley. SF. G. B5d. $2.50

MANNHEIM, Karl. *Vampires of Venus.* 1972. Five Star NN. 1st pb. SF. NF. B6d. $9.00

MANNIN, Ethel. *At Sundown the Tiger.* 1952. Popular 438. 1st pb. VG+. B6d. $12.00

MANNING, Bruce. *Triangle of Sin.* 1952. Intimate 25. PBO. Fi. G+. B5d. $6.50

MANNING, Jane. *Affairs of Leading Lady.* Venue 150. PBO. VG. B3d. $10.00

MANNING, Jane. *City Hotel.* Carnival Book 939. c/Ray Pease: gga. VG+. B6a #74. $97.00

MANNING, Jane. *Young Sinners.* Venus Digest 175. c/Belarski. rare. JD. VG+. B6a #77. $72.00

MANNING, Ray. *Renegade Ranch.* 1950. Pocket 663. 1st edn. PBO. F. F2d. $8.00

MANNING, Steve. *Stallion Among Men.* 1965. Magenta Books M 118. PBO. VG. P6d. $2.50

MANNIX, Daniel P. *Beast.* Ballantine 302. PBO. VG. B3d. $6.00

MANNIX, Daniel P. *Hell Fire Club.* 1959. Ballantine 354K. PBO. NF. G+. B5d. $4.00

MANNIX, Jule. *Eagle in the Bathtub.* 1959. Ballantine 348K. 1st pb. VG. B6d. $6.00

MANOR, Jason. *Girl in the Red.* 1955. Popular EB 42. 1st pb. My. NF. B6d. $12.50

MANOR, Jason. *Red Jaguar.* 1958. Corgi S 515. 1st pb. c/My. VG+. B6d. $10.00

MANOR, Jason. *Too Dead To Run.* Perma M 3002. 2nd prtg. VG. B3d. $4.00

MANTEGAZZA, P. *Sexual Relations of Mankind.* Brandon House 2002. VG. B3d. $5.00

MANTEGAZZA, P. *Strange Sex Practices.* Imperial 732. VG+. B3d. $5.00

MANTELL, Laurie. *Murder & Chips.* 1984. Walker 30728. c/M Fresh. My. VG+. B5d. $4.00

MANTLE, B. edt. *Best Plays of 1943-1944.* Armed Services T 25. VG. B3d. $6.00

MANTLEY, John. *Woman Obsessed.* 1959. Perma M 4146. MTI. c/Susan Hayward: photo. VG+. B4d. $4.00

MANTLEY, John. *27th Day.* 1958. Crest S 209. 1st pb edn. F. M1d. $12.00

MANTLEY, John. *27th Day.* 1958. Crest S 209. 1st prtg. VG+. P7d. $6.00

MANTON, P. *Murder in the Highlands.* Jay 8. VG+. B3d. $8.00

MANVILL, Robert. *Dreamers.* Bantam F 2697. 1st prtg. VG+. S1d. $6.50

MANVILLE, W.H. *Breaking Up.* 1963. Dell 0797. 1st prtg. c/gga. VG. P7d. $3.50

MARA, Bernard. *Bullet for My Lady.* 1955. Gold Medal 472. PBO. My. NF. F2d. $10.00

MARAIS, Claude. *Saskia.* 1952. Lion 116. 1st US edn. c/Geygan: gga. scarce. NF. B6a #75. $53.50

MARCH, Kim. *Bachelor Nurse.* 1962. Beacon B 493F. PBO. Ad. VG. B5d. $6.00

MARCH, Ngaio. *Wreath for Rivera.* 1962. Berkley F 610. c/photo. My. VG. B5d. $3.50

MARCH, William. *Bad Seed.* Dell 847. 1st prtg. My. G+. R5d. $2.25

MARCH, William. *Bad Seed.* 1955. Dell 847. 1st pb. c/Kamp. My. NF. B6d. $18.00

MARCH, William. *Company K.* Lion LB 62. 3rd prtg. VG+. B3d. $5.00

MARCH, William. *Company K.* 1958. Signet S 1522. Fi. VG. B5d. $3.50

MARCHAL, L. *Mesh.* Bantam 862. VG+. B3d. $6.00

MARCOUX, M. *Four-Way Triangle.* Brandon House 1169. VG+. B3d. $6.00

MARCOUX, M. *Image of an Angel.* Brandon House 1128. NF. B3d. $5.50

MARCUS, A.A. *Post-Mark Homicide (The Widow Gay).* Graphic 67. VG. G5d. $3.00

MARCUS, A.A. *Walk the Bloody Boulevard.* 1953. Graphic 64. 2nd edn. My. G+. B5d. $2.50

MARCUS, A.A. *Walk the Bloody Boulevard.* 1953. Graphic 64. 2nd prtg. VG+. B3d. $5.00

MARCUS, Carl. *Arrividerci, Ava.* Newsstand U 132. VG+. B3d. $5.00

MARCUS, Carl. *Lewd Angel.* 1959. Newsstand 501. 1st edn. c/gga. De. F. F2d. $17.00

MARCUS, Robert B. *Shadow on the Stars.* 1977. Laser 57. 1st edn. very scarce. SF. F. F2d. $50.00

MARDAAN, A. *Deva Dasi.* Brandon House 2022. VG. B3d. $4.00

MARDAAN, A. *Kama Houri.* Brandon House 3004. VG+. B3d. $5.50

MARESCA, James. *Mr Taxicab.* Bantam 1756. NF. B3d. $5.00

MARESCA, James. *My Flag Is Down.* Bantam 419. VG+. B3d. $4.50

MARGE. *This Is Little Lulu.* 1956. Dell 1st Edn A 125. VG. B3a #20. $24.00

MARGOLIUS, Sidney. *It's Your Money.* 1951. Gold Medal 191. 1st edn. NF. F2d. $7.00

MARGULIES, Leo. *Get Out of My Sky.* 1960. Crest S 362. SF. VG+. B4d. $5.00

MARGULIES, Leo. *Get Out of My Sky.* 1960. Crest S 362. 1st edn. F. M1d. $10.00

MARGULIES, Leo. *Get Out of My Sky.* 1960. Crest S 362. 1st prtg. G. S1d. $2.50

MARGULIES, Leo. *Get Out of My Sky.* 1964. Crest 728. VG+. B3d. $4.50

MARGULIES, Leo. *Ghost Keepers.* Pyramid G 665. 1st pb edn. F. M1d. $10.00

MARGULIES, Leo. *Ghoul Keeper.* 1961. Pyramid G 665. PBO. c/J Schoenherr. SF. G+. B5d. $5.00

MARGULIES, Leo. *Ghoul Keepers.* Pyramid G 665. VG+. I1d. $8.00

MARGULIES, Leo. *Ghoul Keepers.* Pyramid 1210. 2nd prtg. c/Bloch: sgn. VG. B3d. $4.00

MARGULIES, Leo. *Mike Shayne's Torrid Twelve.* Dell K 109. VG. G5d. $3.00

MARGULIES, Leo. *Mike Shayne's Torrid Twelve.* 1960. Dell K 109. 1st edn. c/McGinnis: gga. My. F. F2d. $10.00

MARGULIES, Leo. *Mink Is for a Minx.* Dell 1st Edn 5642. PBO. c/McGinnis. My. VG+. B6d. $6.00

MARGULIES, Leo. *Mink Is for a Minx.* Dell 5642. PBO. VG. B3d. $4.00

MARGULIES, Leo. *Mink Is for a Minx.* 1964. Dell 5642. 1st edn. My. F. F2d. $10.00

MARGULIES, Leo. *My Best SF Story.* Pocket 1007. VG. I1d. $6.00

MARGULIES, Leo. *My Best SF Story.* 1954. Pocket 1007. SF. VG. B5d. $7.50

MARGULIES, Leo. *My Best SF Story.* 1954. Pocket 1007. 1st pb edn. F. M1d. $20.00

MARGULIES, Leo. *One-Way Street.* 1955. Pyramid 159. 1st prtg. c/gga. VG. P7d. $7.50

MARGULIES, Leo. *Race to the Stars.* 1958. Crest S 245. SF. VG+. W2d. $5.25

MARGULIES, Leo. *Race to the Stars.* 1958. Crest S 245. 1st edn. F. M1d. $10.00

MARGULIES, Leo. *Race to the Stars.* 1958. Crest 5246. NF. P9d. $2.00

MARGULIES, Leo. *Selected Western Stories.* Popular 187. VG. B3d. $4.00

MARGULIES, Leo. *Three From Out There.* 1959. Crest. 1st edn. F. M1d. $10.00

MARGULIES, Leo. *Three in One.* 1963. Pyramid F 899. PBO. c/E Emsh. SF. VG. B5d. $4.00

MARGULIES, Leo. *Three in One.* 1963. Pyramid F 899. 1st prtg. F. S1d. $8.00

MARGULIES, Leo. *Three Times Infinity.* Gold Medal D 1324. 2nd prtg. G+. S1d. $4.00

MARGULIES, Leo. *Three Times Infinity.* Gold Medal D 1680. 1st prtg. SF. VG. R5d. $2.00

MARGULIES, Leo. *Three Times Infinity.* 1958. Gold Medal S 726. PBO. SF. VG+. B3d. $5.00

MARGULIES, Leo. *Three Times Infinity.* Gold Medal 1680. NF. B3d. $4.50

MARGULIES, Leo. *Three Times Infinity.* Redseal 131. VG. B3d. $7.00

MARGULIES, Leo. *Unexpected.* Pyramid 795. 2nd prtg. c/Bloch. VG. B3d. $4.50

MARGULIES, Leo. *Unexpected.* 1961. Pyramid. 1st edn. F. M1d. $20.00

MARGULIES, Leo. *Weird Tales.* Pyramid R 1029. 1st prtg. F. S1d. $15.00

MARGULIES, Leo. *Worlds of Weird.* 1965. Pyramid R 1125. G. P9d. $1.25

MARGULIES, Leo. *Worlds of Weird.* 1965. Pyramid R 1125. SF. VG. B4d. $6.00

MARGULIES, Leo. *Worlds of Weird.* 1965. Pyramid 1125. 1st edn. c/Finlay. SF. F. F2d. $20.00

MARGULIES, Leo. *Young & Deadly.* 1959. Crest S 272. JD. G+. P1d. $7.50

MARGULIES, Leo. *Young & Deadly.* 1959. Crest 272. 1st edn. scarce. My. F. F2d. $40.00

MARGULIES, Leo. *Young Punks.* 1957. Pyramid G 271. PBO. c/Gil Brewer. scarce. JD. VG+. B6a #79. $47.25

MARGULIES, Leo. *Young Punks.* Pyramid 921. 3rd prtg. VG+. B3d. $6.00

MARIE, Therese. *I'm for Hire.* Brandon House 2001. VG. B3d. $4.50

MARINO, Nick. *One-Way Street.* 1952. Pyramid 65. c/gga. FA. VG+. B4d. $12.50

MARINO, Vic. *Paths Are Three.* 1962. Chicago PB House 110. 1st edn. My. F. F2d. $9.00

MARIO, Queena. *Murder Meets Mephisto.* 1945. Bart House. 1st pb ed. F. M1d. $12.00

MARIO, T. *Playboy's Gourmet.* Playboy 16124. VG+. B3d. $5.00

MARK, David. *Neighborhood.* 1960. PopularG 437. JD. VG. P1d. $10.50

MARK, Edwina. *Odd Ones.* 1959. Berkley G 245. 1st edn. F. F2d. $15.00

MARK, Edwina. *Sinful One.* Hillman 121. VG. B3d. $4.50

MARK, Stephen. *Overnight Escapade.* 1949. Newsstand A 24. My. G+. B5d. $3.50

MARK, Stephen. *Overnight Escapade.* 1949. Newsstand A 24. VG. B3d. $6.00

MARK, Ted. *Dr Nyet.* Lancer 73-477. G. G5d. $2.75

MARK, Ted. *Girl From Pussycat.* 1966. Lancer 73-446. 4th edn. My. VG. B5d. $4.00

MARK, Ted. *I Was a Teeny-Bopper for the CIA.* Berkley G 1496. VG. B3d. $4.00

MARK, Ted. *Man From Charisma.* 1970. Dell 05196. 1st prtg. c/photo. VG. P7d. $4.00

MARK, Ted. *Man From ORGY.* 1966. Lancer. F. M1d. $8.00

MARK, Ted. *My Son, the Double Agent.* 1966. Lancer 73-485. 1st prtg. My. VG. W2d. $4.00

MARK, Ted. *Nude Wore Black.* 1967. Lancer 73-546. PBO. My. VG. B5d. $5.50

MARK, Ted. *Pussycat, Pussycat!* 1966. Lancer 73-461. PBO. VG+. B6d. $7.50

MARK, Ted. *Pussycat Transplant.* 1968. Berkley S 1625. PBO. c/Borack. VG+. B6d. $5.00

MARK, Ted. *Room at the Topless.* 1973. Dell 07397. 1st prtg. c/photo. VG. P7d. $4.00

MARK, Ted. *Room at the Topless.* Dell 7397. VG. B3d. $4.00

MARK, Ted. *Unhatched Egghead.* 1966. Lancer 73-527. PBO. VG. B6d/M6d. $5.00

MARKANDAY, Kamala. *Some Inner Fury.* 1958. Signet S 1532. Fi. VG. B5d. $4.00

MARKEY, Gene. *Kentucky Pride.* Perma M 4078. VG+. B3d. $5.00

MARKEY, Morris. *Unhurrying Chase.* Pony 53. VG. B3d. $4.40

MARKHAM, Steve. *Hideout.* Art Publicity NN. VG. B3d. $12.00

MARKHAM, T. *Female Flesh.* Bachelor 542. VG+. B3d. $5.00

MARKLER, John. *Her Avid Desires.* 1967. Saturn SN 1152. Ad. NF. B5d. $8.00

MARKOWITZ, Arthur. *Daughter.* 1957. Pyramid G 295. 1st prtg. c/Nappi: gga. VG. P7d. $7.50

MARKOWITZ, Arthur. *Daughter.* 1951. Signet 886. 2nd prtg. c/Avati. VG+. B3d. $5.00

MARKS & PHILLIPS. *Two Souls, One Body.* 1962. Gold Medal 1234. 1st edn. My. F. F2d. $11.00

MARKS & SCHENCK. *Barquero.* 1970. PB Library 63-386. PBO. MTI. We. VG. B6d. $5.00

MARKSON, David. *Epitaph for a Dead Beat.* 1961. Dell 1st Edn B 189. Beat. VG+. B4d. $12.00

MARKSON, David. *Epitaph for a Dead Beat.* 1961. Dell 1st Edn B 189. G+. G5d. $4.00

MARKSON, David. *Epitaph for a Tramp.* 1959. Dell 1st Edn A 193. PBO. c/McGinnis. My. VG. B6d. $7.50

MARLOWE, Dan J. *Death Deep Down.* 1965. Gold Medal K 1524. c/gga. My. NF. B4d. $6.00

MARLOWE, Dan J. *Doorway to Death.* Avon T 307. VG. G5d. $6.50

MARLOWE, Dan J. *Doorway to Death.* 1959. Avon T 307. 1st prtg. My. G+. R5d. $3.00

MARLOWE, Dan J. *Fatal Frails.* 1960. Avon T 452. 1st edn. c/gga. De/Th. F. F2d. $15.00

MARLOWE, Dan J. *Flashpoint.* Gold Medal R 2283. NF. G5d. $6.50

MARLOWE, Dan J. *Killer With a Key.* 1959. Avon T 349. 1st edn. De. F. F2d. $16.00

MARLOWE, Dan J. *Name of the Game Is Death.* Gold Medal 1184. PBO. VG. B3d. $7.00

MARLOWE, Dan J. *Never Live Twice.* Black Lizard 043. VG. G5d. $6.00

MARLOWE, Dan J. *Operation Breakthrough.* Gold Medal T 2486. VG. G5d. $5.00

MARLOWE, Dan J. *Operation Deathmaker.* 1975. Gold Medal 3171. 1st edn. Th. F. F2d. $10.00

MARLOWE, Dan J. *Operation Drumfire.* Gold Medal 2541. VG+. B3d. $4.50

MARLOWE, Dan J. *Operation Flashpoint.* 1970. Gold Medal 2934. 1st edn. Th. F. F2d. $8.00

MARLOWE, Dan J. *Operation Hammerlock.* 1974. Gold Medal 2974. 1st edn. My. F. F2d. $10.00

MARLOWE, Dan J. *Operation Straglehold.* 1973. Gold Medal T 2723. My. NF. B4d. $3.75

MARLOWE, Dan J. *Operation Whiplash.* 1973. Gold Medal T 2866. My. F. B4d. $3.75

MARLOWE, Dan J. *Strongarm.* Gold Medal 1340. VG. B3d. $4.00

MARLOWE, Derek. *Dandy in Aspic.* 1967. Dell 1665. 1st prtg. G+. R5d. $1.50

MARLOWE, Mona. *Frustration.* 1967. Unique UB 128. PBO. c/Ward. NF. B3a #24. $16.00

MARLOWE, Stephen. *Danger Is My Life.* Gold Medal 947. VG. B3d. $5.50

MARLOWE, Stephen. *Death Is My Comrade.* 1960. Gold Medal 986. 1st prtg. PBO. c/Charles: gga. VG. P7d. $7.50

MARLOWE, Stephen. *Drum Beat: Berlin.* Gold Medal K 1420. PBO. c/S Zuckerbert. My. VG. B5d. $4.50

MARLOWE, Stephen. *Francesca.* 1963. Gold Medal K 1285. 1st prtg. PBO. c/McGinnis: gga. VG. P7d. $7.50

MARLOWE, Stephen. *Mecca for Murder.* 1956. Gold Medal 575. c/gga. My. VG. B4d. $6.00

MARLOWE, Stephen. *Peril Is My Pay.* Gold medal 1018. G+. G5d. $3.00

MARLOWE, Stephen. *Second Longest Night.* 1960. Gold Medal 1003. 2nd edn. c/gga. My. VG+. B4d. $3.00

MARLOWE, Stephen. *Terror Is My Trade.* Gold Medal 813. G+. G5d. $3.50

MARLOWE, Stephen. *Violence Is My Business.* Gold Medal 1413. NF. B3d. $4.50

MARLOWE/O'DELL. *Raven Is a Blood Red Bird.* 1967. Gold Medal D 1874. PBO. VG. M6d. $4.50

MARLOWE/WILSON & WILSON. *Turn Left for Murder/Death Watch.* 1955. Ace D 89. PBO. c/Barton. My. VG. P6d. $6.50

MARMOR, Arnold. *Abnormal Desire.* Merit 642. PBO. VG+. B3d. $4.00

MARMOR, Arnold. *Chinese Streetwalker.* 1965. Playtime 718. PBO. NF. B6d. $15.00

MARMOR, Arnold. *Hell Cat.* 1961. Merit 531. PBO. c/gga. NF. B6a #75. $40.25

MARMOR, Arnold. *House of a Thousand Sins.* Tuxedo 121. PBO. VG+. B3d. $6.00

MARMOR, Arnold. *Sex Seekers.* Saber SA 77. VG+. B3d. $5.00

MARQUAND, John P. *Life at Happy Knoll.* Bantam 1781. VG+. B3d. $4.00

MARQUAND, John P. *Ming Yellow.* Jonathan J 54. VG+. B3d. $6.00

MARQUAND, John P. *Thank You, Mr Moto.* 1957. Bantam A 1691. 1st prtg. My. VG+. R5d. $3.00

MARQUAND, John P. *Think Fast, Mr Moto.* 1958. Bantam 1810. 1st prtg. My.VG. R5d. $2.00

MARQUAND, John P. *Think Fast, Mr Moto.* Bestseller B 124. My. G. B5d. $2.00

MARQUAND, John P. *Think Fast, Mr Moto.* 1985. Little Brown 54703. My. VG+. B5d. $4.00

MARQUAND, John P. *Think Fast, Mr Moto.* Pocket 59. VG. B3d. $10.00

MARQUAND, John P. *Warning Hill.* 1964. Pyramid X 1092. c/R Abbett. My. NF. B5d. $6.50

MARQUAND, John P. *Your Turn Mr Moto.* 1985. Little Brown 54697. My. NF. B5d. $5.00

MARQUIS, Don. *Archy & Mehitabel.* 1960. Dolphin C 26. 1st prtg. VG. P7d. $6.00

MARQUIS, Thomas B. *Warrior.* 1958. Corgi 538. 1st Bristish edn. VG+. B3a #24. $6.05

MARRIC, J.J. *Gideon of Scotland Yard.* Berkley G 122. MTI. G+. G5d. $6.50

MARRIC, J.J. *Gideon's Month.* 1965. Berkley F 1150. 1st prtg. VG+. R5d. $3.50

MARRIC, J.J. *Gideon's Night.* Popular 01429. My. VG. W2d. $3.25

MARRIC, J.J. *Gideon's Night.* 1963. Pyramid R 872. My. VG+. B4d. $6.00

MARRIC, J.J. *Gideon's Ride.* 1964. Berkley F 900. 1st prtg. My. VG. R5d. $4.00

MARRIC, J.J. *Gideon's Vote.* 1966. Berkley F 1193. 1st prtg. My. VG. R5d. $2.75

MARRIC, J.J. *Gideon's Wrath.* Popular 02479. My. VG+. B5d. $4.00

MARSDEN, Marsha. *Intimate.* 1961. Midwood Y 128. Fa. VG+. B4d. $18.00

MARSH, Ngaio. *Dead Water.* 1964. Bantam F 2829. 1st prtg. My. VG+. R5d. $2.50

MARSH, Ngaio. *Death in a White Tie.* 1942. Pocket 137. My. G+. B5d. $4.00

MARSH, Ngaio. *Died in the Wool.* Berkley G 529. VG. B3d. $4.00

MARSH, Ngaio. *Final Curtain.* 1948. Collins CD 371. 1st prtg. My. G+. R5d. $4.00

MARSH, Ngaio. *Hand in Glove.* 1963. Berkley F 777. c/photo. My. VG. B5d. $4.00

MARSH, Ngaio. *Killer Dolphin.* 1967. Berkley X 1441. 1st pb. My. VG+. B6d. $10.00

MARSH, Ngaio. *Man Lay Dead.* Berkley F 630. 1st prtg. My. VG. R5d. $3.25

MARSH, Ngaio. *Night at the Vulcan.* 1963. Berkley F 800. 1st prtg. My. VG. R5d. $4.00

MARSH, Ngaio. *Singing in the Shrouds.* 1964. Berkley F 949. 1st edn. My. VG+. R5d. $4.50

MARSH, Ngaio. *Singing in the Shrouds.* 1960. Berkley G 438. c/photo. My. VG. B5d. $4.00

MARSH, Peter. *Devil's Daughter.* 1949. Lion 16. 1st edn. PBO. c/Shoyer: gga. scarce. My. VG+. B6a #75. $30.25

MARSH, Rebecca. *Nurse of Ward 8.* Pyramid 1001. VG. B3d. $4.00

MARSHAK, Sondra. *Prometheus Design.* 1982. Pocket 83398. SF. F. W2d. $5.00

MARSHALL, Alan. *Bed of Shame.* 1964. Idle Hour IH 405. Ad. VG. B5d. $7.00

MARSHALL, Alan. *Flesh Nest.* 1964. Idle Hour IH 423. Ad. G+. B5d. $4.00

MARSHALL, Alan. *Lust Always Rings Twice.* 1967. Ember Library 391. PBO. c/Bonfils: gga. NF. B6a #76. $59.00

MARSHALL, Alan. *Lust Cure.* Nightstand NB 1758. PBO. c/gga. VG+. P6d. $5.00

MARSHALL, Alan. *Man Hungry.* Midwood 147. reprint. NF. B6d. $15.00

MARSHALL, Alan. *Off Limits.* 1961. Bedside BB 1202. Ad. G. B5d. $3.00

MARSHALL, Alan. *Passion Hunt.* Nightstand NB 174. VG+. I1d. $5.00

MARSHALL, Alan. *Queen of Cruelty.* Pleasure Reader 105. VG+. B3d. $7.50

MARSHALL, Alan. *Sally.* 1959. Midwood 22. PBO. c/Rader: gga. G. B6d. $3.50

MARSHALL, Alan. *Shame Sell.* Ember Library El 394. NF. M6d. $20.00

MARSHALL, Alan. *Shame Sell.* 1967. Ember Library EL 394. VG+. B3a #22. $22.00

MARSHALL, Alan. *Sins of Josh Young.* Nightstand NB 1768. PBO. VG+. P6d. $5.00

MARSHALL, Alan. *Swap Specialist.* 1967. Adult Book 410. PBO. c/Bonfils: gga. VG. B6a #80. $59.00

MARSHALL, Alan. *Swapfest.* 1968. Nightstand 1867. PBO. c/gga. scarce in condition. NF. B6a #74. $48.50

MARSHALL, Alan. *Wife Next Door.* 1960. Midwood 31. PBO. c/Bob Maguire: gga. G+. P6d. $3.50

MARSHALL, C. *Sex in the Family.* Barclay 7479. c/photo. VG+. B3d. $4.50

MARSHALL, C. *Swapping Game.* Barclay 7223. c/photo. NF. B3d. $6.00

MARSHALL, D.J. *Teenage Call Girl Ring.* 1970. Vega Book V 74. PBO. c/gga. NF. B6a #76. $38.50

MARSHALL, Edison. *Benjamin Blake, Son of Fury.* Dell 431. VG+. B3d. $4.50

MARSHALL, Edison. *Castle in the Swamp.* Dell 487. G+. G5d. $3.00

MARSHALL, Edison. *Forlorn Island.* Dell 364. VG. I1d. $4.00

MARSHALL, Edison. *Gentleman.* 1956. Cardinal C 233. 1st prtg. c/Binger: gga. VG+. P7d. $4.00

MARSHALL, Edison. *Gentleman.* 1963. Pyramid X 868. Fa. VG. B4d. $3.00

MARSHALL, Edison. *Jungle Hunting Thrills.* 1950. Dell 468. 1st edn. PBO. F. F2d. $15.00

MARSHALL, Edison. *Last Land.* 1972. Curtis 7227. 1st edn. PBO. F. P9d. $2.50

MARSHALL, Edison. *Riders of the Smoky Land.* 1950. Popular 242. We. VG. B4d. $5.00

MARSHALL, Edison. *Splendid Quest.* Dell 188. c/G Gregg. Fi. VG. B5d. $5.00

MARSHALL, Edison. *Upstart.* Dell 233. Fi. VG+. B5d. $6.00

MARSHALL, Edison. *Viking.* 1954. Dell D 139. c/gga. Fa. VG. B4d. $4.00

MARSHALL, Edison. *Voice of the Pack.* 1947. Popular 128. 1st pb. VG. B6d. $6.00

MARSHALL, Edison. *White Brigand.* 1947. Dell 144. c/E Sherwan. Fi. VG. B5d/I1d. $6.00

MARSHALL, Edison. *Yankee Pasha.* Dell 353. c/R Stanley. Fi. G+. B5d. $3.00

MARSHALL, Edison. *Yankee Pasha.* Dell 422. VG. I1d. $4.00

MARSHALL, J.R. *Carla.* Gold Medal 1173. VG. B3d. $6.00

MARSHALL, Marguerite Mooers. *Wilderness Nurse.* 1950. Pocket 746. c/I Dawson. Fi. VG. B5d. $3.00

MARSHALL, Mel. *Foxx's Herd.* 1981. Dell 12730. 1st edn. F. F2d. $7.00

MARSHALL, Rosamond. *Celeste, Gold Coast Virgin.* 1950. Dell 382. c/gga. Fa. VG. B4d. $8.00

MARSHALL, Rosamond. *Celeste, Gold Coast Virgin.* 1959. Pyramid G 428. reprints. Fa. VG. B4d. $2.50

MARSHALL, Rosamond. *Kitty.* Pocket 469. NF. I1d. $5.00

MARSHALL, Rosamond. *Kitty.* 1944. White Circle 99. Fi. G+. B5d. $3.50

MARSHALL, Rosamond. *Mistress of Rogues.* 1956. Popular 717. c/gga. Fa. G+. B4d. $3.00

MARSHALL, Rosamond. *Rib of the Hawk.* 1958. Popular G 258. 1st pb. c/Maguire. NF. B6d. $9.00

MARSHALL, Rosamond. *Rogue Cavalier.* 1957. Popular G 176. VG+. B3d. $4.50

MARSHALL, Rosamond. *Temptress.* 1952. Signet 976. c/gga. Fa. VG+. B4d. $4.00

MARSHE, Richard. *Woman Called Desire.* 1959. Berkley G 236. c/photo. VG. P6d. $3.50

MARSTEN, Richard. *Murder in the Navy.* Gold Medal 507. G+. G5d. $6.50

MARSTEN, Richard. *Murder in the Navy.* 1955. Gold Medal 507. PBO. My. VG. B6d. $12.50

MARSTEN, Richard. *Spiked Heel.* 1957. Crest S 178. VG. B3d. $6.00

MARSTEN, Richard. *Spiked Heel.* Pan G 192. VG+. B3d. $9.00

MARSTEN, Richard. *Vanishing Ladies.* Perma M 3097. VG. G5d. $4.00

MART, Ian Kennedy. *Regan & the Deal of the Century.* 1976. Futura 7399. TVTI. VG. P1d. $5.00

MARTELL, David. *Old Enough.* 1963. Midwood F 339. PBO. NF. B6d. $12.50

MARTIN, A.E. *Bridal Bed Murders.* Dell 840. c/W Rose. My. VG. B5d. $3.00

MARTIN, A.E. *Bridal Bed Murders.* Dell 840. VG+. G5d. $5.50

MARTIN, Andrew. *Unwilling Switchers.* 1969. Saber Book SA 156. PBO. c/gga. VG. B6a #76. $42.00

MARTIN, Astron Del. *One Against Time.* 1970. PB Library 63-270. PBO. c/Jerry Podwil. VG+. P6d. $2.00

MARTIN, Aylwin Lee. *Crimson Frame.* Gold Medal 253. G+. G5d. $4.00

MARTIN, Aylwin Lee. *Death on a Ferris Wheel.* Gold Medal 170. VG. G5d. $6.00

MARTIN, Aylwin Lee. *Fear Comes Calling.* Gold Medal 214. VG. B3d. $4.50

MARTIN, C. *Star.* Dominion 326. VG+. B3d. $4.50

MARTIN, Charles. *Raw Passion.* Uni-Book 16. VG+. B3d. $8.00

MARTIN, Chuck. *Bloody Kansas.* 1950. Avon 654. 1st edn. Hi. F. F2d. $10.00

MARTIN, Chuck. *Day of Vengeance.* 1959. Avon 841. 1st pb. c/Schaare. We. VG+. B6d. $9.00

MARTIN, Chuck. *Six-Gun Helltown.* Hillman 122. VG. B3d. $3.50

MARTIN, Chuck. *Tall in the Saddle.* 1958. Avon 828. We. F. B4d. $10.00

MARTIN, Chuck. *Texas Pride.* Graphic 86. PBO. VG+. B3d. $4.50

MARTIN, David. *Lie to Me.* 1991. Pocket 73876. 1st pb. F. B6d. $9.00

MARTIN, Don. *Don Martin Drops 13 Stories!* Warner 74-115. VG+. B3d. $4.50

MARTIN, Don. *Mad's Don Martin Bounces Back.* Warner 86-175. VG+. B3d. $4.50

MARTIN, E.A. *Portrait of Torment.* Newsstand U 163. VG. B3d. $4.00

MARTIN, G. *Shame.* Midwood 60513. VG+. B3d. $5.00

MARTIN, George. *Bells of St Mary's.* Bantam 103. MTI. VG+. B3d. $5.00

MARTIN, George. *Bells of St Mary's.* 1947. Bantam 103. MTI. c/Bergman & Crosby: photo. NF. B4d. $7.50

MARTIN, George. *Lady Said Yes.* Avon Monthly Novel 10. G+. B3d. $4.00

MARTIN, George. *Lady Said Yes.* 1949. Novel Library 35. c/photo. VG. P6d. $13.00

MARTIN, George. *Mark It With a Stone.* Eton 120. c/Olson. VG+. B6a #74. $44.00

MARTIN, George. *Song for Lya.* 1976. Avon 27581. 1st edn. SF. F. F2d. $17.00

MARTIN, H. *Lust Has No Bounds.* Saber SA 75. NF. B3d. $6.00

MARTIN, Jack. *Halloween II.* 1986. Zebra 89083. 1st prtg. VG. R5d. $1.25

MARTIN, Jay. *Sexy Egg.* 1969. Lancer. 1st edn. F. M1d. $8.00

MARTIN, John Bartlow. *Break Down the Walls.* Ballantine 77. NF. B3d. $5.00

MARTIN, John Bartlow. *Butcher's Dozen.* 1952. Signet 909. 1st prtg. c/Schaare: gga. VG. P7d. $6.00

MARTIN, John Bartlow. *Jimmy Hoffa's Hot.* 1959. Crest 340. 1st edn. c/photo. F. F2d. $9.00

MARTIN, John Bartlow. *My Life in Crime.* 1953. Signet 1033. c/James Meese. Bio. VG. B4d. $3.00

MARTIN, John Bartlow. *Why Did They Kill?* 1953. Ballantine 14. 1st edn. c/photo. Cr. F. F2d. $8.00

MARTIN, John Bartlow. *Why Did They Kill?* 1966. Bantam H 3258. Fi. VG. B5d. $2.50

MARTIN, Kay. *Bachelor Girl.* MacFadden 50-163. PBO. VG+. B3d. $4.50

MARTIN, Kay. *Divorcees.* Pyramid 750. c/Nappi. VG+. B3d. $5.50

MARTIN, Kay. *Taste of Passion.* 1960. Hillman 158. 1st edn. c/gga. F. F2d. $13.00

MARTIN, L. *Stand-In for Sex.* Bee Line 244. VG+. B3d. $5.00

MARTIN, Linda. *Prowling Wives.* 1967. Chevron 116. c/Bilbrew. VG+. B3a #22. $8.80

MARTIN, Ralph. *Man Who Haunted Himself.* 1970. Award 816. 1st edn. c/Roger Moore: photo. My. F. F2d. $12.50

MARTIN, Robert. *Tears for the Bride.* 1955. Bantam 1372. 1st prtg. My. G+. R5d. $2.00

MARTIN, Thom. *Serenade to Seduction.* 1960. Newsstand 508. Ad. VG. B5d. $4.50

MARTIN & LEWIS. *Naked Eye.* Pocket 770. VG+. G5d. $8.00

MARTIN/TOMPKINS. *Law for a Tombstone/One Against a Bullet Horde.* 1954. Ace D 42. PBO. VG. B3d. $8.00

MARTIN/TOMPKINS. *Law for Tombstone/One Against a Bullet Horde.* 1954. Ace D 42. PBO. c/Sanuders. scarce. NF. B6a #80. $63.50

MARTINEZ, Ray J. *Mysterious Marie Laveau: Voodoo Queen.* Hope. SF. F. W2d. $6.00

MARVIN, Susan. *Women Around RFK.* 1967. Lancer 73-661. NF. VG. B5d. $5.00

MARX, Arthur. *Life With Groucho.* PopularPC 600. c/photo. VG+. B3d. $5.00

MARX, Groucho. *Groucho & Me.* 1960. Dell 1st Edn F 112. c/G Marx photo. NF. VG. B5d. $4.00

MASEFIELD, John. *Selected Poems.* Armed Service S 820. VG. B3d. $5.50

MASIN, Herman L. *Curve Ball Laughs.* 1958. Pyramid G 331. c/W Mullin. NF. G+. B5d. $3.50

MASON, David. *Deep Gods.* 1973. Lancer 78-762. 1st edn. VG. P9d. $1.50

MASON, David. *Kavin's World.* 1969. Lancer 75-372. SF. VG. W2d. $3.25

MASON, David. *Kavin's World.* 1969. Lancer 75-372. 1st edn. F. M1d. $7.00

MASON, Douglas R. *Eight Against Utopia.* 1967. PB Library 52-699. c/J Gaughan. SF. VG+. B5d. $4.00

MASON, Douglas R. *Eight Against Utopia.* 1970. PB Library 63-496. SF. VG. B4d. $3.00

MASON, Douglas R. *Matrix.* Ballantine 01816. PBO. VG+. B3d. $5.00

MASON, Douglas R. *Resurrection of Roger Diment.* 1972. Ballantine 02573. SF. VG+. B4d. $3.00

MASON, Douglas R. *Ring of Violence.* 1969. Avon S 399. PBO. SF. VG. B5d. $2.50

MASON, Douglas R. *Ring of Violence.* 1969. Avon S 399. SF. F. W2d. $6.00

MASON, Douglas R. *Satellite 54-Zero.* 1971. Ballantine 02108. SF. VG+. B4d. $3.75

MASON, Ernst. *Tiberius.* Ballantine 361. PBO. VG. B3d. $4.00

MASON, F. Van Wyck. *Barbarians.* 1954. Pocket 1024. Fa. VG. B4d. $3.00

MASON, F. Van Wyck. *Budapest Parade Murders.* Bestseller Mystery B 63. My. VG+. M3d. $6.00

MASON, F. Van Wyck. *Cairo Garter Murders.* 1945. Century 70. 1st edn. PBO. G+. F2d/I1d. $5.00

MASON, F. Van Wyck. *Captain Judas.* Pocket 1076. PBO. VG+. B3d. $5.00

MASON, F. Van Wyck. *China Sea Murders.* 1958. Pocket 1219. c/gga. My. VG+. B4d. $5.00

MASON, F. Van Wyck. *End of Track.* 1963. Pocket 6203. We. VG+. B5d. $4.00

MASON, F. Van Wyck. *Gracious Lily Affair.* 1958. Pocket 1223. 1st pb. c/Meese. NF. B6d. $12.50

MASON, F. Van Wyck. *Hong Kong Airbase Murders.* 1943. De Novel Classic 9. 1st pb. VG+. B6d. $9.00

MASON, F. Van Wyck. *Lysander.* 1956. Pocket 1143. PBO. c/J Meese. My. VG. B5d. $4.00

MASON, F. Van Wyck. *Manilla Galleon.* Arrow 723. VG+. B3d. $8.00

MASON, F. Van Wyck. *Proud New Flags.* 1954. Cardinal GC 17. 1st prtg. c/Meese: gga. VG. P7d. $4.00

MASON, F. Van Wyck. *Saigon Singer.* 1948. Bantam 311. c/gga. My. VG+. B4d. $8.00

MASON, F. Van Wyck. *Secret Mission to Bangkok.* 1961. Pocket 6065. My. NF. B5d. $5.00

MASON, F. Van Wyck. *Singapore Exile Murders.* Pocket 129. VG. G5d. $8.00

MASON, F. Van Wyck. *Spider House.* Handi-Book 98. VG. I1d. $10.00

MASON, F. Van Wyck. *Sulu Sea Murders.* 1958. Pocket 1201. 1st prtg. c/Meese: gga. VG. P7d. $5.50

MASON, F. Van Wyck. *Three Harbours.* 1952. Cardinal C 57. 1st prtg. c/Chiriaka: gga. VG. P7d. $4.00

MASON, F. Van Wyck. *Wild Drums Beat.* 1954. Pocket 977. c/R Cardiff. Fi. VG. B5d. $4.00

MASON, R. *Forever Is Today.* Gold Medal 237. VG+. B3d. $8.00

MASON, R. *Someone & Felicia Warwick.* Gold Medal 1248. NF. B3d. $6.00

MASON, R. *Wind Cannot Read.* Pan G 119. MTI. VG. B3d. $5.50

MASON, S.E. *Crimson Feather.* Dell 207. VG. B3d. $5.00

MASSON, Rene. *Cage of Darkness.* 1952. Bantam 1054 c/Wm Gropper. JD. VG. P6d. $3.00

MASSON, Rene. *Cage of Darkness.* 1952. Bantam 1054. JD. F. P1d. $27.00

MASSON, Rene. *Cage of Darkness.* 1952. Bantam 1054. VG+. B3d. $6.00

MASTERS, Doug. *TNT: The Beast.* 1985. Charter 05153. 1st edn. My. F. F2d. $7.50

MASTERS, John. *Breaking Strain.* 1968. Dell 0794. 1st prtg. c/Adams: gga. VG. P7d. $4.00

MASTERS, John. *Bugles & a Tiger.* 1958. Bantam F 1714. 1st pb. Bio. VG. B6d. $5.00

MASTERS, John. *Coromandel!* 1956. Bantam F 1416. 1st pb. VG+. B6d. $8.00

MASTERS, John. *Lotus & the Wind.* 1955. Bantam A 1335. 1st pb. c/Barye. NF. B6d. $12.50

MASTERS, John. *To the Coral Strand.* Newstand 1168. c/sgn. VG. B3d. $4.00

MASTERS, L. *Naked Desire.* Bedside 823. VG+. B3d. $6.00

MASTERSON, R. *No Prudes Wanted.* Magenta 111. VG+. B3d. $5.00

MASTERSON, Whit. *Cry in the Night.* 1956. Bantam 1487. 1st pb. My. FN. B6d. $12.50

MASTERSON, Whit. *Dead, She Was Beautiful.* Bantam 1543. 1st pb. G+. M6d. $4.00

MASTERSON, Whit. *Hammer in His Hand.* Bantam J 2513. 1st pb. VG. M6d. $4.50

MASTERSON, Whit. *Warning Shot.* Popular 60-8029. MTI. c/D Janssen: photo. My. VG. B5d. $5.00

MASUR, Harold Q. *Big Money.* 1956. Dell 874. 1st prtg. My. G+. R5d. $1.75

MASUR, Harold Q. *Bury Me Deep.* 1948. Pocket 558. 1st pb. My. VG+. B6d. $12.50

MASUR, Harold Q. *Dolls Are Murder.* 1957. Lion LB 152. PBO. My. VG+. B4d. $16.50

MASUR, Harold Q. *Mourning After.* 1981. Raven 373-60062-3-225. VG. P6d. $2.00

MASUR, Harold Q. *Murder on Broadway (Last Gamble).* Dell D 298. G+. G5d. $3.50

MASUR, Harold Q. *Name Is Jordan.* 1962. Pyramid F 720. 1st prtg. PBO. c/Lesser: gga. VG. P7d. $8.50

MASUR, Harold Q. *Send Another Hearse.* 1965. Dell 1st Edn 7737. My. VG+. B4d. $4.00

MASUR, Harold Q. *Send Another Hearse.* 1965. Dell 1st Edn 7737. 1st pb. My. NF. B6d. $5.00

MASUR, Harold Q. *So Rich, So Lovely, & So Dead.* 1953. Pocket 998. 1st prtg. c/Zuckerberg: gga. VG. P7d. $6.00

MASUR, Harold Q. *Suddenly a Corpse.* Pocket 704. VG. B3d. $4.50

MASUR, Harold Q. *Suddenly a Corpse.* Pocket 704. VG+. I1d. $6.00

MASUR, Harold Q. *Tall, Dark & Deadly.* Dell D 232. VG. G5d. $5.00

MASUR, Harold Q. *You Can't Live Forever.* 1959. Dell D 329. c/McGinnis. VG+. B3d/I1d. $4.00

MASUR, Harold Q. *You Can't Live Forever.* 1959. Dell D 329. 1st prtg. My. G+. R5d. $1.75

MASUR, Harold Q. *You Can't Live Forever.* 1952. Pocket 860. c/F McCarthy. My. VG. B5d. $4.00

MASUR, Harold Q. *You Can't Live Forever.* 1970. Pyramid T 2340. c/gga. My. VG+. B4d. $3.00

MATCHA, Jack. *Prowler in the Night.* 1959. Gold Medal 873. 1st edn. My. F. F2d. $14.00

MATCHA, Jack. *Prowler in the Night.* 1959. Gold Medal 873. VG. B3d. $4.00

MATHER, Berkely. *Genghis Khan.* 1965. Dell 2866. MTI. VG+. B4d. $3.00

MATHESON, Richard. *Beardless Warriors.* Bantam H 3566. MTI. reprint. VG+. B6d. $8.00

MATHESON, Richard. *Fury on Sunday.* 1953. Lion 180. PBO. rarest. VG. B6a #77. $368.50

MATHESON, Richard. *Fury on Sunday.* 1953. Lion 180. PBO. VG. B3a #24. $363.00

MATHESON, Richard. *Hell House.* 1972. Bantam N 7277. 1st edn. PBO. Go. VG. P6d. $2.50

MATHESON, Richard. *I Am Legend.* 1964. Bantam J 2744. 1st prtg. SF. VG. R5d. $4.00

MATHESON, Richard. *I Am Legend.* 1971. Berkley S 2041. 2nd prtg. MTI. SF. VG. R5d. $2.50

MATHESON, Richard. *I Am Legend.* Corgi 854. scarce. NF. B6a #76. $88.25

MATHESON, Richard. *I Am Legend.* 1954. Gold Medal 417. PBO. c/sgn. scarce. SF. VG+. B6a #79. $67.25

MATHESON, Richard. *I Am Legend.* 1954. Gold Medal 417. PBO. c/sgn. VG. B3a #24. $32.30

MATHESON, Richard. *I Am Legend.* 1954. Gold Medal 417. 1st edn. NF. M1d. $85.00

MATHESON, Richard. *I Am Legend.* Gold Medal 643. 2nd prtg. VG. B3d. $6.00

MATHESON, Richard. *Ride the Nightmare.* 1959. Avon 301K. PBO. c/photo. G+. P6d. $32.50

MATHESON, Richard. *Shock II.* Dell 7829. c/sgn. VG. B3d. $8.00

MATHESON, Richard. *Shock II.* Dell 7829. 1st pb. G+. M6d. $3.00

MATHESON, Richard. *Shock II.* 1964. Dell 7829. 1st edn. F. I1d. $20.00

MATHESON, Richard. *Shock III.* 1979. Berkley O 4209. SF. G+. B5d. $3.00

MATHESON, Richard. *Shock III.* 1966. Dell 7830. SF. VG. W2d. $7.50

MATHESON, Richard. *Shock III.* 1966. Dell 7830. 1st edn. F. M1d. $25.00

MATHESON, Richard. *Shock III.* 1966. Dell 7830. 1st edn. NF. I1d. $18.00

MATHESON, Richard. *Shock Waves.* Dell 7831. 1st prtg. G. S1d. $2.00

MATHESON, Richard. *Shock Waves.* 1970. Dell 7831. 1st edn. NF. I1d. $18.00

MATHESON, Richard. *Shock Waves.* 1970. Dell 7831. 1st prtg. SF. VG. W2d. $5.50

MATHESON, Richard. *Shock.* 1979. Berkley 04095. SF. VG+. M3d. $5.00

MATHESON, Richard. *Shock.* 1961. Dell 1st Edn B 195. F. I1d/M1d. $20.00

MATHESON, Richard. *Shock!* Dell 1st Edn B 195. VG. B3d. $6.00

MATHESON, Richard. *Shock!* Dell 7828. VG. M6d. $5.00

MATHESON, Richard. *Shores of Space.* 1957. Bantam A 1571. 1st edn. F. M1d. $30.00

MATHESON, Richard. *Shores of Space.* 1979. Berkley 04024. SF. F. W2d. $5.00

MATHESON, Richard. *Shores of Space.* 1965. Corgi 7230. c/reissue. VG. B3d. $6.00

MATHESON, Richard. *Shrinking Man.* 1979. Berkley O 4021. SF. VG. B5d. $4.50

MATHESON, Richard. *Shrinking Man.* 1956. Gold Medal S 577. PBO. c/Matheson: sgn. rare. SF. NF. B6a #80. $165.00

MATHESON, Richard. *Shrinking Man.* 1956. Gold Medal S 577. 1st edn. F. M1d. $90.00

MATHESON, Richard. *Shrinking Man.* 1956. Gold Medal S 577. 1st prtg. SF. G+. W2d. $25.00

MATHESON, Richard. *Stir of Echoes.* Avon S 392. 1st prtg. VG. S1d. $4.00

MATHESON, Richard. *Stir of Echoes.* 1959. Crest S 308. 1st edn. PBO. c/Matheson: sgn. scarce. Fa. NF. B6a #80. $46.75

MATHESON, Richard. *Stir of Echoes.* 1959. Crest S 308. 1st pb edn. F. M1d. $25.00

MATHESON, Richard. *Third From the Sun.* Bantam J 2487. 1st prtg. VG. S1d. $8.00

MATHESON, Richard. *Third From the Sun.* 1955. Bantam 1294. 1st edn. scarce. SF. F. F2d. $28.00

MATHESON, Richard. *What Dreams May Come.* 1979. Berkley 4202. 1st edn. PBO. scarce. Fa. VG. B6a #75. $43.00

MATHEWS, Willard. *Making It Bigger.* 1972. Berkley 2143. 1st edn. c/photo. F. F2d. $12.00

MATHIESON, Theodore. *Devil & Ben Franklin.* 1962. Popular K 1. 1st prtg. SF. G. W2d. $3.00

MATSON, Norman. *Bats in the Belfry.* 1949. Popular 200. 1st pb. Fa. VG. B6d. $7.50

MATTHEWS, Allen R. *Assault.* Perma S 258. VG+. B3d. $4.50

MATTHEWS, Allen R. *Assault.* 1958. Pocket 1207. c/R Schultz. Fi. VG. B5d. $4.00

MATTHEWS, Clayton. *Corrupter.* 1964. Monarch 461. Ad. G+. B5d. $4.00

MATTHEWS, Clayton. *Corrupter.* 1964. Monarch 461. 1st edn. c/gga. My. F. F2d. $14.00

MATTHEWS, Clayton. *Rage of Desire.* 1960. Monarch 164. Ad. VG. B5d. $6.00

MATTHEWS, Kevin. *Pagan Empress.* 1964. Midwood 348. PBO. VG+. B3a #24. $17.60

MATTHEWS, Leone. *Kind of Marriage.* 1964. Lancer 72-773. 1st edn. c/gga. F. F2d. $12.00

MATTHEWS & ROCHE. *My Name Is Violence.* 1959. Avon 847. PBO. c/gga. Cr. VG+. B6d. $8.00

MATTHIESSEN, Peter. *Passionate Seekers.* Avon 753. VG+. B3d. $4.50

MAUGHAM, Robin. *Line on Ginger.* Avon 333. G. G5d. $7.00

MAUGHAM, Robin. *November Reef.* Monarch 412. NF. B3d. $7.00

MAUGHAM, Robin. *November Reef.* 1964. Monarch 412. Ad. G+. B5d. $3.50

MAUGHAM, Robin. *Rough & the Smooth.* Avon 464. VG+. B3d. $6.00

MAUGHAM, Robin. *Servant.* 1950. Avon 233. c/B Lannon. Fi. G+. B5d. $3.00

MAUGHAM, W. Somerset. *Ashenden or the British Agent.* Avon T 420. c/S Kossim. My. VG. B5d. $2.50

MAUGHAM, W. Somerset. *Ashenden or the British Agent.* Avon T 420. 1st prtg. My. VG+. R5d. $3.25

MAUGHAM, W. Somerset. *Avon Book of W Somerset Maugham.* 1946. Avon 115. Fi. G+. B5d. $4.00

MAUGHAM, W. Somerset. *Beachcomber.* Dell 10¢ 16. VG+. B3d. $8.00

MAUGHAM, W. Somerset. *Cakes & Ale.* Avon 50. VG+. B3d. $7.00

MAUGHAM, W. Somerset. *Favorite Stories.* Avon T 412. c/photo. Fi. VG. B5d. $2.50

MAUGHAM, W. Somerset. *Fools & Their Folly.* 1949. Avon 188. 1st pb. c/Barton: gga. VG. B6d. $8.00

MAUGHAM, W. Somerset. *Gentleman in the Parlour.* 1947. Ace 129. c/gga. Fa. VG. B4d/I1d. $5.00

MAUGHAM, W. Somerset. *Hour Before the Dawn.* Popular SP 75. NF. B3d. $5.00

MAUGHAM, W. Somerset. *Letter & Two Other Plays.* Pan GP 10. VG. B3d. $8.00

MAUGHAM, W. Somerset. *Liza of Lambeth.* 1947. Avon 139. VG. P6d. $2.00

MAUGHAM, W. Somerset. *Moon & Sixpence.* Bantam 810. VG. B3d. $4.00

MAUGHAM, W. Somerset. *Narrow Corner.* Avon 41. VG. B3d. $7.00

MAUGHAM, W. Somerset. *Narrow Corner.* 1944. Avon 42. Fi. G. B5d. $4.00

MAUGHAM, W. Somerset. *Narrow Corner.* Bantam 909. VG+. B3d. $5.00

MAUGHAM, W. Somerset. *Painted Veil.* 1957. Cardinal C 261. MTI. VG. B4d. $2.00

MAUGHAM, W. Somerset. *Point of Honour.* Avon 364. G+. I1d. $4.50

MAUGHAM, W. Somerset. *Quartet.* Avon 203. VG. B3d. $4.50

MAUGHAM, W. Somerset. *Rain.* Dell 10¢ 2. VG. B3d. $5.00

MAUGHAM, W. Somerset. *Romantic Young Lady.* 1950. Avon SSM 51. VG. B3a #24. $26.65

MAUGHAM, W. Somerset. *South Sea Stories.* 1956. Perma M 4056. c/L Manso. Fi. VG. B5d. $3.50

MAUGHAM, W. Somerset. *South Sea Stories.* Perma P 74. VG. I1d. $3.00

MAUGHAM, W. Somerset. *Theatre.* 1944. Avon 56. VG. I1d. $15.00

MAUGHAM, W. Somerset. *Traitor.* Belmont L 511. VG. B3d. $4.00

MAUGHAM, W. Somerset. *Trio.* Avon 331. VG+. I1d. $6.00

MAUGHAM, W. Somerset. *Woman of the World.* 1951. Bantam 949. c/Stahl: gga. Fa. VG+. B4d. $3.00

MAUGHAM, W. Somerset. *29 by Maugham.* Shortstory 1. VG. B3d. $5.00

MAUND, Alfred. *Big Boxcar.* 1957. Ballantine 250. Drug. VG+. B4d. $12.00

MAUND, Alfred. *Blood of a Lion.* 1964. Lancer 74-837. 1st pb. NF. B6d. $8.00

MAURETTE, Marcelle. *Anastasia.* 1956. Signet S 1356. MTI. c/I Bergman & Y Brynner: photo. Nfi. VG. B5d. $5.50

MAURIAC, Francois. *Desert of Love.* Bantam 1039. VG. B3d. $4.00

MAURIAC, Francois. *Flesh & Blood.* 1961. Dell 1st Edn F 138. Fa. VG+. B4d. $3.00

MAUROIS, Andre. *Ariel.* 1938. Penguin 1. 7th edn. dust jacket. Nfi. VG. P1d. $15.00

MAXON, P.B. *Waltz of Death.* 1944. Bart House 9. 1st prtg. c/gga. VG. B3d. $7.00

MAXWELL, A. *Art of Survival.* Bantam 28479. G+. G5d. $6.50

MAXWELL, A. *Change.* Popular 316. SF. VG. B5d. $3.00

MAXWELL, A. *Fire Dancer.* 1982. Signet AE 1939. SF. VG. W2d. $3.50

MAXWELL, A. *Gatsby's Vineyard.* Bantam 27409. VG. G5d. $6.50

MAXWELL, A. *Just Another Day in Paradise.* Bantam. VG. G5d. $5.50

MAXWELL, B. *Forbidden Nectar.* Playtime 648. VG. B3d. $5.50

MAXWELL, Bob. *Jaded Sex.* 1963. Playtime 636S. 1st prtg. PBO. c/gga. VG. P7d. $5.00

MAXWELL, Bob. *Tangled Passions.* 1963. Playtime 632. VG. B3d. $5.00

MAXWELL, Bob. *Tangled Passions.* 1963. Playtime 632. 1st edn. c/gga. F. F2d. $9.00

MAXWELL, G. *Girl From Underground.* Beacon 1036. VG. B3d. $3.50

MAXWELL, J.K. *Flank Assault.* Badger WW 116. VG+. B3d. $7.00

MAY, Julian. *Adversary.* 1985. Ballantine 31422. 1st pb. c/Whelan. SF. VG+. B6d. $3.00

MAYBURY, Anne. *Shadow of a Stranger.* 1966. Ace K 251. 1st prtg. VG. R5d. $1.75

MAYBURY, Anne. *Stay Until Tomorrow.* 1966. Ace K 277. 1st prtg. My. VG. R5d. $1.50

MAYER, Frederick. *Our Troubled Youth.* 1960. Bantam A 2088. JD. VG+. P1d. $15.50

MAYFAIR, Franklin. *Over My Dead Body.* 1965. Book Co of America 009. 1st prtg. My. VG. B5d. $4.00

MAYFIELD, Julian. *Hit.* 1959. Pocket 1229. c/Docktor. My. VG. B5d. $4.00

MAYHAR, Ardath. *Seekers of Shar-Nuhn.* 1982. Ace 75877. SF. VG. W2d. $3.75

MAYHAR, Ardath. *Soul Singer of Tyrnos.* 1983. Ace 77590. SF. F. W2d. $4.50

MAYNELL, Laurence. *Virgin Luck.* Avon G 1295. VG. G5d. $3.00

MAYO, Dallas. *All Together Now.* 1965. Midwood 32-578. 1st edn. c/Rader: gga. F. F2d. $12.50

MAYO, Dallas. *Everybody Welcome.* 1963. Midwood F 267. VG+. P6d. $6.00

MAYO, Dallas. *Lesbian Interlude.* Midwood 60608. VG. B3d. $4.00

MAYO, Dallas. *Pagan Summer.* 1965. Midwood 32-465. PBO. Ad. VG+. B5d. $12.00

MAYO, Dallas. *Preety Puppet.* 1964. Midwood 371. PBO. c/Rader. NF. B3a #21. $27.95

MAYO, Dallas. *Scandal.* Midwood Y 158. PBO. VG. M6d. $8.50

MAYO, Dallas. *Silky.* 1964. Midwood 32-418. 2nd edn. Ad. NF. B5d. $7.00

MAYO, Dallas. *Women's Ecstasy.* Midwood 61447. VG. M6d. $5.00

MAYO, James. *Hammerhead.* 1965. Dell 3391. 1st prtg. MTI. My. VG. R5d. $1.75

MAYO, Jim. *Quickness of the Hand.* 1959. Pan G 203. VG. B3d. $7.00

MAYO, Jim. *Utah Blaine.* 1954. Ace D 48. PBO. c/Saunders. VG. B6d. $40.00

MAYSE, Arthur. *Perilous Passage.* 1950. Pocket 727. c/J Bingham. My. VG. B5d. $4.00

MCALLISTER & RILEY. *Bedside Companion to Agatha Christie.* 1979. Ungar 6733. dust jacket. Nfi. VG. P1d. $15.00

MCBAIN, Ed. *'Til Death.* 1960. Perma M 4166. 1st pb. My. G+. B6d. $3.00

MCBAIN, Ed. *'Til Death.* 1960. Perma M 4166. 1st pb. VG. M6d. $5.00

MCBAIN, Ed. *Ax.* 1965. Pocket 50019. My. VG+. B3d/B4d. $4.00

MCBAIN, Ed. *Blood Relatives.* 1978. Bantam 11759. My. F. W2d. $4.25

MCBAIN, Ed. *Death of a Nurse.* 1964. Perma M 4306. My. NF. B4d. $6.00

MCBAIN, Ed. *Doll.* 1966. Dell 2086. My. VG+. B4d. $6.00

MCBAIN, Ed. *Eight Black Horse.* 1986. Avon 70029. 1st prtg. My. F. W2d. $4.00

MCBAIN, Ed. *Empty Hours.* Pan M 4271. VG. B3d. $4.00

MCBAIN, Ed. *Give the Boys a Great Big Hand.* 1968. Dell 2909. c/gga. My. VG+. B4d. $4.00

MCBAIN, Ed. *Give the Boys a Great Big Hand.* 1960. Perma M 4187. My. VG+. B4d. $8.00

MCBAIN, Ed. *Goldilocks.* 1979. Corgi 11090. VG+. B3d. $6.00

MCBAIN, Ed. *Guns.* 1978. Bantam 11890. My. VG+. W2d. $4.00

MCBAIN, Ed. *Hail to the Chief.* 1987. Avon 70370. 1st prtg. My. F. W2d. $4.25

MCBAIN, Ed. *Heat.* 1983. Ballantine 30673. 1st prtg. My. F. W2d. $4.50

MCBAIN, Ed. *Killer's Choice.* 1975. Ballantine 24443. My. VG. B5d. $3.00

MCBAIN, Ed. *Killer's Payoff.* 1958. Perma M 3113. 1st prtg. PBO. c/Schulz: gga. VG. P7d. $10.00

MCBAIN, Ed. *Killer's Payoff.* 1974. Signet Q 5939. 1st prtg. My. VG. W2d. $3.50

MCBAIN, Ed. *Killer's Wedge.* 1959. Perma M 4150. c/gga. My. VG+. B4d. $7.50

MCBAIN, Ed. *Killer's Wedge.* 1959. Perma M 4150. G+. G5d. $3.00

MCBAIN, Ed. *Killer's Wedge.* 1959. Perma M 4150. 1st pb. VG. M6d. $5.00

MCBAIN, Ed. *King's Ransom.* Perma M 4181. G+. G5d. $4.50

MCBAIN, Ed. *Lady, Lady, I Did It!* 1962. Perma M 4253. c/gga. My. VG. B4d. $6.00

MCBAIN, Ed. *Lady Killer.* 1958. Perma M 3119. PBO. My. VG+. B6d. $13.50

MCBAIN, Ed. *Like Love.* Perma M 4289. NF. l1d. $8.00

MCBAIN, Ed. *Mugger.* 1986. Avon 70384. 3rd prtg. My. F. W2d. $4.00

MCBAIN, Ed. *Mugger.* 1975. Ballantine 24656. My. VG+. B5d. $4.00

MCBAIN, Ed. *Mugger.* 1962. Perma M 4266. 2nd prtg. TVTI. VG. R5d. $2.00

MCBAIN, Ed. *Pusher.* 1973. Signet Q 5705. 1st prtg. My. F. W2d. $4.25

MCBAIN, Ed. *See Them Die.* Perma M 4229. VG+. G5d. $10.00

MCBAIN, Ed. *Ten Plus One.* 1964. Perma M 4304. My. VG+. B4d/P7d. $5.00

MCBAIN, Ed. *80 Million Eyes.* 1975. Ballantine 24604. My. VG. B5d. $3.00

MCCAFFREY, Anne. *Cooking Out of This World.* 1973. Ballantine 23413. PBO. extremely scarce. SF. VG+. B6a #79. $73.00

MCCAFFREY, Anne. *Cooking Out of This World.* 1973. Ballantine 23413. VG+. B3a #22. $33.00

MCCAFFREY, Anne. *Decision at Doona.* 1975. Ballantine 24416. 2nd edn. F. P9d. $3.00

MCCAFFREY, Anne. *Dinosaur Planet.* Ballantine 27245. 1st prtg. VG. S1d. $2.50

MCCAFFREY, Anne. *Dragon Quest.* 1971. Ballantine. 1st edn. NF. M1d. $10.00

MCCAFFREY, Anne. *Dragonflight.* 1968. Ballantine. 1st edn. NF. M1d. $8.00

MCCAFFREY, Anne. *Dragonquest Volume #2.* 1971. Ballantine 2245. 1st edn. PBO. F. P9d. $3.00

MCCAFFREY, Anne. *Dragonsong.* 1977. Bantam 10300. 1st prtg. SF. VG. R5d. $1.50

MCCAFFREY, Anne. *Get Off the Unicorn.* 1980. Ballantine 28508. 6th prtg. SF. F. W2d. $5.00

MCCAFFREY, Anne. *Restoree.* Ballantine U 6108. PBO. VG. B3d. $5.00

MCCAFFREY, Anne. *Restoree.* 1967. Ballantine. 1st edn. F. M1d. $12.00

MCCAFFREY, Anne. *Ring of Fear.* Dell 7445. c/sgn. VG. B3d. $6.50

MCCAFFREY, Anne. *To Ride Pegasus.* 1973. Ballantine. 1st edn. F. M1d. $12.00

MCCAGUE, James. *Big Ivy.* Ace D 184. VG. B3d. $5.00

MCCAIG, Robert. *Burntwood Men.* Ace F 316. VG+. B3d. $4.50

MCCAIG, Robert. *Danger West!* Dell 884. VG. B3d. $4.00

MCCAIG, Robert. *Devil's Band.* 1980. Zebra 89083. 1st edn. We. F. F2d. $7.50

MCCAIG, Robert. *Haywire Town.* 1956. Bantam 1435. 1st pb. We. VG+. B6d. $8.00

MCCAIG, Robert. *Shadow Maker.* 1970. Ace 76015. 1st edn. We. F. F2d. $9.00

MCCAIG, Robert. *Toll Mountain.* 1954. Pennant P 53. My. VG. B5d. $5.00

MCCANN, Edson. *Preferred Risk.* 1962. Dell R 114. 1st edn. F. P9d. $2.50

MCCANN, Edson. *Preferred Risk.* 1955. Dell. 1st pb edn. F. M1d. $15.00

MCCARTHY, Gary. *Silver Shot.* 1981. Bantam 14477. 1st edn. We. F. F2d. $7.50

MCCARTHY, Joe edt. *Fred Allen's Letters.* 1966. Pocket 75110. Nfi. NF. B5d. $4.00

MCCARTHY, Justin. *Well Done, Brother Juniper.* 1965. Pocket 45024. Hu. VG+. B4d. $3.00

MCCARTHY, Justin. *Whimsical World of Brother Juniper.* 1963. Pocket 6216. Hu. VG+. B4d. $3.00

MCCARY, Reed. *Kiss & Kill.* Avon 777. My. VG+. B5d. $5.50

MCCARY, Reed. *Sleep With the Devil.* 1952. Original Digest 713. PBO. c/gga. rare. VG+. B6a #77. $82.50

MCCAULEY, Kirby. *Frights.* 1977. Warner 79815. 1st prtg. SF. VG. W2d. $4.75

MCCLARY, Thomas Calvert. *Rebirth.* 1944. Bart House 6. PBO. SF. G+. B5d. $8.00

MCCLARY, Thomas Calvert. *Rebirth.* 1944. Bart House 6. VG+. B3a #21. $12.90

MCCLARY/ST. CLAIR. *Three Thousand Years/Green Queen.* 1956. Ace D 176. PBO. c/E Valigursky. SF. G+. B5d. $5.00

MCCLARY/ST. CLAIR. *Three Thousand Years/Green Queen.* 1956. Ace D 176. 1st prtg. PBO. c/gga. SF. VG. P7d. $7.50

MCCLINTOCK, Marshall edt. *Women on the Wall.* Pyramid 118. PBO. c/J Paul: Fi. G+. B5d. $7.50

MCCLOY, Helen. *Better Off Dead.* 1951. Dell 34. c/Stanley. My. VG+. B4d. $16.00

MCCLOY, Helen. *Dance of Death.* 1944. Dell 33. G+. G5d. $9.00

MCCLOY, Helen. *Dance of Death.* 1944. Dell 33. 1st edn. PBO. c/G Gregg. scarce. VG+. B6a #80. $55.00

MCCLOY, Helen. *Deadly Truth.* 1946. Dell 107. G+. G5d. $6.50

MCCLOY, Helen. *Deadly Truth.* 1946. Dell 107. 1st prtg. VG. P7d. $12.50

MCCLOY, Helen. *Do Not Disturb.* Dell 261. VG+. B3d. $6.00

MCCLOY, Helen. *Man in the Moonlight.* Dell 72. G. G5d. $3.00

MCCLOY, Helen. *One That Got Away.* Dell 355. VG. G5d. $8.00

MCCLOY, Helen. *Panic.* 1950. Dell 369. My. VG. B4d. $4.00

MCCLOY, Helen. *She Walks Alone.* Dell 430. c/B Fleming. My. VG. B5d. $4.00

MCCLOY, Helen. *Through a Glass, Darkly.* 1950. Dell. 1st pb edn. F. M1d. $10.00

MCCLOY, Helen. *Two-Thirds of a Ghost.* Dell D 228. VG. B3d. $3.50

MCCLOY, Helen. *Unfinished Crime.* Graphic 113. VG. B3d. $4.00

MCCLOY, Helen. *Who's Calling?* 1947. Dell 151. 1st edn. PBO. c/Gregg. scarce. NF. B6a #76. $48.50

MCCLOY, Helen. *Who's Calling?* Dell 151. 1st prtg. My. VG+. R5d. $12.00

MCCLOY, Helen. *Who's Calling?* 1947. Dell 151. 1st prtg. VG. P7d. $9.00

MCCOLLUM, Michael. *Antares Passage.* 1987. Ballantine 32314. 1st prtg. SF. VG+. W2d. $3.25

MCCOLLUM, Michael. *Greater Infinity.* 1982. Ballantine 30167. 1st prtg. SF. VG. R5d. $2.00

MCCOMAS, J. Francis. *Special Wonder: Volume #1.* 1971. Beagle 95044. SF. VG. W2d. $3.50

MCCOMAS & HEALY. *Adventures in Time & Space.* 1954. Pennant P 44. SF. VG. B4d. $6.00

MCCOMB, Katherine. *Princess of White Starch.* 1963. Ace D 571. 1st prtg. PBO. c/gga. VG+. P7d. $4.00

MCCONNAUGHEY, James. *Three for the Money.* 1955. Pocket 1050. c/J Meese. My. VG. B5d. $5.00

MCCONNAUGHEY, Susanne. *Point Venus.* 1952. Popular 112. c/gga. Fa. VG. B4d. $5.00

MCCORD, Carter. *Ask Me No Questions.* Midwood 32-482. PBO. c/Rader. VG. B3d. $5.00

MCCOY, Dean. *Double Up.* 1961. Beacon B 435Y. Ad. G+. B5d. $3.50

MCCOY, Dean. *My Lover, My Neighbor.* Beacon 873. PBO. VG. B3d. $5.00

MCCOY, Dean. *Night It Happened.* Beacon 967. 3rd prtg. VG+. B3d. $6.50

MCCOY, Horace. *Corruption City.* 1959. Dell 1st Edn A 188. PBO. VG. B6d. $18.00

MCCOY, Horace. *I Should Have Stayed Home.* 1951. Signet 884. 1st edn. PBO. c/Pease: gga. rare. NF. B6a #76. $165.00

MCCOY, Horace. *Kiss Tomorrow Good-Bye.* 1948. Signet 754. c/Avati: gga. VG. P6d. $6.00

MCCOY, Horace. *No Pockets in a Shroud.* 1948. Signet 690. Fa. VG+. B4d. $12.00

MCCOY, Horace. *No Pockets in a Shroud.* 1948. Signet 690. G+. G5d. $9.50

MCCRUMB, Sharyn. *Lovely in Her Bones.* Avon 89592. 1st prtg. VG. G5d. $5.00

MCCULLERS, Carson. *Heart Is a Lonely Hunter.* Signet 596. name on fly. VG+. B3d. $7.00

MCCULLERS, Carson. *Reflections in a Golden Eye.* Bantam 821. VG. B3d. $6.00

MCCULLEY, Johnston. *Caballero.* 1959. Signet 1632. 1st prtg. VG+. P7d. $5.50

MCCULLEY, Johnston. *Caballero.* 1948. Signet 669. NF. I1d. $7.00

MCCULLEY, Johnston. *Gunman's Gold.* Pyramid 187. VG. I1d. $5.00

MCCULLEY, Johnston. *Gunsight Showdown.* Avon 748. VG. B3d. $4.50

MCCULLEY, Johnston. *Mark of Zorro.* 1958. New Dell Edition D 204. TVTI. c/Vic Kalin. We. VG. P6d. $4.50

MCCULLOUGH, Colleen. *Creed for the Third Millennium.* Avon 70134. 10th prtg. SF. VG+. W2d. $3.50

MCCULLY, Walbridge. *Doctors Beware!* Detective 53. VG. B3d. $5.00

MCCURTIN, Peter. *Bluebolt One.* 1965. Berkley F 1069. My. VG. B5d. $2.50

MCCURTIN, Peter. *Boston Bust-Out.* 1973. Dell 2108. 1st edn. My. F. F2d. $7.00

MCCURTIN, Peter. *Hit.* Leisure 122. reprint. NF. B6d. $4.50

MCCURTIN, Peter. *Sundance Murders.* Belmont 50-608. VG+. B3d. $4.00

MCCUTCHAN, Philip. *Dead Line.* 1966. Berkley F 1269. 1st prtg. My. VG. R5d. $2.25

MCCUTCHAN, Philip. *Gilbralter Road.* 1965. Berkley F 1050. 1st prtg. My. G+. R5d. $1.75

MCCUTCHAN, Philip. *Man From Moscow.* 1966. Berkley F 1183. 1st prtg. My. VG. R5d. $2.25

MCCUTCHAN, Philip. *Screaming Dead Balloons.* 1969. Berkley X 1695. 1st prtg. My. VG. R5d. $2.25

MCCUTCHAN, Philip. *Warmaster.* 1965. Berkley F 1127. 1st prtg. My. VG. R5d. $2.50

MCDANIEL, David. *Arsenal Out of Time.* Ace G 667. SF. G+. W2d. $3.00

MCDANIEL, David. *Dagger Affair.* Ace G 571. Man From UNCLE #4. VG. B3d. $4.00

MCDANIEL, David. *Dagger Affair.* 1965. Ace G 571. 1st prtg. My. G+. R5d. $1.75

MCDANIEL, David. *Monster Wheel Affair.* 1967. Ace G 613. TVTI. c/photo. UNCLE #8. VG+. B4d. $3.00

MCDANIEL, David. *Prisoner #2.* 1969. Ace 67901. TVTI. NF. B4d. $10.00

MCDANIEL, David. *Prisoner #2.* 1969. Ace 67901. TVTI. VG. B3d. $5.00

MCDANIEL, David. *Rainbow Affair.* Ace G 670. Man From UNCLE #13. VG. G5d. $4.00

MCDANIEL, David. *Utopia Affair.* Ace G 729. Man From UNCLE #15. VG. B3d. $4.00

MCDANIEL, David. *Vampire Affair.* Ace G 590. Man From UNCLE #6. G+. G5d. $3.00

MCDANIEL, David. *Vampire Affair.* 1966. Ace G 590. 1st prtg. My. VG+. R5d. $4.50

MCDERMOTT, C.L. *Yank on Piccadilly.* Popular 417. VG. B3d. $6.00

MCDEVITT, Jack. *Talent for War.* 1989. Ace 79953. SF. F. W2d. $4.50

MCDEW, J. *Primitive Passions.* Bedside BB 810. c/gga. NF. I1d. $6.00

MCDONALD, Greg. *Fletch's Fortune.* 1978. Avon 37978. 13th prtg. My. F. W2d. $3.25

MCDONALD, N.C. *Fish the Strong Waters.* 1956. Ballantine 175. PBO. c/Kelly Freas. VG. B6d. $6.00

MCDONALD, N.C. *Song of the Axe.* 1957. Ballantine 499. 1st edn. Hi. F. F2d. $10.00

MCDONALD, N.C. *Witch Doctor.* Ballantine 312. PBO. VG+. B3d. $5.00

MCDONOUGH, Thomas R. *Architects of Hyperspace.* 1987. Avon 75144. 1st edn. SF. F. F2d. $6.00

MCDOUGALL, Colin. *Execution.* 1961. Crest D 489. 1st prtg. NF. P7d. $5.50

MCDOWELL, Emmett. *Three for the Gallows & Stamped for Death.* 1958. Ace 329. PBO. gga. My. VG. P6d. $5.00

MCDOWELL, Michael. *Blackwater: 1-the Flood.* 1983. Avon 81489. 1st prtg. SF. VG. R5d. $1.50

MCDOWELL, Michael. *Cold Moon Over Babylon.* 1980. Avon 48660. PBO. Ho. NF. B6d. $3.00

MCDOWELL/MCDOWELL. *Bloodline to Murder/In at the Kill.* Ace D 445. VG. M1d. $10.00

MCDOWELL/MCDOWELL. *Bloodline to Murder/In at the Kill.* 1960. Ace D 445. c/gga. My. G+. B4d. $2.00

MCDOWELL/TREAT. *Switcheroo/Over the Edge.* 1954. Ace D 51. 1st prtg. My. G+. R5d. $7.50

MCDOWELL/TREAT. *Switchroo/Over the Edge.* Ace D 51. c/gga. My. VG+. B6d. $16.50

MCELFRESH, Adeline. *Hospital Hill.* 1961. Dell 1st Edn B 201. 1st prtg. c/Abbett. VG+. P7d. $3.50

MCELFRESH, Adeline. *Jeff Benton, MD.* 1962. Dell 1st Edn K 110. 1st prtg. PBO. VG+. P7d. $3.50

MCELFRESH, Adeline. *Jill Nolan, RN.* 1962. Dell 1st Edn K 115. 1st prtg. VG+. P7d. $3.50

MCELFRESH, Adeline. *Kay Manion, MD.* 1959. Dell 1st Edn A 187. 1st prtg. PBO. c/Kalin: gga. VG. P7d. $3.50

MCELFRESH, Adeline. *Night Call.* 1961. Dell 1st Edn B 177. PBO. c/Abbett. VG. B6d. $5.00

MCELFRESH, Adeline. *Young Doctor Randall.* 1959. Bantam 1929. Fa. NF. B4d. $2.00

MCEVOY, Seth. *Monsters of Doorna (Space Games).* 1983. Bantam 23941. Interplanetary Spy #5. SF. G+. W2d. $2.75

MCFEATTERS, Dale. *Strictly Business.* Berkley 349. PBO. cartoons. Nfi. G+. B5d. $3.00

MCFEATTERS, Dale. *Strictly Business.* Berkley 349. VG. B3d. $4.00

MCGERR, Patricia. *Is There a Traitor in the House?* 1966. Avon G 1283. My. VG+. B4d. $4.00

MCGERR, Patricia. *Martha, Martha.* 1962. Dell F 187. c/M Hooks. Fi. NF. B5d. $4.50

MCGERR, Patricia. *Pick Your Victim.* Dell 307. VG. G5d. $8.00

MCGERR, Patricia. *Pick Your Victim.* Dell 307. 1st prtg. My. G+. R5d. $4.50

MCGERR, Patricia. *Seven Deadly Sisters.* Dell 412. c/P Burns. My. G+. B5d. $3.00

MCGERR, Patricia. *Seven Deadly Sisters.* Dell 412. VG. G5d. $6.50

MCGHEE, George. *Desire Under the Sun.* 1961. Midwood F 97. PBO. c/Rader: gga. VG+. B6d. $18.00

MCGILL, Gordon. *Armageddon 2000.* 1982. Signet AE 1818. Omen #4. SF. VG+. W2d. $4.25

MCGILL, Gordon. *Final Conflict.* 1980. Signet E 9584. 1st prtg. Omen #3. VG. R5d. $1.75

MCGILL, Gordon. *Spies Like Us.* 1985. Signet AE 4334. 1st prtg. VG+. R5d. $2.00

MCGINLEY, Phyllis. *New Casserole Cookery.* 1970. Berkley X 1745. NF. VG+. B5d. $3.50

MCGIVERN, William P. *#7 File.* Pocket 1156. G+. G5d. $3.50

MCGIVERN, William P. *Big Heat.* 1954. Pocket 981. VG+. G5d. $8.00

MCGIVERN, William P. *Crooked Frame.* 1953. Pocket 961. c/J Meese. My. VG. B5d. $6.00

MCGIVERN, William P. *Heaven Ran Last.* 1952. Dell 599. 1st pb. c/Meese. My. VG+. B6d. $12.00

MCGIVERN, William P. *Killer on the Turnpike & Other Stories.* 1961. Pocket 6075. 1st edn. My. F. F2d. $13.00

MCGIVERN, William P. *Margin of Terror.* 1955. Pocket 1062. c/J Meese. My. VG+. B5d. $9.50

MCGIVERN, William P. *Night Extra.* Pocket 1193. 1st pb. VG. M6d. $6.50

MCGIVERN, William P. *Rogue Cop.* 1954. Pocket 1030. VG+. G5d. $8.50

MCGIVERN, William P. *Savage Streets.* Pocket 6101. VG. G5d. $5.00

MCGIVERN, William P. *Savage Streets.* 1961. Pocket 6101. JD. F. P1d. $19.50

MCGIVERN, William P. *Shield for Murder.* 1952. Pocket 870. G+. G5d. $6.00

MCGIVERN, William P. *Shield for Murder.* 1952. Pocket 870. 1st pb. My. VG. B6d. $9.00

MCGIVERN, William P. *Very Cold for May.* 1951. Pocket 786. c/K Milroy. My. G+. B5d. $4.00

MCGIVERN, William P. *Waterfront Cop.* Pocket 1105. VG+. G5d. $8.00

MCGIVERN, William P. *Whispering Corpse.* Pocket 693. G+. G5d. $5.00

MCGOVERN, James. *Berlin Couriers.* 1961. Pyramid G 651. 1st edn. PBO. c/gga. F. F2d. $8.00

MCGOVERN, James. *Berlin Couriers.* 1966. Pyramid X 1378. 2nd prtg. My. G. W2d. $2.75

MCGOWAN, N. *My Years With Churchill.* Pan G 307. VG. B3d. $8.00

MCGUIRE, Don. *Day Television Died.* Holloway House HH 165. VG. B3d. $5.00

MCGUIRE/NORTON. *Planet for Texans/Star Born.* Ace D 299. F. M1d. $15.00

MCHARGUE, Georgess. *Meet the Werewolf.* 1983. Dell 96182. 1st prtg. VG. P7d. $4.00

MCHUGH, Vincent. *Edge of the World.* Ballantine 53. PBO. VG. B3d. $4.00

MCINERNY, Ralph. *Body & Soil.* 1991. World Wide 25063. My. F. B5d. $6.00

MCINNES, Graham. *Lost Island.* 1955. Signet S 1215. c/gga. Fa. VG. B4d. $3.00

MCINTOSH, J.T. *Flight From Rebirth.* 1971. Avon V 2411. PBO. SF. VG+. B5d. $3.50

MCINTOSH, J.T. *Million Cities.* 1963. Pyramid F 898. SF. VG. B4d/I1d. $5.00

MCINTOSH, J.T. *Rule of the Pagbeasts.* 1956. Crest 150. 1st pb edn. F. M1d. $8.00

MCINTOSH, J.T. *Ruler of the World.* Laser 24. NF. I1d. $6.00

MCINTOSH, J.T. *Six Gates From Limbo.* 1969. Avon V 2274. PBO. SF. VG. B5d. $3.50

MCINTOSH, J.T. *Snow White & the Giants.* 1968. Avon S 347. PBO. c/C Cassler. SF. VG. B5d. $5.00

MCINTOSH, J.T. *Suiciders.* 1973. Avon 17889. 1st prtg. SF. VG+. R5d. $2.50

MCINTOSH, J.T. *Transmigration.* 1970. Avon V 2375. 1st edn. VG. P9d. $1.75

MCINTOSH, J.T. *World Out of Mind.* 1955. Perma M 3027. 1st edn. PBO. F. M1d. $8.00

MCINTOSH, J.T. *World Out of Mind.* 1955. Perma M 3027. c/R Powers. SF. VG. B5d. $5.50

MCINTOSH, J.T. *Worlds Apart.* Avon T 249. 1st edn. F. M1d. $12.00

MCINTOSH, J.T. *Worlds Apart.* 1958. Avon T 249. VG+. B3d. $4.50

MCINTOSH/SWAIN. *One in 300/Transposed Man.* 1955. Ace D 113. c/E Valigursky. SF. VG. B5d/P7d. $7.50

MCINTOSH/SWAIN. *One in 300/Transposed Man.* 1955. Ace D 113. NF. M1d. $15.00

MCINTYRE, Vonda N. *Bride.* 1985. Dell 10801. 1st prtg. MTI. SF. VG+. R5d. $2.50

MCINTYRE, Vonda N. *Star Trek III: The Search for Spock.* 1984. Pocket 49500. MTI. SF. VG+. W2d. $4.25

MCINTYRE, Vonda N. *Star Trek IV: The Voyage Home.* 1986. Pocket 63266. TVTI. SF. VG+. B5d. $4.00

MCINTYRE, Vonda N. *Star Trek: The Wrath of Khan.* 1982. Pocket 45610. SF. VG. W2d. $4.00

MCINTYRE, Vonda N. *Starfarers.* 1989. Ace 78053. SF. F. W2d. $4.00

MCINTYRE, Vonda N. *Superluminal.* 1984. Pocket 53136. 1st prtg. SF. VG. W2d. $3.50

MCKAYE, Richard. *Portrait of the Damned.* Signet 1110. VG. B3d. $4.00

MCKENNA, Richard. *Casey Agonistes.* 1978. Ace 09227. SF. G+. W2d. $3.00

MCKENNEY, Kenn. *Plants.* 1977. Bantam 02976. SF. F. W2d. $4.50

MCKENZIE, M. *Backstage at Saturday Night Live!* 1980. Scholastic 30919. 1st prtg. G+. R5d. $1.25

MCKILLIP, Patricia A. *Fool's Run.* 1988. Popular 20518. 3rd edn. F. P9d. $2.00

MCKILLIP, Patricia A. *Harpist in the Wind.* 1982. Ballantine 31114. 5th prtg. Morgon Trilogy Volume #3. SF. VG+. W2d. $3.25

MCKILLIP, Patricia A. *Heir of Sea & Fire.* 1978. Ballantine 27468. SF. VG+. W2d. $4.00

MCKILLIP, Patricia A. *Heir of Sea & Fire.* 1982. Ballantine 28882. 12th prtg. Morgon Trilogy Volume #2. SF. VG. W2d. $3.00

MCKILLIP, Patricia A. *Riddle Master of Hed.* 1984. Ballantine 32043. 10th prtg. Morgon Trilogy Volume #1. SF. VG. W2d. $3.00

MCKIMMEY, James. *Cornered!* Dell 1st Edn B 157. VG+. B3d. $5.50

MCKIMMEY, James. *Long Ride.* Dell 1st Edn B 211. G. G5d. $3.50

MCKIMMEY, James. *Long Ride.* 1961. Dell 1st Edn B 211. PBO. c/Abbett. My. VG+. B6d. $10.00

MCKIMMEY, James. *Squeeze Play.* Dell 1st Edn B 230. PBO. VG+. M6d. $6.50

MCKIMMEY, James. *Wrong Ones.* Dell 1st Edn B 192. VG. G5d. $4.00

MCKIMMEY, James. *24 Hours To Kill.* 1961. Dell 1st Edn B 169. PBO. c/McGinnis. My. VG+. B6d. $12.50

MCKINNEY, Jack. *Metal Fire.* 1987. Ballantine 34141. Robotech #8. SF. F. W2d. $4.00

MCKNIGHT, Bob. *Kiss the Babe Goodbye.* Ace D 447. PBO. VG. B3d. $5.00

MCKNIGHT, Bob. *Swamp Sanctuary.* 1959. Ace D 411. c/Maguire: gga. scarce. VG+. B6a #77. $38.00

MCKNIGHT, Evans. *She Made Her Bed.* 1960. Beacon 324. PBO. c/Darcy: gga. NF. B6d. $25.00

MCKNIGHT/POWELL. *Running Scared/ Man-Killer.* 1960. Ace D 469. 1st edn. c/gga. My. F. F2d. $18.00

MCKNIGHT/THIELEN. *Slice of Death/Open Season.* Ace D 419. PBO. VG. B3d. $6.50

MCLANE, Ben V. Jr. *Chasm of Lust.* 1961. Newsstand 161. 1st edn. F2d. $12.00

MCLAUGHLIN, Dean. *Dome World.* 1962. Pyramid F 763. 1st edn. F. M1d. $15.00

MCLAUGHLIN, Dean. *Dome World.* 1962. Pyramid F763. PBO. c/E Emsh. SF. VG. B5d. $4.50

MCLAUGHLIN, Dean. *Fury From Earth.* 1963. Pyramid F 923. PBO. c/J Gaughan. SF. NF. B5d. $6.00

MCLAUGHLIN, Dean. *Fury From Earth.* 1963. Pyramid F 923. 1st edn. SF. F. F2d. $10.00

MCLAUGHLIN, Dean. *Fury From Earth.* 1963. Pyramid F 923. 1st prtg. SF. G+. W2d. $2.75

MCLAUGHLIN, Dean. *Man Who Wanted Stars.* 1965. Lancer 73-441. 1st edn. F. M1d. $8.00

MCLAUGHLIN, Dean. *Man Who Wanted Stars.* 1965. Lancer 73-441. 1st prtg. SF. VG. R5d. $3.50

MCLAUGHLIN, Robert. *Notion of Sin.* 1960. Crest S 380. VG+. P6d. $2.00

MCLENDON, James. *Papa Hemingway in Key West 1928-1940.* Popular 520. 1st prtg. VG+. P7d. $4.50

MCLINTOCK, J.D. *Manipur Road.* Digit D 187. NF. I1d. $5.00

MCMANUS, Virginia *Not for Love.* 1961. Dell F 159. VG+. B3d. $4.50

MCMANUS, Yvonne. *Reunion.* 1965. Award 151. 1st edn. F. F2d. $12.00

MCMULLEN, Richard. *Awake to Darkness.* Popular G 229. VG+. B3d. $5.00

MCMULLEN, Richard. *Awake to Darkness.* 1949. Popular 212. c/Belarski: gga. Fa. VG. B4d. $5.00

MCMULLEN, Richard. *Eager Is the Flesh.* Newsstand 26. VG. B3d. $7.00

MCMURTRY, Larry. *Hud.* 1963. Popular SP 218. MTI. c/Newman & O'Neill: photo. VG+. B3d. $5.00

MCNEIL, George. *Tease.* Beacon 784. PBO. VG. B3d. $4.00

MCNEIL, W.K. *Ghost Stories From the American South.* 1988. Dell 20060. SF. VG. W2d. $3.25

MCNICHOLS, Charles L. *Crazy Weather.* 1954. Bantam 1272. 1st prtg. c/E Means. VG+. P7d. $4.50

MCPARTLAND, John. *Danger for Breakfast.* 1956. Gold Medal 574. 1st edn. c/gga. My. F. F2d. $16.00

MCPARTLAND, John. *Face of Evil.* 1954. Gold Medal 393. 1st prtg. PBO. VG. P7d. $7.50

MCPARTLAND, John. *Kingdom of Johnny Cool.* 1963. Gold Medal 1343. 2nd prtg. MTI. VG+. B3d. $4.00

MCPARTLAND, John. *Last Night.* 1959. Gold Medal 909. 1st edn. My. F. F2d. $20.00

MCPARTLAND, John. *No Down Payment.* 1957. Cardinal C 298. MTI. F. B4d. $3.00

MCPARTLAND, John. *Ripe Fruit.* Gold Medal 732. VG. B3d. $4.50

MCPARTLAND, John. *Tokyo Doll.* 1953. Gold Medal 336. VG+. G5d. $17.50

MCPHEE, James. *Survival 2000.* 1991. Gold Eagle 63201. 1st edn. SF. F. F2d. $6.00

MCQUAY, Mike. *Life-Keeper.* 1985. Bantam. 1st edn. F. M1d. $8.00

MCQUAY, Mike. *Mathew Swain: The Odds Are Murder.* 1983. Bantam 22856. 1st prtg. SF. VG. W2d. $3.50

MCQUAY, Mike. *My Science Project.* 1985. Bantam 25378. 1st edn. c/photo. SF. F. F2d. $10.00

MCSHANE, Mark. *Seance on a Wet Afternoon.* Crest 781. MTI. VG. B3d. $4.50

MCSHANE, Mark. *Singular Case of the Multiple Dead.* Ace 76785. My. VG+. W2d. $4.00

MEAD, Harold. *Bright Phoenix.* 1956. Ballantine 147. 1st edn. F. M1d. $10.00

MEAD, Harold. *Bright Phoenix.* 1956. Ballantine 147. 1st prtg. VG. S1d. $5.00

MEAD, Shepherd. *Big Ball of Wax.* Avon 1129. 1st pb edn. F. M1d. $8.00

MEAD, Shepherd. *Big Ball of Wax.* Avon 1129. 1st prtg. G. S1d. $2.00

MEAD, Shepherd. *Big Ball of Wax.* Ballantine 174. VG+. B3d. $5.00

MEAD, Shepherd. *Big Ball of Wax.* 1954. Ballantine 174. 1st edn. F. M1d. $15.00

MEAD, Shepherd. *How To Succeed in Business.* Ballantine 127. VG+. B3d. $5.00

MEAD, Shepherd. *How To Succeed With Women.* Ballantine 287. VG+. B3d. $5.00

MEAD, Shepherd. *How To Succeed With Women.* Ballantine 576. 2nd prtg. VG+. B3d. $5.00

MEADE, Richard. *Rough Night in Jericho.* Gold Medal R 1846. PBO. MTI. My. VG. B5d. $4.50

MEADE, Richard. *Sword of Morning.* 1969. Signet. 1st edn. F. M1d. $8.00

MEADOWS, A.Y. *Easy Way to Sexual Success.* Barclay 7331. c/photo. F. B3d. $5.00

MEADOWS, A.Y. *Velvet Claw.* Brandon House 6375. VG+. B3d. $5.00

MEAKER, Marijane. *Spring Fire.* 1952. Gold Medal 222. 1st edn. c/gga. F. F2d. $15.00

MEANY, Tom. *Babe Ruth.* Bantam 505. F. I1d. $18.00

MEANY, Tom. *Babe Ruth.* Bantam 505. VG. B3d. $5.00

MEANY, Tom. *Baseball's Great Teams.* 1950. Bantam 763. Nfi. VG. B4d. $7.00

MEANY, Tom. *Baseball's Greatest Players.* Dell 839. VG. B3d. $6.00

MEEKER, Richard. *Torment.* Uni-Book 13. VG. B3d. $7.00

MEHLING, Harold. *Scandalous Scamps.* Ace K 125. VG+. B3d. $5.00

MEIER, Frederick. *Men Under the Sea.* Dell 265. VG+. B3d. $6.00

MEISSNER, Hans-Otto. *Man With Three Faces.* Pan GP 88. VG. I1d. $4.00

MELCHER, H. *This Bed Not For Sleeping.* Brandon House 6041. NF. B3d. $6.00

MELINCOVE, B. edt. *Crossword Puzzle Dictionary.* Crest 654. VG+. B3d. $4.00

MELINE, Frank. *Door to Door Rape!* 1962. France 11. 1st edn. c/gga. F. F2d. $17.50

MELLAN, IBERT, & ELEANOR. *Poisons.* 1962. Pyramid X778. Nfi. VG+. B5d. $7.50

MELONEY, W.B. *Farm Girl.* Pyramid 37. 2nd edn. c/Julian Paul: gga. VG+. I1d. $12.00

MELONEY, W.B. *Mooney.* Popular 391. VG. B3d. $6.00

MELTZER, David. *Agency.* 1976. Essex 102. VG+. B3a #24. $22.00

MELTZER, David. *Agent.* Essex 104. VG. B3d. $15.00

MELTZER, David. *Glue Factory.* 1969. Essex 0134. PBO. VG+. B3a #22. $67.45

MELTZER, David. *Healer.* Essex 122. Brain Plant #2. VG. B3d. $10.00

MELTZER, David. *Lovely.* Essex 117. Brain Plant #1. VG. B3d. $8.00

MELTZER, David. *Out.* Essex 129. Brain Plant Book #3. G+. B3d. $8.00

MELUCH, R.M. *Sovereign.* 1979. Signet F 8715. SF. F. W2d. $4.75

MELVILLE, Herman. *Moby Dick.* 1955. Pocket PL 28. Fa. VG+. B4d. $2.50

MELVILLE, Herman. *Moby Dick.* 1949. Pocket 612. 1st prtg. c/Price. VG+. P7d. $6.50

MELVILLE, Herman. *Moby Dick.* 1955. Signet D 1229. Fi. G+. B5d. $3.00

MEMMI, Albert. *Strangers.* Avon F 163. c/Powers. VG. B3d. $4.00

MENCER, D. *Into Each Life.* Paragon 153. VG+. B3d. $5.00

MENDE, Robert. *Tough Kid From Brooklyn.* 1955. Avon T 99. c/gga. JD. VG. B4d. $3.00

MENDE, Robert. *Tough Kid From Brooklyn.* 1951. Avon 382. Fi. G+. B5d. $4.50

MENDELSOHN, F. Jr. *Club Tycoon Sends Man to Moon.* 1965. Book Co of America 013. 1st prtg. SF. VG. R5d. $4.50

MENDELSON, Drew. *Pilgrimage.* 1981. DAW 430. 1st edn. F. M1d. $6.00

MENEN, Aubrey. *Abode of Love.* 1958. Pocket 1188. c/F Banberry. Fi. VG. B5d. $3.00

MENKE, Frank G. *Encyclopedia of Sports.* 1955. Barnes NN. Nfi. VG. B5d. $2.50

MENNEN, Tad. *Lust Lane.* 1964. Herald HR 102. Ad. G+. B5d. $3.00

MENNIN, Ethel. *Julie.* Jarrolds NN. VG. B3d. $10.00

MERAK, A.J. *Dark Conflict.* ca1950s. Badger SN 29. PBO. VG+. B9a. $53.00

MERCER, Charles. *Promise Morning.* 1967. Avon S 305. Fa. F. B4d. $4.00

MERCER, Fred. *Lustville.* Bedside 1239. VG+. B3d. $5.00

MERCER, Fred. *Room & Broad.* 1963. Bedside 1248. PBO. F. B6d. $10.00

MERCHANT, Paul. *Sex Gang.* 1973. Reed Nightstand 3003. format. JD. VG+. B6a #77. $478.00

MEREDITH, George. *Shaving of Shagpat.* 1970. Ballantine 01958. VG. B3d. $4.00

MEREDITH, George. *Shaving of Shagpat.* 1970. Ballantine 01958. 1st edn. Ad/Fa. F. M1d. $15.00

MEREDITH, Richard C. *Sky Is Filled With Ships.* 1969. Ballantine 01600. SF. VG+. B4d. $2.75

MEREDITH, Richard C. *Sky Is Filled With Ships.* 1969. Ballantine 01600. 1st prtg. PBO. VG. P7d. $4.00

MERGENDAHL, Charles. *Bramble Bush.* Bantam F 1968. 4th edn. MTI. c/Barye. VG+. B6d. $3.50

MERGENDAHL, Charles. *Bramble Bush.* Panther 1107. VG. B3d. $6.50

MERGENDAHL, Charles. *Dreams of April.* 1964. Dell 2161. Fa. VG+. B4d. $2.00

MERGENDAHL, Charles. *Girl Cage.* 1953. Popular 484. c/gga. Fa. VG+. B4d. $8.00

MERGENDAHL, Charles. *This Spring of Love.* Popular EB 18. VG+. B3d. $6.00

MERGENDAHL, Charles. *This Spring of Love.* 1950. Popular 304. c/gga. Fa. G+. B4d. $5.00

MERGENDAHL, Charles. *Tiger by the Tail.* 1958. Popular G 275. PBO. c/gga. My. VG+. B6d. $10.00

MERGENDAHL, Charles. *Tonight Is Forever.* Popular 351. c/Bergey. VG+. B3d. $7.00

MERGENDAHL, Charles. *Tonight Is Forever.* 1951. Popular 351. c/Bergey: gga. Fa. NF. B4d. $15.00

MERIMEE, Prosper. *Loves of Carmen & Other Stories.* Pocket 559. MTI. VG. B3d. $4.00

MERIWETHER, Louise. *Daddy Was a Number Runner.* 1971. Pyramid N 2483. VG. B4d. $2.25

MERRIAM, Robert E. *Battle of the Bulge.* Ballantine 190. VG. B3d. $4.00

MERRICK, Clyde. *Sin Slaves.* 1961. Bedside BB 1203. Ad. G+. B5d. $2.50

MERRICK, Gordon. *Between Darkness & Day.* Popular G 158. VG. B3d. $4.00

MERRIL, Edith. *Year's Greatest SF & Fantasy: 3rd Annual Volume.* 1958. Dell 1st Edn B 119. 1st prtg. SF. VG. W2d. $6.00

MERRIL, Judith. *Beyond Human Ken.* 1954. Pennant P 56. c/C Binger. SF. VG. B5d. $6.50

MERRIL, Judith. *Beyond Human Ken.* 1954. Pennant P 56. NF. I1d. $12.00

MERRIL, Judith. *Beyond Human Ken.* 1954. Pennant P 56. 1st pb edn. F. M1d. $15.00

MERRIL, Judith. *Beyond Human Ken.* 1954. Pennant P 56. 1st prtg. G. S1d. $3.00

MERRIL, Judith. *Daughters of Earth.* 1970. Dell 01705. SF. G+. W2d. $3.25

MERRIL, Judith. *Galaxy of Ghouls.* Lion LL 25. 1st prtg. VG. S1d. $10.00

MERRIL, Judith. *Galaxy of Ghouls.* 1955. Lion LL 25. 1st edn. F. M1d. $20.00

MERRIL, Judith. *Human?* 1954. Lion 205. PBO. SF. VG+. B4d/I1d. $15.00

MERRIL, Judith. *Human?* 1954. Lion 205. 1st edn. F. M1d. $25.00

MERRIL, Judith. *Off the Beaten Orbit.* 1961. Pyramid F 683. c/J Schoenherr. SF. VG. B5d. $4.00

MERRIL, Judith. *Off the Beaten Orbit.* 1961. Pyramid F 683. 1st edn. F. M1d. $23.00

MERRIL, Judith. *Out of Bounds.* 1963. Pyramid F 830. 2nd edn. VG. P9d. $1.50

MERRIL, Judith. *Out of Bounds.* Pyramid G 499. 1st prtg. F. S1d. $8.00

MERRIL, Judith. *SF 12.* 1969. Dell 7815. 1st edn. PBO. NF. P9d. $2.00

MERRIL, Judith. *SF: The Best of the Best.* 1968. Dell 0508. SF. VG+. W2d. $4.50

MERRIL, Judith. *Shot in the Dark.* Bantam 751. VG. B3d. $7.00

MERRIL, Judith. *Tomorrow People.* 1962. Pyramid F 806. c/J Schoenherr. SF. VG+. B5d. $4.50

MERRIL, Judith. *Tomorrow People.* 1960. Pyramid G 502. NF. I1d. $12.00

MERRIL, Judith. *Tomorrow People.* 1968. Pyramid X 1802. 3rd prtg. SF. F. W2d. $5.00

MERRIL, Judith. *Year's Greatest SF & Fantasy.* Dell B 119. NF. I1d. $6.00

MERRIL, Judith. *Year's Greatest SF & Fantasy.* 1959. Dell B 129. 1st prtg. SF. G+. R5d. $3.00

MERRIL, Judith. *Year's Greatest SF & Fantasy.* 1956. Dell EB 103. 1st prtg. F. S1d. $9.00

MERRIL, Judith. *10th-Annual Year's Best SF.* 1966. Dell 8611. 1st edn. PBO. F. P9d. $2.50

MERRIL, Judith. *2nd Annual Year's Greatest SF.* 1957. Dell. 1st pb edn. F. M1d. $10.00

MERRIL, Judith. *3rd Annual Year's Greatest SF.* 1958. Dell. 1st pb edn. F. M1d. $10.00

MERRIL, Judith. *4th Annual Year's Greatest SF.* 1959. Dell B 129. VG. I1d. $4.00

MERRIL, Judith. *4th Annual Year's Greatest SF.* 1959. Dell B 129. 1st pb edn. F. M1d. $8.00

MERRIL, Judith. *5th Annual Year's Best SF.* 1961. Dell F 118. c/R Powers. SF. VG+. B5d. $6.50

MERRIL, Judith. *5th Annual Year's Best SF.* 1961. Dell F 118. SF. VG. W2d. $4.50

MERRIL, Judith. *5th Annual Year's Best SF.* 1961. Dell F 118. 1st prtg. SF. G+. R5d. $2.25

MERRIL, Judith. *5th Annual Year's Greatest SF.* 1961. Dell 118. 1st pb edn. F. M1d. $10.00

MERRIL, Judith. *6th Annual Year's Best SF.* 1962. Dell 9772. 1st prtg. SF. VG. R5d. $2.00

MERRIL, Judith. *7th Annual Year's Best SF.* 1963. Dell 9773. 1st edn. PBO. NF. P9d. $2.00

MERRIL, Judith. *8th Annual Year's Best SF.* 1964. Dell 9774. 1st edn. PBO. VG. P9d. $1.50

MERRIL, Judith. *8th Annual Year's Best SF.* 1964. Dell 9774. 1st prtg. SF. VG. R5d. $2.00

MERRILL, Judith. *Shot in the Dark.* 1950. Bantam 751. PBO. SF. NF. B6a #76. $66.00

MERRIMAN, Chad. *Blood on the Sun.* Gold Medal 271. VG. B3d. $3.50

MERRIMAN, Chad. *Stampede.* Ballantine 343. PBO. VG. B3d. $4.50

MERRITT, A. *Black Wheel.* 1981. Avon 55822. SF. F. W2d. $5.00

MERRITT, A. *Burn, Witch, Burn.* 1951. Avon 392. NF. I1d. $15.00

MERRITT, A. *Burn, Witch, Burn.* 1951. Avon 392. 4th edn. VG. M6d. $7.50

MERRITT, A. *Burn, Witch, Burn.* 1944. Avon 43. 1st prtg. G. W2d. $9.75

MERRITT, A. *Creep, Shadow, Creep.* 1943. Avon Murder My 14. VG. B3a #21. $16.50

MERRITT, A. *Dwellers in the Mirage.* 1973. Avon 14340. 3rd prtg. SF. F. W2d. $5.00

MERRITT, A. *Dwellers in the Mirage.* Avon 413. F. I1d. $35.00

MERRITT, A. *Dwellers in the Mirage.* 1962. PB Library 52142. SF. VG+. W2d. $4.50

MERRITT, A. *Dwellers in the Mirage.* 1962. PB Library 52142. 1st edn. NF. M1d. $7.00

MERRITT, A. *Dwellers in the Mirage.* 1965. PB Library 52516. 2nd prtg. SF. VG. W2d. $6.00

MERRITT, A. *Face in the Abyss.* 1945. Avon Murder My 29. c/P Stahr. SF. G+. B5d. $7.50

MERRITT, A. *Face in the Abyss.* 1957. Avon T 161. 1st prtg. G. S1d. $2.00

MERRITT, A. *Face in the Abyss.* 1978. Avon 37010. SF. VG. W2d. $4.25

MERRITT, A. *Face in the Abyss.* 1961. Collier AS 34X. 1st prtg. SF. VG. R5d. $2.00

MERRITT, A. *Fox Woman.* Avon 214. PBO. VG. B6d. $35.00

MERRITT, A. *Fox Woman.* 1949. Avon 214. PBO. c/gga. scarce. Fa. VG+. B6a #75. $77.00

MERRITT, A. *Fox Woman.* 1977. Avon. 1st edn. F. M1d. $7.00

MERRITT, A. *Metal Monster.* 1946. Avon Murder My 41. PBO. SF. G. B5d. $4.00

MERRITT, A. *Metal Monster.* 1966. Avon S 231. 1st prtg. SF. VG. R5d. $4.00

MERRITT, A. *Metal Monster.* 1957. Avon T 172. c/R Powers. SF. VG. B5d. $3.50

MERRITT, A. *Metal Monster.* 1957. Avon T 172. 1st prtg. VG+. S1d. $6.00

MERRITT, A. *Metal Monster.* 1972. Avon V 2422. 5th prtg. SF. VG. W2d. $3.25

MERRITT, A. *Metal Monster.* Avon 315. VG. B3d. $22.50

MERRITT, A. *Moon Pool.* 1944. Avon Murder My 18. SF. G+. B5d. $7.50

MERRITT, A. *Moon Pool.* 1944. Avon Murder My 18. VG+. B3a #24. $18.00

MERRITT, A. *Moon Pool.* 1956. Avon 135. 1st prtg. G+. S1d. $3.00

MERRITT, A. *Moon Pool.* 1951. Avon 370. NF. P9d. $25.00

MERRITT, A. *Moon Pool.* 1961. Collier AS 103X. 1st prtg. SF. G+. R5d. $1.00

MERRITT, A. *Moon Pool.* 1973. Collins 02287. 4th prtg. SF. F. W2d. $4.50

MERRITT, A. *Seven Footprints to Satan.* 1963. Avon G 1192. 9th prtg. SF. G. W2d. $4.00

MERRITT, A. *Seven Footprints to Satan.* 1942. Avon Murder My 1. SF. G. B5d. $5.00

MERRITT, A. *Seven Footprints to Satan.* 1968. Avon S 280. 11th edn. SF. VG. B5d. $2.50

MERRITT, A. *Seven Footprints to Satan.* Avon T 115. reprint. c/gga. reprint. NF. B6d. $12.50

MERRITT, A. *Seven Footprints to Satan.* 1971. Avon V 2417. 12th prtg. SF. G+. W2d. $3.00

MERRITT, A. *Seven Footprints to Satan.* Avon 235. VG. B6d. $35.00

MERRITT, A. *Seven Footprints to Satan.* 1950. Avon 235. My. G+. B4d. $15.00

MERRITT, A. *Seven Footprints to Satan.* 1950. Avon 235. scarce. VG+. B6a #77. $42.50

MERRITT, A. *Seven Footprints to Satan.* 1950. Avon 235. 1st prtg. SF. G. R5d. $5.00

MERRITT, A. *Seven Footprints to Satan.* 1942. Avon 26. 1st prtg. SF. G+. G5d/W2d. $15.00

MERRITT, A. *Seven Footprints to Satan.* Avon 28209. 13th prtg. SF. F. W2d. $5.00

MERRITT, A. *Ship of Ishtar.* 1966. Avon S 229. 4th prtg. SF. VG+. W2d. $4.25

MERRITT, A. *Ship of Ishtar.* 1973. Avon 14092. 3rd prtg. SF. VG. W2d. $3.75

MERRITT, A. *Ship of Ishtar.* Avon 324. c/classic new. scarce. NF. B6a #74. $93.50

MERRITT, A. *Ship of Ishtar.* Avon 324. NF. I1d. $40.00

MERRITT, A. *Ship of Ishtar.* Avon 324. VG. B6d. $35.00

MERRITT, A. *Ship of Ishtar.* Avon 34 Digest 45. My. VG. B4d. $7.50

MERRITT, A. *Swellers in the Mirage.* 1974. Futura L. 1st prtg. SF. VG. W2d. $6.00

MERSEREAU, John. *Corpse Comes Ashore.* 1945. Atlas Mystery 2. My. G+. B5d. $7.50

MERTON, Thomas. *No Man Is an Island.* Dell D 189. VG. B3d. $4.00

MERTON, Thomas. *Seeds of Contemplation.* Dell 725. c/S Salter. NF. VG. B5d. $2.50

MERWIN, Sam Jr. *Chauvinisto.* 1976. Major. 1st edn. F. M1d. $5.00

MERWIN, Sam Jr. *Creeping Shadow.* Gold Medal 227. PBO. VG+. B3d. $10.00

MERWIN, Sam Jr. *Creeping Shadow.* 1952. Gold Medal 227. PBO. VG+. B3a #20. $12.10

MERWIN, Sam Jr. *Sex War.* Beacon 284. VG. B3d. $6.50

MERWIN, Sam Jr. *Time Shifters.* 1971. Lancer 74776. PBO. SF. VG+. B5d. $4.00

MERWIN/NORTON. *3 Faces of Time/Stars Are Ours!* Ace D 121. F. M1d. $25.00

MERWIN/NORTON. *3 Faces of Time/Stars Are Ours!* Ace D 121. G+. I1d. $5.00

MESSMANN, Jon. *City for Sale.* 1975. Signet 6313. 1st edn. My. F. F2d. $8.00

MESTA, Perle. *Perle, My Story.* Avon G 1066. VG+. B3d. $4.50

METALIOUS, Grace. *Return to Peyton Place.* 1958. Dell F 91. c/V Kalin. Fi. VG. B5d. $3.00

METALIOUS, Grace. *Tight White Collar.* Pan X 197. VG. I1d. $5.00

METZELTHIN, Pearl V. *Avon Improved Cookbook.* Avon 101. VG. B3d. $6.00

METZELTHIN, Pearl V. *Avon Improved Cookbook.* 1950. Avon 261. NF. B3a #22. $28.50

MEYER, J.S. *Handwriting Analyzer.* Avon G 1161. VG. B3d. $4.00

MEYER, Nicholas. *Seven-Per-Cent Solution.* 1975. Ballantine 24550. 1st prtg. My. VG. R5d. $1.50

MEYER, Nicholas. *West End Horror.* 1977. Ballantine 25411. 1st prtg. My. VG+. R5d. $2.50

MEYER & NOURSE. *Invaders Are Coming.* 1959. Ace D 366. 1st prtg. SF. VG. I1d. $4.50

MEYERS, Harold. *Can Can Americana.* Avon 359. PBO. VG. B3d. $8.00

MEYERS, Harold. *Can Can Americana.* 1951. Avon 359. 1st prtg. PBO. VG+. P7d. $12.50

MEYERS, Harold. *Honeymoon Guide.* 1955. Avon T 95. PBO. c/Ward. VG. B6d. $6.00

MEYERS, Harold. *Nudist Cartoons.* 1955. Avon 649. PBO. c/Meyers. VG+. B6a #79. $45.00

MEYERS, Harold. *Smoking-Room Joke Book.* 1956. Avon 698. PBO. VG+. B6d. $40.00

MEYERS, Roy. *Daughters of the Dolphin.* 1968. Ballantine 72001. PBO. SF. VG. B6d. $6.00

MEYERS, Roy. *Daughters of the Dolphin.* 1968. Ballantine 72001. 1st edn. F. M1d. $8.00

MEYERS, Roy. *Destiny & the Dolphins.* 1969. Ballantine 01627. PBO. SF. VG. B6d. $6.00

MEYERS, Roy. *Destiny & the Dolphins.* 1969. Ballantine 01627. 1st edn. F. M1d. $8.00

MEYERS, Roy. *Dolphin Boy.* 1967. Ballantine U 6100. SF. VG. B4d. $4.00

MEZO, Francine. *Fall of Worlds.* 1980. Avon 75564. SF. VG+. W2d. $4.00

MIALL, Robert. *Jason King.* Pan 23165. TVTI. My. VG. W2d. $5.50

MIALL, Robert. *Sporting Blood.* 1973. Warner 75-274. 2nd edn. TVTI. VG+. P1d. $7.50

MIALL, Robert. *UFO.* 1971. Piccolo 02644. 2nd edn. TVTI. VG+. P1d. $5.00

MICHAEL, D.J. *Win: or Else!* 1954. Lion 208. PBO. VG+. B3a #22. $26.85

MICHAEL, Lewis. *No Exit for a Blonde.* 1967. Golden Fleece NN. c/gga. VG. B3d. $8.00

MICHAEL, Marjorie. *I Married a Hunter.* 1958. Pyramid Royal PR 14. My. VG+. M3d. $8.00

MICHAELES, M.M. *Suicide Command.* 1967. Lancer 73-590. PBO. VG. B6d. $6.00

MICHAELS, Dale. *Warring Breed.* Gold Medal 1154. VG+. B3d. $6.00

MICHAELS, Dale. *Warring Breed.* Gold Medal 605. VG+. B3d. $7.00

MICHAELS, J. *Homo in the Guesthouse.* Brandon House 2081. VG+. B3d. $4.00

MICHAELS, Melisa. *Far Harbor.* 1989. TOR 54581. SF. F. W2d. $4.25

MICHAELS, Rea. *Lust Queen.* 1964. Lancer 72-714. 1st edn. c/gga. F. F2d. $11.50

MICHAELS, Rea. *Two-Way Street.* 1964. Lancer 72-741. 1st edn. c/gga. F. F2d. $12.50

MICHAELS, Steve. *Main Attraction.* 1963. Belmont F 92-565. 1st edn. c/Nancy Kwan. My. F. F2d. $10.00

MICHAELS, Steve. *Main Attraction.* 1963. Belmont L 92-565. PBO. MTI. VG. M6d. $5.00

MICHAELSON, John Nairne. *Morning, Winter, & Night.* 1958. Berkley G 166. VG. B3d. $4.00

MICHAELSON, John Nairne. *Morning, Winter, & Night.* 1954. Signet 1116. c/Avati Fa. VG+. B4d. $4.00

MICHAUD, Don. *Beckoning Flame.* 1960. Newsstand 509. Ad. VG. B5d. $4.00

MICHEL, M. Scott. *Sweet Murder.* 1946. Handi-Book 47. 1st edn. PBO. VG+. B6a #77. $75.00

MICHEL, M.S. *Psychiatric Murders.* Black Knight 27. VG. B3d. $8.00

MICHENER, James A. *Bridge at Andau.* 1957. Bantam A 1650. Nfi. VG+. B4d. $3.00

MICHENER, James A. *Kent State.* 1971. Crest P 1626. 1st prtg. c/photo. VG. P7d. $4.00

MICHENER, James A. *Return to Paradise.* Bantam 999. VG. B3d. $5.00

MICHENER, James A. *Sayonara.* Bantam 1318. VG. B3d. $4.00

MICHENER, James A. *Tales of the South Pacific.* 1948. Pocket 516. 1st prtg. c/Kidder: gga. VG. P7d. $5.50

MIDDLETON, Ted. *Operation Tokyo.* 1956. Avon 731. 1st prtg. My. G+. R5d. $3.50

MIKSCH, W.F. *Addams Family Strikes Back.* 1965. Pyramid 1257. PBO. F. M1d. $20.00

MIKSCH, W.F. *Addams Family Strikes Back.* 1965. Pyramid 1257. PBO. TVTI. VG+. B3d. $5.00

MILBURN, George. *Hoboes & Harlots.* 1957. Lion LL 160. reprint. NF. B6d. $12.50

MILBURN, George. *Hoboes & Harlots.* 1954. Lion 191. 1st prtg. PBO. c/gga. VG. P7d. $10.00

MILES, K. *For Lust or Love.* Pallette 102. VG+. B3d. $4.50

MILES, R. *Man in the Boat.* Europa 805. VG+. B3d. $5.00

MILES, Richard. *Angel Loves Nobody.* 1968. Dell 0168. 1st prtg. c/Bama. JD. VG. P7d. $4.00

MILES, William E. *College Female.* 1963. Monarch MB 540. c/photo. Nfi. NF. B5d. $6.00

MILES/ARTHUR. *Dally With a Deadly Doll/Somebody's Walking Over My Grave.* Ace D 489. PBO. VG. B3d. $5.50

MILIUS, John. *Life & Times of Judge Roy Bean.* 1973. Bantam N 7518. 1st prtg. VG. R5d. $2.00

MILIUS, John. *Wind & the Lion.* 1975. Award 1468. PBO. MTI. VG+. B6d. $5.00

MILLAR, George. *Crossbowman's Story.* 1957. Bantam F 1591. 1st pb edn. F. M1d. $5.00

MILLAR, Kenneth. *I Die Slowly.* 1955. Lion LL 52. 2nd prtg. c/Clark Hulings: gga. VG. P6d. $3.50

MILLAR, Kenneth. *Night Train.* Lion LL 40. reprint. My. VG+. B6d. $12.50

MILLAR, Kenneth. *Three Roads.* 1951. Dell 497. 1st prtg. c/Stanley: gga. VG. P7d. $7.50

MILLAR, Kenneth. *Trouble Follows Me.* 1950. Lion 47. 1st edn. PBO. VG+. B6a #79. $61.00

MILLAR, Margaret. *Beast in View.* 1956. Bantam 1542. 1st pb. c/Hooks. My. VG. B6d. $15.00

MILLAR, Margaret. *Do Evil in Return.* Dell 558. VG+. G5d. $6.50

MILLAR, Margaret. *Fire Will Freeze.* 1944. Dell. 1st pb edn. F. M1d. $20.00

MILLAR, Margaret. *Iron Gates.* 1960. Dell D 332. 1st prtg. My. VG. R5d. $2.25

MILLAR, Margaret. *Iron Gates.* Dell 209. c/G Gregg. My. G+. B5d. $5.00

MILLAR, Margaret. *Lively Corpse (Rose's Last Summer).* Dell 920. VG+. G5d. $6.00

MILLAR, Margaret. *Lively Corpse.* Dell 920. 1st prtg. My. G+. R5d. $1.75

MILLAR, Margaret. *Rose's Last Summer.* 1967. Lancer 74-890. 1st pb. My. NF. B6d. $9.00

MILLAR, Margaret. *Vanish in an Distant.* Dell 730. VG. B3d. $6.00

MILLAR, Margaret. *Wall of Eyes.* Dell 110. VG. B3d/l1d. $6.00

MILLAR, Margaret. *Wall of Eyes.* 1966. Lancer 72-994. My. VG. B5d. $4.00

MILLAR, Walter. *Canticle for Leibowitz.* 1961. Bantam. 1st pb edn. F. M1d. $15.00

MILLARD, J. *No Law But Their Own.* Regency 324. VG. B3d. $5.00

MILLARD, J.J. *Sporting Woman.* Magenta 109. VG+. B3d. $5.00

MILLARD, Joseph. *Chato's Land.* Award 1034. MTI. c/Bronson. NF. B3d. $5.00

MILLARD, Joseph. *Cheyenne Wars.* 1964. Monarch MA 402. We. VG+. B4d. $9.00

MILLARD, Joseph. *Gods Hate Kansas.* 1964. Monarch 414. SF. G+. B5d. $5.00

MILLARD, Joseph. *Gods Hate Kansas.* 1964. Monarch 414. 1st prtg. PBO. c/Thurston. NF. P7d. $12.50

MILLARD, Joseph. *Good, the Bad, the Ugly.* Award 1495. 4th prtg. MTI. VG. B3d. $4.50

MILLARD, Joseph. *Good Guys & the Bad Guys.* 1969. Award A 577X. 1st prtg. VG. R5d. $1.50

MILLARD, Joseph. *Hec Ramsey: The Hunted.* Award 1232. NF. B3d. $6.50

MILLARD, Joseph. *Mansion of Evil.* 1950. Gold Medal 129. PBO. rare. all color comics. NF. B6a #74. $137.50

MILLARD, Joseph. *Mansion of Evil.* 1950. Gold Medal 129. PBO. VG+. B6d. $125.00

MILLARD, Joseph. *Thunderbolt & Lightfoot.* 1974. Award AN 1320. 1st prtg. MTI. My. G+. R5d. $1.25

MILLAY, Edna St. Vincent. *Lyrics, 7 Sonnets.* Armed Services 857. VG. B3d. $5.00

MILLEN, Gilmore. *Sweet Man.* 1952. Pyramid G 59. 1st pb. c/Paul. VG. B6d. $9.00

MILLER, Arthur. *After the Fall.* 1965. Bantam W 2884. 1st prtg. VG. P7d. $3.50

MILLER, Arthur. *Focus.* 1950. Popular 230. c/Belarski: gga. Fa. VG. B4d. $10.00

MILLER, Arthur. *Misfits.* 1961. Dell F 115. MTI. c/C Gable & M Monroe: photo. Fi. G+. B5d. $7.50

MILLER, Arthur. *Misfits.* 1961. Dell F 115. MTI. VG+. B4d. $20.00

MILLER, Dallas. *Fathers & Daughters.* 1969. Avon N 180. 1st prtg. c/Avati: gga. VG+. P7d. $4.00

MILLER, Diane Disney. *Story of Walt Disney.* 1959. Dell D 266. 1st pb. NF. M1d. $10.00

MILLER, Diane Disney. *Story of Walt Disney.* 1959. Dell D 266. 1st prtg. Bio. VG. R5d. $6.00

MILLER, Douglas. *You Can't Do Business With Hitler.* 1942. Pocket 139. Nfi. VG+. B5d. $7.00

MILLER, Floyd. *Dream Peddlers.* 1956. Popular 787. PBO. c/gga. scarce. NF. B6a #80. $55.00

MILLER, Floyd. *Savage Streets.* 1956. Popular 746. c/Rafael DeSoto: photo. Fa. VG. B4d. $5.00

MILLER, Frank. *Murder's for the Birds.* 1961. Vega Book 9. PBO. My. VG+. B6d. $9.00

MILLER, Gruber W. *Ellery Queen Mystery Magazine.* 1957. Ellery Queen Mystery 118. VG+. B3a #24. $4.40

MILLER, Helen Topping. *Flame Vine.* Avon 254. VG+. l1d. $10.00

MILLER, Helen Topping. *Wicked Sister.* 1949. Avon 210. c/gga. Fa. VG+. B3d. $5.00

MILLER, Henry. *Devil in Paradise.* 1956. Signet 1317. PBO. Nfi. VG+. B5d. $5.50

MILLER, Henry. *Nights of Love & Laughter.* 1955. Signet 1246. Nfi. VG. B5d. $6.00

MILLER, Henry. *Tropic of Cancer.* 1961. Black Cat BD 10. Ad. G+. B5d. $5.00

MILLER, Henry. *World of Sex.* 1965. Greenleaf Classic 110. 1st US edn. F. F2d. $10.00

MILLER, John A. *Men & Volts at War.* 1948. Bantam A 1. c/photos. Nfi. VG. B5d. $3.00

MILLER, Lee O. *Professor of Sex.* 1965. Playtime 758S. 1st edn. c/gga. F. F2d. $10.00

MILLER, M. *Ask the Cards a Question.* Mis Mystery. c/sgn. VG. B3d. $6.00

MILLER, M. *Broadwalk.* Nightstand 1851. PBO. VG+. B3d. $5.50

MILLER, M. *Edwin of Iron Shoes.* Mis Mystery. c/sgn. VG. B3d. $6.00

MILLER, Merle. *Sure Thing.* 1950. Popular 277. c/gga. Fa. VG+. B4d. $12.00

MILLER, R.D. *Impossible.* Ace F 137. F. M1d. $6.00

MILLER, R.D. *Stranger Than Life.* Ace K 168. NF. B3d. $5.50

MILLER, Rusty. *Jedi Master's Quiz Book.* 1982. Ballantine 30697. 1st prtg. G+. R5d. $1.50

MILLER, S. *H for Horrific!* Sentinel. NF. B3d. $8.00

MILLER, S.V. *Lesbian Lover.* 1964. Playtime 676. 1st edn. c/gga. F. F2d. $12.00

MILLER, Sigmund. *Snow Leopard.* Gold Medal S 1106. PBO. G+. M6d. $6.50

MILLER, Sigmund. *Snow Leopard.* 1961. Gold Medal S 1106. PBO. My. NF. B6d. $16.50

MILLER, Vance. *Uncertain Couple.* 1974. Liverpool TNS 579. Ad. VG. B5d. $3.50

MILLER, Victor. *Girl in the River.* 1975. Pocket 78817. PBO. TVTI. VG+. B6d. $5.00

MILLER, Victor. *Girl in the River.* Star 30088. TVTI. VG. M6d. $5.00

MILLER, Victor. *Requiem for a Cop.* 1974. Pocket 78488. PBO. TVTI. VG+. B6d. $5.00

MILLER, Victor. *Siege.* 1974. Pocket 78487. PBO. TVTI. VG+. B6d. $5.00

MILLER, Victor. *Take-Over.* 1975. Pocket 78996. PBO. TVTI. VG+. B6d. $5.00

MILLER, Victor. *Therapy in Dynamite.* 1975. Pocket 78865. PBO. TVTI. VG+. B6d. $5.00

MILLER, Victor. *Very Deadly Game.* 1975. Pocket 78960. PBO. TVTI. VG+. B6d. $5.00

MILLER, Wade. *Big Guy.* 1959. Gold Medal S 936. 2nd prtg. c/Barye. VG. P6d. $2.00

MILLER, Wade. *Branded Woman.* 1952. Gold Medal 257. 1st prtg. PBO. c/Floherty: gga. G+. P7d. $4.00

MILLER, Wade. *Deadly Weapon.* Pengium 648. VG. G5d. $9.50

MILLER, Wade. *Deadly Weapon.* 1960. Signet S 1805. 3rd prtg. c/Bob Abbett: gga. VG. P6d. $2.25

MILLER, Wade. *Deadly Weapon.* Signet 1805. 3rd reissue. VG. B3d. $4.00

MILLER, Wade. *Deadly Weapon.* 1952. Signet 928. 1st prtg. c/Summers: gga. VG. P7d. $6.00

MILLER, Wade. *Devil May Care.* 1958. Gold Medal 758. 1st prtg. VG. P7d. $5.00

MILLER, Wade. *Fatal Step.* 1948. Signet 695. My. VG+. B4d. $5.00

MILLER, Wade. *Girl From Midnight.* 1962. Gold Medal S 1221. c/Bob Abbett. VG+. P6d. $6.00

MILLER, Wade. *Guilty Bystander.* 1958. Signet 1482. 3rd edn. My. VG. B5d. $4.00

MILLER, Wade. *Killer.* Gold Medal 152. G. G5d. $3.50

MILLER, Wade. *Killer*. Gold Medal 152. VG. lld. $6.00

MILLER, Wade. *Killer*. Gold Medal 214. VG. B3d. $6.00

MILLER, Wade. *Killer*. Phantom 522. NF. B6a #76. $67.25

MILLER, Wade. *Killer's Choice*. 1955. Signet 1235. 1st prtg. c/gga. VG. P7d. $5.00

MILLER, Wade. *Killer's Choice*. 1950. Signet 771. 1st prtg. c/gga. VG. P7d. $6.00

MILLER, Wade. *Kiss Her Goodbye*. 1959. Signet 1662. My. VG. B5d. $4.00

MILLER, Wade. *Kitten With a Whip*. Gold Medal 434. VG. B3d. $8.00

MILLER, Wade. *Mad Baxter*. Gold Medal 1355. 2nd edn. VG. B3d. $5.00

MILLER, Wade. *Mad Baxter*. 1955. Gold Medal 469. 1st prtg. PBO. c/Lu Kimmel: photo. VG. P6d. $6.00

MILLER, Wade. *Murder Charge*. 1951. Signet 908. 1st pb. c/Bobertz. My. VG+. B6d. $13.50

MILLER, Wade. *Nightmare Cruise*. 1961. Ace D 518. PBO. VG+. B6d. $30.00

MILLER, Wade. *Shoot To Kill*. Phantom 612. VG+. B6a #76. $55.00

MILLER, Wade. *Shoot To Kill*. Signet 1013. G+. G5d. $6.00

MILLER, Wade. *Shoot To Kill*. Signet 1013. 1st pb. VG. M6d. $4.50

MILLER, Wade. *Sinner Take All*. 1960. Gold Medal 1027. G. C5d. $3.00

MILLER, Wade. *Stolen Woman*. 1950. Gold Medal 139. c/Barye. VG. P6d. $6.00

MILLER, Wade. *Tiger's Wife*. Gold Medal 173. VG+. B3d. $5.50

MILLER, Wade. *Uneasy Street*. 1949. Signet 722. c/J Avati. My. VG+. B5d. $9.00

MILLER, Wade. *Uneasy Street*. 1949. Signet 722. F. lld. $12.00

MILLER, Walter M. *Canticle for Leibowitz*. 1976. Bantam 02973. SF. VG. W2d. $3.00

MILLER, Walter M. *Conditionally Human*. 1962. Ballantine 626. NF. B3d. $7.00

MILLER, Walter M. *Conditionally Human*. 1962. Ballantine. 1st edn. VG. M1d. $6.00

MILLER, Walter M. *View From the Stars*. Ballantine U 2212. 1st prtg. VG. S1d. $4.00

MILLER, Walter M. *View From the Stars*. Ballantine U 2212. 1st edn. F. M1d. $8.00

MILLER, Warren *Cool World*. Four Square 1319. JD. VG. B3d. $8.50

MILLER, Warren *90 Miles From Home*. Crest 463. VG+. B3d. $5.00

MILLER, Warren. *Cool World*. 1960. Crest S 386. JD. F. P1d. $30.00

MILLER, Warren. *Cool World*. 1960. Crest S 386. JD. VG+. P6d. $4.00

MILLER, Warren. *Way We Live Now*. Crest S 299. 1st pb. VG. M6d. $6.50

MILLER & HUNGER/SOHL. *Man Who Lived Forever/Mars Monopoly*. Ace D 162. F. M1d. $15.00

MILLER & HUNGER/SOHL. *Man Who Lived Forever/Mars Monopoly*. Ace D 162. VG+. B3d. $5.50

MILLER & NORTON. *House of Shadows*. 1985. TOR 54743. SF. F. W2d. $4.50

MILLER & UNDERWOOD. *Fear Itself*. Signet AE 5270. 3rd edn. Nfi. VG. P1d. $4.00

MILLER & WADE. *Murder Queen High*. Graphic 54. 2nd edn. VG+. lld. $5.00

MILLER/SOHL. *Man Who Lived Forever/ Mars Monopoly*. Ace D 162. NF. P9d. $6.00

MILLER/WADE. *Murder: Queen High*. Graphic 11. c/Bob Wade: sgn. VG. B3d. $7.50

MILLS, C. Wright. *Causes of World War Three*. 1961. Ballantine F 568. 3rd edn. NF. VG+. B5d. $3.00

MILLS, H. *Prudence & the Pill*. Popular 60-8060. MTI. c/photo. VG+. B3d. $4.50

MILLS, John. *Electronics -- Today & Tomorrow*. Armed Services 824. VG. P6d. $3.50

MILLS, M. *Long Haul*. Avon T 201. MTI. VG. B3d. $5.50

MILLS, Robert E. *Star Quest*. Belmont 51259. SF. G+. W2d. $2.75

MILLS, Robert P. edt. *Best From Fantasy & SF, 9th Series*. Ace 05448. SF. VG. B5d. $3.00

MILLS, Robert P. edt. *Decade of Fantasy & SF*. Dell X 12. VG+. B3d. $4.50

MILLS, Robert P. edt. *Worlds of SF (Anthology)*. PB Library 54-819. NF. B3d. $6.00

MILNER, Michael. *Hatari!* Cardinal C 437. PBO. MTI. VG+. B3d. $5.00

MILNER, Michael. *Hatari!* 1962. Cardinal C 437. PBO. MTI. NF. B6d. $9.00

MILNER, Michael. *Pocket Guide to Birds*. 1954. Cardinal GC 18. 1st pb. VG+. B6d. $7.50

MILNER, Michael. *Sex on Celluloid*. MacFadden 75-141. PBO. VG. B3d. $6.00

MILTON, George Fort. *Conflict, American Civil War*. 1941. Infantry NN. Nfi. VG+. B4d. $4.00

MILTON, Joseph. *Baron Sinister*. Lancer 72-947. My. F. W2d. $4.25

MILTON, Joseph. *Operation: WWIII*. 1966. Lancer 72-134. My. VG+. B4d. $3.00

MILTON, Joseph. *Worldbreaker*. 1964. Lancer 72-760. 1st edn. My. F. F2d. $11.00

MINTON/ST. JOHN. *Paula -- Shadow of a Witch/Daughter of Evil*. 1967. Belmont B 60-058. Go. VG. P1d. $6.00

MIRBEAU, O. *Diary of a Chambermaid*. Avon T 145. VG+. B3d. $5.50

MIRLEES, Hope. *Lud-In-the-Mist*. 1970. Ballantine. 1st edn. Ad/Fa. F. M1d. $12.00

MIRVISH, Robert F. *Eternal Voyagers*. 1955. Signet S 1222. c/C Hulings. Fi. VG. B5d. $3.00

MIRVISH, Robert F. *Eternal Voyagers*. 1955. Signet S 1222. 1st pb. c/Hulings. VG+. B6d. $7.50

MITCHELL, Francis. *Naked Acre*. 1954. Avon T 84. c/gga. Fa. VG. B4d. $3.00

MITCHELL, Francis. *Naked Acre*. 1954. Avon T 84. 1st pb. c/gga. VG+. B6d. $7.00

MITCHELL, Gordon. *Henry's Wife*. Midwood 137. c/Rader: gga. reprint. VG+. B6d. $12.50

MITCHELL, Jackson. *Desire Under the Palms*. 1960. Kozy Books K 96. PBO. c/gga. VG. B3d. $4.00

MITCHELL, Jackson. *Desire Under the Palms*. 1960. Kozy 96. PBO. NF. B6d. $12.00

MITCHELL, John. *City of Revelation*. 1973. Ballantine 23607. Nfi. VG+. B5d. $3.50

MITCHELL, Kerry. *Cruise Doctor*. 1963. Dell 1st Edn 1632. 1st prtg. PBO. c/Abbett: gga. VG+. P7d. $3.50

MITCHELL, Kerry. *Emergency Doctor*. Dell 1st Edn 2287. VG+. B3d. $4.50

MITCHELL, Kirk. *Procurator*. 1984. Ace. 1st edn. F. M1d. $5.00

MITCHELL, Margaret. *Gone With the Wind*. 1961. Perma M 9501. 4th prtg. G+. R5d. $2.50

MITCHELL, Will. *Goldfish Murders*. Gold Medal 118. VG. M6d. $9.50

MITCHIE, John. *Mountain Sin Camp*. 1966. Dragon Edtition 119. PBO. c/gga. scarce. NF. B6a #76. $46.00

MITCHISON, Naomi. *Memoirs of a Space-woman*. 1973. Berkley O 2345. 1st prtg. SF. VG+. R5d. $2.25

MITCHISON, Naomi. *Memoirs of a Space-woman.* 1973. Berkley. 1st pb edn. F. M1d. $7.00

MITRA, Sisirkumar. *Vision of India.* 1949. Jaico NN. Nfi. G+. B5d. $3.50

MITTELHOLZER, Edgar. *Children of Kaywana.* Ace H 234. 3rd edn. c/gga. VG. B3d. $6.00

MITTELHOLZER, Edgar. *Kaywana Stock.* Ace H 284. VG. B3d. $6.00

MITTELHOLZER, Edgar. *Savage Destiny.* 1960. Dell F 97. c/J Meese. Fi. VG. B5d. $2.50

MITTELHOLZER, Edgar. *Shadows Move Among Them.* 1953. Pocket 918. c/T Dunn. Fi. VG. B5d. $4.00

MIZRAHI, Joseph V. *Solitaire.* 1966. Challenge CB 208. 1st prtg. My. G+. R5d. $1.50

MOLL, E. *Seidman & Son.* Signet 1763. VG. B3d. $4.00

MOMADAY, N. Scott. *House Made of Dawn.* 1969. Signet Q 4065. 1st prtg. VG. P7d. $4.50

MONACO, Richard. *Journey Into the Flame.* 1985. Bantam 25373. SF. VG. W2d. $3.00

MONAHAN, James. *Before I Sleep.* 1963. Signet P 2313. Nfi. VG. B4d. $3.00

MONAHAN, John. *Big Stan.* 1953. Gold Medal 355. PBO. c/Barye. NF. B6a #80. $35.00

MONASH, Paul. *How Brave We Live.* 1952. Avon 405. Fi. VG+. B3d/B5d. $6.00

MONDAY, Billie. *Water Bed Orgy.* 1973. Liverpool TNS 573. Ad. NF. B5d. $5.50

MONSARRAT, Nicholas. *Cruel Sea.* 1953. Cardinal GC 10. 1st prtg. c/Pease. NF. P7d. $4.50

MONSARRAT, Nicholas. *Depends What You Mean by Love.* 1954. Signet 1092. Fi. VG. B5d. $4.00

MONSON & MCLEAN. *On the Ropes.* Belmont 952063. VG+. B3d. $4.00

MONTAGU, Ashley. *Cultured Man.* Perma M 4141. VG. B3d. $3.50

MONTAGUE, J.J. *French Kiss.* Canyon 113. PBO. Black Swan #3. VG+. B3d. $5.00

MONTAGUE, Joseph F. *How To Overcome Nervous Stomach.* Perma P 106. VG. B3d. $4.00

MONTANA, Duke. *Nevada Killing.* 1952. Lion 78. 1st US edn. c/Kunstler. We. VG. B6d. $12.50

MONTELEONE, Thomas F. *Lyrica.* 1987. Berkley 09719. 1st edn. c/sgn. Ho. F. F2d. $12.00

MONTELEONE, Thomas F. *Night Train.* 1984. Pocket 44952. 1st edn. sgn. SF. F. F2d. $13.50

MONTELEONE, Thomas F. *Seeds of Change.* 1975. Laser 00. PBO. c/K Freas. SF. VG+. B5d. $5.00

MONTGOMERY, H. *Loretta.* Merit 613. PBO. VG+. B3d. $6.50

MONTGOMERY, I. *Golden Dress.* Boardman NN GD. VG. B3d. $7.00

MONTGOMERY, R.A. *Choose Your Own Adventure #4: Space & Beyond.* 1982. Bantam 23180. 12th prtg. SF. VG. W2d. $2.75

MONTGOMERY, Rutherford. *Gray Wolf.* 1949. Comet 24. 1st pb. c/Powers. VG. B6d. $5.00

MOON, Bucklin. *Champs & Bums.* 1954. Lion 229. PBO. c/Hemingway. VG. B6d. $12.50

MOON, Bucklin. *Darker Brother.* 1949. Bantam 737. VG. B4d. $3.75

MOONEY, Belle S. *How Shall I Tell My Child.* Perma P 11. VG. I1d. $4.00

MOONEY, Booth. *Here Is My Body.* 1952. Gold Medal 218. 1st edn. My. F. F2d. $15.00

MOONEY, Booth. *Here Is My Body.* Gold Medal 781. 2nd prtg. VG. B3d. $6.00

MOONEY, Booth. *Insiders.* Ace D 292. VG+. B3d. $6.00

MOORCOCK, Michael. *Behold the Man.* 1970. Avon V 2333. 1st edn. NF. P9d. $2.00

MOORCOCK, Michael. *Behold the Man.* 1970. Avon V 2333. 1st edn. VG. P9d. $1.50

MOORCOCK, Michael. *Best SF New Worlds 4.* Berkley S 1943. 1st prtg. F. S1d. $7.50

MOORCOCK, Michael. *Best SF Stories From New Worlds 5.* 1971. Berkley S 2003. 1st prtg. SF. VG+. R5d. $4.00

MOORCOCK, Michael. *Black Corridor.* Ace 06530. c/L & D Dillon: Ace SF Special. $3.50

MOORCOCK, Michael. *Black Corridor.* Ace 06530. 1st prtg. VG. S1d. $3.00

MOORCOCK, Michael. *Black Corridor.* 1974. Mayflower 11640. 3rd prtg. SF. F. W2d. $4.50

MOORCOCK, Michael. *Bull & the Spear.* 1974. Berkley. 1st edn. F. M1d. $10.00

MOORCOCK, Michael. *Chinese Agent.* Ace. 1st pb edn. F. M1d. $10.00

MOORCOCK, Michael. *Chronicles of Corum.* 1978. Berkley. 1st edn. F. M1d. $6.00

MOORCOCK, Michael. *City of the Beast.* 1979. DAW 321. SF. VG. B5d. $3.00

MOORCOCK, Michael. *City of the Beast.* Lancer 74-668. 1st prtg. F. S1d. $6.00

MOORCOCK, Michael. *Count Brass.* 1976. Dell 1541. 1st prtg. SF. VG. R5d. $1.75

MOORCOCK, Michael. *Dreaming City.* 1972. Lancer 75-376. PBO. SF. VG. B5d. $3.50

MOORCOCK, Michael. *Dreaming City.* 1972. Lancer 75-376. 1st edn. F. M1d. $10.00

MOORCOCK, Michael. *Elric of Melnibone.* 1976. DAW 214. SF. VG. B4d. $4.00

MOORCOCK, Michael. *Final Programme.* 1968. Avon S 351. 1st book of Jerry Cornelius. PBO. SF. VG. B5d/M3d. $4.00

MOORCOCK, Michael. *Ice Scooner.* Berkley X 1749. 1st prtg. VG. S1d. $3.50

MOORCOCK, Michael. *Jade Man's Eyes.* 1973. Unicorn Fantasy NN. PBO. scarce. NF. B6a #76. $77.00

MOORCOCK, Michael. *Jewel in the Skull.* 1977. DAW UY 1276. SF. VG. W2d. $3.50

MOORCOCK, Michael. *Jewel in the Skull.* 1967. Lancer 73-688. PBO. c/G Morrow. SF. VG. B5d/R5d. $4.50

MOORCOCK, Michael. *Jewel in the Skull.* 1967. Lancer 73-688. 1st edn. F. M1d. $15.00

MOORCOCK, Michael. *Jewel in the Skull.* Lancer 78-771. SF. VG. B5d. $3.00

MOORCOCK, Michael. *Knight of Swords.* Berkley S 1971. 1st prtg. VG. S1d. $5.50

MOORCOCK, Michael. *Knight of the Swords.* Berkley S 1971 1st edn. F. M1d. $12.00

MOORCOCK, Michael. *Land Leviathan.* 1976. DAW UY 1214. SF. VG. W2d. $3.50

MOORCOCK, Michael. *Land Leviathan.* 1976. DAW 178. 1st edn. PBO. F. P9d. $2.00

MOORCOCK, Michael. *Legends From the End of Time.* 1977. DAW 229. c/B Pepper. SF. VG. B5d. $3.50

MOORCOCK, Michael. *Life & Times of Jerry Cornelius.* Dale 01588. 1st prtg. SF. VG+. R5d. $2.50

MOORCOCK, Michael. *Lord of Spiders.* DAW 325. 1st prtg. VG+. S1d. $4.50

MOORCOCK, Michael. *Lord of Spiders.* Lancer 74-736. 1st edn. F. M1d. $7.00

MOORCOCK, Michael. *Masters of the Pit.* 1979. DAW UW1450. 1st prtg. SF. G+. W2d. $3.00

MOORCOCK, Michael. *Masters of the Pit.* DAW 330. 1st prtg. VG. S1d. $2.00

MOORCOCK, Michael. *Masters of the Pit.* Lancer 75-199. 1st prtg. VG. S1d. $4.50

MOORCOCK, Michael. *Messiah at the End of Time.* 1977. DAW 277. 1st edn. VG. P9d. $1.50

MOORCOCK, Michael. *Mother London.* 1989. Harmony. 1st edn. SF. F. F2d. $25.00

MOORCOCK, Michael. *New Worlds Quarterly #1.* 1971. Berkley. 1st edn. F. M1d. $7.00

MOORCOCK, Michael. *New Worlds Quarterly #2.* Berkley N 2102. 1st prtg. F. S1d. $5.50

MOORCOCK, Michael. *New Worlds Quarterly #3.* 1972. Berkley. 1st edn. F. M1d. $7.00

MOORCOCK, Michael. *New Worlds Quarterly #4.* 1972. Berkley. 1st edn. F. M1d. $6.00

MOORCOCK, Michael. *Oak & the Ram.* 1974. Berkley 2534. c/D Johnson. SF. VG. B5d. $3.00

MOORCOCK, Michael. *Oak & the Ram.* 1974. Berkley 2534. 1st edn. F. M1d. $10.00

MOORCOCK, Michael. *Oak & the Ram.* 1974. Berkley 2534. 1st edn. G. P9d. $1.50

MOORCOCK, Michael. *Queen of the Swords.* Berkley S 1999. 1st prtg. G. S1d. $1.50

MOORCOCK, Michael. *Queen of the Swords.* 1971. Berkley. 1st edn. F. M1d. $10.00

MOORCOCK, Michael. *Sailor on the Seas of Fate.* 1976. DAW 220. 1st edn. F. P9d. $2.00

MOORCOCK, Michael. *Secret of Runestaff.* 1969. Lancer 73-824. 1st edn. F. M1d. $10.00

MOORCOCK, Michael. *Secret of Runestaff.* 1969. Lancer 73-824. 1st prtg. G+. S1d. $4.50

MOORCOCK, Michael. *Silver Warriors.* Dell 7994. 1st prtg. VG+. S1d. $3.75

MOORCOCK, Michael. *Singing Citadel.* 1970. Berkley S 1870. 1st edn. NF. M1d. $20.00

MOORCOCK, Michael. *Singing Citadel.* 1970. Berkley S 1870. 1st US edn. SF. VG+. B6d. $7.50

MOORCOCK, Michael. *Sleeping Sorceress.* 1972. Lancer 75-375. 1st edn. F. M1d. $20.00

MOORCOCK, Michael. *Sorcerer's Amulet.* 1968. Lancer 73-707. 1st edn. F. M1d. $20.00

MOORCOCK, Michael. *Stealer of Souls.* 1967. Lancer 73-545. 1st US edn. F. M1d. $20.00

MOORCOCK, Michael. *Stormbringer.* 1967. Lancer 73-579. 1st prtg. G. S1d. $2.00

MOORCOCK, Michael. *Stormbringer.* 1967. Lancer 73-579. 1st prtg. SF. VG. R5d. $4.50

MOORCOCK, Michael. *Stormbringer.* 1967. Lancer 73-579. 1st US edn. F. M1d. $20.00

MOORCOCK, Michael. *Sundered Worlds.* 1966. PB Library. 1st US edn. F. M1d. $15.00

MOORCOCK, Michael. *Sword & the Stallion.* 1974. Berkley 2548. 1st edn. VG. P9d. $1.50

MOORCOCK, Michael. *Swords Trilogy.* 1977. Berkley. 2nd edn. F. M1d. $3.00

MOORCOCK, Michael. *Vanishing Tower.* 1983. Berkley 06406. SF. F. W2d. $3.75

MOORCOCK, Michael. *Warlord of the Air.* 1971. Ace 87060. 1st edn. SF. F. P9d. $2.00

MOORCOCK, Michael. *Winds of Limbo.* PB Library 63249. 2nd prtg. VG. S1d. $2.00

MOORCOCK/PETAJA. *Wrecks of Time/Tramontane.* 1967. Ace H 36. SF. G+. W2d. $4.00

MOORE, Amanda. *Nude in a Red Chair.* 1963. Midwood F 336. PBO. c/Paul Rader: gga. scarce. NF. B6a #75. $112.50

MOORE, Brian. *Cold Heaven.* 1984. Crest 20602. 1st prtg. c/gga. VG. P7d. $4.00

MOORE, Brian. *Emperor of Ice Cream.* Bantam H 3249. 1st pb. VG. M6d. $6.50

MOORE, Brian. *Executioners.* 1951. Harlequin 117. PBO. rare. VG. B6a. $73.00

MOORE, Brian. *Lonely Passion of Judith Hearne.* 1962. Dell F 165. Fa. VG+. B4d. $2.00

MOORE, Brian. *Lonely Passion of Judith Hearne.* 1962. Dell F 165. 1st prtg. VG+. P7d. $4.50

MOORE, Brian. *Sailor's Leave.* 1953. Pyramid 94. 1st US edn. scarce. VG. B6a #80. $43.00

MOORE, C.L. *Doomsday Morning.* 1968. Avon S 378. 3rd prtg. SF. G+. W2d. $4.25

MOORE, C.L. *Doomsday Morning.* Avon T 297. 1st pb edn. F. M1d. $10.00

MOORE, C.L. *Doomsday Morning.* 1959. Avon T 297. 1st prtg. SF. VG. R5d. $2.50

MOORE, C.L. *Earth's Last Citadel.* Ace F 306. F. M1d. $10.00

MOORE, C.L. *Jirel of Jolry.* 1969. PB Library. 1st edn. F. M1d. $12.00

MOORE, C.L. *Judgment Night.* 1965. PB Library 52-863. 1st edn. PBO. F. M1d. $12.00

MOORE, C.L. *There Shall Be Darkness.* American SF NN. VG+. B3a #22. $13.75

MOORE, Dan T. *Terrible Game.* Berkley G 169. VG. B3d. $4.00

MOORE, Emma. *Shallow Runs the River.* 1967. Belmont B 50-753. 1st prtg. My. G+. R5d. $1.75

MOORE, Hal R. *Naked & the Fair.* 1958. Beacon 183. 1st prtg. PBO. c/Micarelli: gga. VG+. P7d. $9.00

MOORE, Hal R. *Shanty Girl.* 1960. Newsstand U 135. Ad. G+. B5d. $4.00

MOORE, Hal R. *Shanty Girl.* 1960. Newsstand U 135. 1st edn. My. F. F2d. $10.00

MOORE, I. *Challenge for Nurse Melanie.* Ace D 567. PBO. VG. B3d. $4.00

MOORE, L. *Wheel & the Hearth.* Ballantine 15. VG. I1d. $4.00

MOORE, Robin. *Devil To Pay.* 1966. Avon N 134. 1st prtg. c/Bob Abbett: gga. VG. P7d. $4.00

MOORE, Robin. *Fifth Estate.* 1974. Bantam X 8333. 1st prtg. My. VG+. R5d. $1.75

MOORE, Roger E. *Endless Quest #25: Conan the Outlaw.* 1984. TSR 73974. 1st prtg. SF. VG. W2d. $2.75

MOORE, Roger. *Saint & Mr Teal.* Saint Novel K 114. TVTI. c/Roger Moore. VG. M6d. $7.50

MOORE, Ruth. *Deep Waters.* 1948. Pocket 508. 1st prtg. G+. R5d. $3.00

MOORE, Ruth. *Fair Wind Home.* 1955. Pocket 1051. c/C Hulings. Fi. VG+. B5d. $5.00

MOORE, Wallace. *Balzan: The Bloodstone.* Pyramid. F. P9d. $2.00

MOORE, Wallace. *Balzan: The Caves of Madness.* 1975. Pyramid V 3714. 1st edn. F. P9d. $2.00

MOORE, Wallace. *Balzan: The Lights of Zetar.* 1975. Pyramid V 3934. 1st edn. F. P9d. $2.00

MOORE, Ward. *Bring the Jubilee.* 1972. Avon. 1st edn. F. M1d. $6.00

MOORE, Ward. *Bring the Jubilee.* 1953. Ballantine 38. 1st edn. NF. M1d. $12.00

MOORE, Ward. *Greener Than You Think.* Ballantine 527. SF. VG. B5d. $5.00

MOORE, Ward. *Greener Than You Think.* Ballantine 527. 1st pb edn. F. M1d. $15.00

MOORE, William. *Heat Spell.* 1966. Midwood 32-587. 1st edn. F. F2d. $10.00

MOORE, William. *So Dark a Desire.* 1966. Midwood 32-603. Ad. NF. B5d. $6.50

MOORE & MACHLIN. *French Connection II.* 1975. Dell 5262. 1st edn. c/Gene Hackman: photo. My. F. F2d. $15.00

MOORE & PADGETT/NORTON. *Beyond Earth's Gate/Daybreak-2250 AD.* Ace D 69. F. M1d. $25.00

MOORE & PADGETT/NORTON. *Beyond Earth's Gates/Daybreak-2250 AD.* Ace D 69. VG+. B3d. $6.00

MOOREHEAD, Alan. *Blue Nile*. 1963. Dell 0636. Fa. VG+. B4d. $2.00

MOORES, S. *Primrose Path & Perversion*. Royal 120. PBO. VG+. B3d. $5.00

MOORIS, William. *Sundering Flood*. 1973. Ballantine. 1st edn. Ad/Fa. F. M1d. $12.00

MOORIS, William. *Well at the World's End, Vol I & II*. 1972-73. Ballantine. F. M1d. $12.00

MOORIS, William. *Wood Beyond the World*. Ballantine AF 01652. 1st prtg. F. S1d. $9.00

MOORSSY, John. *Extraterritorial*. 1977. Laser 52. 1st edn. NF. P9d. $1.75

MOORSSY, John. *Law for the Stars*. 1976. Laser 21. 1st edn. F. P9d. $2.00

MORAC, J. *My Life Is My Own*. Leisure 1. VG. B3d. $4.00

MORAN, Mike. *Double Cross*. 1953. Popular 494. PBO. My. VG. B3d. $4.00

MORAN, Richard. *Cold Sea Rising*. 1987. Berkley 09558. My. VG+. W2d. $3.25

MORAVIA, Alberto. *Bitter Honeymoon*. Signet 1520. VG+. B3d. $4.50

MORAVIA, Alberto. *Conformist*. 1953. Signet S 1071. 1st pb. c/Zuckerberg. VG. B6d. $7.50

MORAVIA, Alberto. *Conjugal Love*. Ace H 183. VG. B3d. $7.00

MORAVIA, Alberto. *Ghost at Noon*. 1956. Signet S 1306. Fa. VG. B4d. $2.50

MORAVIA, Alberto. *Time of Indifference*. 1955. Signet S 1213. c/gga. Fa. VG+. B4d. $2.00

MORAVIA, Alberto. *Two Women*. 1959. Signet D 1657. 1st prtg. c/Avati: gga. VG. P7d. $5.00

MORAVIA, Alberto. *Two Women*. 1959. Signet D 1657. 1st prtg. G+. R5d. $2.25

MORAVIA, Alberto. *Woman of Rome*. 1951. Signet S 844. c/J Avati. Fi. G+. B5d. $3.00

MORAY, Helga. *Carla*. 1966. Belmont B 60-054. Ad. VG+. B5d. $5.00

MORAY, Helga. *Dark Fury*. Corgi 640. VG. B3d. $7.00

MORAY, Helga. *Untamed*. Corgi 796. Reissue. VG+. B3d. $7.50

MORAY, Helga. *Untamed*. Dell 630. c/B Phillips. Fi. VG+. B5d. $4.00

MOOREHEAD & MOTT-SMITH. *New Quiz Book*. 1948. Penguin Books 652. 1st edn. F. F2d. $10.00

MORELL, Lee. *Mimi*. 1959. Beacon 275. 1st edn. c/Orrie Hitt: blurb. F. F2d. $15.00

MORELL, Lee. *Mimi*. 1959. Beacon 275. 1st prtg. PBO. VG. P7d. $7.50

MORELLI, Al. *Red Tide*. 1949. Foldes Press NN. PBO. c/gga. scarce. VG+. B6a #77. $35.00

MORELLI, Spike. *This Way for Hell*. Leisure 7. 2nd edn. c/gga. Fa. VG+. B4d. $15.00

MOREY, Walt. *Gentle Ben*. 1967. Tempo T 166. 1st prtg. VG. R5d. $2.50

MORGAN, Allan. *Blood #3: The Cat Cay Warrant*. 1974. Award AQ 1395. 1st prtg. My. G. W2d. $2.75

MORGAN, Barry. *Last of the Lonely Breed*. 1968. Greywood 114. TVTI. VG. P1d. $10.00

MORGAN, D. *Midnite Joke Book No 1*. Stravon. VG+. B3d. $8.00

MORGAN, Dan. *High Destiny*. 1973. Berkley 2434. 1st edn. G. P9d. $1.25

MORGAN, Dan. *Inside*. 1974. Berkley N 2734. 1st edn. VG. P9d. $1.50

MORGAN, Dan. *New Minds*. 1969. Avon V 2271. 1st US edn. SF. F. F2d. $11.00

MORGAN, Dan. *Uninhibited*. London. 1st edn. NF. M1d. $4.00

MORGAN, H. *Satana*. Rapture 303. VG. B3d. $6.00

MORGAN, Jason. *Death Is a Swinger*. 1968. Lancer 74-967. 1st edn. c/gga. Cr. F. F2d. $7.50

MORGAN, M.X. *Film Strip*. Tuxedo 119. PBO. VG. B3d. $5.00

MORGAN, Michael. *Blonde Body*. 1949. Lion 11. 1st edn. PBO. c/gga. scarce. My. NF. B6a #75. $33.00

MORGAN, Nancy. *Somebody Loves Me*. 1954. Gold Medal S 433. PBO. c/Erickson. VG+. B6d. $10.00

MORGAN, Wesley. *Dirty Harry: The Enforcer*. Warner 88366. 1st prtg. MTI. My. VG. W2d. $4.00

MORMOR, Arnold. *Lust Lodge*. 1960. Merit 509. PBO. VG+. B3d. $6.00

MORNINGSIDE, M. *Strange But True*. 1954. Gold Medal 450. PBO. VG+. B6d. $9.00

MOROSO, John A. *Passionate Fool*. 1949. Red Circle 2. PBO. c/gga. scarce. VG+. B6a #79. $45.00

MOROSO, John A. *Passionate Fool*. 1949. Red Circle 2. 1st edn. PBO. c/gga. scarce. VG+. B6a #75. $57.75

MORRELL, David. *Rambo First Blood Part II*. 1985. Jove 08399. MTI. My. F. W2d. $4.00

MORRESSY, John. *Frostworld & Dreamfire*. Popular04376. SF. VG. B5d. $3.00

MORRESSY, John. *Kingsbane*. 1982. Playboy Press 21098. 1st edn. c/sgn & inscr. SF. F. F2d. $25.00

MORRESSY, John. *Law for the Stars*. 1976. Laser 21. c/Freas. VG+. B3d. $5.50

MORRIS, Donald R. *China Station*. Corgi 551. VG. B3d. $7.50

MORRIS, Donald R. *Girl in Every Port*. 1956. Berkley G 25. 1st edn. PBO. c/gga. F. F2d. $10.00

MORRIS, Janet. *Dream Dancer*. 1982. Berkley 05232. SF. VG+. W2d. $3.25

MORRIS, John. *Candywine Development*. 1974. Dell 02090. 1st prtg. c/gga. VG+. P7d. $4.50

MORRIS, William. *Well at World's End: Volume #1*. 1973. Ballantine 23515. 3rd prtg. SF. VG. W2d. $4.00

MORRIS, William. *Well At World's End: Volume #2*. 1972. Ballantine 02996. 2nd prtg. SF. VG+. R5d. $5.00

MORRIS, Wright. *In Orbit*. 1968. Signet P 3291. 1st prtg. c/photo. VG. P7d. $5.50

MORRIS, Wright. *Love Among the Cannibals*. 1958. Signet S 1531. c/B Phillips. Fi. VG. B5d. $3.50

MORRIS & MORRIS. *Medusa*. 1986. Baen 65573. SF. VG. W2d. $3.50

MORRISON, Henry edt. *Come Seven, Come Death*. 1965. Pocket 50122. My. VG. B5d. $3.50

MORRISON, Ray. *Angels Camp*. 1950. Bantam 794. JD. VG+. P1d. $21.00

MORRO, Don. *Virgin*. 1959. Beacon 244. 1st edn. PBO. c/gga. NF. B6a #76. $42.50

MORRO, Don. *Virgin*. 1959. Beacon 244. 1st prtg. VG. P7d. $9.00

MORROW, James. *This Is the Way the World Ends*. 1989. Ace 80711. SF. NF. B5d. $5.00

MORROW, James. *Wine of Violence*. 1982. Ace 89441. SF. F. W2d. $4.00

MORSE, Benjamin. *Homosexual*. 1962. Monarch MB 527. Nfi. VG+. B4d. $4.00

MORSE, Benjamin. *Lesbian*. Monarch 513. PBO. VG. B3d. $7.00

MORSE, Benjamin. *Lesbian*. 1963. Monarch 543. 1st edn. F. F2d. $10.00

MORSE, Benjamin. *Sexual Behavior of the American College Girl*. 1963. Lancer 74-822. Nfi. VG+. B4d. $6.00

MORSE, L.A. *Old Dick.* 1981. Avon 78329. 1st prtg. My. VG+. W2d. $3.25

MORTIMER, Lee. *Washington Confidential Today.* 1962. PB Library 52-162. Nfi. VG. B5d. $3.00

MORTIMER, Penelope. *Pumpkin Eater.* 1964. Lancer 72-748. 1st pb. MTI. NF. B6d. $8.00

MORTON, Anthony. *Versus the Baron.* 1959. Jay 66. c/G Benvenuti. My. VG. B5d. $7.50

MORTON, Stanley. *Yankee Trader.* Pyramid G 54. Fi. G+. B5d. $5.50

MOSER & COHEN. *Pied Piper of Tucson.* Signet 3486. VG. B3d. $5.00

MOSKOWITZ, Sam. *Coming of the Robots.* Collier 548. 1st prtg. NF. S1d. $5.00

MOSKOWITZ, Sam. *Doorway Into Time.* MacFadden 50311. 1st prtg. VG. S1d. $5.00

MOSKOWITZ, Sam. *Exploring Other Worlds.* 1963. Collier A 5551. 1st edn. F. M1d/S1d. $5.00

MOSKOWITZ, Sam. *Human Zero & Others.* Tower 43-906. c/Bloch: sgn. VG. B3d. $4.50

MOSKOWITZ, Sam. *Other Worlds, Other Times.* 1969. MacFadden 75-238. 1st edn. NF. P9d. $1.75

MOSKOWITZ, Sam. *Vortex Blasters & Others.* 1968. MacFadden 60-325. VG. B3d. $4.00

MOSKOWITZ & NORTON. *Space Magicians.* Pyramid 2393. c/Bloch: sgn. VG. B3d. $7.50

MOSLEY, Lawrence. *Erotica '74.* 1974. Bee Line 1038. 1st edn. F. F2d. $10.00

MOSLEY, Leonard. *Foxhole in Cairo.* Belmont 225. MTI. c/Rommell. VG+. B3d. $6.00

MOSLEY, Nicholas. *Accident.* 1967. Signet T 2953. MTI. c/photo. VG. B4d. $3.00

MOTLEY, Willard. *Knock on Any Door.* 1962. Signet T 2085. 12th edn. JD. VG. P1d. $8.00

MOTLEY, Willard. *Let No Man Write My Epitaph.* Pan X 65. MTI. c/Peff. VG. B3d. $9.00

MOTLEY, Willard. *Let No Man Write My Epitaph.* 1960. Signet D1693. 3rd edn. Fi. VG. B3d. $5.00

MOTLEY, Willard. *We Fished All Night.* Ace H 324. PBO. VG. B3d. $10.00

MOTLEY, Willard. *We Fished All Night.* 1953. Signet 992. 1st edn. PBO. c/Avati: gga. F. F2d. $6.00

MOULTON, Powers. *Best Jokes for All Occasions.* 1956. Perma M 3060. Nfi. VG. B5d. $4.00

MOUNCE, David R. *Shield Project.* 1971. Pyramid T 2451. My. NF. B4d. $3.00

MOURA & SUTHERLAND. *If It Moves, Kiss It!* 1973. Gold Medal 2741. 1st edn. c/Wenzel. F. F2d. $10.00

MOWAT, Farley. *Dog Who Wouldn't Be.* 1959. Pyramid PR 20. 1st pb. VG+. B6d. $7.50

MOYES, Particia. *Dead Men Don't Ski.* 1965. Ballantine U 2242. 1st prtg. My. VG. R5d. $1.75

MOYES, Patricia. *Black Girl, White Girl.* 1990. Owl 9. c/R Mantel: skull. My. VG+. B5d. $4.00

MOYES, Patricia. *Death on the Agenda.* 1965. Ballantine U 2241. 1st pb. My. NF. B6d. $15.00

MOYES, Patricia. *Down Among the Dead Men.* 1965. Ballantine U 2240. 1st pb. My. VG+. B6d. $9.00

MOYES, Patricia. *Down Among the Dead Men.* 1982. Dell 11627. 1st prtg. My. VG. W2d. $3.00

MOYZISCH, L.C. *Operation Cicero.* Pyramid G 337. G+. I1d. $3.50

MULDOON, Guy. *Leopards in the Night.* 1956. Corgi S 195. 1st pb. Ad. VG. B6d. $5.00

MULFORD, Clarence E. *Bring Me His Ears.* Thrilling Novel 29. VG+. B3d. $10.00

MULFORD, Clarence E. *Hopalong Cassidy Takes Cards.* 1948. Popular 146. PBO. We. VG+. B6d. $12.50

MULFORD, Clarence E. *Mesquite Jenkins, Tumbleweed.* 1946. Popular 104. c/Freidler: cow skull. We. F. B4d. $12.00

MULFORD, Clarence E. *Orphan Outlaw.* 1950. Pyramid 25. 1st pb. We. VG. B6d. $9.00

MULFORD, Clarence E. *Tex.* Graphic 15. VG. B3d. $5.00

MULFORD, Clarence E. *Tex.* Graphic 28. VG+. I1d. $6.00

MULFORD, Clarence E. *Tex.* Graphic 91. 4th prtg. VG+. B3d. $5.00

MULHOLLAND, John. *Art of Illusion.* Armed Services O 3. VG. B3d. $7.00

MULHOLLAND, P.H. *Calypso Murders.* 1957. Avon 781. c/gga. My. F. B4d. $11.00

MULLADY & KOFOED. *Meet the Mob.* 1961. Belmont L 507. Nfi. VG. P6d. $1.50

MULLER, John E. *Beyond the Void.* Badger SF 112. VG. B3d. $9.00

MULLER, John E. *Crimson Planet.* Badger SF60. VG+. B3a #20. $10.50

MULLER, John E. *Dark Continuum.* Badger SF 104. VG. B3d. $6.50

MULLER, John E. *Day of the Beasts.* Badger SF 51. VG. B3d. $12.00

MULLER, John E. *Exorcists.* Badger SN 94. VG. B3d. $6.50

MULLER, John E. *Infinity Machine.* 1960. Badger 72. PBO. c/gga. scarce. SF. NF. B6a #74. $53.50

MULLER, John E. *Special Mission.* Vega. 1st edn. VG. M1d. $15.00

MULVIHILL, William. *Mantrackers.* 1960. Signet 1785. 1st edn. Av. F. F2d. $10.00

MULVIHILL, William. *Sands of Kalahari.* Crest 701. 2nd edn. c/Barye. VC. B3d. $4.00

MUNDY, Talbot. *Caesar Dies.* 1973. Centaur 10. c/F Brunner. SF. NF. B5d. $7.50

MUNDY, Talbot. *Helma.* 1967. Avon S 309. c/D Rosa. SF. VG. B5d. $4.00

MUNDY, Talbot. *Jimgrim Sahib.* Royal Giant 12. NF. I1d. $20.00

MUNDY, Talbot. *Jimgrim.* 1968. Avon V 2220. 1st prtg. VG. R5d. $3.50

MUNDY, Talbot. *Liafail.* 1967. Avon S 316. 1st prtg. Tros of Samothrage #3. SF. G+. R5d. $2.00

MUNDY, Talbot. *Secret of Ahbor Valley.* 1967. Avon V2212. c/J Enderwelt. SF. VG. B5d. $3.50

MUNDY, Talbot. *Trek East.* Royal Giant 19. NF. I1d. $25.00

MUNDY, Talbot. *Tros.* 1967. Avon S 303. 1st prtg. Tros of Samothrage. SF. VG. R5d. $4.00

MUNDY/WILLEFORD. *Full Moon/High Priest of California.* Pyramid 20. VG. I1d. $70.00

MUNN, H. Warner. *King of the World's Edge.* Ace M 152. F. M1d. $13.00

MUNN, H. Warner. *Merlin's Ring.* 1974. Ballantine. 1st edn. F. M1d. $8.00

MUNRO, H.H. *Saki Sampler.* 1945. Superior. 1st edn. VG. M1d. $10.00

MUNRO, H.H. *She-Wolf.* 1945. Bantam 143. 1st edn. PBO. scarce. Fa. NF. B6a #75. $75.00

MUNRO, James. *Die Rich Die Happy.* 1967. Bantam S 3401. 1st prtg. c/photo. NF. P7d. $4.50

MUNRO, James. *Die Rich Die Happy.* 1967. Bantam S 3401. 1st prtg. My. VG. R5d. $2.00

MUNRO, James. *Innocent Bystanders.* 1971. Bantam S 5741. 1st prtg. VG+. P7d. $4.50

MUNRO, James. *Man Who Sold Death.* 1966. Bantam S 3168. 1st prtg. VG+. P7d. $4.00

MUNRO, James. *Money That Money Can't Buy.* 1969. Bantam S3985. My. VG. B5d. $2.50

MURDOCK, Iris. *Unofficial Rose.* 1973. PB Library 76-037. 1st pb. NF. B6d. $7.00

MURPHY, Audie. *To Hell & Back.* 1955. Perma M 4029. c/Audie Murphy. War. VG. B4d. $4.00

MURPHY, Audie. *To Hell & Back.* 1951. Perma P 119. c/Korach. G+. P6d. $2.00

MURPHY, Audie. *To Hell & Back.* 1951. Perma P 119. VG. P6d. $4.00

MURPHY, Audie. *To Hell & Back.* Perma P 214. VG. B3d. $4.50

MURPHY, Dennis. *Sergeant.* 1968. MacFadden 75-201. 1st prtg. MTI. VG+. R5d. $3.25

MURPHY, Pat. *Falling Woman.* 1987. TOR. 1st pb edn. F. M1d. $4.00

MURPHY, Shirley. *Caves of Fire & Ice.* 1982. Avon 58081. SF. VG. W2d. $3.00

MURPHY, Shirley. *Ring of Fire.* Avon 47191. 1st edn. PBO. F. P9d. $2.00

MURPHY, Warren B. *Mystery Writers of America.* Gold Medal S 1046. VG. G5d. $4.00

MURPHY & SAPIR. *Adventure Begins.* 1985. Signet AE 3908. 1st prtg. VG. R5d. $1.50

MURPHY & SAPIR. *Bottom Line.* 1979. Pinnacle 40159. 1st prtg. Destroyer #37. My. VG. W2d. $3.00

MURPHY & SAPIR. *Deadly Seeds.* 1975. Pinnacle 00760. 1st prtg. Destroyer #21. My. VG. W2d. $3.00

MURPHY & SAPIR. *Judgement.* 1974. Pinnacle 00303. Destroyer #14. My. VG+. W2d. $3.25

MURRAY, John. *Hell on Wheels.* 1966. Private Edition PE 395. Ad. VG+. B5d. $4.50

MURRAY, Ken. *Ken Murray's Giant Joke Book.* 1954. Ace D 62. PBO. G. P6d. $2.50

MURRAY, Max. *Doctor & the Corpse.* Penguin 1178. VG. G5d. $6.00

MURRAY, Max. *Good Luck to the Corpse.* Dell 639. c/J Meese. My. VG. B5d. $3.00

MURRAY, Max. *Neat Little Corpse.* Dell 560. VG+. B3d. $6.00

MURRAY, Max. *Queen & the Corpse.* 1951. Dell 485. My. VG. P1d. $9.00

MURRAY, Max. *Right Honorable Corpse.* 1957. Penguin 1203. My. VG. P1d. $7.50

MURRAY, Max. *Voice of the Corpse.* 1948. Bantam 358. My. F. P1d. $25.00

MURRAY, Max. *World's Back Doors.* 1943. Guild Services Edn S 22. Nfi. G+. P1d. $12.50

MURRAY, Stephen. *Cool Killing.* 1989. Fontana 617735. My. VG. P1d. $4.00

MURRAY/MURRAY. *Feud in Piney Flats/ Hellion's Hole.* Ace D 34. PBO. G+. B3d. $4.00

MURRAY/SHADE. *Marilyn: The Last Months.* Pyramid 03616. VG+. B3d. $10.00

MURTAGH, John M. *Cast the First Stone.* 1958. Cardinal C 286. Nfi. F. P1d. $15.00

MYAGKOV, Aleksei. *Inside the KGB.* 1983. Ballantine 29843. 3rd edn. Nfi. VG. P1d. $3.00

MYERS, Amy. *Murder in Pug's Parlour.* 1992. Avon 76587. My. VG. P1d. $4.00

MYERS, Bernard. *50 Great Artists.* Bantam 1692. 2nd prtg. VG. B3d. $5.00

MYERS, Harold. *Animals Are Funnier Than People.* Avon 637. VG+. B3d. $8.50

MYERS, Harriet Kathryn. *Small Town Nurse.* 1962. Ace D 543. Ro. VG. P1d. $6.50

MYERS, John M. *Alamo.* Bantam 2089. VG+. B3d. $4.50

MYERS, John M. *Dead Warrior.* 1959. Hillman 115. 1st prtg. VG+. P7d. $8.50

MYERS, John M. *Silverlock.* Ace A 8. F. M1d. $10.00

MYERS, John M. *Silverlock.* Ace A 8. 1st edn. PBO. G. P9d. $1.25

MYERS, John M. *Silverlock.* 1979. Ace 76671. 3rd prtg. SF. VG. W2d. $3.50

MYERS, Robert J. *Cross of Frankenstein.* 1976. Pocket 80542. SF. VG. W2d. $4.00

MYERS & WILLIAMS. *What, When, Where, How To Drink.* Dell 1st Edn 55. PBO. G+. M6d. $3.50

MYKEL, A.W. *Salamandra Glass.* 1985. Bantam 24660. Th. G+. P1d. $2.50

MYLES, Symon. *Big Hit.* 1975. Everest 48. De. VG. P1d. $4.00

NABARRO, Derrick. *Rod of Anger.* 1955. Penguin 1055. My. VG. P1d. $8.00

NABB, Magdalen. *Death in Autumn.* 1986. Fontana 7172. My. VG. P1d. $4.50

NABB, Magdalen. *Death of a Dutchman.* 1984. Fontana 6775. 2nd edn. My. VG. P1d. $4.00

NABB, Magdalen. *Death of an Englishman.* 1983. Fontana 6776. My. VG. P1d. $4.00

NABLO, James Benson. *Long November.* 1949. Newstand A 2. Fa. VG. B3d. $6.00

NABOKOV, Vladimir. *Laughter in the Dark.* 1950. Signet 777. c/gga. Fa. VG. B4d. $3.50

NABOKOV, Vladimir. *Lolita.* Corgi 1066. VG. B3d. $7.00

NABOKOV, Vladimir. *Lolita.* 1959. Crest D 338. 1st prtg. VG. P7d. $4.00

NAGAI, T. *We of Nagasaki.* Ace H 208. VG. B3d. $8.00

NAHA, Ed. *Paradise Plot.* 1980. Bantam 13979. SF. VG. P1d. $3.50

NAMATH, Joe Willie. *I Can't Wait Until Tomorrow.* 1970. Signet Y 4308. Bio. VG+. B4d. $3.00

NAMES, Gerald W. *Mindblock.* 1981. Leisure 988. My. VG. P1d. $3.50

NAPIER, D. *House Party.* Beacon 993. PBO. VG. B3d. $5.50

NAPIER, Geoffrey. *Very Special Agent.* 1970. Crest T 1489. My. VG. P1d. $4.50

NAPIER, Geoffrey. *Wrong Box.* 1966. Dell 9708. My. VG. P1d. $5.50

NARRAN, Bree. *One Night.* Camden NN. c/gga. VG. B3d. $8.00

NARRAN, Bree. *Seven Nights.* Camden NN. VG. B3d. $8.00

NASH, Anne. *Said With Flowers.* 1945. Bart House 19. My. VG. P1d. $12.50

NASH, Anne. *Said With Flowers.* 1945. Bart House 19. 1st prtg. My. G+. R5d. $4.50

NASH, Jay Robert. *Bloodletters & Bad Men Book 2.* Warner 30-151. 7th edn. Nfi. VG. P1d. $3.50

NASH, Ogden. *Ogden Nash Pocket Book.* 1944. Pocket 251. Hu. VG+. B4d. $4.00

NASH, Simon. *Dead of a Counterplot.* 1985. Perennial P 757. 2nd edn. My. VG. P1d. $3.00

NASH, Simon. *Death Over Deep Water.* 1985. Perennial P 740. My. VG. P1d. $3.50

NATHAN, Robert Stuart. *White Tiger.* 1988. Warner 35206. Th. VG. P1d. $4.00

NATHAN, Robert. *Enchanted Voyage.* Armed Services 737. VG. I1d. $4.00

NATHAN, Robert. *Portrait of Jennie.* Armed Services 655. VG+. I1d. $5.00

NATHAN, Robert. *Portrait of Jennie.* 1967. Popular 60-2439. 1st prtg. VG+. B5d. $3.50

NATHAN, Robert. *Portrait of Jenny.* 1962. Popular G 572. 1st prtg. VG+. R5d. $3.75

NATIONAL DAIRY PRODUCTS CORP. *641 Tested Recipes From the Sealtest Kitchens.* 1964. National Dairy NN. Nfi. VG+. B5d. $3.50

NATIONAL LAMPOON edt. *Job of Sex.* Warner 76-429. NF. B3d. $5.50

NATSUKI, Shizuko. *Death From the Clouds.* 1991. Ballantine 36667. My. VG. P1d. $3.50

NATSUKI, Shizuko. *Innocent Journey.* 1989. Ballantine 35645. 1st edn. My. F. F2d. $6.00

NATSUKI, Shizuko. *Murder at Mt Fuju.* 1987. Ballantine 33761. My. VG. P1d. $3.50

NATSUKI, Shizuko. *Obituary Arrives at Two O'Clock.* 1988. Ballantine 35237. My. VG. P1d. $3.50

NATSUKI, Shizuko. *Portal of the Wind.* 1990. Ballantine 36032. My. VG. P1d. $3.50

NAUGHTON, Bill *Alfio.* 1966. Ballantine U 5061. 1st prtg. VG. R5d. $3.00

NAUGHTON, Edmund. *Case in Madrid.* 1973. Curtis 07285. My. VG. P1d. $3.50

NAUGHTON, Edmund. *Case in Madrid.* 1973. Curtis 07285. 1st edn. My. F. F2d. $7.00

NAUGHTON, Edmund. *Maximum Game.* 1975. Warner 76-584. Th. VG. P1d. $3.50

NAZARIAN, Barry. *Blood Rites.* 1980. Signet E 9203. Ho. VG. P1d. $4.00

NAZEL, Joseph. *Canadian Kill.* 1974. Holloway House BH 462. My. VG. P1d. $3.50

NAZEL, Joseph. *Slick Revenge.* 1974. Holloway House BH 452. My. VG. P1d. $3.50

NAZEL, Joseph. *Sunday Fix: Iceman #4.* Holloway House BH 089. VG. M6d. $4.50

NEARING, H. Jr. *Sinister Researches of CP Ransom.* Curtis 07051. F. M1d. $8.00

NEARING, H. Jr. *Sinister Researches of CP Ransom.* Curtis 07051. 1st prtg. SF. VG. R5d. $2.50

NEBEL, Frederick. *Six Deadly Dames.* 1950. Avon 264. VG. B3a #22. $51.25

NEBEL, Frederick. *Six Deadly Dames.* 1950. Avon 264. 1st edn. PBO. rare. NF. B6a #75. $75.00

NEBEL, Frederick. *Six Deadly Dames.* 1950. Avon 264. 1st edn. PBO. VG. B6d. $50.00

NEBEL, Long John. *Way Out World.* 1962. Lancer 72-644. c/O Leibman. NF. VG. B5d. $4.00

NEEL, Janet. *Death's Bright Angel.* 1989. Penguin 11495. My. VG. P1d. $4.00

NEELY, Richard. *Death to My Beloved.* 1971. Signet T 4774. My. VG. P1d. $4.00

NEELY, Richard. *Innocents With Dirty Hands.* 1976. Star L 39857. 1st prtg. MTI. My. F. W2d. $5.00

NEELY, Richard. *Plastic Nightmare.* 1969. Ace 67095. My. VG. P1d. $4.50

NEELY, Richard. *Sexton Women.* 1974. Berkley 02514. My. G. P1d. $1.50

NEIDERMAN, Andrew. *Illusion.* 1987. World Wide 97044. My. VG. P1d. $3.50

NEILL, R. *Hangman's Cliff.* Arrow 518. VG. B3d. $7.00

NEITZEL, Neal. *Hot-Blooded Blonde.* 1961. Merit Book 529. My. VG+. P1d. $9.50

NEITZEL, Neal. *Over-Passionate Blonde!* 1963. Merit Book 6102. My. VG. P1d. $8.00

NELSON, Hugh Lawrence. *Dead Giveaway.* 1951. Dell 520. My. F. P1d. $18.00

NELSON, Hugh Lawrence. *Fountain of Death.* Bestseller Mystery B 116. My. VG. P1d. $12.50

NELSON, R.F. *Blake's Progress.* 1975. Laser 13. PBO. c/K Freas. SF. NF. B5d. $6.00

NELSON, R.F. *Ecolog.* Laser 53. VG. B3d. $4.00

NELSON, R.F. *Then Beggars Could Ride.* 1976. Laser 32. 1st edn. SF. F. F2d. $10.00

NEMEC, John. *Canary's Combo.* 1964. Nitetime 93. PBO. c/Jazz. VG. B6d. $6.00

NEMEC, John. *Exploiting the Innocent.* 1966. Tropic. 1st edn. My. F. F2d. $15.00

NEMEC, John. *Marriage on the Rocks.* 1963. Midwood F 345. PBO. NF. B6d. $16.50

NEMEC, John. *Spy Who Came to Bed.* 1968. Triumph 319. 1st edn. My. F. F2d. $12.00

NEMEC, John. *Wild for Kicks.* 1961. Novel Books 5062. 1st edn. My. F. F2d. $13.00

NEMEC, John. *Wild for Kicks.* 1961. Nove Booksl 5062. VG. B3d. $4.00

NEMEROV, Howard. *Homecoming Game.* 1960. Avon T 415. Fa. VG. B4d. $2.00

NERN, Daniel D. *Black As Night.* 1960. World Dist 944. VG. B3d. $8.00

NESS, Eliot. *Untouchables.* 1960. Popular G 403. TVTI. VG. P1d. $12.50

NESS, Eliot. *Untouchables.* 1964. Popular SP 258. My. VG. P1d. $10.00

NEUBAUER, William. *Golden Heel.* Lancer 4200-48. My. VG. P1d. $3.50

NEUBAUER, William. *Police Nurse.* 1965. MacFadden 50-248. My. VG. P1d. $5.50

NEUMANN, Alfred. *Strange Conquest.* Ballantine 88. PBO. VG+. B3d. $4.50

NEVILLE, Kris. *Invaders on the Moon.* Belmont 75-1085. VG. B3d. $4.00

NEVILLE, Kris. *Mutants.* 1966. Belmont B 50-730. 1st edn. F. M1d. $10.00

NEVILLE, Kris. *Mutants.* 1966. Belmont B50-730. PBO. SF. VG. B5d/W2d. $4.00

NEVILLE, Kris. *Unearth People.* 1968. Belmont B 50-843. 1st prtg. SF. VG. R5d. $3.00

NEVILLE, Kris. *Unearth People.* 1968. Belmont B 50-843. 2nd edn. F. M1d. $5.00

NEVILLE, Kris. *Unearth People.* 1964. Belmont 92-611. PBO. SF. VG. B5d. $3.50

NEVILLE, M. *Pervert.* Merit 602. VG. B3d. $5.00

NEVILLE, Margot. *Murder in Rockwater.* 1957. Fontana 191. My. VG. P1d. $8.00

NEVILLE, Margot. *Murder of Nymph.* 1951. Pocket 829. My. G+. P1d. $6.50

NEVILLE/VAN ARNAM. *Special Delivery/ Star Gladiator.* 1967. Belmont B 50-788. SF. VG+. B5d. $5.50

NEVILLE/VAN ARNAM. *Special Delivery/ Star Gladiator.* 1967. Belmont B 50-788. 1st prtg. SF. G+. R5d. $2.25

NEVINS, Francis M. edt. *Hitchcock in Prime Time.* Avon 89673. 2nd edn. My. VG. P1d. $9.00

NEVINS, M.D. *Sex Life of a College Girl.* Genell 110. VG. B3d. $4.00

NEW, Christopher. *Shanghai.* 1986. Bantam 25781. My. VG. P1d. $4.00

NEWBURY, Will. *Orgy Town.* 1961. Nightstand NB 1550. Ad. G+. B5d. $3.00

NEWBURY, Will. *Tourist Trap.* 1965. Midwood 32-453. PBO. Ad. VG. B5d. $4.50

NEWBURY, Will. *Tourist Trap.* 1965. Midwood 32-453. 1st edn. c/gga. F. F2d. $12.00

NEWCOMB, R.F. *Abandon Ship!* 1961. Corgi 938. VG. B3d. $8.00

NEWCOMBE, J. *Floyd Patterson.* Sport Magazine 7. PBO. VG+. B3d. $6.00

NEWELL, Audrey. *Murder Is Not Mute.* 1943. My Novel Classic 44. My. VG. P1d. $20.00

NEWELL, Bergen F. *Naked Before My Captors.* 1960. Monarch 161. 1st edn. PBO. c/Maguire: gga. scarce. VG+. B6a #80. $40.25

NEWHAFER, Richard. *Golden Jungle.* 1968. Signet T 3650. 1st prtg. VG+. P7d. $5.50

NEWHAFER, Richard. *Violators.* 1967. Signet T 3231. 1st prtg. VG+. P7d. $4.50

NEWHOUSE, Edward. *Temptation of Roger Heriott.* 1955. Berkley 323. c/photo. Fi. VG. B5d. $3.00

NEWMAN, Andrea. *Evil Streak.* 1979. Pocket 82193. Ho. VG. P1d. $4.00

NEWMAN, Bernard. *Cup Final Murder.* 1959. Jay Books 84. My. G+. P1d. $7.50

NEWMAN, Bernard. *Mussolini Murder Case.* 1939. Mystery Novel Monthly NN. My. VG. P1d. $20.00

NEWMAN, Christopher. *Knock-Off.* 1989. Gold Medal 13294. My. VG. P1d. $4.00

NEWMAN, Christopher. *Manana Man.* 1988. Gold Medal 13173. My. F. P1d. $5.00

NEWMAN, Christopher. *Midtown North.* 1991. Gold Medal 14689. My. VG+. P1d. $5.95

NEWMAN, Christopher. *Midtown South.* 1986. Gold Medal 13064. My. VG. P1d. $3.50

NEWMAN, F.E. *Crossword Puzzle Dictionary.* Perma P 89. VG. B3d. $4.50

NEWMAN, G.F. *Price.* 1975. New English 02516. My. VG. P1d. $4.00

NEWSOM, John D. *Wiped Out.* Dell 165 c/G Gregg. Fi. VG. B5d. $6.00

NEWTON, D.B. *Hideout Valley.* Berkley 1351. c/sgn. NF. B3d. $6.00

NEWTON, D.B. *Judas Horse.* Berkley 1780. NF. B3d. $6.00

NEWTON, D.B. *Maverick Brand.* 1962. Monarch 271. c/Bob Stanley. We. VG. P6d. $3.00

NEWTON, Mike. *Satan Ring.* 1978. Publ Consult Hun 3002. My. VG. P1d. $3.50

NEY, Richard. *Wall Street Jungle.* 1973. Ballantine 23478. c/monkey. Nfi. VG+. B5d. $4.00

NEZELOF, N.P. *Josephine, the Great Lover.* Avon T 166. c/gga. NF. F2d. $6.00

NEZELOF, N.P. *Josephine, the Great Lover.* Avon T 166. Fi. VG. B5d. $3.00

NIALL, Ian. *Tiger Walks.* 1964. Popular SP 271. 1st prtg. G+. R5d. $1.75

NIALL, Michael. *Bad Day at Black Rock.* 1954. Gold Medal 451. My. G+. P1d. $8.00

NIALL, Michael. *Run Like a Thief.* 1964. Monarch 421. JD. VG. P1d. $25.00

NICHOLS, Fan. *Angel Face.* 1955. Popular 706. My. VG. B3d. $4.00

NICHOLS, Fan. *Ask for Linda.* 1959. Popular G 325. My. VG. P1d. $7.50

NICHOLS, Fan. *Ask for Linda.* 1953. Popular 1483. 2nd edn. My. VG. P1d. $7.00

NICHOLS, Fan. *Caged.* 1952. Gold Medal 251. My. F. P1d. $22.50

NICHOLS, Fan. *Caged.* Gold Medal 310. VG+. B3d. $7.50

NICHOLS, Fan. *Count Me In.* 1959. Berkley G243. Fi. VG. B5d. $4.00

NICHOLS, Fan. *Count Me In.* 1953. Popular 536. c/gga. Fa. VG. B4d. $4.00

NICHOLS, Fan. *Count Me In.* 1953. Popular 536. My. F. P1d. $17.00

NICHOLS, Fan. *Devil Take Her.* Popular 586. G+. I1d. $4.00

NICHOLS, Fan. *Devil Take Her.* Popular 586. VG. B3d. $6.00

NICHOLS, Fan. *Devil Take Her.* 1954. Popular 586. My. F. P1d. $17.00

NICHOLS, Fan. *Girl in the Death Seat.* 1961. Ace D 503. My. VG. P1d. $6.50

NICHOLS, Fan. *Girl in the Death Seat.* 1961. Ace D 503. 1st edn. PBO. extremely scarce. VG. B6a #77. $29.75

NICHOLS, Fan. *Girl in the Death Seat.* 1961. Ace D 503. 1st prtg. VG+. P7d. $7.50

NICHOLS, Fan. *He Walks By Night.* 1957. Popular 791. My. VG. P1d. $7.50

NICHOLS, Fan. *I Know My Love.* 1958. Popular G 231. Ad. VG. P1d. $11.00

NICHOLS, Fan. *I Know My Love.* 1958. Popular G 231. 1st edn. c/gga. My. F. F2d. $15.00

NICHOLS, Fan. *I'll Never Let You Go.* 1955. Popular 642. Ad. VG. P1d. $12.00

NICHOLS, Fan. *One By One.* 1953. Popular 1409. 2nd edn. My. VG+. P1d. $10.50

NICHOLS, Fan. *One By One.* 1952. Popular 409. My. VG+. P1d. $13.50

NICHOLS, Fan. *Scandalous Lady.* Beacon 114. VG+. B3d. $6.00

NICHOLS, Fan. *Scandalous.* Beacon 220. c/photo. reprint. VG. B6d. $18.00

NICHOLS, Leigh. *House of Thunder.* 1982. Pocket 43266. My/SF. G+. P1d. $5.00

NICHOLS, Leigh. *Key to Midnight.* 1979. Pocket 80915. My/SF. G+. P1d. $3.00

NICHOLS, Sarah. *Clouded Moon.* 1975. Popular 00293. My/SF. F. P1d. $5.00

NICHOLS, Sarah. *Elspeth.* 1979. Popular 04423. My. G+. P1d. $2.75

NICHOLS, Sarah. *Satan's Spring.* 1974. Popular 00225. Go. VG. P1d. $3.50

NICHOLSON, H. *Some People.* Pan 8. VG. B3d. $6.00

NICKERSON, Kate. *Street of the Blues.* 1953. Original Digest 729. PBO. c/Tauss: gga. extremely scarce. VG+. B6a #77. $93.50

NICOLE, Christopher. *Devil's Own.* 1976. Corgi 10200. Hi. VG. P1d. $4.00

NICOLE, Christopher. *Devil's Own.* 1976. Signet J 7256. Hi. VG. P1d. $3.50

NICOLE, Christopher. *Operation Manhunt.* 1974. Dell 6729. My. VG. P1d. $3.50

NICOLE, Claudette. *Bloodroots Manor.* 1970. Gold Medal T 2731. c/gga. My. NF. B4d. $2.50

NICOLE, Claudette. *Dark Mill.* 1972. Gold Medal T 2514. Go. VG. P1d. $4.00

NICOLE, Claudette. *Haunting of Drumroe.* 1973. Gold Medal T 2717. My. VG. P1d. $3.50

NICOLE, Claudette. *House at Hawk's End.* 1971. Gold Medal R 2418. My. VG. P1d. $4.00

NICOLSON, John U. *Fingers of Fear.* 1966. PB Library 53-976. Go. VG. P1d. $5.50

NIEDERMAN, Andrew. *Brainchild.* 1981. Pocket 42830. SF. VG. W2d. $3.25

NIELSEN, Helen. *Dead on the Level.* 1953. Dell 747. 1st prtg. c/Bobertz: gga. VG. P7d. $5.50

NIELSEN, Helen. *Detour (to Death).* Black Lizard 080. NF. G5d. $5.00

NIELSEN, Helen. *Detour to Death.* 1955. Dell 837. 1st prtg. c/Stanley. VG. P7d. $5.50

NIELSEN, Helen. *False Witness.* 1966. Ballantine U 2150. 2nd edn. My. VG. P1d. $4.50

NIELSEN, Helen. *Killer in the Street.* 1971. Curtis 07168. My. VG. P1d. $4.00

NIELSEN, Helen. *Kind Man.* 1953. Dell 649. G+. G5d. $3.50

NIELSEN, Helen. *Kind Man.* 1953. Dell 649. 1st prtg. c/Foxley: gga. VG. P7d. $5.50

NIELSEN, Helen. *Obit Delayed.* Dell 806. c/J McDermott. My. VG. B5d. $3.00

NIELSEN, Helen. *Seven Days Before Dying (Borrow the Night).* Dell 971. VG. G5d. $3.75

NIELSEN, Helen. *Seven Days Before Dying.* 1958. Dell 971. My. F. P1d. $15.00

NIELSEN, Helen. *Sing Me a Murder.* 1988. Black Lizard 079. My. VG+. P1d. $7.50

NIELSEN, Helen. *Verdict Suspended.* 1970. Curtis 06094. My. VG. P1d. $4.50

NIELSEN, Helen. *Woman on the Roof.* 1956. Dell 900. 1st prtg. c/George: gga. VG+. P7d. $6.50

NIELSEN, Virginia. *Try To Forget Me.* Golden Willow 53. VG. B3d. $8.00

NIESEWAND, Peter. *Fallback.* 1983. Granada 05615. My/SF. VG. P1d. $4.00

NIESEWAND, Peter. *Fallback.* Signet AE 2053. 9th edn. My/SF. VG. P1d. $3.50

NIESEWAND, Peter. *Scimitar.* 1984. Granada 05851. Th. VG. P1d. $4.50

NIESEWAND, Peter. *Scimitar.* 1985. Signet AE 3905. Th. G+. P1d. $3.50

NIESEWAND, Peter. *Undercut.* 1985. Granada 05626. 2nd edn. Th. VG+. P1d. $4.00

NIESEWAND, Peter. *Undergound Connection.* 1979. Pan 25912. Th. VG. P1d. $3.50

NIESEWAND, Peter. *Word of a Gentleman.* 1986. Stein & Day 8296. Th. VG+. P1d. $4.50

NIGHTINGALE, Ursula. *Devil Tower.* 1971. Popular 00271. 1st edn. F. F2d. $10.00

NILE, Dorothea. *Mistress of Farrondale.* 1966. Tower 42-593. Go. F. P1d. $11.00

NILES, Blair. *Strange Brother.* 1952. Avon 407. Fi. G+. B5d. $5.00

NIMOY, Leonard. *I Am Not Spock.* 1977. Ballantine 25719. Nfi. VG. W2d. $8.00

NIN, Anais. *Spy in the House of Love.* Avon 755. VG+. B3d. $8.00

NISSLEY, Charles. *Pocket Book of Vegetable Gardening.* 1942. Pocket 148. 1st pb. VG. B6d. $5.00

NISTLER, Ervin. *Roadside Night.* Pyramid 148. 3rd edn. NF. I1d. $2.00

NISTLER, Ervin. *Roadside Night.* 1951. Pyramid 33. c/Barker: gga. Fa. VG+. B4d. $15.00

NIVEN, Larry. *All the Myriad Ways.* 1971. Ballantine. 1st edn. VG. M1d. $12.00

NIVEN, Larry. *Flight of the Horse.* Ballantine 23487. 1st prtg. VG+. S1d. $4.50

NIVEN, Larry. *Flight of the Horse.* 1973. Ballantine 23487. PBO. SF. F. M1d. $15.00

NIVEN, Larry. *Hole in Space.* 1974. Ballantine 24011. SF. VG+. W2d. $6.25

NIVEN, Larry. *Hole in Space.* 1974. Ballantine 24011. 1st. edn. SF. F. F2d. $15.00

NIVEN, Larry. *Integral Trees.* 1985. Ballantine 32065. 1st pb. c/Whelan. VG+. B6d. $4.50

NIVEN, Larry. *Long Arm of Gil Hamiltom.* 1976. Ballantine. 1st edn. F. M1d. $8.00

NIVEN, Larry. *Magic Goes Away.* Ace 51546. 4th prtg. c/sgn. VG+. B3d. $6.00

NIVEN, Larry. *Magic May Return.* Ace 51549. c/sgn. NF. B3d. $8.00

NIVEN, Larry. *Magic May Return.* 1983. Ace 51549. 1st prtg. SF. F. W2d. $7.00

NIVEN, Larry. *Neutron Star.* 1968. Ballantine U 6120. 1st edn. SF. F. F2d. $20.00

NIVEN, Larry. *Patchwork Girl.* 1980. Ace. 1st pb edn. F. M1d. $8.00

NIVEN, Larry. *Protector.* 1973. Ballantine. 1st edn. NF. M1d. $12.00

NIVEN, Larry. *Ringworld.* 1974. Ballantine. 6th edn. NF. M1d. $4.00

NIVEN, Larry. *Shape of Space.* 1969. Ballantine. 1st edn. F. M1d. $20.00

NIVEN, Larry. *Tales of Known Space.* 1975. Ballantine. 1st edn. F. M1d. $12.00

NIVEN, Larry. *World of Ptavvs.* 1966. Ballantine 04095. author's 1st book. SF. VG+. M3d. $5.00

NIVEN, Larry. *World of Ptavvs.* 1966. Ballantine. 1st edn. F. M1d. $25.00

NIVEN & POURNELLE. *Footfall.* 1986. Ballantine 32344. 1st prtg. SF. VG. W2d. $4.25

NIVEN & POURNELLE. *Inferno.* 1978. Pocket. 1st pb edn. F. M1d. $8.00

NIXON, Henry Lewis. *Bawdy Mrs Grey.* 1959. Newsstand U 105. VG+. B3d. $6.00

NIXON, Henry Lewis. *Bawdy Mrs Grey.* 1959. Newsstand U 105. PBO. Ad. G+. B5d. $3.00

NIXON, Henry Lewis. *Caves.* Ace S 100. VG. B3d. $6.00

NIXON, Henry Lewis. *Caves.* 1955. Ace S 100. 1st edn. My. F. F2d. $20.00

NIXON, Henry Lewis. *Confessions of a Psychiatrist.* 1954. Beacon 120. VG+. B3a #24. $22.00

NIXON, Henry Lewis. *Confessions of a Psychiatrist.* 1954. Beacon 120. 1st prtg. VG. P7d. $7.50

NIXON, Henry Lewis. *Naked Desire.* 1959. Beacon 271. 1st prtg. PBO. VG+. P7d. $12.50

NIXON, Henry Lewis. *Six for Flight 13.* Newsstand U 113. VG+. B3d. $5.50

NIXON, Henry Lewis. *Six for Flight 13.* 1959. Newsstand U 113. 1st edn. My. F. F2d. $12.00

NIXON, Joan Lowery. *Seance.* 1981. Dell 97937. My/SF. VG. P1d. $3.50

NIZER, Louis. *My Life in Court.* 1963. Pyramid N 836. Nfi. VG. P1d. $6.00

NOBUNUG & SCHUMAKER. *Shindai: Japanese Bed-Fighting.* Dell 7826. VG+. B3d. $5.00

NOEL, Jeffrey. *Trouble With Guns.* 1976. Sphere 6398. My. VG. P1d. $4.00

NOEL, Sterling. *Empire of Evil.* 1961. Avon F 112. Fa. VG+. B4d. $3.00

NOEL, Sterling. *Empire of Evil.* 1961. Avon F 112. 1st edn. My. F. F2d. $15.00

NOEL, Sterling. *Few Die Well.* Avon 584. G+. G5d. $4.50

NOEL, Sterling. *Few Die Well.* 1954. Avon 584. My. VG. P1d. $8.50

NOEL, Sterling. *Few Die Well.* 1956. Avon 719. My. VG+. P1d. $12.00

NOEL, Sterling. *I Killed Stalin.* 1952. Eton E 110. SF. G+. P1d. $12.50

NOEL, Sterling. *Intrigue in Paris.* 1957. Avon T 159. My. VG+. G5d. $3.00

NOEL, Sterling. *Intrigue in Paris.* 1960. Avon T 477. My. F. P1d. $15.00

NOEL, Sterling. *Prelude to Murder.* Avon T 290. VG+. I1d. $4.00

NOEL, Sterling. *Run for Your Life!* 1958. Avon T 270. My. F. P1d. $15.00

NOEL, Sterling. *Run for Your Life!* 1958. Avon T 270. 1st prtg. My. VG+. I1d/R5d. $5.00

NOEL, Sterling. *We Who Survived.* 1959. Avon T 360. PBO. SF. VG. B5d. $5.00

NOHL, Johannes. *Black Death.* 1960. Ballantine 379K. PBO. NF. VG+. B5d. $5.00

NOLAN, Frederick. *Algonquin Project.* 1976. Pyramid M 3752. My. VG. P1d. $3.50

NOLAN, Frederick. *Brass Target.* 1978. Jove M 4849. MTI. My. VG+. W2d. $3.50

NOLAN, Frederick. *No Place To Be a Cop.* 1975. Futura 7213. My. VG+. P1d. $4.50

NOLAN, Frederick. *Wolf Trap.* 1986. St Martin 90393. Th. VG. P1d. $3.50

NOLAN, Jeannette Covert. *Final Appearance.* 1944. Atlas NN. 1st pb. c/Hoffman. My. VG. B6d. $12.50

NOLAN, Jeannette Covert. *I Can't Die Here.* Detective 4. My. VG. P1d. $20.00

NOLAN, Jeannette Covert. *Murder Will Out.* Detective 8. My. VG. P1d. $20.00

NOLAN, William F. *Alien Horizons.* Pocket 77928. c/sgn. VG. B3d. $4.00

NOLAN, William F. *Impact-20.* 1966. Corgi UK 7357. 1st edn. c/sgn. SF. F. F2d. $15.00

NOLAN, William F. *Impact-20.* PB Library 52-250. c/Powers: sgn. VG. B3d. $5.00

NOLAN, William F. *Impact-20.* PB Library 52-250. NF. I1d. $6.00

NOLAN, William F. *Impact-20.* 1963. PB Library 52-250. 1st edn. F. M1d. $10.00

NOLAN, William F. *Logan's World.* 1977. Bantam 11418. 1st edn. scarce especially in top condition. SF. F. F2d. $25.00

NOLAN, William F. *Man Against Tomorrow.* Avon G 1278. c/Nolan: sgn. VG. B3d. $4.00

NOLAN, William F. *Man Against Tomorrow.* 1965. Avon G 1278. SF. VG. B4d. $3.00

NOLAN, William F. *Man Against Tomorrow.* 1965. Avon G 1278. 1st edn. F. M1d. $7.00

NOLAN, William F. *Men of Thunder.* 1965. Bantam FP 131. 1st edn. PBO. scarce. NF. B6a #76. $24.25

NOLAN, William F. *Pseudo-People.* Berkley 1437. c/Nolan: sgn. VG. B3d. $4.50

NOLAN, William F. *Sea of Space.* Bantam 4590. c/Bloch & Nolan: sgn. VG+. B3d. $6.00

NOLAN, William F. *Sea of Space.* 1970. Bantam 4590. 1st edn. SF. F. F2d. $12.50

NOLAN, William F. *Sinners & Supermen.* Private 334. c/sgn. VG. B3d. $6.00

NOLAN, William F. *Space for Hire.* Lancer. PBO. c/sgn. VG+. B3d. $6.00

NOLAN, William F. *Steve McQueen: Star on Wheels.* 1972. Berkley S 2160. NF. VG+. B5d. $6.00

NOLAN, William F. *Wilderness of Stars.* Dell 9582. c/Nolan: sgn. VG. B3d. $4.00

NOLAN, William F. *3 to the Highest Power.* 1968. Avon S 336. c/William Nolan: sgn. VG. B3d. $5.00

NOLAN, William F. *3 to the Highest Power.* 1968. Avon S 336. SF. G+. B4d. $2.00

NOLAN, William F. *3 to the Highest Power.* 1970. Avon V 2357. 3rd edn. SF. VG. B5d. $2.50

NOLDER, Ann. *Dream of Danger.* Nord 8030. My. VG. W2d. $3.25

NONWEILER, Arville, *Murder on the Pike.* Hangman House 1. My. G+. P1d. $15.00

NOONE, Carl. *Mind Over Murder.* 1976. New English 26183. My. VG. P1d. $4.00

NOONE, Edwina. *Corridor of Whispers.* 1965. Ace K 223. My. VG. P1d. $5.50

NOONE, Edwina. *Corridor of Whispers.* Ace 11741. My. VG. P1d. $3.50

NOONE, Edwina. *Craghold Creatures.* 1972. Beagle 94209. My/SF. VG. P1d. $4.00

NOONE, Edwina. *Craghold Crypt.* 1973. Curtis 09165. Go. G+. P1d. $3.00

NOONE, Edwina. *Craghold Curse.* 1972. Beagle 94196. Go. VG+. P1d. $4.50

NOONE, Edwina. *Dark Cypress.* 1965. Ace K 213. Go. VG. P1d. $5.50

NOONE, Edwina. *Daughter of Darkness.* 1966. Signet D 2967. Go. VG. P1d. $5.50

NOONE, Edwina. *Daughter of Darkness.* Signet T 5803. 3rd edn. Go. VG. P1d. $3.00

NOONE, Edwina. *Gothic Sampler.* 1966. Award A 199X. Go. VG. P1d. $5.50

NOONE, Edwina. *Heirloom of Tragedy.* 1965. Lancer 72-970. My. F. P1d. $11.00

NOONE, Edwina. *Seacliffe.* 1968. Signet D 3357. My. VG. P1d. $5.00

NOONE, Edwina. *Seacliffe.* Signet P 5301. 3rd edn. My. VG. P1d. $3.00

NOONE, Edwina. *Victorian Crown.* 1966. Belmont B 50-675. c/J Gaughan. Fi. VG. B5d. $5.00

NORDAN, Robert. *All Dressed Up To Die.* 1989. Gold Medal 14576. My. VG. P1d. $3.50

NORDAY, Michael. *Strange Thirsts.* 1959. Beacon 264. 1st pb. c/gga. NF. B6d. $25.00

NORDAY, Michael. *Warped.* 1959. Beacon 280. 1st prtg. c/Micarelli: gga. VG. P7d. $9.00

NORMAN, Barry. *To Nick a Good Body.* 1983. Quartet 3334. My. VG. P1d. $6.00

NORMAN, Charles. *Genteel Murderer.* 1963. Collier AS 490. Nfi. VG. P1d. $6.00

NORMAN, Earl. *Kill Me in Atami.* Berkley Y 676. My. G+. W2d. $4.25

NORMAN, Earl. *Kill Me in Rippongi.* 1967. Erle A 704. 1st pb. My. VG. M6d. $4.50

NORMAN, Earl. *Kill Me in Shimbashi.* 1959. Berkley Diamond D 2010. De. VG+. P1d. $10.50

NORMAN, Earl. *Kill Me in Shinjuku.* Erle A 705. G+. M6d. $6.50

NORMAN, Earl. *Kill Me in Yokohama.* Berkley G 411. PBO. VG. B3d. $5.50

NORMAN, Earl. *Kill Me in Yokohama.* 1960. Berkley G 429. PBO. VG+. B3d. $7.50

NORMAN, Earl. *Kill Me in Yokosuka.* Erle A 701. VG. M6d. $7.50

NORMAN, Earl. *Kill Me in Yoshiwara.* 1961. Berkley G 502. De. VG. B3d/P1d. $7.50

NORMAN, Earl. *Kill Me in Yoshiwara.* Erle A 706. VG. M6d. $4.50

NORMAN, Geoffrey. *Midnight Water.* 1985. Avon 69583. My. F. P1d. $5.00

NORMAN, John. *Assassin of Gor.* 1973. Ballantine 22489. 5th prtg. SF. G+. W2d. $2.75

NORMAN, John. *Assassins of Gor.* 1970. Ballantine 02094. 1st edn. F. M1d. $10.00

NORMAN, John. *Beasts of Gor.* 1978. DAW 280. 1st edn. F. M1d. $7.00

NORMAN, John. *Captive of Gor.* 1972. Ballantine 2994. 1st edn. NF. P9d. $3.00

NORMAN, John. *Captive of Gor.* 1973. Ballantine. 2nd edn. F. M1d. $4.00

NORMAN, John. *Cimarron Trace.* Dell 1st Edn A 119. c/Gross. NF. B3d. $5.50

NORMAN, John. *Danver of Gor.* 1985. DAW 00100. SF. VG+. B5d. $3.50

NORMAN, John. *Explorers of Gor.* 1979. DAW 328. 1st edn. F. M1d. $8.00

NORMAN, John. *Fighting Slave of Gor.* 1980. DAW UE 1522. 1st edn. F. M1d. $7.00

NORMAN, John. *Fighting Slave of Gor.* 1984. DAW 376. NF. P9d. $2.00

NORMAN, John. *Ghost Dance.* 1979. DAW UE 1501. SF. VG+. B5d. $3.50

NORMAN, John. *Ghost Dance.* 1979. DAW UE 1501. 1st edn. F. M1d. $5.00

NORMAN, John. *Gods & Devils From Outer Space.* Lancer 78-749. SF. VG. W2d. $3.75

NORMAN, John. *Guardsman of Gor.* 1981. DAW 456. 1st edn. F. M1d. $7.00

NORMAN, John. *Hunters of Gor.* 1974. DAW 96. 1st edn. F. M1d. $7.00

NORMAN, John. *Kajira of Gor.* 1983. DAW 520. 1st edn. F. P9d. $2.50

NORMAN, John. *Magicians of Gor.* 1988. DAW 746. 1st edn. F. P9d. $2.50

NORMAN, John. *Marauders of Gor.* 1975. DAW. 1st edn. F. M1d. $7.00

NORMAN, John. *Mercenaries of Gor.* 1985. DAW 617. 1st edn. F. P9d. $2.50

NORMAN, John. *Nomads of Gor.* 1969. Ballantine 1765. 1st edn. F. M1d. $12.00

NORMAN, John. *Nomads of Gor.* 1973. Ballantine 22488. 5th prtg. SF. VG. W2d. $4.00

NORMAN, John. *Outlaw of Gor.* 1967. Ballantine. 1st edn. NF. M1d. $9.00

NORMAN, John. *Players of Gor.* 1984. DAW 00914. SF. VG+. B5d. $3.50

NORMAN, John. *Players of Gor.* 1984. DAW 568. 1st prtg. PBO. c/Kelly: gga. VG+. P7d. $4.50

NORMAN, John. *Priest-Kings of Gor.* 1968. Ballantine 72015. 1st edn. F. M1d. $10.00

NORMAN, John. *Priest-Kings of Gor.* 1968. Ballantine 72015. 1st prtg. PBO. c/Foster: gga. VG. P7d. $3.50

NORMAN, John. *Raiders of Gor.* 1971. Ballantine. 1st edn. NF. M1d. $9.00

NORMAN, John. *Renegades of Gor.* 1986. DAW 664. 1st edn. F. P9d. $2.50

NORMAN, John. *Rogue of Gor.* 1981. DAW 424. 1st edn. F. M1d. $7.00

NORMAN, John. *Slave Girl of Gor.* 1977. DAW 232. 1st edn. F. M1d. $6.00

NORMAN, John. *Tarnsman of Gor.* 1972. Ballantine. 4th edn. F. M1d. $4.00

NORMAN, John. *Time Slave.* 1975. DAW. 1st edn. F. M1d. $7.00

NORMAN, John. *Tribesman of Gor.* 1976. DAW. 1st edn. F. M1d. $7.00

NORMAN, John. *Vagabonds of Gor.* 1987. DAW 701. 1st edn. F. P9d. $2.50

NORMAN, Marc. *Oklahoma Crude.* 1973. Popular 08233. MTI. c/Scott & Dunaway. VG+. B4d. $3.00

NORMENT, John edt. *Monkeyshines!* 1960. Berkley G 477. PBO. VG. B6d. $6.00

NORRIS, Kathleen. *Barberry.* 1966. PB Library 54-982. 1st pb. Go. NF. B6d. $6.00

NORRIS, Kathleen. *Burned Fingers.* Pocket 605. VG. B3d. $4.00

NORRIS, Kathleen. *Gabrielle.* 1965. PB Library 53-844. Go. VG. P1d. $5.50

NORRIS, Kathleen. *Motionless Shadows.* 1945. Bart House 20. Fi. VG. P1d. $12.50

NORRIS, Kathleen. *Mystery House.* 1947. Pocket 453. VG+. B3d. $5.50

NORRIS, Kathleen. *Mystery House.* 1947. Pocket 453. 1st pb edn. F. M1d. $15.00

NORRIS, Kathleen. *Second-Hand Wife.* 1946. Pony 55. Fa. VG+. B4d. $9.00

NORRIS, Kathleen. *Secret of the Marshbanks.* 1965. PB Library 53-882. Go. VG. P1d. $5.50

NORRIS, Kathleen. *Secrets of Hillyard House.* 1965. PB Library 53-823. 2nd edn. Go. G+. P1d. $3.50

NORRIS, Kathleen. *Wife for Sale.* Pocket 440. VG. B3d/I1d. $4.00

NORST, Joel. *Colors.* 1988. Pocket 66009. My. VG. P1d. $4.50

NORTH, Andrew. *Sargasso of Space.* 1964. Ace F 279. 1st prtg. c/Emsh. SF. VG. P7d. $4.00

NORTH, Eric. *Ant Men.* 1967. MacFadden 60-277. 1st pb. SF. NF. B6d. $9.00

NORTH, Kevin. *Bed Tramps.* 1962. Merit Book 619. My. G+. P1d. $5.00

NORTH, Kevin. *Bunch of Women.* 1963. Beacon B 646. c/gga. Fa. F. B4d. $14.00

NORTH, Kevin. *Cotton Tramps*. 1962. Playtime 620. 1st edn. c/gga. My. F. F2d. $9.00

NORTH, Kevin. *Cult of the Seven Wenches*. 1963. Playtime 646. PBO. c/gga. VG+. P6d. $6.00

NORTH, Kevin. *Road Show*. 1963. Playtime 627. VG+. B3d. $6.00

NORTH, Kevin. *Road Show*. 1963. Playtime 627. 1st edn. c/gga. F. F2d. $10.00

NORTH, Kevin. *Road Tramps*. Playtime 613. VG. B3d. $4.00

NORTH, Sterling. *So Dear to My Heart*. 1966. Avon ZS 108. Fi. VG+. B5d. $3.50

NORTH, Sterling. *So Dear to My Heart*. Dell 291. c/C Clair. Fi. VG. B5d. $4.00

NORTH/NORTH. *Plague Ship/Voodoo Planet*. Ace D 345. c/Emsh. F. M1d. $15.00

NORTH/NORTH. *Plague Ship/Voodoo Planet*. Ace D 345. VG+. I1d. $7.00

NORTIC, Max. *Obsessed*. 1968. Midwood 33-117. Ad. VG+. B5d. $5.00

NORTON, Alden H. *Hauntings & Horrors*. Berkley X 1674. 3rd edn. Ho. VG+. B6d. $4.50

NORTON, Alden H. *Horror Times Ten*. 1972. Berkley X 1414. 9th prtg. SF. VG+. W2d. $3.75

NORTON, Alden H. *Masters of Horror*. Berkley X 1497. 4th prtg. G+. S1d. $2.00

NORTON, Alden H. *Masters of Horrors*. Berkley X 1497. 4th edn. Ho. VG. B6d. $3.50

NORTON, Andre. *Beast Master*. Ace F 315. F. M1d. $8.00

NORTON, Andre. *Book of Andre Norton*. DAW 165. VG+. B3d. $4.50

NORTON, Andre. *Book of Andre Norton*. 1975. DAW 165. SF. F. B4d. $5.00

NORTON, Andre. *Catseye*. Ace F 167. SF. VG+. B5d. $4.50

NORTON, Andre. *Catseye*. Ace F 167. VG. B3d. $4.00

NORTON, Andre. *Catseye*. 1962. Ace F 167. NF. M1d. $7.00

NORTON, Andre. *Catseye*. Ace G 654. 1st prtg. VG. S1d. $2.00

NORTON, Andre. *Catseye*. Ace 09266. SF. VG. B5d. $2.50

NORTON, Andre. *Crossroads of Time*. Ace D 546. VG. M1d. $7.00

NORTON, Andre. *Crossroads of Time*. Ace F 391. NF. M1d. $7.00

NORTON, Andre. *Crossroads of Time*. Ace F 391. 1st prtg. G+. S1d. $2.50

NORTON, Andre. *Crossroads of Time*. Ace 12311. SF. VG+. B4d. $2.00

NORTON, Andre. *Crystal Gryphon*. DAW 75. NF. I1d. $5.00

NORTON, Andre. *Daybreak-2250 AD*. 1961. Ace D 534. F. M1d. $10.00

NORTON, Andre. *Daybreak-2250 AD*. 1961. Ace D 534. 1st prtg. SF. VG. R5d. $4.50

NORTON, Andre. *Daybreak-2250 AD*. Ace F 323. F. M1d. $8.00

NORTON, Andre. *Daybreak-2250 AD*. Ace F 323. VG+. B3d. $4.50

NORTON, Andre. *Daybreak-2250 AD*. Ace F 323. 3rd prtg. SF. G+. W2d. $3.75

NORTON, Andre. *Daybreak-2250 AD*. Ace G 717. VG. M1d. $5.00

NORTON, Andre. *Daybreak-2250 AD*. Ace 13991. SF. G+. W2d. $3.00

NORTON, Andre. *Defiant Agents*. 1963. Ace F 183. SF. VG+. B5d. $4.00

NORTON, Andre. *Defiant Agents*. 1963. Ace F 183. 1st prtg. SF. G+. R5d. $2.25

NORTON, Andre. *Dragon Magic*. 1973. Ace 16647. 1st edn. PBO. VG. P9d. $1.50

NORTON, Andre. *Forerunner*. Pinnacle 48-500. 1st prtg. G. S1d. $2.00

NORTON, Andre. *Galactic Derelict*. Ace D 498. NF. M1d. $10.00

NORTON, Andre. *Galactic Derelict*. Ace F 310. VG. P9d. $1.50

NORTON, Andre. *Galactic Derelict*. Ace F 310. 1st prtg. NF. S1d. $3.50

NORTON, Andre. *Garan the Eternal*. 1973. DAW 45. c/J Gaughan. SF. VG. B5d. $3.00

NORTON, Andre. *Gryphone in Glory*. 1983. Ballantine 30950. SF. F. W2d. $4.00

NORTON, Andre. *Here Abide Monsters*. DAW 121. 1st prtg. VG. S1d. $2.00

NORTON, Andre. *High Society*. 1979. Ace 33704. 5th prtg. SF. VG+. W2d. $3.50

NORTON, Andre. *High Sorcery*. Ace 33702. 1st prtg. F. S1d. $2.50

NORTON, Andre. *Horn Crown*. 1981. DAW 440. F. P9d. $2.00

NORTON, Andre. *Huon of Horn*. Ace F 226. F. M1d. $10.00

NORTON, Andre. *Ice Crown*. 1970. Ace 35840. c/D Meltzer. SF. VG+. B5d. $3.50

NORTON, Andre. *Jargoon Pard*. 1975. Gold Medal P 2657. SF. VG. W2d. $3.50

NORTON, Andre. *Judgement on Janus*. Ace 41550. 3rd edn. VG. P9d. $1.50

NORTON, Andre. *Judgment on Janus*. Ace F 308. F. M1d. $8.00

NORTON, Andre. *Key Out Time*. Ace F 287. F. M1d. $10.00

NORTON, Andre. *Last Planet*. Ace D 542. F. M1d. $10.00

NORTON, Andre. *Last Planet*. Ace D 96. 1st prtg. G. S1d. $3.50

NORTON, Andre. *Last Planet*. Ace F 366. F. M1d. $8.00

NORTON, Andre. *Last Planet*. Ace F 366. 1st prtg. NF. S1d. $3.50

NORTON, Andre. *Last Planet*. Ace 47161. SF. F. B5d. $6.00

NORTON, Andre. *Lavender-Green Magic*. 1977. Ace 47440. SF. VG+. W2d. $3.75

NORTON, Andre. *Lord of Thunder*. Ace F 243. F. M1d. $8.00

NORTON, Andre. *Lord of Thunder*. Ace 49236. SF. VG. B5d. $3.00

NORTON, Andre. *Merlin's Mirror*. 1975. DAW. 5th edn. F. M1d. $3.00

NORTON, Andre. *Moon of Three Rings*. 1967. Ace H 33. 1st edn. PBO. NF. M1d. $5.00

NORTON, Andre. *Night of Masks*. Ace F 365. F. M1d. $8.00

NORTON, Andre. *Night of Masks*. 1964. Ace F 365. SF. VG. B4d. $3.00

NORTON, Andre. *Nights of Masks*. 1973. Ace 57752. 3rd prtg. SF. F. W2d. $4.50

NORTON, Andre. *Opal-Eyed Fan*. Crest 23814. SF. VG. W2d. $3.00

NORTON, Andre. *Operation Time Search*. Crest 24370. 1st prtg. G. S1d. $1.75

NORTON, Andre. *Ordeal in Otherwhere*. Ace F 325. VG. I1d. $3.50

NORTON, Andre. *Ordeal in Otherwhere*. Ace F 325. 1st prtg. F. S1d. $4.00

NORTON, Andre. *Ordeal in Otherwhere*. Ace 63821. VG+. B3d. $4.00

NORTON, Andre. *Plague Ship*. Ace F 291. NF. M1d. $8.00

NORTON, Andre. *Plague Ship.* Ace F 291. 3rd edn. NF. P9d. $2.00

NORTON, Andre. *Postmarked the Stars.* Ace 67556. SF. VG+. B5d. $4.00

NORTON, Andre. *Sargasso at Space.* Ace F 279. 3rd edn. VG. P9d. $1.50

NORTON, Andre. *Secret of the Lost Race.* Ace 75830. 1st prtg. F. S1d. $2.50

NORTON, Andre. *Shadow Hawk.* Ace G 538. VG. M1d. $4.00

NORTON, Andre. *Shadow Hawk.* 1963. Ace G 538. 1st pb. Hi. NF. B6d. $12.50

NORTON, Andre. *Sioux Spaceman.* 1966. Ace F 408. SF. VG+. B4d. $4.00

NORTON, Andre. *Sorceress of the Witch World.* 1968. Ace H 84. SF. VG+. B4d. $4.00

NORTON, Andre. *Sorceress of the Witch World.* 1978. Ace. F. M1d. $4.00

NORTON, Andre. *Sorceress of Witch World.* 1983. Ace 77556. 4th prtg. SF. VG. W2d. $3.00

NORTON, Andre. *Spell of the Witch World.* DAW 1. VG. I1d. $4.00

NORTON, Andre. *Star Born.* Ace F 192. c/E Emsh. SF. VG. B5d. $3.50

NORTON, Andre. *Star Born.* 1966. Ace M 148. SF. VG+. B4d. $2.00

NORTON, Andre. *Star Gate.* Ace F 231. F. M1d. $10.00

NORTON, Andre. *Star Gate.* Ace F 231. VG+. B3d. $4.00

NORTON, Andre. *Star Gate.* Ace 78071. SF. VG+. B5d. $4.50

NORTON, Andre. *Star Guard.* Ace D 527. F. M1d. $10.00

NORTON, Andre. *Star Guard.* Ace G 599. VG+. B3d. $5.00

NORTON, Andre. *Star Guard.* Ace G 599. 4th edn. G. P9d. $1.25

NORTON, Andre. *Star Guard.* 1984. Ballantine 31624. c/L Schwinger. SF. VG+. B5d. $3.50

NORTON, Andre. *Star Guard.* Gold Medal 23646. SF. G. W2d. $2.75

NORTON, Andre. *Star Hunter & Voodoo Planet.* 1968. Ace G 723. SF. VG. B4d. $2.50

NORTON, Andre. *Star Rangers.* 1985. Ballantine 32308. c/L Schwinger. SF. NF. B5d. $4.00

NORTON, Andre. *Stars Are Ours.* Ace D 121. SF. G+. B5d. $5.50

NORTON, Andre. *Stars Are Ours.* Ace F 207. F. M1d. $10.00

NORTON, Andre. *Stars Are Ours.* Ace F 207. VG. I1d. $4.00

NORTON, Andre. *Stars Are Ours.* Ace M 147. SF. F. W2d. $4.50

NORTON, Andre. *Stars Are Ours.* 1981. Ace 78434. SF. VG. B5d. $4.00

NORTON, Andre. *Storm Over Warlock.* Ace F 109. F. M1d. $10.00

NORTON, Andre. *Storm Over Warlock.* Ace F 109. VG. I1d. $3.00

NORTON, Andre. *Storm Over Warlock.* Ace F 329. NF. I1d. $4.00

NORTON, Andre. *Storm Over Warlock.* Ace 78741. 4th edn. VG. P9d. $1.50

NORTON, Andre. *Three Against the Witch World.* Ace F 332. F. M1d. $12.00

NORTON, Andre. *Three Against the Witch World.* 1965. Ace F 332. 1st prtg. PBO. c/Gaughan. VG+. P7d. $5.00

NORTON, Andre. *Three Against Witch World.* Ace 80800. 1st prtg. VG+. S1d. $2.00

NORTON, Andre. *Time Traders.* Ace D 461. VG. M1d. $8.00

NORTON, Andre. *Trey of Swords.* 1978. Ace. 2nd pb. F. M1d. $3.00

NORTON, Andre. *Victory on Janus.* Ace G 703. VG. M1d. $5.00

NORTON, Andre. *Victory on Janus.* 1973. Ace 86321. 2nd edn. SF. VG+. B5d. $3.50

NORTON, Andre. *Victory on Janus.* 1973. Ace 86321. 2nd prtg. SF. F. W2d. $6.50

NORTON, Andre. *Warlock of Witch World.* Ace G 630. NF. M1d. $13.00

NORTON, Andre. *Warlock of Witch World.* Ace G 630. SF. VG. W2d. $4.50

NORTON, Andre. *Warlock of Witch World.* Ace 87319. SF. F. W2d. $4.00

NORTON, Andre. *Warlock of Witch World.* Ace 87319. 2nd edn. VG. P9d. $1.50

NORTON, Andre. *Web of the Witch World.* 1964. Ace F 263. 1st edn. NF. M1d. $15.00

NORTON, Andre. *Web of the Witch World.* Ace G 716. 1st prtg. VG. S1d. $2.50

NORTON, Andre. *Web of the Witch World.* 1964. Ace 263. SF. VG. W2d. $4.50

NORTON, Andre. *Web of the Witch World.* 1978. Ace 87875. F. M1d. $4.00

NORTON, Andre. *Web of the Witch World.* 1978. Ace 87875. SF. VG. W2d. $3.75

NORTON, Andre. *White Jade Fox.* 1976. Crest Q 2865. My. G+. P1d. $2.50

NORTON, Andre. *Witch World.* 1963. Ace F 197. PBO. c/J Gaughan. SF. VG+. B5d. $6.50

NORTON, Andre. *Witch World.* 1967. Ace G 655. SF. F. W2d. $5.00

NORTON, Andre. *X Factor.* Ace 92551. c/J Gaughan. SF. VG. B5d. $3.00

NORTON, Andre. *Year of the Unicorn.* 1965. Ace F 357. F. M1d. $8.00

NORTON, Andre. *Year of the Unicorn.* 1965. Ace F 357. NF. I1d. $5.00

NORTON, Andre. *Year of the Unicorn.* 1965. Ace F 357. SF. VG. W2d. $4.25

NORTON, Andre. *Year of the Unicorn.* Ace 94251. c/J Gaughan. SF. NF. B5d. $5.00

NORTON, Andre. *Yurth Burden.* 1978. DAW 304. 1st edn. SF. F. F2d. $8.00

NORTON, Andre. *Zarsthor's Bane.* 1978. Ace. 1st edn. F. M1d. $6.00

NORTON, Andre. *Zero Stone.* Ace 95961. c/J Jones. SF. VG. B5d. $3.00

NORTON, Browning. *Tidal Wave.* Ace D 423. PBO. VG. B3d/I1d. $4.00

NORTON, Charles A. *Melville Davisson Post.* 1973. Popular Press. Nfi. Fi. P1d. $12.50

NORTON, Olive. *Speight Street Angle.* 1968. Corgi 07873. My. VG. P1d. $5.00

NORTON/NORTON. *Beast Master/Star Hunter.* Ace D 509. PBO. VG+. B3d. $5.00

NORTON/NORTON. *Beast Master/Star Hunter.* 1961. Ace D 509. PBO. SF. F. W2d. $10.00

NORTON/NORTON. *Eye of the Monster/ Sea Siege.* Ace F 147. VG+. I1d. $4.00

NORTON/NORTON. *Eye of the Monster/ Sea Siege.* 1962. Ace F 147. F. M1d. $10.00

NORTON/NORTON. *Eye of the Monster/ Sea Siege.* 1962. Ace F 147. PBO. c/E Valigursky. SF. VG+. B5d. $5.50

NORTON/NORTON. *Judgement on Janus.* Ace F 308. NF. I1d. $4.00

NORTON/NORTON. *Key Out of Time.* Ace 43761. VG. B3d. $4.50

NORTON/NORTON. *Night of Masks.* Ace F 365. G+. I1d. $4.00

NORTON/SOHL. *Secret of the Lost Race/One Against Herculum.* 1959. Ace D 381. 1st edn. NF. M1d. $10.00

NORTON/SOHL. *Secret of the Lost Race/One Against Herculum.* 1959. Ace D 381. 1st prtg. SF. G+. R5d. $4.00

NORTON/WILSON. *Sioux Spaceman/And Then the Town Took Off.* 1960. Ace D 437. NF. I1d. $8.00

NORTON/WILSON. *Sioux Spaceman/And Then the Town Took Off.* 1960. Ace D 437. 1st edn. F. M1d. $15.00

NORTON/WILSON. *Sioux Spaceman/And Then the Town Took Off.* 1960. Ace D 437. 1st prtg. VG. B6d. $6.00

NORVIL, Manning. *Crown of the Sword God.* 1980. DAW 390. 1st edn. SF. F. F2d. $8.00

NORVIL, Manning. *Dream Chariots.* 1977. DAW 260. 1st edn. F. M1d. $5.00

NORVIL, Manning. *Whetted Bronze.* 1978. DAW 281. 1st edn. M1d. $5.00

NORWAY, Kate. *Nurse Brookes.* 1958. Harlequin 427. VG+. B3d. $5.00

NORWOOD, Warren. *Time Police.* 1988. Lynx 00006. SF. F. B5d. $5.00

NOURSE, Alan E. *Bladerunner.* 1975. Ballantine 24654. 1st pb. SF. NF. B6d. $3.00

NOURSE, Alan E. *Counterfeit Man.* 1967. Scholastic 941. SF. VG. W2d. $3.75

NOURSE, Alan E. *Mercy Men.* Ace 52560. SF. NF. B5d. $5.00

NOURSE, Alan E. *PSI High.* Ace G 730. 1st edn. PBO. G. P9d. $1.25

NOURSE, Alan E. *Raiders From the Rings.* 1963. Pyramid F 933. c/J Gaughan. SF. VG+. B5d. $5.00

NOURSE, Alan E. *Raiders From the Rings.* 1963. Pyramid F 933. 1st pb edn. F. M1d. $15.00

NOURSE, Alan E. *Scavengers in Space.* 1962. Ace D 541. F. M1d. $10.00

NOURSE, Alan E. *Scavengers in Space.* 1962. Ace D 541. VG+. B3d. $4.00

NOURSE, Alan E. *Tiger by the Tail.* 1964. MacFadden 50-199. VG+. B3d. $4.50

NOURSE, Alan E. *Tiger by the Tail.* 1964. MacFadden 50-199. 1st pb. SF. NF. B6d/M1d. $8.00

NOURSE, Alan E. *Trouble on Titan.* 1967. Lancer 72-159. SF. VG. B4d/S1d. $4.00

NOURSE, Alan E. *Universe Between.* 1967. PB Library 52-462. c/J Gaughan. SF. VG. B5d. $3.00

NOURSE, Alan E. *Universe Between.* 1967. PB Library 52-462. 1st edn. PBO. VG+. I1d. $4.00

NOURSE/NORTON. *Man Obsessed/Last Planet.* Ace D 96. G+. I1d. $5.00

NOVAK, D. *Time Out for Sex.* France F 4. VG+. B3d. $5.50

NOVAK, Lorna. *Does It Make Into a Bed?* 1964. Popular SP 283. 1st prtg. c/Zuckerberg: gga. VG. P7d. $4.00

NOVAK, Robert. *B-Girl.* 1956. Ace S 174. PBO. c/Marchetti. VG+. B6a #79. $65.00

NOVAK, Robert. *B-Girl.* 1956. Ace S 174. PBO. c/Marchetti: gga. scarce. NF. B6a #75. $82.50

NOVAK, Robert. *Climb a Broken Ladder.* 1956. Ace S 151. 1st edn. My. F. F2d. $20.00

NOVAK, Robert. *Concrete Cage.* 1974. Belmont Tower 50658. My. VG. P1d. $3.50

NOVAK, Robert. *Thrill Killers.* 1974. Belmont Tower 50709. My. VG. P1d. $3.50

NOWLAN, Philip F. *Armageddon 2419 AD.* Ace F 188. SF. VG+. B5d. $6.00

NOWLAN, Philip F. *Armageddon 2419 AD.* Ace F 188. 1st prtg. G. S1d. $2.00

NOWLAN, Philip F. *Armageddon 2419 AD.* 1978. Ace 02935. F. S1d. $3.50

NOWLAN, Philip F. *Armageddon 2419 AD.* 1978. Ace 02935. SF. VG+. W2d. $4.00

NUETZEL, Charles. *If This Goes On.* Book Co of America 15. sgn. VG. B3d. $6.50

NUETZEL, Charles. *Passionate Trio.* 1961. Epic 120. 1st edn. c/gga. My. F. F2d. $15.00

NUETZEL, Charles. *Swordsmen of Vistar.* 1969. Powell PP 121. PBO. VG+. P6d. $4.50

NUETZEL, Charles. *Warriors of Noomas.* Powell 149. c/sgn. VG. B3d. $7.50

NUETZEL, Charles. *Whodunit? Hollywood Style.* 1965. Book Co of America 008. Nfi. VG. P1d. $7.50

NUNES/REYNOLDS. *Inherit the Earth/Dawnman Planet.* Ace G 580. F. M1d. $9.00

NUNES/TUBB. *Recoil/Lallia.* Ace 71082. c/K Freas & G Barr. SF. VG. B5d. $3.00

NUNES/TUBB. *Recoil/Lallia.* Ace 71082. 1st prtg. G+. S1d. $2.75

NYE, Nelson C. *Arizona Dead-Shot.* Avon 758. VG. B3d. $4.50

NYE, Nelson C. *Bandido.* Signet 1473. PBO. c/Schulz. VG+. B3d. $5.50

NYE, Nelson C. *Bullet for Billy the Kid.* 1950. Avon 267. c/J Bama. We. G. B5d. $5.00

NYE, Nelson C. *Bullet for Billy the Kid.* 1950. Avon 267. VG. I1d. $9.00

NYE, Nelson C. *Desert of the Damned.* Popular 481. VG. B3d. $4.00

NYE, Nelson C. *Gunfighter Brand.* Berkley G 138. VG. B3d. $4.00

NYE, Nelson C. *Hired Hand.* 1955. Pocket 1060. c/T Ryan. We. VG. B5d. $4.00

NYE, Nelson C. *Long Run.* Avon 872. NF. I1d. $4.00

NYE, Nelson C. *Saddle Bow Slim.* 1965. Macfadden 50-247. We. VG. B5d. $2.50

NYE, Nelson C. *Shotgun Law (Tinbadge).* Belmont 50-728. NF. B3d. $5.00

NYE, Nelson C. *Strawberry Roan.* Belmont 90-317. VG. B3d. $4.00

NYE, Nelson C. *Texas Tornado.* 1955. Ace D 98. 1st edn. PBO. c/Saunders. VG+. B6a #79. $53.00

NYE, Nelson C. *Trail of Lost Skulls.* 1966. Ace M 160. We. VG+. B4d. $2.75

NYE, Nelson C. *Wide Loop.* Dell 804. VG. B3d. $3.50

NYE, Robert. *Merlin.* 1981. Bantam 13550. SF. F. W2d. $4.00

NYE/NYE. *Gun Feud at Tiedown/Rogue's Rendezvous.* Ace 30701. We. VG. B5d. $3.00

NYE/NYE. *Hideout Mountain/Rafe.* 1969. Ace 70350. We. VG+. B4d. $2.00

NYE/VANCE. *Plunder/Branded Lawman.* Ace D 6. c/Saunders. We. VG. B6d. $12.00

NYLAND, Gentry. *Hot Bullets for Love.* 1943. Double Action DE 2. My. G+. P1d. $15.00

O. HENRY. *Cabbages & Kings.* 1946. Penguin 595. 1st pb. VG. B6d. $7.50

O. HENRY. *Four Million.* Pan 16. 2nd prtg. VG+. B3d. $7.00

O'BANNON, Brian. *Woman on Fire.* 1964. Midwood F 362. PBO. NF. B6d. $12.50

O'BRIAN, Frank. *Arizona.* 1969. Ballantine 70702. We. VG+. P1d. $5.00

O'BRIEN, Barbara. *Operators & Things.* Ace 63510. Nfi. VG+. B5d. $4.00

O'BRIEN, Eugene. *One-Way Ticket.* 1954. Pennant P 50. c/Barye Phillips. War. VG. P6d. $3.50

O'BRIEN, L.H. *Forget About Calories.* Monarch MS 7. PBO. VG+. B3d. $4.00

O'BRIEN, Robert C. *Mrs Frisby & the Rats of Nihm.* Scholastic 10228. SF. VG. W2d. $3.00

O'BRIEN, Robert C. *Report From Group 17.* 1973. Warner 76-039. My/SF. VG. P1d. $3.50

O'BRIEN, Thomas L. *Witch Finder.* Dell 1st Edition B 135. c/Hooks. VG. B3d. $5.00

O'BRIEN, Tim. *Northern Lights.* 1976. Dell 06493. 1st prtg. VG. P/d. $4.00

O'BRIEN, Toni. *Hippie Harlot.* 1967. Cougar 829. PBO. VG. B6a #76. $20.00

O'BRINE, M. *Dead As a Dodo.* Corgi 64. VG. B3d. $6.00

O'CALLAGHAN, Maxine. *Bogeyman.* 1986. TOR 52350. Ho. VG. P1d. $4.00

O'CALLAGHAN, Maxine. *Hit & Run.* 1991. St Martin 92440. My. VG. P1d. $3.50

O'CALLAGHAN, Maxine. *Run From Nightmare.* Raven House 63047. 2nd edn. De. VG. P1d. $3.00

O'CONNOR, Brian. *One-Shot War.* 1982. Ballantine 29885. My. VG. P1d. $3.50

O'CONNOR, Dermot. *Slender Chance.* 1975. Arrow 909860. My. VG. P1d. $4.00

O'CONNOR, Edwin. *I Was Dancing.* 1965. Bantam S 2924. Fi. NF. B5d. $4.00

O'CONNOR, Edwin. *Oracle.* 1956. Lion Library LL 102. Fa. VG+. B4d. $5.00

O'CONNOR, Flannery. *Good Man Is Hard To Find.* 1956. Signet S 1345. 1st prtg. c/Kokinos. VG. P7d. $5.00

O'CONNOR, Jack. *Boom Town.* Dell D 129. VG. B3d. $4.50

O'CONNOR, L. *American Sexual Revolution in Action.* Brandon House 1001. VG+. B3d. $5.00

O'CONNOR, L. *Memoirs of a Stripper.* Brandon House 1004. VG+. B3d. $5.50

O'CONNOR, Patrick edt. *Monkees Go Mod.* 1967. Popular 60-8046. TVTI. VG+. B4d. $4.00

O'CONNOR, Richard. *Company Q.* Bantam 2136. VG+. B3d. $4.50

O'CONNOR, Richard. *Gould's Millions.* 1962. Ace K 162. Nfi. VG+. B4d. $2.00

O'CONNOR, Richard. *Pat Garrett.* 1963. Ace G 502. We. G+. P6d. $1.50

O'CONNOR, Richard. *Pat Garrett.* 1963. Ace G 502. 1st edn. PBO. We. F. F2d. $5.00

O'CONNOR, Richard. *Wild Bill Hickok.* 1960. Ace D 466. VG+. P6d. $6.00

O'DAIR, Stan. *Family Sex Secrets.* Brandon House 6424. VG+. B3d. $4.50

O'DAIR, Stan. *Lavender Girls.* 1964. Brandon House 907. VG+. B3a #24. $25.30

O'DELL, J.W. *Loan Shark.* 1975. Belmont Tower 50864. My. VG. P1d. $3.50

O'DELL, Scott. *Hill of the Hawk.* 1953. Bantam A 1138. 1st pb. c/Skemp. VG. B6d. $6.00

O'DELL, William C. *Leather Albatross.* 1972. Apollo 00147. Th. VG. P1d. $4.00

O'DONNELL, K.M. *Empty People.* 1969. Lancer 74-546. 1st edn. F. M1d. $8.00

O'DONNELL, K.M. *Empty People.* 1969. Lancer 74-546. 1st prtg. VG. S1d. $4.50

O'DONNELL, K.M. *Universe Day.* 1971. Avon V 2394. PBO. SF. VG. B5d/S1d. $3.00

O'DONNELL, Kevin. *Bander Snatch.* 1979. Bantam 12620. SF. VG+. W2d. $4.00

O'DONNELL, Lillian. *Baby Merchants.* 1976. Bantam 02511. My. VG. P1d. $3.50

O'DONNELL, Lillian. *Children's Zoo.* 1982. Crest 2-4498. My. VG. P1d. $3.50

O'DONNELL, Lillian. *Cop Without a Shield.* 1985. Crest 20534. My. VG. P1d. $3.50

O'DONNELL, Lillian. *Falling Star.* 1987. Crest 21395. My. VG. P1d. $3.50

O'DONNELL, Lillian. *Good Night To Kill.* 1990. Crest 21706. My. VG+. P1d. $4.50

O'DONNELL, Lillian. *No Business Being a Cop.* 1987. Crest 21322. My. VG. P1d. $3.50

O'DONNELL, Lillian. *Other Side of the Door.* 1988. Crest 21598. My. VG+. P1d. $4.50

O'DONNELL, Lillian. *Wreath for the Bride.* 1991. Crest 21867. My. VG. P1d. $3.50

O'DONNELL, Peter. *Dead Man's Handle.* 1986. Pan 29452. My. VG. P1d. $4.50

O'DONNELL, Peter. *Dragon's Claw.* 1979. Pan 25880. My. VG. P1d. $4.50

O'DONNELL, Peter. *I, Lucifer.* 1969. Crest T 1234. My/SF. G+. P1d. $3.25

O'DONNELL, Peter. *I, Lucifer.* 1969. Pan 02286. My/SF. VG. P1d. $4.50

O'DONNELL, Peter. *Impossible Virgin.* 1985. Mysterious Press 100. My. F. P1d. $5.00

O'DONNELL, Peter. *Impossible Virgin.* 1973. Pan 23489. My. G+. P1d. $3.00

O'DONNELL, Peter. *Modesty Blaise.* 1966. Crest R 899. My. VG. P1d. $5.50

O'DONNELL, Peter. *Modesty Blaise.* 1984. Mysterious Press 090. My. VG. P1d. $3.75

O'DONNELL, Peter. *Modesty Blaise.* 1966. Pan X 474. My. VG. P1d. $5.50

O'DONNELL, Peter. *Modesty Blaise.* 1971. Pan 10474. 4th edn. My. VG. P1d. $4.00

O'DONNELL, Peter. *Sabre-Tooth.* 1967. Pan M 204. 1st pb. VG+. B6d. $12.50

O'DONNELL, Peter. *Sabre-Tooth.* 1973. Pan 20204. 2nd edn. My. VG. P1d. $4.00

O'DONNELL, Peter. *Silver Mistress.* 1980. Pan 24360. 3rd edn. My. VG. P1d. $4.00

O'DONNELL/O'DONNELL. *Gates of Time/Dwellers of the Deep.* Ace 27400. PBO. SF. VG. B5d. $3.00

O'DONNELL/O'DONNELL. *Gather in the Hall of Planets/In the Pocket.* Ace 27415. NF. P9d. $1.75

O'DONNELL/O'DONNELL. *Gather in the Hall of Planets/In the Pocket.* Ace 27415. PBO. SF. VG+. B5d. $4.50

O'DONNELL/RACKHAM. *Final War/Treasure of Tau Ceti.* Ace 23775. PBO. SF. VG. B5d/S1d. $3.00

O'DONOHOE, Nick. *April Snow.* 1984. Paperjacks 0305. De. VG. P1d. $3.50

O'DONOHOE, Nick. *April Snow.* 1986. Paperjacks 0464. 2nd edn. De. VG. P1d. $3.00

O'DONOHOE, Nick. *Open Season.* 1986. Paperjacks 0476. De. VG. P1d. $3.50

O'DONOHOE, Nick. *Wind Chill.* 1986. Paperjacks 0465. 3rd edn. De. VG. P1d. $3.00

O'FARRELL, William. *Brandy for a Hero.* 1949. Dell 306. VG. I1d. $5.00

O'FARRELL, William. *Causeway to the Past.* 1951. Dell 555. My. VG. P1d. $9.00

O'FARRELL, William. *Ghost Came Twice.* 1970. Bee Line 655. PBO. Fa. NF. B6d. $15.00

O'FARRELL, William. *Gypsy, Go Home.* 1961. Gold Medal S 1175. My. VG. P1d. $8.00

O'FARRELL, William. *Repeat Performance.* 1954. Pennant P 55. VG. G5d. $3.25

O'FARRELL, William. *Thin Edge of Violence.* 1953. Bantam 1128. 1st US edn. My. VG. B6d. $7.50

O'FARRELL, William. *Thin Edge of Violence.* 1950. White Circle CD 462. My. G+. P1d. $10.00

O'FARRELL, William. *Walk the Dark Bridge.* 1954. Pennant P 35. G+. G5d. $5.50

O'FARRELL, William. *Walk the Dark Bridge.* 1954. Pennant P 35. My. VG. P1d. $8.50

O'FARRELL, William. *Wetback.* 1956. Dell 1st Edition A 120. My. F. P1d. $16.00

O'FARRELL, William. *Wetback.* 1956. Dell 1st Edition A 128. 1st prtg. PBO. c/Hooks: gga. VG. P7d. $5.00

O'FLAHERTY, Liam. *Informer.* 1955. Bantam A 1357. My. G+. P1d. $6.00

O'FLAHERTY, Liam. *Informer.* 1945. Superior M 650. My. VG. P1d. $10.50

O'FLAHERTY, Liam. *Selected Stories.* 1958. Signet S 1553. Fa. VG+. B4d. $7.00

O'GRADY, Rohan. *Let's Kill Uncle.* 1965. Ace G 548. My. G+. P1d. $4.00

O'GRADY, Rohan. *Master of Montrolfe Hall.* 1964. Ace K 215. 1st prtg. My. VG. R5d. $1.75

O'HANLON, J. *As Good As Murdered.* Century 17. VG. B3d. $7.00

O'HARA, Boris. *St Valentine's Day Massacre.* 1967. Dell 7586. MTI. c/White. VG. B3d. $4.00

O'HARA, Boris. *St Valentine's Day Massacre.* 1967. Dell 7586. 1st prtg. G+. R5d. $2.00

O'HARA, Donn. *Fair & the Bold.* 1957. Graphic G 222. 1st prtg. PBO. c/Barye: gga. VG. P7d. $5.00

O'HARA, Donn. *Rogue Royal.* Graphic G 212. c/Maguire. VG+. B3d. $5.00

O'HARA, John. *All the Girls He Wanted.* 1951. Avon 368. VG+. B3d. $6.00

O'HARA, John. *Butterfield 8.* Armed Services 799. VG+. B3d. $8.00

O'HARA, John. *Butterfield 8.* Avon 422. VG. B3d. $4.50

O'HARA, John. *Butterfield 8.* Avon 94. VG. B3d. $5.00

O'HARA, John. *Doctor's Son.* 1961. Avon T 511. Fa. VG. B4d. $2.00

O'HARA, John. *Doctor's Son.* 1943. Avon 31. NF. I1d. $10.00

O'HARA, John. *Famer's Hotel.* 1952. Bantam 1046. 1st prtg. c/Hooks: gga. VG+. P7d. $5.00

O'HARA, John. *Farmer's Hotel.* Panther 1186. VG. B3d. $6.00

O'HARA, John. *Hellbox.* 1951. Avon 293. c/gga. Fa. VG. B4d. $6.00

O'HARA, John. *Hellbox.* 1955. Avon 679. VG. B3d. $4.00

O'HARA, John. *Hope of Heaven.* 1947. Avon 144. c/photo. Fi. VG. B5d. $5.50

O'HARA, John. *Hope of Heaven.* 1950. Avon 259. c/gga. Fa. VG. B4d. $4.00

O'HARA, John. *Pal Joey.* Armed Services 817. VG+. B3d. $6.00

O'HARA, John. *Pal Joey.* 1957. Bantam 1679. 1st prtg. VG. R5d. $2.50

O'HARA, John. *Pal Joey.* Dell 10¢ 24. VG+. B3d. $6.00

O'HARA, John. *Pal Joey.* Panther 1115. VG+. B3d. $8.00

O'HARA, John. *Pipe Night.* Armed Services 74. VG. B3d. $6.00

O'HARA, John. *Stories of Venial Sin.* Avon 661. 3rd edn. Fi. VG. B5d. $4.50

O'HARA, Kenneth. *Bird Cage.* 1968. Zebra Z 1097N. My. VG. P1d. $5.00

O'HARA, R.C. *Divorcee.* 1962. Monarch MB 519. PBO. c/Bob Maguire. Nfi. VG. P6d. $2.00

O'MALLEY, B. *More O'Malley's Nuns.* Perma M 4236. VG+. B3d. $5.00

O'MALLEY, B. *O'Malley's Nuns.* Perma M 3105. NF. B3d. $6.00

O'MALLEY, Frank. *Best Go First.* 1952. Bantam 959. 1st prtg. My. G+. R5d. $2.25

O'MARA, Jim. *Guns of Vengeance.* Popular 465. VG+. I1d. $5.00

O'MARA, Jim. *Wall of Guns.* 1951. Pocket 816. c/H Barton. We. VG. B5d. $4.00

O'MARIE, Sister Carol Anne. *Advent of Dying.* 1987. Dell 10052. My. VG. P1d. $3.50

O'MARIE, Sister Carol Anne. *Novena for Murder.* Dell 16469. 3rd edn. My. VG. P1d. $3.00

O'MEARA, Walter. *Grand Portage.* Bantam 1036. VG. B3d. $3.50

O'NEAL, C. *Gods of Our Time.* Crest 443. VG+. B3d. $6.00

O'NEIL, D. *Green Lantern, Arrow #2.* PB Library 64755. NF. B3d. $7.00

O'NEIL, Dennis. *Bite of Monsters.* Uni-book. SF. VG. W2d. $3.25

O'NEIL, Kerry. *Death at Dakar.* Thriller Novel Class 28. My. VG. P1d. $20.00

O'NEIL, Russell. *Don't Call Back.* 1978. Dell 12124. My. VG. P1d. $3.50

O'NEILL, Archie. *Da Vinci Rose.* 1973. Bantam N 8307. My. VG. P1d. $3.50

O'NEILL, Archie. *Duplicate Stiff.* 1974. Bantam N 8414. My. F. P1d. $2.00

O'NEILL, Archie. *Ginzburg Circle.* 1974. Bantam N 8737. My. VG. P1d. $3.50

O'NEILL, Archie. *High Bid for Murder.* 1974. Bantam N 8539. My. VG. P1d. $3.50

O'NEILL, Archie. *High Bid for Murder.* 1974. Bantam N 8539. 1st prtg. My. G+. W2d. $3.00

O'NEILL & RAFFERTY. *Dell Book of Crossword Puzzles.* 1947. Dell 205. PBO. 2nd rarest Dell. file copy. unread. F. B6a #74. $1,100.00

O'NEILL & RAFFERTY. *2nd Dell Book Crossword Puzzles.* 1949. Dell 278. PBO. rarest Dell. file copy. F. B6a #74. $2,035.00

O'QUINN, Allen. *Woman for Henry.* 1954. Gold Medal 399. PBO. c/Barye. VG+. B6d. $10.00

O'ROURKE, Frank. *Action at Three Peaks.* 1949. Bantam 720. We. VG. B3d. $4.00

O'ROURKE, Frank. *Action at Three Peaks.* 1969. Signet P 4079. We. VG. P1d. $4.50

O'ROURKE, Frank. *Battle Royal.* 1955. Dell 1st Edition 89. PBO. c/G Gross. We. VG. B3d/B5d. $4.00

O'ROURKE, Frank. *Big Fifty.* 1955. Dell 1st Edition 59. PBO. c/G Gross. We. VG+. B5d. $5.50

O'ROURKE, Frank. *Car Deal!* 1955. Ballantine 111. Fi. VG. P1d. $8.00

O'ROURKE, Frank. *Dakota Rifle.* 1955. Dell 1st Edition 41. VG. B3d. $4.00

O'ROURKE, Frank. *Dakota Rifle.* 1968. Signet D 3696. We. VG+. B4d. $2.25

O'ROURKE, Frank. *Desperate Rider.* 1959. Signet 1748. We. VG. P1d. $7.00

O'ROURKE, Frank. *Gold Under Skull Peak.* 1953. Bantam 1149. We. VG+. B3d. $5.00

O'ROURKE, Frank. *Great Bank Robbery.* 1961. Dell 1st Edition B 181. We. VG. P1d. $6.50

O'ROURKE, Frank. *Great Bank Robbery.* 1969. Signet D 3918. 1st prtg. G+. R5d. $1.50

O'ROURKE, Frank. *Gun Hand.* 1953. Ballantine 35. We. VG+. B4d. $7.00

O'ROURKE, Frank. *Gun Hand.* Signet Q 5988. 3rd edn. We. VG. P1d. $3.00

O'ROURKE, Frank. *High Dive.* 1955. Bantam 1344. My. G+. P1d. $6.00

O'ROURKE, Frank. *High Vengeance.* Ballantine 214. 2nd prtg. VG. B3d. $4.00

O'ROURKE, Frank. *Last Chance.* 1956. Dell 1st Edition 104. PBO. c/J McDermott. We. VG. B5d. $3.00

O'ROURKE, Frank. *Latigo.* Signet Q 6036. 3rd edn. We. G+. P1d. $2.00

O'ROURKE, Frank. *Legend in the Dust.* Ballantine 421. 2nd prtg. VG+. B3d. $5.00

O'ROURKE, Frank. *Ride West.* 1953. Ballantine 49. We. VG. B4d. $8.00

O'ROURKE, Frank. *Segundo.* Dell 1st Edition 108. NF. I1d. $6.00

O'ROURKE, Frank. *Segundo.* 1956. Dell 1st Edition 108. PBO. c/S Bates. We. VG. B3d. $4.00

O'ROURKE, Jay. *Summer Lovers.* 1964. Beacon 699. VG+. B3d. $7.00

O'SHEA, Sean. *Nymph Island Affair.* 1967. Belmont B 50-782. My. VG. P1d. $5.00

O'SHEA, Sean. *Topless Kitties.* 1968. Belmont B 60-086. My. VG. P1d. $5.00

O'SHEA, Sean. *What a Way To Go!* 1966. Belmont B 50-707. 1st prtg. My. VG. R5d. $3.25

O'SHEA, Sean. *Win With Sin.* 1967. Belmont B 50-769. My. VG. P1d. $5.00

O'SHELL, Maggie. *Karen Travers Story.* 1981. Pinnacle 41-176. My. VG. P1d. $4.50

O'SULLIVAN, J.B. *Don't Hang Me Too High.* 1956. Pocket 1109. De. VG. P1d. $8.00

O'SULLIVAN, J.B. *I Die Possessed.* 1955. Pocket 1055. c/V Tossey. My. VG. B5d. $4.50

O'TOOLE, George. *Agent on the Other Side.* 1975. Dell 4997. My. VG. P1d. $3.50

OAKLAND, H. *Cocksure Graduate.* Brandon House 6474. NF. B3d. $5.00

OATES, Joyce Carol. *Mysteries of Winterthurn.* 1985. Berkley 08022. My. VG. P1d. $4.00

OBSTFELD, Raymond. *Brain Wave.* 1987. Berkley 10339. My. VG+. P1d. $4.50

OBSTFELD, Raymond. *Dead Bolt.* 1982. Charter 14102. My. VG. P1d. $3.50

OBSTFELD, Raymond. *Dead Heat.* 1981. Ace Charter 14110. My. VG. P1d. $3.50

OBSTFELD, Raymond. *Goulden Fleece.* 1979. Charter 29870. My. VG. P1d. $3.50

OBSTFELD, Raymond. *Masked Dog.* 1986. Gold Eagle 62101. My. VG+. P1d. $4.50

OBSTFELD, Raymond. *Remington Contract.* 1988. World Wide 97095. My. G+. P1d. $3.00

OBSTFELD, Raymond. *Remington Factor.* 1985. Charter 71344. My. VG+. P1d. $4.50

ODLUM, Jerome. *Mirabilis Diamond.* 1949. Dell 303. My. VG. I1d. $9.50

OFFORD, Lenore Glen. *Glass Mask.* 1947. Dell 198. 1st edn. PBO. c/Gerald Gregg. scarce. NF. B6a #75. $38.50

OFFORD, Lenore Glen. *Glass Mask.* 1947. Dell 198. My. VG. P1d. $10.00

OFFORD, Lenore Glen. *My True Love Lies.* 1951. Dell 476. My. VG. P1d. $9.00

OFFORD, Lenore Glen. *Skeleton Key.* 1946. Dell 96. My. G+. I1d. $5.00

OFFUTT, Andrew J. *Ardor on Aros.* 1973. Dell. 1st edn. F. M1d. $10.00

OFFUTT, Andrew J. *Castle Keeps.* Berkley S 2187. 1st prtg. VG. S1d. $5.00

OFFUTT, Andrew J. *Conan & the Sorceror.* 1979. Ace 11684. SF. VG. W2d. $3.75

OFFUTT, Andrew J. *Conan the Mercenary.* 1981. Ace 11659. 1st prtg. SF. F. W2d. $5.00

OFFUTT, Andrew J. *Demon in the Mirror.* Pocket 81720. 1st prtg. F. S1d. $4.00

OFFUTT, Andrew J. *Evil Is Live Spelled Backwards.* 1970. PB Library 64-490. PBO. SF. NF. B6d. $9.00

OFFUTT, Andrew J. *Eyes of Sarsis.* Pocket 82679. 1st prtg. F. S1d. $4.00

OFFUTT, Andrew J. *Iron Lords.* Ace 37363. 1st prtg. VG. S1d. $2.00

OFFUTT, Andrew J. *My Lord Barbarian.* Ballantine 25713. 1st prtg. F. S1d. $4.00

OFFUTT, Andrew J. *Purrfect Plunder.* 1982. Playboy 21148. 1st edn. Spaceways #6. SF. F. F2d. $6.00

OFFUTT, Andrew J. *Shadows Out of Hell.* 1980. Berkley O4447. SF. VG+. B5d. $4.00

OFFUTT, Andrew J. *Sign of the Moonbow.* Zebra 254. VG+. B3d. $5.00

OFFUTT, Andrew J. *Swords Against Darkness IV.* 1979. Zebra. 1st edn. F. M1d. $7.00

OFFUTT, Andrew J. *Swords Against Darkness V.* 1979. Zebra. 1st edn. F. M1d. $7.00

OFFUTT, Andrew J. *Swords Against Darkness.* Zebra 239. 1st prtg. VG. S1d. $4.00

OFFUTT, Andrew J. *Under Twin Suns.* 1982. Playboy 21204. 1st edn. Spaceways #8. SF. F. F2d. $6.00

OFFUTT, Andrew J. *When Death Birds Fly.* Ace 00007. 1st prtg. F. S1d. $4.00

OFFUTT, Andrew J. *When Death Birds Fly.* Ace 88087. 1st prtg. VG+. S1d. $3.00

OGAN & OGAN. *Mistress of Erebus.* 1978. Major 3229. My. VG. P1d. $3.50

OGAN & OGAN. *Murder by Proxy.* 1981. Raven House 60055. My. VG. P1d. $3.50

OGDEN, B. *Sex Crowd.* Barclay 7493. c/photo. NF. B3d. $5.00

OKRAND, Marc. *Klingon Dictionary.* 1985. Pocket 54349. 1st edn. SF. F. F2d. $12.00

OLAY, L. *Dark Corners of the Night.* Signet 1834. c/Barye. VG. B3d. $4.00

OLD SCOUT. *Wild West Weekly.* 1965. Gold Star IL 7-59. reprint. We. VG+. B4d. $4.00

OLDEN, Mark. *Book of Shadows.* 1980. Charter 07075. SF. VG. W2d. $3.50

OLECK, Howard. *Heroic Battles of WW2.* Belmont 92-528. VG. B3d. $4.00

OLECK, Jack. *Messalina.* 1960. Dell F 103. c/J Meese. Fi. VG+. B5d. $3.50

OLECK, Jack. *Tales From the Crypt.* Bantam S 7439. 1st prtg. F. S1d. $4.50

OLECK, Jack. *Tales From the Crypt.* 1972. Bantam 07439. 2nd prtg. SF. VG. W2d. $3.50

OLEMY, P.T. *Clones.* 1968. Flagship 840. 1st prtg. SF. VG. R5d. $3.00

OLENDER, Terry T. *My Life in Crime.* 1966. Holloway House 125. 1st edn. PBO. NF. B3d/F2d. $8.00

OLESKER, Harry. *Exit Dying.* 1960. Dell D 376. 1st prtg. c/McGinnis: gga. VG. P7d. $5.00

OLESKER, Harry. *Now, Will You Try for Murder?* Dell 996. VG. G5d. $5.00

OLIPHANT & PETERSON. *Murder in Blue.* 1974. Pocket 77796. 1st edn. My. F. F2d. $8.00

OLIVE, Harry. *Darkness of Love.* Monarch 131. PBO. VG+. B3d. $4.00

OLIVE, Harry. *Run Naked in the Night.* 1960. Monarch 179. PBO. c/Harry Schaare: gga. scarce. VG. B6a #76. $26.50

OLIVER, Anthony. *Pew Group.* 1985. Crest 20594. 1st prtg. My. VG. W2d. $3.00

OLIVER, Chad. *Another Kind.* 1955. Ballantine 113. NF. I1d. $9.00

OLIVER, Chad. *Another Kind.* 1955. Ballantine 113. 1st edn. F. M1d. $12.00

OLIVER, Chad. *Shadows in the Sun.* 1954. Ballantine 91. VG. I1d. $6.00

OLIVER, Chad. *Shadows in the Sun.* 1954. Ballantine 91. 1st edn. NF. M1d. $9.00

OLIVER, Chad. *Unearthly Neighbors.* 1960. Ballantine 365K. PBO. SF. VG. B5d. $5.00

OLIVER, Chad. *Unearthly Neighbors.* 1960. Ballantine 365K. 1st edn. F. M1d. $12.00

OLIVER, Chad. *Unearthly Neighbors.* 1960. Ballantine 365K. 1st prtg. SF. G+. R5d. $2.75

OLIVER, Chad. *Winds of Time.* 1958. Pocket 1222. c/Powers. VG. B3d. $4.00

OLIVER, Chad. *Winds of Time.* 1958. Pocket 1222. c/R Powers. SF. VG+. B5d. $6.50

OLIVER, Chad. *Winds of Time.* 1958. Pocket 1222. 1st pb. c/Powers. SF. NF. B6d. $12.00

OLIVER, Mark. *Wanton Boys.* 1960. Pyramid G 567. JD. F. P1d. $25.00

OLIVER, W. *Defiance.* Camden Digest. VG. B3d. $8.00

OLIVER. *Meaning of the Blues.* Collier 497. 1st pb. VG+. B6d. $12.50

OLIVIA. *Olivia.* 1957. Berkley G 74. 1st edn. PBO. c/Maguire: gga. NF. B6a #75. $43.50

OLLEY, Jack. *Love Together.* Greenleaf Classic GC 305. VG. M6d. $5.00

OLSEN, D.B. *Cat Saw Murder.* 1944. Dell 35. 1st edn. PBO. c/Gregg. rare. F. B6a #80. $66.00

OLSEN, D.B. *Cat's Claw.* 1946. My Novel Classic 87. 1st pb. My. VG. B6d. $4.00

OLSEN, D.B. *Dead Babes in the Woods.* 1954. Dell 784. 1st prtg. c/Foxley: gga. VG. P7d. $5.50

OLSEN, D.B. *Something About Midnight.* 1951. Pocket 817. c/V Kalin. My. VG. B5d. $4.00

OLSEN, T.V. *Blizzard Pass.* Gold Medal D 2019. We. VG. B5d. $3.50

OLSEN, T.V. *Brand of the Star.* Gold Medal 1168. NF. B3d. $6.00

OLSEN, T.V. *Brothers of the Sword.* 1962. Berkley F 633. Fi. VG. B5d. $3.00

OLSEN, T.V. *Canyon of the Gun.* Gold Medal 1568. NF. B3d. $5.50

OLSEN, T.V. *Gunswift.* 1966. Gold Medal K 1700. We. VG+. B4d. $3.00

OLSEN, T.V. *Gunswift.* Gold Medal 547. VG+. B3d. $8.00

OLSEN, T.V. *Man Called Brazos.* 1964. Gold Medal S 1447. 1st prtg. PBO. VG. P7d. $4.50

OLSEN, T.V. *McGivern.* Gold Medal 509. VG+. B3d. $8.00

OLSEN, T.V. *Ramrod Rider.* Gold Medal 1117. VG. B3d. $4.50

OLSEN, T.V. *Ramrod Rider.* Gold Medal 558. VG. B3d. $6.50

OLSEN, T.V. *Savage Sierra.* 1962. Gold Medal S 1239. We. VG+. B4d. $3.00

OLSEN, T.V. *Savage Sierra.* Gold Medal 1766. NF. B3d. $5.00

OLSON, Donald. *Sky Children.* 1975. Avon 26781. 1st prtg. SF. VG. R5d. $1.50

OLSON, Gene. *Stampede at Blue Springs.* Dell 974. VG. B3d. $4.00

OLSON/SMITH. *Man Who Was Morgan/ Maverick.* Ace D 470. PBO. VG. B3d. $4.50

OLSON/SMITH. *Man Who Was Morgan/ Maverick.* Ace D 470. We. VG+. B6d. $15.00

OMURA, Kimiko. *Diary of a Geisha Girl.* 1959. Avon T 313. PBO. c/Whittington. VG+. B6d. $45.00

ONOPA, Robert. *Pleasure Tube.* 1979. Berkley 03941. PBO. Ad/SF. NF. B6d. $3.00

OPOTOWSKY, Stan. *TV: The Big Picture.* 1962. Collier AS 327X. 1st prtg. VG. R5d. $1.75

OPPENHEIM, E.P. *Great Prince Shan.* 1940. Pocket 54. 40th edn. My. G+. B5d. $3.00

OPPENHEIM, E.P. *Lion & the Lamb.* 1951. Popular 339. 1st pb. c/Belarski. My. VG. B3d. $6.00

OPPENHEIM, E.P. *Season for Passion.* Popular 341. 2nd prtg. VG+. B3d. $5.00

ORAM, John. *Copenhagen Affair.* Ace G 564. Man From UNCLE #3. VG+. G5d. $5.00

ORAM, John. *Copenhagen Affair.* 1965. Ace G 564. Man From UNCLE #3. My. VG+. B3d/B4d. $4.00

ORCZY, Baroness. *Lord Tony's Wife.* Hodder #161. VG. B3d. $8.00

ORCZY, Baroness. *Scarlet Pimpernel.* 1958. Pyramid PR 16. Fa. VG. B4d. $3.75

ORDWAY, Peter. *Face in the Shadows.* 1953. Perma 252. 1st pb. My. VG+. B6d. $10.00

ORKOW, Ben. *When Time Stood Still.* Signet 2150. PBO. VG+. B3d. $5.50

ORKOW, Ben. *When Time Stood Still.* 1962. Signet 2150. 1st edn. NF. M1d. $7.00

ORSI, R. *Rome After Dark.* MacFadden 75-225. 3rd prtg. VG+. B3d. $5.00

ORSI, Roberto. *Rome After Dark.* 1968. MacFadden NN. VG+. B3d. $8.50

ORSI, Roberto. *Rome After Dark.* 1962. MacFadden 50-146. NF. VG. B3d. $4.50

ORWELL, George. *Animal Farm.* 1956. Signet 1289. SF. G+. B5d. $3.00

ORWELL, George. *Animal Farm.* 1956. Signet 1289. 1st pb. Fa. VG+. B6d. $15.00

ORWELL, George. *Burmese Days.* 1952. Popular 459. c/gga. Fa. VG+. B4d. $7.00

ORWELL, George. *Clergyman's Daughter.* 1960. Avon G 1071. Fa. VG+. B4d. $2.00

ORWELL, George. *Coming Up for Air.* 1956. Avon T 144. 1st prtg. c/Marchetti: gga. VG. P7d. $5.00

ORWELL, George. *Down & Out in Paris & London.* Perma P 267. VG. B3d. $4.50

ORWELL, George. *1984.* 1984. Signet 51984. 66th prtg. commeration edn. SF. F. W2d. $4.50

ORWELL, George. *1984.* 1950. Signet 798. 1st edn. PBO. VG. P9d. $1.50

OSBORNE, Dod. *Mission: Danger.* Bantam 839. VG+. B3d. $5.00

OSBORNE, Juanita. *Luther.* Signet 2352. VG+. B3d. $4.50

OSBORNE, O. *Rise & Fall of Dr Carey.* Gold Medal 764. VG+. B3d. $6.00

OTWAY, Howard. *Strangers in Paradise.* 1957. Crest Giant S 171. VG. P6d. $1.50

OURSLER, Fulton. *Greatest Faith Ever Known.* 1955. Perma M 4036. c/R Jonas. Nfi. VG+. B5d. $3.50

OURSLER, Will edt. *As Tough As They Come.* 1951. Perma 118. 1st edn. PBO. F. F2d. $15.00

OURSLER & SMITH. *Hooked.* 1953. Popular 528. 1st edn. PBO. c/DeSoto. VG+. B6a #79. $29.00

OVERHOLSER, Wayne D. *Draw or Drag.* Dell 556. c/R Stanley. We. VG. B5d. $3.00

OVERHOLSER, Wayne D. *Draw or Drag.* Dell 903. c/Gross. VG. B3d. $4.00

OVERHOLSER, Wayne D. *Gun Crazy.* 1950. Readers Choice 17. PBO. c/Saunders. VG. B6d. $8.00

OVERHOLSER, Wayne D. *Steel to the South.* 1957. Dell 948. c/G Gross. We. VG. B5d. $3.00

OVERHOLSER, Wayne D. *Tough Hand.* Dell 846. c/R Schulz. We. VG. B5d. $3.00

OVERSTREET, Harry & Bonaro. *What We Must Know About Communism.* 1960. Pocket 7000. NF. VG+. B5d. $4.00

OWEN, Betty. *11 Great Horror Stories.* 1969. Scholastic 1541. 3rd prtg. SF. VG+. W2d. $4.75

OWEN, Dean. *End of the World.* 1962. Ace D 548. VG. B3d. $5.00

OWEN, Dean. *End of the World.* 1962. Ace D 548. 1st edn. MTI. SF. F. F2d. $15.00

OWEN, Dean. *Guns of Spring.* Banner B 40-106. PBO. VG+. B3d. $5.00

OWEN, Dean. *Guns to the Sunset.* Avon 878. We. VG. B5d. $4.50

OWEN, Dean. *Guns to the Sunset.* 1969. Avon 878. 1st edn. We. NF. F2d. $10.00

OWEN, Dean. *Hec Ramsey.* 1973. Award AN 1169. 1st prtg. TVTI. G+. R5d. $1.50

OWEN, Dean. *Juice Town.* 1962. Monarch 290. PBO. c/DeSoto. G+. P6d. $2.00

OWEN, Dean. *Juice Town.* 1962. Monarch 290. 1st edn. c/gga. Cr. F. F2d. $15.00

OWEN, Dean. *Killer's Bargain.* 1960. Hillman 139. VG+. B3d. $4.50

OWEN, Dean. *Killer's Bargain.* 1960. Hillman 139. 1st edn. We. NF. F2d. $8.00

OWEN, Dean. *Konga.* 1960. Monarch MM 604. PBO. MTI. scarce. VG+. B6a #79. $30.00

OWEN, Dean. *Konga.* 1960. Monarch MM 604. 1st edn. MTI. SF. VG. F2d. $12.00

OWEN, Dean. *Last-Chance Range.* Popular SP 326. VG. B3d. $4.00

OWEN, Dean. *Last-Chance Range.* 1957. Popular 802. 1st edn. We. F. F2d. $10.00

OWEN, Dean. *Lone Trail.* Lancer 74-775. PBO. TVTI. Men From Shiloh #1. VG+. B3d. $6.00

OWEN, Dean. *Point of a Gun.* Popular 538. NF. I1d. $7.00

OWEN, Dean. *Ponderosa Kill.* 1968. PB Library 52-757. PBO. TVTI. c/photo. Bonanza #2. VG. P6d. $3.00

OWEN, Dean. *Rawhider From Texas.* 1963. Monarch 401. c/Jack Thurston. We. VG+. B4d. $6.00

OWEN, Dean. *Reptilicus.* 1961. Monarch MM 605. 1st edn. MTI. SF. VG. F2d. $12.00

OWEN, Dean. *Sam Houston Story.* 1961. Monarch MA 308. Nfi. F. B4d. $10.00

OWEN, Dean. *Sam Houston Story.* 1961. Monarch MA 308. 1st edn. We. NF. F2d. $7.00

OWEN, Hans C. *Fit To Kill.* Hangman 6. My. G. B5d. $2.50

OWEN, John. *Disinformer.* 1968. PB Library 53-773. My. VG. B5d. $4.00

OWEN, R.N. *Drifter in Town.* 1966. Brandon 985. Ad. VG+. B5d. $8.00

OWEN, R.N. *Off-Broadway Casanova.* Brandon House 1000. VG+. B3d. $8.00

OWEN/STEVENS. *Man From Boot Hill/Wild Horse Range.* 1953. Ace D 12. PBO. c/Saunders. We. VG+. P6d. $10.00

OWEN/STEVENS. *Man From Boot Hill/Wild Horse Range.* 1953. Ace D 12. 1st edn. PBO. scarce. NF. B6a #75. $66.00

OWEN/WYNNE. *Rincon Trap/Call Me Hazard.* 1966. Ace M 138. We. VG. P1d. $6.50

OZAKI, Milton K. *Case of the Cop's Wife.* Gold Medal 795. VG. G5d. $7.50

OZAKI, Milton K. *Case of the Deadly Kiss.* 1957. Gold Medal 715. 1st prtg. PBO. VG+. P7d. $9.00

OZAKI, Milton K. *Deadly Pick-Up.* Berkley Diamond D 2038. c/Nappi: gga. scarce. NF. B6a #80. $34.25

OZAKI, Milton K. *Dressed To Kill.* Graphic 141. VG. I1d. $4.00

OZAKI, Milton K. *Dummy Murder Case.* Graphic 33. NF. G5d. $9.00

OZAKI, Milton K. *Fiend in Need.* 1950. Handi-Book 116. 1st prtg. c/gga. VG. P7d. $12.50

PAAR, Jack. *I Kid You Not.* 1961. Cardinal GC 103. 1st prtg. TVTI. G+. R5d. $1.50

PAAR, Jack. *My Saber Is Bent.* 1962. Cardinal GC 148. 1st prtg. TVTI. VG. R5d. $1.75

PACKARD, Edward. *Journey to the Year 2000.* 1987. Bantam 26157. SF. F. W2d. $4.25

PACKARD, Edward. *Mystery of Chimney Rock.* 1982. Bantam 23184. 14th prtg. Choose Your Own Adventure #5. SF. VG. W2d. $2.75

PACKARD, Edward. *Supercomputer (Game Book).* 1984. Bantam 16530. SF. F. W2d. $4.00

PACKARD, Gwenna. *How Come a Nice Girl Like You Isn't Married?* Avon G 1158. Nfi. VG. B5d. $2.50

PACKARD, Vance. *Status Seekers.* 1961. Cardinal GC 601. Nfi. NF. B5d. $3.50

PACKER, Bernard. *Caro.* 1976. Avon 31070. 1st prtg. My. VG. R5d. $1.50

PACKER, Peter. *Dark Surrender.* 1952. Popular 468. Fa. VG+. B4d. $7.50

PACKER, Vin. *Come Destroy Me.* 1954. Gold Medal 363. PBO. My. VG+. B6d. $12.50

PACKER, Vin. *Dark Don't Catch Me.* 1956. Gold Medal S 624. c/Meese. VG+. B6a #74. $73.00

PACKER, Vin. *Hare in March.* 1966. Signet P 3028. 1st prtg. PBO. c/photo. VG. P7d. $5.00

PACKER, Vin. *Something in the Shadows.* Gold Medal 1146. VG. B3d. $5.00

PACKER, Vin. *Something in the Shadows.* MacFadden 75-420. G+. M6d. $6.50

PACKER, Vin. *Spring Fire.* Gold Medal D 1593. lesbian theme. Fi. NF. B5d. $7.50

PACKER, Vin. *Thrill Kids.* Gold Medal 510. VG. B3d. $10.00

PACKER, Vin. *Thrill Kids.* Gold Medal 903. 3rd prtg. VG. B3d. $6.00

PACKER, Vin. *Twisted Ones.* 1959. Gold Medal S 861. 1st prtg. PBO. c/Bob Abbett. JD. VG. P6d. $7.50

PACKER, Vin. *Young & Violent.* 1956. Gold Medal 581. PBO. JD. VG. B6d. $12.00

PACKER, Vin. *5:45 to Suburbia.* 1958. Gold Medal S 731. PBO. c/Charles. VG+. B6d. $10.00

PADGETT, Lewis. *Chessboard Planet.* Galaxy SF 26. VG+. B3d. $7.00

PADGETT, Lewis. *Day He Died.* 1948. Bantam 306. 1st pb. c/Fullington. VG. M1d. $10.00

PADGETT, Lewis. *Line to Tomorrow.* Bantam 1251. c/Hooks. VG. B3d. $4.50

PADGETT, Lewis. *Line to Tomorrow.* 1954. Bantam 1251. 1st edn. F. M1d. $15.00

PADGETT, Lewis. *Murder in Brass.* Bantam 107. VG. B3d. $5.00

PADGETT, Lewis. *Well of the Worlds.* Galaxy 17. NF. B3d. $9.00

PADGETT, Lewis. *Well of the Worlds.* Galaxy 17. 1st prtg. G. S1d. $2.50

PAGANO, Jo. *Condemned.* 1954. Perma 286. My. VG. B4d. $2.75

PAGE, Gerald edt. *Year's Best Horror Stories Series IV.* 1976. DAW 217. 1st edn. VG. M1d. $5.00

PAGE, Gerald edt. *Year's Best Horror Stories Series VI.* 1978. DAW 297. 1st edn. F. M1d. $7.00

PAGE, Gerald edt. *Year's Best Horror Stories Series VII.* 1979. DAW 346. 1st edn. F. M1d. $7.00

PAGE, Marco. *Reclining Figure.* 1953. Pocket 931. 1st pb. c/Tossey. My. VG. B6d. $7.50

PAGE, Marco. *Shadowy Third.* Pocket 537. VG. B3d. $4.50

PAGE, Norvell. *Blue Steel.* 1979. Python 002-7. 1st edn. c/George Gross. My. NF. F2d. $12.00

PAGE, Norvell. *Flame Winds.* 1969. Berkley X 1741. 1st edn. F. M1d. $8.00

PAGE, Norvell. *Flame Winds.* 1978. Berkley 03898. SF. G. W2d. $3.00

PAGE, Norvell. *Sons of the Bear-God.* 1969. Berkley X 1769. 1st edn. F. M1d. $8.00

PAGE, Norvell. *Sons of the Bear-God.* 1969. Berkley 1769. PBO. c/J Jones. SF. VG. B5d/W2d. $4.00

PAGE, Patti. *Once Upon a Dream.* Popular G 496. 2nd prtg. VG+. B3d. $4.50

PAGE, Thomas. *Hephaestus Plague.* 1975. Bantam N 8550. SF. VG+. B5d. $3.50

PAIGE, Satchel. *Pitchin' Man.* 1948. Lebovitz NN. NF. B3a #24. $130.00

PALEY, Frank. *Rumble on the Docks.* 1955. Popular G 146. JF. G+. P1d. $9.00

PALMER, David. *Emergence.* 1984. Bantam. 1st edn. F. M1d. $5.00

PALMER, David. *Threshold.* 1985. Bantam. 1st edn. F. M1d. $4.00

PALMER, Drew. *Moments of Passion.* 1964. Saber SA 53. Ad. G+. B5d. $3.00

PALMER, Michael. *Flashback.* 1988. Bantam 27329. PBO. Th. VG+. B6d. $3.00

PALMER, Michael. *Sisterhood.* 1982. Bantam 22704. 1st prtg. My. VG. W2d. $3.00

PALMER, Stuart. *Cold Poison.* 1964. Pyramid F 1040. My. VG. B5d. $4.00

PALMER, Stuart. *Green Ace (Hild Withers).* 1964. Pyramid R 995. 1st prtg. My. G+. W2d. $3.75

PALMER, Stuart. *Penguin Pool Murder.* Detective 18. VG. B3d. $6.00

PALMER, Stuart. *Puzzle of the Silver Persian.* 1943. Dell 18. 1st edn. PBO. c/G Gregg. scarce. VG. B6a #80. $40.25

PALMER & RICE. *People Vs Withers & Malone.* 1965. Award A 146F. G+. G5d. $4.00

PANGBORN, Edgar. *Davy.* 1964. Ballantine U 6018. 1st US edn. SF. F. F2d. $15.00

PANGBORN, Edgar. *Judgement of Eve.* 1967. Dell 4292. 1st prtg. SF. G+. R5d. $1.25

PANGBORN, Edgar. *Mirror for Observers.* 1958. Dell D 246. 1st pb edn. F. M1d. $10.00

PANGBORN, Edgar. *Still I Persist in Wondering.* 1978. Dell 18277. F. P9d. $2.50

PANGBORN, Edgar. *West of the Sun.* 1980. Dell 19366. VG. P9d. $1.50

PANGBORN, Edgar. *West of the Sun.* 1966. Dell 9442. 1st prtg. SF. VG+. R5d. $3.50

PANGBORN, Edgar. *West of the Sun.* 1966. Dell. 1st pb edn. F. M1d. $5.00

PANGER, Daniel. *Ol' Prophet Nat.* 1968. Gold Medal T 1955. 1st prtg. VG+. P7d. $5.50

PANSHIN, Alexei. *Star Well.* 1968. Ace G 756. 1st edn. Fa. F. F2d. $10.00

PARISE, Goffredo. *Don Gastone & the Women.* 1957. Avon T 209. VG+. B3d. $4.50

PARK, C.S. *Showdown at Pistol Flat.* Popular 50-448. VG+. B3d. $4.50

PARK, Jordan. *Valerie.* 1957. Lion LB 153. c/gga. reprint. VG. B6d. $9.00

PARK, Jordan. *Valerie.* 1957. Lion LB 153. 2nd prtg. c/Charles Copeland: gga. G+. P6d. $2.50

PARK, Jordan. *Valerie.* 1953. Lion 176. c/Maquire. NF. B3a #20. $33.80

PARK/WEST. *Quiet Ones/Nothing But My Gun.* Ace D 418. PBO. VG. B3d. $4.00

PARKER, Dorothy. *Enough Rope.* Pocket 6. 2nd edn. VG. B3d. $7.00

PARKER, Dorothy. *Sunset Gun.* 1940. Pocket 76. PBO. VG. P6d. $2.00

PARKER, Dorothy. *Sunset Gun.* 1940. Pocket 76. VG+. B3d. $5.00

PARKER, Jon. *Pickup.* 1967. Wee Hours 517. VG. B3d. $8.00

PARKER, Jon. *Sex Carnival.* 1965. First Niter 224. 1st edn. F. F2d. $20.00

PARKER, M. *Hot Mouth Cults.* Barclay 7466. NF. B3d. $5.00

PARKER, Robert B. *God Save the Child.* Berkley Z 3037. VG. G5d. $6.50

PARKER, Robert B. *Looking for Rachel Wallace.* 1987. Dell 15316. 1st prtg. My. VG+. W2d. $3.00

PARKER, Robert B. *Love & Glory.* Dell 14629. 1st pb. VG. M6d. $4.00

PARKER, Robert B. *Pale Kings & Princes.* 1988. Dell 20004. 1st prtg. My. VG. W2d. $4.00

PARKER, Robert B. *Passport to Peril.* Dell 568. G+. G5d. $4.00

PARKER, Robert B. *Passport to Peril.* Dell 568. 1st pb. c/Stanley. VG. M6d. $6.50

PARKER, Robert B. *Taming a Sea Horse.* 1987. Dell 18841. 1st prtg. My. F. W2d. $4.50

PARKER, Robert B. *Ticket to Oblivion.* 1951. Bantam 878. My. VG+. B4d. $3.00

PARKES & WYNDHAM. *Outward Urge.* 1959. Ballantine 341K. 1st prtg. SF. G. R5d. $2.00

PARKES & WYNDHAM. *Outward Urge.* 1959. Ballantine 341K. 1st US edn. F. M1d. $12.00

PARKHURST, Helen. *Undertow.* 1965. Monarch 494. JD. VG. P1d. $8.00

PARKINSON, C. Northcote. *Parkinson's Law.* 1964. Ballantine U 2218. Hu. VG+. B4d. $2.50

PARKINSON, Frances. *Station Wagon in Spain.* 1959. Avon G 1054. Fa. VG. B4d. $2.00

PARKSMITH, George. *Your Sins & Mine.* 1961. Midwood 79. PBO. c/gga. NF. B6d. $22.50

PARROTT, Ursula. *Ex-Wife.* 1949. Dell 277. VG+. P6d. $3.50

PARROTT, Ursula. *Strangers May Kiss.* 1950. Dell 409. VG. B3d. $5.00

PARROTT, Ursula. *Strangers May Kiss.* 1950. Dell 409. 1st pb. c/Ray Johnson. VG+. B6d. $9.00

PARRY, Michel. *Countess Dracula.* 1971. Beagle 94081. 1st edn. c/photo. scarce. SF. NF. F2d. $20.00

PARRY, Michel. *Countess Dracula.* 1971. Sphere 67091. PBO. MTI. VG+. B3a #22. $25.00

PARRY, Michel. *Rivals of Dracula.* 1977. Corgi 10410. PBO. VG. B6d. $7.50

PARSONS, A. *Case of Missing GI Bride.* Sexton Blake 121. VG. B3d. $10.00

PARSONS, A. *Case of Stolen Evidence.* Sexton Blake 196. VG+. B3d. $15.00

PARSONS, A. *Case of the Second Crime.* Sexton Blake 314. VG+. B3d. $7.00

PARSONS, A. *Case of Wicked Three.* Sexton Blake 322. VG. B3d. $6.00

PARSONS, A. *Great Dollar Fraud.* Sexton Blake 217. NF. B3d. $8.00

PARSONS, A. *Loot of Pakistan.* Sexton Blake 164. VG. B3d. $7.50

PARSONS, A. *Mystery of 250,000 Rupees.* Sexton Blake 117. VG. B3d. $8.00

PARSONS, A. *Riddle of Indian Alibi.* Sexton Blake 111. VG+. B3d. $12.00

PARSONS, A. *Secret of the Moroccan Bazaar.* Sexton Blake 319. VG+. B3d. $7.50

PARTCH, Virgil. *Here We Go Again & Bottle Fatigue.* Dell 3593. reprint. VG. B3d. $4.00

PARTCH, Virgil. *Man the Beast & the Wild, Wild Women.* 1955. Dell 843. 1st pb. VG. B6d. $6.00

PARTCH, Virgil. *New Faces on the Bar Room Floor.* Crest 548. NF. B3d. $5.00

PARTCH & SHANE. *Bar Guide.* Gold Medal 135. VG+. B3d. $4.50

PARTRIDGE, Bellamy. *Excuse My Dust.* 1951. Popular 320. Fa. VG+. I1d. $6.00

PARTRIDGE, Burgo. *History of Orgies.* 1960. Avon T 456. VG. P6d. $3.50

PASCAL, John. *Jean Harlow Story.* 1964. Popular PC 1043. PBO. VG. P6d. $7.00

PATERSON, Neil. *Man on the Tightrope.* 1953. Avon 552. 1st prtg. My. VG. R5d. $4.50

PATON, Alan. *Too Late the Phalarope.* 1956. Signet S 1290. Fi. VG. B5d. $4.00

PATRICK, Joseph. *King's Arrow.* 1952. Perma P 182. c/gga. Fa. VG. B4d. $2.25

PATRICK, Joseph. *King's Arrow.* 1952. Perma P 182. 1st pb. c/Pioneer. NF. B6d. $12.50

PATRICK, Q. *Girl on the Gallows.* 1954. Gold Medal 397. PBO. VG+. B3a #20. $25.00

PATRICK, Q. *Grindle Nightmare.* Ballantine F 722. 1st prtg. My. VG. R5d. $4.00

PATRICK, Q. *Grindle Nightmare.* 1949. Popular 206. c/Belarski. VG. B3d. $10.00

PATRICK, Q. *Grindle Nightmare.* 1949. Popular 206. c/Belarski. VG+. B3a #21. $14.55

PATRICK, Q. *Murder at Cambridge.* 1950. Popular 263. 1st pb. c/Belarski. My. VG. B6d. $12.50

PATRICK, Q. *Return to the Scene.* 1945. Popular 47. 1st edn. PBO. c/Hoffman. scarce. VG+. B6a #75. $49.00

PATRICK, Q. *SS Murder.* 1944. Popular 23. c/Hoffman. My. VG. P6d. $10.00

PATTEN, Lewis B. *Apache Hostage.* 1970. Signet 4220. 1st edn. We. F. F2d. $8.00

PATTEN, Lewis B. *Five Rode West.* Gold Medal K 1567. We. VG. B5d. $3.00

PATTEN, Lewis B. *Gun Proud.* Graphic 151. c/Stanley. VG. B3d. $4.00

PATTEN, Lewis B. *Home Is the Outlaw.* Gold Medal 1834. VG+. B3d. $4.00

PATTEN, Lewis B. *Home Is the Outlaw.* Gold Medal 373. VG. B3d. $7.00

PATTEN, Lewis B. *Home Is the Outlaw.* 1958. Gold Medal 778. 1st prtg. PBO. c/gga. We. VG. P6d. $3.50

PATTEN, Lewis B. *Massacre at San Pablo.* Gold Medal 706. VG. B3d. $4.50

PATTEN, Lewis B. *Renegade Gun.* Avon I 536. VG. B3d. $4.00

PATTEN, Lewis B. *Rope Law.* Gold Medal 182. VG. B3d. $6.00

PATTEN, Lewis B. *Ruthless Men.* Gold Medal 422. VG+. B3d. $7.50

PATTEN, Lewis B. *Savage Star.* Avon T 331. PBO. VG. B3d. $4.50

PATTEN, Lewis B. *Savage Town.* Avon T 451. PBO. VG+. B3d. $4.50

PATTEN, Lewis B. *Top Man With a Gun.* Gold Medal 1815. VG+. B3d. $4.00

PATTEN, Lewis B. *Vow of Vengeance.* 1975. Signet 6516. 1st edn. We. F. F2d. $8.00

PATTEN, Lewis B. *White Warrior.* Gold Medal 203. VG. B3d. $5.00

PATTERSON, Rod. *Whip Hand.* 1954. Lion 203. PBO. VG. B3d. $4.00

PATTERSON/SHIRREFFS. *Shooting at Sundust/Tumbleweed Trigger.* Ace F 134. We. VG+. B6d. $9.00

PATTI, Ercole. *Roman Affair.* 1959. Pocket 1225. c/B Hofmann. Fi. VG+. B5d. $5.00

PATTON, Blenn. *Couch Game.* 1964. Herald HR 101. Ad. G+. B5d. $4.50

PATTON, Frances Gray. *Good Morning, Miss Dove.* 1956. Pocket 1099. 1st prtg. MTI. VG. R5d. $3.25

PAUL, Barbara. *Bibblings.* 1979. Signet E 8937. NF. P9d. $2.00

PAUL, Elliot. *Ghost Town on the Yellowstone.* Bantam 262. VG. B3d. $4.00

PAUL, Elliot. *Ghost Town on the Yellowstone.* 1949. Bantam 262. c/gga. We. VG+. B4d. $8.00

PAUL, Elliot. *Hugger-Mugger in the Louvre.* Pocket 151. VG. B3d. $4.00

PAUL, Elliot. *Indelible.* Mercury 15. G+. G5d. $6.50

PAUL, Elliot. *Last Time I Saw Paris.* 1945. Bantam 13. Fa. VG+. B4d. $7.00

PAUL, Elliot. *Mayhem in B Flat.* 1950. Bantam 850. VG+. B3d. $5.00

PAUL, Elliot. *Mayhem in B Flat.* 1950. Bantam 850. 1st prtg. My. G+. R5d. $1.75

PAUL, Elliot. *Mysterious Mickey Finn.* 1942. Avon Murder My 2. VG. B3a #22. $22.00

PAUL, Elliot. *Mysterious Mickey Finn.* Avon 243. VG. B3d. $4.50

PAUL, Eugene. *Hungry Eye.* 1962. Ballantine S 650. 1st prtg. c/photo. VG. P7d. $4.00

PAUL, F.W. *Man From Stud Vs the Mafia.* 1972. Lancer 70-403. PBO. VG+. B6d. $9.00

PAUL, F.W. *Tool of the Trade.* 1969. Lancer 73-811. PBO. c/photo. VG. P6d. $3.00

PAUL, Gene. *Big Make.* 1957. Lion Library LL 158. c/Maguire: gga. My. VG+. B4d. $10.00

PAUL, Hugo. *Procurer.* 1965. Lancer 74-842. PBO. VG+. B3d. $6.00

PAUL, Louis. *Breakdown.* Dell 425. VG. B3d. $4.50

PAULL, Jessyca. *Destination: Terror.* Award AN 1282. Passport to Danger #2. My. VG. W2d. $4.00

PAULSEN, Gary. *Meteorite Track 291.* Dell 15583. 1st prtg. G+. S1d. $3.00

PAVESE, C. *Moon & the Bonfires.* Signet 1117. VG. B3d. $4.00

PAYNE, Robert. *Alexander & the Camp Follower.* Ace D 127. VG+. B3d. $5.00

PAYNE, Robert. *Charlie Chaplin.* 1964. Ace K 204. 1st prtg. Bio. G+. R5d. $2.00

PAYNE, Robert. *Deluge.* 1953. Lion 233. VG. B3d. $6.00

PAYNE, Robert. *Deluge.* 1953. Lion 233. VG+. B3a #20. $20.00

PAYNE, Robert. *Great Charlie.* Pan GP 71. VG. B3d. $10.00

PAYNE, Robert. *Lovers in the Sun.* 1964. Pyramid R 985. 2nd edn. c/T Kokinos. Fi. VG+. B5d. $5.00

PAYNE, Robert. *Lovers in the Sun.* Pyramid 143. PBO. VG+. B3d. $5.00

PAYNE, Robert. *Red Lion Inn.* 1952. Popular G 108. 1st pb. c/DeSoto: gga. VG. B6d. $7.00

PAYNE, Robert. *Tormentors.* 1959. Hillman 107. c/P Rader. Fi. G+. B5d. $5.00

PAYTON, Barbara. *I Am Not Ashamed.* Holloway House HH 108. 2nd prtg. VG. B3d. $4.00

PEACE, Frank. *Easy Money.* 1955. Perma M 3026. PBO. c/Schulz. We. NF. B6d. $15.00

PEACOCK, Max. *King's Rogue.* Graphic G 205. VG+. B3d. $6.00

PEAKE, Mervyn. *Gormenhast.* 1973. Ballantine 23519. 4th prtg. SF. VG. W2d. $3.25

PEAKE, Mervyn. *Titus Alone.* 1968. Ballantine 73009. 1st edn. PBO. F. P9d. $2.50

PEAKE, Mervyn. *Titus Groan.* 1974. Ballantine 23518. 5th prtg. SF. VG. W2d. $3.25

PEAKE, Mervyn. *Titus Groan.* 1975. Ballantine 25041. 7th prtg. SF. VG+. W2d. $3.25

PEALE, Norman Vincent. *Art of Living.* Perma P 42. NF. I1d. $4.00

PEALE, Norman Vincent. *Guideposts.* Ace D 281. Nfi. VG+. B5d. $4.00

PEARCE, Dick. *Hell or High Water.* 1949. Bantam 213. VG+. B3d. $6.00

PEARCE, Dick. *Impudent Rifle.* 1952. Popular 418. c/Belarski: gga. Fa. VG. B4d. $6.00

PEARCE, Donn. *Cool Hand Luke.* 1968. Gold Medal T 2444. MTI. c/Paul Newman. VG. B3d. $5.00

PEARCE, Frank. *Easy Money.* 1955. Perma M 3026. We. VG+. B4d. $3.75

PEARL, Cyril. *Girl With the Swansdown Seat.* 1958. Signet D 1561. c/B Phillips: photos. Nfi. B5d. $4.00

PEARL, Jack. *Aerial Dogfights of WW2.* Monarch 322. PBO. NF. B3d. $6.00

PEARL, Jack. *Ambush Bay.* 1966. Signet D 2994. War. VG+. B4d. $3.00

PEARL, Jack. *Crucifixion of Pete McCabe.* Pocket 75277. 1st pb. VG. M6d. $4.50

PEARL, Jack. *Dangerous Assassins.* 1962. Monarch K 74. c/photo. Nfi. VG. B5d. $5.00

PEARL, Jack. *Robin & the 7 Hoods.* 1964. Pocket 50033. MTI. c/photo. VG. B4d/B6d. $3.00

PEARL, Jack. *Stockade.* 1965. Pocket 75133. Fa. VG+. B4d. $2.25

PEARL, Jack. *Yellow Rolls-Royce.* 1965. Pocket 50143. Fi. VG+. B5d. $4.50

PEARLMAN, Gilbert. *Young Frankenstein.* 1974. Ballantine 24268. MTI. SF. VG. W2d. $4.00

PEARLMAN, Gilbert. *Young Frankenstein.* 1974. Ballantine 24268. 1st prtg. MTI. SF. G+. R5d. $1.50

PEARSON, Drew. *Senator.* 1962. Avon W 161. Fi. VG+. B5d. $3.50

PEARSON, John. *Life of Ian Fleming.* 1967. Bantam N 3480. 1st prtg. c/Jim Bama: gga. VG+. P7d. $5.00

PEARSON, William. *Beautiful Frame.* 1954. Pocket 1039. VG. G5d. $5.00

PEARSON, William. *Beautiful Frame.* 1954. Pocket 1039. 1st pb. c/Meese. My. NF. B6d. $15.50

PEARSON, William. *Fever in the Blood.* Avon G 1046. c/L Gregori. Fi. NF. B5d. $4.00

PEARSON, William. *Hunt the Man Down.* 1956. Pocket 1141. c/J Meese. My. VG. B5d. $5.00

PEARSON, William. *Hunt the Man Down.* 1956. Pocket 1141. 1st pb. c/Meese. My. NF. B6d. $16.50

PEARSON & TAYLOR. *Fractured French.* 1956. Perma M 3031. VG. B3d/B4d. $4.00

PEASE, Howard. *Road Kid.* 1953. Bantam 1110. JD. VG+. P1d. $19.00

PECK, Martin W. *Meaning of Psycho Analysis.* Perma P 64. VG. I1d. $3.00

PEDRICK, Jean. *Fascination.* 1949. Bantam 477. VG. B3d. $4.00

PEEPLES, Samuel Anthony. *Gun Feud at Stampede Valley.* Avon 596. PBO. We. VG+. B5d. $6.00

PEEPLES, Samuel Anthony. *Star Trek Photonovel #2.* 1977. Bantam 11346. SF. F. B4d. $20.00

PEI, Mario. *Swords for Charlemagne.* Graphic G 208. VG+. B3d. $4.50

PELRINE & PELRINE. *Ian Fleming: Man With the Golden Pen.* 1966. Swan 112. Nfi. VG. P1d. $9.00

PEN, John. *Temptation.* 1951. Avon G 1008. 1st prtg. c/gga. VG. P7d. $9.00

PENDERGAST, Chuck. *Introduction to Organic Gardening.* 1972. PB Library 65-823. c/photo. Nfi. VG+. B5d. $3.50

PENDLETON, Don. *Black Dice.* 1987. Gold Eagle 61098. 1st prtg. Executioner #98. My. VG+. W2d. $3.25

PENDLETON, Don. *Guns of Terra 10.* 1969. Pinnacle P 006N. 1st edn. VG. P9d. $1.50

PENDLETON, Don. *Split Image.* 1987. Gold Eagle 61102. 1st prtg. Executioner #102. My. F. W2d. $3.75

PENDLETON, Ford. *Hell Rider.* 1955. Graphic 116. We. VG+. B4d. $4.00

PENDLETON, Ford. *Hell Rider.* 1957. Graphic 157. 2nd edn. We. VG. B3d. $4.00

PENDLETON, Ford. *Outlaw Justice.* 1957. Graphic 154. 2nd prtg. We. VG+. B3d/B5d. $5.00

PENDOWER, Jacques. *Betrayed.* 1967. PB Library 53-481. My. VG.+. B5d. $3.50

PENDOWER, Jacques. *Mission in Tunis.* 1967. PB Library 53-496. My. NF. B5d. $4.00

PENIAKOFF, V. *Popski's Private Army.* Pan X 10. VG+. B3d. $8.50

PENTECOST, Hugh. *Brass Chills.* 1945. Popular 44. c/Hoffman. G+. P6d. $2.00

PENTECOST, Hugh. *Cat & Mouse.* Quick Reader 128. VG. B3d. $6.00

PENTECOST, Hugh. *Creeping Hours.* 1974. Zebra 00209. 1st prtg. John Jericho #3. My. F. W2d. $4.00

PENTECOST, Hugh. *I'll Sing at Your Funeral.* Popular 109. VG. I1d. $7.00

PENTECOST, Hugh. *Tarnished Angel.* 1965. Avon G 1276. My. VG+. B4d. $2.00

PENTECOST, Hugh. *24th Horse.* Popular 82. VG+. B3d. $15.00

PENTECOST, Hugh. *24th Horse.* 1946. Popular 82. c/Hoffman. VG+. B3a #24. $14.51

PEPPARD, Harold M. *Sight Without Glasses.* Perma P 14. VG+. I1d. $3.00

PEREDA, P. *All the Girls We Loved.* Signet 691. VG+. I1d. $5.00

PERELMAN, S.J. *Acres & Pains.* 1950. Popular 240. VG+. B3d. $4.50

PERKINS, J.R. *Emperor's Physician.* 1947. Pocket 481. 1st prtg. VG. B4d/P7d. $5.00

PERKINS, Kenneth. *Relentless.* 1948. Bantam 251. c/C Young. We. NF. B5d. $5.00

PERKINS, Michael. *Estelle.* 1969. Essex 0132. PBO. VG+. B3a #21. $30.25

PERO & ROVIN. *Always, Lana.* 1982. Bantam 20805. 1st prtg. Bio. VG. R5d. $1.25

PERRELLI, Nick. *At Dead of Night.* 1954. Milestone NN. PBO. VG. B3d. $12.50

PERRELLI, Nick. *Lady Is a Tiger.* 1953. Milestone 1024. VG. B3d. $9.00

PERRELLI, Nick. *Two Dames Too Many.* 1952. Scion 38499. VG. B3d. $9.00

PERRELLI, Nick. *Who Told the Belle.* 1953. Scion G 448. VG. B3d. $10.00

PERRIN, Forrest V. *Don.* 1971. Award 739. 1st edn. My. F. F2d. $10.00

PERRY, Anne. *Resurrection Row.* 1982. Crest 24566. 1st prtg. My. F. W2d. $3.75

PERRY, George Sessions. *Walls Rise Up.* Pennant P 32. c/Hooks. VG+. I1d. $5.00

PERRY, Steve. *Omega Cage.* 1988. Ace 62382. SF. VG+. W2d. $3.50

PERRY, Steve. *Tularemia Gambit.* Gold Medal 14411. SF. C. W2d. $3.00

PESEK, Ludek. *Earth Is Near.* 1975. Dell 4506. VG. P9d. $1.50

PETAJA, Emil. *Nets of Space.* 1969. Berkley X 1692. 1st edn. F. P9d. $2.00

PETAJA, Emil. *Path Beyond the Stars.* 1969. Dell 6864. 1st edn. G. P9d. $1.25

PETAJA, Emil. *Saga of Lost Earths.* 1966. Ace F 392. F. M1d. $7.00

PETAJA, Emil. *Saga of Lost Earths.* 1966. Ace F 392. 1st edn. sgn. SF. F. F2d. $15.00

PETAJA, Emil. *Saga of Lost Earths.* 1966. Ace F 392. 1st prtg. SF. VG. S1d. $3.75

PETAJA, Emil. *Star Mill.* 1966. Ace F 414. G+. M1d. $4.00

PETAJA, Emil. *Star Mill.* 1966. Ace F 414. 1st edn. sgn. SF. F. F2d. $15.00

PETAJA, Emil. *Time Twister.* 1968. Dell 8911. 1st prtg. SF. VG. R5d. $2.50

PETAJA/PURDOM. *Lord of the Green Planet/Five Against Arlane.* 1967. Ace H 22. F. M1d. $8.00

PETAJA/PURDOM. *Lord of the Green Planet/Five Against Arlane.* 1967. Ace H 22. PBO. c/Freas. NF. B3d. $5.50

PETAJA/STABLEFORD. *Seed of the Dreamers/Blind Worm.* Ace 06707. PBO. SF. VG+. B5d. $4.00

PETER, Field. *Riders of the Outlaw Trail.* 1963. Pocket 6201. We. VG+. B5d. $4.00

PETERS, Elizabeth. *Murders of Richard III.* 1986. Mysterious 40229. 2nd prtg. My. VG+. W2d. $3.50

PETERS, Elizabeth. *Street of Five Moons.* 1987. TOR 50766. 1st prtg. My. F. W2d. $3.75

PETERS, Ellis. *Piper on the Mountain.* 1968. Lancer 73-648. 1st pb. VG+. B6d. $7.50

PETERS, Fritz. *Finistere.* 1952. Signet 930. Fi. VG. B5d. $4.00

PETERS, Fritz. *Sin Professor.* Bedside 1225. PBO. VG+. B3d. $6.00

PETERS, Fritz. *World Next Door.* Signet 813. VG. B3d. $4.50

PETERS, Matthew. *Joys She Chose.* 1954. Dell 1st Edn 24. VG. B3d. $3.50

PETERS, Matthew. *Joys She Chose.* 1954. Dell 1st Edn 24. 1st edn. c/gga. F. F2d. $10.00

PETERSEN, Herman. *Old Bones.* Dell 127. VG. B3d. $4.50

PETERSON, Herman. *Murder RFD.* 1943. Best Detective Select NN. 1st edn. PBO. c/Peter Driben. VG. B6a #76. $17.50

PETRY, Ann. *Country Place.* 1950. Signet 761. 1st prtg. c/Avati: gga. VG. B5d/P7d. $5.50

PETRY, Ann. *Narrows.* 1955. Signet T 1259. 1st pb. c/Hulings. VG. B6d. $3.50

PETTIT, Charles. *Chinese Lover.* 1953. Pyramid 85. c/Nappi: gga. scarce. VG. B6a #74. $22.00

PETTIT, Charles. *Son of the Grand Eunich.* 1949. Avon 197. c/A Cantor. Fi. G+. B5d. $5.00

PETTIT, Charles. *Son of the Grand Eunuch.* Avon 197. VG. I1d. $6.00

PETTIT, Charles. *Unfaithful Lady.* Avon 155. VG. B3d. $4.00

PHILIPPE, Charles-Louis. *Bubu of Montparnasse.* 1948. Avon 172. Fi. G+. B5d. $4.00

PHILIPPE, Charles-Louis. *Bubu of Montparnasse.* 1951. Avon 310. c/gga. Fa. G+. B4d. $3.00

PHILIPS, **Judson** *Nightmare at Dawn.* Pinnacle 00283. VG. G5d. $6.50

PHILIPS, **Judson.** *Murder Clear, Track Fast.* Perma M 4273. VG. G5d. $4.50

PHILIPS, **Judson.** *Odds on the Hot Seat.* 1941. Handi-Book NN 1. PBO. scarce. VG. B6a #75. $33.00

PHILLIFENT, **John T.** *Mad Scientist Affair -- UNCLE #5.* Ace G 581. PBO. TVTI. VG. M6d. $5.00

PHILLIFENT, **John T.** *Ring of Argent.* 1973. DAW 46. 4th edn. F. M1d. $3.00

PHILLIFENT/PISERCHIA. *Hierarchies/Mister Justice.* 1973. Ace 53415. SF. G+. W2d. $4.25

PHILLIFENT/PISERCHIA. *Hierarchies/Mr Justice.* 1973. Ace 53415. 1st edn. SF. F. F2d. $14.00

PHILLIPS, **James Atlee.** *Black Venus Contract.* 1975. Gold Medal 3187. 1st edn. My. F. F2d. $10.00

PHILLIPS, **James Atlee.** *Canadian Bomber Contract.* 1971. Gold Medal 2450. 1st edn. Th. F. F2d. $10.00

PHILLIPS, **James Atlee.** *Deadly Mermaid.* 1954. Dell 1st Edn 26. VG. B3d/I1d. $4.00

PHILLIPS, **James Atlee.** *Deadly Mermaid.* 1954. Dell 1st Edn 26. 1st edn. c/gga. My. NF. F2d. $8.00

PHILLIPS, **James Atlee.** *Judah Lion Contract.* 1972. Gold Medal 2608. 1st edn. My. F. F2d. $10.00

PHILLIPS, **James Atlee.** *Last Domino Contract.* 1976. Gold Medal 3587. 1st edn. My. F. F2d. $10.00

PHILLIPS, **James Atlee.** *Makassar Stait Contract.* 1976. Gold Medal 3477. 1st edn. c/gga. My. F. F2d. $10.00

PHILLIPS, **James Atlee.** *Silken Baroness.* 1964. Gold Medal 1489. 1st edn. Th. NF. F2d. $8.00

PHILLIPS, **James Atlee.** *Spice Route Contract.* 1973. Gold Medal 2697. 1st edn. My. F. F2d. $15.00

PHILLIPS, **James Atlee.** *Suitable for Framing.* Pocket 725. VG. G5d. $4.50

PHILLIPS, **James Atlee.** *Suitable for Framing.* Pocket 725. VG+. B3d. $5.00

PHILLIPS, **James Atlee.** *Underground Cities Contract.* 1974. Gold Medal 2925. 1st edn. My. F. F2d. $14.00

PHILLIPS, **James Atlee.** *White Wolverine Contract.* 1971. Gold Medal 2508. 1st edn. My. F. F2d. $10.00

PHILLIPS, **L.** *Cockleshell Heroes.* Pan GP-59. VG+. B3d. $8.00

PHILLIPS, **Mark.** *Brain Twister.* 1962. Pyramid F 783. PBO. c/J Schoenherr. SF. VG+. B5d. $5.50

PHILLIPS, **Mark.** *Brain Twister.* 1962. Pyramid F 783. 1st edn. NF. M1d. $10.00

PHILLIPS, **Mark.** *Impossibles.* 1963. Pyramid F 875. PBO. c/J Schoenherr. SF. VG. B5d. $4.00

PHILLIPS, **Mark.** *Impossibles.* 1963. Pyramid F 875. 1st edn. Cr. F. F2d. $15.00

PHILLIPS, **Mark.** *Supermind.* 1963. Pyramid F 909. PBO. c/J Schoenherr. SF. VG. B5d. $4.00

PHILLIPS, **Mark.** *Supermind.* 1963. Pyramid F 909. VG+. I1d. $5.00

PHILLIPS, **Mark.** *Supermind.* 1963. Pyramid F 909. 1st edn. SF. F. F2d. $15.00

PHILLIPS, **Rog.** *Hot Canary.* All Star 72. VG+. B3d. $4.50

PHILLIPS, **Rog.** *Time Trap.* 1949. Century 116. PBO. c/Malcolm Smith: gga. SF. VG. B6a #79. $73.00

PHILLIPS, **Rog.** *World of If.* Merit B 13. PBO. VG. B3d. $7.50

PHILLIPS, **Rog.** *World of If.* 1951. Merit B 13. 1st edn. c/gga. SF. F. F2d. $20.00

PHILLIPS, **Rog.** *Worlds Within.* 1950. Century 124. 1st edn. c/gga. Fa. F. F2d. $23.00

PHILLIPS, **Rog.** *Worlds Within.* 1950. Century 124. 1st edn. VG. M1d. $20.00

PHILLIPS, **Rog.** *Worlds Within.* 1950. News Stand Library 142. SF. G. B5d. $75.00

PHILLIPS, **Thomas Hal.** *Bitterweed Path.* 1954. Avon T 83. c/G Fullington. Fi. G+. B5d. $2.00

PHILLIPS, **Tom.** *Beyond All Desire.* 1961. Monarch 212. PBO. VG+. B3d. $4.00

PICANO, **Felice.** *To the Seventh Power.* 1990. Avon 70276. 1st pb. Ho. NF. B6d. $3.00

PICKARD, **Nancy.** *Generous Death.* 1987. Pocket 64614. 2nd prtg. My. VG+. W2d. $3.50

PICKARD, **Sam.** *Notebooks.* Award A 7675. Mission #1. My. VG+. W2d. $3.50

PIERCE, **Hertha.** *Bed Crazy.* 1964. Playtime 687. 1st edn. c/gga. F. F2d. $10.00

PIERCE, **Wade.** *Uncertain Destiny.* 1962. Vega V-W 101. PBO. VG. P6d. $7.00

PILPEL, **Robert H.** *High Anxiety.* Ace 33440. MTI. G5d. $3.50

PINCKNEY, **J.** *Great Mischief.* Popular SP 329. c/Zuckerberg. VG+. B3d. $4.50

PINE, **Jack.** *Untamed Passions.* 1970. Pendulum 0-432. VG+. P6d. $7.50

PINEAU & SAITO. *Japanese Destroyer Captain.* 1961. Ballantine S 457K. NF. VG. B5d. $3.50

PINES, **Ned L.** *Cartoon Fun.* 1948. Popular 186. VG. B3a #20. $11.00

PINES, **Ned L.** *Cartoon Fun.* 1948. Popular 186. VG. B3d. $15.00

PINI, **Wendy & Rick.** *Elfquest Playboy.* Trade PB 21171. 1st prtg. F. S1d. $5.00

PINKUS, **Oscar.** *Friends & Lovers.* 1964. Midwood X 347. 1st pb. VG+. B6d. $12.50

PINTO, **Oreste.** *Friend or Foe?* Popular 629. VG. B3d. $5.00

PINTO, **Oreste.** *Spy Catcher #2.* Four Square 216. TVTI. VG. B3d. $7.00

PINTO, **Oreste.** *Spy Catcher.* Berkley G 67. Nfi. VG+. B5d. $4.50

PIPER, **Evelyn.** *Bunny Lake Is Missing.* 1965. Dell 0859. 1st prtg. MTI. My. NF. F2d. $8.00

PIPER, **Evelyn.** *Nanny.* 1965. Crest 865. 1st edn. PBO. MTI. c/photo. Ho. F. F2d. $20.00

PIPER, **H. Beam.** *Cosmic Computer.* Ace F 274. NF. M1d. $15.00

PIPER, **H. Beam.** *Empire.* 1981. Ace 20557. 1st edn. SF. F. F2d. $7.00

PIPER, **H. Beam.** *First Cycle.* 1982. Ace 23919. SF. F. W2d. $4.00

PIPER, **H. Beam.** *Little Fuzzy.* Ace 48432. SF. VG. B5d. $4.50

PIPER, **H. Beam.** *Little Fuzzy.* Ace 48490. 2nd edn. F. P9d. $2.00

PIPER, **H. Beam.** *Little Fuzzy.* 1962. Avon F 118. c/V Kalln. SF. VG. B5d/M1d. $15.00

PIPER, **H. Beam.** *Lord Kalvan of Otherwhen.* Ace F 342. PBO. VG. B3d. $4.00

PIPER, **H. Beam.** *Lord Kalvan of Otherwhen.* 1965. Ace F 342. SF. VG+. W2d. $6.50

PIPER, **H. Beam.** *Other Human Race.* 1964. Avon. 1st edn. F. M1d. $20.00

PIPER, **H. Beam.** *Space Viking.* Ace F 225. F. M1d. $15.00

PIPER, **H. Beam.** *Space Viking.* 1963. Ace F 225. PBO. SF. VG+. B5d. $7.00

PIRRO, **Ugo.** *Thousand Betrayals.* Perma M 4288. VG+. B3d. $5.00

PISERCHIA, Doris. *Billion Days of Earth.* Bantam 8805. 1st prtg. G+. S1d. $2.00

PISERCHIA, Doris. *Spaceling.* 1979. DAW 338. SF. VG+. B5d. $4.00

PISERCHIA, Doris. *Spinner.* 1980. DAW UJ 1548. SF. VG. W2d. $3.25

PISERCHIA, Doris. *Spinner.* DAW 392. 1st prtg. PBO. VG. S1d. $2.50

PITKIN, Walter B. *Life Begins at 40.* 1941. Pocket 120. c/photo. Nfi. VG. B5d. $6.50

PIZER, Laurette. *Eve's Daughters.* Graphic G 217. VG+. B3d. $5.00

PLAGEMANN, Bentz. *Downfall.* 1952. Pyramid 55. 1st prtg. c/gga. VG. P7d. $9.00

PLAGEMANN, Bentz. *Each Night a Black Desire.* Newsstand 4. VG. B3d. $6.00

PLAGEMANN, Bentz. *Sin Underneath.* 1960. Pyramid G 564. 3rd edn. Fi. VG. B5d. $3.50

PLAIDY, Jean. *Beyond the Blue Mountains.* Harlequin 113. 2nd prtg. VC. B3d. $7.00

PLAIDY, Jean. *Beyond the Blue Mountains.* 1953. Perma P 225. 1st prtg. c/gga. VG. P7d. $5.00

PLAIDY, Jean. *King's Mistress.* 1960. Pyramid R 476. 2nd edn. c/P Rader. Fi. VG. B5d. $5.50

PLAIDY, Jean. *Madame Serpent.* Avon T 54. NF. B3d. $7.50

PLATO, Dominic. *Terry.* 1963. France 63. 1st edn. c/photo. My. F. F2d. $10.00

PLATT, Charles. *Garbage World.* 1967. Berkley S 1470. PBO. SF. VG+. B5d. $7.50

PLATT, Charles. *Garbage World.* Berkley T 51164. 3rd. F. P9d. $2.00

PLATT, F.C. edt. *Great Stars of Hollywood's Golden Age.* 1966. Signet P 2979. 1st prtg. VG. R5d. $3.00

PLATT, Kin. *Dracula, Go Home!* 1981. Dell 92022. SF. VG. W2d. $4.00

PLENN, J.H. *Texas Hellion.* 1955. Signet 1174. 1st edn. Hi. F. F2d. $7.00

PLIEVIER, T. *Berlin.* Ace G 371. VG+. B3d. $5.00

PLIEVIER, T. *Moscow.* Ace D 194. VG+. B3d. $5.00

PLIMPTON, George. *Out of My League.* 1967. Pocket 75256. c/photos. Bio. NF. B4d. $3.00

POE, Edgar Allan *Great Tales & Poems of Edgar Allan Poe.* Pocket 39. VG. B3d. $6.00

POE, Edgar Allan. *Eight Tales of Terror.* 1969. Scholastic 290. 11th prtg. SF. VG. W2d. $3.25

POE, Edgar Allan. *Great Tales & Poems of Edgar Allan Poe.* 1951. Pocket 80626. 51st prtg. SF. VG. W2d. $3.50

POE, Edgar Allan. *Great Tales & Poems of Edgar Allan Poe.* 1960. Washington Square SW 246. SF. G+. W2d. $4.00

POE, Edgar Allan. *Murders in the Rue Morgue.* 1950. Arrow Publishing 118. PBO. Canadian rarity. VG+. B6a #77. $137.50

POE, Edgar Allan. *Poe's Tale of Terror.* Lancer 71-325. PBO. MTI. VG. B3d. $4.00

POE, Edgar Allan. *Selected Stories & Poems.* 1962. Airmont CL 8. 1st prtg. My. G+. R5d. $1.50

POE, Edgar Allan. *Selected Stories of Edgar Allan Poe.* Armed Services J 297. 1st prtg. VG. B3d. $6.00

POE, Edgar Allan. *10 Great Mysteries by Edgar Allan Poe.* 1975. Scholastic 210. 14th prtg. SF. VG+. W2d. $4.00

POE, Edgar Allen. *Pit & the Pendulum.* 1948. Nicholson & Watson. VG+. B3a #21. $32.30

POE & SUDAK. *Raven.* 1963. Lancer 70-034. PBO. MTI. c/Matheson. VG. B6d. $12.50

POHL, Frederik. *Abominable Earthman.* 1963. Ballantine 685. PBO. VG. B3d. $4.00

POHL, Frederik. *Abominable Earthman.* 1963. Ballantine 685. 1st edn. NF. M1d. $9.00

POHL, Frederik. *Age of the Pussyfoot.* 1969. Ballantine 01732. 1st prtg. SF. VG+. W2d. $4.25

POHL, Frederik. *Alternating Currents.* 1956. Ballantine 130. SF. VG. B4d/I1d. $5.00

POHL, Frederik. *Alternating Currents.* 1956. Ballantine 130. 1st edn. F. M1d. $12.00

POHL, Frederik. *Beyond the End of Time.* 1952. Perma. 1st edn. F. M1d. $15.00

POHL, Frederik. *Case Against Tomorrow.* Ballantine 206. F. M1d. $12.00

POHL, Frederik. *Case Against Tomorrow.* Ballantine 206. PBO. c/R Powers. SF. G+. B5d. $4.00

POHL, Frederik. *Digits & Dastards.* Ballantine U 2178. PBO. VG+. B3d. $4.50

POHL, Frederik. *Digits & Dastards.* 1966. Ballantine U 2178. 1st edn. NF. M1d. $9.00

POHL, Frederik. *Drunkard's Walk.* 1960. Ballantine 439K. PBO. SF. VG. B3d/B5d. $4.50

POHL, Frederik. *Edge of the City.* Ballantine 199. 1st prtg. VG. S1d. $6.00

POHL, Frederik. *If Reader of SF.* Ace H 19. NF. M1d. $5.00

POHL, Frederik. *If Reader of SF.* Ace H 19. SF. VG. W2d. $4.00

POHL, Frederik. *Man Who Ate the World.* 1970. Ballantine 01946. 3rd prtg. SF. VG. W2d. $3.50

POHL, Frederik. *Man Who Ate the World.* 1960. Ballantine 397. PBO. VG+. B3d/I1d. $5.00

POHL, Frederik. *Man Who Ate the World.* 1962. Ballantine 597. 1st prtg. SF. G+. R5d. $2.75

POHL, Frederik. *Narabedla, Ltd.* 1989. Ballantine 36026. SF. F. W2d. $4.25

POHL, Frederik. *Ninth Galaxy Reader.* 1967. Pocket 50532. VG+. I1d/S1d. $4.00

POHL, Frederik. *Plague of Pythons.* 1965. Ballantine U 2174. PBO. SF. VG. B6d/S1d. $5.00

POHL, Frederik. *Plague of Pythons.* 1965. Ballantine U 2174. 1st edn. F. M1d. $10.00

POHL, Frederik. *Search for the Sky.* 1954. Ballantine 61. SF. VG+. B4d. $5.00

POHL, Frederik. *Search the Sky.* 1969. Ballantine 01660. 3rd prtg. SF. VG. W2d. $3.50

POHL, Frederik. *Search the Sky.* 1954. Ballantine 61. 1st edn. NF. M1d. $12.00

POHL, Frederik. *Second If Reader of SF.* Ace 36331. SF. VG. B5d. $3.00

POHL, Frederik. *Shadow of Tomorrow.* Perma P 236. VG+. B3d. $5.00

POHL, Frederik. *Shadow of Tomorrow.* 1953. Perma. 1st edn. F. M1d. $12.00

POHL, Frederik. *Slave Ship.* Ballantine U 2177. 3rd edn. G. P9d. $1.25

POHL, Frederik. *Slave Ship.* 1957. Ballantine 192. 1st edn. NF. M1d. $10.00

POHL, Frederik. *Space Merchants.* 1953. Ballantine 21. 1st edn. G+. M1d. $10.00

POHL, Frederik. *Space Merchants.* 1974. Ballantine 24290. 8th prtg. SF. VG. W2d. $3.50

POHL, Frederik. *Space Merchants.* 1981. Ballantine 29697. 12th prtg. SF. VG. W2d. $3.25

POHL, Frederik. *Space Merchants.* Ballantine 381. 3rd prtg. VG. B3d. $4.00

POHL, Frederik. *Space Merchants.* 1960. Ballantine 381K. 3rd edn. SF. VG. B5d. $4.00

POHL, Frederik. *Star SF Stories #1.* 1953. Ballantine 16. PBO. VG. B3d. $7.00

POHL, Frederik. *Star SF Stories #1.* 1961. Ballantine 521K. 3rd edn. c/R Powers. SF. VG. B5d. $3.00

POHL, Frederik. *Star SF Stories #2.* Ballantine 55. PBO. VG. B3d. $6.00

POHL, Frederik. *Star SF Stories #2.* Ballantine 55. VG+. I1d. $10.00

POHL, Frederik. *Star SF Stories #2.* 1953. Ballantine 55. 1st edn. F. M1d. $15.00

POHL, Frederik. *Star SF Stories #2.* Ballantine 612. 1st prtg. F. S1d. $5.00

POHL, Frederik. *Star SF Stories #3.* 1962. Ballantine F 675. 2nd edn. c/R Powers. SF VG+. B5d. $4.00

POHL, Frederik. *Star SF Stories #3.* Ballantine 96. VG+. I1d. $9.00

POHL, Frederik. *Star SF Stories #3.* 1954. Ballantine 96. 1st edn. F. M1d. $15.00

POHL, Frederik. *Star SF Stories #4.* Ballantine 272K. VG+. I1d. $6.00

POHL, Frederik. *Star SF Stories #4.* Ballantine 272K. 1st prtg. G+. S1d. $4.00

POHL, Frederik. *Star SF Stories #4.* 1958. Ballantine 272K. 1st edn. F. M1d. $12.00

POHL, Frederik. *Star SF Stories #5.* Ballantine 308. PBO. VG+. B3d. $6.00

POHL, Frederik. *Star SF Stories #5.* 1959. Ballantine 308K. PBO. SF. VG. B5d. $6.50

POHL, Frederik. *Star SF Stories #5.* 1959. Ballantine 308K. 1st edn. F. M1d. $12.00

POHL, Frederik. *Star SF Stories #6.* 1959. Ballantine 353K. 1st edn. F. M1d. $12.00

POHL, Frederik. *Star SF Stories Volume 1, #1.* 1958. Perma Star 1. c/Bloch: sgn. VG. B3d. $6.50

POHL, Frederik. *Star Short Novels.* Ballantine 89. PBO. VG+. B3d. $4.50

POHL, Frederik. *Star Short Novels.* 1954. Ballantine 89. 1st edn. NF. M1d. $12.00

POHL, Frederik. *Starburst.* 1983. Ballantine 27537. c/D Mattingly. SF. NF. B5d. $4.50

POHL, Frederik. *Tomorrow Times Seven.* 1959. Ballantine 01746. 2nd prtg. SF. VG. R5d. $1.50

POHL, Frederik. *Tomorrow Times Seven.* 1959. Ballantine 325K. PBO. c/R Powers. SF. VG. B5d. $5.00

POHL, Frederik. *Tomorrow Times Seven.* 1959. Ballantine 325K. VG+. I1d. $7.00

POHL, Frederik. *Tomorrow Times Seven.* 1959. Ballantine 325K. 1st edn. F. M1d. $15.00

POHL, Frederik. *Turn Left at Thursday.* 1961. Ballantine F 476K. NF. I1d. $12.00

POHL, Frederik. *Turn Left at Thursday.* 1961. Ballantine F 476K. PBO. SF. G+. B5d. $5.00

POHL, Frederik. *Turn Left at Thursday.* 1969. Ballantine 01747. 2nd prtg. SF. VG+. W2d. $4.00

POHL, Frederik. *Wall Around a Star.* 1983. Ballantine 28995. SF. VG. W2d. $3.50

POHL, Frederik. *Way the Future Was.* 1979. Ballantine 26059. Nfi. VG. P1d. $4.50

POHL, Frederik. *Wolfbane.* 1959. Ballantine. 1st edn. VG. M1d. $8.00

POHL, Fredrik. *Slave Ship.* Ballantine U 2177. 2nd reissue. VG+. B3d. $4.50

POHL, Fredrik. *Slave Ship.* Ballantine 192. G+. I1d. $5.00

POHL & POHL. *Jupiter.* 1973. Ballantine 23662. 1st prtg. SF. VG. R5d. $1.50

POHL & WILLIAMSON. *Reefs of Space.* Ballantine U 2172. VG. B3d. $4.50

POHL & WILLIAMSON. *Rogue Star.* 1969. Ballantine 01797. c/Lehr. SF. VG. B4d. $2.00

POHL & WILLIAMSON. *Rogue Star.* 1973. Ballantine 23450. 2nd edn. c/J Wyrs. SF. VG+. B5d. $3.50

POHL & WILLIAMSON. *Starchild.* 1965. Ballantine U 2176. SF. VG+. M3d. $5.00

POHL & WILLIAMSON. *Starchild.* 1973. Ballantine 23449. 2nd prtg. SF. VG. W2d. $3.25

POHL & WILLIAMSON. *Undersea Quest.* 1971. Ballantine 02207. 1st prtg. SF. VG. R5d. $2.00

POIROT-DELPECH, Bertrand. *Fool's Paradise.* 1961. Popular G550. VG. B3d. $4.50

POITRINE, Belle. *Little Me.* 1962. Crest T 570. 1st prtg. VG+. P7d. $7.50

POLLINI, Francis. *Crown.* 1968. Bantam N 3735. 1st prtg. c/Jim Bama: gga. VG+. P7d. $4.00

POLLOCK, Louis. *Stork Bites Man.* 1963. MacFadden 50-174. 1st pb. NF. B6d. $5.00

POLSKY, Thomas. *Curtains for the Copper.* 1944. Dell 29. c/Gerald Gregg. VG. P6d. $5.50

POLSKY, Thomas. *Curtains for the Copper.* 1944. Dell 29. 1st prtg. My. G. R5d. $3.50

POLSKY, Thomas. *Curtains for the Editor.* 1945. Dell 82. VG. B3d. $6.00

PONICSAN, Darryl. *Cinderella Liberty.* 1974. Bantam Q 8399. 1st prtg. VG. R5d. $1.75

POPENOE, P. *Sex, Love & Marriage.* Belmont 92-563. VG+. B3d. $4.50

POPKES, Steven. *Caliban Landing.* 1989. World Wide 30304. SF. F. W2d. $4.25

POPKIN, Zelda. *Dead Man's Gift.* Dell 190. VG. I1d. $6.00

POPKIN, Zelda. *Death Wears a White Gardenia.* Dell 13. G. G5d. $3.50

POPKIN, Zelda. *Journey Home.* 1946. Pocket 364. 1st prtg. VG. P7d. $5.00

POPKIN, Zelda. *Murder in the Mist.* Dell 71. G. G5d. $3.00

POPKIN, Zelda. *Murder in the Mist.* Dell 71. VG. B3d. $7.50

POPKIN, Zelda. *No Crime for a Lady.* Dell 94. VG. B3d. $7.00

POPKIN, Zelda. *Time Off for Murder.* Century 25. VG. B3d. $6.50

PORCELAIN, Sidney. *Office Tramp.* Midwood F 152. PBO. VG. M6d. $4.50

PORGES, Irwin. *Edgar Rice Burroughs.* 1976. Ballantine 25131. Nfi. VG. P1d. $20.00

PORGES, Irwin. *Violent Americans.* 1963. Monarch MA 384. Nfi. VG. B5d. $5.00

PORTER, J. *Dover One.* Crest 948. VG+. B3d. $4.50

POSTGATE, Raymond *Verdict of Twelve.* Pocket 331. NF. B3d. $7.00

POTTER, C.F. *Lost Years of Jesus Revealed.* Gold Medal 768. 2nd prtg. VG+. B3d. $5.00

POTTS, Jean. *Death of a Stray Cat.* 1961. Berkley G 492. 1st pb. My. VG. B6d. $8.00

POTTS, Jean. *Evil Wish.* 1964. Ace G 541. 1st prtg. My. VG. R5d. $1.75

POURNELLE, Jerry. *Birth of Fire.* 1976. Laser 23. NF. I1d. $6.00

POURNELLE, Jerry. *Birth of Fire.* 1976. Laser 23. 1st edn. SF. F. F2d. $10.00

POURNELLE, Jerry. *Black Holes & Other Marvels.* Crest 3962. 1st prtg. SF. VG. R5d. $1.25

POURNELLE, Jerry. *Clan & Crown.* 1984. Ace. 2nd pb edn. F. M1d. $3.00

POURNELLE, Jerry. *Escape From Planet of the Apes.* 1973. Award 1240. PBO. MTI. NF. B6d. $6.00

POURNELLE, Jerry. *Guns of Darkness.* 1987. TOR 54961. 1st prtg. There Will Be War: Volume VI. SF. VG. W2d. $3.50

POURNELLE, Jerry. *Janissaries.* 1980. Ace 38287. 2nd prtg. SF. VG+. W2d. $4.00

POURNELLE, Jerry. *Mercenary.* 1986. Baen 65594. SF. VG. W2d. $3.75

POURNELLE, Jerry. *Mercenary.* 1977. Pocket 80903. 1st edn. SF. F. F2d. $8.00

POURNELLE, Jerry. *Prince of Mercenaries.* 1989. Baen 698117. SF. F. W2d. $5.00

POURNELLE, Jerry. *Red Heroin.* 1969. Berkley. 1st edn. VG. M1d. $5.00

POURNELLE, Jerry. *Spaceship for the King.* DAW 42. NF. I1d. $5.00

POURNELLE, Jerry. *West of Honor.* Laser 50. c/Freas. VG. B3d. $4.00

POURNELLE, Jerry. *West of Honor.* 1976. Laser 50. 1st edn. SF. F. F2d. $13.00

POURNELLE, Jerry. *West of Honor.* 1978. Pocket 82196. PBO. SF. NF. B6d. $6.00

POWELL, Michael. *Death In the South Atlantic.* 1958. Ace D 269. MTI. Nfi. VG. B5d. $5.00

POWELL, Richard. *All Over But the Shooting.* Popular 92. VG. B3d. $6.00

POWELL, Richard. *Lay That Pistol Down.* Bantam 70. VG. B3d. $4.00

POWELL, Richard. *Masterpiece in Murder.* Dell 915. c/A Sussman. My. VG. B5d. $4.00

POWELL, Richard. *Shot in the Dark.* Graphic 55. NF. I1d. $7.00

POWELL, Talmage. *Girl From Big Pine.* 1961. Monarch 188. Ad. VG+. B5d. $10.00

POWELL, Talmage. *Girl Who Killed Things.* 1960. Zenith 37. 1st edn. c/gga. My. F. F2d. $30.00

POWELL, Talmage. *Girl's Number Doesn't Answer.* 1960. Pocket 6031. 1st edn. My. F. F2d. $10.00

POWELL, Talmage. *Killer Is Mine.* 1959. Pocket 1250. PBO. My. NF. B6d. $15.00

POWELL, Talmage. *Start Screaming Murder.* 1962. Perma M 4251. 1st edn. De. F. F2d. $12.50

POWER, Thomas S. *Design for Survival.* 1965. Pocket 75113. Nfi. VG+. B5d. $3.00

POWERS, Anne. *Ironmaster.* 1952. Perma P 162. 1st pb. c/Victor Olson. VG+. B6d. $9.00

POWERS, Anne. *Ride East! Ride West!* Ace G 454. VG. B3d. $4.00

POWERS, Anne. *Rogue's Honor.* 1952. Perma P 173. VG+. B3d. $4.50

POWERS, R.T. *Incestuous Wives.* Barclay 7020. VG. B3d. $4.00

POWERS, R.T. *Women Who Seduce Virgins.* Barclay 7113. c/photo. VG+. B3d. $4.50

POWERS, S.R. *Willing Flesh.* 1962. Chariot 220. 1st edn. c/Mamie Van Doren. F. F2d. $27.00

POWERS, Timothy. *Dinner at Deviant's Palace.* 1985. Ace 14879. PBO. SF. F. M3d. $20.00

POWERS, Timothy. *Epitaph in Rust.* 1976. Laser 47. 1st edn. c/sgn. scarce. SF. F. F2d. $30.00

POWERS, Timothy. *Epitaph in Rust.* 1976. Laser 72047. SF. VG+. W2d. $5.50

POWERS, Timothy. *On Stranger Tides.* 1987. Ace. 1st edn. c/sgn. dust jacket. Ho. F. F2d. $35.00

POWERS, Timothy. *Skies Discrowned.* 1976. Laser 28. 1st edn. c/sgn. SF. NF. F2d. $30.00

POWERS, Tom. *Virgin With Butterflies.* 1950. Dell 392. 1st pb. c/Roy Price. VG. B6d. $6.00

POYER, Joe. *Operation Malacca.* Curtis 07032. 1st edn. PBO. G. P9d. $1.25

POYER, Joe. *Operation Malacca.* Curtis 07032. 1st prtg. SF. VG+. R5d. $3.50

PRAGNELL, Festus. *Terror From Timorkal.* 1946. Bear Pocket 4. PBO. scarce. VG+. B6a #76. $90.00

PRASKINS & SLATER. *Three Violent People.* 1956. Gold Medal 615. PBO. MTI. We. VG. B6d. $5.00

PRATHER, Richard S. *Always Leave 'Em Dying.* 1959. Gold Medal 849. 1st prtg. VG. P7d. $4.00

PRATHER, Richard S. *Bodies in Bedlam.* Gold Medal P 8. VG+. B3d. $6.00

PRATHER, Richard S. *Bodies in Bedlam.* 1951. Gold Medal 147. c/Barye: gga. My. VG+. B4d. $8.00

PRATHER, Richard S. *Case of the Vanishing Beauty.* Gold Medal 425. 2nd prtg. VG. B3d. $5.50

PRATHER, Richard S. *Case of the Vanishing Beauty.* 1958. Gold Medal 820. My. VG+. B4d. $5.00

PRATHER, Richard S. *Cockeyed Corpse.* Gold Medal 1462. VG. B3d. $4.00

PRATHER, Richard S. *Comfortable Coffin.* Gold Medal S 1046. VG. G5d. $4.50

PRATHER, Richard S. *Comfortable Coffin.* 1960. Gold Medal S 1046. c/gga. My. VG+. B4d. $5.00

PRATHER, Richard S. *Comfortable Coffin.* 1960. Gold Medal S 1046. 1st prtg. PBO. c/Barye: gga. VG. P7d. $7.50

PRATHER, Richard S. *Dagger of Flesh.* 1964. Gold Medal K 1425. My. VG+. B4d. $3.00

PRATHER, Richard S. *Dead Heat.* 1967. Pocket 50519. 4th prtg. My. VG. W2d. $3.25

PRATHER, Richard S. *Dig That Crazy Grave.* 1965. Gold Medal D 1598. 1st prtg. c/Barye: gga. VG. P7d. $4.50

PRATHER, Richard S. *Everybody Had a Gun.* 1951. Gold Medal 165. PBO. c/gga. VG. B6d. $9.00

PRATHER, Richard S. *Find This Woman.* 1966. Gold Medal D 1620. 1st prtg. VG. P7d. $4.00

PRATHER, Richard S. *Find This Woman.* 1958. Gold Medal 821. c/Barye. My. VG+. B4d. $5.00

PRATHER, Richard S. *Gat Heat.* 1968. Pocket 55021. 1st pb. My. NF. B6d. $6.00

PRATHER, Richard S. *Gat Heat.* 1968. Pocket 55021. 3rd prtg. My. VG+. W2d. $4.00

PRATHER, Richard S. *Have Gat-Will Travel.* 1959. Gold Medal 860. My. VG+. B4d. $5.00

PRATHER, Richard S. *Kill Him Twice.* 1965. Pocket 50123. 1st prtg. My. G+. W2d. $3.50

PRATHER, Richard S. *Kill Me Tomorrow.* Pocket 55030. VG+. G5d. $3.00

PRATHER, Richard S. *Kill Me Tomorrow.* 1971. Pocket 75663. 5th prtg. My. G+. W2d. $2.75

PRATHER, Richard S. *Kill the Clown.* 1964. Gold Medal K 1439. 1st prtg. c/Hooks: gga. VG. P7d. $4.50

PRATHER, Richard S. *Kill the Clown.* Gold Medal 1208. PBO. VG+. B3d. $6.00

PRATHER, Richard S. *Kubla Khan Caper.* 1967. Pocket 50535. My. VG+. B4d. $4.00

PRATHER, Richard S. *Lie Down, Killer.* 1956. Crest 132. 1st prtg. My. G. R5d. $1.00

PRATHER, Richard S. *Lie Down, Killer.* 1964. Gold Medal K 1437. 1st prtg. c/Barye: gga. VG+. P7d. $5.00

PRATHER, Richard S. *Lie Down, Killer.* 1952. Lion 85. PBO. c/classic. rare in condition. NF. B6a #74. $99.00

PRATHER, Richard S. *Lie Down, Killer.* 1952. Lion 85. PBO. scarce. VG+. B6a #80. $57.25

PRATHER, Richard S. *Meandering Corpse.* 1969. Pocket 55024. 7th edn. My. VG+. B5d. $4.00

PRATHER, Richard S. Over Her Dear Body. 1959. Gold Medal S 887. c/Barye Phillips: gga. VG. B4d/B5d. $5.00

PRATHER, Richard S. Pattern for Panic. 1958. Berkley G 98. 1st prtg. c/Rader: gga. VG. P7d. $6.00

PRATHER, Richard S. Pattern for Panic. 1955. Berkley 316. 1st pb. VG. B6d. $5.00

PRATHER, Richard S. Pattern for Panic. 1956. Berkley 362. 2nd edn. c/R Maguire. My. VG. B5d. $5.00

PRATHER, Richard S. Peddler. 1966. Gold Medal D 1629. 1st prtg. c/Bennett: gga. VG. P7d. $5.00

PRATHER, Richard S. Peddler. Gold Medal 1277. VG. B3d. $4.00

PRATHER, Richard S. Scrambled Yeggs. 1963. Gold Medal K 1316. 4th edn. My. VG+. B5d. $4.50

PRATHER, Richard S. Scrambled Yeggs. 1958. Gold Medal 770. 1st prtg. c/gga. NF. I1d. $6.00

PRATHER, Richard S. Shell Scott's 7 Slaughters. 1961. Gold Medal S 1072. VG. P6d. $2.00

PRATHER, Richard S. Slab Happy. 1958. Gold Medal S 817. 1st prtg. PBO. c/gga. VG+. P7d. $9.00

PRATHER, Richard S. Take a Murder, Darling. 1967. Gold Medal D 1798. c/gga. My. NF. B4d. $3.00

PRATHER, Richard S. Take a Murder, Darling. Gold Medal 745. PBO. VG. M6d. $3.50

PRATHER, Richard S. Take a Murder, Darling. 1958. Gold Medal 745. My. VG+. B4d. $7.00

PRATHER, Richard S. Take a Murder, Darling. 1958. Gold Medal 745. NF. I1d. $10.00

PRATHER, Richard S. Three's a Shroud. Gold Medal 665. NF. B3d. $4.50

PRATHER, Richard S. Too Many Crooks. Gold Medal R 2173. My. NF. B5d. $5.00

PRATHER, Richard S. Too Many Crooks. 1969. Gold Medal R 2173. 1st prtg. c/Barye: gga. VG. P7d. $4.00

PRATHER, Richard S. Too Many Crooks. Gold Medal 551. 4th prtg. c/Barye. VG+. B3d. $4.50

PRATHER, Richard S. Too Many Crooks. 1959. Gold Medal 850. 1st prtg. c/Barye: gga. VG. P7d. $5.00

PRATHER, Richard S. Trojan Hearse. 1972. Pocket 75705. 10th prtg. My. G+. W2d. $2.75

PRATHER, Richard S. Wailing Frail. 1964. Gold Medal K 1422. 1st prtg. c/Barye: gga. VG. P7d. $4.50

PRATHER, Richard S. Wailing Frail. 1956. Gold Medal 592. My. VG+. B4d. $8.00

PRATHER, Richard S. Wailing Frail. 1959. Gold Medal 851. 3rd edn. reprint. My. VG. B4d. $2.50

PRATHER, Richard S. Way of the Wanton. 1960. Gold Medal S 1032. c/gga. My. VG. B4d. $2.00

PRATOLINI, Vasco. Hero of Our Time. 1953. Signet 969. 1st pb. c/Erickson. VG+. B6d. $9.00

PRATOLINI, Vasco. Naked Streets. Ace H 185. VG. B3d. $7.00

PRATOLINI, Vasco. Tale of Poor Lovers. Ace H 219. VG. B3d. $6.00

PRATT, Fletcher. Alien Planet. Ace F 257. VG. I1d. $3.00

PRATT, Fletcher. Alien Planet. Ace F 257. 1st prtg. F. M1d. $12.00

PRATT, Fletcher. Blue Star. 1969. Ballantine 01602. SF. G+. W2d. $4.50

PRATT, Fletcher. Blue Star. 1969. Ballantine. 1st edn. Ad/Fa. F. M1d. $15.00

PRATT, Fletcher. Double Jeopardy. Curtis 07044. reprint. SF. VG+. B6d. $6.00

PRATT, Fletcher. Double Jeopardy. Curtis 07044. SF. VG. W2d. $4.00

PRATT, Fletcher. Invaders From Rigal. 1964. Airmont SF 4. 1st prtg. VG. S1d. $3.00

PRATT, Fletcher. Invaders From Rigel. 1964. Airmont SF 4. SF. VG+. W2d. $5.00

PRATT, Fletcher. Invaders From Rigel. 1964. Airmont SF 4. 1st pb edn. F. M1d. $10.00

PRATT, Fletcher. Short History of Army & Navy. 1944. Infantry S 224. Nfi. VG+. B4d. $4.00

PRATT, Fletcher. Undying Fire. 1953. Ballantine 25. PBO. SF. VG. B3d/I1d/M3d. $5.00

PRATT, Fletcher. Well of the Unicorn. Ballantine 25012. 1st prtg. NF. S1d. $2.50

PRATT, Fletcher. Well of the Unicorn. 1976. Ballantine. 1st edn. Ad/Fa. F. M1d. $13.00

PRATT, Fletcher. Well of the Unicorn. 1967. Lancer 74-911. c/S Savage. SF. VG. B5d. $4.00

PRATT, Fletcher. Well of the Unicorn. 1967. Lancer 74-911. 1st pb edn. F. M1d. $10.00

PRATT, Rex K. You Tell My Son. 1959. Signet S 1708. Nfi. VG+. B5d. $4.50

PRATT, Theodore. Cocotte. 1951. Gold Medal 153. PBO. VG+. B6d. $10.00

PRATT, Theodore. Golden Sorrow. 1952. Red Seal 16. 1st edn. VG. F2d. $7.50

PRATT, Theodore. Handsome. 1951. Gold Medal G 205. PBO. VG. B6d. $4.00

PRATT, Theodore. Handsome's Seven Women. Crest 289. PBO. c/Barye. VG+. B3d. $6.00

PRATT, Theodore. My Bride in the Storm (Big Blow). Avon 275. VG. B3d. $5.50

PRATT, Theodore. Seminole. 1960. Gold Medal S 1028. VG. P6d. $1.00

PRATT, Theodore. Smash-Up. Gold Medal 867. F. G5d. $8.00

PRATT, Theodore. Tormented. 1950. Gold Medal 119. VG. B3d. $4.50

PRATT, Theodore. Tormented. 1950. Gold Medal 119. 1st prtg. PBO. c/Barye: gga. VG+. P7d. $6.00

PRATT, Theodore. Tropical Disturbance. 1961. Gold Medal S 1143. c/Bob McGinnis: gga. G+. P6d. $1.50

PRATT, Theodore. Tropical Disturbance. 1961. Gold Medal S 1143. F. G5d. $8.00

PRATT, Theodore. Without Consent. 1962. Gold Medal S 1252. Fa. VG. B4d. $2.75

PRATT, Theodore. Without Consent. 1962. Gold Medal S 1252. 1st edn. My. F. F2d. $11.00

PREISS, Byron. Weird Heroes Volume #2. 1975. Pyramid A 04044. SF. G+. W2d. $3.00

PREISS, Byron. Weird Heroes Volume #2. 1975. Pyramid A 4044. SF. VG+. B4d. $5.00

PREISS, Byron. Weird Heroes Volume #4: Night Shade. 1976. Pyramid A 4035. VG. P9d. $1.50

PRENDERGAST, William. Calling All Z-Cars. 1968. Arrow 010. TVTI. VG. P1d. $7.50

PRESCOT, Dray. Beasts of Antares. 1980. DAW 397. PBO. SF. VG+. B5d. $4.00

PRESCOT, Dray. Manhounds & Arena of Antares. 1981. DAW. 1st edn. F. M1d. $5.00

PRESCOT, Dray. Sword for Kregen. 1979. DAW 352. 1st edn. F. P9d. $2.50

PRESCOT, Dray. Victory for Kregen. 1980. DAW 382. PBO. SF. VG+. B5d. $4.00

PRESCOT, Dray. Victory for Kregen. 1980. DAW 382. 1st prtg. VG. S1d. $2.50

PRESCOT, Dray. Witches of Kregen. 1985. DAW 624. 1st edn. F. P9d. $3.00

PRESCOT, John. *Wagon Train.* 1957. Bantam 1654. NF. B3d. $4.50

PRESCOTT, H.F.M. *Dead & Not Buried.* 1965. Collins 02381. 1st prtg. My. G. W2d. $3.00

PRESNELL, Frank G. *Too Hot To Handle.* 1952. Dell 593. c/R Stanley. My. VG. B5d. $3.00

PRESTON, Charles. *Cartoon Guide to the Kinsey Report.* 1954. Avon 559. PBO. cartoons. Nfi. G+. B5d. $3.50

PRESTON, Charles. *Cartoon Guide to the Kinsey Report.* 1954. Avon 559. VG+. B3d. $8.00

PRESTON, Charles. *Choice Cartoons From Sports Illustrated.* Perma M 3083. NF. B3d. $7.00

PRESTON, Charles. *Juvenile Delinquency.* Dell 1st Edn 97. VG. I1d. $3.50

PRESTON, Charles. *Pets: Including Women.* 1956. Perma M 3067. PBO. NF. B6d. $12.00

PRESTON, Lana. *Sensual Heiress.* 1967. Wizzard 409. Ad. G+. B5d. $2.00

PRESTON, Lillian. *Sex Habits of Single Women.* 1964. Beacon 748. VG. B3d. $6.00

PRICE, E. Hoffman. *Operation Exile.* 1986. Ballantine 32599. 1st prtg. SF. VG+. R5d. $2.00

PRICE, E. Hoffman. *Operation Longlife.* 1983. Ballantine 30715. SF. VG. W2d. $3.00

PRICE, George. *Who's in Charge Here?* Berkley 329. VG. B3d. $3.50

PRICE, Jeramie. *Blackbeard's Bride.* 1959. Cardinal C 393. 1st prtg. c/gga. VG. P7d. $3.50

PRICE, Reynolds. *Long & Happy Life.* 1964. Avon S 119. 1st prtg. c/gga. VG. P7d. $4.00

PRICE, Roger. *Three in Three.* 1976. Piccolo 24105. 2nd edn. TVTI. VG. P1d. $4.50

PRICE. *Pursuit of the Phoenix.* 1990. Zebra 8217. PBO. SF. NF. B6d. $3.00

PRIEN, G. *I Sank the Royal Oak.* Badger WW 28. VG. B3d. $7.50

PRIEST, Christopher. *Inverted World.* Popular 00309. SF. VG. B5d. $3.00

PRIESTLEY, J.B. *Black-Out in Gretley.* Armed Services C 75. G+. G5d. $4.50

PRIESTLEY, J.B. *Black-Out on Gretley.* Signet 548. c/Peng. VG. B3d. $5.50

PRIESTLEY, J.B. *Old Dark House.* Penguin 535. G+. G5d. $6.50

PRITCHARD, J.T. *Lady Cop.* 1955. Beacon 112. 1st edn. c/gga. scarce top condition. F. F2d. $30.00

PRITCHIE, Neil. *Savage Kick.* 1977. Gold Medal 1261. 1st edn. c/gga. My. F. F2d. $20.00

PRITCHIE, Neil. *Savage Kick.* Gold Medal 647. VG. B3d. $5.00

PROCTER, Madelyn. *Drama Teacher.* 1973. Liverpool SRS 1019. AD. VG. B5d. $4.00

PROCTER, Maurice. *Hurry the Darkness.* Dell 739. c/R Stanley. My. VG. B5d. $3.00

PROCTER, Maurice. *Murder Somewhere in This City.* 1956. Avon 696. 1st pb. My. VG+. B6d. $12.50

PROCTER, Maurice. *Pub Crawler.* 1958. Berkley G 165. c/R Maquire. My. G+. B5d. $2.50

PROCTER, Maurice. *Ripper Murders.* Avon 794. VG. B3d. $4.00

PROCTOR & VARDEMAN. *To Demons Bound.* 1985. Ace 81464. 1st edn. c/Vardeman: sgn/inscr. SF. F. F2d. $12.50

PROCTOR & VARDEMAN. *Yoke of Magic.* 1985. Ace 94840. 1st edn. c/Vardeman: sgn/inscr. SF. F. F2d. $12.50

PROHIAS. *Mad's Spy Vs Spy.* Signet 3480. VG+. B3d. $5.50

PROHIAS. *Third Spy Vs Spy.* PB Library 64-843. VG. B3d. $5.00

PROKOSCH, Frederic. *Dark Dancer.* 1965. Pocket 50108. c/gga. Fa. F. B4d. $3.00

PROKOSCH, Frederic. *Nine Days to Mukalla.* Avon T 90. Fi. G+. B5d. $2.00

PROKOSCH, Frederic. *Tale for Midnight.* Popular SP 38. VG+. B3d. $5.00

PROLE, Lozania. *Magnificent Courtesan.* Popular 334. c/Belarski. VG. B3d. $6.00

PRONZINI, Bill. *Midnight Specials.* 1978. Avon 37903. SF. VG. W2d. $4.25

PRONZINI, Bill. *Stalker.* 1974. Pocket 77635. 3rd prtg. My. F. W2d. $5.00

PROUTY, Olive Higgins. *Now, Voyager.* 1946. Dell 99. c/G Gregg. Fi. VG+. B3d. $6.00

PROUTY, Olive Higgins. *White Fawn.* 1947. Dell 167. 1st pb. c/Gregg. Ro. VG. B5d/B6d. $6.00

PRUETT, Herbert O. *Back of Town.* 1958. Beacon 161. PBO. c/gga. VG. B3d. $4.00

PRUETT, Herbert O. *Scandal High.* 1960. Beacon 351. PBO. c/Faragasso: gga. VG. B6d. $10.00

PRUITT, Alan. *Typed for a Corpse.* Handi-Book 135. c/Saunders. VG. I1d. $7.00

PUGH, John. *Captain of the Medici.* 1955. Perma M 4032. 1st pb. c/Maguire: gga. VG. B3d. $4.50

PUMA, Fernando. *Arts #2.* Perma P 262. VG. B3d. $4.00

PUNSHON, E.R. *Bathtub Murder Case.* Detective 11. VG. B3d. $4.00

PURDOM, Tom. *Barons of Behavior.* 1972. Ace 04760. SF. VG+. W2d. $4.00

PURDOM, Tom. *Reduction of Arms.* 1971. Berkley S 2088. 1st edn. NF. P9d. $2.00

PURDY, James. *Cabot Wright Begins.* 1965. Avon V 2136. 1st prtg. c/Storey. VG. P7d. $4.00

PURDY, James. *Color of Darkness.* 1970. Bantam N 5866. 1st prtg. VG. P7d. $3.50

PURDY, James. *Malcolm.* 1960. Avon T 465. 1st prtg. c/Richard Powers. VG+. P7d. $5.00

PURDY, James. *Malcolm.* 1965. Avon VS 6. 3rd edn. Fi. VG. B5d. $3.50

PURDY, James. *Nephew.* 1966. Avon SS 12. c/S Lambert. Fi. VG. B5d. $3.50

PURTELL, Joseph. *To a Blindfold Lady.* 1943. Handi-Book 20. 1st edn. PBO. rare. NF. B6a #75. $44.00

PURTILL, Richard. *Golden Gryphon Feather.* 1979. DAW. 1st edn. F. M1d. $5.00

PURTILL, Richard. *Mirror of Helen.* 1983. DAW 549. 1st edn. F. P9d. $2.00

PURTILL, Richard. *Stolen Goddess.* 1980. DAW. 1st edn. F. M1d. $5.00

PUTNAM, A.E. *Eight Years With Congo Pigmies.* Panther 618. c/Heade. VG. B3d. $8.00

PUTNAM, J. Wesley. *Playthings of Desire.* 1949. Novel Library 15. 1st pb edn. c/gga. F. F2d. $20.00

PUZO, Mario. *Dark Arena.* 1985. Bantam 24860. 1st prtg. My. F. W2d. $3.25

PUZO, Mario. *Dark Arena.* Dell D 164. VG. B3d. $5.00

PUZO, Mario. *Fortunate Pilgrim.* 1969. Lancer 75-077. Fi. VG+. B5d. $4.00

PUZO, Mario. *Godfather Papers.* 1973. Crest P 1797. 1st prtg. VG. P7d. $4.00

PUZO, Mario. *Inside Las Vegas.* Charter 47620. 1st prtg. VG+. P7d. $5.50

Q., John. *Bunnies.* 1965. Avon S 176. My. VG. B4d. $2.00

Q., John. *Survivor.* 1965. Avon S 177. My. VG+. B5d. $3.50

QUANDT, Albert L. *Baby Sitter.* 1952. Original Digest 720. PBO. scarce. JD. VG+. B6a #80. $75.00

QUANDT, Albert L. *Big-Time Girl.* 1951. Venus Digest 129. PBO. c/gga. scarce. VG+. B6a #77. $85.00

QUANDT, Albert L. *Desperate Lives.* 1954. Star Books 233. PBO. VG. B3d. $15.00

QUANDT, Albert L. *Gang Moll.* 1952. Original Digest 709. PBO. c/Nappi: gga. rare. VG+. B6a #77. $110.00

QUANDT, Albert L. *Social Club.* 1954. Carnival 930. c/Schulz. VG. B3a #24. $32.30

QUANDT, Albert L. *Social Club.* Carnival 947. c/Schulz. reprint. JD. VG. B6a #74. $55.00

QUANDT, Albert L. *Street Girl.* 1951. Quarter Book 91. PBO. c/George Gross: gga. VG+. B6a #77. $82.50

QUANDT, Albert L. *Zip-Gun Angels.* 1952. Original 721. VG. B3a #20. $82.55

QUANT, M. *Quant by Quant.* Ballantine U 6094. VG+. B3d. $7.00

QUARRY, Nick. *Hoods Come Calling.* 1958. Gold Medal 747. 1st prtg. PBO. c/Barye: gga. VG. P7d. $7.50

QUEEN, Ellery. *Adventures of Ellery Queen.* 1954. Pocket 99. 22nd edn. c/A Sussman. My. VG. B5d. $3.00

QUEEN, Ellery. *American Gun Mystery.* 1959. Avon T 292. c/gga. My. VG. B3d. $5.50

QUEEN, Ellery. *American Gun Mystery.* 1943. Dell 4. VG+. I1d. $20.00

QUEEN, Ellery. *And on the Eighth Day.* 1966. Pocket 50209. 1st prtg. My. VG. B3d/W2d. $4.50

QUEEN, Ellery. *Black Hearts Murder.* 1970. Lancer 74640. My. F. W2d. $4.00

QUEEN, Ellery. *Blow Hot, Blow Cold.* 1964. Pocket 45007. 1st prtg. My. VG. W2d. $4.50

QUEEN, Ellery. *Bordello.* 1963. Dove Book 102. PBO. c/gga. NF. B6a #76. $36.50

QUEEN, Ellery. *Calamity Town.* 1945. Pocket 293. My. VG. B4d. $5.00

QUEEN, Ellery. *Cat of Many Tails.* 1965. Bantam F 3026. 1st pb. My. VG. B6d. $4.50

QUEEN, Ellery. *Chinese Orange Mystery.* 1950. Pocket 17. 12th edn. My. G+. B5d. $2.50

QUEEN, Ellery. *Copper Frame.* Pocket 50490. G+. G5d. $2.75

QUEEN, Ellery. *Crime Carousel.* 1967. Signet P 3267. 1st pb. VG. B6d. $5.00

QUEEN, Ellery. *Dead Man's Tale.* 1961. Pocket 6117. My. VG+. B5d. $4.00

QUEEN, Ellery. *Death Spins the Platter.* 1962. Pocket 6126. My. G+. B5d. $4.00

QUEEN, Ellery. *Devil To Pay.* Pocket 2270. 7th prtg. VG. B3d. $4.00

QUEEN, Ellery. *Double Double.* Dell 2140. VG. B3d. $4.00

QUEEN, Ellery. *Dragon's Teeth.* 1947. Pocket 459. My. VG+. B4d. $9.00

QUEEN, Ellery. *Drury Lane's Last Case.* 1957. Avon T 184. My. VG. B4d. $2.75

QUEEN, Ellery. *Drury Lane's Last Case.* Avon T 381. c/A Sussman: gga. My. VG. B5d. $5.00

QUEEN, Ellery. *Drury Lane's Last Case.* Pocket 669. NF. G5d. $10.00

QUEEN, Ellery. *Drury Lane's Last Case.* Pocket 669. VG. B3d. $4.50

QUEEN, Ellery. *Ellery Queen's Awards.* Perma M 3076. VG. B3d. $4.00

QUEEN, Ellery. *Ellery Queen's Awards.* 1957. Perma M 3076. My. VG. B4d. $4.00

QUEEN, Ellery. *Four Johns.* 1964. Pocket 4706. My. NF. B5d. $5.00

QUEEN, Ellery. *Four of Hearts.* Avon T 242. My. VG. B5d. $3.00

QUEEN, Ellery. *Greek Coffin Mystery.* 1960. Cardinal C 390. 1st prtg. My. VG. R5d. $2.00

QUEEN, Ellery. *Green Turtle Mystery.* 1949. Comet 13. 1st pb. VG+. B6d. $9.00

QUEEN, Ellery. *Halfway House.* 1944. Pocket 259. 1st edn. PBO. rare horizontal cover. VG+. B6a #79. $250.00

QUEEN, Ellery. *Halfway House.* Pocket 6133. reprint. My. VG+. B6d. $5.00

QUEEN, Ellery. *Inspector Queen's Own Case.* 1957. Pocket 1167. 1st pb. My. VG. B6d. $3.50

QUEEN, Ellery. *Kill As Directed.* 1963. Pocket 4704. PBO. My. VG+. B6d. $5.00

QUEEN, Ellery. *King Is Dead.* 1954. Pocket 1005. My. VG. B4d. $3.00

QUEEN, Ellery. *Kiss & Kill.* Dell 4567. VG. G5d. $3.50

QUEEN, Ellery. *Lamp of God.* Dell 10¢ 23. VG+. B3d. $7.00

QUEEN, Ellery. *Last Score.* 1964. Pocket 50486. My. VG+. B5d. $4.00

QUEEN, Ellery. *Murder With a Past.* 1963. Pocket 4700. PBO. My. VG+. B6d. $5.00

QUEEN, Ellery. *Murderer Is a Fox.* 1948. Pocket 517. 1st pb. My. VG+. B6d. $12.50

QUEEN, Ellery. *New Adventures of.* 1945. Pocket. 11th pb edn. NF. M1d. $4.00

QUEEN, Ellery. *Perfect Crime.* 1968. Pyramid R 1814. My. VG+. B4d. $4.00

QUEEN, Ellery. *Queen's Awards Eighth Series.* 1955. Perma M-3015. c/W George. My. VG. B5d. $4.00

QUEEN, Ellery. *Queen's Bureau of Investigation.* Pan G 484. VG. B3d. $5.50

QUEEN, Ellery. *Queen's Bureau of Investigation.* Pocket 1118. VG. G5d. $6.50

QUEEN, Ellery. *Room To Die In.* 1965. Pocket 50492. My. VG+. B5d. $4.00

QUEEN, Ellery. *Scarlet Letters.* 1955. Pocket 1049. c/C Bobertz. My. VG. B5d. $4.50

QUEEN, Ellery. *Siamese Twin Mystery.* Pocket 109. VG. I1d. $5.00

QUEEN, Ellery. *Spanish Cape Mystery.* 1970. Signet T 4343. 1st prtg. My. VG. W2d. $3.50

QUEEN, Ellery. *Superfan.* 1972. Signet T 5136. PBO. c/Jack Davis. VG+. B6d. $9.00

QUEEN, Ellery. *Ten Days' Wonder.* Pocket 740. VG. G5d. $5.00

QUEEN, Ellery. *There Was an Old Woman.* 1946. Pocket 326. 3rd prtg. My. VG+. B3d. $4.50

QUEEN, Ellery. *To Be Read Before Midnight.* Popular SP 237. NF. B3d. $5.00

QUEEN, Ellery. *Tragedy of X.* Avon T 141. reprint. My. VG+. B6d. $10.00

QUEEN, Ellery. *Tragedy of Y.* Avon T 337. c/Gross. VG+. B3d. $4.50

QUEEN, Ellery. *Tragedy of Y.* Avon 450. VG. G5d. $6.50

QUEEN, Ellery. *Tragedy of Z.* Avon 465. My. NF. B6d. $18.00

QUEEN, Ellery. *Vanishing Corpse.* 1976. Pyramid NN. 1st prtg. TVTI. VG. R5d. $1.25

QUEEN, Ellery. *Where Is Bianca?* Popular 50-447. My. VG. B5d. $3.00

QUEEN, Ellery. *Wife or Death.* 1963. Pocket 4703. My. NF. B5d. $5.00

QUEEN, Ellery. *Wife or Death.* 1963. Pocket 4703. 1st prtg. My. G+. W2d. $3.75

QUEEN, Ellery. *Wife or Death.* Signet E 8087. PBO. NF. B6d. $12.50

QUENTIN, Patrick. *Black Widow.* 1954. Dell 759. 1st pb. c/Bill George. My. VG. B6d. $7.00

QUENTIN, Patrick. *Fatal Women.* Pan G 354. VG. B3d. $6.00

QUENTIN, Patrick. *Fate of the Immodest Blonde.* PB Library 676. VG. G5d. $5.00

QUENTIN, Patrick. *Follower.* Dell 710. 1st prtg. My. G+. R5d. $1.75

QUENTIN, Patrick. *Follower.* 1953. Dell 710. 1st prtg. c/Geygan: gga. VG. P7d. $5.50

QUENTIN, Patrick. *Girl on the Gallows.* Gold Medal 397. G+. G5d. $5.00

QUENTIN, Patrick. *Grindle Nightmare.* Popular 206. VG. G5d. $20.00

QUENTIN, Patrick. *Love Is a Deadly Weapon.* Pocket 614. NF. G5d. $9.50

QUENTIN, Patrick. *Puzzle for Fiends.* Ballantine F 778. 1st prtg. My. VG+. R5d. $4.00

QUENTIN, Patrick. *Puzzle for Fools.* Dell D 192. VG. B3d. $3.50

QUENTIN, Patrick. *Puzzle for Players.* 1942. Pocket 164. My. G+. B5d. $4.50

QUENTIN, Patrick. *Run to Death.* Dell 851. c/W George. My. VG. B5d. $3.00

QUENTIN, Patrick. *Slay the Loose Ladies.* Pocket 460. VG. G5d. $6.50

QUENTIN, Patrick. *Suspicious Circumstances.* 1960. Dell D 394. c/Bob Maguire. VG. P6d. $2.00

QUINLAN, Sterling. *Jugger.* 1961. Perma M 4237. Fa. VG+. B4d. $3.00

QUINN, Jake. *Mindbenders.* 1975. Leisure 00226. 1st prtg. Shannon #3. My. G. W2d. $2.75

QUINN, Jake. *Shallow Grave.* 1974. Leisure 00215. 1st prtg. Shannon #2. My. VG. W2d. $3.25

QUINN, Jake. *Undertaker.* 1974. Leisure 203. 1st edn. Shannon #1. My. F. F2d. $10.00

QUINN, John. *Crystal Kill.* 1984. Pinnacle 42065. 1st prtg. Terminator #4. My. VG. W2d. $3.00

R

RABE, Peter. *Anatomy of a Killer*. 1961. Berkley G 541. VG+. B3a #22. $27.00

RABE, Peter. *Box*. Gold Medal S 1262. VG. I1d. $6.00

RABE, Peter. *Bring Me Another Corpse*. 1959. Gold Medal 864. PBO. VG+. B3a #24. $17.70

RABE, Peter. *Code Name Gadget*. 1967. Gold Medal D 1830. 1st prtg. PBO. c/Bennett: gga. VG. P7d. $7.50

RABE, Peter. *Cut of the Whip*. 1958. Ace D 297. c/Barton. VG+. B6d. $45.00

RABE, Peter. *Cut of the Whip*. 1958. Ace D 297. PBO. c/Barton: gga. scarce. VG. B6a #75. $44.00

RABE, Peter. *Dig My Grave Deep*. Black Lizard. NF. G5d. $7.00

RABE, Peter. *Dig My Grave Deep*. 1956. Gold Medal 612. PBO. c/Kimmel. scarce. VG+. B6a #75. $72.00

RABE, Peter. *His Neighbor's Wife*. 1962. Beacon B 542F. PBO. VG. P6d. $10.00

RABE, Peter. *House in Naples*. 1963. Gold Medal K 1337. 2nd edn. c/L Kimmel. My. VG. B5d. $4.50

RABE, Peter. *It's My Funeral*. Gold Medal 678. VG. B3d. $8.00

RABE, Peter. *Journey Into Terror*. Gold Medal 1426. c/Hooks. VG. B3d. $6.00

RABE, Peter. *Journey Into Terror*. 1957. Gold Medal 710. PBO. c/Hooks. My. VG. B6d. $18.00

RABE, Peter. *Kill the Boss Good-By*. 1956. Gold Medal 594. PBO. c/Barye. scarce. VG+. B6a #75. $137.50

RABE, Peter. *Kill the Boss Good-By*. 1956. Gold Medal 594. PBO. My. VG. B6d. $18.00

RABE, Peter. *Mission for Vengeance*. Gold Medal 773. VG. B3d. $5.00

RABE, Peter. *Out Is Death*. Black Lizard. VG. G5d. $5.00

RABE, Peter. *Out Is Death*. 1957. Gold Medal 657. PBO. c/Hooks. My. VG. B6d. $12.50

RABE, Peter. *Shroud for Jesso*. 1955. Gold Medal 528. PBO. VG. B6d. $30.00

RABE, Peter. *Spy Who Was Three-Feet Tall*. 1966. Gold Medal D 1714. NF. I1d. $8.00

RABE, Peter. *Spy Who Was Three-Feet Tall*. 1966. Gold Medal D 1714. VG+. B3d. $7.00

RABE, Peter. *Stop This Man!* 1964. Gold Medal K 1403. c/gga. My. VG. B4d. $7.50

RABE, Peter. *Stop This Man!* 1955. Gold Medal 506. PBO. c/Kimmel. My. VG. B6d. $18.00

RABE, Peter. *Tobruk*. Bantam S 3335. 2nd edn. MTI. VG. M6d. $6.50

RABE, Peter. *War of the Dons*. 1972. Gold Medal M 2592. 1st prtg. PBO. VG. P6d. $2.50

RACE, Philip. *Killer Take All*. 1959. Gold Medal 888. 1st edn. c/gga. My. F. F2d. $15.00

RACE, Philip. *Self-Made Widow*. 1958. Gold Medal S 796. PBO. c/Darcy. My. VG. B6d. $8.00

RACINA, Thom. *Baretta: Sweet Revenge*. 1977. Berkley 03559. 1st edn. TVTI. c/photo. My. F. F2d. $12.00

RACINA, Thom. *Kojak in San Francisco*. 1976. Berkley Z 3237. 1st prtg. TVTI. My. VG+. R5d. $2.00

RACKHAM, John. *Beanstalk*. 1973. DAW 78. PBO. c/K Freas. SF. VG. B5d. $3.00

RACKHAM, John. *Danger From Vega*. Ace G 576. VG+. B3d. $5.00

RACKHAM/SABERHAGEN. *We, the Venusians/Water of Thought*. 1965. Ace M 127. PBO. F. M1d. $10.00

RACKHAM/SABERHAGEN. *We, the Venusians/Water of Thought*. 1965. Ace M 127. PBO. SF. VG+. M3d. $7.50

RACKHAM/STRIKE. *Flower of Doradil/Promising Planet*. Ace 24100. PBO. SF. VG. B5d. $3.00

RACKHAM/TUBB. *Alien Sea/COD Mars*. Ace H 40. 1st prtg. G+. S1d. $3.50

RACKHAM/TUBB. *Alien Sea/COD Mars*. 1968. Ace H 40. SF. VG. W2d. $6.00

RACKOWE, Alec. *My Lord America*. 1952. Perma P 164. 1st pb. c/Geygan. VG. B6d. $7.00

RADCLIFF, J. *They Call Me Lez*. Paraiso 101. VG. B3d. $4.00

RADDALL, T.H. *Give & Take*. Popular 615. VG. B3d. $4.50

RADFORD, R.L. *Crime & Judy*. 1964. Airmont M6. My. VG. B5d. $2.50

RADFORD, R.L. *Prelude to Love*. 1962. Monarch. 1st edn. My. F. F2d. $11.00

RADIGUET, Raymond. *Devil in the Flesh*. Signet 1175. VG. M6d. $5.00

RADIN, E.D. *Beyond the Law*. 1953. Popular 513. PBO. VG+. P6d. $4.50

RADIN, E.D. *Crimes of Passion*. 1954. Popular 605. 1st pb. Cr. VG. B6d. $6.00

RADIN, E.D. *Headline Crimes of the Year*. Popular 470. VG. B3d. $6.00

RADIN, E.D. *Innocents*. Tower 43-514. VG+. B3d. $4.50

RADIN, E.D. *Lizzie Borden: The Untold Story*. Dell 4886. VG. B3d. $4.00

RADIN, E.D. *12 Against Crime*. Bantam 921. VG+. B3d. $5.00

RADIN, E.D. *12 Against the Law*. Bantam 997. VG+. B3d. $5.00

RADWAY, Ann. *Discotheque Doll*. 1966. Brandon House 983. VG+. B3a #24. $6.05

RAE, J. *Custard Boys*. Ace H 525. MTI. VG. B3d. $5.00

RAGSDALE, Clyde B. *Big Fist*. Dell 698. c/C Bobertz. Fi. VG. B5d. $3.00

RAINE, N.R. *Tugboat Annie*. 1947. Dell 192. VG+. B3d. $5.00

RAINE, W.M. *Bandit Trail*. Dell 793. c/R Stanley. We. VG. B5d. $3.00

RAINE, W.M. *Big-Town Roundup*. 1949. Hillman 29. VG+. B3a. $8.30

RAINE, W.M. *Border Breed*. Pocket 721. VG. B3d. $4.00

RAINE, W.M. *Bucky Follows a Cold Trail*. Popular 86. VG+. B3d. $7.00

RAINE, W.M. *Clattering Hoofs*. Signet 758. VG+. B3d. $5.00

RAINE, W.M. *Colorado*. Avon 500. VG. B3d. $4.00

RAINE, W.M. *Fighting Edge*. Pocket 691. c/sgn. scarce sgn. VG. B3d. $6.00

RAINE, W.M. *Fighting Edge*. Pocket 691. VG. B3d. $4.00

RAINE, W.M. *Fighting Tenderfoot*. Signet 712. VG+. B3d. $7.00

RAINE, W.M. *Guns of the Frontier*. Signet 1140. VG. B3d. $4.00

RAINE, W.M. *Gunsight Pass*. Dell 629. c/R Stanley. We. VG. B5d. $2.50

RAINE, W.M. *Gunsmoke Trail*. 1948. Popular 145. 1st pb. We. VG+. B6d. $12.50

RAINE, W.M. *Hell & High Water*. Popular 322. NF. I1d. $9.00

RAINE, W.M. *High Grass Valley*. Popular SP 262. VG+. B3d. $4.50

RAINE, W.M. *On the Dodge*. Pocket 743. VG+. B3d. $5.00

RAINE, W.M. *On the Dodge*. 1945. Western Novel Classic 47. 1st pb. VG+. B6d. $8.00

RAINE, W.M. *Pistol Pardners*. Popular 172. VG. B3d. $5.50

RAINE, W.M. *Powdersmoke Feud (Nettle Danger)*. Signet 1483. 2nd prtg. VG. B3d. $4.50

RAINE, W.M. *Powdersmoke Feud*. Signet 806. VG. B3d. $5.00

RAINE, W.M. *Range Beyond the Law (Broad Arrow)*. Popular 471. VG. B3d. $5.00

RAINE, W.M. *Range Beyond the Law*. 1952. Popular 471. sgn. We. VG+. B4d. $18.00

RAINE, W.M. *River Bend Feud*. Popular 280. VG. I1d. $5.00

RAINE, W.M. *Rustlers' Gap*. Popular 213. VG. B3d. $6.00

RAINE, W.M. *Sheriff's Son*. Pocket 815. VG. B3d. $5.00

RAINE, W.M. *Sheriff's Son*. Western Novel Classic 22. VG+. B3d. $6.00

RAINE, W.M. *Six-Gun Kid*. Signet 973. VG. B3d. $4.50

RAINE, W.M. *Song of the Paddle*. Signet 673. VG. B3d. $5.00

RAINE, W.M. *Square-Shooter*. Pocket 611. VG+. B3d. $5.00

RAINE, W.M. *Steve Yeager*. Hillman 11. VG. B3d. $7.00

RAINE, W.M. *Texas Kid (Damyank)*. Popular 414. VG. B3d. $4.00

RAINE, W.M. *Trail of Danger*. Hillman 24. VG. B3d. $4.50

RAINE, W.M. *Trail's End*. Armed Services G 184. 1st prtg. VG+. P7d. $6.00

RAINE, W.M. *Trail's End*. Dell 179. c/G Gregg. We. VG. B5d. $7.50

RAINE, W.M. *Trail's End*. Dell 359. c/Sherwan. reprint. We. VG. B6d. $7.00

RAINE, W.M. *Trail's End*. Dell 889. VG. B3d. $3.50

RAINE, W.M. *West of the Law*. Popular 531. VG. B3d. $4.50

RAINEY, Rich. *Cult 45*. 1984. Pinnacle 42156. 1st prtg. Protector #4. My. G. W2d. $2.00

RAINEY, Rich. *Dragon Slayings*. 1985. Pinnacle 42160. 1st prtg. Protector #6. My. VG+. W2d. $3.00

RAINEY, Rich. *Hit Parade*. 1983. Pinnacle 42069. 1st edn. My. F. F2d. $7.00

RAINEY, Rich. *Hit Parade*. 1983. Pinnacle 42069. 1st prtg. Protector #3. My. VG. W2d. $3.00

RALD, P. *Bigamists*. Intimate 719. VG+. B3d. $5.00

RALSTON, Gilbert A. *Ben*. 1972. Bantam S 7517. 1st prtg. MTI. c/photo. SF. VG. R5d. $2.00

RAMER, J. *Duke: Story of John Wayne*. Award 1185. PBO. VG+. B3d. $8.00

RAMPA, L. *Doctor From Lhasa*. 1966. Corgi 7146. 4th prtg. VG. B3d. $6.00

RAMSAY, Mark. *Falcon Strikes*. 1982. Signet 1770. 1st edn. Av. F. F2d. $10.00

RAND, Ayn. *Anthem*. Signet 1985. VG. B3d. $4.00

RAND, Ayn. *Atlas Shrugged*. Signet AE 3215. 43rd prtg. SF. VG+. W2d. $4.00

RAND, Max. *Valley Vultures*. Popular 822. VG. B3d. $3.50

RAND, Rick. *Way With Women*. Saber SA 76. NF. B3d. $6.50

RAND, Steve. *So Sweet, So Wicked*. 1961. Monarch 211. Ad. G+. B5d. $4.00

RANDALL, Clay. *Amos Flagg Rides Out*. 1966. Gold Medal K 1677. PBO. We. VG+. B3d. $6.00

RANDALL, Clay. *Boomer*. 1957. Perma M 3077. We. VG. B5d. $4.00

RANDALL, Clay. *Hardcase for Hire*. Gold Medal 1357. PBO. VG+. B3d. $5.00

RANDALL, Clay. *Life, Loves, & Meat Loaf*. Brandon House 704. VG+. B3d. $6.00

RANDALL, Martha. *Journey*. 1978. Pocket 81207. SF. VG. W2d. $3.25

RANDALL, Rona. *Kinight's Keep*. 1968. Ace H 69. 1st prtg. My. VG+. R5d. $2.25

RANDALL, Rona. *Witching Hour*. Ace 89900. SF. G+. W2d. $3.25

RANDAU & ZUGSMITH. *Visitor*. 1946. Dell 132. c/G Gregg. My. G+. B5d. $5.00

RANDAU & ZUGSMITH. *Visitor*. 1946. Dell 132. F. F2d. $10.00

RANDAU & ZUGSMITH. *Visitor*. 1946. Dell 132. VG+. B3d/G5d. $8.00

RANDOLPH, Greg. *Sex Goddess*. Playtime 623. NF. B3d. $7.00

RANDOLPH, Greg. *Web of Evil*. 1963. Playtime 637S. Fa. VG+. B4d. $12.00

RANGELY, O. *Battalion Broads*. Playtime 749. NF. B3d. $6.00

RANK, Mary O. *Dream of Falling*. 1960. Crest 375. My. VG+. B3d. $4.50

RANKINE, John. *Bromius Phenomenon*. Ace 8145. 1st prtg. VG+. S1d. $3.00

RANKINE, John. *Lunar Attack*. 1975. Orbit 7875. MTI. Space: 1999 #5. SF. VG. B5d. $5.00

RANKINE, John. *Moons of Triopus*. 1969. PB Library 63-228. SF. VG+. B5d. $4.00

RANKINE, John. *Operation Umanag*. Ace 63590. 1st prtg. VG. S1d. $3.00

RANSOME, Stephen. *Some Must Watch*. Perma M 4275. G+. G5d. $3.50

RANSOME, Stephen. *Some Must Watch*. Perma M 4275. 1st pb. VG. M6d. $6.50

RANSOME/WHITTINGTON. *I, the Executioner/So Dead My Love!* 1953. Ace D 7. c/DeSoto: gga. My. VG. B6d. $16.50

RASCOVICH, Mark. *Flight of the Dancing Bear*. Popular SP 166. 1st pb. MTI. VG. B6d. $3.75

RATCLIFF, J.D. *Conception, Pregnancy, & Birth*. Pocket 800. VG+. B3d. $5.50

RATTIGAN, Terence. *Prince & the Showgirl*. Signet 1409. MTI. VC. B3d. $5.50

RATTIGAN, Terence. *Separate Tables*. 1959. Signet S 1609. MTI. c/Hayworth, Kerr, Niven & Lancaster. VG+. B4d/B5d. $4.00

RAU, Santha Rama. *Home to India*. 1966. Perennial P 68. Nfi. VG+. B5d. $4.50

RAUCH, Earl Mac. *Buckaroo Banzai*. 1984. Pocket 54058. 1st prtg. VG+. R5d. $2.50

RAVEL, Robert. *Fever Heat*. Newsstand 50. VG. B3d. $5.00

RAVEN, Simon. *Doctors Wear Scarlet*. 1967. Berkley S 1435. c/photo. VG. P6d. $3.00

RAVEN, Simon. *Feathers of Death*. Ace H 411. c/gga. VG. B3d. $7.00

RAWLINGS, M.K. *South Moon Under*. Bantam 10. VG+. B3d. $6.00

RAWSON, Clayton. *Footprints on the Ceiling*. Dell 121. G. G5d. $5.00

RAWSON, Tabor. *I Want To Live*. 1958. Pyramid S 1587. MTI. c/Susan Hayward: photo. VG+. B4d. $4.00

RAY, Wesley. *Damoron's Gun.* Signet 1566. PBQ. VG. B3d. $4.00

RAYMOND, Alex. *Lion Men of Mongo.* Avon 15815. Flash Gordon #1. VG+. B3d. $5.00

RAYMOND, Alex. *Plague of Sound.* Avon 19166. Flash Gordon #2. VG. B3d. $4.00

RAYMOND, Alex. *Space Circus.* 1974. Avon 19695. 1st prtg. Flash Gordon #3. SF. VG. W2d. $3.50

RAYMOND, Alex. *Time Trap of Ming.* Avon 20446. Flash Gordon. VG+. I1d. $5.00

RAYMOND, Alex. *War of the Cybernauts.* 1975. Avon 22335. VG+. P6d. $5.00

RAYMOND, J.K. *Battle Clouds.* Badger WW 133. VG+. B3d. $7.50

RAYMOND, Litzka. *How To Read Palms.* 1950. Perma P 81. PBO. VG+. P6d. $3.75

RAYMOND, R. *AC-DC Sex.* Playtime 666. VG+. B3d. $5.50

RAYNER, D.A. *Enemy Below.* Pocket 1192. MTI. NF. B3d. $5.00

RAYTER, Joe. *Asking for Trouble.* 1956. Pocket 1132. 1st pb. c/Meese. My. NF. B6d. $15.00

RAYTER, Joe. *Stab in the Dark.* 1957. Pocket 1145. c/G Zeil. Fi. G+. B5d. $4.00

RAYTER, Joe. *Stab in the Dark.* 1957. Pocket 1145. 1st pb. c/Ziel. My. VG+. B6d. $12.50

RAYTER, Joe. *Victim Was Important.* 1955. Pocket 1070. 1st pb. c/Meese. My. NF. B6d. $16.50

REACH, James. *Late Last Night.* Graphic 130. 2nd prtg. VG+. I1d. $5.00

REACH, James. *Late Last Night.* Graphic 70. VG. B3d. $6.00

REACH, James. *Sunset Strip.* Popular 828. VG. B3d. $4.50

REACH, James. *Sunset Strip.* 1957. Popular 828. 1st edn. c/striking wraparound gga. My. F. F2d. $20.00

READE, Quinn. *Quest of the Dark Lady.* 1960. Belmont B 60-1067. 1st edn. F. P9d. $2.00

READY, William. *Understanding Tolkien & the Lord of Rings.* 1969. PB Library 64-036. Nfi. VG. P1d. $4.50

REAMY, Tom. *Blind Voice.* 1979. Berkley 04165. SF. G+. W2d. $2.75

REASONER, Harry. *Tell Me About Women.* Dell 417. c/H Barton. Fi. G+. B5d. $3.00

REBECCA, Margaret. *Ceylun.* 1950. Lion 32. 1st pb. c/Julian Paul: gga. VG. B6d. $12.50

REBEL, Adam. *Stable Boy.* 1954. Beacon 107. 1st edn. c/gga. F. F2d. $15.00

REDDING, J. Saunders. *Stranger & Alone.* 1951. Popular 327. VG+. B4d. $9.00

REED, Dana. *Sister Satan.* Leisure 08439. SF. VG. W2d. $3.25

REED, David V. *Murder in Space.* Galaxy SF 23. VG. B3d. $4.50

REED, David V. *Thing That Made Love.* Uni-book 15. VG. B3d. $8.00

REED, Eliot. *Maras Affair.* 1955. Perma M 3025. Fa. VG. B4d. $4.00

REED, Eliot. *Maras Affair.* 1955. Perma M 3025. 1st pb. c/Meese. My. NF. B6d. $15.00

REED, Harry. *Piece of Something Big.* 1972. Lancer 75-286. PBO. c/hypo. My. NF. B6d. $9.00

REED, Kit. *Armed Camps.* 1971. Berkley S2086. c/R Powers. SF. VG. B5d/W2d. $3.50

REED, Kit. *Mister DA V.* Berkley 02380. 1st prtg. VG. S1d. $3.00

REED, Kit. *Other Stories &...Attack of the Giant Baby.* 1981. Berkley 05032. 1st edn. c/sgn & inscr to Clifford Simak. SF. F. F2d. $25.00

REED, Langford. *Perma Rhyming Dictionary.* 1950. Perma P 86. 1st US edn. G. P6d. $1.00

REED, Mark. *Sinners Wild.* 1960. Avon 874. Fa. VG+. B4d. $10.00

REED, R. *Stars & Their Pets.* 1972. Tiger Beat XQ 2007. 1st prtg. TVTI. VG. R5d. $2.50

REED-MARR, P.J. *Hot Saturday.* 1960. Gold Medal 1034. 1st edn. c/gga. My. F. F2d. $17.00

REED-MARR, P.J. *Kurt Vonnegut, Jr.* 1972. PB Library 68-923. Nfi. VG+. P1d. $5.00

REEDER, Colonel. *MacKenzie Raid.* 1955. Ballantine 110. We. VG+. B4d. $3.50

REES, G. *Secret of the Suez Canal.* Sexton Blake 324. c/Heade. VG. B3d. $8.00

REESE, John. *Looters.* 1970. Pyramid T 2142. 1st prtg. MTI. VG. R5d. $1.75

REESE, John. *Sierra Showdown.* Gold Medal 2472. VG. B3d. $4.00

REID, Desmond. *High Heels & Homicide.* Sexton Blake 405. VG+. B3d. $8.00

REID, Desmond. *Roadhouse Girl.* Sexton Blake 386. NF. B3d. $8.50

REID, Desmond. *Something To Kill About.* Sexton Blake 471. VG+. B3d. $8.00

REID, Ed. *Mafia.* 1954. Signet 1151. My. VG+. B5d. $8.00

REID, P.R. *Escape From Colditz.* Berkley G 107. 2nd prtg. VG+. B3d. $4.00

REID, P.R. *Escape From Colditz.* Berkley G 38. VG. B3d. $4.00

REILLY, Helen. *Compartment K.* 1964. Ace G 546. My. VG+. B4d. $2.25

REILLY, Helen. *Day She Died.* Ace G 536. VG. B3d. $3.50

REILLY, Helen. *Dead Man Control.* 1964. MacFadden 50-203. 1st prtg. c/Schultz: gga. VG. P7d. $4.00

REILLY, Helen. *Death Demands an Audience.* 1943. Popular 7. 1st prtg. c/Hoffman. VG+. P7d. $25.00

REILLY, Helen. *Ding-Dong Bell.* 1971. MacFadden 95160. 1st prtg. My. VG+. W2d. $4.00

REILLY, Helen. *Doll's Trunk Murder.* 1949. Popular 211. 1st edn. PBO. c/Belarski: gga. VG. B6a #75. $110.00

REILLY, Helen. *Doll's Trunk Murder.* 1949. Popular 211. 1st edn. PBO. c/Belarski: gga. VG+. B6a #79. $82.50

REILLY, Helen. *Double Man.* Dell 732. c/D Gillon. My. VG. B5d. $3.00

REILLY, Helen. *Double Man.* Dell 732. 1st prtg. My. G+. R5d. $2.25

REILLY, Helen. *Double Man.* 1953. Dell 732. 1st prtg. c/Gillen. VG+. P7d. $6.50

REILLY, Helen. *Farmhouse.* Dell 397. VG. B3d. $4.00

REILLY, Helen. *Lament for the Bride.* Dell 621. G. I1d. $3.00

REILLY, Helen. *Mourned on Sunday.* 1944. Dell 63. c/Greg. G+. F2d. $10.00

REILLY, Helen. *Mr Smith's Hat.* Popular 48. VG. I1d. $10.00

REILLY, Helen. *Mr Smith's Hat.* 1945. Popular 48. 1st pb. c/Hoffman. My. G+. B6d. $6.00

REILLY, Helen. *Murder at Arroways.* Dell 576. VG. B3d. $4.00

REILLY, Helen. *Murder in the Mews.* 1950. Popular 259. 1st pb. My. VG. B6d. $12.00

REILLY, Helen. *Murder on Angler's Island.* Dell 228. VG+. B3d. $6.00

REILLY, Helen. *Name Your Poison.* Dell 148. c/G Gregg. My. G+. B5d. $5.00

REILLY, Helen. *Name Your Poison.* Dell 148. VG. B3d. $7.00

REILLY, Helen. *Opening Door.* Dell 200. VG. B3d. $4.00

REILLY, Helen. *Opening Door.* Dell 917. 1st prtg. My. VG. R5d. $2.75

REILLY, Helen. *Silver Leopard.* Dell 287. c/F Giles. My. G. B5d. $3.50

REILLY, Helen. *Silver Leopard.* 1949. Dell 287. 1st pb. c/Giles. My. VG. B6d. $12.50

REILLY, Helen. *Staircase 4.* 1951. Dell 498. c/B Phillips. My. G+. B5d. $2.50

REILLY, Helen. *Staircase.* 1951. Dell 498. c/Barye Phillips: gga. VG+. P6d. $3.75

REILLY, Helen. *Three Women in Black.* Dell 114. VG. G5d. $14.50

REILLY/REILLY. *Canvas Dagger/Not Me, Inspector.* 1963. Ace G 531. VG. B3d. $4.00

REILLY/REILLY. *Certain Sleep/Ding-Dong-Bell.* 1963. Ace G 528. My. VG+. B4d. $3.00

REILLY/REILLY. *Opening Door/Follow Me.* 1963. Ace G 518. My. VG+. B4d. $4.00

REINER, Carl. *Enter Laughing.* Crest S 279. VG+. I1d. $5.00

REINHARDT, Guenther. *Crime Without Punishment.* 1953. Signet 1067. My. VG+. B5d. $5.50

REISNER, Mary. *Hunted.* 1967. Belmont B 50-742. 1st prtg. My. VG. R5d. $2.50

REISNER, Mary. *Mirror of Delusion.* 1965. Belmont 93-051. 1st prtg. My. VG. R5d. $3.00

REISNER, R. *Great Wall Writing Etc.* Canyon 202. VG. B3d. $4.50

REMARQUE, E.M. *All Quiet on the Western Front.* Lion LL 81. 2nd prtg. VG+. B3d. $4.50

REMARQUE, E.M. *All Quiet on the Western Front.* Lion 49. VG. B3d. $4.00

REMARQUE, E.M. *Night in Lisbon.* 1965. Crest R 794. 1st prtg. NF. P7d. $5.00

REMARQUE, E.M. *Three Comrades.* Popular G 133. VG. B3d. $4.00

REMINGTON, A.R. *Sex & the Singles Bar.* Barclay 7385. NF. B3d. $4.50

REMY. *Bombs Away!* Digit NN. VG. B3d. $6.50

RENARD, Maurice. *Flight of the Aerofix.* Stellar 14. SF. F. W2d. $15.00

RENAULT, Mary. *King Must Die.* 1960. Cardinal GC 78. c/J Hill. Fi. VG+. B5d. $3.50

RENIN, Paul *Bright Young Things.* Verlock NN. G+. B3d. $8.00

RENIN, Paul *Scandal.* 1946. R&L Locker NN. VG+. B3a #21. $20.00

RENIN, Paul *Sin Called Love.* R&L Locker NN. VG. B3d. $7.50

RENIN, Paul. *Daring Diana.* 1948. R&L Locker NN. c/stocking top. VG. B3d. $9.00

RENIN, Paul. *Sex.* 1951. Archer 50. Fa. F. B4d. $25.00

REPP, E.E. *Gun Hawk.* Hillman 17. VG. B3d. $6.00

REPP, E.E. *Hell in the Saddle.* Hillman 13. VG. B3d. $4.00

RESCOVITCH, Mark. *Flight of the Dancing Bear.* 1962. Popular SP 166. 1st prtg. G+. R5d. $1.25

RESKO, John. *Reprieve.* Panther 1066. VG. B3d. $5.00

RESNICK, Michael. *Goddess of Ganymede.* 1968. PB Library 52-687 1st pb edn. F. M1d. $10.00

RESNICK, Michael. *Pursuit on Ganymede.* PB Library 52-760. VG+. B3d. $4.00

RESNICK, Michael. *Redbeard.* 1969. Lancer 74-579. PBO. c/K Freas. SF. VG. B5d. $4.00

RESNICK, Michael. *Redbeard.* 1969. Lancer 74-579. 1st edn. NF. M1d. $10.00

RESNICOW, Herbert. *Seventh Crossword.* 1985. Ballantine 32732. 1st prtg. PBO. VG+. P7d. $5.00

RESNIK, M. *Girl in Turquoise Bikini.* Corgi 7356. 1st English edn. VG. B3d. $6.00

REYBURN, W. *Port of Call.* Panther 953. VG. B3d. $6.00

REYMOND, Henry. *Deadlier Than the Male.* 1967. Signet 3128. 1st edn. c/photo. Th. F. F2d. $15.00

REYNOLDS, Mack. *Ability Quotient.* 1975. Ace 00265. 1st edn. SF. F. F2d. $10.00

REYNOLDS, Mack. *After Some Tomorrow.* 1967. Belmont B 50-795. 1st prtg. SF. G+. R5d. $3.00

REYNOLDS, Mack. *Amazon Planet.* Ace 01950. SF VG+. B5d. $4.00

REYNOLDS, Mack. *Commune 2000 A A.* 1974. Bantam N 8402. 1st prtg. VG. R5d. $1.50

REYNOLDS, Mack. *Cosmic Eye.* 1969. Belmont B 60-1040. 1st edn. SF. F. F2d. $8.00

REYNOLDS, Mack. *Earth War.* 1963. Pyramid F 886. SF. VG+. B4d. $6.00

REYNOLDS, Mack. *Earth War.* 1963. Pyramid F 886. 1st edn. SF. F. F2d. $8.00

REYNOLDS, Mack. *Episode on the Riviera.* Monarch 205. PBO. VG. B3d. $6.00

REYNOLDS, Mack. *Expatriates.* 1963. Regency 321. 1st edn. Av. F. F2d. $25.00

REYNOLDS, Mack. *Jet Set.* 1964. Monarch 405. PBO. c/Tom Miller: gga. VG. P6d. $5.00

REYNOLDS, Mack. *Jet Set.* 1964. Monarch 405. 1st edn. Av. F. F2d. $15.00

REYNOLDS, Mack. *Planetary Agent X.* London. 1st British edn. F. M1d. $5.00

REYNOLDS, Mack. *Planetary Agent X.* Priory 1132. SF. VG. B5d. $3.50

REYNOLDS, Mack. *Rival Rigelians, Planetary Agent X.* Ace 66995. 1st prtg. F. S1d. $2.50

REYNOLDS, Mack. *Satellite City.* 1975. Ace 75045. 1st edn. SF. F. F2d. $10.00

REYNOLDS, Mack. *Space Visitor.* Ace 77782. 1st prtg. F. S1d. $2.50

REYNOLDS, Mack. *Time Gladiator.* 1969. Lancer 74-537. 1st edn. SF. F. F2d. $8.00

REYNOLDS, Mack. *Tomorrow Might Be Different.* Ace 81670. 1st prtg. VG. S1d. $2.50

REYNOLDS, Mack. *Towers of Utopia.* 1973. Bantam. 1st edn. F. M1d. $5.00

REYNOLDS, Quentin. *Courtroom.* Popular G 106. NF. B3d. $6.00

REYNOLDS, Quentin. *Raid at Dieppe.* 1958. Avon T 226. War. VG. B4d. $2.75

REYNOLDS, Quentin. *Smooth & Deadly.* Popular 533. VG. B3d. $4.00

REYNOLDS, Quentin. *70,000 to One.* 1958. Pyramid G 351. c/G McConnell. NF. VG. B5d. $4.50

REYNOLDS, Quentin. *70,000 to One.* Pyramid 545. 2nd prtg. VG+. B3d. $4.50

REYNOLDS, Winston. *Assignment: Lust.* 1964. Gaslight 114. PBO. NF. B6d. $9.00

REYNOLDS/REYNOLDS. *Blackman's Burden/Border, Breed Nor Birth.* 1972. Ace 06612. SF. VG+. W2d. $6.50

REYNOLDS/TUBB. *Computer War/Death Is a Dream.* Ace H 34. 1st prtg. VG. S1d. $4.00

REYNOLDS/TUBB. *Computer War/Death Is a Dream.* 1967. Ace M 127. PBO. SF. G+. M3d. $3.00

RHEINGOLD, Howard. *War of the Gurus.* 1974. Freeway Press FP 2045. 1st prtg. SF. VG+. R5d. $6.50

RHOADES, J. *Over the Fence Is Out.* Mac-Fadden 50-175. VG+. B3d. $4.00

RHOADS, G. *Place To Sleep.* Ballantine 599. PBO. VG. B3d. $4.50

RHODAN, Perry. *Action: Division 3.* Ace 66078. G. P9d. $1.00

RHODAN, Perry. *Again: Atlan!* Ace 66029. VG. P9d. $1.50

RHODAN, Perry. *Ambassadors From Aurigel.* Ace 66047. F. P9d. $2.00

RHODAN, Perry. *Atom Hell of Gravtier.* Ace 66055. VG. P9d. $1.50

RHODAN, Perry. *Attack From the Unseen.* Ace 66033. F. P9d. $2.00

RHODAN, Perry. *Beware the Microbots.* Ace 66018. NF. P9d. $1.75

RHODAN, Perry. *Blazing Sun.* Ace 66070. VG. P9d. $1.50

RHODAN, Perry. *Bonds of Eternity.* Ace 66053. VG. P9d. $1.50

RHODAN, Perry. *Caves of the Druufs.* Ace 66056. VG. P9d. $1.50

RHODAN, Perry. *Challenge of the Unknown.* Ace 60015. VG. P9d. $1.50

RHODAN, Perry. *Checkmate: Universe.* Ace 66058. VG. P9d. $1.50

RHODAN, Perry. *Columbus Affair.* Ace 66064. F. P9d. $2.00

RHODAN, Perry. *Conflict Center: Naator.* Ace 66061. VG. P9d. $1.50

RHODAN, Perry. *Cosmic Decoy.* Ace 66004. VG. P9d. $1.50

RHODAN, Perry. *Cosmic Traitor.* Ace 66009. NF. P9d. $1.75

RHODAN, Perry. *Dead Live.* Ace 66031. F. P9d. $2.00

RHODAN, Perry. *Death Waits in Semi-Space.* Ace 66044. VG. P9d. $1.50

RHODAN, Perry. *Dimension Search.* Ace 66043. VG. P9d. $1.50

RHODAN, Perry. *Earth Dies.* Ace 66024. VG. P9d. $1.50

RHODAN, Perry. *Enterprise Stardust.* Ace 65970. VG. P9d. $1.50

RHODAN, Perry. *Epidemic Center: Avalon.* Ace 66020. F. P9d. $2.00

RHODAN, Perry. *Escape to Venus.* Ace 65984. VG. P9d. $1.50

RHODAN, Perry. *Fleet of the Spingers.* Ace 66005. VG. P9d. $1.50

RHODAN, Perry. *Fortress Atlantis.* Ace 66035. F. P9d. $2.00

RHODAN, Perry. *Friend to Mankind.* Ace 66075. NF. P9d. $1.75

RHODAN, Perry. *Galactic Riddle.* Ace 65977. F. P9d. $2.00

RHODAN, Perry. *Ghosts of Gol.* Ace 65979. NF. P9d. $1.75

RHODAN, Perry. *Giant's Partner.* Ace 66016. F. P9d. $2.00

RHODAN, Perry. *Guardians.* Ace 66041. NF. P9d. $1.75

RHODAN, Perry. *Horror.* Ace 66049. F. P9d. $2.00

RHODAN, Perry. *Idol From Passa.* Ace 66082. NF. P9d. $1.75

RHODAN, Perry. *Infinity Flight.* Ace 66007. NF. P9d. $1.75

RHODAN, Perry. *Interlude on Siliko 5.* Ace 66042. F. P9d. $2.00

RHODAN, Perry. *Last Days at Atlantis.* Ace 66045. F. P9d. $2.00

RHODAN, Perry. *Life Hunt.* Ace 66026. VG. P9d. $1.50

RHODAN, Perry. *Man & Monsters.* Ace 66019. VG. P9d. $1.50

RHODAN, Perry. *Menace of the Mutant Master.* Ace 65988. VG. P9d. $1.50

RHODAN, Perry. *Micro-Techs.* Ace 66038. VG. P9d. $1.50

RHODAN, Perry. *Mutants Vs Mutants.* Ace 65990. F. P9d. $2.00

RHODAN, Perry. *Mystery of the Anti.* Ace 66072. VG. P9d. $1.50

RHODAN, Perry. *Peril on Ice Planet.* Ace 66006. VG. P9d. $1.50

RHODAN, Perry. *Phantom Fleet.* Ace 66081. NF. P9d. $1.75

RHODAN, Perry. *Plague of Oblivian.* Ace 66010. F. P9d. $2.00

RHODAN, Perry. *Planet of the Dying Sun.* Ace 65980. F. P9d. $2.00

RHODAN, Perry. *Planet of the Gods.* Ace 66011. NF. P9d. $1.75

RHODAN, Perry. *Plasma Monster.* Ace 66079. VG. P9d. $1.50

RHODAN, Perry. *Power Key.* Ace 66062. NF. P9d. $1.75

RHODAN, Perry. *Power's Price.* Ace 66073. VG. P9d. $1.50

RHODAN, Perry. *Prisoner of Time.* Ace 66039. F. P9d. $2.00

RHODAN, Perry. *Project: Earthsave.* Ace 66021. F. P9d. $2.00

RHODAN, Perry. *Pseudo One.* Ace 66027. VG. P9d. $1.50

RHODAN, Perry. *Pucky's Greatest Hour.* Ace 66065. NF. P9d. $1.75

RHODAN, Perry. *Realm of the Tri Planets.* Ace 66014. F. P9d. $2.00

RHODAN, Perry. *Rebels of Tuglan.* Ace 65781. F. P9d. $2.00

RHODAN, Perry. *Recruits for Arkon.* Ace 66060. VG. P9d. $1.50

RHODAN, Perry. *Red Eye of Betelgeuse.* Ace 6603. NF. P9d. $1.75

RHODAN, Perry. *Renegades of the Future.* Ace 66048. F. P9d. $2.00

RHODAN, Perry. *Return From the Void.* Ace 66034. G. P9d. $1.00

RHODAN, Perry. *Secret Barrier X.* Ace 65986. VG. P9d. $1.50

RHODAN, Perry. *Shadow of the Mutant Master.* Ace 66030. F. P9d. $2.00

RHODAN, Perry. *Silence of Gom.* Ace 66020. F. P9d. $2.00

RHODAN, Perry. *Sleepers.* Ace 66063. NF. P9d. $1.75

RHODAN, Perry. *Snowman in Flames.* Ace 66008. F. P9d. $2.00

RHODAN, Perry. *Solar Assassins.* Ace 66032. VG. P9d. $1.50

RHODAN, Perry. *SOS: Space Ship Titan.* Ace 66017. VG. P9d. $1.50

RHODAN, Perry. *Spaceship of Ancestors.* Ace 66057. VG. P9d. $1.50

RHODAN, Perry. *Spy Bot!* Ace 66036. VG. P9d. $1.50

RHODAN, Perry. *Starless Realm.* Ace 66071. VG. P9d. $1.50

RHODAN, Perry. *Target Star.* Ace 66076. NF. P9d. $1.75

RHODAN, Perry. *Thora's Sacrifice.* Ace 66054. VG. P9d. $1.50

RHODAN, Perry. *Thrall of Nympho.* Ace 65991. VG. P9d. $1.50

RHODAN, Perry. *Tigris Leaps.* Ace 66046. F. P9d. $2.00

RHODAN, Perry. *Times Lonely One.* Ace 66025. VG. P9d. $1.50

RHODAN, Perry. *To Arkun!* Ace 66013. NF. P9d. $1.75

RHODAN, Perry. *Touch of Eternity.* Ace 66040. F. P9d. $2.00

RHODAN, Perry. *Unknown Sector: Milky Way.* Ace 66028. F. P9d. $2.00

RHODAN, Perry. *Unleashed Powers.* Ace 66074. F. P9d. $2.00

RHODAN, Perry. *Vagabond of Space.* Ace 66077. VG. P9d. $1.50

RHODAN, Perry. *Venus Trap.* Ace 65987. VG. P9d. $1.50

RHODAN, Perry. *Venusin Danger.* Ace 65983. F. P9d. $2.00

RHODAN, Perry. *World Gone Mad.* Ace 66012. VG. P9d. $1.50

RHODE, John. *Book of Modern Crime Stories.* 1942. Avon 21. VG. B3d. $8.00

RHODE, John. *Dead of the Night.* 1946. Popular 99. PBO. My. G+. G5d. $10.00

RHODE, John. *Dead of the Night.* 1946. Popular 99. 1st pb. My. VG. B6d. $12.50

RHODE, John. *Death Sits on the Board.* Popular 12. G. G5d. $15.00

RHODE, John. *Dr Priestley Investigates.* 1941. Avon 5. VG+. B3a #24. $55.00

RHODE, John. *Dr Priestley Investigates.* 1941. Avon 5. 1st edn. PBO. F. F2d. $42.00

RHODE, John. *Dr Priestley Investigates.* 1941. Avon 5. 1st edn. VG. B3d/B6d. $15.00

RHODE, John. *Poison for One.* 1943. Avon 35. VG. B3d. $6.00

RHODE, William. *Give Me a Little Something.* 1956. Pyramid G 226. 1st edn. c/gga. F. F2d. $16.00

RHODES, Eugene. *Proud Sheriff.* 1953. Dell 688. We. VG+. B4d. $6.00

RHODES, H.T.F. *Satanic Mass.* Pedigree Books NN. VG. B3a #24. $30.00

RICCIO & SLOCUM. *All the Way Down.* 1963. Ballantine F 712. JD. VG+. P1d. $13.50

RICE, Anne. *Interview With the Vampire.* 1977. Ballantine 25608. 1st pb edn. SF. VG. M3d. $7.50

RICE, Craig. *Big Midget Murders.* Pocket 528. VG. B3d. $4.00

RICE, Craig. *Corpse Steps Out.* Pocket 476. NF. I1d. $5.00

RICE, Craig. *Fourth Postman.* Pocket 651. VG+. G5d. $8.50

RICE, Craig. *Having Wonderful Crime.* Pocket 289. VG. G5d. $7.50

RICE, Craig. *Lucky Stiff.* Pocket 391. G+. G5d. $6.00

RICE, Craig. *My Kingdom for a Hearse.* 1957. Pocket 1189. c/photo. VG. P6d. $2.50

RICE, Craig. *Name Is Malone.* Pyramid 671. VG. B3d. $4.50

RICE, Craig. *Sunday Pigeon Murders.* Banner 1. VG. B3d. $8.00

RICE, Craig. *Sunday Pigeon Murders.* Pocket 434. reprint. VG+. B6d. $12.50

RICE, Craig. *Trial by Fury.* Dell D 187. VG. B3d. $4.00

RICE, Craig. *Trial by Fury.* 1943. Pocket 237. My. VG+. B4d. $6.00

RICE, Elmer. *Imperial City.* Avon 273. VG. B3d. $5.00

RICE, Jeff. *Night Stalker.* 1973. Pocket 78343. PBO. MTI. c/photo. VG. P6d. $3.00

RICE, Jeff. *Night Stalker.* 1973. Pocket 78343. 1st prtg. TVTI. SF. F. W2d. $6.00

RICE, John Andrew. *Local Color.* 1955. Dell 1st Edn 71. PBO. c/A Shilstone. Fi. VG. B5d. $4.00

RICE & STORY. *Murder in the Family.* Saint My Library 123. PBO. VG. M6d. $9.50

RICHARD, Louis. *And Sex Is the Payoff.* 1962. Beacon B 565F. PBO. VG. P6d. $3.50

RICHARD, R. *Car-Hop Wife.* Gaslight 115. PBO. VG+. B3d. $5.00

RICHARDS, C. *Sex Tools '70.* Barclay 7086. NF. B3d. $5.00

RICHARDS, D. *Women Like Me.* Domino 72-915. PBO. NF. B3d. $6.00

RICHARDS, Donna. *Swivel Hips.* 1963. France 52. 1st edn. c/gga. F. F2d. $10.00

RICHARDS, Donna. *Take Me in Passion.* 1965. Lancer 72-929. PBO. VG+. B6d. $8.00

RICHARDS, I.A. *Republic of Plato.* Armed Services H 217. VG. P6d. $1.50

RICHARDS, Lee. *Punks.* 1964. Beacon B 706X. JD. VG+. P1d. $20.00

RICHARDS, Monty. *Surgeon at Sea.* 1967. Belmont B 50-765. PBO. Fi. NF. B5d. $4.50

RICHARDS, Rick. *Abnormal.* 1962. Midwood 187. 1st edn. c/gga. F. F2d. $15.00

RICHARDS, Robert. *I Can Lick Seven.* 1960. Berkley G 480. Fi. VG+. B5d. $4.00

RICHARDS, Tad. *Blazing Saddles.* 1974. Warner 76-536. 1st prtg. VG. R5d. $2.00

RICHARDS, William. *Dead Man's Tide.* 1953. Graphic 60. G+. G5d. $7.50

RICHARDS, William. *Dead Man's Tide.* 1953. Graphic 60. 1st prtg. PBO. VG. P7d. $9.00

RICHARDS, William. *Money Men.* Popular 60-2379. c/Hooks. VG. B3d. $4.00

RICHARDSON, A. *Wingless Victory.* Pan GP 38. VG. B3d. $6.00

RICHARDSON, G. *Rustlers' Moon.* Boardman 14. VG. B3d. $7.00

RICHARDSON, Humphrey. *Sexual Life of Robinson Crusoe.* 1967. Traveller Companion 205. 1st US edn. F. F2d. $10.00

RICHELSON, G. *Star Wars Storybook.* 1978. Scholastic 4466. 1st prtg. SF. VG+. W2d. $4.25

RICHMOND, Roe. *Hard Men.* 1962. Pyramid G 755. c/J Leone. We. VG. B5d. $3.00

RICHMOND/RICHMOND. *Gallagher's Glacier/Positive Charge.* Ace 27235. c/K Freas. SF. VG. B5d. $3.50

RICHMOND/SHAW. *Shock Wave/Envoy to the Dog Star.* Ace G 614. NF. M1d. $8.00

RICHTER, Conrad. *Light in the Forest.* 1954. Bantam 1264. We. VG+. B4d. $2.50

RICHTER, Conrad. *Sea of Grass.* Bantam 1208. reprint. NF. B6d. $10.00

RICHTER, Conrad. *Sea of Grass.* 1947. Pocket 413. MTI. VG+. B4d. $10.00

RICHTER, H. *Beyond Defeat.* Crest 188. VG+. B3d. $4.00

RICKS, Dave. *Blood Feud.* 1953. Pyramid 78. PBO. We. G+. B5d. $4.00

RICO, Don. *Daisy Dilemma.* 1967. Lancer 73-639. PBO. VG+. B6d. $7.00

RICO, Don. *Daisy Dilemma.* 1967. Lancer 73-639. 1st edn. My. F. F2d. $10.00

RICO, Don. *Last of the Breed.* 1965. Lancer 70-081. c/Stanley. We. F. B4d. $9.00

RICO, Don. *Nikki.* 1963. Midwood 340. c/Schultz. NF. B3a #21. $15.00

RICO, Don. *Unmarried Ones.* 1964. Beacon 713. 1st edn. c/gga. My. F. F2d. $15.00

RIDER, Brett. *Death Stalks the Range.* Pocket 542. VG. B3d. $4.00

RIDER, J.W. *Jersey Tomatoes.* 1987. Pocket 64108. 1st prtg. My. VG. W2d. $3.00

RIDGWAY, Jason. *Hardly a Man Is Now Alive.* 1962. Perma M 4234. 1st prtg. VG. P7d. $4.00

RIDGWAY, Jason. *People in Glass Houses.* 1961. Perma M 4209. 1st prtg. PBO. VG. P7d. $4.00

RIDGWAY, Jason. *Treasure of the Cosa Nostra.* 1966. Pocket 50196. My. VG+. B4d. $4.00

RIEFE, Alan. *Conspirators.* 1975. Popular 00650 1st edn. De. F. F2d. $8.00

RIEFE, Alan. *Silver Puma.* 1975. Popular 00662. 1st edn. De. F. F2d. $9.00

RIENOW, L. & R. *Year of the Last Eagle.* 1970. Ballantine 02065. 1st prtg. SF. VG. R5d. $2.25

RIFKIN, Shepard. *Desire Island.* 1960. Ace D 444. PBO. c/Copeland. VG. B6d. $10.00

RIFKIN, Shepard. *King Fisher's Road.* Gold Medal 1824. VG. B3d. $4.00

RIFKIN, Shepard. *Savage Years.* 1967. Gold Medal 1799. 1st edn. F. F2d. $9.00

RIFKIN, Shepard. *Texas Blood Red.* 1955. Dell 1st Edn 82. PBO. c/G Gross. We. VG+. B5d. $5.00

RIFKIN & NORMAN. *Gutter Girl.* 1960. Beacon 306. PBO. c/gga. scarce. JD. NF. B6a #75. $80.50

RIGBY, Ray. *Hill.* 1965. Dell 3599. 1st prtg. MTI. VG+. B3d. $4.50

RIGSBY, Howard. *Kill & Tell.* 1953. Pocket 934. 1st prtg. c/Meese: gga. VG. P7d. $6.50

RIGSBY, Howard. *Lucinda.* 1954. Gold Medal 400. PBO. c/Mayer. My. VG. B6d. $7.50

RIGSBY, Howard. *Murder for the Holidays.* Pocket 901. G. G5d. $3.50

RIIS, S.M. *Yankee Komisar.* 1939. Red Arrow 7. 1st edn. PBO. very scarce. NF. F2d. $20.00

RILEY, Nord. *Armored Dove.* 1964. Gold Medal K 1435. PBO. VG. B6d. $5.00

RILEY, Nord. *Bedroom Derby.* Gold Medal 1521. VG. B3d. $4.00

RIMANELLI, Giose. *Fall of Night.* 1955. Popular 713. c/gga. Fa. VG. B4d. $3.00

RINEHART, Mary Roberts. *After House.* 1965. Dell 0044. 1st prtg. My. VG. W2d. $4.25

RINEHART, Mary Roberts. *After House.* 1944. Popular 21. 1st pb. c/Hoffman. My. VG. B6d. $9.00

RINEHART, Mary Roberts. *Alibi for Israel.* Dell 10¢ 22. VG. B3d. $4.50

RINEHART, Mary Roberts. *Breaking Point.* 1967. Dell 0795. 5th prtg. My. VG. W2d. $3.75

RINEHART, Mary Roberts. *Case of Jennie Brice.* 1965. Dell 1094. 1st prtg. My. G+. R5d. $1.00

RINEHART, Mary Roberts. *Case of Jennie Brice.* 1944. Dell 40. 1st edn. PBO. c/Gregg. rare. F. B6a #80. $74.00

RINEHART, Mary Roberts. *Case of Jennie Brice.* Dell 404. VG. I1d. $5.00

RINEHART, Mary Roberts. *Door.* 1964. Dell 2138. 1st prtg. c/Kalin. VG. P7d. $4.00

RINEHART, Mary Roberts. *Episode of the Wandering Knife.* 1961. Dell D 433. 1st prtg. My. VG+. R5d. $4.00

RINEHART, Mary Roberts. *Episode of the Wandering Knife.* Dell 541. c/R De Soto. My. VG. B5d. $4.00

RINEHART, Mary Roberts. *Haunted Lady.* Dell 361. c/V Kalin. My. VG. B5d. $5.00

RINEHART, Mary Roberts. *Haunted Lady.* Dell 361. G. I1d. $3.00

RINEHART, Mary Roberts. *Locked Doors.* Dell 10¢ 4. c/Phillips. NF. B3d. $8.00

RINEHART, Mary Roberts. *Locked Doors.* 1951. Dell 10¢ 4. VG+. B3a #20. $5.35

RINEHART, Mary Roberts. *Man in Lower 10.* Dell D 276. c/Muni. VG+. B3d. $5.00

RINEHART, Mary Roberts. *Man in Lower 10.* 1946. Dell 124. My. VG. B4d. $5.00

RINEHART, Mary Roberts. *Man in Lower 10.* Dell 403. c/R Stanley. My. VG. B5d. $5.00

RINEHART, Mary Roberts. *Miss Pinkerton.* Dell Map 494. My. G+. W2d. $4.50

RINEHART, Mary Roberts. *Miss Pinkerton.* 1964. Dell 5679. 1st prtg. My. VG. R5d. $1.50

RINEHART, Mary Roberts. *Miss Pinkerton.* Popular 5. VG. B3d. $6.00

RINEHART, Mary Roberts. *Red Lamp.* 1961. Dell R 103. 1st prtg. My. VG. R5d. $3.25

RINEHART, Mary Roberts. *Red Lamp.* 1946. Dell 131. 1st prtg. VG. P7d. $9.00

RINEHART, Mary Roberts. *Red Lamp.* Dell 782. 1st prtg. My. VG. R5d. $2.75

RINEHART, Mary Roberts. *Sight Unseen.* Avon 83. VG. B3d. $5.00

RINEHART, Mary Roberts. *State Vs Elinor Norton.* Dell R 107. reprint. VG+. B3d. $4.50

RINEHART, Mary Roberts. *State Vs Elinor Norton.* 1947. Dell 203. c/G Gregg. My. VG+. B5d. $10.00

RINEHART, Mary Roberts. *State Vs Elinor Norton.* 1988. Zebra 02412. c/skull. My. VG+. B5d. $5.00

RINEHART, Mary Roberts. *Swimming Pool.* Dell D 126. VG+. B3d. $4.50

RINEHART, Mary Roberts. *Wall.* Dell 166. VG. I1d. $5.00

RINEHART, Mary Roberts. *Wall.* 1963. Dell 9370. My. VG+. B4d. $2.00

RINEHART, Mary Roberts. *Window at the White Cat.* 1957. Dell 506. reprint. VG+. B6d. $12.00

RINEHART, Mary Roberts. *Window at the White Cat.* Dell 57. G+. I1d. $5.00

RINEHART, Mary Roberts. *Window at the White Cat.* Dell 57. 1st pb. c/Gregg. VG. B6d. $12.50

RINEHART, Mary Roberts. *Yellow Room.* 1949. Bantam 314. c/Bernard Barton. VG. P6d. $3.00

RINEHART, Mary Roberts. *Yellow Room.* 1962. Dell 9790. 1st prtg. My. VG+. R5d. $1.50

RIPLEY, Austin. *Minute Mysteries.* 1962. Pocket 6132. 5th edn. My. VG+. B5d. $3.50

RIPLEY, Robert L. *Believe It or Not.* 1970. Gold Key. 1st edn. NF. M1d. $5.00

RIPLEY, Robert L. *Ripley's Believe It or Not! 5th Series.* Pocket 1195. VG+. B3d. $7.00

RIPLEY, Robert L. *Second Believe It or Not!* 1948. Pocket 426. 1st prtg. VG+. P7d. $10.00

RIPLEY, Robert L. *Stars-Space-UFOs.* 1978. Pocket 82064. SF. VG. W2d. $3.00

RIPLEY, Robert. *Ripley's Believe It or Not! 6th Series.* 1958. Pocket 1208. c/Hoffman. Nfi. VG. B5d. $4.00

RITCHIE, Jack. *New Leaf & Other Stories.* 1971. Dell 6381. 1st edn. scarce. My. F. F2d. $35.00

RITTWAGEN, Marjorie. *Sins of Their Fathers.* 1959. Pyramid G 398. JD. VG+. P1d. $15.50

RIVERE, Alec. *Lost City of the Damned.* 1961. Pike 101. PBO. c/sgn. SF. VG+. B6a #79. $110.00

RIVERE, Alec. *Lost City of the Damned.* 1961. Pike 101. VG. B3d. $4.50

RIVERS, S. *Sex Kittens.* Tiger 139. c/sgn. VG+. B3d. $8.00

RIVKIN, J.F. *Dreamstone.* 1991. Ace 73696. 1st edn. F. F2d. $6.00

ROAN, Tom. *Wyoming Gun.* Dell 849. VG+. B3d. $5.00

ROARK, Garland. *Fair Wind to Java.* Perma P 127. VG. B3d/I1d. $4.00

ROARK, Garland. *Rainbow in the Royals.* 1951. Perma P 139. 1st pb. c/Shoyer. VG+. B6d. $9.00

ROARK, Garland. *Slant of the Wild Wind.* 1953. Perma P 198. 1st pb. c/Bobertz. VG. B6d. $7.00

ROARK, Garland. *Wake of the Red Witch.* Dell F 52. VG. B3d. $5.50

ROARK, Garland. *Wreck of the Running Gale.* 1954. Perma P 274. NF. B3d. $6.50

ROARK, Garland. *Wreck of the Running Gale.* 1954. Perma P 274. 1st prtg. c/gga. VG. P7d. $5.00

ROATE, M.C. *New Hotdog Cookbook.* MacFadden 75-196. PBO. NF. B3d. $3.50

ROBBINS, Alan Pitt. *Gilbert & Sullivan.* 1950. Avon 228. VG. B4d. $3.00

ROBBINS, L. *Lesbian Wives.* Barclay 7102. NF. B3d. $5.00

ROBERSON, Jennifer. *Shape Changers.* 1984. DAW 564. 1st edn. NF. P9d. $1.75

ROBERTIELLO, Richard C. *Voyage From Lesbos.* 1960. Avon T 397. Nfi. VG+. B4d. $7.50

ROBERTS, Adam. *Glad To Be Bad.* 1960. Midwood 46. PBO. c/Rader: gga. VG. M6d. $7.50

ROBERTS, Cecil. *One Small Candle.* 1946. Pony 59. NF. I1d. $15.00

ROBERTS, Colette. *Millions for Love.* 1949. Novel 31. c/gga. Fa. G+. B4d. $8.00

ROBERTS, Dorothy. *Enchanted Cup.* Bantam 1319. VG+. B3d. $4.50

ROBERTS, E.M. *Time of Man.* Signet 1133. VG+. B3d. $5.50

ROBERTS, G. *Desperate Moments.* Saber SA 4. VG+. B3d. $6.00

ROBERTS, Herb. *Love in the Shadows.* 1963. Beacon B 589F. PBO. Ad. VG+. B5d. $6.50

ROBERTS, Herb. *These Women.* 1963. Beacon 640. 1st edn. F. F2d. $8.00

ROBERTS, J. Pierpont. *Navy Swappers.* 1972. Liverpool TNS 539. Ad. VG+. B5d. $4.50

ROBERTS, John M. *Spacer: Window of the Mind.* 1988. Ace 77787. SF. VG+. W2d. $3.25

ROBERTS, Keith. *Furies.* 1966. Berkley F 1177. 1st prtg. SF. VG. R5d. $4.50

ROBERTS, Keith. *Inner Wheel.* 1972. Playboy 16143. SF. VG+. B4d. $3.00

ROBERTS, Keith. *Inner Wheel.* 1972. Playboy 16143. 1st prtg. G. S1d. $2.00

ROBERTS, Keith. *Pavane.* 1976. Berkley O3142. c/R Powers. SF. VG+. B5d. $4.00

ROBERTS, Kenneth. *Lively Lady.* Armed Services Q 29. VG+. B3d. $5.00

ROBERTS, Lee. *Death of a Ladies Man.* 1960. Gold Medal 968. My. VG+. B3d. $6.00

ROBERTS, Lee. *Pale Door.* Bantam 1535. VG+. B3d. $5.50

ROBERTS, Lionel. *Time-Echo.* 1959. Badger 23. PBO. SF. VG+. B6a #74. $44.00

ROBERTS, R.E. *Second Time Around.* 1961. Perma M 4246. 1st prtg. VG. R5d. $2.75

ROBERTS, Richard. *Gilded Rooster.* 1949. Bantam 714. 1st pb. c/Skemp. NF. B6d. $12.50

ROBERTS, Steve. *Max Headroom: 20 Minutes Into the Future.* 1986. Vintage 74779. 1st prtg. SF. F. W2d. $10.00

ROBERTS, Susan. *Witches USA.* 1971. Dell 9607. 1st edn. F. F2d. $8.00

ROBERTS, Suzanne. *Campus Nurse.* Ace D 558. PBO. VG. B3d. $4.50

ROBERTS, Suzanne. *Hootenanny Nurse.* 1964. Ace D 579. PBO. VG. P6d. $2.50

ROBERTS, Suzanne. *Prize for Nurse Darci.* 1965. Ace F 341. 1st prtg. PBO. VG. P7d. $3.50

ROBERTS, Wendell. *Leapfrog Swap.* 1969. PEC G 1172. PBO. VG+. B6d. $7.00

ROBERTS, Z. *Sex Circus.* Carousel 506. VG. B3d. $4.00

ROBERTSON, Charley. *Hoodlum.* 1951. Popular 347. c/gga. Fa. VG. B3d. $5.50

ROBERTSON, F.C. *Brand of Open Hand.* Fight West Novel 39. VG+. B3d. $5.00

ROBERTSON, F.C. *Cow Country Law.* 1950s. Thrilling Novel 16. 1st pb. VG+. B6d. $9.00

ROBERTSON, F.C. *Lawman's Pay.* Ballantine 208. PBO. VG+. B3d. $5.50

ROBERTSON, F.C. *Powder Burner.* 1966. Belmont B 45-906. We. VG. B5d. $3.50

ROBERTSON, F.C. *Red Rustlers.* Readers Choice 24. VG. B3d. $7.00

ROBERTSON, F.C. *Roundup in the River.* West Action 1. VG. B3d. $4.50

ROBERTSON, F.C. *Trouble Shootin' Man.* Readers Choice 14. VG. B3d. $4.00

ROBERTSON, T. *Night Raider of Atlantic.* Ace D 244. VG. B3d. $4.00

ROBERTSON, T. *Ship With Two Captains.* Pan G 212. VG. B3d. $7.50

ROBESON, Kenneth. *Angry Ghost.* Bantam 02862. G. G5d. $3.50

ROBESON, Kenneth. *Annihilist.* 1968. Bantam F 3885. Doc Savage #31. SF. F. W2d. $9.00

ROBESON, Kenneth. *Annihilist.* 1968. Bantam F 3885. 1st prtg. SF. VG. R5d. $3.00

ROBESON, Kenneth. *Black Death.* Avenger 22. NF. I1d. $5.00

ROBESON, Kenneth. *Black Spot.* 1974. Bantam S 8305. Doc Savage #76. SF. G+. W2d. $4.50

ROBESON, Kenneth. *Blood Countess.* Warner 75-783. Avenger #33. G. G5d. $5.00

ROBESON, Kenneth. *Blood Ring.* PB Library 64-963. Avenger #6. VG+. B3d. $5.00

ROBESON, Kenneth. *Blood Ring.* 1972. Warner 64963. Avenger #6. SF. G+. W2d. $4.00

ROBESON, Kenneth. *Blood Ring.* Warner 65-943. Avenger. VG. B3d. $4.00

ROBESON, Kenneth. *Brand of the Werewolf.* Doc Savage #5. VG+. I1d. $6.00

ROBESON, Kenneth. *Crimson Serpent.* 1974. Bantam S 8367. 1st prtg. Doc Savage #78. SF. VG+. W2d. $8.00

ROBESON, Kenneth. *Czar of Fear.* Doc Savage #22. VG. I1d. $4.00

ROBESON, Kenneth. *Dagger In the Sky.* Doc Savage #40. G+. I1d. $3.00

ROBESON, Kenneth. *Deadly Dwarf.* Doc Savage #28. NF. I1d. $5.00

ROBESON, Kenneth. *Death in Silver & Mystery Under the Sea.* 1983. Bantam 23648. Doc Savage #26 & #27. SF. F. W2d. $4.00

ROBESON, Kenneth. *Death in Slow Motion.* Warner 74-392. Avenger #18. VG. G5d. $4.00

ROBESON, Kenneth. *Death in Slow Motion.* 1975. Warner 74-392. 1st edn. F. F2d. $7.00

ROBESON, Kenneth. *Demon Island.* Warner 75-858. Avenger #36. G. G5d. $5.00

ROBESON, Kenneth. *Derrick Devil.* 1973. Bantam S 7637. Doc Savage #74. SF. G. W2d. $3.50

ROBESON, Kenneth. *Derrick Devil.* 1973. Bantam S 7637. 1st prtg. Doc Savage #74. SF. F. W2d. $8.50

ROBESON, Kenneth. *Devil Genghis.* 1974. Bantam S 8772. 1st prtg. Doc Savage #79. SF. VG. W2d. $7.50

ROBESON, Kenneth. *Devil's Horns.* PB Library 64-920. Avenger #4. VG+. B3d. $5.00

ROBESON, Kenneth. *Devil's Playground.* 1968. Bantam F 3841. 1st prtg. SF. VG+. R5d. $5.50

ROBESON, Kenneth. *Dr Time.* Avenger #28. G+. I1d. $4.00

ROBESON, Kenneth. *Fear Cay.* 1966. Bantam F 3455. 3rd prtg. Doc Savage #11. SF. F. W2d. $8.00

ROBESON, Kenneth. *Feathered Octopus.* 1970. Bantam H 5367. 1st prtg. Doc Savage #48. SF. VG. W2d. $7.50

ROBESON, Kenneth. *Flaming Falcons.* Doc Savage #30. VG. I1d. $4.00

ROBESON, Kenneth. *Fortress of Solitude.* 1968. Bantam F 3716. 1st prtg. SF. VG. R5d. $3.50

ROBESON, Kenneth. *Freckled Shark.* Bantam S 6923. VG. G5d. $3.75

ROBESON, Kenneth. *Frosted Death.* PB Library 64-939. Avenger #5. VG. B3d. $4.50

ROBESON, Kenneth. *Glass Man.* Avenger #34. VG. I1d. $4.00

ROBESON, Kenneth. *Glass Mountain.* Warner 74-008. Avenger #8. VG+. B3d. $4.50

ROBESON, Kenneth. *Golden Peril.* 1970. Bantam H 5652. Doc Savage #55. SF. VG. W2d. $7.50

ROBESON, Kenneth. *Hate Master.* Warner 74-262. Avenger #16. VG. G5d. $4.00

ROBESON, Kenneth. *House of Death.* 1973. Warner 74-261. Avenger #15. VG. G5d. $6.50

ROBESON, Kenneth. *House of Death.* 1973. Warner 74-261. 1st edn. F. F2d. $10.00

ROBESON, Kenneth. *House of Death.* 1973. Warner 74-261. Avenger #15. SF. VG+. W2d. $5.00

ROBESON, Kenneth. *Iron Skull.* Warner 75-848. Avenger #35. VG+. B3d. $4.50

ROBESON, Kenneth. *Jiu San & The Black, Black Witch.* 1981. Bantam 14901. Doc Savage #107 & #108. SF. VG+. W2d. $4.00

ROBESON, Kenneth. *Justice, Inc.* Warner 64-862. Avenger #1. G. G5d. $4.00

ROBESON, Kenneth. *Land of Always-Night.* 1966. Bantam F 3520. 4th prtg. Doc Savage #13. SF. VG. W2d. $6.00

ROBESON, Kenneth. *Land of Fear.* 1973. Bantam S 7719. 1st prtg. Doc Savage #75. SF. VG+. W2d. $8.00

ROBESON, Kenneth. *Land of Long Juju.* 1970. Bantam H 5309. Doc Savage #47. VG. M6d. $4.00

ROBESON, Kenneth. *Lost Oasis.* 1965. Bantam E 3017. Doc Savage #6. SF. VG. W2d. $7.50

ROBESON, Kenneth. *Lost Oasis.* 1972. Bantam S 7524. 5th prtg. Doc Savage #6. SF. VG+. W2d. $6.50

ROBESON, Kenneth. *Man From Atlantis.* Warner 75-609. Avenger #25. VG. G5d/I1d. $4.00

ROBESON, Kenneth. *Man of Bronze.* 1964. Bantam E 2853. 2nd prtg. Doc Savage #1. SF. VG. W2d. $5.25

ROBESON, Kenneth. *Man Who Shook the Earth.* 1969. Bantam H 4761. 2nd prtg. Doc Savage #43. SF. VG. W2d. $6.50

ROBESON, Kenneth. *Medal Master.* 1973. Bantam S 7229. 2nd prtg. Doc Savage #72. SF. F. W2d. $7.50

ROBESON, Kenneth. *Men Who Smiled No More.* 1970. Bantam H 4875. 2nd prtg. Doc Savage #45. SF. VG. W2d. $6.00

ROBESON, Kenneth. *Merchants of Disaster.* 1969. Bantam H 4689. Doc Savage #41. SF. VG. W2d. $7.50

ROBESON, Kenneth. *Meteor Menace.* 1973. Bantam S 7521. 6th prtg. Doc Savage #3. SF. F. W2d. $7.50

ROBESON, Kenneth. *Monsters.* 1974. Bantam S 8604. 4th prtg. Doc Savage #7. SF. VG. W2d. $6.00

ROBESON, Kenneth. *Motion Menace.* Bantam S 6653. VG. G5d. $3.00

ROBESON, Kenneth. *Motion Menace.* 1971. Bantam S 6653. 2nd prtg. Doc Savage #64. SF. VG+. W2d. $7.00

ROBESON, Kenneth. *Munitions Master.* 1971. Bantam S 5788. 1st prtg. SF. G+. R5d. $1.50

ROBESON, Kenneth. *Murder Melody.* 1967. Bantam F 3296. 2nd prtg. SF. G+. R5d. $1.00

ROBESON, Kenneth. *Murder Mirage.* 1972. Bantam S 7418. 1st prtg. Doc Savage #71. SF. VG. W2d. $7.50

ROBESON, Kenneth. *Mystery Under the Sea.* 1983. Bantam 23648. SF. F. W2d. $4.00

ROBESON, Kenneth. *Mystic Mullah.* 1965. Bantam E 3115. Doc Savage #9. SF. G. W2d. $2.50

ROBESON, Kenneth. *Nevlo.* 1973. Warner 74-391. 1st edn. F. F2d. $7.00

ROBESON, Kenneth. *Nightwitch Devil.* Warner 75-672. Avenger #29. VG+. B3d. $4.50

ROBESON, Kenneth. *Other World.* Bantam F 3877. G. G5d. $3.00

ROBESON, Kenneth. *Poison Island.* Bantam H 5743. G+. G5d. $3.50

ROBESON, Kenneth. *Purple Dragon.* 1978. Bantam 11116. My. VG+. B4d. $4.00

ROBESON, Kenneth. *Purple Zombie.* 1974. Warner 75611. Avenger #27. SF. F. W2d. $9.00

ROBESON, Kenneth. *Quest of Qui.* 1966. Bantam E 3111. Doc Savage #12. SF. F. W2d. $9.00

ROBESON, Kenneth. *Red Moon.* 1974. Warner 75610. Avenger #26. SF. F. W2d. $9.00

ROBESON, Kenneth. *Red Snow.* 1969. Bantam H 4065. SF. VG+. B4d. $3.00

ROBESON, Kenneth. *Red Snow.* 1969. Bantam H 4065. 1st prtg. SF. G+. R5d. $1.50

ROBESON, Kenneth. *Red Spider.* 1979. Bantam 12787X. reprint. Doc Savage #95. VG+. P6d. $3.50

ROBESON, Kenneth. *Red Terrors.* 1976. Bantam 06486. Doc Savage #83. F. G+. W2d. $4.50

ROBESON, Kenneth. *River of Ice.* Warner 74-134. Avenger #11. VG. G5d. $4.00

ROBESON, Kenneth. *River of Ice.* 1973. Warner 74-134. 1st edn. F. F2d. $10.00

ROBESON, Kenneth. *Seven Agate Devils.* 1973. Bantam S 7492. 1st prtg. Avenger #73. SF. VG. W2d. $7.50

ROBESON, Kenneth. *Sky Walker.* PB Library 64-898. Avenger #3. VG. B3d. $4.00

ROBESON, Kenneth. *Sky Walker.* 1973. PB Library 64-898. 3rd prtg. Avenger #3. SF. F. W2d. $7.50

ROBESON, Kenneth. *Smiling Dogs.* 1973. Warner 74-142. 1st edn. F. F2d. $10.00

ROBESON, Kenneth. *South Pole Terror.* Bantam S 7571. VG. G5d. $3.00

ROBESON, Kenneth. *Spook Hole.* 1972. Bantam S 7144. Doc Savage #70. SF. G. W2d. $3.50

ROBESON, Kenneth. *Spook Legion.* 1967. Bantam F 3340. Doc Savage #16. SF. F. W2d. $9.00

ROBESON, Kenneth. *Stockholders in Death.* 1972. Warner 64-985. Avenger #7. SF. F. W2d. $7.50

ROBESON, Kenneth. *Stockholders in Death.* 1972. Warner 64-985. Avenger #7. VG. G5d. $4.50

ROBESON, Kenneth. *Submarine Mystery.* 1971. Bantam S 6552. 1st prtg. SF. VG+. R5d. $4.50

ROBESON, Kenneth. *Submarine Mystery.* 1971. Bantam 6542. reprint. VG. P6d. $2.00

ROBESON, Kenneth. *Terror in the Navy.* 1969. Bantam H 5729. 2nd prtg. Doc Savage #33. SF. F. W2d. $9.00

ROBESON, Kenneth. *Thousand-Headed Man.* 1973. Bantam N 6353. 7th prtg. Doc Savage #2. SF. G. W2d. $3.25

ROBESON, Kenneth. *Thousand-Headed Man.* 1972. Bantam S 7520. 6th prtg. Doc Savage #2. SF. F. W2d. $8.00

ROBESON, Kenneth. *Three Gold Crowns.* Warner 74-260. Avenger #14. VG. G5d. $6.50

ROBESON, Kenneth. *Tuned for Murder.* Warner 74-025. Avenger #9. VG. B5d. $4.50

ROBESON, Kenneth. *Tuned for Murder.* 1973. Warner 74-025. Avenger #9. SF. VG+. W2d. $5.00

ROBESON, Kenneth. *Yellow Cloud.* Bantam 5838. Doc Savage #59. VG+. B3d. $5.00

ROBESON, Kenneth. *Yellow Hoard.* 1972. PB Library 64-881. 1st edn. F. F2d. $10.00

ROBESON/ROBESON. *They Died Twice/ Screaming Man.* Bantam 14916-4. VG. P6d. $10.00

ROBIE, W.F. *Art of Love.* 1967. PB Library 55-215. 9th edn. Nfi. NF. B5d. $4.00

ROBIE, W.F. *Hidden Joys of Love.* 1964. Belmont 95-101. Ad. VG. B5d. $4.00

ROBIE, W.F. *Sex & Life.* Brandon House 993. VG. B3d. $5.00

ROBIE, W.F. *Sex & Life.* Lancer 73-422. VG. B3d. $4.00

ROBINETT, Stephen. *Man Responsible.* 1978. Ace 51899. 1st edn. c/review. review slip. De. F. F2d. $20.00

ROBINS, Denise. *I Should Have Known.* 1970. Gold Medal T 2296. Ro. VG+. B4d. $2.25

ROBINS, Patricia. *Lady Chatterley's Daughter.* Ace K 150. VG+. B3d. $5.00

ROBINSON, Alan. *Wildcat.* 1965. Leisure 672. c/Robert Bonfils: gga. F. B6a #74. $82.50

ROBINSON, Anthony. *Easy Way.* 1964. Cardinal GC 211. 1st prtg. My. VG+. R5d. $3.00

ROBINSON, David. *Confession of Alma Quartier.* 1962. Signet 2103. 1st edn. author's 1st book. c/gga. My. F. F2d. $12.00

ROBINSON, Derek. *Rotten With Honour.* 1976. Pan 24346. My. F. W2d. $5.00

ROBINSON, Frank M. *Power.* Bantam A 1593. 3rd prtg. VG. S1d. $2.00

ROBINSON, Frank M. *Power.* Popular 60-8059. MTI. c/Hamilton & Pleshette. SF. VG. B5d. $3.50

ROBINSON, G.D. *Passion Trip.* Tuxedo 113. VG+. B3d. $6.00

ROBINSON, G.R. *Have Wife Will Trade.* News Stand Library 523. VG+. B3d. $5.00

ROBINSON, Henry Morton. *Great Snow.* 1964. Pyramid R 978. c/R Abbett. Fi. VG+. B5d. $4.00

ROBINSON, Henry Morton. *Water of Life.* 1961. Cardinal GC 951. Fa. VG+. B4d. $3.00

ROBINSON, M.L. *Bitter Forfeit.* Bantam 465. VG+. B3d. $5.00

ROBINSON, Ray. *Baseball Stars of 1958.* 1958. Pyramid G 324. PBO. scarce. NF. B6a #76. $44.00

ROBINSON, Ray. *Baseball Stars of 1965.* 1965. Pyramid R 1148. PBO. c/photo. VG. P6d. $6.00

ROBINSON, Spider. *Best of All Possible Worlds.* 1980. Ace. 1st edn. F. M1d. $6.00

ROBINSON, Spider. *Callahan's Secret.* 1986. Berkley. 1st edn. SF. F. F2d. $10.00

ROBLES, Emmanuel. *Dawn on Our Darkness.* 1954. Avon T 87. c/gga. Fa. VG. B3d. $4.00

ROBLES, Emmanuel. *Dawn on Our Darkness.* 1954. Avon T 87. c/H Rubin. Fi. G+. B5d. $2.00

ROCHE, A.S. *Case Against Mrs Ames.* 1948. Popular 138. 1st prtg. c/Belarski: gga. VG. P7d. $12.50

ROCHEFORT, Christiane. *Warrior's Rest.* 1960. Crest S 407. 1st prtg. c/gga. VG. P7d. $4.00

ROCK, Hote. *Mr Madam.* 1961. Newsstand U 151. Ad. VG. B5d. $4.00

ROCK, Hote. *Mr Madam.* 1961. Newsstand U 151. 1st edn. c/gga. My. F. F2d. $15.00

ROCK, Phillip. *Dirty Harry.* 1971. Bantam S 7329. 1st prtg. MTI. My. VG. R5d. $1.75

ROCKWELL, K. *Hard Man.* Brandon House 6391. NF. B3d. $5.00

RODEN, H.W. *One Angel Less.* Dell 247. VG. B3d. $6.00

RODEN, H.W. *Too Busy To Die.* Dell 185. VG. B3d. $5.50

RODEN, H.W. *Too Busy To Die.* Dell 349. G. G5d. $3.00

RODEN, H.W. *Wake for a Lady.* 1949. Dell 345. 1st prtg. c/gga. VG+. B3d. $6.00

RODEN, H.W. *You Only Hang Once.* 1945. Dell 102. 1st pb. c/Gregg. My. VG+. G5d. $11.00

RODIN, Arnold. *Woman Soldier.* Gold Medal 294. VG. B3d. $6.00

ROE, V.E. *Smoke Along the Plains.* Pyramid 1060. 2nd prtg. NF. B3d. $5.00

ROE, Vingie. *West of Abilene.* 1952. Bantam 1031. We. VG. B4d. $2.25

ROEBURT, John. *Al Capone.* 1959. Pyramid G 405. PBO. MTI. NF. B6d. $12.50

ROEBURT, John. *Al Capoone.* 1959. Pyramid G 405. 1st edn. F. F2d. $15.00

ROEBURT, John. *Corpse on the Town.* 1950. Graphic 27. PBO. scarce in condition. NF. B6a #74. $38.50

ROEBURT, John. *Corpse on the Town.* 1950. Graphic 27. VG+. I1d. $8.00

ROEBURT, John. *Corpse on the Town.* Harlequin 109. c/variant. VG. B6a #74. $33.00

ROEBURT, John. *Corpse on the Town.* Harlequin 109. VG. B3d. $7.50

ROEBURT, John. *Hollow Man.* Graphic 110. NF. I1d. $6.00

ROEBURT, John. *Hollow Man.* Graphic 110. VG. B3d. $4.00

ROEBURT, John. *Long Nightmare.* 1958. Crest 246. 1st prtg. My. G+. R5d. $2.75

ROEBURT, John. *Murder in Manhattan.* Avon 772. 1st prtg. My. G+. R5d. $2.25

ROEBURT, John. *Sing Out Sweet Homicide.* Dell 1st Edn K 105. TVTI. VG+. B3d. $5.00

ROEBURT, John. *There Are Dead Men in Manhattan.* Graphic 42. VG. I1d. $4.00

ROEBURT, John. *Tough Cop.* Graphic 22. VG+. G5d. $8.00

ROEBURT, John. *Tough Cop.* Graphic 38. VG. I1d. $4.00

ROFFMAN, Jan. *Reflection of Evil.* 1964. Ace K 216. 1st prtg. My. G+. R5d. $1.00

ROGERS, Dale Evans. *Angel Unaware.* 1963. Pyramid R 826. c/photo. Nfi. VG. B5d. $3.00

ROGERS, H. *Passion Playground.* Bedside 1234. PBO. VG. B3d. $4.00

ROGERS, James Cass. *Silver Streak.* Ballantine 25458. MTI. G5d. $3.50

ROGERS, Joel Townsley. *Never Leave My Bed.* 1963. Beacon B 600. c/gga. Fa. F. B4d. $12.00

ROGERS, Joel Townsley. *Red Right Hand.* 1957. Dell D 203. My. VG+. B4d. $3.00

ROGERS, L. *Guerilla Surgeon.* Fontana 333. VG. B3d. $6.00

ROGERS, Michael. *Mindfogger.* 1976. Dell 4895. SF. VG+. W2d. $4.00

ROGERS, Mick. *Freakout on Sunset Strip.* 1967. Greenleaf Classic 221. PBO. scarce. NF. B6a #76. $31.00

ROGERS, S. *Don't Look Behind You.* Popular 287. VG. I1d. $6.00

ROGERS, T. *Argosy Book Adventure Stories.* Bantam A 1158. 1st prtg. G. S1d. $2.00

ROGET, M. & H. *Swingers Guide for the Single Girl.* Holloway House HH 156. NF. B3d. $6.00

ROGUE, Male. *Rough Shoot.* Bantam 1019. G+. G5d. $4.00

ROHDE, William. *Help Wanted: For Murder.* 1950. Gold Medal 115. PBO. c/Barye. My. VG. B6d. $3.50

ROHDE, William. *High Red for Dead.* 1951. Gold Medal 145. PBO. My. NF. B6d. $18.00

ROHDE, William. *High Red for Dead.* 1951. Gold Medal 145. VG. B3d. $4.00

ROHMER, Sax. *Bianca in Black.* 1962. Airmont M 3. My. VG+. B4d. $3.00

ROHMER, Sax. *Bianca in Black.* 1962. Airmont NN. 1st prtg. My. G+. R5d. $1.50

ROHMER, Sax. *Bride of Fu Manchu.* 1960. Pyramid F 761. 1st edn. My. F. F2d. $10.00

ROHMER, Sax. *Bride of Fu Manchu.* 1960. Pyramid F 761. 1st prtg. G+. S1d. $3.50

ROHMER, Sax. *Bride of Fu Manchu.* 1969. Pyramid X 2113. 2nd prtg. SF. VG. W2d. $3.75

ROHMER, Sax. *Daughter of Fu Manchu.* 1949. Avon 189. 1st edn. PBO. c/Ann Cantor. scarce. Fa. NF. B6a #75. $82.50

ROHMER, Sax. *Daughter of Fu Manchu.* 1949. Avon 189. 1st edn. PBO. c/Cantor. VG. B6d. $22.50

ROHMER, Sax. *Daughter of Fu Manchu.* 1976. Pyramid V 4024. 3rd prtg. SF. VG. W2d. $3.25

ROHMER, Sax. *Day the World Ended.* Ace F 283. 1st prtg. G+. S1d. $4.00

ROHMER, Sax. *Day the World Ended.* 1964. Ace F 283. 1st edn. PBO. My. F. F2d. $8.00

ROHMER, Sax. *Devil Doctor.* 1966. Consul 1023. 1st edn. PBO. scarce. NF. B6a #76. $44.00

ROHMER, Sax. *Devil Doctor.* Corgic GC 7588. SF. VG. W2d. $5.00

ROHMER, Sax. *Dream Detective.* Pyramid. 1st pb edn. VG. M1d. $10.00

ROHMER, Sax. *Drums of Fu Manchu.* 1971. Pryamid X 2531. 3rd prtg. SF. VG+. W2d. $4.00

ROHMER, Sax. *Drums of Fu Manchu.* 1962. Pyramid F 804. c/H Tauss. SF. VG. B5d. $4.00

ROHMER, Sax. *Drums of Fu Manchu.* 1976. Pyramid V 4030. 2nd prtg. SF. VG. W2d. $3.50

ROHMER, Sax. *Drums of Fu Manchu.* 1985. Zebra 01617. SF. VG+. B5d. $5.50

ROHMER, Sax. *Emperor Fu Manchu.* 1959. Gold Medal S 929. c/Bob Abbett. VG. P6d. $7.00

ROHMER, Sax. *Emperor Fu Manchu.* 1959. Gold Medal S 929. 1st edn. F. F2d. $23.00

ROHMER, Sax. *Emperor Fu Manchu.* Pyramid R 110. G+. G5d. $5.00

ROHMER, Sax. *Emperor Fu Manchu.* 1976. Pyramid V 3946. 2nd prtg. SF. VG+. W2d. $4.25

ROHMER, Sax. *Fire Goddess.* 1952. Gold Medal 283. G. I1d. $6.00

ROHMER, Sax. *Fire Goddess.* 1952. Gold Medal 283. 1st edn. PBO. F. F2d. $25.00

ROHMER, Sax. *Hand of Fu Manchu.* 1962. Pyramid F 688. SF. F. W2d. $11.00

ROHMER, Sax. *Hand of Fu Manchu.* Pyramid R 1306. 1st prtg. VG. S1d. $3.50

ROHMER, Sax. *Hand of Fu Manchu.* 1971. Pyramid X 2342. 3rd prtg. SF. VG+. W2d. $5.00

ROHMER, Sax. *Hangover House.* 1951. Graphic 32. 1st edn. PBO. My. VG. F2d. $15.00

ROHMER, Sax. *Hangover House.* 1954. Graphic 78. My. F. F2d. $25.00

ROHMER, Sax. *Hangover House.* 1954. Graphic 78. My. VG+. P6d. $6.00

ROHMER, Sax. *Insidious Doc Fu Manchu.* 1961. Pyramid G 579. VG. I1d. $7.00

ROHMER, Sax. *Insidious Dr Fu Manchu.* 1961. Pyramid G 579. 1st edn. PBO. My. F. F2d. $10.00

ROHMER, Sax. *Insidious Dr Fu Manchu.* 1961. Pyramid G 579. 1st prtg. G+. S1d. $3.50

ROHMER, Sax. *Insidious Dr Fu Manchu.* 1975. Pyramid J 3945. 5th prtg. SF. F. W2d. $4.50

ROHMER, Sax. *Insidious Dr Fu Manchu.* 1970. Pyramid X 2166. 4th prtg. SF. F. W2d. $7.50

ROHMER, Sax. *Island of Fu Manchu.* 1963. Pyramid F 858. My. NF. B4d. $6.00

ROHMER, Sax. *Island of Fu Manchu.* 1963. Pyramid F 858. SF. VG. B5d. $4.00

ROHMER, Sax. *Island of Fu Manchu.* 1963. Pyramid F 858. 1st edn. My. F. F2d. $10.00

ROHMER, Sax. *Island of Fu Manchu.* 1976. Pyramid V 4055. 4th prtg. SF. G+. W2d. $2.75

ROHMER, Sax. *Mask of Fu Manchu.* 1962. Pyramid F 740. c/gga. My. VG. B4d/S1d. $3.50

ROHMER, Sax. *Mask of Fu Manchu.* 1966. Pyramid R 1303. SF. VG+. W2d. $5.50

ROHMER, Sax. *Mask of Fu Manchu.* 1976. Pyramid V 3942. SF. F. W2d. $4.25

ROHMER, Sax. *Mask of Fu Manchu.* 1970. Pyramid X 2248. SF. VG. W2d. $4.50

ROHMER, Sax. *Mystery of Dr Fu Manchu.* 1960. World Dist 905. 2nd prtg. G+. B3d. $5.50

ROHMER, Sax. *Nude in Mink.* 1950. Gold Medal 105. 1st edn. PBO. My. NF. F2d. $15.00

ROHMER, Sax. *Nude in Mink.* 1950. Gold Medal 105. 1st prtg. PBO. VG. P6d. $7.00

ROHMER, Sax. *Nude in Mink.* 1953. Gold Medal 321. 6th edn. VG. M1d. $5.00

ROHMER, Sax. *President Fu Manchu.* 1963. Pyramid F 946. G+. G5d. $3.75

ROHMER, Sax. *President Fu Manchu.* 1963. Pyramid F 946. My. NF. B4d. $6.00

ROHMER, Sax. *President Fu Manchu.* 1976. Pyramid V 4056. 3rd prtg. SF. F. W2d. $4.25

ROHMER, Sax. *President Fu Manchu.* 1969. Pyramid X 2135. 2nd prtg. SF. VG. B3d/W2d. $4.50

ROHMER, Sax. *Quest of the Sacred Slipper.* 1966. Pyramid R 1313. 1st prtg. SF. VG+. S1d. $4.00

ROHMER, Sax. *Re-Enter Fu Manchu.* 1964. Gold Medal K 1458. c/B Phillips. SF. G+. B5d. $2.50

ROHMER, Sax. *Re-Enter Fu Manchu.* 1964. Gold Medal K 1458. SF. F. W2d. $11.00

ROHMER, Sax. *Re-Enter Fu Manchu*. 1957. Gold Medal S 684. 1st edn. My. F. F2d. $15.00

ROHMER, Sax. *Re-Enter Fu Manchu*. 1976. Pyramid V 3944. 2nd prtg. SF. VG. W2d. $4.00

ROHMER, Sax. *Return of Dr Fu Manchu*. 1965. Pryamid R 1302. 2nd prtg. SF. F. W2d. $6.50

ROHMER, Sax. *Return of Dr Fu Manchu*. 1961. Pyramid G 641. 1st edn. PBO. F. F2d. $10.00

ROHMER, Sax. *Return of Dr Fu Manchu*. 1975. Pyramid V 4943. 4th prtg. SF. VG. W2d. $3.25

ROHMER, Sax. *Return of Dr Fu-Manchu*. 1961. Pyramid G 641. c/R Kohfield. SF. VG. B5d. $6.00

ROHMER, Sax. *Return of Sumuru*. 1954. Gold Medal 408. VG. I1d. $18.00

ROHMER, Sax. *Return of Sumuru*. 1954. Gold Medal 408. 1st edn. My. F. F2d. $20.00

ROHMER, Sax. *Return of Sumuru*. 1959. Gold Medal 868. c/gga. reprint. My. VG. B4d. $2.75

ROHMER, Sax. *Romance of Sorcery*. 1973. Freeway Press. 1st pb. F. M1d. $10.00

ROHMER, Sax. *Secret of Holm Peel*. 1970. Ace. 1st edn. F. M1d. $15.00

ROHMER, Sax. *Shadow of Fu Manchu*. Pyramid F 837. G+. G5d. $4.00

ROHMER, Sax. *Shadow of Fu Manchu*. 1963. Pyramid F 837. SF. VG. M3d/W2d. $6.00

ROHMER, Sax. *Shadow of Fu Manchu*. 1976. Pyramid V 4053. 3rd prtg. SF. F. W2d. $4.25

ROHMER, Sax. *Shadow of Fu Manchu*. 1986. Zebra 08217. SF. F. W2d. $4.75

ROHMER, Sax. *Sinister Madonna*. 1956. Gold Medal 555. c/Charles Binger. VG. P5d. $12.00

ROHMER, Sax. *Sinister Madonna*. 1956. Gold Medal 555. 1st edn. My. F. F2d. $25.00

ROHMER, Sax. *Sumuru*. 1951. Gold Medal 199. 1st edn. c/gga. F. F2d. $40.00

ROHMER, Sax. *Sumuru*. 1951. Gold Medal 199. 1st prtg. PBO. c/Barye: gga. VG. P7d/W2d. $20.00

ROHMER, Sax. *Sumuru*. Gold Medal 757. 2nd edn. NF. G5d. $8.50

ROHMER, Sax. *Tales of Chinatown*. 1950. Popular 217. c/Belarski: gga. G+. P6d. $10.00

ROHMER, Sax. *Tales of Chinatown*. 1950. Popular 217. 1st pb. c/Belarski. My. VG. B6d. $16.50

ROHMER, Sax. *Tales of Secret Egypt*. 1974. Freeway Press 2054. SF. VG. W2d. $5.00

ROHMER, Sax. *Trail of Fu Manchu*. 1963. Consul Books 1227. VG. B3d. $9.00

ROHMER, Sax. *Trail of Fu Manchu*. 1962. Pyramid F 688. SF. F. W2d. $16.50

ROHMER, Sax. *Trail of Fu Manchu*. 1964. Pyramid R 1003. SF. VG. W2d. $8.00

ROHMER, Sax. *Trail of Fu Manchu*. 1964. Pyramid R 1003. 1st edn. PBO. F. F2d. $12.00

ROHMER, Sax. *Trail of Fu Manchu*. 1976. Pyramid V 4070. 4th prtg. SF. VG. W2d. $4.00

ROHMER, Sax. *Trail of Fu Manchu*. 1970. Pyramid X 2192. 3rd prtg. SF. F. W2d. $6.00

ROHMER, Sax. *Trail of Fu Manchu*. 1970. Pyramid X 2192. 3rd prtg. SF. VG+. W2d. $4.75

ROHMER, Sax. *Trail of Fu Manchu*. Pyramid 1308. 2nd prtg. VG. B3d. $4.00

ROHMER, Sax. *Wrath of Fu Manchu*. 1976. DAW UW 1224. SF. VG. W2d. $5.00

ROHMER, Sax. *Wrath of Fu Manchu*. 1976. DAW 186. PBO. VG+. B6a #77. $36.50

ROHMER, Sax. *Wrath of Fu Manchu*. 1976. DAW 186. 1st edn. My. F. F2d. $15.00

ROHMER, Sax. *Yellow Claw*. 1966. Pyramid R 1317. SF. VG+. W2d. $10.00

ROLAND, K. *Cherry Pickers*. Barclay 7359. NF. B3d. $4.50

ROLAND, K. *Swivel Hips*. Barclay 7485. NF. B3d. $4.50

ROLAND, Louis. *Dangerous Affairs*. Chariot CB 130. PBO. VG. M6d. $4.50

ROLPH, C.H. edt. *Women of the Streets*. Ace 515. VG+. B3d. $8.00

ROMAINS, Jules. *Lord God of the Flesh*. 1953. Pocket 919. c/T Dunn. Fi. VG+. B5d. $5.00

ROMANO, Don. *Mafia: Operation Hit Man*. 1974. Pyramid 3444. 1st edn. My. F. F2d. $8.00

ROMANO, Romualdo. *Scirocco*. 1952. Pocket 900. c/Belarski: gga. Fa. VG+. B4d. $5.00

ROME, Anthony. *Miami Mayhem*. Pocket 1269. G+. G5d. $3.00

ROME, Anthony. *My Kind of Game*. Dell 1st Edn B 232. VG. G5d. $5.00

ROMKEY, Michael. *I, Vampire*. 1990. Gold Medal 14638. PBO. NF. B6d. $7.50

RONALD, James. *Angry Woman*. Bantam 749. VG. B3d. $4.50

RONALD, James. *This Way Out*. Popular 389. G+. G5d. $3.00

RONALD/SHARKEY. *Our Man in Space/Ultimatum in 2050 AD*. Ace M 117. F. M1d. $7.00

RONALD/SHARKEY. *Our Man in Space/ Ultimatum in 2050 AD*. Ace M 117. 1st prtg. G+. S1d. $3.00

RONNS, Edward. *Black Orchid*. 1959. Pyramid G 391. PBO. MTI c/S Loren & A Quinn: photo. Fi. VG. B5d/R5d. $7.00

RONNS, Edward. *Catspaw Ordeal*. Gold Medal 766. 2nd prtg. VG. B3d. $4.50

RONNS, Edward. *Cowl of Doom*. Hangman House 13. VG. M6d. $20.00

RONNS, Edward. *Dark Memory*. Harlequin 127. scarce. VG+. B6a #75. $41.25

RONNS, Edward. *Lady Takes a Flyer*. 1958. Avon T 228. PBO. MTI. NF. B6d. $15.00

RONNS, Edward. *Say It With Murder*. Graphic 76. VG. I1d. $4.00

RONNS, Edward. *They All Ran Away*. 1955. Graphic 114. 1st prtg. PBO. c/gga. VG. B3d. $5.50

RONSON, M. *Wild Nympho*. PAD 521. NF. B3d. $6.00

ROOKE, Daphne. *Grove of Fever Trees*. Signet 953. VG. B3d. $4.00

ROOKE, Daphne. *Ratoons*. Ballantine 42. PBO. NF. B3d. $6.00

ROONS, Edward. *Dark Destiny*. Graphic 59. VG. I1d. $4.00

ROOS, H. *Frightened Stiff*. Dell 56. G+. B3d. $5.00

ROOS, Kelley. *Blonde Died Dancing*. 1958. Dell 968. c/V Kalin. My. NF. B5d. $5.50

ROOS, Kelley. *Frightened Stiff*. 1944. Dell 56. 1st edn. PBO. c/Gregg. rare. F. B6a #80. $74.00

ROOS, Kelley. *Frightened Stiff*. Dell 687. G+. G5d. $4.00

ROOS, Kelley. *Ghost of a Chance*. Dell 266. VG+. G5d. $8.00

ROOS, Kelley. *Ghost of a Chance*. 1948. Dell 266. 1st prtg. VG. P7d. $7.50

ROOS, Kelley. *If the Shroud Fits*. 1944. Avon Murder My 13. c/W Forrest. My. G+. B5d. $10.00

ROOS, Kelley. *Made Up To Kill*. 1946. Dell 106. G. G5d. $7.50

ROOS, Kelley. *Made Up To Kill.* 1946. Dell 106. 1st edn. PBO. c/Gerald Gregg. scarce. NF. B6a #75. $36.50

ROOS, Kelley. *Made Up To Kill.* 1946. Dell 106. 1st edn. PBO. c/Gregg. VG+. B6d. $30.00

ROOS, Kelley. *Murder in Any Language.* Dell 398. NF. G5d. $9.00

ROOS, Kelley. *Murder in Any Language.* Dell 398. 1st prtg. My. G+. R5d. $3.50

ROOS, Kelley. *Requiem for a Blonde.* 1960. Dell D 386. 1st prtg. c/McGinnis: gga. VG+. P7d. $6.50

ROOS, Kelley. *Sailor, Take Warning!* Dell 155. G. G5d. $5.00

ROOSEVELT, Eleanor. *On My Own.* 1958. Dell F 86. c/E Roosevelt: photo. NF. VG. B5d. $2.50

RORICK, I.S. *Mr & Mrs Cugat.* Bantam 11. NF. B3d. $5.00

ROSANITH, Olga. *Unholy Flame.* 1952. Gold Medal 273. 1st edn. VG. M1d. $10.00

ROSCOE, Mike. *Death Is a Round Black Ball.* Signet 966. VG. G5d. $6.00

ROSCOE, Mike. *One Tear for My Grave.* Signet 1358. VG. G5d. $3.00

ROSCOE, Mike. *Riddle Me This.* 1953. Signet 1060. 1st pb. My. VG. B3d. $4.00

ROSCOE, Mike. *Slice of Hell.* 1955. Signet 1216. c/MacGuire: gga. My. VG. B4d. $3.00

ROSDICK, H.E. *Man From Nazareth.* Pocket 959. VG+. B3d. $4.00

ROSE, A. *Who's Got the Action?* Crest 572. MTI. VG. B3d. $4.00

ROSEN, V. *Dark Plunder.* Lion LL 11. VG+. B3d. $5.00

ROSEN, V. *Gun in His Hand.* Gold Medal 154. VG. B3d. $5.00

ROSENBERG, Joel. *Sword & the Chain.* 1984. Signet 2883. 1st edn. SF. F. F2d. $10.00

ROSENBERGER, Joseph. *Castro File.* 1974. Pinnacle 00264. 1st prtg. Death Merchant #7. My. VG. W2d. $3.00

ROSENBERGER, Joseph. *Pole Star Secret.* 1977. Pinnancle 40019. 1st prtg. Death Merchant #21. My. VG. W2d. $3.00

ROSENTHAL, H. *Baseball's Best Managers.* Sport 4. PBO. VG+. B3d. $7.00

ROSMANITH, Olga. *Long Thrill.* 1954. Lion 200. Fa. VG. B4d. $7.50

ROSMANITH, Olga. *Unholy Flame.* 1952. Gold Medal 273. 1st edn. VG. M1d. $10.00

ROSNY, J.H. *Quest for Fire.* 1982. Ballantine 30067. MTI. SF. VG+. B5d. $4.50

ROSNY, J.H. *Quest of the Dawn Man.* 1964. Ace F 269. 1st prtg. VG+. S1d. $4.00

ROSS, Angus. *Burgos Contract.* 1986. Walker 31384. c/S Moore. My. NF. B5d. $5.00

ROSS, Angus. *Darlington Jaunt.* 1986. Walker 31546. c/J Jinks. My. NF. B5d. $5.00

ROSS, Barnaby. *Passionate Queen.* Pocket 50497. VG. G5d. $3.00

ROSS, Barnaby. *Strange Kinship.* 1965. Pocket 50493. Fa. VG+. B4d. $4.00

ROSS, Colin. *Mistress.* 1958. Beacon 196. 1st pb. c/George Gross: gga. NF. B6d. $27.50

ROSS, Frank. *Dead Runner.* Crest 23454. My. F. W2d. $4.00

ROSS, Gene. *Two Smart Dames.* Leisure Library 9. VG. B3d. $12.00

ROSS, Gene. *You're Dead, My Lovely.* 1950. Archer Press NN. PBO. VG+. B6a #77. $66.00

ROSS, J. *Hungry for Love!* Merit 659. VG+. B3d. $4.00

ROSS, J. *They Don't Dance Much.* Signet 913. VG+. B3d. $6.00

ROSS, K. *Made Up To Kill.* Dell 106. VG+. B3d. $6.00

ROSS, Leonard Q. *Education of H*Y*M*A*N K*A*P*L*A*N.* HL PPL 29. Fi. NF. B5d. $5.00

ROSS, Leonard Q. *Sleep, My Love.* 1946. Century 66. PBO. MTI. c/photo. rare. VG+. B6a #77. $110.00

ROSS, Lillian. *Portrait of Hemingway.* Avon SS 3. 1st prtg. VG. P7d. $4.00

ROSS, Marilyn. *Assignment: Danger.* 1967. PB Library 53-466. SF. VG. W2d. $3.00

ROSS, Marilyn. *Barnabas, Quentin & the Avenging Ghost #17.* 1970. PB Library 63-338. PBO. TVTI. c/photo. VG+. P6d. $4.00

ROSS, Marilyn. *Barnabas, Quentin & the Avenging Ghost #17.* 1970. PB Library 63-338. 1st prtg. SF. F. W2d. $18.50

ROSS, Marilyn. *Barnabas, Quentin & the Body Snatchers.* 1971. PB Library 63-534. 1st prtg. VG+. R5d. $6.00

ROSS, Marilyn. *Barnabas, Quentin & the Grave Robbers #28.* 1971. PB Library 63-584. SF. VG. W2d. $10.00

ROSS, Marilyn. *Barnabas, Quentin & the Haunted Cave.* PB Library 63-427. VG+. G5d. $4.00

ROSS, Marilyn. *Barnabas, Quentin & the Hidden Tomb #31.* 1971. PB Library 64-772. 1st prtg. SF. VG. W2d. $10.00

ROSS, Marilyn. *Barnabas, Quentin & the Mad Magician #30.* 1971. PB Library 64-714. 1st prtg. SF. VG+. W2d. $15.00

ROSS, Marilyn. *Barnabas, Quentin & the Magic Potion #25.* 1971. PB Library 63-515. SF. F. W2d. $18.50

ROSS, Marilyn. *Barnabas, Quentin & the Mummy's Curse.* PB Library 63-318. VG. G5d. $4.00

ROSS, Marilyn. *Barnabas, Quentin & the Scorpio Curse.* PB Library 63-468. VG. G5d. $4.50

ROSS, Marilyn. *Barnabas, Quentin & the Scorpio Curse.* 1970. PB Library 63-468. SF. VG+. W2d. $15.00

ROSS, Marilyn. *Barnabas, Quentin & the Serpent #24.* 1970. PB Library 63-491. SF. VG. W2d. $10.00

ROSS, Marilyn. *Barnabas, Quentin & the Vampire Beauty.* PB Library 64-824. PBO. TVTI. G+. M6d. $6.50

ROSS, Marilyn. *Barnabas, Quentin & the Witch's Curse #20.* 1970. PB Library 63-402. SF. F. W2d. $18.50

ROSS, Marilyn. *Barnabas, Quentin & the Witch's Curse #20.* 1970. PB Library 63-402. SF. G. W2d. $4.00

ROSS, Marilyn. *Barnabas & Quentin's Demon.* 1970. PB Library 63-275. 1st prtg. VG. R5d. $4.00

ROSS, Marilyn. *Barnabas Collins, Quentin & the Crystal Coffin #19.* 1970. PB Library 63-385. SF. VG. W2d. $10.00

ROSS, Marilyn. *Barnabas Collins & the Mysterious Ghost #13.* 1970. PB Library 63-258. SF. VG. W2d. $10.00

ROSS, Marilyn. *Barnabas Collins & the Warlock #11.* 1969. PB Library 62-212. SF. VG. W2d. $10.00

ROSS, Marilyn. *Barnabas Collins #6.* 1968. PB Library 62-001. SF. F. W2d. $14.50

ROSS, Marilyn. *Barnabas Collins #6.* 1968. PB Library 62-001. SF. VG. M3d. $10.00

ROSS, Marilyn. *Barnabas Collins in a Funny Vein.* 1969. PB Library 62-062. 5th prtg. SF. F. W2d. $6.00

ROSS, Marilyn. *Barnabas Collins: Picture Album of Jonathan Frid.* PB Library 62-210. VG. G5d. $10.00

ROSS, Marilyn. *Behind the Purple Veil.* 1973. Warner 75084. 1st prtg. My. VG. W2d. $3.50

ROSS, Marilyn. *Beware My Love.* 1969. PB Library 63-154. 2nd prtg. SF. G+. W2d. $3.25

ROSS, Marilyn. *Brides of Saturn.* 1976. Berkley D 3273. SF. G+. W2d. $3.00

ROSS, Marilyn. *Cellars of the Dead.* 1976. Popular 00410. SF. VG. W2d. $3.75

ROSS, Marilyn. *Curse of Collinwood.* PB Library 52-608. NF. G5d. $6.50

ROSS, Marilyn. *Curse of Collinwood.* PB Library 52-608. 2nd prtg. VG+. B3d. $4.00

ROSS, Marilyn. *Dark Legend.* 1970. PB Library 63-271. 2nd prtg. SF. VG. W2d. $3.50

ROSS, Marilyn. *Dark Shadows #1.* 1969. PB Library 52-386. 7th prtg. SF. G. W2d. $7.00

ROSS, Marilyn. *Dark Shadows Book of Vampires & Werewolves.* 1970. PB Library 63419. SF. F. W2d. $11.50

ROSS, Marilyn. *Dark Shadows.* 1968. PB Library 52-386. 4th prtg. TVTI. VG. R5d. $1.25

ROSS, Marilyn. *Demon of Barnabas Collins.* 1969. PB Library 62-084. PBO. SF. VG. M3d/R5d. $6.00

ROSS, Marilyn. *Demon of Barnabas Collins.* 1969. PB Library 62-084. PBO. SF. VG+. M3d. $8.00

ROSS, Marilyn. *Desperate Heiress.* 1966. PB Library 52350. SF. G+. W2d. $3.25

ROSS, Marilyn. *Face in the Shadows.* 1973. Warner 75068. 1st prtg. My. VG. W2d. $3.25

ROSS, Marilyn. *Foe of Barnabas Collins.* 1969. PB Library 62-135. PBO. SF. VG. M3d. $6.00

ROSS, Marilyn. *Foe of Barnabas Collins.* 1969. PB Library 62-135. PBO. TVTI. G+. M6d. $3.00

ROSS, Marilyn. *House of Dark Shadows.* 1970. PB Library 64-537. 1st prtg. MTI. VG. R5d. $4.00

ROSS, Marilyn. *House of Ghosts.* 1973. PB Library 75-092. SF. VG. W2d. $3.50

ROSS, Marilyn. *Locked Corridor.* 1965. PB Library 52-870. SF. G+. W2d. $3.00

ROSS, Marilyn. *Locked Corridor.* 1969. PB Library 63-169. 2nd prtg. SF. VG. W2d. $3.50

ROSS, Marilyn. *Memory of Evil.* 1966. PB Library 52-922. 1st prtg. My. VG. W2d. $3.25

ROSS, Marilyn. *Memory of Evil.* 1970. PB Library 53-334. 2nd prtg. SF. VG. W2d. $3.50

ROSS, Marilyn. *Mistress of Moorwood Manor.* 1972. PB Library 65-916. 1st prtg. SF. VG+. W2d. $3.50

ROSS, Marilyn. *Mistress of Ravenswood.* 1970. PB Library 63-358. 2nd prtg. SF. VG. W2d. $3.75

ROSS, Marilyn. *Mystery of Collinwood.* 1968. PB Library 52-610. 1st prtg. VG+. R5d. $6.00

ROSS, Marilyn. *Peril of Barnabas Collins.* 1969. PB Library 62-244. SF. VG. M3d. $7.00

ROSS, Marilyn. *Phantom & Barnabas Collins.* 1969. PB Library 62-195. 1st prtg. G+. R5d. $2.50

ROSS, Marilyn. *Phantom Manor.* PB Library 52-895. PBO. G+. M6d. $3.50

ROSS, Marilyn. *Phantom Manor.* 1970. PB Library 63-372. 2nd prtg. My. G+. W2d. $3.00

ROSS, Marilyn. *Phantom of Fog Island.* 1971. PB Library 64692. 1st prtg. My. VG. W2d. $3.50

ROSS, Marilyn. *Phantom Wedding.* 1976. Popular 08475. 1st prtg. My. VG. W2d. $3.25

ROSS, Marilyn. *Secret of Barnabas Collins #8.* 1969. PB Library 62-039. SF. F. W2d. $18.50

ROSS, Marilyn. *Secret of Barnabas Collins.* 1969. PB Library 62-039. 3rd prtg. PBO. TVTI. c/photo. VG. P6d. $2.00

ROSS, Marilyn. *Shadow Over Emerald Castle.* 1975. Beagle 26708. SF. G+. W2d. $3.00

ROSS, Marilyn. *Step Into Terror.* 1973. Warner 75023. 1st prtg. My. VG. W2d. $3.50

ROSS, Marilyn. *Strangers at Collins House.* PB Library 52-543. VG+. B3d. $4.00

ROSS, Marilyn. *Witch of Dralhavon.* 1973. PB Library 65-894. 2nd prtg. My. VG. W2d. $3.00

ROSS, S. *Half-Way To Hell.* France 41. VG+. B3d. $6.00

ROSS, Sam. *He Ran All the Way.* 1955. Lion Library LL 59. My. VG+. B4d. $7.50

ROSS, Sam. *Hustlers.* 1956. Popular 782. PBO. scarce. JD. VG+. B6a #77. $45.25

ROSS, Sam. *This, Too, Is Love.* 1953. Red Seal 26. 1st edn. F. F2d. $10.00

ROSS, Sam. *Tight Corner.* 1957. Signet 1434. Fi. VG. B5d. $4.00

ROSS, Sam. *You Belong to Me.* 1955. Popular 657. 1st edn. My. F. F2d. $13.00

ROSS, Zola. *Bonanza Queen.* 1950. Readers Choice 25. 1st pb. We. VG. B6d. $6.00

ROSS, W. *Immortal.* Cardinal C 338. VG. B3d. $4.00

ROSSI, Bruno. *Killing Machine.* 1973. Leisure 00134. 1st prtg. Sharpshooter #1. My. VG. W2d. $3.00

ROSSMANN, John F. *Recycled Souls.* 1976. Signet 7145. 1st edn. SF. F. F2d. $12.50

ROTH, Cecil. *Magnificent Rothschilds.* 1962. Pyramid X 757. Nfi. NF. B5d. $5.50

ROTH, Holly. *Mask of Glass.* 1963. Berkley Y 713. 4th prtg. My. G+. W2d. $2.75

ROTH, Holly. *Shocking Secret.* Dell 850. VG. B3d. $4.00

ROTH, Holly. *Sleeper.* 1957. Lion LB 171. 1st edn. PBO. c/gga. NF. B6a #76. $66.00

ROTSLER, William. *Patron of the Arts.* 1974. Ballantine 24062. PBO. c/T Adams. SF. VG. B5d. $3.50

ROTSLER, William. *Return to the Planet of the Apes.* 1976. Ballantine 251220. 1st edn. TVTI. c/photo. SF. F. F2d. $10.00

ROTTENSTEINER, Franz. *SF Book.* 1975. NAL G 9978. Nfi. VG+. P1d. $15.00

ROUECHE, Berton. *Alcohol.* 1962. Black Cat BA 12. Nfi. VG. B5d. $4.50

ROUECHE, Berton. *Incurable Wound.* 1958. Berkley G 188. Nfi. VG+. B4d. $4.00

ROUECHE, Berton. *Last Enemy.* Dell 1st Edn 90. c/Hooks. NF. B3d. $5.00

ROUECHE, Berton. *Rooming House.* 1957. Lion LL 133. Fa. NF. B4d. $15.00

ROUECHE, Berton. *Rooming House.* 1957. Lion LL 133. 2nd prtg. VG+. B3d. $6.00

ROUECHE, Berton. *Rooming House.* 1953. Lion 141. PBO. scarce. NF. B6a #76. $36.50

ROUGVIE, Cameron. *Tangier Assignment.* 1965. Ballantine U 2250. 1st prtg. My. VG. R5d. $2.25

ROURKE, Thomas. *Of All My Sins.* Avon T 255. VG+. B3d. $5.00

ROURKE, Thomas. *Thunder Below.* 1954. Avon 565. 1st pb. c/gga. VG. B6d. $7.50

ROVERE, Richard H. *Weeper & the Blackmailer.* 1950. Signet 763. NF. VG. B5d. $4.00

ROVERE, Richard H. *Weeper & the Blackmailer.* 1950. Signet 763. 1st edn. PBO. c/courtroom scene. F. F2d. $8.00

ROWANS, Virginia. *Loving Couple.* 1957. Perma M 4077. c/H Schaare. Fi. G. B5d. $3.00

ROWE, James. *Artist Colony.* 1962. Playtime 610. PBO. VG. P6d. $1.00

ROWE, Julie. *Psycho Sin.* 1965. Publishers Export G 1101. PBO. c/gga. F. B6a #75. $30.25

ROWENFELD, J.R. *Sex Behind the Iron Curtain.* Brandon House 1016. VG+. B3d. $7.00

ROWLAND, D.S. *Battle Done.* 1958. Digit 203. PBO. VG+. B3d. $7.00

ROWLEY, Chris. *Golden Sunlands.* 1987. Ballantine 33174. SF. VG+. W2d. $3.25

ROY, Claude. *Agony of Love.* Hillman 142. VG. B3d. $4.00

ROY, John Flint. *Guide to Barsoom.* 1976. Ballantine 24722. 1st prtg. SF. F. W2d. $5.00

ROY, Jules. *Unfaithful Wife.* 1957. Signet 1429. 1st pb. VG. B6d. $5.00

ROYAL HIGHNESS. *Confessions of a Princess.* Avon T 106. VG. B3d. $4.00

ROYER, Francis C. *Star Seekers.* Tit-Bits SF Library NN. VG+. B3a #22. $13.20

ROYER, Louis-Charles. *French Doctor.* 1951. Pyramid 35. c/gga. Fa. VG+. B4d. $9.00

ROYER, Louis-Charles. *Harem.* 1954. Pyramid 114. c/Olson: gga. VG+. B6d. $15.00

ROYER, Louis-Charles. *Love Camp.* 1953. Pyramid 84. c/gga. NF. B6a #74. $77.00

ROYER, Louis-Charles. *Man From Paris.* 1956. Pyramid G 217. VG. B3d. $5.00

ROYER, Louis-Charles. *Man From Paris.* 1956. Pyramid G 217. 1st US edn. c/gga. NF. F2d. $8.00

ROYER, Louis-Charles. *Redhead From Chicago.* 1954. Pyramid 110. Fa. VG+. B4d. $9.00

ROYER, Louis-Charles. *Savage Triangle.* 1954. Pyramid 134. Fa. NF. B4d. $12.00

ROYER, Louis-Charles. *Savage Triangle.* 1954. Pyramid 134. Fi. G+. B5d. $4.00

RUBEL, James L. *No Business For a Lady.* 1965. Gold Medal K 1520. My. VG. B5d. $3.50

RUBEL, James L. *No Business for a Lady.* 1950. Gold Medal 114. 1st prtg. PBO. c/gga. VG. P7d. $7.50

RUBEL, James L. *Wanton One.* Newstand U 133. NF. B3d. $6.50

RUBIN, T.I. *Sweet Daddy: Story of a Pimp.* Ballantine 704. PBO. VG+. B3d. $5.50

RUBINSTEIN, S.L. *Battle Done.* EB 64. VG. B3d. $4.50

RUCKER, Rudy. *Software.* 1982. Ace 77408. SF. VG. B5d. $3.00

RUDEL, Hans Ulrich. *Stuka Pilot.* 1958. Ballantine F 276K. War. VG+. B4d. $3.00

RUDEL, Hans Ulrich. *Stuka Pilot.* Ballantine 459. 2nd prtg. VG. B4d. $4.00

RUESCH, Hans. *Racer.* Ballantine 17. PBO. G+. M6d. $3.50

RULE/WELLMAN. *Bow Down to Nul/Dark Destroyers.* 1960. Ace D 443. SF. VG+. B4d. $6.00

RUNNELS, Benny. *Blood on Big Sandy.* Vega W 100. NF. B3d. $6.00

RUNYON, Charles. *Anatomy of Violence.* 1960. Ace D 429. PBO. scarce. VG+. B6a #80. $53.50

RUNYON, Charles. *Anatomy of Violence.* 1960. Ace D 429. PBO. VG+. B3a #24. $17.85

RUNYON, Charles. *Black Moth.* 1967. Gold Medal D 1873. c/gga. My. VG+. B4d. $3.25

RUNYON, Charles. *Color Him Dead.* Gold Medal K 1320. VG. G5d. $3.50

RUNYON, Charles. *Death Cycle.* Gold Medal 1268. VG. B3d. $4.00

RUNYON, Charles. *Pigworld.* 1973. Lancer 75-446. 1st pb. c/Walotsky. NF. B6d. $15.00

RUNYON, Charles. *Power Kill.* 1972. Gold Medal T 2560. My. NF. B4d. $2.75

RUNYON, Damon. *First & Last.* Graphic 30. VG+. I1d. $6.00

RUNYON, Damon. *Guys & Dolls.* 1955. Pocket 1098. 1st prtg. VG+. R5d. $8.00

RUNYON, Damon. *Poems for Men.* Perma P 113. VG. B3d. $3.50

RUNYON, Damon. *Runyon First & Last.* Graphic 69. 2nd prtg. VG+. B3d. $6.00

RUNYON, Damon. *Runyon First & Last.* 1953. Graphic 69. 2nd prtg. VG+. B3d. $6.00

RUNYON, Damon. *Three Wise Guys.* 1946. Avon 102. c/Endris. Fi. G+. B5d. $4.00

RUSE, Gary Alan. *Death Hunt on a Dying Planet.* 1988. Signet AE 5615. SF. VG. W2d. $3.50

RUSH, Ann. *Nell Shannon, RN.* Ace D 561. PBO. VG. B3d. $4.00

RUSS, Joanna. *Adventures of Alyx.* 1986. Baen 65601. 1st edn. SF. F. F2d. $7.50

RUSS, Joanna. *And Chaos Died.* 1970. Ace 02268. 1st edn. SF. F. P9d. $3.50

RUSS, Joanna. *And Chaos Died.* Ace 02269. 2nd edn. VG. P9d. $1.50

RUSS, Joanna. *Picnic on Paradise.* Ace H 72. F. M1d. $6.00

RUSS, Joanna. *We Who Are About To.* 1977. Dell 19428. 1st edn. G. P9d. $1.25

RUSS, Martin. *Last Parallel.* 1958. Signet D 1487. c/R Schulz. Fi VG. B5d. $4.00

RUSSELL, Don. *Swap Knots.* 1969. Companion 614. PBO. c/gga. scarce. NF. B6a #76. $61.00

RUSSELL, Eric Frank. *Deep Space.* 1955. Bantam 1362. 1st pb edn. F. M1d. $12.00

RUSSELL, Eric Frank. *Deep Space.* 1955. Bantam 1362. 1st prtg. SF. G+. R5d. $3.00

RUSSELL, Eric Frank. *Dreadful Sanctuary.* 1967. Lancer 72-149. c/K Freas. SF. VG+. B5d. $5.00

RUSSELL, Eric Frank. *Dreadful Sanctuary.* 1963. Lancer 74-819. SF. VG. R5d. $3.25

RUSSELL, Eric Frank. *Great Explosion.* 1963. Pyramid F 862. c/E Emsh. SF. VG. B5d. $4.00

RUSSELL, Eric Frank. *Men, Martians & Machines.* 1965. Berkley F 1088. F. M1d. $7.00

RUSSELL, Eric Frank. *Men, Martians & Machines.* 1965. Berkley F 1088. 1st prtg. SF. VG. I1d. $4.00

RUSSELL, Eric Frank. *Men, Martians & Machines.* 1958. Berkley G 148. SF. VG+. B5d. $5.00

RUSSELL, Eric Frank. *Mindwarpers.* 1965. Lancer 72-942. PBO. c/R Powers. SF. VG. B5d. $4.00

RUSSELL, Eric Frank. *Rabble Rousers.* 1963. Regency RB 317. 1st edn. very scarce. F. F2d. $40.00

RUSSELL, Eric Frank. *Sentinels From Space.* Ace D 468. VG. M1d. $8.00

RUSSELL, Eric Frank. *Sinister Barrier.* 1966. PB Library 52-384. SF. VG. B4d/B5d. $3.00

RUSSELL, Eric Frank. *Somewhere a Voice.* 1965. Ace F 398. 1st edn. VG+. I1d. $4.00

RUSSELL, Eric Frank. *Wasp.* 1959. Perma M 4120. SF. G+. W2d. $4.00

RUSSELL, Eric Frank. *Wasp.* 1959. Perma M 4120. 1st pb edn. NF. M1d. $10.00

RUSSELL, Fred. *I'll Try Anything Twice.* Armed Services 1017. VG. B3d/B5d. $4.50

RUSSELL, John. *Lost God.* 1946. Pocket 408. PBO. My. VG. M3d. $8.00

RUSSELL, John. *SAR.* 1974. Pocket 77726. SF. G+. W2d. $3.25

RUSSELL, John. *SAR.* 1974. Pocket 77726. 1st prtg. VG. S1d. $4.00

RUSSELL, John. *Short Stories of Adventure.* Armed Services O 20. VG. B3d. $5.00

RUSSELL, Lord. *Scourge of the Swastika.* Ballantine 169. c/photo. VG. B3d. $4.00

RUSSELL, Ray. *Incubus.* 1981. Dell 14129. SF. G+. W2d. $3.00

RUSSELL, Ray. *Sagittarius.* 1971. Playboy 16131. NF. B3d. $5.00

RUSSELL, Ray. *Sagittarius.* 1971. Playboy 16131. SF. VG. B4d. $3.00

RUSSELL, W. *Berlin Embassy.* MacFadden 50-129. VG+. B3d. $5.00

RUSSELL, William. *Love Affair.* 1956. Avon 743. PBO. VG. B3d. $4.50

RUSSELL, William. *Love Affair.* 1956. Avon 743. 1st edn. My. F. F2d. $15.00

RUSSELL, William. *Wind Is Rising.* Belmont 222. VG+. B3d. $5.00

RUSSELL/RUSSELL. *Six Worlds Yonder/ Space Willies.* Ace D 315. F. M1d. $15.00

RUSSELL/RUSSELL. *Six Worlds Yonder/ Space Willies.* Ace 77785. 1st prtg. VG. S1d. $3.75

RUSSELL/WILLIAMS. *Three to Conquor/ Doomsday Eve.* 1957. Ace D 215. PBO. c/E Valigursky. SF. VG+. B5d/M1d. $8.00

RUSSELL/WOLLHEIM. *Sentinels of Space/ Ultimate Invader.* 1954. Ace D 44. PBO. F. M1d. $25.00

RUSSELL/WOLLHEIM. *Sentinels of Space/Ultimate Invader.* 1954. Ace D44. c/S Meltzoff. SF. VG. B5d. $9.00

RUSSO, B. *Uncharted Lust.* Rapture 208. VG+. B3d. $5.50

RUSSO, John. *Bloodsisters.* 1982. Pocket 41692. 1st edn. Ho. F. F2d. $13.00

RUSSO, Paul V. *Image of Evil.* Midwood 328. PBO. VG. B3d. $4.50

RUSSO, Paul V. *One Flesh.* 1961. Midwood 83. PBO. c/Wagner: gga. VG. B6d. $12.50

RUSSO, Paul V. *Restless Virgin.* 1961. Midwood 78. PBO. c/Paul Rader: gga. scarce. NF. B6a #75. $73.00

RUSSO, Paul V. *Satan in Silk.* Midwood 32-499. 2nd prtg. NF. B3d. $7.50

RUSSO, Paul V. *Soft Shoulders.* Midwood 33-788. PBO. c/photo. NF. B3d. $7.00

RUSSO, Paul V. *Stag Starlet.* Midwood F 88. VG. I1d. $5.00

RUSSO, Paul V. *This Yielding Flesh.* 1961. Midwood 94. VG. B3d. $4.00

RUSSO, Paul V. *Without Shame.* Midwood 108. VG. I1d. $7.00

RUSSO, Richard Paul. *Inner Eclipse.* 1988. TOR 55256. PBO. SF. VG+. B6d. $3.00

RUTH, Babe. *Babe Ruth Story.* Pocket 562. VG. B3d. $5.00

RUTH, Mrs. Babe. *Babe & I.* Avon T 513. VG. B3d. $4.00

RUTLEDGE, Deborah. *Natural Beauty Secrets.* 1968. Avon S 282. 3rd edn. Nfi. VG. B5d. $2.50

RYAN, Alan. *Dead White.* 1983. TOR 52451. 1st edn. NF. P9d. $2.00

RYAN, Alan. *Kill.* 1982. TOR 48055. 1st edn. NF. P9d. $2.00

RYAN, Don. *Devil's Brigadier.* 1955. Berkley G 8. c/photo. Fi. VG. B5d. $4.00

RYAN, J.M. *Brooks Wilson Ltd.* Gold Medal 1671. PBO. c/McGinnis. VG+. B3d. $5.00

RYAN, M. *Twisted Loves.* Bedside BB 807. VG. I1d. $5.00

RYAN, Patrick. *How I Won the War (Lennon J.).* Ballantine U 6110. NF. I1d. $10.00

RYAN, Riley. *Gun Hell.* Lion LB 100. VG. B3d. $4.50

RYAN, S. *Fortune Hunter.* Playtime 651. VG+. B3d. $4.00

RYAN, Thomas. *Adolescence of P-1.* 1979. Ace. 1st edn. F. M1d. $4.00

RYERSON. *Gunfire at Purgatory Gate.* 1976. Major 3094. PBO. We. NF. B6d. $7.50

SABATINI, Rafael. *Bardelys the Magnificent.* 1940s. Hillman Classic 2. 1st edn. PBO. F. F2d. $10.00

SABATINI, Rafael. *Black Swan.* 1962. Lancer 72-630. 1st pb. NF. B6d. $9.00

SABATINI, Rafael. *Captain Blood Returns.* 1976. Ballantine 24963. Fi. VG+. B5d. $4.00

SABATINI, Rafael. *Captain Blood Returns.* 1963. Popular. VG. M1d. $6.00

SABATINI, Rafael. *Captain Blood.* 1961. Pyramid R 613. VG. M1d. $6.00

SABATINI, Rafael. *Fortunes of Captain Blood.* 1950. Popular 241. MTI. c/Belarski: gga. VG+. B4d. $8.00

SABATINI, Rafael. *Fortunes of Captain Blood.* 1950. Popular 241. MTI. VG. B3d. $6.00

SABATINI, Rafael. *Fortunes of Captain Blood.* 1950. Popular 241. 1st prtg. G. R5d. $2.50

SABATINI, Rafael. *Mistress Wilding.* 1946. Avon 84. VG. B3d. $5.00

SABATINI, Rafael. *Scaramouche.* 1945. Bantam 5. Fa. VG+. B4d. $9.00

SABATINI, Rafael. *Sea Hawk.* 1961. Popular SP 109. VG+. B3d. $4.50

SABATINI, Rafael. *Sea Hawk.* 1946. Popular 91. 1st pb. Ho. VG+. B6d. $15.00

SABATINI, Rafael. *Trampling of the Lilies.* 1943. Adventure Novel 12. 1st pb. NF. B6d. $12.50

SABER, Robert O. *Dame Called Murder.* Graphic 111. VG. I1d. $5.00

SABER, Robert O. *Time for Murder.* Graphic 123. NF. G5d. $8.00

SABER, Robert O. *Too Young To Die.* Graphic 90. VG+. G5d. $7.00

SABER, W.J. *Devious Defector.* 1967. Banner B 60-108. 1st edn. scarce. My. F. F2d. $20.00

SABER, W.J. *Devious Defector.* 1967. Banner B 60-108. 1st prtg. My. G+. R5d. $3.00

SABERHAGEN, Fred. *After the Fact.* Baen 0671. 1st prtg. G. S1d. $2.00

SABERHAGEN, Fred. *Berserker Wars.* 1985. TOR 55320. 4th prtg. SF. F. W2d. $4.75

SABERHAGEN, Fred. *Berserker.* 1986. Ace 05495. 13th prtg. SF. F. W2d. $4.75

SABERHAGEN, Fred. *Berserker.* 1967. Ballantine U 5063. 1st edn. NF. M1d. $8.00

SABERHAGEN, Fred. *Berserker: Blue Death.* 1987. TOR 55329. SF. VG+. W2d. $4.50

SABERHAGEN, Fred. *Black Mountains.* 1971. Ace 06615. 1st edn. F. P9d. $2.00

SABERHAGEN, Fred. *Broken Lands.* 1968. Ace G 740. 1st prtg. SF. VG. R5d. $2.25

SABERHAGEN, Fred. *Brother Assassin.* 1969. Ballantine 72018. SF. VG+. B4d. $3.00

SABERHAGEN, Fred. *Brother Assassin.* 1969. Ballantine 72018. 1st prtg. SF. VG. R5d. $2.50

SABERHAGEN, Fred. *Dominion.* 1982. TOR 48536. 1st prtg. SF. VG. W2d. $5.00

SABERHAGEN, Fred. *Dracula Tape.* Warner 78-869. VG. G5d. $7.50

SABERHAGEN, Fred. *Empire of the East.* 1980. Ace 20563. 2nd prtg. SF. VG+. W2d. $3.00

SABERHAGEN, Fred. *Holmes-Dracula File.* 1978. Ace 34245. 1st edn. SF. VG. M3d. $7.50

SABERHAGEN, Fred. *Pyramids.* 1987. Baen 65609. SF. F. W2d. $4.25

SABERHAGEN, Fred. *Second Book of Lost Swords: Sightbinder' s Story.* 1988. TOR 55296. 1st prtg. SF. F. W2d. $4.00

SABERHAGEN, Fred. *Third Book of Swords (#2).* 1984. TOR 55303. SF. G+. W2d. $4.00

SABERHAGEN, Fred. *Thorn.* Ace 80744. G+. G5d. $5.00

SABERHAGEN, Fred. *Water of Thought.* 1981. TOR 48501. PBO. SF. NF. B6d. $3.00

SABERHAGEN, Fred. *Water of Thought.* 1985. TOR 55290. 2nd prtg. SF. F. W2d. $4.00

SABERHAGEN/WRIGHT. *Golden People/ Exile From Xanadu.* Ace M 103. F. M1d. $12.00

SABERHAGEN/WRIGHT. *Golden People/ Exile From Xanadu.* 1964. Ace M 103. 1st prtg. SF. VG. R5d. $2.75

SABIN, L. *Basketball Stars of 1972.* Pyramid 2568. c/Alcindor. VG. B3d. $4.50

SACHS, Paul J. *Pocket Book of Great Drawings.* 1961. Washington Square W 730. Nfi. VG. B5d. $3.00

SACKETT, Susan edt. *Letters to Star Trek.* 1977. Ballantine 25522. 1st prtg. VG. R5d. $4.00

SACKVILLE-WEST, V. *Edwardians.* Arrow 562. VG. B3d. $6.50

SADDENS, A. *Blackboard Bordello.* Barclay 7364. VG+. B3d. $4.50

SAFIAN, L.A. edt. *2000 Insults for All Occasions.* Pocket 50287. VG+. B3d. $4.50

SAGAN, Francois. *Bonjour Tristesse.* 1958. Dell D 166. 4th prtg. VG. R5d. $1.25

SAGAN, Francois. *Certain Smile.* Dell D 206. NF. B3d. $5.00

SAGE, Dana. *22 Brothers.* 1951. Pocket 775. c/V Kalin. My. VG. B5d. $4.00

SAGE, Dana. *22 Brothers.* 1951. Pocket 775. NF. I1d. $5.00

SAHA, Arthur. *Year's Best Fantasy #8.* 1982. DAW 501. SF. F. B4d. $6.00

SAHA, Arthur. *Year's Best Fantasy Stories.* 1986. DAW 88677. 1st edn. F. P9d. $2.00

SAINT-LAURENT, C. *Affairs of Caroline Cherie.* Dell 852. VG. B3d. $4.50

SAINTE-CLAIRE, S. *Daisy Chain Swappers.* Barclay 7438. VG+. B3d. $4.00

SAKARI, Saburo. *Samurai!* Ballantine F 248. c/photos. NF. VG. B5d. $4.00

SAKI. *Humor, Horror, & the Supernatural.* 1965. Scholastic 599. 1st prtg. SF. VG. W2d. $5.00

SALE, Richard. *Benefit Performance.* 1948. Dell 252. c/G Gregg. My. VG. B5d. $5.00

SALE, Richard. *Benefit Performance.* 1948. Dell 252. 1st prtg. My. G+. R5d. $3.50

SALE, Richard. *Death at Sea.* 1948. Popular 163. 1st pb. c/Belarski. My. VG. B6d. $12.00

SALE, Richard. *Home Is the Hangman.* 1949. Popular 205. My. VG. B4d. $10.00

SALE, Richard. *Murder at Midnight.* 1950. Popular 275. c/gga. My. VG+. B4d. $10.00

SALE, Richard. *Passing Strange.* 1953. Ace D 23. 1st edn. PBO. Fa. NF. B6a #75. $44.00

SALE, Richard. *Passing Strange.* 1953. Ace D 23. 1st edn. PBO. Fa. VG. B6d. $20.00

SALEM, Randy. *Chris.* 1959. Beacon 223. 1st prtg. PBO. VG+. P7d. $12.50

SALEM, Randy. *Sex Between.* Midwood 219. PBO. VG. B3d. $4.00

SALEM, Randy. *Soft Sin.* 1962. Midwood 196. PBO. VG+. B3a #20. $12.10

SALEM, Randy. *Tender Torment.* 1962. Midwood 172. c/Rader. VG+. B3a #20. $11.90

SALEM, Randy. *Unfortunate Flesh.* Midwood 63. VG+. I1d. $10.00

SALEM, Randy. *Unfortunate Flesh.* 1960. Midwood 63. PBO. c/Rader. VG+. B6a #80. $56.25

SALINGER, J.D. *Catcher in the Rye.* 1961. Signet D 1667. 18th edn. Fa. VG. B4d. $2.00

SALINGER, J.D. *Catcher in the Rye.* 1953. Signet 1001. c/J Avati. Fi. G+. B5d. $4.50

SALINGER, J.D. *Nine Stories.* Signet 1111. VG. B3d. $4.50

SALISBURY, Harrison E. *Shook-Up Generation.* 1959. Crest S 321. JD. VG+. P1d. $25.00

SALISBURY, Harrison E. *Shook-Up Generation.* Crest 775. VG. B3d. $4.00

SALMONSON, J.A. *Amazons II.* 1982. DAW 485. 1st edn. F. P9d. $2.00

SALMONSON, J.A. *Amazons!* 1979. DAW 364. SF. VG. B5d. $4.00

SALTEN, Felix. *Bambi.* 1940. Pocket. 6th pb edn. NF. M1d. $8.00

SALTER, Elizabeth. *Will To Survive.* 1968. Ace G 700. 1st prtg. My. G+. R5d. $1.50

SALTER, James. *Hunters.* 1958. Bantam A 1700. 1st prtg. VG. R5d. $2.00

SALTER, James. *Hunters.* Pan G 151. MTI. VG. B3d. $6.50

SALTUS, Edgar. *Imperial Orgy.* 1947. Avon 111. c/gga. Fa. VG. B4d. $6.00

SAMBROT, William. *Island of Fear & Other SF Stories.* 1963. Perma M 4278. VG. I1d. $4.00

SAMBROT, William. *Island of Fear & Other SF Stories.* 1963. Perma M 4278. 1st prtg. SF. F. W2d. $7.00

SAMUELS, Charles. *Death Was the Bridegroom.* Gold Medal 466. NF. G5d. $10.00

SAMUELS, Charles. *Death Was the Bridegroom.* Gold Medal 466. PBO. G+. M6d. $7.50

SAMUELS, Martin. *Men Want My Flesh.* 1964. Gaslight 102. PBO. NF. B6d. $9.00

SAMUELS, Victor. *Vampire Women.* 1973. Popular 0503. PBO. c/Jeff Jones. VG. B6d. $9.00

SAMUELS & SAMUELS. *Girl in the House of Hate.* 1953. Gold Medal. 1st edn. VG. M1d. $10.00

SAMUELS & SAMUELS. *Night Fell on Georgia.* 1956. Dell 1st Edn 83. 1st prtg. PBO. c/Powers. VG. P7d. $5.00

SAND, D. *Best of the Satyr Library.* Maverick. VG+. B3d. $6.00

SANDBURG, Carl. *Selected Poems of Carl Sandburg.* Armed Services 1122. VG+. B3d. $7.50

SANDERS, B. *Midnight Hazard.* Digit 739. c/Elvis look-alike. VG+. B3d. $8.00

SANDERS, E. *Family.* Avon M 110. VG. B3d. $5.00

SANDERS, George. *Crime on My Hands.* 1940s. Invincible Press NN. 1st edn. PBO. rare. VG. B6a #76. $68.00

SANDERS, J. *Sinking of Troopship Leopoldville.* MacFadden 60-151. VG. B3d. $4.00

SANDERS, Jacquin. *Girls From Goldfield (Fortune Finders).* Popular 807. c/De Soto. VG+. B3d. $5.00

SANDERS, Jacquin. *Look to Your Geese.* Avon T 496. Fi. VG+. B5d. $3.50

SANDERS, L. *Eighth Commandment.* 1987. Berkley 10005. 1st prtg. My. VG+. W2d. $4.00

SANDERS, N. *Adultress.* Bachelor 501. VG. B3d. $4.50

SANDERS, W.F. *Whip Hand.* Gold Medal 1087. VG+. B3d. $8.00

SANDERS & WILLEFORD. *Whip Hand.* 1961. Gold Medal 1087. 1st edn. c/gga. My. F. F2d. $20.00

SANDERSON, Douglas. *Mark It for Murder.* Avon T 309. My. VG. B5d. $3.00

SANDERSON, Ivan. *More Things.* 1969. Pyramid T 2005. Nfi. NF. B4d. $3.50

SANDERSON, Ivan. *Things.* 1967. Pyramid. 1st edn. F. M1d. $10.00

SANDERSON, William. *Horses Are for Warriors.* 1956. Corgi T 192. 1st pb. c/William Sanderson. We. VG+. B6d. $10.00

SANDFORD, K. *Mark of the Lion.* Popular M 2057. VG+. B3d. $4.50

SANDFORD & STEEBER. *Square Jungle.* 1960. Panther 1040. VG. B3d. $8.00

SANDOZ, Mari. *Slogum House.* Dell D 116. NF. B3d. $6.00

SANDS, Curt. *Housecall of Sin.* 1964. Corinth Stardust 112. 1st edn. c/gga. F. F2d. $15.00

SANDSTROM, Flora. *Midwife of Pont Clery.* 1958. Perma M 4097. 1st prtg. c/Knapp: gga. VG+. P7d. $4.50

SANFORD, John. *Make My Bed in Hell.* 1957. Avon T 189. VG. B3d. $4.00

SANFORD, John. *Make My Bed in Hell.* 1954. Avon 574. c/gga. Fa. VG. B4d. $5.00

SANGSTER, Jimmy. *Touchfeather, Too.* 1971. Berkley S 2065. 1st prtg. My. VG. R5d. $1.75

SANTEE, Ross. *Cowboy.* Pocket 732. G+. G5d. $3.50

SANTEE, Ross. *Lost Pony Tracks.* Bantam F 1494. 2nd edn. We. VG+. B6d. $4.00

SANTESSON, H.S. *Gentle Invaders.* 1969. Belmont B 60-1011. 1st prtg. SF. G+. R5d. $2.25

SANTESSON, H.S. *Gods for Tomorrow.* 1967. Award. 1st edn. F. M1d. $5.00

SANTESSON, H.S. *Mighty Barbarians.* 1969. Lancer 74-556. 1st prtg. SF. VG. R5d. $4.50

SANTESSON, H.S. *Mighty Swordsmen.* 1970. Lancer 74-707. c/J Steranko. SF. VG+. B5d. $6.00

SANTESSON, H.S. *Mighty Swordsmen.* 1970. Lancer 74-707. 1st edn. SF. F. F2d. $12.00

SANTESSON, H.S. *Rulers of Men.* 1965. Pyramid R 1227. c/Robert Bloch: sgn. VG. B3d. $7.00

SAPERSTEIN, David. *Cocoon.* 1985. Jove O 8400. SF. VG. B5d. $3.00

SARAC, Roger. *Throwbacks.* 1965. Belmont B 50-642. PBO. SF. VG. B5d/R5d. $4.50

SARAC, Roger. *Throwbacks.* 1965. Belmont B 50-642. 1st edn. F. M1d. $10.00

SARALEGUI, Jorge. *Shadow Stalker.* 1987. Charter. 1st edn. VG. M1d. $4.00

SARBAN. *Doll Maker.* 1960. Ballantine 431D. 1st US edn. NF. M1d. $20.00

SARBAN. *Doll Maker.* 1960. Ballantine 431K. PBO. SF. VG. B5d. $7.50

SARBAN. *Ringstones.* 1961. Ballantine 498K. Ho. VG. B4d. $10.00

SARBAN. *Sound of His Horn.* 1960. Ballantine 377K. PBO. SF. VG+. B5d. $7.50

SARGENT, R. *There Are No Angels.* Kozy 112. VG. B3d. $4.50

SARLAT, Noah. *Handfull of Hell.* Lion LL 73. PBO. VG. B3d. $4.00

SARLAT, Noah. *Rogues & Lovers.* 1956. Lion LL 83. PBO. NF. B6d. $16.50

SARLAT, Noah. *Sintown, USA.* Lion 106. VG. B3d. $4.50

SARLAT, Noah. *Spy in Black Lace.* 1964. Lancer 72-767. 1st prtg. My. VG. W2d. $3.75

SARLAT, Noah. *This Is It!* Lion LL 167. PBO. VG+. B3d. $4.50

SAROYAN, William. *Human Comedy.* 1945. Pocket 282. 1st prtg. c/Freeman. VG. P7d. $5.00

SAROYAN, William. *Rock Wagram.* 1952. Signet 945. c/gga. Fa. VG+. B4d. $4.00

SAROYAN, William. *Secret Story (Laughing Matter).* Popular G 334. VG. B3d. $4.50

SAROYAN, William. *31 by Saroyan.* Short-story 4. VG+. B3d. $6.00

SAROYAN, William. *48 Saroyan Stories.* Avon 19. VG. B3d. $5.00

SARTO, Ben. *Chicago Dames.* Modern Fiction NN. c/Perl. VG. B3d. $10.00

SARTO, Ben. *Gorrila's Moll.* Modern Fiction NN. G+. B3d. $7.50

SARTO, Ben. *Manhattan Terrors.* Modern Fiction NN. VG. B3a #21. $10.00

SARTO, Ben. *Rope for a Lady.* Modern Fiction NN. VG. B3a #20. $22.00

SARTO, Ben. *Soho Spiv.* Modern Fiction NN. c/Perl. G+. B3d. $8.00

SARTRE, J.P. *Intimacy.* 1953. Avon AT 69. 1st pb. VG+. B6d. $6.00

SARTRE, J.P. *Intimacy.* 1956. Berkley G 30. c/Nappi. VG+. B3d. $5.00

SATTERTHWAIT, Walter. *At Ease With the Dead.* 1991. World Wide 26072. c/skull. My. F. B5d. $6.00

SATTON, Jeff. *First on the Moon.* Ace D 327. VG+. B3d. $4.00

SAUL, John. *Unwanted.* 1987. Bantam 26657. SF. F. W2d. $3.75

SAUL, Martin. *Gladiators.* 1967. Signet D 3148. c/gga. Fa. VG+. B4d. $2.50

SAUL, Martin. *Gladiators.* 1967. Signet D 3148. 1st edn. Hi. F. F2d. $10.00

SAUL, Martin. *Last Nights of Pompei.* 1966. Signet D 3051. 1st American edn. VG+. B3d. $4.50

SAUNDERS, Charles R. *Imaro.* 1981. DAW 459. 1st prtg. c/Ken W Kelly. VG. P7d. $4.00

SAUNDERS, D. *Case of Chicago Cop Killers.* Belmont 91-254. TVTI. Mod Squad. VG. B3d. $6.50

SAVAGE, Hardley. *Jetman Meets the Mad Madam.* 1966. Bee Line 118. PBO. scarce. SF. VG. B6a #76. $45.00

SAVAGE, Hardley. *Jetman Meets the Mad Madam.* 1966. Bee Line 118. PBO. scarce. SF. VG+. B6a #79. $50.00

SAVAGE, James. *Girl in a Jam.* 1959. Avon T 356. PBO. My. G+. B5d. $3.00

SAVAGE, Juanita. *Don Lorenzo's Bride.* Dell 360. c/V Kalin. Fi. VG. B5d. $4.00

SAVAGE, Les Jr. *Land of the Lawless.* 1953. Pocket 978. 1st pb. We. VG+. B6d. $10.00

SAVAGE, Les Jr. *Last of the Breed* 1954. Dell 1st Edn 37. PBO. c/S Borack. We. VG. B5d. $4.00

SAVAGE, Les Jr. *Return to Warbow.* 1955. Dell 1st Edn 65. PBO. c/F McCarthy. We. G+. B5d. $2.50

SAVAGE, Les Jr. *Teresa.* 1954. Dell 1st Edn 23. PBO. c/W George. We. VG. B5d. $4.00

SAVAGE, Les Jr. *Treasure of the Brasada.* Dell 253. c/A McWilliams. We. G+. B5d. $4.00

SAVAGE, Thomas. *Lona Hanson.* 1949. Signet 728. Fi. VG. B5d/I1d. $4.00

SAVOY, Willard. *Alien Land.* Signet 767. c/Avati. VG. B3d. $4.00

SAWYER, Gary. *No Man's Land.* 1965. First Niter 219. 1st edn. F. F2d. $17.50

SAWYERS, R. *Flesh Mast.* Brandon House 3073. VG+. B3d. $5.00

SAXBY, C. *Death in the Sun.* Green 10. VG. B3d. $4.50

SAXON, John. *Common Passion.* 1947. Prize 63. c/Malcolm Smith: gga. VG. P6d. $4.00

SAXON, John. *Pushover.* 1949. Newsstand 43. VG. B3d. $6.00

SAXON, John. *Tigress.* 1950s. Novels Inc 10. 1st pb. c/gga. VG+. B6d. $15.00

SAXON, Lyle. *High Yellow.* 1952. Studio Pocket 106. 1st edn. PBO. rare. NF. B6a #76. $43.00

SAXON, Peter. *Act of Violence.* Sexton Blake 388. VG. B3d. $6.00

SAXON, Peter. *Curse of Rathlaw.* Lancer 73-750. SF. VG. W2d. $3.25

SAXON, Peter. *Dark Ways to Death.* Berkley 1712. Guardians #2. VG. B3d. $4.00

SAXON, Peter. *Darkest Night.* 1967. PB Library 52-562. SF. VG. W2d. $4.75

SAXON, Peter. *Darkest Night.* 1967. PB Library 52-562. 1st edn. F. M1d. $10.00

SAXON, Peter. *Darkest Night.* 1967. PB Library 52-562. 1st prtg. VG+. S1d. $6.00

SAXON, Peter. *Haunting of Alan Mais.* Berkley 1727. Guardians #3. VG. B3d. $4.00

SAXON, Peter. *Killing Bone.* Berkley 1703. c/Jones. Guardinas #1. VG+. B3d. $5.00

SAXON, Peter. *Last Days of Berlin.* Sexton Blake 395. VG+. B3d. $8.00

SAXON, Peter. *Satan's Child.* 1968. Lancer 73-784. 1st prtg. c/Jeff Jones: gga. VG. P7d. $6.50

SAXON, Peter. *Sea Tigers.* Sexton Blake 400. VG+. B3d. $8.00

SAXON, Peter. *Torturer.* PB Library 52-469. VG+. B3d. $5.00

SAXON, Peter. *Vampire's Moon.* 1970. Belmont B 75-1095. PBO. VG+. B6d. $8.00

SAXON, Peter. *Vampire's Moon.* 1972. Five Star NN. 1st pb. Ho. NF. B6d. $9.00

SAXON, Peter. *Vampires of Finistere.* 1970. Berkley X 1808. PBO. c/Jeff Jones. Guardians #4. VG. B6d. $5.00

SAXON, Peter. *Violent Hours.* Sexton Blake 393. VG. B3d. $7.00

SAXON, Peter. *Woman of Saigon.* Sexton Blake 369. VG. B3d. $7.50

SAXON, Rex. *Curse of Rathlaw.* 1968. Lancer 73-750. PBO. c/Jeff Jones. Fa. VG+. B6d. $9.00

SAXON, Vin. *Ape Rape.* 1964. Rapture 202. PBO. c/gga. VG+. B6a #79. $74.00

SAXON, Vin. *God of Lust.* 1964. Rapture 103. PBO. c/gga. VG. B6a #79. $73.00

SAXON/STARK. *Liability Limited/Too Many Sinners.* Ace D 81. VG. G5d. $7.50

SAYERS, D. *Stories of the Supernatural.* MacFadden 50-170. VG+. B3d. $5.00

SAYERS, Dorothy L. *Busman's Honeymoon.* 1968. Avon V 2241. c/B Driscoll. My. VG. B5d. $3.00

SAYERS, Dorothy L. *Busman's Honeymoon.* 1946. Pocket 324. 2nd edn. PBO. dust jacket. VG. F2d. $65.00

SAYERS, Dorothy L. *Have His Carcase.* 1968. Avon V 2225. 2nd edn. c/D Crowley. My. VG+. B5d. $4.00

SAYERS, Dorothy L. *Have His Carcase.* Pocket 163. G+. G5d. $6.50

SAYERS, Dorothy L. *In the Teeth of Evidence.* Avon 40. G+. B3d. $5.00

SAYERS, Dorothy L. *In the Teeth of Evidence.* 1943. Avon 40. 1st prtg. VG+. P7d. $27.50

SAYERS, Dorothy L. *Strong Poison.* 1951. Avon 328. VG+. B3a #20. $13.20

SAYERS, Dorothy L. *Strong Poison.* 1951. Avon 328. 1st prtg. My. VG. R5d. $8.00

SAYERS, Dorothy L. *Strong Poison.* 1941. Pocket 130. My. G+. B5d. $5.00

SAYERS, Dorothy L. *Suspicious Characters.* 1943. Avon 23. 1st pb. My. VG. B6d. $16.50

SAYERS, Dorothy L. *Unpleasantness at the Bellona Club.* 1940. Pocket 74. G+. G5d. $9.00

SAYERS, Dorothy L. *Whose Body?* 1948. Avon 176. c/A Cantor. My. G+. B5d. $10.00

SCARBOROUGH, E. *Bronwyn's Bane.* 1983. Bantam 23720. 1st prtg. SF. VG+. W2d. $3.25

SCARM, Arthur N. *Werewolf Vs Vampire Woman.* 1972. Guild-Hartford BG 200. MTI. VG+. B3a #21. $19.40

SCARPETTA, Frank. *Mafia Massacre.* 1974. Belmont 50-686. 1st prtg. My. VG+. R5d. $2.00

SCARPETTA, Frank. *Torture Contract.* 1975. Belmont 50-828. 1st prtg. My. VG. R5d. $1.50

SCHAAF, W.L. *Mathematics for Home & Business.* Perma P 20. VG. I1d. $3.00

SCHACHT, Al. *Clowning Through Baseball.* 1949. Bantam 507. VG+. B3a #22. $4.40

SCHAEFER, J. *Shane.* Bantam 833. VG+. I1d. $10.00

SCHAFER, Kermit edt. *Blooper Blackouts.* 1970. Gold Medal D 2204. Nfi. VG+. B5d. $5.00

SCHAFER, Kermit edt. *Super Bloopers.* Gold Medal 1331. VG. B3d. $4.00

SCHARY, Dore. *Sunrise at Campobello.* 1960. Signet D 1868. MTI. VG+. B4d. $6.00

SCHEER, K.H. *Cosmic Decoy.* 1973. Ace 66004. Perry Rhodan #21. SF. VG. B5d. $3.00

SCHEER, K.H. *Fortress Atlantis.* 1974. Ace 66035. Perry Rhodan #52. SF. F. B5d. $6.00

SCHEER, K.H. *Immortal Unknown.* 1972. Ace 65982. Perry Rhodan #13. SF. NF. B5d. $5.00

SCHEER, K.H. *Realm of the Tri-Planets.* 1973. Ace 66014. Perry Rhodan #31. SF. NF. B5d. $6.00

SCHELLENBERG, W. *Hitler's Secret Service.* Pyramid R 330. VG+. I1d. $5.00

SCHERF, Margaret. *Case of the Kippered Corpse.* 1944. My Novel Classic 75. 1st pb. My. VG+. B6d. $9.00

SCHEUER, Steven H. *Movies on TV.* 1968. Bantam Q 4158. TVTI. VG. P1d. $7.50

SCHIDDEL, Edmund. *Devil in Bucks County.* 1967. Bantam N 3385. 1st prtg. VG. P7d. $3.50

SCHIDDEL, Edmund. *Girl With the Golden Yo-Yo.* 1975. Manor 12262. 1st prtg. c/Edmund Schiddel. VG. P7d. $4.00

SCHIDDEL, Edmund. *Good & Bad Weather.* 1966. Bantam N 3199. 1st prtg. VG. P7d. $3.50

SCHIDDEL, Edmund. *Other Side of the Night.* 1954. Avon 589. c/gga. Fa. VG+. B4d. $8.00

SCHIDDEL, Edmund. *Scandal's Child.* 1963. Cardinal GC 203. 1st prtg. c/gga. VG. P7d. $4.00

SCHLEY, S.M. *Vengeance Pulls Trigger.* Death House 2. G+. B3d. $5.00

SCHLITZ, P.M. *Pleasure Madness.* Barclay 7285. NF. B3d. $5.00

SCHMIDT, H.W. *With Rommel in the Desert.* Ballantine U 5237. VG+. B3d. $4.50

SCHMIDT, H.W. *With Rommel in the Desert.* Panther 508. VG. B3d. $9.00

SCHMITZ, James H. *Agent of Vega.* 1962. Perma M 4242. SF. F. W2d. $5.50

SCHMITZ, James H. *Agent of Vega.* 1972. Tempo. 1st pb edn. F. M1d. $7.00

SCHMITZ, James H. *Lion Game.* 1973. DAW 38. PBO. c/Freas. SF. NF. B6d. $9.00

SCHMITZ, James H. *Tale of Two Clocks.* 1965. Belmont B 50-643. SF. VG+. B5d. $5.50

SCHMITZ, James H. *Telzey Toy.* 1973. DAW 82. 1st edn. F. P9d. $2.50

SCHMITZ, James H. *Universe Against Her.* Ace F 314. VG. M1d. $8.00

SCHMITZ, James H. *Witches of Karres.* Ace A 12. 1st edn. PBO. SF. G. P9d. $1.25

SCHNECK, Stephen. *Nightclerk.* 1966. Grove Press 6376. 1st edn. PBO. c/gga. F. F2d. $10.00

SCHNITZLER, Arthur. *Casanova's Homecoming.* 1948. Avon 160. 1st prtg. c/Biernacki: gga. VG. P7d. $7.50

SCHOELL, William. *Shivers.* Leisure 2235. SF. G+. W2d. $3.00

SCHOFIELD, W.G. *Ashes in the Wilderness.* PB Library 64-862. VG+. B3d. $4.50

SCHOLIFIELD, Alan. *View of Vultures.* 1968. Curtis 7004. 1st pb. VG+. B6d. $4.50

SCHOMBURG, Alex. *Picture Quiz Book.* 1950. Popular 223. PBO. c/Schomburg: gga. rare. NF. B6a #75. $152.00

SCHOONOVER, Lawrence. *Prisoner of Tordesillas.* 1960. Avon T 480. 1st prtg. VG. P7d. $5.00

SCHOONOVER, Lawrence. *Quick Brown Fox.* 1953. Bantam 1178. 1st pb. VG. B6d. $5.00

SCHREIBER, Flora. *Sybil.* Warner 79403. MTI. Nfi. F. W2d. $5.00

SCHROTER, Heinz. *Stalingrad.* Ballantine F 384K. NF. VG. B5d. $3.50

SCHUBBE, C. *Guys & Dolls in Uniform.* Barclay 7327. VG+. B3d. $4.50

SCHULBERG, Budd. *Harder They Fall.* 1949. Bantam 707. 1st prtg. c/Skemp: gga. VG+. P7d. $7.50

SCHULBERG, Budd. *What Makes Sammy Run?* Bantam 18. VG+. B3d. $6.00

SCHULBERG. *Some Faces in the Crowd.* 1965. Mayflower 8097. 1st pb. VG+. B6d. $7.50

SCHULZ, C.M. *Charlie Brown Christmas.* 1967. Signet P 3258. 1st prtg. TVTI. VG+. R5d. $4.00

SCHULZ, C.M. *Dear President Johnson.* 1965. Avon F 225. Hu. VG+. B4d. $3.00

SCHULZ, C.M. *Here Comes Charlie Brown!* Crest 722. NF. B3d. $4.50

SCHULZ, C.M. *Here's to You Charlie Brown.* Crest 1264. PBO. NF. B3d. $5.00

SCHULZ, C.M. *Teenager Is Not a Disease.* 1971. Pyramid X 2360. Hu. NF. B4d. $4.00

SCHULZ, C.M. *This Is Your Life, Charlie Brown.* Crest 1164. NF. B3d. $5.00

SCHUMACHER, Emile. *True Tales of Terror.* 1972. PB Library. 1st edn. F. M1d. $5.00

SCHUSTER, M.L. *Treasury of the World's Great Letters.* Armed Services M 24. VG. P6d. $3.00

SCHWARTZ, Irving. *Fear in the Night.* 1952. Pocket 904. VG+. P6d. $4.00

SCHWEITZER, Albert. *Primeval Forest.* 1963. Pyramid R 856. 1st pb. NF. B6d. $10.00

SCHWEITZER, Gertrude. *Obsessed.* 1950. Gold Medal 125. VG. B3d. $4.00

SCHWEITZER, Gertrude. *Obsessed.* 1958. Gold Medal 754. 2nd prtg. c/Barye. VG. P6d. $2.00

SCHWOB, Marcel. *Imaginary Lives.* Avon G 1162. F. M1d. $5.00

SCIACCA, Tony. *Kennedy & His Women.* 1976. Manor 19110. 1st prtg. c/gga. VG. P7d. $4.00

SCORTIA, Thomas. *Earthwreck!* 1974. Gold Medal. 1st edn. F. M1d. $5.00

SCORTIA, Thomas. *What Mad Oracle?* 1961. Regency RB 111. PBO. VG+. B3a #24. $22.00

SCORTIA & YARBRO edts. *Two Views of Wonder.* 1973. Ballantine 23713. PBO. c/skull. SF. VG. B5d. $3.50

SCOTLAND, Jay. *I, Barbarian.* 1959. Avon T 375. PBO. Fi. G+. B5d. $3.50

SCOTLAND, Jay. *I, Barbarian.* 1959. Avon T 375. PBO. VG+. B3d. $5.00

SCOTLAND, Jay. *Traitor's Legion.* Ace G 532. PBO. VG+. B3d. $5.50

SCOTLAND, Jay. *Veils of Salome.* Avon F 123. VG. B3d. $4.00

SCOTT, Anthony. *Carnival of Love (Mardi Gras Madness).* Lion 13. G+. B3d. $6.00

SCOTT, Anthony. *Carnival of Love.* 1949. Red Circle 13. 1st edn. PBO. c/Johnson: gga. VG. B6a #79. $44.00

SCOTT, Anthony. *Ladies of Chance.* 1949. Novel Library 27. Ad. G+. B5d. $12.50

SCOTT, Anthony. *Ladies of Chance.* 1949. Novel Library 27. VG. B3d. $15.00

SCOTT, Bradford. *Avenger.* 1956. Pyramid 219. We. VG. B4d. $5.00

SCOTT, Bradford. *Averick Showdown.* 1967. Pyramid K 1565. We. VG+. B4d. $3.00

SCOTT, Bradford. *Canyon Killers.* Pyramid 199. NF. I1d. $8.00

SCOTT, Bradford. *Curse of the Dead Man's Gold.* 1967. Pryamid K 1716. We. NF. B4d. $4.00

SCOTT, Bradford. *Dead at Sunset.* 1964. Pyramid F 1059. 1st prtg. PBO. c/Podwil. VG. P7d. $5.00

SCOTT, Bradford. *Dead Man's Trail.* 1957. Pyramid 238. PBO. We. NF. B6d. $12.00

SCOTT, Bradford. *Death Calls the Turn.* 1964. Pyramid F 1075. We. VG+. B4d. $3.00

SCOTT, Bradford. *Death's Harvest.* Pyramid 1605. VG+. B3d. $4.50

SCOTT, Bradford. *Doom Trail.* 1962. Pyramid G 745. PBO. c/Carl Hantman: gga. VG. P6d. $3.00

SCOTT, Bradford. *Gun Law.* Pyramid 1017. 2nd prtg. VG+. B3d. $4.50

SCOTT, Bradford. *Gun Law.* 1959. Pyramid 442. c/Hector Garida: gga. VG. P6d. $3.25

SCOTT, Bradford. *Guns of the Alamo.* 1960. Pyramid G 542. PBO. c/Bob Stanley. We. VG+. P6d. $3.50

SCOTT, Bradford. *Gunsmoke Talk.* 1963. Pyramid G 865. We. VG. B4d. $3.00

SCOTT, Bradford. *Haunted Valley.* 1968. Pyramid R 1776. We. VG+. B4d. $2.75

SCOTT, Bradford. *Masked Riders.* Pyramid 704. VG+. B3d. $4.50

SCOTT, Bradford. *Powder Burn.* 1957. Pyramid 258. PBO. c/M Engel. We. VG. B5d. $4.50

SCOTT, Bradford. *Raiders of the Rio Grande.* 1964. Pyramid F 1046. We. VG+. B4d. $3.00

SCOTT, Bradford. *Range Terror.* Pyramid 1088. 2nd prtg. VG+. B3d. $4.50

SCOTT, Bradford. *Rattlesnake Bandit.* 1963. Pyramid G 888. We. VG+. B4d. $2.75

SCOTT, Bradford. *Rustler's Range.* 1951. Pyramid 34. PBO. We. VG. B5d. $7.50

SCOTT, Bradford. *Rustler's Range.* 1951. Pyramid 34. We. G+. B4d. $4.00

SCOTT, Bradford. *Showdown at Skull Canyon.* Pyramid 953. VG+. B3d. $4.50

SCOTT, Bradford. *Thunder Trail.* 1967. Pyramid K 1705. We. NF. B4d. $5.00

SCOTT, Bradford. *Thundering Guns.* 1965. Pyramid F 1249. We. VG+. B5d. $3.50

SCOTT, Bradford. *Trail of Blood & Bones.* 1962. Pyramid F 807. PBO. c/J Podwill. We. VG. B5d. $3.50

SCOTT, Bradford. *Trail of Guns & Gold.* Pyramid 1102. VG+. B3d. $4.50

SCOTT, Bradford. *Trails of Steel.* 1965. Pyramid F 1142. We. VG+. B4d. $4.00

SCOTT, C. *Pagan Sex-Puritan Sex.* Brandon House 977. VG+. B3d. $4.50

SCOTT, Dennis. *Murder Makes a Villain.* 1945. Croydon 6. VG. B3a #21. $15.00

SCOTT, Glenn. *Farewell My Young Lover.* 1955. Popular 665. Fa. VG. B4d. $4.00

SCOTT, J.M. *Heather Mary.* 1955. Dell 854. 1st prtg. c/Pease: gga. VG+. B3d. $4.50

SCOTT, J.M. *Sea Wife.* 1957. Crest 162. MTI. c/photo. VG. P6d. $2.00

SCOTT, Jack Denton. *Complete Book of Pasta.* 1970. Bantam NE 5347. Nfi. VG+. B5d. $3.50

SCOTT, Jay. *America's War Heroes.* 1961. Monarch MA 314. PBO. Nfi. VG. B5d. $4.00

SCOTT, Jody. *Passing for Human.* 1977. DAW 262. 1st edn. NF. P9d. $2.00

SCOTT, John Anthony. *Ballad of America.* 1966. Bantam NP 154. Nfi. NF. B5d. $4.00

SCOTT, Jos & Len. *Mind Benders.* 1978. Tempo 11198. Close Encounters of the Third Kind. SF. VG. W2d. $4.00

SCOTT, L.K. *Backstairs.* 1953. Pyramid 103. PBO. c/J Bentley. Fi. VG. B5d. $6.00

SCOTT, Mary S. *Crime Hound.* 1944. Dell 34. 1st pb. c/Gregg. My. VG. B6d/I1d. $10.00

SCOTT, Melissa. *Game Beyond.* 1984. Baen 55918. SF. VG. W2d. $3.00

SCOTT, Michael. *Child of Shame.* 1968. Adult Book 420. PBO. c/Bonfils: gga. VG. B6a #80. $58.50

SCOTT, Michael. *Death's Heritage.* Pennant 9. VG+. B3d. $10.00

SCOTT, R.T.M. *Spider Strikes!* 1969. Berkley X 1735. 1st prtg. Spider #1. My. VG+. R5d. $5.00

SCOTT, R.T.M. *Wheel of Death.* 1969. Berkley 01774. Spider #2. SF. VG. W2d. $10.00

SCOTT, Robert L. *Between the Elephant's Eyes.* 1957. Ballantine 217. 1st pb. VG+. B6d. $8.00

SCOTT, Robert L. *God Is My Co-Pilot.* Ballantine 145. VG. B3d. $4.50

SCOTT, Robert L. *Look of the Eagle.* 1957. Ace D 234. 1st pb. c/Tossey. VG+. B6d. $12.00

SCOTT, Robert L. *Tiger in the Sky.* Ballantine 306K. PBO. VG+. B3d. $5.00

SCOTT, Robert L. *Tiger in the Sky.* 1959. Ballantine 306K. PBO. c/photo. NF. VG. B5d. $3.50

SCOTT, Robert L. *Tiger in the Sky.* 1959. Ballantine 306K. PBO. NF. B6d. $10.00

SCOTT, Thurston. *I'll Get Mine.* 1952. Popular 452. JD. VG+. P1d. $45.00

SCOTT, Thurston. *I'll Get Mine.* 1952. Popular 452. 1st edn. PBO. scarce. VG+. B6a #79. $72.50

SCOTT, Warwick. *Cockpit.* 1953. Lion 140. PBO. VG. B6d. $12.50

SCOTT, Warwick. *Doomsday.* 1953. Lion 148. PBO. VG. P6d. $6.00

SCOTT/YOUNG. *Brazos Firebrand/Hell on Hoofs (Quarter Horse).* Ace D 10. PBO. G+. B3d. $5.00

SCULLIN, George. *Paint Your Wagon.* MacFadden 75-304. PBO. MTI. VG. M6d. $6.50

SCULLY, Frank. *Behind the Flying Saucers.* 1951. Popular 326. 1st pb. c/Bergey. VG. B6d. $10.00

SEABROOK, Leslie. *Wexford Co-Eds.* 1967. Signet P 3257. c/gga: photo. Fa. VG+. B4d. $4.00

SEABROOK, William. *Asylum.* 1947. Bantam 106. Nfi. NF. B4d. $7.50

SEARLES, Baird. *Reader's Guide to SF.* 1979. Avon. 1st edn. F. M1d. $7.00

SEARLES, Lin. *Stampede at Houglass.* 1964. Ace D 590. PBO. VG. B3d. $3.50

SEARLS, Hank. *Astronaut.* 1962. Pocket 6093. 1st edn. SF. F. F2d. $10.00

SEARLS, Hank. *Big X.* Four Square 274. VG+. B3d. $6.50

SEARLS, Hank. *Jaws: The Revenge.* 1987. Berkley 10546. 1st edn. My. F. F2d. $8.00

SEARLS, Hank. *Jaws: The Revenge.* 1987. Berkley 10546. 1st prtg. VG+. R5d. $2.00

SEARLS, Hank. *Pilgrim Project.* 1965. Crest R 798. 1st prtg. SF. VG+. B3d. $4.50

SEATON, George John. *Isle of the Damned.* 1952. Popular 444. Fa. VG. B4d. $4.00

SEDGWICK, A.D. *Little French Girl.* Pocket 30. 2nd prtg. VG+. B3d. $7.00

SEEDS, W. *Diary of a Masseuse.* Connoisseur 115. VG+. B3d. $5.00

SEELEY, E.S. *Sorority Sin.* 1959. Beacon 278. 1st prtg. PBO. c/Rodewald: gga. VG. P7d. $9.00

SEELEY, E.S. *Street Walker.* 1959. Beacon 241. 1st prtg. PBO. c/Barton: gga. VG+. P7d. $12.50

SEELEY, M. *Chuckling Fingers.* 1950. Popular 231. 1st pb. c/Belarski. My. VG. B3d. $8.00

SEELEY, M. *Crying Sisters.* Popular 370. VG. B3d. $6.00

SEELEY, M. *Listening House.* Popular 69. VG. B3d. $5.00

SEIFERT, Adele. *Kill Your Own Snakes.* 1947. Boardman NN. VG. B3d. $7.00

SEIFERT, Elizabeth. *Certain Doctor French.* 1947. Bantam 122. c/N Lannon. Fi. G+. B5d. $2.00

SEIFERT, Elizabeth. *Girl Intern.* Harlequin 326. VG. B3d. $4.00

SELA, Owen. *Bearer Plot.* 1975. Dell 0414. 1st prtg. My. VG. W2d. $3.00

SELBY, Curt. *I, Zombie.* 1977. DAW 496. F. P9d. $2.00

SELBY, Hubert Jr. *Last Exit to Brooklyn.* 1965. Grove Press 4663. 1st prtg. VG. P7d. $6.00

SELBY, Hubert Jr. *Room.* Dell 07524. 1st prtg. VG. P7d. $4.00

SELDEN, Neil R. *Drawing the Dead.* 1983. Dell 92141. Twilight Zone #16. SF. VG. W2d. $3.25

SELLERS, Connie. *Animal Broad.* 1960. Novel Books 5025. PBO. VG+. B6d. $10.00

SELLERS, Connie. *Brute.* 1961. Novel Books 5031. 1st edn. Th. F. F2d. $20.00

SELLERS, Connie. *FSC.* 1963. Novel Books 6081. 1st edn. scarce. SF/Fa. F. F2d. $40.00

SELLERS, Connie. *Handful of Death.* 1966. Bee Line 138. Fa. VG. B4d. $2.00

SELLERS, Connie. *Red Rape!* 1960. Headline 105. PBO. scarce. VG+. B6a #77. $51.00

SELLERS, Connie. *Red Rape!* 1960. Headline 105. 1st edn. VG. M1d. $25.00

SELLERS, Connie. *Wench!* 1960. Novel Books 5028. 1st edn. c/photo. F. F2d. $14.00

SELLINGS, Arthur. *Power of X.* 1970. Berkley X 1801. PBO. c/P Lehr. SF. VG+. B5d. $5.00

SELLINGS, Arthur. *Quy Effect.* 1967. Berkley X 1350. PBO. c/R Powers. SF. VG. B5d. $3.00

SELLINGS, Arthur. *Quy Effect.* 1967. Berkley X 1350. 1st edn. F. M1d. $5.00

SELLINGS, Arthur. *Telepath.* 1962. Ballantine F 609. SF. F. W2d. $7.50

SELLINGS, Arthur. *Telepath.* 1962. Ballantine F 609. 1st prtg. SF. VG. R5d. $4.50

SELLINGS, Arthur. *Uncensored Man.* 1967. Berkley X 1379. SF. VG. W2d. $4.00

SELMARD, T. *Bawdy Setup.* Candlelight 105. VG+. B3d. $5.00

SELTZER, Charles Alden. *Arizona Jim.* Popular 204. VG+. B3d. $6.00

SELTZER, Charles Alden. *Drag Harlan.* Armed Services 1030. We. VG. B5d. $4.00

SELTZER, Charles Alden. *Vengeance of Jefferson Gawne.* Armed Services 1071. We. VG. B5d. $4.50

SELTZER, N. *More Sweetie Pie.* Berkley 381. c/cartoons. VG. B3d. $3.00

SELTZER, N. *Sweetie Pie.* Berkley 320. VG. B3d. $3.50

SEMPLE, Gordon. *Life of Pasion.* Stork NN 1. PBO. VG. B3d. $15.00

SEMPLE, Gordon. *Passion's Way.* 1946. Century 94. VG+. B3a #20. $31.90

SEMPLE, Gordon. *Reckless Passion.* 1949. Pyramid 12. c/gga. Fa. VG. B4d. $9.00

SEMPLE, Gordon. *Slave of Desire.* Croyden 18. PBO. VG. B3d. $10.00

SEMPLE, Gordon. *Waterfront Blonde.* 1960. Beacon B 352. PBO. c/gga. Ad. G. B5d. $2.00

SEMPLE, Gordon. *Waterfront Blonde.* 1960. Beacon B 352. 1st edn. c/gga. F. F2d. $15.00

SERAN, V. *Branded Women.* Bee Line 287. VG. B3d. $4.50

SERLING, Rod. *Devils & Demons.* 1967. Bantam H 3324. 1st prtg. My. G. R5d. $1.00

SERLING, Rod. *More Stories From the Twilight Zone.* 1961. Bantam A 2227. TVTI. VG. P1d. $10.00

SERLING, Rod. *New Stories From the Twilight Zone.* 1965. Bantam EP 121. 9th prtg. SF. G+. W2d. $5.50

SERLING, Rod. *Night Gallery #2.* 1972. Bantam SP 7203. 2nd prtg. SF. F. W2d. $10.50

SERLING, Rod. *Other Worlds.* 1978. Bantam 11275. SF. G+. W2d. $3.00

SERLING, Rod. *Season To Be Wary.* 1968. Bantam S 3851. 1st prtg. SF. G+. R5d. $2.00

SERLING, Rod. *Season To Be Wary.* 1968. Bantam S 3851. 1st prtg. VG. P7d. $3.50

SERLING, Rod. *Stories From the Twilight Zone.* 1964. Bantam EP 89. 16th prtg. SF. VG. W2d. $3.25

SERLING, Rod. *Twilight Zone.* 1965. Tempo T 89. NF. P9d. $2.00

SERLING, Rod. *Witches, Warlocks & Werewolves.* 1967. Bantam H 3493. 9th prtg. SF. VG. W2d. $3.50

SERLING, Rod. *Witches, Warlocks & Werewolves.* Bantam J 2623. VG. B3d. $6.00

SERRA, Art. *Lament for a Virgin.* 1961. Midwood 84. PBO. c/Wagner: gga. NF. B6d. $25.00

SERRA, Art. *Tease Me, Baby.* 1962. Epic 134. PBO. VG. B6d. $3.50

SERVISS, Garrett. *Invasion of Mars.* 1969. Powell. 1st pb edn. F. M1d. $20.00

SETON, Anya. *Dragonwyck.* Pocket 365. G+. G5d. $3.50

SETON, Anya. *Dragonwyck.* Pocket 365. VG+. B3d. $5.00

SETON, Anya. *Hearth & Eagle.* Lancer 73-405. Fi. VG+. B5d. $5.00

SETON, Anya. *Hearth & Eagle.* 1950. Pocket 723. c/B Prins. Fi. VG. B5d. $4.00

SETON, Ernest Thompson. *Wild Animals I Have Known.* 1946. Bantam 59. Fa. NF. B4d. $9.00

SETTEL, Irving. *Best Television Humor of the Year.* 1956. Ace D 175. TVTI. VG. P1d. $10.00

SETTLE, M.L. *Fight Night on a Sweet Saturday.* Ballantine U 5040. VG. B3d. $4.00

SEWARD, Jack. *Chinese Pleasure Girl.* 1969. Tower 43209. My. G. W2d. $2.75

SHAARA, Michael. *Soldier Boy.* 1982. Pocket 83342. SF. VG. W2d. $3.00

SHACKLEFORD, JACK D. *Strickland Demon.* 1977. Corgi 10464. 1st UK edn. c/gga. VG. B3d. $9.00

SHAFER, Robert. *Naked & the Damned.* Popular 686. VG. B3d. $5.00

SHAH, Diane K. *As Crime Goes By.* 1990. Bantam 28310. 1st prtg. My. VG. W2d. $3.25

SHAKESPEARE, William. *Age of Kings.* 1961. Pyramid T 37. 1st edn. TVTI. F. F2d. $12.00

SHAKESPEARE, William. *Five Great Comedies.* Pocket 114. VG. I1d. $5.00

SHALLIT, Joseph. *Billion-Dollar Body.* Avon 558. G. G5d. $3.00

SHALLIT, Joseph. *Juvenile Hoods.* 1957. Avon T 170. JD. VG. P1d. $20.00

SHALLIT, Joseph. *Juvenile Hoods.* 1957. Avon T 170. 1st prtg. My. G+. R5d. $3.00

SHALLIT, Joseph. *Lady, Don't Die on My Doorstep.* Avon 461. VG. B3d. $6.00

SHANE, Ted. *Bar Guide.* 1950. Gold Medal 135. Nfi. VG+. B4d. $6.00

SHANNON, Dell. *Blood Count.* 1988. World Wide 26006. 1st prtg. My. VG. W2d. $3.00

SHANNON, Dell. *Cold Trail.* 1989. World Wide 26027. 1st prtg. My. F. W2d. $3.50

SHANNON, Doris. *Seekers.* 1975. Gold Medal M 3226. SF. G+. W2d. $3.00

SHANNON, Fred. *Weightless in Gaza.* 1970. Tower 060-12. 1st edn. SF. F. F2d. $12.00

SHANNON, Jimmy. *Devil's Passkey.* Signet 1027. 1st pb. My. VG. B6d. $12.00

SHANNON, Steve. *Hell-Fire Kid.* Gold Medal 1390. 2nd prtg. VG+. B3d. $5.00

SHAPIRO, Irwin. *Story of Yankee Whaling.* 1965. Perennial P 1013. Nfi. VG+. B5d. $4.00

SHAPIRO, Neil. *Planet Without a Name.* 1976. Major 3099. SF. F. W2d. $4.50

SHAPPIRO, Herbert. *Texan.* Signet 708. VG. B3d. $5.00

SHARKEY, J. *Addams Family.* Pyramid R 1229. PBO. G+. M6d. $5.00

SHARON, S. *No Barriers.* Domino 72-792. PBO. VG+. B3d. $5.00

SHARON, Sylvia. *Murky Underground.* Beacon 1071. VG. B3d. $4.00

SHARON, Sylvia. *Obey Me, My Love.* 1965. Lancer 72-923. PBO. VG+. B6d. $9.00

SHARON, Sylvia. *We Love in Shadow.* Domino 72-782. PBO. VG+. B3d. $5.00

SHARP, Margery. *Cluny Brown.* 1944. Armed Services R 22. Fa. VG. B4d. $6.00

SHARP, Margery. *Miss Bianca.* 1964. Berkley F 1014. 1st pb. Fa. NF. B6d. $12.50

SHARP, Margery. *Nutmeg Tree.* 1942. Pocket 169. 1st pb. c/Salter. VG+. B6d. $6.00

SHARP, Margery. *Stone of Chasity.* Armed Services T 12. VG. B3d. $4.50

SHARP, Margery. *Stone of Chastity.* Avon 165. VG. B3d. $5.00

SHARP, Margery. *Stone of Chastity.* 1955. Avon 624. 3rd edn. SF. G+. B5d. $4.50

SHARPE, William. *Brain Surgeon.* Ballantine 292K. c/photo. NF. VG. B5d. $3.50

SHATTUCK, Richard. *Said the Spider to the Fly.* Popular 125. G+. G5d. $9.00

SHAVER, R.S. *Hidden World (#3).* 1961. Palmer A 3. SF. F. W2d. $20.00

SHAW, Adam. *Buccaneer's Revenge.* 1967. Signet 3174. 1st edn. c/gga. Hi. F. F2d. $10.00

SHAW, Adam. *Shipwrecked on Paradise.* 1967. Signet 3159. 1st edn. c/gga. Av. F. F2d. $10.00

SHAW, Andrew. *Adulterers.* 1960. Nightstand NB 1511. Ad. G+. B5d. $3.00

SHAW, Andrew. *Born To Lust.* Evening Reader ER 746. PBO. NF. M6d. $12.50

SHAW, Andrew. *Corinth Midnight.* 1962. Corinth Midnight 463. 1st edn. c/gga. F. F2d. $13.00

SHAW, Andrew. *Devil's Maidens.* 1973. Nightstand 3056. PBO. c/photo. VG. P6d. $4.00

SHAW, Andrew. *Hot Rod Rogues.* 1967. Ember Library 375. PBO. c/gga. VG+. B6a #77. $88.00

SHAW, Andrew. *Hush-Hush Town.* Ember Library EL 336. PBO. G+. M6d. $12.50

SHAW, Andrew. *Jazz Sinner.* 1966. Leisure 1143. PBO. scarce. NF. B6a #80. $97.00

SHAW, Andrew. *Lover.* 1961. Nightstand NB 1551. Ad. G+. B5d. $3.00

SHAW, Andrew. *Lust Campus.* Midnight Reader MR 408. VG. I1d. $4.00

SHAW, Andrew. *Lust Damned.* Midnight Reader MR 405. VG. I1d. $4.00

SHAW, Andrew. *Mountain of Sin.* 1966. Ember Library 332. PBO. c/Bonfils. NF. B6a #80. $77.00

SHAW, Andrew. *Olympic Orgy.* 1965. Evening Reader ER 1214. PBO. VG. P6d. $3.00

SHAW, Andrew. *Passion in Paint.* Midnight Reader MR 402. G. I1d. $2.00

SHAW, Andrew. *Passion Night Mare.* 1962. Midnight Reader MR 436. VG. P6d. $3.00

SHAW, Andrew. *Voyeur.* Leisure LB 1118. PBO. VG. M6d. $15.00

SHAW, Andrew. *Wild Ones.* Evening Reader ER 713. PBO. VG. P6d. $6.00

SHAW, Bob. *Night Walk.* 1967. Banner B 60-110. 1st edn. c/Frazetta. scarce. SF. F. F2d. $25.00

SHAW, Bob. *One Million Tomorrows.* Ace 62938. PBO. c/L & D Dillion: Ace SF Special. SF. NF. B5d. $6.50

SHAW, Bob. *Palace of Eternity.* 1969. Ace 65050. SF. VG. W2d. $5.00

SHAW, Bob. *Shadow of Heaven.* 1968. Avon S 398. PBO. c/E Soyka. SF. VG. B5d. $3.00

SHAW, Bob. *Shadow of Heaven.* 1969. Avon 5398. 1st edn. VG. P9d. $1.50

SHAW, Bob. *Tomorrow Lies in Ambush.* 1973. Ace 81656. 1st edn. F. M1d. $6.00

SHAW, Bob. *Tomorrow Lies in Ambush.* 1973. Ace 81656. 1st prtg. SF. VG. W2d. $3.50

SHAW, Bob. *Two Timers.* Ace H 79. 1st prtg. G+. S1d. $3.00

SHAW, Bob. *Wreath of Stars.* 1978. Dell 19710. SF. F. W2d. $5.00

SHAW, Charles. *Flesh & the Spirit.* Popular 543. VG. B3d. $5.50

SHAW, Charles. *Heaven Knows, Mr Allison.* 1957. Popular EB 88X. 1st prtg. G+. R5d. $2.25

SHAW, Howard. *Crime of Giovanni Venturi.* Crest 466. VG+. B3d. $5.00

SHAW, Irwin. *Day the War Ends.* Belmont 232. VG. B3d. $4.00

SHAW, Irwin. *Tip on a Dead Jockey.* 1959. Pan G 295. VG. B3d. $8.50

SHAW, Irwin. *Troubled Air.* Four Square 66. VG+. B3d. $8.00

SHAW, Irwin. *Two Weeks in Another Town.* 1961. Signet T 1892. Fa. VG. B4d. $3.00

SHAW, Irwin. *Voices of a Summer's Day.* 1966. Dell 9355. 1st prtg. c/Wohlberg. VG. P7d. $4.00

SHAW, Joseph edt. *Spurs West!* 1951. Perma P 126. 1st pb. We. VG+. B6d. $10.00

SHAW, L. *Rickshaw Boy.* Armed Services 968. Fi. VG+. B5d. $5.50

SHAW, Robert. *Man in the Glass Booth.* Ace 51780. VG+. B3d. $5.00

SHAW, Sam. *Marilyn Monroe As the Girl.* 1955. Ballantine 108. PBO. MTI. VG. B6a #79. $66.00

SHAW, Wilene. *Heat Lightning.* 1954. Ace S 74. PBO. c/Avatl. F. B6a #74. $33.00

SHAW, Wilene. *One Foot in Hell.* 1961. Ace D 520. PBO. My. NI. B6d. $25.00

SHAW, Wilene. *One Foot in Hell.* 1961. Ace D 520. PBO. VG+. B3d. $6.50

SHAW, Wilene. *Tame the Wild Flesh.* 1960. Ace D 464. PBO. c/Copeland. VG+. B6d. $30.00

SHAY, Frank. *Pirate Wench.* 1960. Pyramid G 517. 2nd edn. Fi. VG. B5d. $6.50

SHAYNE, Michael. *Dangerous Dames.* 1955. Dell 1st Edn 77. PBO. c/R Stanley. My. G+. B5d. $3.00

SHAYNE, Michael. *Marked for Murder.* 1951. Dell 503. c/Robert Stanley. VG. P6d. $2.00

SHEA, J.V. edt. *Strange Barriers.* Lion Library LL 47. VG. I1d. $5.00

SHEA, Michael. *Nifft the Lean.* 1982. DAW 508. 1st edn. Ho. F. F2d. $12.00

SHEA, Michael. *Quest for Simbalis.* 1974. DAW 88. 1st edn. SF. NF. F2d. $10.00

SHEA & WILSON. *Illuminatus I -- Eye of the Pyramid.* 1975. Dell 4688. 1st edn. VG. P9d. $1.75

SHEA & WILSON. *Illuminatus II -- The Golden Apple.* 1975. Dell 4691. 1st edn. F. P9d. $2.50

SHEA & WILSON. *Illuminatus III -- Liviathan.* 1975. Dell 4724. 1st edn. F. P9d. $2.50

SHEAR, David. *Cloning.* 1978. Pinnacle 40450. 2nd prtg. SF. VG. W2d. $3.75

SHEARER, J. *Sodom, USA!* Brandon House 954. VG+. B3d. $5.00

SHEARING, Joseph. *Aunt Beardie.* Armed Services 923. My. VG. B5d. $4.50

SHEARING, Joseph. *Golden Violet.* Dell 818. VG. B3d. $5.00

SHEARING, Joseph. *Lady & the Arsenic.* Armed Services L 24. Nfi. G. B5d. $2.50

SHEARING, Joseph. *Moss Rose.* 1965. Berkley X 1067. 1st pb. NF. B6d. $9.00

SHEARING, Joseph. *So Evil My Love.* Pocket 560. VG+. G5d. $6.00

SHEARING, Joseph. *Spectral Bride.* Mercury 99. c/Salter. VG+. B3d. $5.00

SHEARING, Joseph. *Spider in the Cup.* 1963. Berkley X 1105. 1st pb. VG+. B6d. $7.00

SHEARING, Joseph. *Strange Case of Lucille Clery.* Pan 592. VG. B3d. $3.50

SHECKLEY, Robert. *After the Fall.* 1980. Ace 00941. SF. VG. B5d. $3.50

SHECKLEY, Robert. *Citizen in Space.* Ballantine F 648. 1st prtg. F. S1d. $5.50

SHECKLEY, Robert. *Citizen in Space.* Ballantine F 648. 2nd prtg. VG. B3d. $4.00

SHECKLEY, Robert. *Citizen in Space.* Ballantine 126. VG+. I1d. $8.00

SHECKLEY, Robert. *Citizen in Space.* 1955. Ballantine 126. 1st edn. F. M1d. $15.00

SHECKLEY, Robert. *Dimension of Miracles.* 1968. Dell 1940. 1st edn. F. M1d. $8.00

SHECKLEY, Robert. *Dimension of Miracles.* 1968. Dell 1940. 1st prtg. PBO. c/Lehr. VG+. P7d. $4.00

SHECKLEY, Robert. *Game of X.* 1966. Dell. 1st pb edn. VG. M1d. $8.00

SHECKLEY, Robert. *Immortality, Inc.* 1959. Bantam A 1991. SF. VG. B4d. $3.00

SHECKLEY, Robert. *Journey Beyond Infinity.* 1969. Dell. 1st edn. F. M1d. $7.00

SHECKLEY, Robert. *Journey Beyond Tomorrow.* 1962. Signet. 1st edn. F. M1d. $8.00

SHECKLEY, Robert. *Mindswap.* 1978. Ace. 1st pb edn. F. M1d. $4.00

SHECKLEY, Robert. *Notions Unlimited.* Bantam 2003. PBO. c/sgn. VG. B3d. $5.00

SHECKLEY, Robert. *People Trap.* 1968. Dell 6881. 1st edn. NF. M1d. $7.00

SHECKLEY, Robert. *People Trap.* 1968. Dell 6881. 1st prtg. PBO. VG. P7d. $4.00

SHECKLEY, Robert. *Pilgrimage to Earth.* 1957. Bantam A 1672. 1st edn. F. M1d. $12.00

SHECKLEY, Robert. *Pilgrimage to Earth.* 1957. Bantam A 1672. 1st prtg. SF. VG. R5d. $3.50

SHECKLEY, Robert. *Shards of Space.* 1962. Bantam 2443. 1st edn. SF. F. F2d. $17.50

SHECKLEY, Robert. *Shards of Space.* 1962. Bantam 2443. 1st edn. VG. M1d. $8.00

SHECKLEY, Robert. *Status Civilization.* 1968. Dell 8249. SF. NF. M3d. $7.50

SHECKLEY, Robert. *Status Civilization.* 1968. Dell 8249. 1st prtg. VG+. P7d. $4.50

SHECKLEY, Robert. *Status Civilization.* 1960. Signet. 1st edn. F. M1d. $12.00

SHECKLEY, Robert. *Store of Infinity.* 1960. Bantam A 2170. 1st edn. F. M1d. $12.00

SHECKLEY, Robert. *Store of Infinity.* 1960. Bantam A 2170. 1st prtg. VG. P7d. $3.50

SHECKLEY, Robert. *Tenth Victim.* 1979. Ace 80176. SF. G+. W2d. $3.00

SHECKLEY, Robert. *Tenth Victim.* 1965. Ballantine U 5050. 1st edn. SF. F. F2d. $20.00

SHECKLEY, Robert. *Tenth Victim.* Mayflower NN. MTI. VG. B3d. $5.00

SHECKLEY, Robert. *Time Limit.* 1967. Bantam 3001. 1st edn. Th. F. F2d. $15.00

SHECKLEY, Robert. *Untouched by Human Hands.* 1967. Ballantine U 2855. 1st prtg. G+. S1d. $2.00

SHECKLEY, Robert. *Untouched by Human Hands.* 1967. Ballantine U 2855. 67th prtg. SF. VG. W2d. $3.25

SHECKLEY, Robert. *Untouched by Human Hands.* 1960. Ballantine 437K. 2nd edn. SF. VG. B5d. $4.00

SHECKLEY, Robert. *Untouched by Human Hands.* 1954. Ballantine 73. PBO. VG+. B3d. $8.00

SHECKLEY, Robert. *Untouched by Human Hands.* 1954. Ballantine 73. 1st edn. c/Jack Coggins. SF. F. F2d. $25.00

SHECKLEY, Robert. *Untouched by Human Hands.* 1954. Ballantine 73. 1st prtg. VG. S1d. $6.00

SHECKLEY, Robert. *White Death.* 1963. Bantam 2685. 1st edn. My. F. F2d. $15.00

SHECTER, Leonard. *Roger Maris.* 1961. Sport Magazine 11. PBO. VG+. B3a #24. $5.50

SHECTER, Leonard. *Roger Maris: Home Run Hero.* 1961. Sport Magazine 11. PBO. c/photo. Bio. VG. P6d. $10.00

SHEDD, Robert K. *Wicked Wife.* 1961. Newsstand U 141. 2nd edn. AD. VG+. B5d. $5.00

SHEEAN, Vincent. *Rage of the Soul.* 1953. Signet S 1038. c/J Avati. Fi. VG. B5d. $3.50

SHEEN, Fulton J. *Peace of the Soul.* 1955. Perma M 1000. c/Cardinal Sheen: photo. Nfi. VG+. B4d. $3.00

SHEEN, Fulton J. *Three To Get Married.* 1954. Dell D 141. 1st prtg. c/photo. VG. P7d. $4.00

SHEERS, James. *Counterfeit Courier.* 1961. Dell 1st Edn B 186. PBO. My. VG. B6d. $4.50

SHEFF, A.L. *How To Write Letters for All Occasions.* Perma P 2. NF. I1d. $4.00

SHEFFIELD, Charles. *Erasmus Magister.* 1982. Ace 21526. SF. VG+. B5d. $4.00

SHEFFIELD, Charles. *McAndrew Chronicles.* 1983. TOR 48566. SF. VG. W2d. $3.50

SHEFFIELD, Charles. *Proteus Unbound.* 1989. Ballantine 34434. SF. F. W2d. $4.00

SHEFTER, Harry. *6 Minutes to Perfect Spelling.* 1954. Cardinal C 145. Nfi. VG+. B4d. $4.00

SHELDON, R. *Atoms in Action.* Panther 47. VG. B3d. $6.00

SHELDON, Sidney. *Naked Face.* 1984. Warner 34191. 5th prtg. My. VG+. W2d. $3.25

SHELDON, Walt. *Man Who Paid His Way.* 1957. Bantam A 1656. 1st prtg. My. G+. R5d. $1.75

SHELDON, Walt. *Troubling of a Star.* 1954. Bantam 1221. NF. B3d. $5.00

SHELDON, Walter J. *Red Flower Kill.* Gold Medal T 2387. PBO. VG. M6d. $4.50

SHELLABARGER, Samuel. *Captain From Castile.* Bantam 860. VG+. B3d. $6.50

SHELLABARGER, Samuel. *Prince of Foxes.* 1952. Bantam A 973. 1st pb. VG. B6d. $6.00

SHELLEY, Mary *Frankenstein.* 1963. Airmont CL 19. SF. VG. B5d. $2.50

SHELLEY, Mary. *Frankenstein.* 1963. Airmont CL 19. SF. F. W2d. $4.50

SHELLEY, Mary. *Frankenstein.* Dell 2717. 1st prtg. NF. S1d. $2.00

SHELLEY, Mary. *Frankenstein.* Lion 146. VG. B3d. $10.00

SHELLEY, Mary. *Frankenstein.* 1957. Pyramid R 290. F. M1d. $20.00

SHELLEY, Mary. *Frankenstein.* 1957. Pyramid R 290. SF. VG+. B5d. $9.00

SHELLEY, Paul. *Saturday's Harvest.* 1953. Gold Medal 315. PBO. c/Barye. VG+. B6d. $12.00

SHELLEY, Sidney. *Francine.* 1963. Belmont 90-294. Ad. VG+. B5d. $5.00

SHELLEY, Sidney. *McKenzie Break.* 1970. Dell 5128. 1st prtg. VG. R5d. $1.50

SHEPARD, F. *Nurse in Danger.* MacFadden 40-135. VG+. B3d. $4.00

SHEPARD, J. *Coolman.* Belmont 50-732. VG+. B3d. $5.00

SHEPHERD, Billy. *True Story of the Beatles.* 1964. Bantam HZ 2850. Nfi. VG+. B4d. $8.00

SHEPHERD, Eric. *Demise of a Louise.* Belmont 91-248. G+. G5d. $3.00

SHEPPARD, Don. *Flesh Peddlers.* Pike 212. VG+. B3d. $5.50

SHEPPARD, Don. *Scarlet Virgin.* 1962. Pike 215. PBO. c/photo. G+. P6d. $3.00

SHER, Jack. *Love in a Goldfish.* 1961. Cardinal C 409. 1st prtg. VG. R5d. $2.00

SHERBURNE, Zoa. *Girl Who Knew Tomorrow.* Scholastic 1804. SF. VG. W2d. $3.25

SHERF, M. *Case of the Kippered Corpse.* Hillman 75. VG. B3d. $5.00

SHERIDAN, Jack. *Mamie Brandon.* 1951. Popular 312. VG. I1d. $6.00

SHERIDAN, Jack. *Thunderclap.* 1951. Gold Medal 184. PBO. VG+. B3d. $6.00

SHERMAN, D. *Swapped Wives.* Jewel 9501. VG. B3d. $4.50

SHERMAN, Hal. *Fishing for Laughs.* 1964. Ace F 288. PBO. NF. B6d. $18.00

SHERMAN, J. *Lust on Canvas.* Anchor 102. NF. B3d. $6.00

SHERMAN, J. *Reckless.* Venus 113. VG. B3d. $7.00

SHERMAN, J. *Soldier's Girl.* Croyden 86. VG. B3d. $6.00

SHERMAN, J. *Summer Man.* Challenge 209. c/Maguire. VG. B3d. $4.50

SHERMAN, Jane. *Lesbian Queen.* 1964. Playtime 682. 1st edn. F. F2d. $12.00

SHERMAN, Jane. *Twilight Lust.* 1964. Playtime 662. 1st edn. c/gga. F. F2d. $8.00

SHERMAN, Joan. *Suzy.* 1960. Beacon B 364. PBO. Ad. VG. B5d. $6.00

SHERMAN, Joan. *Suzy.* 1964. Beacon B 739. 2nd edn. Ad. VG+. B5d. $5.00

SHERMAN, Joan. *Thrill Me Suzy.* Quarter Book 93. c/Nappi: gga. reprint. scarce. VG+. B6a #77. $71.50

SHERMAN, Jory. *Fires of Autumn.* 1967. All Star AS 139. Ad. VG+. B5d. $5.00

SHERMAN, Richard. *To Mary With Love.* 1947. Bantam 124. c/N Lannon. Fi. VG. B5d. $4.00

SHERMAN, Robert. *Picture Mommy Dead.* 1966. Lancer 72-123. MTI. c/Zsa Zsa: photo. VG+. B4d. $7.00

SHERMAN, Robert. *Picture Mommy Dead.* 1966. Lancer 72-123. 1st edn. c/color photo. SF. F. F2d. $12.00

SHERMAN. *Vegas Vampire.* 1980. Pinnacle 40-223. PBO. NF. B6d. $7.50

SHERRELL, Carl. *Raum.* 1977. Avon 33043. 1st edn. F. P9d. $2.00

SHERRY, Edna. *Defense Does Not Rest.* 1960. Pocket 6033. My. VG. B5d. $3.50

SHERRY, Edna. *Defense Does Not Rest.* 1960. Pocket 6033. 1st pb. My. NF. B6d. $6.00

SHERRY, Edna. *Murder at Nightfall (Backfire).* 1957. Dell 933. G+. G5d. $5.00

SHERRY, Edna. *Sudden Fear.* 1952. Dell 604. 1st prtg. c/Meese: gga. VG. P7d. $5.50

SHERRY, John Olden. *Departure.* 1954. Popular 606. 1st pb. VG+. B5d. $12.00

SHERRY & TRALINS. *Pleasure Was My Business.* 1964. PB Library 52-204. 3rd edn. Nfi. VG. B5d. $3.00

SHERWOOD, Danni. *So Strange a Love.* 1964. Midwood F 363. PBO. NF. B6d. $18.00

SHERWOOD, Deborah. *Young & the Restless.* 1976. Bantam Q 2556. 1st prtg. TVTI. VG+. R5d. $2.00

SHERWOOD, J.S. *Searching Light.* Badger RS 019. VG. I1d. $5.00

SHERWOOD, John. *Dr Bruderstein Vanishes.* Mercury 161. VG. G5d. $5.00

SHERWOOD, Robert E. *Roosevelt & Hopkins, Volume 2.* 1950. Bantam NN. c/photo. Nfi. VG. B5d. $3.00

SHICK & ROSESON. *Care of Your Child.* Dell 340. c/photo. Nfi. VG. B5d. $4.00

SHIEL, M.P. *Purple Cloud.* 1963. PB Library 52-232. 1st pb edn. NF. M1d. $5.00

SHIFFRIN, A.B. *Glitter.* Popular 485. VG. I1d. $4.00

SHIMTH, H. Allen. *Lost in the Horse Latitudes.* Armed Services S 22. Nfi. VG. B5d. $4.00

SHIRAS, Wilmar H. *Children of the Atom.* 1958. Avon T 221. VG. B3d. $4.00

SHIRAS, Wilmar H. *Children of the Atom.* 1958. Avon T 221. 1st pb edn. F. M1d. $8.00

SHIRE, T. *Boy-Loving Woman.* Barclay 7316. VG. B3d. $4.00

SHIRER, William. *Traitor.* 1951. Popular 363. Fa. VG. B4d. $5.00

SHIRLEY, Glenn. *Outlaw Queen.* 1960. Monarch America MA 303. PBO. c/Bob Stanley. G. P6d. $1.50

SHIRLEY, John. *City Come-A-Walkin'.* 1980. Dell 15499. 1st edn. scarce. Ho. F. F2d. $18.00

SHIRREFFS, G.D. *Ambush on the Mesa.* Gold Medal 1071. 2nd prtg. c/sgn. NF. B3d. $8.00

SHIRREFFS, G.D. *Ambush on the Mesa.* Gold Medal 328. c/sgn. VG. B3d. $7.00

SHIRREFFS, G.D. *Apache Butte.* Ace D 412. PBO. c/Shirreffs: sgn. VG. B3d. $6.00

SHIRREFFS, G.D. *Bugles on the Prairie.* Gold Medal 238. c/sgn. VG. B3d. $7.50

SHIRREFFS, G.D. *Five Graves to Boot Hill.* Avon G 1335. c/sgn. VG. B3d. $5.00

SHIRREFFS, G.D. *Lonely Gun.* Avon T 312. c/sgn. VG. B3d. $4.00

SHIRREFFS, G.D. *Massacre Creek.* Popular 832. c/sgn. VG. B3d. $4.50

SHIRREFFS, G.D. *Range Rebel.* 1956. Pyramid 192. We. VG. B4d. $3.75

SHIRREFFS, G.D. *Shadow of a Gunman.* Ace D 400. PBO. c/inscr. VG. B3d. $6.50

SHIRREFFS, G.D. *Shadow Valley.* Popular SP 401. c/sgn. VG+. B3d. $6.00

SHOEMAKER, H. *Good-Bye, Cruel World.* Playboy 16123. VG+. B3d. $4.00

SHOLS, W.W. *Perry Rhodan #16: Secret Barrier X.* 1972. Ace 65986. SF. VG+. B5d. $4.00

SHORT, Luke. *Ambush.* 1950. Bantam 853. We. VG. B3d. $4.50

SHORT, Luke. *And the Wind Blows Free.* Bantam 748. VG. B3d. $4.00

SHORT, Luke. *Barren Land Murders.* Gold Medal 159. G+. G5d. $3.00

SHORT, Luke. *Barren Land Murders.* 1951. Gold Medal 159. 1st edn. Hi. F. F2d. $18.00

SHORT, Luke. *Blood on the Moon.* 1948. Bantam 204. VG+. B3d. $5.00

SHORT, Luke. *Blood on the Moon.* 1948. Bantam 204. We. NF. B4d. $12.00

SHORT, Luke. *Bold Rider.* 1953. Dell 1st Edn 7. PBO. c/W Russwig. We. VG. B5d. $4.00

SHORT, Luke. *Bounty Guns.* Dell 702. c/S Borack. We. NF. B5d. $6.00

SHORT, Luke. *Bounty Guns.* Dell 869. c/S Borack. We. VG. B5d. $3.00

SHORT, Luke. *Brand of Empire.* Dell 769. c/S Borack. We. VG. B5d. $3.00

SHORT, Luke. *Bull-Whip.* Bantam 747. VG. B3d. $5.00

SHORT, Luke. *Coroner Creek.* 1948. Bantam 140. c/B Barton. My. VG. B5d. $4.00

SHORT, Luke. *Fiddlefoot.* Bantam 854. VG. B3d. $4.50

SHORT, Luke. *Hands Off!* 1949. Bantam 703. 1st edn. PBO. c/Stanley. F. F2d. $6.50

SHORT, Luke. *Hard Money.* 1949. Bantam 209. c/Saunders. We. VG+. B3d. $6.00

SHORT, Luke. *Hard Money.* 1949. Bantam 209. We. F. B4d. $12.00

SHORT, Luke. *Hardcase.* Bantam 112. VG+. B3d. $5.00

SHORT, Luke. *Man on the Blue.* 1954. Dell 1st Edn 31. PBO. c/S Borack. We. VG. B5d. $3.00

SHORT, Luke. *Marauder's Moon.* 1955. Dell 70. c/photo back. We. VG+. B4d. $4.25

SHORT, Luke. *Raiders of the Rimrock.* 1949. Bantam 258. c/R Stanley. We. G+. B5d. $5.00

SHORT, Luke. *Raiders of the Rimrock.* 1949. Bantam 258. c/Stanley. We. VG+. B4d. $9.00

SHORT, Luke. *Rawhide & Bob-Wire.* Bantam 1865. NF. B3d. $5.00

SHORT, Luke. *Ride the Man Down.* Bantam 1063. VG. B3d. $4.00

SHORT, Luke. *Ride the Man Down.* Bantam 82. VG+. B3d. $5.00

SHORT, Luke. *Rimrock.* 1956. Bantam 1466. 1st pb. We. NF. B6d. $9.00

SHORT, Luke. *Rustlers.* Bantam 702. VG. B3d. $4.50

SHORT, Luke. *Savage Range.* 1957. Dell 963. c/S Bates. We. VG. B5d. $3.00

SHORT, Luke. *Station West.* 1948. Bantam 139. 1st pb. MTI. We. VG. B6d. $6.00

SHORT, Luke. *Sunset Graze.* 1956. Bantam 1531. We. VG+. B4d. $3.00

SHORT, Luke. *Trumpets West.* Dell 10¢ 1. NF. B3d. $15.00

SHORT, Luke. *War on the Cimarron.* 1950. Bantam 792. 1st pb. We. VG+. B3d. $4.50

SHORT, Luke. *War on the Cimarron.* 1945. We Novel Classic 40. VG. P6d. $3.50

SHRIBER, Ione Sandberg. *As Long As I Live.* 1949. Bantam 320. My. VG+. B4d. $9.00

SHRIBER, Ione Sandberg. *Family Affair.* Superior M 641. G. G5d. $3.50

SHUBIN, Seymour. *Wellville, USA.* Beacon 588F. PBO. Ad. NF. B5d. $6.50

SHULMAN, Irving. *Amboy Dukes.* 1956. Avon T 138. JD. G+. B4d. $2.00

SHULMAN, Irving. *Amboy Dukes.* 1949. Avon 169. Fi. VG. B5d/P7d. $7.50

SHULMAN, Irving. *Amboy Dukes.* Avon 300. VG. B3d. $6.00

SHULMAN, Irving. *Calibre.* 1957. Popular 817. 1st edn. Hi. F. F2d. $15.00

SHULMAN, Irving. *Children of the Dark.* 1957. Popular G 175. JD. VG+. P1d. $35.00

SHULMAN, Irving. *College Confidential.* 1960. Gold Medal 1005. 1st edn. c/photo. F. F2d. $14.00

SHULMAN, Irving. *College Confidential.* Gold Medal 517. c/Mamie Van Doren. VG. B3d. $8.00

SHULMAN, Irving. *Cry Tough!* 1950. Avon 244. c/gga. JD. VG+. B4d/B6d. $15.00

SHULMAN, Irving. *Cry Tough!* 1951. Avon 372. VG. B3d. $4.50

SHULMAN, Irving. *Notorious Landlady.* 1962. Gold Medal S 1197. 1st prtg. VG. R5d. $3.50

SHULMAN, Irving. *Upbeat.* 1965. Lancer 73-433. 1st edn. c/gga. My. F. F2d. $12.00

SHULMAN, Irving. *West Side Story.* 1961. Cardinal GC 122. 1st prtg. VG+. B5d/R5d. $4.00

SHULMAN, Max. *Barefoot Boy With Cheek.* Bantam 1939. VG+. B3d. $4.00

SHULMAN, Max. *Feather Merchants.* Armed Services Q 5. VG+. B3d. $6.00

SHULMAN, Max. *Feather Merchants.* Pocket 728. VG+. B3d. $4.50

SHULMAN, Max. *I Was a Teen-Age Dwarf.* 1960. Bantam F 2140. Hu. VG+. B4d. $3.00

SHULMAN, Max. *I Was a Teen-Age Dwarf.* Pan 630. VG. B3d. $7.00

SHULMAN, Max. *Many Loves of Dobie Gillis.* 1960. Bantam F 2041. 1st prtg. TVTl. VG. R5d. $4.00

SHULMAN, Sandra. *Daughter of Astaroth.* 1968. PB Library 53-689. 1st edn. De. F. F2d. $10.00

SHULMAN & YOUMAN. *Television Years.* 1973. Popular 08215. TVTl. VG. P1d. $5.00

SHUTE, Nevil. *Chequer Board.* Dell D 109. VG+. B3d. $6.00

SHUTE, Nevil. *In the Wet.* 1957. Perma M 4095. SF. VG. B5d. $4.00

SHUTE, Nevil. *Landfall.* 1972. Ballantine 02661. 1st prtg. VG+. P7d. $4.00

SHUTE, Nevil. *Lonely Road.* Pan M 268. 1st pb. reprint. Ad. VG. B6d. $3.50

SHUTE, Nevil. *Most Secret.* 1963. Ballantine X 689. 1st pb. VG. B6d. $5.00

SHUTE, Nevil. *No Highway.* 1951. Dell 516. MTI. VG. B3d. $6.00

SHUTE, Nevil. *No Highway.* 1951. Dell 516. 1st prtg. G+. R5d. $2.50

SHUTE, Nevil. *On the Beach.* 1958. Signet D1562. SF. VG. B5d. $4.00

SHUTE, Nevil. *On the Beach.* 1960. Signet. 6th prtg. MTI. F. M1d. $8.00

SHUTE, Nevil. *Pastoral.* 1945. Pocket Books 281. PBO. VG+. P6d. $3.50

SHUTE, Nevil. *Summer in Salandar.* 1958. Signet S 1602. 1st prtg. c/Powers: gga. VG+. P7d. $5.50

SHUTTON, Henry. *Exhibitionist.* 1968. Crest P 1192. 1st prtg. c/photo. NF. P7d. $5.00

SHWARTZ, Susan. *Hecate's Cauldron.* 1982. DAW 469. 1st prtg. NF. S1d. $3.00

SICHEL, Pierre. *Never Say Love (Such As We).* Popular G 149. VG. B3d. $3.50

SIDNEY, Cynthia. *Love Business.* 1966. Midwood 33-640. Ad. NF. B5d. $6.50

SIDNEY, Gale. *Strange Circle.* 1959. Beacon 281. PBO. c/gga. VG+. B6d. $10.00

SIEGEL, Benjamin. *Witch of Salem.* 1953. Gold Medal 307. PBO. c/Sewell. VG+. B6d. $12.00

SIEGEL, Jerry. *High Camp Superheroes.* 1966. Belmont 50-695. PBO. VG. B3d. $4.50

SIEGEL, Martin. *Agent of Entropy.* 1969. Lancer 74-753. 1st edn. VG. P9d. $1.50

SIEGELS. *Cybil & Bruce: Moonlighting Madness.* 1987. St Martin 90724. 1st prtg. VG. R5d. $1.50

SIEMEL, Sasha. *Tigrero.* 1957. Ace D 218. Fa. VG+. B4d. $5.00

SIEVERT, John. *CADS.* 1985. Zebra 08217. SF. F. W2d. $4.25

SIFAKIS, C. *Catalogue of Crime.* Signet 8821. VG. B3d. $4.00

SILBERSTANG, Edwin. *Rapt in Glory.* 1964. Pocket 50004. My. VG+. B5d. $3.50

SILLIPHANT, Stirling. *Maracaibo.* 1956. Popular EB 74. MTI. c/gga. VG+. B4d. $8.00

SILLIPHANT, Stirling. *Naked City.* 1959. Dell 1st Edn A 180. 1st prtg. TVTl. G+. R5d. $2.50

SILLITOE, Alan. *Counterpoint.* 1968. Avon S 344. MTI. c/Charlton Heston & Maximilian Schell: photo. VG+. B4d. $4.00

SILLITOE, Alan. *Saturday Night & Sunday Morning.* 1960. Pan G 391. 4th prtg. MTI. VG. B3d. $8.00

SILLITOE, Alan. *Saturday Night & Sunday Morning.* 1960. Signet D 1842. 1st prtg. c/Barye. VG. P7d. $5.00

SILONE, I. *Fox & the Camellias.* Popular K 7. c/Hooks. VG+. B3d. $4.50

SILVA & WELLS. *Island of Dr Moreau.* 1971. Ace 37421. 1st prtg. MTI. VG. R5d. $1.75

SILVERBERG, Dan Eliot. *Flesh Flames.* Ember Book EB 912. PBO. VG. M6d. $7.50

SILVERBERG, Dan Eliot. *Lust Lover.* Pillar PB 803. PBO. VG. M6d. $7.50

SILVERBERG, Dan Eliot. *Sin Hellion.* Ember Book EB 913. PBO. VG. M6d. $10.00

SILVERBERG, Robert. *Alpha 2.* 1971. Ballantine 2419. 1st edn. NF. P9d. $1.75

SILVERBERG, Robert. *Alpha 3.* 1972. Ballantine 02883. 1st edn. SF. F. F2d. $10.00

SILVERBERG, Robert. *Alpha 5.* 1974. Ballantine 24140. SF. F. W2d. $4.75

SILVERBERG, Robert. *Alpha 7.* 1977. Berkley 3530. 1st edn. NF. P9d. $1.75

SILVERBERG, Robert. *Alpha.* 1970. Ballantine 2014. 1st edn. F. P9d. $2.00

SILVERBERG, Robert. *Another Night, Another Love.* 1959. Midwood 29. 1st edn. c/gga. F. F2d. $30.00

SILVERBERG, Robert. *Bella on the Roof.* 1967. Banner B 60-109. 1st edn. scarce. My. F. F2d. $20.00

SILVERBERG, Robert. *Best of.* 1976. Pocket. 1st edn. F. M1d. $8.00

SILVERBERG, Robert. *Born With the Dead.* 1988. TOR. 1st edn. F. M1d. $5.00

SILVERBERG, Robert. *Collision Course.* Ace 11510. 1st prtg. VG+. S1d. $2.00

SILVERBERG, Robert. *Convention Girl.* 1961. Corinth NB 1547. 1st edn. c/gga. F. F2d. $17.50

SILVERBERG, Robert. *Cube Root of Uncertainty.* 1971. Collier 02539. 1st prtg. VG. P7d. $5.00

SILVERBERG, Robert. *Deep Space.* Dell 3264. 3rd edn. F. P9d. $2.00

SILVERBERG, Robert. *Earth's Other Shadow.* 1973. Signet Q 5538. 2nd prtg. SF. G+. W2d. $2.75

SILVERBERG, Robert. *Fabulous Rockefellers.* 1963. Monarch K 68. 1st edn. F. M1d. $15.00

SILVERBERG, Robert. *First American Into Space.* 1961. Monarch SP 1. Nfi. VG. B4d. $4.25

SILVERBERG, Robert. *Gilgamesh the King.* 1985. Bantam. 1st pb edn. F. M1d. $5.00

SILVERBERG, Robert. *Godling, Go Home!* 1964. Belmont 92-591. 1st edn. F. M1d. $10.00

SILVERBERG, Robert. *Great Short Novels of SF.* Ballantine 01960. 1st prtg. G+. S1d. $3.00

SILVERBERG, Robert. *Great Short Novels of SF.* 1970. Ballantine. 1st edn. NF. M1d. $4.00

SILVERBERG, Robert. *Hawsbill Station.* 1970. Avon S 411. SF. VG. W2d. $4.00

SILVERBERG, Robert. *How To Spend Money.* 1963. Regency 318. 1st edn. F. F2d. $20.00

SILVERBERG, Robert. *Invaders From Earth.* 1968. Avon S 365. c/D Crowley. SF. VG+. B5d. $3.50

SILVERBERG, Robert. *Lord of Darkness.* 1984. Bantam. 1st pb edn. F. M1d. $5.00

SILVERBERG, Robert. *Masks of Time.* 1968. Ballantine U 6121. SF. VG+. W2d. $4.50

SILVERBERG, Robert. *Master of Life & Death.* 1968. Avon S 329. SF. VG+. W2d. $5.50

SILVERBERG, Robert. *Mind to Mind.* 1974. Dell 5652. 1st prtg. SF. VG. R5d. $1.75

SILVERBERG, Robert. *Moonferns & Starsongs.* Ballantine 02278. PBO. VG+. B3d. $6.00

SILVERBERG, Robert. *Nebula Awards 18.* 1984. Bantam. 1st pb edn. F. M1d. $4.00

SILVERBERG, Robert. *Needle in a Timestack.* Ballantine U 2330. PBO. VG+. B3d. $7.50

SILVERBERG, Robert. *New Dimensions 3.* 1974. Signet Q 5805. SF. VG+. B4d. $2.00

SILVERBERG, Robert. *Next Stop the Stars.* 1977. Ace 57420. SF. VG+. B4d. $4.00

SILVERBERG, Robert. *Reality Trap.* 1972. Ballantine. 1st edn. F. M1d. $6.00

SILVERBERG, Robert. *Recalled to Life.* 1962. Lancer 74-810. PBO. c/E Emsh. SF. VG+. B5d. $6.50

SILVERBERG, Robert. *Seed of Earth.* Ace 75875. 2nd edn. NF. P9d. $1.75

SILVERBERG, Robert. *SF Bestiary.* 1974. Dell 8139. SF. F. W2d. $6.00

SILVERBERG, Robert. *SF Bestiary.* 1974. Dell 8139. 1st prtg. G+. S1d. $3.00

SILVERBERG, Robert. *SF Hall of Fame.* 1971. Avon 00115. SF. G. W2d. $3.00

SILVERBERG, Robert. *Silent Invaders.* 1973. Ace 76390. 2nd edn. SF. VG+. B5d. $4.00

SILVERBERG, Robert. *Stochastic Man.* 1976. Gold Medal 13570. 1st prtg. VG. P7d. $4.00

SILVERBERG, Robert. *Thorns.* 1967. Ballantine U 6097. PBO. c/Foster. SF. VG. B6d. $7.50

SILVERBERG, Robert. *Those Who Watch.* 1967. Signet P 3160. SF. G+. W2d. $3.25

SILVERBERG, Robert. *Time Hoppers.* 1968. Avon S 372. SF. VG. B4d. $2.00

SILVERBERG, Robert. *Time of Changes.* 1979. Berkley 04051. SF. F. W2d. $4.00

SILVERBERG, Robert. *Time of the Great Freeze.* 1966. Dell. 1st pb edn. F. M1d. $5.00

SILVERBERG, Robert. *To Open the Sky.* Ballantine U 6093. PBO. VG+. B3d. $7.00

SILVERBERG, Robert. *To Open the Sky.* 1984. Bantam. 1st edn. F. M1d. $4.00

SILVERBERG, Robert. *Up the Line.* 1969. Ballantine 01680. SF. VG. B4d. $3.00

SILVERBERG, Robert. *Valley Beyond Time.* 1973. Dell 9249. c/sgn. VG+. B3d. $10.00

SILVERBERG, Robert. *Valley Beyond Time.* 1973. Dell 9249. 1st edn. SF. F. F2d. $10.00

SILVERBERG, Robert. *World Inside.* 1978. Panther 04741. SF. VG. B5d. $35.00

SILVERBERG, Robert. *3 Trips in Time & Space.* Dell 8827. 1st prtg. VG. S1d. $4.00

SILVERBERG/SILVERBERG. *Next Stop the Stars/Seed of Earth.* Ace F 145. F. M1d. $9.00

SILVERBERG/SILVERBERG. *Next Stop the Stars/Seed of Earth.* Ace F 145. PBO. VG+. B3d. $6.00

SILVERBERG/SILVERBERG. *Next Stop the Stars/Seed of Earth.* 1962. Ace F 145. 1st prtg. SF. G+. R5d. $2.25

SILVERBERG/TEMPLE. *Silent Invaders/Battle on Venus.* Ace F 195. F. M1d. $8.00

SILVERBERG/TEMPLE. *Silent Invaders/Battle on Venus.* 1963. Ace F 195. PBO. c/E Emsh & E Valigurski. SF. NF. B5d. $7.00

SILVERBERG/WHITE. *Aliens Among Us.* 1969. Ballantine 01545. 1st edn. SF. F. F2d. $12.00

SILVERBERG/WHITE. *Master of Life & Death/Secret Visitors.* 1957. Ace D 237. PBO. c/Emsh. SF. VG+. M3d. $12.00

SILVERBERG/WHITE. *Master of Life & Death/Secret Visitors.* 1957. Ace D 237. 1st edn. SF. F. F2d. $15.00

SILVERBERG/WHITE. *Master of Life & Death/Secret Visitors.* 1957. Ace D 237. 1st prtg. SF. G+. R5d. $4.00

SILVERBERG/WRIGHT. *Stepsons of Terra/Man Called Destiny.* Ace D 311. c/Emsh. F. M1d. $12.00

SILVERBERG/WRIGHT. *Stepsons of Terra/Man Called Destiny.* Ace D 311. VG. B3d. $4.00

SILVERMAN, A. *Warren Spahn: Immortal Southpaw.* 1961. Sport Magazine 9. PBO. VG+. B3d. $7.00

SILVERSTEIN, S. *Grab Your Socks!* Ballantine 163. PBO. VG+. B3d. $12.00

SIMAK, Clifford D. *All Flesh Is Grass.* 1966. Berkley X 1312. 1st pb. SF. VG+. B6d. $7.50

SIMAK, Clifford D. *All the Traps of Earth.* 1963. MacFadden 50-165. 1st edn. PBO. F. P9d. $2.50

SIMAK, Clifford D. *All the Traps of Earth.* 1963. MacFadden 50-165. 1st pb edn. NF. M1d. $8.00

SIMAK, Clifford D. *Cemetery World.* 1983. DAW 00825. SF. VG. B5d. $2.50

SIMAK, Clifford D. *Choice of Gods.* Berkley 02412. 1st prtg. NF. S1d. $3.00

SIMAK, Clifford D. *Choice of Gods.* Berkley 2412. VG. P9d. $1.50

SIMAK, Clifford D. *City.* 1958. Ace D 283. SF. VG. B5d. $6.50

SIMAK, Clifford D. *City.* 1958. Ace D 283. 1st prtg. SF. G+. R5d. $2.75

SIMAK, Clifford D. *City.* 1967. Ace H 30. PBO. SF. F. F2d. $7.50

SIMAK, Clifford D. *City.* 1967. Ace H 30. SF. VG. W2d. $4.00

SIMAK, Clifford D. *City.* Ace 10621. SF. F. W2d. $4.00

SIMAK, Clifford D. *City.* Ace 10621. 1st prtg. VG+. S1d. $3.00

SIMAK, Clifford D. *City.* 1953. Perma 264. 1st edn. PBO. SF. NF. F2d. $12.00

SIMAK, Clifford D. *Cosmic Engineers.* 1970. PB Library 63432. 4th prtg. SF. VG. W2d. $3.50

SIMAK, Clifford D. *Destiny Doll.* Berkley S 2103. 1st prtg. VG+. S1d. $3.00

SIMAK, Clifford D. *Empire.* 1951. Galaxy Novel 7. 1st edn. c/sgn. SF. F. F2d. $60.00

SIMAK, Clifford D. *Enchanted Pilgrimage.* Berkley S 2987. 1st prtg. G+. S1d. $3.00

SIMAK, Clifford D. *First He Died.* 1953. Dell 680. c/W Brooks. SF. VG. B5d. $7.50

SIMAK, Clifford D. *First He Died.* 1953. Dell 680. 1st edn. PBO. SF. F. F2d/M1d. $15.00

SIMAK, Clifford D. *Goblin Reservation.* 1968. Berkley 1671. NF. B3d. $6.00

SIMAK, Clifford D. *Goblin Reservation.* 1968. Berkley 1671. 1st edn. F. M1d. $10.00

SIMAK, Clifford D. *Goblin Reservation.* 1968. Berkley 1671. 1st prtg. G+. S1d. $3.00

SIMAK, Clifford D. *Highway of Eternity.* 1988. Ballantine 32497. 1st prtg. SF. VG. R5d. $1.50

SIMAK, Clifford D. *Other Worlds of.* 1960. Avon. 1st pb edn. F. M1d. $7.00

SIMAK, Clifford D. *Out of Their Minds.* 1970. Berkley S 1879. SF. VG. B4d. $2.00

SIMAK, Clifford D. *Out of Their Minds.* 1970. Berkley S 1879. 1st pb edn. F. M1d. $7.00

SIMAK, Clifford D. *Out of Their Minds.* DAW 514. 1st prtg. NF. S1d. $3.00

SIMAK, Clifford D. *Project Pope*. 1982. Ballantine 29139. SF. VG. W2d. $3.00

SIMAK, Clifford D. *Ring Around the Sun*. Ace 339. VG. I1d. $4.00

SIMAK, Clifford D. *Ring Around the Sun*. Avon S 270. 1st prtg. G+. S1d. $3.50

SIMAK, Clifford D. *Ring Around the Sun*. 1969. Avon V 2317. 3rd prtg. SF. VG. W2d. $3.50

SIMAK, Clifford D. *Shakespeare's Planet*. 1977. Berkley 03394. SF. VG+. W2d. $3.25

SIMAK, Clifford D. *So Bright the Vision*. 1968. Ace H 95. 1st edn. c/sgn. SF. F. F2d. $35.00

SIMAK, Clifford D. *Special Deliverance*. 1982. Ballantine 29140. SF. F. W2d. $4.50

SIMAK, Clifford D. *Special Deliverance*. 1982. Ballantine 29140. 1st prtg. SF. VG+. R5d. $2.50

SIMAK, Clifford D. *Strangers in the Universe*. Berkley F 835. 3rd edn. VG. P9d. $1.50

SIMAK, Clifford D. *Strangers in the Universe*. 1957. Berkley G 71. 1st pb edn. c/Powers. F. M1d. $12.00

SIMAK, Clifford D. *They Walked Like Men*. Avon 52861. 1st prtg. G. S1d. $2.00

SIMAK, Clifford D. *They Walked Like Men*. 1963. MacFadden 50-184. c/R Powers. SF. VG. B3d. $4.00

SIMAK, Clifford D. *They Walked Like Men*. 1963. MacFadden 50-184. 1st pb edn. F. M1d. $12.00

SIMAK, Clifford D. *Time & Again*. 1963. Ace F 239. 1st prtg. c/sgn. SF. F. F2d. $20.00

SIMAK, Clifford D. *Time & Again*. 1963. Ace F 239. 1st prtg. VG. S1d. $4.00

SIMAK, Clifford D. *Time & Again*. Ace 81000. 1st prtg. G+. S1d. $3.00

SIMAK, Clifford D. *Time Is the Simplest Thing*. Crest D 547. 2nd prtg. F. M1d. $5.00

SIMAK, Clifford D. *Time Is the Simplest Thing*. 1963. Crest D 752. 3rd edn. F. P9d. $2.50

SIMAK, Clifford D. *Trouble With Tycho*. Ace 82443. 1st prtg. F. S1d. $2.50

SIMAK, Clifford D. *Way Station*. 1963. MacFadden 60-198. VG+. I1d. $4.00

SIMAK, Clifford D. *Way Station*. 1964. MacFadden 60-198. 1st pb edn. F. M1d. $12.00

SIMAK, Clifford D. *Werewolf Principle*. 1968. Berkley S 1463. SF. VG. B4d. $3.00

SIMAK, Clifford D. *Why Call Them Back From Heaven?* 1968. Ace H 42. 1st edn. PBO. c/sgn. SF. F. F2d. $20.00

SIMAK, Clifford D. *Worlds Without End*. Belmont B 50-791. SF. G. S1d/W2d. $3.00

SIMAK, Clifford D. *Worlds Without End*. 1964. Belmont 92-584. 1st edn. c/sgn. SF. F. F2d. $35.00

SIMAK, Clifford D. *Worlds Without End*. 1964. Belmont 92-584. 1st edn. VG. M1d. $8.00

SIMAK/SUTTON. *So Bright the Vision/Man Who Saw Tomorrow*. Ace H 95. 1st prtg. VG. S1d. $5.50

SIMAK/SUTTON. *So Bright the Vision/Man Who Saw Tomorrow*. 1968. Ace H 95. 1st prtg. SF. G+. R5d. $2.00

SIMENON, Georges. *Accomplices*. Signet 2751. VG. B3d. $4.50

SIMENON, Georges. *Belle*. Signet 1124. c/Zuckerberg. VG+. B3d. $6.00

SIMENON, Georges. *Bottom of the Bottle*. 1954. Signet 1144. Fa. VG. B4d. $3.00

SIMENON, Georges. *Brothers Rico*. 1954. Signet 1109. My. VG. B5d. $4.00

SIMENON, Georges. *Danger Ashore*. Berkley 340. VG+. G5d. $6.50

SIMENON, Georges. *Four Days in a Lifetime*. 1953. Signet 1073. 1st pb. Cr. VG+. B6d. $12.50

SIMENON, Georges. *Fugitive*. 1958. Signet 1465. c/gga. My. VG. B4d. $4.00

SIMENON, Georges. *Girl in His Past*. 1952. Signet 948. c/gga. Fa. VG. B3d/B4d. $4.00

SIMENON, Georges. *Heart of a Man*. 1951. Signet 964. 1st prtg. c/gga. VG. P7d. $6.00

SIMENON, Georges. *In Case of Emergency*. Dell D 279. c/Bardot: photo. VG. B3d. $3.50

SIMENON, Georges. *Inspector Maigret & the Burglar's Wife*. 1957. Dell 964. My. G+. B5d. $2.50

SIMENON, Georges. *Inspector Maigret & the Killers*. Signet 1248. VG. B3d. $4.00

SIMENON, Georges. *Inspector Maigret & the Strangled Stripper*. Signet 1188. VG. G5d. $10.00

SIMENON, Georges. *Madame Maigret's Own Case*. 1963. Pyramid R 825. My. VG. B5d. $4.50

SIMENON, Georges. *Maigret in New York's Underworld*. Curtis 06117. 1st prtg. My. VG+. R5d. $2.25

SIMENON, Georges. *Saint-Fiacre Affair*. Pocket 141. G+. G5d. $5.50

SIMENON, Georges. *Short Cases of Inspector Maigret*. Ace F 198. My. VG. B5d. $4.50

SIMENON, Georges. *Snow Was Black*. Signet 855. VG. I1d. $5.00

SIMENON, Georges. *Strangers in the House*. Signet 1376. VG. G5d. $6.50

SIMENON, Georges. *Versus Inspector Maigret*. Curtis 07143. V.G G5d. $4.50

SIMENON, Georges. *Watchmaker*. Hillman 105. VG. B3d. $4.50

SIMENON, Georges. *Widow*. Popular 724. VG. B3d. $5.00

SIMENON, Georges. *Witnesses*. HB 100. NF. G5d. $9.00

SIMMONS, Blake. *Angry Husband*. 1972. Liverpool TNS 520. Ad. VG. B5d. $3.50

SIMMONS, Blake. *Bride for Bride*. 1972. Liverpool TNS 533. Ad. VG. B5d. $3.50

SIMMONS, Blake. *Eager To Swap*. 1974. Liverpool TNS 590. Ad. VG+. B5d. $4.50

SIMMONS, Blake. *Morning After*. 1974. Liverpool TNS 578. Ad. VG+. B5d. $4.50

SIMMONS, Blake. *Naked Pike-Up*. 1974. Liverpool B 66758. Ad. VG+. B5d. $5.50

SIMMONS, Blake. *Swedish Servants*. 1973. Liverpool TNS 558. Ad. VG. B5d. $3.50

SIMMONS, Geofrey. *Adam Experiment*. 1979. Berkley 04492. SF. VG. W2d. $3.50

SIMMONS, Herbert. *Corner Boy*. 1958. Dell D 245. JD. VG+. P1d. $16.50

SIMMONS, William. *Net of Dreams*. 1990. Popular 21016. 1st edn. sgn. SF. F. F2d. $10.00

SIMON, George. *Bare Skin*. 1962. Chariot 215. PBO. NF. B6d. $10.00

SIMON, George. *Sheer Affair*. 1962. Chariot 222. 1st edn. c/gga. F. F2d. $12.00

SIMON, Njami. *Coffin & Co*. 1987. Black Lizard NN. c/J Kirwan. My. VG. B5d. $4.00

SIMON, Njami. *Coffin & Co*. Black Lizard 049. F. G5d. $4.00

SIMONOV, Konstantine. *Days & Nights*. Ballantine S 412K. c/B Blanchard. Fi. VG. B5d. $4.00

SIMONSON, Sheila. *Larkspur.* 1991. Worldwide 26074. My. F. B5d. $6.00

SIMPSON, Ronald. *End of a Diplomat.* Monarch 413. PBO. VG+. B3d. $6.00

SIMPSON, Ronald. *Make Every Kiss Count.* 1961. Monarch 219. Ad. VG. B5d. $7.50

SIMS, Edward H. *American Aces.* 1959. Ballantine F 349K. War. VG+. B4d. $4.00

SIMS, Edward H. *American Aces.* 1963. Ballantine F 723. reprints F349K. War. VG. B4d. $2.75

SIMS, Edward H. *Greatest Aces.* 1970. Ballantine 02092. 1st prtg. c/photo. VG+. P7d. $4.00

SIMS & WILLIAMS. *Fog.* 1946. Popular 76. G+. G5d. $6.00

SIMS & WILLIAMS. *Fog.* 1946. Popular 76. My. VG. P1d. $15.00

SINCLAIR, Bertrand W. *Gunpowder Lightning.* Dell 437. c/R Stanley. We. VG. B5d. $4.00

SINCLAIR, Bertrand W. *Wild West.* 1949. Popular 180. We. VG. B4d. $6.00

SINCLAIR, Harold. *Horse Soldiers.* 1959. Dell F 76. 1st prtg. VG. R5d. $4.00

SINCLAIR, Marianne. *Corruption of Innocence.* 1964. MacFadden 50-191. Fi. VG+. B5d. $7.50

SINCLAIR, Michael. *How To Steal a Million.* 1966. Signet D 2958. MTI. c/Hepburn & O'Toole; photo. VG+. B4d. $2.75

SINCLAIR, Murray. *Only in LA.* 1988. Black Lizard NN. c/J Kirwan. My. F. B5d. $8.00

SINCLAIR, Murray. *Tough Luck LA.* 1988. Black Lizard NN. c/J Kirwan. My. F. B5d. $8.00

SINCLAIR, Murray. *Tough Luck LA.* 1988. Black Lizard NN. VG. G5d. $4.50

SINCLAIR, Robert B. *11th Hour.* 1952. Pocket 881. 1st prtg. c/Erickson: gga. VG. P7d. $6.00

SINCLAIR, Upton. *Theirs Be the Guilty.* 1960. Hillman 169. Fi. NF. B5d. $6.00

SINGER, Adam. *Platoon.* 1953. Lion 164. PBO. VG. B6d. $7.50

SINGER, Adam. *Platoon.* 1959. Pyramid G 375. Fi. VG. B5d. $5.00

SINGER, Bant. *Blind Alley.* 1954. Pyramid 123. 1st pb. VG+. B6d. $13.50

SINGER, Kurt. *Hemingway: Life & Death of a Giant.* 1961. Holloway House HH 102. Nfi. F. P1d. $20.00

SINGER, Kurt. *Spies Who Changed History.* 1960. Ace K 122. Nfi. VG. B4d. $2.00

SINGER, Kurt. *Tales From the Unknown Planet.* 1971. Pinnacle P 054N. 1st prtg. SF. VG. W2d. $3.50

SINGER, Kurt. *Unearthly.* 1965. Belmont 92-622. VG. B3d. $4.50

SINGER, Kurt. *Unearthly.* 1965. Belmont 92-622. 1st prtg. SF. G+. R5d. $3.00

SINSTADT, Gerald. *Fidelio Score.* 1968. Arrow 033. NF. B3d. $7.50

SINSTADT, Gerald. *Ship of Spies.* 1967. Lancer 73-566. Fa. VG+. B4d. $3.00

SIODMAK, Curt. *City in the Sky.* Pinnacle 00582. c/sgn & inscr. VG. B3d. $5.50

SIODMAK, Curt. *Donovan's Brain.* Armed Services O 9. VG. B3a #21. $12.50

SIODMAK, Curt. *Donovan's Brain.* 1950. Bantam 819. 1st pb edn. VG. M1d. $20.00

SIODMAK, Curt. *Donovan's Brain.* 1969. Berkley X 1716. c/sgn. VG. B3d. $5.00

SIODMAK, Curt. *Donovan's Brain.* 1969. Berkley X 1716. 1st prtg. SF. VG. R5d. $2.50

SIODMAK, Curt. *Donovan's Brain.* Mercury 87. c/Salter. VG. B3d. $8.00

SIODMAK, Curt. *Donovan's Brain.* Mercury 87. c/sgn. VG. B3a #21. $19.80

SIODMAK, Curt. *Donovan's Brain.* Mercury 87. c/sgn. VG. B3a #24. $20.90

SIODMAK, Curt. *For Kings Only.* Dell 2680. c/Bama: sgn. VG+. B3d. $5.00

SIODMAK, Curt. *Hauser's Memory.* 1969. Berkley X 1649. c/sgn. VG. B3d. $6.00

SIODMAK, Curt. *Hauser's Memory.* 1969. Berkley X 1649. SF. G+. W2d. $3.25

SIODMAK, Curt. *Hauser's Memory.* 1969. Berkley X 1649. 1st prtg. F. S1d. $7.50

SIODMAK, Curt. *Riders to the Stars.* 1953. Ballantine 58. NF. I1d. $9.00

SIODMAK, Curt. *Riders to the Stars.* 1953. Ballantine 58. 1st edn. F. M1d. $15.00

SIODMAK, Curt. *Riders to the Stars.* 1953. Ballantine 58. 1st prtg. MTI. SF. VG+. R5d. $8.00

SIODMAK, Curt. *Skyport.* Signet S 1939. 1st prtg. G. S1d. $2.00

SIODMAK, Curt. *Skyport.* 1961. Signet S 1939. c/sgn. VG+. B3d. $6.50

SIODMAK, Curt. *Skyport.* 1961. Signet S 1939. 1st pb edn. F. M1d. $7.00

SIODMAK, Curt. *Third Ear.* Pinnacle 00345. c/sgn. VG+. B3d. $5.00

SIODMAK, Curt. *Whomsoever I Shall Kiss.* 1954. Dell 756. 1st prtg. c/gga. VG. P7d. $7.50

SIRE, Glen. *Deathmakers.* Crest 440. VG. B3d. $4.50

SJOMAN, Vilgot. *I Am Curious (Yellow).* Black Cat BA 184. 8th edn. Fi. VG+. B5d. $7.50

SKELLY, Mike. *Halo for a Heel.* Red Seal 14. PBO. c/Barye. VG. B3d. $6.00

SKINNER, C.O. *Our Hearts Were Young & Gay.* Bantam 105. VG. B3d. $4.50

SKINNER, Mike. *Playground of Violence.* 1961. Novel Book 5035. PBO. c/gga. NF. B6a #74. $61.00

SKINNER, Mike. *Sex Game.* 1962. Midwood 192. PBO. c/Rader. VG+. B3d. $8.00

SKLAR, George. *Promising Young Men.* 1952. Signet S 924. JD. VG. B4d. $3.00

SKLAR, George. *Two Worlds of Johnny Truro.* 1950. Popular 294. Fa. VG+. B4d. $12.00

SKY, Kathleen. *Birthright.* 1975. Laser 14. PBO. c/K Freas. SF. VG+. B3d/I1d. $5.00

SKY, Kathleen. *Birthright.* 1975. Laser 14. 1st edn. SF. F. F2d. $12.00

SKY, Kathleen. *Death's Angel.* 1981. Bantam 14703. SF. VG+. W2d. $4.50

SKY, Kathleen. *Death's Angel.* 1981. Bantam 14703. 1st edn. SF. F. F2d. $12.50

SKY, Kathleen. *Ice Prison.* 1976. Laser 38. 1st edn. SF. F. F2d. $16.00

SLADE, Caroline. *Lilly Crackell.* Signet 829. c/Avati. VG. B3d. $4.50

SLADE, Caroline. *Margaret.* Signet 1267. reprint. VG. B6d. $8.00

SLADEK, John. *Best of John Sladek.* 1981. Pocket 83131. SF. F. W2d. $4.50

SLADEK, John. *Mechasm.* Ace 71435. 1st prtg. F. S1d. $4.00

SLADEK, John. *Roderick.* 1982. Pocket 44886. SF. VG. W2d. $3.50

SLATZER, Robert F. *Hellcats.* 1967. Holloway House 154. PBO. MTI. c/gga. JD. VG+. B6a #79. $38.50

SLAUGHTER, Frank G. *Apalachee Gold.* Ace D 191. VG+. B3d. $4.50

SLAUGHTER, Frank G. *Apalachee Gold.* Ace 01760. F. VG. B5d. $2.50

SLAUGHTER, Frank G. *Battle Surgeon.* Perma M 4048. 6th prtg. VG+. B3d. $4.50

SLAUGHTER, Frank G. *Buccaneer Surgeon.* Perma M 5070. 3rd prtg. VG. B3d. $4.00

SLAUGHTER, Frank G. *Daybreak.* 1959. Perma M 4130. Fa. VG+. B4d. $3.00

SLAUGHTER, Frank G. *Deadly Lady of Madagascar.* Arrow 720. VG. B3d. $7.00

SLAUGHTER, Frank G. *Devil's Harvest.* 1964. Perma M 5085. Fa. VG+. B4d. $4.00

SLAUGHTER, Frank G. *Divine Mistress.* 1956. Perma M 4047. 1st prtg. c/Binger: gga. VG. P7d. $4.00

SLAUGHTER, Frank G. *Epidemic!* 1962. Perma M 5044. Fa. VG. B4d. $3.00

SLAUGHTER, Frank G. *Flight From Natchez.* 1956. Perma 4064. Fi. VG. B5d. $2.50

SLAUGHTER, Frank G. *Fort Everglades.* 1956. Perma M 4054. 1st prtg. c/Meese: gga. VG+. P7d. $7.50

SLAUGHTER, Frank G. *Fort Everglades.* 1952. Perma P 155. c/gga. Fa. VG. B4d. $2.00

SLAUGHTER, Frank G. *Fort Everglades.* 1966. Pocket 50211. 7th edn. Fi. VG+. B5d. $3.00

SLAUGHTER, Frank G. *Galileans.* Perma M 4049. 2nd prtg. c/Schulz. VG. B3d. $4.00

SLAUGHTER, Frank G. *Galileans.* 1954. Perma P 290. Fa. VG. B4d. $2.00

SLAUGHTER, Frank G. *Golden Isle.* 1960. Perma M 4072. 8th edn. Fi. VG+. B5d. $3.00

SLAUGHTER, Frank G. *In a Dark Garden.* Perma P 107. VG+. B3d. $5.00

SLAUGHTER, Frank G. *Jezebel: Queen of Evil.* Arrow 719. VG. B3d. $7.00

SLAUGHTER, Frank G. *Lorena.* 1960. Perma M 4182. c/gga. Fa. VG+. B4d. $4.00

SLAUGHTER, Frank G. *Mapmaker.* Perma M 4111. 2nd prtg. VG+. B3d. $4.00

SLAUGHTER, Frank G. *Pilgrims in Paradise.* 1961. Perma M 5034. c/gga. Fa. VG+. B4d. $3.00

SLAUGHTER, Frank G. *Purple Quest.* 1970. Pocket. 2nd pb prtg. F. M1d. $4.00

SLAUGHTER, Frank G. *Road to Bithynia.* Perma M 4055. 4th prtg. VG. B3d. $4.00

SLAUGHTER, Frank G. *Sangaree.* Popular Giant G 100. VG. I1d. $5.00

SLAUGHTER, Frank G. *Savage Place.* 1965. Pocket 50-148. Fa. VG+. B4d. $5.00

SLAUGHTER, Frank G. *Scarlet Cord.* 1957. Perma M 4069. c/T Dunn. Fi. VG. B5d. $3.00

SLAUGHTER, Frank G. *Storm Haven.* 1955. Perma M 4008. c/R Schulz. Fi. VG. B5d. $3.00

SLAUGHTER, Frank G. *That None Should Die.* Perma M 4026. VG+. B3d. $4.50

SLAUGHTER, Frank G. *That None Should Die.* 1952. Perma P 180. 1st pb. VG+. B6d. $9.00

SLAUGHTER, Frank G. *Tomorrow's Miracle.* 1963. Perma M 5069. Fa. NF. B4d. $2.00

SLAUGHTER, Frank G. *Warrior.* 1957. Perma M 4087. c/Binger. VG+. B3d. $4.50

SLAUGHTER, Frank G. *Your Body & Your Mind.* 1953. Signet 986. c/R Jonas. NF. VG. B5d. $3.50

SLEATOR, William. *House of Stairs.* 1975. Avon 25510. 1st prtg. F. S1d. $4.00

SLEATOR, William. *House of Stairs.* 1975. Avon 25510. 1st prtg. SF. G+. W2d. $3.50

SLEATOR, William. *Interstellar Pig.* 1988. Bantam 25564. 4th prtg. SF. VG+. W2d. $3.50

SLESAR, Henry. *Clean Crimes & Neat Murders.* 1960. Avon T 485. VG. B3d. $5.00

SLESAR, Henry. *Clean Crimes & Neat Murders.* 1960. Avon T 485. 1st edn. very scarce in top condition. My. F. F2d. $30.00

SLESAR, Henry. *Gray Flannel Shroud.* 1959. Zenith 33. 1st pb edn. c/gga. F. F2d. $20.00

SLIDELL, F. *Love Teacher.* Allstar 11. VG+. B3d. $5.00

SLIGH, Nigel. *Copperbelt.* 1951. Popular 365. Fa. VG. B4d. $4.00

SLIM, W. *Defeat Into Victory.* Four Square 58. VG+. B3d. $8.00

SLOAN, G.P. *Negligee.* Newsstand A 1. VG. B3d. $5.00

SLOANE, Willaim. *To Walk the Night.* 1955. Dell 856. G. G5d. $3.00

SLOANE, William. *Edge of Running Water.* Armed Services T 23. VG. B3a #22. $15.00

SLOANE, William. *To Walk the Night.* 1955. Dell 856. 1st pb edn. c/gga: sgn. Fa/Th. VG. F2d. $20.00

SMALL, J.W. *Dance Merchants.* Ace D 300. VG. B3d. $6.00

SMITH, A.C.H. *Dark Crystal.* 1982. Owl 62436. MTI. SF. F. W2d. $5.00

SMITH, A.C.H. *Labyrinth.* 1986. Owl 07322. SF. F. B5d. $5.00

SMITH, A.C.H. *Labyrinth.* 1986. Owl 07332. 1st prtg. MTI. SF. VG+. W2d. $3.50

SMITH, Abbott. *Erotic Spy.* 1968. Pendulum PP 003. 1st edn. My. F. F2d. $22.00

SMITH, Abbott. *Erotic Spy.* 1968. Pendulum PP 003. 1st prtg. VG+. R5d. $15.00

SMITH, Artemis. *Odd Girl.* 1959. Beacon 230. PBO. c/Darcy: gga. VG. B6d. $7.50

SMITH, Artemis. *This Bed We Made.* 1961. Monarch 182. c/De Soto. VG+. B3a #24. $27.50

SMITH, Arthur D. Howden. *Grey Maiden.* 1974. Centaur 12. c/D Ireland. SF. VG+. B5d. $5.50

SMITH, Arthur D. Howden. *Grey Maiden.* 1974. Centaur 12. 1st pb edn. F. M1d. $6.00

SMITH, Ben. *Peril of the Peloncillos.* Monarch 440. PBO. c/Stanley. VG. B3d. $4.00

SMITH, Caesar. *Heat Wave.* 1959. Ballantine 293K. 1st pb. My. NF. B6d. $12.50

SMITH, Carol Sturm. *For Love of Ivy.* 1968. Avon V 2239. 1st prtg. VG+. R5d. $2.25

SMITH, Clark A. *Hyperborea.* 1971. Ballantine. 1st edn. Ad/Fa. F. M1d. $20.00

SMITH, Clark A. *Immortal of Mercury.* Stellar 16. SF. F. W2d. $40.00

SMITH, Clark A. *Xiccarph.* Ballantine 02501. 1st prtg. VG. S1d. $6.00

SMITH, Clark A. *Zothique.* Ballantine 01938. 1st prtg. VG. S1d. $6.50

SMITH, Cordelia. *Great SF Stories.* 1964. Dell 3160 1st edn. F. M1d. $5.00

SMITH, Cordelia. *Great SF Stories.* Dell 3160. 1st prtg. VG. S1d. $4.00

SMITH, Cordwainer. *Best of Cordwainer Smith.* 1985. Ballantine 32302. 3rd prtg. SF. F. W2d. $3.75

SMITH, Cordwainer. *Norstrilia.* 1978. Ballantine 27800. 3rd prtg. SF. VG. W2d. $3.00

SMITH, Cordwainer. *Nostrilia.* Ballantine 24366. 1st prtg. G. S1d. $1.50

SMITH, Cordwainer. *Planet Buyer.* 1964. Pyramid R 1084. PBO. c/J Schoenherr. SF. VG. B3d/B5d. $4.50

SMITH, Cordwainer. *Quest of 3 Worlds.* Ace F 402. F. M1d. $12.00

SMITH, Cordwainer. *Space Lords.* 1965. Pyramid R 1183. PBO. c/Jack Gaughan: gga. SF. VG+. B3d. $5.00

SMITH, Cordwainer. *Space Lords*. 1968. Pyramid X 1911. F. M1d. $12.00

SMITH, Cordwainer. *Underpeople*. 1968. Pyramid X 1910. PBO. c/Gaugham. SF. NF. M3d. $9.00

SMITH, Cordwainer. *Underpeople*. 1968. Pyramid X 1910. 1st edn. F. M1d. $10.00

SMITH, Cordwainer. *You Will Never Be the Same*. 1970. Berkley S 1894. SF. G+. B5d. $3.00

SMITH, Cordwainer. *You Will Never Be the Same*. 1970. Berkley S 1894. SF. VG. W2d. $4.75

SMITH, David. *Witch of the Indies*. 1977. Zebra 267. PBO. NF. B6d. $7.50

SMITH, Don. *Angola*. 1970. Award AN 1153. My. VG. W2d. $3.25

SMITH, Don. *China Coaster*. 1953. Popular 522. 1st prtg. c/gga. VG. B3d/P7d. $5.00

SMITH, Don. *Out of the Sea*. 1952. Red Seal 11. 1st edn. F. F2d. $16.00

SMITH, Don. *Payoff*. 1973. Gold Medal M 2775. 1st prtg. My. G. W2d. $2.75

SMITH, Don. *Peking*. 1968. Award Books. 1st edn. F. M1d. $15.00

SMITH, Don. *Secret Mission: Munich*. 1970. Award A 727S. 1st prtg. My. G+. R5d. $1.25

SMITH, E.E. *Appointment at Bloodstar*. 1978. Jove 91245. SF. VG. W2d. $3.75

SMITH, E.E. *Best of Edward E 'Doc' Smith*. 1979. Jove 04245. 1st edn. Fi/Bio. F. F2d. $15.00

SMITH, E.E. *Children of the Lens*. 1966. Pyramid X 1264. 1st edn. PBO. F. P9d. $2.50

SMITH, E.E. *Clockwork Traitor*. 1977. Pryamid V 4003. SF. G. W2d. $2.75

SMITH, E.E. *First Lensman*. 1973. Pyramid N 2925. 8th prtg. SF. VG+. W2d. $4.00

SMITH, E.E. *First Lensman*. 1964. Pyramid R 1114. SF. G+. W2d. $3.25

SMITH, E.E. *First Lensman*. 1964. Pyramid R 1114. 1st prtg. VG+. S1d. $4.00

SMITH, E.E. *First Lensman*. 1970. Pyramid T 2172. 6th prtg. SF. F. W2d. $5.00

SMITH, E.E. *Galactic Patrol*. 1964. Pyramid R 1103. SF. VG+. B4d. $7.50

SMITH, E.E. *Galactic Patrol*. 1968. Pyramid X 1457. 5th prtg. SF. VG. W2d. $4.25

SMITH, E.E. *Galaxy Primes*. 1965. Ace F 328. F. M1d. $15.00

SMITH, E.E. *Galaxy Primes*. 1965. Ace F 328. 1st edn. NF. I1d. $12.00

SMITH, E.E. *Gray Lensman*. 1965. Pyramid X 1245. SF. VG. B4d. $4.00

SMITH, E.E. *Masters of the Vortex*. Pyramid X 1851. 1st prtg. G+. S1d. $2.50

SMITH, E.E. *Second-Stage Lensmen*. 1965. Pyramid X 1262. SF. VG. B4d. $3.00

SMITH, E.E. *Skylark Duquesne*. 1980. Berkley 04638. SF. F. W2d. $4.50

SMITH, E.E. *Skylark Duquesne*. 1974. Panther 03946. SF. F. W2d. $6.50

SMITH, E.E. *Skylark Duquesne*. 1970. Pyramid T 2238. 5th prtg. SF. G+. W2d. $3.25

SMITH, E.E. *Skylark Duquesne*. 1966. Pyramid X 1539. SF. VG. W2d. $4.00

SMITH, E.E. *Skylark Duquesne*. 1966. Pyramid X 1539. 1st edn. F. M1d. $15.00

SMITH, E.E. *Skylark of Space*. 1984. Berkley 06561. 4th prtg. SF. F. W2d. $3.75

SMITH, E.E. *Skylark of Space*. 1962. Pyramid F 764. 2nd edn. c/R Powers. SF. VG. B5d. $4.00

SMITH, E.E. *Skylark of Space*. 1958. Pyramid G 332. c/R Powers. SF. G+. B5d. $4.50

SMITH, E.E. *Skylark of Space*. 1958. Pyramid G 332. 1st pb edn. F. M1d. $15.00

SMITH, E.E. *Skylark of Space*. 1970. Pyramid T 2232. 7th prtg. SF. VG. W2d. $3.00

SMITH, E.E. *Skylark of Space*. 1966. Pyramid X 1350. 1st prtg. c/Gaughan. VG. P7d. $6.00

SMITH, E.E. *Skylark of Valeron*. 1962. Pyramid F 948. 1st edn. c/Ed Emsh. SF. VG. M3d. $6.00

SMITH, E.E. *Skylark of Valeron*. 1963. Pyramid F 948. 1st pb. c/Emsh. SF. NF. B6d. $10.00

SMITH, E.E. *Skylark of Valeron*. 1970. Pyramid T 2237. 5th prtg. SF. VG. W2d. $3.50

SMITH, E.E. *Skylark Three*. 1963. Pyramid F 924. 1st pb. c/Ed Emsh. SF. VG+. B3d. $5.00

SMITH, E.E. *Spacehounds of IPC*. 1966. Ace F 372. 1st pb. SF. VG. B6d/M1d. $6.00

SMITH, E.E. *Subspace Explorers*. 1968. Ace H 102. 1st prtg. SF. VG+. R5d. $2.75

SMITH, E.E. *Triplanetary*. Pyramid R 1222. 1st prtg. VG. S1d. $3.00

SMITH, E.E. *Triplanetary*. 1970. Pyramid T 2174. 6th prtg. SF. G+. W2d. $3.00

SMITH, E.E. *Triplanetary*. 1972. Pyramid T 2174. 7th prtg. SF. VG. W2d. $3.50

SMITH, E.E. *Triplanetary*. 1968. Pyramid X 1456. 5th prtg. SF. VG. W2d. $3.50

SMITH, Evelyn. *Perfect Planet*. 1963. Lancer 72-679. VG+. B3d. $4.50

SMITH, Evelyn. *Perfect Planet*. 1963. Lancer 72-679. 1st pb edn. F. M1d. $7.00

SMITH, Francis. *Harry Vernon at Prep*. 1960. Signet S 1833. Fa. VG. B4d. $3.50

SMITH, Frank. *Back Alley*. 1958. Beacon 181. 1st prtg. c/Geygan: gga. VG+. P7d. $9.00

SMITH, Frederick E. *Killing for the Hawks*. 1967. Ace A 18. 1st pb. c/Valigursky. NF. B6d. $9.00

SMITH, Garret. *Between Worlds*. Stellar 1. SF. VG+. W2d. $40.00

SMITH, George A. *Coming of the Rats*. 1961. Pike 203. PBO. c/GH Smith: sgn. VG+. B6a #79. $121.00

SMITH, George H. *Brazen Broad*. 1961. Pike 206. 1st edn. c/photo. F. F2d. $18.00

SMITH, George H. *Carnal Cage*. 1962. Novel Book 6045. 1st edn. c/gga. My. F. F2d. $22.00

SMITH, George H. *Doomsday Wing*. 1963. Monarch 388. PBO. c/E Mayan. SF. VG. B5d. $8.00

SMITH, George H. *Doomsday Wing*. 1963. Monarch 388. 1st edn. F. M1d. $15.00

SMITH, George H. *Four-Day Weekend*. 1966. Belmont B 50-699. PBO. SF. VG. M3d. $5.00

SMITH, George H. *Four-Day Weekend*. 1966. Belmont B 50-699. 1st edn. F. M1d. $15.00

SMITH, George H. *Hot Jazz*. 1960. Novel Book 5029. 1st edn. My. F. F2d. $25.00

SMITH, George H. *Lovemakers*. 1965. Beacon 894. 1st edn. c/gga. F. F2d. $20.00

SMITH, George H. *Private Hell*. Pike 210. c/sgn. VG+. B3d. $6.50

SMITH, George H. *Satan's Daughter*. 1961. Epic Book 113. 1st edn. SF. F. F2d. $20.00

SMITH, George H. *Satan's Mate*. Newsstand 507. NF. B3d. $10.00

SMITH, George H. *Satan's Mate*. 1959. Newsstand 507. Fa. G+. B4d. $3.00

SMITH, George H. *Shocking She-Animal*. 1962. Novel Book 6047. 1st edn. My. F. F2d. $20.00

SMITH, George H. *Strange Harem.* 1962. France 24. 1st edn. c/gga. F. F2d. $20.00

SMITH, George H. *Strip Artist.* 1964. Playtime 681. 1st edn. F. F2d. $25.00

SMITH, George H. *Thirst for Love.* 1962. Novel Book 6013. 1st edn. F. F2d. $25.00

SMITH, George H. *Unending Night.* 1964. Monarch 464. PBO. c/R Brillhart. SF. VG+. B5d. $11.00

SMITH, George H. *Unending Night.* 1964. Monarch 464. 1st prtg. PBO. c/Brillhart. VG. P7d. $8.50

SMITH, George H. *Unending Night.* Priory 1088. SF. VG. B5d. $3.50

SMITH, George H. *Virgin Mistress.* 1961. Pike 802. 1st edn. c/sgn. Ho/Fa. F. F2d. $30.00

SMITH, George H. *Who Is Ronald Reagan?* 1968. Pyramid T 1793. c/photo. Bio. VG. B4d. $2.25

SMITH, George H. *Witch Queen of Locklann.* Signet P 40998. 1st prtg. G+. S1d. $4.50

SMITH, George H. *1976: The Year of Terror.* 1961. Epic 103. PBO. rare. SF. NF. B6a #80. $137.50

SMITH, George Malcolm. *Grass Is Always Greener.* Bantam 410. NF. I1d. $5.00

SMITH, George Malcolm. *Handy Book of Indoor Games.* Perma P 55. VG+. I1d. $3.00

SMITH, George O. *Brain Machine.* 1968. Lancer 74-936. 1st prtg. SF. VG. R5d. $3.50

SMITH, George O. *Fourth R.* 1959. Ballantine 316K. PBO. c/R Powers. SF. VG. B5d. $4.50

SMITH, George O. *Fourth R.* 1959. Ballantine 316K. 1st edn. F. M1d. $15.00

SMITH, George O. *Fourth R.* 1979. Dell. F. M1d. $4.00

SMITH, George O. *Highways in Hiding.* 1967. Lancer. 1st edn. F. M1d. $8.00

SMITH, George O. *Space Plague.* Avon G 1154. 3rd edn. G. P9d. $1.25

SMITH, George O. *Space Plague.* 1957. Avon T 180. SF. VG+. B4d. $4.00

SMITH, George O. *Space Plague.* 1957. Avon T 180. 1st pb edn. F. M1d. $10.00

SMITH, George O. *Space Plague.* 1957. Avon T 180. 1st prtg. SF. G+. R5d. $2.25

SMITH, George O. *Troubled Star.* 1959. Beacon 256. VG. B3a #20. $133.50

SMITH, George O. *Troubled Star.* 1959. Beacon 256. VG. B3d. $12.00

SMITH, George O. *Troubled Star.* 1959. Beacon 256. 1st edn. PBO. c/gga. SF. F. F2d. $42.50

SMITH, George O. *Venus Equilateral.* 1967. Pyramid T 1725. 1st edn. PBO. F. P9d. $2.50

SMITH, Guy N. *Crab's Moon.* 1988. Dell 20023. 1st prtg. SF. VG+. R5d. $2.00

SMITH, H. Allen. *Desert Island Decameron.* 1949. Pocket 615. 1st prtg. c/Hershfield: gga. VG+. P7d. $6.00

SMITH, H. Allen. *Don't Get Personel With a Chicken.* 1960. Perma M 4177. Hu. VG+. B4d. $3.00

SMITH, H. Allen. *Low Man on a Totem Pole.* Bantam 409. VG. G5d. $2.00

SMITH, H.M. *Coral & Brass.* Panther 847. 1st English edn. VG+. B3d. $12.00

SMITH, Harvey. *Nine to Five.* 1952. Harlequin 195. VG. B3d. $5.00

SMITH, James W. *Loner.* Pyramid 1607. 3rd prtg. VG+. B3d. $4.50

SMITH, Julie D. *Call of Madness.* 1990. Ballantine 36327. 1st prtg. SF. F. W2d. $3.75

SMITH, L. Neil. *Lando Calrissian & the Flamewind of Oseon.* 1983. Ballantine. 1st edn. F. M1d. $4.00

SMITH, L. Neil. *Lando Calrissian & the Mindharp of Sharu.* 1983. Ballantine 31158. 1st edn. F. M1d. $5.00

SMITH, L. Neil. *Lando Calrissian & the Mindharp of Sharu.* 1983. Ballantine 31158. 1st prtg. SF. VG. W2d. $3.00

SMITH, L. Neil. *Their Majesties' Bucketeers.* 1981. Ballantine 29244. 1st edn. scarce. SF. F. F2d. $20.00

SMITH, Lady Eleanor. *Dark & Splendid Passion.* 1964. Ace K 207. 1st prtg. My. G+. R5d. $1.50

SMITH, Lillian. *Journey.* 1960. Hillman 180. Nfi. VG+. B5d. $5.50

SMITH, Lillian. *Now Is the Time.* Dell 1st Edn 44. VG+. B3d. $4.00

SMITH, Lillian. *Strange Fruit.* 1948. Signet 665. 1st prtg. c/Jonas: gga. VG. P7d. $5.00

SMITH, Martin C. *Polar Star.* 1990. Ballantine 36765. 1st prtg. My. F. W2d. $5.00

SMITH, Phil. *Incredible Melting Man.* 1978. NEL UK 43487. 1st edn. SF/Ho. F. F2d. $15.00

SMITH, Red edt. *Saturday Evening Post Sports Stories.* 1949. Pocket Books 649. VG. P6d. $2.00

SMITH, Robert Paul. *Because of My Love.* 1952. Avon 458. c/Victor Olson: gga. Fa. VG. B4d. $5.00

SMITH, Robert Paul. *Time & the Place.* Avon 534. VG. I1d. $5.00

SMITH, Robert Paul. *Where Did You Go?* Cardinal C 327. VG+. B3d. $4.00

SMITH, Robert. *Baseball's Hall of Fame.* 1965. Bantam S 2932. c/photos. Nfi. VG. B5d. $5.00

SMITH, Shelley. *Crooked Man.* Perma S 287. VG+. B3d. $5.00

SMITH, Shelley. *Shrew Is Dead.* 1959. Dell D 318. 1st prtg. My. VG. R5d. $2.25

SMITH, Son. *Secret Mission: Tibet.* 1969. Award A 522X. 1st prtg. My. VG. R5d. $1.50

SMITH, Stan. *Soldier's Women.* 1959. Hillman 113. PBO. VG+. B3d. $6.00

SMITH, Stan. *Soldiers Women.* 1959. Hillman 113. G+. I1d. $4.00

SMITH, Steven Philip. *First Born.* 1984. Pocket 54765-8. 1st edn. My. F. F2d. $8.00

SMITH, Susy. *ESP.* 1962. Pyramid. 1st edn. F. M1d. $10.00

SMITH, Thorne. *Did She Fall?* 1962. PB Library 52-176. VG. B3d. $4.50

SMITH, Thorne. *Glorious Pool.* 1946. Pocket 409. VG. P6d. $3.00

SMITH, Thorne. *Night Life of the Gods.* 1948. Pocket 428. 7th prtg. SF. VG. W2d. $5.75

SMITH, Thorne. *Night Life of the Gods.* Pyramid 630. VG. B3d. $4.50

SMITH, Thorne. *Stray Lamb.* 1945. Avon 69. 1st prtg. SF. G. R5d. $4.00

SMITH, Thorne. *Stray Lamb.* 1948. Pocket 518. 1st prtg. VG+ P7d. $6.50

SMITH, Thorne. *Topper.* 1939. Pocket 4. 4th pb prtg. NF. M1d. $10.00

SMITH, Thorne. *Turnabout.* 1947. Pocket 447. PBO. VG. P6d. $3.00

SMITH, W. *Finders Keepers: Buried Treasure.* Belmont 60-061. NF. B3d. $4.50

SMITH, W.F. *Chronicle of Diamond Six.* Corgi 1025. VG. B3d. $8.00

SMITH, Wallace. *Bessie Cotter.* Berkley G 21. VG+. B3d. $5.00

SMITH, Warren. *Strange ESP.* Popular 60-2398. VG. B3d. $3.50

SMITH, Warren. *Strange Powers of the Mind.* 1968. Ace K 296. 1st edn. F. F2d. $6.00

SMITH, Warren. *Strange Women of the Occult.* Popular 60-2342. Nfi. VG. B5d. $4.50

SMITH, William Gardner. *Anger at Innocence.* 1951. Signet 907. c/T Dunn. Fi. VG+. B5d. $5.50

SMITH, William Gardner. *Last of the Conquerors.* 1949. Signet 706. 2nd edn. c/Avati: gga. Fa. VG. B3d. $4.50

SMITH & TIERNEY. *When Hell Laughs.* 1982. Ace 71158. 1st edn. c/Tierney: sgn. Fa. F. F2d. $13.00

SMITH & TIERNEY. *Witch of the Mists.* 1978. Zebra 313. PBO. NF. B6d. $7.50

SMITH & VAN VOGT. *Lost in Space/Earth's Last Fortress.* Ace D 431. PBO. c/sgn. VG+. B3d. $7.50

SMITH/VAN VOGT. *Lost in Space/Earth's Last Fortress.* 1960. Ace D 431. PBO. c/Emsh. SF. VG+. M3d. $12.00

SMITH/VAN VOGT. *Lost in Space/Earth's Last Fortress.* 1960. Ace D 431. 1st edn. F. M1d. $15.00

SMITH/WEST. *Guns of Sonora/Black Buzzards of Bueno.* 1969. Ace 30850. We. NF. B5d. $5.00

SMYTHE, David Mynders. *Golden Venus.* 1961. Dell F 145. c/F Elliott. Fi. VG. B5d. $2.50

SMYTHE, Joseph Hilton. *Sex Probers.* 1961. Beacon-Envoy 104F. PBO. Ad. VG. B5d. $5.00

SMYTHE, Reginald. *Andy Capp, the One & Only.* 1971. Gold Medal R 2436. Hu. F. B4d. $4.00

SMYTHE, Reginald. *Hats Off, Andy Capp.* 1968. Gold Medal D 2009. Hu. NF. B4d. $3.00

SMYTHE, Reginald. *Undisputed Andy Capp.* 1972. Gold Medal R 2649. Hu. F. B4d. $4.00

SNAVELY, A. *Big Flick.* Kozy 122. VG+. B3d. $4.50

SNAVELY, A. *Love Drive.* Kozy 181. VG. B3d. $4.50

SNAVELY, A. *Wine, Women & Love.* Kozy 160. VG+. B3d. $5.50

SNAVELY, A. *2: 4 Sex.* Kozy 101. VG+. B3d. $6.00

SNEIDER, Vern. *Teahouse of the August Moon.* 1956. Signet S 1348. MTI. VG+. B4d. $7.00

SNELLING, O.F. *007 James Bond, a Report.* 1965. Signet D 2652. G+. B4d. $3.00

SNELLING, O.F. *007 James Bond, a Report.* 1965. Signet D 2652. Nfi. VG. P1d. $5.50

SNOW, C.H. *Guns Along the Border.* Gunfire 42. VG+. B3d. $5.00

SNOW, C.H. *Outlaws of Sugar Loaf.* Gunfire 52. VG+. B3d. $6.00

SNYDER, Cecil III. *Hawks of Arcturus.* 1974. DAW 103. PBO. c/K Freas SF. NF. B5d. $5.00

SNYDER, Gene. *Mind War.* 1980. Playtime 16612. SF. F. W2d. $6.50

SNYDER, Gene. *Tomb Seven.* 1985. Charter 81643. SF. F. W2d. $5.00

SNYDER, Guy. *Testament XXI.* 1973. DAW 64. 1st edn. NF. I1d. $4.00

SOHL, Jerry. *Altered Ego.* 1954. Pennant P 75. G. I1d. $3.00

SOHL, Jerry. *Altered Ego.* 1954. Pennant P 75. 1st prtg. SF. VG. W2d. $7.00

SOHL, Jerry. *Altered Ego.* 1954. Pennant. 1st pb edn. F. M1d. $15.00

SOHL, Jerry. *Costigan's Needle.* 1968. Avon S 349. SF. VG. B4d. $3.00

SOHL, Jerry. *Costigan's Needle.* 1954. Bantam. 1st pb edn. NF. M1d. $10.00

SOHL, Jerry. *Haploids.* 1953. Lion 118. 1st edn. PBO. c/De Soto. scarce. SF. VG. B6a #75. $58.50

SOHL, Jerry. *Haploids.* 1953. Lion 118. 1st pb edn. NF. M1d. $35.00

SOHL, Jerry. *I, Aloppo.* 1976. Laabor 35. 1st edn. SF. F. F2d. $10.00

SOHL, Jerry. *Night Slaves.* 1965. Gold Medal D 1561. 1st prtg. SF. VG. R6d. $6.50

SOHL, Jerry. *Point Ultimate.* 1959. Bantam A 1952. 1st prtg. SF. G+. R5d. $2.00

SOHL, Jerry. *Point Ultimate.* 1959. Bantam A 1952. 2nd pb prtg. F. M1d. $4.00

SOHL, Jerry. *Time Dissolver.* 1957. Avon I 186. 1st edn. SF. F. F2d. $12.00

SOHL, Jerry. *Time Dissolver.* 1957. Avon T 186. 1st prtg. VG. S1d. $3.00

SOHL, Jerry. *Transcendent Man.* 1959. Bantam A 1971. 1st prtg. SF. VG. R5d. $2.50

SOLLERS, Philippe. *Concha.* Belmont 216. NF. B3d. $7.00

SOLOMAN, Louis. *TV Doctors.* 1974. Scholastic 2457. 1st prtg. VG. R5d. $1.50

SOLOVIEV, M. *When the Gods Are Silent.* Popular G 135. VG. B3d. $4.00

SOLZHENITSYN, A. *1 Day in the Life of Ivan Denisovich.* Lancer 72-663. VG+. B3d. $4.00

SOMERS, Bart. *Beyond the Black Enigma.* 1965. PB Library 52-848. 1st edn. PBO. NF. P9d. $2.00

SOMERS, Bart. *Beyond the Black Enigma.* 1963. PB Library 53-785. 3rd edn. F. P9d. $2.00

SOMERS, S. *Nurse for Doctor Keith.* PB Library 51-182. c/Borack. VG+. B3d. $4.00

SONNICHSEN, C.L. *Roy Bean: Law West of the Pecos.* 1972. Gold Medal M 2547. 1st prtg. VG. R5d. $2.50

SONNICHSEN, C.L. *Roy Bean: Law West of the Pecos.* 1959. Hillman 108. VG. B3d. $4.50

SOREL, Julia. *Rocky.* 1976. Ballantine 25321. 1st prtg. VG. R5d. $1.50

SORKIN, Bernard. *Steel Shivs.* 1962. Pyramid F 731. PBO. JD. VG. M6d. $6.50

SORRELL, Phillip. *Doctor's Women.* 1962. Beacon B 486F. c/gga. Fa. VG+. B4d. $12.00

SOTONA, Wayne. *Hell & High Water.* 1969. Tempo 5319. 1st edn. TVTI. c/color photo. Hi. F. F2d. $15.00

SOUSA, J.P., III. *My Family Right or Wrong.* Armed Services 662. VG+. B3d. $5.00

SOUTHERN, Terry. *Magic Christian.* 1964. Bantam H 2917. 1st pb edn. F. M1d. $6.00

SOUTHERN, Terry. *Magic Christian.* 1964. Bantam H 2917. 1st prtg. VG. P7d. $4.00

SOUTHWORTH, John. *Pirate From Rome.* 1967. Pocket. 1st pb edn. F. M1d. $4.00

SOYA, C.E. *17 (Rites of Spring).* Pyramid 1646. 2nd prtg. MTI. B3d. $4.50

SPAIN, John. *Death Is Like That.* Popular 178. VG+. G5d. $22.50

SPAIN, John. *Dig Me a Grave.* 1951. Bantam 968. 1st prtg. My. VG. R5d. $4.50

SPAIN, John. *Evil Star.* Popular 239. VG. I1d. $5.00

SPAIN, N. *Name Your Vice.* Kozy 189. NF. B3d. $7.50

SPAIN, Terry. *Time To Kill.* 1953. Popular 500. c/gga. Fa. VG. B4d. $5.00

SPARKIA, Roy D. *Vanishing Vixen.* 1959. Crest 268. PBO. c/Barye Phillip. VG. P6d. $2.50

SPARROW, Gerald. *Golden Orchid.* 1968. Arrow 029. 1st pb. c/gga. VG. B6d. $6.00

SPAULDING, H.D. *Yellow Press.* Newsstand Library U 121. VG+. B3d. $5.50

SPAULDING, Michael. *Anything Under the Sun.* 1964. Midwood F 355. PBO. VG. B6d. $7.50

SPELLMAN, F.J. *Road To Victory.* Avon 48. VG. B3d. $10.00

SPENCER, D. *Different Kind of Love.* Brandon House 608. VG+. B3d. $6.00

SPENCER, Elizabeth. *Voice at the Back Door.* 1957. Cardinal C 272. 1st prtg. c/Avati: gga. VG+. P7d. $4.50

SPENCER, Frederic. *Cleo.* 1953. Cameo 327. Fi. G+. B5d. $7.50

SPENCER, Frederic. *Wild Party.* 1953. Carnival 912. VG+. B3a #24. $15.04

SPENCER, John. *Lycanthrope.* Supernatural Vol 1 No 1. c/Ray Cosmic. VG+. B3a #22. $24.00

SPERRY, Margaret. *Sun Way.* 1930. Boni NN. Fa. NF. B4d. $12.00

SPETZ, Steven. *Rat Pack Six.* 1969. Gold Medal 2182. 1st edn. F. F2d. $8.00

SPEWACK, Samuel. *Skyscaper Murder.* 1948. Bleak House 17. VG. I1d. $15.00

SPICER, Bart. *Black Sheep, Run.* 1956. Bantam 1049. VG. B3d. $5.00

SPICER, Bart. *Burned Man.* 1967. Bantam S 3530. My. VG+. B5d. $3.50

SPICER, Bart. *Dark Light.* Corgi 466. VG. B3d. $6.50

SPICER, Bart. *Day of the Dead.* Dell 909. c/A Sussman. My. VG. B5d. $3.00

SPICER, Bart. *Long Green.* 1953. Bantam 1126. G+. G5d. $5.00

SPICER, Bart. *Shadow of Fear.* Corgi 432. VG. B3d. $6.00

SPICER, Bart. *Taming of Carney Wilde.* 1956. Bantam 1409. VG. G5d. $4.50

SPIELBERG, Steven. *Close Encounters of the Third Kind.* 1977. Dell 11433. SF. VG. W2d. $4.00

SPILLANE, Mickey. *Big Kill.* 1951. Signet 915. VG. I1d. $10.00

SPILLANE, Mickey. *Bloody Sunrise.* 1965. Signet D 2718. c/gga. My. VG+. B4d. $3.00

SPILLANE, Mickey. *Body Lovers.* 1967. Signet P 3221. c/gga. My. VG+. B4d. $2.75

SPILLANE, Mickey. *By-Pass Control.* 1967. Signet P 3077. 1st prtg. VG. P7d. $4.50

SPILLANE, Mickey. *Day of the Guns.* Signet 2643. VG+. B3d. $4.00

SPILLANE, Mickey. *Death Dealers.* 1966. Signet D 2886. c/gga. My. VG+. B4d. $2.00

SPILLANE, Mickey. *Deep.* 1962. Signet D 2044. My. VG+. B4d. $2.75

SPILLANE, Mickey. *Deep.* 1962. Signet D 2044. 1st edn. PBO. F. F2d. $12.50

SPILLANE, Mickey. *Delta Factor.* 1968. Signet P 3377. 1st prtg. My. VG. W2d. $4.25

SPILLANE, Mickey. *Girl Hunters.* 1963. Signet T 5515. 3rd prtg. My. VG+. W2d. $4.25

SPILLANE, Mickey. *I, the Jury.* Signet T 3382. 1st prtg. VG. P7d. $4.50

SPILLANE, Mickey. *Killer Mine.* 1968. Signet P 3483. 1st prtg. My. VG. W2d. $4.25

SPILLANE, Mickey. *Killer Mine.* 1968. Signet 3483. 1st edn. My. F. F2d. $12.00

SPILLANE, Mickey. *Killing Man.* 1990. Signet AE 6784. 2nd edn. VG. P1d. $4.50

SPILLANE, Mickey. *Kiss Me, Deadly.* 1962. Corgi SC 996. 2nd edn. De. G+. P1d. $5.00

SPILLANE, Mickey. *Kiss Me, Deadly.* 1953. Signet 1000. De. F. P1d. $20.00

SPILLANE, Mickey. *Kiss Me, Deadly.* 1953. Signet 1000. G. G5d. $3.50

SPILLANE, Mickey. *Kiss Me, Deadly.* 1953. Signet 1000. My. VG. P6d. $6.00

SPILLANE, Mickey. *Last Cop Out.* 1974. Corgi 09577. My. VG. P1d. $4.00

SPILLANE, Mickey. *Last Cop Out.* 1973. Signet Y 5626. 1st prtg. My. VG+. W2d. $3.50

SPILLANE, Mickey. *Long Wait.* 1952. Signet 932. c/Kimmel: gga. My. VG. P1d. $10.00

SPILLANE, Mickey. *Me, Hood!* 1969. Signet D 3759. 1st US edn. My. F. F2d. $13.00

SPILLANE, Mickey. *Me, Hood!* 1969. Signet P 3759. 1st prtg. c/gga. VG. P7d. $5.00

SPILLANE, Mickey. *My Gun Is Quick.* Signet 791. G+. G5d. $3.75

SPILLANE, Mickey. *My Gun Is Quick.* Signet 791. VG. I1d. $5.00

SPILLANE, Mickey. *One Lonely Night.* 1951. Signet 888. De. G+. P1d. $7.00

SPILLANE, Mickey. *Snake.* 1965. Corgi GC-7307. De. VG. P1d. $7.50

SPILLANE, Mickey. *Snake.* 1964. Signet D 2548. De. VG. P1d. $6.00

SPILLANE, Mickey. *Snake.* 1964. Signet D 2548. 1st edn. PBO. F. F2d. $12.50

SPILLANE, Mickey. *Survival. Zero!* 1971. Signet T 4592. De. F. P1d. $5.00

SPILLANE, Mickey. *Twisted Thing.* 1966. Signet D 2949. VG. G5d. $4.50

SPILLANE, Mickey. *Vengeance Is Mine.* 1951. Signet 852. De. G+. P1d. $6.50

SPINELLI, Marcos. *Assignment Without Glory.* 1947. Bantam 95. VG+. B3d. $5.00

SPINELLI, Marcos. *Assignment Without Glory.* 1947. Bantam 95. Th. F. P1d. $20.00

SPINELLI, Marcos. *Mocambu.* 1958. Ace D 310. Ad. VG. P6d. $4.00

SPINGARN, Ed. *Perfect 36.* 1960. Pyramid G 565. c/Maguire. VG+. B3a #21. $31.00

SPINGARN, Ed. *Perfect 36.* 1957. Pyramid G-299. PBO. c/Marchetti. F. F2d. $15.00

SPINRAD, Norman. *Agent of Chaos.* 1967. Belmont B 50-739. PBO. SF. VG+. B5d/M3d. $6.00

SPINRAD, Norman. *Agent of Chaos.* 1967. Belmont B 50-739. SF. VG. B4d. $4.00

SPINRAD, Norman. *Agent of Chaos.* 1967. Belmont B 50-739. 1st prtg. SF. G+. R5d. $3.00

SPINRAD, Norman. *Bug Jack Baron.* 1967. Avon. 1st pb edn. NF. M1d. $8.00

SPINRAD, Norman. *New Tomorrows.* 1971. Belmont B 95-2172. SF. VG. B5d. $5.00

SPINRAD, Norman. *Solarians.* 1966. PB Library 52-985. PBO. SF. VG+. M3d. $5.50

SPINRAD, Norman. *World Between.* 1979. Pocket 82876. 1st prtg. SF. VG+. W2d. $3.50

SPOCK, Benjamin. *Dr Spock Talks With Mothers.* Crest 759. VG+. B3d. $4.00

SPRAGUE, C. *My Fathers & I.* Barclay 7262. NF. B3d. $4.50

SPRAGUE, W.D. *Lesbian in Our Society.* Midwood 154. VG. B3d. $4.00

SPRAGUE, W.D. *Sexual Behavior of American Nurses.* 1963. Lancer 73-420. Nfi. VG+. B4d. $4.00

SPRINGER, Nancy. *Black Beast.* 1982. Pocket 44117. SF. VG+. W2d. $3.25

SPRINGER, Nancy. *Golden Swan.* 1983. Pocket 45253. SF. NF. B5d. $5.00

SPRUILL, Steven. *Keepers of the Gate.* 1978. Dell 14441. 1st pb. c/Boris. SF. VG+. B6d. $3.00

ST LAURENT, C. *Clotilde.* Pan M 7. 3rd prtg. VG. B3d. $7.00

ST. CLAIR, M. *Shadow People.* Dell 7620. 1st prtg. G+. S1d. $3.00

ST. CLAIR, Margaret. *Sign of the Labrys.* 1963. Bantam 2617. 1st edn. NF. M1d. $6.00

ST. CLAIR, Margaret. *Sign of the Labrys.* 1963. Bantam 2617. 1st edn. SF. F. F2d. $13.00

ST. CLAIR, Margaret. *Sign of the Labrys.* 1963. Bantam 2617. 1st prtg. SF. VG. R5d. $2.50

ST. CLAIR/ST. CLAIR. *Message From the Eocene/Three Worlds of Futurity.* Ace M 105. F. M1d. $8.00

ST. CLAIR/ST. CLAIR. *Message From the Eocene/Three Worlds of Futurity.* Ace M 105. VG+. B3d. $4.00

ST. CLAIR/ST. CLAIR. *Message From the Eocene/Three Worlds of Futurity.* Ace M 105. 1st prtg. G. S1d. $1.75

ST. CLARE, Dexter. *Saratoga Mantrap.* Gold Medal 195. G. G5d. $3.00

ST. CLARE, Dexter. *Saratoga Mantrap.* 1951. Gold Medal 195. My. F. P1d. $22.50

ST. CLARE, Dexter. *Saratoga Mantrap.* 1951. Gold Medal 195. PBO. VG. B6d. $6.00

ST. GEORGE, David. *Diamond Doll.* 1960. Bedtime 969. Ad. VG. B5d. $5.00

ST. JAMES, B. *April Thirtieth.* 1980. Raven House 60035. My. VG. P1d. $3.50

ST. JAMES, B. *Christina's Desire.* Playboy 16437. NF. B3d. $7.00

ST. JAMES, B. *Christina's Hunger.* Playboy 16407. VG. B3d. $4.00

ST. JAMES, B. *Christina's Nights.* Playboy 16739. 2nd prtg. VG+. B3d. $5.00

ST. JAMES, B. *Christina's Pleasure.* Playboy 16653. 2nd prtg. NF. B3d. $5.00

ST. JAMES, B. *Christina's Promise.* Playboy 21047. 2nd prtg. VG+. B3d. $5.00

ST. JAMES, Burton. *Christina's Surrender.* Playboy 16520. VG+. B3d. $7.50

ST. JOHN, Burton. *Smoldering Women.* 1963. Beacon B 585F. PBO. c/gga. F. B4d. $12.00

ST. JOHN, Burton. *Smoldering Women.* 1963. Beacon B 585F. PBO. VG. B5d. $4.00

ST. JOHN, Burton. *Twin Taboos.* 1963. Beacon B 576F. c/gga. Fa. F. B4d. $15.00

ST. JOHN, Darby. *Bride Brings Death.* My Novel Classic 50. My. VG+. P1d. $30.00

ST. JOHN, David. *Diabolus.* 1972. Crest T 1725. My/SF. VG. P1d. $4.00

ST. JOHN, David. *On Hazardous Duty.* 1965. Signet D 2684. Fa. VG+. B4d. $2.00

ST. JOHN, David. *Venus Probe.* 1966. Signet D 3005. My. VG. P1d. $5.50

ST. JOHN, Genevieve. *Dark Watch.* 1966. Belmont B 50-667. My. VG. P1d. $5.50

ST. JOHN, Genevieve. *Sinister Voice.* 1967. Belmont B 50-747. My. VG. P1d. $5.00

ST. JOHN, M. *Temptress.* Kozy 116. NF. B3d. $6.50

ST. JOHN/WINSTON. *Night of Evil/Castle of Closing Doors.* 1967. Belmont B 60-062. 1st prtg. My. VG. R5d. $2.00

ST. MICHAELS, Donella. *Prisoner.* 1966. Lancer 72-110. Go. G+. P1d. $4.00

STABLEFORD, Brian M. *Castaways of Tanager.* 1981. DAW 428. 1st edn. F. M1d. $5.00

STABLEFORD, Brian M. *Critical Threshold.* 1977. DAW 230. 1st edn. G. P9d. $1.25

STABLEFORD, Brian M. *Days of Glory.* Ace 14000. c/K Freas. SF. VG+. B5d. $4.00

STABLEFORD, Brian M. *Days of Glory.* 1971. Ace 14000. SF. F. W2d. $7.00

STABLEFORD, Brian M. *Fenris Device.* 1974. DAW 130. 1st edn. G. P9d. $1.25

STABLEFORD, Brian M. *Halcyon Drift.* 1972. DAW 32. 1st prtg. PBO. c/Gaughan. VG. P7d. $4.00

STABLEFORD, Brian M. *In the Kingdom of the Beasts.* Ace 37106. c/K Freas. SF. VG. B5d. $5.00

STABLEFORD, Brian M. *In the Kingdom of the Beasts.* Ace 37106. SF. G+. W2d. $3.00

STABLEFORD, Brian M. *Journey to the Center.* 1982. DAW 492. 1st edn. G. P9d. $1.25

STABLEFORD, Brian M. *Mind-Riders.* 1976. DAW 194. PBO. c/V DiFate. SF. VG+. B5d. $4.00

STABLEFORD, Brian M. *Mind-Riders.* 1976. DAW 194. 1st prtg. PBO. c/DiFate. VG+. P7d. $4.50

STABLEFORD, Brian M. *Optiman.* 1980. DAW 406. 1st prtg. PBO. c/Mariano. VG+. P7d. $4.50

STABLEFORD, Brian M. *Promised Land.* 1973. DAW 92. 1st prtg. VG+. S1d. $3.50

STABLEFORD, Brian M. *Realms of Tartarus.* 1977. DAW 248. 1st edn. F. M1d. $5.00

STABLEFORD, Brian M. *Rhapsody in Black.* 1973. DAW 59. PBO. c/K Freas. SF. VG. B5d. $2.50

STABLEFORD, Brian M. *Swan Song.* 1975. DAW 149. PBO. c/K Freas. SF. VG. B5d. $3.50

STABLEFORD, Brian M. *To Challenge Chaos.* 1972. DAW 7. 1st prtg. SF. VG. R5d. $2.50

STABLEFORD, Brian M. *Wildeblood's Empire.* 1977. DAW UW 1331. 1st prtg. SF. VG. W2d. $3.50

STACEY, J. *Intimate Love & the Stepchild.* Barclay 7233. VG+. B3d. $5.00

STACEY, J. *Seduction of the Stepchild.* Barclay 7480. VG+. B3d. $4.00

STACK, Ben. *Wild Passion.* 1963. Merit 691. My. F. P1d. $15.00

STACKELBERG, Gene. *Double Agent.* 1959. Popular Eagle G 313. My. VG+. P1d. $10.50

STACTON, David. *Dancer in Darkness.* 1963. Ballantine X 726. Fa. VG. B4d. $3.00

STACTON, David. *Sir William.* 1965. Avon N 121. Fi. VG. B5d. $2.50

STACY, Ryder. *Bloody America.* 1985. Zebra 08217. Doomsday Warrior #4. SF. F. W2d. $4.50

STACY, Ryder. *Last American.* 1981. Zebra 14899. 1st prtg. Doomsday Warrior #3. SF. F. W2d. $4.00

STADLEY, Pat. *Black Leather Barbarians.* 1960. Signet S 1963 JD. F. B4d. $12.50

STAGG, D. *Bloody Beaches.* Monarch 210. VG+. B3d. $4.50

STAGG, D. *Glory Jumpers.* Mayflower 3061. 1st English edn. VG. B3d. $6.00

STAGGE, Jonathan. *Assignment in Beirut.* Sexton Blake 367. VG. B3d. $7.00

STAGGE, Jonathan. *Crime of Violence.* Sexton Blake. VG+. B3d. $8.00

STAGGE, Jonathan. *Death, My Darling Daughters.* 1946. LJUS Crime Library 55. dust jacket. My. VG. P1d. $25.00

STAGGE, Jonathan. *Dogs Do Bark.* 1951. Popular 350. 1st pb. My. VG. B6d. $12.00

STAGGE, Jonathan. *Nightmare in Naples.* Sexton Blake 373. VG. B3d. $7.00

STAGGE, Jonathan. *Panic in the Night.* Sexton Blake 377. VG+. B3d. $8.00

STAGGE, Jonathan. *Passport to Danger.* Sexton Blake 391. VG+. B3d. $9.00

STAGGE, Jonathan. *Stars Spell Death.* Popular 40. VG. B3d. $6.00

STAGGE, Jonathan. *Stars Spell Death.* 1944. Popular 40. My. G+. P1d. $8.00

STAGGE, Jonathan. *Time for Murder.* Sexton Blake 428. VG+. B3d. $8.00

STAGGE, Jonathan. *Turn of the Table.* Popular 267. G+. G5d. $7.50

STAGGE, Jonathan. *Turn of the Table.* 1950. Popular 267. My. G. P1d. $4.50

STAGGE, Jonathan. *Turn of the Table.* 1950. Popular 267. 1st edn. PBO. c/Belarski. VG+. B6a #79. $47.75

STAGGE, Jonathan. *Yellow Taxi.* 1945. Popular 62. My. G+. P1d. $10.00

STAGGER, H. *Naked Side of Vice.* Saber SA 100. NF. B3d. $6.00

STAHL, Nancy. *Jelly Side Down.* 1972. Gold Medal T 2562. Nfi. VG+. B5d. $4.00

STAMPER, A. *Glory Squad.* Panther 131. PBO. VG+. B3d. $8.00

STANDISH, Robert. *Bonin.* Armed Services N 24. VG. B3d. $5.00

STANDISH, Robert. *Elephant Walk.* 1963. Ballantine X 732. 1st pb. VG. B6d. $5.00

STANDISH, Robert. *Worthy Man.* 1953. Bantam 1153. My. VG. P1d. $8.50

STANFORD, Don. *Bargain in Blood.* 1951. Gold Medal 162. PBO. My. VG. B6d. $5.00

STANFORD, Don. *Slaughtered Lovelies.* 1950. Gold Medal 116. VG+. G5d. $7.00

STANLEY, Fay Grissom. *Murder Leaves a Ring.* 1953. Dell 662. G. G5d. $4.00

STANLEY, Fay Grissom. *Murder Leaves a Ring.* 1953. Dell 662. 1st prtg. c/Meese: gga. VG. P7d. $5.50

STANLEY, G. *Might of the Emperor.* Digit 344. VG. B3d. $7.50

STANLEY, Jackson. *Florentine Ring.* 1964. PB Library 53-305. Fi. VG. B5d. $3.00

STANLEY, Katheryn. *Country Teacher.* Liverpool SRS 1030. AD. VG+. B5d. $5.00

STANLEY, Katheryn. *Divorcee Teacher.* 1973. Liverpool SRS 1009. Ad. VG. B5d. $4.00

STANLEY, Leo L. *My Most Unforgettable Convicts.* 1967. Greywood 103. Nfi. VG. P1d. $7.50

STANTON, C. *Lip Magic.* Barclay 7442. NF. B3d. $4.50

STANTON, C. *Winners, Losers, & Lovers.* Barclay 7373. NF. B3d. $5.00

STANTON, Ken. *Operation Mermaid.* 1974. Manor 95-364. My. VG. P1d. $3.50

STANTON, Ken. *Operation Steelfish.* 1972. Manor 95-218. My. VG. P1d. $4.00

STANTON, Paul. *Village of Stars.* 1962. Perma M 4230. 1st prtg. VG. P7d. $3.50

STANTON, Vance. *Walking Fingers.* 1972. Curtis 06162. 1st prtg. My. VG+. R5d. $3.00

STANWOOD, Donald A. *Memory of Eva Ryker.* 1979. Dell 15550. My. VG+. P1d. $4.50

STAPLEDON, Olaf. *Odd John.* Galaxy SF 8. VG. B3d. $6.00

STAPLEDON, Olaf. *Starmaker.* 1961. Berkley E 563. PBO. SF. VG+. B5d. $7.50

STAPLETON, Douglas. *Corpse Is Indignant.* 1946. Five Star Mystery 44. My. VG. P1d. $20.00

STAPLETON, Douglas. *Corpse Is Indignant.* 1946. Pony 122. My. VG. P1d. $15.00

STARK, J. *Runaways of Passion.* Imperial 740. NF. B3d. $6.00

STARK, John. *Vice Dolls.* 1963. Midwood F 334. PBO. VG+. B6d. $12.50

STARK, M. *Run for Your Life.* Handi-Book 70. VG. B3d. $4.00

STARK, Richard. *Black Ice Score.* 1968. Gold Medal D 1949. My. VG. P1d. $7.50

STARK, Richard. *Butcher's Moon.* Avon 69907. 1st pb. VG. M6d. $4.50

STARK, Richard. *Damsel.* Signet P 3874. G+. G5d. $6.50

STARK, Richard. *Green Eagle Score.* 1967. Gold Medal D 1861. My. VG. P1d. $7.50

STARK, Richard. *Green Eagle Score.* HF Coronet 4463. G+. G5d. $9.00

STARK, Richard. *Handle.* 1966. Pocket 50220. PBO. VG+. G5d. $7.00

STARK, Richard. *Hunter.* 1984. Avon 68627. My. VG. P1d. $4.00

STARK, Richard. *Hunter.* 1962. Perma M 4272. My. G+. P1d. $5.00

STARK, Richard. *Hunter.* 1962. Perma M 4272. 1st prtg. PBO. c/Bennett. VG. P7d. $10.00

STARK, Richard. *Jugger.* 1965. Pocket 50149. My. VG. P1d. $8.00

STARK, Richard. *Man With the Getaway Face.* 1963. Pocket 6180. My. VG+. P1d. $9.00

STARK, Richard. *Man With the Getaway Face.* 1963. Pocket 6180. PBO. G+. B6d. $5.00

STARK, Richard. *Mourner.* 1963. Perma M 4298. My. F. B4d. $20.00

STARK, Richard. *Mourner.* 1963. Perma M 4298. My. G+. P1d. $5.00

STARK, Richard. *Outfit.* 1963. Perma M 4292. My. G+. P1d. $5.00

STARK, Richard. *Point Blank!* 1967. Coronet 02370. MTI. c/Lee Marvin. VG+. B3d #24. $22.00

STARK, Richard. *Point Blank!* 1967. Gold Medal D 1856. MTI. c/Lee Marvin. VG. M6d. $6.50

STARK, Richard. *Run Lethal.* 1973. Berkley 02479. My. VG. P1d. $5.00

STARK, Richard. *Score.* 1964. Pocket 35014. My. VG. P1d. $7.50

STARK, Richard. *Seventh.* 1966. Pocket 50244. My. VG+. P1d. $8.50

STARK, Richard. *Sour Lemon Score.* Hayakawa 1480. My. VG. P1d. $7.50

STARK, Richard. *Split.* 1966. Gold Medal D1997. MTI. c/R McGinnis. My. VG. M6d. $7.50

STARK/TURNER. *Kill Box/Tobacco Auction Murders.* 1954. Ace D 55. PBO. c/Maguire. VG+. B6d. $35.00

STARK/TURNER. *Kill Box/Tobacco Auction Murders.* 1954. Ace D 55. PBO. c/Maguire: gga. VG+. B6a #75. $49.50

STARK/TURNER. *Kill Box/Tobacco Auction Murders.* 1954. Ace D 55. My. G+. P1d. $8.00

STARK/TURNER. *Kill Box/Tobacco Auction Murders.* 1954. Ace D 55. My. VG. P1d. $15.00

STARKS, Christopher. *Possession.* 1983. Gold Medal 12547. 1st edn. Ho. F. F2d. $10.00

STARNES, Richard. *And When She Was Bad She Was Murdered.* 1951. Pocket 779. My. VG. P1d. $9.00

STARNES, Richard. *Another Mug for the Bier.* 1952. Pocket 858. My. VG. P1d. $9.00

STARNES, Richard. *Other Body in Grant's Tomb.* 1953. Pocket 917. c/G Erickson. My. G+. B5d. $3.00

STARNES, Richard. *Other Body in Grant's Tomb.* 1953. Pocket 917. My. F. P1d. $17.00

STARR, Bill. *Way to Dawnworld.* 1979. Ballantine 28166. 2nd prtg. SF. G+. W2d. $2.75

STARR, Jimmy. *Three Short Biers.* 1945. Bart House 15. VG. B3d. $8.00

STARR, Jimmy. *Three Short Biers.* 1945. Bart House 15. 1st pb edn. F. M1d. $12.00

STARRETT, Vincent. *Private Life of Sherlock Holmes.* 1975. Pinnacle 250695. F. G5d. $18.00

STARRETT, Vincent. *Private Life of Sherlock Holmes.* 1975. Pinnacle 250695. Nfi. G+. P1d. $4.00

STASHEFF, Christopher. *Warlock in Spite of Himself.* 1969. Ace. 1st edn. F. M1d. $15.00

STATEHAM, B.R. *Banners of the Sa'Yen.* 1981. DAW. 1st edn. F. M1d. $5.00

STATTEN, V. *Inferno.* Scion NN. VG+. B3d. $8.00

STEAKLEY, John. *Armor.* 1984. DAW UE 2368. 7th prtg. SF. F. W2d. $4.00

STEARN, Jess. *Edgar Cayne: The Sleeping Prophey.* 1968. Bantam N 3654. 6th prtg. Nfi. F. W2d. $5.00

STEARN, Jess. *Wasted Years.* 1961. Hillman 50-109. JD. VG+. P1d. $14.50

STEBEL, S.L. *Vorovich Affair.* 1977. Penguin 4380. My. VG. P1d. $4.00

STED, Richard. *They All Bleed Red.* Bestseller Mystery B 186. My. VG. P1d. $12.50

STEEL, Kurt. *Judas Incorporated.* 1948. Dell 244. My. F. P1d. $20.00

STEEL, Kurt. *Judas Incorporated.* 1948. Dell 244. VG+. G5d. $10.00

STEEL, Kurt. *Murdor Cocs to College.* 1944. Atlas Mystery. My. VG. P1d. $20.00

STEELE, A. *New People: They Came From the Sea.* 1969. Tempo 5308. 1st prtg. TVTI. VG. R5d. $3.00

STEELE, Addison. *Buck Rogers in the 25th Century.* 1978. Dell. 1st edn. F. M1d. $7.00

STEELE, Addison. *That Man on Beta.* 1979. Dell 10948. Buck Rogers #2. SF. F. W2d. $8.00

STEELE, Curtis. *Army of the Dead.* 1966. Corinth CR 120. My/SF. F. P1d. $20.00

STEELE, Curtis. *Army of the Dead.* 1966. Corinth CR 120. Operator 5. VG+. B3a #24. $6.05

STEELE, Curtis. *Hosts of the Flaming Death.* 1966. Corinth. Operator 5 #5. VG. M1d. $15.00

STEELE, Curtis. *Invasion of the Yellow Warlords.* 1966. Corinth CR 144. 1st edn. SF. F. F2d. $15.00

STEELE, Curtis. *Invisible Empire.* 1966. Corinth CR 124. My/SF. F. P1d. $20.00

STEELE, Curtis. *Invisible Empire.* 1974. Freeway Press. 1st edn. Operator 5 #2. NF. M1d. $8.00

STEELE, Curtis. *Legions of Death Master.* 1966. Corinth. Operator 5 #1. G+. M1d. $10.00

STEELE, Curtis. *Master of Broken Men.* 1966. Corinth CR 128. My/SF. F. P1d. $20.00

STEELE, Curtis. *Yellow Scourge.* 1974. Freeway Press 2056. 1st edn. SF. F. F2d. $15.00

STEELE, Jaclen. *Forbidden Room.* 1952. Gold Medal 221. PBO. c/Barye. NF. B6d. $9.00

STEELE, Jaclen. *Forbidden Room.* 1952. Gold Medal 221. VG+. B3d. $6.00

STEELE, Linda. *Ibis.* 1985. DAW 644. PBO. c/J Chiodo. SF. NF. B6d. $9.00

STEELE, M. *Bachelor Apartment.* Playtime 635. c/gga. VG. B3d. $5.00

STEELE, M. *Clipjoint Cutie.* Playtime 624. NF. B3d. $7.00

STEELE, M. *Jungle of Lust.* 1962. Bedside 1229. 1st edn. c/gga. F. F2d. $15.00

STEELE, M. *Love Champ.* Playtime 664. PBO. c/gga. VG+. B3d. $6.00

STEELE, M. *Passionate Cheat.* Bedside 1246. PBO. VG+. B3d. $5.00

STEELE, M. *Sucker Bait.* Playtime 647. VG. B3d. $4.00

STEELEY, Robert Derek. *Hot Ice.* 1978. Carlyle CS 7021-T. My. VG. P1d. $3.50

STEEVES, Harrison R. *Good Night, Sheriff.* 1945. Superior M 657. My. VG. P1d. $10.50

STEFFANSON, C. *Lion Men of Mongo.* 1974. Avon 18515. SF. VG. W2d. $5.00

STEFFANSON, C. *Plague of Sound.* 1974. Avon 19166. SF. VG. W2d. $5.00

STEFFANSON, C. *Space Circus.* 1974. Avon 19695. SF. G. W2d. $3.00

STEFFERUD, Alfred edt. *Wonderful World of Books.* 1953. Mentor M 82. Nfi. F. P1d. $11.00

STEGER, Shelby. *Desire in the Ozarks.* 1957. Ace D 224. PBO. c/gga. VG. B6d. $12.50

STEIGER, Brad. *Alien Meetings.* 1978. Ace 01571. 1st edn. F. F2d. $6.00

STEIGER, Brad. *Bizarre Honeymoon.* 1964. Merit 6M446. 1st edn. c/gga. scarce. SF. F. F2d. $22.00

STEIGER, Brad. *In My Soul I Am Free.* Lancer 74-952. PBO. Nfi. VG. B5d. $4.00

STEIGER, Brad. *Sex & Satanism.* Ace 75-958. Nfi. NF. VG. $7.50

STEIGER, Brad. *Sex & the Supernatural.* Lancer 75-060. PBO. VG. M6d. $5.00

STEIGER, Brad. *Strange Guests.* Ace K 241. VG+. B3d. $4.50

STEIN, Aaron Marc. *Case of the Absent-Minded Professor.* My Novel Classic 82. My. VG. P1d. $20.00

STEIN, Aaron Marc. *Days of Misfortune.* Bestseller Mystery B 132. My. VG. P1d. $12.50

STEIN, Aaron Marc. *Deadly Delight.* 1968. Popular 60-2287. My. VG. P1d. $5.00

STEIN, Robert. *Singalong Song Book.* 1961. Lancer 72-613. PBO. VG+. B3d. $5.00

STEIN. *Death Meets 400 Rabbits.* 1970. Curtis 6023. 1s tpb. My. NF. B6d. $9.00

STEINBECK, John. *Acts of King Arthur & His Noble Knights.* 1984. Ballantine 28955. 6th prtg. SF. VG. W2d. $4.00

STEINBECK, John. *Cannery Row.* Bantam 75. VG. B3d. $4.00

STEINBECK, John. *Cup of Gold.* 1953. Bantam 1184. 1st prtg. c/Mayan. VG+. P7d. $5.50

STEINBECK, John. *Cup of Gold.* 1950. Popular 216. c/Belarski: gga. Fa. VG+. B4d. $15.00

STEINBECK, John. *Fourteen Great Short Stories.* 1947. Avon 132. PBO. VG. B6d. $6.00

STEINBECK, John. *In Touch.* Dell 4023. VG. B3d. $4.00

STEINBECK, John. *Long Valley.* 1945. Avon 77. 1st prtg. c/La Carrada. NF. P7d. $20.00

STEINBECK, John. *Long Valley.* Corgi 577. VG. B3d. $5.50

STEINBECK, John. *Of Mice & Men.* 1955. Bantam A 1329. Fa. VG+. B4d. $5.00

STEINBECK, John. *Pastures of Heaven.* Bantam 899. VG+. B3d. $4.50

STEINBECK, John. *Pastures of Heaven.* 1951. Bantam 899. c/gga. Fa. VG. B4d. $4.00

STEINBECK, John. *Pearl.* 1947. Bantam 131. MTI. c/gga. VG+. B4d. $10.00

STEINBECK, John. *Red Pony.* 1948. Bantam 402. MTI. VG. B3d. $4.00

STEINBECK, John. *Red Pony.* 1948. Bantam 402. 1st pb. MTI. NF. B6d. $35.00

STEINBECK, John. *Short Reign of Pippin IV.* Bantam 1753. VG+. B3d. $5.00

STEINBECK, John. *Steinbeck Pocket Book.* 1943. Pocket 243. 1st pb. VG. M6d. $9.50

STEINBECK, John. *Sweet Thursday.* 1956. Bantam A 1412. c/Barye: gga. Fa. VG+. B4d. $7.00

STEINBECK, John. *Sweet Thursday.* Pan GP 92. 2nd prtg. c/Heade. VG. B3d. $8.50

STEINBECK, John. *To a God Unknown.* Dell 358. VG+. B3d. $5.50

STEINBECK, John. *Tortilla Flat.* Signet 816. 4th prtg. VG. B3d. $5.00

STEINCROHN, Peter J. *How To Stop Killing Yourself.* 1957. Ace D 213. VG. B5d. $4.50

STEINER, Paul edt. *Bedside Bachelor.* 1957. Lion Library LL 168. 1st prtg. PBO. c/Hawley: gga. VG. P7d. $5.00

STEINER, Paul edt. *Bedtime Laughs.* 1956. Lion Library LL 105. 1st prtg. PBO. c/Hawley: gga. VG. P7d. $6.00

STELL, Aaron. *Angel of Satan.* 1974. Pinnacle 292. PBO. Ho. VG+. B6d. $7.50

STENDHAL. *Charterhouse of Parma.* 1960. Bantam SC 67. Fi. VG. B5d. $2.50

STEPHENS, A. *Sex Offense.* Brandon House 966. VG+. B3d. $4.50

STEPHENS, Reed. *Man Who Risked His Partner.* 1984. Ballantine 31804. 1st pb edn. My. F. B6d. $7.50

STERLING, Brett. *Tenth Planet.* Popular 60-2445. 1st prtg. G. S1d. $2.00

STERLING, R. *Flesh!* Nite Time 108. VG. B3d. $4.50

STERLING, Stewart. *Alibi Baby.* 1955. Avon 685. G+. G5d. $3.00

STERLING, Stewart. *Alibi Baby.* 1955. Avon 685. My. F. P1d. $16.00

STERLING, Stewart. *Alibi Baby.* 1955. Avon 685. PBO. c/gga. My. VG+. B6d. $12.50

STERLING, Stewart. *Blonde in Suite 14.* 1959. Avon T 320. c/gga. My. VG. B4d. $3.00

STERLING, Stewart. *Blonde in Suite 14.* 1959. Avon T 320. My. F. P1d. $14.00

STERLING, Stewart. *Dead of Night.* 1952. Dell 583. 1st prtg. c/Downes: gga. VG. P7d. $5.50

STERLING, Stewart. *Dead Sure.* Dell 420. 1st prtg. My. G+. R5d. $3.50

STERLING, Stewart. *Dead Wrong.* Dell 314. 1st prtg. My. VG. R5d. $5.25

STERLING, Stewart. *Hotel Murders.* 1957. Avon 762. My. F. P1d. $15.00

STERLING, Stewart. *Nightmare at Noon.* 1953. Dell 693. My. F. P1d. $20.00

STERLING, Stewart. *Nightmare at Noon.* 1953. Dell 693. 1st prtg. My. G+. R5d. $3.00

STERLING, Stewart. *Too Hot To Kill.* 1958. Avon 835. c/Darcy. My. VG+. B5d. $5.50

STERLING, Stewart. *Where There's Smoke.* 1949. Dell 275. 1st prtg. VG. P7d. $7.50

STERLING, Thomas. *Evil of the Day.* 1963. Grove Press BA 48. My. VG. P1d. $6.00

STERLING, Thomas. *House Without a Door.* Boardman 133. VG. B3d. $9.00

STERLING, Thomas. *House Without a Door.* 1951. Pocket 774. My. F. P1d. $18.00

STERLING, Thomas. *Murder in Venice.* 1959. Dell D 270. My. F. P1d. $15.00

STERLING/STERLING. *Dying Room Only/ Body in the Bed.* 1960. Ace D 463. VG. B3d. $5.00

STERN, Bill. *Bill Stern's Favorite Boxing Stories.* Pocket 416. PBO. VG+. B3d. $6.00

STERN, Daniel. *Girl With the Glass Heart.* 1955. Perma M 4010. Fi. F. P1d. $16.00

STERN, Daniel. *Suicide Academy.* 1972. Ballantine 02538. My. F. P1d. $5.00

STERN, David. *Francis.* 1951. Dell 507. MTI. c/R Hook. SF. G. B5d. $3.00

STERN, Jill. *Nine Miles to Reno (Not in Our Stars).* Signet 1570. c/Barye. VG. B3d. $4.50

STERN, Philip Van Doren edt. *Pocket Book of America.* 1942. Pocket 182. PBO. Nfi. VG. B5d. $5.50

STERN, Philip Van Doren edt. *Pocket Book of Ghost Stories.* 1947. Pocket 384. 1st edn. VG. B6d. $8.00

STERN, Philip Van Doren edt. *Pocket Reader.* 1941. Pocket 108. Nfi. G+. B5d. $5.50

STERN, Philip Van Doren edt. *Strange Beasts & Unnatural Monsters.* 1968. Crest 1166. 1st edn. PBO. SF. F. F2d. $8.00

STERN, Philip. *Great Tales of Fantasy & Imagination.* Cardinal C 156. VG+. I1d. $5.00

STERN, Richard Martin. *Bright Road To Fear.* 1963. Ballantine F 707. 3rd edn. My. VG+. P1d. $7.50

STERN, Richard Martin. *I Hide, We Seek.* 1967. Lancer 73-581. Th. VG. P1d. $5.00

STERN, Richard Martin. *Search for Tabitha Carr.* MacFadden 60-180. VG. B3d. $4.00

STERN, Richard Martin. *Stanfield Harvest.* 1974. Crest P 2015. Fi. VG. P1d. $3.50

STERN, Richard Martin. *Suspense.* 1959. Ballantine 331K. PBO. My. VG+. B6d. $12.00

STETTINIUS, E.R. *Lend-Lease Weapon for Victory.* Pocket 266. VG. B3d. $4.50

STEVENS, Dale. *In Any Man's Bed.* 1967. Intimate 203. Ad. VG+. B5d. $6.00

STEVENS, Dan J. *Blood Money.* 1956. Perma M 3033. PBO. c/Schulz. We. VG+. B6d. $12.00

STEVENS, Dan J. *Deadline.* Tower 42-622. PBO. VG+. B3d. $4.50

STEVENS, Dan J. *Hangman's Mesa.* 1959. Monarch 135. 1st prtg. PBO. c/Ross. VG. P7d. $5.00

STEVENS, Dan J. *Hangman's Mesa.* 1963. Monarch 383. c/Bob Stanley. We. VG. P6d. $3.00

STEVENS, Dan J. *Oregon Trunk.* 1951. Lion 50. c/gga. scarce in condition. NF. B6a #74. $48.50

STEVENS, Dan J. *Oregon Trunk.* 1951. Lion 50. G+. I1d. $6.00

STEVENS, Dan J. *Oregon Trunk.* 1951. Lion 50. PBO. c/gga. VG. B6d. $9.00

STEVENS, Edmund. *Un-Censored!* 1951. Eton ET 108. VG+. P6d. $3.00

STEVENS, Francis. *Citadel of Fear.* 1970. PB Library 65-401. PBO. c/Steele Savage. SF. VG. B6d. $5.00

STEVENS, G. *Thing About Susan.* Brandon House 985. VG. B3d. $4.50

STEVENS, Gus. *Why Play Games?* 1966. Midwood 33-700. Ad. VG+. B5d. $5.50

STEVENS, Shane. *Go Down Dead.* 1968. Pocket 75242. JD. VG. P1d. $10.00

STEVENS, Troy. *Kiss Her, Kill Her!* 1967. Triumph TNC 303. My. VG. P1d. $5.00

STEVENS/SULLIVAN. *Dry Fork Incident/ Deadly Deputy.* 1969. Ace 17000. We. VG. B5d. $3.00

STEVENSON, Robert Louis. *Dr Jekyll & Mr Hyde.* 1964. Airmont CL 42. SF. VG. B5d. $2.50

STEVENSON, Robert Louis. *Dr Jekyll & Mr Hyde.* 1964. Airmont CL 42. 1st prtg. SF. G+. R5d. $1.00

STEVENSON, Robert Louis. *Dr Jekyll & Mr Hyde.* 1973. Bantam SP 7846. 12th prtg. SF. G+. W2d. $2.75

STEVENSON, Robert Louis. *Dr Jekyll & Mr Hyde.* Lancer 14101. SF. G. W2d. $2.75

STEVENSON, Robert Louis. *Dr Jekyll & Mr Hyde.* 1942. Pocket 123. 5th edn. My/SF. VG+. P1d. $14.50

STEVENSON, Robert Louis. *Dr Jekyll & Mr Hyde.* 1964. Scholastic 550. 2nd prtg. SF. VG. W2d. $3.25

STEVENSON, Robert Louis. *Dr Jekyll & Mr Hyde.* 1950. Zephyr 129. dust jacket. My/SF. VG. P1d. $45.00

STEVENSON, Robert Louis. *Master of Ballantrae.* Popular SP 265. NF. B3d. $5.00

STEVENSON, Robert Louis. *Suicide Club.* 1974. Scholastic 1000. My. VG. P1d. $3.50

STEVENSON, Robert Louis. *Treasure Island.* 1948. Bantam 142. Fa. VG+. B4d. $8.00

STEWARD, Davenport. *Black Spice.* Popular SP 78. VG+. B3d. $5.00

STEWARD, Davenport. *They Had a Glory.* Perma P 181. VG+. B3d. $5.00

STEWARD, Dwight. *Acupuncture Murders.* 1974. Warner 76-575. My. VG. P1d. $3.50

STEWART, Blair. *Delinquents.* 1964. Playtime 685. JD. VG+. P1d. $25.00

STEWART, Desmond. *Leopard in the Grass.* 1953. Signet 997. My. F. P1d. $17.00

STEWART, Desmond. *Stranger in Eden.* 1956. Signet 1357. Th. F. P1d. $16.00

STEWART, Edward. *They've Shot the President's Daughter.* 1974. Signet E 5928. 3rd prtg. My. VG. W2d. $3.25

STEWART, Fred M. *Mephisto Waltz.* 1982. Berkley 05343. 2nd prtg. SF. F. W2d. $4.50

STEWART, Fred M. *Mephisto Waltz.* Signet Q 4184. 1st prtg. F. S1d. $3.50

STEWART, Fred M. *Mephisto Waltz.* 1970. Signet Q 4184. 1st prtg. VG. R5d. $2.50

STEWART, George R. *Names on the Land.* Armed Services 929. Nfi. VG. B5d. $4.00

STEWART, George R. *Ordeal by Hunger.* Armed Services E 134. VG. B3d. $5.00

STEWART, Jack. *Fabulous Fondas.* 1976. Belmont Tower 50896. 1st edn. MTI. Bio. F. F2d. $8.00

STEWART, Jeff. *Sex Singer.* 1962. Bedside 1240. 1st edn. c/gga. F. F2d. $8.00

STEWART, L. *Savage Stronghold.* Gold Medal 327. VG. B3d. $3.50

STEWART, L. *Secret Rider.* Gold Medal 243. VG. B3d. $5.00

STEWART, L. *War Bonnet Pass.* Gold Medal 137. VG. B3d. $5.00

STEWART, L. *War Bonnet Pass.* Gold Medal 313. NF. I1d. $8.00

STEWART, Mary. *Airs Above the Ground.* 1970. Crest M 1360. My. VG+. P1d. $5.00

STEWART, Mary. *Crystal Cave.* 1971. Crest 02173. SF. VG+. W2d. $4.00

STEWART, Mary. *Gabriel Hounds.* 1968. Crest T 1179. My. F. P1d. $10.00

STEWART, Mary. *Madam, Will You Talk?* 1968. Crest T 1212. My. VG. P1d. $5.00

STEWART, Mary. *Thunder on the Right.* 1965. Crest D 609. 4th edn. My. F. P1d. $9.00

STEWART, Mary. *Touch Not The Cat.* 1977. Coronet 21984. My/SF. VG. P1d. $4.00

STEWART, Mary. *Wildfire at Midnight.* 1962. Crest D 563. My. VG. P1d. $6.50

STEWART, Michael. *Far Cry.* 1988. Paperjacks 0785. Ho. VG. P1d. $4.00

STEWART, Michael. *Hello, Dolly!* 1968. Signet I 3651. 1st prtg. VG+. R5d. $2.50

STEWART, Ramona. *Desert Town.* 1948. Pocket 526. My. VG. P1d. $10.00

STEWART, Ramona. *Stars Abide.* 1962. Cardinal GC 156. Fa. VG+. B3d. $4.00

STEWART, Ramona. *Surprise Party Complex.* 1963. Pocket 6214. Fi. VG. B5d. $3.00

STEWART, S.D. *Campus Humor.* Dell 1025. VG+. B3d. $5.00

STEWART, Sam. *McCoy.* 1976. Dell 5293. My. VG. P1d. $5.00

STILES, Bert. *Serenade to the Big Bird.* 1957. Ballantine 216. 1st pb. VG. B6d. $6.00

STILLMAN & BAKER. *Doctor's Quick Teenage Diet.* 1972. PB Library 65-830. Nfi. VG+. B5d. $4.00

STILWELL, Hart. *Border City.* 1950. Bantam 765. NF. I1d. $5.00

STILWELL, Hart. *Campus Town.* 1951. Popular 331. 1st edn. PBO. c/Bergey: gga. VG+. B6a #80. $82.50

STIMSON & BELLAH. *Avenger Tapes.* 1971. Pinnacle P 019-Z. Th. VG. P1d. $4.00

STINE, Bob. *Spaceballs: The Book.* 1987. Scholastic 41226. MTI. SF. VG+. W2d. $4.50

STINE, G.H. *Earth Satellites.* 1957. Ace D 239. VG+. B3d. $4.00

STINE, Hank. *Prisoner #3.* 1970. Ace 67902. TVTI. NF. B4d. $10.00

STINE/STINE. *Journey to Vernico #5.* 1984. Scholastic 33213. 2nd prtg. Twistaplot #12. SF. F. W2d. $3.50

STINE/STINE. *Jungle Quest (Computer Game Book).* Scholastic 33166. Micro Adventure #2. SF. VG+. W2d. $2.75

STINETORF, Louise A. *White Witch Doctor.* 1952. Pocket 851. Nfi. VG. B4d. $3.00

STIRLING, Peter. *Stop Press: Murder!* Black Knight 33. G+. G5d. $4.00

STIX, T.L. *Sporting Gesture.* Armed Services 832. VG. B3d. $5.00

STOCKBRIDGE, Grant. *City Destroyer.* 1974. Pocket 77943. 2nd edn. My/SF. VG. P1d. $6.00

STOCKBRIDGE, Grant. *Death & the Spider.* 1974. Pocket 77953. G. G5d. $6.00

STOCKBRIDGE, Grant. *Death & the Spider.* 1974. Pocket 77953. 2nd edn. My/SF. VG. P1d. $6.00

STOCKBRIDGE, Grant. *Death Reign of the Vampire King.* Pocket 77952. VG. G5d. $7.00

STOCKBRIDGE, Grant. *Hordes of the Red Butcher.* 1975. Pocket 77944. c/Bob Maguire. reprint. Spider Series #2. G. P6d. $2.25

STOCKBRIDGE, Grant. *Spider-Master of Men!* Carroll & Graf. NF. B3d. $6.50

STOCKBRIDGE, Grant. *Wings of the Black Death.* Berkley X 1782. VG. B5d. $9.00

STOCKTON, Frank. *Great Stone of Sardis.* 1976. Belmont-Tower. F. M1d. $4.00

STODDARD, Charles. *Devil's Portage.* 1958. Harlequin 414. Hi. VG. P1d. $20.00

STOILMAN, Richard. *Overflowing Ruin.* 1979. Avon 75019. My. VG. P1d. $3.50

STOKER, Bram. *Dracula.* Armed Services L 25. VG. B3d. $8.00

STOKER, Bram. *Dracula.* 1957. Perma M 4088. VG. I1d. $5.00

STOKER, Bram. *Dracula.* 1957. Perma M 4088. 2nd edn. MTI. NF. B6d. $12.50

STOKER, Bram. *Dracula.* 1947. Pocket 452. VG. M1d. $10.00

STOKER, Bram. *Dracula.* 1947. Pocket 452. 1st edn. PBO. VG+. F2d. $22.00

STOKER, Bram. *Dracula.* 1947. Pocket 452. 1st edn. rare. F. B6a #75. $66.00

STOKER, Bram. *Dracula.* 1974. Tempo 05744. SF. VG+. W2d. $4.50

STOKER, Bram. *Garden of Evil.* 1966. PB Library 53946. SF. VG. W2d. $4.00

STOKER, Bram. *Garden of Evil.* 1969. PB Library 63790. 2nd prtg. SF. G+. W2d. $3.50

STOKER, Bram. *Jewel of Seven Stars.* 1972. Scholastic 970. SF. F. W2d. $5.00

STOKER, Bram. *Lair of the White Worm.* 1960. Arrow 585. VG. B3d. $9.00

STOKER, R. *Nymphets & Their Lovers.* Barclay 7293. c/photo. NF. B3d. $5.00

STOKES, Donald. *Appointment With Fear.* Signet 873. G+. l1d. $5.00

STOKES, Donald. *Appointment With Fear.* 1951. Signet 873. My. VG. P1d. $9.00

STOKES, Donald. *Captive in the Night.* 1956. Crest 126. My. VG. P1d. $8.00

STOKES, Donald. *Captive in the Night.* 1953. Signet 1006. My. G+. P1d. $6.00

STOKES, Manning Lee. *Crooked Circle.* 1951. Graphic 40. G+. G5d. $3.50

STOKES, Manning Lee. *Crooked Circle.* 1951. Graphic 40. My. VG+. P1d. $13.50

STOKES, Manning Lee. *Grave's in the Meadow.* 1961. Dell D 420. 1st prtg. My. VG. R5d. $3.25

STOKES, Manning Lee. *Murder Can't Wait.* 1955. Graphic 117. 1st prtg. PBO. VG. P7d. $6.00

STOKES, Manning Lee. *Too Many Murderers.* 1955. Graphic 98. 2nd edn. My. VG. B5d. $5.00

STOKES, Manning Lee. *Under Cover of Night.* 1958. Dell 1st Edn A 163. My. F. P1d. $15.00

STOKES, Manning Lee. *Under Cover of Night.* 1958. Dell 1st Edn A 163. PBO c/Darcy: gga. My. VG. B6d. $7.50

STOKES, Manning Lee. *Winning.* 1969. Signet T 3827. Fi. VG. P1d. $4.50

STOKES, Manning Lee. *Wolf Howls Murder.* 1946. Prize Mystery 21. My. VG. P1d. $20.00

STOLBERG, Charles edt. *Avon Book of Crossword Puzzles.* 1943. Avon 27. VG. B3a #24. $101.30

STOLZ, Mary. *Oriole's Nest.* 1963. Berkely F 720. PBO. NF. B6d. $12.00

STONE, Andrew L. *Cry Terror.* 1958. Signet 1508. MTI. c/Maguire: sgn. VG+. B3d. $8.50

STONE, Andrew L. *Deck Ran Red.* 1958. Signet 1595. 1st edn. c/gga. My. F. F2d. $15.00

STONE, Grace Zaring. *Cold Journey.* 1946. Bantam 44. Fa. VG+. B4d. $8.00

STONE, Hampton. *Babe With the Twistable Arm.* 1963. Popular K 54. My. VG. P1d. $6.00

STONE, Hampton. *Corpse in the Corner Saloon.* 1950. Dell 464. My. VG. P1d. $9.50

STONE, Hampton. *Corpse That Refused to Stay Dead.* 1954. Dell 790. 1st prtg. VG. P7d. $5.50

STONE, Hampton. *Corpse Who Had Too Many Friends.* Bestseller Mystery B 173. My. VG. P1d. $12.50

STONE, Hampton. *Girl Who Kept Knocking Them Dead.* Dell D 278. c/McGinnis. VG+. B3d. $4.50

STONE, Hampton. *Man Who Had Too Much To Lose.* 1957. Dell 943. c/A Brule. My. VG. B5d. $3.00

STONE, Hampton. *Man Who Looked Death in the Eye.* 1971. PB Library 64-652. My. VG. P1d. $4.00

STONE, Hampton. *Murder That Wouldn't Stay Solved.* 1956. Dell 883. c/W Rose. We. VG. B5d. $4.00

STONE, Idella Purnell edt. *Never in This World.* 1971. Gold Medal T 2406. SF. VG. B5d. $3.50

STONE, Idella Purnell edt. *14 Great Tales of ESP.* 1969. Gold Medal T 2164. 1st prtg. SF. VG. B3d. $4.00

STONE, Irving. *Love Is Eternal.* 1956. Cardinal GC 32. c/T Dunn. Fi. VG. B5d. $2.50

STONE, Patti. *Big Town Nurse.* 1965. Pyramid K 1129. Fa. NF. B4d. $6.00

STONE, Patti. *Pip Night.* 1966. Bantam H 3104. Fi. VG. B5d. $2.50

STONE, Patti. *Sandra, Surgical Nurse.* 1963. Bantam J 2944. Fi. VG. B5d. $2.50

STONE, Peter. *Charade.* 1963. Gold Medal K 1358. My. F. My. P1d. $12.00

STONE, Peter. *Charade.* 1963. Gold Medal K 1358. PBO. MTI. My. VG. B5d. $5.00

STONE, Peter. *Charade.* 1963. Gold Medal K 1358. 1st prtg. G+. R5d. $2.75

STONE, Scott. *Coasts of War.* 1966. Pyramid X 1277. We. VG+. B4d. $2.75

STONE, Scott. *Divorcees.* 1959. Beacon 246. 1st prtg. VG. P7d. $9.00

STONE, Scott. *Dragon's Eye.* 1969. Gold Medal R 2157. My. G+. W2d. $3.00

STONE, Scott. *Dragon's Eye.* 1969. Gold Medal R 2157. My. VG. B5d. $3.50

STONE, Scott. *Margo.* 1959. Beacon 248. 1st prtg. VG+. P7d. $12.50

STONE, Scott. *She Learned the Hard Way.* 1960. Beacon 315. 1st pb. c/gga. VG+. B6d. $16.50

STONE, Thomas. *Doctor by Day.* Harlequin 142. VG. B3d. $6.00

STONE, Thomas. *Ex-Mistress.* 1960. Beacon 285. 1st prtg. PBO. VG. P7d. $7.50

STONE, Thomas. *Help Wanted -- Male.* 1950. Novel Library 41. PBO. c/gga. VG+. B6a #74. $42.00

STONE, Thomas. *Red-Headed Nurse.* Intimate 47. VG+. B3d. $10.00

STONE, Thomas. *Shameful Love (Raging Passions).* 1952. Croydon 102. VG. B3a. $48.00

STONE, Thomas. *Shameless Honeymoon.* 1950. Pyramid 18. 1st pb. c/Barker: gga. VG. B6d. $7.50

STONE, Thomas. *Tramp Girl.* 1960. Beacon 349. 1st edn. c/gga. F. F2d. $13.00

STONEBRAKER, Florence. *Four Men & a Dame.* 1951. Quarter Books 83. PBO. c/Rudy Nappi: gga. NF. B6a #80. $74.00

STONEBRAKER, Florence. *Intimate Affairs of a French Nurse.* 1954. Croydon 79. 1st edn. G+. F2d. $10.00

STONEBRAKER, Florence. *Kept Sisters.* 1961. Beacon B 388. PBO. Ad. G+. B5d. $4.50

STONEBRAKER, Florence. *Lust for Love.* 1960. Beacon B 321. PBO. Ad. G+. B5d. $3.50

STONEBRAKER, Florence. *No Man of Her Own.* 1951. Cameo 300. PBO. c/G Gross. Fi. VG. B5d. $12.50

STONEBRAKER, Florence. *Scarlet Lil.* 1952. Original Digest 706. PBO. c/Nappi: gga. rare. VG+. B6a #77. $90.00

STONEBRAKER, Florence. *Sinful Desires.* Bedside 801. VG+. B3d. $8.00

STONEBRAKER, Florence. *Three Men & a Mistress.* 1951. Quarter Books 92. c/Gross. VG. B3a #24. $20.00

STONEBRAKER, Florence. *Who Knows Love?* 1962. Lancer 72-654. 1st edn. PBO. F. F2d. $8.00

STONER, B. *Hold Me Closer.* Spotlight 316. PBO. VG+. B3d. $6.00

STORER, D. edt. *Amazing But True Animals.* Gold Medal 1359. PBO. NF. B3d. $6.50

STORER, John H. *Web of Life.* 1956. Signet KS 333. Nfi. VG+. B4d. $2.25

STOREY, Ed. *Frustrated.* 1961. Novel Book 5053. 1st edn. My. F. F2d. $15.00

STOREY, Philip. *Four O'Clock on Friday.* 1961. Newsstand U 177. Fa. VG+. B4d. $14.00

STOREY, Philip. *Four O'Clock on Friday.* 1961. Newsstand U 177. PBO. c/Bonfils. VG. M6d. $9.50

STOREY, Philip. *Four O'Clock on Friday.* 1961. Newsstand U 177. PBO. c/gga. VG. P6d. $5.00

STORM, C. *Campus Motel.* Softcover Library B 852X. VG. I1d. $4.00

STORME, Michael. *Made Mine a Harlot.* 1952. Archer 84. My. VG+. P1d. $35.00

STORME, Michael. *Make Mine a Shroud.* 1952. Leisure 4. Fa. VG+. B4d. $45.00

STORME, Peter. *Case of the Thing in the Brook.* 1941. Mystery Novel Monthly 22. My. VG. P1d. $20.00

STORY, J.T. *Collapse of Stout Party.* Sexton Blake 401. VG+. B3d. $8.50

STORY, J.T. *Mix Me a Person.* 1962. Corgi SC 1104. My. VG. P1d. $6.50

STORY, J.T. *Murder -- With Love!* Sexton Blake 372. VG+. B3d. $8.00

STORY, J.T. *Murder in the Sun.* Sexton Blake 412. VG+. B3d. $8.50

STORY, J.T. *Season of the Skylark.* Sexton Blake 374. c/gga. VG+. B3d. $8.50

STOUT, Rex. *Alphabet Hicks.* 1947. Dell 146. My. VG. P1d. $12.50

STOUT, Rex. *And Be a Villain.* 1961. Bantam A 2197. My. VG+. P1d. $10.00

STOUT, Rex. *And Be a Villain.* 1950. Bantam 824. My. VG. P1d. $15.00

STOUT, Rex. *And Four To Go.* 1959. Bantam A 2016. My. VG+. P1d. $10.50

STOUT, Rex. *Bad for Business.* 1949. Dell 299. VG. G5d/P1d. $12.50

STOUT, Rex. *Black Mountain.* 1955. Bantam 1386. My. G+. P1d. $6.00

STOUT, Rex. *Black Mountain.* Bantam 2791. 3rd prtg. VG. B3d. $4.00

STOUT, Rex. *Black Orchids.* 1950. Avon 256. My. G+. P6d. $3.50

STOUT, Rex. *Black Orchids.* 1950. Avon 256. My. VG+. P1d. $14.00

STOUT, Rex. *Black Orchids.* 1946. Avon 95. My. G+. P1d. $7.50

STOUT, Rex. *Black Orchids.* 1946. Avon 95. VG. P6d. $8.50

STOUT, Rex. *Black Orchids.* 1979. Jove M 5085. 1st prtg. My. VG+. W2d. $4.00

STOUT, Rex. *Black Orchids.* 1963. Pyramid R 917. My. G+. P1d. $4.50

STOUT, Rex. *Black Orchids.* 1963. Pyramid R 917. reprint. My. VG+. B6d. $7.50

STOUT, Rex. *Broken Vase.* 1958. Collins Crime Club 270C. My. VG. P1d. $7.50

STOUT, Rex. *Broken Vase.* 1946. Dell 115. My. VG+. P1d. $15.50

STOUT, Rex. *Broken Vase.* Dell 674. M6d. $3.00

STOUT, Rex. *Broken Vase.* Jonathan Press J 9. My. G+. P1d. $9.00

STOUT, Rex. *Broken Vase.* Jonathan Press J 9. My. VG. P1d. $12.50

STOUT, Rex. *Champagne for One.* 1960. Bantam A 2023. My. VG. P1d. $7.00

STOUT, Rex. *Crime & Again.* Fontana 629. VG. B3d. $6.00

STOUT, Rex. *Death of a Doxy.* 1967. Bantam H 5316. 4th edn. My. F. P1d. $8.50

STOUT, Rex. *Death of a Dude.* 1970. Bantam S 5487. My. VG. P1d. $4.50

STOUT, Rex. *Door to Death.* Dell 10¢ 21. G+. G5d. $18.00

STOUT, Rex. *Door to Death.* 1951. Dell 10¢ 21. My. VG. P1d. $25.00

STOUT, Rex. *Doorbell Rang.* Bantam 3254. VG+. B3d. $5.00

STOUT, Rex. *Double for Death.* 1951. Dell 495. c/R Stanley. My. VG. B5d. $4.00

STOUT, Rex. *Double for Death.* 1951. Dell 495. 1st prtg. My. G+. R5d. $2.50

STOUT, Rex. *Double for Death.* 1943. Dell 9. PBO. c/Frederiksen. G+. I1d. $12.00

STOUT, Rex. *Double for Death.* 1943. Dell 9. 1st edn. PBO. VG+. B6d. $50.00

STOUT, Rex. *Double for Death.* 1943. Dell 9. 1st prtg. c/Frederiksen. VG. P7d. $20.00

STOUT, Rex. *Father Hunt.* 1969. Bantam H 4467. My. VG. P1d. $5.00

STOUT, Rex. *Fer-De-Lance.* 1958. Dell D 223. My. VG. P1d. $7.50

STOUT, Rex. *Fer-De-Lance.* 1942. Pocket 112. 6th edn. My. VG. P1d. $9.50

STOUT, Rex. *Fer-De-Lance.* Pyramid R 1370. reprint. My. VG. B6d. $5.00

STOUT, Rex. *Fer-de-Lance.* 1964. Pyramid R 970. My. VG+. B4d. $5.00

STOUT, Rex. *Final Deduction.* 1965. Bantam F 3024. 2nd edn. My. F. P1d. $10.00

STOUT, Rex. *Gambit.* 1964. Bantam F 2731. My. VG. P1d. $7.50

STOUT, Rex. *Golden Spiders.* 1955. Bantam 1387. My. VG. P1d. $10.00

STOUT, Rex. *Golden Spiders.* 1955. Bantam 1387. 1st pb. c/Barye. My. NF. B6d. $18.00

STOUT, Rex. *Hand in the Glove.* 1947. Dell 177. c/G Gregg. My. G. B5d/G5d. $5.00

STOUT, Rex. *Hand in the Glove.* 1947. Dell 177. My. F. P1d. $35.00

STOUT, Rex. *Hand in the Glove.* 1947. Dell 177. VG. G5d. $12.50

STOUT, Rex. *Hand in the Glove.* 1964. Pyramid R 1066. My. VG. B4d. $3.00

STOUT, Rex. *Hand in the Glove.* 1968. Pyramid X 1923. 3rd edn. My. F. P1d. $8.50

STOUT, Rex. *Homicide Trinity.* 1970. Bantam S 5486. My. VG. P1d. $4.50

STOUT, Rex. *How Like a God.* 1955. Lion LL 23. 1st pb. My. VG. B5d. $6.00

STOUT, Rex. *If Death Ever Slept.* 1959. Bantam A 1961. My. VG+. P1d. $10.50

STOUT, Rex. *In the Best Families.* 1953. Bantam 1173. My. VG. P1d. $10.00

STOUT, Rex. *In the Best of Families.* Bantam 3270. 2nd prtg. NF. B3d. $5.00

STOUT, Rex. *Invitation To Murder.* 1956. Avon 738. My. VG. B4d. $3.50

STOUT, Rex. *League of Frightened Men.* Avon 20. VG. B3d. $5.50

STOUT, Rex. *League of Frightened Men.* 1942. Avon 20. 1st edn. My. G+. P1d. $20.00

STOUT, Rex. *Might As Well Be Dead.* 1958. Bantam A 1795. My. VG. P1d. $10.00

STOUT, Rex. *Mother Hunt.* 1964. Bantam F 2828. My. VG. P1d. $6.00

STOUT, Rex. *Mountain Cat Murders.* Dell 1st Edn D 252. reprint. VG. B6d. $4.00

STOUT, Rex. *Mountain Cat Murders.* 1944. Dell 28. c/G Gregg. My. G+. B5d. $7.50

STOUT, Rex. *Mountain Cat Murders.* 1944. Dell 28. My. VG. M3d. $15.00

STOUT, Rex. *Mountain Cat Murders.* 1944. Dell 28. 1st edn. PBO. c/Gregg. rare. F. B6a #80. $99.00

STOUT, Rex. *Mountain Cat Murders*. 1964. Dell 5849. My. F. P1d. $12.00

STOUT, Rex. *Murder by the Book*. 1954. Bantam 1252. My. VG. P1d. $10.00

STOUT, Rex. *Murder by the Book*. Bantam 2666. 2nd prtg. VG. B3d. $4.00

STOUT, Rex. *Murder by the Book*. 1957. Collins Crime Club 259C. My. G+. P1d. $5.50

STOUT, Rex. *Murder by the Book*. 1967. Fontana 1534. My. VG. P1d. $6.00

STOUT, Rex. *Not Quite Dead Enough*. 1946. Armed Services 906. My. VG. P1d. $30.00

STOUT, Rex. *Not Quite Dead Enough*. Jonathan Press J 27. My. VG. P1d. $15.00

STOUT, Rex. *Not Quite Dead Enough*. Pyramid 1361. 2nd reissue. VG. B3d. $4.00

STOUT, Rex. *Over My Dead Body*. 1959. Avon T 296. My. F. P1d. $14.00

STOUT, Rex. *Please Pass the Quilt*. 1974. Bantam Q 8472. My. VG. P1d. $4.00

STOUT, Rex. *Plot It Yourself*. 1960. Bantam A 2156. My. VG. P1d. $10.00

STOUT, Rex. *Plot It Yourself*. 1968. Bantam H 5314. 4th edn. My. F. P1d. $8.50

STOUT, Rex. *President Vanishes*. 1977. Jove V 4390. My. VG+. B5d. $3.50

STOUT, Rex. *Prisoner's Base*. 1955. Bantam 1326. VG. G5d. $6.50

STOUT, Rex. *Red Box*. 1958. Avon T 216. My. G+. P1d. $5.50

STOUT, Rex. *Red Box*. 1958. Avon T 216. reprint. c/gga. My. VG. B6d. $6.00

STOUT, Rex. *Red Box*. 1943. Avon Murder My 9. My. G+. P1d. $20.00

STOUT, Rex. *Red Box*. 1964. Pyramid R 983. My. VG. B4d. $3.75

STOUT, Rex. *Red Bull*. Dell 70. c/G Gregg. My. G+. B5d. $7.50

STOUT, Rex. *Red Bull*. 1945. Dell 70. 1st edn. PBO. VG. B6d. $35.00

STOUT, Rex. *Red Threads*. 1948. Dell 235. My. F. P1d. $20.00

STOUT, Rex. *Red Threads*. 1948. Dell 235. 1st prtg. My. VG. R5d. $8.00

STOUT, Rex. *Red Threads*. 1954. Penguin 976. My. F. P1d. $17.00

STOUT, Rex. *Right To Die*. 1965. Bantam F 3061. My. VG. P1d. $7.50

STOUT, Rex. *Rubber Band*. 1943. Pocket 208. My. VG. P1d. $20.00

STOUT, Rex. *Rubber Band*. 1964. Pyramid R 1053. My. VG+. B4d. $3.75

STOUT, Rex. *Second Confession*. 1952. Bantam 1032. My. VG+. B3d. $4.50

STOUT, Rex. *Silent Speaker*. 1948. Bantam 308. My. F. P1d. $25.00

STOUT, Rex. *Silent Speaker*. 1948. Bantam 308. My. G+. P1d. $7.50

STOUT, Rex. *Silent Speaker*. Bantam 3477. 3rd prtg. VG+. B3d. $4.00

STOUT, Rex. *Some Buried Caesar*. 1979. Jove M 5118. My. VG. P1d. $4.00

STOUT, Rex. *Some Buried Caesar*. 1963. Pyramid R 931. My. VG+. B5d. $6.00

STOUT, Rex. *Sound of Murder*. 1965. Pyramid R 1123. My. VG. P1d. $5.50

STOUT, Rex. *Three Doors to Death*. 1966. Bantam F 3154. 1st prtg. My. VG+. R5d. $2.50

STOUT, Rex. *Three Doors to Death*. 1952. Dell 626. VG. I1d. $4.00

STOUT, Rex. *Three for the Chair*. 1958. Bantam A 1796. My. VG. P1d. $10.00

STOUT, Rex. *Three for the Chair*. Bantam 3120. 4th prtg. NF. B3d. $6.00

STOUT, Rex. *Three Men Out*. Bantam 1388. VG. B3d/I1d. $4.00

STOUT, Rex. *Three Witnesses*. 1957. Bantam A 1633. My. VG+. P1d. $11.00

STOUT, Rex. *Three Witnesses*. Bantam 3155. 3rd prtg. VG+. B3d. $4.50

STOUT, Rex. *To Kill Again*. Hillman 136. NF. I1d. $10.00

STOUT, Rex. *Too Many Clients*. 1962. Bantam J 2334. My. VG. P1d. $8.00

STOUT, Rex. *Too Many Cooks*. 1944. Dell 45. F. F2d. $20.00

STOUT, Rex. *Too Many Cooks*. 1944. Dell 45. My. G+. P1d. $10.00

STOUT, Rex. *Too Many Cooks*. 1951. Dell 540. G+. G5d. $5.00

STOUT, Rex. *Too Many Cooks*. 1963. Pyramid R 894. My. VG+. B4d. $4.00

STOUT, Rex. *Too Many Women*. 1949. Bantam 722. c/Hy Rubin. VG. P6d. $4.00

STOUT, Rex. *Trio for Blunt Instruments*. 1967. Bantam F 3298. My. VG. P1d. $7.50

STOUT, Rex. *Trouble in Triplicate*. 1951. Bantam 925. My. F. P1d. $25.00

STOUT, Rex. *Trouble in Triplicate*. 1951. Bantam 925. 1st prtg. My. VG. R5d. $5.25

STOUT, Rex. *Where There's a Will*. 1946. Avon 103. My. G. B5d. $2.50

STOUT, Rex. *Where There's a Will*. 1946. Avon 103. VG. G5d. $10.00

STOUT. *Hoe Like a God*. Lion LL 23. VG+. I1d. $10.00

STOVER, H. *Eagle & the Wind*. 1954. Popular EB 26. 1st pb. c/DeSoto: gga. VG+. B6d. $9.00

STRABEL, T. *Reap the Wild Wind*. Pennant P 19. VG. B3d. $5.00

STRACHAN, T.S. *Short Weekend*. 1956. Penguin 1140. My. VG. P1d. $8.00

STRACHEY, L. *Elizabeth & Essex*. Pocket 26. VG. B3d. $7.00

STRADT, E. *Fraulein*. PAD 561. VG+. B3d. $5.50

STRAIGHT, Michael. *Carrington*. 1962. Dell F 167. c/J Allison. We. VG. B5d. $2.50

STRAND, Bunny. *Bedroom Imposter*. 1963. Boudoir 1041. Ad. VG. B5d. $6.50

STRANGE, G.R. *Coleridge*. 1959. Dell LB 122. Bio. F. B4d. $3.75

STRANGE, John Stephen. *All Men Are Liars*. 1950. Dell 438. My. VG. P1d. $9.50

STRANGE, John Stephen. *Ballot-Box Murders*. My Novel Classic 53. My. VG. P1d. $20.00

STRANGE, John Stephen. *Let the Dead Past*. Curtis 07148. My. VG. W2d. $3.00

STRANGE, John Stephen. *Make My Bed Soon*. Bestseller Mystery B 107. My. VG. P1d. $12.50

STRANGE, John Stephen. *Murder at World's End*. My Novel Classic 59. My. VG. P1d. $20.00

STRANGE, O. *Marshal of Lawless*. Corgi 975. VG. B3d. $6.00

STRATFORD, Michael. *Sniper*. 1974. Award AN 1266. My. VG. P1d. $6.00

STRATTON, Chris. *Bobby Superstar*. 1971. Curtis 07180. 1st prtg. TVTI. Getting Together #2. VG. R5d. $1.50

STRATTON, Chris. *Change of Mind*. 1969. Pyramid T 2084. My/SF. VG. P1d. $5.00

STRATTON, Chris. *Fine Pair*. 1969. Popular 60-8090. My. F. P1d. $10.00

STRATTON, Chris. *Gunsmoke.* 1970. Popular 08146. 1st prtg. TVTI. VG+. R5d. $2.50

STRATTON, Chris. *Rock!* 1970. Pyramid T 2259. 1st prtg. G+. R5d. $1.50

STRATTON, Chris. *Ticket.* 1970. Pyramid T 2213. TVTI. G+. P1d. $4.50

STRATTON, Thomas. *Invisibility Affair.* 1967. Ace G 645. My/SF. VG. P1d. $7.50

STRATTON, Thomas. *Mind-Twisters Affair.* 1967. Ace G 663. My/SF. VG. P1d. $7.50

STRAUB, Peter. *Mystery.* 1991. Signet AE 6869. My. VG. P1d. $5.00

STRAUB, Peter. *Shadowland.* 1981. Berkley 05056. 1st prtg. SF. VG. R5d. $1.75

STRAUSS, Jack. *What's the Law?* 1972. Gold Medal T 2591. Nfi. VG. B5d. $3.50

STRAUSS, Theodore. *Dark Hunger.* 1951. Bantam 889. My. VG+. P1d. $13.50

STRAUSS, Theodore. *Haters.* 1950. Bantam 857. c/gga. Fa. G+. B4d. $2.00

STRAUSS, Theodore. *Haters.* 1950. Bantam 857. My. VG. P1d. $9.50

STRAUSS, Theodore. *Haters.* 1950. Bantam 857. 1st edn. PBO. scarce. NF. B6a #76. $44.00

STREET, Bradford. *Glass Bottom Boat.* 1966. Dell 2920. My/SF. VG. P1d. $5.50

STREET, Bradford. *In Like Flint.* 1967. Dell 4050. My. VG. P1d. $5.00

STREET, James. *Mingo Dabney.* Pocket 819. VG. B3d. $4.00

STREET, James. *Velvet Doublet.* 1954. Perma M 4005. 1st prtg. VG. P7d. $4.00

STREET & LOTH. *I Was a Drug Addict.* 1954. Pyramid 122. 1st pb edn. scarce. F. F2d. $75.00

STREETCAR, E. *Mr Robbins Rides Again.* PB Library 52-167. VG+. B3d. $4.00

STREETER, E. *Father of the Bride.* Hillman 48. VG. B3d. $4.00

STREIB, Daniel. *Brannon!* 1973. Pinnacle 155N. My. G+. P1d. $3.00

STREIB, Daniel. *House of Silence.* 1970. Powell PP 1007-N. My. VG. P1d. $5.00

STRICK, Marv. *Beatnik Ball.* 1961. Pike 102. VG+. B3a #24. $16.50

STRIEBER, Whit. *Wolfen.* 1981. Bantam 20268. 6th prtg. MTI. SF. F. W2d. $4.00

STRINGER, A. *Wife Traders.* Harlequin 328. VG. B3d. $7.50

STROHEIM, E.V. *Paprika.* Universal Giant Ed 2. VG+. I1d. $15.00

STRONG, R. *Little Boy's Plaything.* Brandon House 6566. PBO. VG. B3d. $4.00

STROUP, William. *Mark of Pak San Ri.* 1965. Book Co of America 010. My. VG. G5d. $3.00

STROUP, William. *Mark of Pak San Ri.* 1965. Book Co of America 010. 1st prtg. My. G+. R5d. $2.25

STRUCK, G.B. *Anglo Saxon & Sex.* Anchor 104. VG+. B3d. $5.00

STRUCK, G.B. *Boozers, Babes & Big Wheels.* Anchor 108. NF. B3d. $6.00

STRUCK, G.B. *Sex Is Everywhere.* Anchor 103. NF. B3d. $5.00

STRUGATSKI, Arkadi & Boris. *Final Circle of Paradise.* 1976. DAW UY 1264. SF. F. W2d. $5.00

STRUGATSKI, Arkadi & Boris. *Hard To Be a God.* 1974. DAW 126. 1st prtg. SF. VG. R5d. $3.25

STRUGATSKI, Arkadi & Boris. *Monday Begins on Saturday.* 1977. DAW 265. 1st edn. F. M1d. $6.00

STRUTHER, J. *Mrs Miniver.* 1942. Pocket 159. NF. B3d. $8.00

STUART, E.B. *Drag Me Down.* 1955. Popular 671. 1st edn. My. F. F2d. $12.50

STUART, Florence. *Hope Wears White.* 1962. Ace D 557. 1st prtg. VG+. P7d. $4.00

STUART, Ian. *Black Shrike.* 1963. Popular SP 208. Th. VG. P1d. $6.00

STUART, Ian. *Satan Bug.* 1963. Popular SP 231. My. G+. W2d. $3.75

STUART, Jeb. *Ordeal of Private Heath.* 1953. Pyramid 106. 1st pb. c/Paul. NF. B6d. $16.50

STUART, Lyle. *God Wears a Bow Tie.* 1950. Avon 305. Fi. G. B5d. $5.00

STUART, Lyle. *God Wears a Bow Tie.* 1950. Avon 305. 1st edn. PBO. VG+. B6d. $30.00

STUART, Matt. *Edge of the Desert.* Lancer 73-833. reprint. VG+. B6d. $6.00

STUART, Matt. *Hackamore Feud.* 1964. Gold Star IL 7-30. PBO. We. VG. P6d. $4.75

STUART, Matt. *Saddle: Man (Gun Smoke Showdown).* Bantam 924. VG. B3d. $6.00

STUART, Matt. *Smoky Trail.* Bantam 1095. VG+. B3d. $5.00

STUART, Matt. *Tough Saddle.* 1961. Pocket 6066. We. VG. B5d. $3.00

STUART, Matt. *Wild Summit.* 1960. Pocket 1268. 1st pb. We. VG+. B6d. $10.00

STUART, S. *Beast With Red Hands.* Popular 01587. VG+. B3d. $6.00

STUART, S. *Night Walker.* Award 124. MTI. VG. B3d. $4.00

STUART, W.J. *Forbidden Planet.* 1956. Bantam A 1443. 1st edn. F. M1d. $30.00

STUART, W.J. *Forbidden Planet.* 1956. Bantam A 1443. 1st edn. PBO. MTI. c/Robot. NF. B6a #76. $40.00

STUART, W.J. *Forbidden Planet.* 1967. PB Library 52-572. c/Robbie the Robot. SF. G+. B5d. $6.00

STUART, William L. *Night Cry.* 1949. Avon 186. My. VG. P1d. $10.00

STUART, William L. *Night Cry.* 1958. Avon 801. 1st prtg. My. G+. R5d. $3.50

STUART, William L. *Night Cry.* 1958. Phantom 779. PBO. VG. B3a #21. $50.50

STUBBS, Jean. *Dear Laura.* 1974. Crest P 2062. My. VG. P1d. $3.50

STUBBS, Jean. *Painted Face.* 1976. Penguin 4173. Ro. VG. P1d. $4.00

STURGEON, T. *Way Home.* Pyramid 184. VG. B3d. $5.00

STURGEON, Theodore. *Aliens 4.* 1959. Avon T 304. SF. VG+. B3d/B4d. $4.00

STURGEON, Theodore. *Aliens 4.* 1959. Avon. 1st edn. F. M1d. $10.00

STURGEON, Theodore. *Away Home.* 1969. Pyrmid X 2030. 1st prtg. c/Hermanson. VG. P7d. $4.00

STURGEON, Theodore. *Baby Is Three.* 1965. Magabook 3. PBO. VG. B6d. $8.00

STURGEON, Theodore. *Beyond.* 1960. Avon T 439. 1st edn. F. M1d. $15.00

STURGEON, Theodore. *Beyond.* 1960. Avon T 439. 1st prtg. G+. S1d. $4.00

STURGEON, Theodore. *Beyond.* 1970. Avon V 2349. 3rd. SF. G+. B5d. $2.50

STURGEON, Theodore. *Cavier.* 1955. Ballantine 119. PBO. c/Powers. SF. VG. B6d/M1d. $12.00

STURGEON, Theodore. *Cosmic Rape.* 1958. Dell 1st Edn B 120. 1st prtg. PBO. c/Powers. VG. P7d. $20.00

STURGEON, Theodore. *Cosmic Rape.* 1968. Dell 1512. F. S1d. $3.00

STURGEON, Theodore. *Cosmic Rape.* 1968. Dell 1512. 2nd edn. NF. P9d. $2.00

STURGEON, Theodore. *Cosmic Rape.* 1977. Pocket 81414. SF. VG. W2d. $3.25

STURGEON, Theodore. *Cosmic Rape.* 1977. Pocket 82934. SF. G+. W2d. $3.00

STURGEON, Theodore. *E Pluribus Unicorn.* 1956. Ballantine 179. SF. G+. B4d. $4.00

STURGEON, Theodore. *E Pluribus Unicorn.* 1956. Ballantine 179. VG+. B3d. $8.00

STURGEON, Theodore. *E Pluribus Unicorn.* 1956. Ballantine 179. 1st edn. NF. M1d. $15.00

STURGEON, Theodore. *King & Four Queens.* Dell 1st Edn A 128. VG. B3d. $5.00

STURGEON, Theodore. *More Than Human.* 1953. Ballantine 46. PBO. VG. G5d. $7.00

STURGEON, Theodore. *More Than Human.* 1953. Ballantine 46. PBO. VG+. I1d. $9.00

STURGEON, Theodore. *More Than Human.* 1953. Ballantine 46. 1st edn. PBO. F. M1d. $25.00

STURGEON, Theodore. *Not Without Sorcery.* Ballantine 506K. SF. G+. B5d. $4.00

STURGEON, Theodore. *Not Without Sorcery.* Ballantine 506K. 1st pb edn. F. M1d. $15.00

STURGEON, Theodore. *Some of Your Blood.* Ballantine 458. PBO. VG. B3d. $6.00

STURGEON, Theodore. *Some of Your Blood.* 1961. Ballantine 458. 1st edn. F. M1d. $35.00

STURGEON, Theodore. *Starshine.* 1978. Jove M 4459. SF. NF. B5d. $5.00

STURGEON, Theodore. *Starshine.* 1961. Pyramid 1543. VG. B3d. $4.50

STURGEON, Theodore. *Sturgeon in Orbit.* 1964. Pyramid F 974. PBO. c/E Emsh. SF. VG. B5d. $6.00

STURGEON, Theodore. *Sturgeon in Orbit.* 1964. Pyramid F 974. 1st edn. F. M1d. $15.00

STURGEON, Theodore. *Sturgeon Is Alive & Well.* 1971. Berkley S 2045. SF. VG. B5d. $4.00

STURGEON, Theodore. *Synthetic Man.* 1957. Pyramid G 247. c/sgn. VG. B3d. $8.00

STURGEON, Theodore. *Synthetic Man.* 1957. Pyramid G 247. VG+. I1d. $10.00

STURGEON, Theodore. *Synthetic Man.* 1965. Pyramid R 1126. 3rd prtg. SF. VG. W2d. $4.00

STURGEON, Theodore. *Touch of Strange.* 1959. Berkley G 280. c/R Powers. SF. G+. B5d. $3.50

STURGEON, Theodore. *Touch of Strange.* 1959. Berkley G 280. 1st pb edn. NF. M1d. $8.00

STURGEON, Theodore. *Touch of Strange.* 1959. Berkley G 280. 1st prtg. SF. VG. B3d. $5.00

STURGEON, Theodore. *Venus Plus X.* 1962. Pyramid F 732. 2nd edn. c/J Schoenherr. SF. VG+. B5d. $5.00

STURGEON, Theodore. *Venus Plus X.* 1960. Pyramid G 544. PBO. c/V Kalin. SF. G+. B5d. $5.50

STURGEON, Theodore. *Venus Plus X.* 1960. Pyramid G 544. 1st edn. F. M1d. $12.00

STURGEON, Theodore. *Venus Plus X.* Pyramid T 2134. 4th edn. F. P9d. $2.50

STURGEON, Theodore. *Visions & Venturers.* 1978. Dell 12648. SF. F. W2d. $5.50

STURGEON, Theodore. *Visions & Venturers.* 1978. Dell 12648. 1st prtg. SF. VG+. R5d. $3.00

STURGEON, Theodore. *Voyage to the Bottom of Sea.* 1961. Pyramid G 622. 1st edn. F. M1d. $18.00

STURGEON, Theodore. *Voyage to the Bottom of the Sea.* 1961. Pyramid G 622. PBO. MTI. SF. VG. B3d. $4.50

STURGEON, Theodore. *Voyage to the Bottom of the Sea.* 1964. Pyramid R 1068. 2nd prtg. MTI. VG+. I1d. $4.00

STURGEON, Theodore. *Way Home.* 1956. Pyramid G 184. VG. I1d. $6.00

STURGEON, Theodore. *Way Home.* 1956. Pyramid G 184. 1st pb edn. F. M1d. $15.00

STURGEON, Theodore. *Way Home.* Pyramid X 2030. 4th edn. F. P9d. $2.50

STURGEON, Theodore. *Way Home.* 1961. Pyramid 673. VG. B3d. $4.00

STURGEON & LEINSTER. *Universe Issue 1.* 1953. Perma Universe 1. c/Bloch: sgn. VG+. B3d. $8.00

STYLES, Showell. *Sea Lord.* 1963. Ballantine 713. 1st edn. PBO. Av. F. F2d. $6.00

SUAREZ, Carreno Jose. *Final Hours.* 1955. Signet 1191. c/J Meese. Fi. VG. B5d. $4.50

SUBLETTE & ROLL. *Perilous Journey.* Armed Services N 30. VG+. B3d. $4.00

SUCHARITKUL, Somtow. *Dawning Shadow: The Light on the Sound.* 1986. Pocket. 1st expanded edn. SF. F. F2d. $6.00

SUCHARITKUL, Somtow. *Utopia Hunters.* 1984. Bantam. 1st edn. F. M1d. $4.00

SUDAK, Eunice. *Icepick in Ollie Birk.* 1966. Lancer 73-467. My. VG. P1d. $5.50

SUDAK, Eunice. *Raven.* 1963. Lancer 70-034. 1st edn. c/Price & Karloff. scarce. SF. F. F2d. $20.00

SUDAK, Eunice. *Story of the Strangest Torture.* Lancer 70-052. PBO. MTI. VG. B3d. $4.00

SUDAK, Eunice. *X.* 1963. Lancer 70-052. PBO. MTI. c/R Milland. SF. VG. B5d. $7.00

SUDAK & MATHESON. *Poe's Tales of Terror.* Lancer 71-325. PBO. MTI. VG. M6d. $9.50

SUEHSDORF, Adie edt. *What To Tell Your Children About Sex.* 1958. Perma M 4106. Nfi. VG+. B4d. $2.25

SUGAR, Andrew. *Enforcer.* 1973. Lancer 75-443. 1st edn. My. F. F2d. $10.00

SUGAR, Andrew. *Kill City.* 1973. Lancer 75-473. My/SF. VG. P1d. $3.50

SUGAR, Andrew. *Kill City.* 1973. Lancer 75-473. 1st edn. My. F. F2d. $10.00

SUGRUE, Thomas. *Stranger in the Earth.* 1971. PB Library 65-456. Nfi. VG+. B5d. $6.00

SULLIVAN, E.S. edt. *Hollwood -- Sin Capital.* Pike 209. VG. B3d. $4.00

SULLIVAN, Katharine. *Girls on Parole.* 1957. Popular G 182. Nfi. VG. P1d. $7.50

SULLIVAN, Lewis W. *Scarlet Cord.* 1977. Major 3137. My. VG. P1d. $3.50

SULLIVAN, Thomas. *Diapason.* 1978. Condor 033. 1st prtg. SF. VG. R5d. $2.00

SULLIVAN, Tim. *V: The Florida Project.* 1985. Pinnacle 42430. SF. VG. W2d. $4.50

SULLIVAN/WYNNE. *Nemesis of Circle A/Mr Sixgun.* Ace 57601. We. G+. P1d. $3.00

SUMMERHILL, A. *Debut of a Belated Lesbian.* RAM 515. VG+. B3d. $4.50

SUMMERS, Charline. *By Lust Possessed.* Saber SA 128. VG. B3d. $3.50

SUMMERS, G. *Mouth Merchants.* Barclay 7345. c/photo. VG+. B3d. $4.50

SUMMERS, G. *Rape '70.* Barclay 7074. VG+. B3d. $4.50

SUMMERS, G. *TGIF Swappers.* Barclay 7358. VG+. B3d. $4.00

SUMMERS, Hollis. *City Limit.* 1949. Bantam 727. JD. VG. P1d. $14.00

SUMMERS, Richard. *Dark Madonna.* Bantam 1025. VG+. B3d. $6.00

SUMMERS, Richard. *Vigilante.* Dell 471. VG+. I1d. $5.00

SUMMERSBY, Kay. *Eisenhower Was My Boss.* Dell 286. VG+. I1d. $5.00

SUMMERTON, Margaret. *Nightingale at Noon.* 1964. Ace K 194. 1st prtg. My. VG. R5d. $2.25

SUMMERTON, Margaret. *Sea House.* 1963. Ace K 181. 1st prtg. My. VG+. R5d. $3.50

SUMNER, Cid Ricketts. *Quality.* 1947. Bantam 126. c/B D'Andrea. Fi. VG. B5d. $3.00

SUMNER, Cid Ricketts. *Quality.* 1947. Bantam 126. VG+. B4d. $4.75

SUMNER, Cid Ricketts. *Tammy Tell Me True.* 1961. Popular PC 1007. 1st prtg. VG. R5d. $2.25

SUMNER, Cid Ricketts. *Tammy Tell Me True.* 1966. Popular 50-439. TVTI. VG. P1d. $6.00

SUMNER, Cid Ricketts. *Tammy Tell Me True.* 1966. Popular 50-439. 1st prtg. TVTI. G+. R5d. $1.50

SUMNER. *Trouble Buster.* 1950. Prize Western 39. 1st pb. c/Popp. VG. B6d. $6.00

SURDEZ, Georges. *Demon Caravan.* Dell 501. c/Stanley. VG. I1d. $5.00

SURDEZ, Georges. *Demon Caravan.* Dell 501. 1st prtg. My. G+. R5d. $2.25

SUSKIND, Patrick. *Perfume.* 1986. Pocket. 1st pb edn. F. M1d. $4.00

SUSKIND, Richard. *Crusades.* 1962. Ballantine F 570. NF. VG. D5d. $35.00

SUTCLIFF, Rosemary. *Shield Ring.* Mayflower 7821. 1st prtg. VG+. S1d. $2.00

SUTCLIFF, Rosemary. *Sword at Sunset.* 1964. Crest M 713. SF. VG. W2d. $5.00

SUTHERLAND, Elizabeth edt. *Letters From Mississippi.* 1966. Signet T 2943. Nfi. VG+. B4d. $3.00

SUTHERLAND, James. *Stormtrack.* 1974. Pyramid N 3297. SF. NF. B4d. $5.00

SUTTER, Larabie. *White Squaw.* 1952. Gold Medal 255. We. VG. P6d. $4.25

SUTTON, Henry. *Vector.* 1971. Dell 9388. 1st prtg. SF. F. W2d. $5.00

SUTTON, Jeff. *Apollo at Go.* 1964. Popular SP 305. 1st edn. PBO. VG+. B3d. $4.00

SUTTON, Jeff. *Atom Conspiracy.* 1966. Ace F 374. NF. M1d. $6.00

SUTTON, Jeff. *Atom Conspiracy.* 1966. Ace F 374. 1st prtg. VG. S1d. $3.50

SUTTON, Jeff. *Bombs in Orbit.* Ace D 377. NF. M1d. $10.00

SUTTON, Jeff. *First on the Moon.* 1953. Ace F 222. c/E Emsh. SF. VG. B5d. $4.00

SUTTON, Jeff. *H Bomb Over America.* 1967. Ace H 18. 1st edn. F. P9d. $2.50

SUTTON, Jeff. *Mindblocked Man.* 1972. DAW 8. PBO. c/J Gaughan. SF. VG+. B5d. $4.00

SUTTON, Jeff. *Mindblocked Man.* 1972. DAW 8. 1st prtg. VG. S1d. $3.00

SUTTON, Jeff. *Missile Lords.* 1964. Dell 5680. 1st prtg. My. VG+. R5d. $3.50

SUTTON, Jeff. *Spacehive.* 1960. Ace D 478. PBO. SF. NF. B6d. $16.50

SUTTON, Jeff. *Spacehive.* 1960. Ace D 478. 1st prtg. G+. S1d. $3.00

SUTTON, Jeff. *Whisper for the Stars.* Dell 9520. SF. VG+. W2d. $4.25

SUTTON, Jeff. *Whisper for the Stars.* Dell 9520. 1st edn. G. P9d. $1.25

SUVIN, Darko edt. *Other Worlds, Other Seas.* 1970. Berkley. 1st edn. F. M1d. $4.00

SUYIN, Han. *Many-Splendored Thing.* 1955. Signet 1183. 3rd prtg. NF. B3d. $4.00

SUYIN, Han. *Mountain Is Young.* 1959. Signet T 1717. Fi. VG. B5d. $3.50

SWADOS, Felice. *House of Fury.* 1950. Avon 298. JD. F. P1d. $75.00

SWADOS, Felice. *House of Fury.* 1952. Avon 430. G+. I1d. $10.00

SWADOS, Felix. *House of Fury.* 1950. Avon 298. NF. B3a #20. $33.90

SWADOS, Felix. *House of Fury.* 1969. Berkley G 240. c/Maguire. NF. B3a #20. $40.00

SWAIN, Lawrence. *Killing.* 1981. Pinnacle 48-004. My. VG. P1d. $3.50

SWAN, A. *Boy & Woman.* Softcover Library B 1007. VG+. I1d. $6.00

SWAN, P. *Campus Lust.* Playtime 667. VG+. B3d. $7.50

SWANBERG, W.A. *Fact Detective Mysteries.* 1949. Dell 332. Nfi. G+. P1d. $7.00

SWANN, T.B. *Will-O-the-Wisp.* 1976. Corgi 10358. 1st English edn. c/gga. VG+. B3d. $10.00

SWANN, Thomas Burnett. *Day of the Minotaur.* Ace F 407. F. M1d. $10.00

SWANN, Thomas Burnett. *Day of the Minotaur.* Ace F 407. PBO. VG. B3d. $4.50

SWANN, Thomas Burnett. *Dolphin & the Deep.* Ace G 694. F. M1d. $10.00

SWANN, Thomas Burnett. *Dolphin & the Deep.* Ace G 694. VG+. B3d. $5.50

SWANN, Thomas Burnett. *Goat Without Horns.* Ballantine 02395. PBO. VG+. B3d. $6.00

SWANN, Thomas Burnett. *Gods Abide.* 1976. DAW 222. PBO. c/G Barr. SF. VG. B5d. $4.00

SWANN, Thomas Burnett. *Green Phoenix.* 1972. DAW 27. 1st edn. F. M1d. $10.00

SWANN, Thomas Burnett. *Lady of the Bees.* 1976. Ace 46850. PBO. Ace SF Special. SF. VG. B5d. $3.00

SWANN, Thomas Burnett. *Moondust.* Ace G 758. NF. M1d. $10.00

SWANN, Thomas Burnett. *Weirwoods.* Ace G 640. F. M1d. $15.00

SWANN, Thomas Burnett. *Wolfwinter.* 1972. Ballantine 02905. PBO. c/Szafran. SF. VG. B3d. $5.00

SWANSON, L. *Earthbound.* Playboy 21144. VG. B3d. $8.00

SWANSON, Neil H. *Phantom Emperor.* 1952. Dell D 113. NF. B3d. $6.00

SWANSON, Neil H. *Unconquered.* 1951. Perma P 108. 1st pb. c/Ken Riley. VG+. B6d. $9.00

SWARTHOUT, Glendon. *They Came to Cordura.* 1959. Signet D 1679. 1st prtg. G+. R5d. $2.75

SWARTHOUT, Glendon. *Where the Boys Are.* 1960. Signet D 1890. Hu. VG+. P1d. $12.50

SWENSON, Peggy. *Blonde.* Midwood Y 160. c/Rader. reprint. VG. B6d. $12.00

SWENSON, Peggy. *Blonde.* 1960. Midwood 56. c/Rader. VG+. B3a #24. $26.25

SWENSON, Peggy. *Unloved.* 1961. Midwood F 110. PBO. c/gga. VG. B6d. $12.50

SWIFT, Jonathan. *Gulliver's Travels.* 1961. Dell LC 164. FA. VG. B4d. $2.25

SWIFT, Jonathan. *Gulliver's Travels.* 1960. Washington Square W 251. SF. VG. B5d. $2.50

SWIGGETT, Howard. *Strong Box.* 1956. Perma M 4045. c/Maguire. G+. G5d. $3.00

SWINSON, Arthur. *Sergeant Cork's Second Casebook.* 1966. Arrow 872. My. VG. P1d. $7.50

SWITZER, R. *Living Idol.* Signet 1335. MTI. c/Maguire. VG+. B3d. $5.00

SWITZER, Robert. *Tent of the Wicked.* 1956. Signet 1313. PBO. NF. B6d. $10.00

SYDELL, Eleanor. *Diplomatic Immunity.* 1966. Lancer 73-534. Th. VG. P1d. $5.50

SYDNEY, Gale. *Strange Circle.* 1959. Beacon 281. 1st prtg. PBO. VG. P7d. $7.50

SYDNEY, Gale. *Strange Circle.* Intimate 49. PBO. VG. B3d. $7.00

SYKES, W. Stanley. *Missing Moneylender.* 1937. Penguin 62. 5th edn. dust jacket. My. VG. P1d. $25.00

SYKES, W. Stanley. *Missing Moneylender.* 1938. Penguin 62. 7th edn. My. G+. P1d. $8.00

SYLVESTER, R. *Dream Street.* Avon 303. VG. B3d. $4.50

SYLVESTER, Robert. *Big Boodle.* 1955. Perma M 3022. c/Schulz. VG. B3d. $4.50

SYLVESTER, Robert. *Big Boodle.* 1955. Perma M 3022. G+. G5d. $3.50

SYLVESTER, Robert. *We Were Strangers.* 1949. Signet 716. Fi. F. P1d. $25.00

SYLVESTER, Robert. *We Were Strangers.* 1949. Signet 716. 1st prtg. VG+. R5d. $8.00

SYMONS, Julian. *Belting Inheritance.* 1966. Signet D 3013. My. VG. P1d. $5.50

SYMONS, Julian. *Bogue's Fortune.* 1961. Dolphin C 290. My. VG. P1d. $6.50

SYMONS, Julian. *Color of Murder.* 1959. Dell D 296. My. F. P1d. $15.00

SYMONS, Julian. *Color of Murder.* 1959. Fontana 343. My. VG. P1d. $7.50

SYMONS, Julian. *Man Who Killed Himself.* 1969. Corgi 08257. My. VG+. P1d. $5.00

SYMONS, Julian. *Narrowing Circle.* 1956. Berkley 354. 1st pb. My. VG+. B6d. $10.00

SYMONS, Julian. *Plot Against Roger Rider.* 1975. Penguin 3949. My. VG. P1d. $4.00

SYMONS, Julian. *31st of February.* 1953. Bantam 1059. My. VG+. B3d. $6.00

SYMS. *Small Talk.* Pocket 682. VG+. B3d. $5.00

SZEDENIK, Alex M. *Anatomy of a Psycho.* 1964. Gold Star IL 7-36. PBO. Nfi. VG. P6d. $2.00

TABER, Gladys. *Heart Has April Too.* Dell 373. c/H Bennett. Fi. VG. B5d. $4.00

TABOR, Michael. *Battle of the Bulge.* 1965. Popular PC 1062. 1st prtg. G+. R5d. $1.75

TABORI, George. *Caravan Passes.* 1952. Signet 963. c/gga. Fa. VG. B4d. $3.00

TABORI, George. *Good One.* 1960. Perma M 4180. My. VG. P1d. $7.00

TABORI, George. *Journey.* 1958. Bantam 1868. 1st edn. c/Kerr & Brynner. My. F. F2d. $11.00

TABORI, Paul. *Doomsday Brain.* 1967. Pyramid X 1564. My/SF. VG. P1d. $5.00

TABORI, Paul. *Green Rain.* 1961. Pyramid G 624. 1st prtg. SF. F. W2d. $15.00

TABORI, Paul. *Green Rain.* 1961. Pyramid G 624. 2nd edn. c/J Schoenherr. SF. VG. B5d/S1d. $6.00

TABORI, Paul. *Green Rain.* 1965. Pyramid R 1152. 3rd edn. SF. G+. P1d. $3.50

TABORI, Paul. *Invisible Eye.* 1967. Pyramid X 1728. 1st edn. My. F. F2d. $8.00

TABORI, Paul. *Invisible Eye.* 1969. Tandem T 2954. My/SF. F. P1d. $6.00

TACK, Alfred. *Forecast Murder.* 1968. Arrow 115. My. VG+. P1d. $7.50

TACK, Alfred. *PA to Murder.* 1967. Arrow 988. My. VG. P1d. $5.00

TADRACK, Moss. *Carnal College!* 1963. Novel Book 6079. Th. F. P1d. $12.00

TAFFRAIL. *Dover: Ostend.* 1953. Hodder & Stoughton C 110. My. VG. P1d. $12.50

TAFFRAIL. *Toby Shad.* 1956. Hodder & Stoughton C 167. My. F. P1d. $16.00

TAINE, John. *Greatest Adventure.* 1960. Ace D 473. VG. B3d. $4.50

TAINE, John. *Greatest Adventure.* 1960. Ace D 473. 1st pb. c/Emsh. SF. NF. M1d. $8.00

TALBOT, Daniel edt. *Damned.* 1954. Lion Library L 16. My. F. P1d. $25.00

TALBOT, Daniel edt. *City of Love.* Dell First Edition 45. VG+. B3d. $4.00

TALBOT, Daniel edt. *Thirteen Great Stories.* Dell First Edition 99. VG. B3d. $4.00

TALBOT, Guy. *Meet Chatty Jones.* 1967. Lancer 73-560. PBO. My. VG. B5d. $4.50

TALBOT, Hake. *Rim of the Pit.* 1947. Dell 173. 1st prtg. My. VG+. R5d. $10.00

TALBOT, Michael. *Delicate Dependency.* 1982. Avon 77982. PBO. SF. VG. M3d. $7.00

TALL, Stephen. *Stardust Voyages.* 1975. Berkley. 1st pb edn. F. M1d. $5.00

TALLANT, Robert. *Mrs Candy & Saturday Night.* 1951. Popular 358. c/Bergey: gga. Fa. VG. B4d. $5.00

TALLANT, Robert. *Voodoo in New Orleans.* Collier AS 481. 1st prtg. c/Peter Max. VG+. P7d. $9.00

TALLIS, Robyn. *Rebel From Alphorion.* 1989. Ivy 0205-8. 1st edn. SF. F. F2d. $7.00

TALLMAN, Robert. *Adios, O'Shaughnessy.* Berkley G 24. c/Jim Davis. NF. B3d. $5.50

TAN, Amy. *Joy Luck Club.* Ivy 0630. VG. G5d. $4.50

TANIZAKI, J. *Key.* Signet 2073. VG. B3d. $4.50

TANNER, J. *Sex Pick-Ups.* Vixceroy 329. VG+. B3d. $4.50

TARKINGTON, Booth. *Monsieur Beaucaire.* 1968. Airmont CL 158. Fi. VG+. B5d. $3.50

TARKINGTON, Booth. *Presenting Lily Mars.* Avon 55. VG. B3d. $5.00

TARKINGTON, Booth. *Seventeen.* Bantam 17. VG. B3d. $4.50

TARR, J.T. *Good Handwriting.* Pan 398. VG. B3d. $7.00

TASKER, W.B. *Just Ask for Margaret.* 1959. Midwood 26. 1st edn. c/Rader: gga. F. F2d. $20.00

TASKER, W.B. *Sex Escort.* 1962. Bedside BB 1216. Ad. VG. B3d/B5d. $4.00

TASKER, W.B. *Without Shame.* 1963. Midwood 254. 1st edn. c/gga. F. F2d. $18.00

TAUBE, Lester S. *Diamond Boomerang.* 1970. Pocket 75450. My. F. P1d. $6.00

TAUBES, Frank. *Run...Run...Run....* 1956. Popular 769. 1st edn. PBO. My. F. F2d. $12.00

TAVER, Robert. *Trouble Shooter.* Bantam 111. VG. M6d. $5.00

TAYLOR, A.J.P. *History of the First World War.* Berkley G 1235. VG+. B3d. $4.50

TAYLOR, Angeline. *Black Jade.* 1949. Pocket 635. F. B4d. $10.00

TAYLOR, Daniel. *All His Women (They Move With the Sun).* 1957. Pyramid 285. VG+. B3d. $5.00

TAYLOR, Daniel. *They Move With the Sun.* 1950. Popular 274. c/gga. Fa. VG+. B4d. $8.00

TAYLOR, Demetria. *Apple Kitchen Cookbook.* Popular 75-8010. Nfi. VG+. B5d. $3.50

TAYLOR, Dyson. *Bitter Love.* 1952. Pyramid G 60. 1st pb. c/Paul. VG+. B6d. $12.00

TAYLOR, E.B. *Sex & Marriage Problems.* Hillman 7. 2nd prtg. VG+. B3d. $5.00

TAYLOR, G. *Hollow Square.* Panther 1049. VG+. B3d. $8.00

TAYLOR, Grant. *Whip Ryder's Way.* 1947. Bantam 129. c/J King. We. VG. B5d. $3.00

TAYLOR, Grant. *Whip Ryder's Way.* 1947. Bantam 129. 1st pb. We. NF. B6d. $10.00

TAYLOR, John G. *Black Holes.* 1975. Avon 46805. 6th prtg. SF. VG+. W2d. $4.75

TAYLOR, Phoebe Atwood. *Octagon House.* 1964. Pyramid F 969. My. VG+. B5d. $5.00

TAYLOR, Phoebe Atwood. *Banbury Bog.* 1948. Dell 251. G+. G5d. $7.50

TAYLOR, Phoebe Atwood. *Banbury Bog.* 1948. Dell 251. My. VG. P1d. $20.00

TAYLOR, Phoebe Atwood. *Cape Cod Mystery.* 1942. Pocket 171. My. G+. P1d. $12.50

TAYLOR, Phoebe Atwood. *Cape Cod Mystery.* 1942. Pocket 171. My. VG. P1d. $20.00

TAYLOR, Phoebe Atwood. *Cape Cod Mystery.* 1965. Pyramid R 1124. My. VG. P1d. $6.00

TAYLOR, Phoebe Atwood. *Criminal COD.* 1943. Popular 14. My. G+. P1d. $17.50

TAYLOR, Phoebe Atwood. *Deadly Sunshade.* 1947. Popular 126. 1st pb. My. VG. B6d. $12.50

TAYLOR, Phoebe Atwood. *Death Lights a Candle.* 1943. Pocket 204. My. VG. P1d. $20.00

TAYLOR, Phoebe Atwood. *Diplomatic Corpse.* 1952. Avon A 439. My. G+. B4d. $2.00

TAYLOR, Phoebe Atwood. *Diplomatic Corpse.* 1952. Avon A 439. My. VG. P1d. $6.00

TAYLOR, Phoebe Atwood. *Octagon House.* 1947. Dell 171. c/G Frederiksen. My. VG. B5d. $7.50

TAYLOR, Phoebe Atwood. *Octagon House.* 1947. Dell 171. My. F. P1d. $25.00

TAYLOR, Phoebe Atwood. *Out of Order.* 1944. Popular 25. My. G+. P1d. $17.50

TAYLOR, Phoebe Atwood. *Perennial Boarder.* 1947. Penguin (US) 618. My. F. P1d. $20.00

TAYLOR, Phoebe Atwood. *Proof of the Pudding.* 1943. Pyramid R 920. VG+. G5d. $7.00

TAYLOR, Phoebe Atwood. *Spring Harrowing.* 1946. Dell 98. My. VG+. P1d. $30.00

TAYLOR, R.W. *She Devil.* Beacon 503. VG. B3d. $4.00

TAYLOR, R.W. *Whiplash.* 1964. Gold Star IL 7-31. My. VG. P1d. $7.50

TAYLOR, Ray Ward. *Doomsday Square.* 1968. PB Library 53-640. My/SF. VG. P1d. $5.00

TAYLOR, Richard. *Better Taylors.* 1947. Avon 119. VG. B6d. $30.00

TAYLOR, Robert L. *Adrift in a Boneyard.* Avon G 1132. 1st pb edn. NF. M1d. $7.00

TAYLOR, Robert W. *Dark Urge.* 1953. Pyramid G 72. PBO. c/gga. NF. B6a #74. $30.00

TAYLOR, Robert W. *Junk Pusher.* 1954. Banner 80. VG+. B3a #22. $56.45

TAYLOR, Robert W. *Junk Pusher.* 1954. Pyramid 126. PBO. c/gga. F. F2d. $40.00

TAYLOR, Robert W. *Junk Pusher.* 1954. Pyramid 126. PBO. rare. VG+. B6a #79. $50.00

TAYLOR, Robert W. *Mimi.* 1953. Pyramid 96. Fa. VG+. B4d. $8.00

TAYLOR, Robert W. *Mimi.* 1953. Pyramid 96. Fi. F. P1d. $17.00

TAYLOR, Robert W. *Scandali.* 1954. Pyramid 107. PBO. c/V Olson. Fi. VG. B5d. $6.00

TAYLOR, Rosemary. *Chicken Every Sunday.* 1945. Pocket 321. 1st pb. MTI. VG. B6d. $18.00

TAYLOR, Rosemary. *Come Clean, My Love.* 1950. Bantam 773. 1st prtg. c/Fink: gga. VG. P7d. $4.50

TAYLOR, Rosemary. *Ridin' the Rainbow.* Armed Services T 19. VG+. B3d. $6.00

TAYLOR, Sam S. *No Head for Her Pillow.* 1953. Signet S 1057. c/G Erickson. My. VG. B5d. $4.00

TAYLOR, Sam S. *Sleep No More.* 1950. Signet 821. My. VG. P1d. $9.50

TAYLOR, Sam S. *So Cold, My Bed.* 1955. Signet 1247. 1st pb. c/Maguire. My. VG. P1d. $10.00

TAYLOR, Theodore. *Body Trade.* 1968. Gold Medal D 1987. My. VG+. P1d. $7.50

TAYLOR, Valerie. *Girls in 3-B.* 1959. Crest S 290. PBO. c/Meese: gga. NF. B6a #74. $44.00

TAYLOR, Valerie. *Hired Girl.* Beacon B 116. VG. I1d. $7.00

TAYLOR, Valerie. *World Without Men.* 1963. Midwood F 346. PBO. F. B6d. $18.00

TAYLOR/VINING. *Grinning Gismo/Too Hot for Hell.* 1952. Ace D 1. My. G. P1d. $35.00

TAYLOR/VINING. *Grinning Gismo/Too Hot for Hell.* 1952. Ace D 1. My. VG. P1d. $100.00

TEALE, Christopher. *Behind These Walls.* 1962. Pyramid R 801. Fi. VG+. B5d. $5.00

TEED, G.H. *Crook's Decoy.* 1933. Sexton Blake 391. My. G+. P1d. $15.00

TEILHET, Darwin L. *Fear Makers.* 1946. Pocket 399. My. F. P1d. $21.00

TEILHET, Darwin L. *Something Wonderful To Happen.* 1948. Bantam 415. Fi. F. P1d. $20.00

TEILHET, Hildegarde Tolman. *Rim of Terror.* 1950. Bantam 856. My. VG+. P1d. $14.00

TELFAIR, Richard. *Bloody Medallion.* 1966. Gold Medal D 1665. 2nd prtg. c/Bill Johnson. VG+. P6d. $3.25

TELFAIR, Richard. *Bloody Medallion.* 1959. Gold Medal 847. My. VG. P1d. $10.00

TELFAIR, Richard. *Corpse That Talked.* 1959. Gold Medal 890. My. VG+. P1d. $15.00

TELFAIR, Richard. *Day of the Gun.* 1958. Gold Medal 827. We. G+. P1d. $7.00

TELFAIR, Richard. *Slavers.* 1961. Gold Medal S 1077. My. G+. P1d. $7.50

TELFAIR, Richard. *Sundance.* 1960. Gold Medal 999. 1st prtg. TVTI. VG. R5d. $5.00

TEMPEL, Earle edt. *Humor in the Headlines.* 1969. Pocket 55101. Nfi. NF. B5d. $4.00

TEMPEST, Rebekah. *Glamour Girls.* Fiction House NN. 2nd edn. c/gga. VG. B3d. $6.00

TEMPLE, Dan. *Love Goddess.* 1962. Beacon B 533F. TVTI. VG+. P1d. $18.00

TEMPLE, W.F. *Shoot at the Moon.* MacFadden 60-239. VG. B3d. $4.00

TEMPLE/TEMPLE. *Automated Goliath/ Three Suns of Amara.* 1962. Ace F 129. F. M1d. $12.00

TEMPLE/TEMPLE. *Automated Goliath/ Three Suns of Amara.* 1962. Ace F 129. PBO. SF. VG+. B5d. $6.00

TEMPLE/TEMPLE. *Automated Goliath/ Three Suns of Amara.* 1962. Ace F 129. PBO. VG. B3d. $4.00

TENN, William. *Human Angle.* 1956. Ballantine 159. 1st edn. F. M1d. $12.00

TENN, William. *Human Angle.* 1956. Ballantine 159. 1st edn. VG. B3d. $4.00

TENN, William. *Of All Possible Things.* 1955. Ballantine 99. 1st edn. F. M1d. $12.00

TENN, William. *Of All Possible Worlds.* 1960. Ballantine 407K. 2nd edn. c/B Blanchard. SF. VG. B5d. $4.00

TENN, William. *Of All Possible Worlds.* 1955. Ballantine 99. G. I1d. $3.00

TENN, William. *Of All Possible Worlds.* 1955. Ballantine 99. PBO. VG. B3d. $5.00

TENN, William. *Of Men & Monsters.* Ballantine 24884. 1st prtg. VG+. S1d. $4.00

TENN, William. *Outsiders: Children of Wonder.* Perma P 291. VG+. B3d. $6.00

TENN, William. *Outsiders: Children of Wonder.* 1954. Perma P 291. 1st pb edn. F. M1d. $10.00

TENN, William. *Seven Sexes.* Ballantine U 6134. 1st prtg. F. S1d. $7.50

TENN, William. *Time in Advance.* 1958. Bantam A 1786. PBO. VG. M1d. $5.00

TENN, William. *Wooden Star.* Ballantine U 6133. PBO. VG+. B3d. $5.50

TENN/VAN ARNAM. *Lamp for Medusa/ Players of Hell.* 1968. Belmont B 60-077. SF. VG. B5d. $4.00

TENNIS, Craig. *Johnny Tonight!* 1980. Pocket 41451. TVTI. VG. P1d. $4.50

TEPPER, Sheri. *After Long Silence.* 1987. Bantam. 1st edn. F. M1d. $4.00

TERASAKI, Gwen. *Bridge to the Sun.* 1961. Dell F 148. 1st prtg. G+. R5d. $1.00

TERRALL, Robert. *Killer Is Loose Among Us.* 1950. Avon 278. G. G5d. $5.00

TERRALL, Robert. *Killer Is Loose Among Us.* 1948. Harlequin 12. My. G+. P1d. $15.00

TERRILL, Rogers. *Argosy Book of Adventure Stories.* Bantam 1158. NF. B3d. $4.50

TERROT, Charles. *Passionate Pilgrim.* Bantam 872. VG+. B3d. $5.00

TERRY, C.V. *Darien Venture.* 1956. Perma M 4057. c/gga. Fa. NF. B4d. $5.00

TERRY, C.V. *Darien Venture.* 1956. Perma M 4057. 1st pb. c/Binger. G+. B6d. $2.50

TERRY, C.V. *Golden Ones.* Perma M 4100. VG+. B3d. $4.50

TERRY, J. William. *Restless Breed.* 1958. Signet S 1603. Fi. VG. B5d. $3.00

TESCH, G. *Never the Same Again.* Pyramid 342. VG+. B3d. $5.50

TESSITORE, John. *For Love or Money.* 1963. Gold Medal K 1341. 1st edn. c/Douglas & Gaynor: color photos. F. F2d. $8.00

TESSITORE, John. *For Love or Money.* 1963. Gold Medal K 1341. 1st prtg. G+. R5d. $3.75

TESSITORE, John. *Nero's Mistress.* Gold Medal 952. PBO. MTI. c/B Bardot. VG. B3d. $4.00

TETA, Jon. *Clock at Ravenswood.* 1969. Pyramid X 1975. PB. c/Marchetti. NF. B6d. $9.00

TETLEY, Roy. *Flip Over the Coin, Lover.* 1964. Spur 102. PBO. VG+. B3d. $4.50

TEVIS, Walter. *Hustler.* Ace H 519. MTI. VG. B3d. $10.00

TEVIS, Walter. *Hustler.* 1961. Dell D 434. 1st prtg. VG. R5d. $4.00

TEVIS, Walter. *Man Who Fell to Earth.* Avon 27276. 1st prtg. G+. S1d. $2.50

TEVIS, Walter. *Man Who Fell to Earth.* 1963. Gold Medal K 1276. 1st edn. NF. M1d. $25.00

TEVIS, Walter. *Man Who Fell to Earth.* 1963. Gold Medal K 1276. 1st prtg. G. S1d. $5.00

TEVIS, Walter. *Man Who Fell to Earth.* Lancer 74-650. SF. VG. B5d. $5.00

TEVIS, Walter. *Mockingbird.* 1981. Bantam. 1st pb edn. F. M1d. $5.00

TEY, Josephine. *Brat Farrar.* 1960. Berkley G 434. My. VG. P1d. $7.00

TEY, Josephine. *Brat Farrar.* 1957. Pan 280. 2nd edn. My. VG. P1d. $6.00

TEY, Josephine. *Come & Kill Me.* 1951. Pocket 784. 1st pb. My. VG. B6d. $7.50

TEY, Josephine. *Daughter of Time.* 1960. Berkley G 265. My. F. P1d. $12.50

TEY, Josephine. *Daughter of Time.* 1956. Penguin 990. My. F. P1d. $13.50

TEY, Josephine. *Franchise Affair.* 1963. Berkley BG 511. 2nd edn. My. VG+. P1d. $7.50

TEY, Josephine. *Franchise Affair.* Pan 671. VG+. B3d. $5.50

TEY, Josephine. *Man in the Queue.* 1965. Berkley F 1100. 1st edn. My. VG. R5d. $2.50

TEY, Josephine. *Man in the Queue.* 1962. Berkley F 657. My. VG+. P1d. $9.50

TEY, Josephine. *Miss Pym Disposes.* 1960. Berkley G 415. My. G+. P1d. $5.00

TEY, Josephine. *Miss Pym Disposes.* 1964. Dell 5677. 1st prtg. My. VG+. R5d. $4.00

TEY, Josephine. *Pocket Guide to Wildflowers.* 1951. Pocket 788. 1st pb. NF. B6d. $10.00

TEY, Josephine. *Shilling for Candles.* 1964. Dell 7823. 1st prtg. My. VG+. R5d. $2.25

TEY, Josephine. *Singing Sands.* 1963. Berkley F 594. 4th edn. My. VG. P1d. $5.00

TEY, Josephine. *Singing Sands.* 1960. Berkley G 298. 1st prtg. My. VG+. R5d. $4.00

TEY, Josephine. *To Love & Be Wise.* 1965. Dell 8940. My. VG. P1d. $5.50

TEY, Josephine. *To Love & Be Wise.* 1953. Pan 259. My. VG. P1d. $10.00

THACHER, Russell. *Tender Age.* 1953. Pocket 969. 1st prtg. c/Dunn: gga. VG. P7d. $5.00

THAYER, Charles W. *Checkpoint.* 1965. Pocket 50181. Th. VG. P1d. $5.50

THAYER, Lee. *Murder Is Out.* 1945. Burl House 16. My. VG. B3d. $6.00

THAYER, Tiffany. *Call Her Savage.* Avon 14. VG. I1d. $45.00

THAYER, Tiffany. *Call Her Savage.* Avon 291. VG. B3d. $4.50

THAYER, Tiffany. *Call Her Savage.* Avon 418. NF. G5d. $9.00

THAYER, Tiffany. *Call Her Savage.* Avon 418. VG. B3d. $6.00

THAYER, Tiffany. *Illustrious Corpse.* 1950. Popular 227. 1st pb. c/Belarski. My. VG. B6d. $12.50

THAYER, Tiffany. *Old Goat.* 1950. Avon 234. Fi. VG. B5d. $5.50

THAYER, Tiffany. *Old Goat.* 1950. Avon 234. VG+. I1d. $8.00

THAYER, Tiffany. *One-Man Show.* 1951. Avon 327. Fa. G+. P1d. $6.50

THAYER, Tiffany. *Three Musketeers & a Lady.* 1950. Signet 772. c/gga. Fa. VG+. B4d. $3.50

THE GORDONS. *Big Frame.* 1958. Bantam 1782. My. VG+. B4d. $2.00

THEROUX, Paul. *O-Zone.* 1987. Ballantine 8047. 1st edn. PBO. NF. P9d. $1.75

THEROUX, Paul. *Picture Palace.* 1987. Washington Square 63844. Fi. F. P1d. $5.00

THIELEN, Benedict. *Lost Men.* 1955. Lion LL 18. G. G5d. $2.50

THIESSEN, Val. *My Brother, Cain.* 1964. Monarch 406. My. VG. P1d. $7.50

THOM, Robert. *Bloody Mama.* 1970. PB Library 63-284. My. VG+. P1d. $7.50

THOM, Robert. *Bloody Mama.* 1970. PB Library 63-284. 1st prtg. G+. R5d. $2.00

THOMAS, B. *Marlon: Portrait of a Rebel As an Artist.* 1975. Ballantine 24400. 1st prtg. Bio. VG+. R5d. $6.00

THOMAS, Bob. *Dead Ringer.* 1964. Gold Medal K 1377. My. VG. B3d. $4.50

THOMAS, Bob. *Flesh Merchants.* 1959. Dell 1st Edn B 133. 1st prtg. PBO. c/McGinnis: gga. VG. P7d. $4.00

THOMAS, Craig. *Emerald Decision.* 1990. Harper 100067. Th. VG. P1d. $5.00

THOMAS, Craig. *Firefox.* 1978. Bantam. Th. VG. P1d. $7.50

THOMAS, Craig. *Wildcat.* 1989. Jove 10186. My. VG. P1d. $4.50

THOMAS, Craig. *Wolfsbane.* 1979. Sphere 8455. Th. VG. P1d. $4.00

THOMAS, Dan. *Seed.* 1968. Ballantine U 6115. PBO. SF. NF. B6d. $10.00

THOMAS, Dylan. *Adventures in the Skin Trade.* 1956. Signet S 1281. Fi. VG. B5d. $6.00

THOMAS, Dylan. *Adventures in the Skin Trade.* 1956. Signet S 1281. G+. B4d. $3.00

THOMAS, Dylan. *Beach of Falesa.* 1965. Ballantine U 5018. VG+. B3d. $4.50

THOMAS, Dylan. *Beach of Falesa.* 1965. Ballantine U 5018. 1st prtg. VG. R5d. $4.00

THOMAS, Frank. *Sherlock Holmes & the Treasure Train.* 1985. Pinnacle 42045. My. VG. P1d. $5.00

THOMAS, Kenneth. *Devil's Mistress.* Gold Medal D 1202. 3rd edn. c/Bardot. VG. M6d. $4.50

THOMAS, Kenneth. *Devil's Mistress.* 1958. Gold Medal S 802. 2nd edn. My. VG. P1d. $10.00

THOMAS, L.H. *No Man's Land.* Carousel 514. VG+. B3d. $5.00

THOMAS, Lee. *Mask of Lesbos.* 1963. Beacon 627. 1st edn. F. F2d. $15.00

THOMAS, Lee. *Woman's Game.* 1962. Beacon B 554F. c/gga. Fa. VG+. B4d. $12.00

THOMAS, Leslie. *Orange Wednesday.* 1969. Pan 02330. My. VG. P1d. $4.50

THOMAS, Leslie. *Virgin Soldiers.* Crest T 1363. 1st prtg. G+. R5d. $1.25

THOMAS, Louis. *Good Children Don't Kill.* 1968. Arrow 090. My. VG. P1d. $5.00

THOMAS, Lowell. *Out of This World to Forbidden Tibet.* 1954. Avon G 1010. Nfi. VG. B5d. $3.00

THOMAS, Lowell. *With Lawrence in Arabia.* 1961. Popular SP 116. 1st prtg. G+. R5d. $1.75

THOMAS, M. *Beyond the Spectrum.* PB Library 52-554. VG+. B3d. $5.00

THOMAS, Martin. *Assignment Doomsday.* 1961. Sexton Blake UK 485. 1st edn. c/gga. SF. F. F2d. $15.00

THOMAS, Martin. *Copy-Cat Killings.* Sexton Blake 392. VG+. B3d. $8.00

THOMAS, Martin. *Laird of Evil.* 1965. Mayflower Dell 4622. My. VG+. P1d. $8.00

THOMAS, Martin. *Shadow of a Gun.* Sexton Blake 425. VG+. B3d. $8.00

THOMAS, Paul. *Cargo = Trouble.* 1960. Avon T 413. My. VG+. P1d. $10.50

THOMAS, Paul. *Code Name: Rubble.* Tower 43763. My. G. W2d. $3.00

THOMAS, Paul. *Defector.* 1967. Tower 42-816. 3rd edn. Th. VG. P1d. $4.50

THOMAS, Ross. *Backup Men.* 1986. Perennial P 833. My. VG. P1d. $3.50

THOMAS, Ross. *Cast a Yellow Shadow.* 1968. Avon S 367. My. VG+. P1d. $7.50

THOMAS, Ross. *Cold War Swap.* 1968. Avon S 302. 3rd edn. Th. VG. P1d. $4.00

THOMAS, Ross. *Porkchoppers.* 1973. Pocket 78289. My. VG+. P1d. $4.50

THOMAS, T.L. *Clone.* 1965. Berkley F 1169. SF. F. W2d. $4.50

THOMAS, W. Craig. *House of Hate.* 1958. Pyramid G 348. My. VG. P1d. $7.50

THOMAS, W. Craig. *Jet Pilot.* 1955. Avon 632. Hi. VG+. P1d. $12.00

THOMAS, W. Craig. *Killer in White.* 1956. Gold Medal 546. My. VG. P1d. $10.00

THOMAS, W. Craig. *Loves of Errol Flynn.* 1962. Monarch K 58. Nfi. VG. P1d. $6.50

THOMAS, W. Craig. *When the Lusting Began.* 1960. Monarch 178. My. F. P1d. $20.00

THOMAS, Wayne. *What's New in Hot Rodding.* 1967. Gold Medal T 1817. PBO. VG. M6d. $6.50

THOMAS, Wayne. *What's New in Hot Rodding.* 1967. Gold Medal 1817. 1st edn. F. F2d. $8.50

THOMASON, June. *Sound Evidence.* 1986. GK Hall Large Print 3986. My. F. P1d. $10.95

THOMEY, Tedd. *And Dream of Evil.* 1954. Avon 614. 1st prtg. c/gga. VG. P7d. $7.50

THOMEY, Tedd. *And Dream of Evil.* 1956. Avon 737. My. VG. B5d. $5.50

THOMEY, Tedd. *And Dream of Evil.* 1956. Avon 737. 1st prtg. My. G+. R5d. $2.50

THOMEY, Tedd. *Flight to Takla-Ma.* 1961. Monarch 216. Fi. G+. B5d. $3.50

THOMEY, Tedd. *Jet Ace.* Avon T 256. PBO. VG. B3d. $4.50

THOMEY, Tedd. *Jet Pilot.* 1955. Avon 632. Fa. VG. B4d. $3.75

THOMEY, Tedd. *Sadist.* 1961. Berkley G 568. 1st edn. c/gga. My. F. F2d. $10.00

THOMEY, Tedd. *Loves of Errol Flynn.* 1962. Monarch K 58. 1st edn. c/color photo. scarce. F. F2d. $30.00

THOMPSON, Arthur. *Starved.* 1965. Belmont 92-616. 1st prtg. My. VG. W2d. $4.00

THOMPSON, B. *Gunman's Spawn.* 1955. Graphic G 210. PBO. VG+. B3d. $5.50

THOMPSON, B. *Gunman's Spawn.* 1957. Graphic G 223. 2nd edn. VG. B3d. $4.00

THOMPSON, B. *Virgins of Veldt.* Kozy 168. VG+. B3d. $6.00

THOMPSON, C.H. *Gun for Billy Reo.* 1955. Dell 1st Edn 49. PBO. c/S Broack. We. VG. B5d. $4.00

THOMPSON, C.H. *Under the Badge.* Dell 1st Edn A 132. VG. B3d. $4.50

THOMPSON, Donald. *Corpse Wore No Shoes.* 1945. Eerie Series 3. My. G+. P1d. $15.00

THOMPSON, Donald. *Next Encounter.* 1982. Gold Medal 44585. 1st prtg. SF. F. W2d. $4.00

THOMPSON, Estelle. *Find a Crooked Sixpence.* 1984. Walker 3042. My. VG+. P1d. $4.50

THOMPSON, G. *Six-Guns Wild!* Graphic 146. VG. B3d. $5.00

THOMPSON, J. *Willie & Phil.* 1980. Coronet 25857. MTI. VG. B3d. $5.00

THOMPSON, Jim. *After Dark, My Sweet.* 1955. Popular 716. Fa. VG. B4d. $135.00

THOMPSON, Jim. *Alcoholics.* 1953. Lion 127. Fa. NF. B4d. $165.00

THOMPSON, Jim. *Alcoholics.* 1953. Lion 127. PBO. VG. B3a #22. $128.50

THOMPSON, Jim. *Bad Boy.* 1953. Lion 149. My. G+. P1d. $100.00

THOMPSON, Jim. *Bad Boy.* 1953. Lion 149. PBO. c/Kunstler. extremely scarce. VG. B6a #77. $110.00

THOMPSON, Jim. *Cropper's Cabin.* 1952. Lion 108. Fa. VG+. B4d. $125.00

THOMPSON, Jim. *Cropper's Cabin.* 1952. Lion 108. PBO. c/gga. scarce. G. B6d. $25.00

THOMPSON, Jim. *Cropper's Cabin.* Pyramid G 336. c/Clark Hulings. scarce. VG+. B6a #75. $100.00

THOMPSON, Jim. *Damned.* 1954. Lion Library LL6. VG+. B4d. $25.00

THOMPSON, Jim. *Getaway.* 1973. Bantam N 7592. 1st prtg. MTI. My. VG. B3d/R5d. $5.00

THOMPSON, Jim. *Getaway.* 1989. Corgi 13350. F. B3d. $10.00

THOMPSON, Jim. *Getaway.* 1973. Sphere 7221. 2nd edn. c/McQueen & MacGraw: photo. My. VG+. B4d. $20.00

THOMPSON, Jim. *Golden Gizmo.* 1954. Lion 192. Fa. G. B4d. $40.00

THOMPSON, Jim. *Golden Gizmo.* Mysterious Press 40671. NF. M6d. $6.50

THOMPSON, Jim. *Grifters.* 1991. Corgi 13351. 2nd edn. My. F. P1d. $10.00

THOMPSON, Jim. *Hell of a Woman.* 1954. Banner 92. G+. B3a #20. $45.00

THOMPSON, Jim. *Hell of a Woman.* Corgi 13240. c/gga. NF. B6a #74. $75.00

THOMPSON, Jim. *Hell of a Woman.* 1956. Lion LB 138. My. NF. B4d. $50.00

THOMPSON, Jim. *Hell of a Woman.* 1956. Lion LB 138. 2nd edn. G+. G5d. $30.00

THOMPSON, Jim. *Hell of a Woman.* 1954. Lion 218. My. G. P1d. $35.00

THOMPSON, Jim. *Hell of a Woman.* 1954. Lion 218. PBO. c/gga. extremely scarce. VG. B6a #77. $91.00

THOMPSON, Jim. *Ironside.* 1967. Popular 60-2244. My. VG. P1d. $30.00

THOMPSON, Jim. *Ironside.* 1967. Popular 60-2244. TVTI. c/Robert Ironside: photo. NF. B4d. $35.00

THOMPSON, Jim. *Ironside.* 1967. Popular 60-2244. 1st prtg. TVTI. G+. R5d. $6.00

THOMPSON, Jim. *Kill-Off.* Corgi 13239. c/gga. NF. B6a #74. $75.00

THOMPSON, Jim. *Kill-Off.* 1957. Lion LL 142. 1st edn. My. F. F2d. $95.00

THOMPSON, Jim. *Kill-Off.* Mysterious Press 40572. NF. M6d. $6.50

THOMPSON, Jim. *Killer Inside Me.* 1965. Gold Medal K 1522. My. VG. P1d. $35.00

THOMPSON, Jim. *Killer Inside Me.* 1965. Gold Medal K 1522. scarce. VG+. B6a #75. $49.00

THOMPSON, Jim. *Killer Inside Me.* 1952. Lion 99. PBO. VG. B6a #77. $225.00

THOMPSON, Jim. *Killer Inside Me.* Quill 03922. NF. M6d. $6.50

THOMPSON, Jim. *Naked in the Dark.* 1953. Lion 154. My. VG+. B4d. $12.50

THOMPSON, Jim. *Nothing But a Man.* 1970. Popular 08116. MTI. VG. B4d. $20.00

THOMPSON, Jim. *Nothing Man.* 1954. Dell 1st Edn 22. My. VG. B4d/P1d. $100.00

THOMPSON, Jim. *Nothing Man.* 1954. Dell 1st Edn 22. PBO. c/Borack. extremely scarce. VG. B6a #79. $61.00

THOMPSON, Jim. *Nothing Man.* 1954. Dell 1st Edn 22. PBO. NF. B3a #22. $92.25

THOMPSON, Jim. *Nothing Man.* Mysterious Press 40570. VG. M6d. $5.00

THOMPSON, Jim. *Nothing More Than Murder.* Black Lizard. G+. G5d. $6.50

THOMPSON, Jim. *Nothing More Than Murder.* 1953. Dell 738. My. VG. B4d. $30.00

THOMPSON, Jim. *Nothing More Than Murder.* 1953. Dell 738. NF. I1d. $40.00

THOMPSON, Jim. *Nothing More Than Murder.* 1953. Dell 738. 1st prtg. My. G+. R5d. $20.00

THOMPSON, Jim. *Nothing More Than Murder.* 1949. Hillman 38. My. NF. B4d. $150.00

THOMPSON, Jim. *Nothing More Than Murder.* 1949. Hillman 38. 1st edn. PBO. extremely scarce. VG. B6a #79. $61.00

THOMPSON, Jim. *Nothing More Than Murder.* 1949. Hillman 38. 1st edn. PBO. rare. VG. B6a #76. $133.25

THOMPSON, Jim. *Pop 1280.* 1964. Gold Medal K 1438. Fa. VG. B4d. $40.00

THOMPSON, Jim. *Pop 1280.* 1964. Gold Medal K 1438. PBO. c/R McGinnis. My. G+. B5d. $27.50

THOMPSON, Jim. *Recoil.* Corgi 13242. c/gga. NF. B6a #74. $75.00

THOMPSON, Jim. *Recoil.* 1953. Lion 120. Fa. G+. B4d. $85.00

THOMPSON, Jim. *Rip-Off.* Mysterious Press 40669. NF. M6d. $6.50

THOMPSON, Jim. *Roughneck.* 1954. Lion 201. My. G+. P1d. $75.00

THOMPSON, Jim. *Roughneck.* 1954. Lion 201. My. VG+. B4d. $125.00

THOMPSON, Jim. *Roughneck.* 1954. Lion 201. PBO. extremely scarce. VG. B6a #77. $137.50

THOMPSON, Jim. *Savage Night.* Corgi 13256. c/gga. NF. B6a #74. $75.00

THOMPSON, Jim. *Savage Night.* 1953. Lion 155. PBO. c/gga. extremely scarce. VG. B6a #77. $125.00

THOMPSON, Jim. *South of Heaven.* 1967. Gold Medal D 1793. My. VG. P1d. $50.00

THOMPSON, Jim. *South of Heaven.* 1967. Gold Medal D 1793. PBO. c/photo. My. G. B5d. $12.50

THOMPSON, Jim. *South of Heaven.* 1967. Gold Medal D 1793. PBO. VG+. B6a #75. $55.00

THOMPSON, Jim. *Swell-Looking Babe.* 1954. Lion 212. My. VG+. B4d. $200.00

THOMPSON, Jim. *Swell-Looking Babe.* 1954. Lion 212. PBO. c/gga. extremely scarce. VG. B6a #77. $121.00

THOMPSON, Jim. *Texas by the Tail.* 1965. Gold Medal K 1502. My. VG. B4d. $40.00

THOMPSON, Jim. *Texas by the Tail.* 1965. Gold Medal K 1502. PBO. c/Barye. scarce. VG+. B6a #75. $61.00

THOMPSON, Jim. *Texas by the Tail.* 1965. Gold Medal K 1502. VG+. I1d. $55.00

THOMPSON, Jim. *Transgressors.* 1961. Signet S 2034. PBO. rare. VG. B6a #75. $55.00

THOMPSON, Jim. *Transgressors.* 1961. Signet 2034. PBO. VG. B3a #20. $113.30

THOMPSON, Jim. *Undefeated.* 1969. Popular 60-8104. MTI. c/John Wayne & Rock Hudson: photo. NF. B4d/F2d. $35.00

THOMPSON, Jim. *Undefeated.* 1969. Popular 60-8104. MTI. c/Wayne & Hudson: photo. VG+. B3d. $22.50

THOMPSON, Jim. *Wild Town.* 1957. Signet 1461. My. NF. B4d. $135.00

THOMPSON, Jim. *Wild Town.* 1957. Signet 1461. PBO. c/Maguire: gga. scarce. VG. B6a #75. $82.50

THOMPSON, John B. *Eager Ones.* 1960. Beacon 329. PBO. c/gga. VG+. B6d. $16.50

THOMPSON, John B. *Girls of the French Quarter.* 1957. Beacon 144. 1st prtg. VG+. P7d. $9.00

THOMPSON, John B. *Half-Caste.* 1959. Beacon 224. 1st prtg. PBO. c/Barton: gga. VG. P7d. $9.00

THOMPSON, John B. *Hot Blood.* 1959. Beacon 265. 1st prtg. PBO. c/Milo: gga. VG. P7d. $9.00

THOMPSON, John B. *Nude in the Sand.* 1959. Beacon 253. PBO. c/Al Rossi: gga. NF. B6a #76. $31.00

THOMPSON, John B. *One More for the Road.* 1960. Beacon 301. PBO. c/Micarelli: gga. VG+. B6d. $15.00

THOMPSON, John B. *Shameless.* 1963. Midwood 304. 1st edn. c/gga. F. F2d. $16.00

THOMPSON, John B. *Spawn of the Bayou.* 1958. Beacon 208. PBO. c/gga. scarce. VG+. B6a #79. $69.50

THOMPSON, John B. *Spawn of the Bayou.* 1958. Beacon 208. 1st prtg. PBO. VG+. P7d. $12.50

THOMPSON, John B. *Swamp Nymph.* Kozy K 150. PBO. VG. M6d. $6.50

THOMPSON, John B. *Tabasco.* 1959. Beacon 219. 1st prtg. PBO. VG+. P7d. $12.50

THOMPSON, Julian F. *Grounding of Group 6.* 1983. Avon Flare 83386. My. F. P1d. $5.00

THOMPSON, Morton. *Cry & the Covenant.* 1955. Signet D 1206. Fa. VG. B4d. $2.00

THOMPSON, Morton. *Joe, the Wounded Tennis Player.* Armed Services 742. VG. B3d. $5.50

THOMPSON, R.W. *Battle for the Rhine.* 1959. Ballantine F 291K. c/photo. NF. VG. B5d. $4.00

THOMPSON, Sharon L. *Lust & His Daughter.* 1965. Tropic Book 918. PBO. c/gga. NF. B6a #76. $38.50

THOMPSON, Thomas. *Brand of a Man.* Signet 2487. 2nd reissue. VG. B3d. $4.00

THOMPSON, Thomas. *Broken Valley.* 1951. Bantam 864. VG+. B3d. $4.00

THOMPSON, Thomas. *Forbidden Valley.* 1960. Popular G 441. 1st pb. VG. M6d. $3.50

THOMPSON, Thomas. *Gunman Brand.* 1952. Bantam 1082. VG+. B3d. $5.00

THOMPSON, Thomas. *Range Drifter.* 1950. Bantam 764. VG. B3d. $4.50

THOMPSON, Thomas. *Shadow of the Butte.* 1954. Pennant P 33. NF. B3d. $8.00

THOMPSON, Thomas. *Trouble Rider.* 1954. Ballantine 74. We. VG+. B4d. $12.00

THOMPSON & WOODFORD. *Honey.* 1956. Beacon 124. 1st prtg. c/Jack Woodford: gga. VG. P7d. $9.00

THOMPSON & WOODFORD. *Male Virgin.* 1960. Beacon 292. 1st edn. F. F2d. $20.00

THOMPSON & WOODFORD. *Passion in the Pines.* Uni-Book 63. VG. B3d. $6.00

THOMPSON & WOODFORD. *Savage Eye.* 1956. Beacon 127. VG. B3d. $5.50

THOMPSON & WOODFORD. *Savage Eye.* 1961. Beacon 381. VG+. B3d. $6.00

THOMPSON & WOODFORD. *Sugar Doll.* 1957. Beacon 140. VG. B3d. $5.00

THOMPSON & WOODFORD. *Swamp Hoyden.* 1956. Beacon B 125. Ad. VG. B5d. $9.00

THOMPSON & WOODFORD. *Swamp Hoyden.* 1956. Beacon 125. c/gga. F. F2d. $20.00

THORN, Ronald Scott. *Dark Shadow.* 1964. MacFadden 60-152. My. VG+. P1d. $9.00

THORNBURG, Newton. *Knockover.* 1968. Gold Medal D 1933. My. VG+. B4d. $3.75

THORNDIKE, Russell. *Dr Syn Returns.* 1974. Ballantine 23785. c/M Johnson. Fi. VG. B5d. $5.00

THORNE, Anthony. *Cabbage Holiday.* 1948. Bantam 452. 1st pb. c/Stahl. VG. B6d. $5.00

THORNE, Anthony. *So Long at the Fair.* 1947. Armed Services 1276. My. VG. P1d. $10.00

THORNE, E.P. *Lady With a Gun.* Special Mystery. My. F. P1d. $15.00

THORPE, Edward. *Night I Caught the Sante Fe Chief.* 1980. Bantam 03913. 2nd prtg. My. F. W2d. $4.00

THORPE, T. *Lightning World.* Badger SF 38. VG. B3a #21. $12.00

THORPE, T. *Lightning World.* Badger SF 38. VG. B3d. $10.00

THURBER, James. *Beast in Me.* 1960. Avon T 437. 1st pb edn. F. M1d. $8.00

THURBER, James. *Let Your Mind Alone.* Armed Services N 7. VG+. B3d. $8.00

THURBER, James. *Men, Women & Dogs.* 1946. Bantam 21. Hu. VG+. B4d. $7.00

THURBER, James. *My Life & Hard Times.* 1947. Bantam 92. Hu. VG. B4d. $2.75

THURBER, James. *Owl in the Attic.* 1965. Perennial 50. 1st pb. F. B6d. $7.50

THURMAN, Steve. *Gun Lightning.* Graphic 153. 2nd edn. VG. B3d. $4.00

THURMAN, Steve. *Hungry Gun.* 1966. PB Library 50-969. PBO. VG+. B3d. $4.50

THURMAN, Steve. *Hungry Gun.* 1966. PB Library 50-969. PBO. We. VG. B5d. $3.00

THURMAN, Steve. *Mad Dog Coll.* 1961. Monarch MM 607. My. VG. P1d. $10.00

THURMAN, Steve. *Night After Night.* 1959. Monarch 142. My. VG+. P1d. $12.50

THURSTON, Robert. *Q Colony.* 1985. Ace 69660. SF. F. W2d. $4.00

TIDYMAN, Ernest. *Shaft Has a Ball.* 1973. Bantam 7699. 1st edn. De. F. F2d. $12.50

TIDYMAN, Ernest. *Shaft.* 1971. Bantam N 6536. My. VG+. P1d. $4.50

TIDYMAN, Ernest. *Shaft's Big Score.* 1972. Bantam N 7540. MTI. My. VG. W2d. $3.75

TIDYMAN, Ernest. *Shaft's Big Score.* 1972. Bantam N 7540. 1st edn. c/photo. De. F. F2d. $17.00

TIDYMAN, Ernest. *Shaft's Carnival of Killers.* 1974. Bantam N 8494. De. VG. P1d. $3.50

TIGER, John. *Code Name: Little Ivan.* 1969. Popular 60-2464. My. VG. P1d. $7.50

TIGER, John. *Countertrap.* 1967. Popular 60-2206. I Spy #5. VG. I1d. $4.00

TIGER, John. *Countertrap.* 1967. Popular 60-2206. 1st edn. c/photo. I Spy #5. My. NF. F2d. $7.00

TIGER, John. *Death Hits a Jackpot.* 1954. Avon 605. Fa. VG. B4d. $4.00

TIGER, John. *Death-Twist.* 1968. Popular 60-2311. 1st edn. c/photo. My. F. F2d. $10.00

TIGER, John. *Death-Twist.* 1968. Popular 60-2311. 1st prtg. VG+. R5d. $6.00

TIGER, John. *Doomdate.* 1967. Popular 60-2237. 1st edn. c/photo. My. F. F2d. $8.00

TIGER, John. *Doomdate.* 1967. Popular 60-2237. 1st prtg. VG+. R5d. $5.00

TIGER, John. *I Spy.* 1965. Popular SP 400. TVTI. c/Culp & Cosby: photo. VG+. B4d. $6.00

TIGER, John. *I Spy.* 1965. Popular SP 400. 1st edn. TVTI. c/photo. My. F. F2d. $10.00

TIGER, John. *I Spy.* 1965. Popular SP 400. 1st prtg. TVTI. G+. R5d. $2.25

TIGER, John. *Masterstroke.* 1966. Popular 60-2127. 1st prtg. I Spy #2. VG. R5d. $3.00

TIGER, John. *Materstroke.* 1966. Popular 60-2127. 1st edn. c/photo. I Spy #2. My. F. F2d. $10.00

TIGER, John. *Mission: Impossible.* 1967. Popular 60-8042. TVTI. c/Martin Landau: photo. VG+. B4d. $3.00

TIGER, John. *Superkill.* Popular 60-2157. PBO. TVTI. c/G Rehberger. My. G+. B5d. $3.50

TIGER, John. *Superkill.* 1967. Popular 60-2157. VG. I1d. $4.00

TIGER, John. *Superkill.* 1967. Popular 60-2157. 1st edn. c/photo. NF. F2d. $7.00

TIGER, John. *Wipeout.* 1967. Popular 60-2180. 1st edn. My. F. F2d. $8.00

TIGER, John. *Wipeout.* 1967. Popular 60-2180. 1st prtg. G+. R5d. $1.50

TIIRA, Ensio. *Raft of Despair.* 1956. Lion Library LL 134. VG. I1d. $4.00

TILLERY, Caryle. *Red Bone Woman.* Avon 334. VG. B3d. $6.00

TILSEY, Frank. *Rage To Love (Fortunate Man).* Popular G 143. VG. B3d. $4.00

TILTON, Alice. *Cold Steal.* Dell 142. VG+. B3d. $7.00

TILTON, Alice. *Hollow Chest.* 1969. Popular 60-2395. My. VG+. P1d. $7.50

TILTON, Lois. *Vampire Winter.* 1990. Pinnacle 55817. PBO. F. B6d. $7.00

TIMLETT, Peter Valentine. *Power of the Serpent.* 1976. Ballantine O 2370. 1st prtg. PBO. VG+. P7d. $4.00

TIMMS, E.V. *Woman in Chains.* 1955. Harlequin 331. My. G+. P1d. $25.00

TINKLE, Lon. *Alamo.* 1960. Signet S1776. MTI. c/B Phillips & J Wayne: photos. Nfi. VG+. R5d. $5.50

TIPTREE, James. *Ten-Thousand Light-Years From Home.* 1978. Ace 80181. 2nd prtg. SF. F. W2d. $4.75

TIPTREE, James. *Ten-Thousand Light-Years From Home.* 1973. Ace. 1st edn. F. M1d. $10.00

TIPTREE, James. *Warm Worlds of Otherwise.* 1975. Ballantine. 1st edn. F. M1d. $10.00

TOBIN, D. *Little Woman.* Pocket 50217. PBO. VG+. B3d. $6.00

TOD, N. *Love on the Rocks.* Kozy 186. VG+. B3d. $7.50

TODAY'S WOMAN. *Marriage & Sex.* Gold Medal 100. VG. B3d. $6.00

TODD, Lucas. *Showdown Creek.* 1956. Perma M 3044. 1st pb. c/Tom Ryan. We. VG+. B6d. $12.00

TOFFLER, Alvin. *Future Shock.* 1974. Bantam Y 6700. 25th prtg. SF. VG. W2d. $3.75

TOFTE, Arthur. *Crash Landing on Iduna.* 1975. Laser 3. PBO. c/K Freas. SF. NF. B5d/I1d. $6.00

TOFTE, Arthur. *Walls Within Walls.* 1975. Laser 5. NF. B3d. $7.00

TOFTE, Arthur. *Walls Within Walls.* 1975. Laser 5. PBO. c/K Freas: sgn. SF. VG. B5d. $4.00

TOLKIEN, J.R.R. *Fellowship of Ring.* 1966. Ace A 4. F. M1d. $15.00

TOLKIEN, J.R.R. *Lord of the Rings Fotonovel.* 1979. Fotonovel 9752. 1st edn. SF. F. F2d. $16.00

TOLKIEN, J.R.R. *Return of the King.* 1979. Ballantine 27260. 63rd prtg. SF. VG. W2d. $3.00

TOLKIEN, J.R.R. *Silmarillion.* 1979. Ballantine 27255. SF. F. W2d. $4.00

TOLKIEN, J.R.R. *Silmarillion.* 1979. Ballantine 27255. 1st prtg. SF. VG. R5d/W2d. $3.00

TOLKIEN, J.R.R. *Smith of Wootton Manor & Farmer Gates of Ham.* 1972. Ballantine 01538. 7th prtg. SF. F. W2d. $4.00

TOLKIEN, J.R.R. *Smith of Wootton Manor & Farmer Gates of Ham.* 1974. Ballantine 21538. 10th prtg. SF. VG. W2d. $3.50

TOLKIEN, J.R.R. *Tolkien Reader.* 1971. Ballantine 01536. 13th prtg. SF. VG+. W2d. $4.00

TOLKIEN, J.R.R. *Two Towers.* 1966. Ace A 5. F. M1d. $15.00

TOLKIEN, J.R.R. *Two Towers.* 1969. Ballantine 01534. 19th prtg. SF. VG. W2d. $3.50

TOLKIEN, J.R.R. *Two Towers.* 1965. Ballantine. 1st edn. F. M1d. $12.00

TOLKIEN, J.R.R. *Unfinished Tales.* 1988. Ballantine 35711. 1st prtg. SF. VG+. R5d. $3.00

TOLSTOY, Leo. *Anna Karenina.* 1948. Pocket 515. 1st prtg. G+. R5d. $3.00

TOM, Gay. *Lion Lover.* 1963. France F 28. VG+. B3d. $5.50

TOM, Gay. *Lion Lover.* 1963. France 28. 1st US edn. NF. B6d. $12.50

TOMERLIN, John. *Return to Vikki.* 1959. Gold Medal 900. My. F. P1d. $17.50

TOMKIES, Mike. *Duke -- The Story of John Wayne.* 1972. Avon N 414. Bio. VG. P6d. $2.50

TOMPKINS, Walker A. *Gold on the Hoof.* Dell 879. VG. B3d. $4.50

TOMPKINS, Walker A. *Manhunt West.* Dell 551. VG. B3d. $4.50

TOMPKINS, Walker A. *Paintin' Pistoleer.* Dell 300. VG. B3d. $4.00

TOMPKINS, Walter A. *Gold on the Hoof.* Dell 879. c/R Stanley. We. VG. B5d. $3.00

TOOLE, John Kennedy. *Confederacy of Dunces.* 1981. Black Cat B 452. c/Sanjulian. Fi. VG. B5d. $5.00

TOOLE, John Kennedy. *Confederacy of Dunces.* 1982. Black Cat B 474. c/Sanjulian. Fi. VG. B5d. $3.50

TOOLE, Rex. *Soft Sell.* Bee Line 157. PBO. VG+. M6d. $9.50

TOOMEY, Robert. *World of Trouble.* 1973. Ballantine 3262. 1st edn. NF. P9d. $2.00

TORGESON, Roy. *Chrysalis 4.* 1979. Zebra 89063. 1st edn. NF. P9d. $2.00

TORRES, Tereska. *Golden Cage.* 1959. Avon T 448. TVTI. c/photo. VG+. P6d. $5.00

TORRES, Tereska. *Not Yet.* Signet 1579. NF. B3d. $5.50

TORRES, Tereska. *Women's Barracks.* 1950. Gold Medal 132. PBO. c/Barye. VG. B6d. $9.00

TORREY, Roger. *42 Days for Murder.* 1949. Hillman 23. My. VG. P1d. $15.00

TORREY, Roger. *42 Days for Murder.* 1939. Mystery Novel Monthly NN. VG. P1d. $20.00

TORRIO, Vincente. *Bootlegger.* 1975. New English 02728. My. VG. P1d. $4.00

TORRIO, Vincente. *Politician.* 1976. New English 27678. 1st prtg. Hoods #3. My. F. W2d. $4.75

TORRO, Pel. *Beyond the Barrier of Space.* Star NN. VG. B3d. $8.50

TORRO, Pel. *Legion of the Lost.* 1950s. Badger Supernatural 66. PBO. c/Fox. NF. B6a #76. $50.00

TORRO, Pel. *Return.* 1963. Vega VSF 10. VG. B3a #24. $12.10

TORRO, Pel. *Strange Ones.* 1960s. Badger Supernatural 70. PBO. c/Fox. scarce. NF. B6a #80. $61.00

TOWARD, George P. *Come Sin With Me.* 1960. Newsstand 138. 1st edn. c/gga. My. F. F2d. $14.00

TOWARD, George P. *Lesbos Hill.* 1960. Newsstand 147. 1st edn. F. F2d. $14.00

TOWER, Diana. *Dark Diamond.* 1975. Beagle 26700. Go. VG. P1d. $3.50

TOWNE, Stuart. *Death From Nowhere.* 1941. Yogi Mystery NN. 1st edn. PBO. rare. NF. B6a #75. $363.00

TOWNSEND, Atwood H. edt. *Good Reading.* 1949. Mentor M 19. 4th edn. Nfi. F. P1d. $10.50

TOWNSEND, Atwood H. edt. *Good Reading.* 1952. Mentor M 76. 6th edn. Nfi. G+. P1d. $3.50

TOWNSEND, Leo. *Young Life.* 1959. Popular G 339. JD. VG+. P1d. $25.00

TOWNSEND, Peter. *Out of Focus.* 1973. Pan 23429. My. VG. P1d. $4.00

TOWNSHEAD, Richard. *Japanese Encounter.* Edwin Self NN. VG+. B3a #21. $12.25

TRACE, John. *Trigger Vengeance.* 1945. Century 22. 1st edn. PBO. F. F2d. $12.00

TRACY, Catherine. *Cotton Moon.* 1951. Popular 852. c/Rozen: gga. Fa. VG+. B4d. $9.00

TRACY, Don *Big X.* 1976. Pocket 80773. 1st edn. De. F. F2d. $10.00

TRACY, Don. *Amber Fire.* 1954. Pocket 1006. c/G Mayers. Fi. VG. B5d. $4.50

TRACY, Don. *Big Blackout.* 1960. Pocket 6006. My. F. P1d. $14.00

TRACY, Don. *Big Blackout.* 1960. Pocket 6006. VG. G5d. $6.00

TRACY, Don. *Black Amulet.* 1968. Pocket 75286. Hi. G+. P1d. $3.50

TRACY, Don. *Carolina Corsair.* 1956. Cardinal C 228. 1st prtg. c/James Meese: gga. VG. P7d. $4.00

TRACY, Don. *Cheat.* 1951. Lion 69. My. F. P1d. $25.00

TRACY, Don. *Chesapeake Cavalier.* 1950. Pocket 729. Fa. VG+. B4d. $3.00

TRACY, Don. *Crimson Is the Eastern Shore.* 1954. Cardinal C 127. 1st prtg. c/Meese: gga. VG+. P7d. $4.50

TRACY, Don. *Criss-Cross.* Mercury 9. G+. G5d. $8.00

TRACY, Don. *Deadly to Bed.* 1960. Perma M 4176. 1st edn. c/gga. My. F. F2d. $12.50

TRACY, Don. *Death Calling Collect.* Pocket 80704. VG. G5d. $3.25

TRACY, Don. *Fun & Deadly Games.* 1968. Pocket 64005. My. VG. P1d. $5.00

TRACY, Don. *Hated One.* Perma M 5094. G+. G5d. $4.00

TRACY, Don. *How Sleeps the Beast.* 1950. Lion 45. My. VG. P1d. $15.00

TRACY, Don. *How Sleeps the Beast.* 1950. Lion 45. VG+. I1d. $18.00

TRACY, Don. *Naked She Died.* 1962. Pocket 6099. My. VG. B5d. $4.00

TRACY, Don. *Roanoke Renegade.* 1955. Cardinal C 189. 1st prtg. c/Hulings: gga. VG+. P7d. $4.50

TRACY, Don. *Strumpet City.* 1952. Pocket 868. c/C Zuckerberg. My. VG. B5d. $4.00

TRACY, Don. *Too Many Girls (Round Trip).* Berkley G 182. VG. G5d. $4.50

TRACY, Don. *White Hell (Last Year's Snow).* Berkley 318. G+. G5d. $4.00

TRAIL, Armitage. *Scarface.* 1959. Dell D 336. My. F. P1d. $15.00

TRAIN, Arthur. *Mr Tutt Finds a Way.* 1945. Armed Services 796. VG. B3d. $7.00

TRAIN, Arthur. *Tutt & Mr Tutt.* 1946. Bantam 55. Fa. VG+. B4d. $12.00

TRAIN, Arthur. *Tutt & Mr Tutt.* 1946. Bantam 55. My. F. P1d. $21.00

TRAIN, Arthur. *Yankee Lawyer.* 1944. Armed Services K 25. My. VG. P1d. $20.00

TRAINER, P.R. *Beast Feast.* 1970. Venice Book 443. 1st edn. c/fantasy-style art. F. F2d. $15.00

TRAINER, R. *Jealous Lover.* Classics Library 13. VG+. B3d. $6.00

TRAINER, Russell. *No Way Back.* Midwood 307. c/Rader. VG. B3d. $4.00

TRAINER, Russell. *Sex, Jealousy, & Conflict.* Brandon House. VG+. B3d. $6.00

TRAINER, Russell. *Three Men for Libby D.* Brandon House 1163. NF. B3d. $7.00

TRAINER, Russell. *Violence of Adultery.* Brandon House 6431. NF. B3d. $5.00

TRAINER, Russell. *Warden's Wife.* 1962. Beacon B 510F. PBO. Ad. VG. B5d. $5.50

TRALINS, Bob. *Colossal Carnality.* 1960. Novel Book 6064. 1st edn. F. F2d. $20.00

TRALINS, Bob. *Miss From SIS.* 1966. Belmont 50-704. VG+. B3d. $6.00

TRALINS, Bob. *Miss From SIS: Chic Chick Spy.* Belmont 50-718. VG+. B3d. $6.00

TRALINS, Bob. *Whisper.* 1965. Beacon 904. 1st edn. SF. VG. F2d. $7.00

TRALINS, Robert. *Black Brute.* 1969. Lancer 75-075. 1st end. Hi. NF. F2d. $10.00

TRALINS, Robert. *Cosmozoids.* 1966. Belmont B 50-692. PBO. SF. VG+. B5d. $5.50

TRALINS, Robert. *Cosmozoids.* 1966. Belmont B 50-692. 1st edn. NF. M1d. $8.00

TRALINS, Robert. *ESP Forewarnings.* 1969. Popular 2427. 1st edn. c/Jack Davis. SF. F. F2d. $10.00

TRALINS, Robert. *Ghoul Lover.* 1972. Popular 1558. 1st edn. Ho. F. F2d. $12.00

TRALINS, Robert. *Torrid Island.* 1961. Novel Book 5046. Ad. VG+. P1d. $14.50

TRANSUE, Jacob. *Twilight of the Basilisks.* 1973. Berkley 02476. SF. VG. W2d. $3.50

TRAPP, M.A. *Story of Trapp Family Singers.* 1960. Dell F 106. 1st prtg. VG. R5d. $2.25

TRAVEN, B. *Death Ship.* 1964. Consul Books 1319. VG+. B3a. $25.30

TRAVEN, B. *March to the Monteria.* 1964. Dell 5350. 1st prtg. c/McCarthy. VG. B3d/P7d. $4.50

TRAVEN, B. *Night Visitor.* 1968. Pocket 75235. Fi. F. P1d. $10.00

TRAVEN, B. *Some Little Blems.* Cardinal GC 121. VG. B3d. $4.00

TRAVEN, B. *Treasure of the Sierra Madre.* 1974. Panther. VG. B3d. $6.50

TRAVEN, B. *Treasure of the Sierra Madre.* 1948. Pocket 455. MTI. c/Barye Phillips: Bogart. VG+. P1d. $20.00

TRAVEN, B. *Treasure of the Sierra Madre.* 1948. Pocket 455. 1st prtg. G. R5d. $3.25

TRAVER, Robert. *Anatomy of a Murder.* 1959. Dell F 75. My. VG. P1d. $7.00

TRAVER, Robert. *Anatomy of a Murder.* 1960. Penguin 1479. My. VG. P1d. $7.50

TRAVER, Robert. *Danny & the Boys.* 1959. Popular G 366. Fi. VG. P1d. $7.00

TRAVER, Robert. *Funeral for Sabella.* 1953. Signet 1065. My. VG. B5d. $4.00

TRAVER, Robert. *Small Town DA.* 1958. Crest S 233. My. VG+. P1d. $11.00

TRAVER, Robert. *Trouble Shooter.* Bantam 111. VG. B3d. $5.00

TRAVER, Robert. *Trouble Shooter.* 1947. Bantam 111. c/J King. My. VG. B3d/B5d. $5.00

TRAVIS, Ben. *Strange Ones.* 1959. Beacon 226. 1st prtg. PBO. c/Darcy: gga. VG. P7d. $9.00

TREAT, Lawrence. *Big Shot.* 1952. Bantam 1026. My. VG. P1d. $9.00

TREAT, Lawrence. *Big Shot.* 1952. Bantam 1026. 1st prtg. My. G+. R5d. $2.25

TREAT, Lawrence. *D As in Dead.* 1943. Atlas NN. 1st pb. My. VG. B6d. $9.00

TREAT, Lawrence. *H As in Hangman.* 1944. Atlas NN. 1st pb. My. VG+. B6d. $12.00

TREAT, Lawrence. *Leather Man Murders.* 1944. Novel Classic 68. My. VG. P1d. $20.00

TREAT, Lawrence. *O As in Omen.* Novel Classic 64. My. VG. P1d. $20.00

TREAT, Lawrence. *Q As in Quicksand.* 1949. Dell 301. My. VG. P1d. $10.00

TREAT, Lawrence. *T As in Trapped.* 1950. Avon 274. My. VG. P1d. $12.50

TREAT, Lawrence. *Wail for the Corpses.* 1943. Best De Selection 6. My. VG. P1d. $20.00

TREE, Gregory. *Case Against Myself.* 1951. Bantam 907. My. VG. P1d. $9.00

TREECE, Henry. *Jason.* 1962. Signet T 2165. Fa. VG. B4d. $3.00

TREECE, Henry. *Pagan Queen.* 1959. Avon T 363. Fa. VG+. B4d. $10.00

TREECE, Henry. *Savage Warriors.* 1959. Avon T 325. VG. B3d. $4.50

TREGASKIS, Richard. *China Bomb.* 1968. Avon N 179. Th. VG. P1d. $5.00

TREGASKIS, Richard. *John F Kennedy: War Hero.* 1962. Dell F 194. 1st prtg. VG+. P7d. $4.50

TREIBICH, S.J. *Burwyck's Wander.* 1967. Lancer 73-589. Go. F. P1d. $10.00

TRELOS, Tony. *Corruption of Linda.* Brandon House 3047. VG+. B3d. $4.00

TRELOS, Tony. *Stray Pussycat.* 1967. Brandon House 1100. PBO. VG+. B6d. $7.50

TREMAYNE, Peter. *Ants.* 1980. Signet 09163. SF. VG. W2d. $3.25

TREMAYNE, Peter. *Bloodmist.* 1988. Baen 65425-X. 1st edn. SF. F. F2d. $8.00

TREMAYNE, Peter. *Bloodright.* 1980. Dell 10509. 1st prtg. SF. F. W2d. $7.50

TREMAYNE, Peter. *Dracula in Love.* 1983. Dell 02138. 1st prtg. VG. P7d. $4.00

TREMAYNE, Peter. *Nicor!* 1987. Sphere UK 8609. 1st edn. SF. F. F2d. $10.00

TREMONT, Victor. *Man Called Kyril.* 1984. Jove. advance reading copy. Th. VG. P1d. $10.00

TREMONT, Victor. *Unconventional Beauty.* 1963. Merit Book 687. My. VG+. P1d. $9.00

TRENCH, Caroline. *Nurse Warding Takes Charge.* Harlequin 419. VG. B3d. $4.00

TRENT, R. *Forbidden Act: Incest.* Copley 195. NF. B3d. $5.00

TRENT, Timothy. *All Dames Are Dynamite.* 1949. Novel Library 29. VG+. B3a #21. $22.70

TREVANIAN. *Eiger Sanction.* 1973. Avon 15404. Th. VG. P1d. $3.50

TREVANIAN. *Loo Sanction.* 1974. Avon 19067. My. VG. P1d. $3.50

TREVANIAN. *Main.* 1977. Jove B 4410. My. VG+. P1d. $4.50

TREVANIAN. *Main.* 1986. Jove 08888. 11th prtg. My. VG. W2d. $3.25

TREVOR, Elleston. *Flight of the Phoenix.* 1966. Avon V 2144. 1st prtg. MTI. My. G+. R5d. $1.50

TREVOR, Elleston. *Gale Force.* 1965. Ballantine U 5044. Fa. VG. B4d. $2.00

TREVOR, Elleston. *Pillars of Midnight.* 1963. Ballantine F 755. 1st prtg. VG. R5d. $2.50

TREVOR, Elleston. *Squadron Airborne.* 1964. Ballantine U 2223. 2nd edn. War. VG+. P1d. $7.50

TREVOR, Elleston. *Tiger Street.* 1954. Lion 207. PBO. Cr. VG. B6d. $15.00

TREVOR, Elleston. *Weave a Rope of Sand.* 1965. Consul 1373. 1st pb. My. VG. B6d. $3.50

TREVOR, Leslie. *Code 1013: Assassin.* 1975. Award AQ 1452. My. VG. P1d. $6.00

TREVOR-ROPER, H.R. *Last Days of Hitler.* 1957. Berkley G 70. VG+. B3d. $4.00

TREVOR-ROPER, H.R. *Last Days of Hitler.* 1960. Berkley S 485. c/photo. Nfi. VG. B5d. $3.00

TREW, Antony. *Two Hours to Darkness.* 1964. Bantam H 2728. MTI. VG+. B4d. $2.00

TREYNOR, A.M. *Hawk of the Desert.* 1944. Aventure Novel 21. 1st pb. VG. B6d. $7.00

TREYNOR, Blair. *She Ate Her Cake.* 1947. Dell 186. VG. B3d/B5d. $6.00

TREYNOR, Blair. *Silver Doll.* 1954. Dell 762. c/S Borack. My. VG+. B5d. $5.00

TREYNOR, Blair. *Silver Doll.* 1954. Dell 762. G+. G5d. $3.00

TREYNOR, Blair. *Silver Doll.* 1954. Dell 762. My. F. P1d. $20.00

TREYNOR, Blair. *Widow's Pique.* 1957. Perma M 3096. c/J Meese. My. VG. B5d. $4.00

TRIMBLE, Louis. *City Machine.* 1972. DAW 24. SF. F. P1d. $5.00

TRIMBLE, Louis. *City Machine.* 1972. DAW 24. 1st prtg. SF. VG. R5d. $3.25

TRIMBLE, Louis. *Date for Murder.* 1943. My Novel Classic 18. My. VG. P1d. $20.00

TRIMBLE, Louis. *Dead & the Deadly.* 1963. Ace F 229. My. VG. P1d. $7.50

TRIMBLE, Louis. *Deadman Canyon.* 1961. Ace F 116. We. VG+. P1d. $12.00

TRIMBLE, Louis. *Design for Dying.* 1946. Bart House 27. My. VG+. P1d. $15.50

TRIMBLE, Louis. *Desperate Deputy of Cougar Hill.* Ace D 594. PBO. VG. B3d. $4.50

TRIMBLE, Louis. *Fighting Cowman.* 1953. Popular 506. We. VG+. B4d. $8.00

TRIMBLE, Louis. *Girl on a Slay Ride.* 1960. Avon T 469. My. F. P1d. $14.00

TRIMBLE, Louis. *Gunsmoke Justice.* 1951. Bantam 892. We. G+. P1d. $6.50

TRIMBLE, Louis. *Hostile Peaks.* 1969. Ace 71372. We. VG. P1d. $5.50

TRIMBLE, Louis. *Murder Trouble.* 1945. Black Cat Detective 18. My. VG. P1d. $20.00

TRIMBLE, Louis. *Till Death Do Us Part.* 1959. Ace D 367. PBO. c/Rader & Maguire: gga. NF. B6a #76. $61.00

TRIMBLE, Louis. *Valley of Violence.* 1950. Bantam 769. We. VG. P1d. $9.50

TRIMBLE, Louis. *Wandering Variables.* 1972. DAW 34. 1st prtg. PBO. VG. P7d. $4.00

TRIMBLE/TRIMBLE. *Duchess of Skid Row/Love Me & Die.* 1960. Ace D 477. My. G+. P1d. $6.50

TRIMBLE/TRIMBLE. *Duchess of Skid Row/Love Me & Die.* 1960. Ace D 477. PBO. VG+. B6d. $40.00

TRIMBLE/WELLS. *Showdown in the Cayuse/Ride a Dim Trail.* 1966. Ace G 579. We. VG. B4d. $1.75

TRIMBLE/WEST. *Siege at High Meadow/ Buzzard's Nest.* Ace F 128. PBO. NF. B3d. $5.00

TRIMBLE/WHITTINGTON. *Corpse Without a Country/Play for Keeps.* 1959. Ace D 347. My. G+. P1d. $10.00

TRIMBLE/WHITTINGTON. *Corpse Without a Country/Play for Keeps.* 1959. Ace D 347. My. VG+. P1d. $35.00

TRIMBLE/WHITTINGTON. *Corpse Without a Country/Play for Keeps.* 1959. Ace D 347. VG+. B3a #22. $27.85

TRINIAN, John. *Big Grab.* 1960. Pyramid G 548. My. VG+. P1d. $10.50

TRINIAN, John. *Game of Flesh.* 1963. Domino 72-678. Ad. VG. P1d. $9.00

TRINIAN, John. *House of Evil.* Pyramid 712. VG+. B3d. $5.00

TRINIAN, John. *North Beach Girl.* 1960. Gold Medal S 1000. Ad. G+. P1d. $9.50

TRINIAN, John. *North Beach Girl.* 1961. Gold Medal 518. VG. B3d. $7.50

TRINIAN, John. *Savage Breast.* Gold Medal 1104. VG+. B3d. $5.50

TRINIAN, John. *Scratch a Thief.* 1961. Ace F 107. My. VG. P1d. $8.00

TRIPP, Miles. *Kilo 40.* 1966. Avon S 194. 1st prtg. My. VG. R5d. $1.75

TROCCHI, Alexander. *Carnal Days of Helen Seferis.* 1967. Brandon House 6028. PBO. VG. P6d. $5.00

TROCCHI, Alexander. *Thongs.* Brandon House 6264. VG+. B3d. $5.00

TRONSON, Robert. *Afternoon of a Counterspy.* 1970. Arrow 002940. My. VG. P1d. $4.50

TROUT, K. *Venus on Half Shell.* Dell 6149. 1st prtg. G. S1d. $2.50

TRUAX, Rhoda. *Joseph Lister.* Armed Services 762. G. P6d. $12.00

TRUDEAU, G.B. *President Is a Lot Smarter Than You Think.* 1973. Popular 445-00607-095. 1st edn. PBO. cartoons. F. F2d. $7.00

TRUE, G.H. *Laugh Oil.* American Humor Guild. c/inscr. VG. B3d. $5.00

TRUE MAGAZINE edt. *True Album of Cartoons.* Crest 498. VG+. B3d. $4.00

TRUESDELL, June. *Be Still My Love.* 1950. Harlequin 39. G+. B3d. $5.00

TRUFFAUT, Francois. *Wild Child.* 1973. Pocket 47893. 1st prtg. VG+. R5d. $1.75

TRUFFAUT, Francois. *400 Blows.* Black Cat B 195. PBO. Fi. NF. B5d. $10.00

TRUMAN, Harry S. *Mr Citizen.* 1961. Popular SP 92. 1st prtg. c/photo. VG+. P7d. $4.00

TRUMAN, Margaret. *Murder in the White House.* 1981. Popular 04661. My. VG+. P1d. $4.50

TRUMBULL, Robert. *Raft.* 1942. Dell 26. Fa. VG. B4d. $10.00

TRUMBULL, Robert. *Raft.* 1942. Dell 26. G+. I1d. $8.00

TRUMBULL, Robert. *Raft.* 1951. Pyramid 38. 1st pb. Ad. VG. B6d. $6.00

TRUMBULL, Robert. *Raft.* 1952. Pyramid 38. Fa. VG+. B4d. $7.50

TRUSS, Seldon. *Draw the Blinds.* Hodder Stoughton 111. My. VG. P1d. $7.50

TRUSS, Seldon. *Never Fight a Lady.* Mercury Mystery 171. My. VG. P1d. $12.50

TRUSS, Seldon. *They Came by Night.* 1936. Crime-Book Society 2. My. G+. P1d. $10.00

TRUSS, Seldon. *Why Slug a Postman.* 1951. Pocket 854. 1st prtg. c/De Soto: gga. VG. P7d. $6.00

TRYON, Mark. *Of G-Strings & Strippers.* 1959. Beacon 273. 1st pb. c/gga. VG. B6d. $6.00

TRYON, Mark. *Sinning Lens.* 1959. Berkley G 206. NF. B3d. $6.00

TRYON, Thomas. *Harvest Home.* 1974. Crest X 2082. SF. F. W2d. $5.00

TRYON, Thomas. *Other.* 1972. Crest P 1668. SF. F. W2d. $5.00

TUBB, E C. *Veruchia.* 1973. Ace 86180. SF. VG. B5d. $3.00

TUBB, E.C. *Breakaway.* 1975. Pocket 80184. 1st prtg. TVTI. Space: 1999 #1. VG. R5d. $3.00

TUBB, E.C. *Century of the Maniken.* 1972. DAW 18. VG+. B3d. $4.50

TUBB, E.C. *Eloise.* 1975. DAW 143. PBO. c/J Barr. SF. VG+. B5d. $4.50

TUBB, E.C. *Genetic Buccaneer.* 1973. DAW 12. 1st edn. SF. F. F2d. $10.00

TUBB, E.C. *Haven of Darkness.* 1977. DAW 242. VG+. I1d. $4.00

TUBB, E.C. *Iduna's Universe.* 1979. DAW 363. 1st edn. SF. F. F2d. $10.00

TUBB, E.C. *Incident on Ath.* 1978. DAW UW 1389. SF. G. W2d. $2.00

TUBB, E.C. *Moon Base.* 1964. Ace F 293. PBO. VG. M1d. $6.00

TUBB, E.C. *Planet of Dread.* 1974. DAW 10. 1st edn. SF. F. F2d. $10.00

TUBB, E.C. *Spawn of Laban.* 1974. DAW 11. 1st edn. SF. F. F2d. $11.00

TUBB, E.C. *Spectrum of a Forgotten Sun.* 1980. Arrow 921420. 1st prtg. SF. VG. R5d. $2.00

TUBB, E.C. *STAR Flight.* 1969. PB Library 62-009. PBO. SF. NF. B5d. $5.00

TUBB, E.C. *STAR Flight.* 1969. PB Library 62-009. 1st prtg. VG. S1d. $2.50

TUBB, E.C. *Terra Data.* 1980. DAW 383. PBO. c/M Mariano. SF. VG. B5d. $3.00

TUBB, E.C. *Veruchia.* 1973. Ace 86180. 1st edn. SF. F. F2d. $10.00

TUBB, E.C. *World Aflame.* 1974. DAW 13. 1st edn. SF. F. F2d. $11.00

TUBB, E.C. *Zenia.* 1974. DAW 115. PBO. c/K Freas. SF. VG+. B5d. $4.50

TUBB/TUBB. *Derai/Winds of Gath.* Ace 89301. VG. P9d. $1.50

TUBB/TUBB. *Derai/Winds of Gath.* 1973. Ace 89301. 2nd edn. c/J Jones. SF. VG+. B5d. $4.50

TUBB/TUBB. *Scatter of Stardust/Technos.* 1972. Ace 79975. PBO. c/Bergman. SF. VG. B5d. $4.50

TUBB/TUBB. *Scatter of Stardust/Technos.* 1972. Ace 79975. SF. F. W2d. $7.50

TUBB/TUBB. *Scatter of Stardust/Technos.* 1972. Ace 79975. 1st prtg. G+. S1d. $3.00

TUCKER, Joan. *Waterfront Club.* Cameo 349. 2nd edn. Fi. VG. B5d. $7.50

TUCKER, Wilson. *Chinese Doll.* 1949. Dell 343. 1st pb. My. VG. B6d. $15.00

TUCKER, Wilson. *Ice & Iron.* 1975. Ballantine 24660. SF. VG+. B5d. $4.50

TUCKER, Wilson. *Lincoln Hunters.* Ace H 62. VG+. B3d. $4.50

TUCKER, Wilson. *Long Loud Silence.* 1954. Dell 791. c/R Powers. SF. VG. B5d. $5.50

TUCKER, Wilson. *Long Loud Silence.* 1954. Dell 791. G+. I1d. $4.00

TUCKER, Wilson. *Long Loud Silence.* 1954. Dell 791. 1st pb edn. F. M1d. $15.00

TUCKER, Wilson. *Man From Tomorrow.* 1955. Bantam 1343. 1st pb edn. F. M1d. $10.00

TUCKER, Wilson. *Man From Tomorrow.* 1955. Bantam 1343. 1st prtg. VG. P7d. $5.50

TUCKER, Wilson. *Resurrection Days.* 1981. Pocket. 1st edn. F. M1d. $5.00

TUCKER, Wilson. *Time Masters.* 1954. Signet 1127. c/J Faragasso. SF. VG+. B5d. $6.50

TUCKER, Wilson. *Time Masters.* 1954. Signet 1127. 1st pb edn. F. M1d. $12.00

TUCKER, Wilson. *Time: X.* 1955. Bantam. 1st pb edn. F. M1d. $12.00

TUCKER, Wilson. *To Keep or Kill.* 1950. Lion 21. My. VG. P1d. $25.00

TUCKER, Wilson. *Tomorrow Plus X (Time Bomb).* Avon T 168. VG+. B3d. $5.00

TUCKER, Wilson. *Tomorrow Plus X.* Avon T 168. 1st pb edn. F. M1d. $10.00

TUCKER, Wilson. *Warlock.* 1969. Avon V 2329. My/SF. VG. P1d. $7.50

TUCKER, Wilson. *Wild Talent.* 1966. Avon G 1301. VG. M6d. $4.50

TUCKER, Wilson. *Year of the Quiet Sun.* Ace 94200 PBO. c/L & D Dillon. SF. VG. B5d. $3.00

TUCKER/WHITTINGTON. *Hired Target/One Deadly Dawn.* 1957. Ace D 241. VG. B3d. $8.00

TULLY, Andrew. *FBI's Most Famous Cases.* 1967. Dell 2501. Nfi. VG+. P1d. $7.50

TULLY, Andrew. *Race of Rebels.* 1961. Popular G 517. Hi. VG. P1d. $6.50

TULLY, Andrew. *Super Spies.* 1970. Pocket 77211. Nfi. VG. P1d. $4.50

TULLY, Jim. *Bruiser.* Corgi 767. VG. B3d. $5.00

TULLY, Jim. *Bruiser.* Pyramid 53. reprint. VG. B6d. $7.00

TUNING, William. *Fuzzy Bones.* 1981. Ace 26181. SF. VG. B5d. $4.00

TUNING, William. *Fuzzy Bones.* 1981. Ace 26181. 1st edn. F. M1d. $5.00

TUNLEY, Roul. *Kids, Crime & Chaos.* 1964. Dell 4449. JD. VG. P1d. $9.00

TURNBULL, Andrew. *F Scott Fitzgerald.* 1971. Ballantine 02334. 2nd edn. Nfi. VG. P1d. $3.00

TURNBULL, Gerry edt. *Star Trek Catalog.* 1979. Ace 78477. 1st prtg. VG+. R5d. $5.00

TURNER, Bill. *Sex Trap.* 1969. New English 00321. My. VG. P1d. $4.50

TURNER, Calvin. *Sinful Love.* Hillman 124. VG+. B3d. $6.00

TURNER, E.S. *Astonishing History of the Medical Profession.* 1961. Ballantine F 469K. NF. NF. B5d. $6.00

TURNER, E.S. *Court of St James's.* 1961. Ballantine S 547K. 1st pb. VG. B6d. $7.50

TURNER, E.S. *History of Courting.* 1960. Ballantine F 415K. NF. VG. B5d. $4.00

TURNER, E.S. *Shocking History of Advertising.* 1960. Ballantine F 403K. 1st prtg. G+. P7d. $5.00

TURNER, John. *Carole Came Back.* 1963. Midwood 308. PBO. VG. B3d. $6.00

TURNER, John. *Dollar Man.* 1961. Pyramid G 589. Fi. VG. B5d. $4.50

TURNER, John. *Sinners.* 1963. Midwood F 325. PBO. NF. B6d. $18.00

TURNER, Robert. *Girl in the Cop's Pocket.* 1956. Ace D 177. My. G+. P1d. $7.50

TURNER, Robert. *Lonely Man.* 1957. Avon 780. We. VG. P1d. $7.50

TURNER, Robert. *Scout.* Pocket 1216. PBO. VG. B3d. $4.00

TURNER, Robert. *Wagonmaster.* Pocket 1196. PBO. TVTI. VG. B3d. $4.00

TURNER, Robert. *Wagons West!* 1958. Pocket 1226. TVTI. VG. B3d. $3.50

TURNER, Russell. *Short Night.* 1957. Hillman 103. My. G+. P1d. $5.50

TURNER, W.O. *Destination Doubtful.* Ballantine U 1050. PBO. VG. B3d. $4.00

TURNER, W.O. *Man Called Jeff.* 1969. Berkley X 1650. We. VG. B5d. $2.50

TURNER, W.O. *Proud Diggers.* Dell 844. VG. B3d. $4.50

TURNER, William W. *Hoover's FBI.* 1971. Dell 3673. Nfi. VG+. P1d. $4.50

TURNEY, Catherine. *Other One.* Dell 695. c/B Hilbert. SF. VG. B3d/B5d. $5.50

TURNGREN, Annette. *By-Line, Mona Knox.* 1962. Belmont 90-268. VG+. G5d. $4.50

TUROW, Scott. *Presumed Innocent.* Warner 35098. VG. G5d. $4.50

TUTE, Warren. *Cruiser.* 1956. Ballantine F 162. War. VG. B4d. $3.00

TUTTLE, W.C. *Ghost Trails.* 1945. Century 15. 1st edn. PBO. F. F2d. $12.00

TUTTLE, W.C. *Gun Feud.* Popular 354. VG. I1d. $5.00

TUTTLE, W.C. *Hashknife of Stormy River.* Hillman 37. VG. B3d. $6.00

TUTTLE, W.C. *Hidden Blood.* Popular 149. VG. B3d. $5.00

TUTTLE, W.C. *Redhead From Sun Dog.* Hillman 28. VG. B3d. $4.00

TUTTLE, W.C. *Shotgun Gold.* Popular 297. VG. B3d. $5.00

TUTTLE, W.C. *Singing River.* 1946. Popular 96. c/Im-Ho. We. VG+. P6d. $4.00

TUTTLE, W.C. *Singing River.* 1946. Popular 96. 1st edn. PBO. F. F2d. $15.00

TUTTLE, W.C. *Thunderbird Range.* 1958. Pyramid G 370. c/V Prezio. We. VG. B5d. $4.00

TUTTLE, W.C. *Trouble Trailer.* Popular 330. VG+. B3d. $6.50

TUTTLE, W.C. *Tumbling River Range.* 1948. Hillman 2. VG+. B3a #24. $8.25

TUTTLE, W.C. *Twisted Trails.* Popular 249. VG+. B3d. $8.00

TUTTLE, W.C. *Valley of Vanishing Herds.* Popular 165. VG. B3d. $5.00

TWAIN, Mark. *Adventures of Huckleberry Finn.* Pocket J 42. VG+. B3d. $5.50

TWAIN, Mark. *Connecticut Yankee in King Arthur's Court.* Airmont CL 29. SF. F. W2d. $5.00

TWAIN, Mark. *Connecticut Yankee in King Arthur's Court.* 1948. Pocket 497. 1st pb. VG. M1d. $12.00

TWAIN, Mark. *Connecticut Yankee in King Arthur's Court.* Signet CD 158. 63rd prtg. SF. F. W2d. $5.00

TWAIN, Mark. *Letter From the Earth.* 1963. Crest R 647. 2nd prtg. SF. F. W2d. $4.75

TWAIN, Mark. *Life on the Mississippi.* 1945. Bantam 1. Nfi. VG+. B4d. $12.50

TWAIN, Mark. *Mysterious Stranger.* Armed Services N 1. VG. B3d. $7.00

TWAIN, Mark. *Stolen White Elephant.* 1928. Tauchitz 2077. My. VG+. P1d. $30.00

TWAIN, Mark. *Tom Sawyer.* Pocket J 37. VG. B3d. $5.00

TWERSKY, Jacob. *Face of the Deep.* 1954. Signet 1132. VG. B3d. $4.00

TWERSKY, Jacob. *Face of the Deep.* 1954. Signet 1132. 1st pb. c/Maguire. NF. B6d. $15.00

TWIST, Peter. *Gilded Hideway.* 1955. Ace S 107. 1st prgt. PBO. c/gga. VG. P7d. $6.00

TYLER, G. *He Kissed Her There.* Uptown 700. VG+. B3d. $5.50

TYLER, John. *You Can't Escape Me!* 1960. Newsstand U 162. c/gga. NF. B3d. $7.00

TYLER, Parker. *Underground Film.* 1970. Black Cat B 260. Nfi. G+. B5d. $5.00

TYLOR, Duncan. *Red Curtain.* 1959. Beacon B 205. PBO. VG+. B6d. $12.50

TYLOR, Duncan. *Red Curtain.* 1959. Beacon B 205. Th. VG. P1d. $10.50

TYNAN, Kathleen. *Agatha.* 1979. Ballantine 27586. 1st prtg. MTI. VG+. R5d. $2.50

TYRE, Nedra. *Reformatory Girls.* 1962. Ace F 151. JD. VG+. P1d. $35.00

TYRE, Nedra. *Reformatory Girls.* 1962. Ace F 151. 1st edn. PBO. c/Johnson. scarce. NF. B6a #80. $82.00

TYRER, W. *Affair of Danny the Dip.* Sexton Blake 226. VG+. B3d. $8.00

TYRER, W. *Crime in Room 37.* Sexton Blake 321. c/Heade. VG. B3d. $8.00

TYRER, W. *Mystery of the Rio Star.* Sexton Blake 230. VG+. B3d. $8.00

TYRER, W. *Mystery of Three Demobbed Men.* Sexton Blake 120. VG+. B3d. $8.50

TZETNIK, Ka. *House of Dolls.* 1958. Pyramid G 326. c/Powell: gga. We. VG+. B4d. $6.00

TZETNIK, Ka. *House of Dolls.* 1960. Pyramid G 503. 2nd edn. c/D Shelton. Fi. VG. B5d. $4.50

U

UCHARD, Mario. *Frenchman in Mohammed's Harem.* 1952. Avon 416. c/gga. Fa. VG. B4d. $7.50

UCHARD, Mario. *Frenchman in Mohammed's Harem.* 1952. Avon 416. NF. I1d. $12.00

UCHARD, Marlo. *Frenchman in Mohammed's Harem.* 1952. Avon 416. c/gga. Fi. G+. B5d. $5.00

UHNAK, Dorothy. *Bait.* 1976. Pocket 82326. 2nd prtg. My. F. W2d. $3.75

UHNAK, Dorothy. *Bait.* 1969. Popular 60-2415. My. VG. P1d. $4.50

UHNAK, Dorothy. *Policewoman.* 1965. MacFadden 60-203. My. VG. P1d. $5.50

ULLMAN, A. *Night Man.* Pyramid 354. VG. B3d. $4.00

ULLMAN, Allan. *Naked Spur.* Pennant P 29. NF. I1d. $6.00

ULLMAN, Allan. *Sorry, Wrong Number.* 1966. MacFadden 50-260. My. G+. P1d. $4.00

ULLMAN, James Michael. *Venus Trap.* 1968. Venus Trap. My. VG. P1d. $5.00

ULLMAN, James Ramsey. *Third Man on the Mountain.* 1959. Cardinal C 391. 1st prtg. VG. R5d. $1.75

ULLMAN, James. *Sands of Kara Korum.* 1953. Bantam 1140. 1st pb edn. F. M1d. $5.00

UNDSET, Sigrid. *Axe.* 1963. Cardinal GC 220. Fa. VG+. B4d. $2.00

UNEKIS, Richard. *Chase.* 1975. Panther 04297. My. F. P1d. $7.50

UNEKIS, Richard. *Pursuit.* 1964. Signet G 2466. My. VG. P1d. $6.00

UNTERMEYER, Louis. *Fireside Book of Verse.* Armed Services T 8. PBO. VG. B3d. $5.00

UNTERMEYER, Louis. *PB of American Poems.* Pocket 529. VG. B3d. $4.00

UNTERMEYER, Walter Jr. *Evil Roots.* 1954. Lion 222. PBO. VG+. B3a. $15.40

UPDIKE, John. *Poorhouse Fair.* 1968. Crest R 1177. 1st prtg. VG+. P7d. $4.00

UPDIKE, John. *Witches of Eastwick.* 1985. Crest 20647. 1st prtg. SF. VG. W2d. $3.50

UPFIELD, Arthur W. *Bachelors of Broken Hill.* 1961. Pan G 424. My. VG. P1d. $7.50

UPFIELD, Arthur W. *Battling Prophet.* 1961. Penguin 1452. 2nd edn. My. VG. P1d. $6.00

UPFIELD, Arthur W. *Death of a Lake.* 1963. Berkley F 831. My. VG+. P1d. $10.00

UPFIELD, Arthur W. *Death of a Swagman.* 1948. Signet 658. My. F. P1d. $25.00

UPFIELD, Arthur W. *Death of a Swagman.* 1948. Signet 658. VG. B3d. $4.50

UPFIELD, Arthur W. *Lake Frome Monster.* 1969. Pan 02348. My. VG. P1d. $5.00

UPFIELD, Arthur W. *Mystery of Swordfish Reef.* 1970. Pan 02571. My. VG. P1d. $5.00

UPFIELD, Arthur W. *Sands of Windee.* 1985. Scribners 18502. My. VG. P1d. $3.50

UPFIELD, Arthur W. *Sinister Stones.* 1964. Berkley F 927. My. F. P1d. $12.50

UPFIELD, Arthur W. *Torn Branch.* 1986. Collier 025930. My. F. P1d. $5.00

UPFIELD, Arthur W. *Will of the Tribe.* 1964. Berkley F 916. My. VG. P1d. $7.50

UPFIELD, Arthur W. *Will of the Tribe.* 1965. Pan X 422. My. VG+. P1d. $10.00

UPFIELD, Arthur W. *Wings Above the Diamantina.* 1965. Penguin C 2301. My. F. P1d. $12.50

UPSHAW, Helen. *Day of the Harvest.* 1954. Perma P 292. 1st prtg. c/gga. VG. P7d. $5.00

USHER, Jack. *Fix.* 1961. Pocket 6053. G+. G5d. $3.75

USHER, Jack. *Fix.* 1961. Pocket 6053. My. F. P1d. $13.00

USHER, Jack. *Reason for Murder.* Pocket 1262. G+. G5d. $3.00

USHER, Jack. *Reason for Murder.* 1959. Pocket 1262. My. VG. P1d. $7.00

USTINOV, Peter. *Add a Dash of Pity.* Signet 1853. VG. B3d. $4.00

UTLEY, Brian R. *Martyr.* 1971. Curtis 07150. 1st edn. SF. F. F2d. $10.00

VACHSS, Andrew. *Flood*. Pocket 61905. VG. G5d. $3.25

VADIM, Roger. *Les Liaisons Dangereuses*. 1962. Ballantine 586. PBO. MTI. VG+. B3d. $7.00

VADIM, Roger. *Les Liaisons Dangereuses*. 1962. Ballantine 586. 1st edn. c/gga. scarce in top condition. F. F2d. $25.00

VAHAN, R. *Truth About the John Birch Society*. MacFadden 50-133. VG+. B3d. $3.50

VAIL, John. *Blonde Savage*. 1955. Gold Medal 476. PBO. c/Barye: gga. Ad. NF. B6d. $12.00

VAIL, John. *Dark Throne*. 1954. Gold Medal 396. PBO. c/Meese. VG+. B6d. $10.00

VAIL, John. *Dark Throne*. 1954. Gold Medal 396. VG. B3d. $5.00

VAIL, John. *Hold Back the Sun*. 1956. Gold Medal 556. VG+. B3d. $5.00

VAIL, John. *Hold Back the Sun*. 1956. Gold Medal 556. 1st edn. Hl. F. F2d. $15.00

VAIL, John. *Sea Waifs*. 1952. Red Seal 13. c/Barye. VG. B3d. $6.00

VAIL, John. *Sea Waifs*. 1952. Red Seal 13. 1st edn. F. F2d. $15.00

VAIL, John. *Sow the Wild Wind*. 1954. Gold Medal 441. PBO. c/Hulings. Ad. NF. B6d. $12.00

VAIL, John. *Sow the Wild Wind*. 1954. Gold Medal 441. VG. B3d. $4.00

VAIL, John. *Sword in His Hand*. 1953. Gold Medal 309. 1st edn. F. M1d. $12.00

VAIL, Thomas. *Anything for Kicks*. 1962. Merit Books 602. PBO. c/photo. VG. P6d. $4.00

VAIL, Thomas. *Blackmail & Old Lace*. 1961. Newsstand U 172. Fa. VG+. B4d. $14.00

VAIL, Thomas. *Blackmail & Old Lace*. 1961. Newsstand U 172. My. G+. P1d. $4.50

VAIL, Thomas. *Blackmail & Old Lace*. 1961. Newsstand U 172. 1st edn. c/gga. My. F. F2d. $15.00

VAIL, Thomas. *Sex Store*. 1964. Rapture Book 405. 1st edn. F. F2d. $8.00

VAIL, Thomas. *Torrid Affair*. 1962. Merit Book 556. My. VG. P1d. $8.00

VAILLAND, Roger. *Law*. 1959. Bantam F 2014. 1st prtg. G+. R5d. $1.50

VALE, Rena. *Beyond the Sealed World*. 1965. PB Library 52-811. PBO. F. M1d. $8.00

VALE, Rena. *Beyond the Sealed World*. 1965. PB Library 52-811. PBO. VG+. B3d. $5.00

VALE, Rena. *Beyond the Sealed World*. 1968. PB Library. 2nd edn. VG. P9d. $1.50

VALE, Rena. *Day After Doomsday*. 1970. PB Library 63-479. PBO. SF. VG+. B5d. $5.00

VALE, Rena. *Taurus Four*. 1970. PB Library 63-253. PBO. SF. VG+. B5d. $4.00

VALENTINE, Jo. *And Sometimes Death*. 1955. Pocket 1083. My. G+. P1d. $6.00

VALENTINE, Victor. *Cure for Death*. 1961. Four Square 328. My. G+. P1d. $4.50

VALIN, Jonathan. *Day of Wrath*. Avon 63917. NF. G5d. $7.00

VALIN, Jonathan. *Dead Letter*. Avon 61366. NF. G5d. $7.50

VALIN, Jonathan. *Final Notice*. Avon 57893. VG. G5d. $5.00

VALIN, Jonathan. *Life's Work*. 1987. Dell 14790. De. VG+. P1d. $4.50

VALTIN, Jan. *Wintertime*. Popular Library 372. VG. I1d. $5.00

VAN ARNAM, Dave. *Lord of Blood*. 1970. Lancer 74-688. SF. VG. W2d. $3.25

VAN ARNAM, Dave. *Lord of Blood*. 1970. Lancer 74-688. 1st edn. F. M1d. $5.00

VAN ARNAM, Dave. *Star Barbarian*. 1969. Lancer 74-509. 1st edn. VG. P9d. $1.50

VAN ARNAM, Dave. *Starmind*. 1969. Ballantine 01626. 1st prtg. SF. G. R5d. $.75

VAN ARNAM/WHITE. *Sideslip*. 1968. Pyramid X 1787. SF. VG+. B4d. $8.00

VAN ASH, Cay. *Fires of Fu Manchu*. 1988. Perennial P 946. 1st prtg. SF. F. W2d. $4.00

VAN ATTA, Winfred. *Shock Treatment*. 1964. Crest K 718. MTI. My. VG+. B3d. $4.50

VAN BUREN, Abigail. *Dear Abby on Marriage*. Crest 637. NF. B3d. $4.00

VAN DE WATER, Frederic F. *Green Cockade*. 1956. Bantam A 1508. Fa. NF. B4d. $3.00

VAN DE WATER, Frederic F. *Hidden Ways*. Dell 67. c/G Gregg. My. G. B5d. $3.00

VAN DE WATER, Frederic F. *Hidden Ways*. 1944. Dell 67. My. F. P1d. $25.00

VAN DE WETERING, Janwillem. *Blond Baboon*. 1979. Pocket 82318. My. VG. P1d. $3.50

VAN DE WETERING, Janwillem. *Death of a Hawker*. 1978. Pocket 81341. My. VG. P1d. $3.50

VAN DER POST, Laurens. *Lost World of the Kalahari*. 1966. Pyramid T 1469. 1st prtg. c/Schoenherr. VG. P7d. $4.00

VAN DINE, S.S. *Benson Murder Case*. 1945. Pocket 333. c/Gillies. My. VG. P1d. $12.50

VAN DINE, S.S. *Bishop Murder Case*. 1969. Gold Medal T 2140. My. VG. P1d. $4.50

VAN DINE, S.S. *Bishop Murder Case*. 1945. Pocket 305. c/Jonas. NF. I1d. $10.00

VAN DINE, S.S. *Bishop Murder Case*. 1945. Pocket 305. G+. G5d. $6.50

VAN DINE, S.S. *Canary Murder Case*. 1968. Gold Medal G 2004. My. VG. P1d. $5.00

VAN DINE, S.S. *Canary Murder Case*. 1943. Pocket 248. 1st pb. My. VG. B6d. $7.50

VAN DINE, S.S. *Dragon Murder Case*. 1949. Bantam 362. My. VG. P1d. $9.50

VAN DINE, S.S. *Greene Murder Case*. 1969. Gold Medal T 2138. My. VG. P1d. $4.50

VAN DINE, S.S. *Greene Murder Case*. Pocket 256. VG. B3d. $4.50

VAN DINE, S.S. *Kennel Murder Case*. 1946. Bantam 60. G+. G5d. $7.00

VAN DINE, S.S. *Kennel Murder Case*. 1946. Bantam 60. My. F. P1d. $21.00

VAN DINE, S.S. *Kennel Murder Case*. 1946. Bantam 60. My. VG+. B4d. $16.00

VAN DINE, S.S. *Kidnap Murder Case*. 1948. Bantam 300. My. VG+. P1d. $20.00

VAN DINE, S.S. *Scarab Murder Case*. 1947. Bantam 96. My. VG. P1d. $12.50

VAN DINE, S.S. *Smell of Murder*. 1950. Bantam 756. 1st prtg. My. G+. R5d. $3.75

VAN DOREN, Mamie. *I Swing*. 1965. Novel Book 769. 1st edn. c/photo. F. F2d. $20.00

VAN DRUFEN, John. *Voice of the Turtle*. Armed Services 815. Nfi. VG. B5d. $4.50

VAN EVERY, Dale. *Bridal Journey*. 1951. Bantam A 871. c/gga. Fa. VG. B3d. $5.00

VAN EVERY, Dale. *Captive Witch*. 1953. Bantam 1090. VG. B3d. $5.50

VAN EVERY, Dale. *Shining Mountains*. 1951. Bantam 981. VG. B3d. $4.00

VAN GULIK, Robert. *Chinese Bell Murders*. 1963. Avon G 1177. My. VG. P1d. $6.00

VAN GULIK, Robert. *Chinese Gold Murders.* 1963. Dell 1265. G+. G5d. $3.50

VAN GULIK, Robert. *Chinese Gold Murders.* 1963. Dell 1265. My. VG+. P1d. $9.00

VAN GULIK, Robert. *Chinese Nail Murders.* 1964. Avon G 1219. 1st prtg. My. VG. G5d. $4.50

VAN GULIK, Robert. *Chinese Nail Murders.* 1977. University of Chicago 84863. 1st edn. My. VG. P1d. $4.50

VAN GULIK, Robert. *Emperor's Pearl.* 1965. Bantam F 3002. My. VG. P1d. $7.50

VAN GULIK, Robert. *Lacquer Screen.* 1968. Penguin C 2826. My. VG. G5d. $4.00

VAN GULIK, Robert. *Necklace & Calabash.* Scribners 16329. My. VG. P1d. $4.50

VAN GULIK, Robert. *Phantom of the Temple.* Scribners 16178. 1st edn. My. F. P1d. $5.00

VAN GULIK, Robert. *Red Pavilion.* Scribners 18142. G5d. $6.50

VAN HEARN, J. *Don't Betray Me.* 1962. Belmont 91-255. PBO. VG+. B3d. $5.00

VAN HELLER, Marcus. *Kidnap.* 1967. Brandon House 2029. My. VG+. P1d. $11.00

VAN HELLER, Marcus. *Wantons.* Brandon House 3006. VG+. B3d. $5.50

VAN HERCK, Paul. *Where Were You Last Pluterday.* 1973. DAW. 2nd edn. F. M1d. $4.00

VAN HISE. *Killing Time.* Pocket 52488. VG. P9d. $1.50

VAN LOON, Hendrik. *Rabelais & Voltaire.* 1940. LA Bantam 20. VG. B3a #20. $28.60

VAN LOON, Hendrik. *Story of Mankind.* 1953. Cardinal GC 5. c/L Manso. NF. VG. B5d. $2.50

VAN LOON, Hendrik. *Story of the Bible.* 1953. Perma P 201S. Fa. VG. B4d. $3.00

VAN OVER, R. *ESP & the Clairvoyants.* Award 672. VG+. B3d. $4.50

VAN PRAAG, V. *Combat.* Pocket 747. VG+. B3d. $4.50

VAN RJNDT, Phil. *Tetramachus Collection.* 1978. Berkley 03516. My. VG. W2d. $3.25

VAN RJNDT, Philippe. *Blueprint.* 1979. Berkley. advance reading copy. Th. VG. P1d. $25.00

VAN ROYEN, Astrid. *Awake Monique.* 1962. Crest D 534. 1st prtg. c/gga. VG+. P7d. $5.00

VAN SAHER, Lilla. *Macamba.* 1950. Popular Library 233. c/gga. Fa. VG. B4d. $7.50

VAN SEYOC, Sydney. *Assignment Nor'Dyren.* 1973. Avon 17160. 1st edn. VG. P9d. $1.50

VAN SEYOC, Sydney. *Saltflower.* 1971. Avon V 2386. SF. VG. W2d. $3.75

VAN TAYLOR, Robert. *Frenzied.* 1962. Monarch 255. PBO. c/Lou Marchetti: gga. G+. P6d. $3.50

VAN VOGT, A E. *Silkie.* 1969. Ace 76500. SF. NF. B5d. $4.00

VAN VOGT, A E. *War Against the Rull.* 1972. Ace 87180. c/J Schoenherr. SF. NF. B5d. $5.00

VAN VOGT, A.E. *Anarchistic Colossus.* 1977. Ace 02255. SF. F. W2d. $4.00

VAN VOGT, A.E. *Anarchistic Colossus.* 1977. Ace 02255. SF. VG. B5d. $3.00

VAN VOGT, A.E. *Away & Beyond.* 1953. Avon 548. 1st pb edn. F. M1d. $10.00

VAN VOGT, A.E. *Away & Beyond.* 1953. Avon 548. 1st prtg. SF. VG. R5d. $5.25

VAN VOGT, A.E. *Away & Beyond.* 1963. Berkley F 812. c/R Powers. SF. VG. B5d. $3.50

VAN VOGT, A.E. *Away & Beyond.* 1959. Berkley G 215. c/R Powers. SF. VG+. B5d. $5.00

VAN VOGT, A.E. *Away & Beyond.* 1959. Berkley G 215. c/sgn. VG+. B3d. $8.00

VAN VOGT, A.E. *Away & Beyond.* 1959. Berkley G 215. 1st prtg. SF. VG. R5d. $4.00

VAN VOGT, A.E. *Battle of Forever.* 1971. Ace 4860. 1st edn. NF. P9d. $1.75

VAN VOGT, A.E. *Battle of Forever.* 1982. DAW 494. c/sgn. VG. B3d. $6.00

VAN VOGT, A.E. *Beast.* 1964. MacFadden 60-169. 1st pb edn. NF. M1d. $8.00

VAN VOGT, A.E. *Beast.* Manor 00479. c/sgn. VG+. B3d. $7.00

VAN VOGT, A.E. *Beast.* Manor 95399. reprint. SF. VG. B6d. $3.75

VAN VOGT, A.E. *Book of Ptath.* 1969. PB Library 63092. 3rd prtg. SF. VG. W2d. $3.50

VAN VOGT, A.E. *Book of Van Vogt.* 1972. DAW 4. c/sgn. VG+. B3d. $6.00

VAN VOGT, A.E. *Book of Van Vogt.* 1972. DAW 4. 1st prtg. F. S1d. $3.50

VAN VOGT, A.E. *Book of Van Vogt.* 1972. DAW 4. 1st prtg. SF. G+. R5d. $2.00

VAN VOGT, A.E. *Changeling.* 1967. MacFadden 50-335. 1st prtg. VG. B3d/P7d. $4.00

VAN VOGT, A.E. *Changling.* 1969. MacFadden 50-335. 1st prtg. G. S1d. $3.25

VAN VOGT, A.E. *Changling.* 1969. MacFadden 60-416. 3rd edn. F. P9d. $2.00

VAN VOGT, A.E. *Children of Tomorrow.* Ace 10410. c/sgn. VG+. B3d. $5.00

VAN VOGT, A.E. *Destination: Universe!* 1964. Berkley 893. c/sgn. VG+. B3d. $5.00

VAN VOGT, A.E. *Destination: Universe!* 1958. Signet S 1558. 3rd prtg. c/sgn. VG+. B3d. $7.00

VAN VOGT, A.E. *Destination: Universe!* 1958. Signet S 1558. 3rd prtg. SF. G. W2d. $3.00

VAN VOGT, A.E. *Destination: Universe!* 1953. Signet 1007. c/sgn. VG+. B3d. $6.50

VAN VOGT, A.E. *Destination: Universe!* 1953. Signet 1007. 1st pb edn. F. M1d. $10.00

VAN VOGT, A.E. *Destination: Universe!* 1953. Signet 1007. 1st prtg. G+. S1d. $3.25

VAN VOGT, A.E. *Destination: Universe!* 1953. Signet 1007. 1st prtg. VG. P7d. $6.00

VAN VOGT, A.E. *Earth Factor X.* 1976. DAW 206. c/sgn. VG. B3d. $6.50

VAN VOGT, A.E. *Future Glitter.* 1973. Ace 25980. SF. VG+. M3d. $7.00

VAN VOGT, A.E. *House That Stood Still.* 1952. Harlequin 177. c/sgn. VG. B3a #22. $69.45

VAN VOGT, A.E. *House That Stood Still.* 1965. PB Library 52-873. c/J Gaughan. SF. VG+. B5d. $4.00

VAN VOGT, A.E. *House That Stood Still.* 1971. PB Library 64-603. 3rd prtg. SF. VG. W2d. $3.00

VAN VOGT, A.E. *House That Stood Still.* 1980. Pocket 83158. SF. VG+. W2d. $3.50

VAN VOGT, A.E. *Man With a Thousand Names.* 1974. DAW 114. 1st edn. SF. F. F2d. $10.00

VAN VOGT, A.E. *Man With a Thousand Names.* 1974. DAW 114. 1st prtg. VG. S1d. $2.00

VAN VOGT, A.E. *Masters of Time.* 1967. MacFadden 50-334. 1st prtg. VG. S1d. $3.00

VAN VOGT, A.E. *Masters of Time.* 1969. MacFadden 60-406. 2nd prtg. SF. F. W2d. $4.00

VAN VOGT, A.E. *Mating Cry.* 1960. Beacon 298. c/sgn. VG. B3a #22. $28.00

VAN VOGT, A.E. *Mating Cry.* 1960. Beacon 298. c/sgn. VG. B3a #24. $33.00

VAN VOGT, A.E. *Mating Cry.* 1960. Beacon 298. 1st edn. VG+. I1d. $45.00

VAN VOGT, A.E. *Mind Cage.* 1958. Avon T 252. 1st edn. PBO. F. M1d. $7.00

VAN VOGT, A.E. *Mind Cage.* 1958. Avon T 252. 1st prtg. SF. G+. R5d. $2.25

VAN VOGT, A.E. *Mission to the Stars.* 1962. Berkley F 704. 4th prtg. c/R Powers. SF. VG+. B5d. $4.00

VAN VOGT, A.E. *Mission to the Stars.* 1962. Berkley F 704. 4th prtg. SF. G. W2d. $3.00

VAN VOGT, A.E. *Mission to the Stars.* 1955. Berkley 344. NF. I1d. $5.00

VAN VOGT, A.E. *Mission to the Stars.* 1955. Berkley 344. 1st prtg. SF. G+. R5d. $2.75

VAN VOGT, A.E. *Mission to the Stars.* 1977. Pocket 81451. SF. VG+. W2d. $4.00

VAN VOGT, A.E. *Mission: Interplanetary.* 1952. Signet 914. c/sgn. VG+. B3d. $6.50

VAN VOGT, A.E. *Mission: Interplanetary.* 1952. Signet 914. SF. VG. B4d. $5.00

VAN VOGT, A.E. *Mission: Interplanetary.* 1952. Signet 914. 1st pb edn. F. M1d. $10.00

VAN VOGT, A.E. *More Than Superhuman.* 1971. Dell 5818. 1st edn. F. M1d. $5.00

VAN VOGT, A.E. *More Than Superhuman.* 1971. Dell 5818. 1st prtg. SF. VG. R5d. $1.50

VAN VOGT, A.E. *M33 in Andromeda.* 1971. PB Library 65584. SF. VG. W2d. $3.50

VAN VOGT, A.E. *Pawns of Null-A.* 1956. Ace D 187. VG+. I1d. $15.00

VAN VOGT, A.E. *Pendulum.* DAW 316. PBO. c/sgn. VG+. B3d. $8.00

VAN VOGT, A.E. *Players of Null-A.* 1966. Berkley F 1195. c/sgn. VG. B3d. $4.00

VAN VOGT, A.E. *Players of Null-A.* 1966. Berkley F 1195. 2nd edn. F. P9d. $3.00

VAN VOGT, A.E. *Players of Null-A.* 1974. Berkley 03368. 4th prtg. SF. G+. W2d. $2.75

VAN VOGT, A.E. *Proxy Intelligence & Other Mind Benders.* 1971. PB Library 64-512. c/sgn. VG. B3d. $6.00

VAN VOGT, A.E. *Proxy Intelligence & Other Mind Benders.* 1971. PB Library 64-512. SF. F. F2d. $12.00

VAN VOGT, A.E. *Ptath.* 1976. Zebra 172. SF. VG+. B5d. $4.00

VAN VOGT, A.E. *Quest for the Future.* 1972. Ace 66970. SF. VG+. B5d. $4.00

VAN VOGT, A.E. *Rogue Ship.* 1966. Berkley F 1292. 1st prtg. SF. VG+. R5d. $4.00

VAN VOGT, A.E. *Rogue Ship.* 1980. DAW 325. 1st edn. F. P9d. $4.00

VAN VOGT, A.E. *SF Monsters.* 1970. PB Library 63-406. c/sgn. VG+. B3d. $6.50

VAN VOGT, A.E. *Slan.* 1961. Ballantine 511K. VG. I1d. $4.00

VAN VOGT, A.E. *Slan.* 1977. Berkley 03352. 9th prtg. SF. VG+. W2d. $2.75

VAN VOGT, A.E. *Slan.* 1953. Dell 696. c/sgn. VG+. B3d. $12.00

VAN VOGT, A.E. *Supermind.* 1977. DAW 224. 1st edn. PBO. NF. M1d. $6.00

VAN VOGT, A.E. *Two-Hundred Million AD.* 1967. PB Library 52-406. 2nd edn. SF. VG+. B5d. $4.50

VAN VOGT, A.E. *Universe Maker.* 1967. Ace G 660. 2nd edn. VG. P9d. $1.75

VAN VOGT, A.E. *Universe Maker.* Ace 84581. SF. VG+. W2d. $3.25

VAN VOGT, A.E. *Violent Man.* 1962. Avon S 139. c/sgn. VG. B3d. $3.50

VAN VOGT, A.E. *Voyage of the Space Beagle.* MacFadden 60-318. reprint. SF. VG+. B6d. $6.00

VAN VOGT, A.E. *War Against the Rull.* Panther 1168. c/sgn. G+. B3d. $3.00

VAN VOGT, A.E. *War Against the Rull.* 1962. Perma M 4263. 1st prtg. VG. P7d. $4.00

VAN VOGT, A.E. *Weapon Makers.* 1966. Ace M 153. VG. M1d. $4.00

VAN VOGT, A.E. *Weapon Makers.* 1979. Pocket 82267. 1st prtg. SF. F. W2d. $4.00

VAN VOGT, A.E. *Weapon Shops of Isher.* 1960. Ace D 482. NF. M1d. $10.00

VAN VOGT, A.E. *Weapon Shops of Isher.* 1973. Ace 87855. c/sgn. VG+. B3d. $6.00

VAN VOGT, A.E. *Weapon Shops of Isher.* 1973. Ace 87855. SF. G. W2d. $2.75

VAN VOGT, A.E. *Winged Man.* 1980. DAW UE 1524. SF. F. W2d. $4.50

VAN VOGT, A.E. *Wizard of Linn.* 1962. Ace F 154. PBO. SF. VG+. B5d. $5.00

VAN VOGT, A.E. *Wizard of Linn.* 1962. Ace F 154. PBO. VG. B3d. $4.00

VAN VOGT, A.E. *Wizard of Linn.* MacFadden 60-366. c/sgn. VG+. B3d. $6.50

VAN VOGT, A.E. *Wizard of Linn.* MacFadden 60-366. 1st prtg. F. S1d. $5.00

VAN VOGT, A.E. *Wizard of Linn.* Manor 12344. 1st prtg. F. S1d. $2.00

VAN VOGT, A.E. *World of Null-A.* 1964. Ace F 295. F. M1d. $8.00

VAN VOGT, A.E. *World of Null-A.* 1964. Ace F 295. G+. I1d. $3.50

VAN VOGT, A.E. *World of Null-A.* 1970. Berkley 51802. SF. G+. W2d. $2.75

VAN VOGT, A.E. *Worlds of AE Van Vogt.* 1974. Ace 22812. 1st edn. SF. F. F2d. $10.00

VAN VOGT/VAN VOGT. *Universe Maker/World of Null-A.* 1953. Ace D 31. G. P9d. $5.00

VAN VOGT/VAN VOGT. *Universe Maker/World of Null-A.* 1953. Ace D 31. PBO. c/Orbaan & R Schulz. SF. VG. B5d. $12.00

VAN VOGT/VAN VOGT. *Universe Maker/World of Null-A.* 1953. Ace D 31. PBO. F. M1d. $25.00

VAN ZYL, P.R. *Prosecutor.* 1975. Berkley Z 2775. My. VG. P1d. $3.50

VANCE, Ethel. *Escape.* 1942. Pocket 149. My. F. P1d. $23.00

VANCE, Ethel. *Escape.* 1942. Pocket 149. VG+. B3d. $6.00

VANCE, Jack. *Anome.* Dell 0441. c/sgn. VG+. B3d. $7.00

VANCE, Jack. *Anome.* Dell 0441. 1st prtg. F. S1d. $3.00

VANCE, Jack. *Asutra.* 1974. Dell 3157. VG+. B3d. $4.50

VANCE, Jack. *Asutra.* 1974. Dell 3157. 1st edn. F. M1d. $10.00

VANCE, Jack. *Big Planet.* Ace G 661. VG. M1d. $5.00

VANCE, Jack. *Blue World.* 1966. Ballantine U 2169. PBO. c/sgn. VG+. B3d. $8.00

VANCE, Jack. *Blue World.* 1966. Ballantine U 2169. 1st edn. F. M1d. $15.00

VANCE, Jack. *Book of Dreams.* 1981. DAW 416. 1st edn. F. P9d. $2.50

VANCE, Jack. *Brave Free Men.* 1973. Dell 1708. c/Vance: sgn. VG+. B3d. $6.00

VANCE, Jack. *Brave Free Men.* 1973. Dell 1708. 1st prtg. F. S1d. $6.00

VANCE, Jack. *Brave Free Men.* 1973. Dell 1708. 1st prtg. SF. VG+. W2d. $4.50

VANCE, Jack. *City of the Chasch.* Ace G 688. F. M1d. $8.00

VANCE, Jack. *City of the Chasch.* DAW 339. c/sgn. VG+. B3d. $7.00

VANCE, Jack. *Deadly Isles.* Ace. 1st pb edn. F. M1d. $15.00

VANCE, Jack. *Die Welten des Magnus Ridolph.* Foreign German 053. c/sgn: German. NF. B3d. $10.00

VANCE, Jack. *Dirdir.* Ace 66901. c/sgn. VG. B3d. $7.00

VANCE, Jack. *Dirdir.* Ace 66901. SF. VG+. B5d. $4.50

VANCE, Jack. *Dirdir.* 1979. DAW 347. c/Jones: sgn. VG+. B3d. $8.00

VANCE, Jack. *Dirdir.* 1979. DAW 347. 1st prtg. SF. VG. R5d. $2.25

VANCE, Jack. *Dying Earth.* 1969. Lancer 74-547. c/E Emsh. SF. G. B5d. $2.50

VANCE, Jack. *Dying Earth.* 1969. Lancer 74-547. F. M1d. $4.00

VANCE, Jack. *Eight Fantasms & Magics.* 1970. Collier. 1st pb edn. F. M1d. $10.00

VANCE, Jack. *Emphyrio.* 1970. Dell 1st Edn 2345. 1st pb. c/Jeff Jones. SF. VG. B6d. $2.50

VANCE, Jack. *Eyes of the Overworld.* Ace M 149. PBO. c/sgn. VG. B3d. $6.00

VANCE, Jack. *Eyes of the Overworld.* Ace M 149. 1st prtg. F. S1d. $7.50

VANCE, Jack. *Face.* 1979. DAW 361. Demon Princess #4. SF. VG+. W2d. $4.00

VANCE, Jack. *Fox Valley Murders.* 1966. Ace 24975. 1st pb. My. VG. B6d. $4.00

VANCE, Jack. *Future Tense.* 1964. Ballantine U 2214. PBO. VG. B3d. $4.50

VANCE, Jack. *Galactic Effectuator.* Ace 27232. 1st prtg. G+. S1d. $2.00

VANCE, Jack. *Gray Prince.* 1975. Avon. 1st pb edn. F. M1d. $10.00

VANCE, Jack. *Gray Prince.* 1981. DAW 473. 1st edn. PBO. VG. P9d. $1.50

VANCE, Jack. *Killing Machine.* 1964. Berkley 1003. VG+. B3d. $5.50

VANCE, Jack. *Killing Machine.* 1964. Berkley 1003. 1st edn. F. M1d. $12.00

VANCE, Jack. *Languages of Pao.* 1966. Ace F 390. NF. M1d. $10.00

VANCE, Jack. *Languages of Pao.* 1966. Ace F 390. 1st edn. PBO. G. P9d. $1.25

VANCE, Jack. *Languages of Pao.* 1966. Ace F 390. 1st prtg. VG+. S1d. $5.00

VANCE, Jack. *Languages of Pao.* Ace 47042. SF. VG. B5d. $3.50

VANCE, Jack. *Languages of Pao.* 1980. DAW 389. NF. P9d. $2.00

VANCE, Jack. *Many Worlds of Magnus Ridolph.* DAW 381. c/sgn. VG+. B3d. $8.00

VANCE, Jack. *Marune: Alastor 933.* 1975. Ballantine 24518. SF. VG+. B5d. $5.00

VANCE, Jack. *Marune: Alastor 993.* Coronet UK. 1st prtg. VG. S1d. $3.00

VANCE, Jack. *Palace of Love.* 1967. Berkley X 1454. 1st edn. F. M1d. $12.00

VANCE, Jack. *Palace of Love.* 1967. Berkley X 1454. 1st prtg. SF. VG. R5d. $5.00

VANCE, Jack. *Place of Love.* 1967. Berkley X 1454. PBO. c/Powers. SF. VG+. I1d. $8.00

VANCE, Jack. *Pleasant Grove Murders.* Ace. 1st pb edn. NF. M1d. $15.00

VANCE, Jack. *Pnume.* 1970. Ace 66902. Planet of Adventure #4. SF. G. W2d. $2.75

VANCE, Jack. *Pnume.* 1970. Ace 66902. SF. VG+. B5d. $4.50

VANCE, Jack. *Pnume.* 1979. DAW 351. c/sgn. VG+. B3d. $8.00

VANCE, Jack. *Pnume.* 1979. DAW 351. 1st prtg. G+. S1d. $2.00

VANCE, Jack. *Pnume.* 1973. Dell. 1st edn. F. M1d. $10.00

VANCE, Jack. *Servants of the Wankh.* Ace 66900. c/Jonas: sgn. VG. B3d. $4.00

VANCE, Jack. *Servants of the Wankh.* 1979. DAW 342. c/sgn. B3d. $9.00

VANCE, Jack. *Showboat World.* Pyramid 3698. c/sgn. VG+. B3d. $8.00

VANCE, Jack. *Space Opera.* 1979. DAW 336. 2nd edn. NF. P9d. $2.00

VANCE, Jack. *Space Opera.* 1965. Pyramid R 1140. PBO. c/J Schoenherr. SF. VG+. B5d/I1d. $8.00

VANCE, Jack. *Space Opera.* 1965. Pyramid R 1140. 1st edn. F. M1d. $15.00

VANCE, Jack. *Space Pirate.* Toby 2. PBO. VG+. B3d. $8.00

VANCE, Jack. *Star King.* 1964. Berkley G 905. c/sgn. VG. B3d. $7.50

VANCE, Jack. *Star King.* 1964. Berkley G 905. 1st edn. NF. M1d. $10.00

VANCE, Jack. *Star King.* 1978. DAW UE 1402. 1st prtg. SF. F. W2d. $5.00

VANCE, Jack. *Star King.* 1978. DAW 305. c/sgn. VG. B3d. $5.00

VANCE, Jack. *Star King.* Mayflower 12102. 2nd prtg. c/sgn. VG+. B3d. $8.00

VANCE, Jack. *To Live Forever.* 1966. Ballantine U 2346. c/sgn. VG. B3d. $7.00

VANCE, Jack. *To Live Forever.* 1966. Ballantine U 2346. SF. VG+. B4d. $2.00

VANCE, Jack. *To Live Forever.* 1966. Ballantine U 2346. 1st prtg. SF. G+. R5d. $1.25

VANCE, Jack. *To Live Forever.* 1956. Ballantine 167. 1st edn. PBO. VG. M1d. $20.00

VANCE, Jack. *Trullion: Alastor 2262.* Ballantine 03308. PBO. NF. B3d. $9.00

VANCE, Jack. *Wyst: Alastor 1716.* 1978. DAW 312. c/sgn. VG+. B3d. $8.00

VANCE, John Holbrook. *Bad Ronald.* 1973. Ballantine 23477. My. F. P1d. $45.00

VANCE, John Holbrook. *Deadly Isles.* Ace 24975. My. VG. P1d. $7.50

VANCE, Jules. *Begum's Fortune.* 1968. Ace H 49. 1st prtg. VG+. S1d. $5.00

VANCE, Jules. *Into the Niger Bend.* 1968. Ace H 41. 1st prtg. NF. S1d. $5.00

VANCE, Louis Joseph. *False Faces.* 1964. Avon G 1235. My. VG. P1d. $6.00

VANCE, Louis Joseph. *Lone Wolf.* 1943. Dell 10. My. VG. P1d. $17.50

VANCE, William. *Day of Blood.* 1961. Monarch 197. Fa. VG+. B4d. $4.00

VANCE, William. *Homicide Lost.* 1956. Graphic 122. My. G+. B4d. $4.00

VANCE, William. *Homicide Lost.* 1956. Graphic 122. My. VG. P1d. $10.00

VANCE/VANCE. *Big Planet/Slaves of the Klau.* 1958. Ace D 295. c/Emsh. F. M1d. $25.00

VANCE/VANCE. *Big Planet/Slaves Of the Klau.* 1958. Ace D 295. PBO. c/E Emsh. SF. VG. I1d. $9.00

VANCE/VANCE. *Brains of Earth/Many Worlds of Magnus Ridolph.* 1966. Ace M 141. NF. M1d. $8.00

VANCE/VANCE. *Brains of Earth/Many Worlds of Magnus Ridolph.* 1966. Ace M 141. PBO. VG+. B3d. $4.50

VANCE/VANCE. *Dragon Masters/Five Gold Bands.* 1962. Ace F 185. c/E Valigursky. SF. NF. B5d. $10.00

VANCE/VANCE. *Dragon Masters/Five Gold Bands.* 1962. Ace F 185. G+. I1d. $5.00

VANCE/VANCE. *Dragon Masters/Last Castle.* 1973. Ace 16641. 3rd prtg. SF. F. W2d. $5.00

VANCE/VANCE. *Houses of Iszm/Son of the Tree.* 1964. Ace F 265. c/Jack Gaughan. SF. VG+. B6d. $9.00

VANCE/VANCE. *Houses of Iszm/Son of the Tree.* 1964. Ace F 265. F. M1d. $12.00

VANCE/VANCE. *Houses of Iszm/Son of the Tree.* 1964. Ace F 265. G+. S1d. $3.50

VANCE/VANCE. *Houses of Iszm/Son of the Tree.* 1964. Ace 77525. SF. VG. B5d. $4.00

VANCE/VANCE. *Monsters in Orbit/World Between & Other Stories.* 1965. Ace M 125. NF. M1d. $8.00

VANCE/VANCE. *Monsters in Orbit/World Between & Other Stories.* 1965. Ace M 125. PBO. VG+. B3d. $4.50

VANCE/WAYMAN. *Last Castle/World of the Sleeper.* 1967. Ace H 21. G+. S1d. $3.50

VANCE/WAYMAN. *Last Castle/World of the Sleeper.* 1967. Ace H 21. NF. M1d. $9.00

VANCE/WAYMAN. *Last Castle/World of the Sleeper.* 1967. Ace H 21. 1st edn. sgn. SF. F. F2d. $25.00

VANCE/WEST. *Crossfire at Barbed M/Raid at Crazy Horse.* 1967. Ace G 648. PBO. VG. B3d. $5.00

VANCE/WYNNE. *Wolf Slayer/Mr Sixgun.* Ace F 276. We. NF. B6d. $12.50

VANCE/WYNNE. *Wolf Slayer/Mr Sixgun.* 1964. Ace F 276. We. VG. P1d. $7.50

VANCE/WYNNE. *Wolf Slayer/Mr Sixgun.* 1964. Ace F 276. We. VG+. B4d. $8.00

VANDERCOOK, John W. *Black Majesty.* 1952. Pocket 857. Nfi. VG. P1d. $9.00

VANDERCOOK, John W. *Murder in Fiji.* 1945. Penguin (US) 560. My. VG. P1d. $10.50

VANDERCOOK, John W. *Murder in Trinidad.* 1944. Penguin (US) 552. My. VG. P1d. $12.50

VANDERCOOK, John W. *Out for a Killing.* 1958. Avon T 278. My. G+. P1d. $5.50

VANDERCOOK, John W. *Out for a Killing.* 1958. Avon T 278. My. VG. B5d. $3.00

VANDIVERT, R. & W. *Wild Animals & Their Young.* Dell LC 105. VG+. B3d. $5.00

VANDORNE, R. *Hungry Socialites.* 1973. Liverpool TNS 557. Ad. VG. B5d. $3.50

VANE, Roland. *Night Haunts of Paris.* 1951. Archer 51. Fa. F. B4d. $20.00

VANE, Roland. *Night Haunts of Paris.* 1951. Archer 51. NF. I1d. $10.00

VANE, Roland. *Pick-Up Girl.* 1952. Leisure 3. Ad. F. P1d. $50.00

VANE, Roland. *Pick-Up Girl.* 1952. Leisure 3. Fa. VG+. B4d. $45.00

VANE, Roland. *Sinful Sisters.* 1951. Archer 52. 2nd edn. Fa. VG+. B4d. $30.00

VANE, Roland. *Vice Rackets of Soho.* 1951. Archer 35. c/Heade: gga. F. B6a #74. $133.25

VANE, Roland. *Vice Rackets of Soho.* 1951. Archer 35. F. I1d. $40.00

VANE, Roland. *Wanton Wife.* 1949. Archer NN. PBO. c/gga. scarce. VG+. B6a #77. $55.00

VANE, Roland. *White Slave Racket.* 1952. Leisure 8. Fa. VG+. B4d. $45.00

VANE, Roland. *Willing Sinner.* Archer 57. VG. I1d. $10.00

VANSITTART, Lord. *Black Record of Germany.* 1944. Avon 45. Nfi. G+. B4d. $6.00

VANSITTART, Lord. *Black Record of Germany.* 1944. Avon 45. VG. B3d. $7.00

VANSON, Bobbi. *Confessions of a Woman Immoral.* 1965. Saber 104. 1st edn. c/gga. F. F2d. $15.00

VARDEMAN, Robert. *Echoes of Chaos.* 1986. Berkley 09295. 1st edn. SF. F. F2d. $7.00

VARDEMAN, Robert. *Fire in Fog.* 1984. Ace 23824. PBO. SF. NF. B6d. $3.00

VARDEMAN, Robert. *In the Shadows of Omizantrium.* 1982. Playtime 16999. SF. F. W2d. $5.00

VARIAN, S. *Slaves to Oral Sex.* Barclay 7275. F. B3d. $5.00

VARLEY, John. *Millennium.* 1985. Berkley 07674. SF. VG. W2d. $3.00

VAST, Jack. *Portraits of Pleasure.* 1965. Exotic 13. 1st edn. c/gga. F. F2d. $10.00

VAST, Jack. *Surprise Swap.* PEC Rapture 232. VG+. B3d. $5.00

VATSEK, Joan. *This Fiery Night.* 1960. Crest D 372. 1st prtg. My. G+. R5d. $2.25

VAUGHAN, R. *Girls of Carnation House.* Saber SA 55. VG+. B3d. $5.00

VAUGHAN, R. *Moulded in Earth.* Signet 991. VG. B3d. $4.00

VELIKOVSKY, I. *Worlds in Collision.* 1967. Dell 9702. Nfi. G. W2d. $3.00

VELIKOVSKY, I. *Worlds in Collision.* 1977. Pocket 81091. SF. VG. W2d. $3.75

VENARCHO, R. *Trucker's Sucker.* Brandon House 6539. PBO. NF. B3d. $5.00

VENDOR, Nick. *Sabrina & the Senator.* 1960. Midwood 58. PBO. c/Rader: gga. scarce. NF. B6a #80. $55.00

VENNING, Michael. *Jethro Hammer.* Jonathan Press J 28. My. G+. P1d. $10.00

VERCORS. *Paths of Love.* Berkley G 579. VG+. B3d. $5.00

VERCORS. *You Shall Know Them.* 1967. Popular Library 60-2202. My/SF. VG. P1d. $5.00

VERNE, Jules *Journey to the Center of the Earth.* 1959. Perma M 4161. 1st prtg. MTI. c/color photo. F. F2d. $10.00

VERNE, Jules. *Around the World in 80 Days.* Airmont CL 24. SF. F. W2d. $5.00

VERNE, Jules. *Around the World in 80 Days.* 1963. Airmont CL 34. SF. VG. B5d. $2.50

VERNE, Jules. *Around the World in 80 Days.* 1956. Avon T 148. 1st prtg. VG+. R5d. $5.00

VERNE, Jules. *Around the World in 80 Days.* Magnum 13415. SF. VG. W2d. $3.25

VERNE, Jules. *Around the World in 80 Days.* 1977. Moby 4512. SF. VG. W2d. $3.75

VERNE, Jules. *Around the World in 80 Days.* 1968. Scholastic 620. 3rd prtg. SF. F. W2d. $4.50

VERNE, Jules. *City in the Sahara.* 1968. Ace H 43. F. M1d. $6.00

VERNE, Jules. *From the Earth to the Moon.* 1958. Crest S 216. 1st edn. F. M1d. $8.00

VERNE, Jules. *From the Earth to the Moon.* 1965. Scholastic T 619. SF. VG+. B5d. $3.50

VERNE, Jules. *Into the Niger Bend.* 1968. Ace H 41. F. VG+. B4d. $2.75

VERNE, Jules. *Into the Niger Bend.* Ace 08041. SF. VG. W2d. $4.00

VERNE, Jules. *Journey to the Center of the Earth.* 1956. Ace D 155. SF. VG. B5d. $6.50

VERNE, Jules. *Journey to the Center of the Earth.* 1959. Ace D 397. 1st prtg. SF. VG. R5d. $3.50

VERNE, Jules. *Journey to the Center of the Earth.* 1963. Ace F 191. SF. VG+. W2d. $6.00

VERNE, Jules. *Journey to the Center of the Earth.* 1966. Ace G 582. SF. VG. W2d. $4.00

VERNE, Jules. *Journey to the Center of the Earth.* 1965. Airmont CL 60. SF. VG. B4d. $2.00

VERNE, Jules. *Journey to the Center of the Earth.* 1959. Perma M 4161. MTI. c/Pat Boone: photo. VG+. B4d. $4.00

VERNE, Jules. *Journey to the Center of the Earth.* 1959. Perma M 4161. 1st prtg. VG. R5d. $2.75

VERNE, Jules. *Journey to the Center of the Earth.* 1973. Scholastic 2525. SF. G+. W2d. $3.75

VERNE, Jules. *Journey to the Center of the Earth.* 1965. Scholastic 618. SF. VG. W2d. $4.25

VERNE, Jules. *Master of the World.* 1961. Ace D 504. MTI. G+. M1d. $8.00

VERNE, Jules. *Master of the World.* 1965. Airmont CL 73. 1st prtg. SF. VG. R5d. $1.50

VERNE, Jules. *Michael Strogoff.* 1957. Pyramid R 300. 1st edn. F. M1d. $15.00

VERNE, Jules. *Mysterious Island.* 1965. Airmont CL 77. SF. VG. B5d. $2.50

VERNE, Jules. *Off on a Comet.* 1957. Ace D 245. c/E Emsh. SF. VG. B5d. $5.50

VERNE, Jules. *Off on a Comet.* 1957. Ace D 245. F. M1d. $10.00

VERNE, Jules. *Propeller Island.* 1965. London. 1st pb edn. NF. M1d. $8.00

VERNE, Jules. *Purchase of the North Pole.* 1960. Ace D 434. VG. M1d. $7.00

VERNE, Jules. *Purchase of the North Pole.* 1960. Ace D 434. 1st prtg. SF. G+. R5d. $2.25

VERNE, Jules. *Round the Moon.* Airmont CL 182. 1st edn. F. P9d. $2.50

VERNE, Jules. *Secret of Wilhelm Storitz.* 1965. London. 1st pb edn. NF. M1d. $8.00

VERNE, Jules. *Village in the Treetops.* 1964. Ace H 67. F. VG+. B4d. $2.00

VERNE, Jules. *20,000 Leagues Under the Sea.* 1962. Scholastic 430. SF. VG+. W2d. $4.50

VERNE, Martin. *Sinister Richard Shale.* 1968. Miracle Library 445. My. VG. P1d. $7.50

VERNER, Gerald. *Crooked Circle.* 1945. Black Cat 16. My. VG. P1d. $20.00

VERNER, Gerald. *Q Squad.* 1944. Domino Mysteries 1. My. VG. P1d. $20.00

VERNON, Roger Lee. *Space Frontiers.* 1955. Signet 1224. SF. VG. B4d. $3.00

VERNON, Roger Lee. *Space Frontiers.* 1955. Signet 1224. 1st edn. F. M1d. $8.00

VERNON, Roger Lee. *Space Frontiers.* 1955. Signet 1224. 1st prtg. VG+. S1d. $4.00

VETTER, Hal. *Women of the Swastika.* Regency 312. VG. B3d. $8.00

VEXIN, Noel. *Murder in Montmartre.* 1960. Dell D 388. My. VG. P1d. $7.00

VIAZZI, Alfred. *Cruel Dawn.* 1952. Popular Library 440. c/gga. Fa. VG+. B4d. $7.00

VIAZZI, Alfred. *Cruel Dawn.* 1952. Popular Library 440. VG. B3d. $5.00

VICARION, Palmiro. *Lust.* 1968. Greenleaf Classic 283. 1st edn. F. F2d. $8.00

VICARY, Jean. *Saverstall.* 1967. Ace G 643. My. VG. P1d. $5.00

VICK, Shelby. *3 Thrill-Hungry Bodies.* 1963. Novel Book 6074. My. G+. P1d. $5.00

VICKER, Angus. *Fever Heat.* Dell 1st Edn 13. VG. B3d/I1d. $4.00

VICKER, Angus. *Fever Heat.* 1961. Gold Medal 1122. 1st prtg. F. F2d. $7.50

VICKERY, Walt. *Cleopatra's Blonde Sex Rival.* 1962. France 15. 1st edn. F. F2d. $15.00

VIDAL, Gore. *Best Television Plays.* 1956. Ballantine 160. TVTI. VG. P1d. $12.50

VIDAL, Gore. *Messiah.* Ballantine 484K. SF. VG. B5d. $4.00

VIDAL, Gore. *Messiah.* 1968. Ballantine 72006. SF. VG+. W2d. $3.25

VIDAL, Gore. *Messiah.* 1954. Ballantine 94. 1st pb edn. F. M1d. $15.00

VIDAL, Gore. *Messiah.* 1954. Ballantine 94. 1st prtg. SF. G+. R5d. $3.50

VIDAL, Gore. *Myra Breckinridge.* Bantam T 5730. 14th prtg. VG. R5d. $1.50

VIDAL, Gore. *Search for the King.* 1967. New English 1964. VG. B3d. $7.50

VIDAL, Gore. *Search for the King.* 1968. Pyramid X 1741. 1st prtg. c/Greene: gga. VG. P7d. $4.50

VIDAL, Gore. *Sex, Death & Money.* 1968. Bantam N 4377. 1st prtg. c/photo. VG. P7d. $3.50

VIDAL, Gore. *Thirsty Evil.* 1958. Signet S 1535. Fi. VG. B5d. $4.00

VIDAL, Gore. *1876.* 1977. Ballantine 25400. 2nd edn. Hi. VG. P1d. $3.00

VIERECK, George Sylvester. *Men Into Beasts.* 1956. Gold Medal 552. 2nd edn. Nfi. G+. P1d. $6.00

VIERECK, George Sylvester. *Nude in the Mirror.* 1959. Beacon 228. 1st prtg. VG. P7d. $25.00

VIERTEL, Peter. *Love Lies Bleeding.* 1966. Pocket 75119. Fi. VG. B5d. $2.50

VILLANOVA, Richard. *Other Kid.* Beacon 619. PBO. VG. B3d. $4.50

VINCENT, G. *Scandal on the Hill.* Award A 218. VG+. B3d. $4.50

VINCENT, H. *Doomsday Planet.* 1966. Tower 42621. SF. VG. W2d. $4.00

VINCENT, Richard. *Portrait in Black.* 1960. Bantam A 2105. My. VG. P1d. $7.50

VINGE, Joan D. *Fireship.* 1978. Dell 15794. F. P9d. $2.00

VINGE, Joan D. *Outcasts of Heaven Belt.* 1978. Signet E 8407. SF. F. M3d. $8.00

VINGE, Joan D. *Outcasts of Heaven Belt.* 1978. Signet E 8407. 1st prtg. VG+. S1d. $3.00

VINGE, Vernor. *Peace War.* 1985. Baen 55965. 1st pb. SF. G+. B6d. $3.00

VINING, Keith. *Family Affair.* 1961. Newsstand U 160. Ad. VG. B5d. $4.00

VINING, Keith. *Family Affair.* 1961. Newsstand U 160. 1st edn. c/gga. F. F2d. $10.00

VINING, Keith. *Keep Running.* 1962. Chicago A 105. My. VG. P1d. $10.00

VINING, Keith. *Too Hot for Hell.* 1952. Ace D 1. PBO. c/Saunders. G+. B6d. $35.00

VIP. *Crazy Cartoons.* 1956. Crest 155. PBO. VG. B3d. $4.50

VIP. *Crazy Cartoons.* 1966. Gold Medal K 1625. PBO. cartoons. Nfi. VG. B5d. $3.50

VIP. *Man the Beast & the Wild, Wild, Women.* 1955. Dell 843. cartoons. NF. VG. B5d. $4.50

VIRMONNE, Claudette. *Valley of No Return.* 1979. Mystique 73058. My. VG. P1d. $3.50

VITTORINI, Elio. *Red Carnation.* 1953. Signet 1042. c/Zuckerberg. Fa. VG+. B4d. $4.00

VIVIAN, Charles. E. *City of Wonder.* 1973. Centaur NN 11. c/D Ireland. SF. F. B5d. $8.00

VIVIAN, Charles. E. *City of Wonder.* 1973. Centaur NN 11. 1st prtg. SF. VG. R5d. $2.75

VOLTAIRE. *Candide.* 1952. Lion 107. PBO. c/gga. NF. B6a #74. $50.00

VOLZ & BRIDGE. *Mafia Talks.* 1969. Gold Medal 2169. c/photos. VG. B3d/B5d. $5.00

VON BLOCK, B.W. *Frustrated American.* 1963. Lancer 73-417. 1st edn. PBO. c/gga. F. F2d. $7.50

VON ELSNER, Don. *Ace of Spies.* 1966. Award A 188F. Th. VG. P1d. $5.50

VON ELSNER, Don. *Countdown for a Spy.* 1966. Signet D 2829. My. VG. P1d. $5.50

VON ELSNER, Don. *Don't Just Stand There Do Someone.* 1962. Signet 2134. 1st edn. De. F. F2d. $16.00

VON ELSNER, Don. *How To Succeed at Murder Without Trying.* 1963. Signet S 2278. My. VG. P1d. $6.00

VON ELSNER, Don. *Jack of Hearts.* 1968. Award A 370X. Th. VG. P1d. $5.00

VON ELSNER, Don. *Jack of Hearts.* 1968. Award A 370X. 1st edn. My. F. F2d. $12.00

VON ELSNER, Don. *Just Not Making Mayhem Like Used To.* 1961. Signet S 2040. G+. G5d. $3.00

VON ELSNER, Don. *Just Not Making Mayhem Like Used To.* 1961. Signet S 2040. My. F. P1d. $13.00

VON ELSNER, Don. *Pour a Swindle Through a Loophole.* 1964. Belmont 92-604. My. VG. P1d. $6.00

VON ELSNER, Don. *Those Who Prey Together Stay Together.* 1961. Signet S 1943. My. F. P1d. $13.00

VON ELSNER, Don. *You Can't Do Business With Murder.* 1962. Signet S 2214. My. VG. P1d. $6.50

VON HARBOU, T. *Metropolis.* Ace F 246. F. M1d. $10.00

VON LUBER, M. *Ladies of Pleasure.* Brandon House 6036. VG+. B3d. $4.50

VON RHAU, Henry. *Big Sol.* 1950. Pocket 701. My. VG. P1d. $9.50

VON STROHEIM, Erich. *Paprika.* Harlequin 150. VG. B3d. $6.00

VON STROHEIM, Erich. *Paprika...the Gypsy Trollop.* Universal. 1st edn. NF. M1d. $25.00

VONNEGUT, Kurt Jr. *Breakfast of Champions.* Dell 3148. 1st prtg. G+. S1d. $3.00

VONNEGUT, Kurt Jr. *Breakfast of Champions.* Delta. 1st prtg. VG. S1d. $3.50

VONNEGUT, Kurt Jr. *Dead-Eye Dick.* 1985. Dell 11765. SF. F. W2d. $5.00

VONNEGUT, Kurt Jr. *Mother Night.* 1979. Dell 15853. 15th prtg. SF. VG. W2d. $2.75

VONNEGUT, Kurt Jr. *Mother Night.* Dell 5853. 1st prtg. VG. S1d. $3.50

VONNEGUT, Kurt Jr. *Mother Night.* 1962. Gold Medal 1191. PBO. VG. B6d. $40.00

VONNEGUT, Kurt Jr. *Sirens of Titan.* 1976. Dell 07948. 26th prtg. SF. G+. W2d. $2.75

VONNEGUT, Kurt Jr. *Sirens of Titan.* 1959. Dell 1st Edn B 138. SF. VG+. B4d. $35.00

VONNEGUT, Kurt Jr. *Sirens of Titan.* 1959. Dell 1st Edn B 138. 1st edn. NF. I1d. $40.00

VONNEGUT, Kurt Jr. *Slapstick.* Dell 18009. 1st prtg. G+. S1d. $3.00

VONNEGUT, Kurt Jr. *Slaughterhouse Five.* 1971. Dell 08029. SF. VG+. W2d. $4.50

VONNEGUT, Kurt Jr. *Slaughterhouse Five.* 1971. Dell 08029. 1st prtg. VG. P7d. $4.00

VONNEGUT, Kurt Jr. *Utopia 14.* 1954. Bantam A 1262. 1st pb edn. F. M1d. $20.00

VONNEGUT, Kurt Jr. *Utopia 14.* 1954. Bantam A 1262. 1st prtg. G+. S1d. $5.00

VONNEGUT, Kurt Jr. *Wapeters, Foma & Granfallons.* 1976. Dell 08533. SF. VG. W2d. $3.25

VONNEGUT, Kurt Jr. *Welcome to the Monkey House.* 1974. Dell 9478. 22nd prtg. SF. VG. W2d. $3.25

VOWELL, David H. *Dragnet 1968.* 1967. Popular 60-8045. My. VG+. P1d. $12.50

VOYNICH, E.L. *Gadfly.* 1961. Pyramid R 599. c/C Egri. Fi. VG. B5d. $4.00

VULLIAMY, C.E. *Don Among the Dead Men.* 1955. Penguin 1073. My. VG+. P1d. $12.00

WADD, Channy. *God's Little Faker.* 1967. Bee Line 162. Ad. VG+. B5d. $10.00

WADE, C. *Sex Perversions & Taboos.* Imperial 707. PBO. VG. B3d. $4.50

WADE, David. *Walk the Evil Street.* 1960. Berkley Diamond D 2028. My. VG. P1d. $7.50

WADE, Harrison. *So Lovely To Kill.* 1956. Graphic 127. My. VG. P1d. $10.00

WADE, Henry. *Too Soon To Die.* 1961. Collier AS 114Y. 1st prtg. My. G+. R5d. $1.25

WADE, T.W. *Sirus Rampart.* Futuristic Science 6. 1st prtg. VG. S1d. $12.00

WADE, Tom. *Voice From Baru.* 1962. London. 1st edn. NF. M1d. $6.00

WADE, Vern. *Karla.* 1960. Saber SA 2. Ad. VG. B5d. $3.50

WADE & MILLER. *Murder: Queen High.* 1949. Graphic 11. My. G+. P1d. $7.00

WADE & MILLER. *Murder: Queen High.* 1952. Graphic 54. 2nd edn. My. VG+. P1d. $11.50

WADELTON, Maggie-Owen. *Sarah Mandrake.* 1966. PB Library 54-977. My/SF. VG. P1d. $5.50

WADLEIGH, J.W. *Bitter Passion.* Hillman 153. VG. B3d. $4.00

WAER, Jack. *Murder in Las Vegas.* 1955. Avon 651. PBO. My. VG. B5d. $4.50

WAER, Jack. *Murder in Las Vegas.* 1955. Avon 651. 1st prtg. My. G+. R5d. $3.50

WAGER, Walter. *Code Name: Judas.* 1967. Popular 2261. 1st edn. c/photo. My. F. F2d. $10.00

WAGER, Walter. *Code Name: Little Ivan.* 1969. Popular 2464. 1st edn. c/photo. My. F. F2d. $10.00

WAGER, Walter. *Death Hits the Jackpot.* Avon T 280. VG+. B3d/B5d. $4.00

WAGER, Walter. *Mission: Impossible.* 1967. Popular 8042. 1st edn. TVTI. c/photo. My. F. F2d. $10.00

WAGER, Walter. *Raw Deal.* 1986. Warner 30201. 1st prtg. VG. R5d. $1.25

WAGER, Walter. *Time of Reckoning.* 1977. Playboy 16469. My. VG. P1d. $3.50

WAGER, Walter. *Viper Three.* 1972. Pocket 77503. Th. VG. P1d. $4.00

WAGNER, Edward. *Death Angel's Shadow.* Warner 75102. NF. P9d. $2.00

WAGNER, Geoffrey. *Dispossessed.* 1959. Beacon B 210. G+. M6d. $6.50

WAGNER, Geoffrey. *Dispossessed.* 1959. Beacon B 210. 1st prtg. c/Walter Popp: gga. VG+. P7d. $9.00

WAGNER, Geoffrey. *Dispossessed.* 1958. Four Square 32. My. VG. P1d. $10.00

WAGNER, Geoffrey. *Passionate Land.* 1959. Beacon 215. 1st pb. c/gga. VG. B6d. $9.00

WAGNER, Geoffrey. *Season of Assassins.* 1961. Gold Medal S 1093. 1st edn. My. F. F2d. $12.00

WAGNER, Geoffrey. *Season of Assassins.* Gold Medal 597. VG+. B3d. $9.00

WAGNER, Geoffrey. *Venables.* 1953. Popular 490. My. VG+. P1d. $12.50

WAGNER, Karl. *Bloodstone.* 1975. Warner. 1st edn. VG. M1d. $5.00

WAGNER, Karl. *Dark Crusade.* 1976. Warner. 1st edn. F. M1d. $6.00

WAGNER, Karl. *Darkness Weaves.* Powell 213. c/sgn. VG. B3d. $6.00

WAGNER, Karl. *Darkness Weaves.* 1978. Warner. 1st of complete text. F. M1d. $5.00

WAGNER, Karl. *Year's Best Horror Stories: Series VIII.* 1980. DAW. 1st edn. NF. M1d. $6.00

WAGNER, Sharon. *Winter Evil.* Lancer 75-269. Go. VG. P1d. $3.50

WAGONER, David. *Money, Money, Money.* 1956. Avon T 147. My. VG. P1d. $8.00

WAGONER, David. *Money, Money, Money.* 1956. Avon T 147. 1st pb. Cr. NF. B6d. $10.00

WAGONER, David. *Rock.* 1959. Bantam A 2020. JD. VG+. P1d. $15.50

WAHLOO, Peter. *Murder on the Thirty-First Floor.* 1970. Sphere 87904. My. VG. P1d. $4.50

WAINWRIGHT, John. *Hard Hit.* 1979. Berkley 04136. My. VG. P1d. $3.50

WAKEFIELD, Dan edt. *Addict.* 1963. Gold Medal D 1332. Nfi. VG. P1d. $6.00

WAKEFIELD, Dan edt. *Addict.* 1963. Gold Medal 1332. 1st edn. F. F2d. $17.00

WAKEFIELD, Dan edt. *Addict.* 1969. Premier T 392. Nfi. VG+. B5d. $5.00

WAKEFIELD, H.R. *Stories From the Clock Strikes Twelve.* 1961. Ballantine 531. c/Powers. VG. B3d. $4.00

WAKEFIELD, H.R. *Stories From the Clock Strikes Twelve.* 1961. Ballantine 531. 1st edn. F. M1d. $12.00

WAKEMAN, Frederic. *Shore Leave.* 1948. Signet 687. Fi. VG. B5d. $4.00

WAKEMAN, Fredric. *Shore Leave.* 1949. Signet 687. VG+. B3d. $5.00

WALDO, Myra. *Dining Out in Any Language.* Bantam 1499. VG+. B3d. $4.40

WALDO, Myra. *Reducing Cookbook for Whole Family.* Perma M 5023. VG. B3d. $4.00

WALDO, Myra. *Round the World Cookbook.* 1956. Bantam A 1427. Nfi. VG+. B4d. $3.00

WALES, Kirk. *6 Were To Die.* 1944. Black Cat Detective 12. My. VG. P1d. $20.00

WALKER, Daniel. *Rights in Conflict.* 1968. Bantam PZ 4273. Nfi. VG+. B5d. $3.50

WALKER, David. *Book of Shai.* 1984. DAW 563. 1st edn. VG. P9d. $1.50

WALKER, David. *Harry Black.* 1958. Bantam A 1828. 1st prtg. VG. R5d. $2.50

WALKER, David. *Lord's Pink Ocean.* 1973. DAW 67. NF. I1d. $4.00

WALKER, David. *Lord's Pink Ocean.* 1973. DAW 67. 1st prtg. VG. S1d. $3.00

WALKER, David. *Storm & the Silence.* 1956. Fontana 127. My. VG. P1d. $8.00

WALKER, David. *Storm & the Silence.* 1955. Lion Library LL 33. Fa. G+. B4d. $2.50

WALKER, David. *Storm & the Silence.* 1955. Lion LL 33. VG+. B3d. $4.50

WALKER, David. *War Gamer's World.* 1978. DAW 314. VG. P9d. $1.50

WALKER, David. *Wire.* 1953. Perma P 204. 1st pb. c/Kampen. NF. B6d. $12.50

WALKER, Gerald. *Cruising.* 1971. Crest M 1603. 1st prtg. VG. P7d. $4.00

WALKER, Gertrude. *So Deadly Fair.* Bestseller Mystery B 105. My. VG. P1d. $12.50

WALKER, Gertrude. *Suspect.* 1979. Major 3244. 2nd edn. My. VG. P1d. $3.00

WALKER, Hugh. *Magira.* 1978-1979. DAW. 3 volumes. set. F. M1d. $15.00

WALKER, L.H. *Lascivious Abbot.* 1967. Greenleaf Classic 303. PBO. c/Bonfils: gga. NF. B6a #76. $44.00

WALKER, Max. *Code Name: Judas.* 1968. Popular 60-2261. My. VG. P1d. $7.50

WALKER, Max. *Code Name: Rapier.* 1968. Popular 60-2325. Mission Impossible #3. My. VG. W2d. $7.00

WALKER, Max. *Code Name: Rapier.* 1968. Popular 60-2325. Th. VG. P1d. $7.50

WALKER, Robert W. *Sub-Zero.* 1979. Belmont Tower 51395. My. VG. P1d. $3.50

WALKER, S. *Girl School Sex.* Barclay 7024. NF. B3d. $5.00

WALKER, Shel. *Man I Killed.* 1952. Lion 112. MY. F. P1d. $22.50

WALKER, Shel. *Man I Killed.* 1952. Lion 112. PBO. VG+. B3a #21. $19.80

WALL, Evans. *Marriage Rite.* Intimate 43. VG+. B3d. $10.00

WALL, Evans. *Wedding Night.* 1960. Beacon 331. PBO. c/Darcy. gga. scarce. NF. B6a #76. $27.50

WALLACE, C.H. *Crashlanding in the Congo.* 1965. Belmont B 50-639. 1st prtg. My. VG+. R5d. $5.00

WALLACE, C.H. *ETA for Death.* 1966. Belmont B 50-734. VG+. B3d. $5.00

WALLACE, C.H. *Highflight to Hell.* 1966. Belmont B 50-722. My. VG. P1d. $5.00

WALLACE, C.H. *Witchcraft in the World Today.* 1967. Award A 269S. 1st prtg. PBO. VG. P7d. $5.00

WALLACE, Edgar. *Again Sanders.* 1952. Hodder & Stoughton C 112. Hi. F. P1d. $18.00

WALLACE, Edgar. *Again the Three.* 1957. Hodder & Stoughton C 114. My. F. P1d. $15.00

WALLACE, Edgar. *Angel of Terror.* 1959. Pan G 270. My. G+. P1d. $5.00

WALLACE, Edgar. *Avenger.* 1958. Arrow 477. 2nd edn. My. VG+. P1d. $10.00

WALLACE, Edgar. *Big Foot.* 1967. Arrow 407. My. VG. P1d. $5.00

WALLACE, Edgar. *Brigand.* 1957. Hodder & Stoughton C 299. My. VG. P1d. $7.50

WALLACE, Edgar. *Clue of the New Pin.* 1962. Hodder & Sfoughton 169. My. VG+. P1d. $9.50

WALLACE, Edgar. *Clue of the Silver Key.* 1956. Harlequin 361. My. VG. P1d. $20.00

WALLACE, Edgar. *Clue of the Silver Key.* 1961. Hodder & Stoughton 492. My. VG+. P1d. $10.00

WALLACE, Edgar. *Coat of Arms.* Arrow 288H. My. G+. P1d. $6.00

WALLACE, Edgar. *Crimson Circle.* 1955. Hodder & Stoughton C 202. My. G+. P1d. $6.00

WALLACE, Edgar. *Death Packs a Suitcase.* 1964. Hodder & Stoughton 632. My. G+. P1d. $4.50

WALLACE, Edgar. *Door With Seven Locks.* 1947. Avon 125. My. G+. P1d. $7.50

WALLACE, Edgar. *Door With Seven Locks.* 1947. Avon 125. VG. B3d. $5.00

WALLACE, Edgar. *Door With Seven Locks.* 1960. Pan G 378. My. VG. P1d. $7.00

WALLACE, Edgar. *Double.* 1965. Pan X 375. My. F. P1d. $11.00

WALLACE, Edgar. *Face in the Night.* Arrow 593. VG+. B3d. $6.00

WALLACE, Edgar. *Feathered Serpent.* 1944. Dell 49. 1st pb. c/Gregg. My. VG. B6d. $18.00

WALLACE, Edgar. *Feathered Serpent.* 1958. Harlequin 418. My. G+. P1d. $7.00

WALLACE, Edgar. *Flat 2.* Hutchinson Cr Book 17. dust jacket. My. VG. P1d. $20.00

WALLACE, Edgar. *Flying Squad.* Pan X 272. My. VG+. P1d. $7.50

WALLACE, Edgar. *Flying Squad.* Pan X 272. VG. B3d. $7.00

WALLACE, Edgar. *Forger.* 1960. Pan G 415. My. G+. P1d. $5.00

WALLACE, Edgar. *Four Just Men.* 1956. Harlequin 349. G+. G5d. $7.50

WALLACE, Edgar. *Four Just Men.* 1956. Harlequin 349. My. VG. P1d. $20.00

WALLACE, Edgar. *Four Just Men.* 1950. Pan 142. My. VG. P1d. $10.00

WALLACE, Edgar. *Four Just Men.* 1938. Penguin 64. 7th edn. dust jacket. My. VG. P1d. $25.00

WALLACE, Edgar. *Golden Hades.* 1962. Hodder & Stoughton 507. My/SF. VG. P1d. $6.50

WALLACE, Edgar. *Green Ribbon.* 1974. Arrow 909570. My. VG. P1d. $4.00

WALLACE, Edgar. *India-Rubber Men.* 1956. Harlequin 352. My. VG. P1d. $20.00

WALLACE, Edgar. *Joker.* 1960. Pan G 370. 4th prtg. VG. B3d. $7.00

WALLACE, Edgar. *Joker.* 1950. Pan 140. My. G+. P1d. $7.00

WALLACE, Edgar. *Law of the Three Just Men.* 1963. Hodder & Stoughton 62. My. VG+. P1d. $9.00

WALLACE, Edgar. *Man at the Carlton.* Hodder & Stoughton 170. My. F. P1d. $10.00

WALLACE, Edgar. *Man Who Bought London.* Digit 765. VG. B3d. $6.00

WALLACE, Edgar. *Man Who Knew.* 1957. Panther 505. 2nd edn. My. G+. P1d. $5.00

WALLACE, Edgar. *Mind of Mr JG Reeder.* 1959. Harlequin 475. My. VG. P1d. $20.00

WALLACE, Edgar. *Missing Million.* 1956. Arrow 418. My. VG. P1d. $8.00

WALLACE, Edgar. *Mixer.* 1962. Arrow 642. My. F. P1d. $13.00

WALLACE, Edgar. *Murder on Yarmouth Yards.* Newnes 010. VG. B3d. $5.00

WALLACE, Edgar. *Nine Bears.* 1950s. Ward Lock NN. 1st pb. My. VG+. B6d. $6.00

WALLACE, Edgar. *Northing Tramp.* 1954. Hodder & Stoughton C 172. My. VG. P1d. $10.00

WALLACE, Edgar. *On the Spot.* Avon Murder My 45. VG. G5d. $20.00

WALLACE, Edgar. *On the Spot.* 1936. Crime Book Society 3. My. VG. P1d. $13.00

WALLACE, Edgar. *Ringer.* 1957. Harlequin 378. My. VG. P1d. $20.00

WALLACE, Edgar. *Ringer.* 1948. Pan 42. My. VG. P1d. $10.00

WALLACE, Edgar. *Room 13.* 1961. Arrow 625. My. G+. P1d. $4.50

WALLACE, Edgar. *Sanders.* 1948. Pan 5. Hi. VG+. P1d. $15.00

WALLACE, Edgar. *Silinski, Master Criminal.* 1942. Avon Murder My 3. My. VG+. P1d. $35.00

WALLACE, Edgar. *Silinski, Master Criminal.* 1942. Avon Murder My 3. VG+. B3a #22. $29.35

WALLACE, Edgar. *Square Emerald.* Harlequin 334. VG. I1d. $15.00

WALLACE, Edgar. *Squeaker.* Harlequin 420. VG+. B3d. $8.00

WALLACE, Edgar. *Squeaker.* 1958. Harlequin 420. My. G+. P1d. $7.50

WALLACE, Edgar. *Squealer.* Avon 112. VG+. B3d. $7.00

WALLACE, Edgar. *Squealer.* 1946. Avon 112. 1st prtg. My. VG. R5d. $7.50

WALLACE, Edgar. *Terror Keep.* 1930. Hodder & Stoughton. My. VG. P1d. $20.00

WALLACE, Edgar. *Twister.* 1966. Arrow 643. My. VG+. P1d. $8.00

WALLACE, Edgar. *Valley of Ghosts.* 1953. Hodder & Stoughton C 125. My. G+. P1d. $7.50

WALLACE, Edgar. *When the Gangs Came to London.* 1959. Arrow 481. 2nd edn. My. VG. P1d. $6.00

WALLACE, Edgar. *White Face.* 1957. Harlequin 387. My. G+. P1d. $7.00

WALLACE, Francis. *Kid Galahad.* 1947. Bantam 133. VG+. B3d. $6.00

WALLACE, Ian. *Dr Orpheus.* 1969. Berkley S 1767. c/P Lehr. SF. VG+ B5d. $5.00

WALLACE, Ian. *Heller's Leap.* 1979. DAW 345. 1st edn. F. M1d. $6.00

WALLACE, Ian. *Rape of the Sun.* 1982. DAW 468. 1st edn. F. M1d. $6.00

WALLACE, Ian. *World Asunder.* 1976. DAW 216. 1st edn. F. M1d. $7.00

WALLACE, Ian. *Z-Sting.* 1979. DAW 308. 1st edn. F. M1d. $7.00

WALLACE, Irving. *Plot.* 1968. Pocket 12508. 3rd edn. My. G+. P1d. $3.00

WALLACE, Irving. *Seventh Secret.* 1986. Signet AE 4557. 2nd edn. My. VG+. P1d. $4.50

WALLACE, Lew. *Ben-Hur.* 1956. Bantam A 1450. VG+. P6d. $3.50

WALLACE, Lew. *Ben-Hur.* 1959. Cardinal GC 75. 1st prtg. VG. R5d. $1.75

WALLACE, Lew. *Ben-Hur.* Pan X 32. 6th edn. MTI. c/Heade. VG+. B3d. $8.50

WALLACE, Robert. *Corpse Parade.* 1966. Corinth CR 139. 1st edn. De. F. F2d. $18.00

WALLACE, Robert. *Curio Murders.* 1966. Corinth CR 113. My/SF. F. P1d. $20.00

WALLACE, Robert. *Death Glow.* 1966. Corinth CR 117. My/SF. F. P1d. $20.00

WALLACE, Robert. *Fangs of Murder.* Corinth CR 112. Phantom Detective. VG. M6d. $7.50

WALLACE, Robert. *Melody Murders.* 1966. Corinth CR 123. My/SF. F. P1d. $20.00

WALLACE, Robert. *Tycoon of Crime.* 1965. Corinth CR 104. My/SF. VG+. P1d. $15.00

WALLACE, Robert. *Uniformed Killers.* 1966. Corinth-Regency CR 127. VG+. B3a #22. $10.00

WALLACE, Robert. *Vampire Murders.* 1965. Corinth CR 101. Phantom Detective #1. NF. M1d. $15.00

WALLACE, Wayne. *His Lesbian Love.* 1965. Brandon House 730. VG+. B3a #20. $16.00

WALLACE, Wolf. *Hive.* 1966. Beacon Softcover 948. 1st edn. c/gga. F. F2d. $7.50

WALLACH, Ira. *Front Page.* 1975. Warner 76-779. 1st edn. My. F. F2d. $10.00

WALLANT, E.L. *Tenants of Moonbloom.* Popular SP 340. c/Zuckerberg. NF. B3d. $6.00

WALLANT, Edward Lewis. *Human Season.* 1964. Berkley G 1005. VG. B3d. $4.50

WALLANT, Edward Lewis. *Pawnbroker.* MacFadden 50-138. 2nd edn. My. VG. P1d. $5.00

WALLANT, Edward Lewis. *Tenants of Moonbloom.* Popular 75-1326. Fi. VG. B5d. $3.50

WALLANT, Lewis. *Pawnbroker.* 1965. MacFadden 50-138. MTI. c/R Stiger & G Fitzgerald: photo. Fi. VG. B5d. $4.00

WALLENSTEIN, Marcel. *Red Canvas.* 1952. Avon 447. 1st pb. VG+. B6d. $12.50

WALLENSTEIN, Marcel. *Tuck's Girl.* 1953. Eton E 124. My. VG. P1d. $8.50

WALLER, Leslie. *Bed She Made.* 1952. Popular 1393. 2nd edn. My. VG. P1d. $7.50

WALLER, Leslie. *K.* 1963. Gold Medal K 1319. My. VG. P1d. $7.50

WALLING, R.A.J. *Corpse in the Green Pyjamas.* 1941. Avon 8. My. VG. P1d. $20.00

WALLING, R.A.J. *Corpse With the Eerie Eye.* Popular 106. VG. I1d. $7.00

WALLING, R.A.J. *Corpse With the Grimy Glove.* 1948. Popular 139. My. G+. P1d. $7.50

WALLING, R.A.J. *Corpse With the Grimy Glove.* 1948. Popular 139. 1st prtg. VG. P7d. $9.00

WALLING, R.A.J. *Corpse With the Red-Headed Friend.* 1946. Pocket 49. VG. P6d. $6.00

WALLING, R.A.J. *Corpse Without a Clue.* Armed Services Q 15. VG. G5d. $3.75

WALLING, R.A.J. *Murder at Midnight.* 1942. Avon 16. G. G5d. $5.00

WALLING, R.A.J. *Murder at Midnight.* 1942. Avon 16. My. NF. B6d. $22.50

WALLING, R.A.J. *Murder at Midnight.* 1942. Avon 16. VG. B3d. $7.00

WALLIS, J.H. *Once Off Guard.* 1951. Popular 385. My. VG. P6d. $1.75

WALLIS, J.H. *Woman in the Window.* 1945. Armed Services 723. My. VG. P1d. $20.00

WALLIS, Ruth Sawtell. *Blood From a Stone.* 1947. Bantam 109. c/Cappello. My. VG. B5d. $4.00

WALLIS, Ruth Sawtell. *Blood From a Stone.* 1947. Bantam 109. c/Cappello: gga. My. NF. B4d. $12.00

WALLIS, Ruth Sawtell. *Blood From a Stone.* 1947. Bantam 109. G+. G5d. $3.00

WALLIS, Ruth Sawtell. *Blood From a Stone.* 1947. Bantam 109. 1st pb. My. VG+. B6d. $9.00

WALLIS, Ruth Sawtell. *No Bones About It.* 1946. Bantam 72. My. VG. I1d. $5.00

WALLIS, Ruth Sawtell. *Too Many Bones.* Dell 123. G+. I1d. $5.00

WALLIS, Ruth Sawtell. *Too Many Bones.* Dell 123. VG+. B3d. $7.00

WALLIS. *Only Lovers Left Alive.* 1966. Pan X 464. 1st pb. SF. VG+. B6d. $15.00

WALLMANN, Jeffrey M. *Clean Sweep.* 1978. Avon 33827. My. F. P1d. $5.00

WALLMANN, Jeffrey M. *Spiral Web.* 1969. Signet T 3830. Th. VG. P1d. $4.50

WALLOP, Douglass. *Dangerous Years.* 1957. Pocket 1146. c/J Meese. Fi. VG. B5d. $5.00

WALLOP, Douglass. *Year the Yankees Lost the Pennant.* 1959. Cardinal C 328. Hu. VG. B4d. $3.00

WALLOP, Douglass. *Year the Yankees Lost the Pennant.* 1959. Cardinal C 328. 1st prtg. G+. R5d. $2.00

WALPOLE, Ellen Wales. *Everyday Encyclopedia.* 1954. Signet KS 311. Nfi. VG+. B4d. $2.00

WALPOLE, Hugh. *Man With Red Hair.* 1949. Avon 204. 1st edn. PBO. VG+. B6d. $25.00

WALPOLE, Hugh. *Portrait of a Man With Red Hair.* 1949. Avon 204. My. VG. P1d. $15.00

WALPOLE, Hugh. *Portrait of a Man With Red Hair.* 1949. Avon 204. 1st edn. PBO. c/Ed Paulsen. scarce. NF. B6a #75. $65.00

WALPOLE, Hugh. *Portrait of a Man With Red Hair.* 1949. Avon 204. 1st prtg. G+. P7d. $10.00

WALPOLE, Hugh. *Portrait of a Man With Red Hair.* 1967. PB Library 53-409. My. VG. B5d. $5.50

WALPOLE, Hugh. *Silver Thorn.* Tauchitz 15. Fi. VG. P1d. $12.50

WALSH, J.M. *Express Delivery.* 1948. White Circle 334. My. VG. P1d. $10.00

WALSH, J.M. *Spies in Pursuit.* 1938. Collins Mystery 224. 7th edn. dust jacket. My. VG. P1d. $20.00

WALSH, J.M. *Vanguard to Neptune.* 1952. Fantasy Book 410. PBO. c/great SF. scarce. SF. VG+. B6a #74. $50.00

WALSH, Maurice. *Blackcock's Feather.* Pennant P 28. NF. B3d. $8.50

WALSH, Paul E. *KKK.* 1956. Avon 742. My. VG+. P1d. $15.00

WALSH, Paul E. *Murder in Baracoa.* 1958. Avon 802. G+. G5d. $3.00

WALSH, Paul E. *Murder in Baracoa.* 1958. Avon 802. My. VG. P1d. $7.50

WALSH, Paul E. *Murder Room.* 1957. Avon 767. My. G+. P1d. $5.50

WALSH, Robert. *Violent Hours.* 1958. Signet 1492. My. VG. P1d. $7.50

WALSH, Robert. *Violent Hours.* 1958. Signet 1492. 1st edn. c/gga. My. VG+. F2d. $13.00

WALSH, Ruth M. *Alcoholic Woman.* 1959. Beacon 229. 1st prtg. VG+. P7d. $9.00

WALSH, Thomas. *Dark Window.* 1958. Bantam 1840. My. VG. P1d. $7.50

WALSH, Thomas. *Dark Window.* 1958. Bantam 1840. 1st prtg. My. G+. R5d. $1.50

WALSH, Thomas. *Night Watch.* 1953. Bantam 1150. 1st prtg. My. VG. R5d. $2.75

WALSH, Thomas. *Nightmare in Manhattan.* 1951. Bantam 895. VG. G5d. $9.00

WALSH, Thomas. *Thief in the Night.* 1965. Award A 126F. My. VG. P1d. $5.50

WALSH, Thomas. *To Hide a Rogue.* 1966. Award A 193F. 1st prtg. My. VG. R5d. $1.75

WALT, Bryce. *Long Night.* 1952. Falcon Books 42. PBO. c/gga: photo. VG. P6d. $15.00

WALTER, A.M. *Moondrop to Gascony.* Pan 165. 2nd prtg. VG+. B3d. $8.00

WALTER, E. *Love You Good, See You Later.* MacFadden 60-217. VG+. B3d. $4.50

WALTER, J. *Dance Merchants.* 1958. Ace D 300. PBO. VG+. B6d. $16.50

WALTERS, Hank. *Dammit: Don't Touch My Board!* 1960. Novel Book 3507. Ad. G+. B5d. $3.00

WALTERS, Hank. *Lucky Rape.* 1960. Novel Book 3505. PBO. Ad. VG. B5d. $4.50

WALTON, Bryce. *Long Night.* 1952. Falcon 42. VG. B3a #24. $41.80

WALTON, Evangeline. *Children of Llyr.* 1971. Ballantine 02332. 1st edn. Ad/Fa. NF. M1d. $12.00

WALTON, Evangeline. *Children of Llyr.* 1971. Ballantine 02332. 1st prtg. VG. S1d. $5.50

WALTON, Evangeline. *Cross & the Sword.* 1960. Bantam. 1st pb edn. F. M1d. $7.00

WALTON, Evangeline. *Island of the Mighty.* 1970. Ballantine 01959 1st edn. Ad/Fa. F. M1d. $12.00

WALTON, Evangeline. *Song of Rhiannon.* 1973. Ballantine. 2nd edn. Ad/Fa. F. M1d. $6.00

WALTON, Evangeline. *Witch House.* Award AN 1246. SF. VG. W2d. $4.00

WALTON, Evangeline. *Witch House.* 1962. Monarch B 264. 1st pb edn. F. M1d. $20.00

WALZ, J. & A. *Bizarre Sisters.* Bantam 1182. F. B3d. $6.00

WAMBAUGH, Joseph. *Black Marble.* 1979. Dell 10647. My. F. P1d. $5.00

WAMBAUGH, Joseph. *Choirboys.* 1976. Dell 1188. My. VG. P1d. $3.50

WAMBAUGH, Joseph. *Lines & Shadows.* 1984. Bantam 24607. My. F. P1d. $5.00

WAMBAUGH, Joseph. *Secrets of Harry Bright.* 1986. Bantam 26021. My. F. P1d. $5.00

WAND, Della. *Devil's Caress.* 1960. Newsstand U 140. Ad. G+. B5d. $3.00

WAND, Della. *Devil's Caress.* 1960. Newsstand U 140. My. VG. P1d. $7.00

WAND, Della. *Devil's Caress.* 1960. Newsstand U 140. 1st edn. c/gga. Cr. F. F2d. $12.50

WAND, Jonas. *Buchanan Gets Mad.* 1958. Gold Medal 803. We. G+. P1d. $7.00

WAND, Jonas. *Buchanan Says No.* 1957. Gold Medal 662. We. G+. P1d. $7.00

WANGERIN, W. Jr. *Book of the Dun Cow.* 1979. Pocket 83217. SF. VG. W2d. $5.00

WARD, Barbara. *Short Year.* 1968. Signet T 3621. c/gga. Fa. VG+. B4d. $4.00

WARD, Brad. *Frontier Street.* Berkley G 989. VG+. B3d. $4.50

WARD, Brad. *Man From Andersonville.* 1956. Ace S 148. PBO. c/Leone. We. G+. B5d. $4.50

WARD, Brad. *Man From Andersonville.* 1956. Ace S 148. PBO. We. VG. B6d. $5.00

WARD, Brad. *Marshal of Medicine Bend.* Ace S 60. We. VG. B5d. $6.00

WARD, Brad. *Missourian.* Berkley G 504. NF. I1d. $4.00

WARD, Brad. *Thirty Notches.* 1958. Signet 1481. We. VG+. B4d. $4.00

WARD, Don edt. *Dark of the Soul.* 1970. Tower T 075-3. PBO. Ho. NF. B6d. $12.50

WARD, Jonas. *Buchanan on the Prod.* Gold Medal P 3472. VG. M6d. $3.50

WARD, Jonas. *Name's Buchanan.* 1960. Gold Medal 1021. 2nd prtg. VG. P6d. $2.00

WARD, Jonas. *Name's Buchanan.* 1966. Gold Medal 1622. VG+. B3d. $4.50

WARD, Jonas. *One-Man Massacre.* 1966. Gold Medal K 1651. We. VG+. B4d. $3.00

WARD, Jonathan. *Bed & Board.* Kozy 172. NF. B3d. $8.00

WARD, Jonathan. *Love Under Glass.* 1962. Kozy 166. PBO. NF. B6d. $12.00

WARD, Maisie. *GK Chesterton.* 1958. Penguin 1070. Nfi. G+. P1d. $5.50

WARD, Mary Jane. *Snake Pit.* 1949. Signet 696. Fa. VG+. B4d. $4.00

WARD, William. *Jeff Clayton's Demon Pursuer.* 1911. Westbrook 86. My. G+. P1d. $13.00

WARD, William. *Jeff Clayton's Lost Ship.* 1911. Westbrook 96. My. G+. P1d. $13.00

WARD, William. *Jeff Clayton's Strong Arm.* 1912. Westbrook 126. My. VG. P1d. $17.50

WARD, William. *Jeff Clayton's Thunderbolt.* 1910. Westbrook 46. My. VG. P1d. $17.50

WARD, William. *Mystery of the Great Ruby.* Westbrook 110. VG. B3a #20. $17.35

WARE, Harlan. *Come, Fill the Cup.* 1953. Bantam A 1097. My. F. P1d. $17.00

WARE, Judith. *Detour to Denmark.* 1967. PB Library 53-480. Th. VG. P1d. $5.00

WARNAK, Tim. *Crossed Swords.* 1978. Ace 67865. 1st edn. c/photo. Hi. F. F2d. $15.00

WARNER, Douglas. *Death on a Warm Wind.* 1973. Penguin 3601. My/SF. VG. P1d. $4.00

WARNER, E. *Seven Days to Lomaland.* Pyramid 1671. VG+. B3d. $4.50

WARNER, Mignon. *Tarot Murders.* 1981. Dell 16162. My. VG+. W2d. $3.50

WARNER, Sylvia. *Lolly Willowes.* Popular 602294. SF. VG. W2d. $4.75

WARNER-CROZETTI, R. *Widderburn Horror.* 1971. Leisure LB 28S. My/SF. VG. P1d. $4.00

WARNOW, Morton. *Forced March.* 1962. Signet 2039. 1st edn. Hi. F. F2d. $10.00

WARREN, Charles. *Valley of the Shadow.* 1949. Bantam 732. We. VG+. B4d. $4.00

WARREN, Doug. *Case of Rape.* 1975. Pyramid 3617. 1st edn. TVTI. c/Elizabeth Montgomery: photo. My. F. F2d. $12.00

WARREN, J. *Stepmothers & Their Stepchildren.* Barclay 7199. F. B3d. $5.00

WARREN, Laura. *No Place in Heaven.* 1949. News Stand Library 13. dust jacket. rare. NF. B6a #76. $102.00

WARREN, Paul. *Next Time Is for Life.* 1953. Dell 1st Edn 6. Nfi. F. P1d. $20.00

WARREN, Paulette. *Caliban's Castle.* 1976. Berkley N 3064. My. VG. P1d. $3.50

WARREN, Paulette. *Ravenkill.* 1965. Lancer 72-945. Go. VG. P1d. $5.50

WARREN, Paulette. *Ravenkill.* 1965. Lancer 72-945. PBO. c/Marchetti. VG+. B6d. $6.00

WARREN, Robert Penn. *All the King's Men.* 1951. Bantam Giant A 939. VG+. P6d. $3.75

WARREN, Robert Penn. *At Heaven's Gate.* 1949. Signet 725. 1st pb. NF. B6d. $18.00

WARREN, Robert Penn. *Unvanquished.* 1952. Signet 977. c/J Avati. Fi. VG. B5d. $4.50

WARREN, Robert Penn. *World Enough & Time.* 1952. Signet D 975. c/Cardiff. Fi. VG. B5d. $6.00

WARREN, Roy. *Space Sex.* 1960. Heart 105. 1st edn. c/gga. SF. F. F2d. $20.00

WARRINER, Thurman. *Doors of Sleep.* 1961. Penguin 1610. Ho. G+. P1d. $6.00

WASHBURN, L.J. *Wild Night.* 1987. TOR 51041. De. VG+. P1d. $4.50

WATERBURY, R. *Elizabeth Taylor: Life, Loves, Future.* Popular PC 1057. VG+. B3d. $4.50

WATERS, Ethel. *His Eye Is on the Sparrow.* 1952. Bantam A 985. 1st pb. Bio. VG+. B3d. $5.00

WATERS, F. *Earp Brothers.* 1963. Corgi 1331. VG. B3d. $6.50

WATERS, T.A. *Blackwood Cult.* 1968. Lancer 73-769. Go. VG. P1d. $5.00

WATERS, T.A. *Centerforce.* 1974. Dell 6191. 1st prtg. SF. VG. R5d. $2.00

WATERS, T.A. *Lost Victim.* 1975. Pyramid V 3562. My. VG. P1d. $3.50

WATERS, T.A. *Psychedelic.* 1967. Lancer 73-656. 1st edn. My. F. F2d. $10.00

WATERS & WISBERG. *Savage Soldiers.* 1956. Avon T 130. 1st pb. c/gga. VG+. B6d. $7.00

WATKINS, Glen. *Sinful Life.* 1950. Stork 3. PBO. c/gga. VG+. B6a #76. $55.00

WATKINS, Glen. *Tavern Girl.* 1950. Pyramid 17. 1st pb. c/Barker: gga. VG. B6d. $7.50

WATKINS, Leslie. *Sleepwalk Killers.* 1976. Everest 3925. Nfi. G+. P1d. $2.50

WATSON, Colin. *Charity Ends at Home.* 1969. Berkley X 1748. My. G+. P1d. $3.25

WATSON, Colin. *Coffin, Scarcely Used.* 1962. Penguin 1754. My. F. P1d. $13.00

WATSON, Colin. *Hopjoy Was Here.* 1966. Penguin C 2404. My. VG. P1d. $5.50

WATSON, Colin. *Lonelyheart 4122.* 1968. Berkley X 1586. 1st pb. My. VG+. B6d. $9.00

WATSON, Colin. *Lonelyheart 4122.* 1977. Methuen Lancer 01880. My. G+. P1d. $2.75

WATSON, Ian. *Martian Inca.* 1978. Ace 50244. SF. F. W2d. $5.00

WATSON, James L. *Agent Orange Affair.* 1971. Apollo 00110. Th. VG. P1d. $4.00

WATSON, Julia. *Winter of the Witch.* 1972. Bantam N 6734. Hi. VG. P1d. $4.00

WATSON, Ken. *Curling With Ken Watson.* Harlequin 442. c/photo. VG. B3d. $4.00

WATSON, Will. *Wolf Dog Range.* Lion 61. VG. I1d. $7.00

WATT-EVANS, Lawrence. *Lure of the Basilisk.* 1980. Ballantine 28624. 1st prtg. SF. VG. R5d. $2.00

WATTS, F. edt. *Pocket Book Magazine #2.* Cardinal C 160. PBO. VG+. B3d. $4.50

WAUGH, Evelyn. *Loved One.* Dell 771. c/S Beckett. Fi. VG. B5d. $3.00

WAUGH, Evelyn. *Vile Bodies.* Dell 807. VG. I1d. $5.00

WAUGH, Hillary. *Born Victim.* 1964. Avon G 1239. My. VG. P1d. $6.00

WAUGH, Hillary. *Case of the Brunette Bobshell.* 1957. Crest 172. c/Abbott. My. VG. P6d. $1.50

WAUGH, Hillary. *Eighth Mrs Bluebeard.* 1959. Crest 292. My. F. P1d. $20.00

WAUGH, Hillary. *Finish Me Off.* 1971. Belmont B 95-2101. My. VG. P1d. $4.00

WAUGH, Hillary. *Girl Who Cried Wolf.* 1960. Dell D 338. VG+. G5d. $7.00

WAUGH, Hillary. *If I Live To Dine.* 1949. Graphic 12. 1st edn. PBO. extremely scarce. VG+. B6a #77. $38.50

WAUGH, Hillary. *Last Seen Wearing.* 1954. Pocket 988. My. G+. P1d. $6.00

WAUGH, Hillary. *Late Mrs D.* 1964. Avon G 1212. My. VG. P1d. $6.00

WAUGH, Hillary. *Rag & a Bone.* 1955. Pocket 1075. My. VG+. B4d. $4.00

WAUGH, Hillary. *Road Block.* 1966. Pan X 616. 2nd edn. My. VG. P1d. $5.00

WAUGH, Hillary. *30 Manhattan East.* 1971. Belmont B 95-2081. My. VG. P1d. $4.00

WAY, F. *Pilotin' Comes Natural.* Armed Services P 14. VG+. B3d. $5.00

WAY, Isabel Stewart. *House on Sky High Road.* 1972. Belmont Tower 50252. Go. VG. P1d. $4.00

WAYLAND, Patrick. *Counterstroke.* 1968. PB Library 52-631. My. VG+. B4d. $3.00

WAYNE, Anderson. *Charlie Dell.* 1953. Popular G 123. VG. B3d. $4.50

WAYNE, Charles. *Way of the Flesh.* 1962. Saber SA 25. Ad. G+. B5d. $3.50

WAYNE, Joseph. *Bunch Grass.* 1956. Signet 1277. 1st pb. We. VG+. B6d. $9.00

WEATHERALL, Ernie. *Rock 'N Roll Gal.* 1957. Beacon 131. PBO. c/Kampen: gga. scarce. JD. VG+. B6a #79. $122.50

WEATHERALL, Ernie. *Rock 'N Roll Gal.* 1961. Beacon 379. c/Kampen. JD. NF. B6a #74. $74.00

WEATHERLY, Max. *Mantis & the Moth.* 1965. Pocket 50183. My. VG. P1d. $5.50

WEAVER, N. *Love or Kill Them All.* Kozy 188. VG+. B3d. $6.00

WEAVER, Ward. *End of the Track.* 1951. Popular 342. VG. I1d. $6.00

WEAVER, Ward. *Hang My Wreath.* 1951. Popular 388. Fa. VG. B4d. $6.00

WEBB, Duncan. *Deadline for Crime.* 1958. Panther 749. Nfi. VG. P1d. $10.00

WEBB, Forrest. *Snowboys.* 1976. Bantam T 6850. My. VG. P1d. $3.50

WEBB, Jack. *Bad Blonde.* 1957. Signet 1422. c/MacGuire: gga. My. VG+. B4d. $5.00

WEBB, Jack. *Badge.* 1959. Crest S 341. My. G+. P1d. $5.00

WEBB, Jack. *Big Sin.* 1953. Signet 1076. My. F. P1d. $17.00

WEBB, Jack. *Big Sin.* 1953. Signet 1076. PBO. c/Tossey. scarce. My. NF. B6a #76. $28.00

WEBB, Jack. *Big Sin.* 1953. Signet 1076. VG. B3d. $4.00

WEBB, Jack. *Brass Halo.* 1958. Signet 1556. c/Maguire. NF. I1d. $6.00

WEBB, Jack. *Brass Halo.* 1958. Signet 1556. My. F. P1d. $15.00

WEBB, Jack. *Brass Halo.* 1958. Signet 1556. VG. B3d. $4.00

WEBB, Jack. *Broken Doll.* 1956. Signet 1311. My. G+. P1d. $6.00

WEBB, Jack. *Broken Doll.* 1956. Signet 1311. 1st pb. c/Maguire. My. VG. B6d. $9.00

WEBB, Jack. *Damned Lovely.* 1955. Signet 1233. c/Bob Maguire: gga. VG. P6d. $5.00

WEBB, Jack. *Deadly Sex.* 1961. Signet S 1988. My. VG. P1d. $6.50

WEBB, Jack. *Delicate Darling.* 1960. Signet S 1816. G+. G5d. $3.50

WEBB, Jack. *Delicate Darling.* 1960. Signet S 1816. My. VG. P1d. $7.00

WEBB, Jack. *Gilded Witch.* 1963. Regency RB 311. My. G+. P1d. $15.00

WEBB, Jack. *Naked Angel.* 1954. Signet 1149. My. F. P1d. $17.00

WEBB, Jean Francis. *Anna Lucasta.* 1949. Dell 331. 1st prtg. VG. R5d. $4.50

WEBB, Jean Francis. *Bride of Cairngore.* 1976. Popular 00376. Go. VG. P1d. $3.50

WEBB, Jean Francis. *Little Women.* Dell 296. MTI. VG. B3d. $4.50

WEBB, Paul. *Mountain Boys.* 1957. Signet 1441. c/P Webb: cartoons. Nfi. VG. B3d/B5d. $4.50

WEBB, Paul. *Mountain Boys.* 1957. Signet 1441. 1st edn. F. F2d. $10.00

WEBB, Sharon. *Ram Song.* 1985. Bantam. 1st pb edn. F. M1d. $4.00

WEBBER, Everett. *Rampart Street.* Pocket 681. VG+. I1d. $5.00

WEBBER, Gordon. *Far Shore.* 1955. Bantam 1345. We. VG. B4d. $2.00

WEBER, Carl. *Pleasures of Pipe Smoking.* 1955. Bantam NN. Nfi. VG. B5d. $3.50

WEBER, J. Sherwood edt. *Good Reading.* 1960. Mentor MT 293. 15th edn. Nfi. VG. P1d. $3.75

WEBER, Ken. *Five-Minute Mysteries.* Running Press 690. 3rd edn. My. VG. P1d. $6.00

WEBER, Rubin. *Grave Maker's House.* 1966. Avon G 1282. My. VG. P1d. $5.50

WEBSTER, John. *Tragedy of the Duchess of Malfi!* 1959. Washington Square W 101. Nfi. VG. B5d. $2.50

WEBSTER, Sam. *Society Doctor.* 1964. Monarch 404. Ad. VG. B5d. $4.00

WECHSBERG, Joseph. *Looking for a Bluebird.* 1947. Penguin 622. 1st pb. VG. B6d. $3.25

WEEKLEY, W.G. *Castaway Island.* Perma P 111. VG. B3d. $4.00

WEEKS, Jack. *Grey Affair.* 1961. Dell F 135. 1st prtg. My. VG+. R5d. $3.25

WEEKS, Jack. *I Detest All My Sins.* 1954. Dell 1st Edn D 20. PBO. c/J McDermott. Fi. VG. B5d. $3.50

WEEKS, William Rawle. *Knock & Wait Awhile.* 1965. Bantam F 2949. 2nd edn. Th. VG. P1d. $4.50

WEEKS, William Rawle. *Knock & Wait Awhile.* 1957. Bantam 1706. VG. B3d. $4.00

WEES, Frances Shelley. *M'Lord, I Am Not Guilty.* 1967. Pyramid X 1625. My. G+. P1d. $3.50

WEES, Frances Shelley. *Someone Called Maggie Lane.* 1948. Bantam 418. VG. B3d. $4.00

WEES, Frances Shelley. *Where Is Jenny Now?* 1970. Pyramid X 2144. My. VG. P1d. $4.50

WEHEN, Joy Deweese. *Golden Hill Mystery.* 1964. Berkley C 898. 1st prtg. My. F. R5d. $4.00

WEIDMAN, Jerome. *Dime a Throw & Other Stories.* 1957. Berkley G 49. PBO. c/gga. G. P6d. $2.00

WEIDMAN, Jerome. *Dime a Throw & Other Stories.* 1957. Berkley G 49. VG. B3d. $4.50

WEIDMAN, Jerome. *I Can Get It for You Wholesale!* Avon T 240. 8th edn. Fi. VG. B5d. $2.50

WEIDMAN, Jerome. *I Can Get It for You Wholesale!* 1949. Avon 226. Fi. VG. B5d. $4.50

WEIDMAN, Jerome. *I Can Get It for You Wholesale!* 1951. Avon 356. MTI. VG+. B3d. $5.50

WEIDMAN, Jerome. *I'll Never Go There Anymore.* 1956. Avon T 153. Fa. VG. B4d. $2.25

WEIDMAN, Jerome. *I'll Never Go There Anymore.* 1963. Cardinal GC 149. Fi. VG+. B5d. $3.50

WEIDMAN, Jerome. *Price Is Right.* 1950. Avon 279. VG+. B3d. $4.50

WEIDMAN, Jerome. *Price Is Right.* 1952. Avon 429. VG+. B3d. $5.50

WEIDMAN, Jerome. *Slipping Beauty.* 1952. Avon 442. VG. B3d. $5.00

WEIDMAN, Jerome. *Third Angel.* 1951. Avon G 1017. VG. B3d. $3.50

WEIDMAN, Jerome. *What's in It for Me?* 1955. Avon T 103. c/gga. Fa. VG. B4d. $2.25

WEIDMAN, Jerome. *What's in It for Me?* 1950. Avon 241. VG. I1d. $4.00

WEIDMAN, Jerome. *What's In It For Me?* 1950. Avon 241. VG+. B3d. $5.00

WEIDMAN, Jerome. *Your Daughter Iris.* Avon G 1026. Fi. VG. B5d. $3.00

WEIDMAN, Jerome. *Your Daughter Iris.* Avon 1086. Fi. VG. B5d. $3.00

WEIL, Jerry. *Naked in Paris.* 1963. Lancer 72-653. VG+. B3d. $5.00

WEIL, Jerry. *Nobody Dies In Paris.* 1957. Signet 1449. PBO. c/Baryc. VG+. B6d. $7.50

WEIL, Jerry. *Nobody Dies in Paris.* 1957. Signet 1449. 1st prtg. c/gga. VG. P7d. $5.00

WEILL, Gus. *Woman's Eyes.* 1976. Ballantine 24774. My. G+. P1d. $2.75

WEIN, Len. *Stalker From the Stars.* 1978. Pocket 82084. Incredible Hulk. SF. F. W2d. $6.00

WEIN & WOLFMAN. *Mayhem in Manhattan.* 1978. Pocket 82044. My/SF. VG. P1d. $4.00

WEINBAUM, Stanley G. *Best of Stanley Weinbaum.* 1974. Ballantine 23890. 1st edn. VG. P9d. $1.50

WEINBAUM, Stanley G. *Black Flame.* 1969. Avon V 2280. SF. G+. R5d. $1.75

WEINBAUM, Stanley G. *Black Flame.* 1967. Avon. F. M1d. $15.00

WEINBAUM, Stanley G. *Black Flame.* 1948. Harlequin 205. VG+. B3a #21. $151.00

WEINBAUM, Stanley G. *Martian Odyssey.* 1966. Lancer 72-146. 1st prtg. SF. VG+. R5d. $6.50

WEINBAUM, Stanley G. *Martian Odyssey.* 1962. Lancer 74-808. SF. VG. B5d. $5.50

WEINBAUM, Stanley G. *New Adam.* 1969. Avon V 2288. 1st pb edn. VG. M1d. $10.00

WEINBAUM, Stanley G. *New Adam.* 1969. Avon V 2288. 1st prtg. SF. G+. W2d. $3.00

WEINER, Ed. *Damon Runyon Story.* 1950. Popular 220. c/gga. Fa. VG. B4d. $7.50

WEINER, Ellis. *Howard the Duck.* 1986. Berkley 09275. PBO. MTI. SF. NF. B6d. $3.00

WEINER, Willard. *Four Boys, a Girl, & a Gun.* 1951. Avon 292. JD. G+. P1d. $10.00

WEINER, Willard. *Four Boys, a Girl, & a Gun.* 1951. Avon 292. JD. VG+. I1d. $12.00

WEINER, Willard. *Young Killers.* 1957. Avon T 174. JD. VG+. B6d. $22.50

WEINSTEIN, Sol. *Deep Domain.* Pocket 63329. F. P9d. $2.25

WEINSTEIN, Sol. *Loxfinger.* 1965. Pocket 10081. 1st edn. My. F. F2d. $15.00

WEINSTEIN, Sol. *Matzohball.* 1966. Pocket 10094. 1st edn. My. F. F2d. $15.00

WEINSTEIN, Sol. *On the Secret Service of His Majesty.* 1966. Pocket 10172. Th. G. P1d. $7.50

WEISS, Arthur. *O'Kelly.* 1969. PB Library 65-056. 1st prtg. MTI. G+. R5d. $1.50

WEISS, J. *Career Girl.* Midwood 33-789. PBO. VG+. B3d. $4.50

WEISS, Joe. *Love Peddler.* 1957. Beacon 141. 1st prtg. c/Kampen: gga. VG+. P7d. $12.50

WEISS, Joe. *Lovely Fraud.* 1957. Beacon 148. 1st prtg. VG+. P7d. $12.50

WEISS, Martin L. *Hate Alley.* 1957. Ace D 214. PBO. JD. VG. B6d. $25.00

WEISS, Peter. *Marat Sade.* 1966. Pocket 75178. MTI. NF. B4d. $4.00

WELCH, K.F. *Sound of Death.* Digit 518. VG. B3d. $6.00

WELCOME, John edt. *Best Crime Stories 2.* 1964. Faber. advance uncorrected proof. My. G+. P1d. $25.00

WELCOME, John edt. *Beware of Midnight.* 1972. Harrow HW 7026. My. VG+. P1d. $4.50

WELCOME, John edt. *Run for Cover.* 1963. Penguin 1881. My. G+. P1d. $4.50

WELCOME, John edt. *Stop at Nothing.* 1983. Perennial P 665. My. VG. P1d. $3.50

WELDON, John Lee. *Naked Heart.* 1954. Signet 1126. VG+. B3d. $5.00

WELDON, John Lee. *Thunder in the Heart.* 1955. Signet 1184. 1st pb. c/Hulings. VG+. B6d. $9.00

WELDON, Rex. *Love Me Wild.* 1965. Brandon House 945. NF. B3a #20. $18.40

WELDON, Rex. *Peculiarly Passionate Pair.* 1963. Novel Book 60115. My. G+. P1d. $5.00

WELDON, Rex. *Round Robin.* 1968. Publishers Export G 1148. PBO. VG. B6d. $6.00

WELLARD, James. *Action of the Tiger.* 1957. Avon T 188. My. VG. P1d. $7.50

WELLARD, James. *Snake in the Grass.* 1945. Handi-Book 35. My. G+. P1d. $15.00

WELLER, R.B. *Acapulco Swap.* 1970. Candid Reader 1019. PBO. c/gga. scarce. NF. B6a #76. $26.50

WELLES, Kermit. *Blood on Boot Hill.* 1960. Pyramid G 563. We. VG+. B4d. $5.00

WELLES, Kermit. *Gambler's Girl.* 1951. Original Digest 704. PBO. c/Nappi: gga. scarce. VG. B6a #79. $75.00

WELLES, Kermit. *Pleasure Bound.* 1952. Cameo Digest 310. PBO. c/George Gross: gga. VG+. B6a #74. $88.00

WELLES, Kermit. *Reformatory Women.* 1959. Bedside 812. 1st edn. c/gga. scarce. F. F2d. $25.00

WELLES, Kermit. *See No Evil.* 1952. Original Digest 710. c/gga. VG+. B6a #80. $82.50

WELLES, Kermit. *Wild Wanton.* Bedside BB 818. VG+. I1d. $6.00

WELLES, Orson. *Invasion From Mars.* 1949. Dell 305. VG. I1d. $8.00

WELLES, Orson. *Invasion From Mars.* 1949. Dell 305. 1st edn. NF. M1d. $20.00

WELLES, Orson. *Invasion From Mars.* 1949. Dell 305. 1st prtg. SF. G. R5d. $3.00

WELLES, Orson. *Mr Arkadin.* 1958. Pyramid G-357. My. VG. P1d. $10.00

WELLMAN, Don. *Flesh Act.* 1963. Ember Book EB 901. VG. B3d. $3.50

WELLMAN, Manly Wade. *After Dark.* Berkley 07103. 1st prtg. VG+. S1d. $3.50

WELLMAN, Manly Wade. *Beasts From Beyond.* 1950. World Fantasy NN. PBO. rare. SF. VG+. B6a #77. $126.50

WELLMAN, Manly Wade. *Beyonders.* 1977. Warner 88202. SF. F. W2d. $4.75

WELLMAN, Manly Wade. *Find My Killer.* Signet 1448. reprint. My. VG. B6d. $6.00

WELLMAN, Manly Wade. *Fort Sun Dance.* 1955. Dell 1st Edn 52. PBO. c/Tossey. We. VG. B6d. $7.50

WELLMAN, Manly Wade. *Invading Asteroid.* Stellar 15. SF. F. W2d. $40.00

WELLMAN, Manly Wade. *Sherlock Holmes' War of the Worlds.* 1975. Warner 982. 1st edn. SF. F. F2d. $20.00

WELLMAN, Manly Wade. *Sojarr of Titan.* 1949. Prize SF 11. PBO. c/sgn. VG+. B3a #22. $45.00

WELLMAN, Manly Wade. *Sojarr of Titan.* 1949. Prize SF 11. PBO. SF. G+. B5d. $12.50

WELLMAN, Manly Wade. *Solar Invasion.* Popular 60-2346. c/F Frazetta. SF. VG+. B5d. $3.50

WELLMAN, Manly Wade. *Twice in Time.* Galaxy SF 34. VG+. B3d. $5.50

WELLMAN, Manly Wade. *Who Fears the Devil?* 1964. Ballantine U 2222. PBO. VG+. B3d. $5.00

WELLMAN, Manly Wade. *Who Fears the Devil?* 1975. London. 1st British edn. F. M1d. $10.00

WELLMAN, Paul I. *Comancheros.* 1961. Perma M 4194. VG. B3d. $4.50

WELLMAN, Paul I. *Comancheros.* 1961. Perma M 4194. 2nd prtg. G+. R5d. $1.50

WELLMAN, Paul I. *Jubal Troop.* 1960. Cardinal GC 91. 1st prtg. VG+. P7d. $4.00

WELLMAN & WELLMAN. *Sherlock Holmes' War of the Worlds.* 1975. Warner 76-982. PBO. SF. G+. M3d. $15.00

WELLS, Anna Mary. *Murderer's Choice.* 1946. Dell 126. My. F. P1d. $30.00

WELLS, Anna Mary. *Murderer's Choice.* 1946. Dell 126. 1st pb. c/Gregg. My. G+. B6d. $4.00

WELLS, Anna Mary. *Talent for Murder.* 1944. Dell 66. My. VG. P1d. $11.00

WELLS, Anna Mary. *Wells, Carolyn.* 1944. Atlas Mystery. My. G+. P1d. $15.00

WELLS, Barry. *Day the Earth Caught Fire.* 1961. Ballantine F 602. PBO. MTI. SF. VG. B5d. $5.50

WELLS, Barry. *Day the Earth Caught Fire.* 1961. Ballantine F 602. 1st US edn. F. M1d. $12.00

WELLS, Charlie. *Last Kill.* 1955. Signet 1225. PBO. c/Maguire: gga. My. VG. P1d. $8.00

WELLS, Charlie. *Last Kill.* 1955. Signet 1225. 1st edn. c/Maguire: gga. My. F. F2d. $30.00

WELLS, Charlie. *Let the Night Cry.* 1954. Signet 1167. 1st pb. VG. M6d. $6.50

WELLS, George. *Three Bites of the Apple.* 1967. Popular 8035. PBO. MTI. VG+. B6d. $7.00

WELLS, H.G. *Empire of the Ants.* 1977. Scholastic 3298. SF. VG. W2d. $3.75

WELLS, H.G. *First Man in the Moon.* 1964. Ballantine U 2232. 3rd prtg. SF. VG. W2d. $4.00

WELLS, H.G. *First Men in the Moon.* 1965. Airmont CL 78. F. P9d. $2.00

WELLS, H.G. *First Men in the Moon.* Ballantine F 687. SF. VG. B5d. $4.00

WELLS, H.G. *First Men in the Moon.* 1967. Berkley F 1398. 1st prtg. SF. VG. R5d. $1.50

WELLS, H.G. *First Men in the Moon.* 1947. Dell 201. c/E Sherwan. SF. G+. B5d/R5d. $7.50

WELLS, H.G. *First Men in the Moon.* 1947. Dell 201. SF. VG+. B4d. $15.00

WELLS, H.G. *First Men in the Moon.* 1947. Dell 201. VG. I1d. $10.00

WELLS, H.G. *First Men in the Moon.* 1947. Dell 201. 1st pb edn. F. M1d. $25.00

WELLS, H.G. *Food of the Gods.* 1963. Ballantine F 725. SF. VG. W2d. $4.50

WELLS, H.G. *Food of the Gods.* 1963. Ballantine 725. 1st prtg. F. F2d. $6.00

WELLS, H.G. *Food of the Gods.* 1964. Popular SP 286. SF. VG+. B4d. $3.00

WELLS, H.G. *Inexperienced Ghost/The New Accelerator.* Vall Pr Ltd. SF. VG+. W2d. $15.00

WELLS, H.G. *Invisible Man.* 1964. Airmont CL 40. SF. VG. B5d. $2.50

WELLS, H.G. *Invisible Man.* 1949. Dell 269. 1st prtg. SF. F. F2d. $20.00

WELLS, H.G. *Invisible Man.* 1956. Pocket 1140. c/R Korn. SF. G+. B5d. $5.00

WELLS, H.G. *Invisible Man.* 1956. Pocket 1140. SF. G. G5d. $4.00

WELLS, H.G. *Invisible Man.* 1956. Pocket 1140. VG+. I1d. $10.00

WELLS, H.G. *Invisible Man.* 1956. Pocket 1140. 1st edn. NF. M1d. $15.00

WELLS, H.G. *Invisible Man.* 1963. Scholastic 540. 1st prtg. SF. F. W2d. $5.00

WELLS, H.G. *Island of Dr Moreau.* Airmont CL 110. SF. F. W2d. $5.00

WELLS, H.G. *Island of Dr Moreau.* 1978. Scholastic 3979. SF. F. W2d. $4.50

WELLS, H.G. *Island of Dr Moreau.* 1977. Signet Y 7495. SF. VG+. W2d. $3.50

WELLS, H.G. *Star Begotten.* Manor 95394. 3rd edn. F. P9d. $2.50

WELLS, H.G. *Time Machine.* 1964. Airmont CL 44. 1st prtg. SF. VG. R5d. $1.50

WELLS, H.G. *Time Machine.* 1960. Berkley G445. 2nd edn. MTI. c/R Powers & R Taylor. SF. VG+. B5d. $5.00

WELLS, H.G. *Time Machine.* 1957. Berkley 380. c/R Powers. SF. VG+. B5d. $4.50

WELLS, H.G. *Time Machine.* 1957. Berkley 380. VG. B3d. $3.50

WELLS, H.G. *Time Machine/War of the Worlds.* 1968. Premier M 491. SF. VG. B5d. $3.00

WELLS, H.G. *Truth About Pyecraft/The Magic Shop/The Valley of Spiders.* Vall Press Ltd. SF. VG. W2d. $12.50

WELLS, H.G. *War of the Worlds.* Lancer 13410. SF. F. W2d. $4.00

WELLS, H.G. *War of the Worlds.* 1953. Pocket 947. VG+. I1d. $12.00

WELLS, H.G. *War of the Worlds.* 1953. Pocket 947. 1st edn. F. M1d. $20.00

WELLS, H.G. *War of the Worlds.* 1968. Scholastic T 1118. 3rd edn. SF. VG+. B5d. $3.00

WELLS, H.G. *War of the Worlds.* 1974. Scholastic 1030. 6th prtg. SF. VG. W2d. $3.00

WELLS, H.G. *When the Sleeper Wakes.* 1959. Ace D 388. 1st edn. PBO. VG. P9d. $1.75

WELLS, L.E. *Devil's Range.* Berkley G 1314. VG. B3d. $4.00

WELLS, L.E. *Naked Land.* Avon T 378. PBO. VG+. B3d. $4.50

WELLS, Michael. *Captives.* 1961. Hillman 186. 1st prtg. PBO. c/Copeland: gga. VG. P7d. $5.00

WELLS, Michael. *Roving Eye.* 1957. Ace D 243. VG. B3d. $6.00

WELLS, Robert. *Candle in the Sun.* 1971. Berkley S 2016. SF. VG+. B5d. $4.00

WELLS, William K. *Chaos.* 1987. TOR 51045. Th. F. P1d. $5.00

WELLSLEY, Julie. *Climb the Dark Mountain.* Lancer 73882. Go. VG. P1d. $3.50

WELTY, Eudora. *Ponder Heart.* Dell 887. c/J Krush. Fi. VG. B5d. $3.00

WENTWORTH, Patricia. *Alington Inheritance.* 1979. Coronet 24171. My. VG. P1d. $4.00

WENTWORTH, Patricia. *Benevent Treasure.* 1966. Pyramid X 1511. My. VG+. P1d. $8.00

WENTWORTH, Patricia. *Blind Side.* 1945. Popular 66. My. G+. P1d. $7.50

WENTWORTH, Patricia. *Blind Side.* 1945. Popular 66. VG. B3d. $8.00

WENTWORTH, Patricia. *Brading Collection.* 1975. Coronet 12361. 2nd edn. My. VG. P1d. $4.00

WENTWORTH, Patricia. *Brading Collection.* 1969. Pyramid T 2096. 2nd edn. My. VG. P1d. $3.50

WENTWORTH, Patricia. *Case Is Closed.* Detective Novel 4. VG. B3d. $4.50

WENTWORTH, Patricia. *Case of William Smith.* 1949. White Circle CD 423. My. G. P1d. $5.00

WENTWORTH, Patricia. *Catherine Wheel.* 1967. Pyramid X 1656. My. G+. P1d. $3.50

WENTWORTH, Patricia. *Chinese Shawl.* 1976. Coronet 10899. 4th edn. My. VG. P1d. $4.00

WENTWORTH, Patricia. *Chinese Shawl.* 1952. Hodder & Stoughton C 116. My. G+. P1d. $8.00

WENTWORTH, Patricia. *Clock Strikes Twelve.* 1974. Coronet 17832. 2nd edn. My. VG+. P1d. $4.00

WENTWORTH, Patricia. *Clock Strikes Twelve.* Popular 131. VG+. B3d. $5.00

WENTWORTH, Patricia. *Dark Threat (Pilgrim's Rest).* 1951. Popular 382. VG+. G5d. $25.00

WENTWORTH, Patricia. *Dark Threat.* 1951. Popular 382. 1st edn. PBO. c/Belarski: gga. NF. B6a #75. $40.00

WENTWORTH, Patricia. *Dead or Alive.* 1943. Dell 2. My. VG. P1d. $50.00

WENTWORTH, Patricia. *Death at Deep End.* 1963. Pyramid R 932. My. VG. P1d. $6.00

WENTWORTH, Patricia. *Fingerprint.* 1974. Coronet 18775. 2nd edn. My. VG. P1d. $4.00

WENTWORTH, Patricia. *Fingerprint.* 1962. Hodder & Stoughton 548. My. VG. P1d. $6.50

WENTWORTH, Patricia. *Fingerprint.* 1966. Pyramid X 1514. 2nd edn. My. VG. P1d. $4.50

WENTWORTH, Patricia. *Grey Mask.* 1952. Pan 218. My. G+. P1d. $6.50

WENTWORTH, Patricia. *In the Balance.* 1944. Popular 39. 1st prtg. c/Hoffman: gga. VG+. P7d. $17.50

WENTWORTH, Patricia. *Ivory Dagger.* 1975. Coronet 10520. 2nd edn. My. VG. P1d. $4.00

WENTWORTH, Patricia. *Key.* 1984. Coronet 02715. 4th edn. My. VG. P1d. $3.00

WENTWORTH, Patricia. *Latter End.* 1979. Coronet 24515. My. VG. P1d. $4.00

WENTWORTH, Patricia. *Listening Eye.* 1977. Coronet 21794. My. VG. P1d. $4.00

WENTWORTH, Patricia. *Lonesome Road.* 1951. Popular 333. My. F. P1d. $25.00

WENTWORTH, Patricia. *Lonesome Road.* 1951. Popular 333. 1st edn. PBO. c/Belarski: gga. NF. B6a #75. $40.25

WENTWORTH, Patricia. *Miss Silver Comes To Stay.* 1972. Coronet 15951. My. VG. P1d. $4.00

WENTWORTH, Patricia. *Miss Silver Comes To Stay.* Pan G 122. VG. B3d. $6.00

WENTWORTH, Patricia. *Out of the Past.* 1971. Berkley S 2027. My. VG. P1d. $4.00

WENTWORTH, Patricia. *Pilgrim's Rest.* 1981. Coronet 25357. 2nd edn. My. VG. P1d. $4.00

WENTWORTH, Patricia. *Poison in the Pen.* 1985. Bantam 25067. 3rd. edn. My. VG. P1d. $3.00

WENTWORTH, Patricia. *Rolling Stone.* 1946. Popular 79. My. G+. P1d. $10.00

WENTWORTH, Patricia. *Rolling Stone.* 1946. Popular 79. PBO. G. G5d. $9.00

WENTWORTH, Patricia. *Rolling Stone.* 1946. Popular 79. 1st pb. c/Hoffman. My. VG. B6d. $12.50

WENTWORTH, Patricia. *Silence in Court.* 1950. Popular 283. G+. I1d. $5.00

WENTWORTH, Patricia. *Silent Pool.* 1976. Coronet 20047. 2nd edn. My. VG+. P1d. $4.00

WENTWORTH, Patricia. *Spotlight.* 1979. Coronet 17833. 3rd edn. My. VG. P1d. $4.50

WENTWORTH, Patricia. *Through the Wall.* 1973. Pyramid N 3118. 2nd edn. My. VG. P1d. $3.25

WENTWORTH, Patricia. *Watersplash.* 1973. Coronet 15950. 3rd edn. My. VG. P1d. $4.00

WENZEL & WOHL. *How To Make a Good Airline Stewardess.* 1972. Gold Medal M 2645. 1st prtg. c/Wenzel: gga. VG+. P7d. $6.00

WENZEL & WOHL. *How To Make a Good Airline Stewardess.* 1972. Gold Medal 2645. 1st edn. c/Wenzel. F. F2d. $10.00

WERNER, George. *One Helluva Blow.* 1964. Gold Star IL 7-27. My. VG+. P1d. $10.00

WERPER, Barton. *Tarzan & the Abominable Snowman.* 1965. Gold Star IL 7-60. SF. F. W2d. $25.00

WERPER, Barton. *Tarzan & the Silver Globe.* 1964. Gold Star IL 7-42. SF. F. W2d. $25.00

WERPER, Barton. *Tarzan & the Snake People.* 1964. Gold Star IL 7-54. SF. F. W2d. $25.00

WERPER, Barton. *Tarzan & the Snake People.* 1964. Gold Star IL 7-54. SF. VG+. B4d. $20.00

WERPER, Barton. *Tarzan & the Snake People.* 1964. Gold Star IL 7-54. 1st prtg. PBO. VG. P7d. $12.50

WERRY, Richard R. *Hammer Me Home.* 1956. Bantam 1506. My. VG. P1d. $8.00

WERSTEIN, Irving. *July, 1863.* 1958. Ace D 325. VG. I1d. $3.00

WERTHAM, Fredric. *Circle of Guilt.* 1961. Four Square 370. c/Mortlemans. VG. B3d. $8.00

WERTHAM, Fredric. *Show of Violence.* 1967. Bantam N 3567. Nfi. VG. P1d. $5.00

WERTHAM, Fredric. *Sign for Cain.* 1969. PB Library 65-033. Nfi. VG+. P6d. $5.00

WESCOTT, Glenway. *Apartment in Athens.* 1947. Bantam 87. My. F. P1d. $20.00

WESLEY, A.D. *Village Madness.* Bedside 963. VG. B3d. $4.00

WEST, Ben. *Loves of a Girl Wrestler.* 1952. Uni-Books 32. PBO. c/Ed Chan: gga. VG. P6d. $7.50

WEST, Edwin. *Brother & Sister.* 1965. Monarch 497. c/Harry Schaare: gga. VG. P6d. $4.25

WEST, Edwin. *Campus Doll.* 1961. Monarch 189. PBO. c/Miller: gga. VG. B6a #77. $30.25

WEST, Edwin. *Wild.* 1962. Zodiac Books ZB 102. VG+. B3a. $51.30

WEST, Elliot. *Man Running.* 1967. Ace K 116. My. VG. P1d. $5.00

WEST, Gloria. *Of Sex & Flesh.* 1968. Saber SA 134. PBO. c/gga. VG+. B6a #76. $37.00

WEST, J. *Friendly Persuasion.* Hodder & Stoughton C 272. 2nd prtg. MTI. c/Gary Cooper. VG+. B3d. $8.00

WEST, John B. *An Eye for an Eye.* 1959. Signet 1642. De. G+. P1d. $7.50

WEST, John B. *Bullets Are My Business.* 1960. Signet S 1852. De. VG. P1d. $12.50

WEST, John B. *Cobra Venom.* 1960. Signet 1755. De. VG+. P1d. $15.00

WEST, John B. *Death on the Rocks.* 1961. Signet S 1883. c/gga. My. VG. B4d. $4.00

WEST, John B. *Never Kill a Cop.* 1961. Signet S 1929. My. G+. P1d. $7.50

WEST, John B. *Taste for Blood.* 1960. Signet S 1800. De. F. P1d. $20.00

WEST, John B. *Taste for Blood.* 1960. Signet S 1800. 1st prtg. c/Barye: gga. VG. P7d. $5.00

WEST, K. *Showdown at Gila Bend.* 1963. Berkley G 836. NF. B3d. $5.00

WEST, Lindsay. *Empire of the Ants.* 1977. Ace 20560. MTI. SF. VG+. W2d. $4.25

WEST, Mae. *Goodness Had Nothing To Do With It.* 1959. Avon G 1047. c/M West. Nfi. VG. B5d. $3.00

WEST, Mae. *Goodness Had Nothing to Do With It.* 1959. Avon G 1047. VG+. I1d. $4.00

WEST, Mae. *Goodness Had Nothing To Do With It.* 1970. MacFadden 95-147. 1st prtg. Auto. G+. R5d. $2.00

WEST, Mae. *Pleasure Man.* 1975. Dell 07074. 1st prtg. c/Mae West. VG+. P7d. $4.50

WEST, Mark. *His Boss's Wife.* 1964. Beacon B 768X. 2nd edn. c/V Olson. Ad. VG. B5d. $4.50

WEST, Mark. *Office Affair.* 1961. Beacon B 421Y. PBO. Ad. VG. B5d. $6.50

WEST, Morris L. *Ambassador.* 1966. Dell 0097. My. VG. P1d. $5.50

WEST, Morris L. *Backlash.* 1959. Perma M 4155. My. VG. P1d. $7.00

WEST, Morris L. *Crooked Road.* 1962. Dell F 178. 1st prtg. My. VG+. R5d. $3.25

WEST, Morris L. *Daughter of Silence.* 1965. Dell 1673. 6th edn. My. VG. P1d. $4.50

WEST, Morris L. *Devil's Advocate.* 1960. Dell S 15. Fi. VG. P1d. $7.00

WEST, Morris L. *Harlequin.* 1975. Pocket 80086. My. VG. P1d. $3.50

WEST, Morris L. *Second Victory.* 1967. Dell 7699. My. VG. P1d. $5.00

WEST, Morris L. *Shoes of the Fisherman.* 1964. Dell 7833. Fi. VG. P1d. $6.00

WEST, Natalie. *Girls in Publishing.* 1974. Ace 28896. 1st edn. c/gga. F. F2d. $5.00

WEST, Nathaniel. *Day of the Locust.* 1957. Bantam A 1704. 1st pb edn. F. M1d. $8.00

WEST, Nathaniel. *Day of the Locust.* 1953. Bantam 1093. VG. B3d. $4.00

WEST, Nathaniel. *Miss Lonelyhearts.* 1959. Avon T 634. Fi. G+. B5d. $2.50

WEST, Nathaniel. *Miss Lonelyhearts.* 1959. Avon T 634. VG. B3d. $4.00

WEST, Token. *Why Get Married?* 1949. Red Circle 12. 1st edn. PBO. c/Altson. scarce. VG+. B6a #80. $59.00

WEST, Tom. *Bucking for Boot Hill.* 1970. Ace 08360. 1st edn. We. F. F2d. $8.00

WEST, Tom. *Buzzard's Nest.* 1962. Ace F 128. We. VG. P1d. $8.00

WEST, Tom. *Outlaw Brand.* 1956. Pyramid 216. PBO. c/Prezio. We. VG+. B6d. $9.00

WEST, Tom. *Toughest Town in the Territory.* 1965. Ace M 118. We. VG+. B4d. $2.25

WEST, Wallace. *Bird of Time.* 1961. Ace F 114. SF. VG. B5d. $4.00

WEST, Wallace. *Bird of Time.* 1961. Ace F 114. 1st pb. SF. NF. M1d. $8.00

WEST, Wallace. *Lords of Atlantis.* 1963. Airmont SF 3. SF. VG+. W2d. $5.25

WEST, Wallace. *Lords of Atlantis.* 1963. Airmont SF 3. 1st pb edn. F. M1d. $10.00

WEST, Wallace. *Memory Bank.* 1962. Airmont SF 1. SF. VG+. B4d. $5.00

WEST/WHITTINGTON. *Dead Man's Double Cross/Wild Sky.* 1962. Ace F 148. We. NF. B6d. $18.00

WEST/WYNNE. *Triggering Texan/Big Snow.* 1963. Ace F 200. We. VG. B5d. $4.50

WESTCOTT, E.N. *David Harum.* 1946. Bantam 41. F. I1d. $6.00

WESTCOTT, Glenway. *Apartment in Athens.* 1947. Bantam 87. Fa. NF. B4d. $9.00

WESTCOTT, Jan. *Border Lord.* 1954. Cardinal C 136. 1st prtg. c/Hulings: gga. VG+. P7d. $4.00

WESTCOTT, Jan. *Border Lord.* 1950. Dell 439. G+. I1d. $3.00

WESTCOTT, Jan. *Captain for Elizabeth.* 1952. Graphic G 101. c/Barye. VG+. B3d. $5.00

WESTCOTT, Jan. *Captain for Elizabeth.* 1952. Harlequin 164. 2nd prtg. VG. B3d. $4.00

WESTHEIMER, David. *Day Into Night.* 1952. Popular 395. Fi. F. P1d. $18.00

WESTHEIMER, David. *Tillie.* 1952. Pyramid G 52. Fi. G+. P1d. $6.50

WESTHEIMER, David. *Von Ryan's Express.* 1965. Signet T 2566. MTI. VG+. B4d. $3.00

WESTLAKE, Donald E. *Adios, Scheherazade.* 1971. Signet Q 4802. Fi. VG. P1d. $7.50

WESTLAKE, Donald E. *Bank Shot.* 1974. Pocket 77643. 5th prtg. VG. R5d. $2.00

WESTLAKE, Donald E. *Busy Body.* 1971. Ballantine 02440. My. F. P1d. $7.50

WESTLAKE, Donald E. *Busy Body.* 1967. Lancer 73-591. My. F. P1d. $10.00

WESTLAKE, Donald E. *Busy Body.* 1967. Penguin C 2718. My. VG. P1d. $7.50

WESTLAKE, Donald E. *China Tramp.* 1962. Corinth MR 459. 1st edn. c/gga. My. F. F2d. $20.00

WESTLAKE, Donald E. *Cops & Robbers.* 1973. Coronet 17839. My. VG. P1d. $5.00

WESTLAKE, Donald E. *Fugitive Pigeon.* 1971. Ballantine 02458. My. G+. P1d. $5.00

WESTLAKE, Donald E. *God Save the Mark.* 1968. Signet T 3625. 1st prtg. VG+. P7d. $6.00

WESTLAKE, Donald E. *Help! I Am Being Held Prisoner.* 1975. Ballantine 24426. My. VG. P1d. $7.50

WESTLAKE, Donald E. *I Gave at the Office.* 1972. Pocket 77504. My. G+. P1d. $3.50

WESTLAKE, Donald E. *Killing Time.* 1972. Ballantine 02604. My. VG. P1d. $5.00

WESTLAKE, Donald E. *Operator.* 1964. Dell 6698. 1st prtg. c/Engle: gga. VG. P7d. $4.00

WESTLAKE, Donald E. *Spy in the Ointment.* 1972. Ballantine 02603. My. F. P1d. $7.50

WESTLAKE, Donald E. *Spy in the Ointment.* 1972. Ballantine 02603. 1st prtg. VG. P7d. $4.00

WESTLAKE, Donald E. *Spy in the Ointment.* 1967. Lancer 73-657. 1st prtg. VG. P7d. $5.00

WESTLAKE, Donald E. *Two Much.* 1976. Crest X 2750. My. VG. P1d. $5.00

WESTLAKE, Donald F. *Curious Facts Preceding My Execution.* Ballantine 03307. VG. G5d. $12.00

WESTLAKE, Donald. *Black Ice Score.* 1968. Gold Medal 1949. 1st edn. My. F. F2d. $15.00

WESTLAKE, Donald. *Handle.* 1966. Pocket 50220. 1st edn. My. NF. F2d. $15.00

WESTLAKE, Donald. *Jugger.* 1965. Pocket 50149. 1st edn. My. F. F2d. $15.00

WESTLAKE, Donald. *Man With the Getaway Face.* 1963. Pocket 6180. 1st edn. My. VG+. F2d. $10.00

WESTLAKE, Donald. *Smashers.* 1962. Dell F 176. 1st edn. PBO. My. F. F2d. $12.00

WESTLAKE, Donald. *Sour Lemon Score.* 1969. Gold Medal 2037. 1st edn. c/gga. My. F. F2d. $15.00

WESTLAKE, Tucker Coe. *Kinds of Love, Kinds of Death.* Charter 44467. 1st pb? VG. M6d. $4.50

WESTLEY, Kirk. *Shanty Boat Girl.* Berkley G 260. c/gga. VG. B6a #77. $49.50

WESTLEY, Kirk. *Shanty Boat Girl.* Cameo Digest 361. c/Whittington: gga. VG. B6a #77. $48.50

WESTLEY, Kirk. *Shanty Boat Girl.* MacFadden 60-282. c/gga. F. B6a #80. $33.00

WESTMACOTT, Mary. *Rose & the Yew Tree.* 1964. Dell 7503. 1st prtg. My. VG. R5d. $2.00

WESTMACOTT, Mary. *Unfinished Portrait.* 1964. Dell 9217. 1st prtg. My. VG+. R5d. $2.50

WESTON, C. *Dark Wood.* Bantam 723. VG. B3d. $4.50

WESTON, Charlton. *Reluctant Husband.* 1973. Liverpool TNS 551. Ad. VG. B5d. $3.50

WESTON, Garnett. *Hidden Portal.* Harlequin 125. G. G5d. $2.50

WESTON, Garnett. *Poldrate Street.* 1950. Harlequin 48. My. G+. P1d. $10.00

WESTON, George. *His First Million Women.* 1952. Avon 396. 1st pb edn. VG. M1d. $15.00

WESTON, J. *Jolly.* Doll 4249. c/McGinnis. VG+. B3d. $4.50

WESTON, J. *Never Sleep Alone.* Spicy Library. VG+. B3d. $4.50

WESTON, Paul B. *Muscle on Broadway.* 1962. Regency RB 117. Nfi. F. P1d. $30.00

WETHERELL, June. *Glorious Three.* 1952. Popular G 109. c/gga. Fa. VG+. B4d. $7.00

WETHERELL, June. *Mahogany House.* 1967. Lancer 73-692. My. VG. P1d. $5.00

WEVERKA, Robert. *Circle of Iron.* 1979. Warner 89-928. Hi. VG. P1d. $4.00

WEVERKA, Robert. *Easter Story.* 1976. Bantam Q 2411. TVTI. VG+. P1d. $7.50

WEVERKA, Robert. *March or Die!* 1977. Bantam 11261. 1st edn. Av. F. F2d. $8.00

WEVERKA, Robert. *Moonrock.* 1973. Bantam N 8306. My/SF. VG. P1d. $6.00

WEVERKA, Robert. *Sting.* 1974. Bantam. 1st edn. MTI. My. F. F2d. $10.00

WEYMOUTH, Anthony. *Tempt Me Not.* 1952. Pocket (British) B 47. My. G+. P1d. $10.00

WHEATLEY, Dennis. *Bill for the Use of a Body.* 1975. Arrow 905940. 4th edn. My. VG. P1d. $4.00

WHEATLEY, Dennis. *Black August.* 1975. Arrow 911150. 6th edn. My/SF. VG. P1d. $4.00

WHEATLEY, Dennis. *Codeword -- Golden Fleece.* 1961. Arrow 622. My. VG. P1d. $6.50

WHEATLEY, Dennis. *Come Into My Parlour.* 1960. Arrow 578. My. VG. P1d. $7.00

WHEATLEY, Dennis. *Come Into My Parlour.* 1960. Arrow 578. VG+. B3d. $8.00

WHEATLEY, Dennis. *Contraband.* 1966. Arrow 582. 2nd edn. My. VG. P1d. $4.50

WHEATLEY, Dennis. *Dark Secret of Josephine.* 1961. Arrow 599. Hi. G+. P1d. $4.50

WHEATLEY, Dennis. *Desperate Measures.* 1976. Arrow 912850. My. VG. P1d. $4.00

WHEATLEY, Dennis. *Eunich of Stamboul.* 1967. PB Library 54-552. Fi. VG+. B5d. $4.00

WHEATLEY, Dennis. *Evil in a Mask.* 1971. Arrow 464. My. VG. P1d. $4.00

WHEATLEY, Dennis. *Fabulous Valley.* 1959. Arrow 284. 4th edn. My. VG. P1d. $6.00

WHEATLEY, Dennis. *Forbidden Territory.* 1973. Ballantine 03305. My. VG. P1d. $3.50

WHEATLEY, Dennis. *Forbidden Territory.* 1946. LJUS Crime Library 53. dust jacket. My. VG. P1d. $25.00

WHEATLEY, Dennis. *Gateway to Hell.* 1973. Ballantine 23550. 1st prtg. SF. VG. R5d. $4.00

WHEATLEY, Dennis. *Gunmen, Gallants & Ghosts.* 1963. Arrow 691. My/SF. VG. P1d. $7.50

WHEATLEY, Dennis. *Haunting of Toby Jugg.* 1961. Arrow 543. 2nd edn. Ho. VG+. P1d. $10.00

WHEATLEY, Dennis. *Island Where Time Stands Still.* 1964. Arrow 563. 2nd edn. My/SF. VG+. P1d. $7.50

WHEATLEY, Dennis. *Ka of Gifford Hillary.* 1964. Arrow 583. 3rd edn. My/SF. VG. P1d. $5.00

WHEATLEY, Dennis. *Launching of Roger Brook.* 1966. Arrow 455. 5th edn. My. VG. P1d. $4.50

WHEATLEY, Dennis. *Mayhem in Greece.* 1968. Arrow 758. 3rd edn. My. VG. P1d. $4.00

WHEATLEY, Dennis. *Old Rowley.* 1962. Arrow 680. Nfi. VG. P1d. $7.50

WHEATLEY, Dennis. *Quest of Julian Day.* 1963. Arrow 632. 2nd edn. My. G+. P1d. $3.50

WHEATLEY, Dennis. *Ravishing of Lady Mary Ware.* 1975. Arrow 907220. My. VG. P1d. $4.00

WHEATLEY, Dennis. *Satanist.* Arrow 653. 4th prtg. VG+. B3d. $7.00

WHEATLEY, Dennis. *Scarlet Imposter.* 1973. Ballantine 03258. My. VG. P1d. $3.50

WHEATLEY, Dennis. *Secret War.* 1961. Arrow 336. 4th edn. My. VG. P1d. $5.50

WHEATLEY, Dennis. *Shadow of Tyburn Tree.* 1958. Arrow 465. 2nd edn. My. G+. P1d. $4.50

WHEATLEY, Dennis. *Star of Ill-Omen.* 1965. Arrow 378. SF. VG. P1d. $5.50

WHEATLEY, Dennis. *Strange Conflict.* 1959. Arrow 549. Ho. F. P1d. $17.50

WHEATLEY, Dennis. *Strange Story of Linda Lee.* 1974. Arrow 908830. My. VG. P1d. $4.50

WHEATLEY, Dennis. *Such Power Is Dangerous.* 1965. Arrow 628. 3rd edn. My. VG. P1d. $4.50

WHEATLEY, Dennis. *Sultan's Daughter.* 1970. Arrow 345. Hi. VG. P1d. $4.50

WHEATLEY, Dennis. *Sword of Fate.* 1954. Arrow 363. My. G+. P1d. $6.00

WHEATLEY, Dennis. *They Found Atlantis.* 1972. Edito-Service. SF. F. P1d. $7.50

WHEATLEY, Dennis. *Three Inquisitive People.* 1960. Arrow 581. My. VG. P1d. $7.00

WHEATLEY, Dennis. *Traitor's Gate.* 1966. Arrow 594. My. VG. P1d. $5.50

WHEATLEY, Dennis. *Unholy Crusade.* 1975. Arrow 910470. SF. VG. P1d. $4.50

WHEELER, Elmer. *Fat Boy's Book.* 1953. Avon 517. VG. B3d. $3.50

WHEELER, Keith. *Reef.* 1952. Popular 403. 1st prtg. c/gga. VG. P7d. $5.00

WHEELER, Paul. *And the Bullets Were Made of Lead.* 1970. Arrow 295. My. VG. P1d. $4.50

WHELAN, Russell. *Flying Tigers.* 1968. PB Library 54-672. 1st pb. c/Peter Caras. NF. B6d. $7.00

WHELTON, Paul. *Call the Lady Indiscreet.* 1949. Graphic 17. G. G5d. $3.00

WHELTON, Paul. *Call the Lady Indiscreet.* 1949. Graphic 17. My. VG. P1d. $10.00

WHELTON, Paul. *Call the Lady Indiscreet.* 1954. Graphic 95. 2nd prtg. VG. B3d. $6.00

WHELTON, Paul. *Death & the Devil.* 1946. Pony 63. G+. G5d. $3.50

WHELTON, Paul. *Death & the Devil.* 1946. Pony 63. My. F. P1d. $21.00

WHELTON, Paul. *Flash-Hold for Murder.* 1949. Graphic 13. G+. G5d. $4.00

WHELTON, Paul. *In Comes Death.* 1952. Graphic 49. G. G5d. $3.00

WHELTON, Paul. *In Comes Death.* 1952. Graphic 49. VG. I1d. $6.00

WHELTON, Paul. *Lures of Death.* 1950. Graphic 19. My. VG. P1d. $10.00

WHELTON, Paul. *Pardon My Blood.* 1951. Graphic 37. G+. G5d. $3.75

WHELTON, Paul. *Pardon My Blood.* 1951. Graphic 37. My. VG. P1d. $10.00

WHELTON, Paul. *Uninvited Corpse.* 1950. Graphic 24. My. G+. P1d. $7.00

WHIPPLE, Chandler. *Lt John F Kennedy: Expendable.* 1962. Beacon-Envoy 107F. PBO. Nfi. VG. B5d. $5.00

WHITAKER, David. *Doctor Who: The Daleks.* 1967. Avon G 1322. VG. P9d. $2.00

WHITCOMB, Catherine. *No Narrow Path.* 1951. Popular 379. c/Belarski. VG+. B3d. $6.50

WHITE, A.S. *Northwest Crossing.* Superior Books. c/gunfight. VG. B3d. $6.00

WHITE, Alice N. *Dirge for a Lady.* 1968. Lancer 73-718. Go. G+. P1d. $3.50

WHITE, B. *Teen-Age Dance Book.* Perma M 5071. VG+. B3d. $5.00

WHITE, Charlene. *Mask of Evil.* 1966. First Niter 226. PBO. VG. B6a #77. $61.00

WHITE, Daniel. *Southern Daughter.* 1953. Avon 547. VG. B3d. $3.50

WHITE, Daniel. *Southern Daughter.* 1956. Avon 750. VG. B3d. $4.00

WHITE, Daniel. *Southern Daughter.* 1960. Avon 870. VG+. I1d. $4.00

WHITE, Ethel Lina. *Fear Stalks the Village.* 1966. PB Library 53-336. Go. VG. G5d/P1d. $5.50

WHITE, Ethel Lina. *Her Heart in Her Throat.* 1945. Popular 54. G+. G5d. $9.00

WHITE, Ethel Lina. *Lady Vanishes.* 1962. Fontana 721. My. VG+. P1d. $9.50

WHITE, Ethel Lina. *Man Who Was Not There.* 1967. PB Library 53-407. My. F. P1d. $10.00

WHITE, Ethel Lina. *Man Who Was Not There.* 1946. White Circle 259. My. VG. P1d. $10.50

WHITE, Ethel Lina. *Put Out the Light.* 1946. Penguin (US) 598. My. G. P1d. $5.00

WHITE, Ethel Lina. *She Faded Into Air.* 1946. Popular 75. My. VG. I1d. $8.00

WHITE, Ethel Lina. *Spiral Staircase.* 1947. Popular 120. G+. G5d. $8.00

WHITE, Ethel Lina. *Spiral Staircase.* 1947. Popular 120. VG+. G5d. $15.00

WHITE, Ethel Lina. *Spiral Staircase.* 1947. Popular 120. 1st pb. MTI. My. VG. B6d. $12.50

WHITE, Ethel Lina. *Step in the Dark.* 1966. PB Library 52-988. Go. F. P1d. $11.00

WHITE, Ethel Lina. *Third Eye.* 1944. Popular 15. Ho. F. F2d. $25.00

WHITE, Ethel Lina. *Unseen.* 1966. PB Library 52-351. My. VG. P1d. $5.50

WHITE, Ethel Lina. *Wax.* 1967. PB Library 53-423. My. VG. P1d. $5.00

WHITE, Ethel Lina. *Wheel Spins.* 1955. Penguin 1104. My. VG. P1d. $8.00

WHITE, Ethel Lina. *Wheel Spins.* 1944. Popular 32. G+. G5d. $7.00

WHITE, Ethel Lina. *While She Sleeps!* Best seller Mystery B 77. My. VG+. P1d. $18.50

WHITE, Ethel Lina. *While She Sleeps!* 1966. PB Library 52-974. 2nd edn. My. F. P1d. $11.00

WHITE, Ethel Lina. *Third Eye.* 1944. Popular 15. c/Hoffman. VG+. B3a #21. $208.00

WHITE, Harry, *Shadow at Noon.* 1955. Pyramid 169. We. VG+. P1d. $20.00

WHITE, James. *All Judgment Fled.* 1979. Ballantine 28025. 2nd edn. c/W Barlowe. SF. VG+. B5d. $3.50

WHITE, James. *Deadly Litter.* 1964. Ballantine U 2224. PBO. VG+. B3d. $4.50

WHITE, James. *Deadly Litter.* 1964. Ballantine U 2224. 1st edn. F. M1d. $9.00

WHITE, James. *Escape Orbit.* Ace F 317. NF. M1d. $7.00

WHITE, James. *Escape Orbit.* 1965. Ace F 317. 1st prtg. SF. VG. R5d. $2.50

WHITE, James. *Grass Is Greener.* Ace H 437. MTI. VG. B3d. $5.00

WHITE, James. *Hospital Station.* 1962. Ballantine F 595. PBO. SF. VG. B5d. $5.00

WHITE, James. *Hospital Station.* 1962. Ballantine F 595. 1st edn. NF. M1d. $9.00

WHITE, James. *Monsters & Medics.* 1977. Ballantine 25623. 1st prtg. SF. VG. R5d. $2.25

WHITE, James. *Secret Visitors.* 1967. Ace G 675. 2nd edn. NF. P9d. $2.00

WHITE, James. *Spoletta Story.* 1957. Pan 422. My. VG. P1d. $7.50

WHITE, James. *Star Surgeon.* 1963. Ballantine F 709. 1st edn. VG. M1d. $8.00

WHITE, James. *Star Surgeon.* 1963. Ballantine F 709. 1st prtg. SF. G+. R5d. $2.75

WHITE, James. *Sweet Evil.* 1970. Arrow 273. 2nd edn. My. VG. P1d. $4.00

WHITE, James. *Watch Below.* 1966. Ballantine U 2285. PBO. VG. B3d. $4.50

WHITE, James. *Watch Below.* 1966. Ballantine U 2285. 1st edn. F. M1d. $8.00

WHITE, Jon Manchip. *Last Race.* 1954. Pocket 1016. Fi. VG. P1d. $8.50

WHITE, Jon Manchip. *Mercenaries.* 1979. Major 3248. My. VG. P1d. $3.50

WHITE, L. *House Next Door.* Signet 1442. VG. B3d. $4.00

WHITE, Leslie Turner. *Highland Hawk.* 1953. Pocket 974. c/G Mayers. Fi. G+. B5d. $3.00

WHITE, Leslie Turner. *Log Jam.* 1961. Ace D 494. 1st pb. NF. B6d. $15.00

WHITE, Leslie Turner. *Lord Johnnie.* Pocket 745. VG. I1d. $5.00

WHITE, Leslie Turner. *Sir Rogue.* 1955. Cardinal C 178. 1st prtg. c/Hulings: gga. VG. P7d. $4.50

WHITE, Leslie Turner. *Vice Squad.* Bestseller Mystery B 165. My. VG. P1d. $12.50

WHITE, Lionel. *Coffin for a Hood.* 1968. Gold Medal 775. My. F. P1d. $30.00

WHITE, Lionel. *Coffin for a Hood.* 1958. Gold Medal 775. My. VG+. B4d. $14.00

WHITE, Lionel. *Coffin for a Hood.* 1958. Gold Medal 775. PBO. c/Darcy. My. VG. B6d. $7.50

WHITE, Lionel. *Death Takes the Bus.* 1957. Gold Medal 663. PBO. VG. M6d. $7.50

WHITE, Lionel. *Flight Into Terror.* 1957. Signet 1378. c/R Maguire. My. VG. B5d. $5.50

WHITE, Lionel. *Flight Into Terror.* 1965. Tower 43-530. My. VG. P1d. $12.50

WHITE, Lionel. *Hijack.* 1969. MacFadden 75-248. My. VG. P1d. $10.00

WHITE, Lionel. *Hijack.* Manor 12347. VG. M6d. $5.00

WHITE, Lionel. *Hostage for a Hood.* 1957. Gold Medal 687. PBO. VG. B6d. $27.50

WHITE, Lionel. *House Next Door.* 1966. Lancer 72-128. My. VG. P1d. $10.00

WHITE, Lionel. *House Next Door.* 1957. Signet 1442. VG. G5d. $4.00

WHITE, Lionel. *Killing.* 1956. Signet 1310. 1st pb. MTI. c/Maguire: gga. VG. B3d. $7.00

WHITE, Lionel. *Killing.* Tower 42-431. VG. B3d. $4.50

WHITE, Lionel. *Love Trap.* 1955. Signet 1204. PBO. VG. P6d. $5.00

WHITE, Lionel. *Marilyn K.* 1960. Monarch 171. PBO. c/Schaare: gga. Cr. VG. P6d. $5.00

WHITE, Lionel. *Merriweather File.* 1961. Bantam A 2247. My. VG. P1d. $12.50

WHITE, Lionel. *Merriweather File.* 1961. Bantam A 2247. 1st prtg. My. G+. R5d. $1.75

WHITE, Lionel. *Mexico Run.* 1974. Gold Medal M 3152. My. F. P1d. $10.00

WHITE, Lionel. *Money Trap.* 1964. Monarch 477. My. VG. P1d. $12.50

WHITE, Lionel. *Murder Volume #1.* 1956. PBO. scarce. NF. B6a #74. $61.00

WHITE, Lionel. *Obsession.* 1963. Monarch 386. My. VG. P1d. $12.50

WHITE, Lionel. *Party to Murder.* 1966. Gold Medal D 1701. My. VG. P1d. $15.00

WHITE, Lionel. *Rafferty.* Bantam 2028. c/Zuckerberg. VG. B3d. $4.00

WHITE, Lionel. *Run, Killer, Run!* 1959. Avon T 361. My. VG+. P1d. $15.00

WHITE, Lionel. *Steal Big.* 1960. Gold Medal 998. 1st edn. c/gga. Cr. F. F2d. $15.00

WHITE, Lionel. *Time of Terror.* 1962. Ace F 155. My. F. P1d. $20.00

WHITE, Lionel. *To Find a Killer.* 1955. Signet 1241. My. VG. P1d. $20.00

WHITE, Lionel. *Too Young To Die.* 1958. Gold Medal 786. My. F. P1d. $35.00

WHITE, Max. *After Dark.* 1954. Pyramid 109. 1st pb. VG. B6d. $8.00

WHITE, Max. *Anna Becker.* Bantam 830. VG+. B3d. $4.50

WHITE, Milton. *Cry Down the Lonely Night.* 1854. Gold Medal 427. c/Barye. VG. B3d. $6.00

WHITE, Robb. *Jungle Fury.* 1956. Berkley G 16. 1st edn. PBO. c/gga. VG+. B6a #79. $44.00

WHITE, Stewart Edward. *Arizona Nights.* Hillman 43. VG+. B3d. $6.00

WHITE, Stewart Edward. *Killer.* 1943. Quick Reader 102. My. G+. P1d. $15.00

WHITE, Stewart Edward. *Long Rifle.* Dell D 147. c/buckskin shirt. VG+. B3d. $5.00

WHITE, T.H. *Book of Merlin.* 1978. Berkley 03826. SF. F. W2d. $3.25

WHITE, T.H. *Master.* Avon ZS 118. 1st prtg. VG. S1d. $3.50

WHITE, T.H. *Mistress Masham's Repose.* 1979. Berkley O4205 SF. VG+. B5d. $5.00

WHITE, T.H. *Mountain Road.* Pan X 53. MTI. VG. B3d. $7.00

WHITE, T.H. *Mountain Road.* 1960. Signet D 1793. 1st prtg. G+. R5d. $3.00

WHITE, T.H. *Once & Future King.* 1967. Berkley N 1320. 4th prtg. MTI. SF. G+. W2d. $3.00

WHITE, T.H. *Once & Future King.* 1961. Dell Y 001. 2nd prtg. VG. R5d. $1.50

WHITE, Ted. *Jewels of Elsewhen.* 1967. Belmont B 50-751. PBO. SF. VG. B5d. $4.50

WHITE, Ted. *Jewels of Elsewhen.* 1967. Belmont B 50-751. 1st edn. F. M1d. $12.00

WHITE, Ted. *Phoenix Prime.* 1966. Lancer 74-593. 1st edn. F. M1d. $8.00

WHITE, Ted. *Phoenix Prime.* 1966. Lancer 74-593. 1st prtg. VG+. S1d. $6.00

WHITE, Ted. *Secret of the Maurauder Satellite.* 1978. Berkley O 3888. SF. VG. B5d. $2.50

WHITE, Ted. *Sorceress of Qar.* 1966. Lancer 73-528. 1st edn. PBO. F. M1d. $8.00

WHITE, Ted. *Sorceress of Qar.* 1969. Lancer 74-592. c/S Stanweis. SF. VG+. B5d. $5.00

WHITE, Ted. *Spawn of the Death Machine.* 1968. PB Library 53680. SF. VG. W2d. $4.00

WHITE, Ted. *Star Wolf!* 1971. Lancer 75-252. PBO. c/Charles Moll. SF. F. M1d. $7.00

WHITE, Ted. *Star Wolf!* 1971. Lancer 75-252. 1st prtg. G. S1d. $2.00

WHITE, W.C. *Pale Blonde of Sands Street.* 1950. Popular 254. c/Earl Bergey: gga. VG. P6d. $12.00

WHITE, W.P. *Hidden Trails.* Thrilling Novel 32. VG. B3d. $4.50

WHITEHEAD, Don. *Border Guard.* 1964. Avon S 144. Nfi. VG. P1d. $6.00

WHITEHEAD, Don. *FBI Story.* 1958. Cardinal GC 45. Nfi. VG. P1d. $7.50

WHITEHEAD, Don. *Journey Into Crime.* 1961. Cardinal GC 110. Nfi. VG. P1d. $6.50

WHITFIELD, Raoul. *Green Ice Murders.* 1957. Avon Murder My 46. 1st edn. PBO. extremely scarce. VG+. B6a #79. $101.00

WHITFIELD, Raoul. *Green Ice Murders.* 1947. Murder My Monthly 46. My. G+. P1d. $55.00

WHITFIELD, Steo. *Making of Star Trek.* 1975. Ballantine 24691. 16th prtg. Nfi. VG. W2d. $5.50

WHITING, Charles. *Decision at St Vith.* 1969. Ballantine 01604. War. VG+. B4d. $3.00

WHITING, Charles. *Hitler's Werewolves.* 1973. Bantam Q 7610. 1st prtg. VG+. P7d. $4.00

WHITING, Charles. *Operation Afrika.* 1975. Pinnacle 220757. My. VG. P1d. $3.50

WHITING, Charles. *48 Hours to Hammelburg.* 1970. Ballantine 02066. 1st prtg. PBO. c/D'Achille. VG+. P7d. $4.00

WHITLATCH, John. *Judas Goat.* 1970. Pocket 75643. 2nd edn. My. VG. P1d. $3.50

WHITLATCH, John. *Lafitte's Legacy.* 1971. Pocket 75670. 2nd edn. My. VG. P1d. $3.50

WHITLATCH, John. *Stunt Man's Holiday.* 1973. Pocket 77660. 1st edn. Cr. F. F2d. $10.00

WHITLATCH, John. *Stunt Man's Holiday.* 1973. Pocket 77660. 2nd edn. My. VG. P1d. $3.25

WHITMAN, Howard. *Let's Tell the Truth About Sex.* 1963. Monarch MB 542. Nfi. VG+. P6d. $4.00

WHITMAN, Howard. *Terror in the Streets.* 1951. Bantam A 964. Nfi. VG+. P1d. $13.50

WHITMAN, S.E. *Black Rock Valley.* 1959. Ballantine 328K. We. VG+. B4d. $5.00

WHITMAN, S.E. *Captain Apache.* Berkley G 1072. NF. B3d. $5.00

WHITMAN, S.E. *Change of Command.* Berkley G 1293. VG+. B3d. $4.50

WHITMAN, Walt. *Leaves of Grass.* 1943. Penguin 523. 1st pb. poetry. VG. B6d. $9.00

WHITNEY, Hallam. *Lisa.* 1965. PB Library 52-816. Fi. F. P1d. $25.00

WHITNEY, Hallam. *Wild Seed.* 1956. Ace S 153. PBO. VG+. B6a #77. $60.00

WHITNEY, Hallam. *Wild Seed.* 1956. Ace S 153. PBO. VG+. B6d. $40.00

WHITNEY, Joseph. *Mirror of Your Mind.* 1956. Avon 700. PBO. Nfi. VG. B5d. $4.00

WHITNEY, Phyllis A. *Black Amber.* 1965. Crest D 786. My. VG. P1d. $5.50

WHITNEY, Phyllis A. *Black Amber.* 1970. Crest M 1514. My. VG. P1d. $4.50

WHITNEY, Phyllis A. *Blue Fire.* 1975. Crest P 2339. My. VG. P1d. $3.50

WHITNEY, Phyllis A. *Domino.* 1980. Crest 2-4350. My. F. P1d. $5.00

WHITNEY, Phyllis A. *Fire & the Gold.* 1974. Signet Y 5772. Ro. VG. P1d. $3.50

WHITNEY, Phyllis A. *Hunter's Green.* 1969. Crest T 1253. My. G+. P1d. $3.25

WHITNEY, Phyllis A. *Lost Island.* 1971. Crest M 1644. My. VG. P1d. $4.00

WHITNEY, Phyllis A. *Moonflower.* 1964. Lancer 72-779. My. F. P1d. $12.00

WHITNEY, Phyllis A. *Moonflower.* 1964. Lancer 73-514. 1st pb. VG+. B6d. $5.00

WHITNEY, Phyllis A. *Mystery of the Crimson Ghost.* 1970. Scholastic 1613. My. VG. P1d. $4.50

WHITNEY, Phyllis A. *Poinciana.* 1981. Crest 2-4447. My. VG. P1d. $3.50

WHITNEY, Phyllis A. *Quicksilver Pool.* 1963. Ace K 178. 1st prtg. My. G+. R5d. $1.50

WHITNEY, Phyllis A. *Quicksilver Pool.* 1963. Ace K 178. My. VG. P1d. $5.00

WHITNEY, Phyllis A. *Red Carnelian.* 1972. PB Library 64-827. 7th edn. Go. VG. P1d. $3.00

WHITNEY, Phyllis A. *Sea Jade.* 1975. Crest Q 2572. My. VG. P1d. $3.50

WHITNEY, Phyllis A. *Seven Tears for Apollo.* 1964. Crest D 721. My. VG. P1d. $6.00

WHITNEY, Phyllis A. *Silverhill.* 1968. Crest T 1135. My. VG+. P1d. $7.50

WHITNEY, Phyllis A. *Skye Cameron.* 1973. Crest M 2010. My. G+. P1d. $3.00

WHITNEY, Phyllis A. *Snowfire.* 1974. Crest P 2041. My. VG. P1d. $3.50

WHITNEY, Phyllis A. *Spindrift.* 1976. Crest C 2746. My. VG. P1d. $3.50

WHITNEY, Phyllis A. *Stone Bull.* Crest 2-3638. My. VG. P1d. $3.50

WHITNEY, Phyllis A. *Thunder Heights.* 1967. Ace K 158. My. VG+. P1d. $7.50

WHITNEY, Phyllis A. *Turquoise Mask.* 1975. Crest Q 2365. My. VG. P1d. $3.50

WHITNEY, Phyllis A. *Window on the Square.* 1973. Crest P 1992. My. VG. P1d. $3.50

WHITNEY, Phyllis A. *Winter People.* 1970. Crest M 1515. My. VG. P1d. $4.50

WHITNEY, Walter. *Take It Out in Trade.* 1957. Ace D 229. PBO. c/Tossey. VG. B3d. $5.00

WHITTAKER, K.P. *Roll Your Tent Flaps, Girls!* Avon H 106. c/R Bugg. Fi. VG. B5d. $3.00

WHITTEMORE, L.H. *Peroff, the Man Who Knew Too Much.* 1976. Ballantine 25104. Nfi. G+. P1d. $2.75

WHITTEMORE, Reed. *Browning.* 1970. Dell LB 147. Bio. VG+. B4d. $3.75

WHITTEN, Leslie H. *Moon of the Wolf.* Ace 54000. SF. VG. B5d. $3.50

WHITTINGTON, Harry. *Across That River.* 1956. Ace D 201. PBO. scarce. NF. B6a. $75.00

WHITTINGTON, Harry. *Burden's Mission.* 1968. Avon S 379. 1st edn. My. NF. F2d. $15.00

WHITTINGTON, Harry. *Burden's Mission.* 1968. Avon S 379. 1st prtg. PBO. c/Prezio: gga. G+. P7d. $3.50

WHITTINGTON, Harry. *Charro!* 1969. Gold Medal R 2063. MTI. VG. M6d. $8.50

WHITTINGTON, Harry. *Charro!* 1969. Gold Medal R 2063. 1st prtg. G+. R5d. $2.50

WHITTINGTON, Harry. *Charro!* Gold Medal 2684. MTI. VG+. B3d. $6.00

WHITTINGTON, Harry. *Connolly's Woman.* 1960. Gold Medal 1058. PBO. My. VG. B3d. $8.00

WHITTINGTON, Harry. *Cracker Girl.* Uni-Book 58. Ad. G+. P1d. $30.00

WHITTINGTON, Harry. *Desert Stake-Out.* 1968. Gold Medal D 1961. We. VG. B4d. $5.00

WHITTINGTON, Harry. *Desert Stake-Out.* 1965. Gold Medal K 1603. 2nd edn. We. VG. P1d. $12.50

WHITTINGTON, Harry. *Desire in the Dust.* 1960. Gold Medal 1050. 2nd edn. My. F. P1d. $20.00

WHITTINGTON, Harry. *Desire in the Dust.* 1956. Gold Medal 611. My. G+. P1d. $12.50

WHITTINGTON, Harry. *Don't Speak to Strange Girls.* 1963. Gold Medal K 1303. My. VG. P1d. $15.00

WHITTINGTON, Harry. *Don't Speak to Strange Girls.* 1963. Gold Medal 680. VG. B3d. $12.00

WHITTINGTON, Harry. *Doomsday Affair.* 1965. Ace G 560. Man From UNCLE #2. VG+. W2d. $14.00

WHITTINGTON, Harry. *Doomsday Affair.* 1965. Ace G 560. PBO. TVTI. G+. M6d. $7.50

WHITTINGTON, Harry. *Doomsday Affair.* 1966. Four Square 1466. 3rd edn. My/SF. VG. P1d. $10.00

WHITTINGTON, Harry. *Doomsday Mission.* 1967. Banner B 60-106. My. VG. P1d. $15.00

WHITTINGTON, Harry. *Drawn to Evil.* 1952. Ace D 5. PBO. c/Saunders. VG. B6d. $45.00

WHITTINGTON, Harry. *Fall of the Roman Empire.* 1964. Gold Medal D 1385. Hi. F. P1d. $35.00

WHITTINGTON, Harry. *Fall of the Roman Empire.* 1964. Gold Medal D 1385. MTI. c/photo. VG+. B3d. $6.50

WHITTINGTON, Harry. *Fall of the Roman Empire.* 1964. Gold Medal D 1385. 1st prtg. PBO. MTI. c/photo. VG. P6d. $5.00

WHITTINGTON, Harry. *Fires That Destroy.* 1988. Black Lizard NN. c/J Kirwan. My. F. B5d. $10.00

WHITTINGTON, Harry. *Fires That Destroy.* Black Lizard 34. VG. M6d. $5.00

WHITTINGTON, Harry. *Fires That Destroy.* 1958. Gold Medal 831. 2nd prtg. VG. B3d. $7.50

WHITTINGTON, Harry. *Forgive Me, Killer.* 1987. Black Lizard NN. c/J Kirwan. My. VG. B5d. $5.00

WHITTINGTON, Harry. *Guerilla Girls.* 1961. Pyramid G 600. My. VG. P1d. $15.00

WHITTINGTON, Harry. *Halfway to Hell.* 1959. Avon T 299. JD. VG. P1d. $35.00

WHITTINGTON, Harry. *Halfway to Hell.* 1959. Avon T 299. PBO. scarce. JD. VG+. B6a #77. $101.00

WHITTINGTON, Harry. *Halfway to Hell.* 1959. Avon T 299. 1st edn. c/gga. scarce. My. F. F2d. $50.00

WHITTINGTON, Harry. *Hangrope Town.* 1964. Ballantine U 1021. We. VG. B4d/ M6d. $5.00

WHITTINGTON, Harry. *Hangrope Town.* 1970. Ballantine 01190. 2nd edn. c/Hantman. reprints U1021. We. VG. B4d. $3.25

WHITTINGTON, Harry. *Hell Can Wait.* 1960. Gold Medal 1044. Fa. F. B4d. $40.00

WHITTINGTON, Harry. *High Fury.* 1964. Ballantine U 1020. We. VG+. B4d. $6.00

WHITTINGTON, Harry. *Lady Was a Tramp.* 1951. Handi-Book 131. PBO. c/gga. scarce. VG+. B6a #75. $75.00

WHITTINGTON, Harry. *Love Cult.* 1952. Lancer 71-315. c/gga. VG. B6a #79. $33.00

WHITTINGTON, Harry. *Lust for Love.* 1959. Bedside BB 804. PBO. VG+. B6a #80. $46.75

WHITTINGTON, Harry. *Lust for Love.* 1959. Bedside BB 804. 1st edn. VG+. I1d. $40.00

WHITTINGTON, Harry. *Man in the Shadow.* 1957. Avon T 196. PBO. MTI. c/photo. scarce. NF. B6a #80. $50.00

WHITTINGTON, Harry. *Man in the Shadow.* 1957. Avon T 196. 1st prtg. MTI. G+. R5d. $4.50

WHITTINGTON, Harry. *Moment To Prey.* Black Lizard NN. VG+. G5d. $5.00

WHITTINGTON, Harry. *Mourn the Hangman.* 1952. Graphic 46. My. VG+. P1d. $40.00

WHITTINGTON, Harry. *Murder Is My Mistress.* 1951. Graphic 41. My. G+. P1d. $25.00

WHITTINGTON, Harry. *Naked Jungle.* 1955. Ace S 95. Hi. G+. P1d. $10.00

WHITTINGTON, Harry. *Naked Jungle.* 1955. Ace S 95. PBO. VG. B6d. $22.50

WHITTINGTON, Harry. *Native Girl.* 1956. Berkley G 250. 1st edn. c/gga. F. F2d. $45.00

WHITTINGTON, Harry. *Night for Screaming.* 1960. Ace D 472. PBO. c/Maguire. scarce. VG. B6a #80. $36.50

WHITTINGTON, Harry. *Nita's Place.* Pyramid 972. 2nd prtg. VG. B3d. $8.00

WHITTINGTON, Harry. *Prime Sucker.* 1960. Beacon 337. VG. B3a #24. $20.50

WHITTINGTON, Harry. *Rebel Woman.* 1960. Avon T 403. PBO. extremely scarce. VG+. B6a #77. $66.00

WHITTINGTON, Harry. *Shack Road Girl.* Berkley Diamond D 2004. c/McGinnis. VG. B6a #80. $42.00

WHITTINGTON, Harry. *Sicilian Woman.* 1979. Gold Medal 1-4286. Fi. VG. P1d. $5.00

WHITTINGTON, Harry. *Slay Ride for a Lady.* 1950. Handi-Book Mystery 120. PBO. VG. B3a #21. $38.50

WHITTINGTON, Harry. *So Dead My Love!* 1953. Ace D 7. PBO. c/De Soto. VG. B6d. $40.00

WHITTINGTON, Harry. *Strange Bargain.* 1959. Avon T 347. G+. M6d. $6.50

WHITTINGTON, Harry. *Strange Bargain.* 1959. Avon T 347. PBO. scarce. NF. B6a #76. $67.25

WHITTINGTON, Harry. *Strange Bargain.* 1959. Avon T 347. PBO. VG+. B6d. $25.00

WHITTINGTON, Harry. *Teen-Age Jungle.* 1958. Avon T 241. extremely scarce. VG. B6a #74. $39.00

WHITTINGTON, Harry. *Temptations of Valerie.* 1957. Avon T 187. MTI. c/photo. scarce. NF. B6a #80. $46.75

WHITTINGTON, Harry. *Ticket to Hell.* 1987. Black Lizard NN. c/J Kirwan. My. F. B5d. $10.00

WHITTINGTON, Harry. *Ticket to Hell.* 1959. Gold Medal 862. NF. G5d. $22.50

WHITTINGTON, Harry. *Ticket to Hell.* 1959. Gold Medal 862. VG. B3d. $9.00

WHITTINGTON, Harry. *Web of Murder.* Bridbooks NN. VG. M6d. $5.00

WHITTINGTON, Harry. *Web of Murder.* 1958. Gold Medal 740. PBO. VG. M6d. $6.50

WHITTINGTON, Harry. *Wild Lonesome.* 1965. Ballantine U 1022. PBO. VG. M6d. $4.50

WHITTINGTON, Harry. *Wild Oats.* Uni-Book 70. Ad. G+. P1d. $30.00

WHITTINGTON, Harry. *Woman Is Mine.* 1954. Gold Medal 366. My. G+. P1d. $15.00

WHITTINGTON, Harry. *Woman on the Place.* 1956. Ace S 143. PBO. c/Marchetti. VG. B6d. $27.50

WHITTINGTON, Harry. *Woman on the Place.* 1956. Ace S 143. PBO. VG. B3a #21. $172.50

WHITTINGTON, Harry. *You'll Die Next.* Red Seal 138. G+. B3a #20. $16.00

WHYTE, H. Walter. *Deep Freeze.* 1977. Manor 12527. SF. VG. W2d. $3.75

WIBBERLEY, Leonard. *Mouse on the Moon.* Bantam F 2641. 2nd prtg. VG. R5d. $1.50

WIBBERLEY, Leonard. *Mouse on the Moon.* 1965. Bantam FP 104. 7th prtg. SF. F. W2d. $4.75

WIBBERLEY, Leonard. *Mouse That Roared.* 1959. Bantam A 1982. 1st pb. MTI. NF. B3d. $4.50

WIBBERLEY, Leonard. *Mouse That Roared.* 1959. Bantam A 1982. 1st prtg. SF. VG. R5d. $2.00

WICHELNS, Lee. *Rip Tide.* Popular 439. VG+. B3d. $5.00

WICHELNS, Lee. *Rip Tide.* 1952. Popular 439. 1st edn. PBO. c/sgn presentation inscr. NF. F2d. $16.00

WICKWARE, Francis Sill. *Dangerous Ground.* 1948. Dell 248. My. F. P1d. $20.00

WICKWARE, Francis Sill. *Tuesday to Bed.* 1951. Popular 316. VG+. B3d. $7.00

WIDDEMER, M. *Lani.* Pocket 601. VG. B3d. $4.50

WIDDEMER, Margaret. *Golden Wildcat.* 1955. Popular G 152. 1st pb. VG. B6d. $6.00

WIDDEMER, Margaret. *Red Castle Women.* 1970. Popular 75-1324. Go. VG. P1d. $4.50

WIDMER, Andy. *Passion.* 1964. Prize PV 101. Ad. F. B5d. $7.00

WIDMER, Harry edt. *Hardboiled Lineup.* 1956. Lion 130. 1st edn. My. F. F2d. $20.00

WIEGAND, William. *At Last, Mr Tolliver.* 1953. Dell 697. My. VG. P1d. $8.50

WIEGAND, William. *Incorrigibles.* 1960. Belmont L 502. My. VG. P1d. $7.00

WIENER, Willard. *Four Boys, a Girl, & a Gun.* Avon 444. VG. B3d. $4.00

WIGGAM, Albert E. *Let's Explore Your Mind.* Pocket 598. 1st pb. VG+. M6d. $6.50

WIGHTON, C. *Dope International.* 1964. Four Square 1145. VG. B3d. $7.50

WILCOX, Collin. *Hiding Place.* 1979. Jove M 5193. My. G+. P1d. $2.75

WILCOX, Collin. *Long Way Down.* 1979. Jove M 5195. My. VG. P1d. $3.50

WILCOX, Collin. *McCloud.* 1973. Award AN 1203. My. VG. P1d. $6.00

WILCOX, Collin. *New Mexico Connection.* Award AN 1259. TVTI. McCloud #2. VG+. B3d. $5.00

WILCOX, Collin. *New Mexico Connection.* Award AN 1259. TVTI. NF. G5d. $6.00

WILDE, Oscar. *Picture of Dorian Gray.* 1964. Airmont CL 39. SF. VG+. B5d. $3.50

WILDE, Oscar. *Picture of Dorian Gray.* 1953. Dell 681. c/G Foxley. SF. VG. B5d. $5.00

WILDE, Oscar. *Picture of Dorian Gray.* 1953. Dell 681. G+. G5d. $3.00

WILDE, Oscar. *Picture of Dorian Gray.* Pyramid 584. VG. B3d. $4.00

WILDE, Percival. *Design for Murder.* De Novel Classic 13. VG+. B3d. $6.00

WILDE, Percival. *Inquest.* 1945. Superior M 647. My. VG. P1d. $10.50

WILDE, Ray. *I've Got a Thing for Him.* 1963. Publishers Export N 154. Ad. VG+. B5d. $4.00

WILDE, Ray. *Resort Stud.* 1966. Publishers Export N 150. PBO. c/gga. NF. B6a #75. $30.25

WILDER, Joan. *Jewel of the Nile.* 1985. Avon 89984. My. VG. P1d. $3.50

WILDER, Robert. *And Ride a Tiger.* 1953. Bantam A 1162. 1st pb. c/Hooks. NF. B6d. $18.00

WILDER, Robert. *Autumn Thunder.* 1954. Bantam A 1258. 1st prtg. VG. P7d. $4.00

WILDER, Robert. *Flamingo Road.* 1951. Bantam A 928. Fi. VG+. P1d. $13.50

WILDER, Robert. *Flamingo Road.* 1951. Bantam A 928. VG. B3d. $6.00

WILDER, Robert. *Fruit of the Poppy.* Bantam S 3169. My. VG. R5d. $2.00

WILDER, Robert. *God Has a Long Face.* Bantam 983. VG. B3d. $5.00

WILDER, Robert. *Sun Is My Shadow.* 1961. Bantam H 2264. 1st prtg. c/Zuckerberg: gga. VG. P7d. $3.50

WILDER, Robert. *Wait for Tomorrow.* 1953. Bantam A 1181. Fi. VG. B3d. $4.50

WILDER, Robert. *Walk With Evil.* 1957. Crest 179. My. VG+. P1d. $11.00

WILDER, Robert. *Walk With Evil.* 1957. Crest 179. 1st edn. scarce in top condition. My. F. F2d. $20.00

WILDER, Thornton. *Bridge of San Luis Rey.* 1959. Washington Square W 236. Fi. VG. B5d. $2.50

WILDER, Thornton. *Heaven's My Destination.* 1945. Avon 59. VG. B3d. $5.00

WILDER, Thornton. *Heaven's My Destination.* 1945. Avon 59. VG+. B3a #22. $13.55

WILDER, Thornton. *Our Town.* 1940. Pocket 55. Nfi. G+. B5d. $10.00

WILDING, Philip. *Murder With Merit.* 1959. Banner 103. G+. B3d. $6.00

WILEY, Hugh. *Murder by the Dozen.* 1951. Popular 325. My. VG. P1d. $15.00

WILHEIM, Kate. *Mile-Long Spaceship.* 1963. Berkley F 862. PBO. c/R Powers. SF. VG+. B5d. $5.00

WILHELM, Gale. *Strange Path.* 1953. Lion 121. 1st edn. PBO. rare. NF. B6a #75. $49.50

WILHELM, Gale. *We Too Are Drifting.* Berkley 327. reprint. NF. B6d. $20.00

WILHELM, Kate. *Killer Thing.* 1969. Dell 4496. SF. F. W2d. $5.00

WILHELM, Kate. *Margaret & I.* 1978. Pocket. 1st pb edn. F. M1d. $5.00

WILHELM, Kate. *Mile-Long Spaceship.* 1963. Berkley F 862. 1st edn. F. M1d. $10.00

WILK, Max. *Don't Raise the Bridge (Lower the River).* 1968. Berkley S 1556. Fi. VG+. B5d. $4.00

WILKERSON, David. *Cross & the Switchblade.* 1977. Jove A 4591. JD. VG. P1d. $5.00

WILKERSON, David. *Hey Preach. You're Comin' Through!* 1971. Pyramid T 2419. Nfi. NF. B4d. $4.00

WILKINSON, Burke. *Night of the Short Knives.* 1966. Popular 60-2108. Th. VG. P1d. $5.50

WILKINSON, G.K. *Monkeys, Go Home.* 1967. Avon S 251. 3rd edn. MTI. c/M Chevalier & Y Mimieux. Fi. VG+. B5d. $4.00

WILKINSON, L. *High-Flying Hookers.* Barclay 7355. VG+. B3d. $5.00

WILLARD, J. *Thorne Theater Mystery.* Prize Mystery 25. VG. B3d. $4.50

WILLEFORD, Charles. *Cockfighter.* Avon 20495. MTI. scarce. NF. B6a #80. $88.00

WILLEFORD, Charles. *Cockfighter.* 1974. Avon 20495. 2nd edn. MTI. VG. P6d. $13.00

WILLEFORD, Charles. *Cockfighter.* Black Lizard 26. VG. M6d. $6.00

WILLEFORD, Charles. *Cockfighter.* 1987. Black Lizard 88739. 1st prtg. c/Kirwan. NF. P7d. $7.50

WILLEFORD, Charles. *Cockfighter.* 1962. Chicago PB House B 120. My. VG+. P1d. $125.00

WILLEFORD, Charles. *Cockfighter.* 1962. Chicago PB House B 120. PBO. scarce. NF. B6a #75. $110.50

WILLEFORD, Charles. *Cockfighter.* Vintage 73471. NF. M6d. $9.50

WILLEFORD, Charles. *Honey Gal.* 1958. Beacon 160. PBO. VG+. B6a #79. $363.00

WILLEFORD, Charles. *Honey Gal.* 1958. Beacon 160. 1st prtg. PBO. c/gga. VG+. P7d. $175.00

WILLEFORD, Charles. *Lust Is a Woman.* 1958. Beacon 175. PBO. c/Micarelli: gga. rare. VG+. B6a #79. $400.00

WILLEFORD, Charles. *Lust Is a Woman.* 1958. Beacon 175. 1st prtg. PBO. c/Micarelli: gga. VG+. P7d. $140.00

WILLEFORD, Charles. *Machine in Ward Eleven.* 1963. Belmont 90-286. PBO. c/Maguire. NF. B6a #75. $40.25

WILLEFORD, Charles. *Machine in Ward Eleven.* 1963. Belmont 90-286. 1st prtg. My. G+. R5d. $15.00

WILLEFORD, Charles. *Miami Blues.* Ballantine 32016. 1st pb. VG. M6d. $6.50

WILLEFORD, Charles. *Pick-Up.* 1955. Beacon 109. PBO. extremely scarce. VG+. B6a #79. $302.50

WILLEFORD, Charles. *Woman Chaser.* Carroll & Graf 556. NF. M6d. $5.00

WILLEFORD, Charles. *Woman Chaser.* 1960. Newsstand U 137. NF. B3a #22. $62.75

WILLEFORD, Charles. *Woman Chaser.* 1960. Newsstand U 137. 1st edn. My. F. F2d. $95.00

WILLIAM, Peter. *Death at Abu Mina.* Thriller Novel 35. My. VG. P1d. $20.00

WILLIAMS, Alan. *Shah-Mak.* 1977. Panther 04640. Th. VG. P1d. $4.00

WILLIAMS, Ben Ames. *All the Brothers Were Valiant.* 1949. Avon 215. Fi. G+. B5d. $2.50

WILLIAMS, Ben Ames. *All the Brothers Were Valiant.* 1949. Avon 215. Hi. VG. P1d. $9.50

WILLIAMS, Ben Ames. *Crucible.* 1947. Popular 113. My. F. P1d. $25.00

WILLIAMS, Ben Ames. *Crucible.* 1947. Popular 113. VG. B3d. $4.50

WILLIAMS, Ben Ames. *Death on Scurvy Street.* 1949. Popular 194. G. G5d. $6.00

WILLIAMS, Ben Ames. *Death on Scurvy Street.* 1949. Popular 194. 1st prtg. c/Belarski: gga. VG. P1d/P7d. $12.50

WILLIAMS, Ben Ames. *Dreadful Night.* 1948. Popular 155. VG. I1d. $5.00

WILLIAMS, Ben Ames. *Great Oaks.* 1952. Harlequin 152. 2nd edn. Hi. VG. P1d. $9.50

WILLIAMS, Ben Ames. *It's a Free Country.* 1951. Popular 308. c/Rozen: gga. Fa. VG+. B4d. $12.00

WILLIAMS, Ben Ames. *Killer Among Us.* 1957. Lion LL 149. My. VG. P1d. $10.00

WILLIAMS, Ben Ames. *Leave Her to Heaven.* 1950. Bantam Giants A 771. c/Schaare. VG. P6d. $2.50

WILLIAMS, Ben Ames. *Silver Forest.* 1949. Popular 215. c/Belarski. VG. B3d. $9.00

WILLIAMS, Ben Ames. *Strange Woman.* 1950. Bantam A 847. Hi. VG+. P1d. $14.00

WILLIAMS, Ben Ames. *Strumpet Sea.* Popular 371. VG. B3d. $5.00

WILLIAMS, Ben Ames. *Valley Vixen.* 1948. Avon 153. c/gga. Fa. VG. B4d/I1d. $6.00

WILLIAMS, C.A. *Mix Yourself Redhead (Touch of Death).* 1967. Pan C 685. VG. B3d. $7.50

WILLIAMS, Charles. *Aground.* 1961. Crest S 471. My. VG+. P1d. $12.00

WILLIAMS, Charles. *Aground.* 1961. Crest S 471. 1st pb. G+. M6d. $4.50

WILLIAMS, Charles. *All Hallow's Eve.* 1969. Avon YQ 13. 1st prtg. SF. VG+. R5d. $3.00

WILLIAMS, Charles. *All the Way.* 1958. Dell 1st Edn A 165. PBO. c/Darcy. My. G+. B6d. $6.00

WILLIAMS, Charles. *And the Deep Blue Sea.* 1971. Signet Q 4515. My. VG. P1d. $7.50

WILLIAMS, Charles. *Big Bite.* 1956. Dell A 114. PBO. c/Sussman. scarce. NF. B6a #80. $55.00

WILLIAMS, Charles. *Big Bite.* 1973. Pocket 77506. c/Stanley Borack. reprint. VG. P6d. $3.00

WILLIAMS, Charles. *Big City Girl.* Gold Medal 651. 4th prtg. c/Barye. VG. B3d. $8.00

WILLIAMS, Charles. *Dead Calm.* 1965. Avon G 1255. My. VG. P1d. $10.00

WILLIAMS, Charles. *Dead Calm.* Perennial P 655. VG. M6d. $5.00

WILLIAMS, Charles. *Dead Calm.* 1971. Pocket 77365. My. F. P1d. $12.50

WILLIAMS, Charles. *Diamond Bikini.* 1956. Gold Medal S 607. Fi. G+. P1d. $10.00

WILLIAMS, Charles. *Fires of Youth.* 1960. Magnet 309. PBO. c/Nappi. VG+. B6a #74. $55.00

WILLIAMS, Charles. *Girl Out Back.* 1958. Dell 1st Edn B 114. PBO. c/Darcy. scarce. NF. B6a #80. $53.50

WILLIAMS, Charles. *Girl Out Back.* 1958. Dell 1st Edn B 114. VG. B3d. $12.50

WILLIAMS, Charles. *Go Home, Stranger.* Gold Medal 1344. 3rd prtg. c/Barye. VG+. B3d. $6.00

WILLIAMS, Charles. *Go Home, Stranger.* 1954. Gold Medal 371. PBO. c/gga. extremely scarce. VG. B6a #74. $47.50

WILLIAMS, Charles. *Go Home, Stranger.* 1956. Gold Medal 625. 2nd edn. My. VG. P1d. $12.50

WILLIAMS, Charles. *Go Home, Stranger.* 1956. Gold Medal 625. 2nd prtg. reprint. VG+. B3a #24. $13.35

WILLIAMS, Charles. *Gulf Coast Girl.* 1956. Dell 898. My. G+. P1d. $10.00

WILLIAMS, Charles. *Gulf Coast Girl.* 1956. Dell 898. 1st edn. PBO. c/Maguire. scarce. NF. B6a #80. $68.50

WILLIAMS, Charles. *Hell Hath No Fury.* 1960. Gold Medal S 1012. My. VG+. B4d. $4.00

WILLIAMS, Charles. *Hill Girl.* 1951. Gold Medal 141. My. F. P1d. $45.00

WILLIAMS, Charles. *Hot Spot.* Vintage 73329. NF. M6d. $8.50

WILLIAMS, Charles. *Long Saturday Night.* 1962. Gold Medal S 1200. c/Darcy. G+. P6d. $5.00

WILLIAMS, Charles. *Man on the Run.* Gold Medal 822. VG. B3d. $12.00

WILLIAMS, Charles. *Nothing in Her Way.* Gold Medal K 1289. 2nd edn. G+. M6d. $6.50

WILLIAMS, Charles. *Nothing in Her Way.* 1953. Gold Medal 340. My. F. P1d. $12.50

WILLIAMS, Charles. *River Girl.* 1951. Gold Medal 207. c/Barye. VG+. B3a #24. $30.25

WILLIAMS, Charles. *Sailcloth Shroud.* 1961. Dell D 410. My. VG. P1d. $10.00

WILLIAMS, Charles. *Sailcloth Shroud.* 1964. Pan G 679. 1st pb. My. VG. B6d. $7.50

WILLIAMS, Charles. *Sailcloth Shroud.* Perennial P 654. VG. M6d. $5.00

WILLIAMS, Charles. *Scorpion Reef.* 1972. Pocket 77428. My. VG+. P1d. $9.00

WILLIAMS, Charles. *Talk of the Town.* 1958. Dell 1st Edn A 164. My. VG. P1d. $15.00

WILLIAMS, Charles. *Talk of the Town.* 1958. Dell 1st Edn A 164. PBO. c/Darcy. scarce. NF. B6a #80. $42.50

WILLIAMS, Charles. *Touch of Death.* Gold Medal K 1353. 2nd edn. VG. M6d. $7.50

WILLIAMS, Charles. *Touch of Death.* 1954. Gold Medal 434. My. G+. G5d. $9.00

WILLIAMS, Charles. *Touch of Death.* 1954. Gold Medal 434. PBO. c/Saul Teeper. scarce. VG+. B6a #77. $55.00

WILLIAMS, Charles. *Wrong Venus.* 1983. Perennial P 656. My. VG. P1d. $6.00

WILLIAMS, Coe. *Go for Your Gun.* Popular EB 39. VG. B3d. $4.00

WILLIAMS, Coe. *Trouble Trail.* Popular EB 25. VG. B3d. $4.00

WILLIAMS, Eric. *Wooden Horse.* 1951. Bantam 842. MTI. VG. B4d. $3.00

WILLIAMS, Gordon. *Last Day of Lincoln Charles.* 1967. Ballantine U 5069. 1st prtg. My. VG. R5d. $1.75

WILLIAMS, Gordon. *Revolt of the Micronauts.* 1981. Bantam 20107. PBO. SF. NF. B6d. $3.00

WILLIAMS, H. *New Kind of Love.* Dell 6329. MTI. VG. B3d. $4.00

WILLIAMS, H.H. *Oral Sex & the Teenager.* Barclay 7060. VG+. B3d. $4.50

WILLIAMS, H.H. *Teenage S-M.* Barclay 7029. NF. B3d. $5.00

WILLIAMS, Henry. *Ensign.* 1964. Dell 2364. 1st prtg. VG+. R5d. $2.50

WILLIAMS, Henry. *How To Murder Your Wife.* 1965. Dell 3921. 1st prtg. VG+. R5d. $2.75

WILLIAMS, Idabel. *Hussy.* Beacon BB 117. G+. M6d. $7.50

WILLIAMS, Idabel. *Hussy.* Beacon 221. c/gga. reprint. NF. B6d. $16.50

WILLIAMS, J.H. *Elephant Bill.* Pennant P36. NF. B3d. $7.50

WILLIAMS, J.X. *Esctasy, Inc.* 1969. Candid Reader 982. PBO. c/Bonfils: gga. F. B6a #76. $54.00

WILLIAMS, J.X. *Flesh Castle.* 1964. Evening Reader ER 755. PBO. c/gga. VG. P6d. $3.50

WILLIAMS, J.X. *Flesh Countess.* Leisure LB 654. VG+. I1d. $5.00

WILLIAMS, J.X. *Gutterlust.* 1962. Bedside BB 1214. Ad. VG. B5d. $4.00

WILLIAMS, J.X. *How-To Hustler.* Pleasure Reader 123. NF. B3d. $6.00

WILLIAMS, J.X. *Lust Tycoon.* 1965. Nightstand NB 1727. Ad. NF. B5d. $6.50

WILLIAMS, J.X. *Nudist Nympho.* Late-Hour Library LL 726. PBO. VG. M6d. $5.00

WILLIAMS, J.X. *Orgy Weekend.* Leisure LB 658. VG. B3d. $4.00

WILLIAMS, J.X. *Passion Proxy.* Ember Book EB 923. VG. B3d. $4.00

WILLIAMS, J.X. *Passion Rap.* 1966. Ember Library 357. PBO. c/Bonfils: gga. NF. B6a #76. $45.00

WILLIAMS, J.X. *Passion's Princess.* 1968. Candid Reader CA 914. PBO. VG. P6d. $3.75

WILLIAMS, J.X. *Sex Pill.* 1968. Pleasure Reader 172. PBO. scarce. SF. VG+. B6a #77. $68.25

WILLIAMS, J.X. *Sex Spy.* 1961. Nightstand NB 1552. Ad. G+. B5d. $2.50

WILLIAMS, J.X. *Sex Toy.* 1968. Adult Book 425. PBO. c/gga. NF. B6a #80. $148.50

WILLIAMS, J.X. *Suburb Wanton.* 1965. Leisure 670. PBO. c/Bonfils: gga. F. B6a #76. $53.50

WILLIAMS, J.X. *Tamara's Lust.* 1966. Idle Hour IH 485. Ad. G+. B5d. $3.50

WILLIAMS, J.X. *Twincest.* 1967. Leisure 1199. PBO. c/Bonfils: gga. NF. B6a #76. $41.00

WILLIAMS, J.X. *Wanton Wife.* 1973. Reed Nightstand 3006. NF. B3a #21. $24.20

WILLIAMS, J.X. *Wheel of Sin.* 1967. Leisure 1190. PBO. c/Bonfils: gga. NF. B6a #76. $48.50

WILLIAMS, Jack. *Dragon's Island.* Tower 43531. 3rd edn. F. P9d. $2.50

WILLIAMS, Jack. *Legion of Space.* Pyramid X 1576. 3rd edn. F. P9d. $2.50

WILLIAMS, James. *Never To Belong.* Fabian Z 135. VG+. B3d. $8.00

WILLIAMS, Jay. *Witches.* 1959. Bantam A 1937. Fa. VG+. B4d. $3.00

WILLIAMS, Jeffrey. *Nymphomaniac.* 1965. Midwood 32-498. VG+. B3d. $5.00

WILLIAMS, John A. *Angry Ones.* 1960. Ace D 420. c/Copeland. VG. B6d. $18.00

WILLIAMS, John A. *Night Song.* Dell 6406. VG. B3d. $4.00

WILLIAMS, John A. *Stoner.* Lancer 73-455. VG. B3d. $4.00

WILLIAMS, Lawrence. *Fiery Furnace.* 1961. Avon T 497. Fa. VG+. B4d. $2.50

WILLIAMS, Lon. *Adulteress.* 1959. Beacon 214. 1st prtg. c/Darcy: gga. NF. P7d. $12.50

WILLIAMS, Lon. *Hill Hellion!* 1958. Beacon 177. 1st prtg. PBO. VG+. P7d. $9.00

WILLIAMS, Lon. *Hill Hoyden.* 1958. Beacon 162. PBO. c/gga. VG. B6d. $9.00

WILLIAMS, Lon. *Hill Hoyden.* 1958. Beacon 162. 1st prtg. PBO. VG+. P7d. $12.50

WILLIAMS, Michael. *Sorcerer's Apprentice.* 1990. Popular 21054. 1st edn. SF. F. F2d. $6.00

WILLIAMS, Mona. *Company Girls.* Gold Medal K 1503. PBO. VG. M6d. $5.00

WILLIAMS, R. *Hard Way.* Popular 515. VG. B3d. $6.00

WILLIAMS, Richard L. *Zanthar of the Many Worlds.* 1967. Lancer 73-694. 1st prtg. SF. VG+. R5d. $5.00

WILLIAMS, Richard. *Sniper.* 1965. Mayflower-Dell 8051. My. VG. P1d. $6.00

WILLIAMS, Robert Moore. *Beachhead Planet.* 1970. Dell 0462. 1st edn. VG. M1d. $6.00

WILLIAMS, Robert Moore. *Bell From Infinity.* 1968. Lancer 73-766. PBO. SF. VG+. B6d. $7.50

WILLIAMS, Robert Moore. *Bell From Infinity.* 1968. Lancer 73-766. 1st edn. F. M1d. $10.00

WILLIAMS, Robert Moore. *Bell From Infinity.* 1968. Lancer 73-766. 1st prtg. SF. VG. R5d. $4.50

WILLIAMS, Robert Moore. *Day They H-Bombed LA.* 1961. Ace D 530. F. M1d. $22.00

WILLIAMS, Robert Moore. *Easy Eye.* 1968. Lancer 74-941. PBO. c/Ed Emsh. VG+. P6d. $2.25

WILLIAMS, Robert Moore. *Jongor Fights Back.* 1970. Popular. 1st edn. F. M1d. $10.00

WILLIAMS, Robert Moore. *Jongor of the Lost Land.* 1970. Popular. 1st edn. F. M1d. $10.00

WILLIAMS, Robert Moore. *Return of Jongor.* 1970. Popular 2511. 1st edn. F. M1d. $10.00

WILLIAMS, Robert Moore. *Second Atlantis.* 1965. Ace F 335. PBO. c/Gray Morrow. SF. VG. P6d. $1.75

WILLIAMS, Robert Moore. *Seven Tickets to Hell.* 1972. Popular. 1st edn. F. M1d. $10.00

WILLIAMS, Robert Moore. *Star Wasps.* 1960s. Priory 1108. 1st pb. SF. VG+. B6d. $4.50

WILLIAMS, Robert Moore. *Vigilante 21st Century.* 1967. Lancer 73-644. SF. VG+. P4d. $4.00

WILLIAMS, Robert Moore. *Zanthar at Moon's Madness.* 1968. Lancer. 1st edn. F. M1d. $10.00

WILLIAMS, Robert Moore. *Zanthar at the Edge of Never.* 1968. Lancer 74-941. PBO. c/Ed Emsh. VG. P6d. $3.00

WILLIAMS, Robert Moore. *Zanthar at the Edge of Never.* 1968. Lancer 74-941. 1st edn. F. M1d. $8.00

WILLIAMS, Robert Moore. *Zanthar at Trip's End.* 1969. Lancer 73-836. 1st edn. c/Jeff Jones. SF. F. F2d. $12.00

WILLIAMS, Robert Moore. *Zanthar of the Many Worlds.* 1967. Lancer. 1st edn. F. M1d. $8.00

WILLIAMS, Rose. *Nurse in Jeopardy.* 1967. Lancer 72-165. c/gga. Fa. NF. B4d. $4.00

WILLIAMS, Roswell. *Woman Without Love?* 1949. Novel Library 10. VG+. B3a #20. $16.20

WILLIAMS, Roswell. *Women Without Love?* 1949. Novel Library 10. G+. I1d. $5.00

WILLIAMS, Roy. *Secret World of Roy Williams.* Bantam 1697. VG. B3d. $4.00

WILLIAMS, Sidney. *Blood Hunter.* 1990. Pinnacle 55817. 1st prtg. Ho. VG. W2d. $3.25

WILLIAMS, T. *Strangler.* 1979. Bantam 12305. My. VG. P1d. $3.50

WILLIAMS, Tennessee. *Baby Doll.* 1956. Signet S 1334. MTI. c/Carroll Baker: photo. VG+. B4d. $7.00

WILLIAMS, Tennessee. *Baby Doll.* 1956. Signet S 1334. 1st pb. MTI. NF. B6d. $15.00

WILLIAMS, Tennessee. *Cat on Hot Tin Roof.* 1958. Signet S 1590. MTI. VG+. B4d. $8.00

WILLIAMS, Tennessee. *Fugitive Kind.* 1960. Signet S 1745. 1st prtg. VG+. R5d. $5.25

WILLIAMS, Tennessee. *Night of the Iguana.* 1964. Signet D 2481. MTI. VG+. B4d. $4.00

WILLIAMS, Tennessee. *Night of the Iguana.* 1964. Signet D 2481. 1st prtg. G+. R5d. $2.50

WILLIAMS, Tennessee. *Roman Spring of Mrs Stone.* Signet 955. c/Avati. VG. B3d. $4.00

WILLIAMS, Tennessee. *Rose Tattoo.* 1955. Signet 1236. MTI. VG+. B4d. $8.00

WILLIAMS, Tennessee. *Rose Tattoo.* 1955. Signet 1236. 1st prtg. VG. R5d. $5.50

WILLIAMS, Tennessee. *Streetcar Named Desire.* 1953. Signet 917. 6th prtg. G+. R5d. $1.00

WILLIAMS, Tennessee. *Suddenly Last Summer.* 1960. Signet S 1757. MTI. c/photo. Nfi. VG. B5d. $4.00

WILLIAMS, Tennessee. *Suddenly Last Summer.* 1960. Signet S 1757. MTI. VG+. B4d. $7.00

WILLIAMS, Tennessee. *Suddenly Last Summer.* 1960. Signet S 1757. 1st edn. PBO. c/Liz Taylor photo. F. F2d. $10.00

WILLIAMS, Tennessee. *Summer & Smoke.* 1961. Signet D 2019. 1st prtg. VG. R5d. $3.50

WILLIAMS, Thomas. *Ceremony of Love.* 1956. Perma M 4044. Fi. VG. B5d. $3.00

WILLIAMS, Valentine. *Orange Divan.* 1945. Pony 47. My. VG. P1d. $10.50

WILLIAMS, W. *Blue Angel.* Signet 1720. MTI. VG. B3d. $4.50

WILLIAMS, Wright. *Play for Pay.* 1958. Beacon 167. 1st prtg. c/photo. VG+. P7d. $9.00

WILLIAMS, Wright. *Side Street.* Beacon B 391. Ad. G+. B5d. $3.50

WILLIAMS, Wright. *Side Street.* Uni-Book 20. VG. B3d. $5.00

WILLIAMS, Wynn. *Take the Money & Die.* 1980. Raven House 60014. My. F. P1d. $5.00

WILLIAMS. *Chaos Fighters.* Ace S 90. VG. M1d. $10.00

WILLIAMS. *Odd Girl Out.* 1966. Ember Library 344. PBO. c/gga. unread. F. B6a #74. $82.50

WILLIAMS-HELLER, Ann. *Thrifty Gourmet's Meat Cookbook.* 1971. Gold Medal M 2413. Nfi. VG+. B5d. $3.50

WILLIAMS/WILLIAMS. *Blue Atom/Void Beyond & Other Stories.* 1958. Ace D 322. F. M1d. $15.00

WILLIAMS/WILLIAMS. *Blue Atom/Void Beyond & Other Stories.* 1958. Ace D 322. PBO. SF. VG+. P6d. $4.75

WILLIAMS/WILLIAMS. *World of the Masterminds/To the End of Time & Other Stories.* 1960. Ace D 427. PBO. VG. B3d. $4.00

WILLIAMS/WILLIAMS. *World of the Masterminds/To the End of Time & Other Stories.* 1960. Ace D 427. 1st edn. NF. M1d. $12.00

WILLIAMS/WOODCOTT. *Darkness Before Tomorrow/Ladder in the Sky.* 1962. Ace F 141. F. M1d. $9.00

WILLIAMS/WOODCOTT. *Darkness Before Tomorrow/Ladder in the Sky.* 1962. Ace F 141. G. S1d. $3.50

WILLIAMS/WOODCOTT. *Darkness Before Tomorrow/Ladder in the Sky.* 1962. Ace F 141. PBO. c/E Valigursky. SF. VG+. B5d. $6.00

WILLIAMSON, Jack. *Cometeers.* 1967. Pyramid X 1634. c/sgn. VG. B3d. $5.00

WILLIAMSON, Jack. *Cometeers.* 1967. Pyramid X 1634. 1st prtg. G+. S1d. $2.50

WILLIAMSON, Jack. *Darker Than You Think.* Lancer 73421. 1st prtg. F. S1d. $9.00

WILLIAMSON, Jack. *Dragon's Island.* 1952. Popular 447. c/Bergey: gga. SF. VG+. B4d. $12.50

WILLIAMSON, Jack. *Dragon's Island.* 1952. Popular 447. c/Earle Bergey: gga. SF. VG. B4d. $7.00

WILLIAMSON, Jack. *Dragon's Island.* 1952. Popular 447. 1st edn. PBO. c/Williamson: sgn. F. F2d. $25.00

WILLIAMSON, Jack. *Dragon's Island.* 1952. Popular 447. 1st pb edn. F. M1d. $20.00

WILLIAMSON, Jack. *Dragon's Island.* 1952. Popular 447. 1st prtg. G+. S1d. $5.00

WILLIAMSON, Jack. *Dragon's Island.* Tower 43531. 1st prtg. VG. S1d. $2.50

WILLIAMSON, Jack. *Golden Blood.* 1964. Lancer 72-740. c/E Emsh. SF. VG. B5d. $7.50

WILLIAMSON, Jack. *Golden Blood.* 1964. Lancer 72-740. c/sgn. VG+. B3d. $9.00

WILLIAMSON, Jack. *Golden Blood.* 1964. Lancer 72-740. 1st edn. F. M1d. $20.00

WILLIAMSON, Jack. *Golden Blood.* 1964. Lancer 72-740. 1st prtg. SF. G+. R5d. $5.50

WILLIAMSON, Jack. *Golden Blood.* 1967. Lancer 73-630. c/S Savage. SF. VG. B5d. $4.50

WILLIAMSON, Jack. *Green Girl.* 1950. Avon Fantasy Novels 2. PBO. c/gga. NF. B6a #74. $133.50

WILLIAMSON, Jack. *Green Girl.* 1950. Avon Fantasy Novels 2. 1st edn. NF. I1d. $70.00

WILLIAMSON, Jack. *Horror House.* Leisure 2492. SF. VG. W2d. $3.50

WILLIAMSON, Jack. *Humanoids.* 1954. Galaxy 21. c/Emsh: sgn. VG+. B3a #24. $16.50

WILLIAMSON, Jack. *Humanoids.* 1963. Lancer 72-129. c/E Emsh. SF. VG+ B5d. $5.50

WILLIAMSON, Jack. *Humanoids.* 1963. Lancer 72-129. 1st prtg. G. S1d. $2.50

WILLIAMSON, Jack. *Humanoids.* 1963. Lancer 74-812. c/E Emsh: hypo. SF. VG. B5d. $7.00

WILLIAMSON, Jack. *Humanoids.* Lancer 75-362. SF. VG. B5d. $3.50

WILLIAMSON, Jack. *Legion of Space.* Galaxy SF 2. NF. B3d. $8.00

WILLIAMSON, Jack. *Legion of Space.* 1967. Pyramid X 1576. 1st prtg. c/Gauhan. VG. P7d. $4.00

WILLIAMSON, Jack. *One Against the Legion.* Pyramid X 1657. 1st prtg. G+. S1d. $2.50

WILLIAMSON, Jack. *Pandora Effect.* Ace 65125. SF. VG. B5d. $3.00

WILLIAMSON, Jack. *Reign of Wizardry.* 1964. Lancer 72-761. 1st edn. F. M1d. $20.00

WILLIAMSON, Jack. *Reign of Wizardry.* 1964. Lancer 72-761. 1st prtg. c/Frazetta. NF. P7d. $15.00

WILLIAMSON, Jack. *Reign of Wizardry.* 1968. Lancer 73-748. 1st prtg. SF. VG. R5d. $3.50

WILLIAMSON, Jack. *Seetee Ship.* 1968. Lancer 73-732. SF. VG. B4d. $4.00

WILLIAMSON, Jack. *Seetee Shock.* 1968. Lancer 73-733. 1st prtg. SF. VG+. R5d. $5.00

WILLIAMSON, Jack. *Star Bridge.* 1963. Ace F 241. 1st prtg. G+. S1d. $2.50

WILLIAMSON, Jack. *Trapped in Space.* 1970. Scholastic 1749. SF. VG+. W2d. $4.00

WILLIAMSON, Jack. *Trial of Terra.* 1962. Ace D 555. PBO. VG. B3d. $4.00

WILLIAMSON, Jack. *Trial of Terra.* 1962. Ace D 555. 1st prtg. F. S1d. $9.00

WILLIAMSON, S.G. *Torment.* 1953. Popular 479. VG. B3d. $6.00

WILLIAMSON, Thames. *Gladiator.* 1953. Perma P 215. 1st pb. VG+. B6d. $9.00

WILLIAMSON, Tony. *Technicians of Death.* 1979. Fontana 5577. My. VG. P1d. $4.00

WILLIAMSON. *After Worlds End.* 1963. Magabook 2. PBO. VG+. B6d. $12.50

WILLIE, Ennis. *Code of Vengeance.* Merit 492. VG. B3d. $4.00

WILLIE, Ennis. *Scarlet Goddess.* Merit 683. PBO. VG. B3d. $3.50

WILLIFORD, Charles. *Cockfighter.* 1987. Black Lizard NN. c/J Kirwan. My. G+. B5d. $6.50

WILLIFORD, Charles. *High Priest.* 1956. Beacon 130. PBO. extremely scarce. VG+. B6a #79. $363.00

WILLINGHAM, Calder. *End As a Man.* 1950. Avon 240. VG. I1d. $6.00

WILLINGHAM, Calder. *Geraldine Bradshaw.* 1951. Avon G 1005. Fi. G+. B5d. $5.00

WILLINGHAM, Calder. *Natural Child.* Lancer 70-004. c/photo. Fi. VG. B5d. $3.50

WILLINGHAM, Calder. *Natural Child.* 1953. Signet S 1062. c/J Avati. Fi. G+. B5d. $3.00

WILLINGHAM, Calder. *Reach to the Stars.* Signet 987. VG. B3d. $5.00

WILLIS, G. *Hungry for Love.* Uni-Book 62. VG+. B3d. $9.00

WILLIS, W.N. *Girl of London Town.* Camden NN. VG. B3d. $8.50

WILLOCK, Colin. *Death in Covert.* 1963. Penguin 1934. My. VG. P1d. $6.00

WILLOW, Peter. *Extra Duty.* 1967. Uni-Book UB 140. PBO. c/Ward. NF. B3a #21. $21.60

WILLOW, Peter. *Just Friends.* 1967. Wee Hours 511. PBO. NF. B3a #24. $36.65

WILLOW, Peter. *Pay the Devil.* 1966. After Hours 128. PBO. VG+. B6a #77. $74.00

WILLOW, Peter. *Proper Respect.* 1967. Wee Hours 552. c/Stanton. VG+. B3a #21. $8.80

WILLS, Thomas. *Mine To Avenge.* 1955. Gold Medal 490. My. G+. P1d. $10.00

WILLS, Thomas. *You'll Get Yours.* Lion LB 129. 2nd prtg. NF. B3d. $5.00

WILLSON, Meredith. *Music Man.* 1962. Pyramid X 736. MTI. c/photo. VG+. B4d. $3.75

WILMER, Dale. *Dead Fall.* 1956. Bantam 1420. My. VG. P1d. $8.00

WILMER, Dale. *Dead Fall.* 1956. Bantam 1420. 1st prtg. My. G+. R5d. $1.50

WILMOT, Robert Patrick. *Blood in Your Eye.* 1953. Pocket 975. My. VG. P1d. $8.50

WILMOT, Robert Patrick. *Murder on Monday.* Pocket 997. NF. G5d. $9.00

WILSON, Carolyn. *Scent of Lilacs.* 1966. Ace G 603. 1st prtg. My. G+. R5d. $1.50

WILSON, Colin. *Adrift in Soho.* 1964. Pan X 297. Fi. VG+. P1d. $9.00

WILSON, Colin. *Killer.* 1970. New English 2792. My. VG. P1d. $6.00

WILSON, Colin. *Lifeforce.* 1985. Warner. 1st pb edn. F. M1d. $8.00

WILSON, Colin. *Mind Parasites.* 1968. Bantam F 3905. 1st prtg. SF. VG. R5d. $3.00

WILSON, Colin. *Necessary Doubt.* 1966. Pocket 75066. 1st prtg. My. F. W2d. $4.00

WILSON, Colin. *Outsider.* 1970. Pan 23001. 3rd edn. Nfi. VG. P1d. $5.00

WILSON, Colin. *Quest for Wilhelm Reich.* 1982. Granada 04852. Nfi. VG. P1d. $4.00

WILSON, Colin. *Schoolgirl Murder Case.* 1975. Panther 04232. My. VG. P1d. $6.00

WILSON, Colin. *Space Vampires.* 1977. Pocket 80916. Ho. VG. P1d. $7.50

WILSON, Dana. *Uneasy Virtue.* Novel Library 12. VG+. I1d. $18.00

WILSON, David. *Corpse Maker.* Award AN 1365. McCloud #4. VG. M6d. $7.50

WILSON, David. *Dangerous Place To Die.* 1975. Award AN 1386. My. VG+. P1d. $10.00

WILSON, David. *Dangerous Place To Die.* 1975. Award AN 1386. PBO. TVTI. McCloud #5. G+. M6d. $6.50

WILSON, David. *Park Avenue Executioner.* 1975. Award AQ 1463. My. VG. P1d. $6.00

WILSON, Donald Powell. *My Six Convicts.* 1952. Cardinal C 77. 2nd edn. Nfi. VG+. P1d. $11.50

WILSON, Earl. *Pike's Peek or Bust.* Popular 236. VG. B3d. $6.00

WILSON, Edmund. *I Thought of Daisy.* 1953. Ballantine 20. PBO. VG+. B6d. $8.00

WILSON, Edmund. *Memoirs of Hecate County.* 1976. Bantam O 2794. 1st prtg. c/gga. VG. P7d. $4.00

WILSON, Ethel. *Lilly's Story.* 1956. Avon 721. Fa. VG+. B4d. $4.00

WILSON, G. *Feared & the Fearless.* Corgi 141. VG. B3d. $8.00

WILSON, Gahan. *Harry, the Fat Bear Spy.* 1978. Dell 43824. 2nd edn. My/SF. VG. P1d. $5.00

WILSON, Harry Leon. *Ruggles of Red Gap.* 1951. Pocket 772. Fa. NF. B4d. $6.00

WILSON, Herbert Emerson. *I Stole $16,000,000.* 1956. Signet 1293. Nfi. G+. P1d. $6.00

WILSON, John H. *Nell Gwyn: Royal Mistress.* Dell 766. c/G Foxley. Fi. VG+. B5d. $4.50

WILSON, Margaret. *Able McLaughlins.* Avon G 1094. Fi. VG. B5d. $2.50

WILSON, Margery. *Pocket Book of Etiquette.* 1941. Pocket 107. c/photo. Nfi. G+. B5d. $3.00

WILSON, Meredith. *Music Man.* 1962. Pyramid R 736. MTI. c/photo. VG+. B4d. $3.75

WILSON, Mitchell. *Live With Lightning.* 1952. Bantam A 1035. Fi. VG+. P1d. $13.50

WILSON, Mitchell. *None So Blind.* 1960. Hillman 182. Fi. F. P1d. $14.00

WILSON, Mitchell. *Panic-Stricken.* 1948. Dell 263. My. VG+. P1d. $20.00

WILSON, Mitchell. *Panic-Stricken.* 1948. Dell 263. NF. B3a #22. $22.00

WILSON, Mitchell. *Panic-Stricken.* 1948. Dell 263. 1st prtg. My. G+. R5d. $4.50

WILSON, Mitchell. *Stalk the Hunter.* 1945. Pocket 315. My. G+. P1d. $7.50

WILSON, Paul F. *Tery.* 1990. Baen 69855-9. 1st edn. Fa. F. F2d. $8.00

WILSON, R. *Sex After Forty.* Viceroy 232. VG+. B3d. $4.50

WILSON, Richard. *Girls From Planet 5.* 1955. Ballantine 117. G+. I1d. $6.00

WILSON, Richard. *Girls From Planet 5.* 1955. Ballantine 117. 1st edn. F. M1d. $18.00

WILSON, Richard. *Girls From Planet 5.* 1967. Lancer 75-550. 3rd edn. NF. P9d. $2.00

WILSON, Richard. *Those Idiots From Earth.* 1957. Ballantine 237. PBO. VG+. B3d. $5.50

WILSON, Richard. *Those Idiots From Earth.* 1957. Ballantine 237. 1st edn. F. M1d. $15.00

WILSON, Richard. *Time Out for Tomorrow.* 1962. Ballantine F 658. PBO. c/R Powers. SF. VG. B5d. $4.50

WILSON, Richard. *Time Out for Tomorrow.* 1962. Ballantine F 658. 1st edn. F. M1d. $20.00

WILSON, Richard. *30-Day Wonder.* 1960. Ballantine 434K. NF. I1d. $8.00

WILSON, Richard. *30-Day Wonder.* 1960. Ballantine 434K. PBO. c/R Powers. SF. VG. B5d. $5.00

WILSON, Richard. *30-Day Wonder.* 1960. Ballantine 434K. 1st edn. F. M1d. $15.00

WILSON, Richard. *30-Day Wonder.* 1962. Ballantine 631. 1st prtg. SF. G+. R5d. $2.00

WILSON, Sloan. *Man in the Gray Flannel Suit.* 1956. Cardinal C 230. VG. B3d. $4.00

WILSON, Sloan. *Sense of Values.* 1962. Cardinal GC 129. Fi. VG+. B5d. $3.50

WILSON, Sloan. *Summer Place.* 1959. Cardinal GC 65. c/D Green. Fi. VG. B5d. $2.50

WILSON, William. *Detour.* 1975. Berkley Z 2790. 1st prtg. My. VG. W2d. $3.25

WILSON, William. *Strangers.* Dell 834. c/G Erickson. Fi. VG. B5d. $3.00

WILSTACH, John. *Bedtime Blonde.* 1950. Quarter Book 56. PBO. c/Rodewald: gga. VG+. B6a #77. $77.00

WILSTACH, John. *Night Club Girl.* 1951. Avon Special NN. PBO. c/gga. VG+. B6a #77. $62.75

WINDHAM, Donald. *Dog Star.* 1951. Signet 871. 1st pb. VG. B6d. $7.00

WINDHAM, Donald. *Let Me Alone.* 1956. Popular 754. JD. VG. P1d. $12.00

WINSKI, Norman. *Nevada Nightmare.* 1984. Pinnacle 41929. My. VG. P1d. $3.50

WINSKI, Norman. *Sword & the Sorceror.* 1982. Pinnacle 41787. 1st prtg. MTI. SF. VG. W2d. $3.50

WINSLOW, Pauline Glen. *Copper Gold.* 1981. Dell 11130. My. VG. P1d. $3.50

WINSOR, Kathleen. *Star Money.* 1951. Signet 868AB. c/J Avati. Fi. VG. B5d. $4.00

WINSOR, Roy. *Always Lock Your Bedroom Door.* 1976. Gold Medal 3674. 1st edn. De. F. F2d. $8.00

WINSOR, Roy. *Corpse That Walked.* 1974. Gold Medal P 3278. My. VG. P1d. $3.50

WINSTEAD, Rebecca Noyes. *Tunnel of Darkness.* 1974. Canyon 119. My. G+. P1d. $3.00

WINSTON, Daoma. *Bracken's World.* 1969. PB Library 64-237. Fi. VG. P1d. $7.50

WINSTON, Daoma. *Devil's Princess.* 1971. Lancer 75-220. Go. VG. P1d. $4.50

WINSTON, Daoma. *Flight of a Fallen Angel.* 1977. Pocket 80953. My. VG. P1d. $3.50

WINSTON, Daoma. *Golden Tramp.* 1959. Beacon 272. PBO. VG. B3d. $3.50

WINSTON, Daoma. *Golden Valley.* 1976. Pocket 80469. 2nd edn. Fi. VG. P1d. $3.00

WINSTON, Daoma. *High Country.* 1970. PB Library 64-279. Fi. VG. P1d. $7.50

WINSTON, Daoma. *Long & Living Shadow.* 1968. Belmont B 50-847. Go. VG. P1d. $5.00

WINSTON, Daoma. *Mansion of Smiling Masks.* 1967. Signet P 3136. Go. VG. P1d. $5.00

WINSTON, Daoma. *Other Stranger.* 1958. Beacon 193. 1st pb. c/Levine: gga. VG. B6d/P7d. $9.00

WINSTON, Daoma. *Seminar in Evil.* 1972. Lancer 75-392. Go. VG. P1d. $4.00

WINSTON, Daoma. *Sound Stage.* PB Library 64-364. IVTI. Bracken's World #3. VG. B3d. $4.00

WINSTON, Daoma. *Visit After Dark.* 1975. Ace 86512. Go. VG. P1d. $3.50

WINSTON, Daoma. *Woman He Wanted.* 1956. Beacon B 118. Ad. G+. P1d. $9.00

WINSTON, Daoma. *Woman He Wanted.* 1958. Beacon 172. 1st prtg. c/gga. VG+. P7d. $12.50

WINTER, Alice. *Velvet Bubble.* 1978. Belmont Tower 51-325. Ho. VG. P1d. $4.00

WINTER, Douglas E. *Prime Evil.* 1988. Signet 5909. 1st edn. PBO. F. P9d. $3.00

WINTER, Douglas E. *Stephen King: The Art of Darkness.* Signet AE 5866. 4th edn. Nfi. VG. P1d. $4.50

WINTERBOTHAM, Russ. *Red Planet.* 1962. Monarch 270. PBO. VG. M6d. $8.50

WINTERBOTHAM, Russ. *Red Planet.* 1962. Monarch 270. 1st edn. SF. F. F2d. $16.00

WINTERBOTHAM, Russ. *Red Planet.* Priory 1094. 2nd edn. SF. VG. B4d. $3.00

WINTERBOTHAM, Russ. *Space Egg.* 1962. Monarch 252. SF. VG. B5d. $8.00

WINTERBOTHAM, Russ. *Space Egg.* 1962. Monarch 252. 1st pb edn. F. M1d. $20.00

WINTERBOTHAM, Russ. *Space Egg.* Priory 1126. SF. VG. W2d. $3.00

WINTERS, Jon. *Drakov Memoranda.* 1979. Avon 47563. My. VG. P1d. $3.50

WINTHROP, Wilma. *Island of the Accursed.* 1969. Lancer 74-535. 2nd edn. My. VG. P1d. $3.50

WINTHROP, Wilma. *Tryst With Terror.* 1965. Lancer 72-927. Go. VG+. P1d. $8.00

WINTON, John. *Fighting Temeraire.* 1973. Pan 23520. Th. G+. P1d. $3.00

WINWAR, Frances. *Joan of Arc.* 1948. Bantam 459. MTI. c/Ingrid Bergman. VG. B4d. $3.00

WINWAR, Frances. *Joan of Arc.* 1948. Bantam 459. MTI. VG+. B4d. $6.00

WINWAR, Frances. *Joan of Arc.* 1948. Bantam 459. NF. I1d. $8.00

WIRE, H.C. *Trail Boss of Indian Beef.* 1945. Dell 97. VG+. I1d. $10.00

WISE, William. *Death's Head.* 1965. Penguin C 2353. My. G+. P1d. $4.00

WISEMAN, William R. *Drawn by Desire.* 1961. Newsstand 179. 1st edn. c/gga. F. F2d. $15.00

WISTER, Owen. *Virginian.* 1964. Scholastic T 610. We. VG. B5d. $2.50

WITCOVER, Jules. *85 Days: The Last Campaign of Robert F Kennedy.* 1969. Ace 19660. Nfi. VG+. B5d. $3.50

WITHERELL, June. *Mahogany House.* 1967. Lancer 73-692. PBO. VG. B6d. $5.00

WITHERS, E.L. *Diminishing Returns.* 1961. Perma M 4203. My. VG. P1d. $6.50

WITHERS, E.L. *House on the Beach.* Crest 252. c/Powers. VG+. B3d. $4.00

WITHERSPOON, Bill. *Death Row.* 1968. Pyramid X 1742. Nfi. F. P1d. $10.00

WITHERSPOON, Bill. *Death Row.* Pyramid 1742. VG. B3d. $5.00

WLASCHIN, Ken. *Italian Job.* 1969. Signet T4093. My. VG. P1d. $5.00

WOBIG/WRIGHT. *Youth Monopoly/Pictures of Pavanne.* Ace H 48. VG. P9d. $2.00

WODEHOUSE, P.G. *Blandings Castle.* 1966. Penguin 985. 2nd edn. TVTI. VG+. P1d. $8.50

WODEHOUSE, P.G. *Code of the Woosters.* Dell 393. F. F2d. $10.00

WODEHOUSE, P.G. *Code of the Woosters.* Dell 393. VG. B3d. $4.50

WODEHOUSE, P.G. *Code of the Woosters.* 1950. Dell 393. c/V Kaufman. Fi. G+. B5d. $3.00

WODEHOUSE, P.G. *Galahad at Blandings.* 1966. Penguin 2570. TVTI. VG. P1d. $6.50

WODEHOUSE, P.G. *Leave It to Psmith.* Dell 357. NF. F2d. $10.00

WODEHOUSE/WODEHOUSE. *Quick Service/Code of the Woosters.* 1953. Ace D 25. c/Saunders. NF. I1d. $15.00

WODEHOUSE/WODEHOUSE. *Quick Service/Code of the Woosters.* 1953. Ace D 25. VG. B3d. $5.00

WOHL, Burton. *China Syndrome.* 1979. Bantam 13017. My. VG. P1d. $4.00

WOHL, Burton. *Cold Wind in August.* 1961. Dell 1st Edn C 120. My. VG. P1d. $5.50

WOIWODE, L. *What I'm Going To Do, I Think.* 1970. Ballantine 01916. 1st prtg. c/Duncan: gga. VG+. P7d. $5.00

WOJCIECHOWSKA, Mayo. *Tuned Out.* 1969. Dell 09139. 1st prtg. VG. P7d. $4.00

WOLD, Allen. *V: The Pursuit of Diana.* 1984. Pinnacle 42401. SF. G+. W2d. $3.75

WOLF, Gary. *Who Censored Roger Rabbit?* 1982. Ballantine 30325. 1st prtg. My. VG+. W2d. $4.00

WOLF, Leonard. *Dream of Dracula: In Search of the Living Dead.* 1972. Popular 00159. Nfi. F. W2d. $4.00

WOLF, Mari. *Golden Frame.* 1961. Perma M 4227. My. VG. P1d. $6.50

WOLFE, Aaron. *Invasion.* 1975. Laser 9. PBO. c/K Freas. SF. G+. M3d. $12.00

WOLFE, Bernard. *Limbo.* Ace A 3. VG. M1d. $8.00

WOLFE, Bernard. *Magic of Their Singing.* 1962. MacFadden 50-151. c/Leo & Diane Dillon. JD. F. B4d. $9.00

WOLFE, Bernard. *Magic of Their Singing.* 1962. MacFadden 50-151. VG. B3d. $4.00

WOLFE, Charles X. *Education of Lydia.* 1963. Beacon 672. 1st edn. c/gga. F. F2d. $12.00

WOLFE, Don. *New Voices: American Writing Today.* Perma P 213. VG+. B3d. $5.00

WOLFE, Gene. *Operation Ares.* 1970. Berkley. 1st edn. F. M1d. $7.00

WOLFE, John. *Wrong Target.* Major 3200. My. F. W2d. $5.00

WOLFE, Louis. *Journey of the Oceanauts.* Pyramid T 2299. 1st prtg. G+. S1d. $3.00

WOLFE, Peter. *Beams Falling: Art of Dashimill Hammett.* 1980. Popular 140. Nfi. VG. P1d. $15.00

WOLFE, Thomas. *Hills Beyond.* Pyramid 321. VG. B3d. $3.50

WOLFE, Thomas. *Look Homeward, Angel.* 1948. Signet 697. Fi. G+. B5d. $3.00

WOLFE, Thomas. *Look Homeward, Angel: Part II.* Signet 697. VG. B3d. $4.50

WOLFE, Thomas. *Of Time & the River.* Armed Services 1013. VG. B3d. $5.00

WOLFE, Thomas. *Selected Great Stories.* 1944. Avon Monthly Mystery 17. Fi. G. B5d. $2.00

WOLFE, Winifred. *Ask Any Girl.* 1959. Bantam A 1983. 1st prtg. VG. R5d. $2.00

WOLFE, Winifred. *If a Man Answers.* 1962. Dell 3966. MTI. F. B4d. $4.00

WOLFE & VEILLER. *Trail of Mary Dugan.* 1949. Pocket 647. My. F. P1d. $19.00

WOLFERT, Ira. *Act of Love.* 1955. Cardinal GC 29. c/T Dunn. Fi. VG+. B5d. $3.50

WOLFERT, Ira. *Underworld.* 1950. Bantam A 798. My. VG+. P1d. $14.00

WOLFF, D. *Fishing Tackle & Techniques.* Popular PC 1022. VG+. B3d. $4.50

WOLFF, Leon. *In Flanders Field.* Ballantine F 390K. NF. VG. B5d. $4.00

WOLFF, Maritta M. *Big Nickelodeon.* 1958. Bantam A 1721. Fa. VG+. B4d. $3.00

WOLFF, Maritta M. *Whistle Stop.* 1950. Popular 257. c/Rozen: gga. Fa. VG+. B4d. $7.50

WOLFF, Maritta M. *Whistle Stop.* 1950. Popular 257. VG. I1d. $6.00

WOLFF, Ruth. *Hawthorne.* 1969. PB Library 63-150. reprint. Go. NF. B6d. $7.50

WOLFFE, Charles X. *Education of Lydia.* 1963. Beacon B 672X. PBO. Ad. VG+. B5d. $6.50

WOLFFE, Charles X. *High-School Scandal.* 1963. Beacon 651. VG. B3d. $4.50

WOLFORD, C. *Blow-Up at Three Springs.* Berkley G 1101. VG. B3d. $3.50

WOLFORD, Nelson & Shirley. *Long Ride Home.* 1967. Pocket 50548. 2nd prtg. VG+. R5d. $1.50

WOLFSON, P.J. *Flesh Baron.* 1955. Lion Library LL 4. Fa. VG+. B4d. $7.50

WOLFSON, P.J. *Hell Cop.* 1960. Berkley Diamond D 2036. My. VG. P1d. $7.50

WOLFSON, P.J. *Is My Flesh of Brass?*
Berkley G 181. VG. B3d. $5.00

WOLFSON, P.J. *Is My Flesh of Brass?* 1948.
Newsstand 13. My. VG. P1d. $20.00

WOLFSON, P.J. *Pay for Her Passion.* 1949.
Newsstand 3A. VG. B3d. $7.00

WOLFSON, P.J. *Pay for Her Passion.* 1949.
Newsstand 3A. Fi. G+. B5d. $3.50

WOLFSON, P.J. *This Woman Is Mine (All Women Die).* Popular 356. VG. B3d. $3.50

WOLFSON, P.J. *Three of a Kind.* 1959.
Berkley G 248. Fa. VG+. B4d. $6.00

WOLFSON, P.J. *Three of a Kind.* 1957.
Berkley G 85. Fi. VG+. P1d. $11.00

WOLFSON, P.J. *Three of a Kind.* Berkley
598. VG. B3d. $4.50

WOLK, George. *Man Who Dealt in Blood.*
1974. Warner 59-267. My. VG. P1d. $3.50

WOLLCOTT, Alexander. *Long, Long Ago.*
Bantam 39. VG+. B3d. $4.50

WOLLCOTT, Alexander. *While Rome Burns.*
1941. Pocket 131. Nfi. VG. B5d. $5.00

WOLLHEIM, Donald A. *Ace SF Reader.*
1971. Ace 00275. SF. VG. W2d. $3.50

WOLLHEIM, Donald A. *Ace SF Reader.*
1971. Ace 00275. VG+. B3d. $4.50

WOLLHEIM, Donald A. *Ace SF Reader.*
1971. Ace 00275. 1st prtg. G. S1d. $2.00

WOLLHEIM, Donald A. *Adventures on Other Planets.* Ace D 490. NF. M1d. $10.00

WOLLHEIM, Donald A. *Adventures on Other Planets.* Ace D 490. 1st prtg. VG. S1d. $4.00

WOLLHEIM, Donald A. *Adventures on Other Planets.* 1955. Ace S 133. NF. M1d. $12.00

WOLLHEIM, Donald A. *Adventures on Other Planets.* 1955. Ace S 133. SF. VG. B5d. $7.50

WOLLHEIM, Donald A. *Avon Fanstasy Reader #11.* 1950. Avon. c/Ray Bradbury: sgn. VG+. B3a #20. $16.20

WOLLHEIM, Donald A. *Avon Fantasy Reader #14.* 1950. Avon. c/Ray Bradbury: sgn. VG+. B3a #20. $25.30

WOLLHEIM, Donald A. *Avon Fantasy Reader #2: City of the Living Dead.* 1947.
Avon. VG+. B3a #24. $3.30

WOLLHEIM, Donald A. *Avon Fantasy Reader #5: Scarlett Dream.* 1947. Avon.
c/Bloch: sgn. VG+. B3a #24. $19.25

WOLLHEIM, Donald A. *Avon Fantasy Reader.*
1969. Avon S 384. 1st edn. F. M1d. $10.00

WOLLHEIM, Donald A. *Avon Fantasy Reader.* 1969. Avon S 384. 1st prtg. SF. VG. W2d. $4.00

WOLLHEIM, Donald A. *DAW SF Reader.*
1976. DAW 200. VG. I1d. $3.00

WOLLHEIM, Donald A. *End of the World.*
1956. Ace S 183. F. M1d. $15.00

WOLLHEIM, Donald A. *End of the World.*
1956. Ace S 183. 1st edn. G. P9d. $1.25

WOLLHEIM, Donald A. *End of the World.*
1956. Ace S 183. 1st prtg. SF. VG. B5d/R5d. $5.00

WOLLHEIM, Donald A. *Hidden Planet.* Ace
D 354. F. M1d. $12.00

WOLLHEIM, Donald A. *Hidden Planet.* Ace
D 354. NF. I1d. $8.00

WOLLHEIM, Donald A. *Hidden Planet.* Ace
D 354. 1st prtg. VG. S1d. $5.00

WOLLHEIM, Donald A. *Macabre Reader.*
Ace D 353. c/Bloch: sgn. VG. B3d. $7.50

WOLLHEIM, Donald A. *Macabre Reader.*
Ace D 353. F. M1d. $25.00

WOLLHEIM, Donald A. *Men on the Moon.*
Ace 52470. c/G Morrow. SF. VG+. B5d. $4.00

WOLLHEIM, Donald A. *Mike Mars & the Mystery Satellite.* 1966. PB Library 56-369.
c/Hanke. SF. VG+. B5d. $4.00

WOLLHEIM, Donald A. *Mike Mars at Cape Kennedy.* 1966. PB Library 56-961. 1st edn.
PBO. VG. P9d. $1.50

WOLLHEIM, Donald A. *More Adventures on Other Planets.* Ace F 178. NF. M1d. $6.00

WOLLHEIM, Donald A. *More Macabre.*
Ace D 508. F. M1d. $25.00

WOLLHEIM, Donald A. *Pocket Book of SF.*
1943. Pocket 214. VG. I1d. $15.00

WOLLHEIM, Donald A. *Secret of Saturn's Rings.* 1966. PB Library 52-996. c/Hanke.
SF. VG. B5d. $3.00

WOLLHEIM, Donald A. *Secret of the Martian Moons.* 1963. Tempo T 28. 1st prtg. SF.
F. W2d. $5.50

WOLLHEIM, Donald A. *Secret of the Ninth Planet.* 1965. PB Library 52-874. 1st edn.
PBO. VG. P9d. $1.50

WOLLHEIM, Donald A. *Secret of the Ninth Planet.* 1965. PB Library 52-874. 1st pb edn. F. M1d. $7.00

WOLLHEIM, Donald A. *Swords in Sky.* Ace
F 311. F. M1d. $8.00

WOLLHEIM, Donald A. *1972 Annual World's Best SF.* 1972. DAW 5. PBO. SF. VG. B5d. $2.50

WOLLHEIM, Donald A. *1973 Annual World's Best SF.* 1973. DAW 53. c/J Gaughan. SF. VG. B5d. $2.50

WOLLHEIM, Donald A. *1974 Annual World's Best SF.* 1974. DAW 101. 1st prtg. SF. G+. R5d. $1.75

WOLLHEIM, Donald A. *1975 Annual World's Best SF.* DAW 148. VG. I1d. $3.00

WOLLHEIM, Donald A. *1977 Annual World's Best SF.* 1977. DAW 87997. 1st prtg. SF. VG. W2d. $3.25

WOLLHEIM, Donald A. *1978 Annual World's Best SF.* 1978. DAW 288. 1st edn. F. P9d. $2.00

WOLLHEIM, Donald A. *1986 Annual World's Best SF.* DAW 675. F. P9d. $2.00

WOLLHEIM, Donald A. *1987 Annual World's Best SF.* 1987. DAW 88677. 1st prtg. SF. VG+. W2d. $4.00

WOLLHEIM, Donald A. *2nd Avon Fantasy Reader.* 1969. Avon S 385. 1st edn. F. M1d. $10.00

WOLLHEIM, Donald A. *2nd Avon Fantasy Reader.* 1969. Avon S 385. 1st prtg. SF. VG. B5d. $7.50

WOLLHEIM/WOLLHEIM. *Adventures in the Far Future/Tales of Outer Space.* 1954.
Ace D 73. VG+. B3a #22. $6.50

WOLLHEIM/WOLLHEIM. *Adventures in the Far Future/Tales of Outer Space.* 1954.
Ace D 73. 1st edn. SF. F. F2d. $15.00

WOLLHEIM/WRIGHT. *Earth in Peril/Who Speaks of Conquest?* Ace D 205. G+. I1d. $4.00

WOLLHEIM/WRIGHT. *Earth in Peril/Who Speaks of Conquest?* 1957. Ace D 205.
PBO. c/Emsh. SF. VG. B5d. $6.00

WOLPERT, Stanley. *Nine Hours to Rama.*
1963. Bantam S 2474. My. VG. P1d. $6.00

WOLPERT, Stanley. *Nine Hours to Rama.*
1963. Bantam S 2474. 1st prtg. MTI. My. G+. R5d. $1.25

WOOD, Clement. *Studio Affair.* 1958. Beacon 189. 1st prtg. c/Micarelli: gga. VG. P7d. $9.00

WOOD, Ed Jr. *Raped in the the Grass.*
1968. Pendulum Pictorial 2. 1st edn. c/color photo. F. F2d. $65.00

WOOD, Ed Jr. *Watts After.* 1967. Pad Library 578. PBO. c/great hippie. scarce. VG+. B6a #74. $55.00

WOOD, Ed Jr. *Watts...The Difference.* 1967. Pad Library 564. VG. B3a #20. $26.40

WOOD, S. Andrew. *Sinner's Castle.* 1944. Prize Mystery 13. My. VG. P1d. $20.00

WOOD, Ted. *Corkscrew.* 1989. World Wide 26024. My. VG. W2d. $3.00

WOOD, Ted. *Live Bait.* 1986. Bantam 25558. 1st prtg. My. F. W2d. $4.00

WOODCOTT, Keith. *Martian Sphinx.* 1965. Ace F 320. G+. M1d. $4.00

WOODFORD, Jack. *Abortive Hussy.* 1947. Avon 146. c/Strick. Fi. G+. B5d. $4.00

WOODFORD, Jack. *Abortive Hussy.* 1967. Avon 146. c/gga. Fa. VG. B4d. $6.00

WOODFORD, Jack. *Ecstasy Girl.* 1948. Novel Library 2. 1st prtg. c/gga. VG. P7d. $9.00

WOODFORD, Jack. *Free Lovers.* 1951. Avon Special NN. c/Driben. VG+. B6d. $75.00

WOODFORD, Jack. *Free Lovers.* 1948. Novel Library 3. VG. I1d. $6.00

WOODFORD, Jack. *Grounds for Divorce.* Avon 4. scarce. VG+. B6a. $49.50

WOODFORD, Jack. *Grounds for Divorce.* 1948. Novel Library 7. Ad. VG. B5d. $12.00

WOODFORD, Jack. *Grounds for Divorce.* 1948. Novel Library 7. F. I1d. $20.00

WOODFORD, Jack. *Grounds for Divorce.* 1948. Novel Library 7. 1st prtg. c/gga. VG+. P7d. $15.00

WOODFORD, Jack. *Hard-Boiled Virgin.* 1947. Avon 138. c/Barye: gga. Fa. VG. B4d. $5.00

WOODFORD, Jack. *Hard-Boiled Virgin.* 1947. Avon 138. VG+. I1d. $6.00

WOODFORD, Jack. *Home Away From Home.* 1962. Chicago PB House B 130. Nfi. F. P1d. $13.00

WOODFORD, Jack. *Illegitimate.* 1963. Beacon B 607F. PBO. Ad. G+. B5d. $3.00

WOODFORD, Jack. *Male & Female.* 1950. Novel Library 36. 1st prtg. c/gga. VG. P7d. $15.00

WOODFORD, Jack. *Passionate Princess.* Avon 6. c/Driben. VG+. B6d. $75.00

WOODFORD, Jack. *Passionate Princess.* 1948. Novel Library 4. Ad. G+. B5d. $7.50

WOODFORD, Jack. *Passionate Princess.* 1948. Novel Library 4. 1st prtg. c/gga. VG. P7d. $10.00

WOODFORD, Jack. *Peeping Tom.* 1948. Novel Library 6. 1st prtg. c/gga. G+. P7d. $10.00

WOODFORD, Jack. *Possess Me Not.* 1951. Avon 346. 1st edn. PBO. Fa. VG. B6d. $18.00

WOODFORD, Jack. *Rites of Love.* 1950. Avon Bedside Novel 1. PBO. 1st edn. c/gga. VG. B6a #77. $50.00

WOODFORD, Jack. *Teach Me To Love.* 1951. Avon Book Dividend 6. 1st edn. PBO. c/Driben: gga. rare. VG+. B6a #77. $75.00

WOODFORD, Jack. *Three Gorgeous Hussies.* Avon Special NN. scarce. VG+. B6a #80. $55.00

WOODFORD, Jack. *Three Gorgeous Hussies.* 1948. Novel Library 1. Ad. G. B5d. $5.00

WOODFORD, Jack. *Three Gorgeous Hussies.* 1948. Novel Library 1. 1st prtg. c/gga. VG. P7d. $9.00

WOODHALL, Edwin T. *Detective & Secret Service Days.* Mellifont. dust jacket in fair condition. Nfi. VG. P1d. $20.00

WOODHOUSE, Martin. *Bush Baby.* 1969. Berkley S 1726. Th. VG. P1d. $4.50

WOODLEY, Demmos R. *Blacklace Girls.* Chariot 907. VG. B3d. $4.50

WOODLEY, Richard. *Dealer.* 1972. PB Library 66-897. Nfi. VG+. B5d. $5.00

WOODLEY, Richard. *Death Scouts.* 1977. Dell 15369. 1st edn. TVTI. c/photo. SF. F. F2d. $12.50

WOODLEY, Richard. *Man From Atlantis #1.* 1977. Dell 15368. My/SF. VG. P1d. $5.00

WOODLEY, Richard. *Man From Atlantis #1.* 1977. Dell 15368. 2nd prtg. SF. G+. W2d. $4.00

WOODLEY, Richard. *Slap Shot.* 1977. Berkley 03339. 1st prtg. VG+. R5d. $2.00

WOODMAN, Michael. *Medusa Kiss.* 1971. Beagle 95125. My. VG. P1d. $4.50

WOODS, Merry. *Sweet Revenge.* 1966. Midwood 32-586. Ad. NF. B5d. $6.00

WOODS, Sara. *Bloody Instructions.* 1970. Popular 02495. My. VG. P1d. $4.50

WOODS, Sara. *Knives Have Edges.* 1973. Dell 4579. My. VG+. P1d. $4.50

WOODS, Sara. *Third Encounter.* 1970. Popular 02496. My. VG. P1d. $4.50

WOODS, Sara. *Though I Know She Lies.* 1980. Raven House 62nd edn. My. VG. P1d. $3.00

WOODS, Stuart. *Deep Lie.* Pan 29378. Th. VG. P1d. $4.00

WOODWARD, David. *Secret Raiders.* 1958. Avon T 236. c/photo. Nfi. VG. B5d. $2.50

WOODWARD, L.T. *Deceivers.* 1962. Beacon B529F. PBO. Ad. NF. B5d. $12.50

WOODWARD, L.T. *Sadism.* 1964. Lancer 74-835. VG+. B3d. $5.50

WOODWARD, L.T. *Sex & Hypnosis.* Monarch 516. VG. B3d. $4.00

WOODWARD, L.T. *Sex & the Divorced Woman.* 1964. Lancer 73-424. PBO. NF. G+. B5d. $5.00

WOODWARD, L.T. *Twilight Women.* 1963. Lancer 74-821. PBO. NF. P6d. $2.50

WOOLF, Virginia. *Orlando.* 1946. Penguin 590. 1st prtg. c/Salter. VG. P7d. $5.00

WOOLFE, Byron. *Animal Urge.* 1960. Vega Book 1. PBO. VG. B6d. $6.00

WOOLFE, Byron. *Bold Desires.* Saber SA 10. VG. B3d. $5.00

WOOLFE, Byron. *Lust at the Waterfront.* 1965. Saber SA 80. PBO. c/Elaine: gga. NF. B6a #76. $33.00

WOOLFE, Byron. *Sex Addict.* Playtime 668. VG+. B3d. $5.50

WOOLFOLK, William. *My Name Is Morgan.* 1964. Perma M 7513. Fi. VG. P1d. $6.00

WOOLFOLK, William. *Naked Hunter.* 1960. Berkley Diamond D 2032. My. F. P1d. $14.00

WOOLFOLK, William. *Overlords.* 1973. Crest P 2008. My. F. P1d. $5.00

WOOLFOLK, William. *President's Doctor.* 1975. Playboy 16283. My. VG. P1d. $3.50

WOOLFOLK, William. *Run While You Can.* 1956. Popular 790. PBO. My. VG. B6d. $7.00

WOOLFOLK, William. *Run While You Can.* 1956. Popular 790. 1st edn. My. F. F2d. $14.00

WOOLFOLK, William. *Way of the Wicked.* 1959. Monarch 118. My. VG. P1d. $10.00

WOOLLCOTT, Alexander. *Long, Long Ago.* 1946. Bantam 39. Nfi. VG+. B4d. $4.00

WOOLRICH, Cornell. *Beware the Lady (Bride Wore Black).* 1953. Pyramid 80. VG+. B3a #21. $109.85

WOOLRICH, Cornell. *Beware the Lady.* 1953. Pyramid 80. rare. VG+. B6a #79. $82.50

WOOLRICH, Cornell. *Beyond the Night.* 1959. Avon T 354. SF. VG. W2d. $5.50

WOOLRICH, Cornell. *Beyond the Night.* 1959. Avon T 354. 1st edn. NF. M1d. $30.00

WOOLRICH, Cornell. *Black Alibi.* 1982. Ballantine 30707. My. VG. B5d. $7.50

WOOLRICH, Cornell. *Black Alibi*. 1965. Collier 02665. 1st prtg. My. VG+. R5d. $6.00

WOOLRICH, Cornell. *Black Angel*. 1946. Avon 96. My. VG+. P1d. $55.00

WOOLRICH, Cornell. *Black Angel*. 1946. Avon 96. scarce. VG+. B6a #80. $82.50

WOOLRICH, Cornell. *Black Curtain*. 1968. Ace H 104. My. VG. P1d. $6.00

WOOLRICH, Cornell. *Black Curtain*. 1948. Dell 208. 1st edn. PBO. c/Frederiksen. VG. B6d. $27.50

WOOLRICH, Cornell. *Black Path of Fear*. 1968. Ace H 66. My. VG. P1d. $6.00

WOOLRICH, Cornell. *Black Path of Fear*. 1946. Avon 106. My. VG+. P1d. $35.00

WOOLRICH, Cornell. *Black Path of Fear*. Thriller 29. VG. G5d. $20.00

WOOLRICH, Cornell. *Bride Wore Black*. 1968. Ace G 699. VG. P6d. $2.00

WOOLRICH, Cornell. *Bride Wore Black*. Ace 07921. My. VG. B5d. $4.50

WOOLRICH, Cornell. *Bride Wore Black*. 1957. Dell D 186. G+. P6d. $1.50

WOOLRICH, Cornell. *Bride Wore Black*. 1957. Dell D 186. My. VG. P1d. $10.00

WOOLRICH, Cornell. *Bride Wore Black*. 1945. Pocket 271. 2nd edn. My. VG. P1d. $12.50

WOOLRICH, Cornell. *Deadline at Dawn*. Ace 14153. My. G+. B5d. $3.50

WOOLRICH, Cornell. *Death Is My Dancing Partner*. 1959. Pyramid G 374. My. G+. P1d. $25.00

WOOLRICH, Cornell. *Death Is My Dancing Partner*. 1959. Pyramid G 374. PBO. c/Schmidt. extremely scarce. VG+. B6a #79. $88.00

WOOLRICH, Cornell. *Doom Stone*. 1960. Avon T 408. 1st edn. F. F2d. $26.00

WOOLRICH, Cornell. *Night Has a Thousand Eyes*. 1967. PB Library 54-438. My. G+. P1d. $7.50

WOOLRICH, Cornell. *Phantom Lady*. Ace 66050. My. VG+. P1d. $7.50

WOOLRICH, Cornell. *Rear Window*. 1984. Ballantine 30668. Fi. VG. B5d. $7.50

WOOLRICH, Cornell. *Rendezvous in Black*. 1949. Pocket 570. NF. G5d. $15.00

WOOLRICH, Cornell. *Savage Bride*. 1950. Gold Medal 136. My/SF. F. P1d $50.00

WOOLRICH, Cornell. *Savage Bride*. 1950. Gold Medal 136. PBO. VG+. B3a #20. $24.00

WOOLRICH, Cornell. *Savage Bride*. 1950. Gold Medal 136. VG. B3d. $20.00

WOOLRICH, Cornell. *Six Times Death*. 1948. Popular 137. 1st edn. PBO. My. F. F2d. $45.00

WORKMAN, James. *Shock Stories*. 1962. Horwitz 119. PBO. VG+. B6a #79. $73.00

WORLEY, William. *My Dead Wife*. 1951. Pocket 773. G. G5d. $3.50

WORLEY, William. *My Dead Wife*. 1951. Pocket 773. My. VG+. P1d. $13.50

WORMSER, Richard. *Bedtime Story*. 1964. Gold Medal K 1427. 1st prtg. VG. R5d. $3.50

WORMSER, Richard. *Body Looks Familiar*. 1958. Dell 1st Edn A 156. My. VG. P1d. $7.50

WORMSER, Richard. *Drive East on 66*. 1961. Gold Medal S 1133. My. VG. P1d. $8.00

WORMSER, Richard. *Hanging Heiress*. 1950. Signet 787. My. VG. P1d. $10.00

WORMSER, Richard. *Hanging Heiress*. 1950. Signet 787. 1st pb. My. VG+. B6d. $13.50

WORMSER, Richard. *Invader*. 1972. Gold Medal T 2524. My. VG. P1d. $4.00

WORMSER, Richard. *Last Days of Sodom & Gomorrah*. 1962. Gold Medal K 1245. MTI. VG+. B3d. $6.00

WORMSER, Richard. *Last Days of Sodom & Gomorrah*. 1962. Gold Medal K 1245. 1st edn. F. F2d. $14.00

WORMSER, Richard. *Last Days of Sodom & Gomorrah*. 1962. Gold Medal K 1245. 1st prtg. VG. P1d/R5d. $8.00

WORMSER, Richard. *Lonesome Quarter*. 1952. Bantam 1056. Fi. F. P1d. $18.00

WORMSER, Richard. *Longhorn Trail*. 1955. Ace D 92. We. VG. P1d. $10.00

WORMSER, Richard. *McLintock*. 1963. Gold Medal 1350. c/John Wayne: photo. VG. B3d. $5.00

WORMSER, Richard. *Operation Crossbow*. 1965. Dell 6697. My. VG. P1d. $5.50

WORMSER, Richard. *Pan Satyrus*. 1963. Avon G 1191. SF. F. P1d. $12.00

WORMSER, Richard. *Pan Satyrus*. 1963. Avon G 1191. 1st edn. VG. M1d. $7.00

WORMSER, Richard. *Perfect Pigeon*. 1962. Gold Medal S 1201. G. G5d. $3.50

WORMSER, Richard. *Perfect Pigeon*. 1962. Gold Medal S 1201. VG. B3d. $6.00

WORMSER, Richard. *Torn Curtain*. 1966. Dell 8980. 1st prtg. VG. R5d. $2.00

WORMSER, Richard. *Widow Wore Red*. Crest 230. VG. B3d. $4.00

WORMSER, Richard. *Wild Wild West*. 1966. Signet D 2836. PBO. TVTI. VG. P6d. $3.25

WORSLEY-GOUGH, Barbara. *Alibi Innings*. 1958. Penguin 1321. My. VG. P1d. $7.50

WORTHY, K. *Sexual Deviation & Law*. Imperial 715. NF. B3d. $5.00

WORTS, George F. *Blue Lacquer Box*. 1947. Popular 93. My. VG+. P1d. $20.00

WORTS, George F. *House of Creeping Horror*. Hart Book K 1. My. VG. P1d. $30.00

WORTS, George F. *Overboard*. 1950. Popular 292. My. VG. P1d. $75.00

WORTS, George F. *Overboard*. 1950. Popular 292. 1st edn. PBO. c/Belarski; gga. VG. B6a #79. $44.00

WOUK, Herman. *City Boy*. 1964. Dell 1297. 1st prtg. c/Liebman. VG. P7d. $4.00

WOUK, Herman. *Marjorie Morningstar*. 1957. Signet T 1454. MTI. c/G Kelly & N Wood. Fi. VG. B5d. $4.00

WREDE, Patricia C. *Talking to Dragons*. 1985. Tempo 79591. 1st edn. c/sgn. SF. F. F2d. $13.00

WREN, Percival C. *Beau Geste*. 1960. Perma M 4190. Fa. VG. B4d. $3.00

WREN, Percival C. *Beau Sabreur*. Perma P 232. VG+. B3d. $4.50

WREN, Percival C. *Stories of the Foreign Legion*. 1955. Perma M 4011. 1st prtg. VG. P7d. $5.00

WREN, Percival C. *Wages of Virtue*. 1961. John Murray NN. VG. B3d. $8.00

WRIGHT, C. *Sex Wasn't Love*. Saber SA 194. VG+. B3d. $6.00

WRIGHT, Harold Bill. *Shepherd of the Hills*. 1947. Pocket 441. VG+. B3d. $6.50

WRIGHT, Harold Bill. *Shepherd of the Hills*. 1947. Pocket 441. 1st prtg. VG. P7d. $5.00

WRIGHT, Ian. *Last Hope of Earth*. 1965. Ace F 347. 1st prtg. VG+. S1d. $3.00

WRIGHT, Ian. *Last Hope of Earth*. 1965. Ace F 347. 1st prtg. SF. VG. R5d. $2.50

WRIGHT, Lee edt. *Pocket Book of Great Detectives*. 1941. Pocket 103. My. G+. P1d. $8.50

WRIGHT, Lee edt. *Pocket Book of Mystery Stories.* 1941. Pocket 117. 2nd edn. My/SF. F. P1d. $19.50

WRIGHT, Lee edt. *Pocket Book of Mystery Stories.* 1945. Pocket 117. 11th edn. My/SF. VG. P1d. $8.50

WRIGHT, Lee edt. *Pocket Mystery Reader.* 1942. Pocket 172. 2nd edn. My. G+. P1d. $7.00

WRIGHT, Lee edt. *Wicked Women.* 1959. Pocket 1263. PBO. c/Morgan Kane: gga. VG. P6d. $2.50

WRIGHT, M. *Swinging Singles.* Brandon House 1116. NF. B3d. $7.00

WRIGHT, Richard. *Black Boy.* 1951. Signet 841. 1st edn. PBO. VG+. B6a #79. $40.25

WRIGHT, Richard. *Lawd Today.* Avon S 126. VG. B3d. $4.50

WRIGHT, Richard. *Outsider.* 1954. Signet S 1114. 1st pb. VG+. B6d. $12.50

WRIGHT, Richard. *Uncle Tom's Children.* 1947. Signet 647. 1st prtg. c/Jonas. VG. B3d/P7d. $5.00

WRIGHT, S. Fowler. *Amphibians.* Galaxy SF 4. VG+. B3d. $6.00

WRIGHT, S. Fowler. *World Below.* Galaxy SF 5. VG. B3d. $4.00

WRIGHT, Sewell Peaslee edt. *Chicago Murders.* Armed Services 992. VG. B3d. $5.00

WRIGHT, Sewell Peaslee edt. *Chicago Murders.* 1947. Bantam 127. Nfi. VG. P1d. $10.00

WRIGHT, W.E. *Borrowed Ecstasy.* Carnival 904. VG. B3d. $6.50

WYATT. *Of Ermine & Vermin.* 1967. Edka 123. PBO. NF. B6d. $10.00

WYLER, Richard. *Savage Journey.* 1968. Avon G 1342. We. VG. B4d. $2.25

WYLIE, John. *Johnny Purple.* Zenith 3. VG. B3d. $5.00

WYLIE, Philip. *After Worlds Collide.* 1973. PB Library 74-219. 6th prtg. SF. VG. W2d. $3.25

WYLIE, Philip. *Answer.* 1961. PB Library 52-205. 4th edn. SF. VG. B5d. $3.00

WYLIE, Philip. *As They Reveled.* 1951. Avon 360. Fi. VG. B5d. $6.50

WYLIE, Philip. *Babes & Sucklings.* Avon 375. NF. I1d. $10.00

WYLIE, Philip. *Best of Chunch & Des.* 1958. Crest S 240. c/Barye Phillips: gga. reprint. VG. P6d. $2.50

WYLIE, Philip. *Danger Mansion.* LA Bantam 27. G. P6d. $30.00

WYLIE, Philip. *Experiment in Crime.* 1956. Avon 711. My. VG. B3d. $5.00

WYLIE, Philip. *Experiment in Crime.* 1967. Lancer 73-675. My. VG. B5d. $4.00

WYLIE, Philip. *Finnley Wren.* 1958. Berkley BA 100. VG. B3d. $4.50

WYLIE, Philip. *Finnley Wren.* 1958. Berkley BG 100. VG+. I1d. $6.00

WYLIE, Philip. *Finnley Wren.* 1949. Signet 701. Fa. F. B4d. $16.00

WYLIE, Philip. *Finnley Wren.* 1949. Signet 701. Fi. VG. B3d. $6.00

WYLIE, Philip. *Footprint of Cinderella.* Dell 140. VG+. B3d. $10.00

WYLIE, Philip. *Generation of Vipers.* Cardinal GC 93. G. G5d. $3.00

WYLIE, Philip. *Gladiator.* 1957. Avon T 155. VG. B3d. $4.50

WYLIE, Philip. *Gladiator.* 1949. Avon 216. G+. B4d. $3.00

WYLIE, Philip. *Gladiator.* 1949. Avon 216. SF. F. W2d. $12.50

WYLIE, Philip. *Gladiator.* 1949. Avon 216. VG. B3d. $4.50

WYLIE, Philip. *Gladiator.* 1965. Lancer 72-937. c/S Borack. SF. VG. B5d. $4.00

WYLIE, Philip. *Los Angeles: AD 2017.* 1975. Popular 00272. My/SF. VG. P1d. $6.00

WYLIE, Philip. *Night Unto Night.* Popular W 1132. VG+. B3d. $5.00

WYLIE, Philip. *Savage Gentleman.* 1951. Avon 390. c/gga. Ga. VG+. B4d. $18.00

WYLIE, Philip. *Savage Gentleman.* 1945. Dell 85. c/gga. G+. P6d. $4.50

WYLIE, Philip. *Smuggled Atom Bomb.* 1956. Avon 727. SF. VG. B5d. $5.00

WYLIE, Philip. *Smuggled Atom Bomb.* 1965. Lancer 72-916. My. F. P1d. $11.00

WYLIE, Philip. *Spy Who Spoke Porpoise.* 1970. Pyramid N 2315. Th. VG. P1d. $4.50

WYLIE, Philip. *Tomorrow!* 1956. Popular G 156. 1st edn. PBO. G. P9d. $1.25

WYLIE, Philip. *Tomorrow!* 1956. Popular G 156. 1st pb edn. NF. M1d. $8.00

WYLIE, Philip. *Triumph.* 1964. Crest R 675. SF. VG. W2d. $4.50

WYLIE, Philip. *Truimph.* 1967. Crest R 1033. 1st prtg. SF. G+. R5d. $1.50

WYNDHAM, John. *Chocky.* 1968. Ballantine U 6119. 2nd prtg. MTI. SF. G+. R5d. $1.25

WYNDHAM, John. *Day of the Triffids.* Crest M 1932. SF. G+. W2d. $3.00

WYNDHAM, John. *Day of the Triffids.* 1970. Crest T 1322. 1st prtg. VG. P7d. $4.00

WYNDHAM, John. *Day of the Triffids.* Crest 1049. NF. B3d. $5.00

WYNDHAM, John. *Day of the Triffids.* Crest 741. NF. B3d. $5.00

WYNDHAM, John. *Infinite Moment.* 1961. Ballantine 546. PBO. c/R Powers. SF. VG. B5d. $7.50

WYNDHAM, John. *Infinite Moment.* 1961. Ballantine 546. 1st edn. F. M1d. $12.00

WYNDHAM, John. *Midwich Cuckoos.* 1980. Ballantine 28821. 9th edn. SF. VG+. B5d. $3.50

WYNDHAM, John. *Midwich Cuckoos.* 1959. Ballantine 299K. 1st prtg. VG+. P7d. $7.50

WYNDHAM, John. *Out of the Deeps.* 1953. Ballantine 50. PBO. G+. I1d. $5.00

WYNDHAM, John. *Out of the Deeps.* 1953. Ballantine 50. 1st edn. F. M1d. $20.00

WYNDHAM, John. *Out of the Deeps.* 1953. Ballantine 50. 1st prtg. SF. VG. R5d. $7.00

WYNDHAM, John. *Out of the Deeps.* 1961. Ballantine 545. 1st prtg. SF. VG. R5d. $4.00

WYNDHAM, John. *Out of the Deeps.* 1961. Ballantine 545. 2nd edn. c/R Powers. SF. VG+. B5d. $5.50

WYNDHAM, John. *Outward Urge.* 1959. Ballantine 341K. 1st US edn. SF. G+. M3d. $4.00

WYNDHAM, John. *Re-Birth.* 1955. Ballantine 104. 1st edn. F. M1d. $20.00

WYNDHAM, John. *Re-Birth.* 1960. Ballantine 423K. 1st prtg. c/Richard Powers. VG. P7d. $4.50

WYNDHAM, John. *Revolt of the Triffids.* 1952. Popular 411. VG. B3d. $7.00

WYNDHAM, John. *Revolt of the Triffids.* 1952. Popular 411. 1st pb edn. NF. M1d. $30.00

WYNDHAM, John. *Stowaway to Mars.* 1972. Gold Medal T 2646. 1st prtg. SF. VG. B3d. $4.50

WYNDHAM, John. *Tales of Gooseflesh & Laughter.* 1956. Ballantine 182. 1st edn. F. M1d. $15.00

WYNDHAM, John. *Trouble With Lichen.* 1960. Ballantine 449K. PBO. c/R Powers. SF. VG. B5d. $5.00

WYNDHAM, John. *Trouble With Lichen.* 1960. Ballantine 449K. 1st edn. F. M1d. $12.00

WYNDHAM, John. *Village of the Damned.* Ballantine 453K. MTI. c/G Sanders & B Shelley. SF. VG. B5d. $7.50

WYNNE, Andrew. *Have Heels, Will Travel.* 1964. Midwood F 337. PBO. VG+. B6d. $12.50

WYNNE, Anthony. *Death of a Banker.* 1938. Crime-Book Society 34. dust jacket. My. VG. P1d. $30.00

WYNNE, Anthony. *Murder in the Morning.* 1942. De Novel Classic 14. My. VG. P1d. $20.00

WYNNE, B. *Man Who Refused To Die.* PB Library 52-569. NF. B3d. $4.50

WYNNE, Brian. *Night It Rained Bullets.* 1965. Ace M 128. We. VG. P1d. $6.50

WYNNE, Frank. *Dragoon Pass.* 1964. Ace F 302. We. VG. P1d. $6.00

WYNNE, Nancy Blue. *Agatha Christie Chronology.* 1976. Ace 10445. Nfi. VG. P1d. $4.00

YARDLEY, James. *Kiss a Day Keeps the Corpses Away.* 1973. Pan 23456. My. VG. P1d. $4.00

YARNELL, Duane. *Mantrap.* 1960. Crest 346. 2nd edn. My. VG. P1d. $6.00

YARNELL, Duane. *Murder Bait.* 1958. Crest 253. 1st prtg. My. VG+. R5d. $6.00

YATES, Alan. *Coriolanus, the Chariot!* 1978. Ace 11739. SF. VG. B5d. $3.00

YATES, Dornford. *And Berry Came Too.* 1945. Penguin (US) 570. My. VG. P1d. $10.50

YATES, Dornford. *Blind Corner.* 1965. Tandem T 20. My. VG. P1d. $6.00

YATES, Dornford. *Devil in Satin.* Mercury 23. G+. G5d. $9.50

YATES, George Worthing. *Body That Wasn't Uncle.* 1944. Dell 52. VG. F2d. $12.00

YATES, George Worthing. *Body That Wasn't Uncle.* 1952. Dell 645. G+. G5d. $3.00

YATES, George Worthing. *Body That Wasn't Uncle.* 1952. Dell 645. 1st prtg. VG. P7d. $5.50

YATES, George Worthing. *If a Body.* 1947. Dell 159. My. VG. P1d. $10.00

YATES, Peter. *Curtain Call for Murder.* 1945. Vulcan 6. My. G+. P1d. $15.00

YATES, Peter. *Death in the Hands of Talent.* 1945. Five Star 7. My. VG+. P1d. $30.00

YEATS-BROWN, Francis. *Lives of a Bengal Lancer.* 1946. Bantam 43. c/Cal Diehl. Fa. VG+. B4d. $7.50

YERBY, Frank. *Captain Rebel.* 1957. Cardinal C 249. 1st prtg. c/Binger: gga. VG+. P7d. $4.00

YERBY, Frank. *Devil's Laughter.* 1954. Cardinal C 142. 1st prtg. c/Hulings: gga. VG. P7d. $4.50

YERBY, Frank. *Foxes of Harrow.* 1964. Cardinal 50009. 4th edn. Fi. VG+. B5d. $3.50

YERBY, Frank. *Foxes of Harrow.* 1949. Pocket 577. 1st pb. VG. B3d. $4.50

YERBY, Frank. *Golden Hawk.* Cardinal C 54. c/gga. NF. B6d. $9.00

YERBY, Frank. *Griffin's Way.* 1963. Cardinal GC 173. Fa. VG+. B4d. $2.50

YERBY, Frank. *Jarrett's Jade.* 1960. Cardinal GC 101. c/gga. VG+. B4d. $2.50

YERBY, Frank. *Jarrett's Jade.* 1960. Cardinal GC 101. F. B5d. $4.50

YERBY, Frank. *Old Gods Laugh.* 1965. Pocket 50120. Fa. NF. B4d. $2.00

YERBY, Frank. *Saracen Blade.* 1953. Cardinal C 124. 1st prtg. c/James Meese: gga. VG+. P7d. $5.50

YERBY, Frank. *Treasure of Pleasant Valley.* Pocket 1131. VG. B3d. $4.50

YERBY, Frank. *Woman Called Fancy.* 1962. Cardinal GC 125. Fi. VG. B5d. $2.50

YORDAN, Philip. *King of Kings.* 1961. Perma M 5036. 1st prtg. VG+. R5d. $4.00

YORE, Clem. *Age of Consent.* Dell 622. c/R Stanley. Fi. VG+. B5d. $3.50

YORK, Alix. *Love Pirate.* 1965. Midwood 32-455. PBO. c/Rader: gga. scarce. NF. B6a #75. $55.00

YORK, Andrew. *Eliminator.* 1967. Arrow 002. Th. VG. P1d. $5.00

YORK, Carol Beach. *Takers & Returners.* 1973. Tempo 5661. My. F. P1d. $5.00

YORK, J. *Hide & Kill.* Consul 1041. VG+. B3d. $7.00

YORK, J. *Sentence of Death.* Jay Suspense 4. VG+. B3d. $8.00

YORK, Jeremy. *So Soon To Die.* 1959. Pyramid G 382. My. VG. P1d. $7.00

YORKE, Margaret. *Cast for Death.* 1979. Arrow 919580. My. VG. P1d. $4.00

YORKE, Margaret. *Dead in the Morning.* 1976. Arrow 913170. My. VG. P1d. $4.00

YORKE, Margaret. *Grave Matters.* 1976. Arrow 913180. My. VG+. P1d. $4.50

YORKE, Susan. *Agency House Malaya.* 1969. MacFadden 60-380. 2nd edn. My. VG. P1d. $3.50

YORKE, Veline. *Brides of the Devil.* 1949. Panther Book NN. PBO. extremely scarce. VG+. B6a #77. $59.00

YOUNG, Chic. *Blondie Dagwood.* 1947. Dell NN. PBO. extremely scarce. VG. B6a #79. $54.00

YOUNG, Desmond. *Rommel, the Desert Fox.* 1958. Berkley G 96. PBO. c/photo. Nfi. VG. B5d. $3.50

YOUNG, Desmond. *Rommel, the Desert Fox.* 1958. Berkley G 96. VG+. B3d. $4.50

YOUNG, Edward. *Hospital Doctor.* 1952. Pyramid G 67. 1st pb. VG+. B6d. $12.50

YOUNG, Gordon. *Range Boss (Red Clark, Range Boss).* Popular 384. VG. B3d. $4.50

YOUNG, Gordon. *Trouble on the Border.* 1951. Popular 321. VG. P6d. $3.50

YOUNG, Jefferson. *Good Man.* 1954. Bantam A 1245. VG+. B3d. $4.50

YOUNG, Robert F. *Eridahn.* 1983. Ballantine 30854. 1st edn. SF. F. F2d. $10.00

YOUNG, S. *So Red the Rose.* Popular W 1135. c/McGinnis. VG. B3d. $4.50

YOUNG, T. *Brothers' Wives.* Barclay 7314. c/photo. F. B3d. $6.00

YUILL, P.B. *Hazell & the Menacing Jester.* 1977. Penguin 4400. De. VG. P1d. $5.00

YUILL, P.B. *Hazell Plays Solomon.* 1976. Penguin 4214. 2nd edn. De. G+. P1d. $2.75

YURICK, Sol. *Fertig.* 1967. Pocket 75225. My. VG+. P1d. $7.50

YURICK, Sol. *Warriors.* 1966. Pyramid X 1466. JD. G+. P1d. $6.00

YURKA, Blanche edt. *Three Scandinavian Plays.* 1962. Washington Square W 657. Nfi. VG+. B5d. $3.50

ZACHARY, Hugh. *Gwen in Green.* 1974. Gold Medal M 2982. SF. VG. W2d. $3.50

ZACHARY, Hugh. *One Day in Hell.* 1961. Newsstand U 158. My. VG+. P1d. $9.50

ZACHARY, Hugh. *Revenant.* 1988. Onyx 40092. 1st edn. Ho. F. F2d. $8.00

ZACHERLEY. *Vulture Stew.* 1960. Ballantine 417K PBO. c/R Powers. SF. VG. B5d. $9.00

ZACKEL, Fred. *Cocaine & Blue Eyes.* 1979. Berkley 04456. De. VG+. P1d. $4.50

ZAHN, Timothy. *Backlash Mission.* 1986. DAW 683. PBO. c/DiFate. SF. NF. B6d. $9.00

ZAHN, Timothy. *Black Collar.* 1983. DAW 556. 1st edn. VG. P9d. $1.50

ZAHN, Timothy. *Triplet.* 1987. Baen. 1st edn. F. M1d. $4.00

ZAMMIT, Gina. *Nights of Malta.* 1969. Holloway House HH 169. My. VG. P1d. $4.50

ZAMYATIN, Yevgeny. *We.* 1972. Bantam X 7271. 1st prtg. SF. VG. R5d. $1.75

ZANE, H. *They Always Take Their Secrets Etc.* Signet 2353. PBO. VG. B3d. $5.00

ZANE, Lohl. *Bronda.* 1952. Gold Medal 264. 1st prtg. PBO. VG. P6d. $4.25

ZARUBICA, Mladin. *Scutari.* 1969. PB Library 64-067. My. VG. P1d. $4.50

ZATTERIN, Ugo. *Revolt of the Sinners.* 1956. Popular 727. c/gga. Fa. NF. B4d. $12.00

ZATTERIN, Ugo. *Revolt of the Sinners.* 1956. Popular 727. My. VG. P1d. $8.00

ZEBROWSKI, George. *Ashes & Stars.* 1977. Ace 87269. SF. VG. B5d. $3.00

ZEBROWSKI, George. *Omega Point.* 1972. Ace 62380. SF. VG+. B4d. $3.00

ZEBROWSKI, George. *Star Web.* Laser 15. NF. B3d. $6.00

ZEIGER, Henry A. *Ian Fleming: The Spy Who Came in With the Gold.* 1966. Popular 60-2131. VG. P1d. $5.50

ZEIGFREID, Karl. *Escape to Infinity.* 1960. Badger SF 82. PBO. c/classic. SF. VG. B6a #74. $33.00

ZEIGFREID, Karl. *Projection Infinity.* 1960. Badger 103. PBO. c/Fox. scarce. SF. VG+. B6a #74. $48.50

ZEIGFREID, Karl. *Projection Infinity.* Vega SF 12. VG. B3d. $7.00

ZEIGFREID, Karl. *Radar Alert.* Badger SF 83. VG. B3d. $8.00

ZEIGFREID, Karl. *Walk Through Tomorrow.* Badger SF 78. VG+. B3a #22. $17.75

ZEIGFREID, Karl. *Zero Minus X.* Badger SF 81. VG+. B3a #22. $16.50

ZEISER, Benno. *Road to Stalingrad.* 1956. Ballantine 168. 1st edn. VG+. B3d. $5.00

ZELAZNY, Roger. *Bridge of Ashes.* 1976. Signet. 1st edn. F. M1d. $7.00

ZELAZNY, Roger. *Changing Land.* 1981. Ballantine 25389. 1st edn. SF. F. F2d. $10.00

ZELAZNY, Roger. *Courts of Chaos.* 1979. Avon 47175. 1st prtg. SF. VG+. R5d. $1.75

ZELAZNY, Roger. *Creatures of Light & Darkness.* 1970. Avon U 2362. 1st edn. PBO. NF. P9d. $2.00

ZELAZNY, Roger. *Damnation Alley.* 1970. Berkley S 1846. 1st pb. c/Lehr. SF. VG+. B6d. $9.00

ZELAZNY, Roger. *Damnation Alley.* 1977. Berkley 03641. SF. F. W2d. $6.00

ZELAZNY, Roger. *Doors of His Face.* 1975. Corgi 10021. 1st prtg. SF. VG. R5d. $3.00

ZELAZNY, Roger. *Dream Master.* Ace F 403. PBO. c/sgn. VG+. B3d. $10.00

ZELAZNY, Roger. *Dream Master.* Ace F 403. NF. M1d. $8.00

ZELAZNY, Roger. *Dream Master.* 1966. Ace 16701. SF. VG. B5d. $3.00

ZELAZNY, Roger. *Dream Master.* 1966. Ace 16701. 1st prtg. NF. S1d. $4.00

ZELAZNY, Roger. *Four for Tomorrow.* Ace M 155. NF. M1d. $8.00

ZELAZNY, Roger. *Four for Tomorrow.* Ace M 155. PBO. c/sgn. VG+. B3d. $8.00

ZELAZNY, Roger. *Guns of Avalon.* 1974. Avon 20032. 1st pb edn. F. M1d. $7.00

ZELAZNY, Roger. *Guns of Avalon.* 1974. Avon 20032. 1st prtg. SF. VG. R5d. $1.50

ZELAZNY, Roger. *Hand of Oberon.* 1977. Avon 51318. 5th prtg. SF. F. W2d. $4.00

ZELAZNY, Roger. *Nebula Awards Stories #3.* 1970. Pocket 75420. SF. VG. B5d. $3.00

ZELAZNY, Roger. *Roadmarks.* 1980. Ballantine 25388. SF. VG. W2d. $3.25

ZELAZNY, Roger. *Roadmarks.* 1980. Ballantine 25388. 1st prtg. SF. F. W2d. $5.25

ZELAZNY, Roger. *This Immortal.* 1966. Ace F 393. F. M1d. $10.00

ZELAZNY, Roger. *This Immortal.* 1966. Ace F 393. 1st edn. c/sgn. SF. F. F2d. $30.00

ZELAZNY, Roger. *This Immortal.* 1966. Ace 80691. SF. VG. B4d. $2.00

ZELAZNY, Roger. *Trumps of Doom.* 1986. Avon 89635. PBO. Amber #6. c/sgn. SF. F. M3d. $10.00

ZENO. *Grab.* 1972. Pan 02925. My. G+. P1d. $3.00

ZETFORD, Tully. *Whirlpool of Stars.* 1975. Pinnacle 220528. 1st prtg. Hook #1. SF. VG. W2d. $3.50

ZIMMER, Paul E. *King Chondos' Ride.* 1983. Berkley 06430. 3rd prtg. Dark Border Volume #2. SF. VG. W2d. $3.75

ZIMMER, Paul E. *Lost Prince.* 1982. Playtime 21147. Dark Border Volume #1. SF. VG. W2d. $3.75

ZINBERG, Len. *Walk Hard -- Talk Loud.* 1950. Lion 29. Fi. G. P1d. $6.00

ZINBERG, Len. *What D'Ya Know for Sure?* 1955. Avon T 93. 3rd edn. Fi. VG. B5d. $3.00

ZINBERG, Len. *What D'Ya Know for Sure?* Berkley 225. c/Maguire. VG. B3d. $4.00

ZINDEL, Paul. *Undertaker's Gone Bananas.* 1979. Bantam 12801. 2nd edn. My. VG. P1d. $3.00

ZINSSER, Hans. *Rats, Lice & History.* 1945. Pocket 309. 1st pb. VG+. B6d. $7.00

ZOLA, Emile. *Human Beast.* Avon G 1013. VG. B3d. $4.00

ZOLA, Emile. *Kill.* 1955. Bantam A 1290. My. VG+. P1d. $12.00

ZOLA, Emile. *Lesson in Love.* 1953. Pyramid 105. c/Jim Bentley; gga. VG. P6d. $7.50

ZOLA, Emile. *Love Episode.* 1948. Avon 150. 1st US edn. c/Maxwell; gga. VG. P7d. $7.50

ZOLA, Emile. *Nana.* 1945. Pocket 104. 15th edn. Fi. VG. B5d. $3.00

ZOLA, Emile. *Nana's Mother.* 1950. Avon 271. 1st prtg. c/gga. VG+. P7d. $10.00

ZOLA, Emile. *Piping Hot.* 1948. Avon 167. VG. B3d. $4.00

ZOLA, Emile. *Restless House.* 1954. Bantam A 1244. Fa. VG+. B4d. $2.00

ZOLA, Emile. *Shame.* 1954. Ace S 76. 1st US edn. c/gga. VG+. B6d. $15.00

ZOLA/ZOLA. *Shame/Therese Raquin.* 1956. Ace D 182. VG. P6d. $4.50

ZORRO. *12 Must Die.* 1966. Corinth CR 118. My/SF. VG+. P1d. $20.00

ZWEIG, Arnold. *Case of Sergeant Grischa.* Royal Books Giant 23. VG+. I1d. $10.00

Pseudonyms

Listed below are pseudonyms of many paperback and hardcover authors. This information was shared with us by some of our many contributors, and we offer it here as a reference for our readers. This section is organized alphabetically by the author's actual name (given in bold) followed by the pseudonyms he or she has been known to use. (It is interesting to note that 'house names' were common with more than one author using the same name for a particular magazine or publishing house).

If you have any information (or corrections), please let us hear from you so we can expand this section in future editions.

Aarons, Edward S.
Ayres, Paul
Ronns, Edward

Albert, Marvin H.
Conroy, Albert
Jason, Stuart
Quarry, Nick
Rome, Anthony

Ard, William
Ward, Jonas (some)

Avallone, Mike
Carter, Nick (a few)
Conway, Troy (a few)
Dalton, Priscilla
Jason, Stuart
Noone, Edwina
Stuart, Sidney
Walker, Max

Ballard, W.T.
Hunter, D'Allard
MacNeil, Neil
Shepherd, John

Ballinger, Bill
Sanborn, B.X.

Blake, Roger
Sade, Mark

Blassingame, Lurton
Duncan, Peter

Beaumont, Charles
Grantland, Keith

Beck, Robert
Iceberg Slim

Bedford-Jones, H.
Feval, Paul
Pemjion, L.

Bloch, Robert
Young, Collier

Block, Lawrence
Ard, William
Emerson, Jill
Harrison, Chip
Lord, Sheldon
Morse, Benjamin, M.D.
Shaw, Andrew

Bradley, Marion Zimmer
Chapman, Lee
Dexter, John (some)
Gardner, Miriam
Graves, Valerie
Ives, Morgan

Brunner, John
Woodcott, Keith

Bulmer, Kenneth
Hardy, Adam
Norvil, Manning
Prescot, Dray

Burnett, W.R.
Monachan, John
Updyke, James

Burroughs, William S.
Lee, William

Byrne, Stuart
Bloodstone, John

Campbell, Ramsey
Dreadstone, Carl
Ramsay, Jay

Carr, John Dickson
Dickson, Carter
Fairbairn, Roger

Cooper, Basil
Falk, Lee

Cooper, Clarence
Chestnut, Robert

Cross, David
Chesbro, George B.

Creasey, John
Ashe, Gordon
Frazier, Robert Caine
Gill, Patrick
Holliday, Michael
Hope, Brian
Hughes, Colin
Hunt, Kyle
Marric, J.J.

Daniels, Norman
Daniels, Dorothy
Wade, David

Davidson, Avram
Queen, Ellery
(about 2 titles only)

Derleth, August
Grendon, Stephen

Dewey, Thomas B.
Brandt, Tom
Cord Wainer

Disch, Thomas
Demijohn, Thomas
Cassandra, Knye
(both names with Sladek, John)

Ellis, Peter
Tremayne, Peter

Ellison, Harlan
Merchant, Paul

Etchison, Dennis
Martin, Jack

Fairman, Paul
Paul, F.W.

Farmer, Philip Jose
Norfolk, William
Trout, Kilgore

Fearn, John Russell
Del Martia, Aston

Fox, Gardner F.
Chase, Glen
Cooper, Jefferson
Gardner, Jeffrey
Gardner, Matt
Gray, James Kendricks
Jennings, Dean
Majors, Simon
Matthews, Kevin
Morgan, John Medford
Morgan, Rod
Summers, Bart

Gardner, Earle Stanley
Fair, A.A.
Kendrake, Carleton
Kinney, Charles

Garrett, Randall
Bupp, Walter
Gordon, David
1/2 of Mark Phillips and Robert
Randall

Geis, Richard
Owen, Robert
Swenson, Peggy

Gibson, Walter B.
Brown, Douglas
Grant, Maxwell

Goulart, Ron
Falk, Lee
Kains, Josephine
Kearney, Julian
Robeson, Kenneth
Shaw(n), Frank S.
Silva, Joseph

Grant, Charles L.
Andrew, Felicia
Lewis, Deborah

Haas, Ben
Meade, Richard

Haldeman, Joe
Graham, Robert

Halliday, Brett
Shayne, Mike

Hansen, Joseph
Brock, Rose
Colton, James

Harknett, Terry
Hedges, Joseph
Stone, Thomas H.

Harris, Timothy
Hyde, Harris

Hochstein, Peter
Short, Jack

Hodder-Williams, C.
Brogan, James

Holt, John Robert
Giles, Elizabeth
Giles, Raymond

Hunt, E. Howard
St.John, David

Hunter, Evan
Cannon, Curt
Collins, Hunt
Hannon, Ezra
Marsten, Richard
McBain, Ed

Jakes, John
Ard, William
Payne, Alan
Scotland, Jay

Jenkins, Will F.
Leinster, Murray

Jones, H. Bedford
Pemjean, Lucien

Kane, Frank
Boyd, Frank

Kane, Henry
McCall, Anthony

Kavanagh, Dan
Barnes, Julian

Kent, Hal
Davis, Ron

King, Stephen
Bachman, Richard

Klass, Philip
Tenn, William

Knowles, William
Allison, Clyde
Ames, Clyde

Koontz, Dean R.
Axton, David
Coffey, Brian
Dwyer, Deanna
Dwyer, K.R.
Hill, John
Nichols, Leigh
North, Anthony
Paige, Richard
West, Owen
Wolfe, Aaron

Kornbluth, Cyril
Eisner, Simon
Park, Jordan

Kosinski, Jerzy
Somers, Jane

Kubis, P.
Scott, Casey

Kurland, Michael
Plum, Jennifer

L'Amour, Louis
Mayo, Jim

Laumer, Keith
LeBaron, Anthony

Lesser, Milton
Marlowe, Stephen

Lessing, Doris
Somers, Jane

Linebarger, Paul
Smith, Cordwainer

Long, Frank Belknap
Long, Lyda Belknap

Lucas, Mark
Palmer, Drew

Ludlum, Robert
Ryder, Jonathan

Lupoff, Richard
Steele, Adison

Lynds, Dennis
Collins, Michael
Crowe, John
Grant, Maxwell (some)
Sadler, Mark

Malzberg, Barry
Berry, Mike
Dumas, Claudine
Johnson, Mel
Johnson, M.L.
O'Donnell, Barrett
O'Donnell, K.M.

Marshall, Mel
Tayler, Zack

Martin, Robert
Roberts, Lee

Mason, Van Wyck
Coffin, Geoffrey

Masterton, Graham
Luke, Thomas

Matheson, Richard
Swanson, Logan

McGaughy, Dudley
Owen, Dean

Meaker, Marijane
Aldrich, Ann
Packer, Vin

Millar, Kenneth
MacDonald, Ross
MacDonald, John Ross

Moorcock, Michael
Bradbury, Edward P.
Barclay, Bill

Moore, Brian
Michael, Bryan
Mara, Bernard

Morris, James
Morris, Jan (after sex change)

Norton, Alice
North, Andrew
Norton, Andre

Nuetzel, Charles
Augustus, Albert Jr.
Davidson, John
English, Charles
Rivere, Alec

Oates, Joyce Carol
Smith, Rosamond

Offutt, Andrew
Cleve, John
Giles, Baxter
Williams, J.X. (some)

Patterson, Henry
Fallon, Martin
Graham, James
Higgins, Jack
Patterson, Harry
Marlowe, Hugh

Philips, James Atlee
Atlee, Philip

Phillips, Dennis
Chambers, Peter
Chester, Peter

Phillips, Judson
Pentecost, Hugh

Posner, Richard
Foster, Iris
Murray, Beatrice
Todd, Paul

Prather, Richard
Knight, David
Ring, Douglas

Radford, R.L.
Ford, Marcia

Pronzini, Bill
Foxx, Jack

Rabe, Peter
MacCargo, J.T.

Rawson, Clayton
Towne, Stuart

Reynolds, Mack
Belmont, Bob
Harding, Todd
Reynolds, Maxine

Rice, Anne
Rampling, Anne

Rosenblum, Robert
Maxxe, Robert

Ross, W.E.D.
Dana, Rose
Daniels, Jan
Ross, Clarissa
Ross, Dan
Ross, Dana
Ross, Marilyn

Rossi, Jean-Baptiste
Japrisot, Sebastien

Sellers, Con
Bannion, Della

Silverberg, Robert
Beauchamp, Loren
Burnett, W.R. (some only)
Drummond, Walter
Elliott, Don (some)
Ford, Hilary
Hamilton, Franklin
Knox, Calvin
Lt. Woodard, M.D.

Smith, George H.
Deer, J.M.
Hudson, Jan
Jason, Jerry
Knerr, M.E.
Queen, Ellery (some)
Summers, Diana

Stacton, David
Clifton, Bud

Sturgeon, Theodore
Ewing, Frederick R.
Ellery Queen (1 book only)

Thomas, Ross
Bleeck, Oliver

Tracy, Don
Fuller, Roger

Tralins, Bob
Miles, Keith
O'Shea, Sean

Tubb, E.C.
Kern, Gregory

Vance, Jack
Held, Peter;
Queen, Ellery (some/few)

Vidal, Gore
Box, Edgar

Wager, Walter
Tiger, John
Walker, Max

Ward, Harold
Zorro

Webb, Jack
Farr, John

Weiss, Joe
Anatole, Ray
Dauphine, Claude
Mirbeau, Ken

Westlake, Donald E.
Allan, John B.
Clark, Curt
Culver, Timothy
Cunningham, J. Morgan
Holt, Samuel
Marshall, Alan
Stark, Richard
West, Edwin

Williams, Gordon
Yuill, P.B

Whittington, Harry
Harrison, Whit
Shepherd, Shep

Williamson, Jack
Stewart, Will

Wollheim, Don
Grinnell, David

Woolrich, Cornell
Hopley, George
Irish, William

Worts, George F.
Brent, Loring

Book Buyers

In this section of the book we have listed buyers of books and related material. When you correspond with these dealers, be sure to enclose a self-addressed stamped envelope if you want a reply. Do not send lists of books for appraisal. If you wish to sell your books, quote the price you want or send a list and ask if there are any on the list they might be interested in and the price they would be willing to pay. If you want the list back, be sure to send a SASE large enough for the listing to be returned. When you list your books, do so by author, full title, publisher and number, date, edition, and condition, noting any defects on cover or contents.

Adult

1960s
Footstool Detective Books
3148 Holmes Ave. S
Minneapolis, MN 55408-2629

All Genre

Books Are Everything
P.O. Box 5068
Richmond, KY 40475
606-624-9176

Jeff Patton
3621 Carolina St. NW
Massillon, OH 44646-3201

Americana

Ardent Books
1110 Park Dr.
Ft. Lauderdale, FL 33312
305-792-8845 or FAX 305-467-0959

Auction Service

Black Ace Books
1658 Griffith Park Blvd.
Los Angeles, CA 90026
213-661-5052

Robert Fisher
1631 Sheridan St.
Williamsport, PA 17701

Autographs

For Collectors Only
2028B Ford Pkwy. #136
St. Paul, MN 55116

Beat Literature

Black Ace Books
1658 Griffith Park Blvd.
Los Angeles, CA 90026
213-661-5052

Biography

Ardent Books
1110 Park Dr.
Ft. Lauderdale, FL 33312
305-792-8845 or FAX 305-467-0959

Children's

Popek's
R.D. 3, Box 44C
Oneonta, NY 13820
607-432-8036

Comic

Allen
10218 Dovercrest
St. Louis, MO 63128

Jeff Patton
3621 Carolina St. NW
Massillon, OH 44646-3201

Counterculture

Black Ace Books
1658 Griffith Park Blvd.
Los Angeles, CA 90026
213-661-5052

Detective

Don Crawford
3210 Eastlake
Elkhart, IN 46514
219-264-2784

For Collectors Only
2028B Ford Pkwy. #136
St. Paul, MN 55116

Murder by the Book
1281 N Main St.
Providence, RI 02904

Marvin Sommer, Bookseller
Box 442 Bridge Station
Niagara Falls, NY 14305

Disney

Robert Fisher
1631 Sheridan St.
Williamsport, PA 17701

General

Popek's
R.D. 3, Box 44C
Oneonta, NY 13820
607-432-8036

Hippie

Black Ace Books
1658 Griffith Park Blvd.
Los Angeles, CA 90026
213-661-5052

Horror

For Collectors Only
2028B Ford Pkwy. #136
St. Paul, MN 55116

Literature

Bob Fisher
1631 Sheridan St.
Williamsport, PA 17701

Popek's
R.D. 3, Box 44C
Oneonta, NY 13820
607-432-8036

Magazines

Jeff Patton
3621 Carolina St. NW
Massillon, OH 44646-3201

Manuscripts

For Collectors Only
2028B Ford Pkwy. #136
St. Paul, MN 55116

Media

For Collectors Only
2028B Ford Pkwy. #136
St. Paul, MN 55116

Movie Tie-Ins

Allen
10218 Dovercrest
St. Louis, MO 63128

Arnie Davis
HCR 72, Box 3418
E Waterboro, ME 04030
207-247-4222

Robert Fisher
1631 Sheridan St.
Williamsport, PA 17701

Joseph Patton Rare Books
Box 95
Galax, VA 24333
703-744-3572

Robert Murphy, Bookseller
3113 Bunker Hill Rd.
Marietta, GA 30062-5421

Mystery

Don Crawford
3210 Eastlake
Elkhart, IN 46514
219-264-2784

Footstool Detective Books
3148 Holmes Ave. S
Minneapolis, MN 55408-2629

Originals
Mordida Books
P.O. Box 79322
Houston, TX 77279
713-467-4280

Popek's
R.D. 3, Box 44C
Oneonta, NY 13820
607-432-8036

Negro

Ardent Books
1110 Park Dr.
Ft. Lauderdale, FL 33312
305-792-8845 or FAX 305-467-0959

Science Fiction

Ardent Books
1110 Park Dr.
Ft. Lauderdale, FL 33312
305-792-8845 or FAX 305-467-0959

Don Crawford
3210 Eastlake
Elkhart, IN 46514
217-264-2784

Footstool Detective Books
3148 Holmes Ave. S
Minneapolis, MN 44508-2629

For Collectors Only
2028B Ford Pkwy. #136
St. Paul, MN 55116

Popek's
R.D. 3, Box 44C
Oneonta, NY 13820
607-432-8036

J. Waters
Box 459
Morristown, AZ 85342

Trades Books

Americana Books
P.O. Box 14
Decatur, IN 46733

TV Tie-In

Allen
10218 Dovercrest
St. Louis, MO 63128

Robert Murphy, Bookseller
3113 Bunker Hill Rd.
Marietta, GA 30062-5421

Vintage

1930s-70s
Attic Books
707 S Loudoun St.
Winchester, VA 22601

Black Ace Books
1658 Griffith Park Blvd.
Los Angeles, CA 90026
213-661-5052

Book Rack
4840 Irvine Blvd., Ste. 108
Irvine, CA 92720
714-669-1844

Books Are Everything
P.O. Box 5068
Richmond, KY 40475
606-624-9176

from 1939-65
Buck Creek Books, Ltd.
838 Main St.
Lafayette, IN 47901
317-742-6618

Don Crawford
3210 Eastlake
Elkhart, IN 46514
219-264-2784

A.F. Kokol
5 Jamaica Ave.
Plainview, NY 11803

For Collectors Only
2028B Ford Pkwy. #136
St. Paul, MN 55116

Lynn Munroe Books
P.O. Box 1736
Orange, CA 92668

Paper Treasures
9595 Congress St.
New Market, VA 22844

Pauper's Books
206 N Main St.
Bowling Green, OH 43402-2420

Jeffrey L. Pressman, Bookseller
3246 Ettie St.
Oakland, CA 94608
510-652-6232

Marvin Sommer, Bookseller
Box 442 Bridge Station
Niagara Falls, NY 14305

C. Townsend
44 Edgedale Dr. NW
Calgary, AB T3A 2R4
Canada

Want Lists Serviced

For Collectors Only
2028B Ford Pkwy. #136
St. Paul, MN 55116

Westerns

Ardent Books
1110 Park Dr.
Ft. Lauderdale, FL 33312
305-792-8845 or FAX 305-467-0959